# COMPARATIVE POLITICS

# COMPARATIVE POLITICS

## A Global Introduction

THIRD EDITION

Michael J. Sodaro
The George Washington University

With contributions by:

Dean W. Collinwood
University of Utah

Bruce J. Dickson
The George Washington University

Joseph L. Klesner
Kenyon College

Timothy D. Sisk
University of Denver

Boston Burr Ridge, IL Dubuque, IA New York San Francisco St. Louis
Bangkok Bogotá Caracas Kuala Lumpur Lisbon London Madrid Mexico City
Milan Montreal New Delhi Santiago Seoul Singapore Sydney Taipei Toronto

Published by McGraw-Hill, an imprint of The McGraw-Hill Companies Inc., 1221 Avenue of the Americas, New York, NY 10020. 

This book is printed on acid-free paper.

4 5 6 7 8 9 0 CCW 10

ISBN: 978-0-07-352631-7
MHID: 0-07-352631-2

Editor-in-chief: *Emily Barosse*
Publisher: *Frank Mortimer*
Sponsoring editor: *Monica Eckman*
Developmental editor: *Kate Scheinman*
Marketing manager: *Simon Heathcote*
Production editor: *Anne Fuzellier*
Production supervisor: *Tandra Jorgensen*
Design manager: *Preston Thomas*
Cover designer: *Kay Lieberherr*
Production service: *Melanie Field*
Photo research coordinator: *Christine A. Pullo*
Compositor: *10/12 Palatino by ICC Macmillan Inc.*
Printing: 45# New Era Matte Plus, Courier, Westford

Cover image: *Stock Illustration Source, Inc.*

Credits: The credits section for this book begins on page 799 and is considered an extension of the copyright page.

**Library of Congress Cataloging-in-Publication Data**

Sodaro, Michael J.
Comparative politics : a global introduction / Michael J. Sodaro; with contributions by Dean W. Collinwood . . . [et al.]. — 3rd ed.
p. cm.
Includes bibliographical references and index.
ISBN 0-07-352631-2
1. Comparative government—Textbooks. I. Collinwood, Dean Walter, 1949– II. Title.
JF51.S547 2007
320.3—dc22 2007009508



**www.mhhe.com**

# ABOUT THE AUTHORS

MICHAEL JOSEPH SODARO (chapters 1–18 and 20) is the principal author and editor of *Comparative Politics: A Global Introduction.* As Professor of Political Science and International Affairs at the George Washington University, where he has been on the faculty since 1977, he is the Director of the European and Eurasian Studies program at the Elliott School of International Affairs and a member of the Institute for European, Russian, and Eurasian Studies. He has a BA from Fordham University, an MA from the School of Advanced International Studies of the Johns Hopkins University, and a PhD from Columbia University. He earned a certificate at the Institut d'études politiques in Paris and studied in Berlin. He has conducted research in Britain, France, Germany, Italy, and Russia, and has taught at Georgetown, John Hopkins, and the U.S. Foreign Service Institute. In addition to publishing numerous articles and book chapters and a co-edited volume, he is the recipient of the Marshall Shulman prize for *Moscow, Germany, and the West from Khrushchev to Gorbachev* (Cornell, 1990). In 1992 he was awarded the Oscar and Shoshana Trachtenberg prize for excellence in teaching at George Washington University.

DEAN W. COLLINWOOD (chapter 19, "Japan") is Director of the Global Business Development Center and of the U.S.-Japan and China Centers in Salt Lake City, Utah, where he also teaches in the Political Science Department at the University of Utah and serves on the board of the Salt Lake Committee on Foreign Relations and the Asia-Pacific Council. He has a BA from Brigham Young University, an MSc from the University of London, and a PhD from the University of Chicago. He was a Fulbright scholar at the University of Tokyo in 1986–87 and is a past president of the Western Conference of the Association for Asian Studies. He is the author of the Global Studies series volumes *Japan and the Pacific Rim,* published by Dushkin/McGraw-Hill.

BRUCE J. DICKSON (chapter 21, "China") is Professor of Political Science and International Affairs at the George Washington University. He obtained his BA, MA, and PhD from the University of Michigan. He is the author of *China's Red Capitalists: The Party, Private Entrepreneurs, and Prospects for Political Change* (Cambridge, 2003) and *Democratization in China and Taiwan: The Adaptability of Leninist Parties* (Oxford, 1998). He is co-editor of three other books and author of articles appearing in *Asian Survey, China Quarterly, Comparative Politics,* and other leading journals.

JOSEPH L. KLESNER (chapter 22, "Mexico and Brazil") is Professor and Chair in the Department of Political Science at Kenyon College. He received his BA at Central College and his SM and PhD at the Massachusetts Institute of Technology. The author of articles appearing in *Comparative Politics, Mexican Studies, Electoral Studies,* and the *Latin American Research Review,* in addition to many book chapters, he has worked on politics in Mexico and on public opinion and political culture in Latin America. His research has been funded by Fulbright grants to Mexico, South America, and most recently, Ireland and by funding from the National Science Foundation and the National Endowment for the Humanities.

TIMOTHY D. SISK (chapter 23, "Nigeria and South Africa") is Associate Professor in the Graduate School of International Studies at the University of Denver, where he also serves as a faculty member in the MA program in Conflict Resolution and as Director of the BA program in International Studies. He obtained his BA and MA from Baylor University and his PhD from the George Washington University. After experience as a journalist in South Africa and a legislative assistant in the U.S. Senate, he served as a program officer and research scholar at the federally chartered United States Institute of Peace in Washington, D.C. Sisk is just completing a major new scholarly book titled *Pursuing Peace in Civil Wars: From Escalation to Sustainable Settlement.* He is also the author of a new book for policy practitioners titled *Democracy, Conflict and Human Security* (with Judith Large; International IDEA, 2006). He has written five other books and many articles, including *Democracy at the Local Level* (IDEA, 2000), *Democratization in South Africa* (Princeton, 1995), and *Power Sharing and International Mediation in Ethnic Conflicts* (Carnegie Commission on Preventing Deadly Conflict, 1995).

# BRIEF CONTENTS

PART TWO

## COUNTRIES AND LEADERS

# CONTENTS

PART TWO

# COUNTRIES AND LEADERS

# PREFACE

The enormous success of the second edition of *Comparative Politics: A Global Introduction* was extremely gratifying. The book was adopted by professors at a large number of colleges and universities and by high school teachers throughout the United States. It was also used at various universities around the world. In 2006 a Spanish version of the book, *Polìtica y Ciencia Polìtica: Una Introducción,* was published under the supervision of Professor José Ignacio Torreblanca of the Universidad Nacional de Educación a Distancia in Madrid. We are very grateful for the positive reactions we have received from instructors and students alike, and we are grateful as well for the suggestions we have received for improving the book's content. In view of the encouraging feedback—and valid criticisms—the second edition received, the present edition retains the basic structure of the last edition while adding a considerable amount of new material.

### What's the Same?

**A Global Approach** This book takes a "global" approach to comparative politics not only with respect to the number of countries that are treated but also with respect to the topics and analytical techniques that we explore. Like the first two editions of *Comparative Politics: A Global Introduction*, the third edition has three ambitious goals: (1) to introduce readers to the *conceptual foundations* of comparative politics; (2) to enhance their *analytical and critical-thinking skills* through an introduction to some of the basic empirical techniques of political science; and (3) to promote their understanding of a wide range of *countries and political leaders*.

**Concepts** Unlike some introductory texts on comparative politics, this book is not limited to just a chapter-by-chapter treatment of individual countries. We believe that comparative politics needs to be understood conceptually, with a clear treatment of core concepts and theories and a firm grounding in academic scholarship. The fifteen chapters that make up Part One ("Concepts and Critical Thinking") therefore address such fundamental topics of comparative politics as *democracy* and *democratization; human rights; authoritarianism; class, ethnicity, gender, religion,* and other aspects of *political sociology; power; state institutions; nationalism; supranationalism; electoral systems; voting behavior; parties, interest groups, NGOs,* and *social movements; political culture; ideology; dissent* and *revolution; political economy; political development*, and other key concepts. Drawn from classic works of political science and political philosophy as well as from some of the latest scholarly literature, these ideas come to life through numerous illustrative examples reflecting recent events around the world.

*Democracy* and *democratization* occupy an especially prominent place throughout the book. In addition to defining these concepts in a way that illuminates their various components and variations, we present a list of ten conditions for democracy whose presence often contributes to the creation and consolidation of democracy and whose absence can thwart democracy's very emergence or undermine its chances for long-term success. These ten factors provide a framework for the comparative analysis of democracies and nondemocracies of all kinds. We have also retained our *eclectic approach* to comparative politics by exposing readers to a wide range of conceptual and theoretical orientations, both traditional and contemporary. This book does not confine itself to just one approach, such as structural-functionalism.

**Critical Thinking** One of this book's unique features is that it seeks to enhance the *critical-thinking skills* of its readers by exposing them to some of the ways that scientific logic applies to the study of politics. In addition to introducing students to the study of comparative politics, this volume introduces them to various *analytical techniques of political science*. We believe that today's students need to take every available opportunity to improve their ability to think logically and systematically, irrespective of where their main interests may lie or where their career paths may take them. Political science offers a superb opportunity to sharpen analytical thinking. Our approach to political analysis is elementary and understandable; this book is *not* a text on quantitative methods or research methodology. At a rudimentary level and in a clearly written fashion, it explains the application of such elementary scientific concepts as *theories, hypotheses, dependent and independent variables, correlations, models,* and *paradigms* to the study of political phenomena. It also walks students through the logic of qualitative hypothesis testing and provides numerous examples of how it is done. To drive home the step-by-step logic of this analytical technique, virtually every chapter in the book contains a *hypothesis-testing exercise*. Like the conceptual definitions introduced in Part One, these exercises are taken from real-world political events and from influential works by scholars and political thinkers.

**Countries and Leaders** *Comparative Politics: A Global Introduction,* third edition, seeks to provide as much breadth and depth as possible in covering an assortment of countries around the world. In every case we strive to integrate our treatment of these countries with the conceptual and analytical frameworks we employ. Part One includes sections on a number of countries or regions with the aim of illustrating particular concepts treated in individual chapters. Part Two ("Countries and Leaders") consists of eight chapters covering ten major states: *the United Kingdom, France, Germany, Japan, Russia, China, Mexico, Brazil, Nigeria,* and *South Africa.* Each of these chapters highlights key historical events in the country under investigation and describes its political system in detail. To enliven these accounts and illustrate how personalities interact with institutions, all these chapters contain vivid biographical profiles of important political leaders. These capsule biographies provide substantial material for core courses focused on political *leadership.* The country chapters also treat some of the most controversial issues affecting political developments in these states—such as human rights, ethnic or religious conflict, and economic policy—and they invite readers to make comparisons with the ways roughly similar issues are dealt with in their own country. Although there is no chapter devoted specifically to the United States, this book makes numerous explicit comparisons between other countries and the U.S. political system with respect to political institutions and policy issues.

**Clarity and Readability** Like the first two editions, this third edition of our book seeks to unite high scholarly standards with an engaging style. This is not a dumbed-down textbook, nor is it excessively advanced for introductory students. All the contributors are accomplished scholars with a commitment to educating students. We want our readers to appreciate the relevance of concepts and ideas to the events they read about and see on television. We also want this book to be interesting, clear, and readable. The responses we have received to the first two editions have convinced us that there is a wide audience for a conceptually sophisticated introduction to comparative politics. We have worked hard to make the third edition of *Comparative Politics: A Global Introduction* even better.

## What's New?

The most challenging aspect of writing a survey of comparative politics is the volatile nature of the subject matter. Political realities are changing all the time, despite the persistence of long-term trends and tendencies. The first edition of *Comparative Politics: A Global Introduction* came out in late 2000. Less than a year later, the United States was shaken by the events of September 11, 2001—events that were to have lingering repercussions around the world. The second edition was completed in 2003, only months after the U.S.-led invasion of Iraq. These occurrences, which took place just as much of the world was getting used to the end of the Cold War and looking forward to the future with fresh optimism, inevitably gave rise to new political priorities around the globe. Among other things, they heightened the significance of the relationship between Islam and the non-Islamic world, they focused new attention on the Middle East, and they raised pressing questions about the prospects for democracy in nondemocratic countries. Inevitably, the new edition of this book reflects the salience of these and related issues. Meanwhile, academic scholarship has added new insights and ideas on just about every aspect of comparative politics. Although it is of course impossible to refer to every new development in this vast field, our global approach has required us to pay close attention to some of the most important advances in the scholarly literature.

The third edition of *Comparative Politics: A Global Introduction* updates our coverage through the end of 2006. It also includes the following new features:

- A revised presentation of the concept of democracy in chapter 7 ("Democracy: What Is It?") that graphically illustrates democracy's various components in the form of a Greek temple—the *Temple of Democracy*
- A new chapter that compares *Afghanistan* and *Iraq* to the ten conditions for democracy, thoroughly covering important historical developments in these countries as well as the main events of recent years
- New sections in Part One on *Egypt, Indonesia, Lebanon, Sudan,* and *Ukraine*
- Revised and expanded sections that deal with the *European Union, India, Iran, Israel, Pakistan, the Palestinian Authority, South Korea, Turkey,* and the former *Yugoslavia*
- New or updated conceptual material on *civil wars, failed states, globalization, human development theory, human rights, Islam, nation-building, terrorism, torture, transnational social movements, welfare states, women in politics, world values,* and other subjects

We have made a few additional changes and adjustments in Part One as well. Our analyses of the large countries covered in Part Two have also been updated to take account of the most important developments occurring up to the end of 2006.

# ACKNOWLEDGMENTS

This book is the product of many hands, and I am very grateful to a number of people whose commitment and hard work have proved invaluable.

To begin with, it is once again a privilege for me to thank the four contributors to this volume: Dean Collinwood (who wrote chapter 19, on Japan); Bruce Dickson (chapter 21, on China); Joseph Klesner (chapter 22, on Mexico and Brazil); and Timothy Sisk (chapter 23, on Nigeria and South Africa). The scholarly quality and readability of their chapters attest to their expertise and their dedication to high educational standards.

All of us are extremely thankful for our families and loved ones, and I join with the other authors in expressing our deepest appreciation for their continuing love and encouragement. On a personal note, I wish to thank my mother, Ellen DeVincentiis Sodaro, for her devotion and selflessness (and also for her sketch of the Temple of Democracy in chapter 7).

My thanks also go to the following reviewers whose critiques were very helpful in revising this third edition: Maria Hsia Chang, University of Nevada, Reno; Terry D. Clark, Creighton University; Louise K. Davidson-Schmich, University of Miami; Vilma Elisa Fuentes, Santa Fe Community College; Matthew T. Kenney, Austin Peay State University; Catherine H. Keyser, Drew University; Denise V. Powers, University of Iowa; George D. Price, Santa Fe Community College; Christoph H. Stefes, University of Colorado at Denver; and Nikolaos Zahariadis, University of Alabama at Birmingham.

The contributors and I are indebted to a number of people associated with McGraw-Hill, including Monica Eckman, Anne Fuzellier, and Melanie Field. Developmental editor Kate Scheinman deserves special kudos for her unstinting support during the long months that went into the preparation of this volume. Wendy Nelson was once again a superb manuscript editor, matching the fine quality of the work she did on the second edition.

I wish to thank the Institute for European, Russian, and Eurasian Studies at the Elliott School of International Affairs for continuing to provide me with a stimulating academic home base at the George Washington University. Thanks also to Mike Brown, the dean of the Elliott School, for supporting my work, and to my colleagues on the GW faculty for their continuing friendship and inspiration. As a result of George Washington's generosity I have been able to count on the indispensable assistance of several research assistants, including Lawrence Bryant, Sviatlana Francis, and Krista Vogt. Alex Wilson also provided important assistance, especially during the 2005 British elections. My gratitude extends as well to a number of friends and colleagues who provided advice, research material, or other timely help, above all Heinrich Bortfeldt, Susan Fridy, Shoshana and Brian Foster, and Ann Rogers. And my heart goes out to more than ten thousand students who have taken my introductory course on comparative politics at George Washington since I began teaching it in 1978. This book is for them and for those incoming students I hope to have the privilege to teach in the years ahead.

The contributors and I together dedicate this book to you, our students. As eternally youthful sources of information, advice, inspiration, amusement, and—occasionally—consternation, you keep us young (by our own standards, at least) and you keep us going. You will inherit the prospects and problems we lay out in this book, and we thank you for inspiring us to share with you our hopes, our concerns, and our love of the world.

Michael J. Sodaro

PART ONE

# CONCEPTS AND CRITICAL THINKING

CHAPTER 1

# COMPARATIVE POLITICS: WHAT IS IT? WHY STUDY IT?

Since the early 1990s, an international team of archeologists has been carefully excavating Patara, an ancient town on the Mediterranean coast of what is now Turkey. Among the treasures they have unearthed are the remains of a building that once housed the world's first representative parliament. In its heyday, Patara was the center of the Lycian League, a group of more than twenty Greek city-states that together formed history's first federated government more than two thousand years ago. Each city-state, in proportion to its size, sent one or more delegates to a federal assembly to elect the federation's principal leader and other officials. The representatives deliberated on common problems and made decisions on such vital matters as war and peace on the basis of democratic voting procedures.

After the Lycian League fell apart and the sands of time settled over its monuments, it took more than a thousand years for representative parliaments and elected governments to take firm root once again, first in England and then in America. Democracy is difficult. Throughout history, it has been conspicuous around the world mainly by its absence. Until the post–World War II period, democratic forms of government were more prone to failure than to long-term success. Nevertheless, the Lycian League's parliament building and the ideas that emanated from it were destined to have an influence that spanned the centuries. James Madison and Alexander Hamilton referred to the League in *The Federalist*, the publication that laid the intellectual groundwork for the federal form of government that was later established under the U.S. Constitution. The Lycian parliament's semicircular rows of seats served as a model for the Capitol building in Washington, D.C., home of the U.S. Congress. More broadly, the Lycian League's guiding premise that political issues should be addressed on the basis of fair representation and democratic voting processes set an early precedent for the more elaborate representative democracies of the future. As Mark Twain put it, "The ancients stole our best ideas."[1]

While work continued on the dig in Patara in the first years of the new millennium, another attempt at building a representative governmental system was taking place only a few hundred miles away, in Iraq. In March 2003, American and British forces spearheaded an invasion that quickly toppled Saddam Hussein, the dictator who had ruled Iraq with an iron fist for decades. Although President George W. Bush and Prime Minister Tony Blair argued that the invasion was necessary in order to

**Afghanistan's President Hamid Karzai**

locate and destroy the chemical and biological weapons of mass destruction that they believed Saddam's government possessed, they made it abundantly clear that an ulterior aim of the incursion was "regime change": the deliberate attempt to replace dictatorial rule in Iraq once and for all with democracy. Months of careful searching uncovered no weapons of mass destruction. But the work of creating a democracy was still going on, with alternating successes and setbacks, as these pages went to press in the final months of 2006. The process was marked by elections and car-bombings, coalition building and sectarian violence, Iraqi self-assertion and foreign occupation.

Half a world away, another attempt to establish democracy on the ruins of a toppled dictatorship was under way in Afghanistan. Like Iraq, Afghanistan initiated its rapid push for democracy after its dictatorial regime was destroyed by an American-led military assault. In October 2001, scarcely two months after the September 11 terrorist attacks on the World Trade Center buildings and the Pentagon that shocked the world, the United States and several of its key allies unleashed a massive aerial bombardment campaign against Afghanistan's government, which was under the control of a militant Islamic organization known as the Taliban. The Taliban government, for its part, was heavily financed and supported by al Qaeda, the international terrorist movement headed by Osama bin Laden. With the Taliban's encouragement, bin Laden had turned Afghanistan into al Qaeda's principal headquarters, complete with training camps for Islamic terrorists from all over the world. The nineteen terrorists who perpetrated the September 11 attacks in the United States all worked with al Qaeda, whose leaders had planned and organized the operation. Thus the U.S.-led offensive in Afghanistan was simultaneously a strike against the Taliban and a strike against al Qaeda.

Buttressed by Western troops on the ground and by Afghan militias opposed to Taliban rule, the bombing missions drove the Taliban from power in December 2001. As bin Laden fled for his life and al Qaeda's main operations in the country were shut down, an international conference established a provisional Afghan government dedicated to laying the foundations of democracy in a country that had never before established truly democratic institutions. As in Iraq, the task of creating democracy under difficult conditions is still proceeding in Afghanistan by fits and starts, punctuated by singular achievements and ominous failings.

To be sure, Iraq and Afghanistan are very different from each other, and very different as well from most other countries around the world. Moreover, the circumstances surrounding their attempts to build democracy—including military intervention from abroad and the absence of a strong pro-democracy movement at home—were really quite unusual. Nevertheless, some of the challenges that these two countries are encountering are very similar to those facing many other populations today as they confront the choice between democracy and dictatorship. From Latin America to the Middle East, from Eurasia to Africa, and from South Asia to the Far East, in the past two decades dozens of countries have been making the transition from nondemocratic regimes to democratic governments. One prominent scholar, Samuel Huntington, has characterized this ongoing process as history's "third wave" of democratization.[2] The first wave occurred in the period extending from the 1820s to the 1920s, when democracy emerged or matured in about thirty countries. The second wave began during World War II and lasted until the early 1960s. The current wave has its roots in democratic movements that gathered force in southern Europe (specifically, in Greece, Portugal, and Spain) and in Latin America in the 1970s and 1980s. The collapse of communism in the Soviet Union and East Central Europe in the early 1990s added a powerful impetus to the third wave's forward progress, engulfing much of the globe in a spirit of optimism about the prospects for worldwide democracy and lasting peace. At the time, some observers regarded the advance of human rights and democratic government as virtually unstoppable. Others, however, cautioned that democracy's triumph was by no means inevitable. Huntington himself noted that the first two waves of democratization had been followed in some countries by "reverse waves" in the direction of dictatorship. Another scholar warned that "movements of rage" might rear up in an uncertain future.[3]

In fact, the triumph of democracy in recent years has been far from universal. Dictatorships of various kinds remain well entrenched, and democracy's foes are openly active. For one thing, Islamic fundamentalism—and the terrorism it sometimes spawns—pose serious threats to democracy's ideals. In addition, some countries have been rendered ungovernable by civil war, pervasive corruption, or other forms of internal decay. Others have little control over their own destinies because of outside interference. Both Iraq and Afghanistan have been affected by several of these antidemocratic tendencies, including terrorism, violent religious or ethnic rivalries, and a continuing dependence on foreign troops.

The experiences of Iraq, Afghanistan, and other countries that are currently making efforts to establish democracy—efforts that may perhaps fail to produce lasting democracy—inevitably capture our interest as students of world affairs. To understand these transitional processes, we need to raise our sights above a few specific cases and look at broader issues that concern the concept of democracy itself and the numerous ways democracy has developed, or failed to develop, in a variety of countries and historical contexts. Viewed from this wider perspective, the struggles taking place on the proving grounds of democracy today raise a number of questions that are central to the study of comparative politics. For example:

- What is democracy? How do we know it when we see it? What are its defining principles and features? Chapter 7 describes democracy as consisting of three central components: *popular sovereignty*, or the notion that government must emanate from the people and remain effectively accountable to them; guaranteed *civil rights and liberties*; and the *economic well-being* of the population. These three components are all based on fundamental democratic *values* (such as freedom, tolerance, and equality) and on the principle of *the rule of law*. One implication of this multifaceted definition is that *elections alone are not sufficient to constitute a democracy*. There are many dictatorial governments in today's world that keep a grip on power while staging manipulated or fraudulent elections, denying fundamental civil rights and freedoms, and violating or ignoring other democratic precepts.
- What are the various forms that democracy can take? Chapter 8 delineates the main ways that democracies tend to organize their institutions: *presidentialism* (as in the United States); *parliamentary government* (as in Britain); and the mixed *presidential-parliamentary* system (as in France). Each of these approaches has numerous variants, as we shall see. And each of them has its own advantages and disadvantages.
- Are there certain basic conditions that a country must fulfill for democracy to develop and prosper there? Are some countries simply *not ready* for democracy? Chapter 9 lists ten factors that are especially important in raising the chances for democracy's success.
- Are there any observable patterns in the ways democracies get established? Developments in Iraq, Afghanistan, and other countries suggest that before democratic institutions and practices can work effectively, at the very least the country's key leaders must agree that they accept the fundamental values of democracy and must seek to maximize cooperation in their political interactions. In most instances these leaders will represent the country's principal ethnic and religious groups and socioeconomic classes; its chief political parties and other political associations

(if they exist); the military; and perhaps other groups as well. This *democratic bargain* among society's leading elements—its so-called political elites—necessitates above all a willingness to share power fairly and deal with conflicts peacefully on the basis of agreed-upon decision-making procedures, enforceable laws, mutual respect, and compromise. Without this "agreement to govern by agreement"—as opposed to intransigence, intimidation, and violence—such things as elections, constitutions, and other essentials of democracy may prove meaningless. How do democracies-in-the-making go about addressing these and other challenges they encounter in the very first stages of creating a democracy?

- To what extent do democracies live up to their proclaimed ideals, and to what extent do they violate or ignore them, whether inadvertently or hypocritically? Is there such a thing as *partial* democracy? Can a country have a mixture of democratic and nondemocratic institutions and practices?
- Is democracy essentially a Western concept, one that is ill-suited to countries with other cultures and other historical traditions? Or does it really have universal appeal and global applicability?
- Why did it take so long for Britain and the United States, the contemporary world's oldest surviving democracies, to move from the earliest phases of democratic development—characterized by very limited voting rights and accompanied by slavery, discrimination, and other distortions of democratic principles—to the full-blown mass democracies they became in the twentieth century? What are the implications of such a lengthy evolution for countries that have just recently embarked on the path of democracy?
- Why do many countries that manage to establish functioning democracies fail to keep them, reverting to some form of nondemocratic rule? Argentina, Brazil, Chile, France, Germany, Italy, Lebanon, Nigeria, Pakistan, South Korea, and Spain, to name just a few, all tried democracy and failed at certain points in their history. Some of them were subsequently able to create a successful democracy on the second or third try; others still have nondemocratic, or only partially democratic, regimes. Is it possible that democracy cannot succeed over the long run unless it collapses at least once, and sometimes more than once, forcing a country's leaders and population to learn from their mistakes?
- Why is it that some countries with long records as centrally governed states have come to democracy either very late in their history or not at all? Japan, Russia, and China, for example, have governmental traditions that stretch back a thousand years or more. Yet Japan did not develop a democracy until after its defeat in World War II, Russia did not start democratizing until the early 1990s, and China is still governed dictatorially by the Communist Party.
- Can democracy be imposed on a country by outsiders, or must it have homegrown roots in order to emerge?
- For democracy to succeed, *people must want it.* What happens when large numbers of people—perhaps a majority—simply do not want democracy as we know it? What happens when deeply cherished religious beliefs, male-dominant gender roles, or the power enjoyed by a particular social or political group over other groups in society make nondemocratic government more popular, or at least more acceptable, than democracy for significant segments of the population? What happens if a strong dictator is genuinely admired? Does democracy have a chance under these circumstances? Should democratic countries actively seek to promote democracy in such places, or should they back off?
- What happens if people take advantage of free elections, press freedoms, and other democratic opportunities in order to promote nondemocratic causes or the destruction of democracy? A famous example occurred in Germany, when more than half the voters in 1932 voted for either Adolph Hitler's Nazi Party or the German Communist Party, the two most outspokenly antidemocratic parties in the country. Hitler took power the following year and quickly abolished democracy. In today's world, this question has immediate relevance in places where Islamic militants and other groups hostile to democracy have shown that they can win seats in legislatures and perhaps win election to governing power. Should democratic countries promote democracy in such conditions? Or should they let the existing dictatorships stay in power,

especially if they are friendly—as allies in the war on terrorism, for instance, or providers of desirable resources like oil?

- More broadly, what are some of the root causes of nondemocratic government? Why have monarchies, fascist regimes, communist governments, military dictatorships, and other forms of dictatorial rule remained in power, at times for decades?
- Will a democratic world necessarily be a more peaceful world? Or will the spread of democracy perhaps open the floodgates in some places to mass-supported religious or racial intolerance, to unrestrained greed, or to hatreds and resentments that make war, civil strife, and even terrorism *more* likely rather than less?
- How do *political* factors affect a country's ability to develop its economy, improve its population's health and education, and safeguard the Earth's delicate environment? Do democracies accomplish these tasks more successfully than nondemocracies?
- Finally, is there an overall trend in the direction of democracy in the world we live in? Or will some democracies flourish while others disintegrate, leaving behind only the remnants of once-proud structures for future excavators to pick over?

These and a host of related questions make front-page news almost every day and command the attention of government officials, political activists, and average citizens in virtually every country on our planet. They assume life-and-death importance for millions of people caught up in the turmoil of political conflict. Of course, we cannot answer all these questions in this book. It is far more important that you think about your own answers. The world needs people of goodwill who are capable of making independent judgments on the basis of a wide knowledge of global realities and an ability to think clearly and logically. That is why the study of comparative politics is more necessary and challenging than ever. What, then, is comparative politics all about?

> **Comparative politics** ***examines political realities in countries all over the world. It looks at the many ways governments operate and the ways people behave in political life.***

**Toppling of Saddam Hussein Statue on April 9, 2003**

The importance of *government* as a primary topic of comparative politics is self-evident. Governments around the globe play a central role in virtually every field of human endeavor, from science and the economy to public health and the environment. It is governments that make war or negotiate peace, fight crime or breed corruption, grant human rights or stifle opposing voices. The numerous ways governments are constituted, and the wide variety of their procedures and operations, occupy a prominent place in the study of comparative politics. Similarly, the individuals who assume leadership roles in governmental affairs also deserve careful attention. What kinds of men and women seek political power? How do they act once they have risen to peak positions of governmental authority? What policies do they choose, and how do they go about implementing them? Policy orientations, leadership styles, and other attributes of these *political elites* are also vital components of comparative politics. *It matters who governs!*

But if governments and political leaders are important, so are the people they govern. Comparative politics looks at far more than just the activities of governments and political elites. It also pays close attention to the ways ordinary people behave in their interactions with governments and in other aspects of political life. People can hold their leaders accountable for their actions or—whether willingly or unwillingly—they can endure the most extreme forms of tyranny. They can participate in political life by voting regularly and joining organizations, or they can withdraw into apathy. They can cooperate with one another for mutual benefit, or they can hunker down into uncompromising confrontation. They can support their constitution, thumb their nose at the law, or rise up in revolution. What accounts for these behaviors? Comparative politics is very interested in "people politics."

Given this wide range of topics, comparative politics examines such specific things as the following:

- How governments are structured and how they function, including different forms of democracy and various forms of nondemocratic government. This area of inquiry focuses mainly on *governmental institutions.*
- How governments interact with their populations in pursuing community goals (such as improving health care, reducing unemployment, and so on) and in dealing with conflicts that arise over a variety of political, economic, and social issues. Here the emphasis is on *public policy,* such as health policy, economic policy, and the like.
- How political leaders and the population behave in politics, including the ideas they have about politics and the ways they participate in political life through such mechanisms as elections, parties, interest groups, and other modes of political activity. The focus here is on *elite and mass political behavior* and includes such things as *political ideologies* and *political participation.*
- How political leaders and the mass public think and feel about politics, and how these attitudes affect their behavior. This topic is known as *political culture.*

## A GLOBAL INTRODUCTION

True to its subtitle, this book is introductory in nature. It assumes you have little or no background in studying the politics of different countries on a systematic basis. Our approach is "global" in three senses of the term: (1) it provides *broad coverage of countries around the world,* (2) it offers *conceptual comprehensiveness,* and (3) it promotes *critical thinking.*

### Countries

In the most literal sense, this book is global in its coverage of a representative selection of countries spread across all the world's geographic regions. Chapters 16 through 23 are devoted to specific countries. In addition, chapters 1 through 15 present a considerable amount of information about other states not covered in subsequent chapters—Afghanistan, Egypt, India, Indonesia, Iran, Iraq, Pakistan, and Turkey, among others—for the purpose of illustrating various concepts in comparative politics. Though there is no chapter devoted specifically to the United States, there are numerous references to it throughout the book for comparative purposes.

We also provide biographical *profiles of world leaders.* Portraits of leaders can tell us a great deal not only about political developments in their respective countries but also about the nature of political leadership.

### Concepts

This book is also global in its comprehensive *conceptual* treatment of the field of comparative politics. In order to understand political life in the United States, Japan, or any other country, we must not only examine relevant facts concerning the country's history, political institutions, public opinion, and other essential features of its political system; we must also pay close attention to the ways *general political processes and concepts* apply to them. For example, in order to understand the way democracy works in specific countries like Israel, France, or South Africa, we need to know something about democracy in general. What is it? How does it come about? These and other questions we raised at the start of this chapter address some critical aspects of democracy in general terms. Whether the topic is democracy or some other feature of political reality, *comparative politics almost always involves the interaction of the specific and the general.*

There are numerous additional concepts and categories of political phenomena that must also be examined if we want to get a good grasp of political reality around the world. Accordingly, chapters 4 through 15 are specifically designed to introduce you to some of the main concepts in comparative politics. They include such things as *power, the state, nationalism, ideology, political culture,* and *political economy.* These chapters provide material drawn from a vast array of countries as well as from a broad sampling of scholarly literature produced by some of the top specialists in comparative politics. They also present some of the core ideas of prominent political thinkers whose theories have helped shape political history and the ways we think about politics. In sum, our approach is not confined to giving you just "a bunch of facts" about individual countries. It actively seeks to deepen your understanding of politics in general.

## Critical Thinking

The third sense in which this text is global relates to critical thinking. Relevant facts and key concepts are necessary, but to appreciate the complexities of political reality more fully, we need to know *how to think* about politics and *how to analyze* it in a logical and systematic manner.

Comparative politics is a subfield of political science. Students often ask, "Is political science *really* a science?" The answer to this question obviously requires an understanding of what science is. While the term *science* may conjure up images of people in lab coats measuring chemicals or observing mice, in fact science is primarily a system of logic. *Science is a set of rules and methods for investigating reality logically and systematically.* Political science is therefore a science to the extent that it observes the cardinal rules of scientific logic. To be more specific, political science is "scientific" when it engages in the following operations: *definition, description, explanation, prediction,* and *prescription.*

**Definition** Any science must define its terms as precisely as possible, and political science is no different. Definitional clarity is especially necessary in politics because terms like *democracy, socialism, liberalism,* and other commonly used political concepts often have more than one meaning and are frequently misused or misunderstood. We therefore need precise and consistent definitions of political terms as well as a subtle appreciation of their variations and shades of meaning in particular contexts.

**Description** Like physicists and biologists, political scientists need to describe the phenomena they are examining as accurately as possible. How does the U.S. system of checks and balances among the three branches of government actually work? How is the British parliamentary system organized? How can we categorize various types of democracy and nondemocratic regimes? These and other political phenomena need to be described carefully so that we can understand them clearly.

**Explanation** *Why* do things happen the way they do? Why, for example, does democracy succeed in some countries but not in others? Why did the Communist Party dictatorship collapse in the Soviet Union but not in China? The list of political phenomena begging for explanation is practically endless.

In an effort to explain the things they find intriguing, scientists frequently make *generalizations* about the phenomena they seek to understand. Very often these generalizations are expressed as *theories* or *hypotheses* that posit a *cause-and-effect relationship* between things. Political scientists formulate generalizations that seek to address the causes of democracy, war, voter turnout, fascism, and other political realities. And like natural scientists, political scientists are frequently engaged in *testing* their generalizations against the hard facts of reality to determine whether they are true or false, or whether perhaps they are true under some conditions but not in others.

> *Hypothesis testing* is a central activity of political science. One of the main aims of this book is to teach you to think about politics in terms of hypotheses that can be tested against relevant evidence.

**Prediction** Political scientists have a spotty record when it comes to predicting the future. Today's highly sophisticated statistical models can sometimes forecast election results with impressive accuracy—but not always. Most statistical models predicted that Al Gore would win the 2000 presidential election. The realities of human behavior and political life are so variegated that we have very little ability to foretell what will happen in any particular country over the near term, let alone the long term. The world is full of surprises. Nevertheless, we can observe *trends* and *patterns* in various aspects of political life. Sometimes we can extrapolate from these observable trends and suggest, however tentatively, what broad tendencies are *possible,* or even *probable,* assuming that certain conditions hold.

While we cannot say with certainty that democracy is bound to succeed or doomed to fail in Iraq or Russia or somewhere else, we can at least specify the factors that may make democracy's success or failure more probable. In other words, prediction in political science is *probabilistic* in nature. It can sketch out alternative possibilities and probabilities, while modestly desisting from claims to foolproof reliability.

**Prescription** Doctors can prescribe medicines on the basis of the findings of research biologists and pharmacologists. Can political science prescribe remedies to the political problems besetting the nations of the world?

Yes and no. In some instances we can provide recommendations that, if followed, may increase the probability that a desirable outcome will ensue at some indeterminate point in time. We can prescribe, for example, a set of actions that need to be taken in order to establish a democracy and enhance its prospects for success. We can urge the adoption of a body of laws ensuring fair elections, civil rights, an independent judiciary, and so forth. But no political advisor can compel any country to take her advice, and no one can guarantee that, even if all the prescribed steps are followed, democracy will inevitably succeed. The particularities of each individual country and the unforeseeability of future events may dash even the most determined efforts to make democracy work. Still, our prescriptions for democracy can at least increase the *chances* that democracy will succeed.

Many readers of this book may be drawn to the study of politics in order to have an impact on the real world. Whether you seek to embark on a political career, to be an activist in a political cause, or simply to become a better informed citizen, a scientific approach to politics can help you formulate your own ideas and better assess the recommendations offered by politicians, government officials, and others engaged in political action and debate. *Sound government policies rest on sound analysis.* A scientific approach to politics contributes to intelligent policy prescription.

Thus the analytical aspect of this book is designed to teach you how political scientists think when they study comparative politics in accordance with scientific rules and methods. In the process, this book explicitly seeks to *improve your own critical-thinking skills.* The value of taking a scientific approach to the study of politics extends well beyond the field of political science. The ability to think logically and coherently is a vitally necessary skill in a large number of academic disciplines and non-academic careers. It deserves the highest priority in your education. The analytical techniques employed in this volume, while rudimentary, can be applied across a wide spectrum of intellectual and professional endeavors. In helping you understand the world of politics, this book enhances your general education by helping you think more sharply and effectively. It also seeks to help you make up your own mind about some of the world's most pressing issues. Learning *how* to think will help you figure out *what* to think.

The scientific approach to comparative politics is spelled out in chapter 3. In addition, every subsequent chapter contains at least one *hypothesis-testing exercise* designed to bolster your comprehension of how scientific analysis can be applied to the study of politics.

## COMPARATIVE POLITICS AND INTERNATIONAL POLITICS

Political scientists make a basic distinction between two areas of inquiry: *comparative politics* and *international politics.*

*Comparative politics* examines political activities *within* individual countries. It looks at politics inside, say, the United States, Russia, Japan, Mexico, or South Africa. It then compares the domestic experiences of particular countries with the domestic experiences of others. The focus is on each country's *internal* politics, with a view to making generalizations about politics in a variety of domestic settings. For example, we can compare various democracies with one another to learn more about democracy. We can also compare various nondemocratic governments to learn more about how they work, such as communist countries or military dictatorships.

**International politics**, by contrast, ***concerns relations* between *countries*.** Here the focus is on the *external* relationships of individual countries. Diplomacy, international law, international economic relations, war, and peacemaking are among the chief topics studied by political scientists concerned with international affairs. Their task is to look at relationships between, say, the United States and Russia, Israel and Egypt, and so on. Such investigations explain how these relationships work and provide us with a more theoretical understanding of international politics in general.

The dividing line between comparative and international politics is razor thin, however, and it's getting thinner all the time. Domestic and international politics are increasingly intertwined within virtually every country in the world today. We cannot really understand the domestic politics of most nations without some reference to their international relationships. What goes on internally is often affected by events occurring externally, beyond the country's borders. Conversely, we cannot fully comprehend international affairs without a good look inside the domestic political systems of individual countries. The actions of individual governments frequently have a powerful impact on other countries or on the world as a whole. Somewhat like biology and chemistry, comparative politics and international politics are complementary: though they are separate fields of analysis, they are intimately interrelated. The politics of energy relationships provides vivid examples of some of the ways international and domestic factors intersect.

## ENERGY AND POLITICS

The world's hunger for energy resources like oil and natural gas is insatiable. These assets are finite in quantity, and the fact that only a few countries have abundant supplies of petroleum or gas makes for very close interdependencies between the resource-rich suppliers and the countries that must import their energy supplies. Some countries have very limited energy sources of their own, or none at all, and they must import most or all of the energy they consume. Others—like the United States—have their own energy sources, but not enough to satisfy domestic demand; they must import whatever additional energy they need. (The United States imported 58 percent of its petroleum in 2005; its two main suppliers were Canada and Mexico.) The imbalance between the energy-exporting countries and energy-importing countries can sometimes lead to sharp political frictions. In some cases, oil-exporting countries can exert external influences on the internal economic, and sometimes political, conditions of oil-importing countries. The relationship between Russia and Ukraine provides an example.

### Russia and Ukraine

When the Soviet Union—known more formally as the Union of Soviet Socialist Republics (the USSR)—disintegrated at the end of 1991, Russia and the other fourteen "union republics" that constituted the USSR became independent countries. The second-largest of these constituent republics after Russia was Ukraine, a largely Slavic country with a thousand-year history of interaction with the Russians marked by close cooperation as well as intense conflict. After Ukraine became independent, it began the difficult transition from a communist dictatorship to a new democracy, but corruption and abuses of power became commonplace. When Leonid Kuchma was reelected Ukraine's president in 1999, his campaign was marred by a number of illegal machinations. Subsequently President Kuchma was caught on tape ordering the murder of a prominent pro-democracy journalist who was critical of his administration. By the time the 2004 elections rolled around, many Ukrainians were eager for change.

Because Kuchma was barred by the constitution from seeking a third term, one of his cronies, Viktor Yanukovich (yah-noo-KOH-vihch), ran in his place. Yanukovich's chief opponent was Viktor Yushchenko (YOOSH-chehn-kaw), a vocal proponent of democratic accountability and the rule of law. As polls showed rising support for Yushchenko, the Kuchma-Yanukovich team pulled out all the stops to block their opponent's election. In one of several assassination attempts, state security agents peppered Yushchenko with dioxin, a poison that almost killed the candidate and permanently disfigured his face. The incident infuriated Yushchenko's supporters, and the crowds that thronged his campaign stops grew larger.

Interest in the election was by no means limited to Ukrainians. With democracy on the line in Ukraine, the United States and the European Union (EU) denounced the Kuchma government's attempts to harass Yushchenko. The United States was incensed at Kuchma, not only because of his assassination schemes, but also because he had sold military equipment to

**Yushchenko supporters demonstrate during Ukraine's "Orange Revolution" of 2004.**

Saddam Hussein. The EU had its own stake in Ukraine. It had recently expanded its membership from 15 West European countries to 25 countries that included eight former communist states in Central and Eastern Europe. Many Europeans regarded Ukraine as a potential EU member, but only if its government were solidly democratic. For its part, Russia's government under President Vladimir Putin openly sided with the Kuchma-Yanukovich forces. Putin was determined to retain Russia's traditional influence in Ukraine, if not through outright subjugation as in the past, then at least by making sure that Ukraine was governed by leaders who regarded Russia as their country's principal partner and took Russia's interests into account.

When the state electoral commission announced preliminary results showing that the Russian-backed Yanukovich had defeated the pro-Western Yushchenko in a head-to-head runoff election by barely 3 percent, an uproar followed. Yushchenko's supporters found indisputable evidence of fraudulent vote counts, along with incriminating tapes proving a government conspiracy to misrepresent the actual vote. Millions of Ukrainians staged daily demonstrations and demanded a fair recount or new elections. Many waved flags and banners in bright orange, the official color of the Yushchenko campaign. The "Orange Revolution" was under way.

The enormous popular upheaval in Yushchenko's favor could not be denied: Ukraine's Supreme Court invalidated the election results and mandated a new runoff contest. Money and campaign advice from American and EU sources poured into Yushchenko's campaign, while Russia provided assistance to the Kuchma-Yanukovich camp—each side providing graphic examples of external influences on Ukraine's internal politics. On December 26, Yushchenko defeated Yanukovich by winning 51.99 percent of the vote. The Orange Revolution had triumphed.

President Putin's disappointment at Yushchenko's victory did not die down easily. In early 2006, less than three months before crucial parliamentary elections in Ukraine, Putin's government announced that it was raising Ukraine's gas bill by 400 percent. Russia increased the pressure by cutting back gas deliveries to

Ukraine, and to European countries as well, at the height of a frigid winter. (Russia supplied 30 percent of Ukraine's natural gas, and about one-fourth of Europe's supply.) Concerned about Russia's use of energy as a political weapon, European governments convinced Putin to back down: he resumed gas exports and cut a deal with Ukraine limiting the price increase to 90 percent. But the agreement obliged the Ukrainian government to purchase the gas through a Swiss company rumored to be under the control of corrupt Russian business magnates and crime figures. In the end, it appeared that President Putin had succeeded in heightening Ukraine's vulnerability to Russian energy pressures.

Now let's take a look at external–internal relationships from another vantage point: How can *internal* conditions within energy-exporting countries have *external* effects on importing countries?

As anyone who drives a car or pays for home heating fuel knows, the prices for these indispensable products have risen appreciably in recent years. At the start of 1999, the world market price for crude oil was only slightly higher than $10 per barrel. In 2006 it frequently exceeded $70 a barrel, approaching $80 during the conflagration involving Israel and Lebanon. The price of home heating oil in the United States jumped from a national average of $1.13 per gallon in 2002 to $2.33 per gallon by the end of 2005, with still higher prices to follow.[4] To some extent, these price hikes are attributable to rising energy demands in the world's two largest countries, China and India, whose hot economies require ever-increasing fuel imports from abroad. As world demand for energy goes up, oil companies—whether government owned or privately owned—can get away with charging higher prices. But energy price increases also depend in part on fears about the reliability of supplies in countries that are, or could become, politically unstable. Some of the main oil-exporting countries in the world with a potential for instability include Algeria, Iran, Iraq, Kuwait, Nigeria, Saudi Arabia, the United Arab Emirates, and Venezuela (see table 1.1). Who governs these countries, and how reliable are their energy supplies?

**TABLE 1.1**

**The Top 11 Petroleum-Exporting Countries**

| Country | Oil Exports (million barrels per day, 2004) | Share (%) of Total U.S. Oil Imports, 2005[a] |
|---|---|---|
| Saudi Arabia | 8.73 | 11.3 |
| Russia | 6.67 | 3.0 |
| Norway | 2.91 | 2.0 |
| Iran | 2.55 | 0.0 |
| Venezuela | 2.36 | 11.1 |
| United Arab Emirates | 2.33 | 0.1 |
| Kuwait | 2.20 | 1.7 |
| Nigeria | 2.19 | 8.5 |
| Mexico | 1.80 | 12.2 |
| Algeria | 1.68 | 3.5 |
| Iraq | 1.48 | 3.9 |

[a]Canada supplied 16.1 percent of U.S. oil imports in 2005.
*Source:* Energy Information Administration, U.S. Department of Energy, www.eia.doe.gov.

## Algeria

After more than 130 years as a French colony, Algeria achieved its independence in 1962. Since then it has been governed mainly by a succession of military leaders and military-backed civilian dictators. Most of them have had little interest in democracy. Elections to the presidency and legislature have tended to be manipulated by the main ruling party. By the late 1980s, as the government began to permit a bit more democracy, the chief opposition to the ruling clique was a collection of Islamic groups organized as the Islamic Salvation Front. Some of these Islamic groups were relatively moderate, but others were more extreme in their assertion of fundamentalist Islamic doctrines at variance with democratic freedoms and practices. In the first round of parliamentary elections held in 1991, the Islamic Salvation Front won 188 seats in the national legislature and appeared poised to win a commanding two-thirds majority of seats in the second round. Rather than allow this Islamic victory, the military staged a coup at the start of 1992 and canceled the second round of voting. Islamic groups then went on the offensive, and a bloody civil war ensued. It is estimated that, over the course of the next ten years or so, about 150,000 Algerians were killed as the more extreme Islamic elements engaged in wholesale massacres and urban terrorism, while militias loyal to the government went on killing sprees against the oppositionists. In 1999, Abdelaziz Bouteflika (boo-tah-FLEE-kah), a former foreign minister with close ties to the military, won the presidency in an election marred by fraud and the withdrawal of the leading challengers. Bouteflika immediately sought to calm the country through a "civil harmony" law granting amnesty to Islamic fighters who were willing to reject violence. The civil war gradually abated, though sporadic outbursts of fighting killed thousands during the next several years. In 2004, Bouteflika was returned to power in an election deemed relatively clean by official international observers. His government announced a new amnesty program for Islamic militants in 2006. Algeria was now more peaceful than it had been in many years, and oil exports to the United States and other countries increased significantly after 2000. But widespread unemployment and other problems persisted, nurturing opposition to the governing elite that could ignite more instability in the future. And with about 700 armed Islamic extremists still at large, a new eruption of violence could jeopardize Algeria's reliability as one of the world's leading oil suppliers.

### Iran

When Iran's democratically elected prime minister engineered the government's takeover of a largely British-owned oil company in the 1950s, Britain and the United States forcibly removed him from power and replaced him with the shah, who was the son of the country's former ruler. The shah established a powerful dictatorship, but a succession of U.S. presidents nevertheless supported him as a key ally in the oil-rich Persian Gulf region. The United States continued to support the shah until a revolution led by the Islamic cleric Ayatollah Khomeini (ho-may-NEE) toppled him in 1979. From the start, Iran's Islamic Republic was militantly anti-American—and anti-Western—and it has remained so. The United States no longer imports oil from that country. In recent years, the Iranian government's attempt to build nuclear weapons has seriously aggravated its relations with the United States and Europe. While the Western allies sought to block Iran's nuclear bid through diplomacy and the prospect of economic sanctions, hints of possible U.S. military action against Iran provoked defiant responses from Iran's leaders, including threats of raising oil prices still higher or cutting back exports to Europe. When Iran test-fired a missile in the spring of 2006, the price of oil futures on world markets jumped $2 a barrel. Iran's support for Hezbollah, the militant Islamic group that launched rockets at Israel from Lebanon in 2006, contributed to raising oil prices even higher. Iran has the second-largest share of the world's total known petroleum reserves (11.1 percent of the total in 2004), and concerns about the availability of oil from Iran's largely isolated Islamic government inevitably have a chilling effect on the global petroleum market.

### Iraq

When Saddam Hussein ordered his forces to invade Kuwait in 1990, one of his principal motives was to gain control over Kuwait's valuable oil fields. The United States and its main allies condemned the unprovoked attack as a brazen violation of international law. They feared that if Saddam were allowed to get away with this move, he might be tempted to invade Saudi Arabia next. Iraq has 9.7 percent of the world's total known petroleum reserves, the third-largest share in the world. Control over Kuwait (which has 8.3 percent of the world's proven oil reserves) and Saudi Arabia (22.1 percent) would have made Saddam the proprietor of 40 percent of the world's oil reserves, allowing him to virtually dictate international oil prices. The Western allies—and other countries as well—regarded such a prospect as unacceptable; together they formed an anti-Iraq coalition consisting of more than thirty countries. Coalition forces ejected Iraqi troops from Kuwait in 1991. Subsequently, an "oil for food" program was established under the United Nations that allowed Saddam's government to sell oil on world markets, while requiring it to use most of the proceeds to feed the Iraqi population and take care of its health needs and other vital requirements. The UN program was riddled with corruption, however, as detailed by an official investigation panel.[5]

Some critics of the 2003 U.S.-led invasion of Iraq have charged that the Bush administration's primary aim all along was to gain control of Iraq's oil wealth. Whether or not this claim was true, it cannot be doubted that Iraq's oil will play a vital role not only inside Iraq but around the world as well. Proceeds from oil revenues can help pay for the country's post-invasion rebuilding and modernization. And a reliable flow of oil from Iraq at reasonable prices may have a stabilizing effect on world prices. Since the invasion, antiquated oilfield equipment and periodic attacks on pipelines by anti-American insurgents have made Iraq's oil exports fall below their 2003 level, resulting in a shortfall of 2 to 5 million barrels of oil a day. Whatever the future may bring, whoever controls Iraq's government is bound to have a palpable effect on the international energy market.

### Kuwait

Since the Persian Gulf War of 1990–91, Kuwait's leaders have drawn closer to the United States. In 2003 they permitted U.S. forces to base most of their contingents on Kuwaiti territory prior to the invasion of Iraq. Since 1992, Kuwait's monarchical government under the Al-Sabah family has allowed the national parliament to play a role in overruling some of the decisions taken by the royal family, and the leadership has recently granted women full voting rights and other civil rights. To date, the government's pro-Western orientation and its ability to export large quantities of oil have made it a reliable source of energy in the global marketplace. Even so, its precarious location makes its long-term outlook dependent to some extent on what happens in Iraq.

### Nigeria

A British colony from the nineteenth century until 1960, Nigeria has only recently returned to the path of democracy after more than thirty years of military dictatorship. From the mid-1960s until 1999, military rulers were responsible for massive corruption and government inefficiency, squandering an estimated $280 billion in oil revenues. The election of General Olusegun Obasanjo (o-BAH-san-jo) as president in 1999 opened the way to the restoration of democracy. Despite his avowed commitment to the rule of law and political equality, Obasanjo had a difficult time establishing democratic practices in a country seething with ethnic and religious conflict and suffering from endemic poverty. Long-standing animosities between Muslims and Christians periodically exploded into violence, and the acute maldistribution of Nigeria's national income (including its oil revenues) among its various regions and its 250 ethnolinguistic groups exacerbated socioeconomic disparities.

Not long after assuming power, Obasanjo's government announced the elimination of state subsidies for domestically consumed fuel. The subsidies had kept energy prices relatively low for Nigerian citizens, but they contributed to the government's budget deficits. The removal of the subsidies sparked nationwide strikes and protests. In 2003 violence escalated in the oil-rich Niger Delta, where an ethnically based militia warned that it would kill foreign oil workers in the region if its demands for local self-rule and a greater share of oil income were not given to its core ethnic group. The turbulence resulted in a 40 percent reduction in oil production in the region. In 2006 the Movement for the Emancipation of the Niger Delta (MEND) kidnapped foreign oil workers and shut down part of an oil facility, among other violent activities. Nigeria's oil exports fell by 25 percent and world oil prices spiked ever higher as a result. With presidential elections set for 2007, Nigeria's internal turmoil was expected to intensify.

### Saudi Arabia

Thanks to its control over the world's largest petroleum reserves, Saudi Arabia is a principal energy supplier for many countries around the world. In 2004 it banked more than $100 billion in oil revenues. Ever since the country was constituted as a unified state in 1932, it has been governed by the large Al Saud family, which has based its rule on a fairly strict interpretation of Islamic law. Despite the fact that this monarchical regime is about as far removed as any political system can be from democracy, with practically no electoral or civil liberties guaranteed to the citizenry, Saudi leaders have been cultivated by every American president from Franklin D. Roosevelt to the Bushes, as well as by the leaders of other democracies around the world. In recent years the foundations of Saudi rule have been rocked by terrorism. Osama bin Laden, who came from one of Saudi Arabia's wealthiest and most influential families, has made it clear that his ultimate aim is to bring down Al Saud rule and replace it with an even more stringent—and more anti-Western—Islamic state. Fifteen of the nineteen perpetrators of September 11 came from Saudi Arabia, and Saudi donors have provided millions of dollars in contributions to al Qaeda.

In 2003 and 2004, terrorists stepped up their attacks on foreign oil companies and other targets in Saudi Arabia, driving up world oil prices. In early 2006 a daring attempt by suicide bombers to blow up the world's largest oil-processing plant was foiled at the last minute by Saudi security forces. The plant processes two-thirds of the country's oil and affects 10 percent of the world's oil supplies. Fears of such attacks in the future instantly raised world oil prices by more than $2 a barrel. Any disruption in the flow of Saudi Arabia's oil to the outside world is bound to cause a major escalation in the prices the world must pay for petroleum products.

### The United Arab Emirates (UAE)

The UAE, which possesses 8.2 percent of the world's known oil reserves, is a confederation of seven small Persian Gulf states. Governed by conservative emirs who have shown little inclination to introduce democratic rights and liberties, the UAE has been internally stable. Nevertheless, the UAE's location in the Middle East makes it vulnerable to regional conflicts. Prior to September 11, terrorist organizations used banks and financial services in the UAE, but since then the confederation has generally complied with U.S. requests to stop these practices. When the U.S. government made a deal with a UAE company to provide security for seven American ports in 2006, vocal opposition to the agreement in the port cities and in Congress, based on fears of potential terrorism, pressured the UAE to cancel the deal.

### Venezuela

From the early 1960s to the late 1990s, Venezuela was governed mainly by civilian parties that did little to restrain official corruption or relieve acute poverty. In 1999 Hugo Chávez was elected president on a platform promising an attack on government malfeasance and a more equitable economic policy. Upon assuming the presidency, Chávez immediately set to work reorganizing Venezuela's main political institutions. A new constitution that was approved by the voters in a referendum allowed Chávez to restructure the national legislature and the Supreme Court, reducing their independence and subjecting them to his leadership. Although Chávez enjoyed broad support in the reshaped legislature and among millions of Venezuela's poor, his opponents mounted a campaign to remove him from the presidency. Elements of the military managed to oust him in 2002, but Chávez returned to office two days later with the help of his backers in the military ranks. Massive demonstrations and a 62-day strike staged by the president's opposition in 2003 failed to unseat him, and a recall referendum in 2004 resulted in yet another Chávez victory. Chávez retaliated by stepping up the prosecution of opposition leaders, including political figures and human rights activists.

Chávez has been openly critical of the United States, denouncing U.S. hegemony in the global economic system and lambasting the invasion of Iraq. Despite these frictions, the United States was still a major importer of Venezuela's oil. With 6.5 percent of the world's oil reserves—the sixth-largest supply in the world—Venezuela has reaped windfall income gains as world oil prices have risen in recent years. Chávez has injected large infusions of these oil profits into social services for Venezuela's poor, firming up his base of support in this large segment of the population. Nevertheless, Chávez has accused the U.S. government of undermining his regime and has threatened to cut off oil exports to the United States. In 2006 his government called on the oil-producing countries to cut their exports by up to a million barrels a day. In advance of the 2006 presidential elections, he ordered trials for political oppositionists on trumped-up criminal charges. But as expected, Chávez handily won reelection in December 2006, winning 56.2 percent of the popular vote. The possibility of more instability in Venezuela may affect its reliability as an oil supplier in the international economy.

The oil-exporting countries we have just reviewed provide considerable evidence that events occurring *inside* individual countries can indeed have an enormous impact on the outside world, as represented in this case by the *international economy* (more specifically, by world energy prices). In each case, we have shown that *it matters who governs* the energy-exporting countries of the world.

The connections between domestic and international affairs are especially noticeable in two of the most powerful tendencies at work in today's world: *globalization* and *democratization.*

## GLOBALIZATION

**Globalization** ***refers to the growing interconnectedness of governments, non-state actors, and populations throughout the world through a variety of political, economic, technological, cultural, environmental, and other interactions.***

Although globalization is a multifaceted phenomenon, and its components interact in all sorts of ways, economic factors stand out as its principal motor force. Technology provides its thrust. Computers, software, fax machines, fiber optics, the Internet, satellites, e-mail, cell phones—these and other technological advances have energized the unprecedented speed and breadth of global transactions. If economics is the engine of globalization, technology is its fuel.

We are now living in a truly global economy. International trade and other forms of economic exchange have risen exponentially in the past two decades. Exports of merchandise around the world rose from \$1.8 trillion in 1983 to \$6.2 trillion in 2000. Exports of services like banking and insurance went from \$357 billion to more than \$1.4 trillion in roughly the same time span. Private and government investment in foreign countries also rose dramatically. The creation of the *World Trade Organization* (WTO) in 1995 was designed to facilitate these global economic links. By 2006 the WTO consisted of 149 member countries. Businesses are not only selling their goods in a vast and highly competitive global marketplace; they are setting up factories and offices outside the borders of their home countries to an extent unimaginable even a few decades ago. Powered by the Internet and other communications technologies, they can move inventories, jobs, and money around the world at a dizzying pace. The average "American" car typifies these global connections. No longer "made in Detroit," it most likely consists of parts that have been manufactured in a half-dozen or more countries.

Some are hurt by these transformations. When companies close their plants in one locality and relocate in countries that offer cheaper wages, lower taxes, or other profitable advantages, or when they outsource jobs to those countries, the people who are left behind must often cope with unemployment or other harsh consequences of economic change. Similarly, when global investors pull their money out of countries with struggling economies, the results can be catastrophic for employees, businesses, and governments in those countries that are suddenly deprived of vitally necessary financial infusions. And when an economic slowdown affects large economies like those of the United States, Japan, and Germany, other economies that are linked to them in the global marketplace are bound to experience problems when trade and investment dry up. "When the U.S. economy sneezes, the rest of the world catches cold."

Undeniably, economic globalization has its dark side. Its critics have pointed not only to the trade disadvantages that developing economies experience in their dealings with the more developed states and powerful global corporations, but also to such widespread afflictions as subsistence-level poverty, child labor, the marginalization of women, environmental degradation, and other troubling realities. But proponents of world trade observe that the fastest-growing economies in the world are almost without exception the very ones that are tightly plugged into the global economy. Poor countries that joined in the globalization process by increasing their foreign trade in proportion to their domestic economy reaped a substantial 5 percent annual growth in income during the 1990s—double the rate of rich countries. But poor countries that did not "globalize" ended up with *no* income growth in this period. Quite a few countries have registered significant economic gains from doing business with private enterprises. Between 1990 and 1998, for example, direct investment in the developing world by foreign private companies skyrocketed from $24.5 billion to $155 billion. As the international economist Jagdish Bhagwati has argued, globalization certainly has its downsides, but it also has a "human face"—trade and private investment definitely increase economic growth in developing countries, and growth in turn reduces poverty. It can also reduce child labor and enhance opportunities for women and the quality of the environment. Asserting that "globalization must be managed so that its fundamentally benign effects are ensured and reinforced," Bhagwati calls for energetic efforts on the part of governments, international agencies like the World Bank, and citizen organizations concerned with social and environmental issues to devise and implement effective remedies for the negative features of the global economic order. Otherwise, he warns, globalization itself may be imperiled.[6]

Other students of globalization note that it is producing unprecedented career opportunities. As *New York Times* columnist Thomas Friedman writes in his book *The World Is Flat*, the development of the Internet, powerful search engines, and other tools of global collaboration have created a "flattened" worldwide economic playing field that is open to millions of new participants, many of them in erstwhile thickets of poverty like India. "In the future globalization is going to be increasingly driven by the *individuals* who understand the flat world, adapt themselves quickly to its processes and technologies, and start to march forward. They will be every color of the rainbow and come from every corner of the world."[7]

What do all these economic tendencies have to do with comparative politics? A great deal, as it turns out. The forces of economic globalization are by no means limited to private companies. Governments around the world are also enveloped in the globalization process, whether as active promoters of international trade or as sources of jobs, unemployment compensation, retraining, and other forms of assistance to those whose livelihood is jeopardized by the maelstrom of global economic activity. *It therefore matters who governs.* Some political leaders may deal with the effects of economic globalization differently from others. Studying comparative politics helps us understand these differences and why they occur. The global financial crisis of 1997–99 is a striking example of how external factors—such as developments in the international economy—can have direct effects on economic and political processes *inside* individual countries.

## THE GLOBAL FINANCIAL CRISIS OF 1997–99

It all started on July 2, 1997, when domestic economic difficulties forced the government of Thailand to announce that it could no longer support the value of its currency, the baht.

The currencies of the world—U.S. dollars, Japanese yen, the euro and so on—are like stocks and bonds: they are traded on world markets every business day. As a consequence, the value of individual currencies relative to other currencies is constantly shifting. If the dollar is strong and the yen is growing weaker, for example, people involved in currency exchanges, whether they are Japanese tourists visiting the United States or professional currency traders, will have to pay out more yen for each dollar they wish to buy. On a typical day the value of most currencies against other currencies does not change very much, usually by a small fraction of 1 percent. But if a country's economy is in crisis, the value of its currency may plummet very quickly as the world's currency speculators rapidly sell their holdings of that currency. When that happens, the government must usually come to its own currency's rescue by buying it in world currency markets. But when the government cannot afford to take such remedial action, as in Thailand's case, its currency may go into a tailspin. Immediately after the Thai government made its announcement, the value of the baht fell a whopping 20 percent against the dollar.

Although Thailand is a small country, the effects of its currency crisis had global repercussions. Because the economies of Southeast Asia are closely linked, Thailand's neighbors Malaysia, Singapore, and Indonesia immediately experienced currency troubles of their own. A ripple of currency devaluations and stock market slides spread to Hong Kong, Taiwan, and South Korea over the following weeks and months. Japan and South Korea witnessed the collapse of several of their largest banks in late 1997.

The deterioration of East Asia's previously dynamic economies sent shock waves throughout the global economy. Because private companies and governments around the world, from the United States and Canada to Latin America and Europe, were heavily involved in trade and other economic transactions with Asia, it was not long before their economies felt the effects of the Asian crisis. On October 27, 1997, the New York Stock Exchange fell 554 points, until then its biggest one-day loss in history. The sudden plunge reflected the fears of investors that Asia would no longer be able to purchase American-made goods as actively as in the past, thereby reducing the profits of U.S. corporations. Wall Street quickly recovered from this drop, but other countries were not so fortunate. Some were affected by a substantial loss of revenue from trade with Asian partners. A number of countries were also affected by a decline of foreign investments as the Asian crisis made many international investors squeamish about placing their funds in risky economies known in the investment world as "emerging markets." India and South Africa, for example, experienced severe economic problems before too long. So did Russia, whose government in August 1998 declared its inability to prop up the ruble. Within a week Russia's currency lost about a third of its value against the dollar and plunged considerably lower by year's end. Brazil also experienced problems as nervous investors began pulling money out of the Brazilian economy. Brazil's government could no longer support the country's currency—the real—whose value dipped 20 percent against the dollar in early 1999. By mid 1999, much of Latin America was in a deep economic slump.

The ramifications of these multiple financial shocks were by no means limited to economics. Political changes also ensued in a number of places. Indonesia's financial crunch precipitated riots and student demonstrations that ultimately brought about the resignation of President Suharto, who had ruled the country as its unchallenged dictator since 1965. South Korea's economic woes paved the way for the election of a new government under President Kim Dae Jung, a courageous advocate of democracy and an outspoken opponent of his country's previous military governments. In elections held in July 1998, Japan's ruling party received a rude jolt from an electorate worried about continuing stagnation in the world's second largest economy. The prime minister resigned and a new government came to power. Russian President Boris Yeltsin fired his prime minister as the ruble disintegrated. In Brazil, President Fernando Henrique Cardoso managed to gain parliamentary approval for the main elements of his economic reform program, but only after protracted negotiations. For these and other governments around the world, the turmoil showed that economic globalization can forcefully intrude into the subject matter of comparative politics.

When governments contending with currency fluctuations and other economic problems do not have enough money to cover their budgets, they must frequently borrow what they need from other governments or from commercial (private) banks around the world. Like other borrowers, they are expected not only to repay their loans but also to service their debts by paying interest on them. As one difficult year follows another, some governments may accumulate international debts amounting to tens of billions of dollars, requiring interest payments that can also run into the billions every year. When a financially strapped government cannot repay its debts or even meet its debt-servicing obligations, it can apply to the *International Monetary Fund (IMF)* for help. The IMF is a specialized agency of the United Nations. Its chief purpose is to provide financial assistance to governments that have currency problems or difficulty repaying their debts or making interest payments. The IMF's membership currently consists of 184 governments, all of which contribute to the organization's lending resources.

Before providing any assistance, IMF officials tend to impose fairly stringent conditions on the recipient government, pressuring it to put its domestic finances in order so as to reduce its dependency on future loans. Typically they may require it to cut its budget deficits by raising taxes or reducing government spending. Such measures are likely to bring unwelcome domestic consequences. Raising taxes invariably sparks protests, and slashing spending may terminate jobs for bureaucrats and drastically reduce the money available for food, health care, education, and other government programs that materially affect people's lives. Few politicians make these decisions gladly, especially if they fear riots or other manifestations of public disapproval.

As the 1997–99 financial crises unfolded, the IMF pledged a $17 billion rescue package for Thailand, $23 billion for Indonesia, $57 billion for South Korea, $22.6 billion for Russia, and $41.5 billion for Brazil. While the recipient governments gratefully welcomed the money, they did not look forward to making the politically painful economic adjustments the IMF demanded in return for its disbursements. Some countries in similar straits have actually declined the IMF's assistance rather than accept its conditions. Critics of the IMF contend that the organization can do more harm than good. One of them, Joseph Stiglitz, a Nobel Prize winner and former presidential adviser, has rebuked the IMF for imposing excessively harsh conditions on indebted countries. The IMF's defenders counter that, without these difficult adjustments, economies in trouble will only get worse.[8]

In recent years there has been a worldwide movement to cancel all the international debts of the developing countries. In 2002 those debts totaled approximately $460 billion. The IMF rejected the idea as too costly. In the 1990s it created the Heavily Indebted Poor Countries Initiative, which by 2006 had provided $35 billion in debt relief to 29 countries as a "first step" toward stabilizing their economies. In 2005 the Group of 8 (G-8) industrial countries (the United States, Canada, Britain, France, Germany, Italy, Japan, and Russia) proposed canceling all the debts of especially indebted countries, and later that year the IMF selected nineteen countries for this Multilateral Debt Relief Initiative.[9]

Economic globalization is by no means the only form of expanding interconnectedness in today's world; additional forms of globalization abound. Each one of these issue areas is characterized by the dynamic interaction of international and domestic factors.

*International security* is another important aspect of globalization. *Nuclear proliferation,* potentially the most destructive of all security threats, is a decades-old problem. By its very nature it is a global one. Nuclear explosions do not observe boundaries: an open blast in any part of the world is likely to spread radioactive contaminants over a wide swath. Security against a nuclear blast anywhere is therefore a matter of concern everywhere.

Ever since the United States exploded two nuclear bombs over Japan in 1945, several other states have joined the nuclear club. At the height of the Cold War, the United States, the Soviet Union, Britain, France, and China together possessed tens of thousands of nuclear warheads (bombs), most of which could be delivered to their targets hundreds or thousands of miles away by guided missiles. The winding down of the Cold War resulted in substantial reductions in most of these arsenals. With a view to preventing the spread of nuclear weapons to other states, the main nuclear powers drafted the Nuclear Non-Proliferation Treaty (NPT) in 1968. The NPT obligates signatory states that do not officially possess nuclear weapons to pledge that they will not acquire them. Israel, India, and Pakistan never signed the NPT, and all three are known to possess nuclear weapons and missile delivery systems.[10]

North Korea signed the NPT in 1985 under its hardline communist dictator, Kim Il Sung. After international inspectors discovered treaty violations, the United States pressured North Korea to sign an agreement in 1994 pledging to cease its nuclear weapons program. In early 2003 Kim Il Sung's successor, his son Kim Jong Il, withdrew from the NPT after announcing that his government was reopening its nuclear production facilities. Official U.S. sources believed at the time that North Korea had the capability to build one or two nuclear bombs. In July 2006 North Korea tested a missile allegedly capable of hitting the U.S. west coast. Later in the year, it test-fired a nuclear bomb underground. The United States and North Korea's neighbors—South Korea, China, Japan, and Russia—expressed considerable uneasiness about Kim Jong Il's intentions.

Iran is also a signatory of the NPT, but there are signs that it is trying to develop nuclear weapons. In 2006 the country's president announced that Iran already had "the full gamut of nuclear technology at its disposal." The United States and its chief European allies did not accept the government's assertions that it had no intentions of building nuclear weapons, assuming instead that Iran would be ready to build nuclear bombs in five to ten years.

One of the fears associated with nuclear weapons in recent years is the possibility that radioactive material may fall into the hands of terrorists. The commitment of countries possessing radioactive material to keep it secure against theft and to prevent its transfer or sale to terrorists is therefore imperative. To no small extent this commitment is political: its fulfillment depends on the ability of those in power to keep their country's nuclear devices—from weapons and power plants to hospital radiology equipment—under firm control. Once again, *it matters who governs.*

Terrorism itself, of course, is the most widely feared security threat in many parts of today's world. Historically, most terrorist groups have confined themselves to a particular country or region. What is notable about al Qaeda is its global reach. At the time of the September 11 attacks in the United States, al Qaeda—which means "the Base"—was active either directly or indirectly (through affiliated terror organizations) in as many as seventy countries. An estimated 15,000 to 25,000 of its adherents had learned terrorist techniques in its training camps.

Although Osama bin Laden and the al Qaeda leadership are rabid enemies of certain aspects of globalization, especially the far-flung influences of the American economy and American culture, they have taken considerable advantage of global telecommunications and transportation networks and the tightly interconnected world economy. They have deftly used the Internet, airline vulnerabilities, international financial markets, and the global arms trade to pursue their stated goals of combating the West and promoting the establishment of Islamic states. Al Qaeda's philosophy may reject key features of the modern world, but its operations reflect a keen awareness of how to enlist globalization in the cause of terrorism.

The topic of security in general raises a host of questions that reflect the close connections between international relations and comparative politics. Whether it is a matter of nuclear weapons, biochemical substances, terrorists, or some other source of international danger, who governs the countries where they are located? Who makes diplomatic and security policy decisions? Do the country's leaders believe in the peaceful resolution of disputes, a concept traditionally associated with democracy? These and similar questions suggest that one of the most important reasons for studying comparative politics is to examine the *domestic sources of foreign policy and security policy* in individual countries. To understand what's going on between countries, we have to understand what's going on inside them.

The *environment* provides additional examples of the political implications of globalization. Ecological developments occurring inside one country can have immediate and long-term repercussions in neighboring areas as well as in countries clear across the planet. In recent decades the unabated rise in industrial emissions, the destruction of rain forests, and the release of greenhouse gases like carbon dioxide and methane have heightened concerns about global warming, the ozone layer, and other components of the Earth's ecological balance. These environmental hazards have multiplied as a result of globalization. As private companies seek the most profitable locations for their operations around the world, they frequently select countries where environmental regulations are lax. Conversely, the governments in charge of these countries have strong economic incentives to ignore environmental considerations precisely in order to attract foreign investment.

In 1997, representatives of 150 countries hammered out the *Kyoto Protocol* to the 1992 United Nations Framework Convention on Climate Change. The Protocol obliges them to reduce the emission of six greenhouse gases by a global average of 5 percent of 1990 levels by 2008–2012. The United States, which produces one-fourth of the world's greenhouse gas emissions, was obligated to implement a 7 percent emissions cut. The terms of the accord became a controversial political issue in a number of countries. In the United States, the Clinton administration signed the treaty in 1998, but congressional opposition induced the president to postpone asking the Senate to ratify it. By a vote of 95–0, the Senate had already passed a resolution in 1997 expressing its opposition to some of the protocol's provisions, especially the ones exempting large polluters like China and India from its requirements. Shortly after taking office in 2001, President George W. Bush declared that the United States would not observe the protocol on the grounds that its terms placed too large a burden on the U.S. economy while providing unwarranted exemptions for other countries. Without U.S. participation, the protocol did not take effect until February 2005, following its ratification by countries that together accounted for at least 55 percent of carbon dioxide emissions in 1990. The Kyoto Protocol expires in 2012. At a major follow-up conference held in Montreal in December 2005, participant governments decided to start discussions on a second commitment period for the protocol, to extend from 2013 to 2017. The United States agreed to participate in talks on global warming as long as they were nonbinding.

*Culture* is a particularly controversial aspect of globalization. By culture we mean a pattern of beliefs, values, attitudes, and lifestyles that people tend to share in large groups (such as the majority of an entire country or region). Though the world is characterized by a diversity of cultures, it is hard to deny that signature aspects of American culture have expanded their global presence over the past twenty to thirty years. Examples include the use of English as the lingua franca of international business, diplomacy, and scientific research; made-in-USA trademarks like Coca-Cola and McDonald's; Hollywood films and television shows, hip-hop, and other distinctly American modes of entertainment; American approaches to individual expression, feminism, Protestantism, human rights, anti-smoking campaigns, and so on. These and other symbols of the American way of life have proven their appeal throughout the world. But they are sometimes resented as an unwelcome imposition of American wealth and power, or as a disturbing threat to countries with different cultural traditions or political priorities. Some governments—like North Korea and Iran—have sought to prevent the penetration of American culture completely. Others—like China and France—have tried to limit the inflow of some products of American culture while promoting their own alternatives. Some societies have adapted American fads to their own tastes or behavioral customs. And some have successfully promoted the globalization of their own cultural hallmarks, such as Japanese quality-control techniques, Asian New Age ideas, and various religious beliefs. Though the icons of American culture may be the most pervasive throughout the world, when it comes to cultural influences there are truly "many globalizations."[11]

Globalization has been enormously affected by developments in *telecommunications.* Internet hosts grew from virtually zero at the start of the 1990s to more than 40 million worldwide by 2000. The use of e-mail, cell phones, and other modes of communication has also risen meteorically. Although there currently exists an international "digital divide" in computer literacy and Web access between rich and poor countries, and between democracies and dictatorships, that split is expected to diminish appreciably in the coming decades. The communications revolution not only creates extraordinary opportunities for governments, businesses, political activists, and other globally engaged organizations and individuals; it also poses serious problems for rulers who seek to limit their population's exposure to the outside world. From China to Cuba, from Iran to North Korea, dictatorial regimes are finding it increasingly difficult to censor or block out information in today's tightly wired global village, a reality that may catalyze real political change.

The *media* are similarly active in penetrating the barriers that divide the world. Global television networks like CNN and the BBC transmit real-time information to anyone with access to cable or satellite TV. Al-Jazeera, a Muslim-oriented network based in Qatar, broadcasts news and politically sensitive discussions that may be taboo in countries where the media are controlled by a dictatorial state. Organizations like Reporters Without Borders are constantly at work to make sure that journalists have access to information and are allowed to report their stories without government interference.[12] Efforts to restrict freedom of the press by nondemocratic regimes, or even by governments that claim to be committed to democracy, are increasingly challenged by the globalization of information.

*Refugee flows* have intensified in recent years as civil wars, political repression, ethnic antagonisms, and other problems occurring inside particularly troubled countries cascade into other states where refugees seek shelter, asylum, or simply a chance to build a better life. The United Nations estimated that there were nearly 20 million refugees, asylum seekers, internally displaced persons, and other "populations of concern" in 2004. At times the new arrivals create economic distress in countries that lack the means to adequately shelter or employ them. Whereas some refugees take flight so as to escape political violence at home, people who wish to migrate from one country to another primarily in order to improve their economic opportunities are also on the move around the world. The resulting surge in *migration flows* sometimes produces serious political backlashes, as the rise of anti-immigrant parties in Western Europe in recent years attests. By 2000 there were an estimated 175 million immigrants worldwide.[13]

*Public health* issues are also assuming a more pronounced global scope, often with significant political repercussions. The scourge of HIV/AIDS, resulting in more than 2 million deaths annually, requires intense international cooperation among governments, scientists, and pharmaceutical companies to contain and eventually conquer the epidemic. In some cases the disease's spread has widened because of inadequate responses by national governments. In 2003 the sudden appearance of SARS (severe acute respiratory syndrome), which was initially covered up by Chinese officials, prompted quick reactions by governments and world health authorities while temporarily stifling travel between Asia and the rest of the world. And bird flu (the H5N1 avian virus), which initially broke out in China in 1996 and then reemerged with a vengeance in Thailand and South Korea in 2003, spread across much of the globe by 2006, resulting in approximately 100 human fatalities. In an effort to halt the strain, governments and world health agencies cooperated in killing some 200 million birds.

*Law enforcement* has also broadened its global horizons as drug trafficking, organized crime, and terrorism present growing cross-border challenges to societies and governments around the world.

In sum, just about every domain of organized activity has a global dimension in today's closely linked international community.

## DEMOCRATIZATION

Along with globalization, the second powerful tendency in world affairs today is *democratization.*

**Democratization** ***is the transition from nondemocratic to democratic forms of government.***

As we noted at the start of this chapter, we are now in the midst of a "third wave" of democratization, a process that has accelerated since the second half of the 1980s. In 1987 there were 66 countries that permitted democratic elections. By the end of 2005 there were 123, including a number of former communist countries that had been involved in nearly fifty years of Cold War confrontation with the United States and its allies. Some 89 of these 123 countries, comprising 46 percent of the world's 6.1 billion people, buttressed their democratic election procedures with a solid respect for human rights and the rule of law, compared with only 43 countries thirty years earlier. A majority of the world's Muslims now live under governments that have been elected democratically in countries like Indonesia, Turkey, India, and Nigeria. Although it is far too early to assess democracy's prospects in Afghanistan and Iraq, the recent removal of their nondemocratic regimes holds out at least a glimmer of hope that democracy may gain a footing in those countries, however great the challenges may be.[14]

Many proponents of democracy contend that the clash between advocates and opponents of democracy is the central political struggle of our times. It lies at the heart of such recent developments as the collapse of communism, the proliferation of civil wars and interstate conflicts, and the global confrontation with terrorism. No one can foresee the ultimate outcome of this historic confrontation or the course the latest wave of democratization will take. But the record convincingly shows that democracy, though by no means perfect, offers humanity its best chance of escaping tyranny, poverty, and relentless political violence. We will discuss democratization further in chapter 9. ("Transition countries" that have embarked on democratization since the mid-1980s are listed in tables 9.4, 9.5, and 9.6.)[15]

**What Can You Do?** There are numerous opportunities for concerned citizens to participate in the advance of democratic rights and freedoms wherever they may be suppressed. For example, people can get involved with human rights organizations like Amnesty International, Freedom House, and Human Rights Watch. These and similar associations often pressure governments to observe human rights, and they publish critical reports and important informational material.[16]

In the 1980s the U.S. government created the National Endowment for Democracy to promote democracy around the world. At the same time, four affiliated institutions were also created with similar goals: the National Democratic Institute for International Affairs, the National Republican Institute for International Affairs, the Free Trade Union Institute (later renamed the American Institute for International Labor Solidarity), and the Center for International Private Enterprise. Strictly speaking, these organizations are independent of the U.S. government and the main American political parties, but they receive substantial funding from Congress and government agencies, and their governing boards include prominent American political figures. All are heavily engaged in democracy-building projects around the world, with outreach programs for democracy activists in the United States and internationally. Other democracies have analogous organizations.[17]

Another way of taking part in international prodemocracy campaigns is by joining a nongovernmental organization. **Nongovernmental organizations (NGOs)** ***are typically organizations of concerned citizens and experts who seek to inform the public and influence governments, international institutions, private corporations, or other relevant bodies to take action in addressing particular problems.*** It is estimated that there are now some 2 million NGOs around the world, dedicated to such causes as women's rights, environmental protection, the eradication of child labor, fair trade, and countless other issues. There are NGOs of both the left and the right. As long as they are committed to democracy they are expected to promote their goals without recourse to violence. NGOs are a fundamental building block of "civil society"—the citizenry organized for political action independently of governments. And civil society, in turn, is an essential building block of democracy.

Activism by ordinary citizens can be highly effective. As Margaret Keck and Kathryn Sikkink demonstrate in their prize-winning book, *Activists Beyond Borders,* transnational advocacy networks of organizations and individuals, linked across the globe through e-mail and the Internet, have scored major successes in publicizing a variety of causes.[18] In a number of cases their efforts have produced significant changes in governmental policies. Jody Williams, for example, helped launch from her home in Vermont an international campaign against land mines. A treaty banning the weapons was signed in 1997, and Ms. Williams shared the Nobel Peace Prize.

What are human rights? Over the centuries there have been numerous attempts to identify the most important rights and freedoms that people should enjoy, starting with such landmarks as the parliamentary bill of rights passed by the British Parliament in 1689; the Declaration of the Rights of Man, drafted during the French Revolution in 1789; Thomas Paine's tract, *The Rights of Man,* published in 1790; and the U.S. Bill of Rights (the first ten amendments to the Constitution), adopted in 1791. Perhaps the best-known human rights document in modern times is the Universal Declaration of Human Rights, approved by the United Nations in 1948.

## THE UNIVERSAL DECLARATION OF HUMAN RIGHTS

The Declaration's thirty articles begin by proclaiming that "all human beings are born free and equal in dignity and rights" and that everyone is entitled without discrimination to the political, economic, and social rights spelled out in the document. As paraphrased here, the Declaration's provisions include the following rights and freedoms:

- The right to life, liberty, and security of person.
- Freedom from slavery or servitude.
- Freedom from torture and from cruel, inhuman, or degrading treatment or punishment.
- The right to equality before the law, to equal protection of the law, to the presumption of innocence until proven guilty, and to a fair public hearing by an independent and impartial tribunal if one is accused of a penal offense. Freedom from arbitrary arrest, detention, or exile.
- Freedom from arbitrary interference with one's privacy, family, home, or correspondence and from attacks upon one's honor and reputation.
- Freedom of movement and residence within one's own country. The right to leave any country, to return to one's own country, and to seek asylum from political persecution.
- The right to a nationality. No one shall be arbitrarily deprived of nationality nor required to change it.
- The right to marry and found a family, with the free and full consent of the intending spouses. Equal rights during marriage and at its dissolution. The family is the natural and fundamental group unit of society and is entitled to social and state protection.
- The right to own property alone or with others. Freedom from arbitrary deprivation of property.
- Freedom of thought, conscience, and religion, including the right to manifest religion or belief in teaching, practice, worship, and observance.
- Freedom of opinion and expression, and the right to receive and impart information and ideas through any media and regardless of frontiers.
- Freedom of peaceful assembly and association. No one may be compelled to belong to an association.
- The right to take part in the government of one's country, directly or through freely chosen representatives, and the right of equal access to public service. The will of the people shall be the basis of the authority of government, as expressed in periodic and genuine elections by universal and equal suffrage and a secret vote (or equivalent free voting procedures).
- The right to social security and to the economic, social, and cultural rights that are indispensable for one's dignity and the free development of one's personality.
- The right to work, to free choice of employment, to just and favorable conditions of work, and to protection against unemployment. The right to equal pay for equal work, without discrimination. The right to just and favorable remuneration so as to ensure for oneself and one's family an existence worthy of human dignity and supplemented, if necessary, by other means of social protection. The right to form and join trade unions.
- The right to rest and leisure, including a reasonable limitation of working hours and periodic holidays with pay.
- The right to a standard of living adequate for the health and well-being of oneself and one's family (including food, clothing, housing, medical care, and necessary social services). The right to security in the event of unemployment, sickness, disability, widowhood, old age, or other lack of livelihood in circumstances beyond one's control. Motherhood and childhood are entitled to special care and assistance. All children, born in or out of wedlock, shall enjoy the same social protection.
- The right to education, which shall be free and compulsory at the elementary stages. Technical and professional education shall be generally made available, and higher education shall be equally accessible to all on the basis of merit. Education shall be directed to the full development of the personality and to the strengthening of respect for human rights and fundamental freedoms. It shall promote understanding, tolerance, and friendship among all nations and racial or religious groups, and shall further the activities of the United Nations for the maintenance of peace. Parents have the right to choose the kind of education that shall be given to their children.
- The right to participate freely in the community's cultural life, to enjoy the arts, and to share in scientific advancement and its benefits. The right to the protection of the moral and material interests resulting from any scientific, literary, or artistic production of which one is the author.
- The right to a social and international order in which the Declaration's rights and freedoms can be realized.
- Everyone has duties to the community in which alone the free and full development of one's personality is possible. Everyone's rights and liberties shall be subject only to such limitations as are determined

by law solely to secure due recognition and respect for the rights of others and to meet the just requirements of morality, public order, and the general welfare in a democratic society. These rights and freedoms may not be exercised contrary to the purposes and principles of the United Nations.

- Nothing in the Declaration may be interpreted as implying for any state, group, or person the right to engage in any activity or to perform any act aimed at the destruction of any of the rights and freedoms set forth above.

*Source:* http://www.un.org/Overview/rights.html

Despite the Declaration's claim to universality, many of its provisions have been routinely flouted by governments that have signed the document. One of its framers was the Soviet Union, whose dictatorial practices at home made a mockery of the Universal Declaration's terms. Other framers whose governments are democratic—including the United States, Britain, and France—have failed to incorporate many of the Declaration's principles into their own constitutional structures. Moreover, the United Nations has no effective enforcement mechanisms to ensure the Declaration's observance. In spite of these limitations, the Universal Declaration provides what many human rights advocates around the world regard as a comprehensive list of aspirations that the governments of the world should strive to achieve.[19]

A number of additional human rights conventions have followed in the wake of the Universal Declaration. In 1950 a group of West European countries drafted a Convention for the Protection of Human Rights and Fundamental Freedoms. Modeled on the UN's Universal Declaration, it provides for a more effective method of enforcement: the European Court of Human Rights, a judicial body whose rulings must be observed by the signatory states.[20] The United Nations has produced several additional documents that have amplified the provisions of the Universal Declaration. They include the International Covenant on Civil and Political Rights and the Covenant on Economic, Social and Cultural Rights, among others.[21]

The democratization tendencies that are unfolding before our very eyes, and the struggle for human rights that accompanies them, provide more examples of the connections linking comparative and international politics. Another example of this linkage centers on the relationship between democracy and peace: Are democracies inherently more peaceful than nondemocracies?

## DEMOCRACY AND PEACE

President Woodrow Wilson was a firm believer in the hypothesis that democracies are inherently more peaceful than nondemocracies. "A steadfast concert of peace can never be maintained," he said, "except by a partnership of democratic nations." For that reason, Wilson justified American involvement in World War I on the grounds that American troops in Europe would be fighting to "make the world safe for democracy." If democracies could be set up throughout Europe after the war, Wilson believed, World War I would turn out to be the "war to end all wars."

Was Wilson right? If we look at the historical evidence, we find that democracies can be very aggressive once attacked. Of course, a nation can defend itself against attack and still be fundamentally peace loving. The real test of whether democracies are peaceful by nature centers on the question of whether they refrain from launching unprovoked attacks on others.

In fact, democratic governments have at times taken the initiative in starting military conflicts. When the French Revolution replaced the monarchy in the 1790s with a government that was more representative of popular sentiments, France attacked its neighbors on the European continent with the aim of bringing the blessings of "liberty, equality, fraternity" to the Germans, the Austrians, and other people who still lived under monarchies of one form or another. British and French imperialism provide additional examples of unprovoked aggression by democracies. Both Britain and France had democratically elected governments in the latter decades of the nineteenth century when they sent troops to Africa and other parts of the world to impose their imperial rule on the peoples they conquered. These and other historical examples suggest that democracies can sometimes be just as aggressive as nondemocracies in *starting* military conflicts, even when they are not militarily threatened.

But the historical record also indicates that *democracies generally do not fight one another.* The world's leading democracies, such as the United States, Britain, and France, have tended to be allies rather than enemies. Why haven't these democracies gone to war against one another? One reason is that a fundamental principle of democracy asserts that conflicts should be settled peacefully, through negotiation and compromise, rather than by force. Another reason is that democratic governments require popular consent in order to govern. If a majority of the people are opposed to war, a democratically elected government may find it difficult to engage military forces abroad. President Franklin D. Roosevelt, who opposed Germany's aggression in Europe and Japan's aggression in Asia, could not take military action against those countries as long as most Americans opposed it. Only when public sentiment turned around after Pearl Harbor was Roosevelt able to get Congress to declare war. In later years, the U.S. government sought negotiated settlements to end American military involvement in the Korean War (1950–53) and the Vietnam War (1961–73) once a majority of Americans turned against armed intervention.

Still, there are exceptions to the rule that democracies do not fight one another. The United States and Britain clashed in the War of 1812, for example, and the American Civil War pitted the North against the South in a four-year conflict that left over six hundred thousand dead. Both the northern Republic and the southern Confederacy were governed by democratically elected officials (though the right to vote was restricted to white males).

We must therefore conclude that President Wilson's hypothesis is only partially correct. Democracies are not always peaceful by nature; they have at times launched unprovoked attacks against nondemocracies, and they have even gone to war against one another. War can be a popular choice; it can be supported by a majority of the people, at times with considerable patriotic passion. Nevertheless, the record also shows that democracies *usually* do not go to war against one another. Hence we may accept *as a general tendency* Wilson's idealistic proposition that "a partnership of democratic nations" will promote world peace.

As in virtually all human affairs, nothing can be guaranteed. Nevertheless, it appears that *democracy increases the probability of peace, at least among democratic nations.* Thus, peace *among* the nations of the world may ultimately depend on the fate of democracy *within* the nations of the world.[22]

---

If there is evidence both for and against the notion that democracy promotes peace, what about the relationship between democracy and globalization? Does globalization help or hinder the cause of democracy? The jury is still out on this one; we need to observe world trends for a number of years before we can come to any firm conclusions. Nevertheless, analysts are already voicing strong arguments on either side of this issue. Thomas Friedman, for example, maintains that globalization tends to promote democracy. He agrees with those who say that, in order to attract foreign investments, nondemocratic countries need to assure investors that corruption will be punished by an independent judiciary, that information will flow freely, and that the government will hold itself accountable for its actions both to outside investors and to its own population. These requirements tend to push governments in a democratic direction.[23]

Benjamin Barber draws a more pessimistic picture. In his view, the contemporary world is torn between two contending forces. On one side stand the forces of "jihad"—a term he uses as a blanket designation for groups and movements that reject international cooperation, technological advancement, the market economy, and other features of the modern world. They prefer instead to pursue unending warfare against rival cultures, religions, ethnic groups, or other enemies. Arrayed against them are the influences of "McWorld": the very tendencies toward worldwide economic integration, technology, and pop culture that epitomize globalization. Both of these warring forces undermine democracy, Barber asserts. "Jihad" preaches hatred and the primacy of one's own tribal identity. "McWorld" threatens to immerse the world in profit-driven consumerism, reducing it to a "homogenous global theme park" where democratic governments turn their backs on the public interest and the common good. To combat these antidemocratic tendencies, Barber calls for the creation of an international network of concerned citizens—a "global civil society" dedicated to promoting greater citizen participation in the affairs of government throughout the world.[24]

And Zbigniew Brzezinski, the former national security advisor to President Jimmy Carter, warns that the global spread of Western (especially American) economic and cultural influences may actually undermine the appeal of democracy around the world unless the West infuses its democratic message with positive moral values. If the market economy and

Western popular culture convey little more than an obsession with greed, sexual gratification, and other forms of self-indulgence, Brzezinski argues, then millions of people across the globe who are offended by these tendencies may turn their backs on democracy itself, ignoring its core values of intellectual freedom, the rule of law, scientific rationality, and compromise.[25]

While the debate over globalization's impact will surely rage for quite some time, we should leave open the possibility that different aspects of globalization may have different effects in different countries. Because it is a multifaceted phenomenon, globalization may be neither exclusively conducive to democracy nor entirely antithetical to it in all countries. It will often cut in both directions at once. Hypothetically, we can imagine a devout Muslim man in Iraq or Iran who may welcome economic investments from the United States but reject the open sexual behaviors displayed in Hollywood movies or on MTV. He may therefore favor limitations on freedom of expression. Similarly, a woman in the developing world may champion the egalitarian impulses of Western feminism but object to the practices of profit-driven Western companies, thus favoring restraints on private enterprise and international trade. Will these and other aspects of globalization nip democracy in the bud? Or will they foster creative attempts to hybridize democratic principles with local traditions and prevailing values? How will they affect economic development, a vital requirement for democracy's long-term success? Time will tell, of course. And studying comparative politics can illuminate these complicated interrelationships as they unfold.

In fact, one of the principal intentions of this book is to help you see how the parts relate to the whole. Comparative politics teaches us how to relate the particularities of individual countries to broader trends and processes. As we have already seen, these general tendencies include not just purely political phenomena like democracy and tyranny; they also encompass aspects of economics, culture, the environment, and other domains that have their own dynamics and defining features. And they include not just domestic phenomena but also external concerns like international security and world trade. As Henry Nau has argued, a country's foreign policy is more than just the product of its military power or economic interests. At a more basic level, it reflects the country's *national identity*—its self-image as shaped by its history, its ethnic (or multiethnic) population, and its core ideological, religious, or other values. The various ways in which people define their national identity—whether as citizens of a democracy, as Muslims, or what have you—profoundly affect their views of both domestic and international affairs, including their attitudes toward the use of force at home and abroad.[26]

We therefore need what Friedman calls a "globalist" perspective on today's realities. We need to recognize that the world is a web where everything is interconnected. "The dominant trend within universities and think tanks is toward ever-narrower specialization," Friedman warns. "But we need more students, professors, diplomats, journalists, spies and social scientists trained as globalists"—people who are sensitive to the many interconnections that tie the world together.[27] Of course, we cannot possibly trace all these interconnections in this book. But our comprehensive approach to comparative politics can certainly help you understand how a good many of the world's most important political relationships and events fit together.

## THE PURPOSES OF COMPARISON

What exactly is "comparative" about comparative politics? What are we comparing, and for what aims?

To understand politics comprehensively, we must compare. We cannot possibly understand democracy, for example, by simply concentrating on one example of a democratic government, such as the United States or Britain. Democracies organize their executive, legislative, and judicial institutions in different ways. Some have encouraged free enterprise while others have favored greater government interference in the economy. Some democracies have succeeded while others have failed. Democracy is not a single phenomenon; it has many manifestations. The same is true of nondemocratic regimes. To fully grasp how these governmental systems work, we need to look at a diversity of cases and systematically examine their similarities and differences.

Another reason for making systematic comparisons between different countries and political systems is that we can learn a great deal more about any one particular case (country X) by comparing it with other relevant cases (countries A, B, and C). If you are interested in South Africa, China, Russia, or any other country, you will acquire a deeper appreciation of its history and politics by holding it up against the experiences of other nations. This simple idea is central to the logic of comparative analysis. And it strikes very close to home: we can learn a lot more about politics in our *own* country by comparing it with other countries. Specialists in comparative politics are fond of quoting Rudyard Kipling in this regard. "And what should they know of England," the poet inquired, "who only England know?" Presumably, not much. At least, not as much as they would know if they ventured outside their homeland and savored life's possibilities in other places.

To a considerable extent, studying comparative politics is like traveling abroad. It awakens us to the varieties of human experience and shows us that there are different ways of doing things than what we are used to in our own country. In the end we come home with a greater sensitivity to both the positive and negative features of our homeland as well as an enhanced appreciation of why other people do things differently.

Thus for people in the United States, a comparative analysis of Britain, Japan, Israel, or other established democracies can shed light on how the American political system actually works. Both the similarities the United States shares with these countries and the peculiarities that set America apart from them will stand out in sharp relief. For example:

- The U.S. system of government is based on *a separation of powers* and *checks and balances.* But how does this system compare with the British system? Or the Russian, French, or South African? In fact, these and other democracies are organized quite differently. The U.S. system is unique in many of its most essential features. What are the advantages and disadvantages of the U.S. system, compared with other democratic systems of government?
- One of the most frequent criticisms Americans level at their own system of government is that it is prone to *gridlock:* between Congress and the president, major decisions often do not get made effectively. Is gridlock a peculiarly American phenomenon, or do other governments have it, too? Can the United States reduce or eliminate gridlock by adopting constitutional procedures used in other democracies?
- Some of the most controversial political issues in the United States center on such topics as voting procedures, health care, and opportunities for women. How do other democracies handle these problems? Can the United States learn anything from these countries, or vice versa?

The principal purposes of studying comparative politics may therefore be summarized as follows:

- *to widen our understanding of politics in other countries*
- *to increase our appreciation of the advantages and disadvantages of our own political system and to enable us to learn from other countries*
- *to develop a more sophisticated understanding of politics in general, including the nature of democracy and nondemocratic governments, the relationships between governments and people, and other concepts and processes*
- *to help us understand the linkages between domestic affairs and international affairs*
- *to help us see the relationship between politics and such fields as science, technology, the environment, public health, law, business, religion, ethnicity, culture, and others*
- *to enable us to become more informed citizens, so that we can more effectively develop our own political opinions, participate in political life, evaluate the actions and proposals of political leaders, and make our own political decisions and electoral choices*
- *to sharpen our critical-thinking skills by applying scientific logic and coherent argumentation to our understanding of political phenomena*

Of course, you may have your own special reasons for studying comparative politics. But whatever your main field of study may be and whatever your personal goals, you will gain a better understanding of how you fit into the web of global interrelationships. You will truly be studying *yourself* in relation to the rest of humanity.

## KEY TERMS
### (In bold and underlined in the text)

Comparative politics
International politics
Globalization
Democratization
Nongovernmental organizations (NGOs)

## NOTES

1. *New York Times*, September 19, 2005, and www.lycianturkey.com.
2. Samuel P. Huntington, *The Third Wave: Democratization in the Late Twentieth Century* (Norman: University of Oklahoma Press, 1991).
3. Kenneth Jowitt, *New World Disorder: The Leninist Extinction* (Berkeley: University of California Press, 1992). For an optimistic appraisal of democracy's future, see Francis Fukuyama, *The End of History and the Last Man* (New York: Free Press, 1992).
4. Energy Information Administration of the U.S. Department of Energy, www.eia.doe.gov.
5. *Manipulation of the Oil-for-Food Programme by the Iraqi Regime*, www.iic-offp.org. See also Brian Urquhart, "The UN Oil-for-Food Program: Who Is Guilty?" *New York Review of Books*, February 9, 2006, 45–50.
6. Jagdish Bhagwati, *In Defense of Globalization* (New York: Oxford University Press, 2004), 35. For contending views on globalization, see Martin Wolf, *Why Globalization Works* (New Haven, Conn.: Yale University Press, 2004); Daniel Cohen, *Globalization and Its Enemies,* trans. Jessica B. Baker (Cambridge, Mass.: MIT Press, 2006); Peter Singer, *One World: The Ethics of Globalization,* 2nd ed. (New Haven, Conn.: Yale University Press, 2004); John Cavanaugh and Jerry Mander, eds., *Alternatives to Economic Globalization: A Better World Is Possible* (San Francisco: Berrett-Koehler, 2004); Paul Blustein, *The Chastening: Inside the Crisis That Rocked the Global Financial System* (New York: Public Affairs, 2003) (on the 1997–98 financial crisis); and David Held and Anthony McGrew, *Globalization/Anti-Globalization* (Cambridge: Polity, 2002). Also Vijay Joshi and Robert Skidelsky, "One World?" *New York Review of Books*, March 25, 2004, 19–21; John Gray, "The Global Delusion," *New York Review of Books*, April 27, 2006, 18–23; and Sebastian Mallaby, "Making Globalization Work," *Washington Post*, February 28, 2005.
7. Thomas L. Friedman, *The World Is Flat* (New York: Farrar, Straus & Giroux, 2005), 183.
8. Joseph E. Stiglitz, *Globalization and Its Discontents* (New York: W. W. Norton, 2002).
9. The IMF's website is www.imf.org.
10. By mid 2003 it was reliably estimated that the United States possessed 7,295 strategic (i.e., long-range deliverable) warheads; Russia had 6,094 strategic warheads deployed. China had about 300 warheads; France, less than 500; and the United Kingdom, less than 200. Israel was believed to have 75 to 125 warheads; India, 45 to 95; and Pakistan, 30 to 50. See the Arms Control Association's website, www.armscontrol.org.
11. Peter L. Berger and Samuel P. Huntington, eds., *Many Globalizations: Cultural Diversity in the Contemporary World* (Oxford: Oxford University Press, 2002). For a critical view of the globalization of American culture, see Walter LaFeber, *Michael Jordan and the New Global Capitalism*, rev. ed. (New York: Norton, 2002).
12. Reporters Without Borders, based in France, can be accessed at www.rsf.org. See also the annual Freedom House publication, *Freedom of the Press: A Global Survey of Media Independence* (consult www.freedomhouse.org).
13. It is estimated that about 150 million people now live outside their own countries. About 1 million people enter the United States legally every year, along with about a half million illegal immigrants. The European Union has similar numbers of legal and illegal immigrants annually. *The Economist,* March 3, 2001 and November 2, 2002. See also *The State of the World's Refugees*, published annually by the United Nations High Commissioner for Refugees and available at www.unhcr.org.
14. Freedom House, *Freedom in the World 2006* (New York: Freedom House, 2006), 3, 4.
15. On transitional countries, see the following publications by Freedom House: *Freedom in the World 2006; Countries at the Crossroads* (2004 and 2005); and *Nations in Transit 2005*.

**16.** Amnesty International's website is www.amnesty.org. Freedom House can be accessed at www.freedomhouse.org. The website of Human Rights Watch is www.hrw.org. Numerous additional organizations and causes can be located by looking under "Human Rights" in most large search engines. The U.S. State Department publishes an annual human rights report, available on its website at www.state.gov.

**17.** The National Endowment for Democracy can be accessed at www.ned.org; the National Democratic Institute for International Affairs at www.ndi.org; the International Republican Institute at www.iri.org; the International Labor Solidarity organization at www.solidaritycenter.org; the Center for International Private Enterprise at www.cipe.org. In 1998, NED created the World Movement for Democracy, a global network of democracy activists, accessible at www.wmd.org.

**18.** Margaret E. Keck and Kathryn Sikkink, *Activists Beyond Borders* (Ithaca, N.Y.: Cornell University Press, 1998).

**19.** For a history of the Universal Declaration that focuses on Eleanor Roosevelt's role in its drafting and adoption, see Mary Ann Glendon, *A World Made New: Eleanor Roosevelt and the Universal Declaration of Human Rights* (New York: Random House, 2001).

**20.** Both the Convention and the Court were created by the Council of Europe, an organization that is separate from the European Union. For documentation, see www.coe.int.

**21.** The texts can be accessed through the United Nations website, www.un.org.

**22.** For arguments supporting the proposition that democracies are peaceful, see Immanuel Kant, *Perpetual Peace,* published in 1795; Bruce Russett, *Grasping the Democratic Peace* (Princeton: Princeton University Press, 1993); Michael W. Doyle, "Liberalism and World Politics," *American Political Science Review* 80, no. 4 (December 1986): 1151–69. For counterarguments, see Christopher Layne, "Kant or Cant: The Myth of the Democratic Peace," *International Security* 19, no. 2 (Fall 1994): 5–49; and David E. Spiro, "The Insignificance of the Liberal Peace," *International Security* 19, no. 2 (Fall 1994): 50–86.

**23.** Thomas L. Friedman, *The Lexus and the Olive Tree: Understanding Globalization* (New York: Anchor, 2000), 187–190.

**24.** Benjamin R. Barber, *Jihad vs. McWorld: How Globalism and Tribalism Are Reshaping the World* (New York: Ballantine, 1996).

**25.** Zbigniew Brzezinski, *Out of Control: Global Turmoil on the Eve of the 21st* Century (New York: Collier, 1994).

**26.** Henry R. Nau, *At Home Abroad: Identity and Power in American Foreign Policy* (Ithaca, N.Y.: Cornell University Press, 2002).

**27.** Friedman, *Lexus and Olive Tree,* 26, 28.

CHAPTER 2

# MAJOR TOPICS OF COMPARATIVE POLITICS

As we noted in chapter 1, science requires us to define our terms as accurately as possible. It therefore makes sense to begin this overview of major topics of comparative politics by defining politics itself. Though most people have a general idea of what politics is all about, and though you can find valid definitions of the term in dictionaries and textbooks, we present our own working definition here for the sake of clarity and consistency.

## WHAT IS POLITICS?

**Politics** ***is the process by which people pursue collective goals and deal with their conflicts authoritatively by means of government.***

When we say that politics is a *process*, we mean that it is a continuing sequence of events and interactions among various individuals, groups, and governments. The concept of process also implies that these political interactions generally take place within a structure of rules, procedures, and institutions rather than haphazardly.

*People* is an all-encompassing term that includes individuals and all sorts of groups and organizations. The emphasis, however, is on *collective* activity. Though individuals certainly matter in political life, politics is largely a collective endeavor. Each of us may have political ideas, hopes, and passions, but it is practically impossible for you or me to realize our personal political goals by acting alone—unless, of course, our goal is to avoid politics altogether and retreat into apathetic or cynical isolation. Even the most powerful leaders must pursue their agendas by working with others, including other government officials and, at least in democracies, the populations they govern. And solitary bloggers must reach out to a wide world of Web surfers if they want to spread their political messages.

What kinds of groups and organizations are involved in politics? The ever-growing list includes large, relatively unorganized *social groupings* like socioeconomic classes (the middle class and the working class, for example), ethnic groups like Korean Americans and Kurds, and adherents of religions like Catholics and Muslims. It includes fairly broad-based, goal-oriented *social movements* such as the feminist movement or the Islamic fundamentalist movement. It also includes relatively well-organized *non-state associations*, a category broad enough to encompass political parties; traditional interest groups with a large core following (such as trade unions, business and professional associations, and ethnic organizations like the NAACP); smaller and more narrowly focused NGOs (like human rights or environmental policy organizations); private business corporations; and terrorist organizations like al Qaeda. And it includes *governmental institutions* at any level of community life, from the smallest town to an entire country to the world as a whole—the global community. Governmental actors range from elected or unelected officials to institutions like executive agencies (the U.S. Department of Agriculture or Japan's Ministry of Finance), legislative bodies (the British Parliament), judicial organs (the U.S. Supreme Court), and multinational organizations (like the United Nations or the European Union). In this book our main focus is on national communities, that is, entire countries and their national governments. We'll devote less attention to subnational administrative units (such as counties or cities) or to international organizations (such as the United Nations).

Whichever size the community may be, human beings from time immemorial have found ways to organize their interactions in order to promote various *collective goals* or endeavors. Perhaps the most basic goals sought by just about every country in the world are physical security and material well-being. Virtually all nations want to secure the safety of their population and territory against outside aggression, and most would want to improve their living standards. Beyond these basic goals, people can choose from a long list of potential ones, from maximizing individual freedom to improving social welfare, from cleaning up the environment to building powerful military establishments. "To govern is to choose" is an old adage.

In the best of circumstances, people are able to define and accomplish their goals on the basis of cooperation. But few communities are so fortunate as to be without conflict. Even if there is wide consensus on what a community's goals should be, conflicts frequently arise over how to go about achieving them. Many political observers would assert that conflict is the driving force of politics. At times these conflicts are fairly mild and can be dealt with in a peaceful manner through negotiation, bargaining, and compromise. But under less propitious circumstances political conflict may turn violent, exploding into bloody demonstrations, terrorism, or outright warfare.

Note that our definition says that politics involves "dealing with" conflict; it does not say "resolving" conflict. In some cases people do manage to resolve certain conflicts fairly decisively: government authorities broker a strike settlement, racial segregation is outlawed, a contentious tax bill becomes law. But in many cases the conflicts are not resolved or are settled only partially or temporarily: labor disputes keep flaring up, racial tensions persist, tax codes are made to be rewritten. Some conflicts are so intractable that they must be "dealt with" on a continuing basis over years or even decades. It may even happen that a society is so internally divided that *no* enduring settlement can be achieved. The result may be stalemate, civil war, or a one-sided dictatorship that imposes its will on the population.

The most important part of our definition refers to the manner in which people pursue their goals and deal with their conflicts: they do so *authoritatively by means of government*. Actually, this phrase is a bit redundant: "authoritative action" in politics *means* "action taken by government." Governments are "authoritative" to the extent that they make laws and enforce them. In effect they have the final say in political matters and do not allow citizens to take the law into their own hands. We employ the redundancy in order to emphasize the central importance of government in political life. The term *politics*, after all, has all sorts of everyday usages, such as campus politics, office politics, and the like. But *politics as we study it in political science ultimately involves government in one way or another.*

It is government that makes authoritative decisions on the people's goals, whatever those goals may be. And it is to governments that people turn for authoritative decisions in dealing with their conflicts. Even those who want the government to stay out of a particular matter and leave the citizens free to deal with it on their own, or those who attack a government in order to harm or destroy it, are still engaged in a political process insofar as they seek to define the scope and direction of government authority. Whatever their nature, conflicts are "political" to the extent that governments are somehow involved, whether directly or indirectly, immediately or potentially, extensively or minimally.

How governments are organized, how they work, how people interact with them, and, in some cases, how they break down are topics of critical significance in comparative politics. So let's take a look at the two main forms of government in the modern world: *democracy* and *authoritarianism*.

## DEMOCRACY AND AUTHORITARIANISM

There is a fundamental distinction between two broad types of governmental system: *democracies and authoritarian governments*. (The term *regime* means, among other things, *a form of government*.)

> ***The essential idea of democracy is that the people have the right to determine who governs them. In most cases they elect the principal governing officials and hold them accountable for their actions. Democracies also impose legal limits on the government's authority by guaranteeing certain rights and freedoms to their citizens.***

Whereas democracy places the people above the government, **authoritarianism (or dictatorship)** ***places the governing authorities above the people.*** The people have little, if any, say in who governs them or how they are governed. Authoritarian regimes thus tend to be the principal violators of fundamental human rights.

There are several different types of authoritarian government. Perhaps the oldest is the traditional monarchy, in which a king, queen, emperor, or prince, often flanked by blood-related aristocrats, wields effective power. Contemporary variants of monarchal government include Saudi Arabia and several other countries in the Middle East. Another form of authoritarianism is a dictatorship run by a single political party headed by an all-powerful leader or a small committee of leaders. The most extreme variant of such a regime is *totalitarianism*, a political system in which the state's domination of the individual and society as a whole is virtually total, permeating almost every aspect of political and social life. Historically, Hitler's Nazi regime in Germany, Mussolini's fascist dictatorship in Italy, Joseph Stalin's brutal rule over the Soviet Union, and China under Mao Zedong in the 1950s and 1960s were prime examples of totalitarian regimes. North Korea is still totalitarian today. Military governments run directly by the military high command constitute yet another form of authoritarianism. Burma (Myanmar) is a contemporary example. Some authoritarian governments are headed by civilians whose power is heavily protected by the military leadership; others are based on a combination of a dominant party and the military (as in Egypt and in Iraq under Saddam Hussein). ***A state run by religious authorities is called a* theocracy.** Contemporary Iran, whose Islamic government is strongly authoritarian, is a prominent example.

Although democracy and authoritarianism in their purest forms are antithetical, in fact both forms of government come in shades of gray. *There are varying degrees of democracy and authoritarianism.* Quite a few countries in today's world are *mixed regimes*. **Mixed regimes** ***combine elements of democracy and authoritarianism.***

The experts who produce *Freedom in the World*, an annual publication that evaluates democracies and nondemocracies around the globe, provide some useful criteria for making distinctions among governments that are predominantly democratic, those that are predominantly authoritarian, and those that fall in between. Every year they investigate how nearly two hundred countries measure up against a *political rights checklist* and a *civil liberties checklist*. (Table 2.1 presents the main questions on the checklists used in 2005.) Every country is given a score for its performance in meeting the requirements of each checklist. The most democratic performance merits a grade of 1; the most authoritarian gets a grade of 7. (These numbers are not based on rigorous statistical calculations, but reflect the experts' judgments of how each country should be graded.) A country's scores on each list are then averaged to produce a combined score. Countries are considered "free" if they have an average combined score of 1 to 2.5. Those whose scores range from 3 to 5 are considered "partly free." And most of those whose scores run from 5.5 to 7 are categorized as "not free."[1] A list of most of the governments covered in the 2006 edition of *Freedom in the World* can be found in chapter 3.

Obviously, countries with a combined score of 1 are the most democratic, and those bottoming out with a grade of 7 are the most authoritarian. *Freedom in the World* reported that by the end of 2005 there were 51 countries that topped the list with an overall score of 1, and 8 countries brought up the rear with a score of 7. But 135 countries had scores ranging from 1.5 to 6.5, and 58 of these countries were rated "partly free." Many of them are

**TABLE 2.1**

**Checklists from *Freedom in the World***

**Political Rights Checklist***

- Is the head of government or other chief national authority elected through free and fair elections?
- Are the national legislative representatives elected through free and fair elections?
- Are the electoral laws and framework fair?
- Do people have the right to organize in different political parties or other competitive political groupings of their choice, and is the system open to the rise and fall of these competing parties and groupings?
- Is there a significant opposition vote and a realistic possibility for the opposition to increase its support or gain power through elections?
- Are the people's political choices free from domination by the military, foreign powers, totalitarian parties, religious hierarchies, economic oligarchies, or any other powerful group?
- Do cultural, ethnic, religious, and other minorities have full political rights and electoral opportunities?
- Do the freely elected head of government and national legislative representatives determine the policies of the government?
- Is the government free from pervasive corruption?
- Is the government accountable to the electorate between elections, and does it operate with openness and transparency?
- For traditional monarchies that have no parties or electoral process, does the system provide genuine, meaningful consultation with the people, encourage public discussion of policy choices, and allow the right to petition the ruler?
- Is the government or occupying power deliberately changing the ethnic composition of a country or territory so as to destroy a culture or tip the political balance in favor of another group?

**Civil Liberties Checklist***

- Are there free and independent media and other forms of cultural expression?
- Are religious institutions and communities free to practice their faith and express themselves in public and private?
- Is there academic freedom and is the educational system free of extensive political indoctrination?
- Is there open and free private discussion?
- Is there freedom of assembly, demonstration, and open public discussion?
- Is there freedom for nongovernmental organizations (including civic organizations, interest groups, foundations, etc.)?
- Are there free trade unions and peasant organizations or equivalents, and is there effective collective bargaining? Are there free professional and other private organizations?
- Is there an independent judiciary?
- Does the rule of law prevail in civil and criminal matters? Are police under direct civilian control?
- Is there protection from political terror, unjustified imprisonment, exile, or torture, whether by groups that support or oppose the system? Is there freedom from war and insurgencies?
- Do laws, policies, and practices guarantee equal treatment of various segments of the population?
- Does the state control travel or choice of residence, employment, or institution of higher education?
- Do citizens have the right to own property and establish private businesses? Is private business activity unduly influenced by government officials, the security forces, political parties/organizations, or organized crime?
- Are there personal social freedoms, including gender equality, choice of marriage partners, and size of family?
- Is there quality of opportunity and the absence of economic exploitation?

*The full checklist includes sub-questions under the questions listed here.
*Source: Freedom in the World 2006* (Landham, Md.: Rowman & Littlefield, 2006), 878–89.

transitional countries listed in tables 9.4, 9.5, and 9.6. How should we apply the terms *democratic* and *authoritarian* to these intermediate regimes?

To keep it simple, we label the countries classified as "free" in *Freedom in the World* as "democratic," and the countries classified "not free" as "authoritarian." This categorization acknowledges that some democracies are more democratic than others. Countries with a composite score of 2 or 2.5 have problems meeting all the criteria fulfilled by countries with a "perfect" score of 1. (As we'll see in later chapters, even countries with the highest score—like Britain and France—are less than perfect when it comes to providing equal democratic

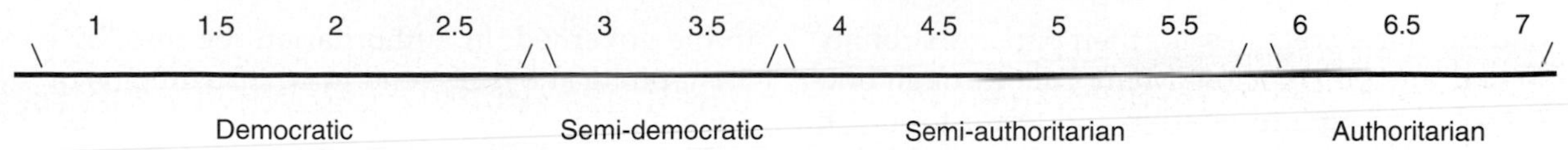


**FIGURE 2.1 Democracy–Authoritarianism Continuum**
The numbers represent a country's combined score of political rights and civil liberties, as reported in *Freedom in the World, 2006*.

rights to all their citizens.) It also acknowledges that authoritarian countries with a score of 6.5 or 6 may not be quite as tyrannical as those with a score of 7. We categorize countries labeled "partly free" in *Freedom in the World* as *mixed regimes.* They can be considered either *semi-democratic* or *semi-authoritarian,* depending on whether one regards the proverbial glass as mostly full or mostly empty (i.e., as *mostly* democratic or *mostly* authoritarian). In raw numbers, we classify countries with a combined score of 3 or 3.5 as semi-democratic, and those with a score ranging from 4 to 5.5 as semi-authoritarian. It seems proper that a high standard should be set for semi-democratic governments; that is why we place countries with a grade of 4 closer to authoritarianism than to democracy. Viewed in these terms, the relationship between democracy and authoritarianism should be seen as a continuum, with intermediate gradations between the extremes. (See figure 2.1.)

What do these labels mean in practice? According to the *Freedom in the World* checklists, a country with an overall rating of 3 or 3.5 might have such democratic procedures as free and fair elections and an independent judiciary, but is penalized for having rampant corruption, pervasive discrimination against women or ethnic minorities, limitations on press freedom, the use of torture, or other nondemocratic practices. Countries with grades ranging from 4 to 5.5 may or may not have democratic elections; in either case, political power tends to be heavily concentrated in the hands of a small elite that evades legal controls and real accountability to the populace. Countries with a grade of 6 or 6.5 may be fundamentally authoritarian in political terms, with an unelected hierarchy that wields power without much accountability to the citizenry; but there may be some redeeming democratic features such as elections to a legislature (though it is controlled by the authorities), a quasi-independent judiciary, or private enterprise. In each case, aspects of democracy coexist with aspects of authoritarianism. The distinction between these two types of government is not always clear-cut.[2]

## POLITICAL PROCESSES

As we've indicated, politics is a process that takes place within a structure of rules and procedures. Viewed in the broadest of terms, the political process typically consists of *bargaining* or *coercion* or some combination of the two. *Bargaining* is a process in which individuals and groups pursue their goals and deal with their conflicts through direct negotiation or indirect forms of exchange. Bargaining typically involves compromise, deal-making, or other forms of give-and-take. It can also involve efforts by one party to exert pressure on other parties. In most instances bargaining is a relatively peaceful process.

*Coercion,* by contrast, means the use of force or the threat to use it. In a coercive political process, A *forces* B to do something, often against B's will.

Democracies and authoritarian regimes employ both bargaining as well as coercion in their political processes. Democracies tend to favor bargaining. Voting, for example, is essentially a bargaining process in which candidates for office make various promises to the voters in exchange for their votes. Once in office, government officials in democracies routinely bargain with one another at various levels—in the legislature, in the executive branch, or between the two—to work out laws and policies. Bargaining is not the only process democracies employ, however; they also engage in coercion. In its most extreme application, the enforcement of the law ultimately depends on force, even in a democracy. The police, the courts, and the penal system are all coercive institutions. It should not surprise us that the word *politics* derives from the same Latin and Greek roots as the word *police.*

Authoritarian regimes, for their part, are strongly oriented toward coercion. Many rule through outright force, using intimidation and terror to stay in power. The military, the secret police, and other forms of coercive power may be displayed quite demonstratively to keep the population and potential opposition groups in line. Still, even authoritarian regimes sometimes engage in bargaining. The mightiest dictators may seek to gain the people's acquiescence by providing economic and social benefits, in effect exchanging such goods for the population's tacit acceptance of the regime. Within the councils of government, meanwhile, the individuals who rule authoritarian regimes may bargain with one another over how to share power at the top or how to govern the country.

In many authoritarian states, the intimidating strength of the regime's coercive power, when combined perhaps with economic benefits or other rewards to key segments of society, such as the business community or a favored religious or ethnic group, may be quite sufficient to keep the general population quiet and opponents of the regime in line. Until the late 1980s, the Soviet Union under communist rule fell into this category: most Soviet citizens (especially ethnic Russians) accepted the regime, and millions were proud of the USSR's superpower status. But some dictatorships have to deal with unruly populations that are not afraid to demonstrate their discontent in spite of the government's coercive strength. Poland under communist rule is a good example. From the earliest stages of Soviet-imposed communism at the end of World War II until the ultimate collapse of Polish communism in 1989–90, millions of Poles dared to defy the governing authorities by openly supporting the Catholic Church, staging demonstrations and strikes, and organizing an independent trade union (Solidarity) that proved instrumental in bringing down the communist regime.

Democracies and authoritarian regimes tend to differ in certain other aspects of the political process as well. The roles of political parties and elections are good examples. In democracies, the main role of parties is to field candidates for elective office, and the main function of elections is to enable citizens to choose those who govern them, thereby ensuring the government's accountability to the governed. In authoritarian regimes, by contrast, political parties tend to be instruments of the government's domination over the populace. The Nazi party of Hitler's Germany, the Communist Party of the former Soviet Union, and Saddam Hussein's Baath party, for example, all had the express aim of keeping the population under the strict control of the governing authorities while endeavoring to cultivate the public's support for their dictatorial rule. In today's world the Chinese Communist Party maintains a monopoly of political power in the People's Republic of China.

Most authoritarian regimes do not permit truly competitive elections. They are generally unwilling to allow a multiplicity of candidates and parties to express their opinions openly or organize their campaigns freely, and they are very reluctant to empower the citizens to vote them out of power. When authoritarian regimes hold elections, they usually rig them with the express purpose of guaranteeing that the ruling authorities win a lopsided victory in some way or other—whether by preventing their main challengers from running for office, harassing those who are allowed to run, dominating the media, reporting false vote tallies, or using other manipulative techniques. These deceptive elections are intended to convey the false impression that the rulers have been confirmed in power by a majority of the population, allegedly by as many as 99 percent of the voters. Some semi-authoritarian regimes may permit competitive elections involving real opposition candidates, but they frequently find ways to limit the opposition's power and reassert their own dominance. For example, they may permit elections to a national legislature, but then deprive the legislators of real lawmaking power.

Whether we are looking at democracies or nondemocracies, parties and elections are central features of *political participation*, an important area of investigation in comparative politics. The various ways elites and masses behave in both types of regimes form the broader topic of *political behavior.*

## SOURCES OF POLITICAL CONFLICT

What kinds of conflicts do people and their governments typically face in political life, and how do democracies and authoritarian regimes deal with them? If we think about it, we can probably come up with a long list of real or potential issues that spark political controversy. In this book, we focus on *five main sources of political conflict: power, resources, identity, ideas,* and *values*. These sources of conflict often overlap with one another.

### Power

In just about every country in the world, some people at one time or another have dominated others. Masters have subjugated slaves, aristocrats have lorded it over commoners, majorities have discriminated against minorities, and so on. Whenever governments get involved in these social relationships, the question of who has power in society becomes a question of *political power*. If a particular group gains control of the state apparatus—including the executive, the police, the courts, and the military—it may be able to get its way all or most of the time, exercising real dominance over the entire population. By contrast, if no group is able to impose its dominance on everyone else, a certain balance of power may exist. In that case, the government may play a mediating role as the various groups that compose society (businesspeople, employees, religious groups, ethnic minorities, and so forth) seek to influence the governing authorities to help them out or favor them in one way or another. In politics, *the state is the prize:* whoever controls the government and its institutions—whether in a dictatorship or a democracy—plays the central role in dominating or influencing political realities.

As we'll see in chapter 4, *dominance* and *influence* are both forms of political power. Democracy is based on *power sharing*, and the main mode of exercising political power in most democracies tends to be the exercise of influence. In authoritarian regimes, dominance tends to prevail. But there can be elements of both dominance and influence in democracies and nondemocracies alike. Regardless of the nature of the regime, politics invariably involves a conflict over *who controls or influences the state*. At its very core, politics is thus a conflict over power itself.

### Resources

*Resources* are another source of political contention. Natural resources like land, oil, and water have ignited conflicts ranging in severity from legislative wrangling to mortal combat. Money itself is also a resource that sparks political controversy. How much will the government spend on the military, the elderly, students, big business, the sick, the poor, the middle class? Which policies will the government adopt to stimulate economic growth, reduce prices, or alleviate poverty? Such bread-and-butter issues are the raw stuff of political controversy in virtually every country in the world.

Conflicts of these kinds are typically *economic* conflicts. **Political economy** ***refers broadly to the relationship between politics and economics.*** It constitutes yet another major topic in comparative politics. Students of political economy look at the various ways economic resources are dealt with through the political process.

In some countries the government plays a relatively small or indirect role in the economy, leaving the better part of economic activity in the hands of private businesses and workers. Democracies tend to grant considerable latitude to private enterprise. But most democratic governments in today's world also play a major role in the national economy, raising taxes, regulating private businesses, enhancing social welfare, and in some cases owning corporations.

Authoritarian regimes, for their part, are generally prone to restrict the freedoms of private enterprises. Control over the country's population requires control over its economy. A comparison of the economic policies of various authoritarian regimes, however, reveals considerable variability. In the most extreme cases, the government may own and operate the entire economy, as was the case in the former USSR. Such a system is called a *centrally planned economy*. But even dictatorships sometimes allow private enterprise, though the government usually keeps a watchful eye on the private sector and may impose regulations to make sure that its activities conform to the government's general policy objectives. Hitler's dictatorship in Nazi Germany, communist China since the 1980s, and various military dictatorships around the world have permitted private enterprise but have usually taken measures to ensure that the business sector complies with the government's economic and political goals.

*The private sector and its activities—including the production of goods and services by businesses and their sale to consumers—are broadly referred to as the* **market economy**, *or simply as* **the marketplace or markets.** *Government in general is frequently referred to as* **the state.**

*One of the most important questions in comparative politics centers on the relationship between states and markets.* How much economic activity should be controlled or regulated by the state, and how much should be left to the free play of market forces? This question is controversial in democracies as well as in nondemocracies.

### Identity

*Identity* constitutes a third source of political conflict. **Identity** ***refers to the ways in which individuals and groups are defined in society.*** (Here we define society in simple terms as a country's population.) Every individual consists of a multiplicity of identities. Everyone has a *gender identity*, a *racial* or *ethnic identity*, and a *generational* identity. Many people also identify themselves with some form of *religion*, whether it is an organized religion or a set of religious beliefs. (A nonreligious or antireligious attitude may also define one's religious identity.) Most people acquire an *occupational identity:* as a student, for example, or a factory worker, a lawyer, or an unemployed person. Educational attainments establish a person's *educational identity* as poorly educated, highly educated, or some intermediate category. Many people also belong to a particular socioeconomic *class*, such as the upper class, the middle class, or the poor. Some people may strongly identify themselves with the area or region in which they live. Southerners, rural folk, suburbanites, and city dwellers exemplify various types of *regional identity*. Some people may identify themselves with a particular language group (or *ethno-linguistic* group), such as English-speaking Canadians and French-speaking Canadians. Some may have strong attachments to a tribe, a clan, or an extended family. And most people share a *national identity* with their compatriots (Americans, Japanese, Swiss, and so on).

The branch of comparative politics that focuses on how the groups associated with these various social identities behave in the political process is known as *political sociology*.

**Political sociology** *is the study of the relationship between social identity and political behavior, and of how political power is distributed among social groups.*

All too often, conflict is the central behavior that arises from these different group identities. Conflicts over opportunities for women and homosexuals, racial or ethnic antagonisms, the clash of generations, religious strife or intolerance, class struggles, or regional rivalries can be found in almost every country in the world. Whenever governments get involved in taking sides or mediating among conflicting identity groups, these conflicts become political conflicts over who has power or how the economy operates.

At a deeper and more personal level, however, identity conflicts can be far more intense than issues that involve just power or resources. They can be a matter of fundamental dignity and respect, qualities to which all human beings feel rightfully entitled. When our basic human worth is at stake, when the essence of who we are and how we live is bound up with profound emotional attachments to our ethnic group, our religion, or some other identity group, we can become fiercely determined to defend ourselves whenever our group is discriminated against or threatened by antagonistic forces. For this reason, identity conflicts are often extremely difficult to resolve. Unlike conflicts over money, we cannot always "split the difference" in conflicts over identity.

Democracies and authoritarian regimes tend to deal with identity conflicts, as with most other matters, in different ways. Democracies approach social conflicts through the ground rules of the democratic process: electoral competition, political bargaining, and the right to organize interest groups. In the most successful cases, democratic governments manage to reduce social antagonisms by helping the contending parties compromise their differences and cooperate on the basis of tolerance and nondiscrimination. If cooperation proves impossible, governments may at least manage to keep the opposing groups from harming each other. Unfortunately, these ground rules are not always observed with scrupulous fairness. Democracies are not immune to social discrimination. Electoral majorities can find ways to subjugate minorities by supporting discriminatory laws. For much of its history, the United States has wrestled with the question of how—and at times even whether—to integrate African Americans into the democratic process on an equal basis with whites. Until multiracial elections were held in 1994, South Africa's government represented the white minority, which comprised only 18 percent of the population, against the country's massive nonwhite majority. Other democracies have had their own difficulties implementing the ideals of democratic nondiscrimination with respect to various social groups.

Still, for all their problems, democracies are usually better disposed than authoritarian regimes to dealing with social conflicts with relative fairness. Fairness is a democratic ideal that many authoritarian regimes cynically spurn. Quite a few dictatorships have rested on privileged social groups such as the upper class or a dominant ethnic or religious group. Most communist governments paid lip service to social equality but were actually ruled by a privileged Communist Party elite. At times the ruling elites have oppressed subjugated groups with cold-blooded ruthlessness, taking full advantage of the government's coercive powers. Under more chaotic conditions, civil tranquillity may break down altogether if the government cannot prevent rival social groups from assailing one another. In recent decades such violent turmoil has plagued both democracies and authoritarian regimes alike, especially in countries torn apart by intractable ethnic or religious divisions.

To get a better understanding of how comparative politics addresses identity, let's take a brief look at some issues connected with *class, ethnicity, religion, gender, tribal* or *clan*, and *generational* identities. We'll be looking at these and other forms of identity conflict in greater detail at various points in this volume.

**Class** The concept of class usually refers to the economic position of an individual or group in society. Class thus refers to a person's *socioeconomic identity*. The division of a country's population into socioeconomic classes is called *social stratification*.

TABLE 2.2

**Socioeconomic Classes in the United States**

| Money Income of Families in 2000: Percent Distributions | |
|---|---|
| **Family Income in 2003** | **% of All Families[a]** |
| Under $15,000 | 15.9 |
| $15,000–24,999 | 13.1 |
| $25,000–34,999 | 11.9 |
| $35,000–49,999 | 15.0 |
| $50,000–74,999 | 18.0 |
| $75,000–99,999 | 11.0 |
| $100,000 and over | 15.1 |

[a]112,000,000 families.

*Source:* U.S. Bureau of the Census, *Statistical Abstract of the United States:* 2006 (Washington, D.C., 2006), 460.

There are two main ways of determining socioeconomic class. One way is the subjective approach: we simply ask people which class they think they belong to. As a general rule, people act on their *perceptions* of reality. If they perceive themselves as middle class or working class, they are likely to behave accordingly, such as by voting for candidates who represent their perceived class interests.

The other way is the objective approach, which employs various quantitative measures. For example, we can divide the population in terms of the annual earnings of families, as illustrated in table 2.2. Alternatively, we can calculate what percentage of a country's annual income goes to the richest 20 percent of the population, what percentage goes to the poorest 20 percent, and how much the three intermediate quintiles share, as indicated in table 2.3. (Of course, we can also divide the population into tenths or some other fraction.) Another objective measure is the **Gini coefficient** (or **Gini index**). This figure ***measures the ratio of rich people to poor people*** and is thus a measure of ***the relative degree of socioeconomic inequality*** within a particular country. *Perfect equality equals zero:* all individuals (or households) receive the same annual income; there is zero inequality. *Maximum inequality equals 100:* only one individual (or household) monopolizes all (100 percent) of society's income while everybody else gets nothing. Any number between 0 and 100 represents the degree to which a society's income distribution pattern deviates from perfect equality.

The significance of the Gini index figures is largely relative: they show that some countries

TABLE 2.3

**Gini Coefficients and Income Distribution in Selected Countries**

| Country | Year | Gini Coefficient | Lowest 20% | Second 20% | Third 20% | Fourth 20% | Highest 20% |
|---|---|---|---|---|---|---|---|
| Denmark | 1997 | 24.7 | 8.3 | 14.7 | 18.2 | 22.9 | 35.8 |
| Japan | 1993 | 24.9 | 10.6 | 14.2 | 17.6 | 22.0 | 35.7 |
| Sweden | 2000 | 25.0 | 9.1 | 14.0 | 17.6 | 22.7 | 36.6 |
| Norway | 2000 | 25.8 | 9.6 | 14.0 | 17.2 | 22.0 | 37.2 |
| Finland | 2000 | 26.9 | 9.6 | 14.1 | 17.5 | 22.1 | 36.7 |
| Hungary | 2002 | 26.9 | 9.5 | 13.9 | 17.6 | 22.4 | 36.5 |
| Germany | 2000 | 28.3 | 8.5 | 13.7 | 17.8 | 23.1 | 36.9 |
| Slovenia | 1999–2000 | 28.4 | 9.1 | 14.2 | 18.1 | 22.9 | 35.7 |
| Ukraine | 2003 | 28.1 | 9.2 | 13.6 | 17.3 | 22.4 | 37.5 |
| Austria | 2000 | 29.1 | 8.6 | 13.3 | 17.4 | 22.9 | 37.8 |
| Netherlands | 1999 | 30.9 | 7.6 | 13.2 | 17.2 | 23.3 | 38.7 |
| Pakistan | 2002 | 30.6 | 9.3 | 13.0 | 16.3 | 21.1 | 40.3 |
| South Korea | 1998 | 31.6 | 7.9 | 13.6 | 18.0 | 23.1 | 37.5 |
| Bangladesh | 2000 | 31.8 | 9.0 | 12.5 | 15.9 | 21.2 | 41.3 |
| India | 1999–2000 | 32.5 | 8.9 | 12.3 | 16.0 | 21.2 | 43.3 |
| Indonesia | 2002 | 32.5 | 8.4 | 11.9 | 15.4 | 21.0 | 43.3 |
| Canada | 2000 | 32.6 | 7.2 | 12.7 | 17.2 | 23.0 | 39.9 |
| France | 1995 | 32.7 | 7.2 | 12.6 | 17.2 | 22.8 | 40.2 |
| Egypt | 1999–2000 | 34.4 | 8.6 | 12.1 | 15.4 | 20.4 | 43.6 |
| United Kingdom | 1999 | 36.0 | 6.1 | 11.4 | 16.0 | 22.5 | 44.0 |
| Israel | 2001 | 39.2 | 5.7 | 10.5 | 15.9 | 23.0 | 44.9 |
| Russia | 2002 | 39.9 | 6.1 | 10.5 | 14.9 | 21.8 | 46.6 |
| United States | 2000 | 40.8 | 5.4 | 10.7 | 15.7 | 22.4 | 45.8 |
| Nigeria | 2003 | 43.7 | 5.0 | 9.6 | 14.5 | 21.7 | 49.2 |
| Iran | 1998 | 43.0 | 5.1 | 9.4 | 14.1 | 21.5 | 49.9 |
| Turkey | 2003 | 43.6 | 5.3 | 9.7 | 14.2 | 21.5 | 47.5 |
| China | 2001 | 44.7 | 4.7 | 9.0 | 14.2 | 22.1 | 50.0 |
| Venezuela | 2000 | 44.1 | 4.7 | 9.4 | 14.5 | 22.1 | 49.3 |
| Mexico | 2002 | 49.5 | 4.3 | 8.3 | 12.6 | 19.7 | 55.1 |
| South Africa | 2000 | 57.8 | 3.5 | 6.3 | 10.0 | 18.0 | 62.2 |
| Brazil | 2003 | 58.0 | 2.6 | 6.2 | 10.7 | 18.4 | 62.1 |
| Haiti | 2001 | 59.2 | 2.4 | 6.2 | 10.4 | 17.7 | 63.4 |
| Bolivia | 2002 | 60.1 | 1.5 | 5.9 | 10.9 | 18.7 | 63.0 |

*Source:* World Bank, *World Development Indicators 2006*, 76–78.

have a more equal sharing of wealth than others do. *The lower the Gini index, the greater the degree of socioeconomic equality; the higher the number, the greater the degree of inequality.* As table 2.3 shows, no country comes even close to perfect equality (zero); but among the countries selected here, real differences are evident. In Denmark, which tops the list, the richest 20 percent shared 35.8 percent of the country's total income in 1997; the poorest quintile shared 8.3 percent. In Bolivia, at the bottom, the gap between rich and poor in 2002 was much greater.

The figures displayed in tables 2.2 and 2.3 demonstrate that *all* countries are socially stratified. In democracies and nondemocracies alike, class distinctions are often a powerful influence on political behavior and government policies. In democracies, class is one of the main factors affecting the way people vote. The game of politics in most democracies revolves to a considerable degree around conflicts between the rich, the poor, and the middle classes over the budget and the government's economic policies. Dictatorships of various kinds must also pay heed to class distinctions, and they often base their rule on alliances with one or more favored socioeconomic groups. Conflicts over class identity thus frequently overlap with conflicts over power and resources.

Social class often goes a long way to explaining how democracy itself comes about and endures over the long run. As many observers have pointed out, democracies tend to flourish when there is a vibrant middle class. Countries that are sharply polarized between a small number of extremely rich people and masses of impoverished laborers and peasants, with few middle-class professionals or private business people in between, are more likely to succumb to authoritarianism.[3]

**Ethnicity** Ethnicity *is a form of group identification or distinctiveness often based on a* **common biological ancestry** *in the distant past. More accurately, it is typically based on the* **belief** *in such a common biological ancestry,* because the fact itself cannot normally be proven with scientific accuracy.

The terms *ethnicity* and *ethnic group* sometimes refer to *race*. Traditionally, anthropologists and other scientists have applied the term *race* to only a few large groupings of human beings who are assumed to have various biological commonalities. Caucasians (whites), Negroids (blacks), Mongoloids (East Asians), and three or four other such groupings have often been characterized as the main racial categories. Despite certain noticeable physical differences, there is no such thing as a completely distinct race that is biologically separate from all other races. Each of these groups contains a mixture of biological characteristics, including blood types and DNA.

The same can be said for the many subgroups that fall within these larger racial categories. Caucasians, for example, include Indo-Europeans, a category that is further subdivided into such groupings as Scandinavians, Anglo-Saxons, Slavs, and others. These latter groups in turn can be further divided into smaller groupings. Slavs, for example, would include Russians, Poles, Czechs, Slovaks, Ukrainians, Serbs, Croats, and still others. Although each of these groups is typically defined as an ethnic group, none is biologically distinct. Any racial or ethnic group that is defined in biological terms is bound to consist of a mixture of biological influences—the result of mass migrations, invasions, and other forms of intergroup contact—stretching far back into unrecorded time. The notion that individual races or other biologically defined groupings are fundamentally distinct is symptomatic of *racism*, which falsely exalts some ethnic groups as genetically superior while demeaning others as fundamentally inferior.

To say that no ethnic group is biologically homogeneous, however, is not to deny the reality of kinship patterns within identifiable groups. Centuries of living together within relatively circumscribed geographical boundaries and intramarriage among members of the same group can create real biological bonds among its members. These bonds explain why so many ethnic groups define themselves on the basis of blood ties. Japanese, Germans, Koreans, Russians, and hundreds of other collectivities regard themselves as distinctive ethnic groups largely on the basis of kinship ties, forged in the course of a long history of living together. In some cases these ties foster a people's sense of constituting a distinctive "nation," as we'll see in chapter 6. It is therefore perfectly acceptable to acknowledge that ethnicity often has a genuine biological basis, at least to some extent, as long as we also recognize that no ethnic group can certify an unbroken lineage from a unique set of identifiable common ancestors. As Donald Horowitz, a noted scholar of ethno-politics, puts it, ethnicity is frequently based on the "myth of collective ancestry." Myths can be powerful integrative forces in ethnic identity, however.[4]

Kinship ties are not the only defining features of ethnicity. Ethnographers and other students of ethnicity also point to such nonbiological phenomena as language, social customs, cuisine, clothing, art, and other cultural phenomena as factors that may distinguish one ethnic group from another. In some cases the concept of ethnicity may even include the group's predominant religious beliefs. More typically, however, ethnicity and religion are separate identities.

Despite the complexities of defining ethnicity, most people in today's world identify themselves with an ethnic group. It also happens that some people *are defined by others* as belonging to a particular ethnic group. In some countries, persons of mixed race, for example black and white, may be considered black (or, in some countries, "colored") by others in society, irrespective of how such individuals might prefer to define themselves. Social scientists therefore say that ethnic identity is *socially constructed:* it is created or defined by people in the course of their social interactions rather than being determined by objective criteria like biology. Ethnic self-definitions, along with the definitions imposed on people by others, can have a profound effect on political behavior. Tragically, they can also lead to intractable political conflicts, at times with violent results.

**Religion** Religion is another social identity that can have a demonstrable impact on the way people behave in politics. In the most tranquil of circumstances, societies divided along religious lines find a way to permit adherents of different religions to live peacefully side by side. The United States, for example, was established on the basis of the separation of church and state, and its traditions of religious tolerance have made a vital contribution to its success as a democracy. Many people came to America precisely in order to escape religious persecution at home. Most of them practiced religious tolerance to ensure their own religious freedom.[5]

But religious identity often gives rise to sharp political conflict. (Religious conflict is sometimes called *sectarian* conflict, from "sect.") The separation of church and state does not necessarily mean the separation of religion and politics. In the United States, for example, controversies abound over the interpretation of the clauses of the First Amendment of the Constitution which state that "Congress shall make no law respecting the establishment of religion, or prohibiting the free exercise thereof." In accordance with the most literal meaning of these clauses, the United States does not have an official (or "established") state religion or church, and Americans are generally free to practice any religion they want, subject to laws against bigamy, drug use, and the like. Beyond a general agreement on these basic principles, however, there has been considerable disagreement among American citizens, politicians, and jurists on the extent to which the U.S. government, or state and local governments, may permit religious beliefs, practices, and symbols to cross the boundary separating church and state. Quite often the courts determine where that boundary lies, though court rulings rarely end debate on these matters. More broadly, religious doctrines and values are central to the deep disagreements dividing Americans over such issues as abortion, gay marriage, euthanasia, creationism, school prayer, and related issues. Inevitably such conflicts spill over into the political process, directly affecting the votes people cast, the laws passed by legislatures, and the cases brought before the courts.

The relationship between religion and the state has been a source of controversy in other countries as well, resulting in a wide variety of constitutional arrangements. Some countries have an *established church*—that is, an official state religion or church. The United Kingdom has two established churches: the Church of England, which is the Episcopalian (or Anglican) church that was founded by King Henry VIII in the sixteenth century, and which is still headed by the reigning monarch; and the Church of Scotland, which is Presbyterian. British citizens enjoy freedom of religion, however, and may worship as they wish. Moreover, British citizens enjoy political and legal equality regardless of their religious faith. Iran takes the concept of an established religion more literally. The Islamic Republic's theocratic government is run by hardline clerics; more moderate clerics have been harassed. The Iranian legal system is based on Islamic law (*shariah*). Christians and Jews may worship freely but they are denied political and legal equality, encountering systematic discrimination in both government and nongovernment employment, property rights, and education. In stark contrast, other countries go even further than the United States in proclaiming the separation of church and state. France, for example, passed a law on secularity (*laïcité*) in 1905 mandating the government's complete neutrality in religious matters. This law was fiercely opposed by many French Catholics at the time, in part because it limited public funding for Catholic schools. More recently the tradition of French secularism has created animosity in the country's growing Muslim community, following the government's 2004 ban on the wearing of headscarves and other religious attire in public schools. Turkey has its own concept of secularity, despite the fact that its population is 99 percent Muslim. We'll discuss Turkey in chapter 6.

In addition to sparking constitutional conflicts over church–state relations, religion is frequently the source of conflict between different elements of a country's population. In some cases these conflicts involve adherents of different religions.

Anti-Semitism, for example, has a particularly long history in Christian Europe and Russia, producing the Holocaust during World War II. Nigeria experiences intense strife between its Muslims and Christians. India has seen periodic outbreaks of violence between Muslims and Hindus. Other countries have witnessed sharp inter-religious contention as well. In still other instances there has been antagonism between different denominations of the same religion. Sectarian violence in Northern Ireland between Protestants and Catholics has claimed more than 3,200 lives since 1969. Contemporary Iraq is seething with religious tensions between *Sunni* and *Shiite* (or Shia) Muslims, a dispute that goes back nearly 1,400 years to the formative decades of Islam. (Sunnis reject the Shiites' claim that the Prophet Muhammad's son-in-law Ali was the legitimately chosen fourth successor to Muhammad as the leader of the Muslim faith.) There are internecine feuds between various doctrinal orientations within the Sunni and Shia traditions as well.

Still other countries suffer from conflicts both between and within religions. Lebanon is a particularly tortured example.

## LEBANON

A country with eighteen officially recognized religious groups, Lebanon has been caught in the crossfire of Middle East conflicts for much of the past forty years. After gaining its independence from France in 1943–44, Lebanon established a democracy on the basis of an artfully constructed power-sharing arrangement among its three largest religious communities: Christians (mostly Maronites), Sunni Muslims, and Shiite Muslims. A National Covenant worked out in 1943 provided that the country's president would always be a Christian, its prime minister a Sunni, and the speaker of its parliament, the National Assembly, a Shiite. Initially, Christians constituted a slight majority of the population, and Sunnis outnumbered Shiites. But more than 100,000 Palestinians (mostly Sunni) fled to Lebanon after the creation of Israel in 1948, and their numbers rose to more than 300,000 by the mid-1970s. Lebanese Muslims outnumbered Christians by the early 1960s. By 1975 the Shia population had tripled, constituting 30 percent of the population. These population trends reinforced Muslim grievances against Christians, and Shiite grievances against both Christians and Sunnis.

As long as peace prevailed, Beirut prospered as the "Paris of the Middle East." But the tensions simmering between the three main religious groups erupted into a brutal civil war that dragged on from 1975 to 1991. The war was fought mainly between Muslims and Christians, but it was exacerbated by rivalries within each religion. The conflict resulted in more than 100,000 deaths and the demolition of the country's fragile democracy. Meanwhile, the Palestine Liberation Organization under Yasser Arafat increasingly used southern Lebanon, which borders Israel, as a base for attacks against the Israelis starting in the late 1960s, following Israel's victory in the Six-Day War of 1967 (see chapter 6). As these attacks persisted, Israeli troops entered southern Lebanon in 1979 and 1980. In 1982 Israel launched a major invasion of Lebanon, and Palestinian forces were compelled to leave the country. Subsequently, after Lebanon's new Maronite president was assassinated, Israel collaborated with Maronite militias that massacred between seven hundred and eight hundred Palestinians in the Sabra and Shatila refugee camps in September 1982. Israel would occupy southern Lebanon for the next eighteen years. Meanwhile, Syria had traditionally regarded Lebanon as falling within its sphere of influence. Under two successive dictators—Hafez al-Assad, who ruled from 1970 until his death in 2000, and his son Bashar al-Assad—Syria maintained as many as sixteen thousand troops in Lebanon starting in 1976. After the United States, France, and other Western countries sent troops to Beirut to enforce a ceasefire in the civil war, suicide bombers killed 241 U.S. marines and 59 French soldiers in 1983.

Iran began its intervention in Lebanese affairs in this period. Iran's Islamic Republic, a theocracy led by an intensely anti-Western and anti-Israeli government of Shiite clerics, collaborated with a group of Lebanese Shiite clerics to establish a new organization called *Hezbollah* ("Party of God") in 1982. Lebanon's Shiites, numbering 1.4 million, were now the largest religious denomination in the country. Traditionally given the short end of the stick in both political and economic terms, they were largely poor and were heavily concentrated in the villages of southern Lebanon, in parts of the Bekaa Valley neighboring Syria, and in Beirut's southern suburbs. Hezbollah, with Iranian assistance, was determined to raise the Shiites' political influence in Lebanon and to work against the Israeli occupation. The organization's declared goal was the ultimate elimination of Israel as a Jewish state. To these ends it created a well-armed militia along with a network of hospitals, schools, and social services for Lebanese Shiites, constituting a state within a state. It was also a political party engaged in electoral politics, and it ran an international terror network responsible for attacks as far away as Argentina. Iran supplied Hezbollah with arms and financial support.

Lebanon's nightmarish civil war began winding down with the conclusion of the Taif accords, brokered in 1989 by the Arab League, which represented the region's main Arab governments. Lebanese Christians and Muslims agreed to share power on a 50–50 basis. Not all Maronites and Muslims accepted this arrangement; political assassinations and civil violence continued until 1991. Gradually, however, Lebanon started to rebuild its shattered political, social, and economic infrastructure. These efforts gained ground under Rafiq Hariri, a Sunni Muslim and self-made billionaire, who served as prime minister from 1992 to 1998, and then again from 2000 to 2004. Hariri turned against Syrian interference in Lebanese politics and focused on rebuilding Beirut and other parts of the war-ravaged country. Syria threw its support behind Emile Lahoud, a Maronite who was elected Lebanon's president in 1998.

In 2000, Israel withdrew its troops from all of southern Lebanon except for a small area known as the Shebaa Farms, strategically located at the juncture of Israel, Lebanon, and Syria. Pressures were also building among many Lebanese for the withdrawal of Syrian troops and the disarmament of Hezbollah, measures that pro-democracy forces regarded as essential for the Lebanese government to gain control over all its territory. In September 2004 the United Nations Security Council passed Resolution 1559, which called upon "all remaining foreign forces to withdraw from Lebanon" and for "the disbanding and disarmament of all Lebanese and non-Lebanese militias." In the same month Syria pressured Lebanon's National Assembly to extend President Lahoud's term in office by an additional three years. In protest, Hariri resigned as prime minister the following month. In February 2005, Hariri and twenty-two others were killed in a car-bomb explosion. A UN report blamed Syrian and Lebanese security officials for the attack. Over the course of 2005, ten more bombings were aimed at politicians, journalists, and other Lebanese with anti-Syrian views.

Growing indignation at Syria triggered massive anti-Syrian demonstrations and an upsurge in pro-democracy sentiments known as the "Cedar Revolution." Elections to the National Assembly in the spring of 2005 returned a large anti-Syrian majority. In July, Fouad Siniora—a graduate of American University in Beirut and a former business partner of Hariri's—became prime minister. Siniora's election was warmly greeted by the United States, as he vowed to keep Lebanon on the path of democracy. In an effort to build national unity, Siniora's new multiparty government included two Hezbollah cabinet ministers. Meanwhile, Syria withdrew its remaining troops in 2005, under intense pressure from the United States and its European allies.

In the summer of 2006, Hezbollah forces entered northern Israel and captured two Israeli soldiers, killing three others. On the same day, Hezbollah launched rocket attacks on Israeli forces in Shebaa Farms and on the Israeli town of Shlomi. Israel retaliated with troop and tank incursions into southern Lebanon, which had been a heavily fortified Hezbollah stronghold since 2000. These events triggered a new round of violence in the region, as Hezbollah—with support from Syria and Iran—unleashed rocket attacks on Haifa and smaller Israeli towns, killing and wounding civilians. Israel bombed suspected Hezbollah targets throughout Lebanon, inflicting hundreds of civilian casualties, and sent thousands of troops into southern Lebanon to clear out Hezbollah military outposts. The Israelis also bombed runways, bridges, and highways in an effort to prevent Iran and Syria from resupplying Hezbollah, and they devastated Shiite neighborhoods in Beirut and other cities and towns. (Hezbollah launched many of its short-range Katyusha rockets from houses and apartment buildings.) Nearly a million Lebanese and at least a hundred thousand Israelis left their homes in search of safety, and a major humanitarian disaster occurred in Lebanon. Efforts to achieve a cease-fire through the United Nations took weeks. By the end of 2006, a tenuous truce was in place. But instability continued as Pierre Gemayel, the descendent of a politically prominent Maronite family and an outspokenly anti-Syrian member of Siniora's cabinet, was assassinated, and Hezbollah staged mass demonstrations aimed at toppling the pro-democracy government.

---

The relationship between religion and democracy has often been a source of controversy and, at times, sharp conflict. Democracy is essentially a secular idea. It does not derive directly from any of the world's great religions. Historically, most religions have tended to be exclusionary, each one regarding itself as the main repository of divine inspiration and as the primary executor of God's will, however it may conceive of the deity (or deities). These exclusionary attitudes have often produced intolerance of other religions and, in the worst of cases, incessant bloodshed, as evidenced not only in the examples we have just cited but also in the Crusades, Europe's Wars of Religion, Islamic terrorism, and other outbursts of religious violence. Modern democracy, by contrast, derives mainly from the European Enlightenment of the seventeenth and eighteenth centuries, an intellectual movement that exalted tolerance, scientific reasoning, and political liberty in an era when these ideals were still exceedingly rare. By advocating tolerance of all religions, democracy makes peace between religions possible by preventing the domination of one religion over all the others. But religious tolerance, like racial tolerance, can be very difficult for some people to accept.

One of the burning issues of the contemporary world is the question of whether Islam is compatible with democracy. We'll address this question more thoroughly in chapter 14. For now, it is worth noting that today the Muslim world—consisting of approximately 1.5 billion adherents and fifty countries with a Muslim majority—is characterized by considerable religious and political diversity. From Iran's Shiite theocracy to Indonesia's electoral democracy, from al Qaeda's network of terror to Turkey's membership in NATO (the U.S.-led North Atlantic Treaty Organization), the Muslim community presents a vast panorama of political orientations, alliances, and leaders. The patterns of conflict and cooperation that arise from these differences are equally variegated. Conflicts between Muslims and non-Muslims in some areas coexist with ties of cooperation in others. Universal Muslim reverence for the Koran coexists with disagreements over its meaning and disputes about Muhammad's rightful heirs. Like other major religions, Islam is the source of intense bonds of community, but also of acute dissension.

Can religious leaders change their attitudes toward democracy? The history of the Roman Catholic Church hierarchy provides some instructive answers to this still-timely question.

## CATHOLICISM AND DEMOCRACY

One of the most profound observers of American politics, the French political theorist Alexis de Tocqueville, noted during his visit to the United States in the 1830s that America's Roman Catholics were "the most republican and democratic of all classes in the United States." Later in the century, however, the Catholic hierarchy in Rome adopted a decidedly negative stance on democracy, especially in Italy. Until 1860, Italy lacked a central government; its territory was carved up into a multiplicity of political entities answering to different rulers. At the time, the pope was not only the spiritual head of world Catholicism but also the temporal ruler of a large part of the Italian peninsula known as the Papal States. Efforts by Italian nationalists to unite the country under a single monarch and an elected parliament achieved their first success in 1860, when most of the country was united under the new Kingdom of Italy. In the process, the papacy lost half the Papal States to the new government. With the completion of the unification process ten years later, the Church lost the rest of its territorial domains with the exception of the small enclave that became known as Vatican City.

From the outset, the papacy opposed not only Italy's unification but also the ideas of political liberty and a secular state that accompanied it. All these tendencies were regarded as a direct challenge to papal authority. In the *Syllabus of Errors* (1864), Pope Pius IX flatly dismissed any compromise "with progress, with liberalism, and with modern civilization." He refused to recognize the unified Italian state, and he excommunicated Italy's king from the Catholic Church. In the early 1870s the Vatican issued declarations sternly forbidding Italian Catholics from voting in parliamentary elections and from participating in national politics. Meanwhile, many supporters of the new Italy embraced *anticlericalism*, a position of strict opposition to the influence of religious clergy in public life. Even Catholic proponents of this view demanded the formal separation of church and state.

In the decades that followed, the papacy's opposition to democracy mellowed. As the Italian state and its elected parliament showed no signs of disintegrating, and as Italian political parties that were hostile to the Church—such as the anticlerical parties and the Marxist-oriented Socialist Party—remained popular, subsequent popes reversed course and relaxed the Church's earlier antidemocracy declarations. Following World War I, Pope Benedict XV rescinded the ban on Catholic political participation. He also encouraged the formation of a Catholic political party, the Popular Party, which scored impressive gains in the 1919 parliamentary elections. After the destruction of Benito Mussolini's fascist dictatorship and the end of World War II, the Catholic Church renewed its support for democracy, providing moral and material support for a new Catholic party, the Christian Democrats, whose leaders dominated Italian politics until the early 1990s.

The Catholic Church hierarchy's evolution from opposition to democracy to support for its basic principles provides striking evidence that organized religions can change their attitudes toward democracy. Of course, the conditions under which the papacy changed its views were rooted in the specific circumstances of Italian politics and the specific international milieu of those times. The world today is very different in many fundamental respects. Moreover, the Catholic Church is much more centralized than other religions such as Islam, which has no universally accepted authority figure like the pope. Nevertheless, the papacy's experience demonstrates that a highly antidemocratic religious hierarchy can embrace democracy if support for democracy in the surrounding society is strong, and if the religion can find a role of its own in a democratic political system.

**Gender** It took a long time for women to win the most elementary political rights in the world's democracies. Women first won a general right to vote in New Zealand in 1893. Despite their long histories as electoral democracies, Britain did not grant women the vote until 1918, the United States did not adopt a constitutional amendment according all its female citizens the right to vote until 1920, France did not extend the franchise to women until 1944, and Switzerland not until 1971. Ever since the 1960s and 1970s, feminist movements around the world have vigorously promoted public awareness of the subordinate status of women in various spheres of social and political life. Gender issues overlap with conflicts over political power and economic resources, and—in many countries—religion.

In some cases, governments have responded. Legislation has been passed to address such issues as job discrimination and sexual harassment. In other cases, governmental action has not been as effective as many women would wish, even in democracies. In most nondemocracies, women have few or no opportunities to speak up for a more equitable status in society. In India, Bangladesh, and other countries, killings and suicides over dowries are common. The deliberate abortion and infanticide of girls is practiced in India, Pakistan, China and other countries, resulting in abnormally low female-to-male sex ratios. Various African groups engage in the ritual genital mutilation of women. Rape and domestic violence are common around the world, and in many countries such acts routinely go unpunished.

In most of the developing world, especially in authoritarian regimes, women generally have less schooling and lower literacy rates than men. In the developing world and even in the most economically developed democracies of North America, Europe, and elsewhere, women have lower levels of economic activity and lower levels of political participation than men, at times substantially so.[6] Women are still underrepresented in the governmental structures of most democracies today; that is, their share of governmental positions is less than their share of the population, which is usually about 50 percent. As table 2.4 illustrates, they do better in some national parliaments than in others.[7]

Another indicator of the status of women relative to men is the Gender Empowerment Measure (GEM), which is a composite measure of men's and women's political and economic participation and decision-making and their power over resources. Countries with a high GEM value have greater political and economic gender equality than countries with a lower value. Table 2.5 on page 48 is a list of selected countries that are rank-ordered according to their GEM values.

Women are especially disadvantaged in the Muslim world. A recent Freedom House survey of sixteen states in the Middle East and North Africa (including the Palestinian Authority)—states with large Muslim majorities and with little or no real democracy—found that women were routinely discriminated against in every category of political, economic, and social rights. Using a rigorous scientific methodology, the team of regional experts who conducted the study found that, on a scale of 1 to 5 (with 1 constituting the lowest level of women's rights and 5 the highest), not one of these countries scored a 4 or 5 in any of five separate categories of rights. Most of these countries fell below a score of 3 in all five categories, reflecting major restrictions by the government and non-state actors on women's rights to equal justice and nondiscrimination, to personal freedom and security, to economic freedom and opportunity, to political participation, and to social and cultural opportunities.[8] In another study, Steven Fish found that the status of women in traditionally Muslim countries is the

**TABLE 2.4**

**Percentage of Female Members of Lower House or Unicameral Legislature in Selected Countries (November 30, 2006)**

| Country | % | Country | % | Country | % | Country | % |
|---|---|---|---|---|---|---|---|
| Sweden | 45.3 | Bulgaria | 22.1 | Chile | 15.0 | Malta | 9.2 |
| Costa Rica | 38.6 | Moldova | 21.8 | Bosnia- | | Malaysia | 9.1 |
| Finland | 38.0 | Croatia | 21.7 | Herzegovina | 14.3 | Brazil | 8.8 |
| Norway | 37.9 | Pakistan | 21.3 | Cyprus | 14.3 | Ukraine | 8.7 |
| Denmark | 36.9 | Portugal | 21.3 | Israel | 14.2 | Montenegro | 8.6 |
| Netherlands | 36.7 | Singapore | 21.2 | South Korea | 13.4 | India | 8.3 |
| Spain | 36.0 | Canada | 20.8 | Ireland | 13.3 | Kenya | 7.3 |
| Argentina | 35.0 | Poland | 20.4 | Greece | 13.0 | Benin | 7.2 |
| Mozambique | 34.8 | Bahamas | 20.0 | Liberia | 12.5 | Albania | 7.1 |
| Belgium | 34.7 | Slovakia | 20.0 | Niger | 12.4 | Mongolia | 6.6 |
| Iceland | 33.3 | United Kingdom | 19.7 | France | 12.2 | Algeria | 6.2 |
| South Africa | 32.8 | Dominican Republic | 19.7 | Slovenia | 12.2 | Nigeria | 6.1 |
| Austria | 32.2 | Senegal | 19.2 | Serbia | 12.0 | Jordan | 5.5 |
| New Zealand | 32.2 | Latvia | 19.0 | Jamaica | 11.7 | Sri Lanka | 4.9 |
| Germany | 31.6 | Estonia | 18.8 | Lesotho | 11.7 | Lebanon | 4.7 |
| Burundi | 30.5 | Venezuela | 18.0 | Indonesia | 11.3 | Turkey | 4.4 |
| Peru | 29.2 | Italy | 17.3 | Romania | 11.2 | Bahrain | 4.2 |
| Macedonia | 28.3 | Bolivia | 16.9 | Botswana | 11.1 | Iran | 4.1 |
| Afghanistan | 27.3 | El Salvador | 16.7 | Uruguay | 11.1 | Haiti | 2.3 |
| Namibia | 26.9 | Panama | 16.7 | Ghana | 10.9 | Egypt | 2.0 |
| Iraq | 25.5 | United States | 16.2 | Hungary | 10.4 | Kuwait | 1.5 |
| Switzerland | 25.0 | Czech Republic | 15.5 | Mali | 10.2 | Yemen | 0.3 |
| Lithuania | 24.8 | Cape Verde | 15.3 | Paraguay | 10.0 | Kyrgyzstan | 0.0 |
| Australia | 24.7 | Philippines | 15.3 | Russia | 9.8 | Saudi Arabia | 0.0 |
| Luxembourg | 23.3 | Nicaragua | 15.2 | Georgia | 9.4 | United Arab Emirates | 0.0 |
| Mexico | 22.6 | Bangladesh | 15.1 | Japan | 9.4 | | |

[a]The 100-member US Senate had 16 women.
*Source:* Inter-Parliamentary Union, www.ipu.org/wmn-e/classif.htm

single most important variable associated with authoritarianism in the Islamic world—more significant than levels of political violence or the degree of state secularism. Fish used a variety of statistical measures to show that women are considerably more disadvantaged in Muslim countries than in non-Muslim countries.[9] Quite clearly, the subaltern status of women is a major factor obstructing democracy in the Muslim world.

Even though politics is a male-dominated enterprise in every country in the world, the number of women who have succeeded in gaining positions in the executive, legislative, or judicial branches of government has nevertheless risen appreciably since the 1970s in most economically advanced democracies. In a few cases women have risen to the apex of the political pyramid, even in predominantly Muslim countries like Bangladesh, Indonesia, Pakistan, and Turkey. A list of women who have occupied the post of elected head of state or government in democracies is provided in table 2.6.

When political scientists look at the role that gender plays in shaping political behavior, one of the essential questions they ask is, to what extent is the political activity of women determined *mainly* by their identity as women? Are the political opinions and attitudes of women shaped fundamentally by their gender, or do women behave essentially the same as men? In most democracies the answers are mixed. Some women place gender above all other considerations in their political activity, but many other women agree with men on the same topics and vote accordingly. Nevertheless, in virtually every country in the world, gender is a social identity that has important political implications, even

**TABLE 2.5**

**Selected Countries Rank-Ordered by Gender Empowerment Measure (GEM) Values**

| Rank | Country | GEM Value | Rank | Country | GEM Value | Rank | Country | GEM Value |
|---|---|---|---|---|---|---|---|---|
| 1. | Norway | 0.928 | 28. | Latvia | 0.606 | 55. | Ecuador | 0.490 |
| 2. | Denmark | 0.860 | 29. | Bulgaria | 0.604 | 56. | Romania | 0.488 |
| 3. | Sweden | 0.852 | 30. | Slovenia | 0.603 | 57. | Belize | 0.486 |
| 4. | Iceland | 0.834 | 31. | Namibia | 0.603 | 58. | Malta | 0.486 |
| 5. | Finland | 0.833 | 32. | Croatia | 0.599 | 59. | South Korea | 0.479 |
| 6. | Belgium | 0.828 | 33. | Slovakia | 0.597 | 60. | Russia | 0.477 |
| 7. | Australia | 0.826 | 34. | Czech Republic | 0.595 | 61. | Chile | 0.475 |
| 8. | Netherlands | 0.814 | 35. | Estonia | 0.595 | 62. | El Salvador | 0.467 |
| 9. | Germany | 0.813 | 36. | Greece | 0.594 | 63. | Thailand | 0.452 |
| 10. | Canada | 0.807 | 37. | Italy | 0.589 | 64. | Venezuela | 0.441 |
| 11. | Switzerland | 0.795 | 38. | Mexico | 0.583 | 65. | Paraguay | 0.427 |
| 12. | United States | 0.793 | 39. | Cyprus | 0.571 | 66. | Ukraine | 0.417 |
| 13. | Austria | 0.779 | 40. | Panama | 0.563 | 67. | Georgia | 0.416 |
| 14. | New Zealand | 0.769 | 41. | Macedonia | 0.555 | 68. | Bahrain | 0.393 |
| 15. | Spain | 0.745 | 42. | Tanzania | 0.538 | 69. | Mongolia | 0.388 |
| 16. | Ireland | 0.724 | 43. | Japan | 0.534 | 70. | Fiji | 0.381 |
| 17. | Bahamas | 0.719 | 44. | Hungary | 0.528 | 71. | Pakistan | 0.379 |
| 18. | United Kingdom | 0.716 | 45. | Dominican Republic | 0.527 | 72. | Sri Lanka | 0.370 |
| 19. | Costa Rica | 0.668 | 46. | Philippines | 0.526 | 73. | Cambodia | 0.364 |
| 20. | Argentina | 0.665 | 47. | Bolivia | 0.525 | 74. | Honduras | 0.356 |
| 21. | Portugal | 0.656 | 48. | Peru | 0.511 | 75. | Iran | 0.316 |
| 22. | Singapore | 0.654 | 49. | Botswana | 0.505 | 76. | Turkey | 0.285 |
| 23. | Trinidad and Tobago | 0.650 | 50. | Uruguay | 0.504 | 77. | Egypt | 0.274 |
| 24. | Israel | 0.622 | 51. | Malaysia | 0.502 | 78. | Saudi Arabia | 0.253 |
| 25. | Barbados | 0.615 | 52. | Colombia | 0.500 | 79. | Bangladesh | 0.218 |
| 26. | Lithuania | 0.614 | 53. | Moldova | 0.494 | 80. | Yemen | 0.123 |
| 27. | Poland | 0.612 | 54. | Swaziland | 0.492 | | | |

*Note:* The GEM value is calculated on the basis of percentage shares of seats in parliament held by men and women; shares of male and female legislators; shares of senior officials and managers; shares of professional and technical positions; and women's and men's estimated earned income. A score of 1.0 indicates equality of men and women based on these measures.
*Source:* United Nations Development Program's *Human Development Report 2005* (New York: UNDP, 2005), 303–306, 345.

in those countries where women's voices are largely silenced. We'll look at women's issues further in the countries to be examined in Part Two of this book, as well as in a number of countries treated later in Part One.

**Ellen Johnson-Sirleaf Elected President of Liberia in 2005**

**Tribes, Clans, and Families** Close kinship ties are perhaps the most tightly knit forms of identity. In some countries they play important political roles, providing a strong basis of group self-interest, social and political organization, and even political power. The distinction between tribes, clans, and families is not always precise. All three involve kinship relationships, and their differences are based mainly on size. *Tribes* are typically the largest of the three groups, often consisting of interrelated

TABLE 2.6

**Female Heads of State or Government in Democracies**

| Name | Country | Office | Years in Office |
|---|---|---|---|
| Corazón Aquino | Philippines | President | 1986–92 |
| Michelle Bachelet | Chile | President | 2006 to present |
| Sirimavo Bandaranaike | Sri Lanka | Prime minister | 1960–65, 1970–77, 1994–2001 |
| Benazir Bhutto | Pakistan | Prime minister | 1988–90, 1993–96 |
| Gro Harlem Brundtland | Norway | Prime minister | 1981, 1986–89 |
| Kim Campbell | Canada | Prime minister | 1993 |
| Violeta Chamorro | Nicaragua | President | 1990–97 |
| Mary Eugenia Charles | Dominica | Prime minister | 1980–95 |
| Tansu Ciller | Turkey | Prime minister | 1993–96 |
| Helen Clark | New Zealand | Prime minister | 1999 to present |
| Edith Cresson | France | Prime minister | 1991–92 |
| Ruth Dreifuss | Switzerland | President | 1999 |
| Vigdis Finnbogadottir | Iceland | President | 1980–96 |
| Indira Gandhi | India | Prime minister | 1966–77, 1980–84 |
| Tarja Halonen | Finland | President | 2000 to present |
| Sheik Hasina | Bangladesh | Prime minister | 1996–2001 |
| Janet Jagan | Guyana | President | 1997–99 |
| Ellen Johnson-Sirleaf | Liberia | President | 2006 to present |
| Chandrika Bandaranaike Kumaratunga | Sri Lanka | President | 1994–2005 |
| Gloria Macapagal-Arroyo | Philippines | President | 1999 to present |
| Mary McAleese | Ireland | President | 1997 to present |
| Golda Meir | Israel | Prime minister | 1969–74 |
| Angela Merkel | Germany | Chancellor | 2005 to present |
| Mireya Elisa Moscoso | Panama | President | 1999–2004 |
| Isabel Perón | Argentina | President | 1974–76 |
| Mary Robinson | Ireland | President | 1990–97 |
| Hanna Suchocka | Poland | Prime minister | 1992–93 |
| Megawati Sukarnoputri | Indonesia | President | 2001–04 |
| Margaret Thatcher | United Kingdom | Prime minister | 1979–90 |
| Vaira Vike-Freiberga | Latvia | President | 1999 to present |
| Khaleda Zia | Bangladesh | Prime minister | 1991–96, 2001–06 |

*Note:* Usually the president is head of state, and the prime minister is head of government. The distinction is explained in chapter 6.

families or communities that speak the same dialect and share various cultural characteristics. Native American Indian tribes are obvious examples, but roughly similar groups can be found in such diverse places as Africa and Afghanistan. Tribes tend to be smaller than ethnic groups but bigger than clans. *Clans* tend to be built around closer family ties than tribes. (In some cases they are subgroups of tribes.) Scotland, Ireland, China, and Japan are historically known for their clan-based societies, though the clan warfare that once characterized the struggle for power in these countries is now a thing of the past. Clan rivalries can still be highly volatile, however. Somalia, for example, has been seized by intermittent clan violence since 1991, rendering the country ungovernable. Clans also play an important political role in contemporary Iraq and other countries. *Families* are the smallest of the three kinship groups. Some modern political leaders have based their rule at least in part on their family connections, assigning important positions of power either to a close circle of immediate family members (like the Assad family in Syria) or to a more extended family (like Saddam Hussein, who drew on a large family centered in his home town of Tikrit).

**Age** "Never trust anyone over 30!" was the battle cry echoed by millions of young Americans who came of political age in the 1960s, the decade in which the term *generation gap* captured the clash of attitudes between the young and their elders on a spectrum of issues ranging from the Vietnam War to sex. Although this tumultuous period has receded into history, generational factors have always played a prominent role in the political life of most countries. According to one hypothesis, every generation tends to be stamped by the political and social events of its youth. The attitudes that most people take through life, in this view, are substantially molded by the political experiences they encountered in their teens and twenties.

As a general rule, different generations are likely to have different political outlooks. Throughout history, young people—especially students—have frequently been in the forefront of movements for political transformation in numerous countries around the world, waving the banners of such contradictory causes as democracy and fascism, global harmony and national assertiveness, peaceful reform and violent revolution. In recent years courageous young activists, boldly risking incarceration or death, have pressed their demands for democracy against entrenched dictatorships in Indonesia, Iran, Nigeria, Egypt, and elsewhere.

On a somewhat more mundane economic level, demographic trends in recent years have set the stage for what may turn out to be significant generational conflicts in a number of countries. As the elderly come to constitute a rising percentage of the population, younger people may have to pay higher taxes and make other sacrifices in order to satisfy the needs of older generations for adequate pensions, health care, and other necessities. Table 2.7 shows some of these trends.[10]

**TABLE 2.7**

**Generational Trends in Selected Countries**

| | Population over 65 (%) | | | |
|---|---|---|---|---|
| | 1950 | 1975 | 2000 | 2025 |
| United States | 8 | 10 | 12 | 16 |
| United Kingdom | 10 | 14 | 15 | 17 |
| Sweden | 10 | 15 | 16 | 20 |
| Japan | 5 | 7 | 15 | 23 |
| China | 5 | 5 | 6 | 11 |

| | Workers per Retiree | |
|---|---|---|
| | 1995 | 2025 |
| United States[a] | 4.7 | 3.3 |
| Canada | 5.2 | 2.7 |
| Japan | 2.8 | 2.1 |
| France | 2.8 | 1.7 |
| Germany | 3.1 | 2.3 |
| Italy | 2.4 | 1.8 |

[a]In the 1930s, the ratio of workers per retiree in the United States was 42:1.

*Sources:* United Nations; *Washington Post*, 31 October 1995 and 20 December 1995.

**Cross-Cutting and Polarizing Cleavages** As we examine these and other identity conflicts in the ensuing chapters, we should keep in mind the distinction between *cross-cutting cleavages* and *polarizing cleavages.* Cleavages are social divisions. **Cross-cutting cleavages** ***occur when the various factors that make up an individual's social identity tend to pull that person in* different *political directions.*** Take, for example, a twenty-year-old African American female student in New York City who is a devout Catholic opposed to abortion, whose parents together earn $100,000 a year, and who hopes to pursue a career in the military. Public opinion polls and voting studies demonstrate that most African Americans, most females, most college students, and most New Yorkers in the 1990s tended to vote for Democrats in presidential and congressional elections, whereas most opponents of abortion, most upper-income families, and most military officers tended to vote Republican. This individual's ethnic, gender, generational, and regional identities are said to *cut across* her class, religious, and career identities, leading her to support Democrats on some issues and Republicans on others.

**Polarizing cleavages** ***occur when the factors composing one's social identity tend to pull in the same political direction.*** Consider a forty-five-year-old white male corporate executive who earns $250,000 a year and who is a born-again evangelical Protestant residing in Charleston, South Carolina. Every one of his separate social identities reinforces the others in a cumulative fashion to pull him toward the Republicans and away from Democratic candidates. By contrast, a twenty-five-year-old Hispanic female agnostic earning $30,000 a year as a temp in New York City has all the attributes of a typical Democratic voter. In terms of their various social identities, these two people are polar opposites. Of course, they are both free individuals and may vote any way they please. There is nothing to

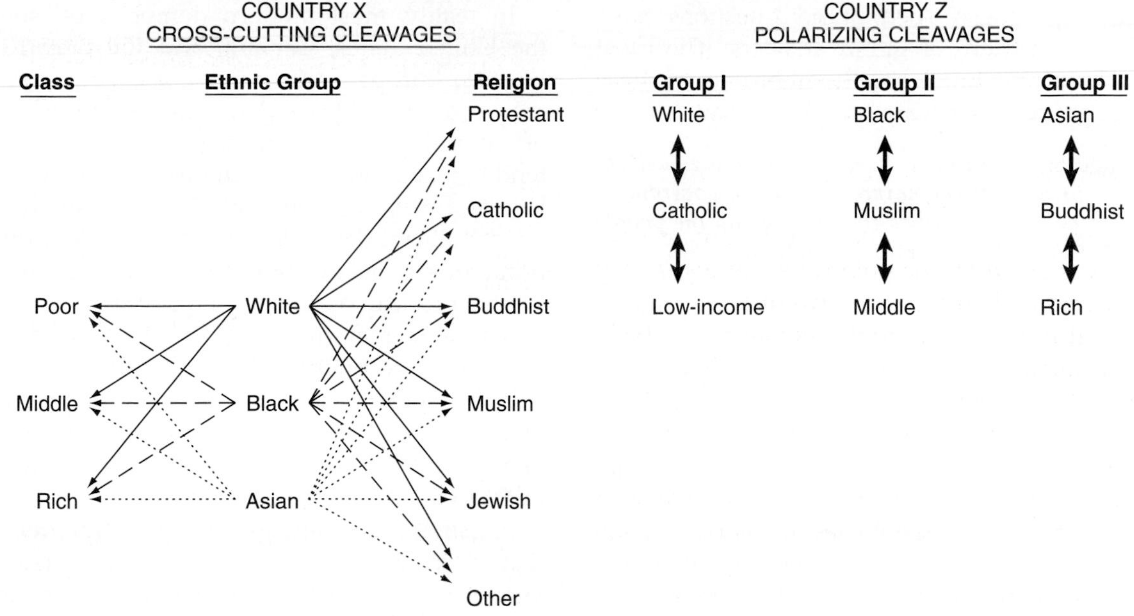


**FIGURE 2.2 Cross-Cutting and Polarizing Social Cleavages**

prevent the former from voting for Democrats or the latter from voting solely for Republicans. All we can do as political scientists is *hypothesize* how these individuals *may* vote, given the general voting patterns of the population. Once people have voted, however, and all the votes are counted, real voting patterns invariably emerge.

Now let's move from individual cases to entire countries. Suppose Country X has a highly complex society with a diversity of ethnic groups (white, black, Asian, etc.). *Each one* of these ethnic groups has members at different socioeconomic levels (low-income, middle class, rich), and *each one* has members who profess different religions (Catholic, Muslim, Buddhist, Protestant, etc.). This society as a whole is characterized by *cross-cutting cleavages:* ethnicity cuts across class and religion in a multiplicity of ways (see figure 2.2).

Country Z, by contrast, consists of three *completely unique* groups, each with a distinctive combination of social identities. For example, all the whites are impoverished Catholics, all the blacks are middle-class Muslims, and all the Asians are rich Buddhists. There are no other combinations of ethnicity, class, and religion. Within each group, the key factors of social identity combine in such a way as to create three polarized groups with virtually nothing in common.

Most political scientists would hypothesize that the society of Country X, characterized by cross-cutting cleavages, is better suited for democracy and cooperative interaction than deeply polarized societies. In view of its extreme polarization, Country Z is a prime candidate for prolonged social confrontation, political stalemate, and, in the worst of scenarios, a civil war that might only be terminated by the dictatorial domination of one group over the other two. As a general rule, whenever two or more identities reinforce each other, social conflicts are likely to be all the more intense.[11]

## Ideas

Some of the oldest and most contentious conflicts in world history have centered on political *ideas.* In some cases these conflicts have revolved around what may be called the "grand questions" of politics: What is the best form of government? What should the community's most important goals be? freedom? equality? social welfare? military strength?

Not surprisingly, such grand questions have provoked a variety of grand answers. The most far-reaching and intellectually ambitious of these political grand designs are called *ideologies.*

***An ideology is a coherent set of ideas and guidelines that defines what the nature and role of government should be and prescribes the main goals the people should pursue through political action.***

*Democracy, socialism,* and *fascism* are among the most influential political ideologies that have emerged over the course of humankind's political development. Other political ideologies have derived from various religions, such as *Christian Democracy, Zionism* (which derives from Judaism), and various ideological orientations that stem from Islam. Each of these ideologies spells out certain ideas about the proper role of government and the relationship between the ruling authorities and the population. Whereas some ideologies and their variants favor democracy, others espouse authoritarianism. Each one of these broad ideologies, moreover, has important variations.

Democracy as an ideology has at least two main tendencies:

- ***Liberal democracy tends to emphasize the freedom of the individual.*** Intellectual and religious freedom, freedom of speech, freedom to participate in political life, and the freedom to own and operate one's own private business are among the chief liberties celebrated in the liberal-democratic tradition. As a rule, liberal democracy favors serious limitations on the powers of government so as to maximize personal liberty.
- ***Social democracy tends to emphasize the collective welfare of society as a whole.*** Although it also favors freedom of thought, speech, religious worship, and political activity, and although it may favor private enterprise, social democracy seeks to ensure a certain minimum level of economic welfare for all members of society while striving to improve general welfare as much as possible. To this end, social-democratic ideology favors expanding the powers of government and limiting the liberties of private enterprise so as to provide the population with such benefits as education, adequate health care, unemployment insurance, and retirement pensions.

In reality, most modern democracies, such as the United States, Canada, and the countries of Western Europe, seek to strike a balance between the freedoms of liberal democracy and the benefits of social democracy. Still, some of these countries tend to lean more heavily in one of these two ideological directions. The United States usually leans toward liberal democracy (though it also provides numerous social welfare benefits), whereas most West European countries typically lean toward social democracy (though they also provide basic political and economic liberties). Although the differences between the two orientations are not as great today as they once were, the tension between liberty and welfare produces serious policy disputes in most democracies today.

*Socialism* is an ideology whose central premise is that an economy based on private enterprise (also known as *capitalism*) places excessive economic and political power in the hands of a small band of private entrepreneurs. Socialists contend that this capitalist elite, driven exclusively by greed for profits, uses its powers to exploit the working masses who constitute the vast majority of the population. Socialist ideology maintains that humanity would be better off if the free-enterprise system were abolished altogether. In its place, a socialist economy would put control over factories, farms, banks, stores, and other economic enterprises in the hands of the people as a whole.

While generally agreeing on these basic axioms, socialists have historically disagreed over *how* the ideals of socialism should be put into practice. *Karl Marx* (1818–83), the most influential theorist of socialist ideology, believed that a socialist society would not require any government at all. Marx did not view socialism in authoritarian terms; he saw it as a liberating force that would free the masses from economic exploitation.

Soviet-style communists, by contrast, believed in an all-powerful government operated by a well-organized Communist Party claiming to represent the workers. Under such leaders as *V. I. Lenin* (1870–1924) and *Joseph Stalin* (1879–1953) in the Soviet Union, and *Mao Zedong* (1893–1976) in China, communists of this type set up oppressive authoritarian regimes that placed exclusive political and economic power in the hands of a small party elite that administered a huge bureaucracy.

| Radical left | Communism, socialism | Democracy | Conservative authoritarian regimes (monarchies, military governments, etc.) | Fascism |
|---|---|---|---|---|

**FIGURE 2.3 The Left-Right Spectrum**

Additional variants of socialist ideology have been advanced by other theoreticians and political activists.

*Fascism* is an ideology that emerged in various parts of Europe in the 1920s and 1930s. Its most malignant manifestations were *Adolph Hitler* and his Nazi movement, which ruled Germany from 1933 to 1945, and the Italian fascist party under *Benito Mussolini,* who held power from 1922 to 1943. Fascism's essential features include an aggressive nationalism that glorifies one's own people above all others; intense racism; and devotion to an all-powerful, heavily militarized state. Efforts to whip up popular support through mass propaganda campaigns accompanied these orientations.

Although ideologies may constitute the grand ideas of politics, they are not the only examples of how ideas can stir up political conflict. On a more routine level, ideas are constantly at the heart of political debates and controversies in both democracies and authoritarian regimes. In democracies, people are constantly debating such issues as what the proper role of government should be and which policies the government should adopt in addressing the community's problems. Even authoritarian regimes must decide from a menu of alternative ways of pursuing the ruling elite's chosen goals.

Political ideologies can be placed along a left–right spectrum. (See figure 2.3.) The terms *left* and *right* in politics derive from the French Revolution. When the French legislature known as the Convention convened in 1792, revolutionaries who favored replacing the monarchy with a fundamentally different political system took their seats to the left of the presiding officer, and conservatives who wished to preserve the monarchy were seated to his right. Moderates who sought some kind of compromise gathered in the center. These seating arrangements endured and so did the political alignments associated with them. Accordingly, proponents of political change became known as *leftists* (or the *left wing*), conservative advocates of the status quo became known as *rightists* (or *right-wingers*), and those in the middle became identified, quite appropriately, as *centrists*. The most extreme right-wingers are often called *reactionaries* because they want to turn the clock back to some previously existing (or idealized) governmental system or concept of government.

We'll examine these and other ideological issues further in chapter 13.

## Values

***Values** may be defined as spiritual or moral principles, ideals, or qualities of life that people favor for their own sake.*

Among the most important values to be found in political life are *freedom, justice, equality, security, order*, and *community*. People often cherish these principles and ideals because of their intrinsic merit in promoting human dignity and civilized relationships, not simply because they may confer wealth or power. In addition, people may attach a special value to certain qualities of life. A healthy environment, for example, or "family values" may be prized for their own sake as conditions of civilized existence. Religion is also a major source of values, and value conflicts often overlap with religious conflicts. On the whole, values make a major contribution to a country's *political culture*, the complex of attitudes and beliefs that shape political mentalities and behavior. As we'll see in chapter 12, the World Values Survey and other studies clarify value orientations around the world.

Some political values tend to promote democracy; others are often invoked to justify authoritarian rule. Freedom is one of the most hallowed democratic values, one that is seldom, if ever, embraced by dictators. People who support authoritarian regimes attach a higher value to order than to freedom and justify the use of dictatorial rule and unrestrained force as necessary to ensure domestic tranquillity. Indeed, democracy ultimately rests on certain core values that include not only freedom but also the notion that human dignity and equality are impossible under dictatorial oppression and require the state's full accountability to the people. The clash between democracy and dictatorship is thus in large measure a clash over values, not simply a conflict over power or resources.

Political conflicts may arise over values for a variety of reasons. Sometimes the multiple values that a society favors may clash with one another, making it difficult or impossible to fulfill one value without limiting another. Freedom and equality are frequently in conflict, for example. The freedom to operate a business without any governmental interference may clash with employees' demands for a just wage and social welfare benefits or for the nondiscriminatory treatment of females or ethnic minorities in the workplace. To ensure a measure of social fairness, governments may infringe on the freedoms of the private entrepreneur.

On a global scale, some of the most contentious issues in today's world center around values. Whereas proponents of democracy and private enterprise cherish freedom and individualism, some people reject these ideals as "Western values" that they regard as incompatible with the cultural norms and value systems of their own societies. They tend to view the West's exaltation of individual freedom as dangerously excessive and argue that it leads to decadent egoism and social breakdown. In its place they stress the individual's responsibilities to the community and the need for deference to established political or religious authorities. Variants of these arguments have been put forward by certain East Asian authoritarian leaders who assert the superiority of "Asian values," highly conservative Muslims who want Islamic law to replace civil law in Islamic countries, and various others.[12] Advocates of democracy insist that its basic values and procedures are universally applicable and can be adapted to local cultures and value systems.

In asserting our support for democracy, we argue that when people are denied the possibility to elect their government or speak out freely, many of them will know that they are being politically oppressed, regardless of their culture. When people are subjected to systematic discrimination, arbitrary arrest, or brutal torture because of their political views, religious beliefs, ethnic identity, gender, or for some similar reason, they know that they are being deprived of fundamental human rights, regardless of their culture. The forms that human societies take are incredibly diverse; cultural differences abound. Nevertheless, we believe that the values that distinguish democratic rights and liberties from authoritarian repression are everywhere the same, and that they are universally recognized by those who seek a genuine alternative to exclusion, persecution, and the suppression of human dignity. Hard evidence from non-Western cultures backs up these idealistic assertions. In recent surveys, an average of 69 percent of Africans and 59 percent of East Asians in participating countries favored democracy.[13]

## GAMES PEOPLE PLAY

What explains why conflict occurs? If political contention causes so much turmoil and bloodshed, why can't people just compromise their differences and learn to cooperate? The answers to these questions can be hugely complicated. If we want really comprehensive answers, we have to probe specific conflicts in considerable detail, analyzing their historical, social, economic, and other dynamics as thoroughly as we can. But we can also look for broad theoretical answers to the puzzles of conflict and cooperation. *Game theory* provides a conceptual approach to understanding how humans behave in conflict situations in general.

Game theory is a form of rational choice theory. *Rational choice theory* (or *rational actor theory*) in political science is derived from economics. It stems from the assumption that human beings are motivated in their economic behavior primarily by material self-interest: they strive to acquire money and other possessions aimed at enhancing their well-being. Behavior aimed at achieving these objectives is considered rational. Of course, people do not always succeed at making money: life has its uncertainties, and sometimes we miscalculate or have bad luck. But economic behavior is still considered rational as long as people consciously try to increase their gains in the *expectation* of succeeding rather than failing.

Political scientists have adapted these notions of rational economic behavior in an effort to explain *political* behavior. How do voters choose their favored candidates on election day? Why do the vast majority of people living in a democracy decline to get actively involved in politics? Why are some populations willing to tolerate a repressive authoritarian regime, while others—like the Poles under communism—are unafraid of rising up in defiance of their rulers? For proponents of rational choice theory, the short answer to these questions is that, regardless of the situation, people tend to act rationally. That is, they calculate the expected gains and the anticipated costs or risks of a particular action—voting, volunteering for a political cause, or demonstrating against a dictatorship—and they choose accordingly. Most rational choice theorists today would add that this rational calculation does not necessarily have to be limited to maximizing one's *material* benefits; rather, one can rationally seek such nonmaterial gains as a cleaner environment, security against terrorism, or the promotion of one's religious values. What matters is that rational behavior is based on the individual's personal desires and priorities. In short, **rational choice theory** ***maintains that individuals behave in politics on the basis of self-interest, seeking to increase their expected gains and minimize their expected costs and risks on the basis of their personal preferences.***

The merits of rational choice theory as a general explanation of political behavior are hotly debated. We'll take up this topic in more detail in chapter 11. For now, let's focus on game theory as it applies to explaining political conflict.

Like rational choice theory, game theory originated in economics. Initially it was created to explain in abstract terms how business executives make decisions in a competitive market economy. Many of the problems executives face can be likened to various games of strategy. Political scientists picked up on the fact that quite a few political situations can also be understood in terms of games.[14]

One type of game is the **zero-sum game**. ***This is a two-person (or two-sided) game in which one player's loss is the other player's gain in equal measure.*** If I jump two of your checkers, my gain is +2 and your loss is −2. The sum equals zero. Real-life examples include situations in which an invading country grabs a piece of another country's territory, one party loses voters to a competing party, or a certain amount of money in the national budget is transferred from your favorite program (education, for example) to mine (space exploration). Zero-sum games usually reflect all-out conflict: one side wins and the other loses. Zero-sum games can most easily be understood as battles over scarce resources like territory or money. But sometimes the parties to a conflict are so entrenched in their enmity that they *perceive* their conflict in zero-sum terms, even when the issues at stake are not finite objects that can be divided up. Ethnic or religious antagonisms often involve such perceptions. If you are very distrustful of me, you may not be willing to make *any* compromises—not even a symbolic gesture of reconciliation—for fear that any such move would be a psychological gain for me and hence a loss for you. When people are caught up in the logic of zero-sum games, conflict is intractable and cooperation is practically impossible.

But not all games are so one-sided. In *variable-sum games,* the outcome can at times be beneficial for all or most of the players. If you and I find ways to resolve our disputes and cooperate, we both may win something. Instead of fighting fruitlessly over scarce resources, for example, we might work together to increase our economic production, raising incomes for ourselves as well as for our fellow citizens. In this positive-sum game, your gain (+10) is my gain (+5), even if we don't necessarily share our winnings equally. But if we do not cooperate, or if other factors conspire against us (if we lose a war, for example, or if we are hurt by an economic downturn), we may both lose out. In this case, the variable-sum game is a negative-sum game: you lose −5 and I lose −10. Obviously, such negative-sum outcomes should be avoided like the plague. But strange as it may seem, it can be exceedingly difficult to avoid outcomes in which everyone loses, as the intriguing game of *Prisoner's Dilemma* illustrates.

Prisoner's Dilemma is presented as an appendix to this chapter. With ingenious simplicity it explains why conflicts are so hard to resolve: *conflict can be a rational choice.* But the game also provides a way out, showing how cooperation can lead to mutually beneficial results if the parties are willing to make riskier decisions.

The game offers a mixture of zero-sum, positive-sum, and negative-sum outcomes. And it is a metaphor for a host of real-world conflicts, including ethnic and religious disputes, state-to-state conflicts, and a variety of other political confrontations. Play it with a partner (if you don't mind jeopardizing your friendship!) and with a third person who acts as your go-between (the "prosecutor"). Play it ten or twenty times in succession to see if your choices change with repeated plays.[15]

In sum, all governments have to deal with conflicts of one kind or another. One of the chief differences between democratic governments and authoritarian ones is that democracies deal with their conflicts out in the open, through procedures that guarantee the government's accountability to the public, whereas authoritarian regimes typically deal with their conflicts behind closed doors and with little or no accountability. *Democracy is not a recipe for eliminating conflict; rather, it is a mechanism for dealing with it in accordance with generally accepted rules.*

**Conclusion** This chapter has shown that comparative politics covers a wide array of topics. Not surprisingly, comparativists have come up with a wide array of approaches to understanding these phenomena. "Institutionalists" focus on how governmental institutions work and how they affect political outcomes. Rational choice theorists zero in on the decisions people make on the basis of calculations of anticipated gains and risks. "Culturalists" look at the attitudes and values of various populations. Other approaches have their own perspectives. Each approach has its strengths and limitations; when it comes to the complexities of politics, no single theory or school of thought can explain everything. That is why this book does not confine itself to just one approach to comparative politics. It seeks to be eclectic, exposing you to several different ways of examining political realities. Our premise is that any theory or analytical orientation must ultimately answer two basic questions: What does it tell us about politics in general? How well can it explain specific phenomena? To figure out how to address these questions, we need to know something about how scientific methods can be applied to politics. We now turn to that subject in chapter 3.

## KEY TERMS
**(In bold and underlined in the text)**

Politics
Democracy
Authoritarianism (dictatorship)
Theocracy
Mixed regimes
Political economy
Market economy
Identity
Political sociology
Gini coefficient/index
Ethnicity
Cross-cutting cleavages
Polarizing cleavages
Ideology
Liberal democracy
Social democracy
Values
Rational choice theory
Zero-sum game

## APPENDIX

### Prisoner's Dilemma

Two partners who collaborated in an armed robbery are arrested. The police put them into separate cells. The prosecutor would like to convict them both, but there are no witnesses to the crime who can identify them. To get a conviction, the prosecutor needs the testimony of the robbers themselves. In separate conversations, she offers each prisoner the same deal: "If you squeal on your partner and say he's guilty, but your partner keeps silent, I'll set you free and give you a $25,000 reward; your partner will get fifty years in the slammer. But if he squeals on you and you keep silent, he goes free and gets the money, and you will get fifty years. If each of you accuses the other, I'll get two convictions, and in thanks, I'll see to it that each of you gets only ten years. If you both keep silent, I'll have to set you both free, but neither one of you will get any reward." If you are one of the prisoners, what is your "rational choice"?

Note the underlying premises of the game. First, whatever choice you make, the outcome will not be determined entirely by your decision. It will also be determined by what your partner does. Second,

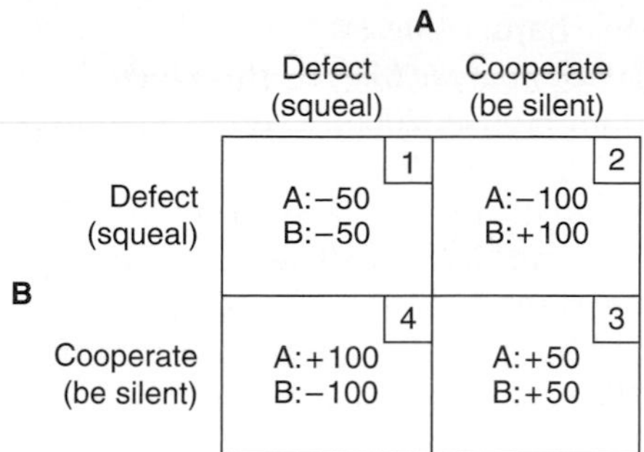


FIGURE 2.4

you cannot be certain in advance what your partner will do, and you cannot communicate with him. Third, your partner is just like you: a criminal, not Mother Teresa. Can you trust him? Can you figure out what *his* rational choice will be?

In order to visualize the various options before you and their potential consequences, it is useful to construct a *decision matrix* (figure 2.4). The matrix consists of four boxes that correspond to the four possible decision outcomes: (1) you both squeal; (2) you keep silent but your partner squeals; (3) you both keep silent; (4) you squeal but your partner keeps silent. Inside each box are two numbers. The numbers are purely arbitrary, but they represent the *relative value* to you and your partner of the possible consequences of your decisions. Since the best outcome for you (or your partner) would be to go free with the $25,000 reward, let's assign that outcome a value of +100. The worst possible outcome for you (or your partner) would be to get a fifty-year prison sentence; let's assign this worst outcome a value of −100. The other possible outcomes lie in between these extremes. Let's say that a ten-year sentence is worth −50, and going free without the reward is worth +50.

You are Prisoner A and your partner is Prisoner B. To translate your decision options into the jargon of game theory, we'll call squealing on one's partner "defection" and keeping silent "cooperation."

In Box 1, you and your partner both squeal on each other (i.e., you both "defect"). Thus you both end up with ten-year prison terms (−50 each). In Box 2, your partner squeals (defects) and you keep silent (cooperate). As a result, your partner gets the maximum payoff (+100) and you end up with the maximum punishment (−100). (To put it another way, B gets the better of the two possible positive outcomes and you get the worse of the two possible negative outcomes.) In Box 3, you both keep silent. You are both set free, but you get no reward. Each of you ends up with +50. Finally, Box 4 is the reverse image of Box 2: you defect by squealing, while your partner cooperates by keeping silent. Consequently, you get +100 and your partner gets −100.

The prosecutor has made her offers, and you and your partner are now deliberating what to do. From the prosecutor's standpoint, does this game have a "solution" that she can predict? Is there a single choice whose potential consequences offer the highest possible gain at the lowest possible risk?

Consider your options. If you choose to defect (i.e., squeal), depending on what Prisoner B does, you will end up with either −50 (Box 1) or +100 (Box 4). If you choose to cooperate (keep silent), you will end up with either −100 (Box 2) or +50 (Box 3). Most game theoreticians, playing the prosecutor's role, would say that the rational choice would be for you to defect. Defection offers the highest possible gain (+100) and the less costly of the two negative outcomes (−50). By contrast, cooperation offers the lower of the two positive outcomes (+50) and the more costly of the negative outcomes (−100). If you are rational, therefore, you will choose to defect. So will your partner. From the prosecutor's vantage point, the rational "solution" to the game is Box 1. She can reasonably predict that you and your partner will both squeal.

Viewed in political terms, the chief implication of Prisoner's Dilemma is that *it is more rational for each individual to be uncooperative than cooperative.* If this is indeed the case, it would follow that political conflict is inevitable and cooperation virtually impossible. This conclusion appears to hold even if *individual* rationality leaves both players *worse off* than they would be if they had cooperated. Hence the dilemma.

How valid are these conclusions? As game theorists themselves are aware, Prisoner's Dilemma is likely to lead to the negative-sum solution of mutual defection only if it is played once or a few times. But real-life political interactions rarely involve a single, one-shot decision. Remember, politics is a *process:* it usually involves an ongoing series of interactions, decisions, reconsiderations, and new decisions. Moreover, the two prisoners in the game were not allowed to communicate with each other. But in actual practice, people usually do communicate; even enemies negotiate. Hence it is at least possible that the rational tendency to be uncooperative, as reflected in Prisoner's Dilemma, can be overcome through repeated interactions and communications among individuals, groups, or countries in conflict. Repeated plays of the game are called *iterations*.

When Prisoner's Dilemma is played out in a laboratory setting, it frequently turns out that players A and B start out by defecting, but they increasingly cooperate the more they play the game. They learn that when *both* defect, neither one gets +100; both get jail time (−50). With more iterations they learn to trust each other and come to realize that, if both cooperate, both will get out of prison (+50). The result of mutual cooperation, therefore, is a positive payoff for each player; the result of mutual defection is a cost for each one. Still, both players are always aware that cooperation carries huge risks: if you cooperate and your partner suddenly defects, you could end up with the worst possible outcome.

The main point of Prisoner's Dilemma as applied to politics is simply this: it graphically demonstrates why cooperation is so difficult to achieve by showing how conflict can be a *rational choice*. It also demonstrates that, over time, people can *learn* that the benefits of cooperation can outweigh the risks of continued conflict.

## NOTES

1. *Freedom in the World 2006* (New York: Freedom House, 2006). A large set of data on political regimes since 1800, known as Polity IV, is available online at cidcm.umd.edu/inscr.polity.
2. See Marina Ottoway, *Democracy Challenged: The Rise of Semi-Authoritarianism* (Washington, D.C.: Carnegie Endowment for International Peace, 2003).
3. For an overview, see Patrick Joyce, ed., *Class* (Oxford: Oxford University Press, 1995).
4. Donald L. Horowitz, *Ethnic Groups in Conflict* (Berkeley: University of California Press, 1985), 52.
5. See Jon Meacham, *American Gospel: God, the Founding Fathers, and the Making of a Nation* (New York: Random House, 2006); David L. Holmes, *The Faiths of the Founding Fathers* (New York: Oxford University Press, 2006); and Gordon S. Wood, "American Religion: The Great Retreat," *New York Review of Books*, June 8, 2006, 60–63.
6. See the data in United Nations Development Program, *Human Development Report 2005* (New York: UNDP, 2005), 299–302, 307–19.
7. See Monique Leijenaar, *The Political Empowerment of Women: The Netherlands and Other Countries* (Leiden and Boston: Martinus Nijhoff, 2004); Michael A. Genovese, *Women as National Leaders: The Political Performance of Women as Heads of Government* (Newbury Park, Calif.: Sage, 1993), and Barbara J. Nelson and Najma Chowdhury, *Women and Politics Worldwide* (New Haven: Yale University Press, 1994). See also the annual *Global Gender Gap Report* published by the World Economic Forum, www.weforum.org
8. Sameena Nazir and Leigh Tomppert, eds., *Women's Rights in the Middle East and North Africa: Citizenship and Justice* (Lanham, Md.: Rowman and Littlefield, 2005). See also World Bank, *Gender and Development in the Middle East and North Africa: Women in the Public Sphere* (Washington, D.C.: World Bank, 2004).
9. M. Steven Fish, "Islam and Authoritarianism," *World Politics* 55, no. 1 (October 2002): 4–37. See also Daniela Donno and Bruce Russett, "Islam, Authoritarianism, and Female Empowerment: What Are the Linkages?" *World Politics* 56, no. 4 (July 2004): 582–607.
10. One estimate by the U.S. Health Care Financing Agency, which administers Medicare, predicted that there will be 3.9 million new Medicare enrollees in 2020, with lifetime Medicare expenses likely to reach $210 billion. In 1990 there were only 2.1 million new Medicare enrollees, whose total Medicare expenses expected to be $112 billion (*Washington Post*, 13 April 1995). It is estimated that in 2025 there will be two persons in the United States over age 65 for every one teenager.
11. See Amy Gutmann, *Identity in Democracy* (Princeton: Princeton University Press, 2003).
12. On Asian values as conceived in Singapore, see Kishore Mahbubani, "The United States:

'Go East, Young Man,'" *Washington Quarterly* 17, no. 2 (spring 1994): 5–23. On the views of Malaysia's leader Mohamad Mahathir, see Khoo Boo Teik, *Paradoxes of Mahathirism* (Oxford: Oxford University Press, 1995).

**13.** See www.afrobarometer.org/survey1.html and www.globalbarometter.org.

**14.** The seminal work on game theory is John von Neumann and Oskar Morgenstern, *Theory of Games and Economic Behaviour* (New York: Wiley, 1944). For recent applications, see James D. Morrow, *Game Theory for Political Scientists* (Princeton: Princeton University Press, 1994).

**15.** Jon Elster has commented that politics is essentially about "ways of transcending the Prisoner's Dilemma." See also Anatol Rapoport and Alber M. Chammah, *Prisoner's Dilemma* (Ann Arbor: University of Michigan Press, 1965), and Robert Axelrod, *The Evolution of Cooperation* (New York: Basic Books, 1984).

CHAPTER 3

# CRITICAL THINKING ABOUT POLITICS

## Analytical Techniques of Political Science— The Logic of Hypothesis Testing

As we pointed out in chapter 1, comparative politics is a subfield of political science. Political science, in turn, is a science to the extent that its practitioners engage in the tasks of *definition, description, explanation, probabilistic prediction,* and *prescription*. This chapter explains how we can apply these scientific operations to the study of politics. The first part defines important terms and provides examples of how they are used. The second part walks you through a hypothesis-testing exercise, using a step-by-step procedure that is utilized in all the chapters that follow. Both parts demonstrate how the logic of scientific analysis can help you understand reality, enhancing critical-thinking skills that you can apply in a variety of academic and professional contexts. As a major leaguer once said about baseball, "Ninety percent of this game is half mental."

## I. ANALYTICAL TECHNIQUES OF POLITICAL SCIENCE

### *Ought*-Questions and *Is*-Questions

As a general rule, political science asks two broad types of questions: *is*-questions (What *is* political reality?) and *ought*-questions (What *ought* to be done about political reality?). The two sets of questions are intimately related: we cannot adequately determine what we ought to do through practical political activity without a thorough comprehension of the realities we are facing. *Good policy prescription requires good analysis!* We must always keep in mind, however, that is-questions and ought-questions are basically different. Is-questions concentrate on *facts* and *explanations* of facts, whereas ought-questions mostly deal with *personal preferences* and *values*. The systematic analysis of facts is called *empirical analysis*. This chapter is mainly concerned with the logic of empirical analysis. Before we move on to that subject, however, we need to clarify the relationship between is-questions and ought-questions a bit further.

### *Ought*-Questions and Policy Prescription

Because one of the purposes of studying comparative politics is to decide what we ought to do through political action, comparative politics is, at least in part, a *policy science:* it helps us devise and select governmental policies aimed at improving things. In this sense, comparative politics can be used to serve *prescriptive* and *meliorative* purposes: it helps us choose the right policy prescriptions with the aim of making the world a better place.

(The Latin word *melior* means "better.") One of the problems with determining what ought to be done in politics, of course, is that people often disagree over personal preferences and values. Although we can use the analytical tools of science to dig up facts and explain how they fit together, science cannot determine the rightness or wrongness of *value judgments*.

**Value judgments** ***are evaluations that we make on the basis of values, standards, or ideals.*** They are based on such things as ethical principles, aesthetic standards, or personal tastes. Value judgments thus reflect personal preferences about what is moral or immoral, beautiful or ugly, good or bad. Value judgments are not simply statements of fact, nor are they explanations of how various facts come about or interact. When we say, "Democracy is morally superior to authoritarianism," we are making a value judgment. When we say, "In today's world there is a trend toward more democracies," we are making a statement of fact, not a value judgment.

In principle, facts and explanations can be proved or disproved as true or false with reference to the facts themselves. We can look at reality and see if there is—or is not—a trend toward democracy, for example. Facts are independent of the individual observer and are therefore considered *objective* (that is, they are the *object* of the individual's observations). But value judgments cannot be proved or disproved as true or false. They represent the *preferences* or *ideals* of the individual and are therefore considered *subjective* (that is, they are rooted in the mind of the individual *subject*). We can study the origins and development of democracies objectively by examining the relevant facts. But whether you or I prefer liberal democracy to social democracy, or the Republicans to the Democrats, may involve a considerable amount of subjective preference.

Although is-questions and ought-questions are different, they are frequently related. Political arguments resting on value judgments cannot be completely oblivious to knowable facts. If we want to argue that democracies are morally superior to dictatorships *because* they maximize political participation, freedom, and human dignity, we had better be sure that democracies in fact really do these things. If someone can point out that democracies have at times permitted the majority to dominate and exploit a minority (as occurred in the United States when slavery was permitted), we may have to modify our position to take account of this factually verifiable reality. The facts may force us to admit that democracy does not necessarily maximize freedom and dignity in all cases. It may do so only when specific measures are taken to prevent the majority from subjugating the minority. By the same token, apologists for authoritarianism who argue that an enlightened dictator may know better than the masses what is best for the country must acknowledge the fact that dictatorships are often characterized by brutality, corruption, and economic stagnation.

It can be quite disconcerting to change our cherished political opinions in the face of contradictory evidence, no matter how indisputable the evidence might be. But a scientific approach to politics may sometimes force us to make that change. Learning how to adjust our political views to verifiable realities may be difficult at times, but it is one of the principal purposes—and benefits—of studying politics scientifically.

Within the academic traditions of political science, ought-questions are the special province of two fields of the discipline: *political philosophy* and *public policy analysis*.

*Political philosophy*, which is also called *political thought*, is perhaps the oldest form of systematic thinking about politics. Its roots in the Western tradition go back to ancient Greece and such thinkers as *Plato* (427–347 B.C.E.) and *Aristotle* (384–322 B.C.E.). Non-Western philosophers like *Confucius* (557?–479 B.C.E.) and religious visionaries like *Muhammad* (570–632) have also propounded ideas about life and society that have had a profound impact on political developments around the world down to the present day. For most political philosophers, the central question of political philosophy has traditionally been, "What is the best form of government?" This broad question has inspired a chorus of related ones: "What ought to be the main goals of political action: freedom? order? equality? justice?" "How do we define these goals in practical circumstances?" These and similar questions are characterized above all by their concern with political values and with optimal standards of political organization and behavior. Such values and standards are called *norms*. Consequently, the field of political philosophy is also called *normative political theory*.[1]

*Public policy analysis* is the other subfield of political science that is primarily concerned with ought-questions, but it also employs a lot of empirical analysis to assess the impact of policy decisions. *Public* policy essentially means *governmental* policy. Public policy analysis is concerned with the decisions that governments make (or should make) in order to reach certain goals. Public policy analysts who pursue their careers in government agencies or in nongovernmental organizations, such as public watchdog groups, take a hard look at specific issues such as health care, homeland security, or defense policy, and propose specific governmental programs or decisions. Once policies are adopted through the political process, these analysts monitor the results and recommend pertinent adjustments and corrections. These tasks require strong analytical skills as well as a personal dedication to improving government performance.[2]

This textbook concentrates on comparative politics, not on political philosophy or public policy analysis per se. But comparative politics cannot be properly understood in isolation from some of the leading traditions of political thought. We cannot understand such prominent features of the contemporary world as democratization or political culture unless we examine their normative foundations in the thought of various political philosophers, even though some of them may have lived hundreds or even thousands of years ago. We are also interested in various public policy issues confronting the governments of the world, such as economic policies, women's issues, and immigration. By studying public policy comparatively, we may be able to figure out what our own government ought to be doing in grappling with similar problems.

## "WHAT IS?": A GUIDE TO EMPIRICAL POLITICAL ANALYSIS

In addition to being interested in what people ought to do in the realm of politics, political science is concerned with *describing* and *explaining* political realities. To this end it takes a close look at the facts of political life and searches for patterns or relationships that help explain the facts. What is democracy and how does it work? What is a military dictatorship? Why does it tend to occur in some countries but not in others? Questions such as these probe the *what*, the *how*, and the *why* of political reality.

> **Empirical analysis** ***is centered on facts. It seeks to discover, describe, and explain facts and factual relationships, to the extent that the facts are knowable.***

The term *empirical* derives from the ancient Greek word for *experience*. Empirical analysis is based strictly on what we can experience or perceive through our senses: namely, *facts*. Empirical analysis is not concerned with our values, ideals, or preferences. It does not make value judgments. And it cannot probe spiritual phenomena, such as God or the human soul. We cannot empirically prove or disprove God's existence or demonstrate the intentions or actions of any deity.

At least in principle, when we study politics empirically we are supposed to put aside our personal preferences and religious faith and just stick to the observable facts. As a consequence, empirical political science is sometimes called *value-free* political science: it requires us to keep our investigations of political reality free from our own particular values and biases, no matter how well-intentioned or well-reasoned our convictions may be. If we favor democracy, for example, we must not allow this preference to intrude into our efforts to understand how democracies work in actual fact. Otherwise, we may blind ourselves to certain realities about democracies that we may find unpalatable. The same admonition applies to adherents of all political persuasions. In practice, however, it can be quite difficult to keep our subjective inclinations completely separate from our fact-centered analyses. Personal values and preferences sometimes creep into the way we select the topics we are interested in and the ways we look at them. But the canons of science require us to acknowledge our biases and make sure that they do not get in the way of our quest for objective truth when conducting empirical investigations.

The principal approach of this book is empirical. Its main purposes are to present and explain facts about politics and to teach you various ways of analyzing political reality from an empirical perspective. At the same time, the authors freely acknowledge that we are not unbiased. To put our cards on the table, we unabashedly proclaim that we favor democracy over any known form of authoritarianism. Though we may differ among ourselves about how to promote democracy in the world or how democracies should be run in actual practice, we favor democracy as a general principle because it provides far more opportunities for human dignity and self-expression than authoritarian regimes, which either limit these opportunities substantially or deny them altogether. Beyond this normative commitment to the principle of democracy, we agree and disagree on a wide range of political issues. Nevertheless, we make a sincere effort in this volume to be as objective as possible in presenting comparative politics as an empirical science.

### Definition

All sciences must strive for definitional clarity. Unless we are clear about the terms we use, we may end up in a conceptual muddle. The same terms may mean different things to different people, or they may have several different meanings depending on the context in which they are used.

As political scientists, we must define our concepts and refine our definitions so that they apply to reality as accurately as possible. A *concept* is a word, a term, or a label that applies to a whole class or category of phenomena or ideas. In political science, such terms as freedom, power, democracy, liberalism, conservatism, socialism, and globalization are concepts whose meanings need to be spelled out carefully so that we can talk about them intelligibly and consistently. Like many political concepts, each of them can be defined in more than one way. For James Madison and the framers of the U.S. Constitution, for example, freedom meant above all freedom from the tyranny of an excessively powerful state and freedom to engage in private economic activity. For Karl Marx, however, it meant freedom from economic exploitation by private industrialists. In early twentieth-century Germany, a conservative was a staunch opponent of democracy who favored a militarily powerful authoritarian state. Conservatives in contemporary Germany, by contrast, favor both democracy and civilian control over the military. Conceptual clarity is imperative whether we are discussing political values (e.g., freedom) or describing political facts (e.g., German conservatism). Achieving such clarity is one of the main tasks of political science.

### Description: Observing, Collecting, Comparing

Natural scientists must look very closely at natural phenomena, record their observations, and gather them together in some systematic fashion. One of the oldest ways of studying the natural world has involved the *comparative method*. Biologists, for example, compare various forms of animal and plant life and group them into categories such as kingdom, genus, and species. In a roughly similar manner, political scientists examine systems of government, describe their similarities and differences, and classify them in various categories. Starting with democracy and authoritarianism as the two broadest categories, we can group different types of democracy under the first rubric and different forms of authoritarian government under the second. Gabriel Almond, a pioneering figure in the study of comparative politics, once suggested that it is especially useful to look for *dissimilarities* between *similar* forms of government (such as democracies) and *similarities* between *dissimilar* forms of government (such as democracies and non-democracies). By employing these descriptive and comparative techniques, we can get a better understanding of how governments work—and ought to work.

The precise methods we use to carry out our observations and comparisons will vary from case to case. If we are interested in the way people vote, we will want to gather election returns as well as relevant information about the voters, such as their social class, religion, ethnicity, and the like. If we want to understand how political elites view politics, it may be helpful to conduct interviews with relevant officials, such as parliamentarians or bureaucrats, to see how they perceive politics and their own role in political affairs. To increase the breadth and depth of these observations, we may want to examine voting patterns or elite attitudes in a variety of countries over extended periods of time. The more information we observe, the more likely patterns will emerge that will permit us to go beyond merely describing reality. It will then be possible to make generalizations about reality with the aim of explaining it.

### Explanation and Generalization

Are Americans increasingly fed up with their political parties? Are similar tendencies occurring in other democracies? If so, then why? Do political leaders in democratizing countries share similar conceptions of human rights or do they differ? What accounts for these similarities or differences? Are these attitudes conducive to stabilizing democracy or might they tend to undermine it?

Questions like these take us beyond merely isolated facts about politics in this or that country, however intriguing they may be. They prompt us to generalize from those facts in order to gain a broader perspective on political reality. By themselves, facts are not especially meaningful. (As one wag put it, "History is just one damned thing after another!") The facts of political life assume meaning only when we visualize them as general patterns, tendencies, or relationships.

Therefore, if we want to understand the significance of discrete facts or events in political life, we must integrate them into larger analytical frameworks. Today's headlines, for example, may announce that the prime minister of a major democratic country has resigned, that the government's central bank in a leading trading nation has just raised interest rates, and that the military in a country struggling to establish democracy has seized power in a coup d'état. Governments, private businesses, journalists, and other interested parties around the world must pay instant attention to these occurrences and assess their implications for decision makers or average citizens. As political scientists, we too may be interested in the immediate practical effects of these events. But we will also be interested in what they tell us about politics more generally.

What does the prime minister's resignation tell us about how democracies work? What does the central bank's actions tell us about the relationship between politics and economics? What does the latest coup tell us about military intervention in politics? Our aim here is to deepen our understanding of democracy in general, political economy in general, and military authoritarianism in general. *Generalization is a central purpose of science.* At the same time, we can apply our understanding of these general processes and tendencies to sharpen our understanding of the specific events at hand.

In order to construct meaningful generalizations from a wealth of political information and in order to determine how accurate these generalizations are, we must use scientific methods of analyzing facts and testing general propositions. Many students of science maintain that *the essence of science lies in its methods of analysis.*[3]

*Analysis* is simply the quest for understanding through close observation and broad generalization. In pursuit of this objective, scientific analysis has a toolbox of concepts and procedural operations. *Variables, correlations, laws, theories, hypotheses, models,* and *paradigms* are some of the most important ones, and they are particularly important in political science. What follows is a brief explanation of each of these terms, coupled with some elementary examples of how they can be employed in political science.

#### Variables

> ***A* <u>variable</u> *is something that can vary or change. That is, it can take* different forms *or be a* changeable characteristic *of a phenomenon.***

Suppose we want to understand democracy. Democracy has many different characteristics that can vary or come in different forms. For example, there are *stable* democracies that endure over long periods of time with few major alterations (such as the United States); there are *unstable* democracies that experience frequent changes of government (like Italy, which has had more than sixty governments since World War II) or that alternate over time with nondemocratic modes of government (like Brazil, which has alternated between democracy and dictatorship). *Stability* is thus a characteristic of democracy that can vary. We can focus on stability as one among several variables about democracy that can be analyzed systematically. We can define exactly what we mean by stability and instability, we can collect information on stable and unstable democracies, compare different cases of each variant, and look for possible explanations of why some democracies are stable and others are not. The factors that account for stability or instability are also variables. For example, we may find that, of all the possible characteristics of a given country, national wealth is the variable that best explains democratic stability: rich democracies may turn out to be the most stable, poor ones the most unstable.

Suppose we want to figure out why people vote the way they do. The choices voters make can vary. People can vote for different parties or candidates, or they can stay home and not vote at all. The voters themselves also have variable characteristics. The electorate consists of different social classes, ethnic groups, religions, and other social categories. Like election-year political consultants, we can systematically gather information on all these variables and analyze the extent to which the various characteristics of the electorate account for the population's electoral choices.

Just about any general topic in political science has characteristics that can vary, such as types of government (e.g., democracy, authoritarianism), governmental institutions (e.g., unicameral and bicameral legislatures), or the political behavior of people (e.g., mass voting behavior, elite decision-making behavior). When we engage in the scientific study of politics, it is variables like these that occupy our direct attention. In some cases we may wish simply to observe these phenomena, collecting information about them and perhaps classifying them in some way. Things get especially interesting, however, when we find relationships between two or more observed variables.

Is there perhaps a relationship between democratic stability and a country's level of economic development? (Are stable democracies predominantly rich countries? Are poor countries doomed to authoritarianism?) Is there a relationship between voting for conservative candidates and the voters' income level or religion or ethnic group or gender? (Do upper-income voters, whether in the United States or other countries, tend to vote mainly for conservatives?) One of the first ways of generalizing about politics is to look for relationships of these kinds.

**Dependent and Independent Variables** Whenever we are looking for patterns or connections between two variables, one variable is the *dependent variable* and the other is the *independent variable*.

> ***The <u>dependent variable</u> is the variable we are most interested in examining or explaining; it is the main object of our study. It is the* effect or outcome *that is influenced or caused by another variable or variables. It is the variable whose value changes in response to changes in the value of other variables (viz., independent variables).***

Let's say that we are interested in understanding voting behavior in the United States and other democracies. One variable characteristic of voting behavior is *turnout*, the number of people who turn out to vote. Some voters go to the polls but others stay home. Electoral statistics over the past fifty years show that Americans tend to vote at consistently lower rates than West Europeans. What explains these differences? Are there any patterns we can find that might be associated with the level of voter turnout? Put another way, on what factors is turnout *dependent*? Turnout is thus our *dependent* variable. It is the variable we seek to explain; we want to see what it *depends* on.

> ***The <u>independent variable</u> is the factor or characteristic that influences or causes the dependent variable. In cause-and-effect relationships, it is the* causal *or* explanatory variable. *Changes in the value of the independent variable may produce changes in the value of the dependent variable.***

In our hypothetical study of voting behavior, the independent variables are various characteristics of the electorate that may help account for variations in voter turnout. These characteristics would include income level, age, education level, ideological proclivities, and other pertinent factors. For example, low-income voters may be less inclined to vote than upper-income voters; younger voters may be less inclined to turn out than older ones; and so on. Independent variables could also include different attitudes about politics, as evidenced in public opinion surveys. Some people may not vote because they believe their vote doesn't really matter and that voters can't change anything for the better; they therefore have a low sense of *political efficacy* and feel alienated from the political system. By contrast, others may have a high sense of political efficacy: they believe that "every vote counts" and that voters can in fact influence

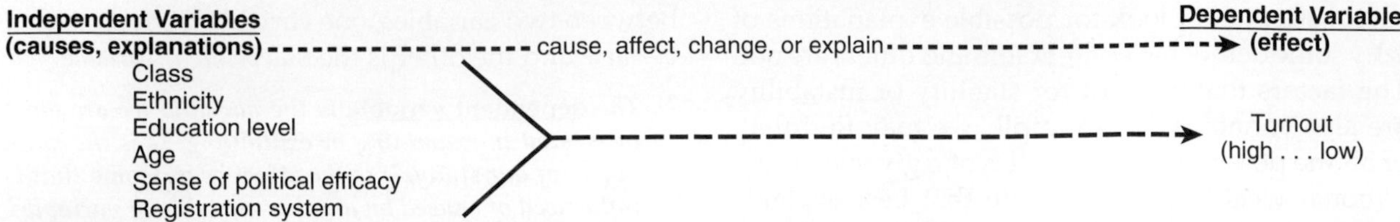


**FIGURE 3.1 Independent and Dependent Variables**

politicians to make desirable decisions while in office. Turnout might also hinge on registration procedures: it may be higher in countries where registering to vote is easy and lower where it is more inconvenient (as in the United States). Just about anything that might affect turnout can be an independent variable in our investigation. Figure 3.1 illustrates these variables.

In short, in the statement "A causes B," A is the *independent variable* and B is the *dependent variable.* B is dependent on A.

We can try out our independent variables individually to see to what extent each one is associated with our dependent variable, or we can try different combinations of independent variables. For example, we can focus first on the relationship between ethnicity and turnout in the United States, examining turnout levels for whites, blacks, Asians, Hispanics, and so on. We can do the same for the income-level variable, the religious variable, and so on. In these instances we are engaging in *single-variable analysis.* We can also examine two or more independent variables in combination against the dependent variable (e.g., rich whites, poor blacks; Protestants who attend church regularly and Protestants who do not attend church regularly, and so on). Such analyses are *multivariable analyses.*

Our aim in this study is to determine whether, or to what extent, there are any connections between the independent variables and our dependent variable, voter turnout. Such connections between variables are called *correlations,* or *associations.*

### Correlations

> ***A*** **correlation** ***(or*** **association*****) is a relationship in which two or more variables change together.***

*Correlates* are variables that are associated with each other in some way. For example, such things as a high level of national wealth, a large middle class, and a well-educated populace are often correlates of democracy: as a general tendency they go together with democratic forms of government.

*Variables are positively correlated when they vary in the same direction.* Two variables are positively correlated when they go up or down together (i.e., they *increase together* or *decrease together*).

If our variables are quantifiable, we can plot them on a graph. Usually we plot the dependent variable along the y-axis (vertical axis), and the independent variable along the x-axis (horizontal axis). Let's measure the relationship between turnout and the electorate's income levels in a hypothetical country. Figure 3.2 illustrates a *positive correlation* between the voters' income levels (the independent variable) and the percentage of people who turn out to vote (the dependent variable). The higher the income level, the higher the turnout; the lower the income level, the lower the turnout. Eighty percent of people in the highest income bracket turn out to vote, but only 5 percent of the people in the lowest income level show up at the polls. Note that when the correlation is positive, the plotted line goes from bottom left to top right.

*Variables are inversely correlated when they vary in opposite or reverse directions.* In quantitative terms, an inverse correlation occurs when one variable *increases* and the other variable *decreases,* or vice versa. We can grasp an inverse correlation rather easily by looking at the relationship between turnout (the dependent variable) and the voters' sense of *alienation* from the political system (the independent variable). (Alienation means a low sense of political efficacy and a basic distrust of politicians and government officials.) As figure 3.3 illustrates, voters with the lowest sense of alienation have the highest turnout rates; voters with the highest sense of alienation have the lowest turnout rates. Thus there is an *inverse correlation*

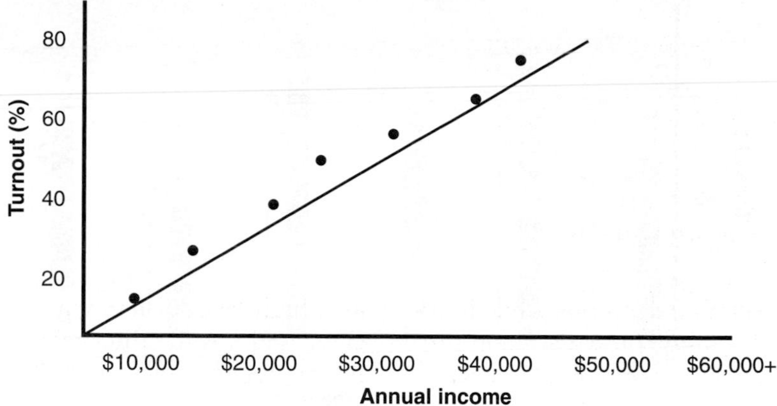


**FIGURE 3.2 Positive Correlation Between Income Levels and Turnout**

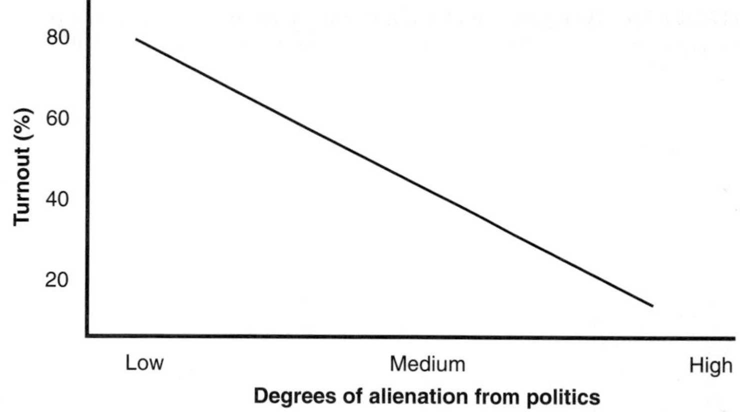


**FIGURE 3.3 Inverse (Negative) Correlation Between Alienation and Turnout**

between alienation and turnout. Inverse correlations are also called *negative correlations*. Note that when the correlation is negative, the plotted line goes from top left to bottom right.

In some cases we cannot chart quantifiable degrees of variation on a graph, but we can display different examples of the variable on a *histogram*. Figure 3.4 shows the relationship between turnout and voter registration in the United States. Because we cannot distinguish among different magnitudes of "registered-ness," we cannot plot variations in turnout rates *within* these two groups. The histogram compares the percentage of registered voters who have turned out to vote in elections to the House of Representatives with the percentage of all potential voters—registered and unregistered—who have turned out.

Conceivably, we could undertake a different research project by taking one of the independent variables just listed and making it our dependent variable. Suppose, for example, we are primarily interested in focusing on the phenomenon of political alienation: what factors might affect or cause it? In this study, political alienation becomes the dependent variable, and we then try out various independent variables to see if they are correlated with it. To what extent (if any) is political alienation dependent on race or ethnicity? on religious orientation? on income level? on education level? on psychological factors? on other variables? on some combination of variables? Figure 3.5 shows a negative (inverse) correlation between alienation (the dependent variable) and education level (the independent variable). The less educated people are,

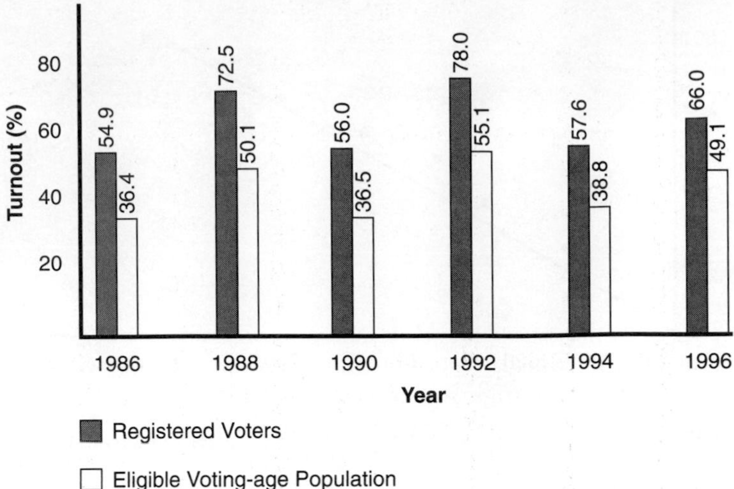


**FIGURE 3.4 Histogram Comparing Turnout Rates of Registered and All Potential U.S. Voters (Elections to House of Representatives, 1986–96)**

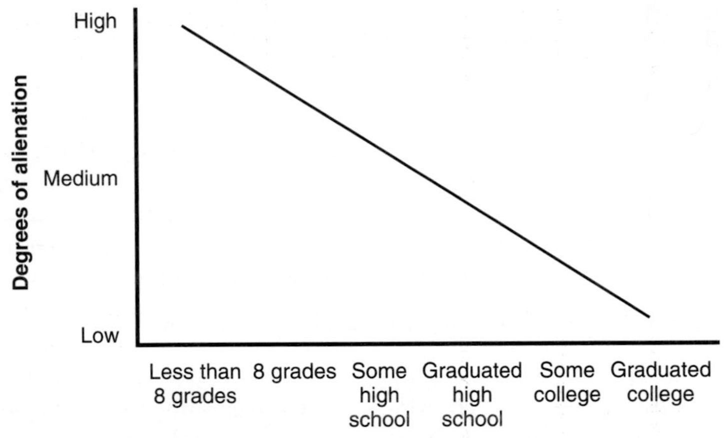


**FIGURE 3.5 Correlation Between Alienation and Education Level**

the higher their sense of alienation; the more educated people are, the lower their sense of alienation. Our point here is that, depending on the main focus of our analysis—that is, the main *effect* we wish to understand or explain—alienation can be either an independent variable or a dependent variable. Many other variables can also be used either way.

Keep in mind that *correlations are not explanations.* Even though our data may show a clear correlation, positive or negative, between the dependent and independent variables, they do not explain *why* the variables are related. Let's take another look at figure 3.2, which shows a positive correlation between voter turnout and income levels. *Why* do higher-income people vote at higher rates than less well-off citizens? We cannot get answers to this question just by looking at the graph depicting the correlation.

To find out why higher-income voters come out on election day at higher rates than the less well-to-do voters do, we will have to extend our investigations by conducting surveys of voter attributes and attitudes. These surveys may reveal that wealthier citizens tend to be better educated than

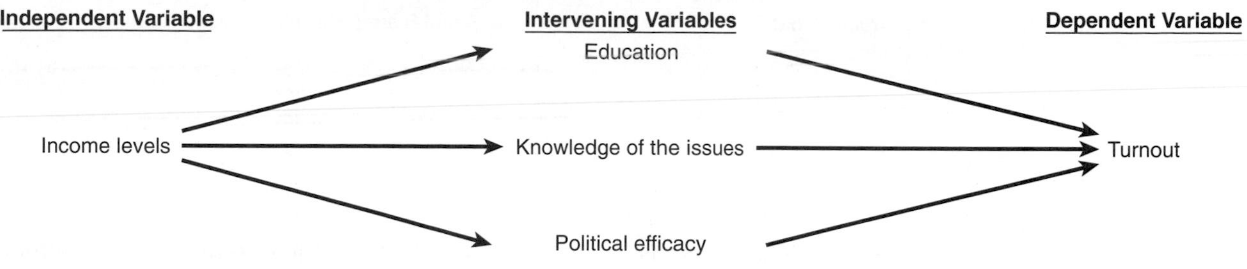


**FIGURE 3.6 Intervening Variables**

poorer ones and thus more knowledgeable about political issues. They may also have a higher sense of their own political efficacy, that is, their ability to have a real impact on government policies. The surveys may further reveal that poor citizens tend to be poorly educated, display less knowledge of the issues of the day, and have a markedly lower sense of political efficacy. These results suggest that income levels (the independent variable) affect election-day turnout (the dependent variable) by working through such intermediary factors as education, knowledge of the issues, and a citizen's sense of political efficacy. These intermediary factors are called **intervening variables.** As figure 3.6 shows, intervening variables ***are located in between the independent and dependent variables.***

As a general rule, *correlations do not prove that one variable* (i.e., income level) *actually* causes *the other variable* (i.e., voter turnout). In other words, *correlations do not conclusively demonstrate* causality. All a correlation does is suggest or imply that there *may* be a cause-and-effect relationship between the variables under observation. Of course, in order to show that a causal relationship does in fact exist, it is first necessary to demonstrate that a correlation exists. Correlations are *necessary* to demonstrate causality, but by themselves they are not *sufficient* to do so.

Sometimes variables may be positively or negatively correlated but it turns out on further investigation that there is no direct cause-and-effect relationship between them. We then have a *spurious correlation*.

One type of spurious correlation occurs when there *appears* to be a correlation between the variables but in fact no real relationship of any kind exists. One of the most famous examples concerns the fairy tale that babies are delivered by storks. The story comes from actual statistical data from northern Europe that showed an increase in human births whenever stork births increased. When stork births declined, so did human births. No one ever came up with any verifiable explanations as to why human and stork birthrates were positively correlated. Obviously, the one event could not have caused the other, but neither was there any evidence that some other variable (climactic patterns? lunar cycles?) caused the two birthrates to rise and fall together. Until someone brings forward convincing evidence of a causative variable, we can assume that the correlation between human births and stork births is entirely fortuitous. Thus a spurious correlation can at times be a matter of pure coincidence, with *no* causal factors at work.

In other circumstances, a spurious correlation can be said to exist when two apparently correlated variables (let's say A and B) are not *directly* linked in a cause-and-effect relationship (A does not cause B, and B does not cause A); rather, they are *indirectly* linked because some other variable is causing one or the other, or both (C causes both A and B, or just one of them). In other words, the stork-and-baby correlation would still be considered spurious even if it could be shown that some third factor (like climactic patterns) caused the two infant populations to increase and decrease together.

> ***In sum, a* spurious correlation *occurs when two variables appear to be directly linked in a cause-and-effect relationship but in fact (a) there is no causal linkage whatsoever, or (b) they are linked indirectly by some other causative variable or variables.*** Figure 3.7 depicts the logic of spurious correlations.

As political scientists we must constantly be on guard against spurious correlations when conducting or examining scientific research. We should be similarly vigilant as citizens. In the rough-and-tumble

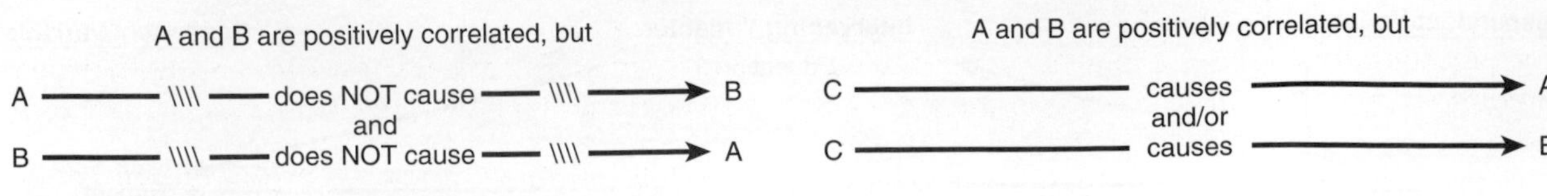


**FIGURE 3.7 Spurious Correlations**

world of politics, it is commonplace for politicians seeking to oust their opponents from office in the next elections to blame the incumbents for virtually everything that has gone wrong in the country during the government's term in office. In some cases, the elected officials may indeed be responsible for the problems they are accused of creating. But not always. It could happen, for example, that a downturn in the national economy that occurs when the Freedom Party is in power actually had its causative roots in policies pursued several years earlier when the Independence Party was in office. The correlation between the Freedom Party's incumbency and the deterioration of the economy is spurious because a third variable, the Independence Party, actually caused the economic tailspin.

Alternatively, it could happen that the actions of neither party were responsible for the economic decline. Other factors over which the two rival parties had little or no control while in office may have been at fault, such as unfavorable international economic conditions or the effects of disastrous weather on the national economy. Examples of spurious correlations in the real world of politics are rarely in short supply.

### Laws

***In science, a law is a regularly occurring association (or correlation) between two or more variables.***

A *deterministic law* means that whenever X occurs, Y *always* occurs. The laws of gravity are an example. Starting with the simple observation that what goes up *must* come down (at least within the Earth's atmosphere), Sir Isaac Newton showed with mathematical precision that physical bodies have a general tendency to be pulled toward one another in patterns determined by their mass and distance. Albert Einstein's famous equation, $E = mc^2$, is a law specifying that energy *always* occurs as the product of mass times the square of the speed of light. The physical world has a number of deterministic laws, many of them translatable into timeless mathematical equations. As Einstein put it, "God does not play dice with the universe!"

A less stringent type of scientific law is a *probabilistic law.* In this case, whenever A occurs, B *sometimes* occurs. Occasionally we can calculate the *degree of probability* with which B is likely to occur. In the natural world, weather predictions are frequently based on probabilistic laws. Given certain temperatures, humidity levels, and other atmospheric conditions, we can predict when snow will probably fall. Depending on the accuracy of our weather data and the sophistication of our computer models, we may be able to make accurate forecasts with a very high degree of probability. Nevertheless, so many variables are at work that we cannot be absolutely certain when it will snow, or if it does, we cannot be completely sure how much will fall on which spots.

Human behavior is not as law-bound as inanimate nature. Unlike the planets or atomic particles, human beings are capable of conscious volitional behavior and completely erratic irrational behavior. We can make decisions about how we wish to behave by choosing from a menu of alternative courses of action. We can change our minds. We can act singly or in all sorts of groups. We can act cooperatively or at cross-purposes. Moreover, our social or political behavior can be affected by a multitude of variables (our ethnic group, religion, economic interests, parents, peers, etc.). Sometimes we miscalculate, acting on the basis of false assumptions, inadequate information, or faulty logic. Sometimes we may not even be consciously aware of the factors that induce us to behave in certain ways, as when our biases, emotions, or subconscious impulses intrude on our actions.

As a consequence, human behavior is extremely variable and unpredictable. Hence the social sciences, which focus on human behavior (especially in large social groups), cannot predict the future with unfailing accuracy. Whereas the planets and other celestial bodies obligingly conform to the laws of gravitational motion, making it possible to pinpoint with mathematical precision the position of the moon or Halley's comet hundreds or even thousands of years from now, human behavior is so variegated that no one can foretell what political, social, or economic realities will look like ten years from now or even ten months from now. Perhaps for this reason Einstein also declared, "Politics is more difficult than physics."

Hence there are no *deterministic* laws in political science. Nevertheless, in political science as in other social sciences (such as sociology, economics, and social psychology), researchers can frequently discern real patterns and tendencies in human social activity. And even though we cannot foretell with any degree of certainty exactly what the future will bring, social scientists can sometimes suggest which future developments are more probable or less probable, at least in the near term.

Prediction of the future in the social sciences is thus suggestive or *probabilistic* in nature. If we can identify regularities in a population's voting patterns, for example, we can *suggest* how people *may* vote in the next elections. The closer we get to election day, the greater the confidence we may have in our estimation of *probable* outcomes. Even the most sophisticated statistical analyses of the most comprehensive polling data we can obtain, however, may not be sufficient to predict the way people actually will vote the very next day. Many pollsters were as surprised as virtually everyone else by Harry Truman's upset victory over Thomas Dewey in 1948, and most statistical models predicted that Al Gore would beat George W. Bush in 2000.[4] Similarly, experts on the Soviet Union were shocked at the USSR's complete collapse in 1991; veteran China-watchers did not foresee the eruption of prodemocracy student demonstrations in Beijing in 1989; and specialists on South Africa could scarcely have predicted in the early 1980s that the white minority would finally allow multiracial elections to take place there in the early 1990s, bringing Nelson Mandela, a black man, to the presidency.

Only in a suggestive and probabilistic sense, therefore, can we speak of laws in social science. Actually, social scientists rarely use the term *law* at all. In a few cases, they apply the term to certain patterns of social behavior that occur with considerable frequency and in a relatively regularized manner. Even these cases, however, are probabilistic rather than deterministic laws.

> In economics, for example, the *law of supply and demand* states that, as a general rule, prices in a market economy will rise whenever the supply of goods is low or the demand for goods rises. Conversely, prices tend to fall whenever supply increases or demand declines. Thus, prices are positively correlated with demand and negatively correlated with supply.
>
> In political science, *Duverger's law*, named after a French political scientist, stipulates that an electoral system in which the voters choose competing candidates by a simple majority (i.e., the highest number of votes) in a single ballot tends to produce a two-party system. Examples would include elections to the U.S. House of Representatives and the British House of Commons.

Just about every scientific law has its exceptions, as even natural scientists acknowledge with respect to nature. This reality is especially true in the social sciences. Economists recognize that the law of supply and demand, although a general tendency, does not always operate perfectly. Even in a market economy, factors such as monopolies or fluctuating consumer demands may interfere with it. Similarly, Duverger's law may not apply in all circumstances, as Duverger himself acknowledged. (Britain, for example, has more than two parties represented in the House of Commons.)[5] Any so-called law in the social sciences must be constantly put to the test against the evidence of reality to determine whether, or to what extent, it holds true. In social science as in the physical sciences, laws are occasionally broken.

Moreover, laws—like correlations—are not *explanations.* They simply point out that two or more variables generally go together, but they do not explain why. To find out why these patterns exist, social scientists must conduct other exploratory investigations. The principal ways of explaining political realities scientifically are by formulating *theories* and *hypotheses.*

**Theories** The term **theory** can have several different meanings in political science.

1. In its broadest sense, theory simply refers to ***thinking about politics as opposed to practicing***

***it.*** As such, it is an ***abstract intellectual exercise.*** Theorizing can mean nothing more than ***making generalizations*** about politics ("Majorities always discriminate against minorities!"), whether in accordance with strict scientific rules ("And I can prove it!") or far more informally, as in late-night political discussions with friends ("Now don't try to reason with me!").

In this elementary definition of the term, theory also refers to ***general principles or abstract ideas*** that may not necessarily be true in actual fact. For example, when we say, "In theory, democracy is government by the people," we are referring to some general principle or idea of democracy; we are not explaining how democracy actually works in practice.

2. More restrictively, theory can mean ***normative theory:*** that is, value-centered political philosophy (or political thought), as we defined these terms earlier in this chapter.
3. In the natural and social sciences, theory most frequently means ***a generalization, or set of generalizations, that seeks to* explain, *and perhaps* predict, *relationships among variables. This is* explanatory theory.**

*Explanation is the main aim of theory in empirical political science.* The word *because* is stated or implied in just about every explanatory theory.

**Parsimonious and Middle-Range Theories** Scientists use the term *parsimonious theory* to refer to a *theory that explains a vast range of phenomena in very succinct terms.* Charles Darwin's theory of evolution is an example of parsimonious theory. His theory states that all animal life evolved from lower animal forms through a process of natural selection. In just one brief sentence, Darwin's theory purports to account for all animal species. Parsimonious theories are said to have a high level of *explanatory power*.

Political science has few parsimonious theories. (Some political scientists maintain that it has none.) Instead of enunciating bold generalizations capable of explaining all or even most political phenomena in a sentence or two, political science largely confines itself to so-called *middle-range theories*. These are theories that explain specific categories, or segments, of political reality. Typically, middle-range theories in political science are sets of statements and hypotheses that are strung together to explain a particular subfield of political reality.

*Democratic theory* consists of descriptions of how democracies are supposed to work in principle and how they work in practice, along with various explanations of how democracies emerge or endure.

*Elite theory* describes the roles that political elites play and makes a variety of explanatory generalizations about their social backgrounds, their political perceptions, their relationships with the masses, and so on.

*Rational choice theory* explains political behavior by regarding virtually all individuals as "rational actors" who seek to increase their personal gains and minimize their losses or risks. As in Prisoner's Dilemma, rational choice theories present the logic of a process or behavior in general (conflict, for example), without immediate reference to specific cases. But the logic can be used to explain specific cases (like the Palestinian–Israeli conflict). Some proponents of rational choice theory assert that it is a parsimonious theory that can explain a vast array of political phenomena. Others, however, insist that it is just another middle-range theory that has its limits.

Middle-range theories also exist on a host of other political phenomena, such as *electoral behavior, the state, revolution, and war*. Subsequent chapters in this book examine a number of these theories.

As a general rule, explanations that merit the term theory have usually gained wide acceptance over long periods of time because their ability to explain the facts has been confirmed in repeated scientific investigations. Theories thus tend to be more solidly grounded in empirical reality than hypotheses, which are typically assumptions that have yet to be sufficiently tested. Nevertheless, even the most widely respected theories are not unchallengeable truths. They are meant to be constantly challenged against the hard facts of reality. In political science as in the natural sciences, *explanatory theories are not abstractions that are divorced from reality; on the contrary, they seek to* explain *reality*. Theories are valid only as long as they are consistent with the facts they endeavor to explain. If new evidence comes to light that contradicts the theory, then the theory is probably either partially or entirely wrong. It must then be modified or discarded and replaced by a better theory that fits the facts. All explanatory theories need to be repeatedly subjected to verification against the hard data of reality. The main way of accomplishing this task is by breaking theories down into hypotheses and testing them against the available evidence.

### Hypotheses

***A <u>hypothesis</u> is an assumption or supposition that needs to be tested against relevant evidence.***

In some cases, hypotheses can be purely *descriptive* in nature. For example, we can hypothesize that democracy has broad popular support in Russia. We can then test this hypothesis by surveying a large number of Russians and asking them whether they support democracy, and if so, how strongly. After we've collected and analyzed our research data we will end up with a description, a picture, of mass attitudes toward Russian democracy. The data will permit us to describe the Russian electorate as mostly supportive of democracy or mostly unsupportive of it by providing statistical readings of the proportion of the voters who support it strongly, the percentage of those who support it with less conviction, and the percentage of those who don't support it very much or not at all.

This descriptive hypothesis simply proposes certain facts about the Russian electorate, and the hypothesis-testing survey seeks to determine whether and to what extent those facts are really occurring. The descriptive hypothesis does not suggest an *explanation* as to *why* the proposed phenomena might be occurring, however. It is not an *explanatory* hypothesis that explains *why* Russians feel as they do about democracy. But in political science as in the physical sciences, *explanation is the ultimate goal.*

*Explanatory hypotheses* posit a cause-and-effect relationship between dependent and independent variables that can be tested empirically (i.e., against factual evidence). By formulating explanatory hypotheses about politics, we force ourselves to specify our dependent and independent variables and to be clear about the sharp difference between cause and effect. By *testing* hypotheses empirically, we submit them to a reality check: we take a close look at all the available facts to see if they substantiate or contradict the relationships we propose in our hypotheses. For example, we might find that, contrary to our hypothesis, popular support for democracy in Russia is in fact much weaker than we had originally surmised. We must then formulate explanatory hypotheses that might suggest possible reasons for this phenomenon. We could hypothesize that public dissatisfaction with the economy is causing people to turn against democracy; or we could hypothesize that disgust at political corruption may be the main explanatory variable accounting for Russian attitudes; or we could assume that public ignorance about democracy may be the explanation; or we could develop a host of other possible explanations, whether singly or in combination.

We could then test these various explanatory hypotheses by going back to Russia and resurveying the electorate, asking them more specific questions about their attitudes on the economy, corruption, and so forth. After analyzing our survey data, we can then come to some conclusions about which of these explanatory variables explain why many Russians are suspicious of democracy. We may find, for example, that *all* of them play a role, albeit to varying degrees, among the voters. In these explanatory hypotheses, *"negative attitudes toward democracy"* is the *dependent variable.* The *possible explanations* to be tested are the *independent variables.* (See figure 3.8.)

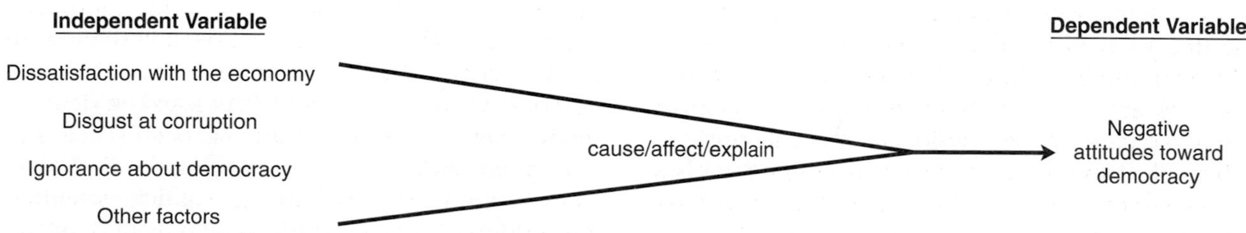


**FIGURE 3.8 Independent Variables Affecting Negative Attitudes Toward Democracy**

The second part of this chapter is devoted to an extended exercise in testing the proposition that *"national wealth promotes democracy."* Is this hypothesis correct? Is it only partially correct? Or is it perhaps just plain wrong? Reading Part Two attentively will give you a more comprehensive idea of how the logic of hypothesis testing applies to the study of politics.

**Scientific Generalization and Practical Politics** Explanatory theories and hypotheses in political science greatly enhance our understanding of the real world of politics. They can also help us work out our own positions on the political problems of our times. Indeed, many of the practical policy choices facing government decision makers and average citizens are rooted in some overarching theory. Debates over the decision to invade Iraq in 2003 are connected with theories about U.S. foreign policy, with some favoring "regime change" to create a democracy as an immediate goal and others placing national security ahead of democratization as the country's number-one foreign policy priority, even when it means putting up with a vile dictator. Debates on tax policy are connected with theories about how or whether governments can stimulate economic growth while cutting budget deficits and keeping inflation low. The list of theory-related policy issues could be extended indefinitely.

Although some people dismiss theory as completely detached from the real world, in fact most individuals act in political life on the basis of certain assumptions and understandings about politics that are the equivalent of theoretical generalizations, even if they do not always realize it. As the British economist John Maynard Keynes once observed, "Practical men, who believe themselves to be exempt from any intellectual influences, are usually the slaves of some defunct economist." By the same token, politicians and the people they govern can be the slaves of political ideas they accept uncritically. An intelligent approach to politics requires a keen understanding of the relevance of explanatory theory and hypothesis testing to the real world of political action. To put it succinctly, the scientific approach to politics requires us to support our political generalizations with relevant evidence and systematic logic.

**Models**

***In political science, a <u>model</u> is a simplified representation of reality in descriptive or abstract form.***

A scale model of a Stealth bomber can neither fly nor drop bombs. Its sleek proportions, however, provide some understanding of how the real aircraft is able to avoid radar detection. An auto designer's computer model of next year's dream car indicates how all its components will mesh together in perfect harmony once the vehicle hits the road. Environmental scientists have built a large model of the Chesapeake Bay designed to replicate the bay's complex ecological system. Economists construct graphical and mathematical models of various dynamic economic processes, such as a perfectly competitive market economy or a global free trade system.

Though the composition of these models is different, they all serve the same function: they enable us to understand some aspect of reality, whether aerodynamics or the economy, by *representing* some of its essential features in a simplified or idealized form. Obviously, these scaled-down physical or mathematical models cannot be perfect copies of the realities they represent. The car designer does not plan for the car to malfunction, but at some point it probably will. Economists know that purely free market systems, which are devoid of any governmental interference or monopolies, exist nowhere in today's world.

The purpose of a model is not to represent reality perfectly but to enable us to understand reality by allowing us to compare it against some standard or pattern. If the car has stalling problems, the computer design can help us find the source. If world trade is declining, the mathematical model of how a free trade system works in theory may help us understand how to deal with existing trade barriers in the global economy. When viewed against the model, the complexities of the real world stand out all the more prominently by comparison with the simplified version. As one economist put it, "Models are to be used, not believed." As learning devices, models serve a *heuristic* purpose, a term that derives from the Greek word meaning "to find out."

In roughly similar fashion, political scientists use models of various kinds to help us understand political realities. Sometimes these models are purely descriptive. For example, we can construct a model of democracy just by listing its characteristic features: a competitive electoral system, legal guarantees of certain freedoms and rights, and so forth. Although many democracies in today's world may actually diverge from this model of an "ideal" democracy in one way or another, these divergences will tend to stand out when compared with the model, prompting us to investigate how and why they occur.

A descriptive model of this sort is known as an *ideal type*. An **ideal type** ***is a model of a political or social phenomenon that describes its main characteristic features.*** The term was coined by the German sociologist *Max Weber* (1864–1920), one of the founders of modern sociology. Weber was among the first students of modern bureaucracy. Based on his observations of European bureaucracies in the early twentieth century, Weber devised an ideal type of a modern bureaucracy that specified the features most commonly found in them. He described this standard (or ideal-typical) bureaucracy as a highly impersonal organization run in accordance with strict rules and legal procedures. Not all bureaucracies in Europe conformed exactly to this standard type in every respect, however. For Weber, an ideal type is not just a carbon copy of one or two real-world examples of the phenomenon it represents. Rather, it is an abstract conception constructed from a variety of observations and trends. Weber used it as a conceptual standard against which social scientists could study and compare the world's bureaucracies and come to a better understanding of the phenomenon of bureaucracy itself. The concept of the ideal type is very useful in describing all sorts of political phenomena.

In addition to ideal types, political science makes use of several other types of models. *Static models* simply define the fundamental attributes of a phenomenon (like ideal types), but they do not describe how those attributes change or develop over time. By contrast, *dynamic models* describe processes of change. For example, the *modernization model* describes how so-called "traditional societies" develop into "modern societies" through the process of industrialization. As a nation's economy becomes more industrialized, people tend to move from the countryside into the cities, communications networks expand, educational opportunities improve, and traditional religious practices and superstitions give way to more secularized lifestyles and beliefs. Modernization theorists base this model on the historical development of Europe and the United States, and they believe that most countries of the world sooner or later will move in much the same directions. The modernization model of political development has provoked considerable controversy. Its critics contend that it is too narrowly based on European and American experiences and that it pays inadequate attention to the special experiences and cultures of Asia, Africa, the Middle East, and other regions of the developing world. Some of these critics propose alternative models of political development that combine elements of both modern and traditional societies. We shall return to this issue in chapters 12 and 15.

Some models are *analogies*. In these cases, political scientists clarify political phenomena by comparing them to something else. For example, one scholar likens democracy to a market economy, with voters choosing candidates in the political "marketplace" on the basis of considerations very similar to those motivating consumers shopping for a good buy.[6] Another political scientist compares the ways governments work to cybernetic processes, complete with feedback mechanisms, communications loops, and other features of computer technology.[7] As we saw in chapter 2, some analysts regard many forms of political behavior as analogous to games like Prisoner's Dilemma.

Some models are simply *diagrams*, or schematic depictions of processes and relationships. Figures 3.9 and 3.10 diagram two alternative forms of democracy: *direct democracy* and *representative democracy*. Under direct democracy, the citizens themselves assemble and make authoritative decisions for their community. Under representative democracy, as the term implies, the citizens elect their representatives to the legislative and executive branches of government and entrust the elected

**FIGURE 3.9 Model of Direct Democracy**

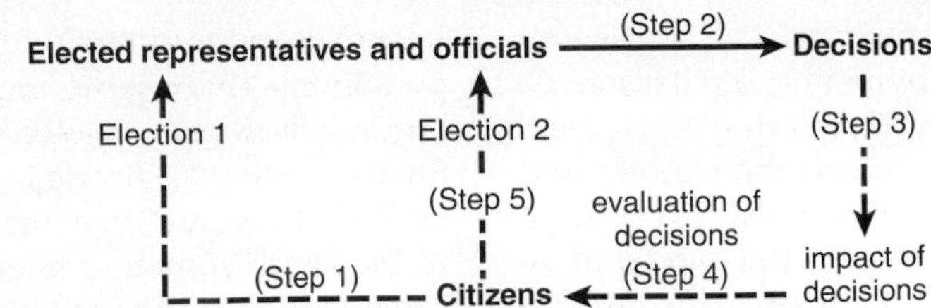


FIGURE 3.10 Model of Representative Democracy

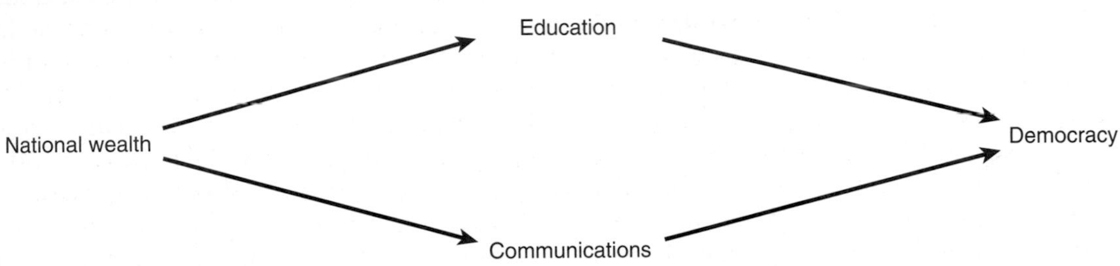


FIGURE 3.11 Model Depicting Causes of Democracy

officials and their appointees to make governmental decisions on their behalf. Once some of these decisions take effect, the citizens have the opportunity to evaluate their impact and to hold their elected representatives accountable in the next elections by voting them out of office or reelecting them.

Finally, like economists and natural scientists, political scientists sometimes construct complex mathematical models in an effort to represent various political phenomena as precisely as possible. This book will not examine such statistically advanced modeling techniques.

Strictly speaking, a model is not an explanatory theory. Whereas explanatory theory *explains* reality, models *represent* and *describe* reality. However simplified or sophisticated its form may be, a model is just a picture, not an explanation. Very frequently, however, we use the term *theoretical model* (or *conceptual model*). This term can have two meanings.

In one meaning, a model is said to be theoretical if it is an intellectual abstraction as opposed to a physical representation of something. Computer models, mathematical models, diagrams, and even ideal types are theoretical models in this sense of the term. They are *intellectual* or *abstract* representations of reality, not physical objects.

In the second meaning of the term, a theoretical model *represents* explanatory theories. A theory that states, for example, that national wealth *causes* democracies to come about by promoting education and communication can be depicted in a diagram. Figure 3.11 is a *causal model* that graphically represents this theory. Causal models can be a useful way of specifying causal relationships and clarifying our thinking about how different variables interact.

Moreover, models can stimulate explanatory theory. Just as environmental scientists use their model of the Chesapeake Bay to develop theories about how marine life develops or why so much of it is dying prematurely, political scientists can use their models to come up with explanatory theories about how and why various political phenomena occur as they do. Models, in short, are yet another useful method for generalizing systematically about politics.

**Paradigms** The term *paradigm* has two meanings in political science:

> **In one sense, *a* <u>paradigm</u> *is a prime example of a particular phenomenon or pattern.***

For example, the British system of government is a *paradigm* of parliamentary democracy. This is not to say that all parliamentary governments are exactly like Britain's in every respect. Italy, Israel, and other parliamentary political systems differ from the British version (and from one another) in various ways. Still, they are all close to the British example in certain fundamental respects. We can understand how these various governments work more clearly by comparing them to the British paradigm.

Paradigms are quite useful in comparative politics because they help us observe and analyze variations on a theme (such as parliamentary democracy). In this respect they serve the same purpose as models. The difference is that whereas models tend to be abstract or intellectually idealized representations of reality, paradigms are usually real-world phenomena (like Britain's governmental system).

**In another sense, *a <u>paradigm</u> is a particular way of looking at phenomena, formulating questions and generalizations, and conducting research.***

This second definition of paradigm construes it as a particular form of intellectual inquiry or a specific approach to scientific investigation. This meaning of the term was popularized by Thomas Kuhn, a philosopher interested in the nature of scientific thought. Kuhn argued that over the centuries Western science developed several radically different paradigms of scientific thinking, based on very different assumptions about the natural world and about how to study it. Ptolemaic astronomy, for example, held that the sun and planets revolve around the Earth. Only in the sixteenth century did Ptolemy's ancient paradigm give way to the heliocentric astronomy of Copernicus, based on more precise methods of observing the solar system. Similarly, Aristotle's views on physics were eventually supplanted by Newton's laws of mechanics; Newton's paradigm gave way to twentieth-century relativity theory and quantum mechanics; and so on.[8]

This meaning of paradigm also applies to political science. The paradigm of political science presented in this chapter conforms in its essential features to the rules of scientific logic that emerged from the empirical approach to scientific inquiry pioneered by Copernicus, Newton, and other seminal contributors to modern science. This scientific approach to studying politics is a fairly recent development, however. It emerged slowly in the United States in the 1930s and 1940s and increasingly shaped the way American political scientists were trained to think about politics in the 1950s and subsequently. Earlier, the dominant paradigm of political science research was largely descriptive and tended to concentrate on governmental institutions and constitutional law. It was less concerned with studying how people behave in political life, and it did not employ such concepts as variables, hypotheses, correlations, and other nuts and bolts of modern scientific thinking. It was also considerably less quantitative. Even today, many important books and articles are written about politics that employ the more traditional descriptive approach. But the scientific paradigm presented in this book is currently the leading one in most American universities.

## QUANTITATIVE AND QUALITATIVE POLITICAL SCIENCE

Political science offers two basic approaches to investigating relationships among variables: *quantitative* approaches and *qualitative* approaches.

*Quantitative* political science is "by the numbers." It looks mainly at phenomena that can vary in measurable degrees or quantities, such as the number of votes cast in an election or in legislative balloting, or the percentages of people who express various opinions in a public opinion survey. Statisticians have developed a variety of sophisticated techniques and software programs for performing different types of measurements involving quantifiable dependent and independent variables, and many of these tools can be adapted to research on politics.[9]

We will not use any of these sophisticated statistical techniques in this book, but they can be quite useful in the study of political science at more advanced levels, depending on the nature of the problem being investigated.

Statistical rigor is not always possible in the study of politics, however. Sometimes we would like to have relevant statistical information but it is not available, or if available, it is unreliable. Authoritarian regimes, for example, rarely permit contested elections or release public opinion poll information, and the statistics they do publish (such as economic data) may be untrustworthy. At least in these cases, Mark Twain was right when he quipped, "There are lies, damned lies, and statistics." At other times we may have statistical information available that can be quite useful in helping us understand a situation, but all we need do is report this information in tables or graphs without getting into highly sophisticated calculations. Economic statistics, election returns, and other relevant quantitative data are often used in this uncomplicated but vitally important way in political science, and we shall employ such raw data quite extensively in subsequent chapters. Finally, in some cases statistical analysis is only partially helpful in enabling us to understand political reality and must be combined with other factual information that is not readily quantifiable, such as historical accounts or other descriptions of political events, processes, or ideas.

Research and analysis in political science that is not primarily quantitative in nature is called *qualitative* political science. Political scientists who are engaged in qualitative research rely largely on descriptive accounts of the political realities they study. In seeking to explain political processes and interactions, analysts frequently use qualitative research to provide detailed (or "thick") descriptions of such things as how governmental institutions work, or how parties and interest groups are organized, or how political ideas and ideologies define the issues facing the country. These and similar political phenomena cannot be fully understood if we confine ourselves strictly to statistical analysis; descriptive detail may also be necessary.

Many qualitatively oriented analysts are especially sensitive to the broader historical and contemporary contexts within which political life takes place in any given country. Qualitative analysts often remind us that the specific details of politics—such as a recent leadership change or the latest elections—do not occur in a vacuum. These events have historical roots, and they may also be related to complex social, cultural, economic, or other conditions in ways that cannot be adequately explained just by referring to numerical data or by performing statistical operations. Statistics, such analysts would argue, can't explain everything. We need to immerse ourselves in the history, culture, and languages of individual countries if we want to understand their political systems.

Advocates of quantitative and qualitative approaches to political science have engaged in sharp debates about which mode of analysis is superior. Quantitatively oriented analysts cherish the precision and neatness of statistical rigor; they often accuse qualitatively oriented researchers of being vague or mushy. Qualitatively inclined political scientists, for their part, tend to accuse their number-crunching colleagues of ignoring everything about politics that cannot be reduced to mere statistics. They contend that quantifiers fail to appreciate the full scope of political reality in all its complexity.

A substantial number of political scientists today would admit that quantitative and qualitative approaches are complementary and that the approach an analyst chooses depends on the nature of the problem being studied. Most important, both quantitative and qualitative approaches must observe the same ground rules of scientific logic that we cover in this chapter.[10]

## LOGICAL FALLACIES

To round out this chapter's introduction to critical thinking about politics, we must warn against certain logical fallacies that are commonly committed in political argumentation. Our list can be only a partial one, and it cannot substitute for a book on logic. Nevertheless, the fallacies presented here are common enough to warrant special attention.

**Fallacy of composition** ***This fallacy assumes that the whole is exactly the same as its parts.*** Beware of ascribing attributes (such as attitudes, behaviors, etc.) to an entire class or group when those attributes may apply only to a portion of that group. For example, do not say, "The Germans are highly disciplined" or "Americans are well off," when in fact only *some* Germans may be highly disciplined and *not all* Americans are well off. This fallacy is the basis of *stereotyping*, that is, regarding all individuals of a particular group as similar while overlooking their differences.

**Tautology (circular reasoning)** ***ascribes causation to the very phenomenon whose causes we are trying to explain.*** To put it another way, beware of using your dependent variable as an independent variable that accounts for it. The term comes from the ancient Greek word for "the same." For example, the statement "Armed conflict among Yugoslavia's contending groups produced a bitter civil war" is tautological because civil war *is* armed conflict among a country's contending groups. The two points are essentially the same thing; hence, the one cannot cause the other. To ascertain the causes of the civil war, we must look at real explanatory variables such as ethnic and religious hatreds. One of the most famous tautologies attributed to a politician was the remark allegedly uttered by President Calvin Coolidge, "When a great many people are unable to find work, unemployment results."

*Post hoc ergo propter hoc* ("After it, therefore because of it") is the fallacy of concluding that A *caused* B just because A *preceded* B. For example, "The U.S.-led victory over Iraq in the Persian Gulf War at the start of 1991 precipitated the collapse of the Soviet Union later that same year." In fact, the war had no demonstrable effect on the Soviet collapse.

*The inevitability fallacy.* Just because things turn out a certain way, beware of assuming that they necessarily *had to* turn out as they did. As a rule, political outcomes are *path dependent*: they follow from the paths charted by history. But the course of events is often contingent on numerous factors—decisions, interactions, fortuitous occurrences, and the like—that are capable of leading to multiple possible results. Many things that appear inevitable after they happen were unforeseeable before they happened.

*A fortiori* ("All the more") assumes that what is true of a phenomenon at one level or degree is automatically true of the same phenomenon at larger levels or degrees. The statement "The more private enterprise there is in the economy, the more democracy will flourish" assumes that, just because a certain amount of private enterprise may be good for democracy, then a totally private economy, with no government involvement in economic affairs whatsoever, will be even better for democracy. It overlooks the possibility that a completely private economy, with no government-sponsored safety net to help the poor and the middle class, could create great disparities in wealth and perhaps lead to intense social conflicts capable of destroying democracy.

*False analogy* is the fallacy of making inappropriate or inexact analogies or comparisons between one phenomenon or situation and another. One example is the statement "Political systems are like organisms: they are born, they grow, and they inevitably decay and die." This "organic" analogy does not stand up to the facts. Historical analogies are also frequently misused. For example, prior to the successful U.S.-led attack against Iraqi troops occupying Kuwait in 1991, some people warned that such an invasion would result in a protracted military standoff similar to the Vietnam War. The analogy proved incorrect: the Persian Gulf War lasted only a few weeks. In fact, no two historical cases are ever *exactly* alike in all respects, and one must pay as much attention to dissimilarities as to similarities when comparing them.[11]

A *nonfalsifiable hypothesis* is a hypothesis that cannot be tested empirically. The only kind of hypothesis that can be tested empirically is one that is capable of being *contradicted* by factual evidence. An example of a nonfalsifiable hypothesis is, "Our country's fate is in God's hands." Because we cannot physically see or hear God, we have no empirical evidence enabling us to *disprove* the hypothesis; everything that happens to our country, good or bad, can be interpreted as consistent with it. Another example: "The laws of history make the collapse of authoritarianism inevitable in the long run, though it may succeed in the short run." Because we cannot have empirical evidence on the future, we have no basis for proving that the hypothesis is wrong (or right). Both hypotheses are articles of faith and cannot be empirically tested against hard evidence.

*False inference* is the fallacy of making unwarranted inferences from statistical data or other facts, especially when trying to establish causation. *Reductivism* is the fallacy of explaining something in terms of one sole cause when other causes could also be at work. Both fallacies are covered in the second part of this chapter.

## II. THE LOGIC OF HYPOTHESIS TESTING

Hypothesis testing is a central activity of political science. It is one of the things that makes it a science in the formal meaning of the word. By learning how to formulate and test hypotheses we can learn a lot about both political science and, not incidentally, political reality itself.

By learning some of the main rules of hypothesis testing, we can also learn a great deal about how to think logically and coherently. One of our most important tasks in this regard is to learn some of the cardinal *rules of causation*. Just what do we really know about politics for sure, and what are we less sure about? To what extent can we really "prove" that one thing actually causes another? How valid are our generalizations? Questions like these lie at the heart of *epistemology*, the field of inquiry that seeks to clarify the scope and limits of our ability to know. Epistemological issues are of fundamental importance in all the sciences, including political science, and they are vital to the development of critical reasoning skills more generally.

### SOURCES OF HYPOTHESES

Hypotheses about politics can spring from a variety of sources. In some instances they may derive from questions that pop into our minds from our observations of reality. Just from reading the newspaper, for example, we may notice the rather obvious fact that some countries have democratic systems of government and others do not. How come? From a superficial survey of these news accounts, a few possible answers may come to mind. One possible explanation centers on economics: the world's most successful and enduring democracies, we observe, are among the richest countries of the world. We notice, in particular, that such well-to-do countries as the United States, Canada, Britain, France, Germany, and Japan are successful democracies. Countries that lack democracy and countries that are currently engaged in the process of building democracy following the collapse of an authoritarian regime appear for the most part to be less economically developed. Many countries in Latin America and Africa fall into these latter categories.

A cursory glance at these facts prompts us to formulate the following hypothesis: *"National wealth promotes democracy."* This hypothesis implies a cause-and-effect relationship: national wealth somehow *causes* democracy to come about and endure, whereas national poverty precludes or undermines democracy.

The technique we have just used to formulate our hypothesis is called *induction*. **Induction** ***is a reasoning process that goes from the specific to the general.*** We begin with some *specific facts or observations*, and on the basis of these specifics we devise an overarching *generalization* that applies to the phenomena we have observed as well as to related phenomena that we have not as yet observed, as depicted in figure 3.12. (*Induction* derives from the Latin word for "lead into"; in essence, specific facts lead into a generalization.) Thus our observation of a few specific wealthy democracies and a few specific poor nondemocracies leads us to suspect that national wealth is perhaps associated with *all* democracies and national poverty is perhaps associated with *all* nondemocracies. We say "perhaps" because at this point these broad generalizations are only suspicions or guesses that we have made on the basis of a small number of observations. That is precisely what hypotheses frequently are: suspicions, educated guesses, or hunches. We don't know yet if our hunch is true or false in reality. Only when

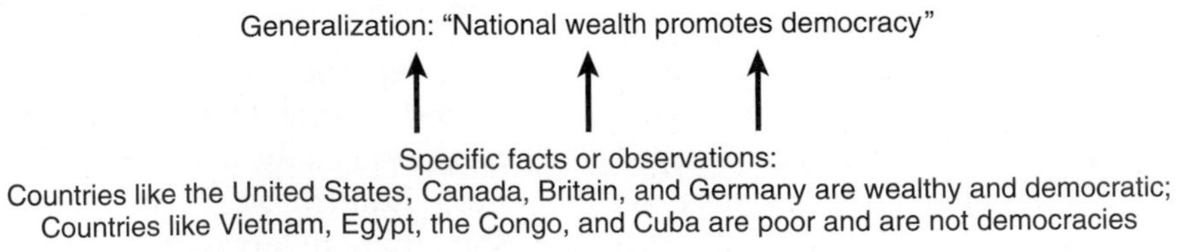

Specific facts or observations:
Countries like the United States, Canada, Britain, and Germany are wealthy and democratic;
Countries like Vietnam, Egypt, the Congo, and Cuba are poor and are not democracies

**FIGURE 3.12 Diagram of Inductive Reasoning**

we have tested our hypothesis by looking at a far wider number of democracies and nondemocracies will we have a better idea of whether, or to what extent, our proposed generalization is valid.

Another source of hypotheses consists of generalizations that have already been formulated. In the course of our newspaper gleanings we may have come across an editorial arguing in favor of major international efforts to promote the economic development of nascent democracies like Russia and South Africa. The editorialist justifies this policy recommendation on the basis of a broad generalization: *"National wealth,"* she writes, *"promotes democracy."*

The editorialist then sets forth a number of reasons explaining why national wealth promotes democracy. One reason is that democracy requires an educated populace that understands political issues and actively participates in the electoral process and other opportunities for political involvement. Educated people, she argues, are more likely than the uneducated to take part in political affairs. But an educated electorate requires a good mass education system, and that costs money. Wealthy countries are in a better position than poor ones to provide their citizens with a good education. Democracy, we are told, also requires a well-developed mass communications system so that people can keep themselves informed about political developments. That too costs money.

Furthermore, the writer maintains, democracy requires a fairly sizable middle class that is eager to have a say in the way the country is governed. The middle class, she believes, is a prime source of pro-democracy activism. By contrast, the rich may be perfectly content with an authoritarian regime that allows them to retain their wealth, while the poor may be insufficiently educated or too unorganized to push for democratic reforms. Wealthy countries are more likely than impoverished ones to have a sizable middle class.

In addition, the writer notes, wealthy countries are better equipped than poor ones to meet their citizens' demands for government services. Democracy gives the mass public an opportunity to demand such benefits as education, decent housing, health care, job training, and pensions. Poor countries are less able to meet these popular demands, and their rulers therefore deny their populations a chance to articulate them in an open democratic process. A repressive authoritarian government is the likely result. Thus, if we want democracy to succeed around the world, the writer concludes, the wealthy democracies must do whatever they can to assist the less developed nations of the world in overcoming their poverty.

In this particular case, the editorialist did not look at specific democratic and nondemocratic countries, as we did in our perusal of newspaper articles. Rather, she derived her hypothesis from *generalizations* about what causes democracies to come about. Her supposition that national wealth promotes democracy is based on a general explanation of various factors needed to build a democratic regime, all of which ultimately depend on national wealth. Thus *generalizations themselves*, not just specific facts, can also be a source of hypotheses.

## STEPS OF HYPOTHESIS TESTING

Are the editorialist's sweeping generalizations correct? In order to find out, we need to break them down into testable propositions and test them against hard evidence. Let's concentrate on her central hypothesis, "National wealth promotes democracy." How do we go about testing this proposition?

We can choose from a variety of methods, depending on whether we are relying mainly on quantitative or qualitative analysis (or some combination of the two) and on whether we want to examine a large number of countries or confine ourselves to a few particularly illustrative ones. In most cases, however, the logic of hypothesis testing will involve the following five steps:

1. Defining key terms
2. Identifying the variables
3. Specifying the expectations of the hypothesis
4. Collecting and examining the evidence
5. Drawing conclusions from the evidence

### Defining Key Terms

Because our hypothesis is about democracy, we must define the term. *Democracy* is a multifaceted concept that includes regular elections, civil liberties, and a host of other elements. The Freedom

House lists of political and civil rights that we presented in chapter 2 encompass just about all of democracy's essential components. Moreover, the numerical rating system that Freedom House employs, with the most democratic countries meriting a grade of 1 and the most authoritarian states getting a 7, provides a useful estimate of the extent to which the countries of the world fulfill these numerous criteria, despite the system's lack of statistical precision. We shall therefore use the Freedom House criteria here as our operative definition of democracy, and we'll use the Freedom House composite political and civil rights index as a measure of each country's relative degree of democracy. In addition, we'll sort the countries of the world into the categories we introduced in chapter 2. Accordingly, *democracies* are countries with a political/civil rights index from 1 to 2.5; *semi-democracies*, 3 or 3.5; *semi-authoritarian regimes*, from 4 to 5.5; and *authoritarian regimes*, from 6 to 7.[12]

We can narrow our conception of democracy even further by singling out *successful* democracies, the ones that endure over fairly lengthy periods of time. For the purposes of this exercise, we'll define a *long-term democracy* as one that has existed for at least forty years in succession.

Because we are looking for a relationship between democracy and national wealth, we must also specify what we mean by *wealth* and *poverty*. There are several different ways of measuring a country's annual income, but we need not go into those details here. We'll simply rely on the gross national income (GNI) statistics reported by the World Bank in *World Development Report 2007*. That publication divides the world's countries into four categories by their per capita GNI in 2005: *high-income* countries, $10,726 or more; *upper-middle-income* countries, $3,466 to $10,725; *lower-middle-income* countries, $876 to $3,465; and *low-income* countries, $875 or less.[13]

Finally, what do we mean when we hypothesize that national wealth *"promotes"* democracy? Here we need to specify that national wealth somehow "causes" democracy. More specifically, we mean that (a) wealth *causes* democracy to come into existence, replacing authoritarian modes of government, and (b) it *causes* democracies already in existence to succeed over protracted periods of time.

### Identifying Our Variables

The next step we must take is to identify our dependent and independent variables. Because the *existence of democracy* is the effect we wish to explain, it is our *dependent variable*.

Our *independent variable* is the *level of national wealth*. We want to see how varying levels of national wealth, as specified in the per capita GNI categories listed earlier, relate to democratic and nondemocratic systems of government. This independent variable is our presumed *explanatory* variable. We can *manipulate* it by observing how different gradations of national wealth are related to democracy.

### Specifying the Expectations of the Hypothesis

Hypotheses are usually stated as declarative propositions. Thus far we have stated our hypothesis as a declarative sentence: *"National wealth promotes democracy."* To test a hypothesis systematically, we must restate it in terms that will indicate what we should look for as we hunt for evidence that might confirm or contradict its validity: *if* the hypothesis is valid, *then* what would we *expect* to find as we sift through the available facts? In other words, what *expectations* does the hypothesis generate? To guide our research, therefore, *it is helpful to restate our hypothesis in "if . . . then" form:*

> *If* national wealth promotes democracy, *then* we would expect to find that (a) relatively wealthy states are democracies and (b) relatively poor states are not.

Logically, we would also expect to find that (c) democracies will be relatively wealthy, and (d) authoritarian regimes will be relatively poor. The more wealth a country has, the greater is the likelihood that it will be democratic; a country with poor economic fortunes has a poor prospect for democracy and a greater likelihood for some degree of authoritarianism. We would therefore expect to find that high-income and upper-middle-income countries will be either democracies or semi-democracies, and that lower-middle-income and low-income countries will have either semi-authoritarian or authoritarian regimes.

The process of translating our hypothesis into "if . . . then" form is an example of *deduction*. **Deduction** ***is a reasoning process that proceeds***

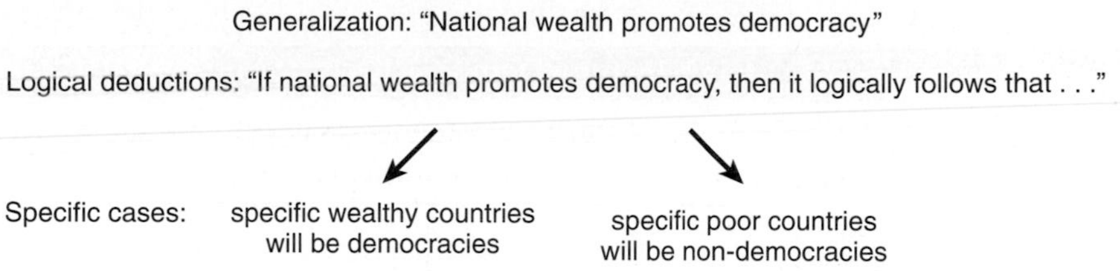

Generalization: "National wealth promotes democracy"

Logical deductions: "If national wealth promotes democracy, then it logically follows that . . ."

Specific cases: specific wealthy countries will be democracies | specific poor countries will be non-democracies

**FIGURE 3.13 Diagram of Deductive Reasoning**

***from the general to the specific.*** It begins with a generalization that covers a wide range or class of phenomena and then applies that generalization to specific cases (see figure 3.13). In our example, we start with our hypothesis, which proposes that national wealth promotes democracy *in general*, and we apply that generalization to specific countries. In deductive logic, the applications of the generalization to specific cases *must follow with logical necessity*. In other words, *if* A is true, *then* B *must* be true; if B is true, it follows that C is true; and so on. ("Deduction" comes from the Latin term for "lead from": each conclusion leads from the preceding one with logical necessity.) As we've already suggested, *if* national wealth promotes democracy, *then* it is only logical that specific countries that are relatively wealthy should be democracies, while specific countries that are relatively poor should be nondemocracies. When phrased in "if . . . then" terms, a hypothesis *predicts* a certain research result as a logical outcome.

The deductions we have just drawn from our hypothesis tell us what we should *expect* to find in reality. But whether we actually *will* find these results is another matter. If the facts that we gather in our hypothesis-testing research are consistent with these predicted results, then the hypothesis itself may be factually correct. But if the facts deviate from the expected results, the hypothesis may be wrong. We must now look at the facts to see if the predicted outcomes occur.

### Collecting and Examining the Evidence

Empirical analysis, as we've already pointed out, is based on facts. Unless there is a sufficient body of factual evidence bearing on our hypothesis, we cannot properly test it. Suppose, for example, that there is only one democracy in the world, and it happens to be quite rich. All the other governments of the world are nondemocracies, and all are economically undeveloped. On the basis of this evidence, we can conclude that the available evidence is *consistent* with our hypothesis linking democracy with a relatively high level of national wealth. But one case is scarcely enough to warrant high confidence in the generality of this conclusion. It does not convince us that national wealth is really necessary to *promote* democracies elsewhere. Other factors may be more important (such as the degree of social harmony, the nature of religious beliefs, and so on). The fact that our lone democracy is wealthy may be purely coincidental and have nothing whatsoever to do with causing or promoting democracy. Our confidence in the validity of a generalization tends to rise with the number of cases we have in its support.

As it happens, quite a few democracies in the world meet our definition of the term. We must now identify them and see if they meet our criteria of national wealth. The countries listed in table 3.1 meet these criteria: they are among the richest countries of the world, and all are bona fide democracies with combined political and civil rights ratings of 1 to 2.5. All but a few are also long-term democracies that have sustained democratic institutions for at least forty years. (There were no high-income semi-democracies.)

There is also a large number of upper-middle-income countries that can be classified as either democracies or semi-democracies, once again in conformity with our expectations (table 3.2 on page 85). Unlike the majority of high-income countries, however, only two of these countries—Costa Rica and Botswana—qualify as long-term democracies that have maintained democratic institutions and practices for at least forty years without interruption.

**TABLE 3.1**

**High-Income Democracies**

(2005 Political/Civil Rights Index of 1 to 2.5; Per Capita GNI of $10,726 and Above)

| Country | Per Capita GNI | Political/Civil Rights Index | Long-Term Democracy (X) |
|---|---|---|---|
| Luxembourg | $65,630 | 1 | X |
| Norway | 59,590 | 1 | X |
| Switzerland | 54,930 | 1 | X |
| Denmark | 47,390 | 1 | X |
| Iceland | 46,320 | 1 | X |
| United States | 43,740 | 1 | X |
| Sweden | 41,060 | 1 | X |
| Ireland | 40,150 | 1 | X |
| Japan | 38,980 | 1 | X |
| United Kingdom | 37,600 | 1 | X |
| Finland | 37,460 | 1 | X |
| Austria | 36,980 | 1 | X |
| Netherlands | 36,620 | 1 | X |
| Belgium | 35,700 | 1 | X |
| France | 34,810 | 1 | X |
| Germany | 34,580 | 1 | X |
| Canada | 32,600 | 1 | X |
| Australia | 32,220 | 1 | X |
| Italy | 30,010 | 1 | X |
| New Zealand | 25,960 | 1 | X |
| Spain | 25,360 | 1 | |
| Greece | 19,670 | 1.5 | |
| Israel | 18,620 | 1.5 | X |
| Slovenia | 17,350 | 1 | |
| Portugal | 16,170 | 1 | |
| South Korea | 15,830 | 1.5 | |
| Malta | 13,590 | 1 | X |
| Antigua and Barbuda | 10,920 | 2 | X |
| Andorra | Estimated high income | 1 | |
| Bahamas | Estimated high income | 1 | X |
| Barbados | Estimated high income | 1 | X |
| Cyprus | Estimated high income | 1 | |
| Liechtenstein | Estimated high income | 1 | |
| Monaco | Estimated high income | 1.5 | |
| San Marino | Estimated high income | 1 | X |
| Taiwan | Estimated high income | 1 | |

Although there seems to be abundant evidence confirming our expectation that wealthy and upper-middle-income countries tend to be democracies, or semi-democracies, there is also evidence in support of our assumption that, conversely, poor countries tend to be semi-authoritarian or authoritarian regimes. Take a look at table 3.3 on page 86.

Our expectation that lower-middle-income countries will tend to be either semi-authoritarian or authoritarian regimes also has evidence in its support, as table 3.4 on page 87 demonstrates.

These data support the expectations of our hypothesis that the poorer a country is, the less democratic it is likely to be.

We have now found quite a few contemporary democracies and semi-democracies classified as wealthy or relatively wealthy (the latter having upper-middle-level incomes) and a large number of nondemocracies classified as poor or relatively poor (the latter having lower-middle-level incomes). Countries with the highest score on the political/civil rights index are predominantly in the wealthy category, as are all the long-term

TABLE 3.2

**Upper-Middle-Income Democracies and Semi-Democracies**

(2005 Political/Civil Rights Index of 1 to 2.5 for Democracies, 3 to 3.5 for Semi-Democracies; 2005 Per Capita GNI of $3,466 to $10,725)

| Democracies | | | Semi-Democracies | | |
|---|---|---|---|---|---|
| **Country** | **Per Capita GNI** | **Political/Civil Rights Index** | **Country** | **Per Capita GNI** | **Political/Civil Rights Index** |
| Czech Republic | $10,710 | 1 | Seychelles | $8,290 | 3 |
| Trinidad and Tobago | 10,440 | 2.5 | Turkey | 4,710 | 3 |
| Hungary | 10,030 | 1 | | | |
| Estonia | 9,100 | 1 | | | |
| St. Kitts and Nevis | 8,210 | 1 | | | |
| Croatia | 8,060 | 2 | | | |
| Slovakia | 7,950 | 1 | | | |
| Palau | 7,630 | 1 | | | |
| Mexico | 7,310 | 2 | | | |
| Poland | 7,110 | 1 | | | |
| Lithuania | 7,050 | 1 | | | |
| Latvia | 6,180 | 1 | | | |
| Chile | 5,870 | 1 | | | |
| Mauritius | 5,260 | 1 | | | |
| Costa Rica[a] | 5,490 | 1 | | | |
| Botswana[a] | 5,180 | 2 | | | |
| South Africa | 4,960 | 1.5 | | | |
| St. Lucia | 4,900 | 1 | | | |
| Panama | 4,630 | 1.5 | | | |
| Argentina | 4,470 | 2 | | | |
| Uruguay | 4,360 | 1 | | | |
| Grenada | 3,920 | 1.5 | | | |
| Romania | 3,830 | 2 | | | |
| Dominica | 3,790 | 1 | | | |
| St. Vincent and Grenadines | 3,590 | 1.5 | | | |
| Belize | 3,500 | 1.5 | | | |
| Brazil | 3,460 | 2 | | | |
| Jamaica | 3,400 | 2.5 | | | |

[a]Long-term democracy

democracies. These data are *consistent* with what our hypothesis predicted we would find.

Our collection of evidence bearing on the hypothesis is by no means finished, however.

> In scientific hypothesis testing, it is never sufficient just to look for evidence that *confirms* the hypothesis or to terminate our research after finding such evidence. We must also look for evidence that might *contradict* the hypothesis.

The quest for information contrary to our prevailing assumptions is vital to all forms of logical argumentation. Most scientists would go even further and say that science itself consists above all in the formulation and testing of generalizations that are capable of being empirically *falsified*.[14]

We must therefore try to find evidence of (a) democracies that are *not* wealthy or relatively wealthy, and (b) nondemocracies that *are* wealthy or relatively wealthy.

As it happens, quite a few democracies (with a combined political and civil rights index of 1 to 2.5) are categorized as lower-middle-income or low-income economies, as indicated in table 3.5 on page 87. One of the poorest (and largest) countries in the world—India—has sustained democratic procedures for most of its existence as an independent country since 1947. (Democracy in India was briefly suspended in the 1970s. See chapter 15 for an outline of India's political development.) There are also more than a dozen lower-middle-income and low-income countries classified as semi-democracies (see table 3.6 on page 88).

The existence of so many democracies and semi-democracies in the lower-middle and low-income

TABLE 3.3

## Low-Income Semi-Authoritarian and Authoritarian Regimes

(2005 Political/Civil Rights Index of 4 to 5.5 for Semi-Authoritarian Regimes, 6 to 7 for Authoritarian Regimes; 2005 Per Capita GNI of $875 or Less)

**Semi-Authoritarian Regimes**

| Country | Per Capita GNI | Political/Civil Rights Index |
|---|---|---|
| Bangladesh | $970 | 4 |
| Republic of Congo | 950 | 5 |
| Bhutan | 870 | 5.5 |
| Pakistan | 690 | 5.5 |
| Comoros | 640 | 4 |
| Yemen | 600 | 5 |
| Mauritania | 560 | 5 |
| Nigeria | 560 | 4 |
| Zambia | 490 | 4 |
| Kyrgyzstan | 440 | 4.5 |
| Burkina Faso | 400 | 4 |
| Chad | 400 | 5.5 |
| Cambodia | 380 | 5.5 |
| Guinea | 370 | 5.5 |
| Central African Republic | 350 | 4.5 |
| Togo | 350 | 5.5 |
| Tajikistan | 330 | 5.5 |
| Gambia | 290 | 4.5 |
| Uganda | 280 | 4.5 |
| Nepal | 270 | 5.5 |
| Rwanda | 230 | 5.5 |
| Ethiopia | 160 | 5 |
| Malawi | 160 | 4 |
| Liberia | 130 | 4 |
| Burundi | 100 | 4 |
| Afghanistan | Estimated low income | 4.5 |

**Authoritarian Regimes**

| Country | Per Capita GNI | Political/Civil Rights Index |
|---|---|---|
| Ivory Coast | $840 | 6 |
| Sudan | 640 | 7 |
| Vietnam | 620 | 6 |
| Uzbekistan | 510 | 7 |
| Haiti | 450 | 6.5 |
| Laos | 440 | 6.5 |
| Zimbabwe | 340 | 6.5 |
| Eritrea | 220 | 6.5 |
| Democratic Republic of Congo | 120 | 6 |
| Burma (Myanmar) | Estimated low income | 7 |
| Equatorial Guinea | Estimated low income | 6.5 |
| Somalia | Estimated low income | 6.5 |

categories runs counter to our expectations. This mundane analytical detail contains a powerful real-world lesson: the countries listed in tables 3.5 and 3.6 provide incontrovertible evidence that *poverty does not constitute an insurmountable barrier to democracy.* Whereas a relatively low-income economy may indeed make it more difficult for a country to build and sustain democratic institutions and practices, by no means does it doom its chances irreparably.

An equally important political lesson emerges from table 3.7 on page 88. It lists high-income and upper-middle-income countries that were *not* full-fledged democracies or even semi-democracies in 2005. The information presented in this table *contradicts* our expectation that wealthy countries are likely to be democracies that guarantee a high level of political and civil rights. These data also contradict our expectation that upper-middle-income countries are likely to be democratic or at least semi-democratic. The obvious lesson to be gleaned from these figures is that *national wealth provides no guarantee of democracy.* It doesn't even provide a guarantee against highly repressive authoritarianism and

**TABLE 3.4**

**Lower-Middle-Income Semi-Authoritarian and Authoritarian Regimes**

(2005 Political/Civil Rights Index of 4 to 4.5 for Semi-Authoritarian Regimes, 6 to 7 for Authoritarian Regimes; 2005 Per Capita GNI of $876 to $3,465)

**Semi-Authoritarian Regimes**

| Country | Per Capita GNI | Political/Civil Rights Index |
|---|---|---|
| Kazakhstan | $2,930 | 5.5 |
| Tunisia | 2,890 | 5.5 |
| Algeria | 2,730 | 5.5 |
| Jordan | 2,500 | 4.5 |
| Guatemala | 2,400 | 4 |
| Maldives | 2,390 | 5.5 |
| Tonga | 2,190 | 4 |
| Morocco | 1,730 | 4.5 |
| Armenia | 1,470 | 4.5 |
| Egypt | 1,250 | 5.5 |
| Azerbaijan | 1,240 | 5.5 |
| Angola | 1,350 | 5.5 |
| Djibouti | 1,020 | 5 |
| Iraq | Estimated low income | 5.5 |

**Authoritarian Regimes**

| Country | Per Capita GNI | Political/Civil Rights Index |
|---|---|---|
| Iran | $2,770 | 6 |
| Belarus | 2,760 | 6.5 |
| Swaziland | 2,280 | 6 |
| China | 1,740 | 6.5 |
| Syria | 1,380 | 7 |
| Cameroon | 1,010 | 6 |
| Turkmenistan | Estimated low income | 7 |
| Cuba | Estimated low income | 7 |
| North Korea | Estimated low income | 7 |

**TABLE 3.5**

**Lower-Middle-Income and Low-Income Democracies**

(2005 Political/Civil Rights Index of 1 to 2.5)

**Lower-Middle-Income (2005 Per Capita GNI of $876 to $3,465)**

| Country | Per Capita GNI | Political/Civil Rights Index |
|---|---|---|
| Bulgaria | $3,340 | 1.5 |
| Namibia | 2,990 | 2 |
| Marshall Islands | 2,930 | 1 |
| Serbia and Montenegro | 2,680 | 2.5 |
| Peru | 2,610 | 2.5 |
| El Salvador | 2,450 | 2.5 |
| Micronesia | 2,300 | 1 |
| Suriname | 2,280 | 2 |
| Dominican Republic | 2,370 | 2 |
| Samoa | 2,090 | 2 |
| Cape Verde | 1,870 | 1 |
| Vanuatu | 1,600 | 2 |
| Ukraine | 1,520 | 2.5 |
| Kiribati | 1,390 | 1 |
| Indonesia | 1,280 | 2.5 |

**Low-Income (2005 Per Capita GNI of $875 or Less)**

| Country | Per Capita GNI | Political/Civil Rights Index |
|---|---|---|
| Lesotho | $960 | 2.5 |
| India | 720 | 2.5 |
| Senegal | 710 | 2.5 |
| Mongolia | 690 | 2 |
| Benin | 510 | 2 |
| Ghana | 450 | 1.5 |
| Sao Tome and Principe | 390 | 2 |
| Mali | 380 | 2 |

TABLE 3.6

**Lower-Middle-Income and Low-Income Semi-Democracies**

(2005 Political/Civil Rights Index of 3 and 3.5)

| Lower-Middle-Income (2005 Per Capita GNI of $876 to $3,465) | | | Low-Income (2005 Per Capita GNI of $875 or Less) | | |
|---|---|---|---|---|---|
| **Country** | **Per Capita GNI** | **Political/Civil Rights Index** | **Country** | **Per Capita GNI** | **Political/Civil Rights Index** |
| Fiji | $3,280 | 3.5 | Moldova | $880 | 3.5 |
| Macedonia | 2,830 | 3 | East Timor | 750 | 3 |
| Thailand | 2,750 | 3 | Papua-New Guinea | 660 | 3 |
| Ecuador | 2,630 | 3 | Solomon Islands | 590 | 3 |
| Albania | 2,580 | 3 | Kenya | 530 | 3 |
| Bosnia-Herzegovina | 2,440 | 3.5 | Tanzania | 340 | 3.5 |
| Colombia | 2,290 | 3 | Mozambique | 310 | 3.5 |
| Georgia | 1,350 | 3 | Madagascar | 290 | 3 |
| Philippines | 1,300 | 3 | Niger | 240 | 3 |
| Paraguay | 1,280 | 3 | Sierra Leone | 220 | 3.5 |
| Honduras | 1,190 | 3 | Guinea-Bissau | 180 | 3.5 |
| Sri Lanka | 1,160 | 3 | | | |
| Bolivia | 1,010 | 3 | | | |
| Guyana | 1,010 | 3 | | | |
| Nicaragua | 910 | 3 | | | |

TABLE 3.7

**Upper-Middle-Income and High-Income Semi-Authoritarian and Authoritarian Regimes**

(2005 Political/Civil Rights Index of 4 to 4.5 for Semi-Authoritarian Regimes, 6 to 7 for Authoritarian Regimes)

| Upper-Middle-Income (2005 Per Capita GNI of $3,466 to $10,725) | | | High-Income (2005 Per Capita GNI of $10,726 and Above) | | |
|---|---|---|---|---|---|
| **Country** | **Per Capita GNI** | **Political/Civil Rights Index** | **Country** | **Per Capita GNI** | **Political/Civil Rights Index** |
| Oman | $9,070 | 5.5 | Singapore | $27,490 | 4.5 |
| Lebanon | 6,180 | 4.5 | Kuwait | 24,040 | 4.5 |
| Libya | 5,530 | 7 | Saudi Arabia | 11,770 | 6.5 |
| Gabon | 5,010 | 5 | Bahrain | Estimated high income | 5 |
| Malaysia | 4,960 | 4 | Brunei Darussalem | Estimated high income | 5.5 |
| Venezuela | 4,810 | 4 | Qatar | Estimated high income | 6 |
| Russia | 4,460 | 5.5 | United Arab Emirates | Estimated high income | 6 |

flagrant abuses of fundamental political and civil rights.

We now have conflicting evidence bearing on our hypothesis. Most of the high-income countries of the world are democracies; indeed, this income category has by far the highest concentration of long-term democracies. Moreover, a large number of lower-middle-income and poor countries are semi-authoritarian or authoritarian. These facts are *consistent* with our hypothesis.

But some high-income countries and a few upper-middle-income countries are not democracies or even semi-democracies. In addition, a substantial list of lower-middle-income and even poor countries *are* democracies or semi-democracies. These data are *inconsistent* with our hypothesis: they contradict our expectations. Our next step is to determine what conclusions we can draw from this conflicting evidence.

### Drawing Conclusions from the Evidence

The first question we are tempted to ask when drawing conclusions from the available evidence is whether we have "proved" that our hypothesis is correct. The term *proof* implies absolute certitude, however, and most scientists doubt that we can ever prove anything with complete certainty. For one thing, the evidence we collect, no matter how exhaustive our search, may not be enough to permit a final verdict on the *universal* validity of our conclusions. (A proposition is *universally* valid if it applies to *all* relevant cases.) Even if all the evidence at our disposal confirms our hypothesis, there may still exist contrary evidence of which we are unaware. Instead of boasting that the evidence conclusively "proves" that a hypothesis is correct, therefore, we'll have to settle for the more modest conclusion that the evidence is *consistent* with the hypothesis. Any conclusion that a hypothesized relationship is "true" can only be tentative.

It is easier to *disprove* the universal validity of a hypothesis than to prove it. If we can find any evidence at all that is contrary to the results predicted by the hypothesis, we can demonstrate that the hypothesized relationship is not *universally* valid. The relationship may be valid sometimes, but not always. In some instances we can show that the hypothesis is *never* valid. In any event, evidence that is contrary to the results predicted by the hypothesis is designated simply as *inconsistent* with the hypothesis.

> When drawing conclusions from our evidence, we have to distinguish between evidence that is *consistent* with our hypothesis and evidence that is *inconsistent* with it.

In some cases our evidence will be entirely one or the other. But in many cases it will cut both ways: some of it will be consistent with the hypothesis, some inconsistent. In these cases the results of our research are *mixed* and lead us to conclude that the hypothesis appears to be partly true and partly false. (At times the evidence may be *mostly* true or *mostly* false.) If possible, we then need to specify the conditions under which the hypothesis is correct and those under which it is not.

In yet another set of cases, the evidence may be so evenly mixed, confusing, or simply inadequate as to be *inconclusive:* we cannot really be sure whether our hypothesis is true or false, or to what extent it is the one or the other. In these cases, our final conclusion must be "we don't know." Frustrating though it may be, "we don't know" is sometimes the right answer in science. *Science is characterized not by the certitude of its results but by the logic of its methods.* Its value is just as great when it shows us what we do *not* know as when it points out what we do know with considerable confidence.

Taking these general observations into account, let's now draw some conclusions from the evidence we've garnered on democracies and national wealth. To begin with, we have evidence that is both consistent and inconsistent with the hypothesized relationship between democracy and national wealth. There are relatively wealthy democracies as well as nondemocracies; there are relatively poor democracies as well as nondemocracies. Taken in its entirety, therefore, the evidence we have examined is *mixed:* some of it supports the hypothesis, some contradicts it. The evidence we have seen does not consistently and exclusively link relative wealth with democracy, nor does it conclusively rule out a relationship between these two variables.

Nevertheless, we can still discern some broad patterns. The overwhelming majority of the highest-scoring long-term democracies are clustered in the high-income category. Very authoritarian regimes (with a rating of 6 or 7) tend to be clustered in the low-income category. These data tell us that, *as a general tendency*, national wealth is a correlate of democracy (but not always).

Establishing a correlation between variables is a vital first step in the direction of demonstrating a causal relationship between them. If there is no evident relationship of any kind, obviously there can be no causal one. Keep in mind, however, that *a correlation does not by itself establish causality.* To what extent does our evidence demonstrate that national wealth "promotes" democracy in the sense that it actually *causes* democracy to come about or endure? At this point we need to consider a few basic principles of causal inference and the process of reasoning by induction.

**Induction** As we noted earlier, *induction proceeds from the specific to the general. It is the process of drawing conclusions or generalizations from specific information or evidence.* The inductive process is also characterized by the fact that, unlike deduction, *the evidence does not lead to logically determined conclusions.* Rather, the facts may be consistent with two or more possible conclusions, some perhaps closer to the actual truth than others. Our specific information on democracy and national wealth, for example, does not logically compel us to conclude that national wealth always promotes democracy. It merely suggests that wealth *may* promote democracy, but only in certain cases, if then. Drawing conclusions from empirical tests of hypotheses in political science is often an inductive process. In these cases, whatever conclusions we are able to draw from our evidence can only be tentative and uncertain; the laws of logic provide no ironclad guarantee of their validity.

**Indirect Hypothesis Testing** Notice that we did not test our hypothesis, "National wealth promotes democracy," directly. We did not directly observe a single case in which national wealth clearly caused a democracy to come about when none existed before or caused an existing democracy to remain in existence over a protracted period of time. All we did was to categorize the countries of the contemporary world by income group and type of government to see if any patterns emerged. We did not undertake in-depth investigations of these countries individually to see if wealth really does account for the presence or absence of democracy in each case, and if it does, *how* it does so. We never directly looked for evidence demonstrating the editorialist's contention that wealth promotes democracy by promoting education, mass communications, a middle class, or a government responsive to its citizens' demands.

Although the data we presented on nearly 200 countries displays a general pattern linking wealth and successful, long-term democracies, they do not permit us to conclude that wealth *always* promotes democracy. They don't even permit us to conclude that wealth is definitely responsible for creating or sustaining democracy in any of the wealthiest democracies listed in table 3.2. The data simply tell us that wealth is *associated* (or *correlated*) with the most successful democracies as a general rule. Although this correlation is consistent with the hypothesis that national wealth promotes democracy, the evidence does not *definitively* demonstrate that the hypothesis is true. That conclusion would be a *false inference.*

Most of the hypotheses we test in political science are tested indirectly, not directly. Especially when we look at aggregate data for a variety of countries, the best we can do is draw tentative inferences from whichever general patterns we can discern. Case studies of individual countries would give us deeper, more detailed information about whether, and how, national wealth actually promotes democracy in practice. In other words, we would have to undertake in-depth examinations of the relationship between national wealth and democracy in, say, the United States, Japan, or other democracies to see if (and how) wealth actually *promotes* democracy. But individual case studies are usually too narrowly focused to enable us to draw grand conclusions about the relationship between wealth and democracy *in general.* Such studies typically cannot show us how this relationship might apply to all or most of the nations of the world in different historical periods. Once again, we are forced to be very modest about the scope and certitude of our knowledge.

**Multicausality** Sometimes a phenomenon has only one cause. Heat alone, for example, causes ice to melt. But far more often, even in the natural world, events occur because of a multiplicity of causes. These multiple causes can work simultaneously or in different sequences; they can work in a variety of combinations and quantities. Political and social phenomena, in particular, rarely have only one cause; in human affairs, *multicausality* is far more likely than monocausality. Whether we are trying to explain democracy, dictatorship, voter turnout, economic growth, or why nations go to war, two or more independent variables typically account for the dependent variable we are trying to explain. Thus the level of national wealth *by itself* may not account for democracy or its absence in any of the countries listed in our tables.

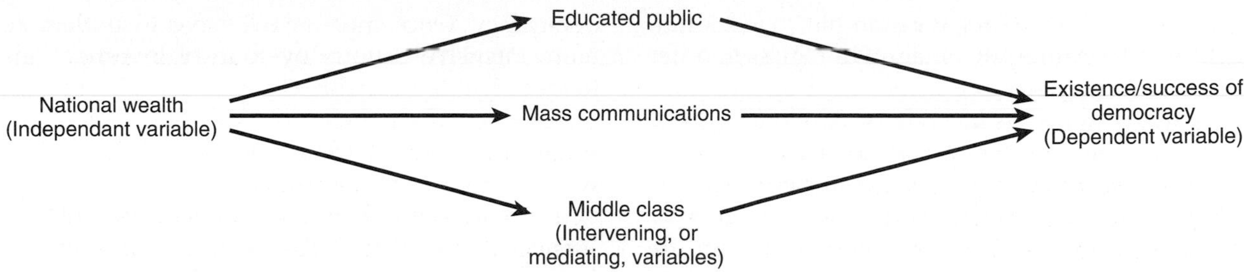


**FIGURE 3.14 Intervening Variables Between National Wealth and Democracy**

Conceivably, national wealth may promote democracy by working through other variables that may play a more direct role in stimulating the birth of a democracy or in undergirding a successful democracy over time. In a major work on this topic, Seymour Martin Lipset suggested that such variables as an educated public, mass communications, and a politically active middle class may ultimately depend on the size of a nation's wealth, but it is these intervening variables, not wealth per se, that may have a more immediate impact on the fate of democracy. These variables intervene between national wealth and democracy, enabling the one to exert a causative effect on the other, as illustrated in figure 3.14.[15]

The recipe for a successful democracy has so many ingredients that it is virtually impossible to specify which ones are more important than others. In addition to national wealth and the intervening variables it can buy, democracies may need such things as a general respect for the law, a tradition of cooperation and compromise among social groups, a political elite that respects the rights and liberties of the population, and a host of additional factors as well. The precise mixture of these ingredients may vary from democracy to democracy. Rarely, if ever, is democracy simply the product of one sole causal variable. Although the analysis we have just conducted shows a strong association between national wealth and successful democracy, it by no means rules out the possibility that *additional* independent variables (other than those connected with wealth) may also be of crucial significance in accounting for the existence or long-term success of democracies.

In trying to understand political reality, we must always be sensitive to the possibility (indeed the likelihood) of multicausality. Reducing complex realities to just one explanatory variable while paying insufficient attention to other contributing explanations is a logical fallacy called *reductivism*. Reductivism is just as fallacious in everyday political discourse as it is in political science. When we make such statements as "In U.S. politics, race determines everything" or "Big business runs the country," we may be just as reductivist in our reasoning as is someone who would suggest that national wealth alone explains the existence or success of democracy. Before we single out one particular variable as the sole explanation of the phenomenon at hand, therefore, we had better make certain that we have systematically ruled out all other potential explanatory variables. A scientific approach to politics requires us to be on the lookout at all times for multiple sources of explanation and causation in political life and to pay close attention to the ways they interact. To do otherwise is to engage in illogical argumentation and oversimplification.

**Necessary and Sufficient Conditions** One of the most basic distinctions in the logic of causation is the distinction between *necessary* and *sufficient* conditions.

A **necessary condition** *is one that* **must** *be present in order for some phenomenon or event to occur; without it, the event cannot occur.* A certain amount of sunlight is a necessary condition for most plant growth. By itself, however, sunlight may not be sufficient to ensure the steady growth of a plant to maturity. Anyone who raises tomatoes or houseplants knows that regular watering may also be necessary.

A **sufficient condition** *is one that* **by itself** *suffices for the phenomenon to occur.* When a sufficient condition is present, the phenomenon *must* occur. It is not necessary, for example, to focus sunlight on paper through a magnifying glass in order to ignite a fire. Striking a match or spontaneous combustion is just as incendiary. Any one of these methods, however, is *sufficient* to start a fire.

Some causative agents are both necessary *and* sufficient conditions simultaneously. The gravitational attraction of the Earth and the moon are both necessary and sufficient to cause the tides to change.

Other agents may exert a discernible causative effect on phenomena, but are neither necessary nor sufficient to cause the observed outcomes. Numerous studies show that smokers contract lung cancer at significantly higher rates than nonsmokers. Yet smoking is not a necessary condition for lung cancer, since nonsmokers also contract the disease. Nor is smoking a sufficient cause for lung cancer, since smoking does not always result in cancer; many lifelong smokers remain cancer-free all their lives. As a consequence, scientists prefer to call smoking a "risk factor" that is "strongly correlated" with cancer.

Is a high level of national wealth a necessary or sufficient condition for democracy? The data presented in the tables show that it is neither. Costa Rica, a lower-middle-income country, has been relatively successful in maintaining democratic electoral procedures since 1949. This country provides evidence that a relatively high level of wealth is not absolutely *necessary* to build and sustain electoral democracy. By implication, factors other than those that depend on national wealth may be very important in creating a democracy and even sustaining it over many decades. We'll have to look specifically at fairly poor democracies like India to find out exactly what these democracy-sustaining forces are.

At the same time, our data show that wealth is not *sufficient* to establish or maintain democracy. Fairly rich countries like Saudi Arabia, Singapore, Kuwait, and the United Arab Emirates are not democracies, nor are several countries in the upper-middle-income category, as indicated in table 3.7. The Soviet Union at its peak had the world's second largest GNP after the United States, yet it was never a democracy. Again, by implication, factors in addition to those that depend on national wealth may be necessary to build and sustain democracy. Once more, we'll have to undertake more intensive country-by-country investigations to identify these variables.

To what extent, then, does the information presented here permit us to conclude that national wealth "promotes" (or "causes") democracy? The best answer we can give is that *national wealth is strongly correlated with democracy and therefore increases the likelihood of democracy.* As Lipset concluded in his pioneering work, "The more well-to-do a nation, the greater the chances that it will sustain democracy." Conversely, the poorer a country is, the *less likely* it is that it will have or sustain democracy. The correlation is not perfect, however; as we have seen, there are exceptions to it.

Furthermore, the data do not tell us exactly when a new democracy will come into existence, replacing some form of authoritarianism. As Adam Przeworski and his co-researchers have demonstrated in a study that looks at the relationship between wealth and democracy over a forty-year period, democracy by no means arises automatically once a country passes a certain threshold of national wealth. Factors other than wealth—such as concrete actions taken by political forces that want democracy—can be even more important than economic factors in forging a democracy where none existed previously. Wealth is important primarily in sustaining democracy over the long term in countries where it already exists, the study concludes.[16]

The evidence at hand tells us that national wealth *tends* to promote and sustain democracy and increases the *chances* for democracy. But it does not *determine* that democracy will actually come about, or even necessarily succeed, over the long run.

## PARADOXES OF CAUSATIVE LOGIC

As the preceding hypothesis-testing exercise has shown, demonstrating causation is not easy. We now come to a great paradox of scientific logic: *although one of the most important aims of science is to discover the causes of things, causation is one of the most difficult of all phenomena to demonstrate conclusively.* This paradox is especially evident in political science, where we are dealing with so many interacting variables. Only rarely in political life do we

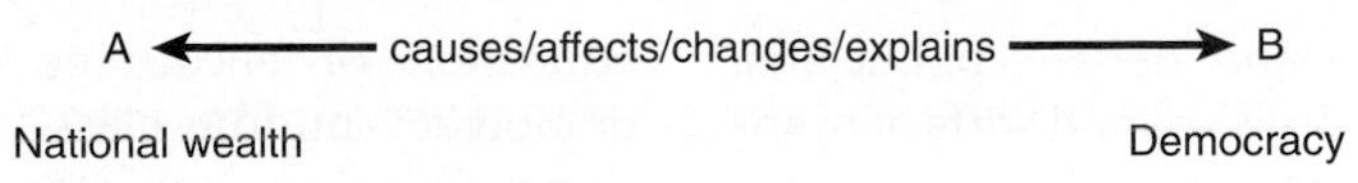


**FIGURE 3.15 Reciprocal Causation**

come upon an instance in which A demonstrably causes B, necessarily and sufficiently. It is far more likely that B is caused by more than one factor.

To make things even more complicated, we may confront the conundrum of the chicken and the egg. Evidence indicating a strong correlation between A and B does not necessarily mean that A is a cause of B; it could mean that B is a cause of A. Thus the data presented in this chapter may not be telling us that national wealth tends to promote democracy; rather, it may be indicating that democracy promotes national wealth. Alternatively, A and B could be related in a mutually reinforcing *interactive* process known as *reciprocal causation*. In that case, national wealth promotes democracy, and democracy in turn raises national wealth (see figure 3.15). To learn exactly which is causing which, and *how* these processes work, we have to look more deeply into specific cases and observe the relationship between national wealth and democracy in individual countries, and then compare the results. The systematic comparison of such individual cases is one of the main activities of comparative politics.

Political science must also contend with another problem: *it is rarely able to test its hypotheses under controlled laboratory conditions*. Whereas natural scientists can frequently test their hypotheses in scrupulously controlled experiments by manipulating their lab rats, chemicals, and atom-smashing devices as they wish, political scientists are seldom so fortunate. In some cases we can exercise a modicum of control over our variables. We can conduct focus group surveys or elite interviews with a manageable number of individuals, for example, and derive some generalizations about politics from their responses to our questionnaires. Even these kinds of studies have problems. Our respondents may misinterpret our questions, or their responses may be ambiguous and hard to interpret. Still more problematically, we must often test our hypotheses against whatever factual information we can dig up from the uneven ground of historical and contemporary reality. The information we may need in order to come to reliable conclusions may be insufficient or unreliable. The generalizations we make from this patchy evidence are all the more uncertain as a result.

And so we come to another paradox: *political science seeks to generalize about politics, but most of our generalizations are at best tentative or only partially valid.* It often happens in political science that our efforts to make clear-cut, universally valid generalizations run into empirical evidence of considerable complexity. Some of our generalizations apply only under certain conditions; there are exceptions to most every rule. It is vitally important to specify what these conditions are and why the exceptions occur. Paradoxically yet again, *defining the limits of our generalizations is a major purpose of scientific generalization itself.*

Thus the scientific approach to politics cautions us to be modest in our claims to political certitude. Political science teaches us that, when it comes to making explanatory generalizations about politics, *uncertainty is more likely than certainty.* This lesson is an important one. In every science, recognizing the limits of our knowledge is the start of wisdom.

## THE PRACTICAL IMPORTANCE OF HYPOTHESIS TESTING

In spite of the difficulties of causative logic, hypothesis testing is still a powerful analytical mechanism for understanding politics. It compels us to be explicit in our use of political terminology. It makes us check our generalizations against available evidence. It forces us to consider evidence *against* our prevailing assumptions and biases, not just evidence supporting them. It requires us to be systematic and logical in analyzing the evidence and drawing conclusions from it. It clarifies what we know, and what we don't know, about political life.

The logic of hypothesis testing is therefore essential to political science. But the benefits of hypothesis testing are by no means confined to the ivory-tower world of academic abstractions. They have an immense practical value as well. In the real world of political action and debate, politicians, pundits, and ordinary people hold all sorts of opinions on all sorts of political issues. Not uncommonly, people cling to their most cherished political beliefs with unshakable obstinacy, regarding their certainty as beyond question. In actuality, however, a great deal of what people know (or think they know) about politics really amounts to *hypotheses:* assumptions, impressions, or hunches that in many instances are only vaguely articulated or insufficiently examined. Many of us, for example, have heard such platitudes as "The longer politicians stay in office, the more they are out of touch with public opinion," or "Governments just waste money," or "Foreign aid does not work," or countless other generalizations about politics that animate everyday political discussion. Political scientists are not the only ones who like to generalize about politics; politicians and average citizens do, too. Such generalizations frequently provide the underlying rationale for important decisions political leaders make and for the way people behave within their respective political systems. But are those generalizations true? Only a systematic analysis of the evidence can tell us.

Consider as an example the editorialist's recommendation that wealthy democracies should provide economic assistance to newly democratizing countries. How do our findings about the relationship between national wealth and democracy help us formulate our own opinion on this practical policy issue? As we saw, national wealth is strongly—but not perfectly—correlated with democracy. But we also saw that national wealth per se does not necessarily promote democracy; only when it is funneled into such intervening variables as education, an open communications system, or a middle class is wealth more likely to strengthen the conditions for democratic rule. And we also concluded that factors *other than* wealth may also be necessary to build and maintain democratic modes of government.

Thus our empirical analysis compels the conclusion that economic assistance aimed at raising the national wealth of democratizing countries may indeed be very helpful in supporting democracy, but it provides no guarantee that democracy will actually succeed. A great deal depends on how the money is spent. Will it be used to expand education or encourage the growth of a pro-democracy middle class? Or will it be spent on things that do not necessarily increase the chances for democracy, such as higher salaries for bureaucrats or graft for corrupt politicians? In any event, if key elites or broad segments of the population simply do not want democracy or do not try to make it work, wealth alone may not save the democratic cause.

Unfortunately, not everybody subjects their generalizations to a systematic reality check as we've just done. As a consequence, the generalizations people commonly make about politics often tend to oversimplify matters. But testing our political assumptions against reality is precisely what a scientific approach to politics demands. Applying scientific logic to the study of politics helps us avoid oversimplification and enables us to appreciate the complexities of the real world.

Accordingly, one of the most important "scientific" questions we can ask about any political generalization is, *"What is the evidence to support it?"* Another is, *"What is the evidence against it?"* We must then be very cautious and scrupulously logical in interpreting the results of these inquiries.

## COUNTERINTUITIVE RESULTS

Systematic hypothesis testing is especially interesting when its results are *counterintuitive.* **Counterintuitive results** ***are those that run counter to what we expect.*** Not infrequently, they contradict widely held preconceptions or what "everybody knows" on the basis of "common sense." For centuries, "everybody knew" that the Earth is flat. Evidence to the contrary was counterintuitive. Though perhaps less dramatic, hypothesis testing in political science can also yield counterintuitive outcomes. Quite a few generalizations people make about politics on the basis of "common sense" or personal experience turn out, on examination, to be either completely false or true only in certain instances. Here are a few examples:

- Democracy, it is widely assumed, is government "by the people," not by elites. Comparative studies of democracies show, however, that elites may be even more important than the people are in creating and sustaining democratic modes of government. In some cases, elites are more respectful of democratic values—such as tolerance and freedom of speech—than the general public is.

- Another widely held assumption about democracy is that people will take full advantage of the opportunities it offers to stand up for their rights and actively promote their interests through the political process. In fact, however, most people in democracies do *not* engage in such "collective action," even when their own economic interests or other concerns are at stake. Ironically, they are far more likely to believe that their personal interests are best served by doing nothing.
- It is often assumed that revolutions and mass uprisings against unpopular governments are most likely to take place when the population hits bottom, that is, when poverty and political subjugation reach intolerable extremes. In reality, however, revolutions and mass unrest are more likely to take place after a noticeable improvement has taken place in living conditions. It is not the extremely poor who most often rebel, but people who are experiencing "rising expectations" of still more improvements. Their anger may reach the boiling point when these expectations are then frustrated.

Scientific hypothesis testing is also important for another practical reason: *it can help you examine your own political assumptions in a rational and coherent manner.* One of the main objectives of your political science education should be to learn how to spell out your own political ideas in terms of propositions that can be put to a systematic test against the facts. Critical-thinking skills of this kind are invaluable in dealing not only with empirical questions about politics but with normative issues as well. As we noted earlier in this chapter, our political values and ideals need to be addressed with reference to the realities of political life. The rules of hypothesis testing provide a method for determining what those realities are and for clarifying how well we know them.

## SOME CONCLUDING THOUGHTS

Now that you have examined some key scientific terminology in political science and walked through a hypothesis-testing exercise, you should have a better idea of what political science is. Of course, you won't get a deeper feel for it until you've studied it more thoroughly, but you should at least be in a position to appreciate some generalizations about what political science tries to do.

Let's emphasize what political science is *not.* First, it is not "just opinion." Although the study of politics usually provides ample opportunities to formulate and express one's personal political views, political science *as an empirical science* insists on the observance of strict rules of collecting, analyzing, and interpreting the facts. It requires us to support our opinions with relevant evidence and to modify our opinions (or perhaps discard them entirely) in the light of contrary information. Thus political science does not regard all political opinions as equally valid. Those opinions that can meet the acid test of empirical reality checks based on the rigors of scientific logic are generally more valid than are those based on insufficient evidence or faulty logic.

Of course, sometimes we just do not have the evidence we need to draw a reasoned, "scientific" conclusion. At times the information we need does not exist; at times it may not be readily available. In these cases, it is incumbent on us to *acknowledge* that the evidence we need to substantiate our case is lacking.

Even though the canons of empirical science are demanding, there is still plenty of room for rational debate and disagreement over controversial political issues. Subjective value judgments and preferences invariably play—indeed *must* play—a major role in political thinking. Just as important, the rules of scientific logic open up a vast realm of empirical uncertainty with respect to many political questions. By itself, empirical political science cannot compel you to be a liberal or a conservative, a moderate or a radical. It simply tells you that, whatever your personal political predilections, you must take the rules of scientific logic into account when shaping and defending your political views.

Second, political science is not "just current events," nor is it "just facts" or "just stories." As we indicated in chapter 1, political science is an effort to understand current events as well as the past (and, to some extent, the future) by generalizing about humanity's political experience. Political science *uses* facts to formulate and test these generalizations. Political scientists are just as fascinated or amused as anyone else by stories and anecdotes about politics, but as social scientists we are mainly concerned with connecting particular incidents to broader trends and processes. In telling stories about politics, we are especially interested in what the stories tell us about politics. Moreover, random facts or *anecdotal evidence* may not be enough to sustain a political generalization. We may need to analyze a vast array of available evidence before we can come to any reliable conclusions. And if the evidence available is incomplete or merely anecdotal, we must say so.

More than anything else, political science is a *mode of thinking* about politics. It is an academic "discipline" in that it disciplines our minds to think in certain ways, in accordance with a specified logic and systematic methods of analysis.

### Developing Critical-Thinking Skills

Depending on the career path you take, you may need more advanced analytical skills than we can provide in this book. This volume is purely introductory. In the pages that follow, we do not engage in formal statistical hypothesis testing, nor do we teach you how to design a research project of your own. Rather, we present numerous examples of hypotheses that have been advanced by political scientists who have written on the topics and countries covered in this volume. Along the way we introduce you to key concepts in political science, and to prominent theories and models as they apply to comparative politics. We also expose you to some of the most influential scholarship in the field. Throughout this enterprise, we are guided by one overriding aim: to help you *think for yourself* about politics in terms of the scientific terminology and logic presented in this chapter.

Accordingly, this book provides numerous synopses of scholarly arguments that use the five-step hypothesis-testing logic presented here:

1. Definition of key terms
2. Identification of the variables
3. Expectations of the hypothesis in "if . . . then" form
4. Collection and examination of the evidence
5. Conclusions (*consistent* with the hypothesis, *inconsistent*, *mixed*, or *inconclusive*)

*Every chapter that follows contains a hypothesis-testing exercise that employs this format.* We hope that by learning how these logical steps are used in comparative politics, you will learn not only how to think like a political scientist but also how to apply these steps yourself to analytical tasks in other areas of inquiry.

## KEY TERMS
**(In bold and underlined in the text)**

Value judgments
Empirical analysis
Variable
Dependent variable
Independent variable
Correlation (association)
Intervening variables
Spurious correlation
Law
Theory
Hypothesis
Model
Ideal type
Paradigm
Fallacy of composition
Tautology
Induction
Deduction
Necessary condition
Sufficient condition
Counterintuitive results

## NOTES

1. For an introduction to some of the timeless themes of political philosophy, see Glenn Tinder, *Political Thinking: The Perennial Questions*, 6th ed. (New York: Longman, 2003).
2. For an overview of the field, see Michael E. Kraft and Scott R. Furlong, *Public Policy: Politics, Analysis, and Alternatives*, 2nd ed. (Washington, D.C.: CQ Press, 2006).
3. In *The Grammar of Science*, written in 1892, the scientist and philosopher Karl Pearson wrote, "The unity of all science consists alone in its method, not its material."
4. For postmortem reappraisals of election predictions in 2000, see *PS: Political Science and Politics* 34, no. 1 (March 2001).

5. Maurice Duverger, *Political Parties*, 2nd English ed., rev., trans. Barbara and Robert North (London: Methuen, 1959), 217. See also Duverger's *Party Politics and Pressure Groups*, trans. David Wagoner (New York: Crowell, 1972), and *Introduction à la politique* (Paris: Gallimard, 1964).
6. Anthony Downs, *An Economic Theory of Democracy* (New York: Harper & Row, 1957).
7. Karl W. Deutsch, *The Nerves of Government* (New York: Free Press, 1966).
8. Thomas Kuhn, *The Structure of Scientific Revolutions*, 2nd ed. (Chicago: University of Chicago Press, 1970).
9. For example, there exist rigorous tests for determining the *statistical significance* of particular statistical results. In addition, the relative *strength* of a correlation between dependent and independent variables can be calculated and specified in numerical terms. The resulting *correlation coefficient* is a very useful tool in political analysis. Another statistical technique that is widely used in political science is *regression analysis*, which permits analysts to measure the probable effect of a change (or *variance*) in one or more independent variables on a dependent variable. It is very useful in analyzing voting patterns and other quantifiable relationships.
10. For a concise outline of the scientific approach, see Stephen Van Evera, *Guide to Methods for Students of Political Science* (Ithaca, N.Y.: Cornell University Press, 1997). A more advanced text is Gary King, Robert O. Keohane, and Sidney Verba, *Designing Social Inquiry* (Princeton: Princeton University Press, 1994).
11. For a study of the dangers of false historical analogies, see Richard E. Neustadt and Ernest R. May, *Thinking in Time: The Uses of History for Decision-Makers* (New York: Free Press, 1986).
12. *Freedom in the World 2006* (New York: Freedom House, 2006).
13. World Bank, *World Development Report 2007* (New York: Oxford University Press, 2006), 249–52. The national income statistics reported in this publication, published in September 2006, are preliminary figures for 2005. The World Bank's method for calculating gross national income (formerly gross national product) is in ibid., 265 and 270–71.
14. The philosopher Karl Popper popularized the notion that the essence of the scientific method is empirical falsifiability. See *The Logic of Scientific Discovery* (New York: Harper & Row, 1968).
15. Seymour Martin Lipset, "Economic Development and Democracy," in *Political Man* (New York: Doubleday, 1960), chap. 2.
16. Adam Przeworski, Michael E. Alvarez, Jose Antonio Cheibub, and Fernando Limongi, *Democracy and Development: Political Institution and Well-Being in the World, 1950–1990* (Cambridge: Cambridge University Press, 2000).

CHAPTER 4

# POWER

Readers of the *New York Times* on a Sunday in May 2006 did not have to look very far for examples of the varieties of power in political affairs. The lead story reported on the formation of a national-unity government in Iraq, a power-sharing arrangement that included the country's three main groups—Arab Sunnis, Arab Shiites, and Kurds. (Most Kurds are Sunnis, some are Shiites.) The new prime minister was expected to have "overall authority over the government." American officials hoped he would show more "decisiveness" than his predecessor, whose leadership had been reined in by rival political parties. The U.S. ambassador in Iraq had reportedly "played a muscular role" in influencing the composition of the new cabinet, but his influence was not strong enough to get the coalition partners to agree on key ministerial appointments and touchy constitutional issues. This disappointment was an "embarrassing blow" to the United States, which was forced to "punt" on these matters, postponing their settlement to a later date. Nevertheless, the new coalition government represented a major shift in power from the days of Saddam Hussein's police state. Saddam, a Sunni, had built up Iraq's "elitist Sunni ruling class," enabling it to enjoy a "dominant perch in Iraqi society" over Shiites and Kurds, who were brutally persecuted under his rule.

Another article reported on the failure of the American occupation regime to form an effective Iraqi police force in the aftermath of the 2003 invasion. It quoted former U.S. ambassador L. Paul Bremer III as asserting that "the most fundamental role of government is [maintaining] law and order," a task he admitted the U.S. authorities had failed to accomplish in the immediate post-invasion period. The result was widespread chaos and the growth of a deadly insurgent movement. Three years after the invasion, the Iraqi state was still "virtually powerless to stop insurgent attacks," one Iraqi complained, deploring the killing of Shiites by illegal Sunni militias. "In order to dominate" the Shiites, he said, the Sunnis "have to eliminate them." "There is no government," another Iraqi lamented. "I can't feel safe." Meanwhile, the *Times* reported that "corruption was rampant" in the new Iraqi police force.

Still another story referred to a pro-democracy dissident in Iran who was sentenced to death "after questioning the authority of high-ranking clerics" who governed the country. Iranian political prisoners, the report added, "were forced to make false confessions." Another piece reported that the president of the Palestinian Authority "has the power to dismiss the prime minister, but not necessarily to call new elections." An article on political turmoil in Nepal cited a rebel leader who questioned whether the Royal Nepalese Army was "legal and legitimate." The reporter noted that the recently installed interim government in Nepal had "stripped the king of his authority over the military." Another report reminded readers that a pro-democracy party in Burma (Myanmar) had won a landslide election victory in 1990, "only to be denied power by the army." Another alluded to Italy's political corruption investigations of the early 1990s and quoted an Italian journalist's description of Italy today as "a country where the law may be written but those who don't have respect can succeed in getting away with it." And another recalled that Peru's government had collapsed in 2000 because it was "engulfed by corruption scandals."[1]

## DEFINING POWER

*Power, authority, dominance, influence, elite, ruling class, leadership, law and order, force, legitimacy, corruption, powerlessness:* these and similar terms are the stuff of politics just about everywhere. Not surprisingly, power and its attributes are major topics of comparative politics. In chapter 2 we put power at the top of our list of five main sources of political conflict. The concept of power goes straight to the question of who is strong and who is weak in political life. Power is as central in the world of politics as money is in economics.[2] Let's begin by defining power and political power, and then move on to discuss some related concepts.

In its most general sense, power is *the capacity to effect outcomes.* To *effect* means to *cause* or *bring about.* Outcomes are *actions* or *results.* Power is thus *the capacity to cause or bring about actions or results.*

Power is above all a *capability* or a *potential.* The words *power* and *potent* derive from the Latin *potere,* "to be able." Power is not any specific thing (such as a law, a fist, or an atomic bomb), nor is it any specific action (a veto, a punch, an explosion). Rather, it is an *ability* that someone possesses or that inheres in something. Depending on its specific form, this ability can be held by inanimate objects (the sun, the atom), animals (as in horsepower), individuals (a strong leader), groups (a dominant class), or institutions (the U.S. presidency). Moreover, power does not have to be exercised. It is a potential that can exist without being used.

In chapter 2 we defined *politics* as *the process by which people pursue collective goals and deal with their conflicts authoritatively by means of government.* In keeping with this definition, *political power is the capacity to effect outcomes by controlling or influencing the state.* "State" means government at any level. To put it more precisely,

> **political power** ***means the ability to determine or influence the decisions or behavior of government officials.***

In some cases the terms *power* and *authority* are used interchangeably to refer to the *legal right* of the state and its officials to take certain actions—to make and enforce legally binding laws and decisions, for example. (As we've seen, the president of the Palestinian Authority has the legal authority to dismiss the prime minister.) In other cases, power can refer more broadly to the ability of *nongovernmental individuals or groups* (like the "elitist Sunni ruling class" under Saddam) to have an impact on what state officials do.

In comparative politics we focus on the various ways power can be used *within* countries. Students of international politics tend to focus on the ways power is used in relations *between* countries and other international actors.[3]

## WHO HAS POWER? AND HOW MUCH?

All societies are divided between *elites* and *masses.*

The term *elites* can refer to socially prominent people in general, but it typically implies the possession of a fairly high degree of political power. We define **political elites** as ***people who have prominent positions either in government or in nongovernmental organizations and professions that have a real effect on government actions.*** Government officials who have significant decision-making authority—presidents, cabinet ministers, legislators, and the like—obviously top the list of political elites. This top elite, or *primary elite,* may comprise no more than 1 percent of a country's population. The concept of political elites also includes people who are not in government but who may nevertheless have a significant impact on government decisions. Heads of major corporations and business associations, leaders of trade unions and other important interest groups, religious authorities, politically influential journalists and academics—these and similarly prominent people constitute a society's *secondary elite*. Together the primary and secondary elites typically comprise about 2 to 5 percent of the population. The term *political society* is sometimes used to refer to the most politically active members of the population—government officials, party activists, and the like. These highly politicized individuals include elements of both the primary and secondary elites and comprise a very small percentage of a country's population.

The term *masses* refers broadly to the rest of the population. It by no means implies, however, that the masses always constitute a homogeneous group. As we saw in chapter 2, societies can be quite diverse, consisting of a multiplicity of identity groups based on such markers as ethnicity, religion, and class. In most countries—even in democracies—one or more of these groups may be more politically powerful than others.

The concept of power assumes that some people have more of it than others have. More precisely, some people get more than others through government action. We live in a world of scarce resources, and governments are uniquely positioned to make authoritative decisions about how society's resources—money, land, food, medical facilities, and so on—get distributed among the population and the various groupings that compose it. Positions of governmental authority—cabinet posts, seats in the legislature, and the like—are also scarce resources even in democracies. The political process often determines who has the power to distribute and acquire these various resources. Appropriately, one of the classics of political science is Harold Lasswell's book, *Politics: Who Gets What, When, and How*—a title that neatly captures the centrality of power in political life.[4]

In practice, *power is relational:* it involves a relationship between a power holder (A) and someone else (B) over whom A has some kind of power. Power relationships can take a number of different forms. For example, A has power over B to the extent that:

- A beats B (in a war, for example).
- A can influence B's behavior.
- A can cause B to do something that B would not otherwise do.
- A can compel B to do something, even if B would do it anyway.
- A can affect B in a manner contrary to B's interests.
- A can prevent B from doing something contrary to A's wishes, in effect exercising a kind of veto power over B's actions.
- B believes that A is more powerful.

These and other conceptualizations of power relationships must take account of varying degrees of power. Power comes in different sizes. One way of refining the concept is to distinguish between *dominance* and *influence*. Both are forms of power in that they can cause political outcomes; their difference is mainly one of degree. We can think of them as representing two *dimensions* of power.

### Power as Dominance

The ability to *determine* or *control* political outcomes—especially when it exists on a regular or continuing basis rather than just occasionally—is the ability to exercise *dominance* in political life. **Dominance** ***is the maximum degree of political power.*** Those who possess power-as-dominance can usually get whatever they want from the government. This type of political power can be exercised either by government officials who enjoy an exceptionally large measure of legal authority (such as powerful dictators) or by nongovernmental groups or individuals who possess a large capacity to determine how the government operates or what its main policy orientations must be. South Africa's white minority was such a dominant social group prior to the historic elections of 1994. Until then, the whites completely dominated the nonwhite majority, denying them voting rights and enforcing strict racial segregation laws.

### Power as Influence

The term *influence,* like many terms in political science, is itself a source of considerable controversy. Some scholars have used *power* and *influence* interchangeably while others have stressed their differences. As the eminent political scientist Robert Dahl rightly acknowledged, "One writer's 'influence' is another's 'power.'"[5] As defined here, political influence is a *form* of power, not something different from it. More specifically, it is a degree or dimension of power, one that is less all-encompassing than domination.

We define *influence as the capacity to effect outcomes indirectly or partially*. Accordingly, **political influence** ***means the capacity to* affect *government decisions, actions, or behavior without fully controlling them.*** Depending on the particular circumstances, the ability to influence the outcomes of state activity is usually less direct, or less decisive or definitive, than the capacity to determine them. To have power-as-influence over a particular governmental decision means to have some say in the matter without necessarily being able to dictate the ultimate outcome. It frequently means that one has some access to state decision makers but not complete control over their decisions.

As in the case of the capacity to determine political outcomes, the capacity to influence them can be held by either government officials or nongovernmental individuals or groups. The president of the United States provides a good example of a government official who has more influence than dominance when it comes to exercising official power. Although the U.S. Constitution gives the president the legal authority to veto acts of Congress and make certain other decisions on his own, in many other instances the president must share power with Congress or other institutions. In most cases the president does not "determine" the final outcome of the legislation; he can only *influence* legislative outcomes by bargaining with congressional leaders. To different degrees, governing executives in most democracies must bargain with legislators and other officials (not to mention the voters) in order to get their way. For even the most powerful executives in democratic countries, power is exercised largely as influence rather than as dominance.

By contrast, authoritarian rulers tend to exert dominance over the population, but their degree of power within the state tends to differ. Some individual dictators are able to impose virtually complete dominance over other government officials (Saddam Hussein, for example), while others must share power with other officials and bargain with them over state decisions.

Similarly, groups or individuals outside government may also have the capacity to influence the outcomes of governmental activities without being able to determine or dictate whatever they want or to exercise a pervasive dominance over the state's activities. Such people possess political influence to the extent that they are able to persuade or pressure authoritative state officials or agencies to do favors for them or meet their demands, if only partially or in specific cases. Invariably, some people are more politically influential than others—even in democracies, where the egalitarian principle "one person, one vote" by no means ensures equality of political influence.

The distinction between *dominance* and *influence* is not always clear-cut. Problems often arise when we try to differentiate "dominant" government officials and non-government groups from "influential" or "highly influential" ones. The long-running debate over whether the United States is dominated by a "power elite" reflects these ambiguities.

## IS THE UNITED STATES DOMINATED BY A "POWER ELITE"?

In the 1950s, sociologist C. Wright Mills set off a lively debate when he argued that the U.S. political system was dominated by a *power elite.* These "higher circles" of powerful politicians, corporate executives, and military leaders, in his view, formed a unified and organized network of "interlocking directorates" that dominated the decision-making levers of American political and economic life. They consisted almost exclusively of white males, mostly Protestant. Beneath them, the middle layers of American society were considerably less influential, while the overwhelming majority of the population constituted a fragmented "mass society" with practically no power of any kind. Roughly similar views have been expressed by various students of power relationships in the United States and other countries.

These provocative arguments ignited counterattacks by scholars who have maintained that, while various elite groups may indeed enjoy considerable political power in the United States, they do not form as cohesive and well-organized a clique as the power-elite theorists contend. Sometimes these politically powerful people disagree among themselves on matters of government policy. Moreover, they do not leave the rest of the population utterly powerless;

public opinion and election results *do* have an impact on what the government does. Most critics of the power-elite hypothesis maintain, in effect, that while some individuals and groups may indeed be exceptionally *influential* in American political life, they do not necessarily *dominate* it to the exclusion of everyone else. Furthermore, their influence over government actions tends to vary with the issue: corporate executives of firms that manufacture military equipment may influence the government's military expenditures, but they may not have much influence over environmental or health care policy.

Many of these critics of the power-elite concept are known as *pluralists*. The concept of *pluralism* contends that political power in the United States and other democracies is shared by a plurality of social classes, political parties, interest groups, voters, and other participants in the political process and is not dominated by a single, all-powerful elite. In other words, pluralism means *power sharing*.[6]

## POWER AND ELITES

Let's go back to the top of the political heap, to the powerful governmental decision makers who constitute a country's primary elite.

**Who Are They?** Examining the biographies of prominent leaders can tell us a lot about why they went into politics in the first place and how they succeeded in climbing to "the top of the greasy pole" of political power. It can also tell us about the relationship between individual leaders and the political system, the larger society, and the historical context in which they rose to power. In some cases we can catch revealing glimpses into psychological idiosyncracies.[7]

Most importantly, a focus on individual leaders helps us understand *leadership* in general. Many leaders can be quite successful at managing the routine transactions of day-to-day politics, bargaining with other decision makers and perhaps currying favor with key segments of the population, all for the overriding purpose of staying in office. But truly great leadership rises above the self-serving deal cutting and vote counting of "transactional" politics. What James MacGregor Burns has called "transforming" leadership requires a leader to summon the population to achieve more elevated goals—such as an expansion of freedom or justice—or to surmount severe challenges such as an economic crisis or war. Transforming leaders are not afraid to take on unpopular causes, even at the risk of losing power. The most successful leaders are the ones who possess a special aura of *personal authority*. Personal authority is leadership ability: the capacity to effect outcomes by getting others to acknowledge and follow one's leadership. When we speak of "strong leaders" we refer not just to their legal powers but also to their ability to inspire trust and confidence and to command the respect of those they lead. Especially magnetic leaders are said to possess *charisma* (Greek for "divine gift").[8]

The most morally uplifting form of leadership obliges leaders to put the interests of the people they lead ahead of their own personal interests, fully respecting the population's basic human rights. Leadership of this quality usually requires some form of democracy. But leaders can also establish their personal authority by compelling others to submit to their rule. Such leaders are more interested in cultivating the respect and fear of those they rule than in eliciting their love or trust. A famous exponent of this leadership style was the Italian statesman and philosopher Niccolò Machiavelli (1469–1527). In *The Prince* (1513), Machiavelli asserted that a leader must be willing to use violence against the population and ruthlessly employ deceit to ensure the preservation and prosperity of the state. A wise leader "should not deviate from what is good, if that is possible, but he should know how to do evil, if that is necessary," Machiavelli counseled.[9]

**What Are the Sources of Their Power?** No matter how persuasive or intimidating they may be, even the most successful political leaders do not achieve power alone. Some may enjoy the backing of prominent social groups—such as an ethnic group, religious organizations and their adherents, or major corporations and economically prominent families. Some may ride to power on the basis of broad popular support, whether through institutionalized election procedures or through some other manifestation of the popular will, such as a revolutionary upheaval. Others may gain power through the barrel of a gun, seizing it in a military coup or through victory in a civil war. Monarchs have traditionally inherited power as their birthright. Whatever the origin of their power, the top political elites invariably cultivate the support of certain segments of the population when seeking power, and they invariably need to sustain—and perhaps widen—their support base in the course of governing. Saddam Hussein based his rule on his family ties, Iraq's Sunni minority, the Baath Party, and the fearsome military and police forces he built up.

An important source of any governing elite's power is its *legitimacy*. **Legitimacy *means the right to rule.*** By what right do some human beings rule over others? This question is as old as organized civilization and as current as today's headlines. The term *legitimacy*—or *legitimate authority*—is usually attached to an entire system of government rather than to just an individual ruler or ruling coalition. When people become disenchanted with a particular leader, it is sometimes said that the person in question has lost his or her legitimacy. But in a more formal sense, legitimacy has a wider application. It refers to whether a country's political regime—such as a democracy of some kind, a military dictatorship, or a monarchy—is regarded as a proper or acceptable form of government.

Who determines whether or not a government is legitimate, and how is this determination made? In other words, what is the *source* of a government's legitimacy?

Many theorists regard democracy as the only truly legitimate form of government, on the grounds that democracy is explicitly based on the consent of the governed. *In democracies, the people are the source of the state's legitimacy.* Because the people, either directly or through their elected representatives, can adopt the constitution and laws they want, and because they have the opportunity to change these laws as well as their leaders through periodic elections and related procedures, democracies provide observable evidence of popular approval or disapproval of the political system itself. Democracies place their legitimacy on the line on a continuing basis.

Not all political theorists or practitioners have regarded the people as the chief source of legitimacy, however. Throughout most of the Middle Ages in Europe, monarchs ruled on the basis of the "divine right of kings," the notion that God—not human beings—conferred legitimacy on the reigning kings, queens, and emperors. A roughly similar view held sway in China, where for nearly two thousand years a succession of dynasties claimed that their right to govern derived from "the mandate of heaven." Japan's emperors also traced their legitimacy to divine sources, claiming that they all descended from the Sun Goddess, whose grandson allegedly came down to Earth in antiquity. Following Japan's capitulation at the end of World War II, Emperor Hirohito issued a declaration admitting that he himself was not a god, but he pointedly refrained from denying his ancestry from the Sun Goddess.[10] For his part, Karl Marx believed that the laws of history determined legitimacy. Although he did not tend to use the term *legitimacy* explicitly, in effect he maintained that the laws of historical development (which he claimed to have discovered) determined the illegitimacy of capitalism and the legitimacy of communism as economic and political systems.

Is it possible for nondemocratic regimes to be considered legitimate? One answer to this question was provided by a prolific contributor to modern political science, the German sociologist Max Weber (1864–1920).

## WEBER'S THREE TYPES OF LEGITIMATE AUTHORITY

Max Weber argued that, even when democratic procedures for legally removing governments from office do not exist, some political regimes are still regarded as legitimate by their populations. Weber defined *authority* as occurring when there is a probability that people will obey a specific command. He defined *legitimate authority* as occurring when people obey the authority because they regarded it as obligatory or exemplary. In his view there have been essentially three ways in which political leaders throughout history have convinced their populations to accept their authority as legitimate.

The first way is *traditional authority*. This type of legitimacy rests on "an established belief in the sanctity of immemorial traditions." Over vast stretches of time, people come to accept the existing political realities simply because they have been there for prolonged periods. Centuries-old monarchies, such as those that once held sway in Britain, China, Japan, and elsewhere, are examples of tradition-based legitimacy.

The second type of legitimacy is *legal-rational authority.* This type is rooted in "the belief in the legality of rules and in the right of those who occupy positions by virtue of those rules to issue commands." This type of legitimacy is most prominent in democracies, which establish very rigorous rules for determining who has the right to issue governmental commands. Conceivably, some nondemocracies may also be based on at least an element of legal-rational authority. Over the centuries, Britain's monarchs gradually came to accept the notion that they too were subject to certain laws.

The third type of legitimate authority was what Weber called *charismatic authority.* This type of legitimacy attaches itself to a certain uniquely magnetic or inspiring leader and "rests upon the devotion" of his followers to his "extraordinary sanctity, heroism or exemplary character" as well as to the "patterns of order revealed or ordained by him." In these rare cases, the charismatic leader is perceived by others as "set apart from ordinary men" and as "endowed with supernatural, superhuman, or at least specifically exceptional powers or qualities." Religious figures like Moses, Jesus, Muhammad, and Buddha clearly fit this description. So, too, do certain political figures. For good or ill, such riveting personalities as Napoleon, Hitler, Stalin, Franklin D. Roosevelt, and a few other notable leaders were able to exert a charismatic effect on their followers.

Charismatic authority, in Weber's view, is the most unstable form of legitimacy. Once charismatic leaders die, their ideas and support can die with them. To prevent this from happening, the charismatic leader and successive generations of followers must institutionalize (or "routinize") the leader's charisma by building institutions that will survive, such as an organized religion, a political party, or a state. These efforts are not always successful, however.

Ultimately Weber argued that political legitimacy is grounded in the *beliefs* of those who are governed. If the masses believe that their rulers are legitimate, for whatever reason, then the rulers *are* legitimate. And if the masses believe in their leaders' legitimacy, they are more likely to comply with the laws of the land voluntarily rather than because they are forced to do so. Government based on legitimacy is therefore likely to be more stable and enduring than one based on sheer coercion.[11]

---

One reason many democracies have endured for long periods of time is that their legitimacy is rooted in the consent of the governed. When leaders and the regimes they control are viewed as illegitimate in the eyes of the majority, they must usually rule with an iron fist or face the potential of serious instability. But democracies are by no means immune from legitimacy problems of their own. Large segments of the population may favor democracy in principle but object to the way it works in practice. And if democracy fails to deliver what most people expect in terms of adequate living standards or domestic tranquillity, the people may turn to authoritarians who promise them a better life. History is strewn with the wreckage of failed democracies, and the countries that are struggling to build new democracies today have no guarantees of long-term success.

**How Much Power Do the Governing Elites Have?** A critical question concerning the power of primary elites is whether their ability to make decisions is limited or unconstrained. Are government officials and the institutions they operate subject to the jurisdiction of laws that limit their power? Or are they—like Saddam Hussein—above the law? These questions focus on *the legal authority of the state*—the governing elite's capacity to make, implement, and enforce the law. Whereas legitimacy refers to the *right* to rule, *legal authority* is the *ability* to rule. No one doubted that Saddam Hussein and his government apparatus had the ability to make and enforce the laws they wanted; whether they had the *right* to do so in the eyes of the population was another matter.

Democracies are based on the principle of the *rule of law.* The *rule of law* means that the legal authority of the state and its officials is limited by the law, and that no one is above the law. Even the most powerful government officials must observe the laws that define and limit their decision-making authority. In the United States, for example, the Constitution prescribes that the legal powers of the president, the Congress, and the Supreme Court are to be balanced roughly evenly. Under a system of *checks and balances,* the legal authority of each of these branches of the national government is more or less equal. Other democracies distribute legal powers among their respective governmental institutions in a variety of ways, but as a general rule these powers are limited by the law.

Although authoritarian rulers tend to rule above the law rather than under it, sometimes they recognize certain legal limits to their governmental power. For instance, when Britain was ruled by monarchs prior to the advent of parliamentary democracy, the crown's legal authority was progressively subjected to limitations. One of the landmarks in this development was *Magna Carta* (the Great Charter), signed in 1215 by King John and a group of powerful barons and churchmen anxious to protect their privileges against excessive monarchal power. Faced with a veritable rebellion, the king agreed to respect certain baronial rights and to observe limits to the crown's powers in such matters as taxation and property ownership. Magna Carta's terms plainly implied that the monarchy itself was not above the law, but was bound by it. Over time this principle led to the development of electoral democracy in Britain. Other authoritarian regimes have also observed legal limitations on their power, but only rarely. The most authoritarian governments in modern times have tended to be less constrained by legal obligations. As we noted in chapter 2, however, quite a few governments in today's world are mixed regimes that combine elements of authoritarianism with varying degrees of democracy, at times providing certain legal rights to the population and perhaps some legal constraints on those who govern.

Some authoritarian regimes are *autocracies.* **Autocracy** ***means one-person rule:*** one individual exercises supreme governing authority and is acknowledged as the maximum leader by the country's dominant cliques or groups. Of course, no single person can make all the decisions, and most autocrats must rely on institutions like the army, the bureaucracy, or a political party to carry out their demands. Autocrats may also take advice from trusted loyalists or accommodate the wishes of certain key figures or groups. Despite these limitations, an autocrat still has considerable latitude to make final decisions. Hitler and Stalin were both autocrats. Some autocrats have been called *sultanistic* rulers, a term coined by Max Weber in reference to the sultans of the Ottoman Empire. Sultanistic leaders exercise highly concentrated personal power, often appointing trusted family members and cronies to positions of political responsibility. Saddam Hussein is an example.

Other authoritarian regimes are *oligarchies.* **Oligarchy** ***means rule by a few:*** a small number of individuals—usually no more than twenty—at the top of the ruling elite share power among themselves. These arrangements involve compromises and understandings on the part of extremely powerful officials who believe that it is in their own best interest to exercise power collectively as a committee rather than tolerate an autocrat. After the death of the autocrat Stalin in 1953, the Soviet Union was governed by oligarchies led by less powerful figures like Nikita Khrushchev, who was "first among equals" in the Soviet leadership until his ouster in 1964, and Leonid Brezhnev, who headed the collective leadership from 1964 until his death in 1982. Similarly, contemporary China is governed by a Communist Party oligarchy.

In the most severe regimes, the government controls or regulates almost every aspect of social life—the economy, religion, education, the media, culture, leisure activities, and so on. These political systems are called *totalitarian.*

> **Totalitarianism** ***is a form of authoritarianism in which the government's domination of politics, the economy, and society is virtually total. Individuals have few, if any, rights or freedoms.***

Nazi Germany, the Soviet Union (especially under Stalin), and North Korea today are examples.[12]

Whether the state is authoritarian or democratic, coercion is often necessary to ensure the state's authority—that is, its legal right and ability to apply its laws. *Coercion* is the act of compelling people to so something, usually by threatening or implementing some kind of punishment if they fail to comply. In all countries, the authority of the governing elite ultimately rests on force. If the state becomes ineffective at using coercive force to curb lawlessness or direct challenges to its legitimacy, its ability to govern may very well be in jeopardy.

**How Do the Masses Relate to the Elites?** Throughout history a number of political theorists have been very pessimistic about the people's ability to govern themselves in any kind of democratic fashion. Some theorists have argued that the masses are better off under some form of elite rule, provided that the elites govern for the good of society as a whole rather than pursuing power for its own sake. In *The Republic,* Plato favored the creation of a ruling caste of "guardians," well schooled in the liberal and martial arts, who would preside over society. Aristotle in *The Politics* favored a "middle way" between a ruling elite and popular opinion, though he did not translate this principle into a specific constitutional design. (James Madison and other authors of the U.S. Constitution of 1789 believed that their document embodied Aristotle's ideals.) Thomas Hobbes argued in *Leviathan* (1651) that the people have a natural right to determine how they are governed by forming a "covenant" with their leaders. But he warned that humanity's aggressive impulses make democracy impossible, inevitably leading to a war "of every man against every man." To guarantee the social tranquillity necessary for the advancement of civilization, Hobbes proposed that the people voluntarily "confer all their power and strength upon one man, or upon one assembly of men," who would wield supreme authority. In essence, Hobbes favored dictatorship by consent of the governed. Other skeptics of popular democracy have voiced concerns about mass tendencies to follow totalitarian pied pipers, to be duped or manipulated by ruling cliques, or to abandon the responsibilities of self-government altogether in an "escape from freedom." Chilling evidence of these tendencies was plainly visible in 1932, when 52 percent of German voters cast their ballots for either the Nazis or the Communists, the two most outspokenly antidemocratic parties in what was still a democratic country.[13]

Some observers who are generally pessimistic about the masses' willingness to take seriously their political obligations in a democracy maintain that democracy can still work, provided that the governing elites observe the rule of law and stick to the rules of democratic procedures. In this view, elites are not only compatible with democracy, they are indispensable to it. Such were the views of James Madison (1751–1836) and most other founders of the American system of government. Fearing that the uneducated masses could not be trusted with a democracy, they preferred to characterize the U.S. political system as a "republic." The Constitution of 1789—which does not contain the word "democracy"—therefore combined limited electoral procedures (initially confined to property-owning males) with day-to-day governance by an enlightened, freedom-loving elite.[14] In more recent times, several political theorists contributed to what became known as the theory of **democratic elitism**. This is the notion that ***modern democracies are governed in practice by elites who are accountable to the people.*** The political economist Joseph Schumpeter (1883–1950) succinctly summarized this idea by saying that real-world democracy is not "government by the people," but rather "government *chosen* by the people." At election time, Schumpeter observed, the people essentially choose between competing sets of political elites.[15] Empirical evidence confirming the critical role of prodemocracy elites is persuasive. A massive survey of political attitudes conducted in the late 1970s showed that local elites in the United States (including elected officials, judges, civic activists, and others involved in the political process) were more supportive of civil liberties and constitutional rights than the mass public was.[16] And as we shall see in chapter 9 and elsewhere in this book, elites can play a pivotal role in saving troubled democracies from collapse and in guiding the delicate transition from authoritarian rule to democratic institutions and practices.

Students of mass behavior who are more optimistic insist that successful democracies are usually propped up by a dependable core of political and social activists, organized in nongovernmental associations of various kinds that foster cooperation and good citizenship. People who come together in such organizations—whether for explicitly political purposes, for charitable aims, or just for fun—are known collectively as *civil society.* As the experiences of the United States and other democracies illustrate, the more vibrant the civil society, the stronger and more lasting the democracy is likely to be. In some cases a more or less organized civil society can even exist under a dictatorship, whether legally or surreptitiously. Chapter 9 will discuss civil society in more detail.

## HYPOTHESES ON POWER

### Economics and Power

Does economic strength automatically lead to political power? Does individual wealth, or control over large corporations, inevitably confer a correspondingly large amount of influence over government decision makers? Political scientists who have studied these questions have found a variety of real-world relationships between economic and political power, some with expected results and some not so expected. A prominent example is Robert Dahl's classic study of power in New Haven, Connecticut.

## HYPOTHESIS-TESTING EXERCISE: Power in New Haven

### Hypothesis and Variables

In his widely read book *Who Governs?*, Robert Dahl of Yale University tested the hypothesis that economic power confers political power on the wealthiest segments of society. In this hypothesis, *economic power* is the *independent variable* and *political power* is the *dependent variable.* In the 1950s Dahl decided to see if this hypothesis applied in New Haven, Yale's hometown.[17]

### Expectations

Dahl's initial expectation was that, if economics determines politics, then the richest families of New Haven and the city's most successful businesspeople should always get their way any time they needed the local government to make a decision in their behalf. Another expectation was that their dominance of the local economy would provide them with a general control over the city's governmental affairs. If that were true, then New Haven's mayor and other elected officials, along with their parties, would be expected to pay more attention to the needs and demands of the city's economic elite than to the voters who elected them to office. Indeed, the hypothesis plainly implies that electoral democracy is a sham: in the end, the wealthy minority always enjoys considerably more political power than the voting majority.

### Evidence

Dahl focused his research on key decisions taken by local politicians in three issue areas: public education, urban redevelopment, and nominations for public office by the Democratic and Republican parties. He found that New Haven's most well-established wealthy families in fact possessed very little political influence on these issues. Many of them were not even interested in politics at all. He also found that the most prominent local business leaders—the so-called "economic notables"—had no real influence on any of these issues, either. Although they occasionally succeeded in getting what they wanted through the political process, economic power did not confer on this small group a general control over the city. Even on issues of vital importance to the business community, New Haven's elected officials were able to make major decisions without undue interference by business leaders. Moreover, less powerful groups, such as factory workers and the lower middle class, had significant political resources that they could utilize to influence governmental policy on a host of questions. By electing city officials sympathetic to their views, they could often succeed in getting the local government to decide certain questions in their favor.

### Conclusions

Dahl therefore concluded that the evidence was *inconsistent* with the hypothesis: New Haven was not ruled by "the hidden hand of an economic elite," but was governed by a *plurality* of social classes, political parties, and public and private institutions. These conclusions contradicted the assertions of C. Wright Mills and other proponents of the power-elite hypothesis and supported the concept of *pluralism* in American political life.[18]

---

Dahl's book and the debates it provoked prompted a number of political scientists to undertake their own studies of the relationship between economic and political power in various communities. In most cases it has been found that economic power in democracies definitely provides political influence, but rarely does it confer complete domination over political life.

## The Abuse of Power

Another topic under the heading of power concerns the *abuse of power:* how can it be prevented? This age-old question was of vital importance to the founding fathers of the American Revolution. James Madison was especially interested in creating a system of government that protected individual liberties from the encroachments of an obtrusive and all-powerful state. "If men were angels," he wrote in *The Federalist,* "neither external nor internal controls on government would be necessary. In framing a government to be administered by men over men, the great difficulty lies in this: You must first enable the government to control the governed; and in the next place, oblige it to control itself." Accordingly, "to control the abuses of government," Madison reasoned that a carefully constructed constitutional system in which the various branches of the state—the legislature, the executive, and the judiciary—checked and balanced each other's legal authority would prevent the abuse of power by any one of these branches. Madison's design, of course, became the basis of the U.S. Constitution that took effect in 1789.[19]

The abuse of governmental power by political leaders is only one form of the abuse of power to be found in political life. Madison and other political theorists have also cautioned against the *tyranny of the majority*. Even in a democracy with a narrowly circumscribed governmental system, it is possible that a large majority of voters, exercising their constitutional rights, may find ways to restrict the rights and opportunities of minority groups in society. In the same passage from *The Federalist* just cited, Madison wrote that it was important not only to guard society against the oppression of its rulers, but also "to guard one part of the society against the injustice of the other part."

To this end, Madison favored a large, "extended" American republic whose laws would cover all the various states of the union. Arguing that large societies are likely to be divided into a wide variety of social groups and interests that provide minorities with an opportunity to forge effective coalitions in defense of their rights, Madison hypothesized that "the larger the society, . . . the more duly capable it will be of self government."

One astute observer of the United States in its formative decades singled out the tyranny of the majority as a particularly grave threat to America's fledgling democracy. Alexis de Tocqueville (1805–59) was a perceptive Frenchman who traveled around the United States at the age of 26 in 1831. De Tocqueville heaped praise on the young republic but warned against tendencies to intellectual conformity and mediocrity in American life as a result of the majority's vulgarizing influences. "If ever freedom is lost in America," he predicted, "that will be due to the omnipotence of the majority driving the minorities to desperation and forcing them to appeal to physical force." De Tocqueville's magisterial work, *Democracy in America,* still stands as one of the most insightful examinations ever undertaken of American politics and, more broadly, of democracy itself.

### Corruption

"Power corrupts; absolute power corrupts absolutely." This oft-quoted phrase of the British historian Robert Acton appears to have a timeless validity. Corruption is one of the most widespread examples of the abuse of power; scarcely any country in the world is immune to it (see table 4.1).

We define **political corruption** ***as the illegal or unethical use of a political position to provide special advantages for individuals or groups.*** Though the present age is probably no more or less corrupt than prior eras, recent years have witnessed a rash of sensational cases of corrupt practices by political figures in authoritarian regimes and democracies alike. Here are just two examples:

- In the 1990s the entire Italian political system was rocked by political scandals that devastated the country's political elites and reshaped its political parties and electoral system. More than eight thousand political figures, including some of the most respected leaders of the post–World War II decades, were indicted for accepting bribes and other favors from the Mafia, private businesses, and various other sources. The scandals led to the collapse of established political parties and to major electoral reforms.
- Mobutu Sese Seko was the dictator of Zaire from 1965 to 1997. During his long reign he was regarded as one of the world's most corrupt political leaders. Though the overwhelming majority of Zaire's population of approximately 43 million were mired in poverty, the country's profitable copper, cobalt, and diamond exports provided a rich source of income for Mobutu and his cronies. The national bank printed money at the dictator's whims. As a consequence, Zaire had the highest inflation rate in the world in 1994: 12,500 percent. Under Mobutu's direction, Zaire had become a veritable *kleptocracy:* a state ruled by thieves. Mobutu fled the country in 1997 as rebel forces ousted him in a bloody civil war. The new government, which changed the country's name to the Democratic Republic of Congo, claimed that Mobutu had squirreled away $8 billion in Swiss banks.

Among many other countries, Japan, Russia, Mexico, and Nigeria have all had major corruption problems, as we'll see in Part Two.

**TABLE 4.1**

**Corruption Perceptions Index for Selected Countries, 2006**

Transparency International annually ranks countries on the basis of businesspeople's perceptions of the corruption they encounter when dealing with government and nongovernment personnel. The Corruption Perceptions Index (CPI) ranges from a score of 10 for "highly clean" countries to 0 for "highly corrupt" countries.

| Rank | Country | CPI Score |
|---|---|---|
| 1. | Finland | 9.6 |
| 1. | Iceland | 9.6 |
| 1. | New Zealand | 9.6 |
| 4. | Denmark | 9.5 |
| 5. | Singapore | 9.4 |
| 6. | Sweden | 9.2 |
| 11. | United Kingdom | 8.6 |
| 14. | Canada | 8.5 |
| 16. | Germany | 8.0 |
| 17. | Japan | 7.6 |
| 18. | France | 7.4 |
| 20. | Chile | 7.3 |
| 20. | United States | 7.3 |
| 34. | Israel | 5.9 |
| 34. | Taiwan | 5.9 |
| 42. | South Korea | 5.1 |
| 45. | Italy | 4.9 |
| 51. | South Africa | 4.6 |
| 57. | Bulgaria | 4.0 |
| 60. | Turkey | 3.8 |
| 61. | Poland | 3.7 |
| 70. | Brazil | 3.3 |
| 70. | China | 3.3 |
| 70. | Egypt | 3.3 |
| 70. | India | 3.3 |
| 70. | Mexico | 3.3 |
| 70. | Saudi Arabia | 3.3 |
| 84. | Romania | 3.1 |
| 93. | Argentina | 2.9 |
| 99. | Georgia | 2.8 |
| 99. | Ukraine | 2.8 |
| 105. | Bolivia | 2.7 |
| 105. | Iran | 2.7 |
| 111. | Kazakhstan | 2.6 |
| 121. | Philippines | 2.5 |
| 121. | Russia | 2.5 |
| 130. | Indonesia | 2.4 |
| 130. | Zimbabwe | 2.4 |
| 138. | Venezuela | 2.3 |
| 142. | Kenya | 2.2 |
| 142. | Kyrgyzstan | 2.2 |
| 142. | Nigeria | 2.2 |
| 142. | Pakistan | 2.2 |
| 151. | Belarus | 2.1 |
| 156. | Bangladesh | 2.0 |
| 156. | Chad | 2.0 |
| 156. | Congo (Dem.Rep.) | 2.0 |
| 156. | Sudan | 2.0 |
| 160. | Burma | 1.9 |
| 160. | Iraq | 1.9 |
| 163. | Haiti | 1.8 |

*Source:* Transparency International, www.transparency.org.

Corruption can be the Achilles' heel of democracy. It can antagonize citizens in well-established democracies like Italy, and it can undermine democracy's chances in newly democratizing countries if elected officials or their appointees break the public's fragile trust.

What causes political corruption? Even if we assume that its root cause lies in the acquisitive appetites of individuals who demand wealth and power, are there any *political* variables that may help explain how corruption manifests itself and perhaps shed some light on how it might be reduced or discouraged?

Among the many independent variables that might account for political corruption, one of the more obvious ones is *the absence of the rule of law.* Quite clearly, authoritarian regimes in which the leaders are unrestrained by any higher law are especially susceptible to personal greed and the lust for power. Even when the rule of law prevails as a general principle, as it does in democracies, corruption may still exist if it is not adequately detected and the law is not properly enforced. Effective detection and enforcement mechanisms are therefore essential to discourage corrupt practices in democratic states.

Another troubling problem arises in democracies when the law permits activities that, in the minds of some people, should be regarded as corrupt. The weakness of campaign financing laws is regarded by many observers as a major weakness of democracy. Most of the world's democracies permit private political contributions to the election campaign war chests of individual candidates or political parties. Although some countries place limits on these allowable contributions, ample opportunities still remain for private campaign funding. Unquestionably, the purpose of many of these contributions is to extract political favors from the recipients should they get elected. The controversy illustrates the difficulty of defining "corruption" in a manner that suits everybody, even in a democracy. Practices that are currently *legal* may be regarded by some people as *unethical* and should, in their view, be outlawed.

A second independent variable impinging on corruption is the *lack of alternation in power.* If the highest government officials are not rotated by the electorate on a periodic basis and if they have good reason to believe that they will not be removed from their positions in the foreseeable future, the likelihood rises that they will engage in corrupt activities. Authoritarian rulers are particularly well-armed against removal from power; hence they feel free to engage in extreme forms of corruption. But democracies can also experience inadequate alternation in power.

Italy and Japan provide telling examples. Prior to the elections of 1994, Italy had been governed by coalition cabinets consisting of the same four or five parties for over thirty years. Because these governing parties could be quite certain that they would not be voted out of office by opposition parties, they felt relatively free to enjoy the spoils of political corruption without fearing the wrath of an angry electorate large enough to vote them out of office. (The chief opposition party was the Italian Communist Party, which was never sufficiently popular to unseat the ruling coalitions.) As we'll see in chapter 19, Japan has experienced similar problems. The evidence from Italy and Japan is thus quite consistent with the hypothesis that *the likelihood of corruption varies inversely with the likelihood of alternation in power:* the less likely it is that a government will be removed from office, the more likely it is that it will engage in illegal corruption.

Some students of political corruption have hypothesized that political corruption is a "normal," routine part of governing in most political systems. Such practices as vote-buying, embezzlement, and *nepotism* (i.e., favoritism shown to the family members of public officials) can be found in both democracies and nondemocracies. In some cases certain types of corruption, such as providing favors to one's political friends while in office, may even be necessary for the survival of society's basic arrangements for dealing with the demands of its social groups.[20]

### Torture

Torture is arguably the most perverse form of abuse of state power. The use of techniques designed to inflict severe physical pain or psychological stress on victims held captive by state authorities has a long history. And despite efforts by international organizations, governments, and human rights activists to ban it, torture is still widely practiced around the world. An Amnesty International investigation covering the period from 1997 to mid 2000 uncovered reports of torture or ill treatment by state officials in more than 150 countries.

Whether it is used to elicit confessions from suspected criminals, to intimidate political opponents, or to extract information from spies or terrorists, state-practiced torture is outlawed by several international agreements. The Universal Declaration of Human Rights (1948) upholds freedom from "torture and from cruel, inhuman, or degrading treatment or punishment" (see chapter 1). The Geneva Conventions of 1949 and the International Covenant on Civil and Political Rights (1966) also banned torture, and in 1984 the United Nations General Assembly adopted the Convention Against Torture and Other Cruel, Inhuman, or Degrading Treatment or Punishment. The Convention established a Committee Against Torture to which states adhering to the treaty must submit reports. The U.S. Senate ratified the Convention in 1994.

One might expect that democracies would be constitutionally averse to torture, given their commitment to human rights. But this hypothesis is at times contradicted in democratic countries by practices that at the very least border on torture, as well as by some notorious cases of unmistakable torture. France used torture tactics when fighting to maintain colonial rule in Indochina and Algeria in the 1950s. Israel used physical torture against suspected Palestinian terrorists in the 1970s and 1980s. After September 11 the United States subjected certain al Qaeda suspects to acute physical and mental distress under interrogation. During its occupation of Iraq, U.S. military officers were exposed to international condemnation for subjecting Iraqi detainees to painful and humiliating treatment at the infamous Abu Ghraib prison, the site of Saddam Hussein's former torture chambers. And in 2006 the Council of Europe, an intergovernmental human rights organization, concluded that there were "serious indications" that the U.S. Central Intelligence Agency was secretly cooperating with European governments to apprehend and detain suspected terrorists illegally. In some cases the CIA, allegedly with European assistance, engaged in the "rendition" of detainees to countries outside Europe that were known to practice torture.

On the positive side, democracies tend to observe the international agreements they have signed to outlaw torture and other, presumably less grievous, forms of "inhuman and degrading punishment." Israel's Supreme Court outlawed the government's harsh interrogation methods in 1999. The U.S. military prosecuted and convicted officers involved in the Abu Ghraib incidents; all received prison sentences. But the threats to mass populations posed by terrorists have raised difficult legal and moral questions about the differences that may exist between "torture," which is wrong, and "coercive interrogation," which is routinely practiced by police and investigative authorities. A related question is whether torture is justified if it is necessary to prevent a "ticking bomb" from going off. As human rights scholar Michael Ignatieff has argued, the age of terror confronts us with tough choices between the rights of prisoners and the security of the community.[21]

### Powerlessness

Thus far we have looked almost exclusively at those who wield power. But what of the powerless? Are the weak who must endure the hegemony of all-powerful governments or dominant social groups doomed to pure submission? The weak may have subtle weapons of their own.

## WEAPONS OF THE WEAK

History provides striking evidence that subjugated peoples can sometimes find effective ways to turn the tables on their masters. Although successful revolutions are relatively rare, it was as recently as 1989 and 1990 that the people of East Germany, Poland, Czechoslovakia, and other countries of East-Central Europe managed to cast off decades of communist rule. In other places, groups that do not accept their subservient status have found attention-grabbing ways to express their dissatisfaction: car-bombings, insurrections, and other acts of violence often capture world headlines. But do there exist instances of discontent that are too quiet or hidden to stir public notice?

In *Weapons of the Weak,* James C. Scott observed the subtle dynamics of class relationships between Malaysian peasants and the landowners and officials who controlled their world. When the landlords began imposing new rice production techniques that worked to the peasants' disadvantage, the peasants did not openly rebel. But even though they appeared outwardly deferential when speaking publicly with their social superiors, they could be highly critical of their overlords when speaking about them in private. Some peasants also engaged in clandestine acts of poaching or minor property destruction aimed directly at the landlords. These and similar insubordinate actions, Scott concluded, constituted deliberate *political* acts of defiance that expressed the peasants' opposition to the prevailing power structures in Malaysia.

In a subsequent work, *Domination and the Arts of Resistance,* Scott widened his analysis into a comparative study of low-level political defiance in a variety of countries and historical eras. Drawing on accounts of slavery in the United States, serfdom in nineteenth-century Russia, British colonialism in Burma, castes in India, communist rule in the Soviet Union and Eastern Europe, and numerous other instances of relations between dominant and powerless groups, Scott probed the hypothesis that "relations of dominance are, at the same time, relations of resistance." Even when resistance is not overt or violently confrontational, he suggested, it is present nonetheless. In addition to expressing their resentments privately, oppressed groups engage in low-profile forms of public resistance: pilfering, foot-dragging, sabotaging crops or machinery, squatting, withholding taxes or food deliveries, shoddy workmanship, arson, and the like. Through gossip, rumors, jokes, folk tales, and other modes of coded or symbolic public discourse, they cleverly employ elliptical modes of mocking or vilifying the ruling groups that oppress them.

"Every subordinate group," Scott writes, "creates, out of its ordeal, a 'hidden transcript' that represents a critique of power spoken behind the back of the dominant." Far from being a *substitute* for resistance, these hidden transcripts are themselves a *form* of resistance. The cumulative effects of seemingly petty acts of defiance can exact a heavy toll in economic and other costs to the dominant classes. In some cases, they can also pave the way to a more explosive mass uprising. If we want to understand the realities of power relations, therefore, we must penetrate the veneer of outward appearances and explore the many ways the weak "speak truth to power."[22]

---

Contemporary Iran provides a fascinating case of how these various aspects of power can operate in a country that combines authoritarian rule with rising pressures for democracy.

## POWER IN IRAN

In an eighteen-page letter addressed to President George W. Bush, President *Mahmoud Ahmadinejad* (mah-MOOD ah-mah-dih-nee-ZHAHD) of Iran accused his American counterpart of violating the teachings of Jesus Christ by invading Afghanistan and Iraq. He also bluntly spelled out his opposition to democracy as it is practiced in the West. "Liberalism and Western-style democracy have not been able to realize the ideals of humanity," Ahmadinejad wrote. "Today these two concepts have failed." In their place, Iran's president called for a return to the teachings of the "divine prophets"—Moses, Jesus, and Muhammad—as "the only road leading to salvation."[23] Written at a time of escalating international tensions over Iran's efforts to build facilities that might be capable of producing nuclear weapons, the letter was instantly dismissed by the U.S. government as mere rhetoric. But there was little doubt that the missive's direct, nondiplomatic tone and its ardent religious content accurately reflected the political style and convictions of President Ahmadinejad, the man chosen by a large majority of Iranian voters in 2005 as their principal elected leader. Whether Ahmadinejad's ideas on democracy, religion, and relations with the United States accurately reflected the views of most Iranians was less certain, however, despite his landslide win.

Ahmadinejad's come-from-behind electoral victory surprised most observers of Iranian politics, including many Iranian citizens. As the most hardline Islamic candidate in a field of seven presidential contenders, Ahmadinejad did not appear to represent the views of most Iranians on vital issues of domestic and foreign policy. According to polls and other gauges of

**President Mahmoud Ahmadinejad stands before Ayatollah Khomeini's portrait.**

public opinion, most Iranians preferred a loosening of religious controls over their lives, real democratic representation, and an improvement in Iran's ties with the United States. It was estimated that only about 10 to 20 percent of Iranians were dyed-in-the-wool supporters of the Islamic hardliners who favored stringent codes of dress and comportment between the sexes in public, a tightly regulated election system that keeps democratic reformers off the ballots, and a confrontationist stance vis-à-vis the United States and cultural "Westoxication."[24] Ahmadinejad's election had come about in part because several potential candidates committed to democratic reforms were prevented from running for the presidency by the religious authorities who have the final say in determining who gets to compete for elective office in Iran. Although he was not himself a cleric, Ahmadinejad was the clearly preferred choice of the conservative Shiite clerics who control Iran's theocratic state. They used the full force of the state-controlled media and their influence over pro-regime militants to boost Ahmadinejad's candidacy. One of Ahmadinejad's defeated opponents claimed that religious authorities had intimidated voters and manipulated the voting process to make sure that Ahmadinejad finished as one of the top two contenders in the first round of the presidential election, thereby guaranteeing him a spot in the decisive two-candidate showdown in the second round. At the same time, Ahmadinejad struck a responsive chord among large elements of Iran's working class. With his unassuming manner, modest lifestyle, and sincere promises to improve the lot of underprivileged Iranians, Ahmadinejad came across as more humane and genuine than his second-round opponent, former president Ali Akbar Hashemi Rafsanjani, a veteran clerical leader reputed to be the richest man in Iran. Ahmadinejad thus owed his triumph at the polls to a combination of nondemocratic elite favoritism and class-based popular appeal—an ambivalent basis for legitimate authority.

Ahmadinejad's actual power was also a matter of ambivalence. Although the president is the country's top elected official, Ahmadinejad quickly found out how circumscribed presidential authority can be in Iran's theocracy. In fact the number one political decision maker in Iran is not the president but the country's chief religious figure, *Ayatollah Ali Khamenei* (hah-mehn-a-EE). In his capacity as Iran's Supreme Leader, chosen by an elected body of mostly conservative Shiite clerics, Khamenei has the power to appoint Iran's chief judge, its military high command, and members of two powerful institutions, the Council of Guardians and the Expediency Council. The Guardians certify candidates for elections, and they have the right to strike down legislation passed by Iran's parliament if they believe it is contrary to Islamic law. The Expediency Council was originally created to adjudicate conflicts between the Council of Guardians and Iran's elected parliament, the Majles. But several months after Ahmadinejad's election victory, Khamenei unilaterally granted the Expediency Council new oversight authority over the president's cabinet and the parliament. Khamenei's move was clearly intended to limit the power of archconservatives in Ahmadinejad's government and the Majles, and to elevate the authority of Rafsanjani, the defeated presidential candidate who headed the Expediency Council.

It also reflected persisting rivalries within the ruling Islamic hierarchy between several competing tendencies. The contending camps include *hardline Islamists* like Ahmadinejad, who have a puritanical approach to Islamic law and hostile attitudes toward the West; *traditional conservatives*, represented mainly by clerics who are not politically active and who are more interested in Islamic culture; *neoconservatives*, who combine Islamic religiosity with an emphasis on developing the private sector, a view widely shared in the ruling elite; and *pragmatic conservatives*, who are flexible on religious ideology and culture, and who favor political and economic openings to the outside world.[25]

Iran's Islamic theocracy is fundamentally authoritarian in nature, with a composite Freedom House rating of 6 in 2005. But this tightly controlled political system has not eliminated conflict over power or policy. Conflicts take place within the religious-political elite, between the elite and reformist political activists, and between the elite and reform-minded segments of the mass population. How did Iran get to this point? A brief review of the country's checkered history can help us understand its current predicament and—perhaps—its possible paths to the future.

As the heir to Persia and its storied empires, Iran has deep roots in antiquity. Following more than two millennia of monarchal regimes, Iran also has democratic roots that stretch back a hundred years. After centuries of rule from the "Peacock Throne" by the Qajar dynasty, proponents of liberal democracy forced the crown to convene an elected assembly in 1906. The delegates drafted a new constitution creating a Western-style limited monarchy: the monarch (the shah) was forced to share power with a parliament and acknowledge that his authority derived from the people rather than from God. When the shah resisted, he lost power completely in a civil war (1908–09). Political parties sprang into existence, running the left–right gamut. A National Assembly (*Majles*) was elected periodically, and the right to vote was eventually extended to all adult males. By 1911, Iran's first revolution—a democratic revolution—had triumphed. But social and political conflicts were intense. Moderates favoring democracy, rooted mainly in the middle class, had to contend with revolutionary communists, the armed forces, Islamic clerics, and other nondemocratic groups with political priorities of their own. The country's social fabric was further strained by ethnic tensions: about a third of the population was not Persian. And Iran was subjected to continuing pressure from Britain to share its oil reserves and keep out Russian influences.

As the country threatened to come apart, a colonel from a little-known Turkish-speaking military family, Reza Khan, staged a coup d'état in 1921. He used his new post as chief of the army to manipulate election results, eventually packing the Majles with his supporters. In 1925 a majority of deputies voted to depose the last Qajar monarch and elected Reza as the new shah. He had recently changed his family name to Pahlavi, an old Persian name. *Reza Shah* ruled with the authority of an absolute monarch, relying principally on the army and relegating the Majles to an insignificant role. Although he alienated most of Iran's social groups and his regime lacked popular legitimacy, it was his openly pro-German sympathies that cost him his rule. As World War II got under way, Britain and the Soviet Union agreed to partition Iran between them until the war ended so as to keep the Nazis out. The British unseated Reza and replaced him with his young son, Muhammad Reza Pahlavi.

The new shah initially cooperated with the parties in the Majles, while building close ties with Britain and the United States. But a confrontation ensued when Muhammad Mossadeq, a constitutional lawyer, was elected prime minister in 1951. Mossadeq sought to reduce the shah's powers, and he struck a blow at British oil interests when his government took over the Anglo-Iranian oil company. Mossadeq enjoyed widespread popular support, but the United States and Britain collaborated to remove him from office. As pro-Mossadeq crowds gathered in the streets of Tehran in 1953, the shah left the country. He returned after elements of the military, backed by the CIA, arrested Mossadeq. From this point on, Muhammad Reza Shah asserted his monarchal authority, reestablishing strong authoritarian rule.[26]

American pressures for reforms resulted in the shah's "White Revolution" in the 1960s. In addition to effecting some economic changes, the reforms gave Iranian women the right to vote. But they did not touch the shah's expanding powers. Seeking support primarily from Iran's wealthiest classes and from elements of the middle class, the shah enjoyed little popularity among the millions who constituted the working class and the peasantry. In the early 1960s a Shiite cleric, *Ayatollah Ruhollah Khomeini* (ho-may-NEE) openly criticized the shah for corruption, election fraud, violations of press freedoms, and insensitivity to the economic needs of the lower and middle classes. These ideas had wide support among Iran's masses. (Iranians are overwhelmingly Shiite Muslims.) After anti-shah riots broke out in 1963, the shah exiled Khomeini. Later in the decade, while living in Iraq, Khomeini called for an Islamic government to replace the shah's regime.

During the 1970s, the shah played a key role in U.S. security designs, guarding the Persian Gulf against potential Soviet encroachments and supplying aid to Israel. He also joined with other oil-producing countries in actively promoting steep increases in world oil prices. The result was a sudden bonanza of oil wealth for Iran. Some of these revenues were used to build schools, hospitals, and other features of the "White Revolution." But large amounts went into the private coffers of the Pahlavis and other well-heeled families, and spending was lavished on the military. By the end of the decade, Iran was still one of the most inegalitarian societies in the world. Illiteracy and housing shortages grew during the oil boom, agriculture stagnated, the middle class saw its income eaten away by inflation, and millions of the very poorest were left destitute.

A series of anti-shah demonstrations and strikes rocked Iran in 1977 and 1978. Harsh reprisals by the shah's hated security forces only intensified the population's outrage. A broad coalition of forces came together in favor of the shah's removal; they included students, the middle class, the working class, and the Islamic clergy. Elements of the army began deserting the shah as well, refusing to shoot at demonstrators and in some cases joining them. As the United States tried to arrange the shah's graceful exit and his replacement by a group of democratically inclined politicians, Ayatollah Khomeini—whose taped speeches had won a huge audience inside Iran—returned to Tehran to a rapturous welcome by his supporters in February 1979. Less than two weeks later, the shah's security apparatus collapsed. The shah left the country on February 11, and in March more than 98 percent of Iranian voters approved the creation of a theocratic Islamic republic. In November, pro-Khomeini militants stormed the U.S. embassy in Tehran; they were to hold their captives hostage for more than a year. Iran's second revolution had triumphed. But it quickly turned out to be far less democratic than its first revolution of 1906–11.[27]

Khomeini radiated charismatic authority. His father, a religious scholar descended from the prophet Muhammad, was murdered when the boy was an infant. Khomeini became an ardent mystic and adopted a stern asceticism that was later translated into his government's ban on popular music and its insistence that women wear the body-covering *chador* in public. But he combined his intense spirituality with a politically activist approach to religious doctrine, breaking with traditional Shiite reluctance to mix religion and politics. His bold denunciation of the shah in the 1960s won him wide notoriety. During his years in exile, he broadened his religious perspective by incorporating leftist ideological notions that were current among intellectuals in the developing world, including the need for radical social and economic change and a rejection of Western influences. By the time Khomeini returned to Iran in 1979, he was hailed by his followers as their preeminent religious guide, and he was accorded the title of Object of Emulation. But Khomeini's amalgam of piety and activism resulted in a multifaceted, and at times internally contradictory, set of views on the relationship between religious authority and the exercise of political power.

Using Max Weber's concepts, Daniel Brumberg has shown that Khomeini's charismatic authority, rooted in his status as a widely acknowledged holy man, was combined with a "rational" and "utilitarian" concept of authority, focused squarely on the practicalities of government decision making. Khomeini fulfilled his charismatic-religious role in his capacity as Supreme Leader, an extraordinary position that made him the highest official in Iran's theocracy by virtue of his sacred bond with millions of Iranians. He addressed his rational-utilitarian role by working to establish enduring laws and state institutions and by allowing office-holders to formulate policies and make day-to-day decisions. At times these two roles—the charismatic and the utilitarian—were in conflict, and this contradiction was mirrored in the Islamic Republic's first constitution.[28]

A majority of Iranians acknowledged Khomeini's charismatic authority by electing him their Supreme Leader. The new regime's first constitution also permitted the people to elect a consultative assembly, the Majles; the president of Iran; and an Assembly of Experts, consisting of about eighty clerics authorized to choose Khomeini's successors in the event that no one was worthy of popular election as Supreme Leader. All prospective candidates to these positions, however, had to be approved by the Council of Guardians. In addition to the regular military, an armed organization called the Islamic Revolutionary Guard Corps was created for the purpose of enforcing the regime's stern interpretation of Islamic law, including dress codes and relations between the sexes in public. The Supreme Leader was empowered to select the heads of the army and the Revolutionary Guards, the head of the judiciary, and six clerical members of the Council of Guardians. (The remaining six Guardians would be judges chosen by the Majles from a list provided by the head of the judiciary.) The ultimate purpose of this constitutional scheme was to permit a limited amount of electoral democracy while guaranteeing that, however the people might vote, decision-making power would rest firmly in the hands of the country's religious elite.

The document was vague, however, about what would happen if disagreements arose among these institutions. While identifying God as the ultimate source of the regime's authority, the constitution stated that the country's affairs would be administered "in accordance with public opinion, expressed through elections," thus implying a measure of democracy. (The preamble links the Islamic Republic to "democratic movements" around the world.) Khomeini himself declared that the Majles was higher than all the other institutions; but he was repeatedly called upon to render the final decision when the Majles got into disputes with the Council of Guardians. As long as Khomeini was around, he was able to impose his will on the Islamic Republic's squabbling factions. Policy differences within the governing elite were in fact quite profound on such issues as relations with the United States (centering initially on the hostage crisis), economic policy, the 1980–88 war with Iraq, and other matters. With an eye to stabilizing Iran's political system after his death, Khomeini in 1988 created the Expediency Discernment Council (known simply as the Expediency Council), a 31-member body chosen by the Supreme Leader for the purpose of adjudicating conflicts that might arise if the Council of Guardians vetoed legislation passed by the Majles. Sure enough, policy conflicts and power struggles intensified significantly after Khomeini died in 1989.

As we've seen, Max Weber argued that a charismatic leader must find ways to institutionalize (or "routinize") his personal authority in order to pass on his legacy to succeeding generations. After Khomeini died, the question of how to ensure the survival of the Islamic Republic by institutionalizing his personal authority became an urgent problem for his followers. Recognizing that no one could match Khomeini's

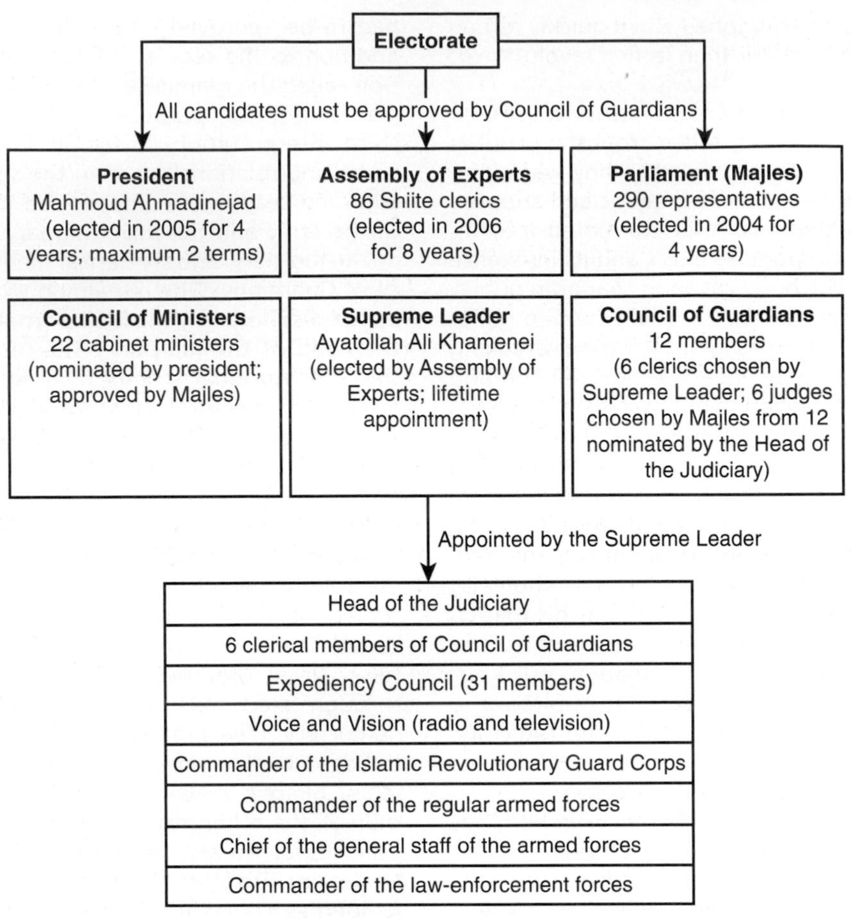


**FIGURE 4.1 Iran's Main State Institutions**
*Source:* Based on *The Economist,* January 18, 2003, and Wilfried Buchta, *Who Rules Iran?* (Washington, D.C.: Washington Institute, 2000).

religious preeminence, Iran's leaders amended the constitution in 1989 and reduced the position of Supreme Leader to a more human dimension. Instead of having to be recognized by the people as a source of religious emulation, the occupant of that position would henceforth be chosen by the Assembly of Experts primarily on the basis of his *political* skills—in other words, on the basis of rational and utilitarian criteria (Can he govern?) instead of charismatic-religious criteria (Is he a great holy man?). On this basis, Ayatollah Ali Khamenei, a conservative cleric who was not among the clergy's most esteemed Objects of Emulation, was selected to serve as the new Supreme Leader for life. (For Iran's main institutions, see figure 4.1.)

Since Khomeini's passing, Iran has been shaken by open disagreements among its key religious leaders over the very nature of the Islamic regime. How much power should be held by the religious authorities, and how much should be held by secular legislators and government officials? How much cultural freedom and freedom of the press should there be? How should the country relate to the rest of the world, in particular to the United States, which was vilified by Khomeini as "the Great Satan"? Many of these critical issues were in play in 1997, when 90 percent of the eligible voters turned out for a hotly contested presidential election. The contest pitted several government-backed candidates against a more liberal cleric, *Ayatollah Muhammad Khatami* (hah-tah-ME). Though Khatami's candidacy was approved by the Council of Guardians, he was regarded as an opponent of the ruling clique because of his increasingly outspoken advocacy of press freedom, women's rights, greater openness to Western cultural influences, and a possible resumption of friendly ties with the United States. (Khatami would later call for a "dialogue among civilizations.") Khatami's main audience was Iran's youth. By the middle of the 1990s, half the Iranian population had been born after the 1979 revolution. Surveys showed massive disaffection with Iran's political system on the part of young people, with more than 80 percent expressing minimal religious inclinations and a greater interest in trendy fashions and sex. Unexpectedly, Khatami captured 70 percent of the vote.

The new president assumed office with little decision-making power. The judiciary, the military, the Revolutionary Guards, and other instruments of coercive power answered to the Supreme Leader, not to Khatami. Iran's conservative clerics continued to exercise dominant power. A number of the new president's followers were harassed, tortured, and even murdered on orders from the religious hierarchy. One of them, the former mayor of Tehran, was convicted of graft and sentenced to sixty lashes and five years in prison. Other reformers were gunned down by officially sanctioned murder squads. Still, President Khatami's popularity held steady, enabling him to wring a few concessions from the ruling authorities. Women, for example, were increasingly allowed to ignore the official Islamic dress code. But when the Majles passed a law limiting press freedoms on July 8, 1999, and a pro-reform newspaper was shut down, two hundred students staged a public protest.

At 2:30 the next morning, government security forces burst into a student housing compound at the University of Tehran. A rampage ensued as the invading units, accompanied by pro-regime vigilantes, set fire to dorm rooms and bludgeoned students as they slept. As word of the assault got around town during the day, crowds of students and their supporters swarmed into the streets, setting tires ablaze and erecting barricades. Students launched a counterattack on the university compound, driving out the police forces. The student uprising lasted a week. After spreading to other campuses around the country, it ran into the determination of the ruling authorities to stop it. The hardline leadership denounced the demonstrations as the work of "infiltrators" and American spies. As hundreds of thousands of armed supporters of the regime took over the streets of Tehran—shouting "Death to counterrevolutionaries!"—the government clamped martial law on the city. Five students were reportedly killed in the weeklong confrontation and 1,400 were arrested.[29]

Khatami did not join in the conservatives' denunciations of the protesters as spies. But his call for law and order disappointed some of his young supporters and demonstrated the limits of his ability—or willingness—to defy the religious conservatives. Nevertheless, in early 2000 the pro-reform Iran Participation Front and other reformers won a resounding victory in parliamentary elections, giving the forces for change a decisive majority in the 290-member Majles. About 4 percent of the members of the new Majles were women.

In June 2001, Khatami was reelected president, handily defeating nine other handpicked candidates with 76 percent of the vote. Once again, youth and women flocked to his candidacy. Two-thirds of Iran's population of 65 million were now under 30, and the minimum voting age of 16 made young voters the majority of the electorate. Young people were also better educated than their parents' generation. But the religious authorities made it clear that they would retain the upper hand. Soon after the election, they ordered public floggings of young men who were caught consuming alcohol, owning Western CDs, or associating in public with women to whom they were not related. Khatami condemned the bloody spectacles, but he continued to temper his calls for the rule of law and democratic principles with pleas for patience and moderation. His ultimate goal appeared to be a kind of religious democracy, combining democratic freedoms with some role for religious authority.

President Khatami had a difficult time getting the more powerful clerics to approve his proposals for reform, however. Iran's conservative religious hierarchy dealt the president a particularly harsh blow in June 2003 when the Council of Guardians rejected a bill passed by the Majles that would have given Khatami the authority to call referendums on measures aimed at strengthening his own presidential powers and at eliminating the Council's right to screen all candidates running for the parliament.

By the time preparations were under way for the 2004 parliamentary elections, advocates of democratic reforms were more dispirited than ever. Many of them expressed open disdain for President Khatami's preference for dialogue with regime hardliners as opposed to more emphatic confrontation. As a pall of resignation set in, the Council of Guardians dealt the reformers another setback by barring 3,600 out of 8,000 potential candidates for the 290-seat national legislature, the Majles. Later the number of banned applicants was reduced to about 2,400, a minor concession that still prevented most reform-oriented hopefuls from running, including 80 Majles incumbents. President Khatami's own brother, the leader of Iran's largest reform party, was among those stricken from the applicant lists. Declaring that the elections would not be "legal and free," the would-be candidate announced that his party would boycott the elections. President Khatami himself proclaimed that the vote would not be fair, but he agreed to go ahead with the balloting anyway, disappointing those who urged him to cancel the "sham" elections. More than 120 Majles deputies resigned even before the elections took place. A number of them addressed a letter to Supreme Leader Khamenei, accusing him of running "a system in which legitimate freedoms and the rights of the people are being trampled in the name of Islam."

When election day arrived in February, only half the country's 46 million eligible voters trooped to the polls, a steep drop from the 67 percent turnout in 2000. In Tehran, fewer than 30 percent bothered to vote. As expected, conservatives opposed to fundamental change won a decisive majority in the Majles. But the widespread boycott of the vote undermined the ruling elite's claim to popular legitimacy. Following their victory, the conservatives launched a new offensive against the advocates of reform, closing down more pro-reform newspapers (bringing the total of closures in recent years to more than a hundred), imposing new censorship laws on Internet usage, and sequestering satellite dishes. With the aid of pro-regime vigilante groups like Ansar-i-Hezbollah and the Basij, the government cracked down anew on "social corruption" by arresting women who were not covered in Islamic attire and harassing unmarried men and women seen together in public.

The twelve women represented in the new Majles—all allied with the conservative hierarchy—joined with the majority in voting down bills aimed at improving the legal status of Iranian women in accordance with the United Nations convention banning discrimination against women. At least one female deputy spoke out in favor of polygamy, which is permitted under Islamic law in Iran but widely scorned by the population. The precarious status of women in Iran was underscored in August 2004 when a sixteen-year-old girl was hanged on charges of adultery. The man who was her alleged partner was sentenced to a hundred lashes. Nevertheless, 60 percent of Iran's university students are women. Quite a few women take advantage of periodic lulls in the authorities' enforcement of Islamic social codes by dressing as they wish and associating with men in public, defying the most puritanical authorities. And one of Iran's most prominent women, human rights lawyer Chirine Ebadi, won the Nobel Peace Prize in 2003, much to the consternation of the archconservatives.[30]

The 2005 presidential elections enabled the religious conservatives to press their freshly won advantages. More than a thousand people applied to run in the first round of the two-round election, but the Council of Guardians initially rejected all but six, accepting only one moderately reformist candidate. Outgoing president Khatami warned that "only a large turnout can give legitimacy to the regime," a fact that may have induced Supreme Leader Khamenei to pressure the Guardians into putting two previously disqualified applicants onto the first-round ballot. After a conservative candidate dropped out, seven candidates remained in contention on election day. The results of the first round of voting were a shock even to election officials. As expected, former president Rafsanjani, who sank $5 million into his campaigns, came in first, garnering 21 percent of the vote. But Tehran's hardline mayor, Mahmoud Ahmadinejad, stunned the field by finishing second with 19.5 percent. As the vote count proceeded through the night, the main reformist candidate, Mostafa Moin, was running second behind Rafsanjani, as projected by exit polls. But with the Council of Guardians carefully supervising the secret count, Ahmadinejad jumped into second place by dawn, prompting President Khatami to accuse "some centers of power" of "violating the law" by using the Guardians to boost Ahmadinejad's candidacy. Another candidate charged that the government's ultraconservative Revolutionary Guards and armed pro-regime militias had intimidated voters on election day into voting for Ahmadinejad.

The second-round runoff between Ahmadinejad and Rafsanjani gave reformists nothing to cheer about. Rafsanjani sought to portray himself as a pragmatic reformer, but his record as a conservative president in the 1990s—a period marked by Islamic puritanism as well as official corruption—undermined his reformist credentials. Students subjected him to tough questions about his past record when he appeared at the University of Tehran during the campaign. When the final ballots were tallied after the June 24 vote, Ahmadinejad had won 61.7 percent and Rafsanjani 35.9 percent. Turnout was about 60 percent—higher than expected but lower than in the two previous presidential elections.[31]

Ahmadinejad had started out as a pro-Khomeini militant in 1979. (It was unclear whether he had played any role in the U.S. embassy hostage crisis.) He was the only candidate to refer to the 1979 revolution during the campaign. Subsequently he served with the Revolutionary Guards—the regime's watchdogs of Islamic purity—during the war with Iraq, and he later worked as an instructor for a pro-regime militia, the Basij. He was appointed mayor of Tehran in 2003. After assuming the presidency, Ahmadinejad quickly caught the world's attention with a hard-hitting speech at the United Nations, brusquely rebuffing U.S. and European attempts to stop Iran from producing enriched uranium. The following month he captured headlines again by repeating Ayatollah Khomeini's assertion that "Israel must be wiped off the map." Later he said that the Holocaust was a "myth."

Although Ahmadinejad's determination to stand up to the world's great powers may stoke Iranian national pride, ultimately his presidency may stand or fall on his handling of the economy. Ahmadinejad owed his election not so much to his fervent religious orthodoxy or foreign policy stance, but rather to his populist appeal to Iran's vast working-class and lower-middle-class populations, most of whom live in poverty. (*Populism* is a political orientation aimed at addressing the anti-elitist resentments of the underprivileged.) He was the only candidate to bash the country's rich minority and extol the Islamic virtues of economic equality and social justice. His campaign video, which displayed his modest house and furnishings, stood in marked contrast to the lavish lifestyles of Rafsanjani and other highly placed clerics, winning him votes among millions of ordinary Iranians. In his first year in office, President Ahmadinejad barnstormed the country, speaking to throngs of citizens who voiced grateful approval of his promises to improve their living standards. "It's good to have a very kind person near you, caring about your problems," said one devoted follower. Ahmadinejad has raised high expectations for economic change—for better health care, more housing loans, and higher incomes—that could backfire on him if he fails to deliver.

The president has his work cut out for him. Although rising world oil prices produced a one-year windfall of about $50 billion by mid-2006—double the 2004 figure—Iran's annual economic growth was only about 5 percent, not enough to meet the country's anticipated needs. The inflation rate (the average rate of price increases) topped 13 percent in 2006. Ahmadinejad's budget proposal for 2007 was ripped apart in the conservative-dominated parliament. Lawmakers feared that his plans to siphon large sums of state money into development projects around the country, combined with his generous funding of the Revolutionary Guards, would only increase the government's bulging deficit. Increased government spending also increases the demand for various goods, and higher demand produces higher prices. A steeper inflation rate would further weaken the average Iranian's meager purchasing power. The Iranian government already spends $25 billion a year on subsidies to reduce consumer prices for staples like rice, flour, and even gasoline. Any substantial increase in prices for these or other essentials could provoke an outburst of public discontent.

Unemployment is another problem. The country's official unemployment rate of 12 percent (representing 3 million unemployed) is probably lower than the true figure. Bleak job prospects for many young Iranians, both the educated and the poorly educated, have fostered boredom and the world's highest opium addiction rate. The private sector, which employs 80 percent of Iranians, is starved for investment funds. But the bulk of the economy is controlled by the theocratic state, which has not provided enough loans to energize private businesses so that they can expand and hire more people. Legislation passed by the conservative Majles since 2004 has made the investment climate in Iran quite unattractive to foreign companies that might want to do business there, and this has also limited the creation of new jobs.[32]

As debates on how to improve the economy intensify, ideological differences appear to be deepening, even at the top of the country's religious hierarchy. The most zealous Islamic conservatives stand behind Ahmadinejad. One ayatollah with close ties to the president created a furor when he said that Iran's voters were irrelevant because the government has God's approval; future elections, he suggested, were therefore unnecessary. A more moderate official allied with Supreme Leader Khamenei condemned this view, likening its proponents to the Taliban and al Qaeda. Pragmatic conservatives with flexible ideas on the rights of women and relations with the West are present not only in the upper reaches of state officialdom but also among the clergy. Several respected ayatollahs residing in the holy city of Qom have come out openly in favor of democracy, including the rights of women. They are pinning their hopes on Iran's youth, who are the vast majority of the population. Pro-democracy sentiments are rife in this rising generation, as attested by the growing number of bloggers who are building networks inside Iran and disseminating their calls for change at home and around the world. (It is estimated that there are 75,000 bloggers in Iran.) Meanwhile, efforts by the Bush administration to promote democracy in Iran via a proposed new satellite television station and educational activities have run up against resistance from the Iranian government. In 2006 the authorities jailed two democracy activists who attended a U.S-sponsored human rights workshop in Dubai the previous year.[33]

With political and economic pressures on the theocratic regime mounting inside Iran, international pressures are growing as well. The confrontation between Iran and the world's nuclear powers over the development of uranium enrichment capabilities has oscillated between threats of intransigence and hints of a negotiated agreement. The West fears that a hostile Iranian regime armed with nuclear weapons would be a serious danger, especially if it gave nuclear devices to terrorist groups. (Iran was expected to have the ability to build a nuclear bomb by around 2011.) Iran's official position is that it is seeking to develop its own nuclear capacity solely for peaceful purposes, in accordance with the Nuclear Non-Proliferation Treaty. Despite its vast oil reserves, Iran lacks adequate refineries, and it consumes nearly half of the 4 million barrels of oil it produces each day. As a consequence, Iranian officials maintain that Iran needs nuclear reactors to generate electricity. In recent years, however, Iran has concealed certain aspects of its nuclear development program from the International Atomic Energy Agency, raising suspicions that it is producing weapons-grade nuclear material.

Although the Bush administration has refused to rule out possible military action against an Iranian nuclear-weapons capacity, in the spring of 2006 the United States joined with Britain, France, Germany, Russia, and China in offering Iran a deal. Reportedly, the offer involved a number of economic rewards—including assistance in developing nuclear energy for electricity—in exchange for Iran's agreement to refrain from producing nuclear weapons. It also specified a number of punitive measures that might be undertaken by the United Nations should Iran move ahead with the production of nuclear weapons. (Apparently the proposal did not threaten an oil embargo, considering that Europe and China import some of their oil from Iran.) Shortly after Iran received these proposals, Supreme Leader Khamenei created a new advisory organ, the Strategic Committee for Foreign Policy, to facilitate decision making and "find new horizons" in the government's approach to foreign affairs. Khamenei's action was interpreted as a victory for moderates in the Iranian hierarchy and a blow against President Ahmadinejad and his hardline faction. But speculation about an impending positive response to the proposed deal on nuclear power came to an abrupt halt in midsummer amid an eruption of hostilities in the Middle East.

On July 12, members of the Hezbollah militia in Lebanon crossed the border into Israel, killing three Israeli soldiers and kidnapping two others. Hezbollah also launched rocket attacks on Israel's last remaining military outpost in Lebanon and on an Israeli town. Israel responded immediately by moving troops and tanks into southern Lebanon and bombing bridges connecting the region to the rest of the country. The next day, Hezbollah fired more rockets into Israel, killing two civilians. Dozens of Lebanese civilians were killed in Israel's initial operations. A full-scale war suddenly exploded.

Hezbollah ("Party of God") had been established in 1982 through the collaboration of militant Lebanese Shiite clerics and Iran's Ayatollah Khomeini. Both sides were determined to oppose the recent Israeli invasion of Lebanon and raise the political clout of Lebanon's large Shiite population (see the section on Lebanon in chapter 2). Over the ensuing decades Iran remained Hezbollah's principal sponsor, supplying its vast military arsenal (including some fourteen thousand short-range Katyusha rockets) along with generous funding for the organization's network of hospitals, schools, and other services for Lebanon's Shia population. Iran also provided military training for Hezbollah fighters.

As hostilities quickly escalated in the summer of 2006, it was not clear why Iran might have prompted Hezbollah to initiate the conflict. (Hezbollah's leader, Hassan Nasrallah, stated at the start of the fighting that he did not want a war, but just an exchange of the kidnapped Israeli soldiers for three Hezbollah prisoners in Israel.) Conceivably the hardliners around President Ahmadinejad were seeking to torpedo a potential agreement with the West on nuclear power. After a cease-fire brokered by the United Nations Security Council took effect in Lebanon in late summer, Iran presented its long-awaited counterproposal. The Iranians rejected the main elements of the deal they had been offered in the spring. Instead, they proposed a plan that would allow them to proceed with their uranium enrichment program without providing any firm guarantee that they would refrain from building nuclear weapons. By the end of 2006 the issue still was not resolved to the satisfaction of the United States and its partners. Meanwhile, the United States was concerned not only about a potential Iranian nuclear weapons capacity and Iran's support of Hezbollah, but also about Iran's support for Shiite militants in Iraq who are opposed to cooperating with the United States or with other Iraqis in building a viable democracy there (see the section on Iraq in chapter 10).

How these various domestic and international problems are dealt with will depend in great measure on who has power in Iran in the coming years. Will the most extreme Islamic elements widen their grip on decision making, or will more flexible conservatives overrule them? Will the regime be paralyzed by continuous infighting? Will truly democratic forces gain the upper hand, or precipitate mass unrest? What should the United States and its allies do with respect to Iran? Should they openly support the democratic forces, or will such a proactive approach create an adverse reaction against outside interference? Will tough action against Iran's nuclear program drive the reformist forces and the conservative clerics closer together in defense of their country? However these questions are answered in the years ahead, it is unquestionable that the struggle for power inside Iran will have major implications for the rest of the world.

---

This chapter has shown that power permeates political life. In one way or another, it plays a vital role in all the countries we will examine in this book.

## KEY TERMS
## (In bold and underlined in the text)

Political power
Political elites
Dominance
Political influence
Legitimacy
Autocracy
Oligarchy
Totalitarianism
Democratic elitism
Political corruption

## NOTES

1. *New York Times*, 21 May 2006.
2. For a comparison of power and money, see Karl W. Deutsch, *The Nerves of Government* (New York: Free Press, 1966), 120–22; and Robert E. Lane, "Experiencing Money and Experiencing Power," in *Power, Inequality, and Democratic Politics*, ed. Ian Shapiro and Grant Reeher (Boulder, Colo.: Westview Press, 1988), 80–105.
3. For books that deal with power in international relations, see the classic study by Hans J. Morgenthau, *Politics Among Nations*, 6th ed. (New York: Knopf, 1985); Michael P. Sullivan, *Power in Contemporary International Politics* (Columbia: University of South Carolina Press, 1990); and Joseph S. Nye, Jr., *Soft Power: The Means to Success in World Politics* (New York: Public Affairs, 2004).
4. Harold Lasswell, *Politics: Who Gets What, When, and How* (New York: McGraw-Hill, 1936).
5. Robert A. Dahl, *Modern Political Analysis*, 5th ed. (Englewood Cliffs, N.J.: 1991), 12, 32. Dahl stresses the similarities between power and influence. See his discussion in chapters 2–4. For a contrary view emphasizing the distinctions between power and influence, see Peter Morriss, *Power: A Philosophical Analysis* (New York: St. Martin's Press, 1987), 8–13, 23–24. Edward C. Banfield defines influence as "the ability to get others to act, think, or feel as one intends" and power as "the ability to exercise control over another." He regards the term *influence* as "a generic term including authority, control, and power." See his *Political Influence* (New York: Free Press, 1961), 3, 348n. For a sophisticated attempt to measure power in quantitative terms, see Jack H. Nagel, *The Descriptive Analysis of Power* (New Haven: Yale University Press, 1975). See also Harold Lasswell and Abraham Kaplan, *Power in Society: A Framework for Inquiry* (New Haven: Yale University Press, 1950).
6. C. Wright Mills, *The Power Elite* (London: Oxford University Press, 1956); and G. William Domhoff, *Who Rules America? A View for the '80s* (Englewood Cliffs, N.J.: Prentice Hall, 1983), *The Power Elite and the State* (New York: Aldine de Gruyter, 1990), *State Autonomy or Class Dominance?* (New York: Aldine de Gruyter, 1996), and *Who Rules America? Power and Politics in the Year 2000*, 3rd ed. (Mountain View, Calif.: Mayfield, 1998). See also Albrecht Rothacher, *The Japanese Power Elite* (New York: St. Martin's Press, 1993). For more generalized critiques of power elites in democracies, see Steven Lukes, *Power: A Radical View* (London: Macmillan, 1974); and Thomas E. Wartenberg, ed., *Rethinking Power* (Albany: State University of New York Press, 1992). For some opposing views, see Nelson Polsby, *Community Power and Political Theory* (New Haven: Yale University Press, 1963), and Jack E. Walker, "A Critique of the Elitist Theory of Democracy," *American Political Science Review* 60 (1966): 285–95.

7. Harold Lasswell hypothesized that people seek political power to overcome low self-esteem brought on by unloving or excessively demanding parents, physical handicaps, economic deprivation, or other psychological factors. See *Power and Personality* (New York: W. W. Norton, 1948) and *Psychopathology and Politics* (New York: Viking, 1960).
8. James MacGregor Burns, *Leadership* (New York: Harper & Row, 1978). See also F. G. Baily, *Humbuggery and Manipulation: The Art of Leadership* (Ithaca, N.Y.: Cornell University Press, 1988), and Ruth Ann Wilner, *The Spellbinders: Charismatic Political Leadership* (New Haven: Yale University Press, 1984).
9. Niccolò Machiavelli, *The Prince,* trans. George Bull (Baltimore, Md.: Penguin, 1961), 101.
10. Herbert P. Bix, *Hirohito and the Making of Modern Japan* (New York: HarperCollins, 2000), 560ff.; John W. Dower, *Embracing Defeat: Japan in the Wake of World War II* (New York: W. W. Norton, 1999), 308ff.
11. Max Weber, *On Charisma and Institution Building: Selected Papers,* ed. S. N. Eisenstadt (Chicago: University of Chicago Press, 1968).
12. On the concept of totalitarianism, see Abbott Gleason, *Totalitarianism: The Inner History of the Cold War* (New York: Oxford University Press, 1995); Hannah Arendt, *The Origins of Totalitarianism* (New York: Harcourt, Brace, & World, 1968); and Carl J. Friedrich and Zbigniew K. Brzezinski, *Totalitarian Dictatorship and Autocracy* (New York: Praeger, 1961).
13. Classics include José Ortega y Gasset, *The Revolt of the Masses* (New York: Norton, 1957); Erich Fromm, *Escape from Freedom* (New York: Avon, 1971); and William Kornhauser, *The Politics of Mass Society* (New York: Free Press, 1969).
14. See Joseph J. Ellis, *Founding Brothers: The Revolutionary Generation* (New York: Knopf, 2001); and Robert A. Dahl, *How Democratic Is the American Constitution?* (New Haven: Yale University Press, 2002).
15. Peter Bachrach, *The Theory of Democratic Elitism: A Critique* (Boston: Little, Brown, 1967); Joseph Schumpeter, *Capitalism, Socialism, and Democracy,* 3rd ed. (New York: Harper & Row, 1950).
16. Herbert McCloskey and Alida Brill, *Dimensions of Tolerance: What Americans Believe About Civil Liberties* (New York: Russell Sage Foundation, 1983).
17. Robert Dahl, *Who Governs?* (New Haven: Yale University Press, 1961).
18. Dahl's findings did not go unchallenged. Peter Bachrach and Morton S. Baratz argued that Dahl had failed to consider decisions that the New Haven government did *not* make because the local business elite would have disapproved of them. Such behind-the-scenes influence, they argued, constitutes a real form of power that can result in "nondecisions" by government officials. See Peter Bachrach and Morton S. Baratz, "Two Faces of Power," *American Political Science Review* 56, no. 4 (December 1962): 947–52. See also, by the same authors, "Decisions and Nondecisions: An Analytical Framework," *American Political Science Review* 57, no. 3 (September 1963): 632–42. See also Geoffrey Debnam, "Nondecisions and Power: The Two Faces of Bachrach and Baratz," *American Political Science Review* 69, no. 3 (September 1975): 889–904, followed by replies.
19. The passage quoted here is from *The Federalist,* Number 51.
20. James C. Scott, *Comparative Political Corruption* (Englewood Cliffs, N.J.: Prentice Hall, 1972). Also Susan Rose-Ackerman, *Corruption and Government* (Cambridge: Cambridge University Press, 1999).
21. See the discussion of torture on Amnesty International's website at www.amnestyusa.org/stoptorture/about.html. For the 1984 UN Convention, consult www.ohchr.org. Consult also the World Organization Against Torture at www.omct.org. See the Human Rights Watch report on Abu Ghraib at hrw.org/reports/2005/us0905; also Karen J. Greenberg and Joshua L. Dratel, *The Torture Papers* (New York: Cambridge University Press, 2005). On rendition, see the *Washington Post,* June 8, 2006. Also Kenneth Roth and Minky Worden, eds., *Torture: Does It Make Us Safer? Is It Ever OK? A Human Rights Perspective* (New York: New Press, 2005), and Michael Ignatieff, *The Lesser Evil: Political Ethics in an Age of Terror* (Princeton: Princeton University Press, 2004).

**22.** James C. Scott, *Weapons of the Weak: Everyday Forms of Peasant Resistance* (New Haven: Yale University Press, 1985) and *Domination and the Arts of Resistance: Hidden Transcripts* (New Haven: Yale University Press, 1990).

**23.** *Financial Times*, May 10, 2006.

**24.** *Washington Post*, June 17, 2005.

**25.** See Robin Wright's analysis in the *Washington Post*, November 29, 2004. Also Mehdi Moslem, *Factional Politics in Post-Khomeini Iran* (Syracuse, N.Y.: Syracuse University Press, 2002), and "God's Rule, or Man's? A Survey of Iran," *The Economist*, January 18, 2003.

**26.** Stephen Kinzer, *All the Shah's Men: An American Coup and the Roots of Middle East Terror* (New York: John Wiley, 2003); Kermit Roosevelt, *Countercoup: The Struggle for the Control of Iran* (New York: McGraw-Hill, 1979).

**27.** Ervand Abrahamian, *Iran Between Two Revolutions* (Princeton: Princeton University Press, 1982); Gary Sick, *All Fall Down: America's Fateful Encounter with Iran* (New York: Random House, 1985).

**28.** Daniel Brumberg, *Reinventing Khomeini: The Struggle for Reform in Iran* (Chicago: University of Chicago Press, 2001).

**29.** For an eyewitness account, see Behzad Yaghmaian, *Social Change in Iran* (Albany: State University of New York Press, 2002).

**30.** *New York Times*, September 19, 2004; *Washington Post*, September 12, 2004. On women's issues, see Azar Nafisi, *Reading Lolita in Tehran: A Memoir in Books* (New York: Random House, 2003); Jane Mary Howard, *Inside Iran: Women's Lives* (Washington, D.C.: Mage, 2002); Hammed Shahidan, *Women in Iran: Gender Politics in the Islamic Republic* (Westport, Conn.: Greenwood, 2002); and Mahnaz Kousha, *Voices from Iran: Changing Lives of Iranian Women* (Syracuse, N.Y.: Syracuse University Press, 2002). See also Elaine Sciolino, *Persian Mirrors: The Elusive Face of Iran* (New York: Simon and Schuster, 2000), and Robin Wright, *The Last Great Revolution: Turmoil and Transformation in Iran* (New York: Vintage, 2001).

**31.** See the discussion "Iran's Peculiar Election," *Journal of Democracy* 16, no. 4 (October 2005): 9–82.

**32.** *Washington Post*, November 14 and 19, 2004, November 24, 2005, March 6 and April 21, 2006; *Financial Times*, July 12, 2005, and March 2, 2006; and *The Economist*, May 6, 2006.

**33.** *Washington Post*, March 14, March 26, and May 11, 2006. Also see Nasrin Alavi, ed. and trans., *We Are Iran: The Persian Blogs* (Brooklyn, N.Y.: Soft Skull Press, 2005).

CHAPTER 5

# THE STATE AND ITS INSTITUTIONS

## DEFINING THE STATE

Thus far we have used the term *government* as a synonym for the state. When discussing government in general, political scientists tend to prefer the *state* as a generic term encompassing all the governmental institutions within an individual country. As we shall see, defining the state can be complicated, and scholars offer a variety of definitional approaches. In its simplest, most commonly understood definition,

> ***The <u>state</u> is the totality of a country's governmental institutions and officials, together with the laws and procedures that structure their activities.***

The state's *institutions* are governmental organizations that typically perform specified functions on the basis of laws, rules, directives, and other authoritative procedures and practices. Cabinets, legislatures, courts, the bureaucracy, the military, the police, public schools and colleges, your local trash removal department—these and similar bodies are all parts of the state and act as its agents. The regulations and operating principles that guide their operations are also part of the state. These include such things as the country's constitution and laws; the rules and customary practices that specify how the legislature and courts work; the procedures governing how bureaucrats are recruited and what they do; military command procedures; and so on.

The most important feature of the state that distinguishes it from other entities—such as social groups or private firms—is that *the state monopolizes legal authority.* In other words, *only the state possesses the legal authority to make, and coercively enforce, laws that are binding on the population.* This legal authority makes the state's decisions "authoritative." By "coercively enforce," we mean that the state has the legal authority to use physical force, if it has to, to compel the population to obey the law. To this end it seeks to monopolize the main means of coercive power—the police, the courts, the penal system, and the military.

If the state loses its monopoly of coercive power and is seriously challenged by domestic groups or individuals who routinely ignore its laws, then it is a *failed state.* A **<u>failed state</u>** ***is a state that has little or no ability to govern its entire territory.*** In most cases, failed states do not provide basic security or services for large parts of the population. They are often confronted by organized groups that possess their own means of violence. Civil war or random chaos rages as central authority breaks down. A sizable element of the population may reject the legitimacy of the government in power or the political regime in its entirety. In some instances, what

**TABLE 5.1**

**States in Critical Condition**

The Failed States Index ranks countries in order of their vulnerability to failure, based on twelve sets of indicators that include demographic pressures, refugees and human flight, economic problems, the delegitimization of the state, factionalized elites, the degradation of public services, human rights violations, security problems, and external intervention. The rankings presented here were based on 2005 data. The Index was prepared by the Fund for Peace and *Foreign Policy* magazine. Part of the 2005 list was published in *Foreign Policy*, May–June 2006. For updates and further information, consult www.fundforpeace.org and www.ForegnPolicy.com. Three states that share the same rank on the list below have identical scores.

1. Sudan
2. Democratic Republic of Congo
3. Ivory Coast
4. Iraq
5. Zimbabwe
6. Chad
6. Somalia
8. Haiti
9. Pakistan
10. Afghanistan
11. Guinea
11. Liberia
13. Central African Republic
14. North Korea
15. Burundi
16. Yemen
16. Sierra Leone
18. Burma
19. Bangladesh
20. Nepal

remains of the state may be captured by gangster-like elements who plunder its resources and use deadly force to impose their rule over the population. Local warlords, drug cartels, rogue militias, or bandits may carve up the countryside and assert their control over local territories. Table 5.1 lists twenty countries, ranked in order of their vulnerability to failure on the basis of the Failed States Index. Out of 148 countries covered in 2005, the twenty listed here were in "critical" condition: they met most or all of the criteria for a failed state. Forty additional states were categorized as being either "in danger" of failure or "borderline"—states that we may describe generically as "weak states." Although the distinction between a "failed state" and a "weak state" may be fuzzy at times, the fact that so many states in today's world are highly vulnerable to some form of breakdown is strikingly evident.[1]

Although governmental institutions form the core of our basic definition of the state, some political scientists argue for a more expansive conception that would include certain nongovernmental organizations or groups that are very closely connected to governmental authorities and have a major impact on what they do. In Saddam Hussein's Iraq, for example, the Baath Party was not, strictly speaking, a governmental institution; yet it was so tightly integrated into Saddam's regime that it was for all practical purposes a part of his state apparatus. In contemporary China, the Chinese Communist Party is tightly intertwined with the country's governmental institutions and activities and exercises superior authority over them.

Marxists traditionally contend that, in capitalist countries, the big-business elite so completely dominates government decision makers that the state is essentially "the guardian and protector" of this economically powerful social class. At least some Marxists contend that the capitalist "ruling class" is part of the "state system."[2] Many non-Marxists would dispute this co-identification of the state and the capitalist class. Nevertheless, as all the preceding cases demonstrate, the dividing line between "state" and "non-state" may sometimes be blurry.

## THREE MEANINGS OF "STATE"

The definition of the "state" as the totality of a country's governmental institutions and officials represents only one way in which the term *state* is used in political science. As we pointed out in chapter 1, *state* is also used as a synonym for an entire country. Strictly speaking, a state in international affairs is a government that has authority over a national population living in a specified territory. In this sense, the United States, Japan, Mexico, and South Africa are all "states"; relations between their respective governments are "interstate relations." In a third usage, *state* is sometimes used to designate an administrative subdivision within certain countries. The United States of America has fifty states. Germany has sixteen *Laender*, a term translated into English as "states."

## SOVEREIGNTY, LEGITIMACY, AUTONOMY, AND PURPOSES OF THE STATE

**Sovereignty** One of the key attributes of a state is *sovereignty*. In its classic definition,

> **sovereignty** ***means the exclusive legal authority of a government over its population and territory, independent of external authorities.***

In other words, a state is sovereign to the extent that it monopolizes the exercise of governmental authority at home, rejecting the right of foreign states or other external actors to impose their own laws from the outside or interfere in its domestic political order. Traditionally, one of the most common ways for a state to bolster its sovereignty is by entering into formal diplomatic relations with other states on the basis of the mutual recognition of each other's sovereign rights.

This conception of sovereignty, which has its roots in the emergence of the modern state system in seventeenth- and eighteenth-century Europe, is accepted by most governments in today's world as a fundamental principle of international law. The officials of most national governments will vigorously defend their state's sovereignty when they feel it is being undermined. But like the European state system from which it sprang, sovereignty isn't what it used to be. Sovereignty is not a timeless concept that never changes. On the contrary, sovereignty is "socially constructed": it is shaped and defined by the specific mixture of domestic and international factors that affect individual countries, or groups of countries, at different periods of history. Europe itself provides a vivid illustration of how sovereignty has changed in today's lattice-like, interdependent world. Since the 1950s, a growing number of European states have voluntarily relinquished some of their sovereign rights to determine their own economic policy and other policies that were formerly reserved to the exclusive competence of domestic authorities. In an effort to promote economic growth, environmental cooperation, and other mutual benefits, European governments have established integrated Europe-wide institutions and engaged in joint decision-making procedures, establishing what has been described as a system of "pooled sovereignty." These efforts culminated in the formation of the European Union (EU), which in 2007 included twenty-seven countries. (We'll describe the EU in greater detail in chapter 6.) Other states around the world have not gone quite as far as the EU in the direction of shared sovereignty. Nevertheless, most governments find it increasingly difficult to keep out unwanted foreign influences like information on the Internet or pressures from foreign states. For many states it is also difficult to avoid the intrusion of international organizations (like the International Monetary Fund) or rules (like World Trade Organization rulings). Though sovereignty is still highly valued around the world—even in EU countries, which still retain sovereign rights in sensitive areas like foreign policy—the forces of globalization are constantly chipping away at its walls.[3]

**Legitimacy** Another important aspect of states is *legitimacy*. As we noted in chapter 4, *legitimacy is the right to rule*. For Max Weber, legitimacy is central to the very definition of the state. In his famous formulation, the state "is a human community that (successfully) claims the *monopoly of the legitimate use of physical force* within a given territory."[4] Weber's use of the term *legitimate* implies that only the state has the *right* to employ force or to authorize others to use it. Thus the state may outlaw private militias and regulate private security companies. But what if the state is regarded as illegitimate in the eyes of its people? Weber's definition suggests that the people may have a right to use force against a government that they cannot remove in any other way. His notion that the state "claims" a monopoly on the legitimate use of force further suggests that it may not be successful in getting the people (or perhaps some component of the population) to accept its claim.

**Autonomy** The concept of the **autonomy of the state** refers to the *relative independence of state authorities from the population*. If the state enjoys a high degree of autonomy, then state officials are quite free to do what they please when it comes to governing the populace. By contrast, a low degree of state autonomy means that state officials have very little room to create laws or make decisions independently of the population as a whole or—as is more likely—independently of its politically most powerful groups. Both extremes have dangers. Maximum state autonomy means dictatorship: the people have little or no say in what their rulers do. Minimum state autonomy implies that state officials have few opportunities to use their expertise and concern for the country's common good to formulate and implement the policies they think best. Instead, they may have to cater to the wishes of society's dominant or most influential individuals and groups. A truly representative democracy, by contrast, would seek to avoid the pitfalls of too much or not enough state autonomy, giving state decision makers enough latitude to govern effectively while holding them accountable to the population for their actions.

**The Purposes of the State** Why have a state? What should it do? The question of the state's ultimate purposes has provoked considerable debate down through the centuries. Some theorists have argued that the state's primary function should be to guarantee order and security. To this end *Thomas Hobbes* (1588–1679) proposed that the people should form a kind of social contract ("covenant") with the leaders of an all-powerful state, which he called "Leviathan." The state's main purpose would be to leave humanity free to pursue science, art, exploration, and other aspects of civilization without the pressures of "continual fear, and danger of violent death."[5]

*John Locke* (1632–1704)—like Hobbes, an Oxford graduate—also favored the idea of a social contract between the people and state authorities, but for aims that were very different from those laid out by Hobbes. Locke argued in his *Second Treatise of Government* (1689) that human beings are born free. Individuals enjoy a natural right to life, liberty, and "estate" (their possessions)—assets that together constitute, in Locke's formulation, one's "property." "The great and *chief end,* therefore, of men's putting themselves under government," Locke declared, *"is the preservation of their property."* Any state that failed to safeguard these natural rights was illegitimate. Accordingly, Locke favored a representative democracy established "by common consent," with an elected legislature constituting the highest political authority. Locke placed special emphasis on the state's responsibility to safeguard the rights and freedoms of the individual. His ideas had an enormous impact on the founding fathers of the American Revolution.[6]

Swiss philosopher *Jean-Jacques Rousseau* (1712–78), a third great "social contract" theorist, advanced yet another set of ideas about the ultimate aims of government. In contrast to Locke's emphasis on individual rights and freedoms, Rousseau stressed the *collective* rights and freedoms of the community. In his view, the people—not the state—are "the sovereign"; together they form an organic "body politic" on the basis of a "general will," which is the common good. For each individual to be free from tyranny, the community as a whole must be free. The liberty of each depends on the liberty of all, a notion that requires each individual to conform to the general will. Rousseau recommended that "whoever refuses to obey the general will shall be constrained to do so by the whole body; which means nothing else than that he shall be forced to be free." Even the individual's right to private property "is always subordinate to the right which the community has over all." In Rousseau's vision, the chief purpose of the state is to enable the sovereign people to express and carry out their general will. In practical terms, he believed that this goal could be accomplished by a small elite making day-to-day decisions, as long as the citizens (which in his day meant property-owning males) exercised their supervisory authority by meeting periodically in popular assemblies.[7]

In contrast to the prescriptions of the social contract theorists, most modern states were fashioned out of brute force rather than the consent of the governed. Countries like China, Japan, Russia, France, and England developed into powerful, centralized states over the course of centuries of internal turmoil, with rival clans, dynasties, warlords, or other combatants clashing over the ultimate prize—the government of the realm. Violent contention for control of the state did not die down until the eighteenth century in Britain, the nineteenth century in Japan and France, and the twentieth century in China and Russia. Once the winning faction was entrenched in power, its chief purpose was to use the state to expand its control over the domestic population and, in many cases, to make war on foreign adversaries. The early modern state was in large measure an authoritarian warfare state.[8]

Over time, states acquired purposes that were more attuned to the wishes of the population, or at least to the wishes of its most politically influential parts. *Adam Smith* (1723–90), the Scottish philosopher who is considered the father of modern free-market economics, argued in *The Wealth of Nations* (1776) that the state's chief purpose should be to promote private enterprise and allow the forces of the market economy to work without excessive government interference. In Smith's view, the state should limit itself to providing a legal system designed to enable commerce to flow smoothly and to undertaking large projects that are too unprofitable for private entrepreneurs to take on themselves, such as building bridges and canals and funding public education and cultural activities. Over the course of the following century, Britain and the United States adopted philosophies of government that conformed quite closely to Smith's proposals. But as democracy expanded in these countries, and the vote was extended to larger segments of the populace, the state was increasingly pressured by mass publics to enhance their economic and social welfare. During the twentieth century, the state in large democracies took on a growing number of welfare functions, from expanding public education to providing pensions, unemployment compensation, health care, housing, and the like. Countries that had once been governed as warfare states evolved into welfare states. Authoritarian regimes like Nazi Germany and the Soviet Union also cultivated mass support through a cornucopia of welfare programs. Even welfare states, however, must regard their domestic and international security as a top priority.

The main goals pursued by states in today's world run a wide gamut; everything depends on who gets to define these goals. Democracies, military regimes, states based on Islamic law—these and other states will define their main goals differently. Perhaps the one universal reality is that **anarchism**, ***which is the notion that the people are better off without an organized government***, has not been adopted as a viable option. *Anarchy* comes from the ancient Greek word meaning "without a ruler." Although fairly large anarchist movements were active in Europe and Russia in the nineteenth century and in Spain the first half of the twentieth century, anarchism has never triumphed anywhere long enough to undergo a trial run. The political world as we know it is a world built on states.[9]

## STATE INSTITUTIONS

Ultimately the topic of the state centers on governmental institutions. *Institutionalism* (or *neo-institutionalism*, in its recent variants) is the branch of comparative politics that looks at how state institutions are set up and how they shape the political decision-making process. Its central hypothesis is that political outcomes—such as governmental decisions that determine "who gets what"—are often decisively affected by a country's institutional framework, and not simply by the direct impact of influential social groups or nongovernmental organizations. As we shall see in this and subsequent chapters, different outcomes may result depending on how a country organizes its executive branch, its legislature, its judiciary, and other institutions, and on how these organs function in practice."[10]

In most countries the legal competence of governmental institutions is spelled out in a national constitution, which is usually a single written document. The United States was the first country to establish itself from scratch on the basis of a written constitution; in this sense, it was "the first new nation."[11] The U.S. Constitution, which has been amended twenty-six times, is the oldest constitution in the world in the form of a single document. The constitutions of most other states are much more recent. Germany, Italy, and Japan, for instance, adopted new constitutional arrangements after World War II. France's present constitution dates from 1958. Most of the countries that abandoned communism after 1989 have written new constitutions, and some are still in the process of revising them. South Africa, Brazil, and a host of other states are also engaged in inaugurating relatively new constitutional orders.

Not all constitutions are single documents. Britain has one of the oldest continuous constitutional traditions in the world, but its constitution consists of thousands of laws and practices that have been developed over the course of centuries of parliamentary interactions with the crown and courts. Israel, established in 1948, also has no formal constitution but a set of Basic Laws and other legislation that substitute for one. The same is true of Germany.

In addition to looking at the constitutionally determined ground rules of governmental authority, political scientists also like to investigate the ways state institutions operate in real life. Quite often a constitution provides only the skeletal structure of a governmental system. It doesn't necessarily indicate how the system's institutional parts really work or how effectively the laws of the land are implemented. Constitutions can also be vague or silent on certain aspects of governmental authority or can be subject to conflicting interpretations. Authoritarian rulers sometimes ignore their country's constitution altogether and rule by fiat. Many Latin American constitutions in past decades were modeled on the U.S. system of separation of powers. In practice, however, those provisions were largely ignored, and state authority tilted heavily in the direction of highly personalized presidential power.[12]

There are several important governmental institutions that we need to look at in order to understand political realities in a variety of settings.

### The Executive

The executive branch is of primary importance in all political systems. Presidents, prime ministers, dictators, governing monarchs, and other officials at the apex of the governmental pyramid are typically the individuals who decide government policy and who hold ultimate responsibility for the state's successes and failures.

As we look at the role of political executives in the chapters that follow, it is important to keep in mind a basic distinction between two distinct executive functions: *head of state* and *head of government*. In most countries, these are two separate offices occupied by two different people who are selected in separate procedures. Although there are some notable exceptions, ***usually the* head of state *is a* ceremonial *position that carries little or no real decision-making power.*** In these cases the head of state is often an individual who stands above the country's ongoing political battles and personifies the nation's unity or the continuity of its history. In some instances the person occupying this symbolically prestigious but politically neutral post is an unelected figure such as a hereditary monarch in a democracy. A **constitutional monarchy** (or **limited monarchy**) is a regime in which the monarch is head of state, but real decision-making power is in the hands of other institutional authorities such as legislators, the prime minister, and other officials who answer to them. A number of countries that once had powerful monarchs but subsequently became democracies have retained the monarchy in order to preserve their historical traditions, while radically diminishing the crown's actual power. Belgium, Britain, Denmark, Japan, the Netherlands, Norway, and Sweden are a few examples. Spain's King Juan Carlos I has played a more active political role, personally shepherding the transition from Francisco Franco's decades-long dictatorship to a successful democracy starting in the late 1970s. In 2006, Thailand's popular monarch made a rare political intervention when he called on the country's courts to invalidate recent parliamentary elections that were boycotted by opponents of the controversial prime minister, Thaksin Shinawatra. The constitutional court complied and ordered new elections. In other cases, the head of state may be an elected civilian who enjoys the respect of the country's population and political elites, including those from opposing parties. The head of state's main duties in such cases are generally limited to making speeches on ceremonial occasions, representing the state at nonpolitical functions, and greeting foreign dignitaries. In some countries the head of state has limited powers of intervention in the political process, in other countries none.

By contrast, the **head of government** ***is usually the country's chief political officer and is responsible for presenting and conducting its principal policies.*** Unlike a ceremonial head of state, the head of government has real decision-making authority. He or she normally supervises the entire executive branch of the state, including its senior ministers (who together comprise the cabinet) and their respective ministries, as well as a host of executive-level agencies designed to propose and execute government policies. In many countries, the term *government*, in addition to being a synonym for the state as we defined it earlier, also refers more specifically to just the head of government and the cabinet ministries. In this context it is used much the way the term *administration* is used in the United

States to refer to a particular president and his executive-level colleagues: "Tony Blair's government" in Britain and "the Bush administration" are analogous designations.

In Britain, the head of state is the monarch; the head of government is the prime minister. In Japan, the head of state is the emperor; the head of government is the prime minister. In Germany, the head of state is the president; the head of government is the chancellor. Many countries make roughly similar distinctions.

But as we noted, there are exceptions. In the United States, the president is both head of state *and* head of government. Another exception is France, which has an unusual "dual executive." In the French system, the president, who is the head of state, often has even greater decision-making authority than the prime minister, who is the head of government. Post-communist Russia and other countries also combine a politically powerful head of state (the president) with an active head of government (the prime minister). Not all heads of state, in other words, are purely ceremonial; some have real power. These and other variants are common, and we will look at some of them in later chapters.

## The Legislature

Legislatures (or *parliaments* with a small *p*) are also important state institutions. Their chief functions, especially in democracies, are to make laws (sometimes in conjunction with the executive branch) and to represent the people in the lawmaking process. In some cases, legislatures also keep a check on the executive branch and its bureaucratic departments by holding inquiries and investigations into their activities. This latter function is known as *legislative oversight*.

Some democracies have a *parliamentary system* of government. In these countries the national legislature actually elects (or approves) the head of government and holds that person, along with the entire cabinet, continuously accountable for their actions. Canada, Britain, Germany, Italy, Japan, Israel, India—these and a host of other countries all have one form or another of parliamentary government. We'll look at this system more closely in chapter 8.

The United States has a different system entirely, one in which the constitutional powers of Congress and the president are balanced more or less evenly. Even authoritarian regimes often have legislative bodies that play a certain role in the political system, though their real lawmaking powers may be negligible or nonexistent. Iran stands out as an example. Conceivably, an elected legislature in a predominantly authoritarian political system could serve as an incubator of democracy, providing an opportunity for popularly chosen representatives to demand wider decision-making powers. We'll explore this possibility further in chapter 9.

Like the executive branch of government, legislatures around the world display considerable variation. Some countries (like Israel and Denmark) have a **unicameral legislature**, ***consisting of only one house (or chamber) of parliament.*** Most others have a **bicameral legislature**, ***consisting of two houses.*** Typically one of these chambers is considered the *lower house* (e.g., the U.S. House of Representatives) and the second is regarded as the *upper house* (e.g., the U.S. Senate). The advantage of a unicameral legislature is that it does not have to share authority with a second legislative chamber in making laws. At least in principle, this arrangement is supposed to reduce the possibility of excessive legislative wrangling, delay, and gridlock. The main advantages of a bicameral legislature, again in principle, are that it provides greater representation for the population and requires greater deliberation in the lawmaking process. In actual practice, however, bicameral legislatures vary in terms of their representative function and their actual role.

Legislatures around the world differ in a variety of ways, including the voting systems used to elect them, their relative power, their lawmaking procedures, and so on. Subsequent chapters will discuss national legislatures in various countries around the world.[13]

## The Judiciary

The judiciary represents a third institution whose significance, while usually considerable, varies from place to place. All states have some form of legal structure, and the role of the judiciary is rarely limited to such routine tasks as adjudicating civil and criminal cases. Inevitably the system of justice is intimately bound up with the state's political essence. Justice is not always blind; it is often keenly political. The political importance of the judiciary was especially evident when the U.S. Supreme Court decided the outcome of the 2000 presidential election. When a dispute arose over whether George W. Bush or Al Gore should be awarded Florida's Electoral College votes, the Court sided with Bush by a 5–4 vote.

In some states the judiciary is relatively *independent* of the political authorities in the executive and legislative branches. It may even possess the legal competence to impose restrictions on what these political leaders may do. In others (especially authoritarian ones), the legal system is often highly politicized and remains tightly controlled by the ruling clique, which manipulates the courts in an effort to keep the population in line. In some countries the legal system is based on secular law, in others on religious law like *shariah* (Islamic law), which is itself subject to various interpretations. In yet another category of cases, the judiciary may play a critical role in defining and even widening the scope of civil rights and liberties for the population when these rights are limited or violated by other branches of government. The courts have played this quasi-independent role (or have at least attempted to play it) in such countries as Egypt, where the central executives have used heavy-handed methods of repression against political opponents, and in various countries in transition to democracy, where the formal definition of the executive's authority and the population's rights are still being worked out.[14]

Some countries, like the United States, have constitutional courts with fairly wide latitude to interpret the highest laws of the land. In some cases these high courts have the power of **judicial review**, ***which is the right to invalidate laws made by the legislature and executive bodies as unconstitutional.*** Other countries have different patterns. In Britain, for instance, the House of Lords—the upper house of the legislature—functions as the country's highest constitutional court.[15]

### The Bureaucracy

The bureaucracy, or *civil service*, is an indispensable part of government in virtually every country in the world. Without a well-developed network of state organs charged with advising political decision makers about different policy options and implementing policies once they have been decided upon, governments could not govern. The modern state invariably includes a vast array of ministries, departments, agencies, bureaus, and other officiously titled institutions whose purview may range from the domestic economy to education, health, the environment, international trade, foreign relations, and so on. The growth of bureaucracies has been a long-term political phenomenon in most countries, as have more recent efforts in some countries (including the United States) to trim their size to less costly proportions.

Although just about all large states are endowed with imposing bureaucratic structures, they differ significantly with respect to the roles their bureaucracies play. In some cases the ability of civil servants to issue regulations on their own authority is kept within fairly narrow limits. Legislative bodies, and in some cases the courts, exercise oversight functions in an effort to rein in the decision-making independence of these fairly restricted bureaucracies. The United States is an example. In other instances, bureaucrats enjoy wider discretionary powers when it comes to specifying how the government's policy aims, which may be sketched out in broad guidelines, are to be interpreted and implemented. Such broad rule-making authority can be found in democracies like Japan and France, as well as in nondemocracies like the former Soviet Union and certain military dictatorships in Latin America. Measures to ensure democratic controls over the bureaucracy are among the most important tasks of newly democratizing countries that have inherited authoritarian bureaucratic structures from the old regime.[16]

Some bureaucracies consist of a fairly stable core of career civil servants who take pride in their technical professionalism and political neutrality. These *technocrats* provide government decision makers with indispensable information and policy analysis in their respective areas of expertise, such as economics, defense, technology, social welfare, and the like. Although the federal bureaucracy in the United States is populated with well-trained and dedicated careerists, the U.S. government has reserved a growing number of bureaucratic positions for political appointees, more so than in most other democracies. One of the chief spoils of political power in Washington is the opportunity given each new presidential administration to appoint faithful supporters to choice government jobs. As George

W. Bush's incoming administration prepared to assume office following the 2000 presidential election, it was authorized to fill 6,500 positions, most of which were advertised in the government's aptly named "plum book."

Bureaucracies can also differ in terms of their operating procedures, the class and educational backgrounds of their personnel, their propensity to corruption, and so on. In subsequent chapters we'll glance at the shape of bureaucratic structures in several countries.[17]

### The Military

Military establishments can have a formidable impact of their own on the organization of institutional authority. Quite a few contemporary political systems are run directly by elements of the military command. (The Spanish term *junta* refers to the leaders of a military government.) Others may be influenced indirectly by military officials who lurk in the background, keeping civilian governments dependent on their approval. A considerable number of states currently in transition to democracy were ruled by military officials, either directly or indirectly, just prior to embarking on the democratic path. These include such disparate countries as Spain, Portugal, Greece, South Korea, and a host of countries in Latin America and Africa. Some countries have undergone so many cyclical oscillations between military rule and democracy that one can say with only slight exaggeration that the alternation between these two regime types in effect *is* their system of government.[18] Between 1825 and 1982, for example, Bolivia experienced periods of civilian rule interspersed with more than 180 military seizures of power. Costa Rica abolished its army in 1949 precisely to prevent military intervention in politics; it has been a successful democracy ever since. In 1973 the Nixon administration ordered the U.S. Central Intelligence Agency to assist Gen. Augusto Pinochet and other Chilean military leaders in ousting the legitimately elected government of President Salvador Allende, a leftist who had nationalized U.S.-owned copper mines. Pinochet's harsh military dictatorship ended when a referendum went against him in 1988, leading to the restoration of democracy in Chile. One of the main tasks these countries face as they seek to stabilize democracy is to ensure civilian control of the military.

When is a **coup d'état**—***a forceful takeover of state power by the military***—most likely to occur? How is it that some countries are more prone to military coups than others? Political scientists who have studied *praetorianism*—the phenomenon of military intervention in a country's domestic politics—have identified a multiplicity of variables that answer these and related questions. Studies have shown that the likelihood and frequency of coups can be explained by such independent variables as economic stagnation, poorly developed political institutions and poor governmental performance, low levels of popular support for civilian politicians, a breakdown in law and order, and other identifiable factors. The precise mixture of these explanatory variables will vary from country to country and from one period of time to another, but certain patterns are discernible.[19]

The military's role in politics can take a variety of forms, as the cases of Turkey and Pakistan—two of the largest Muslim countries in the world—vividly illustrate.

## THE MILITARY IN POLITICS: Turkey and Pakistan

### Turkey

As the Bush administration geared up to invade Iraq in the spring of 2003, the Turkish parliament did something unexpected: it rebuffed intense pressures from the United States, its NATO ally, to station more than 60,000 American troops on Turkish soil for use in the impending combat. With public opinion in Turkey running overwhelmingly against the war, and with U.S. offers of financial assistance falling below the Turkish government's proposed figures, a critical mass of Turkish legislators turned down the American request. The parliament's action was a turning point in the development of Turkish democracy: the Islamic party that had won two-thirds of the seats in the recently elected legislature had survived a controversial vote without serious interference from the Turkish military. In an equally momentous event, the military lifted its ban on the party's leader, *Tayyip Erdogan* (ERR-dough-ahn), allowing the parliamentary majority to elect him prime minister. Only three years earlier the military had sentenced Erdogan to prison for "Islamic sedition" and banned him permanently from holding political office.

These developments were the latest in a series of uneasy encounters between the three most powerful forces in Turkish politics—Islam, democracy, and the military. Turkey's population of 70 million is 99.8 percent Muslim (mostly Sunni). For all but a few years, Turkey has been a multiparty democracy since the end of World War II. But the Turkish military command has intervened in the country's democratic processes on several occasions, removing prime ministers, outlawing parties, and even suspending democracy itself by imposing direct military rule on the population. In justifying these interventions, Turkey's military leaders have claimed a special responsibility for maintaining a secular government and preventing the state from being taken over by proponents of an overtly Islamic political orientation. They have also regarded their interventions as attempts to defend democracy rather than subvert it (or allow others to subvert it). The military's special role as the guardian of Turkey's secular and democratic principles is not a recent phenomenon. It is rooted in the very foundations of the country's post-Ottoman regime and in the ideology of its charismatic founding father, *Mustafa Kemal Atatürk* (1880/1–1938).

Mustafa Kemal was himself a military man. Although he defended the Ottoman Empire as a heroic commander in World War I, he also believed that the time had come for the 600-year-old dynasty to end. From its glory days in the sixteenth century, when it ruled a vast realm that encompassed much of the Balkans, the Middle East, the Caucasus, and parts of Persia, the Ottoman sultanate had progressively declined to the status of "the sick man of Europe" by the nineteenth century. Turkish liberals adopted a constitution in 1876 that required the sultan to share power with a parliament. When successive sultans ignored it, a rebellion by reformers known as the Young Turks forced its acceptance in 1908. The government's decision to support Germany and Austria-Hungary in the First World War proved disastrous and was followed by major territorial losses. As Britain, France, Greece, and Armenia moved to carve up what remained of Turkey and its possessions, Mustafa Kemal took charge of a revolt against the sultanate in 1919. By the following year he headed a rival government in Ankara, backed by rising national sentiment against the weak Ottoman regime in Constantinople (Istanbul). In 1921 he was named commander-in-chief of the army by Turkey's Grand National Assembly, which formally abolished the sultanate in 1922. In 1923, after Turkey's troops had reclaimed some of its lost territory, Mustafa Kemal's ascent to power was completed as the Assembly proclaimed a republic and elected him president.

From the outset, Mustafa Kemal was determined to modernize Turkey's political, social, and cultural foundations. The principal ideas of what became known as *Kemalism* included a secular state and a commitment to raising Turkey to the ranks of the European powers. A constitution adopted in 1924 incorporated the main principles of Kemalist doctrine. In the same year, his government abolished the Caliphate, the spiritual center of Islam that the Ottoman sultans had claimed as their patrimony. In accordance with the concept of *laïcité* (secularity) inscribed in the constitution, Kemalism demanded a strict separation of church and state. Over the next decade Islam was deprived of its constitutional status as the country's official religion, religious courts were closed, and women's headscarves and men's clerical dress were banned outside mosques. To this day, the government's Directorate of Religious Affairs regulates many religious activities, at times even dictating the content of sermons. Women saw their civil and political rights gradually enlarged; in 1934 they won the right to vote in parliamentary elections and run for the national legislature. In 1928 the government replaced the Arabic script with the Roman alphabet for written Turkish. Mustafa Kemal moved Turkey closer to the West in other ways as well, joining the League of Nations in 1932 and signing various border agreements affirming Turkey's role as a European state. In 1934 he adopted the surname Atatürk ("Father Turk").[20]

Atatürk expected the military to be the guardian of his political legacy, but he clearly preferred civilian government to military rule. He did not want the military to play a direct role in politics. Nevertheless, events after his death induced the military to intervene several times in the political fray. During Atatürk's lifetime, Turkey was essentially a one-party state. The ruling party was the Republican People's Party (CHP), founded by Atatürk himself. After World War II, Turkey evolved into a multiparty democracy. Until 1961 there were two main parties: the Kemalist CHP and a right-wing party, the Democrat Party (DP), led by Adnan Menderes, who became prime minister. When violent unrest developed in 1960 after the government limited press freedoms and displayed other authoritarian tendencies, Menderes imposed martial law. (*Martial law* substitutes various military rules of justice for civil law. It typically suspends the presumption of innocence, the right to protection against arbitrary search and arrest, and other civil rights.) The military responded in May 1960 by taking power. Charging that the government was violating Kemalist precepts and that its policies were bringing the country to the brink of disintegration, the chief of the army general staff ordered troops to seize official buildings. The prime minister, the president, and numerous members of parliament were arrested. Menderes himself, who was accused of trying to establish a dictatorship, was later hanged. In 1961 the military leadership formed a constituent assembly to write a new constitution, which was approved in a referendum. Following parliamentary elections later in the year in which fourteen parties participated, the military relinquished power.

In 1971 the military stepped into the political arena again. When rising frustration over the government's failure to adopt the economic, social, and land reforms promised in the new constitution provoked violent protests, the military leadership sent a memo to the president calling for a "strong and credible government" capable of implementing the reforms. The memo warned of military intervention if no action was taken. The prime minister promptly resigned and a new government was formed in response to what was called the "coup by memo."

The Turkish military intervened in domestic politics once again in 1980. Discontent was growing over the failure of a succession of weak center-right and center-left governments to deal with the economic problems generated by the rise in world oil prices in the 1970s. In addition, a growing number of Turkish Muslims, represented by the National Salvation Party led by Necmettin Erbakan, were demanding an end to the restrictions on religious dress and were calling for the adoption of Islamic law. There was also mounting violence in Turkey's Kurdish areas, where an independence movement was gathering strength. Strikes were occurring with increasing frequency, often with the support of the small Turkish Communist Party. And an extreme right-wing party was resorting to street violence and terrorism against its opponents, provoking the government to impose martial law. Sensing that Turkey was heading toward chaos and that the government was violating Kemalist principles, the military seized power. The Islamic party leader Erbakan was sentenced to two years in prison.

The military-appointed government stabilized the economy somewhat, and in 1982 a new constitution was approved by 91 percent of the voters in a referendum. A ten-year ban on political activity was placed on all politicians who were active before the 1980 military intervention. The military did not give up power until 1983, when elections were held for a new parliament. Only three parties were permitted to run in those elections (though more parties were permitted the following year). Martial law was finally lifted in 1984.

In 1993 Tansu Ciller became Turkey's first female prime minister. Corruption charges forced her to resign in 1995, and elections held at the end of the year produced a parliamentary plurality for the Welfare Party (Refah), an ideologically Islamic party led by Erbakan, the veteran political leader. In 1996 Erbakan became prime minister. His efforts to ease restrictions on Islamic dress and steer Turkey's foreign policy away from its close attachment to the United States and from its long-standing cooperation with Israel provoked the military leadership into action. In 1997 the military-dominated National Security Council pressured Erbakan to resign. It subsequently banned the Welfare Party, accusing it of "conspiring against the secular order." The constitutional court barred Erbakan and five other party officials from political life for five years. Although the military's intervention was technically not a coup, it forcefully demonstrated that the military hierarchy was still the guardian of Kemalist ideals and remained the final arbiter of Turkish politics, exercising ultimate authority.

In 1998 a group of parliamentary delegates from the outlawed Welfare Party put together a new Islamic party, the Virtue Party. But in June 2001 the constitutional court disbanded it for taking positions at variance with the regime's secularist orientation. Islamic leaders then formed two new parties, the Felicity Party, with a fundamentalist orientation, and the more moderate Justice and Development Party (AKP) under the leadership of Istanbul's popular former mayor, Tayyip Erdogan. At the time, Erdogan was on record as favoring the adoption of Islamic law in place of Turkey's civil law. At a rally in 1998, he read out a well-known poem that described Islam in militant terms. In response, the government had him arrested and sentenced to ten months in prison. Although he was released after four months, he was barred from holding political office for life.

In parliamentary elections held in November 2002, Erdogan's Justice and Development Party won a resounding victory, capturing 363 (66 percent) of the Grand National Assembly's 550 seats. The only other party to win seats in the new parliament was Atatürk's Republican People's Party. In view of the fate of previous Islamic parties, the leadership of the Justice and Development Party was determined to avoid the radical Islamic label associated with those outlawed parties. Erdogan, its principal leader, conveyed an unmistakably moderate message during the election campaign, asserting that the AKP was a

Tayyip Erdogan

"conservative democratic party" that regarded "secularism as the guarantee of all religious faiths." He also vowed to maintain Turkey's ties with the United States, its "natural ally," and to press for Turkey's admission into the European Union. Because Erdogan was not permitted to become prime minister, his party's deputy leader assumed that office after the elections. But in March 2003, as American pressures on Turkey mounted during the buildup to war in Iraq, Turkish military authorities lifted the ban on Erdogan's right to hold office. Shortly after he assumed his parliamentary seat, his party's large majority in the legislature elected Erdogan prime minister.

Although Erdogan tried to come to an agreement with the United States as the impending invasion of Iraq grew near, public opposition to war and to the economic assistance package offered by the Bush administration was overwhelming. Many Turks were worried that a war with Iraq might unleash a repetition of what had happened during the Persian Gulf War of 1991, when some 350,000 Kurds had fled from Iraq into Turkey, creating a massive refugee problem for the Turkish government. In addition, Turkey claimed that it had lost close to $100 billion in revenue in the years following the Persian Gulf War because of the embargo on Iraqi oil exports that was imposed on Saddam's regime by the United Nations. Economic relations with Iraq, much of it centered on the oil industry, was an important source of income for the Turks. When the Bush administration in 2003 offered $6 billion in direct assistance, a large number of Turkish legislators—many of them in Erdogan's own party—opposed the offer as insufficient. After the parliament turned down the U.S. request to position its troops on Turkish territory, an official in Erdogan's party remarked, "This democracy they (the Americans) did so much to encourage over the years, this is the result of it."

In the months that followed the fall of Baghdad in April 2003, Prime Minister Erdogan patched up his government's relationship with the United States. His pro-democracy Islamic party was viewed by many in Washington as a role model for the Islamic world. Although Erdogan hewed to the moderate course he had promised during the election campaign, Turkey's military high command made it known that it was watching from the wings. It still retained five votes on the nine-member National Security Council, the secretive body that had a powerful behind-the-scenes influence on government decisions. But in the summer of 2003, Erdogan's government got the parliament to pass an unprecedented law declaring that the National Security Council was purely an advisory body with no decision-making authority at all. The legislation further stipulated that the NSC's secretary-general, typically a four-star general, could be a civilian in the future, and it opened up the military budget to parliamentary oversight.

Erdogan's government took these actions at the behest of the European Union, which had been pressuring the Turkish government to curb the military's power. Turkey has had an "association agreement" with the European community since 1963, and it applied for full membership in 1987. In 2002 the EU laid down guidelines requiring major civil rights and other reforms as prerequisites for Turkey's admission. Since then, Erdogan's government has reformed Turkey's penal code, outlawed torture and the death penalty, and extended women's rights. It has also sought to improve the government's relations with Turkey's 15 million Kurds. (Until the late 1990s, the Turkish military had fought a fifteen-year war with Kurdish rebels that resulted in 35,000 deaths and more than a million left homeless.) The EU responded positively to Erdogan's reforms, and negotiations on Turkey's possible accession to the EU began in early 2005. Misgivings among many Europeans about Turkey's prospective membership are considerable, however, and the negotiations are expected to drag on for as long as fifteen years.

By the end of 2005, Turkey had a composite Freedom House rating of 3, qualifying it as a "semi-democracy" in this book. But its recent political stability was by no means unassailable. In 2006 a gunman who was infuriated at an administrative court's decision to uphold the ban on head scarves for female state employees opened fire on the judges, killing one of them. Erdogan deplored the incident. But after tens of thousands of demonstrators marched in Ankara in support of Turkey's secular laws, a leading general called for more such demonstrations. These signs of tension between Erdogan's moderate Islamic government and the Turkish military were expected to intensify as Turkey prepared for parliamentary and presidential elections scheduled for 2007.

### Pakistan

Several hours after the terrorist attacks on New York and Washington of September 11, 2001, Pakistan's ambassador to the United States was asked to attend a meeting at the U.S. State Department early the next morning. In the company of the chief of Pakistan's main military intelligence agency, the ambassador was told by a high-ranking U.S. official, "You are either 100 percent with us or 100 percent against us." For the United States, Pakistan's cooperation in the looming assault on Osama bin Laden's al Qaeda terror network, and on the Taliban regime in Afghanistan that protected it, was critical. Pakistan's porous border with Afghanistan was a breeding ground of al Qaeda and Taliban sympathizers, providing hiding places and other sources of support for terrorists. A succession of Pakistani governments, moreover, had openly supported the Taliban in the past. Until September 11 the military regime of *Gen. Pervez Musharraf* was pursuing the same policy. The Bush administration was determined to stop that cooperation and swing Musharraf decisively to the American side.

Pervez Musharraf

The Taliban movement had its very roots in Pakistan. It emerged there after thousands of Afghans fled their country in the 1980s while it was engulfed in a brutal war against the Soviet Union. The Soviets had invaded Afghanistan at the end of 1979 in hopes of quickly installing a more friendly government. But they became bogged down in a bloody quagmire as Afghan fighters put up fierce resistance. Fatefully, the United States, which opposed Soviet aggression in any form, supported the Afghan resistance. So, too, did the government of Pakistan, which wanted stability in the region and cooperative ties between the large Pashtun ethnic communities that inhabited areas on both sides of the border. And so did Osama bin Laden, a young Islamic militant from Saudi Arabia who was eager to join fellow Muslims in a jihad (holy war) against the invading Soviet infidels. Although the three collaborators each had their own reasons for supporting the Afghan cause, they worked together to funnel American arms and money to the Afghan fighters. Pakistan's secretive military intelligence agency, Inter-Services Intelligence (ISI), served as the main conduit between the United States and the resistance movement. The collaboration was a resounding success: the Soviets gave up and withdrew from Afghanistan by 1989. But as the United States subsequently diverted its attention from the region, the ultraconservative Taliban movement gradually took over Afghanistan, imposing a strict code of Islamic law on the population and providing a home base for al Qaeda.

For a variety of reasons, a succession of civilian and military leaders in Pakistan supported the Taliban government. Some officials sympathized with its Islamic ideology, some identified with the Taliban as fellow Pashtuns, and some wanted a friendly Afghanistan so that Pakistan could concentrate on its more important strategic relationship with India. The events of September 11 radically altered these dynamics. The United States urgently needed Pakistan's support, and that reality required it to cooperate with Musharraf's military government.

Musharraf had taken power in a coup d'état in 1999, ejecting an elected civilian government. Such occurrences were not new in Pakistan. Pakistan's military establishment has intervened in domestic politics far more often—and more directly—than Turkey's military. Military leaders have governed Pakistan for half of its history as an independent state since 1947. Even during periods of nonmilitary rule, the military has often imposed its priorities on the civilian leadership, exercising decisive influence on such policies as relations with India and the development of nuclear weapons. In addition, some of Pakistan's military brass have been far more sympathetic than Turkey's military secularists to the social doctrines and political programs of Islamic radicals.

From the nineteenth century until 1947, Pakistan was ruled by the British as part of colonial India. Mohandas Gandhi, who led India's successful independence movement, hoped to keep postcolonial India as a single state, based on religious harmony between its large Hindu and Muslim populations. But Mohammad Ali Jinnah, the leader of the Muslim League, demanded a separate state for the predominantly Muslim areas in the north. The British acquiesced, and India and Pakistan gained their independence as separate countries.

Things went awry from the start. As Muslims moved north to resettle in Pakistan and Hindus moved south into India, violent conflagrations ignited sectarian bloodletting in both new states. By the time the mayhem subsided, approximately 200,000 people lay dead. The 1947 independence settlement brokered by the British government created the basis for still more antagonisms. Pakistan initially consisted of two parts: western and eastern Pakistan were a thousand miles apart, separated by Indian territory. In 1971, India invaded East Pakistan and presided over its conversion into the independent state of Bangladesh. A more protracted problem centered on the territory of Kashmir and Jammu. Despite its Muslim majority, the area had traditionally been governed by a Hindu prince, and the British awarded it to India. Pakistan never accepted this arrangement and managed to recover only a small portion of the disputed region. Several Pakistani leaders, civilian as well as military, have sponsored Muslim insurgents seeking to detach the rest of the area from India. The acquisition of nuclear weapons by India in the 1970s and by Pakistan in the 1980s added the prospect of massive devastation to the conflict. In 1998 and again in 2002, India and Pakistan engaged in dangerous nuclear saber-rattling over Kashmir, pushing their dispute to the brink of war. Intense diplomatic intervention by the United States and Britain helped defuse these crises, but the underlying problem remained.

In spite of these tensions, India has managed to maintain democratic institutions and practices for all but a couple of years since 1947. (Chapter 15 discusses India in greater detail.) Pakistan has been less successful. The country's first leader, Jinnah, paid lip service to democratic principles but gathered the reins of power in his own hands. After his death in 1948, Pakistan drifted toward chaos. There were seven prime ministers during the next ten years, all of them ineffective. All relied heavily on the bureaucracy and the military to deal with the country's problems, which included widespread poverty, deep ethnic divisions, and doctrinal disputes between rival Muslim groups. In ethnic terms, the new country was divided among Mohajirs (immigrants from India), Punjabis, Sindhis, Bengalis, Parthans (Pashtuns), and Baluchis, along with several smaller groups. Most Pakistanis were Sunni Muslims, but Shiites constituted a sizable minority. The Sunnis themselves were divided into diverse camps, including moderates willing to support a secular state as well as radicals who favored an Islamic theocracy. The Shiites were also divided into various sub-sects. Intense rivalries for political power and economic benefits involving these disparate ethnic and religious groups plagued Pakistan from its very foundation as an independent state. At one time or another virtually all the country's main ethnic groups demanded greater autonomy or outright secession. But though the creation of a unified Pakistani national identity proved difficult internally, most Pakistanis were able to agree on a policy of nationalism that was directed externally against India.

In an effort to impose order on an unruly country, General Ayub Khan seized power in a military coup in 1958 and declared martial law. Ayub Khan favored a secular state and sought to pattern the Pakistani army on the American model of a professional military. But his failure to keep order in East Pakistan, where the largely Bengali population resented the West Pakistani political elite, prompted his resignation in 1969. He was followed by another general, Yahya Khan. Pakistan's new military boss proved far more liberal than his predecessor, permitting free elections in 1970. But when the Bengali opposition movement unleashed demands for East Pakistan's independence, Yahya Khan sent troops to the restive area. As millions of Bengalis fled into India, the Indian government invaded East Pakistan in November 1971, setting the stage for East Pakistan's transformation into the independent country of Bangladesh. Following this disastrous loss, Yahya Khan stepped down and kept his promise to allow civilian government to return.

His successor was Zulfikar Ali Bhutto, the civilian leader of the Pakistan People's Party. Bhutto spearheaded a popular movement dedicated to democracy, economic development, and respect for Islamic ideals within a secular state. But once in power, he ruled with the ruthlessness of an autocrat, bullying the bureaucracy, the military, and local governments to accept his dictates and rigging elections to retain power. When demonstrations against his rule proliferated after the tainted 1977 elections, the military under General Zia ul Haq turned against the beleaguered leader and forced him out. Bhutto was convicted of complicity in a murder and executed in 1979.

Zia's attitudes toward Islam were profoundly different from those of Pakistan's two previous military rulers. Whereas his predecessors had favored a secular army, Zia actively integrated Islamic teachings into military life. He permitted one of Pakistan's most militant Islamic organizations to indoctrinate troops, and he reoriented military strategy to conform with the Koran and the concept of jihad (holy war). He also vigorously pursued the development of a nuclear "Islamic bomb" and cooperated with the United States in supporting the Afghan insurgents' resistance to the Soviet occupation. Although he sought to promote the "Islamization" of Pakistani society, Zia was a Sunni whose doctrinal positions offended the country's Shiites. And as a Punjabi, Zia tended to favor his own ethnic group while discriminating against Sindhis and brutally suppressing a Baluchi separatist movement. Zia's rule came to an abrupt end when he died in a plane crash in 1988.

Civilian government returned following elections held soon after Zia's death. The next prime minister was Benazir Bhutto, daughter of the former president. Educated in the West, Bhutto advocated democracy but did little to curb the influence of the military or the restiveness of Islamic parties and organizations. Her stature suffered further damage with accusations that her husband was pocketing money that belonged to the national treasury. Following the dismissal of her government and fresh elections in 1990, Bhutto was succeeded by Nawaz Sharif, the scion of a wealthy family with long-standing grudges against the Bhuttos. Sharif's first government lasted three years. Ms. Bhutto returned to power in 1993, and in 1997 Sharif replaced her once again. Corruption in the executive, the legislature, and the judiciary was rampant throughout these years of civilian rule under Ms. Bhutto and Sharif. During his second term, Sharif's government put Benazir Bhutto and her husband on trial for receiving millions of dollars in illegal kickbacks, but their conviction was overturned when it was revealed that the government had fixed the case with the presiding judge. Meanwhile, the military and its intelligence services controlled key foreign and defense policy decisions. When Sharif fired the chief of the army, Gen. Musharraf, for aiding Kashmiri rebels, Musharraf ousted him in a coup in 1999.

Like other military rulers before him, Musharraf pledged to restore democracy some day. He also promised to reinvigorate the economy and combat corruption. (Sharif was tried and convicted on corruption charges and exiled to Saudi Arabia.) But Musharraf departed from Gen. Zia's Islamic orientation and adopted a pronouncedly secularist line, explicitly embracing Mustafa Kemal Atatürk as his role model. In his first address after seizing power, Musharraf enjoined Pakistan's religious leaders to disavow intolerance and violence in favor of Islam's traditions of brotherhood and progress. After September 11 he immediately opted for solidarity with the United States in the struggle against the Taliban and al Qaeda, fully recognizing that his own vision of a "progressive and dynamic Islamic welfare state," led by secular figures, required a "day of reckoning" with the advocates of an ultraconservative Islamic theocracy. To this end his government banned two Islamic organizations and rounded up some 500 suspected terrorists by 2003. Musharraf also announced plans to modernize the curriculum of Pakistan's madrassas, the religious schools where as many as 800,000 Pakistani youths—mostly boys from hopelessly destitute backgrounds—get an exclusively Islamic education that is often tinged with extreme anti-Western attitudes.

Having appointed himself president of Pakistan, Musharraf staged a referendum on his tenure in the spring of 2002. The government claimed that 98 percent of those who turned out to vote approved the prolongation of Musharraf's presidency by an additional five years. But a low turnout and charges of vote-rigging detracted from the referendum's credibility. In October Musharraf permitted parliamentary elections. Although his own party finished first, Benazir Bhutto's party came in second, even though Ms. Bhutto was not permitted to return to Pakistan from her exile abroad. Sharif's party also won seats. Most disturbing from Musharraf's point of view, however, were the unexpected gains registered by a coalition of six Islamic parties (the MMF), which finished third after campaigning hard against Musharraf's cooperation with the United States. Together the six parties won 59 out of 342 seats in the National Assembly.

At the end of 2003, Musharraf cut a deal with the Islamic parties: in exchange for the MMF's acknowledgment of Musharraf as Pakistan's legitimate president, Musharraf agreed to relinquish his other post as chief of the army. Both sides backed out of the deal, however. Musharraf got the parliament to approve the creation of a powerful National Security Council under his leadership, giving him the authority to dismiss the parliament and the prime minister. Musharraf's parliamentary backers then extended his tenure as head of the army for three more years.

Since 2003 Musharraf has substantially reinforced his own power in Pakistan while buttressing the political power of the military. He has also sought to maintain the military's secular orientation, even though leading officers and elements of the rank-and-file favor a more pronouncedly Islamic ethos, with some harboring sympathies for al Qaeda and the Taliban. Musharraf has also taken positions that are popular with the military brass even if they fly in the face of U.S. interests. For example, when compelling evidence forced Pakistan's top nuclear scientist, A. Q. Khan, to confess that he had made a fortune selling nuclear technology illegally to Iran, North Korea, and Libya, Musharraf pardoned him, asserting that Khan was still his "hero" for his role in developing Pakistan's nuclear bomb. At the same time, Musharraf has engaged in a delicate balancing act in his approach to Islamic fundamentalism. On the one hand, he has tried to placate the United States by pursuing al Qaeda and Taliban militants active in Pakistan. Between 2001 and 2005, his government killed or arrested more than seven hundred suspected al Qaeda members. On the other hand, Musharraf has refrained from confronting Islamic leaders head-on, preferring to cooperate with the Islamic parties on certain issues and allowing tribal leaders in Pakistan's border regions considerable latitude to implement Islamic law and local customs, including the severe treatment of women accused of adultery or of violating family honor codes. (Musharraf himself was widely criticized for suggesting in a *Washington Post* interview in 2005 that Pakistani women who wish to emigrate to the United States or Canada in order to get rich falsely claim that they were raped in Pakistan.)

In 2005, Pakistan was a semi-authoritarian state, with a Freedom House rating of 5.5. Musharraf's imperious rule faced the challenge of parliamentary elections set for 2007—elections that were once intended to restore democracy. But after narrowly escaping several assassination attempts, and with no obvious successor standing next in line, Gen. Musharraf could offer few certainties about Pakistan's future as election day neared.[21]

---

In sum, Turkey's military hierarchy has acted collectively to preserve secularism and limit the political influence of Islam. In Pakistan, by contrast, the military's relationship with Islam has varied with individual military rulers.

## HOW STATES ARE ORGANIZED

Thus far our survey of state institutions has focused exclusively on the national government—that is, on the central organs (usually located in the capital city) that have responsibility for the country as a whole. But local governments can also be of fundamental importance in determining how the political system works in this or that country. Just how important these subnational governmental bodies are can vary considerably from one place to the next.

Some countries provide relatively little room for subnational authorities to govern independently of the national government. In a **unitary state**, ***decision-making authority and disposition over revenues tend to be concentrated in the central institutions.*** France and Japan are examples.

By contrast, a **federation** ***seeks to combine a relatively strong central government with real authority for various administrative units below the national level.*** These sub-units may be regions, states (e.g., California), counties, municipalities, and the like. In these federal systems the subnational units usually have their own locally selected officials and, in some cases, the right to raise their own revenue through local taxes of various kinds. At the same time, they are usually dependent on the national government for some of their budgetary funding, and they must conform to certain national laws. Examples of federalism include the United States, Germany, the Russian Federation, and India. Until 1999, the United Kingdom of Great Britain and Northern Ireland used to be a classic example of a unitary state, but the establishment of local legislatures in Scotland, Wales, and Northern Ireland signified a historic shift toward a federal system.

A **confederation** ***is an even looser arrangement characterized by a weak central government and a group of constituent subnational elements that enjoy significant local autonomy or even independence as sovereign states.*** In confederal systems the central government's functions are mainly confined to such basic tasks as providing for the national defense, issuing the currency, and delivering the mail. In many issues the central government cannot act at all without the express consent of the subnational governments. Switzerland is an example. The Swiss Confederation's central government possesses only those powers explicitly ceded to it by the twenty cantons and six half-cantons that make up the country.[22] The United

Arab Emirates, consisting of seven monarchies, is another contemporary confederation. Prior to the adoption of the U.S. Constitution in 1789, the thirteen states were organized under the Articles of Confederation of 1777. That system proved to be too decentralized for many Americans, and at the urging of "federalists" like James Madison and Alexander Hamilton, a federal system was established in its place.

## HYPOTHESES ON THE STATE

"Why can't the government get it right?" Anyone who has ever asked this question has probably experienced the frustration of watching government officials or agencies fail to respond adequately to some problem affecting the population. Sometimes the state takes too long to legislate or make authoritative decisions on pressing issues. At other times government officials make bad decisions that fail to resolve the problem or only make matters worse.

Sometimes laws or regulations are not implemented in accordance with their intended purposes. In some cases, local governments may not have the resources needed to carry out decisions imposed on them by the national government ("unfunded mandates"). In others, enforcement officials deliberately refuse to carry out laws they do not like, a phenomenon that has occurred in the United States over such issues as civil rights and gun control. Sometimes laws and regulations work at cross-purposes. (The U.S. government has routinely subsidized tobacco growers while simultaneously conducting antismoking campaigns.) And sometimes governmental institutions are unable to make *any* kind of decision in response to well-known problems, especially when the alternative solutions are politically controversial. Bureaucratic red tape, wasteful government spending, inefficient managerial practices—the catalog of complaints is a long one, and the complaints themselves are strikingly common throughout the world.[23]

To be sure, sometimes governments do get things right; people often take for granted the positive things that governmental actions actually accomplish. Nevertheless, governments seldom operate at optimal levels of efficiency or effectiveness.

> **Efficiency** ***is the process of making decisions in a smooth and timely fashion.***

> **Effectiveness** ***means resolving problems successfully.***

Though we cannot possibly look into all the reasons for these inadequacies here, we can at least briefly examine a few hypotheses concerning the ways governments formulate and implement their policies.

**Divided Government** A **divided government** ***exists when the executive branch is controlled by one political party and the legislature is controlled by the opposition party or parties.*** The United States is frequently singled out in this regard. When the president is a Republican and the congressional majority is in the hands of the Democrats, or vice versa, gridlock—the inability to agree on legislation—may result. In a comprehensive study, Sarah Binder found that gridlock is likely to occur at statistically significant levels under conditions of divided government in the United States.[24] Nevertheless, there is no guarantee that laws will be passed quickly when the president and the congressional majority represent the same party. Democratic presidents like Carter and Clinton, to name just two, did not always get what they wanted out of Democrat-controlled Congresses. France and Brazil have their own variants of divided government, as we shall see in Part Two. So do other countries.

In contrast to the American or French-style political system, in which the chief executive and the national legislature are elected separately, some people extol the British-style parliamentary system as more efficient and less prone to gridlock. In a parliamentary system, the party or parties that have the majority of seats in the legislature decide who the head of government will be. As a consequence, the executive branch and the legislative majority usually represent the same party or parties. Divided government occurs only in rare exceptions to this general rule. For example, Britain's Labor Party won 63 percent of the seats in the House of Commons in the 1997 elections. Labor's leader, Tony Blair, was promptly installed as the country's new prime minister as a result. Blair's government consequently managed to get virtually all its legislation passed by the Labor majority in the Commons with considerable efficiency.

As we'll see in subsequent chapters, however, the parliamentary system does not always produce this happy outcome. In some countries the parliamentary majority consists of two or more parties, resulting in a coalition government that represents these multiple parties. It often happens that, the more parties there are in the cabinet, the harder it is for them to come to agreement on government policies. Gridlock frequently results. We'll discuss the parliamentary system and coalition governments in greater detail in chapter 8. Even Britain's one-party governments can be so internally divided that they find it equally difficult to legislate, as we'll see in chapter 16. The evidence is therefore quite mixed when it comes to determining whether parliamentary government is decisively better than divided government in the lawmaking process.

**Rational Decision Making Versus "Satisficing"** The process of transforming ideas into laws through executive-legislative interaction is invariably a complicated one, especially in democracies. Government decision makers must consider a diversity of competing demands and interests and measure what needs to be done against the resources available to do it. It should hardly be surprising that the lawmaking process does not always result in the "best" laws, if by "best" we mean the most rational solutions to specific problems or the most effective ways of improving the general well-being of the population. In a great number of cases, the laws that emerge from the executive-legislative process reflect such things as the priorities of legislative majorities, the pressures of highly influential lobbies or social groups, and the outcomes of bargaining and compromises among elected officials, most of whom are motivated largely by the desire to get reelected. Instead of "the best" or the most rational laws, the lawmaking process in democracies frequently produces laws that are *the most politically acceptable* to a majority of legislators and to relevant executive branch decision makers.

The term that most often describes this process is *satisficing*. It comes from the old English word *satisfice,* which meant "to satisfy." In contemporary political science, **satisficing** ***means making decisions that are satisfactory, or "good enough," rather than the best of all available options.*** In large organizations like governments, satisficing reflects the central reality that decisions must often be reached through a bargaining process involving negotiation and compromise. Decisions reached through a process of satisficing are not necessarily the "best" decisions because those who make them cannot agree on what the best decision is, or because the best decision for the community at large may damage the interests of some specific segment of it.

What is best for the national economy? Economists may tell us that we need to reduce or eliminate budget deficits, and they may supply all sorts of statistical analyses charting the widespread benefits to be gained from such measures. Analytical studies may also provide convincing evidence that the most efficient and rational way to cut the deficit is to raise taxes *and* curtail government spending simultaneously. But if some people do not want to pay higher taxes and others don't want to give up their government jobs or welfare benefits, how can the elected officials who represent them manage to take the "best" and most appropriate action? All too often, they cannot. Rather than raising taxes and reducing expenditures in the most economically efficient manner, cabinets and legislatures may decide to raise taxes only slightly (or not at all) and to curtail government spending only slightly (or not at all).

Elected legislatures are especially prone to satisficing. Legislators are often divided among themselves for the simple reason that the people who elected them are divided. But what about the executive branch and its bureaucracies? Shouldn't we expect the cabinet, which generally consists of a small number of relatively like-minded individuals chosen by the president or prime minister, to make policy decisions far more efficiently than a fractious legislature?

One model suggests that the executive branch of government does in fact operate in a relatively efficient and unified manner. As already noted, the German sociologist Max Weber was one of the first students of modern bureaucracy. Drawing his information largely from Germany's bureaucracy at the start of the twentieth century, Weber developed a hypothetical *ideal type* of bureaucratic structure and behavior emphasizing the following characteristics:

- *Hierarchy*. Bureaucracies, in Weber's model, are structured in a hierarchical fashion from the top down, with a clear chain of command enabling them to respond efficiently to directives.

- *Specialization.* There is a clearly demarcated, stable division of labor among the bureaucracy's organizational components, and the bureaucrats themselves are chosen solely on the basis of their professional competence.
- *Impersonal rules.* Bureaucracies are run in accordance with carefully spelled out rules and regulations, another factor that makes for efficient and predictable operations. The modern bureaucracy applies these rules impersonally, without granting special favors to privileged individuals or groups.
- *Rationality.* "Bureaucracy," Weber wrote, "has a 'rational' character: rules, means, ends, and matter-of-factness dominate its bearing." The whole bureaucratic process is highly organized to achieve the state's objectives efficiently and effectively. "Precision, speed, unambiguity, knowledge of the files, continuity, discretion, unity, strict subordination, reduction of friction and of material and personal costs—these are raised to the optimum point in the strictly bureaucratic administration."[25]

Weber's model is known as the **unitary actor model** of decision making, ***a process in which all the elements of a state's bureaucracy work together as though they were a single actor.*** But do modern governments actually function this way?

A far different picture of executive-level policy making emerges from more recent studies of organizational behavior. The pioneering work of economists James March and Herbert Simon demonstrated that large organizations, whether private corporations or government bureaucracies, rarely operate as rationally and efficiently as Weber maintained. Hierarchical chains of command are frequently ignored. Critical information may not be available. The "best" alternative solutions are not always carefully considered, let alone chosen. On the contrary, bureaucracies, like legislatures, often indulge in satisficing, with executives and staff personnel engaging in negotiations and compromises that lead to decisions that are good enough to win a large consensus, but are not necessarily the most effective ways to resolve the problem under consideration. Moreover, bureaucrats tend to stick to familiar "standard operating procedures": they don't like to take bold initiatives whose results are unpredictable or ambiguous. New approaches to dealing with society's problems therefore tend to differ very little from past approaches, even if they haven't worked very well.

The result is *incrementalism:* change, if it comes at all, is marginal rather than radical. Experimentation is discouraged. If asked by the head of government or cabinet chiefs to come up with innovative solutions to problems or if ordered to implement unfamiliar directives or rules, bureaucracies may misunderstand, ignore, or even sabotage the new commands.[26]

President Harry Truman probably would have recognized this model of bureaucratic unresponsiveness. Sympathizing with the problems Dwight D. Eisenhower would inherit on assuming the presidency, Truman predicted, "He'll sit here, and he'll say, 'Do this! Do that!' And nothing will happen. Poor Ike—it won't be a bit like the Army. He'll find it very frustrating."[27]

A gripping account of how bureaucratic behavior and executive-level decision making can go awry is Graham Allison's analysis of the Cuban missile crisis of 1962.

## HYPOTHESIS-TESTING EXERCISE: The Cuban Missile Crisis

In October 1962, American spy planes flying over Fidel Castro's communist Cuba noticed Soviet construction crews building missile sites on the island. The discovery came several weeks after the missile construction program had begun. It did not occur earlier because the U.S. State Department had temporarily suspended aerial surveillance of Cuba after a U.S. spy plane was shot down over China. The delay was further protracted when the U.S. Air Force and the Central Intelligence Agency became snarled in a bureaucratic battle over whose pilots would fly a new U-2 reconnaissance aircraft. The dispute took a week to resolve. Had it dragged on longer, the United States might not have uncovered Soviet operations in Cuba until after all the missiles were already in place. This delay was one of many bureaucratic bungles and misunderstandings that complicated President John F. Kennedy's

**President Kennedy meets with the National Security Council during the Cuban missile crisis.**

attempts to get the Soviets to remove the missiles while at the same time avoiding a full-scale nuclear war.

### Hypothesis and Variables

In a classic analysis of the crisis, Graham Allison tested the hypothesis that bureaucratic rationality, as characterized by the unitary actor model of decision making, explained U.S. government behavior in the Cuban missile crisis. In this hypothesis, the *dependent variable* is *U.S. government behavior*, and the *independent variable* is *bureaucratic rationality*.

### Expectations

If the unitary actor model is an accurate representation of how the U.S. government operated during the Cuban missile crisis, then we would expect to find that the president, his key advisors, and the various agencies of the U.S. government involved in making and implementing policy decisions possessed all the information they needed to make well-considered, rational decisions; that they were essentially unified in their analysis of the situation and on the measures that needed to be taken; and that these measures were implemented smoothly and effectively, following established lines of command.

### Evidence

Whereas rational decision making requires relatively complete information about the problem at hand, Allison showed that Kennedy and his advisors did not have *any* information about Soviet activities in Cuba until it was almost too late. Moreover, they had no clear information about Soviet motives. Were the Soviets putting missiles in Cuba in order to bomb or threaten the United States? Were they trying to set up a bargaining situation in hopes of inducing the United States to remove its missiles from Turkey, a NATO ally located on the USSR's borders, in exchange for withdrawing the new missiles from Cuba? Were they simply trying to defend Castro's regime against a potential U.S. attack? The administration was similarly in the dark about Soviet resolve. Would Kremlin leaders back down if the United States used military force to compel Moscow to remove the missiles, or would they risk mutual nuclear annihilation rather than give in? These questions epitomized a general dilemma in governmental decision making: all too often, the decision makers do not have the information they need to make informed, "rational" choices. Sometimes they just have to guess; reality can be a mysterious black box.

The evidence also showed that the key government agencies involved in the crisis did not act in a unified fashion. The tug-of-war between the Air Force and the CIA over the U-2 flights was one example. In addition, the military chiefs of the Air Force and the Navy had their own ideas about how to implement a possible "surgical" air strike of the missile sites and a naval blockade of Cuba, ideas that differed considerably from the ways the president, the secretary of defense, and other top decision makers understood those policy options. "Established, rather boring organizational routines," Allison concluded, "determined hundreds of additional, seemingly unimportant details—any one of which might have served as a fuse for disaster."

Even the Soviets were not immune from their own organizational problems. Allison noted that the U.S. spy flights were able to detect the missile sites largely because Soviet construction crews had cleared the surrounding forests. Such behavior reflected the standard operating procedures of a missile construction bureaucracy accustomed to building missile sites in the flat, treeless plains of the USSR. By sticking to organizational routine, the missile builders in Cuba failed to take advantage of the natural camouflage provided by the forests.

In looking at the fourteen key individuals involved in the decision-making process, Allison once again saw no evidence of unity. Each of these individuals had his own set of perceptions of what the Soviets were up to and how best to deal with them. Some of these individuals were influenced by the nature of their professional roles. In accordance with the adage "Where you stand depends on where you sit," the chief military advisors favored military solutions, including bombardment of the missile sites and an invasion of Cuba. Others, like the president and his brother Attorney General Robert Kennedy, feared that this approach might lead to all-out nuclear war. They favored a political solution. Over the course of the two-week-long crisis, this team of decision makers engaged in a continuing process of negotiating, bargaining, and coalition building. Some changed their minds in the process.

Ultimately the president decided on a naval blockade of the island to prevent more missile shipments from coming in. The world breathed a sigh of relief when the Soviet leadership decided to remove the missiles from Cuba. President Kennedy pledged never to invade the island. Decades later it became known that he had also agreed to remove the U.S. missiles from Turkey.

### Conclusions

The evidence Allison uncovered was largely *inconsistent* with the hypothesis of rational decision-making as predicted by the unitary actor model. Allison concluded that two other models offered more accurate depictions of decision making in the Cuban missile crisis. One of them, the *organizational process* model, describes decision making as a more disjointed process involving miscommunication, insufficient information, poor coordination, and other "irrational" phenomena described by analysts like March and Simon. The other one, which Allison called the *bureaucratic politics* (or *governmental politics*) model, emphasizes the different viewpoints that divided President Kennedy and the thirteen other key individuals involved in finding a solution to the crisis. Allison's analysis provides important generalizations about state decision-making processes that have a far wider application than just this particular incident. Variants of the organizational process model and the bureaucratic politics model have been used by a variety of scholars to study governmental policy processes in a number of countries and settings.[28]

---

Far from being a smooth, "rational" undertaking, the policy process in most countries is often a disjointed affair. One political scientist famously referred to governing as "the science of muddling through."[29]

In conclusion, the state—government—is the central reality of political life. How states are organized, how they operate, and how people interact with them are issues that we will examine in most of the chapters that follow.

## KEY TERMS
## (In bold and underlined in the text)

State
Failed state
Sovereignty
Anarchism
Head of state
Constitutional (limited) monarchy
Head of government
Unicameral legislature
Bicameral legislature
Judicial review
Coup d'état
Unitary state
Federation
Confederation
Efficiency
Effectiveness
Divided government
Satisficing
Unitary actor model

## NOTES

1. See also Robert I. Rotberg, *When States Fail: Causes and Consequences* (Princeton: Princeton University Press, 2004). The World Bank has its own quality-of-governance indicators; see chapter 15.
2. Ralph Miliband, *The State in Capitalist Society* (New York: Basic Books, 1969); and David Wells, *Marxism and the Modern State* (Brighton, UK: Harvester, 1981). For discussions of different conceptions of the state, see James A. Caporaso, ed., *The Elusive State: International and Comparative Perspectives* (Newbury Park, Calif.: Sage, 1989).
3. Thomas J. Biersteker and Cynthia Weber, eds. *State Sovereignty as Social Construct* (Cambridge: Cambridge University Press, 1996); and Stephen D. Krasner, *Sovereignty: Organized Hypocrisy* (Princeton: Princeton University Press, 1999).
4. "Politics as a Vocation," in *From Max Weber: Essays in Sociology*, trans., and ed. H. Gerth and C. Wright Mills (New York: Oxford University Press, 1946), 78.
5. Thomas Hobbes, *Leviathan* (New York: Cambridge University Press, 1991); Deborah Baumgold, *Hobbes's Political Theory* (New York: Cambridge University Press, 1988); Arnold A.

Rogow, *Thomas Hobbes: Radical in the Service of Reaction* (New York: W. W. Norton, 1986).

6. John Locke, *Two Treatises of Government* (New York: Cambridge University Press, 1988); Ruth Grant, *John Locke's Liberalism* (Chicago: University of Chicago Press, 1987); Maurice Cranston, *John Locke: A Biography* (New York: Macmillan, 1967).
7. Jean-Jacques Rousseau, *The Collected Works of Jean-Jacques Rousseau* (Hanover, N.H.: University Press of New England, 1990); Leo Damrosch, *Jean-Jacques Rousseau: Restless Genius* (Boston: Houghton-Mifflin, 2005); Maurice Cranston, *Jean-Jacques: The Early Life and Work of Jean-Jacques Rousseau* (Chicago: University of Chicago Press, 1983), and *The Noble Savage: Jean-Jacques Rousseau, 1754–1762* (University of Chicago Press, 1991); Hilail Gildin, *Rousseau's "Social Contract": The Design of the Argument* (Chicago: University of Chicago Press, 1983); Richard Fralin, *Rousseau and Representation* (New York: Columbia University Press, 1978); Judith N. Shklar, *Men and Citizens: A Study of Rousseau's Social Theory* (Cambridge: Cambridge University Press, 1969).
8. Some scholars have likened these tactics to the activities of bandits or modern-day mobsters engaged in protection rackets. In exchange for supplying "protection" to the population against foreign invaders or local marauders, those in authority demand obedience, loyalty, and tribute (i.e., taxes) in return. See Charles Tilly, "War Making and State Making as Organized Crime," in *Bringing the State Back In*, ed. Peter B. Evans, Dietrich Rueschemeyer, and Theda Skocpol, pp. 169–91; Mancur Olson, "Dictatorship, Democracy, and Development," *American Political Science Review*, vol. 87, no. 3 (September 1993): 567–76. Also Charles Tilly, ed., *The Formation of National States in Western Europe* (Princeton: Princeton University Press, 1975), and Martin van Creveld, *The Rise and Decline of the State* (Cambridge: Cambridge University Press, 1999).
9. Robert Nozick, *Anarchy, the State, and Utopia* (New York: Basic Books, 1974); April Carter, *The Political Theory of Anarchism* (New York: Harper & Row, 1971); Emma Goldman, *Anarchism, and Other Essays* (New York: Dover, 1969) and *Living My Life* (New York: AMS Press, 1970); Marian J. Morton, *Emma Goldman and the American Left: "Nowhere At Home"* (New York: Twayne, 1992); Robert Paul Wolff, *In Defense of Anarchism* (New York: Harper & Row, 1970).
10. For a good overview, see R. Kent Weaver and Bert A. Rockman, *Do Institutions Matter?* (Washington, D.C.: Brookings Institution, 1993).
11. See Seymour Martin Lipset, *The First New Nation: The United States in Historical and Comparative Perspective* (New York: Basic Books, 1963).
12. See Giovanni Sartori, *Comparative Constitutional Engineering: An Inquiry into Structures, Incentives, and Outcomes* (New York: New York University Press, 1997).
13. For a sophisticated game-theoretic analysis of legislative voting, see George Tsebelis, *Veto Players: How Political Institutions Work* (New York: Russell Sage Foundation, 2002). See also Gerhard Loewenberg, Peverill Squire, and D. Roderick Kiewiet, eds., *Legislatures: Comparative Perspectives on Representative Assemblies* (Ann Arbor: University of Michigan Press, 2002); Jean Blondel, *Comparative Legislatures* (Englewood Cliffs, N.J.: Prentice Hall, 1973); Gerhard Loewenberg and Samuel C. Patterson, *Comparing Legislatures* (Boston: Little, Brown, 1979); Michael L. Mezey, *Comparative Legislatures* (Durham, N.C.: Duke University Press, 1979); Hannah F. Pitkin, *The Concept of Representation* (Berkeley: University of California Press, 1972).
14. Nathan J. Brown, *The Rule of Law in the Arab World* (Cambridge: Cambridge University Press, 1997).
15. For some comparative approaches to the judiciary, see Mauro Cappelletti, *The Judicial Process in a Comparative Perspective* (New York: Oxford University Press, 1989); Alan M. Katz., ed., *Legal Traditions and Systems: An International Handbook* (Westport, Conn.: Greenwood Press, 1986); Jerold L. Waltman and Kenneth M. Holland, eds., *The Political Role of the Law Courts in Modern Democracies* (New York: St. Martin's Press, 1988).
16. Randall Baker, ed., *Transitions from Authoritarianism: The Role of the Bureaucracy* (Westport, Conn.: Praeger, 2002).

17. On the U.S. bureaucracy, see James Q. Wilson, *Bureaucracy: What Government Agencies Do and Why They Do It* (New York: Basic Books, 1989); and William T. Gormley, Jr., *Taming the Bureaucracy* (Princeton, N.J.: Princeton University Press, 1989). For comparative studies, see B. Guy Peters, *The Politics of Bureaucracy: A Comparative Perspective*, 3rd ed. (White Plains, N.Y.: Longman, 1989); Frank Fischer, *Technocracy and the Politics of Expertise* (Newbury Park, Calif.: Sage, 1990); Jon Pierre, *Bureaucracy in the Modern State: An Introduction to Comparative Public Administration* (Aldershot, England: E. Elgar, 1995); Joel D. Auerbach, Robert A. Putnam, and Bert A. Rockman, *Bureaucrats and Politicians in Western Democracies* (Cambridge, Mass.: Harvard University Press, 1981).
18. Samuel P. Huntington, *The Third Wave: Democratization in the Late Twentieth Century* (Norman: University of Oklahoma Press, 1991), 42.
19. Three classic studies are Morris Janowitz, *The Professional Soldier: A Social and Political Portrait* (Glencoe, Ill.: Free Press, 1960); Samuel P. Huntington, *The Soldier and the State: The Theory and Politics of Civil-Military Relations* (New York: Vintage, 1964); and Samuel E. Finer, *The Man on Horseback* (Oxford: Pall Mall Press, 1962). For a sweeping comparative analysis, see Eric A. Nordlinger, *Soldiers in Politics: Military Coups and Governments* (Englewood Cliffs, N.J.: Prentice Hall, 1977). For an advanced statistical study, see Robert W. Jackman, "The Predictability of Coups d'État: A Model with African Data," *American Political Science Review*, vol. 72, no. 4 (December 1978): 1262–75.
20. Andrew Mango, *Atatürk* (Woodstock, N.Y.: Overlook, 1999).
21. Stephen P. Cohen, *The Idea of Pakistan*, rev. ed. (Washington, D.C.: Brookings Institution, 2006); Christophe Jaffrelot, ed., *Pakistan: Nationalism without a Nation?* (London: Zed, 2002); Owen Bennett Jones, *Pakistan: Eye of the Storm* (New Haven: Yale University Press, 2002); Mary Anne Weaver, *Pakistan: In the Shadow of Jihad and Afghanistan* (New York: Farrar, Straus & Giroux, 2002); Feroz Ahmed, *Ethnicity and Politics in Pakistan* (Oxford: Oxford University Press, 1999); Stephen Cohen, *The Pakistan Army* (Oxford: Oxford University Press, 1998); Benazir Bhutto, *Daughter of Destiny: An Autobiography* (New York: Simon & Schuster, 1989); Pervez Musharraf, *In the Line of Fire: A Memoir* (New York: Free Press, 2006).
22. Wolf Linder, *Swiss Democracy: Possible Solutions to Conflict in Multicultural Societies* (New York: St. Martin's Press, 1994).
23. On policy implementation in the United States, see Jeffrey Pressman and Aaron Wildavsky, *Implementation: How Great Expectations in Washington Are Dashed in Oakland*, 3rd ed. (Berkeley: University of California Press, 1984).
24. Sarah Binder, *Stalemate: Causes and Consequences of Legislative Gridlock* (Washington, D.C.: Brookings Institution, 2003). See also Robert Elgie, ed., *Divided Government in Comparative Perspective* (Oxford: Oxford University Press, 2001).
25. Max Weber, *From Max Weber: Essays in Sociology*, ed. H. H. Gerth and C. Wright Mills (New York: Oxford University Press, 1971), 196–244.
26. James G. March and Herbert A. Simon, *Organizations* (New York: Wiley, 1958); Herbert A. Simon, *Administrative Behavior*, 3rd ed. (New York: Free Press, 1975), and *Models of Man: Social and Rational* (New York: Wiley, 1957); James G. March, *Decisions and Organizations* (Oxford: Blackwell, 1989).
27. Cited in Richard Neustadt, *Presidential Power* (New York: Wiley, 1960), 9.
28. Graham T. Allison, *Essence of Decision* (Boston: Little, Brown, 1971). The notion that "where you stand depends upon where you sit" is attributed to Rufus Miles, a former U.S. assistant secretary of Health, Education and Welfare, and is known as "Miles's law."
29. Charles E. Lindblom, "The Science of 'Muddling Through,'" *Public Administration Review* 19 (1959): 79–88, and "Still Muddling, Not Yet Through," *Public Administration Review* 39 (1979): 517–26. See also Brian Hogwood, *From Crisis to Complacency: Shaping Public Policy* (Oxford: Oxford University Press, 1987), and Charles E. Lindblom and Edward J. Woodhouse, *The Policy-Making Process*, 3rd ed. (Englewood Cliffs, N.J.: Prentice Hall, 1993).

CHAPTER 6

# STATES AND NATIONS

## Nationalism—Nation Building—Supranationalism

In chapter 5 we looked at states as governments. We identified their main institutions and examined some of the ways they work. Of course, states do not hang loosely in the air; they must be connected with the people under their jurisdiction if they are to serve a meaningful purpose and endure over time. We've already noted the importance of legitimacy as a central element in the relationship between governments and populations. This chapter explores another feature of state–society relationships: the concept of *nation*.

When we speak of "national interests" in reference to a state's vital concerns in world affairs, or of "nation building" with regard to the tasks of reconstructing post-Taliban Afghanistan or post-Saddam Iraq, we imply that the "nation" has something to do with governments. In everyday discourse, the terms *nation* and *state* are frequently used interchangeably as synonyms for a country. The members of the United Nations, for example, are governments of countries; the term *national government* refers to a country's central government. But political scientists also use narrower definitions that highlight the distinction between states and nations. Strictly speaking, states and nations are different. *State* usually refers to a country's governmental framework, as detailed in chapter 5. In contrast,

**a <u>nation</u> *is a group of people whose members share a common identity on the basis of distinguishing characteristics and a claim to a territorial homeland.***

A key distinction between *nation* and *state* is that *a nation may not necessarily have a state of its own,* with its own self-governing institutions. To take just one example, the Ibos of Nigeria have demonstrated that they conceive of themselves as a nation, based on tribal bonds, language patterns, religious affiliations, a territorial base in Nigeria's southeastern region, and other factors. But their alienation from the Nigerian state, which has been largely controlled by groups with different tribal, linguistic, regional, and religious affiliations, prompted the Ibos to rise up in revolt in the 1960s and fight for their own independent state (country), which they planned to call Biafra. The revolt was crushed by Nigeria's military government, and the Ibos were compelled to remain part of Nigeria. But as far as a great many of them were concerned, they remained a nation nevertheless.

For its part, **<u>national identity</u>** is an important component of the very definition of a nation. By itself, it refers to ***a people's conscious belief that they collectively constitute a nation.*** It is a shared understanding that they belong together on the basis of certain characteristics that, in their own minds, transcend their differences and set them apart from other national groups. In other words, national identity reflects a people's *sense of nationhood.* Nations with a strong sense of national identity are bound together by widely diffused, and often deeply felt, attachments and loyalties on the part of the vast majority of their members. Citizens of countries with lower levels of national identity may have stronger identity attachments to smaller groups *within* the nation, such as a clan, an ethnic group, or a religious sect. Severe identity conflicts often result. The Ibos have a strong sense of their own identity as a nation. Nigerians, by contrast, have a weak sense of national identity *as Nigerians:* many of them identify more directly with their own respective tribal, linguistic, regional, or religious group, or some combination of these identity markers. The weakness of the Nigerian identity stems from the fact that the state of Nigeria and its boundaries were created by the British, not by the local people (see chapter 23).

What are the distinguishing characteristics of a people that define their identity as a nation?

One source of national identity is *ethnicity*. As indicated in chapter 2, ethnicity is a form of group identification that is usually rooted in a common biological ancestry—or, more precisely, in a people's *belief* in such a common ancestry. Most ethnic groups trace their roots to a historic homeland. Most remain attached to that ancestral territory over the centuries, either physically or—in the case of émigrés or exiles—sentimentally. Ethnicity frequently includes one or more additional marks of group distinctiveness, such as language, religion, social customs, or artistic expression. Even so, it is mainly a family affair: the ethnic group sees itself as an extended family that has survived through the ages. Ethnic attachments can be reinforced by political factors such as common governmental institutions (a monarch, a legal code, a tribal council) as well as by patterns of economic interaction. Nevertheless, ethnicity is separate from government and the economy. Using these defining criteria for ethnicity, James Fearon counted 822 ethnic groups that each made up at least 1 percent of the population in 160 countries in the 1990s.[1]

Although ethnicity can provide a basis for nationhood, "nation" is not simply another term for "ethnic group." What distinguishes the two is that *the members of a nation lay claim to a more or less clearly defined territory.* They see this territory as belonging to them in some way, whether or not they actually govern it independently of some other governing authority. African Americans in the United States, Hispanic whites in Mexico, and East Indians in Malaysia are all ethnic groups, but they do not claim a specific territory within their country of residence. Nations that have defined their national identity in ethnic *and territorial* terms include the Japanese, Chinese, and Germans, as well as smaller groups such as Basques and Catalonians in Spain, Pashtuns in Pakistan and Afghanistan, Scots in Scotland, and dozens of others around the world.[2]

Another source of national identity is a shared *civic community*. In this pattern, people feel that they constitute a nation on the basis of certain *shared principles* or *ideals* or *community goals,* however broadly they may be defined. The United States provides a good example. Some 300 million people representing a wide diversity of ethnic groups and backgrounds identify themselves as Americans largely because of their shared involvement in an American way of life that includes democratic rights and freedoms, private enterprise, and various cultural attitudes and behaviors. Korean Americans, Italian Americans, and other "hyphenated" Americans tend to see themselves as part of a larger American nation, while at the same time feeling connected to their respective ethnic groups. The country's history as a land of immigrants and imported slaves helps account for these identity patterns. Switzerland is another example. Its inhabitants speak four languages but nevertheless identify themselves as "Swiss," a national identity that was forged in medieval times and solidified in the nineteenth century. As in the case of ethnically based nationalism, civic forms of national identity include a territorial dimension: the American and Swiss nations both reside within demarcated boundaries.

In some cases a people's identity can be split between an identification with their territorial ethnic group (e.g., Tatars in Russia) and their *citizenship* as members of a *state* (such as the Russian Federation). If asked to identify their nation (or *nationality*), such people would most likely respond that they are

Tatar. When asked to identify their state or country, they would probably say Russia. (When the USSR existed, they would have said "the Soviet Union" and called themselves Soviet citizens.) Only ethnic Russians would likely identify their *nationality* as Russian. The Russian Federation is a *multinational state:* it consists of a variety of peoples who have their own separate national identities but are also citizens of the Russian state. Most of the non-Russians were incorporated into the Russian empire in earlier centuries as it expanded across the vast Eurasian landmass, and they became citizens of the Soviet Union (or "Soviets") under communist rule. Multinational states can have serious problems staying together because some of their citizens may be more loyal to their own nationality group than to the central state. Yugoslavia provides a glaring example, and we'll look at it later in this chapter.

One scholar has argued that national identity results from shared *patterns of social communication.* According to Karl Deutsch, membership in a people "essentially consists in the ability to communicate more effectively, and over a wider range of subjects, with members of one large group than with outsiders." The bonds that tie people together as a nation typically include group myths, historical memories, and emotive symbols like flags, anthems, and hallowed battlefields. Another scholar has suggested that nations are *imagined political communities.* The nation is imagined, writes Benedict Anderson, "because the members of even the smallest nation will never know most of their fellow-members, meet them, or even hear of them, yet in the minds of each lives the image of their communion.[3]

Students of identity like David Laitin and Russell Hardin have pointed out that national identity is not fixed forever in some primordial state; to a significant degree it is socially constructed. Individuals cannot change their DNA or their blood relations, but they can change their national identity, making choices that vary with the social and political circumstances in which they find themselves. A Russian-speaking Tatar who lived in the Ukrainian Soviet Republic in the days of the Soviet Union, and who now finds herself living in independent Ukraine, can no longer identify herself ambivalently as "Soviet." She must now decide whether to identify herself as Tatar, Russian, Ukrainian, or some composite of these national identities. For their part, some Ukrainians may "construct" this person's identity as Russian or Tatar (or both), but not necessarily Ukrainian ("She's not one of us!"). The intensity of national identity can also vary with circumstances. If our group is threatened by another, we can choose negotiation or violence, depending on the situation. But our response is not predetermined by our ethnicity or by past history: *we have choices.* When we think about national identity, we should be wary of fixed categories and open to the possibilities of choice, change, and ambiguity in the ways identities are formed.[4]

## NATIONALISM

The concepts of *nation* and *national identity* are usually steeped in emotional, psychological, and cultural attachments to one's people and their historic homeland. By contrast, the concept of *nationalism* is essentially political and is more explicitly articulated. Scholars have defined nationalism in a variety of ways.[5] Moreover, nationalism can have different connotations, depending on the context. In some instances nationalism connotes a *people's* resolve to take political action in behalf of their group, whether by getting an existing government to respect their rights or by insisting on some form of self-government. In other instances nationalism connotes a *state's* resolve in international affairs to affirm or defend the country's "national interests" (meaning state interests) in its diplomatic, military, and economic dealings with the outside world. The definition we offer here combines both of these dimensions:

> **Nationalism** ***is a consciously formulated set of*** **political ideas** ***emphasizing the distinctiveness and unity of one's nation, specifying common interests, and prescribing goals for action.***

Whereas national identity proclaims, "We are a people and we belong together in this territory," the idea of nationalism adds, "We must therefore act together to achieve our common political aims." Whereas national identity is largely a social and cultural construct (with a territorial component), nationalism is assertively political in nature: it is a call to action that invariably involves government in some way or another. And whereas national identity evokes sentiments and emotions, nationalism combines these affective inclinations—such as feelings of pride or resentment—with a more or less clearly elaborated political program. National identity answers the question "Who am I?" Nationalism addresses the question "What should we do?" and it responds with a project.

Because nationalism involves political ideas and goals, it can be regarded as a political *ideology.* As such, its defining principle is that the nation must be a high political priority in its own right. For the most ardent nationalists, the nation is the supreme political value, outweighing all other political, social, and economic considerations. The nation's unity, in this view, must be constantly maintained so as to permit decisive collective action. The ties that bind the nation together must therefore take precedence over the class conflicts, religious affiliations, and other fissures that keep its members apart. The nation's distinctiveness vis-à-vis other nations or groups must also be clearly asserted. One of the chief purposes of a nationalist ideology is to define who belongs to the nation and who does not.

In its benign variant, nationalism calls for *patriotism,* which typically means love of one's country and a general loyalty to its laws and institutions. But in some cases the assertion of national distinctiveness can take the more extreme forms of xenophobia and chauvinism. *Xenophobia* means distrust and hatred of foreigners. *Chauvinism* is wildly exaggerated, fanatical patriotism. These attitudes often involve claims that one's own nation is superior to other groups, and they may lead to regarding outside groups as enemies. Adolph Hitler's ideology of fascism, for instance, proclaimed the superiority of the "Aryan race" (a bogus racial category), and it relegated Jews, Slavs, and others to the level of "subhumans." Hitler's Nazi government pursued a policy of *hypernationalism,* an extreme form of nationalism that unleashed Germany's military aggression and the subjugation of its defeated victims in World War II.

Like most ideologies, nationalism is propagated by political elites—professional political activists and intellectuals, for the most part—who take it upon themselves to promote a national culture and design programs for political action. Some nationalist elites may wish to secure the nation's aims through peaceful means; others do not shrink from violent confrontation. Some may favor democracy while others combine nationalism with fascism, communism, or some other authoritarian ideology. Some are exclusively concerned with the good of the nation, while others exploit a people's hopes and grievances in a cynical play for power, whipping up national passions in the process. Whatever the case, the relationship between nationalist elites and the nation—the people whose cause they lead—is central to the ways nationalism is conceived and practiced in specific circumstances. It ultimately determines just how "national" a nationalist movement is.

If a nationalist program is formulated by a small elite, such as the leaders of a political party or a military organization, and if they exclude other representatives of the national community from participating on a roughly equal basis in the nationalist cause, then the people who actually *are* the nation may have little input into defining their common aspirations. If the elite monopolizes power once an independent government is formed, the nation as a whole may end up having little say in its own destiny. Many a national cause has been hijacked by dictators—from Napoleon and Hitler to Mao Zedong and Saddam Hussein—who imposed their own will on the nation they claimed to represent. To be truly "national," nationalism as a political process must be democratically open to the masses who compose the nation and to their chosen representatives. The United States, for example, has managed to build a fairly high level of national unity around its Constitution (with the exception of the Civil War) while expanding democracy among its citizens. In quite a few other countries, by contrast, the process of defining the nation's goals and mobilizing the means to achieve them has been directed from above by an authoritarian elite. That elite often holds power dictatorially after self-government has been achieved.[6]

## Constituting the Nation as a Political Actor

What kinds of goals do groups that consider themselves nations typically seek? What do we mean by "nationalist projects"?

Let's start with a minority group that occupies a fairly well-defined region within a country. If this group is subjected to discrimination at the hands of the majority, it will want the central government to do something about it—especially if the government is perpetrating discriminatory practices itself or permitting others to get away with it. The members of the minority nationality may also want the central government to guarantee their people's rights to economic assistance and other benefits (schools, hospitals, and so on) that other citizens of the country receive. In addition, they may want the right to use their own language in local schools, public offices, and media. In these and similar instances, the group's main aim is to get certain rights legally protected by higher state authorities within its recognized geographical area. Examples include the Hungarian minority in the Transylvanian region of Romania, historically discriminated against by Romanian governments; the Indians of the Chiapas region in Mexico (as described in chapter 22); and the Baluchis in Pakistan, who have recently resorted to violence in order to gain a bigger share of the country's oil revenues and other benefits.[7]

Some nationalists may want more than just an end to discrimination, however; they may want some form of self-determination. **Self-determination** ***usually means self-government.*** It can take different forms. In some cases a regionally based movement may want **territorial autonomy**, ***which means self-government over its own territory within the structure of a larger state.*** Autonomy in this sense amounts to local self-administration, encompassing the group's right to elect its own local officials and administer its own laws with limited interference from the central government. Spain, for example, grants special rights of autonomy to regions whose inhabitants have a strong sense of their own national identity, such as the Basques and the Catalonians. In 2006, Catalonia adopted a new autonomy statute that defined the region as a "nation." In a process known as "devolution," the United Kingdom in recent years has granted new powers of self-administration to three of its four regional components—Scotland, Wales, and Northern Ireland. The population of each of these regions has its own ethnically rooted national identity. (England, the UK's historic heart, does not have similar autonomous powers.) The central governments of both Spain and the United Kingdom have been careful, however, to maintain higher authority over these autonomous units on certain issues, such as foreign policy and the country's economy.

More assertively, a nationalist movement may want outright *independence*. In this case the nation wants its own state (country), fully sovereign over its population and territory and formally recognized by other states around the globe. Achieving this goal may require a revolt against the central government and secession from the existing state, a cause known as *separatism*. In 2002, following decades of conflict that cost more than 200,000 lives, East Timorese seceded from Indonesia and created the new state of East Timor under the auspices of the United Nations. In Russia, Chechen separatists have waged a bloody war for an independent Chechnya since the 1990s. In other cases the drive for independence may require a confrontation with an external power, such as an imperial state like the British, Habsburg, or Ottoman empires. Frequently the struggle turns violent, as in the American colonies' battle for liberation from England or Algeria's fight for independence from France in the 1950s and 1960s. But India and Pakistan gained their freedom from Britain peacefully, thanks to the pacifist ideology of the independence movement's principal leader, Mohandas Gandhi.

At a country-wide level (as opposed to a regional level), a common national identity can be an important unifying force, establishing a measure of homogeneity among a people who may be otherwise divided into different religions, social classes, linguistic groups, or other identity formations. If the group's members can at least agree that they share an overarching identity as a nation (as Americans, as Pakistanis, as Iraqis, and the like), they may be able to overcome the internal differences that provoke dissension in their ranks, at least on the issues that concern their common welfare. Nationalism can thus play a *constitutive* role: it can help constitute the nation as an effective political actor, galvanizing its members' common interests and empowering them to realize their common aims.

But if people do not share a common national identity, the chances that they will be able to act in concert on the basis of a common program, such as an independence movement or a democratization process, are slim. If the inhabitants of a particular country devote their primary loyalties to their respective tribe, linguistic group, religion, or some other parochial identity group as opposed to the larger "nation," they may not be able to govern themselves effectively at all or achieve other "national" goals. A weak national identity reduces the likelihood of a constitutive nationalism through which the various units of society can act together. In the absence of any national homogeneity, a divisive—and perhaps highly conflictual—social heterogeneity takes over. Chronic disunity can result in paralytic gridlock or civil war. Under these circumstances it is not likely that the population will agree on a central government that all can regard as legitimate. It is even less likely that they will be able to put together a stable, successful democracy. The lack of a strong, unifying national identity, in short, has a ripple effect on nationalism, the state, legitimacy, and democracy. All of these things come together under the concept of *nation building*.

## NATION BUILDING

The term *nation building*, like many other entries in the lexicon of politics, means different things to different people. As Francis Fukuyama has observed, "What Americans mean by *nation-building* is usually state-building coupled with economic development."[8] *State building* essentially means the effort to develop an effective government at the political decision-making level, along with supportive bureaucratic agencies that can implement government policies and programs. In a world of failed states and weak states, the task of creating and sustaining states with sufficient "institutional capacity" to maintain order and deliver human services is an urgent one. Promoting "good governance" has thus become a central goal of international development agencies. But states and nations, as we've indicated, are not the same. Accordingly, this book provides an expansive definition of nation building that combines the three tasks of forging a national identity, building an effective state, and developing democratic legitimacy.

> **Nation building** ***is the process of developing a widely shared national identity among a country's population and an effective, legitimate state.***

In some countries the population may already have a broadly shared national identity but lack an effective state that is accepted as legitimate by the key elements of the citizenry. In these cases, the task of "nation building" is essentially confined to state building: it centers on creating a functioning state machinery and on shoring up the state's legitimacy in the eyes of the people through democratic mechanisms and economic progress. But when a dysfunctional government with dubious legitimacy rests on a shaky foundation of national identity, as it does in a large number of countries around the world, the nation-building process becomes all the more challenging. In these cases, programs designed to construct a viable state and democracy will almost certainly require simultaneous efforts to build a common national identity capable of bridging over the population's volatile divisions. If these divisions cannot be overcome, then the only way to achieve either state effectiveness or democracy may be to loosen the country into a federation or confederation (like Switzerland) that grants wide autonomy to its constituent units, or to permit the outright independence of one or more of its parts (like Yugoslavia, as we'll see later in this chapter).

Of course, all of this is easier said than done. Surmounting deeply rooted conflicts and completing the tasks of nation building can take a very long time, as demonstrated in numerous countries around the world—from Afghanistan to Iraq, from Russia to Mexico. These tasks may also require the country's main groups and their leaders to play the leading role in forming a shared identity. It is an open question whether external forces—such as the United States and its allies, or international mediators like the United Nations—can successfully induce a country's diverse elements to bury their hatchets and cement bonds of identity that must, in the end, be self-sustaining. The international community has found it hard enough to build effective states, as Fukuyama notes.[9] Building national identity from the outside is even more problematic. Moreover, success in building a national identity and a state may not be enough to build a functioning democracy. Democracy depends on a host of factors, as we'll see in chapter 9.

**Civil War** When internally divided countries fail at the multiple tasks of forging a broad-based national identity, solidifying an effective government, and building democratic institutions and practices, the results can be devastating. Civil war can ravage a society for years on end. Between 1945 and 1999, approximately 127 civil wars took place inside 73 countries around the globe. At least a thousand people died in each conflict, with the total loss of life amounting to more than sixteen million fatalities. The average war lasted about six years.

What has been the primary cause of these conflicts? In a systematic study, James Fearon and David Laitin found that ethnic, religious, and other forms of cultural diversity are *not* the principal cause of civil wars. Many countries are culturally divided, but not all of them succumb to internal warfare. Fearon and Laitin identify civil wars as insurgencies that are conducted by fairly small, lightly armed guerilla bands based in relatively well-protected rural areas, often in remote mountain ranges. Although the grievances expressed by these rebel groups may at times have an ethnic or religious basis, the wars themselves tend to occur when the central government is too weak, both financially and institutionally, to crush the armed uprising quickly. Corruption and brutal counterinsurgency tactics only prolong civil strife and raise new grievances. Even democratically elected governments can exhibit these tendencies, allowing civil insurgencies to develop. Fearon and Laitin call on the international community to provide financial insistence to beleaguered governments with the aim of enhancing their competence and holding them accountable for their actions. "Good governance" thus appears essential to stopping civil wars.[10]

Fortunately, the number of civil wars and other violent internal conflicts has been declining since the early 1990s. Scholars at the University of Maryland's Center for International Development and Crisis Management, using their Minorities at Risk database and other sources, report that the number of armed conflicts for self-determination (that is, self-governance) fell from forty-nine cases in 1991 to twenty-five by the end of 2004. Most of these conflicts were settled by granting the rebellious groups more autonomy and greater opportunities to secure their collective rights through bargaining with the central government. Ethnonational wars for outright independence in 2004 were down to their lowest level since 1960. In addition, more than seventy territorially concentrated groups around the world were seeking greater self-government *without* recourse to armed violence, relying instead on democratic procedures. Significant reductions in discrimination against minorities have also occurred in the past several decades, especially in the world's democracies.

Despite these successes, 18 countries were embroiled in armed conflicts by early 2005, most of them civil wars. Out of 161 countries, 31 were "red-flagged" for being at severe risk for civil war and 18 were at risk for potential genocide or mass political murder in the near future.[11]

Africa has seen more than its share of protracted civil wars. One of the most horrific examples occurred in Rwanda and Burundi, where approximately 800,000 people lost their lives in ethnic warfare between the Hutus and Tutsis in 1994. Some four million have perished in the Democratic Republic of Congo since 1998, the largest loss of life in warfare since World War II. Uganda has been wracked by a civil rebellion since the mid-1980s. These and other armed conflicts in Africa have shown signs of winding down in recent years, but it is hard to say if peace will endure. Meanwhile, a new round of civil strife broke out in Sudan in 2003.

## SUDAN

In the past several years Sudan (figure 6.1) has become notorious for the continuing catastrophe in its *Darfur* region, a desert area the size of France located in the western part of Africa's largest country. Since 2003 a brutal civil war in Darfur has claimed as many as 450,000 lives and displaced 2.5 million people, in addition to victimizing countless women, children, and other noncombatants. The recent hostilities began when two rebel groups from Darfur's mostly black African population attacked military and police units stationed in the region by Sudan's central government. Blacks form the majority (about 52 percent) of Sudan's population of 39 million. But ever since Sudan gained independence from Britain in 1956, the central government in Khartoum has been dominated by a political and military elite drawn from the country's Arab minority, which constitutes 39 percent of the population. Sudanese Arabs are mostly Sunni Muslims, and they tend to reside in the northern part of the country. For years Darfur's African villagers and farmers—who are themselves also Muslims—experienced systematic

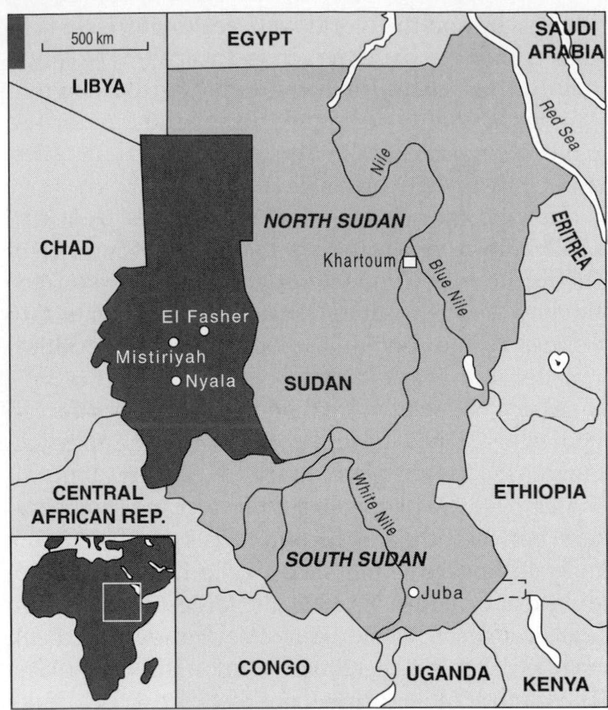


**FIGURE 6.1 Sudan. Darfur is the darkest shaded region in the west.**
*Source: The Economist,* February 11, 2006, p. 44. Copyright 2006 The Economist Newspaper Ltd. www.economist.com

discrimination at the hands of the Arab-led central government, together with a lack of economic opportunity and property rights. They were also subjected to periodic raids by Arab militias in Darfur known as the Janjaweed.

In early 2004, government forces and the Janjaweed stepped up a series of coordinated attacks on Darfur's blacks, concentrating on three African tribal groups. Airstrikes were followed by militia onslaughts that were accompanied by gang rapes, mass murders, and the burning of villages. Turmoil ensued as hundreds of thousands of terrorized people fled their homes, many of them ending up in refugee camps established by international organizations in Darfur and in neighboring Chad. In 2004 the U.S. government condemned the attacks as genocide. A contingent of seven thousand troops was sent to Darfur by the African Union (which represents the continent's fifty-three countries). The Bush administration called for a NATO force to be dispatched to the region, and the United Nations Security Council approved the deployment of a peacekeeping force of 22,500 troops to replace the African Union forces. But Sudan's president resisted the introduction of the UN peacekeepers. In May 2006 the Sudanese government signed a peace agreement with one of Darfur's three rebel groups. The conflict only intensified, however, as government troops joined with the signatories of the peace deal to support the Janjaweed's brutality. The killing, raping, and looting of Darfur's hapless victims continued as the months wore on.

Darfur has not been Sudan's only internal conflict. Right from its inception as an independent state, the country has been ripped apart by a confrontation between Arabs in the north and the black African population in the south. Unlike Darfur's Africans, who are mostly Muslim, Sudan's population in the south is largely animist, with some Christians. Between 1956 and 1972, the two sides were locked in the "Anyanya war," named after a poison used by black fighters. That conflict ended in an agreement that granted the south considerable autonomy plus representation in the central government. But fighting flared up anew in 1984 after Sudan's Muslim-dominated government imposed Islamic law on the non-Muslim south. The revived civil war lasted twenty-one years, leaving two million dead and four million homeless. In January 2005 a peace agreement was signed that promised to end the conflict. The deal removed the application of Islamic law from the south and gave the region a six-year period of autonomous government. The leader of the main black rebel group became Sudan's vice president. In 2011 the southerners will hold a referendum to decide whether to remain in Sudan or establish an independent state of their own.

Sudan has also experienced divisive power struggles at the peak of its Arab-dominated leadership pyramid. The country's elected government was toppled in a military coup in 1969. In 1989 Lieutenant-General Omar al-Bashir took power in another coup. In the 1990s al-Bashir formed an alliance with Hassan al-Turabi, a Muslim cleric who headed the National Congress Party, Sudan's ruling party. Al-Turabi had close links with Islamic terrorists: between 1991 and 1996, Osama bin Laden resided in Sudan under his protection. Rivalries between al-Bashir and al-Turabi intensified over time, prompting al-Bashir to rescind some of al-Turabi's power. In 2001, al-Turabi was arrested after calling for an uprising against the government. After being released in 2003, the cleric was arrested once again. Meanwhile, al-Bashir has sought to mend fences with the United States since September 11, 2001, offering his cooperation in the global war on terrorism.

Sudan tops the list of countries in critical condition shown in chapter 5 in table 5.1. By virtually every measure, it is a failed state. Clearly, the absence of a common Sudanese national identity capable of overarching the country's festering divisions has been a major source of Sudan's troubles.[12]

## WHEN THE NATION AND THE STATE DON'T FIT TOGETHER

Historically, the development of nationalism followed the creation of states in some cases, but preceded or accompanied the creation of new states in others. In England and France, powerful monarchal states existed for several centuries before the creation of a distinct English or French nationalism. When it came, nationalism in these countries tended to be defined in highly political terms, reflecting the development of English parliamentary processes in the one case and the French Revolution in the other.[13] In later centuries, nationalist programs were purposely elaborated to establish new states. Germans formed a central German state in the nineteenth century. At approximately the same time, Italian nationalists created a new state of Italy, putting an end to the peninsula's centuries-long fragmentation into a mosaic of different regimes and foreign occupiers. ("We have made Italy; now we must make Italians," a nationalist leader proclaimed, anticipating the need for nation building.) Across the high seas, new independent states were born in Latin America as liberation movements freed their respective territories from Spain or Brazil. As the century wore on, nationalist movements within the Austro-Hungarian (Habsburg), Ottoman, and Russian empires militated for independent states of their own, processes that accelerated as these imperial regimes collapsed during or after World War I.

In most of these cases of new state creation, the overriding aim of nationalist movements was to create a *nation-state:* a sovereign state consisting of one "nation" within internationally recognized boundaries. And in most instances, the nation was characterized largely in ethnic terms. Germans, Italians, Serbs, Romanians, Poles, and a variety of other ethnically defined groups ultimately succeeded in forming new states whose populations consisted overwhelmingly of their own ethnic group. Over time, the term *nation-state* came to be used as a common synonym for *state* or *country.*[14]

In fact, however, the perfect symmetry of one state and one nation is rare. States are social constructs: they do not exist in nature. The process of state formation is invariably a complicated affair, involving internal clashes, wars, imperialism, foreign occupations, revolutions, liberation struggles, peace treaties, and other domestic and international determinants. As a consequence, the term *nation-state,* in its most literal meaning, is usually a misnomer. A 1971 investigation showed that out of 132 countries, only 12 (9.1 percent) met the strict criterion of one nation and one state.[15] The situation is not much different today. Our survey of 172 countries with populations of at least 200,000 in 2001 revealed that 53 countries (30.8 percent) had a dominant ethnic group that comprised at least 90 percent of the population. (Granted, an ethnic group is not always the same as a nation, but it often forms the basis of one.) Of these 53 states, quite a few have nationhood problems in spite of the fact that one ethnic group constitutes the overwhelming majority of the population. West European countries like Denmark, Germany, France, and the Netherlands have witnessed a rise in immigration from North Africa, the Middle East, and elsewhere in recent decades, resulting in the growth of anti-immigrant sentiment and political parties. These West European countries have historically defined their nationhood in ethnic terms, and the growing number of immigrants and their descendants who seek permanent residence in them has prompted a reexamination of traditional concepts of nation and citizenship. China, whose population is 92 percent Han Chinese, has continuing problems over Tibet, which was forcibly annexed in the 1950s by the Communist Chinese government, and additional problems with its large Uighur minority, which is mostly Muslim. Romania has tensions with Hungarian and Roma minorities. Similar difficulties can be found in other countries with a large dominant ethnic group. On a more positive note, a Freedom House survey in 2001 found that countries with a dominant ethnic group comprising at least two-thirds of the population were more likely to observe political and civil rights than countries that were more ethnically divided. Political allegiances in the latter countries tended to cluster around ethnic identities, often resulting in discriminatory political practices.[16]

Today's world consists of states with more than one nation, and nations without their own states. *Canada* is a good example of the first category. Discord between elements of the country's English and French communities has persisted since the earliest stages of Canadian history. The predominantly French-speaking province of Quebec, originally settled in 1608, has 7 million people, roughly one-fourth of Canada's total population. In the 1960s a separatist movement became increasingly vocal, its leaders calling for an independent Quebec. Not all Quebecers were willing to secede from Canada, however. In 1980, 60 percent of Quebec voters (many of whom were primarily English speakers) rejected a proposal that would have given their leaders the right to negotiate an agreement establishing Quebec's sovereignty. Another referendum conducted in 1995 offered Quebec's voters the possibility of secession in the event that a new autonomy agreement could not be worked out. This time the result was much closer than before: 50.25 percent voted no, barely enough to defeat the proposal. In 2003 the pro-independence Parti Quebecois lost its bid for a third consecutive term in charge of Quebec's provincial government. Although the new governing party was opposed to secession, polls show that a solid core of about 40 percent of Quebec's populace favor an independent Quebec.

Like Canada, *Sri Lanka* is also a state with more than one nation. But unlike Canada, which has dealt with the Quebec issue peacefully and democratically, Sri Lanka (formerly known as Ceylon) has been ravaged by civil war since 1983. The conflict has raged between the majority group, the Sinhalese, who are mostly Buddhists, and their main rivals, the Tamils, who are mostly Hindus. The Tamils constitute about 18 percent of the country's population of 20 million. In addition to practicing different religions, the two groups are ethnically distinct and speak different languages. The Tamils reside mainly in the island's northern and eastern provinces. They claim that they have been systematically oppressed since the 1950s, when Sinhalese-led governments initiated the first in a series of discriminatory laws suppressing Tamil language rights and other basic political and civil rights. The Tamils' fight against the central government is led by the Liberation Tigers of Tamil Elam, a guerilla group that demands full independence for the Tamil region. (Although the organization's leaders tend to come from Hindu families, most of them are inspired by communist ideology rather than by religion.) More than 64,000 people have been killed since the conflict erupted. A cease-fire was arranged in 2002, but fighting continued sporadically. After the powerful tsunami of December 2004 devastated the island's coastal areas, the Tamil Liberation Tigers took charge of international relief efforts in the territories under their control. Large-scale violence broke out once again in 2006.[17]

Just as there are states with more than one nation, there are also nations without a state. The *Kurds,* for example, are a nation of some 25 million people occupying more than seventy thousand square miles of territory that spills across several countries (see figure 6.2). Though they were promised a state of their own after World War I, there is still no independent Kurdistan. Today most Kurds live in Turkey (about 10 million), Iran (5.5 million), and Iraq (about 4 million), with smaller communities in Syria, Armenia, and Azerbaijan. Kurdish fighters have been engaged in virtually continuous conflict for decades, mostly with the governments of Turkey and Iraq.

**FIGURE 6.2 Kurdish Areas (shown in gray)**

Persistent attacks by Saddam Hussein's government prompted the United States, Britain, and France to provide aerial protection for Kurds in Iraq. Iraq's Kurds celebrated Saddam's fall in 2003, but it was still not clear three years later whether they would cooperate with the Arab majority in the post-Saddam nation-building process or would seek some form of autonomy. Turkey has been repeatedly condemned by Western governments for violating the Kurds' rights. In response, the Turkish government initiated a reconciliation program in 2000, and in 2002 it lifted its fifteen-year state of emergency in the Kurdish areas. A Kurdish separatist group announced in 2006 that it would no longer observe the truce. For their part, Iran's Kurds complain of continuing discrimination at the hands of the country's theocratic government. Some Iranian Kurds have crossed the border into Iraq to work with the Party for Free Life in Kurdistan, which is outlawed in Iran.

Perhaps the most tortured conflict over competing visions of nation and state in the modern world is the dispute between Israel, a state with territorial problems, and the Palestinians, a nation without a state.

## ISRAEL AND THE PALESTINIANS

Following the collapse of the Ottoman Empire's dominions in the Middle East during World War I and its aftermath, the British assumed responsibility for the territory of Palestine. Britain's task under a League of Nations mandate was to prepare Palestine for independence, but the population—consisting of a half million Arabs and roughly 70,000 Jews—was divided on how the new state was to be constituted. The Arab majority wanted their own Palestinian state. But proponents of *Zionism,* a Jewish nationalist movement originating in Europe, demanded a state for the Jewish people, whose roots in Palestine reached back two thousand years. In 1917, Foreign Secretary Arthur Balfour committed the British government to the creation of a "national home for the Jewish people" in Palestine, but without prejudice to the rights of local Arabs. The Balfour Declaration's twin goals—statehood for Jews as well as for Arabs—were to prove incompatible.

Jewish emigration to Palestine grew steadily: by the time Adolph Hitler took power in Germany in 1933, Jews constituted about 20 percent of the Palestinian population. In 1939 there were about a half million Jews in Palestine (about a third of the total populace), and their well-organized businesses, farms, trade unions, and social organizations provoked an Arab backlash that occasionally turned violent. The British quelled an Arab revolt against Jewish immigration in 1936–39, but a broad-based Palestinian national movement emerged in the process, led by prominent Arab families opposed to the creation of a Jewish state. To appease the Arabs, the British clamped restrictions on the influx of Jews from abroad. But the tragedy of the Holocaust, in which 6 million European Jews perished under the Nazis' genocidal onslaught, reawakened Jewish nationalism and convinced Jews the world over that it was time for a state of their own in Palestine. As Jewish terrorist organizations blew up British targets in hopes of forcing the British out, Britain in 1947 asked the United Nations to propose a solution to Palestine's status. After considering two plans, the UN General Assembly in November 1947 adopted a resolution calling for the partition of Palestine into separate Jewish and Arab states. Palestinians initiated hostilities the next day, killing Jewish bus passengers and aiming sniper fire at civilians in Tel-Aviv. Palestinian attacks intensified during the next several months, but the better-organized Jewish fighters retaliated. Zionist leaders had already assumed for decades that the creation of a state with a Jewish majority would require the peaceful "transfer" of Arabs out of Jewish territory. A number of them were displeased that the UN partition plan would have left the new Jewish state with a population of a half million Jews and 400,000 Arabs, a large and potentially violent minority. After the fighting began, many Palestinians fled their homes on their own. By the end of March 1948, about 100,000 Arabs had decided to leave. But as Jewish troops took the offensive, they expelled large numbers of Palestinians by force. After Jewish forces killed more than a hundred men, women, and children in the village of Dayr Yasin in April, raping and mutilating others, still more Arabs took flight. By the middle of May, Jewish fighters had captured nearly two hundred Arab villages and towns; more than 300,000 Arab Palestinians were now dispersed. At this point, the British pulled out of Palestine, ending their mandate over the disputed territory. On May 14, Palestine's Jewish community—now numbering 650,000—proclaimed the state of Israel.

The new Jewish state was immediately attacked by its Arab neighbors. But by early 1949 it had achieved a decisive military victory, ending up with more territory than it had been awarded under the UN partition plan. A substantial number of Arabs, estimated at approximately 700,000, had fled the area or were forcibly evicted during the fighting, a mass exodus that Palestinians called "the Disaster." In all, about 150,000 Arabs stayed in Israel.[18] In 1949, the neighboring Arab kingdom of Transjordan (later known as Jordan) annexed the Arab parts of Palestine, consisting of the West Bank of the Jordan River and the eastern part of Jerusalem. Between 1948 and 1950, about 510,000 new Jewish immigrants moved into the freshly created Israeli state. In 1950, Israel enacted the "Law of the Return," which invited Jews from all over the world to settle there. An additional 600,000 arrived between 1950 and 1953. In 1955, the UN refugee organization estimated that 940,000 Arab refugees from Palestine were living in neighboring Arab countries, many of them confined to squalid refugee camps.

The hostilities surrounding Israel's emergence set the stage for the bitter Arab-Israeli conflict that persists to this day. Following Col. Gamal Abdel Nasser's military takeover of Egypt in 1952, cross-border skirmishes between Egyptian and Israeli forces became increasingly common. In 1956, Israel attacked Egypt in conjunction with British and French landings at the Suez Canal, which Nasser had recently taken over. The United States induced the belligerents to withdraw and peace was restored, but clashes along Israel's borders with Egypt and Syria erupted periodically over the ensuing years. In June 1967, as Nasser made visible preparations for war, Israel launched a preemptive strike against Egypt, Syria, and Jordan. Following its rapid victory in the *Six Day War,* Israel captured the Sinai Peninsula and the Gaza Strip from Egypt, the West Bank and East Jerusalem from Jordan, and the Golan Heights from Syria (see figure 6.3).

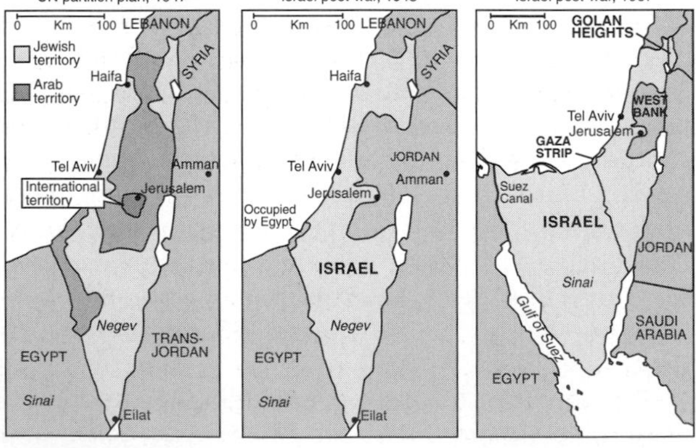


**FIGURE 6.3 The Expansion of the Israeli State**
*Source: New York Times*, February 28, 1988. Copyright © 1988 by The New York Times Company.

After Nasser's death in 1970, Anwar Sadat became Egypt's president. Seeking to recover their lost territories, Egypt and Syria attacked Israel in October 1973. The armies fought to a standstill, and the United States brokered a cease-fire. Israel came away from the *Yom Kippur War* with additional territory, but Egypt recovered the Sinai peninsula by negotiation. Sadat then made a bold gesture for peace, traveling to Jerusalem in 1977 for talks with Israel's hardline prime minister, Menachem Begin. Two years later President Jimmy Carter invited Sadat and Begin to Camp David, where the Egyptian and Israeli leaders came to terms on a peace treaty. Egypt became the first Arab state to establish diplomatic relations with Israel. Sadat paid for his reconciliation policy with his life: in 1981 he was assassinated by Islamic radicals. In later years, some of the assassination plotters would make common cause with Osama bin Laden and al Qaeda.

As these events unfolded, Israeli governments encouraged Jewish settlers to establish communities in the West Bank, which was home to more than a million Palestinians. Though some Israeli politicians cautioned against the settlement policy, warning that it would obstruct an eventual resolution of the Arab-Israeli conflict (a view shared by a succession of U.S. presidents), others favored the settlements, especially very conservative religious Jews and nationalists who regarded the West Bank as the ancient lands of Samaria and Judea, granted by God to the Jewish people. In their view, the West Bank and East Jerusalem needed to be formally incorporated into Israel, but Israeli governments refrained from taking this irrevocable step.[19]

These controversies reflected a broader issue of national identity: who, exactly, was an Israeli? The answer depended in part on how various Jews defined what it meant to be a Jew. Orthodox Jews and other religious conservatives have conceived of Jewish identity primarily in religious terms. They have interpreted that identity as requiring the implementation of religious laws and traditions governing the Sabbath, marriage, dietary practices, and the like. Secular Jews, by contrast, have defined Jewishness in cultural rather than religious terms, and have viewed the Jewish state in secular and national terms rather than in conformity with Biblical precepts. Initially, the Zionist movement was largely secularist. But the early Zionists were split ideologically between socialists, many of whom took part in the creation of farm cooperatives (*kibbutzim*), and revisionists, who opposed socialist doctrines and advocated a more militant brand of Jewish nationalism. All these groups favored democracy.

Nevertheless, unresolvable disagreements over identity issues prevented the elaboration of an Israeli constitution. In its place, Israel adopted "Basic Laws" establishing its secular state institutions and governing principles.

These ideological divisions in Israeli society were accompanied by a changing ethnic mix. After the 1967 war, Jews from the Middle East increasingly outnumbered Jews of European origin. The former group tended to resent the latter's continuing grip on political power. Then in the 1970s and 1980s, successive waves of Jews from the Soviet Union emigrated to Israel, usually on the basis of laboriously negotiated agreements between the U.S. government and the Soviet leadership, which was highly resistant to permitting mass emigration from the USSR. More Jews came to Israel after the Soviet Union's collapse at the end of 1991. Finally, some 20 percent of Israel's citizenry have consisted of non-Jews—mostly Arabs (Palestinians) who remained in Israel after the 1948 war and their descendants. Today about 1.2 million Israeli citizens are Arabs. The vast majority are Muslim, but some are Christian. Throughout Israel's history, the country's sizable Arab minority has complained of discrimination at the hands of the Jewish majority, and they have had a difficult time reconciling their Israeli citizenship with their Arab ethnicity and religious affiliations.[20]

These myriad ideological orientations and geographic or ethnic backgrounds have found their political expression in a vibrant multiparty system. Socialist-oriented Zionists gravitated toward the Labor Party, while revisionists formed the basis of the Likud bloc. Other groupings formed their own parties. The existence of so many parties made for a rich and variegated democracy, but it also complicated the process of forming coherent, stable governments. We'll look at Israel's party system in greater detail in chapter 8.

The Palestinians, for their part, have remained a stateless people. After 1948, a Palestinian diaspora fanned across the Middle East and spread into Europe and North America as well. In 2004 there were nearly 3.8 million registered Palestinian refugees (5 million in all, according to Palestinian authorities). Hundreds of thousands lived in Jordan. The largest concentrations of Palestinians were in the West Bank, where an estimated 2.39 million resided in 2004, and in the Gaza Strip (approximately 1.38 million). Of these, most were Sunni Muslims; about 100,000 were Christians.

The absence of states in most of the Arab world during the centuries of Ottoman rule delayed the growth of a distinct Palestinian national identity. Until the birth of Israel, most Palestinians regarded themselves simply as Arabs, and Palestinian nationalism was articulated mainly by the leaders of prominent Arab families, both Muslim and Christian, in the context of a traditional agricultural society. In the wake of the 1948 Disaster and the mass dispersal of Palestinian Arabs to refugee camps and foreign countries, Palestinian nationalism waned, but it revived in the years just before and after the 1967 Six-Day War. A new generation of Palestinians who grew up in the poverty-stricken camps or abroad formed the social base of a more assertive national identity, led by a growing core of educated young people. This nationalist reawakening was fueled by antagonism toward Israel and by a sense that the collective experiences of the Palestinians marked them as a distinct people in the Arab world.[21]

Meanwhile, the Palestinians remained in political limbo, with no territory under their juridical authority. To provide Palestinian nationalism with an institutional foundation, Palestinian leaders formed the *Palestine Liberation Organization (PLO)* in 1964. The PLO's National Charter affirmed that the establishment of the state of Israel was illegal, that Jews did not "constitute a single nation with an identity of its own," and that the liberation of Palestine in its 1947 borders was a "national duty" that could be achieved only through armed struggle. At the end of the decade the PLO chose *Yasser Arafat* as its chief. Arafat was the leader of Fatah, one of the PLO's most militant factions. Arafat steered the organization in the direction of terrorism against Israelis and got drawn into a bloody—and unsuccessful—attempt to topple the Jordanian monarchy in 1970. The PLO next moved to Lebanon, but it was evicted by the Israeli invasion of 1982. Israeli troops occupied southern Lebanon for the next eighteen years. Casualties mounted as Hezbollah, a Lebanese Shiite organization funded by Iran, repeatedly attacked Israeli forces in the region.

Although the PLO in these years was militantly anti-Zionist, its platform was basically secular, not Islamic. It favored the creation of a Palestinian state on the basis of civil law, not Muslim shariah. The same was largely true of several splinter groups that broke off from Arafat's Fatah movement in the 1960s, asserting an even more militant approach to international terrorism that included airline hijackings and other spectacular operations. Fatah's Black September terrorists perpetrated the murder of Israeli athletes at the 1972 Olympic Games in Munich and other atrocities. But in reaction to harsh Israeli reprisals and international condemnation, Arafat later distanced himself publicly from terror tactics while simultaneously encouraging the development of new terror groups like

Fatah's al-Aqsa Martyrs Brigade. Since the 1980s, Palestinian nationalist organizations with a more Islamic cast have become increasingly vocal, inspired by the success of Ayatollah Khomeini's Islamic revolution in Iran. The most prominent of these groups is *Hamas* (the Islamic Resistance Movement, whose acronym means "zeal"). *Islamic Jihad* emerged as a smaller organization. Hezbollah has also engaged in terrorist activities against Israel. All three groups have rejected Fatah's vision of a secular Palestinian state with religious pluralism, calling instead for an Islamic state based on shariah. All are also militantly opposed to Israel, advocating violence as well as a patient confidence that the day will ultimately come when Israel will cease to exist as a Jewish state.

In 1987, mounting frustration at Israel's refusal to come to terms on a Palestinian state exploded into a violent uprising (*intifada*) conducted mainly by young stone-throwing Palestinians. The continuing stalemate, aggravated by casualties on both sides, led to a modest breakthrough. Starting in 1993, a series of agreements brokered in part by the government of Finland, and known as the *Oslo accords,* provided for Palestinian self-government over the Gaza Strip and parts of the West Bank for five years. A new entity, the *Palestinian Authority (PA),* was created to exercise jurisdiction over the designated areas. Israeli Prime Minister Yitzhak Rabin and Foreign Minister Shimon Peres shared the Nobel Peace Prize with Arafat for their efforts, but Rabin was murdered in 1994 by a rabid Israeli nationalist opposed to the Oslo peace process. As a sign of its commitment to peace, the PLO abrogated the clauses in its National Charter calling for Israel's destruction. (The Israelis, however, insisted on new clauses in the Charter explicitly affirming the PLO's acceptance of Israel's right to exist.) Arafat moved quickly to assert his prominence in the new Palestinian government. In the Palestinians' first-ever free elections, held in January 1996, Arafat handily defeated his opponent in the race for president of the PA, and his Fatah faction won 49 out of 88 seats in the newly created Palestinian Legislative Council. At the same time, a pro-democracy civil society was taking shape in the Palestinian population.[22]

Although the Palestinian Authority gradually gained jurisdiction over 40 percent of the West Bank and two-thirds of Gaza, the PA was a government unconnected to a real state. Meanwhile, Israel continued to build new settlements in the West Bank and Gaza and to encourage new housing for Jews in East Jerusalem, historically the Arab part of the city. At the end of the 1990s there were about 180,000 Jewish settlers in communities scattered across the West Bank, an area the size of Delaware. Another 5,000 Jews had settled in Gaza, and roughly 175,000 Jews were living in East Jerusalem.

In hopes of encouraging a bold leap to a comprehensive Middle East peace agreement, President Bill Clinton in 2000 invited President Arafat and Israel's prime minister, former general Ehud Barak, to a round of talks at Camp David. Barak had by now decided to withdraw Israel's forces from southern Lebanon. The two sides inched toward agreement on several outstanding issues, with Barak offering to cede Gaza and 95 percent of the West Bank to the Palestinians and to accept a limited form of Palestinian sovereignty over East Jerusalem. But in the end neither Barak nor Arafat was ready to make difficult compromises on such sticking points as the Palestinians' demand for full sovereignty over the West Bank, Gaza, and East Jerusalem; Israel's concern for Jewish settlers in these areas; and the fate of Palestinian refugees longing to return to their lost property in Israel. In fact, both Barak and Arafat were under intense pressure from within their own ranks to walk away from a final agreement. Barak's fragile coalition government was falling apart while he was away at Camp David. And Arafat was pressured by hardliners in the PLO as well as by terrorist groups like Hamas, which continued to oppose Israel's right to exist. Quite a few Israelis believed that Arafat himself still clung to that same intransigent position.

Shortly after the Camp David summit broke up, Ariel Sharon—the Likud leader who had made no secret of his opposition to the Oslo peace process and to the Camp David meeting—made a demonstrative visit to Jerusalem's Temple Mount. The site is revered by Jews as the location of the city's ancient temple and by Muslims as Harem al-Sharif, the location of the storied al-Aqsa mosque. Many Muslims regarded Sharon's visit as a deliberate provocation. Before long, Palestinians responded with the first assaults of a new *intifada* against the Israelis. Together these actions unleashed a cycle of violence that was to take a heavy toll in civilian casualties on both sides over the coming years. Sharon defeated Barak in an election held in 2001 and took over as prime minister. In 2003 Sharon's Likud party won a resounding victory at the polls, but was still compelled to form a multiparty coalition government. As Palestinian suicide bombers blew up buses and restaurants in Israel, and as Israeli military strikes assaulted the West Bank and Gaza, casualties mounted on both sides. During three years of turmoil, nearly 900 Israelis and 2,500 Palestinians were killed. The Palestinian Authority lost control over areas it had acquired under the Oslo accords. Arafat himself was confined by Israeli troops to his shelled-out headquarters, and Sharon hinted that the Palestinian leader should be exiled or perhaps eliminated altogether.

With the Sharon government and the Bush administration refusing to talk with Arafat, the Palestinian Authority created the new position of prime minister in 2003 in an effort to resume diplomatic contacts. For its part, the Sharon government began constructing a protective barrier—a wall and other fortifications designed to seal off Israel proper and most Jewish settlers in the West Bank and East Jerusalem from terrorists. The International Court of Justice declared the barrier illegal, and an Israeli court ordered modifications in its route to accommodate Palestinians, but 200 miles of circuitous fencing were completed by mid 2006 and an additional 250 miles were planned. Many Palestinians have been inconvenienced by the barrier, which cuts off neighboring towns and villages and obliges motorists to be cleared at Israeli checkpoints; but terrorist attacks have abated since it was built.[23]

In a major policy turnabout, Prime Minister Sharon in 2004 announced plans to withdraw all Jewish settlers from Gaza. The bombshell decision, coming from an erstwhile ardent advocate of settlements in the occupied territories, was motivated in part by demographic considerations: Palestinians had a higher birth rate than Jewish families, and any future move to incorporate Gaza and the West Bank into Israel could only dilute the Jewish identity of the state. (Demographers predicted that by 2020, the Jewish population of Israel, the West Bank, and Gaza would be around 42 percent of the total, compared with about 50 percent in 2004.) And like a growing number of Israelis, Sharon hoped that a negotiated arrangement with the Palestinians would end the bloodshed and bring peace. Sharon's announcement instantly divided the Likud bloc, a majority of whose members rejected the Gaza pullout in a nonbinding party referendum. But with polls showing 70 percent of Israelis in favor of the move, Sharon went ahead with it. By August 2005 some seven thousand Jewish settlers in Gaza either left voluntarily or were escorted out by Israeli troops; a few hundred put up token resistance and were carried off. In November, Sharon bolted from Likud and formed a new party called Kalima (Forward), dedicated to seeking a settlement with the Palestinians. Veteran Labor Party leader Shimon Peres and like-minded politicians from Likud and other parties soon joined him.

By this time major changes were also occurring in the Palestinian leadership. Yasser Arafat died in November 2004. Elections to choose his successor as president of the Palestinian Authority took place in January 2005. The winner by a wide margin was *Mahmoud Abbas*, a veteran Fatah leader and former PA prime minister. Abbas was a pragmatist who favored renewed negotiations with Israel aimed at achieving a two-state solution to the Israeli–Palestinian conflict. His renunciation of terrorism was welcomed by Israel and its Western allies, and a cease-fire took effect. But Abbas ran into problems trying to build a consensus in an increasingly fractious Fatah movement. And he could not make much headway in wringing major concessions from Israel or in attracting badly needed foreign investment. He soon found himself challenged by Hamas, which had already proved its militancy by organizing or supporting a number of suicide bombings in Israel. (Israeli forces assassinated the organization's top two leaders in 2004, and in the following year Hamas announced a period of "calm" in its use of violence.) Hamas entered the electoral lists for the first time in 2005, winning local council seats in Gaza and the West Bank.

Hamas scored an even more stunning victory in January 2006 when it unexpectedly won a clear majority of seats in elections to the PA's legislature (74 out of 132). Although Hamas's charter contained a pledge to "obliterate" Israel, and its leadership continued to favor Islamic law, the organization played down these themes during the election campaign. Polls showed that a majority of Palestinians favored a negotiated peace agreement with Israel and a secular Palestinian state. Hamas changed the name of its political wing to the "Change and Reform Party" and capitalized on widespread public antipathy to Fatah's endemic corruption and slipshod administration, promising significant improvements in education, health care, law and order, and other bread-and-butter issues of concern to Palestinian voters. Hamas also owed its surprise victory to its deft use of the electoral system, which we will describe in chapter 8.

President Abbas bowed to electoral realities and appointed a Hamas leader as prime minister. But he urged Hamas to abandon its intransigent positions on Israel and accept the principle of a negotiated two-state settlement. Hamas's unwillingness to do so prompted the United States and the European Union to suspend nearly $1 billion in vitally needed annual assistance to the Palestinian Authority, leaving 140,000 PA employees without paychecks. (The United States officially regarded Hamas as a terrorist organization.)

Only weeks before Hamas's election triumph, the political scene in Israel experienced a shock of its own when Prime Minister Sharon suffered a stroke and went into a coma. In elections to Israel's unicameral parliament, the Knesset, that took place in March 2006, Kalima emerged as the largest party, winning 28 out of 120 seats. *Ehud Olmert*, the former mayor of Jerusalem who succeeded Sharon as Kalima's leader, stitched together a four-party coalition government and was sworn in as prime minister in April. (We'll describe Israel's election system and governmental structure as well in chapter 8.)

Olmert's leadership was quickly tested in June 2006. After a Palestinian family was killed on a beach in Gaza, a tragedy for which the Israeli government denied responsibility, Hamas militia troops crossed the border into Israel, killing two soldiers and kidnapping another. These actions effectively ended the "calm" with Israel that had been in effect since 2005. Two days later, Israel responded with major attacks in Gaza. On July 12, Hezbollah forces in southern Lebanon launched Katyusha rockets and mortar fire on Israeli military outposts and border villages. Simultaneously, Hezbollah troops breached the border and kidnapped two Israeli soldiers. Eight Israeli troops were killed on the first day of action. Hezbollah's leader, Hassan Nasrallah, announced that he wanted to exchange the captured Israelis for Arab captives in Israeli prisons. Israel immediately responded with airstrikes and artillery fire on Hezbollah targets in southern Lebanon and the suburbs of Beirut. A major war ensued, lasting thirty-three days.

Hezbollah kept up a steady barrage of rockets aimed at towns and cities in northern Israel, while Israeli warplanes and drones unleashed punishing assaults on Hezbollah targets. Israel also bombed roads, bridges, and airport runways that could be used by Iran and Syria to resupply Hezbollah. In the process, Israeli airstrikes destroyed a considerable amount of civilian housing. Israeli troops also entered southern Lebanon to root out Hezbollah forces, which had built up its arms and fortifications in the six years since the departure of Israeli troops from the area. Caught in the crossfire were close to a million Lebanese civilians who fled their homes in search of safety, along with about 500,000 Israelis who did the same. Also under siege was Lebanon's government under Prime Minister Fouad Siniora, who had come to power in 2005 on a wave of democratic sentiment known as the "Cedar Revolution" (see chapter 2). Siniora had little control over Hezbollah, which had built up a powerful militia that was independent from the Lebanese government.

As the United States and its key European allies discussed a United Nations–sponsored cease-fire, a humanitarian crisis loomed in Lebanon. In Israel, Olmert's policy of retaliation was widely supported, but as the conflict dragged on with little sign that Israel would be able to defeat Hezbollah decisively or even stop the daily rocket attacks, Olmert came under pressure to launch a full-scale invasion of southern Lebanon. Unlike several previous prime ministers, Olmert had no experience as a military commander. Olmert ordered a major call-up of Israeli reserve forces and approved a sizable invasion of southern Lebanon. But a cease-fire went into effect a few days later, on August 14. Siniora's government agreed to send fifteen thousand Lebanese army troops to the Hezbollah-controlled region of southern Lebanon, while Italy, France, and other countries agreed to provide an additional fifteen thousand troops to patrol the area. Although Siniora and the international community agreed in principle that Hezbollah should be disarmed, there were no indications by late 2006 as to how this task would be undertaken.

In the end, neither side had achieved a significant victory. Hezbollah remained powerfully armed and expanded its popularity in Lebanon for standing up to Israel; but it had not expected such a devastating Israeli response, nor did it succeed in intimidating the Israeli government or population. Israel failed to achieve its declared aim of destroying Hezbollah. Nearly twelve hundred Lebanese civilians were killed in the war, and a quarter million were still displaced after the fighting ended. Israel lost 119 troops and 44 civilians. Thousands were injured on both sides. Olmert's government suffered a setback, as some Israelis argued that the army should have invaded Lebanon more aggressively at the start of the war. In the immediate aftermath of the fighting, Olmert shelved, at least temporarily, his plan to withdraw as many as seventy thousand Jewish settlers from their West Bank settlements.

In the fall of 2006 Olmert broadened his coalition government by naming the head of a right-wing party as deputy prime minister. But as Olmert's approval ratings sank below 15 percent, it was not clear how long his government would survive. Meanwhile, sharp conflicts between Fatah and Hamas divided the Palestinians, at times turning violent. As instability prevailed, Israel remained a state with uncertain borders, and the Palestinians still had no state of their own.[24]

---

Though we may be tempted to think of states as enduring entities, they are by no means always so. Like geological formations, states may undergo all sorts of seismic convulsions. They can grow, disintegrate, become reconstituted, or get absorbed into larger states. One of the most volcanic examples of the disintegration of a multinational state is the former Yugoslavia. Its explosive self-destruction in the 1990s was accompanied by the killing of over 250,000 people and the forcible expulsion of more than 2 million from their homes and villages.

## THE DISINTEGRATION OF YUGOSLAVIA

### Origins

The roots of this region's intense conflicts extend more than a thousand years into the past. Starting in the late sixth century, successive waves of Slavic tribes from the eastern steppes, located in what is now Russia and Central Asia, gradually moved into the peninsula whose spine is formed by the Balkan mountains. Their subsequent histories took very divergent paths.

***Slovenes*** occupied the northernmost part of the area. In the eighth century the majority of Slovenes were converted to Roman Catholicism. Most of what is now Slovenia was part of the Austrian-led Habsburg empire from 1335 to 1918. ***Croats*** became Roman Catholics in the tenth century and are still mostly Catholic today. Most of what is now Croatia gradually came under the control of Austria and Hungary and remained part of the Habsburg empire until the end of World War I. ***Serbs*** initially occupied the valleys where Bosnia, Montenegro, and Kosovo meet. In the ninth century they were converted to the eastern rite of Orthodox Christianity—the basis of the Russian Orthodox church—by Saints Cyril and Methodius. Cyril was the founder of what evolved into the Russian (Cyrillic) alphabet. These religious and linguistic developments established a close connection between Serbs and Russians that still endures. The Turks held much of this region from the fourteenth century to the late nineteenth century. Under Russia's patronage, the kingdom of Serbia was established in 1882. Russia's support for Serbia against Austria-Hungary in 1914 was one of the key events that led to World War I.

***Montenegrins*** were originally Serbs. They broke off from the rest of the Serbs in the early fifteenth century in order to escape the advancing Turks, establishing their own monarchy in an inaccessible mountainous region. Montenegro (the Black Mountain) remained an independent state until 1918. ***Bosnians*** were also originally Serbs. They fled Serbia proper in the fourteenth century in advance of the Turks and established their own kingdom in what eventually became known as Bosnia. In 1463 the Turks overran all of Bosnia except a small area around Mostar that was ruled by the duke (*herzeg*) of St. Sava. This area, known as Herzegovina, fell to the Turks twenty years later. Over the course of the next several centuries under Ottoman rule, most Bosnians became Muslims and became known as *Bosniaks*. But others retained their Serbian identity as Orthodox Christians; they became known as *Bosnian Serbs*. The Austro-Hungarian empire took over Bosnia from the Turks in 1878. It was a Bosnian Serb who assassinated Austria's Archduke Franz Ferdinand in Sarajevo in 1914, igniting World War I. ***Macedonians*** probably stemmed from Slavic tribes but they also had close ancestral ties with the non-Slavic Bulgars. In the ninth century a Macedo-Bulgarian empire was formed, but the Ottomans took over most of its territory in the following century, ruling it almost uninterruptedly until 1913. Parts of Macedonia were taken by Serbia, Greece, and Bulgaria in the course of two Balkan wars fought in 1912 and 1913. ***Albanians*** are a non-Slavic people who were ruled by the Ottomans for 450 years until 1912, when Albania became an independent country. Most Albanians became Muslims. Though the majority of them live in Albania, many Albanians have lived for centuries in the region of Kosovo, which is part of Serbia.

Following World War I these diverse peoples gradually formed a new country, which took the name Yugoslavia, "the land of the southern Slavs." (Albania retained its independence.) Intense rivalries virtually doomed the new Yugoslav state from the start. Efforts to establish a stable democracy foundered on the uncompromising attitudes of the various nationality groups and their leaders. In 1934 Yugoslavia's constitutional monarch, who was a Serb, was murdered by Croatian assassins.

Internal turmoil was exacerbated by external intervention. In 1941 Nazi Germany took over Yugoslavia and occupied the country until 1944. While thousands of Yugoslavs took up arms against the Germans in resistance movements, the conflicts among the various Yugoslav nationalities erupted into civil war. Fighting between Serbs and Croats was especially intense. Approximately 1.75 million Yugoslavs lost their lives during World War II. About half were killed by the Germans; the other half died at the hands of other Yugoslavs.

The most successful anti-German resistance movement during the war years was organized by Yugoslav communists. Their leader was Josip Broz, known by his pseudonym, *Tito*. Tito's communists swiftly took control of Yugoslavia following the Germans' withdrawal. Initially, the Yugoslav communists attempted to reorganize the country along the lines of Stalin's harsh Soviet dictatorship. But in 1948 Tito and Stalin got into a feud when the Yugoslav communists expressed their resentment at Soviet interference in their internal affairs. "We are good communists," Tito said, "but we are good Yugoslavs first." Yugoslavia and the Soviet Union broke off their alliance and Tito steered a more neutral course, pursuing economic ties with the West.

As long as Tito remained the country's supreme leader, the ethnic antagonisms simmering just below the surface of Yugoslavia's authoritarian regime did not explode into violence. But they did not disappear entirely. Tito, who was part Croat and part Slovene, occasionally had to take personal action to prevent excessive displays of ethnic nationalism by Serbs, Croats, and other groups. It was Tito's towering presence that held the country together. His death in 1980 at the age of 88 compelled Yugoslavia's nationalities to confront their rivalries anew.

Shortly before his death, Tito bequeathed Yugoslavia a new constitution that required the communist leaders of the country's main nationality groups to share power after his departure. This shaky arrangement lasted little more than ten years. As the winds of freedom fanned across the Soviet Union and Eastern Europe in the late 1980s and early 1990s, Yugoslavs of every nationality demanded similar liberties. For most Yugoslavs, democratic self-expression meant ethnic self-assertion.

Following referendums that showed vast majorities in favor of independence, Slovenia and Croatia seceded from Yugoslavia and declared their sovereignty in June 1991. Macedonia followed suit in September, and the Muslim leaders of Bosnia-Herzegovina declared independence in December. Serbia and Montenegro did not declare their independence but together formed what remained of Yugoslavia. (For a map of the Balkans today, see figure 6.4.) Serbia dominated this partnership under the leadership of *Slobodan Milosevic* (mee-LOW-sheh-vihch), a former communist functionary who advocated the goal of uniting all the region's Serbs into a "Greater Serbia."

Though he appeared to be a typical communist party bureaucrat with no charismatic flair, Milosevic had a keen eye for power. Significantly, he sought to solidify his own power base by deliberately stirring up Serbian national passions. In 1989 Milosevic became president of Serbia, the most populous republic of Yugoslavia. Shortly after taking office, he addressed a throng of Serbs on the site of Kosovo Pole, the "Field

**FIGURE 6.4 The Balkans Today**

of Blackbirds," where the Serbian army had been defeated by the Turks exactly six hundred years earlier. Milosevic's fiery speech promised that Serbia would never again relinquish its control over Kosovo, the province revered as the historic birthplace of the Serbian nation. Hundreds of years of Turkish occupation had left Kosovo with a large ethnic Albanian majority, virtually all of them Muslims. Of the province's 2.2 million residents, more than 80 percent were Albanians. Tito had granted the Albanian Kosovars a number of rights and privileges, and between the 1960s and mid 1980s as many as three hundred thousand Serbs left Kosovo because of local Albanian domination. Milosevic was determined to reverse this process. In 1989 he began terminating the rights of the Albanian Kosovars, removing them from their jobs by the hundreds of thousands. In their place came Serbs determined to reclaim control of the province. The antagonisms set off by these actions ultimately culminated in a wholesale Serbian onslaught in Kosovo, but Milosevic first had to deal with the secession movements in Slovenia, Croatia, and Bosnia.

## The Balkan Wars of the 1990s

Fighting broke out in Slovenia, Croatia, and Bosnia shortly after the initial declarations of independence. Milosevic deployed the Yugoslav army, led predominantly by Serb officers, in an effort to halt Yugoslavia's disintegration. Slovenia quickly repulsed these forces and retained its independence. Croatia and Bosnia-Herzegovina, however, became mired in lengthy conflicts. Not only were they attacked by the Serb-controlled Yugoslav army; they were also assaulted by local Serbs, many of whom were armed by Milosevic's Serbian government. Croatian Serbs seized control of the Krajina, a portion of Croatia where Serbs had lived since the eighteenth century.

By early 1995 Bosnian Serbs, backed by the Yugoslav government, were in control of 70 percent of Bosnia-Herzegovina. Mass murders, gang rapes, and house burnings became routine occurrences as the Bosnian Serbs carried out a policy they called "ethnic cleansing": the removal of Bosnian Muslims from areas claimed exclusively by Serbs. Between 1992 and 1995 the Bosnian capital of Sarajevo, once a model of multiethnic harmony, was besieged by Serb artillery.

Efforts by the United Nations and the NATO alliance to promote a settlement of these disputes proved ineffective until the summer of 1995. In August the Croatian government launched a massive assault on Krajina, evicting more than 150,000 Serbs. Prodded into action by a new wave of Bosnian Serb atrocities, including the murder of thousands of men and boys and their burial in mass graves, the U.S. government and its NATO allies launched a series of air attacks on Serb positions throughout Bosnia-Herzegovina. Bosniak forces took the offensive and regained control of several areas from the Bosnian Serbs. At the same time, fresh diplomatic initiatives succeeded in convincing Serbia's Milosevic to curtail his support for the Bosnian Serbs and come to the peace table.

Peace talks involving the leaders of Croatia, Bosnia-Herzegovina, and Serbia took place under U.S. auspices at the Wright-Patterson Air Force Base outside Dayton, Ohio. After three weeks of intense bargaining, the main parties initialed a comprehensive peace agreement on November 21, 1995. The Dayton Accords divided Bosnia-Herzegovina into a Muslim-Croat Federation and a Serbian zone known as the Serb Republic. This agreement was initially policed by a NATO force of some sixty thousand troops, of whom twenty thousand were Americans.

After the Dayton Accords, attention turned once more to Kosovo. Starting in 1997, a force of ethnic Albanians known as the Kosovo Liberation Army (KLA) took up arms against Serbian forces in an effort to gain the province's complete independence. Serbian reprisals were intense, and by the summer of 1998 some seven hundred thousand refugees had fled the province. As Serb forces pressed their campaign against the KLA and civilian noncombatants, the NATO alliance began an intensive bombing campaign in April 1999. Swarms of refugees streamed out of Kosovo into neighboring Albania and Macedonia, many bearing tales of summary murders, rapes, extortion, and other atrocities committed by Serbian military and special police forces. The ethnic cleansing of Kosovo by some forty thousand Serbian troops and paramilitary fighters was in full swing. After eleven weeks of bombing, which destroyed power plants, bridges, and other facilities in Belgrade and other parts of Serbia and Montenegro, Milosevic suddenly gave up and accepted NATO peace terms. All Yugoslav troops were compelled to leave Kosovo and a fifty-thousand-strong international peacekeeping force led by NATO took their place. By the end of 1999 most of the Kosovar Albanian refugees had returned to Kosovo, often to find their loved ones killed and their property destroyed. About one hundred thousand Serbs have left the province, about half the number who lived there before the bombing campaign.

After giving in to NATO, Milosevic remained in office until a spontaneous revolution forced his resignation. In September 2000 it appeared he had lost the presidential election to Vojislav Kostunica, a constitutional lawyer. When Milosevic tried to suppress the election results, hundreds of thousands of protesters stormed Belgrade, seizing official buildings and media outlets on October 5. Milosevic resigned the next day. He was later handed over to the International Criminal Tribunal for the Former Yugoslavia in The Hague. Milosevic died in jail in 2006 while his trial was still in progress.[25]

Since the end of the Balkan wars, the independent states that once composed Yugoslavia have taken divergent paths. *Slovenia* has developed a stable democratic system, and it joined the European Union and NATO in 2004. *Croatia* has made substantial progress in stabilizing its democracy. In 2004 it was invited to begin talks on joining the European Union. *Bosnia-Herzegovina* was making only slow progress toward democracy and reconciliation among the Muslims, Serbs, and Croatians who live in the two parts of the country's federated system. With the party system fragmented along ethnic lines, nationalistic antagonisms dominated the elections of 2002 and 2006, while international peacekeepers and advisors propped up the country's fragile stability. The European Union planned to start withdrawing its seven thousand troops in 2007.

*Macedonia* was wracked by violent conflict between its Macedonian majority and ethnic Albanians, who compose 23 percent of the population. The Albanians demanded wider language rights, civil service jobs, and constitutional changes in their favor. As Albanian guerillas and Macedonian armed forces squared off, NATO interposed a peacekeeping force. A settlement was reached in the same year, permitting elections to take place in 2002. In 2005 Macedonia was invited to begin negotiations on entering the European Union. What remained of Yugoslavia formally changed its name to the State Union of *Serbia and Montenegro* in 2002. The newly named state was making slow advances toward democracy. But in a 2006 referendum, 55 percent of Montenegrin voters approved independence, setting the stage for the creation of a new state of Montenegro. In the same year, international negotiations on *Kosovo* got under way, with the region's full independence regarded as a possible outcome.

## SUPRANATIONALISM

The state remains the central form of political organization in today's world. To be sure, the forces of globalization—economic interactions, communications links, environmental spillovers, and the like—are driving sovereign governments to cooperate with one another more than at any other time in history, placing the very concept of national sovereignty in doubt. The realities of international relationships have in some cases led to highly structured attempts to promote cooperation across state boundaries. The most far-reaching of these efforts thus far has been the *European Union*.

The European Union (EU) is a prime example of supranationalism at work. **Supranationalism** ***refers to efforts on the part of two or more countries to limit their sovereignty by establishing decision-making structures over and above their national governments.*** In the case of the EU, these supranational bodies have the authority to make laws that are binding on the member states.

## THE EUROPEAN UNION

In 1957, six West European countries signed a historic agreement designed to expand their economic cooperation. Those countries were *France, West Germany, Italy,* and the three Benelux countries (*Belgium,* the *Netherlands,* and *Luxembourg*). At the start of the following year the terms of their agreement, known as the Treaty of Rome, took effect and the European Economic Community (EEC) became a reality. Its principal aim was to promote economic growth among the member states by eliminating tariffs and other trade barriers and by jointly concluding trade agreements with nonmember states. In the early 1960s the EEC members set up a *Common Agricultural Policy (CAP)* to protect their farmers from adverse world trading patterns.

Over time, the EEC was enlarged to include new members. *Britain, Ireland,* and *Denmark* joined in 1973; *Greece* joined in 1981; *Spain* and *Portugal* became members in 1986. As it took on both new members and new tasks, the organization changed its name to the European Union in 1993. Two years later, *Austria, Sweden,* and *Finland* brought the total number of EU members to fifteen. Membership rose to twenty-five in 2004, with the addition of ten more new members: the *Czech Republic, Estonia, Hungary, Latvia, Lithuania, Poland, Slovakia,* and *Slovenia*—all once ruled by communist governments—along with *Cyprus* and *Malta*. *Bulgaria* and *Romania,* two more former communist states, became EU members in 2007. The EU began accession negotiations with Croatia in 2004, with Turkey in 2005, and with Macedonia in 2006.

From the outset, Europeans have been divided between those who have wanted to accelerate the process of economic and political integration and those who have wished to keep integration within stricter limits in order to preserve greater freedom of action for their own national governments. Proponents of greater supranationalism have continuously sparred with advocates of state sovereignty. These debates still take place today, but there has always been a general consensus that varying degrees of both tendencies should coexist. As a consequence, the organization's institutions were set up to permit significant levels of supranational activity while simultaneously preserving the member governments' rights to make important EU decisions and even to opt out of EU activities that they do not like. Following deliberations by a special convention and protracted negogiations, in 2004 the EU completed the drafting of a constitution designed to reform its institutions and clarify their powers. But the document was put on hold after French and Dutch voters rejected it in referendums held in 2006.

The European Union in 2006 retained essentially the same organizational structure created in the Treaty of Rome, with the following key institutions:

- The *European Commission* is one of the EU's most supranational bodies. As such it is authorized to propose and enforce common EU laws and policies. It may also negotiate certain international treaties. However, the Commission is not empowered to make final decisions in creating new EU law, a prerogative that remains in the hands of the EU governments. At present there are twenty-seven Commission members (one from each member state), including the *president of the Commission.* Since 2004 the Commission's president has been José Manuel Barroso. Although the president and the commissioners are appointed by the EU states (and must be approved by the European Parliament), they are expected to act independently of national governments, taking a pledge to place "the general interest of the Community" ahead of the interests of any member country.

- The *Council of the European Union* is the EU's main decision-making body. It consists of regular meetings of cabinet ministers of the member states, broken down into nine functional committees. If general topics or foreign affairs are being discussed, the foreign affairs ministers meet as the General Affairs and External Relations Council. If agricultural matters are being discussed, the Council consists of the agriculture ministers, and so on. The main purpose of the Council is to protect the sovereign rights of the member states through a decision-making process of *intergovernmentalism,* which gives each national government a say in the making of common EU laws and policies. Some Council decisions are taken under a system of weighted majority voting, in which the larger states get more votes than the smaller ones. Other decisions require unanimity, giving each country veto power. The twenty-seven member governments take turns holding the *presidency of the Council of the EU* for a period of six months. In that capacity, that member government's key cabinet ministers chair Council meetings and set their agendas.
- The *European Council* consists of the heads of government of the member countries (plus the heads of state of three of them), along with the president of the European Commission. These powerful individuals meet as a group several times a year to make final decisions on important EU matters and chart the Union's future path. The chief executives of the member countries take special responsibility for the EU's "Common Foreign and Security Policy." Although they sometimes agree to act unanimously, each member country carefully guards its sovereign independence when serious disputes arise. In 2003, as the EU states were being pressured by the United States to support its impending invasion of Iraq, the European Council was split between supporters of the U.S. action, led by British Prime Minister Tony Blair, and its chief opponents, France and Germany. Lacking a consensus, the European Council took no common action.
- The *European Parliament (EP)* has been directly elected by the people of the member countries since 1979. In 2007 it had 738 delegates representing twenty-seven EU members. The EP's approval is required in a number of specified areas before a measure can become EU law, but it still has very limited authority in foreign affairs and agricultural policy, and it has no right to raise revenue. Although these and other restrictions prevent the EP from being a powerful supranational legislature that democratically represents the people of Europe, it won new respect in 1999 when it pressured the entire Commission and its president to resign over a corruption scandal.
- The *European Court of Justice (ECJ)* consists of judges appointed by the member states. It is empowered to issue rulings and legal interpretations in cases involving other EU institutions, member governments, private businesses, associations (such as labor unions), and individuals in matters concerning European community law. In many instances, the laws of the European Union take precedence over the national laws of the member states. As a result, the ECJ plays an important role in the supranational aspects of EU activities.

In addition to these core institutions, the EU has numerous additional organs that serve as advisory bodies, policy implementation agencies, and the like. One of the most important of these institutions is the *European Central Bank,* which coordinates the monetary policies of the twelve EU states that have adopted the euro as their common currency. (Britain, Denmark, Sweden, and the new members admitted in 2004 and 2007 use their own national currency instead of the euro.) All the member states are included in the EU's single market, which promotes the free movement of goods, services, money, and people throughout the region (though newer members are being phased into the single market gradually). On average, about 85 percent of the member countries' business laws are now determined by the EU. In addition, the EU is engaged in coordinating immigration policies, anti-crime and anti-terrorism activities, environmental standards, and a plethora of other matters, with supranational laws often superseding domestic laws and policies. The EU has also played a vital role in promoting democracy in its recently admitted states, most of which were under communist rule less than twenty years ago.

As Europe faces the challenges of a twenty-seven-member Union, with a population topping 450 million, controversies continue to swirl over the central issue of supranationalism versus state sovereignty. Just about everyone wants a measure of both, but they disagree on the right mix. Supranationalists contend that individual EU member states can gain more political influence by cooperating in Europe-wide institutions than by acting alone. They also point to the economic rewards of a highly integrated European economy that had a combined gross domestic product of approximately $12.2 trillion in 2005 among its twenty-five EU members (as compared with $12.4 trillion for the United States). The EU was collectively the number one trading partner of the United States, China, and Russia. Proponents of sovereignty warn that a "democratic deficit" is developing as national governments in Paris, London, and other European capitals lose control over their own domestic and foreign policy choices to community-wide decision-making bodies. They object to ceding vast regulatory authority to some 25,000 EU bureaucrats based mostly in Brussels, the EU's headquarters. Attitudes like these motivated large numbers of French and Dutch voters to turn against the proposed constitution in the 2005 referendums.

As European leaders and citizens continued to debate these issues, one thing was certain: supranationalism would continue to bind the Europeans together in an unprecedented web of interdependencies, but it would not completely replace the sovereign state any time soon.[26]

---

Other regions of the world have also embarked on closer attempts at economic cooperation, though none have gone as far in the direction of supranational institutions as the European Union. Meanwhile, even the EU countries have not entirely dispensed with their own national identities, as the following hypothesis-testing exercise shows.

## HYPOTHESIS-TESTING EXERCISE: Are Europeans Developing a Common Supranational Identity?

### Hypothesis

Let's hypothesize that supranational political and economic institutions and practices are creating a common European identity that is replacing national and regional identities among the people of the member states.

### Variables

In this hypothesis, the *dependent variable* is *a common European identity.* The *independent variable* is *the EU's supranational institutions and practices.*

### Expectations

If our hypothesis is correct, then we'd expect the evidence to show that, over time, the citizens of the EU countries have exhibited on average (1) a noticeable decline in their national and regional attachments; and (2) a correspondingly greater inclination to identify themselves as "European" rather than as French, Italian, Polish, and so on.

### Evidence

The evidence bearing on our hypothesis comes mainly from public opinion surveys conducted by the EU over the years and published in *Eurobarometer.* It does not corroborate our expectations. Instead of diminishing their national or local attachments, people living in most EU countries have continued to affirm these loyalties. A survey in 1990 revealed that, on average, 88 percent felt attached to their country, 87 percent to their region, 85 percent to their town or village, and only 47 percent to 48 percent to the European Community or to Europe as a whole. In 2002, regional and local attachments remained much the same, but attachment to country rose to an EU-average of 90 percent and attachment to the EU dropped to 45 percent.

Similarly, the evidence contradicts our second expectation, that a common European identity is replacing separate national identities. A series of *Eurobarometer* surveys has asked people in the EU countries if they saw themselves in the near future as their "nationality only"; their "nationality and European"; "European and their nationality"; or "European only." The results were precisely the opposite of what our hypothesis would predict. The percentage of people who defined themselves in terms of their "nationality only" actually rose between 1994 and 2004 to an EU-average of 40 percent. The percentage of those who defined themselves in terms of a "nationality and European" identity, *placing nationality first,* rose from an average of 46 percent to 49 percent in 2004. Those who combined national and European identities and *placed Europe first* ("European and nationality") declined, from 10 percent to 4 percent in 2004. Most telling of all, the percentage of people who saw themselves as "European only" was small to begin with in 1994 (7 percent), and their share of the total fell to 3 percent by 2002 and to 2 percent in 2004.

### Conclusions

Evidence indicating growing levels of national identity and declining levels of European identity completely contradicts our expected outcome. Although the percentage of people who expressed at least some degree of European identity, either exclusively or in combination with their nationality, stood at 63 percent in 1994, their ranks fell to 59 percent by 2002 and to 55 percent in 2004. Even though the populations of some countries exhibited higher than EU-average attachments to the European Union in 1994 and 2004, these figures did not grow enough during the interval to alter our basic findings, and in a couple of cases they actually fell. We must therefore conclude that the evidence is *inconsistent* with our hypothesis that European integration is replacing national identities with a broader European identity. Most people in the EU countries profess multiple identities, with national and local identities coexisting with attachment to Europe.[27]

---

In short, states and nations retain their importance in today's global system. In chapter 7 we'll begin examining what has lately become the most widely used method for the governance of states: *democracy*.

## KEY TERMS
## (In bold and underlined in the text)

Nation
National identity
Nationalism
Self-determination
Territorial autonomy
Nation building
Supranationalism

## NOTES

1. James D. Fearon, "Ethnic and Cultural Diversity by Country," *Journal of Economic Growth* 8 (2003): 195–222.
2. Lowell W. Barrington, "'Nation' and 'Nationalism': The Misuse of Key Concepts in Political Science," *PS: Political Science and Politics*, vol. 30, no. 4 (December 1997), 712–16.
3. Karl Deutsch, *Nationalism and Social Communication*, 2nd ed. (Cambridge, Mass.: MIT Press, 1966), 96–98; Benedict Anderson, *Imagined Communities*, rev. ed. (London: Verso, 1991), 6, 7.
4. David D. Laitin, *Identity in Formation: The Russian-Speaking Populations in the Near Abroad* (Ithaca, N.Y.: Cornell University Press, 1998), and *Language Repertoires and State Construction in Africa* (New York: Cambridge University Press, 1992); and Russell Hardin, *One for All: The Logic of Group Conflict* (Princeton: Princeton University Press, 1995).
5. For scholarly views on nationalism, see John Hutchinson and Anthony D. Smith, eds., *Nationalism* (Oxford: Oxford University Press, 1994). Also, Anthony D. Smith, *National Identity* (Reno: University of Nevada Press, 1991); Eric Hobsbawm, *Nations and Nationalism Since 1870* (New York: Cambridge University Press, 1970); Adrian Hastings, *The Construction of Nationhood* (New York: Cambridge University Press, 1997); and Ernest Gellner, *Nationalism* (New York: New York University Press, 1997).
6. For a comparison of German and American nationalism, see Liah Greenfield, *Nationalism: Five Roads to Modernity* (Cambridge, Mass.: Harvard University Press, 1992), ch. 4 and 5.
7. On recent efforts to deal with "linguistic territoriality" in East Central Europe, see Zsuzsa Csergo, *Language, Division, and Integration: Lessons from Post-Communist Romania and Slovakia* (Ithaca, N.Y.: Cornell University Press, 2007).
8. Francis Fukuyama, ed., *Nation-Building: Beyond Afghanistan and Iraq* (Baltimore: Johns Hopkins University Press, 2006), 3.
9. Francis Fukuyama, *State-Building: Governance and World Order in the 21st Century* (Ithaca, N.Y.: Cornell University Press, 2004).
10. James D. Fearon and David D. Laitin, "Ethnicity, Insurgency, and Civil War," *American Political Science Review* 97, no. 1 (February 2003): 75–90.
11. Monty G. Marshall, Ted Robert Gurr, et al., *Peace and Conflict 2005* (College Park: University of Maryland, Center for International Development and Crisis Management, 2005). Annual editions of this report can be accessed at www.cidcm.umd.edu.
12. Julie Flint and Alex de Waal, *Darfur: A Short History of a Long War* (London: Zed, 2005); Gérard Prunier, *Darfur: The Ambiguous Genocide* (Ithaca, N.Y.: Cornell University Press, 2005).
13. Greenfield, *Nationalism*, ch. 1 and 2.
14. Nationalism has also been defined accordingly. Ernest Gellner defined it as the political principle "which holds that the political and national unit should be congruent." See his *Nations and*

*Nationalism* (Ithaca, N.Y.: Cornell University Press, 1983), 1. Elie Kedourie wrote, "Nationalism holds that the only legitimate type of government is national self-determination." See his *Nationalism*, 4th ed. (Oxford: Blackwell, 1993), 1.

**15.** Cited by Walker Connor in Hutchinson and Smith, *Nationalism*, 39.

**16.** *Freedom in the World 2001–2002* (New York: Freedom House, 2002), 15.

**17.** Sumantra Bose, "The Implications of Ethno-National Conflict," in *Freedom in the World 2003* (New York: Freedom House, 2003), 21–23. See also Partha S. Ghosh, *Ethnicity versus Nationalism: The Devolution Discourse in Sri Lanka* (Thousand Oaks, Calif.: Sage, 2003).

**18.** Benny Morris, *The Birth of the Palestinian Refugee Problem Revisited* (Cambridge: Cambridge University Press, 2004); Peter Rodgers, *Herzl's Nightmare: One Land, Two Peoples* (New York: Nation, 2005).

**19.** Gershom Gorenberg, *The Accidental Empire: Israel and the Birth of the Settlements, 1967–1977* (New York: Henry Holt, 2006).

**20.** See Nissim Rejwan, *Israel in Search of Identity: Reading the Formative Years* (Gainesville: University Press of Florida, 1999); Howard M. Sachar, *A History of Israel: From the Rise of Zionism to Our Times* (New York: Alfred A. Knopf, 1976), *A History of Israel II: From the Aftermath of the Yom Kippur War* (Oxford: Oxford University Press, 1987), and *Dreamland: European Jews in the Aftermath of the Great War* (New York: Alfred A. Knopf, 2002).

**21.** Baruch Kimmerling and Joel S. Migdal, *The Palestinian People: A History* (Cambridge, Mass.: Harvard University Press, 2003). See also Rashid Khalidi, *Palestinian National Identity: The Construction of Modern National Consciousness* (New York: Columbia University Press, 1997); Christina E. Zacharia, *Palestine and the Palestinians* (Boulder, Colo.: Westview, 1997); Glenn E. Robinson, *Building a Palestinian State: The Incomplete Revolution* (Bloomington: Indiana University Press, 1997); Yezid Sayigh, *Armed Struggle and the Search for a State: The Palestinian National Movement 1949–1993* (Oxford: Clarendon Press, 1997); and Joel S. Migdal, *Palestinians: The Making of a People* (Cambridge, Mass.: Harvard University Press, 1994).

**22.** Nathan Brown, *Palestinian Politics After the Oslo Accords: Resuming Arab Palestine* (Berkeley: University of California Press, 2003).

**23.** Isabel Kershner, *Barrier: The Seam of the Israeli-Palestinian Conflict* (New York: Palgrave/Macmillan, 2005); *Washington Post*, May 30, 2006.

**24.** See Shlomo Ben-Ami, *Scars of War, Wounds of Peace: The Israeli-Arab Tragedy* (New York: Oxford University Press, 2006); Bernard Wasserstein, *Israelis and Palestinians: Why Do They Fight? Can They Stop?* 2nd ed. (New Haven: Yale University Press, 2003); Bernard Wasserstein, *Divided Jerusalem: The Struggle for the Holy City*, 2nd ed. (New Haven: Yale University Press, 2002); Amira Hass, *Reporting from Ramallah: An Israeli Journalist in an Occupied Land*, ed. and trans. Rachel Leah Jones (Los Angeles: Semiotext(e), 2003); Daphna Golan-Agnon, *Next Year in Jerusalem: Everyday Life in a Divided Land*, trans. Janine Woolfson (New York: New Press, 2005); and Matthew Levitt, *Hamas: Politics, Charity, and Terrorism in the Service of Jihad* (New Haven: Yale University Press, 2006).

**25.** On Milosevic, see Dusko Doder and Louise Branson, *Milosevic: Portrait of a Tyrant* (New York: Simon & Schuster, 1999); Lenard J. Cohen, *Serpent in the Bosom: The Rise and Fall of Slobodan Milosevic* (Boulder, Colo.: Westview, 2000); Louis Sell, *Slobodan Milosevic and the Destruction of Yugoslavia* (Durham, N.C.: Duke University Press, 2000); and Slavoljub Djukic, *Milosevic and Markovic: A Lust for Power*, trans. by Alex Dubinsky (Montreal: McGill-Queen's University Press, 2001).

**26.** For an overview of the history and structure of the EU, see Desmond Dinan, *Ever Closer Union*, 3rd ed. (Boulder, Colo.: Lynne Rienner, 2005); also Neill Nugent, *The Government and Politics of the European Union*, 6th ed. (Durham, N.C.: Duke University Press, 2006); John Van Oudenaren, *Uniting Europe*, 2nd ed. (Lanham, Md.: Rowman & Littlefield, 2004).

**27.** *Eurobarometer* is published periodically by the European Commission and can be accessed through the EU's website, www.europa.eu.int. See, in particular, *Trends 1974–1993* (published in May 1994) and numbers 40 (1993), 41 (1994), 42 (1995), 51 (1999), 58 (2002), and 61 (2004).

CHAPTER 7

# DEMOCRACY: WHAT IS IT?

Thus far we have talked about democracy quite a bit without providing more than a rudimentary definition of the term. In chapter 2 we put it this way:

> *The essential idea of democracy is that the people have the right to determine who governs them. In most cases they elect the principal governing officials and hold them accountable for their actions. Democracies also impose legal limits on the government's authority by guaranteeing certain rights and freedoms to their citizens.*

But like many dictionary-style definitions, this one oversimplifies a highly complex phenomenon. In fact, democracy can take a variety of forms. It can mean different things to different people. For some theorists of democracy, representation based on free, fair, competitive elections is the main defining principle of democratic governance. Many theorists contend that a country with these features at least meets the minimum requirements of an *electoral democracy*. Freedom House estimates that there were 123 electoral democracies around the world by the end of 2005, representing 64 percent of 192 sovereign states. But elections, while vitally important, are by no means sufficient to establish a full-fledged democracy. Democracy also requires certain legally protected rights and liberties for the population. Without such things as freedom of speech, freedom of assembly, and other basic liberties that the government must not infringe, elections are meaningless. Freedom House ranked 89 countries as "free" in 2005, reflecting their success in combining electoral democracy with a wide range of rights and liberties. Countries that guarantee these basic liberties are often called *liberal democracies*. As Fareed Zakaria has suggested, governments that hold elections but withhold fundamental rights and liberties can be considered "illiberal democracies."[1] Illiberal democracies are not true democracies. In this book we classify most of them as either semi-democracies or semi-authoritarian regimes.

What, then, is democracy?

## THE TEMPLE OF DEMOCRACY

The concept of democracy that we employ in this book is built around five core ideas or sets of principles that we regard as essential to any democracy worthy of the name. To understand how these five elements relate to one another, let's visualize democracy in the form of a Greek temple. As depicted in figure 7.1, the facade of the Temple of Democracy has three pillars that stand on a foundation with two steps.

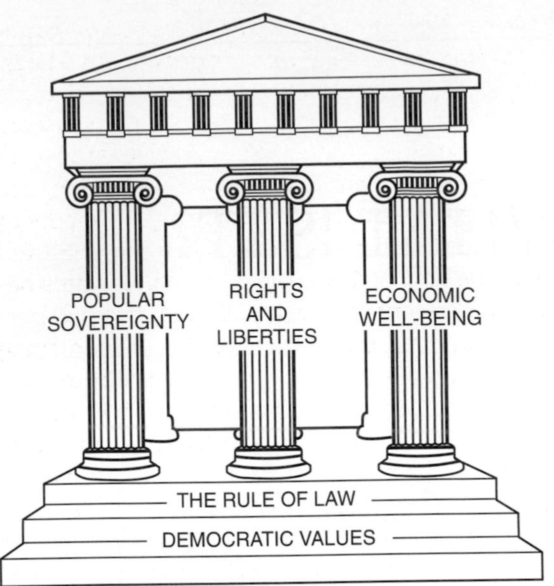


**FIGURE 7.1 The Temple of Democracy**
*Source:* Adapted from a drawing by Ellen DeVincentiis Sodaro.

The two steps represent the foundational base of democracy. The bottom step is a set of *democratic values*, such as *freedom, inclusion, equality, equity, respect, tolerance, compromise,* and *trust*. These basic values undergird the entire structure of democracy. They also provide democracy with a profoundly moral dimension. The next step represents the principle of *the rule of law*, the legal foundation on which democracy rests. These two steps are tightly interconnected. Without the underlying basic values, it is not likely that the builders of a democracy will agree to govern themselves on the basis of mutually agreed-upon laws. And without the rule of law, it is not likely that democracy's essential values will be clearly spelled out to the population in a codified fashion and effectively enforced. In other words, values underlie the law, and the law implements the values.

How are these values and the rule of law put into practice? It is the responsibility of democratic governments to act on the basis of these ideals and implement them in their practical activities. To these ends, democratic governments have three essential functions: to respect *popular sovereignty;* to guarantee specific *rights and liberties;* and to enhance the *economic well-being* of the population. These three governmental tasks are what we call the *functional components* of democracy. They are represented by the three pillars of our Temple of Democracy. Pillar I is the concept of *popular sovereignty*. This is the notion that people govern themselves. Pillar II represents essential *rights and liberties*. These rights are so important that they must not be taken away either by the state or by the people. And Pillar III stands for *economic well-being,* reflecting the idea that democracies must provide people with effective opportunities to escape poverty and improve their quality of life, while also providing basic social welfare benefits.

As we'll see, these three functional components of democracy can take different forms in the real world and exist in varying degrees. In other words, there are different ways of establishing popular sovereignty, defining rights and liberties, and providing economic well-being. In much the same way, the pillars of a temple can come in different sizes and in different architectural styles. But all three pillars must stand on the temple's two-step foundation. That is, the three functional components of democracy—popular sovereignty, rights and liberties, and economic well-being—must be firmly grounded in democratic values and the rule of law. Values help determine what these components look like in practice and what they are intended to do; the rule of law guarantees that these components will be effectively defined and enforced.

We regard all these structural elements of the Temple of Democracy—the two foundational steps and the three pillars—as indispensable to the very definition of what constitutes a democracy in today's world. If one or more of them is weak or missing, the temple cannot stand steadily and democracy is either partial at best or absent altogether.

Now that we've sketched our concept of democracy in architectural terms, let's explain what these steps and pillars mean and how they interact in practice. Let's start with the two steps that form the temple's base.

### Step 1. Democratic Values

As we said in chapter 2, values are *spiritual or moral principles, ideals, or qualities of life that people favor for their own sake.* Democracy is rooted in several key values, or *norms*. These values supply democracy's moral content and give its institutions and procedures their normative purpose.

*Freedom* is perhaps the most cherished value of democracy. Although the term can be defined in a variety of ways, freedom from authoritarian rule is probably the most fundamental and most widely understood aspect of freedom. To be free from dictatorial government and from the application of its arbitrary and repressive laws is what it means to be free in the most elementary *political* sense of the word. Democracy as we know it generally begins with the will to freedom on the part of those who do not wish to live under subjugation in any of its forms. Freedom also has other meanings and connotations that have political relevance, such as freedom of expression, freedom of religion, freedom of movement, and so on. We'll look at some of these specific freedoms when we discuss the rights and liberties associated with Pillar II of our Temple of Democracy. These forms and manifestations of freedom, however, are all rooted in the general principle of freedom as an underlying value of democracy.

*Inclusion* is another key democratic value.

> **Inclusion** ***means that democratic rights and freedoms must be for everyone.***

If a country has such democratic procedures as the right to vote, the right to free speech, and other explicitly defined political rights, these rights must not be denied or limited on a discriminatory basis to particular segments of the population, such as women, ethnic groups, or adherents of a religion. *All* must be included; otherwise, the political system can be considered at most only partially democratic. Even then, some people may regard a partial democracy as no democracy at all.

Inclusion also means that all the main social groups that comprise the population—ethnic groups, religious groups, social classes, and so on—should have reason to feel that they are better off under a democracy than under some nondemocratic form of government. Every group should have a realistic chance to gain something from abiding by democratic rules and procedures.[2] If the "rules of the game" in a democracy are rigged against specific social groups, it is questionable whether such a system may legitimately be considered a democracy.

Recent examples of how democracies can violate the principle of inclusion have occurred in Estonia and Latvia. Prior to World War II, these two countries on the Baltic Sea were independent states. During the war they were overrun by Hitler's Germany and then taken over by the Soviet Union, which incorporated them into the USSR along with the neighboring state of Lithuania. During the next four decades of Soviet rule, large numbers of Russians settled in these areas. When the USSR fell apart at the end of 1991, the three Baltic states became independent once again. By that time, 30 percent of Estonia's population of 1.6 million were Russians, and 34 percent of Latvia's 2.5 million people were Russians. Although the governments of these countries were committed to democracy, most ethnic Estonians and Latvians were reluctant to include the large Russian minorities in the political process. Laws were passed granting voting rights and other democratic privileges on an equal basis to all Estonian and Latvian citizens. But Russians and others who had emigrated to these countries after 1940, along with their descendants, were excluded from citizenship. (In Estonia the Russians were categorized as "aliens.") To become naturalized citizens, the Russians had to meet lengthy residency requirements and overcome other legal obstacles. Under pressure from the United States and the European Union, Estonia and Latvia relaxed some of their restrictions on the targeted Russian minorities. Both countries joined the EU in 2004. But neither country has fully included their sizable Russian minorities in the full rights of citizenship that are enjoyed by ethnic Estonians and Latvians.

A thorny question arises regarding the inclusion of groups that oppose democracy in principle: should they be granted full political rights? If a party proclaims its opposition to democracy's basic tenets—fair elections, freedom of speech, religious tolerance, and so on—should it be given the same rights of assembly and organization as parties that do subscribe to democratic principles? If such a party plans to abrogate basic democratic rights and liberties or abolish democracy in its entirety, should it be allowed to field candidates for public office? Should such parties be included in the democratic process in the hope that their participation will encourage them to accept democracy unreservedly? Every country must answer these questions for itself, of course. Germany's interwar democracy (1919–33) granted full political rights to Adolph

Hitler's Nazi party and to the German Communist party, even though both parties explicitly opposed democracy while taking full advantage of its opportunities. The Nazis eventually became the largest party elected to the German legislature. Hitler subsequently put out the lights of democracy after being appointed chief of Germany's government in accordance with constitutional procedures. For Germany's first democracy, the political inclusion of the Nazi party proved suicidal. Since World War II, democratic Germany has banned the Nazis and other overtly antidemocratic parties.

Several countries today accord political rights to parties that are avowedly hostile to basic features of democracy. As we've seen, Islamic parties with dubious democratic credentials have had electoral successes in places like Pakistan and Palestine. Similar parties have run for office in other countries as well. In some cases the governments that include these parties in the political system abuse the rules of democracy themselves. They may permit elections to legislative bodies but sharply circumscribe the right to legislate, concentrating real power in the hands of dictators. These realities inevitably confront the world's democracies with a serious dilemma: should they encourage the development of democracy in countries where antidemocratic (and militantly anti-Western) parties enjoy significant popularity? Or should they support semi-authoritarian or authoritarian regimes that keep these parties under control while limiting democracy for everyone else as well? The question of who is included in political life and who is excluded frequently ignites major controversy.

Another core democratic value is *equality*.

> **Equality** ***means that democratic rights and freedoms must be accorded to everyone on the same basis.***

Whereas the principle of inclusiveness asserts that democratic rights and freedoms must be for *everyone*, the principle of equality asserts that these same rights and freedoms must be distributed to everyone *equally*. No group or segment of the population should get more rights or freedoms than others. One example of inclusion without equality occurred in Britain. Until 1918, the right to vote was restricted to males who owned a home—a small minority of British adults. A reform in that year conferred voting rights on all British males starting at age twenty-one, and on all females starting at age twenty-eight. Women were included in the voting system for the first time, but not on an equal footing with men. Only in 1928 was the voting age for women lowered to twenty-one.

Theoretically, the concept of equality for all implies inclusion. But in reality, just as there can be inclusion without equality, there can also be a formal legal equality without real inclusion. In the United States, the Constitution's Fourteenth Amendment, ratified in 1868, guaranteed full citizenship rights to all people born in the United States, including former slaves. It explicitly granted the right to vote to all males starting at the age of twenty-one. In actual practice, however, African Americans faced racially motivated limitations on their right to vote in a number of states until the U.S. Congress barred such practices nearly a century later. Despite the amendment's guarantee of "equal protection of the laws," black Americans have been subjected to a variety of discriminatory practices aimed at excluding them from real political and social equality. Other groups around the world can also attest to the kinds of political and social exclusion that sometimes occur in democracies behind the veneer of formal equality.

To be sure, equality is a high standard. It implies that everybody should be exactly or approximately equal. In some cases it's not too difficult to meet this demand. For example, we can grant everyone over eighteen equal voting rights on the basis of "one person, one vote." But this egalitarian principle does not mean that everybody has equal political power. Not everyone is president. And political influence over decision makers is not shared equally across the population, not even in democracies. When it is difficult or impossible to meet the requirements of pure equality, *equity* is the next best thing.

**Equity** ***means fairness.*** It requires that a political system accord people at least a reasonably fair chance to participate in politics without prejudice to their gender, race, religion, income level, or other social attribute. Of course, the playing field is never completely level. Women, minorities, poor people, and other historically disadvantaged groups may have to overcome discrimination and other barriers to getting elected to office or getting the attention of important decision makers. The principle of equity demands that the disadvantaged have sufficient opportunity to surmount these hurdles and join in the political process with a reasonable chance of success.

The principle of equity applies not only to political participation; it is especially applicable in the sphere of economic and social relations. As we noted above, economic well-being is one of the main components of democracy. But if it proves impossible for even the most well-intentioned democracy to achieve real socioeconomic equality among its population (that is, equal wealth for all), it may be possible to promote greater socioeconomic equity (fair opportunities to increase one's wealth). We'll discuss these issues further when we examine Pillar III.

Needless to say, equity is hard to measure. What seems fair to one person may be considered grossly unfair by another. Despite its imprecision, equity is a valid and important legal principle in democracies when equality fails.

*Respect* is another basic value of democracy, one that is closely related to equality. Respect entitles everyone to be treated with equal regard for their dignity as human beings, starting with the sanctity of their lives.

*Tolerance* is yet another essential democratic value. Tolerance means acceptance of those who are different from ourselves and a willingness to live in harmony with them *on the basis of full inclusion and legal equality.* Those italicized words are extremely important. Tolerance in politics means more than just putting up with people we don't like. The Shia-dominated Islamic Republic of Iran "tolerates" Sunnis, Christians, and Jews by allowing them to worship more or less freely; but it does not grant them the right to run for elective office or to enjoy the same educational, employment, or other opportunities that Shiites have. As a value of democracy, tolerance requires the state to grant all individuals and groups in society the same rights and freedoms as everyone else.

At the very least, the state must observe the principle of nondiscrimination in all its activities, including the hiring of its personnel and the lawmaking process. The state may also have to step into the private sector to prohibit blatant discrimination in hiring practices, the housing market, and other areas of the economy. In the United States, legal action was necessary in the 1960s to stop discriminatory practices by the owners of "public accommodations," such as restaurants and hotels, that refused to accommodate African Americans. Such forms of intervention may infringe upon the freedom of private business owners to dispose of their property as they wish. When a clash of values like this occurs, democracies must make hard choices when trying to reconcile their commitment to freedom with the imperative of tolerance. In some cases, democracies may expand their concept of tolerance even wider by making special efforts to favor groups that are the targets of discriminatory abuse or to make up for past discrimination. In the United States, "affirmative action" practices have been introduced to help Native Americans, African Americans, and Hispanic Americans achieve their educational and career goals.

*Welfare* is an additional democratic value. It includes the economic welfare of individuals, groups, and society as a whole.

*Cooperation* is a very important democratic value. For democracy to take hold and survive over the long run, the various organizations and leaders involved in the political process must share a common commitment to cooperate with one another as much as possible through patient bargaining and accommodation. Democracy requires an "agreement to agree." Excessive obstinacy may lead nowhere. In a society with competing principles and goals, intransigence can paralyze effective decision-making. In extreme cases, it can spark deadly violence. Cooperation must go hand in hand with a spirit of *compromise*, another major value of democracy. Compromise requires individuals and groups to reconcile their differences on the basis of fair bargaining and a mutual willingness to make concessions, however painful they may be. Without cooperation and a widely shared spirit of compromise, democracy may falter where it already exists and fail to get off the ground where it is just emerging.

Another critical democratic value is *trust*. Trust requires politicians and government officials, along with the leaders of important social groups, to behave in ways that inspire confidence in their dependability and honesty. Trust can be a very rare commodity in societies that are trying to build democracy after years of dictatorship. Most authoritarian regimes are up to their necks in lies, duplicity, and hypocrisy. These perverse behaviors spread suspicion and untrustworthiness throughout society, habits that may persist long after a dictatorship has disappeared. Unfortunately, even the most successful democracies today display a diminishing sense of public trust in elected leaders, as we'll observe in chapter 12.[3]

*Security* is also a democratic value. Citizens of a democracy are entitled to social peace. They must hold their governments responsible for ensuring their physical safety and the security of their possessions against criminals, terrorists, and any others who threaten the civilized conduct of social life.

Taken together, the values of cooperation, compromise, trust, and security build bonds of *community*, a basic value of democracy in its own right.

When it comes to foreign relations, democracies should be committed to the *peaceful resolution of disputes* with other countries as a fundamental value. Force should be used only as a last resort to preserve the country's security.

These and other core values we could add to this list exemplify the "spirit of democracy." Some people may espouse these democratic values simply because they regard them as morally right. Others whose moral aspirations are not so lofty might adopt these values purely out of self-interest. They may recognize that they cannot have freedom and respect or fairness for themselves unless they are willing to grant the same benefits to others in society, including people they may intensely dislike. Without these mutual accords, society's conflicts may become insurmountable, and then everybody loses. If civil war or dictatorship takes over, we may all lose freedom, respect, and equality. Democracy can even exist in the absence of widespread trust, as long as the rule of law is applied fairly and antagonistic groups are willing to observe the values of tolerance and compromise to protect their own interests ("I'll cooperate with you if you cooperate with me"). In the best of all worlds, people will learn over the course of time to internalize these values so that they become ingrained habits. A democracy built on a moral commitment to its core values is likely to stand stronger than one built on the tenuous grounds of raw self-interest and pervasive distrust.

Some political theorists relegate democratic values to a secondary importance. They maintain that democracy exists as long as there are fair elections and basic civil rights. Values, in their view, "are better thought of as a *product* and not a producer of democracy."[4] But a contrary view asserts that democratic values are vital to the fundamental concept of democracy. One such argument was advanced more than a century and a half ago by Alexis de Tocqueville, who attributed the success of America's young republic in the early 1830s primarily to values that derived from such sources as religion, higher education, and the experience of interpersonal cooperation in local governments and nongovernmental associations. These values, which included the love of liberty and the spirit of cooperation, constituted what Tocqueville called the "mores" of society, "the sum of ideas that shape mental habits." Mores, in his opinion, are even more important than laws in establishing a viable democracy. "Laws are always unsteady when unsupported by mores," he wrote; "mores are the only tough and durable power in a nation." Tocqueville contended that democratic values, far from being the end product of long experience with elections and other institutional aspects of democracy, are part of the very essence of democracy. As a Frenchman, Tocqueville exalted the values proclaimed in the credo of the French Revolution: "Liberty! Equality! Fraternity!"[5]

A more recent variant of this argument has been advanced by Robert Putnam. In a study that sought to explain why some regions in Italy were more successful than others at maintaining stable local governments and delivering basic services to the population, Putnam and his associates found that the principal variable accounting for these differences was the extent to which civic values like high levels of interpersonal trust and cooperativeness were shared by the local citizenry. In some regions these diverging patterns can be traced back hundreds of years. "Effective and responsive institutions depend," Putnam asserts, "on republican virtues and practices."[6]

The problems that countries like Iraq and Afghanistan have encountered in their attempts to create viable democracies provide powerful confirmation of the importance of democratic values—especially freedom, respect, tolerance, and compromise—at the very start of the democratization process. As we'll see in chapter 10, the outright rejection of these values by rival groups and their leaders has pushed both countries to the precipice of civil war, threatening to destroy democracy while it is still under construction. These events, together with the experiences of other countries that have sought to construct democracy on the rough terrain of domestic discord, show conclusively that democratic values must accompany the other initial requirements of democratization. Ideally, *values should come first*. Without them, the tasks of writing a constitution, holding elections, and building effective governmental institutions may prove laboriously difficult, if not impossible.

### Step 2. The Rule of Law

As we noted in chapter 4,

> ***the* <u>rule of law</u> *is the principle that the power of the state and its officials must be limited by the law and that no one is above the law.***

Stated simply, the rule of law means that those who govern, including the most powerful figures in the government, must be under the law rather than above it. It also means that the power of government to make and enforce laws must be limited by legal restraints as opposed to being unlimited. And it means that the state must scrupulously avoid such practices as arbitrary arrest, torture, fixed trials, corruption, nepotism, and other abuses of power.

These notions are captured in the famous description of the American system as "a government of laws, not of men." The rule of law requires the state to spell out the limitations to its authority in official documents, such as a constitution, or in some other explicit form, such as legislation, court rulings, or publicly acknowledged understandings of what the law is. It also requires an *independent judiciary*—that is, judges and prosecutors who are sufficiently independent of elected and unelected officials that they can apply the laws of the land to them without undue pressure or fear of retribution. Unless the rule of law is enshrined as the first principle of government, democracy cannot exist. And unless it is routinely observed by governing officials, democracy may not survive.

As we noted earlier, the two steps at the base of our temple—democratic values and the rule of law—are tightly connected. The rule of law is based on values, and one of its main purposes is to ensure the implementation of those values. What that means in practice is that the law must be formulated and applied so as to promote such things as freedom, respect, and tolerance on an inclusive and equal (or at least equitable) basis for all. Democracies may differ in the precise ways they go about accomplishing these tasks, as we'll see in subsequent chapters. But all democracies must be built on a solid foundation of democratic values and the primacy of the law over those who wield power.

Having inspected the two steps at the base of the Temple of Democracy, we will now look at the three pillars that represent the functional components of democracy.

## Minimum and Maximum Forms of Democracy

As we have pointed out, all three functions of democracy come in different forms and degrees. To understand these various possibilities, we should think of each function as having a *minimum* as well as a *maximum* variant. In order to have a democracy at all, a country must meet certain minimum levels or standards of popular sovereignty, civil rights and liberties, and economic well-being. But people will inevitably differ over what these minimum criteria should be. Consequently, our discussion of minimal forms of democracy is intended mainly to spark your own thinking about democracy and provide you with a framework for organizing your ideas.

Maximum conceptions widen the scope of democracy to the greatest feasible extent. In general, maximum forms of democracy may be viewed as desirable but *not absolutely necessary* for democracy to exist. Inevitably, what some people may regard as maximum forms of democracy may be regarded by others as minimal forms of democracy and thus as essential to the very existence of democracy itself. Additional forms and gradations of democracy can also exist in each of the three functional components of democracy, situated along a continuum in between these minimum and maximum variants (see figure 7.2). These distinctions will become clearer as we examine each pillar of democracy in turn.

| Representative democracy | Plebiscitary democracy | Techno-democracy | Direct democracy |
|---|---|---|---|
| Minimum | | | Maximum |

**FIGURE 7.2 Continuum of Popular Sovereignty**

## Pillar I. Popular Sovereignty

**Popular sovereignty** ***is the idea that the people determine how they are governed.*** The people themselves, in other words, are the source of the state's legitimacy; they are sovereign over their governing institutions and officials. They have the right to determine the type of governmental institutions and actions they want, along with other aspects of their political system. The concept of popular sovereignty is conveyed in such phrases as "government by consent of the governed" and Abraham Lincoln's famous characterization of democracy as "government of the people, by the people, and for the people."

Popular sovereignty is an essential aspect of democracy. Without it, democracy would be impossible. The very word *democracy* derives from the Greek words *demos,* which means "the people," and *kratia,* which means "authority" or "rule." Taken literally, democracy means "rule by the people."

Popular sovereignty has two key aspects: *participation* and *accountability.* If the people are sovereign, they have the right to participate in politics themselves. They also possess the right to hold those who govern them accountable for their actions. Popular sovereignty applies the rule of law by asserting the government's accountability to the people, thereby imposing constraints on the power of the state and its officials. Democracies must make sure that participation and accountability are guaranteed by the laws of the land. And the principles of inclusion, equality, and equity require that everyone share equally—or at least fairly—in these key aspects of popular sovereignty.

But how do the people participate in political life? How do they exercise accountability? Over more than two thousand years the experiences of numerous democratic political systems and the ideas of democratic theorists have produced a number of different responses to these questions. We'll concentrate on two of them here: *representative democracy* and *direct democracy.*

**Representative Democracy** In a **representative democracy**, ***the people elect state officials to represent them and make decisions on their behalf.*** Representative democracy may be regarded as the *minimum* form of popular sovereignty. The main form of participation in this type of democracy is voting, in accordance with the principle of "one person, one vote." The single most important form of accountability in a representative democracy also centers on voting: the people can approve or remove state officials—executives, legislators, and at least some judicial figures—on election day. These electoral rights must be guaranteed by law on an equal basis. Representative democracy is thus based on the rule of law, inclusion, and equality. Elections are typically conducted on the basis of *majority rule.* (As we'll see in chapter 8, however, there are different ways of counting the votes.) Legislatures generally operate on the same principle. Majority rule is thus a key feature of popular sovereignty.

To fulfill their task of ensuring citizen participation and accountability effectively, electoral procedures must meet certain basic criteria. They must be:

- *Meaningful:* The positions to be filled through the electoral process must be positions of serious governmental authority, including responsibility for making laws and for appointing senior-level state authorities.
- *Competitive:* There must be genuine competition for positions of elective office. At a minimum, there must be no laws or practices that might preclude competition or guarantee that candidates run unopposed.
- *Free:* Voters must have the freedom to vote as they see fit. They must not be subjected to any forms of coercion or intimidation by state authorities or by individuals or organizations outside the state.
- *Secret:* To protect the confidentiality of the voters' choices, elections must be held by secret ballot. The secret ballot is known as the *Australian ballot.*[7]
- *Fair:* The processes used for selecting candidates, conducting elections, and counting the votes

must be untainted by favoritism, discrimination, fraud, or any other form of unfairness to the participants or to the population as a whole.

- *Frequent:* Elections must be held at regular intervals, at least every four to five years, so that voters can exercise their rights of accountability and losers can have a chance to run again.
- *Inclusive:* All adults above a certain age (say, eighteen) must have the right to vote, with exceptions kept to a reasonable minimum, while protecting democracy against its enemies.
- *Equal:* Voting rights should be distributed equally to individuals in accordance with the principle of "one person, one vote."

Over the centuries, dictators have dipped into a large bag of tricks intended to create the appearance of electoral accountability while subverting its true substance. They run unopposed in stage-managed elections, depriving the voters of real choice. They hold referendums asking the people to approve or disapprove their rule, then proclaim they won close to 100 percent approval. They handpick the candidates who are allowed to run, excluding the government's opponents. They intimidate voters, report false vote counts, and engage in all sorts of additional forms of electoral deceit. These fraudulent practices violate the most rudimentary notions of popular sovereignty. Elections without popular sovereignty are inherently undemocratic.

In addition to voting in elections, people can take part in electoral politics by taking an active role in a political party or by working for a candidate at election time. They can also take part in the political process by publicly expressing their opinions on issues facing their community to public officials and by joining or supporting policy advocacy organizations. People can also respond to public opinion polls and attitude surveys conducted by polling organizations. These and other mechanisms of public expression serve, however indirectly, the important function of *agenda setting.* They give the population a chance to participate in formulating the agenda of issues and priorities that government officials will be expected to address when drafting legislation or making decisions. In the process, they permit the citizenry to have an input into the political decision-making process.

Popular sovereignty thus requires *political openness* and *transparency.* To the greatest possible extent, state officials must share information with the general population regarding the decisions they make. The sphere of government secretiveness, although at times necessary for reasons of national security, should be kept as narrow as possible while the sphere of open, transparent government should be spread as wide as possible. Officials who violate this vitally important requirement by engaging in illegal or unethical acts of secret or deceitful conduct strike a harsh blow against democracy itself. Democracies must therefore keep a watchful eye on all elements of the government and probe allegations of wrongdoing. Parliaments should have *legislative oversight* capacity over the executive branch, such as the right to question officials or investigate government practices.

By the same token, openness requires the free flow of information. Freedom of the press and freedom of access to multiple sources of information bearing on governmental decisions are fundamental elements of popular sovereignty. Censorship and the deliberate spread of misinformation are typical governing techniques of authoritarian regimes; they have no place in a democracy.

*How Democratic Is Representative Democracy?* The essence of representative democracy lies in the delegation of governmental power and responsibility to a small number of people by the citizenry as a whole. In every democracy in the contemporary world, the actual work of government is carried on by an extremely small portion of the country's population. *Representative democracies, in other words, are governed by political elites.* As a practical necessity these governing elites enjoy a considerable amount of discretion when it comes to managing the community's affairs. As we noted in chapter 4, modern democracy operates on the principle of *democratic elitism.* Rather than being based on the concept of "government *by* the people," democracy as we know it today is government *by elites who are accountable to the people.* It involves a complicated mixture of popular sovereignty and elite decision making.

Robert Dahl, one of the foremost theorists of modern democracy, devised the term *polyarchy* to capture these realities. Whereas democracy means "rule by the people," **polyarchy** ***means "rule by the many."*** Dahl uses the term as a synonym for modern democracy as it emerged in the nineteenth century and developed in the twentieth century. Polyarchies are large-scale democracies, governing entire countries. They combine elite decision making with mass participation, meaningful competition for power, and the accountability of the governing elites to the governed.[8]

**Direct Democracy** In contrast to representative democracy, **direct democracy** ***is characterized by the direct exercise of governmental power by the people themselves.*** It is "government *by* the people" in the most literal sense. Real-world examples of direct democracies are exceedingly rare. In the ancient world a few Greek city-states, most notably Athens, had their own variants of this form of government. During the peak years of Athenian democracy, from roughly 500 to 300 B.C.E., citizens had the right to participate in public debates on the issues facing the city and to vote on alternative proposals for dealing with them. In effect, the citizens were the legislature. The political executive was largely an administrative body charged with implementing the citizenry's wishes; it had little authority to undertake major policy initiatives on its own, and its officials were usually chosen from among the qualified citizenry by lot for a one-year term. The city-state of Geneva in the eighteenth century provided another version of direct democracy.

Neither of these examples of classical direct democracy met very high standards of inclusion or equality, however. Both ancient Athens and eighteenth-century Geneva denied citizenship rights to women. Certain categories of males were also excluded. Slaves, foreign-born "aliens," and men who did not meet property-owning qualifications were not included in the self-governing procedures of Athens. It is estimated that only about two in five adult Athenian males enjoyed the rights of citizenship. Geneva similarly imposed property requirements for citizenship. Moreover, Geneva's democracy conferred considerable decision-making powers on the elites who operated the political executive on a day-to-day basis.[9] The right to participate in direct democratic procedures was only slightly more open in town meetings in the United States, a form of direct democracy prevalent in nineteenth-century New England.[10] Even with such limited participatory rights, these direct democracies of the past could not have functioned except on a very small scale.

Though direct democracies do not exist in today's world, there still exist several possibilities for expanding the immediacy of citizen participation in decision making in between the extremes of representative democracy and direct democracy. One is *plebiscitary democracy,* a concept that has been in use for about a century. The other is a much newer possibility, one that is evolving before our very eyes thanks to the latest developments in communications technology. We call it *techno-democracy.*

*Plebiscitary Democracy* The term *plebiscitary* derives from the Latin word *plebs,* which referred to the common people of ancient Rome as opposed to the patrician elite. Over the course of the twentieth century, a number of representative democracies have provided their citizens the opportunity to vote on specific policy questions in a *referendum* (or *plebiscite*). In the United States, referendums are quite common at state and local levels of government, but they have not been employed at the national level. In Canada, as we have seen, referendums have been held in Quebec on secession. Several West European countries have held referendums on the European Union and other issues. A number of other democracies have also held nationwide referendums on various questions.

In some cases the results of a referendum are binding on government officials; in others the results are merely a popular recommendation with no binding force on official decision makers. In either case, referendums and plebiscites constitute an electoral mechanism located in between representative democracy and full-scale direct democracy.

*Techno-Democracy* Today's exciting advances in communications technologies provide unprecedented opportunities for enhancing the citizenry's abilities to transmit their wishes to their representatives directly and instantaneously. Telephone call-ins, fax transmissions, websites, blogs, e-mail, chat rooms, and similar devices open up the extraordinary possibility of creating a kind of high-tech semi-direct democracy within today's polyarchies. Just consider the following scenario.

## TECHNO-DEMOCRACY

At 9:00 A.M. you turn your TV set to C-SPAN, the cable channel that broadcasts live from the U.S. Congress. On your screen is a schedule of the bills that are expected to come up for a floor vote today. One of them, concerning government-sponsored student loans, is of particular interest to you. For the last several weeks you've been following this bill, reading newspaper articles on it and occasionally tuning in to C-SPAN's coverage of committee hearings and floor debate in the House and Senate. A final vote is scheduled in the House of Representatives at 4:00 P.M. You expect to be tied up all day in class and at your job, so you won't be able to watch the final proceedings or the vote itself. But your screen indicates that you have until 12:00 noon to contact the member of Congress who represents your district, Representitive James "Biff" Peopleman, to indicate whether you support or oppose the bill. Every fifteen minutes C-SPAN displays the main points of the bill that will be voted on later in the day. It also displays a web page you can access in order to get the bill's full text, along with all congressional discussion on it as recorded in the *Congressional Record*.

At frequent intervals, the screen also displays a telephone number you can call to find out your representative's Voter Opinion Number. Every member of Congress has a toll-free telephone number, a fax number, and an e-mail address specifically designed to record incoming popular votes on congressional bills. As a frequent caller, you know Representative Peopleman's toll-free number by heart. You also know from perusing his home page on the Web that Peopleman does not support the bill in its present form. Just before heading off to class, you dial the toll-free number. A recorded message instructs you to enter your Social Security number. After a few seconds, the voice announces that your right to vote has been confirmed and reminds you that the system will record only one phone-vote per registered voter on any individual bill. The recorded speaker then presents you with a menu of bills that are due to come up for a House vote over the next several days. "If you would like to vote on HR 23170, the School Loan Bill, press 3 now," the speaker says. After pressing 3, you are instructed to press 1 if you favor the School Loan Bill, 2 if you oppose it. After you've punched in your choice, the ever-cheerful voice confirms your selection, offers you a chance to change it, then thanks you on Biff Peopleman's behalf.

At approximately 12:30 a member of Representative Peopleman's staff scans her computer and learns that 4,675 people in his district have communicated their support for the School Loan Bill, while 1,520 have voted against it. Some constituents have voted by phone; others have contacted the Congressman's office by fax or e-mail. (Once again, only one vote per individual is recorded.) "I guess that settles it," the Congressman declares on hearing the news. "While I still have my reservations about the present bill, the people have spoken and Peopleman listens. I'm voting for it."

---

Far-fetched? Since the 1990s, the number of people who have contacted their representatives' offices by telephone, fax, and e-mail in the United States has risen dramatically. Assuming that a vote-recording system similar to the one we've described here is technologically feasible, should democracies institute such a system? The notion that legislators should faithfully carry out the wishes of their constituents is known as the *instructed delegate* model of representation. In effect, the people instruct their delegates how to vote on legislation. *Edmund Burke* (1729–97), an influential British political theorist as well as an elected member of Parliament, rejected this concept. In a famous speech, Burke informed his constituents that he would represent their *interests* as he saw fit, not necessarily their *will* on every issue. Burke saw himself as the "trustee" of the people he represented: he expected the voters to trust him to use his "mature judgment" in serving them. This *trustee model* of representation accords legislators considerable autonomy from their constituents. In practice, most legislators in today's democracies probably try to combine the delegate and trustee models of representation. They need to be very attentive to public opinion on key issues in order to get reelected. But they also want a measure of latitude to vote as they think best on specific pieces of legislation.[11]

### Pillar II. Rights and Liberties

We hold these truths to be self-evident, that all men are created equal, that they are endowed by their Creator with certain unalienable rights, that among these are life, liberty, and the pursuit of happiness.

—*Declaration of Independence*
*July 4, 1776*

For the founding fathers of the United States, the single most important purpose of government was to guarantee certain individual rights and liberties through the rule of law, safeguarding the citizenry against potential tyranny. They favored a limited suffrage, reserving the "consent of the governed" to property-owning males. (Initially, about one in thirty adults had the right to vote.) In the founders' view, a mass democracy based on universal suffrage actually threatened the survival of political liberty because the uneducated majority might misuse their voting rights by electing a tyrant. Consequently, the word *democracy* does not appear in the U.S. Constitution. The best form of government that the founders could imagine was a "republic."

Historically, a *republic* was often regarded as a form of government that did not have a monarch. Over time, the term increasingly became understood as a political system under some form of control by the people. (The word derives from the Latin *res publica*—"the people's thing.") The founding fathers of the United States regarded their newly constituted republic as a government of strictly limited powers, with elected representatives and appointed officials held accountable to citizens very much like themselves: enlightened, socially respectable, and utterly devoted to civic virtue and the prevention of despotic rule. Their conception of republican government was an elitist version of popular sovereignty. Of course, the founding fathers could not have foreseen that the term *republic* would be adopted in subsequent centuries by a wide variety of governmental systems, including manifestly authoritarian regimes like the People's Republic of China, the Democratic People's Republic of (North) Korea, and the Islamic Republic of Iran.[12]

It was not until 1791 that the founding fathers codified into law the specific rights and liberties they regarded as sacrosanct. Known as the *Bill of Rights,* these legal guarantees against excessive governmental power were ratified by the end of that year as the first ten amendments of the new U.S. Constitution, which had taken effect only two years earlier. These rights include such things as the freedoms of religion, speech, press, and assembly (First Amendment); the right to bear arms, considered necessary for "a well regulated Militia" (Second Amendment); the right of security against unreasonable searches and seizures (Fourth Amendment); the right to protection against double jeopardy and self-incrimination and the right not to be "deprived of life, liberty, or property without due process of law" (Fifth Amendment); and freedom from "cruel and unusual punishments" (Eighth Amendment). Nowhere in the original U.S. Constitution or its first ten amendments is there an explicit right to vote.

As America's elitist republic evolved over the course of the next two centuries into a mass-based democracy, American conceptions of basic rights and liberties evolved with it. Today the United States—and most other democracies around the world—are committed to providing a broad range of rights and freedoms to their citizens on the basis of the rule of law, the inclusion of virtually the entire populace, and legal equality. Although many of these rights are much the same in most democratic countries, there are some differences from one democracy to the next in the specific rights that are guaranteed and in the ways they are codified into law. We'll look at some of these differences in the countries we examine in Part Two.

One of the most important aspects of basic rights and liberties is that *they must not be removed or infringed by the state or by the people*. Although governments and the people have the right to determine how these rights and freedoms are interpreted and applied to particular cases or situations (as we'll discuss below), they may not eliminate them entirely. A political system that has little or no press freedom, religious freedom, or any of the other rights and liberties that may be considered fundamental to democracy cannot be regarded as truly democratic. Thus there is an inherent tension between popular sovereignty (Pillar I), with its procedures of majority rule, and the basic rights and liberties of Pillar II, which the popular majority must neither eradicate nor evade. There is ample evidence that large segments of the general public may not be willing to accept the full range of rights and liberties that are guaranteed by their own laws. When majorities discriminate against minorities and their governments let them get away with it, the dominant groups are often denying legally guaranteed rights and liberties to the minorities. And as we noted in chapter 4, public attitude surveys conducted in the United States in the 1970s

**TABLE 7.1**

**Democratic Rights and Liberties: A Minimal List**

1. The right to life and the security of one's person and property against government interference without probable cause of illegal activity
2. Freedom of conscience, thought, and expression (including freedom of the press)
3. Freedom of religion
4. The right to vote in meaningful, fair, competitive elections and to hold governing officials accountable
5. The right to assemble and organize peacefully for political purposes
6. Freedom of movement, that is, the right to travel freely within and outside the country's borders and to live where one chooses
7. The right to equal treatment under the law and to the due process of law, including the right to a fair trial and humane forms of punishment
8. The right to own and alienate (i.e., buy and sell) private property and to engage in private business activity
9. The right to publicly funded education

revealed resistance to legally accepted applications of freedom of speech, the right of peaceful assembly, and other provisions of the Bill of Rights on the part of average citizens, at times numbering in the majority. More recent surveys have revealed similar attitudes. In 2002, 49 percent of Americans surveyed agreed that the "First Amendment goes too far in the rights it guarantees."[13]

What are the rights and liberties that, at a minimum, *must* be guaranteed to the population in order for the political system to be considered a democracy? The minimal list we present in table 7.1 is not intended to be the final word on the subject. In heuristic fashion, its main purpose is to provoke you to think for yourself about the rights and liberties you regard as *absolutely essential* for democracy. Our list includes political, juridical, and social rights. You may wish to add one or more items, such as the right to bear arms or the economic and social rights spelled out in the Universal Declaration of Human Rights (see chapter 1). And you may want to delete an item or two from the list provided here.

Whatever one's list of minimal democratic rights and liberties may contain, most democracies provide an expanding number of rights as demanded by their populations. These include such things as the right to privacy, the right to enjoy public accommodations like restaurants and hotels without discrimination; various forms of gay rights, the right to a smoke-free environment, and so on. Some people may regard these or other rights as essential for the very existence of democracy; others may regard them as desirable but not essential. And some may not even regard certain of these rights as desirable.

As you draft your own charter of minimal rights and liberties, keep in mind that the items in table 7.1 are stated in very general terms. Each item is subject to interpretation—very often by the courts—when it comes to their actual application. The same can be said of the U.S. Bill of Rights and similar charters around the world. What does "the right to life" mean in item 1 of our list? Does it apply in the first trimester of pregnancy, as opponents of abortion would contend? The wording in table 7.1 does not answer that question. It simply says that there is a "right to life," as opposed to *no* right to life. If there were no right to life, then presumably the state could take our lives arbitrarily. It is up to the sovereign people and their governments to determine what "life" means according to the law. Similarly, the guarantee of freedom of expression and a free press in item 2 of our minimal list does not tell us whether child pornography or incitement to riot should be allowed. In 2006, Muslims around the world rose up in indignation after a Danish newspaper published a political cartoonist's derogatory caricatures of Muhammad and other European publications reprinted them. (Islamic law forbids pictorial portrayals of the Prophet.) Should democracy protect the cartoonist's right to offend people? If a freely elected government in a Muslim country banned such images, with the approval of a majority of its people and its independent judiciary, would it be a democracy?

If democracies must ensure basic rights, shouldn't they also mandate certain obligations? Should democracies require military service, or some other form of national or community service, as an obligation of citizenship? If such a duty were required by law, how should it be applied inclusively and equally? Advocates of *communitarianism* like Amitai Etzioni argue that democracy requires the acceptance of mutual obligations and responsibilities on the part of its members, including community service.[14]

### Pillar III. Economic Well-Being

One of the most controversial issues surrounding the definition of democracy centers on the relationship between the citizenry and the economy. Some people may legitimately wonder whether the concept of economic well-being properly belongs in the definition of a political concept like democracy. In fact, however, welfare is a democratic value, and the economy has long been a top priority of practically every government in the world. The preamble of the U.S. Constitution states that one of the principal purposes of the American republic is to "promote the general welfare." Millions of Americans expect their government to stimulate economic growth, widen economic opportunity, alleviate poverty, and provide generous welfare benefits ranging from educational assistance and unemployment relief to medical care and Social Security. Most Americans regard these benefits as basic *political* rights to which they feel entitled as citizens of a democracy. Similar views are shared by vast majorities in other democracies as well. Many people also believe that the maldistribution of wealth, with wide gaps between rich and poor, is inherently undemocratic, especially when the poor have little or no chance of improving their lot in life.

Convincing evidence of the importance of economic well-being as a central aspect of democracy comes from public attitude surveys conducted in Eastern Europe in the 1990s. This was the crucial decade when the construction of democracy in that region was still in its initial phases following the collapse of communism. When asked to select "the most important elements of a democracy" from a list of political and economic categories, large numbers of Eastern Europeans—usually a substantial majority—tended to view democracy primarily in economic terms. They regarded such things as an improved economy, greater economic equality, and guarantees that their basic needs would be met as more important than political liberties like freedom of speech and an impartial judiciary. Most Western Europeans surveyed attached a higher priority to political factors, but large minorities placed economic issues first.[15]

Economic well-being is thus a widely recognized component of democracy in the minds of average citizens. Political leaders who seek their votes and who govern in their behalf are keenly aware that the voters will surely hold them accountable for the economy's performance. How, then, do democracies deal with the challenges of economic well-being?

Just about every democracy in today's world features a mixture of private enterprise and various forms of governmental intervention in the economy. These economic systems are therefore called *mixed economies.* Although private companies tend to be the primary engines of economic production and employment, the state plays a major economic role. Governments collect taxes, purchase equipment, employ bureaucrats, and transfer huge sums of money to schools, hospitals, the military, pensioners, and other beneficiaries of the treasury's largesse. The private sector, moreover, is usually subject to the rule of law. Without laws regulating contracts, stock markets, corporate finances, and the like, modern private enterprise could not function. And without laws to safeguard the rights of employees and consumers and to protect the public's health and the environment, private enterprise would have few legal responsibilities to the citizenry. The rule of law and the policies of elected governments thus act as democratic constraints on private enterprise. Whether these constraints should be reduced or increased is a matter of continuing debate in many democracies.

How do democracies observe the values of inclusion and equality (or equity) when dealing with the economy? How can they distribute society's resources—money, food, jobs, housing, medical care, education, and so on—in a fair and inclusive fashion, while at the same time preserving the value of freedom for business and property owners to dispose of their possessions as they wish? Is there a trade-off between equality and liberty in a democratic political economy?

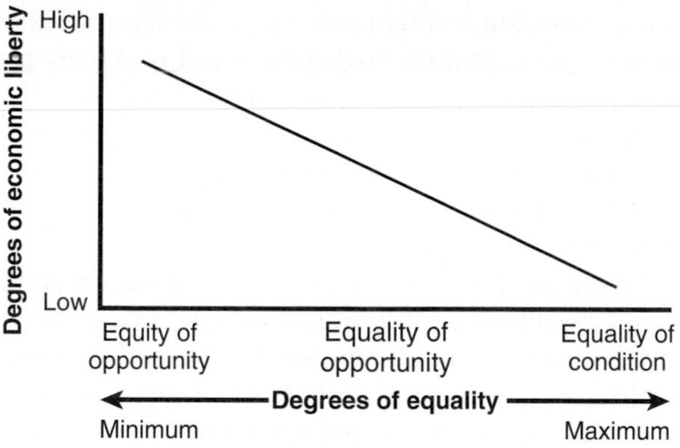


**FIGURE 7.3 Trade-offs Between Liberty and Equality**

Like the first two pillars of democracy, Pillar III can be viewed in terms of a continuum (see figure 7.3). Some people would argue that, at a minimum, a democracy must strive to implement the principle of *equitable opportunity* for all. As noted earlier in this chapter, equitable means fair. Under this principle, political leaders as well as others actively involved in a country's political or economic life would work toward ensuring everyone in society a relatively fair chance at achieving economic security and advancement. Even the very poor, by this standard, should at least have a fair chance at climbing out of poverty, working their way into the middle class, and perhaps even getting rich. To be sure, different societies and individuals will measure fairness differently. Some people will say it is fair enough if the government provides free education through high school to all its citizens; others will insist that the state has an obligation to provide tuition-free education all the way to the top of the academic ladder.

The concept of fair opportunity allows ample room for economic liberty. It would permit individuals and private corporations to run their own businesses and dispose of their private possessions with considerable freedom. The government would have to impose some limitations on these private activities, but the economy could function largely in accordance with rules of the private marketplace and still meet the basic criteria for equitable opportunity.

Another possibility along our continuum is *equality of opportunity.* Equality is a more exacting standard than fairness. Fairness implies that inequalities will still exist as people start out in life and pursue their careers. Equality of opportunity, by contrast, requires efforts by the state and the private sector to make sure that everyone in society is relatively or truly equal when it comes to sharing opportunities for economic advancement. In this highly inclusive approach, no one would have a significant social advantage over anyone else in enjoying access to education or employment.

One way of moving toward greater equality of opportunity is to prohibit, or severely restrict, the right of inheritance, thereby preventing vast concentrations of wealth in the hands of particularly successful families. In an effort to provide greater equality of opportunity in the job market, the government might require businesses to set aside certain jobs on a quota basis for particular segments of the population, such as women and various minority groups. Whether such measures can actually succeed in achieving real equality of opportunity is another question; some people may still enjoy more opportunities than others. One thing, however, is certain: the scope of government intrusion in the private economy would have to be much larger in the quest for greater *equality* of opportunity than would be the case when the goal is simply *equity* of opportunity. As a general rule, the range of economic liberty for individuals and businesses declines as the pursuit of equality intensifies.

At the maximum end of our continuum is the goal of *equality of condition.* Whereas the concept of opportunity suggests that, at the end of the day, some individuals will come out ahead of others in their pursuit of economic well-being, equality of condition means that everyone will ultimately enjoy roughly the same amount of wealth. Obviously the pursuit of such an outcome would require the state to undertake major efforts to redistribute wealth throughout society and perhaps to control incomes as well. Tax policies and other modes of government intervention in the economy would be explicitly aimed at preventing the stratification of society into upper, middle, and lower classes in order to ensure that all citizens belong to the same socioeconomic class. Under these conditions the freedom of individuals and private businesses to conduct their economic affairs as they wish would be severely constricted. Once again, as the scope of economic equality widens, the scope of economic liberty narrows.

Thus we are faced with a real dilemma in our efforts to establish a "democratic" distribution of resources and opportunities. Democracy requires both equality and liberty, but the more equality we want, the less liberty we are likely to get (figure 7.3 shows the inverse correlation between them).

One of the most highly charged controversies in virtually every modern democracy is the clash between two conceptions of how to achieve economic well-being. Some people tend to define economic democracy primarily in terms of *equality.* Others prefer to define economic democracy primarily in terms of the *liberties* of the marketplace. Most democracies strive to resolve this conflict by striking a balance between equality and liberty. They may, for example, emphasize the concept of equity rather than full equality. (When people in the United States speak of "equality of opportunity," they generally mean "equity of opportunity.") At the same time, they may seek to harmonize state intervention in the economy with ample freedom for private enterprise. The modern *democratic welfare state* is the product of this balancing act; it is the most widely adopted form of political economy among the world's economically advanced democracies. Variations in the application of the welfare state model abound, however. Some countries (like the United States) place greater accents on economic liberty; others (like the Scandinavian countries) stress egalitarian and welfarist ideals. We'll take up these issues again in chapter 14.

We can summarize our overview of democracy very simply as follows:

> <u>**Democracy**</u> ***is a system of government that consists of certain core values, the rule of law, popular sovereignty, guaranteed rights and liberties, and the economic well-being of the populace.***

This definition captures the key elements of the definition we presented at the start of this chapter, while adding a few more points as discussed in the preceding pages.

## Dilemmas of Democracy

So much for the idea and ideals of democracy. Are they always realized in practice? The quality of democracy, after all, is only as good as the human beings who are its lifeblood. The central paradox of democracy is that its institutions and practices can be neglected, subverted, or manipulated in ways that contradict its basic purposes, *even when its rules and procedures are being followed.* In some cases democracy can backfire, producing results that are the very opposite of its objectives.

Democracy's core values, for example, promote a variety of freedoms while seeking to reduce social antagonisms through tolerance and compromise. But there is a danger that democracy may intensify and perpetuate social conflicts rather than attenuate them. Freedom of speech gives social groups the opportunity not only to articulate their grievances openly but also to criticize one another, at times provoking further conflict. The right to associate for political purposes may result in the formation of political parties and other organizations that are based exclusively on one ethnic or religious group, or a group devoted to a single issue, thereby entrenching society's divisions and making compromise all the harder.

The rule of law seeks to constrain government power. But constraining power can prove difficult. Once elected, governing elites and their appointees often enjoy considerable autonomy to make unpopular or blatantly discriminatory decisions before facing the voters in the next elections. The very nature of electoral democracy practically dictates that victorious politicians will favor the constituencies that voted for them and will pay less attention to the rest of the electorate. Institutions like the bureaucracy and the courts may possess virtually unchecked authority. The political influence of privileged social groups or giant corporations on elected legislators and executives may also be hard to contain. The financing of political parties and candidates by wealthy donors in some democracies inflates the power of money in the political process and greases the wheels of corruption. Keeping one's supporters on board and reaching out to potential new voters may tempt officeholders to spend money from state coffers on projects that favor their own political "clients," contrary to the interests of the general public. Lying and other forms of deception on the part of public officials can go unpunished or even undetected. The abuse of power may be less flagrant in a democracy than in a dictatorship, but it does not disappear entirely.

Popular sovereignty (Pillar I) aims at establishing self-government by permitting meaningful participation in political life. But political participation can fall well below its potential. Most people in fact do not take part in political life, except perhaps to vote every few years. Many don't even bother to vote. Whether accurately or inaccurately, people may feel that their votes don't count for very much, and so they retreat into apathy or cynicism. Many voters believe, at times justifiably, that important issues are ignored by politicians who prefer soundbites and slogans to real debate, or that there are inadequate opportunities for citizens to discuss politics intelligently in open forums. Manipulation of the issues by elites often substitutes for deliberation by citizens. Meanwhile, nonvoting by many eligible voters confers greater political influence on those who do vote, undermining democratic equality.[16]

Popular sovereignty also enables citizens to express their opinions and demands openly so that politicians can ascertain the wishes of the community and carry out the public will. But in practice it may sometimes be very difficult to implement what the people want. Modern democracies are often seriously divided on important questions. Sometimes a population is so divided on a controversial issue that *no* majority consensus can be achieved. People frequently criticize elected officials for failing to get things done, but *politicians are often divided because the people who elected them are divided.* Institutional complications can magnify these problems. The U.S. Constitution, with its governmental checks and balances, was intentionally crafted to make it difficult to enact laws. Other democracies have their own problems making decisions. The "deadlock of democracy" is a frequent phenomenon. Under some circumstances, either no effective decision can be taken or a decision may have to be imposed on the population "dictatorially"—by the courts, perhaps, or by executive decree. (This phenomenon is explained by Condorcet's "paradox of voting" and Kenneth Arrow's "general possibility theorem."[17]) In other instances, the opinion of the majority may be all too clear: it may reflect their desire to discriminate against minorities. The democratic principle of majority rule thus risks producing the tyranny of the majority, violating democracy's core values of inclusion, equality, and tolerance.

Rights and liberties (Pillar II) may be formally enshrined in legal statutes. But as we've already noted in this chapter, formal legal guarantees can be breached or circumvented in practice. There can also be intense conflicts over basic rights, such as abortion rights, gay rights, religious rights, and the like. In some cases these conflicts may be impossible to resolve to everyone's satisfaction through the normal democratic mechanisms of elections, legislation, bargaining, and mutual compromise. The courts, at times consisting of unelected judges, may have to impose decisions on a divided citizenry and its elected representatives.

The task of enhancing everyone's economic well-being (Pillar III) poses problems of its own. As we've seen, it is impossible to provide true equality of condition, or even true equality of opportunity, without imposing major governmental infringements on private enterprise and on the property rights of individuals and their families. Equity of opportunity may be a more feasible objective, but even that can be hard to achieve in practice. In many democracies there is a serious conflict between economic freedom and economic welfare. Proponents of free enterprise and private property rights expect democracy to maximize their freedom. In their view, an intrusive state with broad powers of intervention in economic and social affairs is undemocratic because it limits the population's right to control its property (including its money, if taxes are high). But others believe that democracy necessitates certain fundamental economic and social rights for the whole population, including medical care, housing, a fair minimum wage, and employment (or full compensation for the unemployed). Any society built on glaring social inequalities is inherently undemocratic, according to this perspective. Its proponents would therefore favor an interventionist state with the authority—and tax revenue—to ensure a decent standard of living for all. Historically, proponents of "democratic socialism" and "participatory democracy" have argued that a true democracy should limit private enterprise significantly, giving the people themselves the power to decide how factories and other workplaces should be run.[18] Even though such views are rarely heard these days, most democracies today still have sharp divisions over the state's proper role in the economy. As with many other issues, these divisions reflect conflicts between democracy's multiple aims and aspirations.

Real-world democracies are far from perfect. Even the best of them have flaws and shortcomings. To their credit, however, democracies are works in progress. They can always be improved through the efforts of citizens and their governments. Dictatorships, by contrast, resist change. Fittingly, Winston Churchill observed that "democracy is the worst form of government—except for all the other forms which have been tried from time to time."

To understand how a deeply divided society can build and sustain a successful democracy, let's take a look at the Netherlands. In order to save democracy, the Dutch developed a new form of democratic governance: *consociational democracy*.

## HYPOTHESIS-TESTING EXERCISE: Consociational Democracy

### Hypothesis

Some theorists hypothesize that a stable, effective democracy requires a relatively homogeneous population. They assume that a society whose people share a common ethnic background, a common religion, compatible economic interests, and fairly similar political outlooks is more likely to sustain democratic institutions and make governmental decisions effectively than heterogeneous societies, which are characterized by a plurality of ethnic groups, religious affiliations, economic interests, or political ideologies. Social diversity, in this view, can be expected to produce permanent political animosity rather than a viable democracy.

### Variables

Actually, we have two interrelated hypotheses here. In the "homogeneity hypothesis," the *dependent variable* is a *stable and effective democracy;* the *independent variable* is a *homogeneous population.* In the "heterogeneity hypothesis," which is the converse of the first one, the *dependent variable* is an *unstable, ineffective democracy;* the *independent variable* is a *heterogeneous population.*

### Expectations

The hypotheses suggest that heterogeneous societies are essentially doomed to failure in their attempts to build and maintain a stable and effective democracy. Because the Netherlands has a politically and socially heterogeneous population, we would expect democracy to fail in that country or at least to be highly unstable and ineffective in its lawmaking processes.

### Evidence

Arend Lijphart pointed out that, for much of its modern history, the Netherlands has exhibited some of the distinctive hallmarks of a highly fragmented society. The Dutch share a common national identity, but they have been divided along religious lines into Roman Catholics and Protestants (mostly Calvinists) ever since the sixteenth century. In addition, starting in the nineteenth century the population became divided along economic and ideological lines. Middle- and upper-class liberals who favored wide freedoms to pursue their private business activities vied with working-class socialists who preferred restrictions on private enterprise along with policies designed to enhance the bargaining power of labor unions and to provide social welfare benefits to workers and their families. By the twentieth century, four well-organized "camps" had formed in Dutch society: Catholics, Protestants, liberals, and socialists. Each camp had its own political party, interest groups, newspapers, and other forms of association. Moreover, the four camps were relatively isolated from one another: their respective members did not cross over into the organizations of the other camps or interact with one another very much. Even intermarriage between camps was rare.

And yet, defying the odds, the Netherlands emerged in the twentieth century as one of the most stable democracies in the world. Competitive elections have taken place on a regular basis; political liberties flourish; the rule of law is not in doubt. Most Dutch governments have proven quite effective in making decisions that address the country's principal problems.

### Conclusions

Lijphart concluded that the evidence of modern Dutch history was *inconsistent* with the heterogeneity hypothesis. Instead of disintegrating into instability and ineffectiveness, Dutch democracy was a stellar success. What accounted for this seemingly paradoxical combination of social fragmentation and healthy democracy? According to Lijphart's explanation, Holland's success was attributable above all to the value its elites attached to *tolerance* and *compromise*. Recognizing that democratic institutions and political liberties might well founder if their respective groups did not get along, the leaders of the four camps made special efforts to tolerate their differences and accommodate their conflicting interests and demands on the basis of inclusion and equity. Through patient negotiation they worked out compromises aimed at providing each group with a fair chance at political power and a relatively equitable distribution of state revenues. Such things as educational funding and civil service jobs were divided up in approximate proportion to each group's share of the population. At the same time, the leaders of all four groups maintained an outspoken commitment to democracy and a determination to implement their agreements effectively.

For their part, most Dutch citizens deferred to their leaders, granting them considerable latitude to strike bargains with the leaders of the competing camps without pressuring them into adopting rigidly uncompromising positions. What Lijphart calls "the politics of accommodation" in the Netherlands was thus a highly elitist form of democracy. It ultimately depended on the ability of the leading personalities representing the four camps to overcome their differences and reach effective bargains, sometimes in secret, for the good of the general population. In other words, Dutch elites saved democracy by observing basic democratic *values.*

**Consociational democracy** is the term Lijphart applied to this system of ***elite accommodation in a socially heterogeneous society.*** In the Netherlands it emerged around 1917 and reached its peak in the 1950s and early 1960s. After the mid 1960s, Dutch society no longer needed the special accommodationist practices of previous years. Democracy remains secure in Holland, perhaps in large part because of the firm foundation it acquired during the long decades of consociationalism. Lijphart argues that consociational democracy, either in its pure form as it once existed in Holland or in some modified variant, constitutes a distinct model of democracy that may be highly applicable in deeply divided societies. It demonstrates that "deep, mutually reinforcing social cleavages do not form an insuperable barrier to viable democracy." Variants of consociational democracy have been used in India and are being tried out in contemporary Bosnia, Afghanistan, and Iraq. But its critics warn that its procedures can become so routine that they may harden a society's divisions instead of reducing them.

Meanwhile, the Netherlands is facing new challenges to its democratic order. Recently arrived immigrants, many of them Muslims who do not fit easily into Holland's freewheeling lifestyles, have provoked a backlash by Dutch voters. In response, the government has tightened restrictions on further immigration and required immigrants to take classes in the Dutch language and culture. Contacts between government officials and leaders of the Muslim community raise interesting parallels with consociational democracy.[19]

---

Now let's apply to Egypt the concepts of democracy we've examined in this chapter.

## IS EGYPT DEMOCRATIZING?

"Egypt, which showed the way toward peace in the Middle East, can show the way toward democracy in the Middle East." With this challenge issued to the region's most populous Arab country, President George W. Bush used his State of the Union message to Congress in January 2005 to promote his campaign for democratization in this historically undemocratic part of the world. In the view of Bush administration strategists (especially neoconservatives), democracy could provide an effective antidote to terrorism. By overcoming dictatorships and giving citizens a say in their own destiny, democracy in their view would relieve the political frustrations and sense of powerlessness that were thought to spawn terrorists in predominantly Muslim countries. Egypt was seen as playing a potentially pivotal role in turning the greater Middle East in democracy's direction.

In calling on the Egyptian government to democratize, President Bush took the risk of undermining one of America's key partners in the region, President *Hosni Mubarak*. At 76, Mubarak was only the third ruler to govern Egypt in more than half a century. The first was Gamal Abdel Nasser, who took power in a military coup against the Egyptian monarchy in 1952. After losing the Sinai Peninsula and the Gaza Strip to Israel in the Six-Day War of 1967, Nasser died in 1970. He was succeeded by his adjutant, Anwar Sadat. Sadat attacked Israel in October 1973 and subsequently recovered the Sinai after protracted negotiations. Having redeemed Egypt's honor on the battlefield, Sadat then turned an about-face and made peace with Israel, sealing the deal in marathon talks with Israeli prime minister Menachem Begin and U.S. president Jimmy Carter at Camp David in 1979. Sadat paid the ultimate price for his peace policy: in 1981 he was assassinated by Islamic extremists. Mubarak, Sadat's right-hand man, quietly assumed power with the backing of Egypt's military command.

Mubarak ordered a swift crackdown on Islamic militants. He soon issued a new Emergency Law that severely restricted the right of political organization, the right of peaceful assembly, and other rights that were supposedly guaranteed by Egypt's constitution. From then on, Mubarak ruled unchallenged. Asserting that competitive elections were unnecessary and possibly destabilizing, Egypt's president staged four successive referendums on his rule, winning upward of 95 percent of the votes each time, according to his government's official tabulations. Meanwhile, Mubarak's regime became the second largest recipient of American military and economic aid after Israel. A succession of U.S. presidents rewarded Egypt with financial incentives to maintain its peaceful relationship with the Israelis, providing its government with $60 billion in American aid between 1979 and 2005. More than half that sum consisted of military assistance.

In response to President Bush's appeal, Mubarak announced that Egypt would hold multicandidate presidential elections with the aim of consolidating "more freedom and democracy." By this time, opponents of Mubarak's grip on power were becoming increasingly outspoken. Demonstrations that started out as protests against the U.S.-led invasion of Iraq in 2003 took a sudden anti-Mubarak turn. In the following year, left-leaning intellectuals and political activists formed an organization called "Enough" (Kifaya) and boldly demanded Mubarak's resignation. A growing number of nongovernmental organizations dedicated to human rights and democracy signaled the emergence of an assertive civil society. (Mubarak's government rebuffed Bush administration efforts to fund some of these NGOs, insisting on the right to block American money from going to groups it considered threatening.) At the same time, one of Egypt's oldest political organizations, the Muslim Brotherhood, stepped up its political activity. Formed in 1924, the Muslim Brotherhood favored a more conservative implementation of Islamic law than the secular Mubarak government implemented, but it renounced the use of violence in the 1970s. Although the Brotherhood had been banned since Nasser's days, Mubarak allowed a small number of its members to serve in Egypt's parliament as independent (nonparty) deputies.

Ten parties were permitted to field candidates in the 2005 presidential elections. Most Egyptians regarded Mubarak's eventual victory as a foregone conclusion, despite the trappings of a competition. The government retained full control of the broadcast media and kept tight restrictions on the press, forbidding "libel" against the ruling authorities. Mubarak's campaign was managed by his forty-one-year-old son Gamal, a leader of the National Democratic Party (NDP), the regime's ruling party. President Mubarak's most vocal opponent was Ayman Nour, a former Mubarak supporter who now favored democracy and a market-oriented economy, together with a pro-Western foreign policy. The Muslim Brotherhood did not run a candidate, but it announced its acceptance of democracy and called on its members to vote for anybody but Mubarak.

Despite the predictable outcome, the three-week campaign featured an unprecedented amount of open criticism of President Mubarak and his government. As the balloting took place on September 7, Nour and other candidates accused Mubarak's backers of vote buying and voter intimidation at the polls. The government refused to permit neutral election monitors inside the polling stations, and officials took several days to count the votes in secret. As anticipated, Mubarak was declared the winner. According to the government's count, he garnered 88.6 percent of the vote. Nour came in second with 7.3 percent. The official turnout figure was a mere 23 percent of the eligible electorate, but election observers claimed the true turnout was even lower. Mubarak thus won the votes of barely 20 percent of Egypt's eligible voters.

Mubarak's next challenge was the three-round parliamentary elections held in November and December. In the past, Mubarak's NDP was assured of winning sweeping majorities in the 454-seat People's Assembly, Egypt's lower house, in carefully controlled elections. Under American and European influence, Mubarak was expected to hold a more open contest in 2005. Instead of acceding to these outside pressures, however, Mubarak embarked on a strategy of crushing the main secular opposition parties while cutting a deal with the Muslim Brotherhood. The Brotherhood was invited to run candidates as "independents" for about 140 of the 444 seats up for election. (Ten seats were unelected.) Nour and other candidates were subjected to harassment and voter manipulation. Nour himself lost his seat in the Assembly when the NDP bused two thousand illegally registered voters into his district to ensure his defeat. Mubarak's apparent aim was to convince the Bush administration that his strong presence at the helm of Egypt's government was the only alternative to Islamic extremism and terrorism. (Egyptian terrorists had set off a series of bombings in coastal resort areas in October 2004 and July 2005.) To Mubarak's surprise, candidates associated with the Muslim Brotherhood, running under the slogan "Islam is the Solution," did better than expected in the first two rounds of voting. Alarmed, the government had the police fire rubber bullets and live ammunition at voters waiting to cast their third-round ballots in Muslim Brotherhood strongholds. Eleven people were killed.

As predicted, Mubarak's National Democratic Party once again took more than two-thirds of the Assembly's seats. But the NDP lost 90 seats, and the "independents" representing the Muslim Brotherhood raised their total from 13 seats in the previous legislature to 88 seats in the new one. Nour's party, Tomorrow, won only 1 seat. Kifaya (Enough) fielded no candidates.

Mubarak wasted no time following up his electoral victories by cracking down hard on his opponents. Muslim Brotherhood members were rounded up and arrested by the hundreds. Ayman Nour was arrested on charges that he had falsified signatures on the petitions needed to qualify for the presidential election. Nour strenuously denied the charges, and a government witness against Nour recanted his testimony, declaring that it had been extracted under torture. With U.S. and European diplomats present in the courtroom, a judge sentenced Nour to five years at hard labor. Nour's appeal was denied in early 2006, prompting the U.S. State Department to label his case a "miscarriage of justice." Meanwhile, two magistrates were prosecuted for accusing other judges of complicity in the government's efforts to defraud the voters during the recent elections. Riot police wielding clubs charged at demonstrators who gathered in support of the magistrates. (One of the magistrates was later given a reprimand, and the other's charges were dismissed.) President Mubarak canceled local elections for two years. In the spring of 2006, several days after another round of bombings in tourist areas by Egyptian terrorists, Mubarak extended the Emergency Law for up to two more years, despite U.S. calls for a relaxation of its restrictions on peaceful political assembly. Anti-regime bloggers were the regime's next target, with Mubarak himself accusing them of "libel and blasphemy."

At the end of 2005, Egypt had a Freedom House rating of 5.5, classifying it as a semi-authoritarian regime. And by the end of 2006, Egypt still had a long way to go before meeting the minimal criteria for democracy that we have identified in this chapter. Starting with the bottom step of our Temple of Democracy, Egypt was seriously lacking in democratic values. Its government showed little interest in a permanent expansion of political freedom. It violated the values of inclusion and equality by excluding prodemocracy opposition parties from participating in the political process on an equal plane with President Mubarak's dominant elite. Women held only 2 percent of the seats in the National Assembly. Tolerance was also in short supply as the government persistently discriminated against non-Muslims. Christians—mostly affiliated with the Coptic Orthodox Church—formed about 10 percent of the country's population, but they had only six seats in the National Assembly (five of which were unelected), and few public-sector leadership positions. Mubarak's regime also showed no inclination to compromise with its main opponents. For its part, the Muslim Brotherhood was suspected of sticking to its demands for an Islamic state in the event that it came to power, a position that implied intolerance of non-Muslims and other nondemocratic attitudes. In addition, the Mubarak regime flagrantly violated the rule of law, including the requirement of an independent judiciary. As a law professor at Cairo University stated, "The president is the law." The Egyptian Organization for Human Rights documented nearly three hundred cases of torture between 1993 and 2004, of which 120 resulted in death. Arbitrary arrests, rigged trials, corruption, nepotism, and other abuses of power were glaringly evident.

President Mubarak's government also infringed the most basic notions of popular sovereignty (Pillar I) and failed to safeguard political rights and liberties (Pillar II). For its part, Egypt's economy had serious problems providing economic well-being (Pillar III) for the mass of the country's population of 72 million. Egypt is ranked by the World Bank as a lower-middle-income economy. Its growth fell from an average annual rate of 4.7 percent in 1999–2000 to 3.4 percent in 2000–2004. Approximately 5 million were unemployed; the unemployment rate rose from 9 percent in 1990–92 to 11 percent in 2000–2004. (During the election campaign, Mubarak promised to create 4.5 million new jobs during his new six-year term as president.) More than 40 percent of the population lived on less than $2 a day, requiring major government subsidies. Egypt's large state sector employed about 7 million people—nearly 10 percent of the population. Maldistributon of income was also relatively high (see chapter 2, table 2.3).

Egypt's next presidential election is set for 2011. It is widely anticipated that Gamal Mubarak will be the odds-on favorite to succeed his father some day. In 2006 the younger Mubarak reportedly told Bush administration officials that he was committed to building democracy, but it would be a long-term process marked by setbacks.[20]

---

This chapter has presented a multifaceted concept of democracy that conforms to the views of most theorists and democracy activists in the world today. Chapter 8 looks at various ways democracies are organized.

## KEY TERMS
## (In bold and underlined in the text)

Inclusion
Equality
Equity
Rule of law
Popular sovereignty
Representative democracy
Polyarchy
Direct democracy
Democracy
Consociational democracy

## NOTES

1. *Freedom in the World 2006* (New York: Freedom House, 2006), 3, 4. These figures compare with 66 electoral democracies recorded in the 1987–88 survey and 91 recorded in 1991–92. In 1972 there were 150 sovereign states, of which 43 were ranked "free." There were 54 "free" states in 1983 and 75 in 1993. Fareed Zakaria, *The Future of Freedom: Illiberal Democracy at Home and Abroad* (New York: Norton, 2003).
2. Adam Przeworski suggests that democracy works "when all the relevant political forces have some specific minimum probability of doing well," and that those who lose elections or fail to have their demands fulfilled "may stay with the democratic game if they believe that even losing repeatedly under democracy is better for them than a future under an alternative system." *Democracy and the Market* (Cambridge: Cambridge University Press, 1991), 30, 31.
3. On respect, see Francis Fukuyama, *The End of History and the Last Man* (New York: Free Press, 1992). On trust, see idem, *Trust: The Social Virtues and the Creation of Prosperity* (New York: Free Press, 1995). For a rational choice perspective, see Russell Hardin, *Trust and Trustworthiness* (New York: Russell Sage Foundation, 2002).
4. Philippe C. Schmitter and Terry Lynn Karl, "What Democracy Is . . . and Is Not," in *The Global Resurgence of Democracy,* 2nd ed., ed. Larry Diamond and Marc F. Plattner (Baltimore, Md.: Johns Hopkins University Press, 1996), 57.
5. Alexis de Tocqueville, *Democracy in America,* ed. J. P. Mayer, trans. George Lawrence (New York: Harper & Row, 1966).
6. Robert D. Putnam, with Robert Leonardi and Raffaella Y. Nanetti, *Making Democracy Work* (Princeton: Princeton University Press, 1993), 182.
7. Secret voting was first employed in South Australia in 1858. It was adopted for general use in Britain in 1872 and in U.S. presidential elections only after the fraud-tainted contest of 1884. Prior to these dates, various forms of nonsecret balloting were the rule, such as a voice vote or show of hands at a public election meeting.
8. Among Dahl's voluminous writings, see *Polyarchy: Participation and Opposition* (New Haven: Yale University Press, 1971), *Dilemmas of Pluralist Democracy* (New Haven: Yale University Press, 1982), *Democracy and Its Critics* (New Haven: Yale University Press, 1989), *On Democracy* (New Haven: Yale University Press, 1999), and *How Democratic Is the American Constitution?* (New Haven: Yale University Press, 2002).
9. The population of Athens probably included 25,000 to 40,000 adult males who were classified as citizens during the fifth century B.C.E. Perhaps a few thousand actually took part in the deliberative assemblies that decided the city-state's laws and policies. Geneva in 1760 had a population of approximately 25,000; only about 1,500 males were qualified to take part in the town's general assembly. On Athenian democracy, see David Stockton, *The Classical Athenian Democracy* (Oxford: Oxford University Press, 1990); M. I. Finley, *Politics in the Ancient World* (Cambridge: Cambridge University Press, 1983), and A. H. M. Jones, *Athenian Democracy* (Oxford: Basil Blackwell, 1969). On Geneva, see R. R. Palmer, *The Age of the Democratic Revolution*, vol. 1 (Princeton: Princeton University Press, 1959), 111, 127–28.
10. Joseph F. Zimmerman, *The Massachusetts Town Meeting: A Tenacious Institution* (Albany: State University of New York Press, Graduate School of Public Affairs, 1967), and *Participatory Democracy* (New York: Praeger, 1986).
11. On "techno-democracy," see Lawrence K. Grossman, *The Electronic Republic: Reshaping*

*Democracy in the Information Age* (New York: Viking, 1995); Cass Sunstein, *republic.com* (Princeton: Princeton University Press, 2002); and Steve Davis, Larry Elin, and Grant Reeher, *Click on Democracy* (Boulder, Colo.: Westview Press, 2002). See Burke's speech to the electors of Bristol in 1774 in *The Portable Edmund Burke*, ed. Isaac Kramnick (New York: Penguin, 1999), 155–57.

**12.** Martin van Gelderen and Quentin Skinner, eds., *Republicanism: A Shared European Heritage*, 2 vols. (New York: Cambridge University Press, 2002); Philip Pettit, *Republicanism: A Theory of Freedom and Government* (New York: Oxford University Press, 1997).

**13.** Herbert McCloskey and Alida Brill, *Dimensions of Tolerance: What Americans Believe About Civil Liberties* (New York: Russell Sage Foundation, 1983). The survey figure fell to 30 percent in agreement in 2004 and 23 percent in 2005. See the annual "State of the First Amendment Survey" conducted by the First Amendment Center, affiliated with Vanderbilt University, at firstamendmentcenter.org.

**14.** Amitai Etzioni, *The Common Good* (Cambridge, UK: Polity, 2004); idem, *Spirit of Community: Rights, Responsibilities, and the Communitarian Agenda* (New York: Crown, 1993); idem, ed., *The Essential Communitarian Reader* (Lanham, Md.: Rowman and Littlefield, 1998); and idem, Andrew Volmert, and Elanit Rothschild, eds., *The Communitarian Reader: Beyond the Essentials* (Lanham, Md.: Rowman and Littlefield, 2004).

**15.** *The People Have Spoken: Global Views of Democracy*, no. 2 (Washington, D.C.: U.S. Information Agency, 1999), 32–35.

**16.** For arguments in behalf of greater citizen participation in the decision-making process, see Benjamin R. Barber, *Strong Democracy* (Berkeley: University of California Press, 1984), and *A Place for Us* (New York: Hill & Wang, 1998); and James S. Fishkin, *Democracy and Deliberation: New Directions for Democratic Reform* (New Haven: Yale University Press, 1991).

**17.** In his famous "paradox of voting," the French philosopher Condorcet reasoned that if three individuals (I, II, and III) are faced with three different choices (A, B, and C), it is possible that no majority can be found for any of the available choices. This result would occur if I prefers A to B and B to C (and thus A to C); II prefers B to C and C to A (and thus B to A); and III prefers C to A and A to B (and thus C to B). Two out of the three people prefer A to B and B to C. However, two out of three prefer C to A! With no majority for any of the three alternatives, gridlock ensues. Nobel Prize–winning economist Kenneth Arrow showed that, when Condorcet's paradox applies to a community trying to choose from among at least three proposals for enhancing its economic welfare, and no majority can be found for any of them, it may be impossible to make a decision at all, or the policy choice must be imposed on the community dictatorially by state authorities. See Kenneth J. Arrow, *Social Change and Individual Values*, 2nd ed. (New Haven: Yale University Press, 1951).

**18.** Robert A. Dahl, *A Preface to Economic Democracy* (Berkeley: University of California Press, 1985). See also the "Porf Huron Statement" adopted by the Students for a Democratic Society in 1962, excerpted in Robert A. Goldwin, ed., *How Democratic Is America? Responses to the New Left Challenge* (Chicago: Rand McNally, 1971), 1–15. For a recent approach, see William Greider, *The Soul of Capitalism: Opening Paths to a Moral Economy* (New York: Simon and Schuster, 2003).

**19.** Arend Lijphart, *The Politics of Accommodation*, 2nd ed. (Berkeley: University of California Press, 1975).

**20.** Saad Ibrahim, "Promises to Keep in Egypt," *Washington Post*, September 24, 2005; Jackson Diehl, "Mubarak Outdoes Himself," *Washington Post*, December 5, 2005; *Washington Post*, May 16, 2006; *New York Times*, December 25, 2005; *Financial Times*, May 19, 2006. See also Maha M. Abdelrahman, *Civil Society Exposed: The Politics of NGOs in Egypt* (New York: Tauris, 2004); the annual country reports on Egypt prepared by the U.S. State Department's Bureau of Democracy, Human Rights, and Labor, at www.state.gov; and *World Development Indicators 2006* (Washington, D.C.: World Bank, 2006).

CHAPTER 8

# DEMOCRACY: HOW DOES IT WORK?

## State Institutions and Electoral Systems

How do modern democratic governments work? This is a huge question with as many answers as there are democracies. In this chapter we address it by focusing on two key aspects of democratic government: *state institutions* and *electoral systems.*

### STATE INSTITUTIONS

In the course of history there have emerged three leading models of representative democracy: (1) the *presidential* system, a variant of which is used in the United States; (2) the *parliamentary system* that initially evolved in Britain, and (3) the mixed *presidential-parliamentary system*, which is currently utilized in France, Russia, and elsewhere. Each model prescribes a set of methods for selecting the *three main branches* of national government—the *executive*, the *legislative*, and *judicial*—and stipulates how legal authority is to be distributed among these three branches. All three models have experienced important evolutionary transformations in the countries where they first emerged. In addition, variants of all three have appeared in other countries as political leaders have sought to copy their essential features while adjusting them to the contours of their own national history and specific political conditions. Our aim in this chapter is to help you understand these three institutional forms of democracy by comparing their main characteristics side by side. We'll concentrate here on the essential features of these systems, leaving the details of how they work in specific countries to subsequent chapters.

Some democracies have institutional arrangements that differ from the three models we are about to describe. The governmental structures of these divergent democratic systems tend to vary from one country to another, following no common patterns. Consequently, they all tend to get lumped together under the general rubric *hybrid democratic regimes.* South Africa is one example that we will examine in this book (see chapter 23).

#### Presidentialism

In the *presidential* system of democracy—also known as **presidentialism**—***the president is the sole effective head of government, constitutionally armed with real decision-making powers.*** Presidents in this type of system are not limited to purely ceremonial duties, and they do not share real executive power with a second executive, such as a prime minister. In most cases the president in this type of regime is not only the formal head of government but also head of state. In many countries with this type of system, the president is elected directly by the people, but in

**TABLE 8.1**

| Selected Presidential Democracies | | | | |
|---|---|---|---|---|
| Afghanistan | Chile | El Salvador | Nigeria | Philippines |
| Argentina | Colombia | Honduras | Panama | Taiwan |
| Bolivia | Costa Rica | Mexico | Paraguay | United States |
| Brazil | Ecuador | Nicaragua | Peru | Uruguay |

the United States the people elect the president indirectly through the electoral college.

In presidential democracies the president must share power with a separately elected national legislature (whether unicameral or bicameral) and must typically respect the authority of the highest courts in the judicial branch of government. The legislature's role can vary across presidential regimes: some legislatures are fairly strong, as in the United States; others are weaker and concede more power to the executive branch. Table 8.1 provides a list of some presidential democracies in today's world.

The United States has a particular form of presidentialism. Its basic features are worth summarizing here for the sake of permitting explicit comparisons with other democracies. The U.S. system was instituted with the Constitution, which was drafted in 1787 and ratified in 1789. The United States has a federal system, with legal authority shared between the national government and the fifty states. At the national level, which is our principal focus here, the three main institutions are the *presidency,* the centerpiece of the executive branch of government; the *Congress,* which is the national legislature; and the *Supreme Court,* which is the highest judicial authority in the land.

The main architects of this system did not want any of these three branches to dominate the other two. They therefore endowed each branch with certain powers designed to check, or counterbalance, the legal authority of the others. In constructing this system of *separation of powers* and *checks and balances,* James Madison and other founding fathers were profoundly influenced by the writings of Aristotle, who believed that the best constitution required a mixture of elite rule and responsible citizens. While he was vague as to details, Aristotle clearly distrusted mass electoral democracy, fearing it would degenerate into mob rule.[1] Another notable influence was the French philosopher Montesquieu (1689–1755). In *The Spirit of Laws* (1748), Montesquieu argued in favor of a carefully constructed separation of powers between the executive, the legislative, and the judicial branches of government so that the same individuals would not be able to dominate two or more of these branches. He hypothesized that such a system would reduce opportunities for the abuse of power.[2] For Madison and other framers of the Constitution, preventing the abuse of state power was the most important priority of the U.S. system of government.

Although certain aspects of American government have evolved since the Constitution took effect in 1789, it is based today on these core principles, centering on the following features (see figure 8.1):

- *The president and the Congress are elected separately.* The president is elected by the electoral college, which in practice is elected by the voters in each state. The two houses of Congress—the Senate and the House of Representatives—are elected by the voters. Congress does not elect the president. Members of Congress may vote to remove the president from office only for "high crimes and misdemeanors," not because they do not like his policies.
- *Lawmaking depends on a balance of Congressional and presidential powers.* Strictly speaking, only members of Congress have the right to propose bills for adoption as law. The president's own legislative proposals are submitted to the Congress by members acting in his behalf. Laws are enacted when both houses of Congress pass bills by majority vote and the president signs the legislation. The president may veto congressional legislation. Congress may override the president's veto by a two-thirds majority.

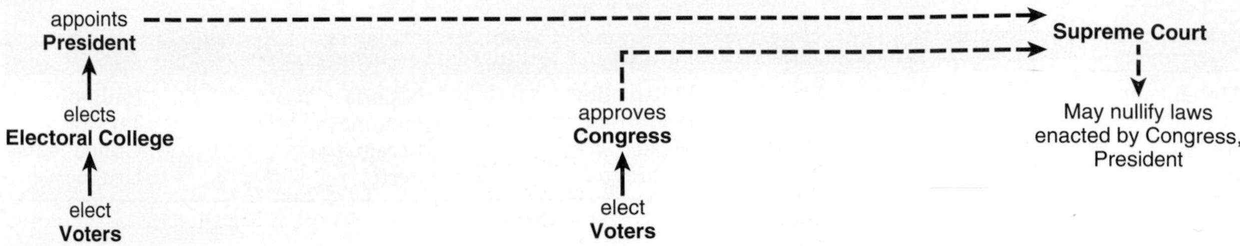


**FIGURE 8.1 U.S. System**

- *The Supreme Court may strike down laws as unconstitutional.* Although this right of *judicial review* is not explicitly contained in the Constitution, ever since the case of *Marbury vs. Madison* in 1803 the Supreme Court has asserted the right to nullify laws on the grounds that they violate the Constitution.
- *The president, the Congress, and the states can together override decisions of the Supreme Court.* The justices of the Supreme Court are selected by the president, with the "advice and consent" of the Senate. If the Court strikes down a law as unconstitutional, the constitution can be amended. Constitutional amendments require a vote of two-thirds of the members of each house of Congress and the approval of three-fourths of the state legislatures.

In keeping with the intentions of the founding fathers, the primary advantage of this system is that neither the president, the Congress, nor the Supreme Court can dominate American government. The primary disadvantage of the checks-and-balances system, however, is its potential for gridlock. Separate elections for the president and Congress make it possible for the president to be a Democrat and the congressional majority to be Republican (or, of course, vice versa), a condition known as *divided government.* If the two sides disagree, it can be very difficult to enact legislation or concur on appointments to the Supreme Court. A more positive view of this situation, however, stresses its potential for compromise. Those who regard compromise as a good thing argue that the possibility of gridlock exerts pressure on both the president and Congress to work out mutually acceptable legislation. Madison himself shared this perspective, arguing that a slow and deliberate process of making laws was preferable to one in which laws are enacted too swiftly and without sufficient scrutiny.

### Parliamentary Government

The *parliamentary system* of democracy, also known as *parliamentary government,* is the most widely used form of democracy in the world today. (For a partial listing of countries using the parliamentary system, see table 8.2.)

In most parliamentary systems of democracy, the term *government* is used in its narrow sense: it refers to the head of government (usually called the *prime minister* or *premier*) and the various ministers of the executive branch (foreign minister, finance minister, etc.), plus the bureaucracies directed by respective cabinet ministers (the foreign ministry, the finance ministry, etc.). The head of government is the chief executive decision maker in the country. Many parliamentary regimes also have a *ceremonial head of state:* a constitutional monarch or president who possesses few, if any, real decision-making powers and whose main job is to symbolize the country's unity or the continuity of its history.

There are numerous versions of parliamentary government, and virtually every country that has this form of democracy has one or more unique features that are not to be found in other parliamentary systems in quite the same way. Nevertheless, the basic institutions of parliamentarism tend to be widely shared. Simply put, the defining principle of **parliamentary government** is that ***the government is selected in a two-step process:***

1. ***The people elect the national legislature.***
2. ***The national legislature (usually the lower house in bicameral legislatures) elects or approves the government.***

TABLE 8.2

**Selected Countries Using the Parliamentary System**

| | | | |
|---|---|---|---|
| Australia | Germany | Jamaica | Norway |
| Bangladesh | Greece | Japan | Slovenia |
| Belgium | Hungary | Latvia | Spain |
| Botswana | India | Luxembourg | Sweden |
| Canada | Iraq | Netherlands | Thailand |
| Denmark | Israel | New Zealand | United Kingdom |
| Estonia | Italy | | |

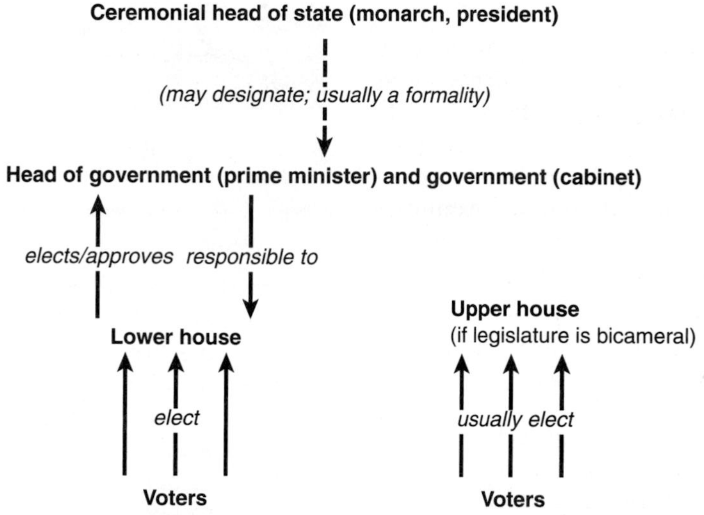


FIGURE 8.2 Parliamentary Government

In this system, there is no separation of powers between the legislative and executive branches as in the United States; rather, there is *a fusion of powers* between the legislature and the executive. To put it another way, *the government in a parliamentary system stems from the legislature and is formally accountable to it.* This fusion of powers and accountability are achieved in the following ways (see figure 8.2):

- As just indicated, *the legislature elects (or approves) the government.* In most examples of the parliamentary system, the people do not directly vote for the prime minister; they vote for candidates running for the national legislature, who in turn have the opportunity to vote for (or approve) the prime minister and cabinet. Some countries provide for a formal vote of the legislature, called an *investiture* vote, to formally approve ("elect") a new government.
- *The prime minister and other government ministers serve simultaneously as members of the legislature.* This dual responsibility, observed in most parliamentary systems, tightens the connection between the executive and the legislature.
- *The government must present and defend its policies before the legislature.* Typically the prime minister and other cabinet ministers must regularly appear before the legislature to present their policies and defend them in open debate. They may also have to answer questions posed by members of the legislature in open session. In the United States, by contrast, the president is not required to answer questions in Congress but is required only to deliver an annual "state of the union" message explaining his policies.
- *The legislature can vote the government out of office.* Just as the legislature "makes" the government

by voting it into office, it can also "unmake" the government by voting it out of office. Typically it exercises this prerogative through a *vote of confidence.*

A **vote of confidence** ***is a showdown vote in the legislature to determine if the government still has the support (confidence) of a voting majority of legislators.*** If the government loses this vote it must usually resign and the legislature must vote a new government into office. If it cannot, the people must vote for a new legislature.

The essential features of parliamentarism provide for a system of *governmental dependence on the legislature* that differs fundamentally from the U.S. system of separation of powers.

Let's clarify how typical parliamentary systems of government work by providing a few examples of *how the legislature elects or approves the government.* Several outcomes are possible, and we'll focus here on three of them. They are (1) *single-party majoritarian government;* (2) *majority coalition government;* and (3) *minority government.*

**Single-Party Majoritarian Government** In a **single-party majoritarian government**, ***one party wins an absolute majority of seats in the national legislature and forms the government.*** (An *absolute majority* means 50 percent plus one.)

An illustration is the British election for the House of Commons of 1997 (see table 8.3). In these elections the Labour Party won 419 of the 659 seats in the House, or 63.6 percent of the total. After the House assembled following the popular elections, the Labour Members of Parliament (MPs) used their majority to establish a government consisting entirely of Labour Party ministers, led by Prime Minister Tony Blair. The other parties in the House

TABLE 8.3

**British House of Commons Elections, 1997**

**(659 Seats)**

| Party | No. of Seats | % of Seats |
|---|---|---|
| Labour | 419 | 63.6 |
| Conservatives | 165 | 25.0 |
| Liberal Democrats | 46 | 7.0 |
| Eight others | 29 | 4.4 |

**British Prime Minister Tony Blair Answering Questions in the House of Commons**

assumed the role of *opposition parties.* (The Labour Party retained its single-party majority in the 2001 and 2005 elections.)

With the Labour Party possessing 179 more seats than the combined total of the opposition parties, Mr. Blair's majoritarian government was now in the position of being able to pass its legislative proposals into law with relative ease. However, this enviable position required the willingness of Labour MPs to maintain *party discipline.* **Party discipline** ***is maintained when the parliamentary deputies of a particular party vote together unanimously as a bloc.*** Party discipline is more likely to occur in parliamentary systems than in the United States, where a tradition of greater independence on the part of individual members of Congress flourishes. Even though unanimous party discipline in Britain by no means occurs all the time, it still occurs more often than in the United States.

As long as the governing party manages to "whip" its legislative delegation into concerted action, a single-party majoritarian government can exhibit remarkable *efficiency:* it can get its legislative proposals passed quickly and smoothly. The opposition parties, lacking the votes against a highly disciplined governing party, simply cannot muster a majority to defeat the government's bills. In the case of Britain, single-party majoritarian governments typically manage to win passage of 97 percent of the bills they propose in the House of

**TABLE 8.4**

**German Bundestag Elections, 1998**

**(669 Seats)**

| Party | No. of Seats | % of Seats |
|---|---|---|
| Social Democrats | 298 | 44.5 |
| Christian Democrats | 245 | 36.7 |
| Greens | 47 | 7.0 |
| Free Democrats | 44 | 6.6 |
| Party of Democratic Socialism | 35 | 5.2 |

Commons, an extraordinarily high degree of governmental efficiency.

***If* no *party succeeds in winning an absolute majority of legislative seats,*** we then have a **hung parliament.** The alternatives are a *majority coalition government* or, failing that, a *minority government.*

**Majority Coalition Government** ***A coalition government consists of two or more parties that agree to share cabinet posts, usually in order to form a voting majority in the legislature.*** An example derives from the results of the elections to the Bundestag, Germany's lower house, in 1998.

As we can see in table 8.4, no party won an absolute majority of the Bundestag's 669 seats (i.e., 335 seats). How, then, can a government be formed? In this case the Social Democrats cut a deal with the Greens to form a coalition government. The Social Democrats, being the larger of the two coalition partners, took the most important cabinet position, that of *chancellor.* (In Germany the head of government is called the chancellor rather than prime minister.) Of the remaining fifteen cabinet slots, ten went to Social Democrats, including the key ministries of finance, justice, and defense. For their part, the Greens got four cabinet posts, including that of foreign minister, the second most prestigious cabinet position after the head of government. One minister had no party affiliation. By joining forces to govern the country, the Social Democrats and the Greens together had 51.5 percent of the seats in the Bundestag, a slender ten-vote majority. As long as their respective Bundestag delegations maintained party discipline, the bills the coalition partners proposed to the legislature would safely win passage.

Quite clearly, the Greens had good reason to feel satisfied with this arrangement. With only 7 percent of the seats in the Bundestag they managed to capture a considerable share of power in the national government. This example illustrates one of the most characteristic features of coalition government: *it provides small parties with an opportunity to participate in the executive branch of government.* Rather than being relegated to the status of a weak opposition party in the Bundestag with little influence on the course of government policy, the Greens negotiated their way into the pinnacle of policy-making power, the cabinet. Their presence in the government meant that they would be able to exert direct influence on practically every major political issue facing the country. (The Social Democrats and Greens formed another coalition government following the 2002 elections. But they lost the 2005 elections, which produced a so-called "Grand Coalition" government between the Social Democrats and their chief rivals, the Christian Democrats. See chapter 18 for details.)

By its very nature, coalition government invariably involves ongoing negotiations among the parties that take part in it. The policies pursued by the cabinet are usually the product of agreements and bargains that are struck between the coalition partners. In the example shown here, the Social Democrats and the Greens had to agree on the bills they proposed to the legislature as well as on other decisions their government made in the day-to-day task of running the national government. Coalition government is government by bargaining par excellence.

What are the chief advantages and disadvantages of coalition government?

One advantage is that coalitions *expand representation in the executive branch of government.* As our example illustrates, coalition governments can permit a small party like the Greens to participate directly in the executive branch of state decision making, giving the people who voted for that party a far greater influence on what their government could do than if the Greens had been simply a minuscule opposition party in the national legislature.

Another advantage of coalition governments is that *they increase the level of bargaining and compromise in the executive branch of government.* By compelling the coalition partners to constantly work together on the policies they pursue, coalitions promote the democratic ideals of negotiation and accommodation. Unlike single-party majoritarian governments, which allow one party to monopolize the executive branch as well as the legislative agenda, coalitions force the largest party to take account of the concerns and preferences of other parties. In the process they provide a mechanism for bridging over the divergences and conflicts that separate the diverse elements of the electorate that these parties represent. At least in principle, coalition governments may increase the likelihood that politics will follow the path of moderation and compromise rather than the dominance of a single party's point of view.

A third advantage of coalition government is its *flexibility and adaptability.* As we've seen, the parliamentary form of democracy permits the legislature to unmake governments as well as make them. If the parties that form a governing coalition have a falling out and cannot patch up their political disagreements, it may be possible to form a new coalition government *without having to wait for the next elections.* The leaders of the various parties have a chance to cobble together a new majority coalition. This happened in Germany in 1982, for example, when the existing coalition government of the Social Democrats and Free Democrats fell apart over irreconcilable differences. A new coalition government was soon formed by the Christian Democrats and Free Democrats, with Helmut Kohl as chancellor. This coalition survived several subsequent elections and governed until 1998, giving Kohl sixteen years in power.

As it happens, the disadvantages of coalition government are closely related to its advantages. Whereas the inclusion of more than one party in a coalition cabinet expands the level of representation in the executive branch, the involvement of too many parties may prove unwieldy. As a general rule, the greater the number of parties represented in a coalition government, the more difficult it is to reach common accord on policies and decisions. The German examples we have just examined are fairly simple ones involving two-party coalition governments. But some democracies have multiparty coalitions involving three or more parties. Throughout much of the 1970s, 1980s, and 1990s, for example, Italy was governed by a succession of coalition governments consisting of four to nine parties. Prolonged negotiations, stalemate, and policy turmoil were often the result. Between 1996 and 2004, India had coalition governments consisting of nineteen to twenty-four parties. Multiparty coalitions can sometimes produce considerable governmental *inefficiency.* It is simply harder for two or more parties to formulate policies and implement decisions as efficiently and effectively as a single party that commands a majority of the legislature's seats. They can also produce governmental *ineffectiveness:* because the coalition partners must usually agree on major policies, their decisions may reflect the lowest common denominator of interparty consensus rather than the most effective ways of addressing the country's goals and problems.[3]

Another potential disadvantage is that small parties may gain a level of influence in the government that far outweighs their share of electoral support. As we saw in the German case, the Greens in 1998 acquired key cabinet positions even though they garnered only 7 percent of Bundestag seats. While some people may applaud a political system that allows a minority party to make its way into the highest reaches of decision-making power, others may regard such a prospect as unfair because it confers excessive influence on parties with small, sometimes very small, constituencies. In 1981–82, Italy's prime minister—the most powerful political figure in the country—came from a party that had captured only 1.9 percent of the vote!

A third disadvantage derives from the very flexibility and adaptability of coalition government that we highlighted earlier as one of its advantages. Whereas the institutions of parliamentary democracy and coalition government can be valuable tools enabling party leaders and legislators to remove ineffective governments, there often exists the potential for abusing these opportunities. In some democracies, ***governing coalitions fall apart and must be replaced fairly frequently.*** This phenomenon is known as **governmental instability.** Once again, Italy provides a cautionary example of what can go wrong in a parliamentary democracy. Between 1945 and 2006, Italy had no fewer than sixty-one governments! A large number of them were coalitions involving three or more parties. Some of these multiparty cabinets lasted no more than a few months or even weeks. Other countries have also had periods of turbulent governmental instability.[4]

**Minority Government** What if no party has an absolute majority of seats in the legislature, and the leaders of the various parties cannot come to terms on forming a coalition government that enjoys the backing of the majority of legislators? Under these difficult circumstances a *minority government* may have to be formed. As its name implies, a **minority government** ***consists of one or more parties whose delegates do not constitute a majority of the legislative house.*** Since it takes a voting majority to pass bills into law, how can such a government legislate? There are several possibilities.

One possibility is a *parliamentary alliance.* In this case, *two or more parties agree that they will not share cabinet posts, but their legislators will vote together to support the government and pass legislation.* Britain provides an example. In 1977 the Labour Party government of Prime Minister James Callaghan lost its majority when several Labour members of Parliament switched parties. Callaghan then got the Liberal Party, which had thirteen members in the House of Commons, to support his government in exchange for joint consultation on all bills brought up for a vote. This arrangement eventually broke down, but Callaghan managed to work out a similar parliamentary alliance with other parties. Agreements of this kind can be quite unstable, as Callaghan found out in 1979 when he lost a vote of confidence in the Commons by only one vote. His government thereupon resigned and new parliamentary elections were held. Callaghan and the Labour Party lost the 1979 elections to their archrivals, the Conservatives, who governed Britain for the next eighteen years.

Sweden's government elected in 2002 provides another example (see table 8.5). Sweden's Social Democrats formed a single-party minority government by negotiating a parliamentary alliance with the Left Party and the Greens. As long as their members voted together unanimously, the three parties could amass 191 votes, more than enough for a majority (175 votes). But the three did not necessarily agree on everything. If a minority party cannot count on votes from its parliamentary alliance partners, it may still be able to form a legislative majority by garnering support from other parties on a vote-by-vote basis.

**TABLE 8.5**

**Swedish Riksdag Elections, 2002**

**(349 Seats)**

| Party | No. of Seats | % of Seats |
|---|---|---|
| Social Democrats | 144 | 41.3 |
| Moderates | 55 | 15.8 |
| People's Liberal Party | 48 | 13.8 |
| Christian Democrats | 33 | 9.5 |
| Left Party | 30 | 8.6 |
| Center Party | 22 | 6.3 |
| Greens | 17 | 4.9 |

Obviously, a minority government's dependence on other parties in the legislature—whether in a parliamentary alliance or on a vote-by-vote basis—can give the cooperating parties a considerable amount of negotiating power. These parties are then in a position to extract benefits from the government that they might not otherwise receive if the governing party possessed its own voting majority. If this ongoing negotiating process bogs down, the result can be gridlock. The U.S. system of government is therefore not the only type of democracy that is gridlock-prone.

A third possible way a minority government can govern is to ask the opposition parties to *abstain* from voting against it whenever it presents its bills to the legislature for a vote. In most democracies, all that is needed to confirm a government in power or pass a bill into law is a majority of those *present and voting.* If some legislators abstain on a given vote or are not present in the chamber when the vote takes place, their "nonvotes" are not counted as votes against the government or against a particular piece of legislation. Minority governments of this type are usually highly unstable: the abstaining parties may not be willing to tolerate for very long a government in which they do not participate or from which they derive few, if any, benefits. Whatever form they may take, minority governments constitute a fragile basis for stable rule over the long run. Nevertheless, they are a relatively common occurrence in today's parliamentary systems.

But what if the parties in the legislature are unable to form *any* government, whether a majoritarian or a minority government? In that case their only recourse is to go to the voters and ask them to elect a new legislature.

**Anticipated Elections** Every democracy requires elections to the national legislature at regular intervals. In the United States, elections are held every two years for the entire House of Representatives and one-third of the Senate. In Britain, elections to the House of Commons must take place every five years. The German Bundestag has a four-year statutory term, and so on. In contrast to the United States, however, most parliamentary forms of democracy permit the possibility of holding parliamentary elections *prior to* the expiration of the legislature's full term in office. The British, for example, do not necessarily have to wait five years before holding elections to the House of Commons; elections to the Commons can take place before the expiration of this statutory term. And once these elections occur, a new full five-year term for the newly elected House of Commons begins. Similar possibilities obtain in other parliamentary democracies.

***Parliamentary elections that take place before the expiration of the legislature's full term are called <u>anticipated elections</u>.*** (They are also informally known as **<u>snap elections</u>**.) Anticipated elections play an important role in realizing the potential of representative democracy. They provide the voters with a valuable mechanism for registering their opinions and influencing political decision makers more often than would be the case if no such mechanism existed. And because snap elections can be called at especially critical junctures in the nation's political life, during a national crisis or in the midst of severe political gridlock, they permit the citizens to have a say in the resolution of the problem in a timely fashion.

Under what circumstances, then, are anticipated elections most likely to take place? The most frequent occasions are the following:

- *No government can be formed in the national legislature.* As explained earlier, it is possible that no single party possesses a majority of seats in the legislature, and it may prove impossible to form a majority coalition government or a minority government. In some instances the government loses a vote of confidence, and the legislators are unable to form a new one. Faced with total gridlock, the nation's political leaders now have no choice but to call the voters to the polls to elect a new parliament.
- *Public pressure demands immediate elections.* Suppose there is a major crisis and the existing government is in trouble. Polls show that public confidence is waning considerably. Even key leaders of the governing party or parties begin calling for change. Under these circumstances the government may feel pressured by public opinion to resign and call new elections, allowing the people an opportunity to vote for a new legislature. Even though the government is *not obliged by law* to call new elections just because the public demands them, it may do so anyway if it feels it can no longer govern effectively.

  For example, in the early 1990s the Italian government was jolted by such shocking revelations of corruption that it responded to the public's disgust by calling anticipated elections in 1994. Because corruption continued even after those elections, another round of snap elections took place only two years later.
- *The government wants snap elections so as to solidify a parliamentary majority.* Sometimes an existing government will want to call anticipated elections because public opinion polls show that, if elections are held right away instead of a year or more later, the governing party (or parties) would win. Every politician knows that the public is fickle and political fortunes cannot be predicted. A government that enjoys popular favor today may lose it next month or next year. Consequently it may be in the government's interest to call snap elections while it still enjoys enough public support to be reelected.

  British Prime Minister Margaret Thatcher, for example, called snap elections in 1983, one year ahead of schedule, to capitalize on her rising popularity following Britain's victory over Argentina in the Falklands War. Her party, the Conservatives, increased its House of Commons majority from 53 percent to 61 percent. Tony Blair called snap elections in 2001 and 2005, retaining the Labour Party's majority in Parliament each time.

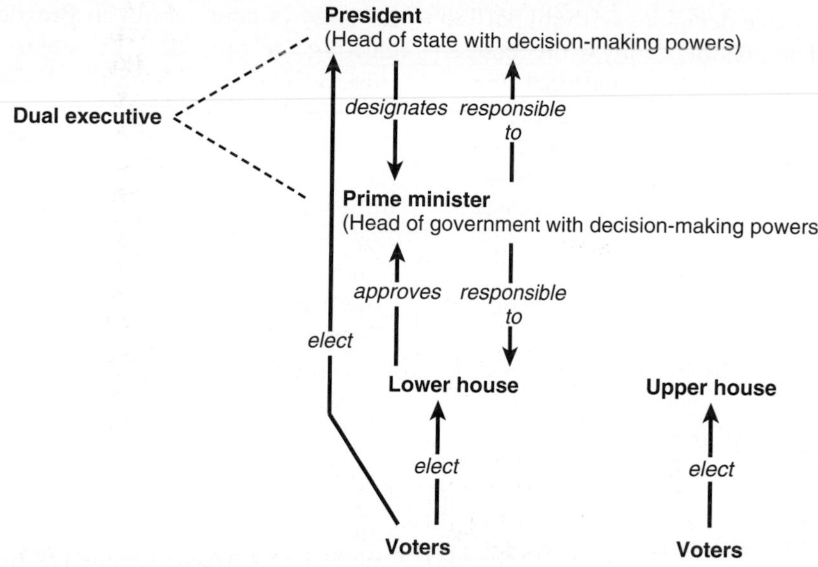


FIGURE 8.3 Presidential-Parliamentary System

TABLE 8.6

**Selected Countries Using the Presidential-Parliamentary Form of Democracy**

| | | | |
|---|---|---|---|
| Bulgaria | Lithuania | Niger | Russia |
| Croatia | Macedonia | Palestinian Authority | Senegal |
| Finland | Madagascar | Poland | Sri Lanka |
| France | Mali | Portugal | Ukraine |
| South Korea | Mozambique | Romania | |

Most politicians understand that they risk alienating the voters if they abuse their right to call anticipated elections. Voters may react angrily if they feel they are being called out to vote too frequently or if they believe that their leaders are not trying hard enough to form a workable government. A number of democracies have rules that limit the number of times snap elections may be held within a given period of time. With or without such rules, political leaders tend to call them fairly rarely, with a keen eye to the public mood.

### Presidential-Parliamentary Democracies

The third type of modern democracy to be sketched out here is the mixed **presidential-parliamentary system**. This system is also known as *semi-presidentialism*. ***It features a president and a prime minister who each have significant decision-making powers.*** The president typically is elected by the voters. The prime minister usually must be approved by the parliament (the lower house in bicameral legislatures). In other words, this is a *dual-executive system*. Figure 8.3 provides a general model of the presidential-parliamentary system. Table 8.6 lists some of the countries that use it in one form or another.

In some cases, as in France and Russia, the president has even greater constitutional powers than the president of the United States, while the legislature has fewer powers than the U.S. Congress. The French or Russian president, for example, may issue decrees or other executive decisions without parliamentary approval. The president may even possess the authority to declare a state of national emergency and govern with little or no parliamentary check on his authority. The parliament, for its part, can be constitutionally forbidden to propose or pass laws in certain areas that are the exclusive preserve of presidential or cabinet authority.

The main purpose of this type of regime is to expedite the process of making governmental decisions. By conferring a significant measure of legal authority on the president, it may be possible to avoid the protracted wrangling that often ensues when lawmaking is dominated by legislators. Presidential-parliamentary democracies are thus intended above all to maximize the *efficiency* of the decision-making process and the *stability* of executive authority. France adopted this system in 1958 precisely in order to avoid the persistent instability and gridlock that had plagued its parliamentary system of government from 1946 to 1958. Russia adopted its own variant of this system in 1993–94 with a view to managing the difficult transition from communism to democracy through strong executive power. President Boris Yeltsin, who was committed to democracy, wanted a free hand to make fundamental political and economic reforms that were opposed by the legislature's majority of Communists and other opponents of change.

The danger arises, however, that a president with too much power may abuse it, perhaps threatening the very principles of negotiation, accommodation, and compromise on which democracy ultimately rests. Russian presidents Yeltsin and Vladimir Putin have been accused of wielding quasi-dictatorial powers, and French President Charles de Gaulle occasionally exceeded his constitutional authority. Some countries not listed in table 8.6 have a presidential-parliamentary system that is authoritarian or semi-authoritarian. They include former parts of the Soviet Union like Armenia, Azerbaijan, Belarus, Kazakhstan, Kyrgyzstan, and Uzbekistan, along with other countries like Haiti and Togo. Presidential-parliamentary regimes tend to walk a fine line between stable, efficient rule on the one hand and the abuse of executive power on the other.

Meanwhile, an efficient decision-making process firmly concentrated in the president's hands may not always come about in practice. In addition to electing the president, the voters elect the legislature. If the president represents one political party and the majority of legislators represent rival parties, divided government and gridlock may ensue. It can even happen that the president and the prime minister represent opposing parties, a prospect that can severely complicate the process of decision making at the highest executive levels of national government. In this system, the president may usually name the prime minister but the legislature has the right to reject the president's choice. As a consequence, the president may be forced to name a prime minister of an opposing party so as to satisfy the legislative majority.

France has experienced this problem several times since the 1980s and most recently between 1997 and 2002 (see chapter 17). Ironically, while the mixed presidential-parliamentary system is designed to streamline executive decision making, it can sometimes end up severely complicating it.[5]

### Comparisons

Of the three types of democracy we have just examined, which one is "the best"? Seeking an unequivocal answer to this question is an exercise in futility. All three systems have advantages and disadvantages. Presidentialism can be an efficient, effective, and stable form of government, provided that the executive and legislative branches work in harmony. But it risks the potential abuse of presidential power, which can reach dictatorial proportions if left unchecked by legislative and judicial authority. (Until 2000 Mexico had this problem, as described in chapter 22.) Another potential problem is gridlock—the paralysis of the lawmaking process—in the event of a standoff between the president and the legislature. Parliamentary government can at times function more efficiently and flexibly than the presidential system, but these advantages are most likely to occur when one party enjoys an absolute majority of seats. When this condition does not prevail, majority coalition governments and minority governments can sometimes cause just as much gridlock as in presidential systems, if not more. Finally, presidential-parliamentary systems may at times ensure stable and effective government, but they can enable the executive branch to run roughshod over the legislature, and they risk crossing the thin line that separates presidential democracy from the abuse of executive power. Far from being *semi-presidential* systems, they can turn out to be *super-presidential* systems. At other times, the decision-making powers of the presidency in this system can shrink considerably if opposing parties control the legislature and the president's chief opponent becomes prime minister.

Every system of government exists in the real-world context of an individual country's unique blend of historical, economic, social, and other characteristics. No two countries are ever exactly alike, and their political institutions are bound to emerge and develop in accordance with their own distinctive features. The U.S. system of separation of powers has evolved over more than two hundred years in a country whose experiences have been very different from those of Europe, Latin America, and other parts of the world. The factors that account for the durability of this system in the United States may not be present in other countries, where other types of democracy may be more suitable or desirable.

Similarly, the factors that account for the way parliamentary government works in Britain are quite different from those that affect its operation in Japan, Israel, India, or elsewhere. The attributes of the mixed presidential-parliamentary system may be appropriate in some countries at particular stages in their history, but not at other times or in other countries. These national particularities will stand out more clearly when we examine the ways parliamentarism and the presidential-parliamentary system work in specific countries in later chapters.[6]

## ELECTORAL SYSTEMS

Regular elections constitute one of the most indispensable components of modern democracy. Not all democracies have the same electoral systems, however. *There are different ways of counting the votes.* As a consequence, *there are different ways of making the votes count* in terms of who wins governing power and who does not. Vote counting is an aspect of political science that has attracted close attention for centuries. It poses some tantalizing theoretical puzzles while at the same time exerting a profound effect on the way political power is distributed in the real world of politics.

First we'll look at two methods for electing a president: the *direct election* system used in France, Russia, and some other countries, and the *electoral college* system used in the United States. Next we'll look at two methods for electing a chamber of the national legislature: the *single-member district/plurality* system and *proportional representation.* These respective electoral systems by no means exhaust the range of vote-counting methods that are in use in the world today or that have been used in the past. With all their variants, however, the systems we describe here are the most widely used electoral systems in today's democracies.

### Electing a President

In some democracies, the process of electing a president is straightforward: the people vote directly for individual candidates. In France and Russia this electoral process can be decided in a single election, or it may require two rounds of voting. In the first round of balloting, virtually any number of candidates may run, subject to certain requirements for candidacy. If one candidate gets an absolute majority of popular votes (50 percent plus one vote) in the first round, that person is declared the winner. If no one gets an absolute majority, a second round of balloting is held a week or two later between the top two finishers of the first round. The winner of this runoff election is elected president.

This direct-election system tends to give voters a wide assortment of choices in the first round. In effect, it amounts to a national primary election in which all the eligible candidates run on the same day. This system also compels the voters to choose between two individuals in the event that a second round is necessary. If one's favorite candidate does not survive into the second round, the voter must decide whether to vote for one of the two remaining candidates or not vote at all. The results of presidential elections in France and Russia show that this system encourages a fairly large turnout in round one and a similar (or even higher) turnout in round two (see table 8.7). At least in France, it also guarantees that the person elected president is the choice of an absolute majority of those who turn

**TABLE 8.7**

**Direct Election Systems in France and Russia**

**French Presidential Elections, 1995**

| Round 1 (April 23) (Turnout: 76.4%) | | | Round 2 (May 7) (Turnout: 77.7%) | |
|---|---|---|---|---|
| **Candidate** | **Party** | **% of Vote** | **Candidate** | **% of Vote** |
| Lionel Jospin | Socialist | 23.3 | Chirac | 52.6 |
| Jacques Chirac | Rally for the Republic | 20.8 | Jospin | 47.4 |
| Edouard Balladur | Rally for the Republic | 18.6 | | |
| Jean-Marie Le Pen | National Front | 15.0 | | |
| Robert Hue | Communist | 8.6 | | |
| Arlette Laguiller | Trotskyite | 5.3 | | |
| Philippe de Villiers | Struggle for Values | 4.8 | | |
| Dominique Voynet | Greens | 3.3 | | |
| Jacques Cheminade | Federation for a New Solidarity | 0.3 | | |

**Russian Presidential Elections, 1996**

| Round 1 (June 16) (Turnout: 69%) | | | Round 2 (July 3) (Turnout: 69%) | |
|---|---|---|---|---|
| **Candidate** | **Party** | **% of Vote** | **Candidate** | **% of Vote** |
| Boris Yeltsin | (No party affiliation) | 34.8 | Yeltsin | 53.8 |
| Gennady Zyuganov | Communist | 32.1 | Zyuganov | 40.3 |
| Alexander Lebed | Congress of Russian Communities | 14.7 | Against both | 4.8 |
| Grigory Yavlinsky | Yabloko | 7.4 | | |
| Vladimir Zhirinovsky | Liberal Democratic Party | 5.8 | | |
| Svyatoslav Fyodorov | (No party affiliation) | 0.9 | | |
| Mikhail Gorbachev | (No party affiliation) | 0.5 | | |
| Martin Shakkum | Russian Popular Socialist Party | 0.35 | | |
| Yuri Vlasov | (No party affiliation) | 0.2 | | |
| Vladimir Bryntsalov | (No party affiliation) | 0.16 | | |
| Against all candidates | | 3.0 | | |

out to vote. The Russians have an opportunity in both rounds to cast a vote *against all* candidates. (See chapter 17 for the results of the 2002 elections in France, and chapter 21 for the 2000 and 2004 elections in Russia.)

The U.S. system is considerably more complicated. Many of the framers of the Constitution did not want the direct election of the president by the voters because they were skeptical about the political wisdom of the population. They preferred a system that gave the final say in choosing the chief executive to a politically sophisticated elite. They therefore introduced a procedure in which voters in each state choose presidential *electors,* who in turn elect the president. The number of electors assigned to each state varies with the size of its population and equals the number of delegates it sends to the House of Representatives plus two for its U.S. Senators. Article II of the U.S. Constitution authorizes each state to choose its presidential electors "in such manner as the Legislature thereof may direct." Individual U.S. citizens do not have a federal constitutional right to vote for the president, but their state legislature may decide to hold a popular election to determine how the state's electors will be chosen. Initially, the legislatures of most states picked the presidential electors themselves. After the Civil War, all the state legislatures allowed the citizens of their respective states to vote for presidential candidates. In actuality, the voters are selecting electors who are pledged to individual candidates (though in some states this unspoken "pledge" is still not legally binding on the electors).

TABLE 8.8

**Minimum Number of States Needed to Win 270 Electoral College Votes (Since 2004)**

| State | Electoral Votes |
|---|---|
| California | 55 |
| Texas | 34 |
| New York | 31 |
| Florida | 27 |
| Illinois | 21 |
| Pennsylvania | 21 |
| Ohio | 20 |
| Michigan | 17 |
| Georgia | 15 |
| New Jersey | 15 |
| North Carolina | 15 |
| TOTAL: | 271 |

Several weeks after the popular elections take place, the chosen electors assemble separately within each state as the *electoral college* and vote for the president. To be elected, the winning candidate must win an absolute majority of the total number of votes in the electoral college. In 2004 there were 538 electoral college votes; the winning majority was 270 votes.

One peculiarity of this system is that, in most states, whoever wins the highest popular vote total automatically wins *all* that state's electoral votes. The U.S. presidential election system thus consists of *winner-take-all* elections in almost all the fifty states plus the District of Columbia. Moreover, as table 8.8 shows, starting in 2004 a candidate could win the presidency by winning a popular majority in just eleven states. Even if that candidate did not win a single *popular* vote in any of the other states, he or she could still win the presidency. And as the controversial 2000 election showed, it is possible for a candidate to win the popular vote but lose the presidency in the electoral college. Al Gore won 48.38 percent of the popular vote and George W. Bush won 47.87 percent; but Bush won 271 electoral college votes to Gore's 266 electoral college votes. Similar anomalies have occurred in the past.[7]

### Legislative Elections

As we pointed out in chapter 5, a country's national legislature is either *unicameral,* consisting of only one house, or *bicameral,* consisting of two. There are several different methods for electing these legislative chambers. The two methods we'll examine here—the *single-member district/plurality* method and *proportional representation*—each has several different variants. In this chapter we'll simply describe the main principles of these two electoral systems using a few illustrative examples, but we'll defer a more detailed explanation of how they work in specific countries to later chapters.

**The Single-Member District/Plurality Method** In the **single-member district/plurality** electoral system, ***the country is divided into electoral districts for elections to a particular legislative chamber.*** The United States, for example, is divided into 435 electoral districts for the House of Representatives. The United Kingdom is now divided into 646 districts for elections to the House of Commons. ***One person is elected to represent each district; hence the term*** **single-member district (SMD).** Because the individual who is elected is said to have a direct mandate from the voters, the SMD system is sometimes called the *mandate* system. ***In each district, the candidate who wins a plurality of votes—that is, the most votes—wins the legislative seat.*** (A *plurality,* or *simple majority,* is the highest number of a set.)

One advantage of this system is that, with only one representative per district, the voters should have an easier time identifying their legislative deputy than would be the case if their district were a *multimember district.* A multimember district sends two or more representatives to the national legislature. Single-member districts are supposed to be more personalized than multimember districts. With only one representative per district, citizens should be able to know the name of the person who represents them in the legislature. This system is designed to promote greater public awareness of politics and greater accountability on the part of the elected representative to his or her constituency. In fact, however, most Americans do *not* know the name of their representative in the House of Representatives.

If there are only two candidates running in each district, the winner automatically wins by an absolute majority. (An *absolute majority* is more than 50 percent.) This result frequently occurs in the United States, where most congressional races are

TABLE 8.9

**Hypothetical Election in a British Electoral District (House of Commons)**

| Candidate | Party | No. of Votes | % of Vote |
|---|---|---|---|
| Jean Smith | Labour | 12,000 | 37.5 |
| Jack Jones | Conservative | 10,000 | 31.3 |
| Martha Brown | Liberal Democrat | 8,000 | 25.0 |
| George Martin | Green | 2,000 | 6.2 |

TABLE 8.10

**Hypothetical Election to the U.S. House of Representatives**

| Party | % of Total Vote Nationwide | % of Seats Won |
|---|---|---|
| Republicans | 51 | 100 |
| Democrats | 49 | 0 |

TABLE 8.11

**Elections to U.S. House of Representatives, 1992**

| Party | % of Popular Vote Nationwide | % of Seats Won |
|---|---|---|
| Democrats | 50.8 | 59.3 |
| Republicans | 45.6 | 40.5 |
| Others | 3.6 | (1 seat) |

traditionally limited to a Democrat competing against a Republican. In Britain and several other countries that have the SMD voting system, however, three or more candidates routinely compete in each district. In some of these races the winning candidate will win an absolute majority of the votes cast, but it is not necessary to win an absolute majority to be elected the district's representative. A simple majority—the highest number of votes among the competing candidates—is sufficient to win. As a consequence, plurality election systems are also called *majoritarian* electoral systems. The candidate who wins the highest number of votes in this system is often said to be "first past the post." In the hypothetical British example shown in table 8.9, Jean Smith, the Labour Party candidate, is the winner with 37.5 percent of the vote in her district. The other candidates simply lose. *The SMD/plurality electoral system is a "winner-take-all" system.* France has a two-round variant of this system.

This electoral system's main advantages lie in its relative simplicity and the chances it offers to promote name recognition on the part of incumbent representatives and their challengers. But it has some potential problems. For one thing, *the SMD/plurality system can lead to a disparity between a party's share of the vote on a nationwide basis and its share of the seats in the legislature.* To understand this possibility, simply consider the outcome of a hypothetical race for one seat in the U.S. House of Representatives. In our example, the Republican candidate gets 51 percent of the votes cast and the Democrat gets 49 percent. There are no other candidates running in this district. The Republican is elected to Congress; the Democrat will have to wait two more years for another opportunity to campaign for the seat.

Now suppose that this result, by odd coincidence, occurs in *all 435 House districts.* If we add up all the votes cast throughout the country for the House of Representatives, it is evident that the Republican candidates together captured 51 percent of the vote nationwide while the Democratic candidates together garnered 49 percent. Because the Republican candidate won each separate House contest, however, the Republicans end up with *all* 435 House seats; the Democrats get none. The bottom line is that the Republicans have won slightly more than half the national vote but 100 percent of the seats. The Democrats have won slightly less than half the vote but come away with no representation in the House at all. Table 8.10 displays this result.

Obviously this is an extreme example that is not likely to occur any time soon. But it illustrates a general point: under the SMD system, a significant difference between a party's share of the national vote and its share of legislative seats *can* occur. Table 8.11 provides a real example. Even more glaring examples of this phenomenon occurred in the

TABLE 8.12

**Elections to the British House of Commons**

| | 1992 | | | 1997 | | |
|---|---|---|---|---|---|---|
| **Party** | **% of Popular Vote** | **% of Seats** | **No. of Seats** | **% of Popular Vote** | **% of Seats** | **No. of Seats** |
| Conservatives | 41.9 | 51.6 | 336 | 30.7 | 25.0 | 165 |
| Labour | 34.4 | 41.6 | 271 | 43.2 | 63.6 | 419 |
| Liberal Democrats | 17.8 | 3.1 | 20 | 16.8 | 7.0 | 46 |
| Others | 5.9 | 3.7 | 24 | 9.3 | 4.4 | 29 |

1992 and 1997 elections to the British House of Commons. (See table 8.12.) At times the anomalies of the SMD system can be truly bizarre, as the following figures show.

## HOW ANOMALIES CAN OCCUR IN THE SMD SYSTEM

Consider a state that elects three members to the U.S. House of Representatives. In each race, a Democrat runs against a Republican. Conceivably, voter turnout and the margin of victory could vary considerably from one district to another, resulting in the following hypothetical result:

| | Candidate | Votes |
|---|---|---|
| 1st District | Democrat | 100,000 |
| | Republican | 10,000 |
| 2nd District | Democrat | 50,000 |
| | Republican | 50,020 |
| 3rd District | Democrat | 10,000 |
| | Republican | 20,000 |
| Totals | Democrats | 160,000 |
| | Republicans | 80,020 |
| | | 240,020 |

As you can see, the three Democrats together captured approximately two-thirds of the votes, but the Republicans won two of the three districts. Anomalies of this sort have actually occurred in real elections.

Another characteristic problem of the SMD/plurality electoral system is that *it tends to punish small parties.* To win a significant share of seats in the U.S. House of Representatives or the British House of Commons, a party must be able to field viable candidates throughout the country, in virtually all districts. Parties that are not large enough to mount such extensive campaigns are not likely to win many legislative seats. The SMD system, in other words, is a major reason why the United States has a two-party system. Other parties are too weak within the individual districts, as well as nationally, to elect their candidates to the House.

Elections to the British House of Commons provide a vivid illustration of how difficult it is for small parties to win a share of parliamentary seats commensurate with their share of the popular vote. Note in table 8.12 that in 1992 and 1997, the Liberal Democrats, Britain's third-largest party, won nearly 20 percent of the vote nationwide but a mere 3.1 percent of the seats in the Commons in 1992 and 7 percent in 1997. (That is, they won only 3.1 percent of the 651 individual district races in 1992 and 7 percent of 659 races in 1997.) Their voter support was spread out widely across the country, but it was sufficiently concentrated to win a plurality in only a few districts. Other parties fared even more poorly. Roughly similar results occurred in 2001 and 2005, as noted in chapter 16.

One of the chief problems of the SMD/plurality system, then, is that *a result that is fair at the local level may turn out to be unfair at the national level.* "Winner take all" may be a fair way to elect someone to represent your district in the national legislature. But when all the votes are counted nationwide, there may be a significant gap between the parties' respective share of legislative seats and their share of the national vote. Statistical measures of these disparities show that they can remain quite significant over many years.

Yet another problem with the SMD/plurality system is that, in some countries, the boundaries of legislative districts can be redrawn to ensure a large majority of voters for a particular party. This practice is known in the United States as "gerrymandering." (The term is named after Elbridge Gerry, a governor of Massachusetts, who in 1811 signed a bill permitting this kind of redistricting.) It often gives incumbents an unfair advantage over their opponents, preventing serious competition on election day. By creating "safe seats," gerrymandering can discourage potential opposition candidates from running against an entrenched incumbent, and it can turn voters away from the polls if they know they have no chance of defeating an incumbent they oppose.

The *proportional representation* system is designed to overcome some of the defects of the single-member-district/plurality electoral system.

**Proportional Representation** ***Under proportional representation (PR), a party's share (percentage) of its seats in the legislature exactly or approximately equals its share of the popular vote nationwide.*** To put it very simply, if a party gets 25 percent of the popular vote in legislative elections, it will get 25 percent (exactly or approximately) of the seats in the legislature. Various statistical formulas are employed to ensure these results. There are numerous variants of the PR principle. Most of those in use today are approximate PR systems. In the *party list* variant, parties draw up lists of candidates, rank-ordering their names in accordance with their political prominence. Typically, if a party is entitled to 200 legislative seats, the first 200 people on its list will get the seats.

If a party so chooses, it can promote the election of women or minority candidates in this type of electoral system by putting the names of those candidates at or near the top of its list, so that they will be among the candidates most likely to win seats. Another feature of this system is that people who run for the legislature usually do not have to raise money to pay for their campaigns. Because they run on their party's list rather than as individual candidates, the party raises and spends campaign money in behalf of *all* the candidates on its list running collectively. In the United States, by contrast, running for Congress can require individual candidates to raise a million dollars or more to run a campaign, even though they may run as Democrats or Republicans. Figure 8.4 illustrates how a party-list PR system works in principle. But it bears repeating that there are quite a few real-world variants of the PR system. Many of them deviate from our illustrative model in particular ways while adhering to PR's essential principles.[8]

*Proportional Representation in Israel* Israel provides a specific example of how a PR system can work. The country as a whole constitutes one large electoral district for the Knesset, its 120-member unicameral legislature. Voters vote for a party, not for individual candidates. Table 8.13 reports the results for the 1999, 2003, and 2006 elections.

The first thing to observe in these results is the close approximation between each party's share of the national vote and its share of the seats in the Knesset. Each party won a share of legislative seats *in rough proportion* to its share of the national vote. We do not see the wide disparities in these two figures that are possible—and that sometimes actually occur—in the SMD/plurality system.[9]

Perhaps the most striking observation is the large number of parties elected to the Knesset. Indeed, *PR can lead to a fairly wide proliferation of political parties represented in the legislature.* Under these conditions, it is not likely that a single party will win an absolute majority of legislative seats. As a consequence, *PR often results in a multiparty coalition government or a minority government.* If the parties that participate in these arrangements get along, such a system can work smoothly in establishing stable and effective governments. But as we've already noted, multiparty governments can also be highly unstable and inefficient. One of the drawbacks of PR, therefore, is that it increases the chances of instability and inefficiency.

Israel is a case in point. The 120-member Knesset elected in 1999 included fourteen party groupings; the Knesset elected in 2003 had thirteen; and the Knesset elected in 2006 had twelve party groupings. These diverse parties reflected the wide range of ethnic, religious, class, and ideological distinctions to be found in Israeli society, as noted in chapter 6.

The center-left Labor Party is one of Israel's oldest surviving parties. It has produced a number of prime ministers, including Golda Meir (1969–74), Yitzhak Rabin (1974–77 and 1992–95), Shimon Peres (1984–86 and 1995–96), and Ehud Barak (1999–2000). Likud (Consolidation), the country's largest right-wing party, has produced Prime Ministers Menachem Begin (1977–83), Yitzhak Shamir

## MODEL OF A PARTY-LIST PROPORTIONAL REPRESENTATION SYSTEM

(100 seats in the legislature)

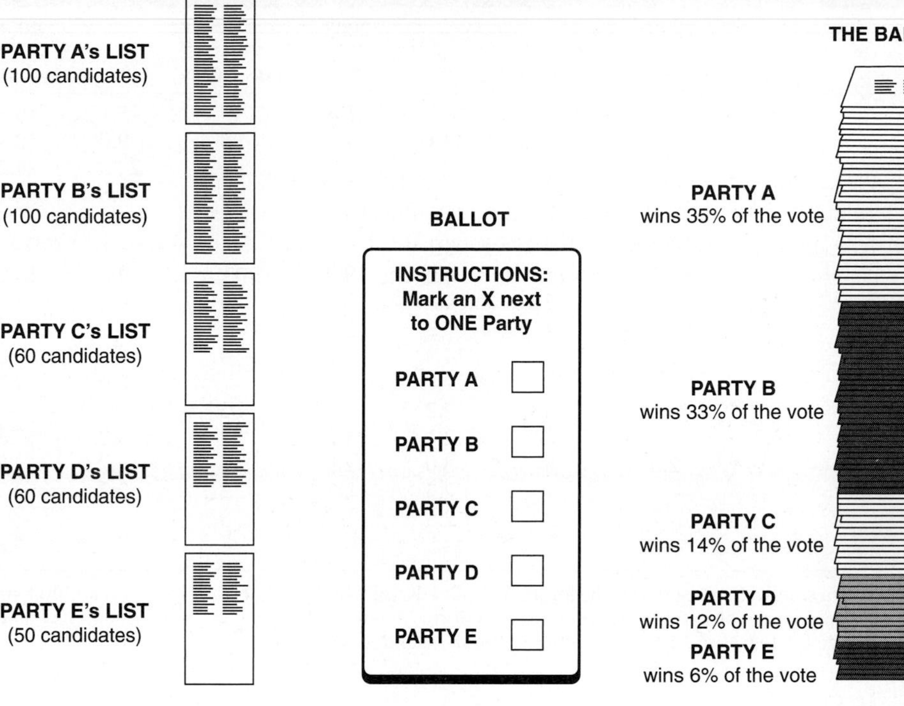


**Step 1. Party lists.**

Each party draws up a list of its candidates, ranked in order of importance. Half the candidates in Parties A and B are women. The largest parties decide to run as many candidates as there are seats; the smaller parties list fewer candidates.

**Step 2. The ballot.**

Each voter votes for 1 party.

**Step 3. The votes are counted.**

Each party wins a percentage of the nationwide popular vote.

**LEGISLATURE**
(100 seats)

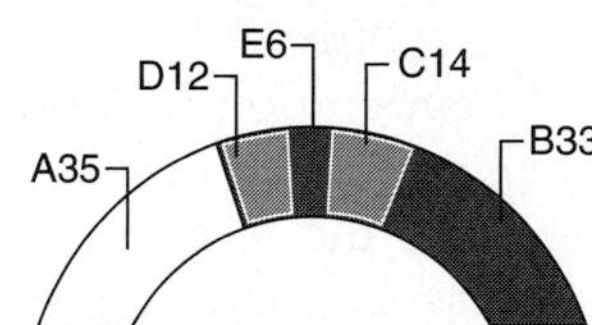


**Step 4. The seats are apportioned according to the popular vote.**

Party A wins 35% of the seats; the top 35 candidates on its list get the seats. Party B wins 33% of the seats; the top 33 candidates on its list get the seats, and so on for C, D and E. It's a hung parliament: no party has a majority. Party A has a plurality.

**COALITION GOVERNMENT**
(20 cabinet ministers)

**PARTY A** (PM + 11 ministers) **+ PARTY D** (6) **+ PARTY E** (2)

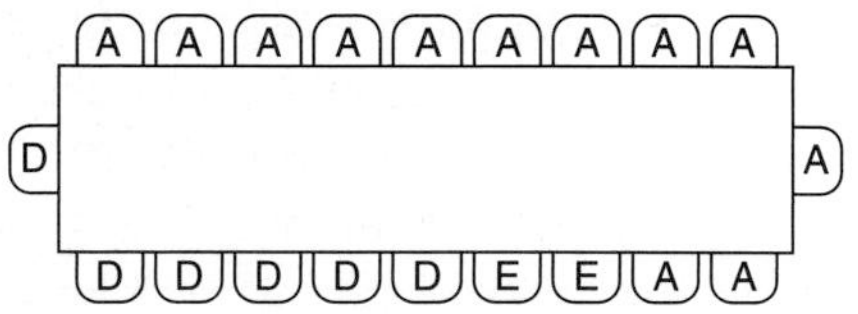


**Step 5. Forming a coalition government.**

The country's head of state (president or monarch) asks the head of Party A to form a government. Party A cannot agree on a governing program with B or C, but comes to terms with D and E. Together Parties A, D, and E have 53 seats, a majority. They agree on how to share 20 cabinet posts. The head of Party A is prime minister, the head of D foreign minister, the head of E finance minister. All ministers are also members of the legislature. If Party A fails to form a government, the head of state asks the head of Party B to try.

**FIGURE 8.4**

**TABLE 8.13**

**Elections to Israel's Knesset, 1999, 2003, and 2006**

| | 1999 | | | 2003 | | | 2006 | | |
|---|---|---|---|---|---|---|---|---|---|
| **Party** | **% Vote** | **% Seats** | **No. Seats** | **% Vote** | **% Seats** | **No. Seats** | **% Vote** | **% Seats** | **No. Seats** |
| Labor[a] | 20.2 | 21.7 | 26 | 14.5 | 15.8 | 19 | 15.1 | 15.8 | 19 |
| Likud | 14.1 | 15.8 | 19 | 29.4 | 31.7 | 38 | 9.0 | 10.0 | 12 |
| Kadima | — | — | — | — | — | — | 22.0 | 24.2 | 29 |
| Meretz-Yachad | 7.6 | 8.3 | 10 | 5.2 | 5.0 | 6 | 3.8 | 4.2 | 5 |
| Shinui | 5.0 | 5.0 | 6 | 12.3 | 12.5 | 15 | — | — | — |
| Center | 5.0 | 5.0 | 6 | 0.1 | — | — | — | — | — |
| Shas | 13.0 | 14.2 | 17 | 8.2 | 9.2 | 11 | 9.5 | 10.0 | 12 |
| National Religious Party | 4.2 | 4.2 | 5 | 4.2 | 5.0 | 6 | — | — | — |
| National Union | 3.0 | 3.3 | 4 | 5.5 | 5.8 | 7 | 7.1 | 7.5 | 9 |
| United Torah Judaism | 3.7 | 4.2 | 5 | 4.3 | 4.2 | 5 | 4.7 | 5.0 | 6 |
| Yisrael Beitenu | 2.6 | 3.3 | 4 | — | — | — | 8.9 | 9.2 | 11 |
| Yisrael Ba'Aliya | 5.1 | 5.0 | 6 | 2.2 | 1.7 | 2 | — | — | — |
| United Arab List | 5.3 | 5.8 | 7 | 2.1 | 1.7 | 2 | 3.0 | 3.3 | 4 |
| Hadash | 2.6 | 2.5 | 3 | 3.0 | 2.5 | 3 | 2.7 | 2.5 | 3 |
| Balad | — | — | — | 2.3 | 2.5 | 3 | 2.3 | 2.5 | 3 |
| One Nation | 1.9 | 1.7 | 2 | 2.8 | 2.5 | 3 | — | — | — |
| Gil (Pensioners) | — | — | — | — | — | — | 5.9 | 5.8 | 7 |

[a] In 1997, Labor ran with two smaller parties under the joint label "One Israel." In 2003, Labor joined with another small party to form Labor-Meimad. In 2006, Meretz joined with another group to form Meretz-Yachad; the National Religious Party ran together with National Union; and the United Arab List ran together with the Arab Renewal Movement.
*Source*: israel-mfa.gov.il.

(1983–84 and 1986–92), Binyamin Netanyahu (1996–99), and Ariel Sharon (2000–2006). Meretz-Yachad (Vigor-Together) is a secular center-left party favoring compromise with the Palestinians. Its name reflects the merger of two previously separate parties. Shinui (Change) and the Center Party were also secular center-left parties, but they suffered internal leadership splits and did not win Knesset seats in 2006. Shas (the Sephardi Religious Party) is a religious right-wing party that mostly represents Jews from Morocco and other parts of North Africa and the Middle East. It is reluctant to give up Jewish settlements in the occupied territories. The National Religious Party and National Union are hardline right-wing religious parties that strongly support Jewish settlements in the West Bank and East Jerusalem, opposing any agreement to give up the occupied territories. The two parties ran together in 2006. United Torah Judaism (also called Torah and Sabbath Judaism) is an Orthodox religious party that appeals largely to Ashkenazic Jews; but it is opposed to Zionism as a nationalist ideology, and it is fairly flexible in its approach to the occupied territories. As a general rule, Israel's religious parties favor public funding for religious schools and strongly support Israel's use of religious law in such things as marriage and family law. (Despite these and other religious influences, Israel is a secular state based on English civil law, not Talmudic law.) Secular parties tend to oppose public funding for religious schools.

Yisrael Beitenu (Our Home Is Israel) and Yisrael Ba'Aliya have represented Jews from the former Soviet Union, mostly from Russia and Ukraine. ("Aliya" refers to emigration to Israel.) From the start, both were hardline right-wing parties that favored holding on to the settlements in the occupied territories. Yisrael Ba'Aliya, which was founded by the former Soviet dissident Natan Sharansky, fell apart after Sharansky and other party leaders merged into the Likud party. The United Arab List, which ran jointly with the Arab Renewal Movement in 2006, appeals to Israel's large Arab minority, a group of Palestinian Muslims and Christians that compose about 20 percent of the population of Israel proper (i.e., not counting the occupied territories). The two Arab parties include Islamists as well as secular Palestinian nationalists. They favor an end to discrimination against Arabs inside Israel as well as a peace settlement with the Palestinian Authority. Balad appeals to secular Arab nationalists. Hadash is a left-wing party that appeals to secular Jewish and Arab voters. One Nation was also a secular leftist party that did not run in 2006.

Two parties were elected to the Knesset for the first time in 2006. As indicated in chapter 6, Kadima (Forward) was the new center-left party created by Prime Minister Ariel Sharon after the Likud Party resisted Sharon's decision to pull Jewish settlers out of Gaza. Ehud Olmert succeeded Sharon as the party's chief after Sharon suffered a debilitating stroke in early 2006, and he became prime minister after the March 2006 elections. Gil (Age) is also known as the Pensioners Party of Israel. As its name implies, it is primarily concerned with Israel's elderly population.

Shortly after the 1999 elections, Ehud Barak of the One Israel bloc (which consisted of the Labor Party and two smaller allies) put together a coalition government that included five other parties, including centrists (Meretz and the Center Party), conservative religious parties (Shas and the National Religious Party), and the conservative Israel Ba'Aliya. The old adage "Politics makes strange bedfellows" could not have been more appropriate for this agglomeration of widely divergent parties. Major differences among the coalition partners broke out not only over domestic matters, such as the question of state funding for religious schools, but also over vital foreign policy issues. Whereas the Labor Party, Meretz, and the Center Party were willing to make new concessions in an effort to achieve peace with the Palestinians, other coalition parties were averse to any agreement that might jeopardize the status of Jewish settlements in the West Bank or other key Israeli interests. They also remained deeply suspicious of Palestinian leader Yasser Arafat's ultimate intentions. When Barak flew to the United States in the summer of 2000 to meet with President Clinton and Arafat at Camp David (as described in chapter 6), the three conservative parties in his government withdrew their support, as did Barak's own foreign minister. Barak returned home to find his government in shards. Unable to stitch together a new coalition, he resigned.

Opposition to Barak's peace initiatives was equally vocal in the Likud Party, Labor's principal opponent. Likud's leader, Ariel Sharon, took advantage of Barak's political tribulations and pushed hard for a change in government. As Israelis and Palestinians entered a new phase of violence, Sharon soundly defeated Barak in a head-to-head election for prime minister in February 2001, winning 62.4 percent of the vote against Barak's 37.6 percent. This election was Israel's second and last attempt to hold separate elections for prime minister and the Knesset.[10]

Upon becoming prime minister, Sharon inherited the fragmented Knesset elected in 1999. In search of enough votes in the Knesset to form a viable government, Sharon reached out to the archrival Labor Party, which agreed to join Likud and a few smaller parties in a new coalition. This combination proved difficult, however, especially with the two largest contending parties in Israeli politics—Likud and Labor—cosseted together in the same government. Meanwhile, over the next two years the spiral of Israeli-Palestinian violence only accelerated. In an atmosphere of acute anxiety, Israelis went to the polls in January 2003 to elect a new Knesset. The result, shown in table 8.13, was another highly fragmented legislature. Though Likud increased its delegation from 19 to 37 seats, it was still far short of an absolute majority (61). With Labor unwilling to rejoin the cabinet, Prime Minister Sharon had little choice but to fashion a new multiparty coalition government that consisted initially of Likud and four smaller parties. Together they held 66 seats in the assembly—a slim 5-seat majority.

To be sure, Israel's proportional representation election system is by no means the principal cause of the intractable conflict with the Palestinians. As we noted in chapter 6, there are deep-seated grounds for distrust and hostility on both sides. Moreover, the PR system does not *create* political divisions within society; like a mirror, it *reflects* them. In fact, it is a highly democratic method for representing in Israel's national legislature the numerous identities, interests, and attitudes to be found in the country's multifaceted society. At the same time, however, PR actively encourages very small Israeli parties to field their own candidates instead of coalescing into "wide-tent" parties like the Democrats and Republicans in the United States. And by making it practically impossible to establish a single-party government with a coherent policy design, PR virtually guarantees that any Israeli cabinet will consist of disparate parties that are bound to disagree on this or that policy decision—including, at times, the most vital questions affecting Israel's security and the Middle East's deadly conflicts.

In effect, very small parties in Israel's government often have a veto over policy initiatives that are favored by the prime minister and the largest party in the government. The new government formed under Ehud Olmert after the 2006 elections, for example, consisted of Kadima, the Labor Party, Shas, and the Pensioners Party. Together these four parties held 67 seats, a slim 7-seat majority. Shas immediately announced that it would not support Prime Minister Olmert's plan to eventually evacuate some eighty thousand Jewish settlers who had established unauthorized settlements in the West Bank. The governing parties pulled together in the summer of 2006 during the fighting with Hezbollah in Lebanon (see chapter 6). But as his approval ratings plummeted, Olmert later invited the head of the hardline Yisrael Beitenu party (which had 11 Knesset seats) to join the cabinet. It was unclear at the end of 2006 how long this expanded coalition government would survive, however. Proportional representation in Israel may not be a catalyst of the Middle East crisis; but it certainly hampers the decision-making process in the Israeli government, adding one more burden to an already overburdened region.

*Variants of PR* Despite these complications—which occur in other democracies besides Israel's—supporters of proportional representation insist that it is far more representative of a country's political divisions than the single-member district/plurality system. The latter may produce more coherent and stable governments, but it may fail to represent fairly the various political orientations to be found in the electorate. PR systems are never two-party systems; they are highly inclusive of a wide spectrum of political opinion. Their advocates assert that by squeezing the voters into two or perhaps three main parties, majoritarian voting systems like SMD unduly limit voter choice and create false legislative majorities (like the British Labour Party's 63 percent majority in Parliament, achieved in 1997 with only 40 percent of the popular vote). Americans who complain that their own views are not adequately addressed by their two-party system might ponder the fact that the adoption of a proportional representation voting system would quite probably increase the number of parties capable of winning seats in Congress. Another advantage of proportional representation is that gerrymandering is not possible in PR systems that do not have electoral districts (as in Israel and the Netherlands).

Critics of PR contend that it can lead to such a large number of parties in the national legislature that governing becomes next to impossible. But some democracies with PR systems have found a way to cut back on the number of parties elected to the legislature. A *hurdle* (or *threshold*) can be used to require a party to win a certain percentage of the national vote in order to acquire legislative seats. Parties falling below this hurdle usually do not get any seats. Sweden has a 4 percent threshold, for example, and Germany has a 5 percent threshold. Israel employed a 1.5 percent threshold in 1999 and 2003, then raised it to 2 percent in the 2006 elections. These hurdles were low enough to allow several small parties to jump over them and enter the Knesset, but they were still high enough to keep out a number of even smaller parties. (In 2003, fifteen parties fell below the 1.5 percent hurdle; in 2006, nineteen fell below the 2 percent hurdle.) Poland imposed a hurdle after the PR system that was used in 1991, in the earliest stages of the country's transition from communism to democracy, returned thirty parties to the legislature. Following the imposition of a 5 percent hurdle for single parties and 8 percent for parties running jointly, the number of elected parties fell to seven in 1993 and five in 1997. (The model displayed in figure 8.4 has no threshold.)

Another criticism that is often leveled at PR is that it tends to be more impersonal than the SMD system. Voters in an SMD system have a chance to identify the competing candidates by name, but in most PR systems the voters vote for a party, not an individual candidate. Each party provides a list of the candidates it puts up for election, but the names on these lists are not likely to be highly publicized in the media. Except for the most prominent leaders in each party, candidates for the legislature in most PR systems do not have a high degree of name recognition among the voters. In addition, some countries with PR systems have multimember districts, with as many as eight or ten legislators elected to serve each district. Although some voters may like having a multiplicity of representatives catering to their district's needs, others may find it difficult to recall the name of any of them. It may therefore be more difficult to hold individual legislators accountable to their local constituents in such circumstances.

Germany tries to get around these problems by combining PR with the SMD system. Half of the Bundestag's seats are elected by PR, the other half by SMD. A statistical formula ensures that the final distribution of seats in that chamber approximates PR. Japan, Russia, and some other countries have also used a combination of PR and SMD in electing a legislative house. The combination of PR and SMD is called a *mixed-member electoral system.*[11] The choice of electoral system has weighty political implications. Russia scrapped its mixed-member system because the single member districts produced many independent legislators with little or no party affiliation. In order to bring the legislature under greater presidential control, President Vladimir Putin and his allies changed the system to proportional representation in time for the 2007 elections. In the early 1990s, Italy replaced its complicated variant of proportional representation with a mixed-member system in order to break the power of corrupt political parties that had used the PR system to dominate Italian governments for more than forty years. But Prime Minister Silvio Berlusconi, hoping to win reelection in 2006, had the system switched back to a new variant of proportional representation. His coalition lost nevertheless.

In sum, the main advantages of PR are (1) its *fairness* in translating popular support for political parties into equivalent shares of legislative seats; (2) its ability to *help small parties*—and perhaps women and minorities—to win a fair share of legislative seats (and maybe cabinet posts); and (3) its tendency to *enhance voter choice* by providing the electorate with a wide array of parties from which to choose. PR's disadvantages include (1) its tendency to promote the *proliferation of a large number of parties;* (2) its tendency thereby to increase the likelihood of *hung parliaments, governmental instability, inefficiency,* and *ineffectiveness;* and (3) its *impersonal character.*

Just as we cannot identify with any confidence "the best" institutional form of representative democracy, it is equally difficult to pick either the SMD/plurality system or PR as the better legislative electoral system. As we've seen, both systems have advantages and disadvantages. Most important, how these systems work in actual practice tends to differ from country to country.

One question is immensely relevant to average citizens in all democracies: do voters turn out at the polls at consistently higher rates under one of these systems as opposed to the other? Theoretically, one would think that the PR system would attract more voters than plurality systems on the grounds that PR gives the voters a greater chance to elect representatives of their favorite party into the legislature. Under plurality systems, as in the United States or Britain, the two largest parties are likely to win the overwhelming majority of the seats. Hypothetically, PR systems thus tend to entice a greater number of parties to run candidates, giving the voters a wider array of choice on election day than they are likely to get under a plurality system.

Following these assumptions, we'll hypothesize that PR electoral systems tend to result in higher voter turnout rates than plurality systems on a fairly consistent basis. Does the available evidence support this supposition?

## HYPOTHESIS-TESTING EXERCISE: Do PR Systems Have Higher Turnout Than Plurality Systems?

### Hypothesis

Proportional representation produces higher voter turnouts than plurality systems in legislative elections.

### Variables

The *dependent variable* is *voter turnout.* The *independent variables* are *PR* and *plurality voting systems.*

### Expectations

If our hypothesis is correct, we would expect to find that democracies with PR will have consistently higher turnout rates than those with plurality systems.

### Evidence

Table 8.14 lists twenty countries that held democratic elections between 1945 and 1997. Most of them

TABLE 8.14

**Turnout in PR and Plurality Electoral Systems**

| PR Systems | | Plurality Systems | |
|---|---|---|---|
| Country | Average Turnout, 1945–1997 | Country | Average Turnout, 1945–1997 |
| Iceland | 89.5% | New Zealand | 86.2% |
| Austria | 85.1 | Australia | 84.4 |
| Belgium | 84.9 | United Kingdom | 74.9 |
| Netherlands | 84.8 | Canada | 68.4 |
| Denmark | 83.6 | France, Vth Republic | 65.3 |
| Sweden | 83.4 | India | 60.6 |
| Germany | 80.6 | United States | 48.3 |
| Israel | 80.0 | | |
| Norway | 79.8 | | |
| Finland | 79.0 | | |
| Ireland | 74.9 | | |
| France, IVth Republic | 72.2 | | |
| Luxembourg | 64.1 | | |
| Switzerland | 49.3 | | |

*Source:* International Institute for Democracy and Electoral Assistance, *Voter Turnout from 1945 to 1997: A Global Report.*

retained the same parliamentary electoral system throughout the decades, the chief exception being France. Though the various PR systems differed in specific details, in principle they were sufficiently similar to justify grouping them together for comparative purposes. The same was true of the plurality systems.

It is immediately apparent that a large number of countries with PR systems had average turnout rates of 79 percent or higher; only two of the states with plurality systems attracted more voters. Turnout in the PR countries from 1945 to 1997 averaged out to 78 percent; in the plurality countries the average was 69.5 percent. These figures are consistent with our hypothesis.

### Conclusions

Higher average turnout rates for PR systems were obviously the rule. Nevertheless, we should not lose sight of some interesting details. Notice that average turnout rates were higher in New Zealand, Australia, the United Kingdom, and Canada—countries with variants of the plurality system—than in Japan, Luxembourg, and Switzerland, which have variants of PR. Plurality systems thus do not *always* have lower turnout rates than PR systems. Our overall evidence is therefore *mixed.*

If we dig into some data not shown here, we can occasionally find significant variations in voter turnout within the same country, despite the fact that no change has occurred in its electoral system. In Switzerland, for example, turnout plunged from 63 percent in 1951 to 35.7 percent in 1995.[12] In the United States, turnout for House elections is typically higher in years when a presidential election takes place than in off years (see figure 3.4).[13] Germany's electoral system combines PR *and* SMD/plurality: though the final result is always approximate proportional representation, voters may be lured to the polls at least in part to vote for a single member to represent their voting district.

These and other departures from the general validity of our hypothesis serve as reminders that virtually every generalization in political science has its exceptions. Also, a correlation between two variables does not by itself explain *why* it occurs. People vote—or stay at home—for all sorts of reasons. Although people show a general tendency to vote in PR systems at higher rates than in countries with plurality systems, it would be a mistake to assume that electoral systems alone account for voter turnout. Voters can decide to troop to the polls or stay home for a variety of reasons, even though the electoral system is the same. Voter turnout in Israel, for example, fell from 78.7 percent in 1999 to 68.9 percent in 2003 and to 63.2 percent in 2006. Perhaps we should remind ourselves of another generalization: more often than not, multicausality is more likely to explain the complex phenomena of political reality than is reductivist monocausality.

*Elections in the Palestinian Authority* To understand the impact of electoral systems on the course of political events, we need to combine a firm theoretical understanding of how these systems *can* work with detailed empirical examinations of how they actually *do* work in real-world circumstances. We've already seen how proportional representation affects politics and policy making in Israel. For another dramatic example of how important the technicalities of electoral systems can be in translating voters' choices into political power, let's go back to the Middle East.

In January 2006, elections were held for the Palestinian Legislative Council, the Palestinian Authority's legislature. The future of Palestinian ties with Israel hung in the balance. Mahmoud Abbas, the PA's president, had already committed himself to seeking a negotiated settlement with Israel based on the "two-state solution": Israel would recognize a Palestinian state, and Palestine would recognize the state of Israel. Abbas hoped to lead his Fatah party—the organization once headed by his predecessor, the late Yasser Arafat—to a solid legislative victory so as to bolster his negotiating position. Polls showed that a majority of Palestinians supported a fair peace deal with Israel. The United States and the European Union pinned their hopes on a Fatah victory in hopes of promoting the Middle East peace process. The Bush administration was particularly interested in advancing the cause of democracy in the Middle East. But Fatah faced a serious challenge from Hamas, the Islamist party that the United States and the EU condemned as a terrorist organization. Hamas rejected the "two-state solution," denying Israel's right to exist. And Hamas was well aware that large numbers of Palestinians were fed up with the ineffectiveness and corruption of the Fatah government. Over the years, Hamas had won widespread approval for its educational activities, medical services, and other forms of social support that the Palestinian Authority had neglected to provide its population. Its leaders were now ready to participate in legislative elections for the first time.

Voter turnout was strong: approximately 990,000 people voted, representing 75 percent of the eligible electorate. After all the votes were counted following the balloting on January 25, Fatah and Hamas finished quite close in the popular count. Hamas won a plurality, garnering 45.5 percent of the total vote. Fatah won 41.7 percent of the vote. But what mattered more than the popular vote was the distribution of legislative seats. If a pure proportional representation electoral system had been in use, each party would have won a share of seats roughly equivalent to their respective shares of the popular vote. In these circumstances, neither party would have had a majority (67 out of 132 seats). Hamas would have won 60 seats, Fatah 55 seats. But Fatah would have been more likely than Hamas to put together a majority coalition government with smaller parties that shared President Abbas's political agenda.

Rather than using a PR system, however, the Palestinians instead adopted a fairly complicated mixed-member voting system. Half the legislature's seats (66) were elected by proportional representation. In this vote, Hamas won 29 seats and Fatah won 28. (Other parties together won 9 PR seats.) The remaining half of the Legislative Council's seats were elected on the basis of a rarely used system called the "bloc vote." For this half of the election, the Palestinian Authority's territories were divided into sixteen districts. Each district got a number of legislative representatives based on its population: Small districts got 1 seat, the largest districts got 9 seats. Each voter was entitled to cast a corresponding number of votes. The district of Ramallah, for example, had 5 seats in the legislature, so each voter in Ramallah got to cast five votes. Jerusalem (i.e., East Jerusalem) had 6 legislative seats, so each resident of the Jerusalem district got six votes.

Hamas shrewdly took advantage of the bloc voting system by giving its voters a simple choice: In each district, Hamas ran only about as many candidates as the number of seats up for grabs. As a result, Hamas voters concentrated their votes on just a few candidates. But Fatah, a larger and less disciplined party with multiple factions, put up far more candidates per district than Hamas. Fatah voters therefore split their votes among a multiplicity of Fatah candidates who were running not only against Hamas but also against one another. The vote totals of individual Fatah candidates got diluted in the process. As table 8.15 shows, Hamas put up four candidates in Ramallah, and all four won. Fatah fielded eighteen candidates there, but only one got enough votes to win the fifth seat. Seventeen Fatah candidates lost out, even though more people in Ramallah voted

**TABLE 8.15**

**Palestinian National Council Elections, 2006**

| Party | % PR Vote | No. PR Seats | % District Votes[a] | No. District Seats | % Total Vote | % Seats | No. Seats |
|---|---|---|---|---|---|---|---|
| Hamas (Change and Reform) | 44.5 | 29 | 45 | 45 | 45.5 | 56 | 74 |
| Fatah | 41.4 | 28 | 44 | 17 | 41.7 | 34 | 45 |
| Others | 14.1 | 9 | NA[b] | 4 | 12.9 | 10 | 13 |

**Ramallah and Jerusalem Districts**

| | Ramallah | | | Jerusalem | | |
|---|---|---|---|---|---|---|
| | Candidates | Votes | Seats Won | Candidates | Votes | Seats Won |
| Fatah | 18 | 169,734 | 1 | 26 | 93,556 | 2 |
| Hamas | 4 | 134,858 | 4 | 4 | 58,144 | 4 |

[a]Includes candidates affiliated with Hamas and Fatah
[b]Not available
*Sources:* Palestinian Authority Central Elections Commission; Jarrett Blanc, "Rules Do Matter: What the Iraqi and Palestinian Elections Tell Us," *Democracy at Large*, vol. 2, 2 (2006): 12–14; *New York Times*, February 19, 2006.

for Fatah than for Hamas candidates. In Jerusalem, Hamas ran four candidates; all four won seats. Fatah ran twenty-six candidates, who together garnered more than 93,000 votes, far more than the 58,144 votes cast for the Hamas candidates. But with twenty-six choices, Fatah voters spread their votes so thin among these candidates that only two Fatah contenders won enough votes to finish among the top six vote-getters. Similar voting patterns occurred in other districts.

The consequences were stunning. Fatah and its affiliated parties won 44 percent of the popular vote for the 66 bloc-vote seats, but Fatah came away with only 17 of these seats. Hamas and its affiliates won 45 percent of the popular vote in this part of the election; but Hamas won 45 out of the 66 bloc-vote seats outright, and three independent candidates affiliated with Hamas also won seats. Even though the Hamas and Fatah forces each won roughly the same percentage of the popular vote in this half of the election, Hamas and its allies won close to three out of four of the 66 bloc-vote seats. Fatah won more *votes* than Hamas in eleven of the PA's sixteen voting districts; but it won more *seats* than Hamas in only three of those districts.

In the end, Hamas won 74 out of the Palestinian Legislative Council's 132 seats—56 percent of the total, a robust majority. Fatah ended up with 45 seats (34 percent). Smaller parties and independents divided up the remaining 13 seats. (See table 8.15.)

Hamas's unexpected triumph compelled President Abbas to appoint a Hamas leader, Ismail Haniyeh, as prime minister. (The Palestinian Authority has a variant of the presidential-parliamentary system.) Haniyeh in turn formed a Hamas-dominated government. The immediate repercussions of these developments were discouraging. The United States, Europe, and Israel cut off vitally necessary financial assistance to the Palestinian Authority's new Hamas government. They also refused to negotiate with Hamas. In the summer of 2006, Hamas supporters launched rocket attacks on Israel from Gaza and kidnapped an Israeli soldier. Israel retaliated with attacks on Gaza. These events were soon followed by a war between Israel and the Lebanon-based Hezbollah militia. American hopes that democracy in the Middle East would promote peace in the region suffered a setback. As Fatah and Hamas militias clashed, Hamas rebuffed Abba's call at the end of 2006 for new elections. But the possibility of a coalition government could not be excluded. Meanwhile, it was clear to everyone that what counts in elections is not just how many votes are counted, but *how* they are counted.[14]

Chapter 7 identified democracy's defining elements. This chapter has shown how democratic governments can be organized and how various election systems work. The next chapter looks at some of the main factors that account for how democracies come about and succeed in the long run.

## KEY TERMS
### (In bold and underlined in the text)

Presidentialism
Parliamentary government
Vote of confidence
Single-party majoritarian government
Party discipline
Hung parliament
Coalition government
Governmental instability
Minority government
Anticipated (snap) elections
Presidential-parliamentary system
Single-member-district/plurality electoral system
Proportional representation

## NOTES

1. Aristotle, *The Politics,* rev. ed., trans. T. A. Sinclair and Trevor J. Saunders (London: Penguin, 1981), bk. 4, sec. 11–12, pp. 264–72.
2. Charles Louis de Secondat, Baron de Montesquieu, *The Spirit of Laws,* 2 vols., trans. Thomas Nugent (New York: Colonial Press, 1900), especially pt. 2, bk. 11. On his influence, see Paul Merrill Spurlin, *Montesquieu in America 1760–1801* (New York: Octagon, 1969).
3. William H. Riker suggests that coalition partners often find that it is in their own best interest to share the spoils of a coalition government with as few parties as possible. They therefore tend to favor a "minimum winning coalition" as opposed to one that maximizes parliamentary support. See *The Theory of Political Coalitions* (New Haven: Yale University Press, 1962).
4. See Wolfgang C. Müller and Kaare Strødom, eds., *Coalition Governments in Western Europe* (Oxford: Oxford University Press, 2000); and Michael Laver and Norman Schofield, *Multiparty Government: The Politics of Coalition in Europe* (Oxford: Oxford University Press, 1991).
5. See Robert Elgie, ed., *Semi-Presidentialism in Europe* (Oxford: Oxford University Press, 1999).
6. For debates on these issues, see Juan J. Linz, "The Perils of Presidentialism," and "The Virtues of Parliamentarism," in *The Global Resurgence of Democracy,* 2nd ed., ed. Larry Diamond and Marc F. Plattner (Baltimore, Md.: Johns Hopkins University Press, 1996), 108–126 and 138–45; Donald L. Horowitz, "Comparing Democratic Systems," in Diamond and Plattner, 127–33; Seymour Martin Lipset, "The Centrality of Political Culture," *The Global Resurgence of Democracy,* 134–37; and the essays in Arendt Lijphart, ed., *Parliamentary Versus Presidential Government* (Oxford: Oxford University Press, 1992). See also Lijphart's study *Patterns of Democracy: Government Forms and Performance in Thirty-Six Countries* (New Haven: Yale University Press, 1999); and Juan J. Linz and Arturo Valenzuela, eds., *The Failure of Presidential Democracy* (Baltimore: Johns Hopkins University Press, 1994). On recent trends toward the "presidentialization" of the prime minister's office in parliamentary democracies, see Thomas Poguntke and Paul Webb, eds., *The Presidentialization of Politics: A Comparative Study of Modern Democracies* (New York: Oxford University Press, 2005).
7. Gore's plurality over Bush was 537,179 votes. Other candidates won the remaining share of the popular vote. In 1876, Rutherford B. Hayes (Republican) won 48 percent of the popular vote and 285 electoral college votes, beating Samuel J. Tilden (Democrat), who won 51 percent of the popular vote but only 184 electoral college votes. In 1888, Benjamin Harrison (R) won 47.8 percent of the popular vote and 233 votes in the electoral college, defeating Grover Cleveland (D), who got 48.6 percent of the popular vote but 168 electoral votes. In 1824, no candidate won a majority of electoral college votes. The election was thrown into the U.S. House of Representatives, with each state's delegation receiving one vote. John Quincy Adams won the election in the House, even though he had won only 30.9 percent of the popular vote to Andrew Jackson's 41.3 percent.
8. For an explanation of various statistical methods for distributing seats in proportional representation systems, see *Electoral Systems: A World-wide Comparative Study* (Geneva: Inter-Parliamentary Union, n.d.), 7–11. The same publication explains variants of other electoral systems as well.
9. "Disproportionality" in voting systems—the difference between a party's share of seats in the legislature and its share of the popular

vote—is consistently higher in plurality systems than under proportional representation. Statistical calculations in which 1.0 equals the lowest level of disproportionality show that Italy's system scored an average of 1.1 over a period of three decades, while Britain's plurality system averaged 19.5 and those of Canada, Australia, and New Zealand together averaged 10.7. See Arend Lijphart et al., *Electoral Systems and Party Systems* (Oxford: Oxford University Press, 1994).

**10.** In an effort to consolidate Israel's multiparty system into something closer to a two-party system, Israel in 1999 held separate elections for the Knesset and for prime minister. Barak defeated Likud's candidate, Prime Minister Netanyahu.

**11.** See Matthew Soberg Shugart and Martin P. Wattenberg, eds., *Mixed-Member Electoral Systems: The Best of Both Worlds?* (Oxford: Oxford University Press, 2001).

**12.** For a debate on legislative electoral systems, see the essays by Lijphart, Lardeyret, and Quade in Diamond and Plattner, *The Global Resurgence of Democracy,* 146–77. See also Rein Taagepera and Matthew Soberg Shugart, *Seats and Votes* (New Haven: Yale University Press, 1989); and G. Bingham Powell, Jr., *Elections as Instruments of Democracy: Majoritarian and Proportional Visions* (New Haven: Yale University Press, 2000).

**13.** *Voter Turnout from 1945 to 1997: A Global Report on Political Participation* (Stockholm: International Institute for Democracy and Electoral Assistance, 1997).

**14.** On the development of Hamas, see Matthew Levitt, *Hamas: Politics, Charity, and Terrorism in the Service of Jihad.* (New Haven: Yale University Press, 2006); Khalid Harub, *Hamas: Political Thought and Practice* (Washington, D.C.: Institute for Palestine Studies, 2000); and Shaul Mishal and Avraham Sela, *The Palestinian Hamas: Vision, Violence, and Coexistence* (New York: Columbia University Press, 2000). On the 2006 elections, see Henry Siegman, "Hamas: The Last Chance for Peace?" *New York Review of Books,* April 27, 2006, 42–48; and Hussein Agha and Robert Malley, "Hamas: The Perils of Power," *New York Review of Books,* March 9, 2006, 22–24.

CHAPTER 9

# DEMOCRACY: WHAT DOES IT TAKE?

## Ten Conditions

Why is it that some countries succeed in establishing democracies and sustaining them over long periods of time, whereas others cannot even build a functioning democracy or keep one for very long? What must countries do in order to make a successful transition from a nondemocratic regime to an enduring democracy? In this chapter we'll look at a number of factors that have helped account for the success of some of the oldest democracies in the world, such as the United States and Britain. These same factors provide guidelines for countries that are now engaged in the difficult but crucially important process of democratization. As we noted in chapter 1, *democratization* is the transition from nondemocratic to democratic forms of government.

Of course, the hope of democracy's advocates is that the democratization processes now going on around the world will succeed and that countries on the verge of democracy will find a way to overcome authoritarian rule. The ultimate aim of all these efforts is the **consolidation** of democracy. Countries that embark on the democratization process need to complete it by ***building a strong and lasting democracy that withstands the tests of time.*** States cross the dividing line between democratization and consolidation when their institutions are so widely accepted and their democratic practices are so ingrained that their populations and elites—including the military and former dictatorial parties—cannot imagine replacing democracy with an authoritarian government. Democracy becomes "the only game in town." It may be difficult, however, to pinpoint when this threshold is reached. Some democracies have appeared to be consolidated, only to collapse and give way to dictatorship.[1] The achievement of a consolidated democracy may require decades of perseverance and hard work. The factors we enumerate in this chapter can help countries proceed from authoritarianism to democratization, and from democratization to the consolidation of a lasting democracy. Success, however, is by no means a sure thing.

### TEN CONDITIONS FOR DEMOCRACY

The ten factors that follow are not a magic formula. They cannot guarantee that a democracy will come about or, if it does, that it will survive over the long run. Every country must find its own path to a democratic system based on its own idiosyncracies. Very few successful democracies or democratizing countries will possess all the factors on our list. Some, in fact, may even display characteristics that are precisely the opposite of some of these factors, yet they may nevertheless succeed in building and sustaining other democratic structures and processes. Hence we regard these factors as "conditions" for democracy in a fairly loose, rather than a deterministic, sense: it is not necessary for a country to have all ten factors in order to be a democracy, and having most of the factors does not ensure a democracy's success.

Rather than constituting a foolproof recipe for "how to build a democracy," what follows is simply a list of *independent variables* in *hypotheses* that we can formulate about how democracies emerge and why they endure. Of course, these are two distinct processes: creating a democracy where none exists is one thing, and consolidating a democracy that is getting off the ground is another. Nevertheless, the two processes are close enough that the same ten variables apply to both of them in one way or another. In each case our *dependent variables* are *democratization* and the *consolidation of democracy.* And in each case our chief *expectation* is that the independent variables promote processes that are conducive to the emergence and long-term survival of democracy. This chapter is therefore an extended *hypothesis-testing exercise* that tests some variables against relevant evidence. Our basic assumption is that each of the ten independent variables on our list *increases the chances* for successful democratization and democratic consolidation.

At the same time, we need to emphasize that how these variables work will tend to differ from one country to the next. Not all countries follow the same path from authoritarianism to democracy, and not all successful democracies manage their consolidation processes in quite the same ways or in the same amount of time. In other words, our ten factors do not cause democracy to come about, or to become consolidated, by interacting in some universally applicable pattern.

The factors on our list *condition* democracy, but they do not actually *cause* a democratization process to occur. No combination of the ten conditions, not even all ten of them acting together, can actually "make" a nondemocratic regime collapse or "make" a democracy emerge and survive. The transformation of a country's governmental system from nondemocracy to democracy results from a specific set of events—political actions, economic developments, social transformations, and the like. The sequence in which these events occur will vary from country to country. In some cases they will unfold in a slow evolutionary process (as in England). In others the accretion of events over time may culminate in a sudden revolutionary eruption, with the "old regime" literally collapsing before everyone's eyes and a new form of government marching into power (as in the French Revolution). In other countries there may be a protracted struggle between a nondemocratic regime and its opponents. In these cases, democratization usually begins when the ruling elites give up power and their pro-democracy opposition takes over (as in Mexico, Nigeria, South Africa, and other countries). Such a transfer of power may result from a negotiated agreement, elections, mass demonstrations, the death of a charismatic dictator, a civil war, foreign intervention, or some other event or combination of events.

Rather than constituting the immediate causes of democratization and consolidation, our ten conditions of democracy are general factors that can *support the emergence* of democratic ideas and movements under nondemocratic regimes; they can *sustain a democratization process* once it has already begun; they can *help a new democracy become consolidated* in its first decade or two of life; and they can *help democracy survive* and flourish in the decades that follow. We say that these factors "can" do these things because we cannot say for sure *whether* a democratization process will actually take place in any specific country, nor can we say *when* or *how* it will take place. Democracy does not automatically "kick in" when some combination of these ten conditions exists. The victory and consolidation of democracy require specific actions in specific historical contexts, and these things inevitably vary across countries. Nevertheless, there are some general patterns of democratization, as we'll see later in this chapter.

Strictly speaking, the "conditions" of democracy that we are about to examine as our independent variables are really *correlates* of democracy. That is, their presence tends to be *associated* with democracy. The more of these conditions that are present, the more *likely* it is that a democratization process will succeed once it has been initiated, and the more likely it is that a long-term consolidation process will prove enduring.

After we describe our ten conditions, we'll look at some patterns of democratization around the world, both in the past and more recently. In chapter 10 we'll apply the ten conditions to two countries where the struggle for democracy is at the center of international attention: Afghanistan and Iraq. And in Part Two we'll relate these conditions to other countries as well.

### 1. Elites Committed to Democracy

For democracy to succeed, *people must want it*. What that means in practice is that people must want to adopt the defining features of modern democracy as we described them in chapter 7. In constructing the Temple of Democracy (see figure 7.1), they must accept democracy's core *values*, above all *freedom, inclusion, equality, equity, tolerance,* and *compromise*. They must want to be governed under the *rule of law*. And they must want to erect the main functional pillars of democracy—*popular sovereignty,* guaranteed *rights and liberties,* and *economic well-being*—in accordance with these underlying values and a law-bound government.

It goes without saying that democracy is most likely to arise and succeed when its main tenets are embraced by the whole population. Mass support for democratic values and institutions makes for a powerful, well-grounded democracy. And pro-democracy forces are more likely to topple a non-democratic regime when large numbers of people openly proclaim their desire for democratization—by forming democracy movements and parties (perhaps illegally), or by coming out into the streets spontaneously to demonstrate their defiance of the ruling authorities. Realistically, however, it is not "the people" who do the nitty-gritty work creating a democratic political order. As we've noted before, modern democracy is not "government *by* the people," but government *by elites* who are accountable to the people. The role of elites in building and sustaining democracy is crucial.

The actions of elites are especially important in the earliest stages of democratization, when a non-democratic regime is weakening and a chance for democracy opens up. It is the task of a country's political, economic, and social elites to take advantage of this opening by joining together and pressing for democracy. Even when there is a mass movement clamoring for democracy outside the door, it is the country's key elites who must sit at the table and hammer out the details of a new democratic system.

In some countries this process can take a very long time. In England it took centuries to move from an all-powerful monarchy to a system in which the monarch shared a certain amount of power with Parliament. It took even more centuries before Parliament was truly supreme and the monarch was reduced to a purely symbolic role. And it took many more decades from that point to develop a mass-based democracy that gives all adult men and women the vote. Throughout this long evolution, it was England's political elites who managed the process of building each successive expansion of democracy, though they tended to move too slowly for many British citizens. In France, the Revolution that exploded in the late eighteenth century was propelled by a popular uprising for democracy, but it was organized by political leaders. Ironically, it was some of these same revolutionary elites who asphyxiated French democracy in its infancy, imposing a harsh dictatorship on the population. Democracy in France had tumultuous ups and downs for more than 150 years before finally taking hold in the decades after World War II. As we'll see in chapter 17, France's political elites—led by a few charismatic individuals—played central roles in the country's long political drama.

In other countries, the creation of democracy has been faster. But even in most of these cases, elites have spearheaded the democratization process. In the United States, the founding fathers, representing the cream of American society, led a popular revolution against British rule and then drafted the country's governing charters, first the Articles of Confederation and then the U.S. Constitution. As we saw in chapter 7, Dutch elites stabilized democracy in the Netherlands on the basis of a consociational democracy. More recently it was two South African leaders—President F. W. de Klerk, the leader of the predominantly white National Party, and Nelson Mandela, the incarcerated leader of the largely black African National Congress—who made the critical agreement to cooperate in establishing a multiracial democracy, producing South Africa's first truly democratic elections on the basis of "one person, one vote" in 1994. And it was reform-minded Communist Party leaders in Russia, Lithuania, Hungary, and other parts of communist Europe who were instrumental in moving their governments from communism to democracy in the 1980s and early 1990s.

In some cases of democratization, society's elites may have to negotiate a "democratic bargain" on which to establish the foundations of democracy. At times their efforts will be supported by the vast majority of the people. In other instances the elites may be hampered by serious divisions in the population, with the values of inclusion and tolerance having weak moorings in society. Many people may approach democracy by bluntly asking, "What's in it for me and my group?" Whatever the attitudes of the masses may be, democracy may not come about in the first place, or survive in the longer run, unless the country's key elites agree to govern by agreement. This "agreement to agree" does not necessarily put an end to society's conflicts. It simply means that conflicts will henceforth be dealt with peacefully through the give-and-take of democratic procedures.

Inevitably, the true test of the elites' leadership skills comes when the leaders must convince their followers to accept whatever compromises may be necessary to establish democracy for all. In the most fortunate cases, their followers won't need to be convinced. They may be so weary of arbitrary rule, economic hardship, and civil strife that they recognize that striking a democratic bargain with their opponents is the only way out of widely shared misery. Even the supporters of a decaying nondemocratic regime, recognizing the futility of their policies, may come to the same conclusions and agree to give up power rather than face unending civil unrest. But when large segments of the population reject the deals their leaders have cut, democracy's chances are likely to diminish appreciably.

Political leaders—government officials, party chiefs, high-profile dissidents, and the like—are not the only ones who must accept whatever democratic bargains are struck. The leaders of a country's principal social groups—such as ethnic groups, religions, labor, farmers, and the business community—must also be on board, as must the leaders of important state institutions like the military, the judiciary, and the administrative bureaucracy. Many of these people may have worked for the outgoing authoritarian regime. It is vitally important to win their loyalty to democracy. Otherwise, they may constitute what Juan Linz has called a "semiloyal opposition," waiting in the wings for an opportunity to scuttle a fledgling democratic regime. Intellectuals and journalists need to support democracy by insisting on freedom of thought and expression, and they must be devoted to speaking and writing the truth.

We hypothesize that elite support for democracy is a vitally important condition both for the democratization process right from its earliest stages and for democracy's long-term consolidation. We regard it as a sine qua non: without broad elite support for democracy's core ideals and procedures, there is little likelihood that democracy will arise from the debris of a discredited nondemocratic regime. And if it does, it probably won't last very long without elite support. The evidence presented in various parts of this book, and in other countries is well, is largely *consistent* with this hypothesis. But even though elite support is a *necessary* condition for democracy, it is by no means sufficient.[2]

### 2. State Institutions

Even before a democratic state has been established, sometimes the institutions of a nondemocratic state can stimulate a democratization process. England's Parliament is the classic example. From its foundations in the first decades of the thirteenth century, Parliament was an incubator of democracy, challenging the powers of the crown with escalating boldness as time went on. The past few decades have witnessed additional examples of state institutions serving as incubators of democracy—or potential democracy—in authoritarian or semiauthoritarian regimes. Sometimes members of the judiciary take it upon themselves to uphold human rights in countries whose constitutions formally guarantee such rights but whose governments routinely violate them. Sometimes nondemocratic governments allow their opponents to form political parties and compete in elections to legislative institutions, all in an attempt by the ruling authorities to legitimize their own rule and perhaps co-opt their opponents into accepting the existing regime in exchange for a few minor concessions. To remain in power, however, the rulers may have to rig the elections or severely limit the lawmaking authority of the elected legislatures, actions that invariably inflame anti-regime passions all the more. As we'll observe in Part Two, the Soviet Union's last leader, Mikhail Gorbachev, and Mexico's long-ruling party, the PRI, dug their own political graves by permitting contested elections to legislative bodies. Theirs were not the only nondemocratic regimes to initiate the institutional processes that ultimately produced their downfall. Time will tell if contemporary regimes like Musharraf's government in Pakistan, Mubarak's in Egypt, and Iran's Islamic theocracy are treading down the same path.

However a country's democratization process may unfold, one of the first tasks—quite often *the* first task—facing the creators of a new democracy is to construct democratic state institutions. For the long haul, thoroughly democratized state institutions are essential for democracy's consolidation. A successful democracy requires a state that has sovereignty over a defined territory and whose boundaries are accepted by the population. Its governing elites and basic institutions must also be viewed as legitimate. As Juan Linz and Alfred Stepan have pointed out, this phenomenon of "stateness" is a prerequisite of democratic development. "Without a state," they note, "there can be no citizenship; without citizenship, there can be no democracy."[3]

The *legitimacy* of the state is crucial. Countries where major elements of the population do not accept the state's boundaries but instead demand independence—like Yugoslavia on the eve of its dissolution in the 1990s—are bound to have serious problems. Problems are also likely to occur in countries where a significant portion of the population categorically rejects the new democratic authorities or established state institutions. If large segments of the populace believe that their leaders have assumed power improperly (through unwelcome outside intervention, for example) or maintain it through phony elections, corruption, or other manipulative stratagems, democracy will be in trouble because the state itself rests on shaky foundations.

To an extraordinary degree, democracy stands or falls on state institutions and procedures. To complete the democratization and consolidation processes successfully, democracy needs governmental institutions that will ensure *popular sovereignty* and basic *civil rights and liberties,* much as we characterized them in chapter 7. From the start, the state must be organized on the basis of the *rule of law.* Those who govern must be *accountable* to the population, with fair, competitive elections permitting the *removability* of key officials on a regular basis. The *transparency* of the governing process must permit the citizenry to keep a watchful eye on state officials so as to detect corruption and punish those who perpetrate it. Corruption can strangle a democracy at any stage of its development, but especially in its formative period, when the population is eager to see if their new leaders are any better than their former dictators. *Legislatures* must have real lawmaking powers as well as the right to hold the executive up to scrutiny. The *judiciary* must be independent of political manipulation by the executive and legislative branches. The *bureaucracy* must be bound by legal procedures, while at the same time possessing sufficient resources to assist elected officials in the policy making and policy implementation processes. The *military* must abide by the rules of democratic governance and accept civilian controls. The lawmaking process must be reasonably *efficient* (timely) and *effective,* successfully addressing the country's problems. Governments need to be *stable* rather than constantly breaking down from petty squabbling among coalition partners.

Democracies must also have sufficient state power to protect themselves against their opponents. Hence there must be a single national military whose officers and troops are loyal to the democratic state. Militias or paramilitary forces that are not answerable to the central government constitute an intolerable danger. The state must also keep a watchful eye on the political foes of democracy. Antidemocratic forces may utilize elections, parliaments, and other democratic institutions for the ulterior purpose of taking power for themselves and then terminating democracy. History is replete with such forces, from Nazis and communists to generals and demagogues. Democratic states

**F. W. de Klerk and Nelson Mandela at Mandela's Inauguration as President of South Africa, May 10, 1994**

may therefore be justified in limiting the rights and freedoms of democracy's adversaries in order to safeguard democracy for those who truly want it. For example, they might ban particularly threatening antidemocratic parties and organizations.

Countries that are building democracy on the ruins of authoritarian regimes must also deal with former dictators and the remnants of their regimes, including once-powerful officials, secret police agents, judges, and torturers. A number of high-level figures from the communist era were put on trial and imprisoned after communism disintegrated in East Germany, Poland, and other parts of Central and Eastern Europe, but the extent of these efforts varied from one country to another. South Africa's first multiracial government following all-white rule set up "truth and reconciliation commissions" to investigate past abuses and hold the perpetrators accountable. The desire for retribution may be understandable when it comes to the most reprehensible figures of the old regime, and even necessary in order to effect a clean break with the past, but newly democratizing countries may also feel a need to put the past behind them and get on with the task of building the future. They might therefore offer a measure of forgiveness and a chance for rehabilitation to lower-level officials who are willing to abide by the rules of democracy.[4]

Evidence that can be gleaned from around the world over long stretches of history appears to be amply *consistent* with the hypothesis that thoroughly democratized state institutions, rather than partially or inconsistently democratized ones, are vitally necessary for the stability and long-term success of democratic principles and processes. *Democratic state building* is thus a primary task of newly democratizing countries, and the strengthening of democratically controlled state institutions is vital to the consolidation process over the long run.

### 3. National Unity

Some theorists contend that democracy is most likely to succeed when it rests on a socially homogeneous society. In this view, fragmented societies that are torn by deep ethnic, religious, class, or other divisions are too unstable for steady democratic governance.

The contemporary world is not lacking in deeply polarized societies that have found it difficult or impossible to establish democratic institutions or maintain them for very long. Information gathered by Freedom House analysts shows that countries in which a dominant ethnic group constitutes at least two-thirds of the population are twice as likely to be rated as "free" as multiethnic ones.[5] But some countries have found ways to make democracy succeed despite serious social cleavages. The United States, Switzerland, and the Netherlands are prominent examples. Few successful democracies in today's world, in fact, are without social cleavages of one kind or another, at times quite severe. Indeed, social heterogeneity may at times *increase* the likelihood of democracy, because democracy provides the most acceptable method for a highly divided people to reconcile their differences and live peacefully together. Conversely, in Japan and Germany, where there was historically a relatively high degree of ethnic homogeneity, democracy did not succeed until after it was imposed by victorious occupation powers after World War II.

Social homogeneity is thus no guarantor of democracy. And though social polarization can make it more difficult for democracy to flower and mature, it does not by any means make it impossible. For one thing, some societies find ways to bridge their social divisions by maintaining an overarching *national unity.* As we pointed out in chapter 6, a *common national identity* can sometimes provide a country's population with a sufficient level of homogeneity to hold its people together *as a nation* in spite of deep-seated divisions based on ethnicity, language, religion, class, and other sources of differentiation. Thanks in part to the unifying web of a shared national identity, the Swiss were able to put together their artfully constructed confederation and the Dutch contrived their consociational democracy. National unity in the United States was founded on a desire for independence from British rule and, simultaneously, on an agreement to construct a limited government dedicated to preserving individual liberties. That unity was shattered in the events that culminated in the Civil War. But after the war was over, and a more widely shared sense of national identity gradually solidified, democracy in the United States was progressively enlarged to incorporate former slaves, women, and successive waves of immigrants from the world over.

National unity thus played a major contributing role in helping to create and sustain viable democratic systems in these otherwise highly heterogeneous countries. Where a common national identity is lacking—as in countries like Nigeria, Sri Lanka, Iraq, and Afghanistan—the forces of social heterogeneity are less restrained. Without a common nationhood to fall back on, socially polarized societies have a difficult time making the compromises necessary to build or sustain democracy.

Dankwart Rustow has argued that national unity is the *sole* "background condition" of democracy, "in the sense that it must precede all other phases of democratization."[6] To be sure, any rule has its exceptions. The United Kingdom of Great Britain and Northern Ireland, for example, became a thriving democracy even though it has lacked a strong, unifying "British" national identity. English, Irish, Scottish, and Welsh national identities remain robust to this very day, but the rules of democracy are accepted throughout the realm (except perhaps by violence-prone Catholic and Protestant extremists in Northern Ireland). They are also accepted in Canada, despite wide support for independence in Quebec. Of course, the United Kingdom and Canada have been democracies for a long time. Younger democracies tend to be more fragile, and more susceptible to the damaging effects of national disunity. For them, national unity is very important, especially if the population is divided into contending social groups.

The evidence for the *homogeneity* hypothesis is mixed. Having a population that is socially homogeneous (in terms of ethnicity, religion, and class) is not an absolute requirement for democracy, but it certainly helps. But evidence from around the world appears to be mainly *consistent* with the *national unity* hypothesis, despite some exceptions. When national unity bridges over social and political differences, the chances for democracy are higher. National unity can be especially important in the early years of a democracy, when democratic institutions and practices are at their most vulnerable. But it can also help sustain a democracy that faces problems even after the consolidation process is completed.

### 4. National Wealth

We examined the correlation between national wealth and democracy at considerable length in chapter 3. That evidence is *mixed.* Though national wealth strongly correlates with established democracies, and most poor countries have not had much success in building or sustaining democracy, there are some striking exceptions. A number of relatively well off countries have failed at democracy; some poor countries have at least embarked on democratization and—in cases like India and Botswana—have registered long-term successes. Studies have shown that economic development can enhance the chances for democracy in some (though not all) countries, but it does not by itself "cause" democracy to come about. Democracy does not inevitably arrive when a country reaches a certain level of per capita income; political elites and elements of the mass public must take action for democracy to arise and survive. However, as Adam Przeworski and his colleagues have demonstrated, once a democracy is already established, its prospects for survival rise as the country's wealth rises.[7]

### 5. Private Enterprise

The connection between private enterprise and democracy reflects the idea that economic freedom promotes political freedom. People who own their own businesses or who work in privately owned companies, according to this hypothesis, will want to have a say in how the government treats them. They will especially want a say in how the government deals with property rights, taxes, business regulations, and so on. "Having a say" in what the government does and holding it accountable is what popular sovereignty is all about. In this conception, democracy emerges as a mechanism for protecting property rights. The reverse side of this hypothesis contends that the absence of economic liberty promotes authoritarianism. When the government controls the economy, it reduces the opportunities for citizens to organize themselves and take care of their economic needs independently of the state, effectively snuffing out citizen controls on state power.

One of the most influential studies of these tendencies is Barrington Moore's *Social Origins of Dictatorship and Democracy*.[8] Moore argued that democracy emerged in Britain and the United States largely because of the early appearance in those countries of a successful capitalist elite, the *bourgeoisie*, who made private industry and agriculture the dominant elements of the economy. They also demanded a say in the governance of their respective countries in order to ensure the state's protection of their property rights. By contrast, countries that failed to develop a strong entrepreneurial class did not produce successful democracies until the second half of the twentieth century, if at all. Historically, countries like Germany, China, and Russia had a comparatively weak private business class and an undeveloped commercial agricultural class in the nineteenth and early twentieth centuries. Instead, they had a land-poor peasantry and powerful state intervention in most facets of economic life. Japan also had a landless peasantry, while its powerful business elite was closely tied to the imperial state.

As a consequence, Moore observed, Russia and China fell to the communists, Germany got a fascist dictatorship, and Japan came under an aggressive military elite prior to World War II. Moore concluded that a thriving capitalist class is essential to the emergence of democratic institutions. He summed up this point in the pithy phrase "No bourgeois, no democracy." Stated another way, Moore's thesis is that private enterprise stimulates the growth of a middle class that does not depend directly on the state for its livelihood. As we'll see in the next section, the middle class itself can provide essential backing for a democratic regime.

While there is ample evidence consistent with these hypotheses, there is also a considerable amount of evidence indicating that private enterprise does not necessarily promote democracy. Quite a few countries have had a thriving private sector in tandem with repressive political institutions. In some cases the owners of large corporations have actively supported nondemocratic political authority, as exemplified at various times in Latin American countries like Mexico, Argentina, Brazil, and Chile and in Asian states like Singapore and the Philippines. Communist China today combines a vibrant private sector with unrelenting one-party dictatorship. It is still not entirely evident that the expansion of private enterprise in that country is stimulating pressures for democracy; to some extent it may actually be buttressing communist rule.[9] In postcommunist Russia the rapid introduction of private enterprise has been accompanied by the emergence of a small clique of politically influential multimillionaires and, simultaneously, by a drastic decline in living standards for large segments of the population. Some of the most disadvantaged people have responded to their plight by rejecting democracy itself, as have some entrepreneurs. As one Russian businessman put it, "If people tell me that for the sake of symbolic democracy I must give up my property—well, democracy is not worth that much to me."[10]

The evidence is therefore *mixed*. Though capitalism has acted to promote democratic tendencies in some countries, it has retarded, undermined, or suppressed them in others.

### 6. A Middle Class

A related hypothesis suggests that countries that are sharply divided into a small class of rich people and a large mass of poor, with no substantial middle class between them, are not likely to establish democracy. The rich will use their control of the economy to dominate the poor, while the poor will be mainly interested in expropriating the rich. Presumably, each of these opposing classes would be willing to use authoritarianism to impose its will on the other. A middle class, according to this hypothesis, is more favorable to democracy because its members seek to establish their own economic security on the basis of private enterprise, the rule of law, and an accountable government. These ideas are as old as Aristotle and as timely as the still-new millennium.

There is substantial historical and contemporary evidence linking the middle class with attitudes favorable to democracy. The democratic tendencies that blossomed in Britain, the United States, and France in the eighteenth and nineteenth centuries were largely the product of middle-class pressures against decaying monarchies and economically stagnant aristocracies. To this very day the middle class is the backbone of democracy in all three countries as well as in other democracies that have emerged and flourished in the twentieth century. In recent years key elements of the middle class have played a leading role in militating for civil rights and democratic procedures in Latin America and in countries like South Korea and Taiwan, where military regimes or one-party governments held sway for decades. In former communist countries like Russia, where the middle class still consists largely of state employees, a new middle class tied to the emerging private sector is just beginning to make its appearance. Thus far it appears to favor democracy.

But does the middle class always support democracy? There is evidence that large elements of the middle class can turn their backs on democratic institutions and throw their support to dictators if they feel that democracy is jeopardizing their well-being. Such was the attitude of millions of middle-class Germans who were devastated by a succession of economic crises in the 1920s and early 1930s, when Germany had a democratic system of government. Having concluded that democracy itself was the source of their woes, major segments of the middle class voted for Hitler and the Nazis. "No prosperity, no democracy" may be a widespread middle-class attitude in other democracies as well. Even if a sizable middle class supports democracy in a given country, there is no guarantee that its support alone can bring democracy about where it does not already exist or sustain it where it does exist. In many cases democracy may require the backing of other classes as well, both rich and poor.

On balance, then, the evidence for this hypothesis is largely consistent with the notion that middle-class support for democracy can be very important in promoting a democratization process right from its earliest stages and in helping sustain democracy as it matures. Middle-class support definitely enhances democracy's chances. But there are mixed results in answer to the question, Does the middle class support democracy? Sometimes members of the middle class do support democracy, sometimes they don't. Much depends on their economic circumstances. If they see an opportunity to prosper under democracy, they will tend to support it; but if their fortunes diminish under a democratic government, they might turn to an authoritarian regime if they feel it can deliver prosperity. Meanwhile, we need to keep in mind that the middle class consists of numerous individuals who do not all behave the same way.

### 7. Support of the Disadvantaged for Democracy

According to this hypothesis, the commitment of society's elites and the middle class may greatly enhance prospects for democracy, but if society's most disadvantaged elements feel they are left out of the democratic process or have nothing to gain from it, they could pose a serious threat to the country's democratic institutions and processes. Typically, the "disadvantaged" consist of the poorest members of the population, a group that in some countries comprises millions of people clinging desperately to survival. But other groups can also be counted among society's economically or socially disadvantaged, such as women and minorities. If democracy offers no real hope of overcoming poverty or discrimination, how can it claim to represent all the people inclusively? One result may be mass indifference on the part of the destitute and the oppressed. More ominously, seething mass discontent could provide a base of support for antidemocratic political movements and might even erupt into politically motivated violence.

Evidence relating to this hypothesis comes from a variety of countries at various stages of their historical development. Britain, for example, managed to solidify democracy while significantly expanding mass political participation in the late nineteenth and early twentieth centuries by gradually giving the working class the right to vote. As a consequence the workers, who constituted the largest and poorest segment of British society, accepted democracy as the only legitimate method for seeking redress of their grievances, rejecting violent revolution and dictatorship. In France and Germany, by contrast, the development of democracy was slower and more turbulent than in Britain. The vast majority of workers in these countries had reason to feel shut out of the political process. The result was a greater sense of disillusionment with democracy on the part of large elements of the working masses, a sense of alienation that in the twentieth century found expression in significant working-class support for communist or fascist parties.

The support of underprivileged groups for democracy is by no means automatic, even when they are given opportunities to take part in the democratic process. Large elements of the impoverished masses, for example, may actually support an existing dictatorship if they believe the government will address their needs. As we saw in chapter 4, millions of poor Iranians voted for the Islamic hardliner Mahmoud Ahmadinejad for president in 2005 in hopes that he would make good on his campaign promise to spend substantial amounts of Iran's oil revenues on social welfare and economic development projects for the country's underprivileged. For similar reasons, the poorer classes of oil-rich Venezuela provide a strong source of support for President Hugo Chávez, despite his authoritarian tendencies. Chávez has vigorously reached out to the poor with generous spending programs. The leaders of other authoritarian or semi-authoritarian regimes around the world have also managed to prolong their stay in power by providing economic benefits to the underprivileged, practicing a form of *populist authoritarianism*. In countries where a nondemocratic regime cannot afford to subsidize its economically deprived populations, or where it chooses not to, the ruling elites risk alienating a potentially threatening source of opposition.

Much depends on how well an elected government deals with the problems of disadvantaged groups, especially those spawned by the private marketplace. Private enterprise may stimulate extraordinary economic growth and thereby foster democratic tendencies on the part of those who profit by it. But the market economy can also produce prolonged slowdowns and deep depressions, persistent unemployment, inflation, acute poverty, and long-term financial insecurity. Those most affected by these hardships will usually look to their government for relief. To maintain mass support for democracy, therefore, elected governments must provide a panoply of social welfare measures designed to help the disadvantaged cope with economic distress.

Even in some democracies or semi-democracies, disadvantaged groups may turn to nondemocratic parties or engage in antigovernment violence if they feel that their basic needs are not being met. Nigeria and Palestine are two examples already mentioned in earlier chapters. In the Palestinian Authority, large numbers of Palestinians in 2006 voted for Hamas, which favors Islamic law, mainly because the Fatah-dominated PA government had failed to improve their economic conditions. Hamas won support in part because of the social services it provides to Palestinians in need (see chapter 8). In Nigeria, members of the Movement for the Emancipation of the Niger Delta (MEND) engaged in continuing violence against the elected government of President Olusegun Obasanjo, as well as against foreign oil companies, in hopes of getting a greater share of Nigeria's oil wealth for their destitute region (see chapters 1 and 23).

In less developed countries, where the disadvantaged are often inhabitants of impoverished rural areas or overcrowded shanty towns, mass support for democracy tends to be weak or nonexistent where the masses of the population are either unable to organize broad-based democratic movements or unwilling to support democratic parties that do not adequately address their problems. It tends to be stronger where democratic parties and interest groups go out of their way to appeal to the underprivileged and make determined efforts to deal with their problems when in government.

While admittedly sketchy, the evidence presented here appears to be generally *consistent* with the notion that the support of the disadvantaged is critical for democracy. Unless these segments of the population believe they can improve their lot by supporting democratic movements and parties, democracy will probably rest on shaky foundations. If democracy is not open to all, it may not succeed for anyone.

## 8. Citizen Participation, Civil Society, and a Democratic Political Culture

To give democracy life, people must participate. Political *parties* play a critical role in the participatory process, providing the main organizational link between politicians who run for office and the mass public. In most democracies, this link may be indirect at best. Typically the public has very little connection with parties except on election day; internal party affairs tend to be controlled by professional politicians and their staffs. However, some parties in the democratic world allow its members to take part in meetings to discuss policy issues and perhaps vote for the party's top leader or its candidates for office. Such parties provide a space for political participation by ordinary citizens at the grassroots level. To be sure, only small segments of the electorate may avail themselves of these opportunities. Partisanship—the extent to which voters actively identify themselves with a particular party—is in decline in most established democracies. Nevertheless, parties remain indispensable to democracy. At the very least, they provide voters with real election-day choices, and they permit legislatures and governments to function on the basis of coherent organizations. Newly democratizing countries therefore need strong parties that can be readily identified by the voters and that accurately represent the diversity of mass opinion on political issues.

To maximize citizen participation, democracy also requires a strong *civil society*. **Civil society** ***refers to the population organized into associations independently of the state.*** Some students of comparative politics say that civil society does not include political parties or the market economy. We prefer a broader conception of civil society that encompasses most democratic political parties—particularly those that permit ordinary citizens to participate in party affairs—and other forms of citizen activity. Civil society includes traditional *interest groups* that are concerned primarily with issues arising out of the market economy, such as trade unions and business associations. It includes *nongovernmental organizations (NGOs)*, which in recent decades have played an increasingly important role in democracies and even in some nondemocracies where they are able to function more or less openly. And it includes *social movements* of various kinds, such as the feminist movement or peasant movements, which may attract adherents outside the frameworks of formal organizations.

The key point is that civil society is *marked off from the state:* it consists of organizations that citizens create and join on their own, without any prompting or interference by government. Some of these associations may have overtly political purposes, such as interest groups that try to influence politicians and government officials to help their cause. In addition to unions and business associations, such groups would include ethnic and religious organizations, as well as single-issue organizations like those advocating or opposing abortion, gun control, and the like. Other associations may be less explicitly political but may still take an interest in relevant public policy issues; examples include organizations concerned with education or health matters. And there are civic associations that have no political agenda at all, such as various charitable organizations, social clubs, or bowling leagues.[11]

The more the citizenry is involved in such voluntary associations, according to a widely held hypothesis, the more likely they will succeed in building and maintaining democracy. By freely entering into groups and associations, individuals learn habits of organization, cooperation, and trust that are vital to the sustenance of democratic institutions and procedures, creating patterns of interaction that link society together at the grassroots level. In the process, they learn how to deal with many of the community's problems on their own, independently of government. Civil society is thus a primary source of a *democratic political culture*—a pattern of widely shared attitudes and values supportive of democratic institutions and procedures. It is the social web that underlies democratic government, making it possible to limit the state's power and keeping it accountable to a self-organized citizenry. At its best, civil society promotes tolerance of other ethnic groups and religions, compromise, and a willingness to trust others and cooperate with them. Of course, citizens can also form organizations that categorically reject democratic principles, such as terrorist organizations, hate groups, or criminal gangs. We do not regard such organizations as part of civil society. On the contrary, they literally constitute an "uncivil society." Our definition of civil society is confined strictly to citizen associations that abide by the rules and values of democracy.

In his famous treatise on democracy in America in the 1830s, Alexis de Tocqueville placed special emphasis on the broad range of private associations that knitted Americans together in the early decades of their republic. This burgeoning network of business groups, religious societies, temperance leagues, and other forums for citizen-to-citizen contact outside the formal boundaries of government was, in his view, of fundamental importance in accounting for the success of the new nation's bold democratic experiment, providing a social bulwark against a tyrannical or domineering state. "The morals and intelligence of a democratic people would be in danger," Tocqueville warned, "if ever a government wholly usurped the place of private associations."[12]

In the 1990s another political scientist painted a more unsettling portrait of the state of American civil society. In *Bowling Alone,* Robert Putnam provides statistical evidence of a steady decline in membership in all sorts of associations in the United States, from PTAs to bowling leagues, from charitable groups to bridge clubs, starting in the late 1960s. The result has been a serious depletion of America's **social capital,** which Putnam defines as ***"social networks and the norms of reciprocity and trustworthiness that arise from them."*** Societies that have networks of people capable of working together will have large amounts of social capital that they can draw on—somewhat like a bank account—to accomplish their goals efficiently.[13]

While Putnam's hypothesis has stimulated considerable debate, few observers would question that a vibrant civil society has played a major role in building and sustaining democracy in America and other successful democracies. Striking confirmation of this reality comes from Central and Eastern Europe, where a number of countries have been consolidating democracy in the wake of communism's collapse. Poland and the Czech Republic have made rapid strides in their transition processes, while Romania and Bulgaria have moved more haltingly. These differences can be explained at least in part by the presence of a real civil society in the first two countries during the years of communist rule. In Poland, more than ten million people joined Solidarity, an anticommunist trade union movement that openly challenged communist authoritarianism. In Czechoslovakia, a smaller but highly active group of political dissidents militated for democratic change starting in the 1960s. Romania and Bulgaria lacked such organizations, and they have taken a more circuitous route to democracy as a result.[14]

As a general rule, there is considerable corroborative evidence linking civil society with democracy. There is also strong evidence correlating a democratic political culture with successful democracy. On the whole, the evidence is *consistent* with the hypothesis.

### 9. Education and Freedom of Information

According to this hypothesis, the prospects for democracy rise with society's education levels: the more educated the populace, the greater the support there will be for democratic values and procedures. Conversely, societies with high levels of illiteracy and a poorly educated populace are less likely to create or sustain democracy. Democracy requires the free flow of information and freedom of expression. Without the ability to discuss politics openly and debate contending points of view, it will be difficult for proponents of democracy to get organized under a dictatorship, a factor that may stall or completely prevent a democracy from coming into being. Even after democratic institutions are set in place, the level of citizen participation in political life will depend to a considerable degree on the ready availability of relevant facts about the community's affairs and on opportunities for public discussion and citizen education about complicated political and economic issues.

There is considerable evidence in support of this hypothesis. When democracy emerged in Britain and the United States, for example, it was pushed forward primarily by society's most highly educated elites. British and American universities in

TABLE 9.1

**Conditions for Democracy**

| Independent Variable | Evidence Is Mainly . . . |
|---|---|
| 1. Elites committed to democracy | Consistent |
| 2. State institutions | Consistent |
| 3. National unity | Consistent |
| 4. National wealth | Mixed: generally consistent, but with major exceptions |
| 5. Private enterprise | Mixed: evidence for and against |
| 6. Middle class | Consistent |
| 7. Support of the disadvantaged | Consistent |
| 8. Citizen participation, civil society, and democratic political culture | Consistent |
| 9. Education and freedom of information | Consistent |
| 10. Favorable international environment | Consistent |

the eighteenth and nineteenth centuries permitted the study of political philosophy and encouraged rigorous debate. In addition, the British monarchy permitted a certain amount of press freedom and open political discussion, a factor that was critical to the expansion of Parliament's role in Britain and to the spread of democratic ideas in the American colonies. Conversely, democratic tendencies in these centuries were stultified in countries like Russia, Japan, and China, where the study of political philosophy was not encouraged and where oppressive state censorship smothered the open exchange of information and ideas. Meanwhile, in today's world, the most successful democracies tend to have higher literacy and secondary school graduation rates than nondemocracies.

Even when educational opportunities are widened and increasing numbers of people finish high school or enter universities, much depends on the *content* of what is taught and discussed. The Soviet Union, for example, greatly expanded educational opportunities for the masses, but the free discussion of political ideas was strictly forbidden. Many other dictatorships have exhibited similar patterns of restricted discussion and official censorship. Whether they can endure in the new millennium, with political information and open discussion accessible across national boundaries via the Internet, e-mail, and satellite television, is a fascinating question. A related development, in countries like India, Pakistan, and Saudi Arabia, is the spread of Hindu or Islamic religious schools where the concept of religious tolerance is rejected, all-out opposition to other religions is inculcated in young minds, and students are given little or no instruction in other subjects. Religious intolerance can strike a death blow to democracy, regardless of who preaches it.

As a general rule, there is a close correlation between democracy, on the one hand, and high educational levels and multiple sources of information on the other. This positive correlation is *consistent* with our hypothesis that education and free information can help promote democracy.

### 10. A Favorable International Environment

The conditions for democracy we have examined thus far are located within individual countries. But at times the external environment can have a significant impact on the prospects for democracy's emergence and subsequent development. War and its consequences can have either negative or positive effects on democracy. On the negative side, war generally requires firm centralized leadership and an influential role for the military command in the highest political councils. Under these circumstances there may be little room for interparty squabbling, an intrusive free press, or the open expression of public opinion. Not all countries involved in dangerous international conflicts have succumbed to the temptation of militaristic authoritarianism, however. The United States and its West European allies, for example, maintained their democratic institutions throughout the Cold War despite the hair-trigger nuclear standoff with the Soviet Union. On a more positive note, World War II produced democracy in West Germany and Japan, thanks to the direct influence of Western occupation authorities. Whether countries like Afghanistan and Iraq will have similar outcomes remains an open question, however.

Global economic conditions can at times exert an equally profound impact on the prospects for democracy in particular countries. The Great Depression of the early 1930s was a major contributing factor in the collapse of Germany's democracy and the rising popularity of the Nazis. In our own day and age, the chances for a successful transition to democracy in countries that have lately cast off dictatorship in Latin America, Africa, or Asia may depend in considerable measure on the willingness of the economically advanced democracies to provide timely economic assistance or to open up their markets to mutually beneficial trade. The European Union is playing a crucial role in Central and Eastern Europe by holding out EU membership to the region's former communist states. And the EU, the World Bank, and other sources of outside assistance are increasingly insisting on *good governance*. Good-governance projects tend to focus initially on getting governments to eliminate corruption and effectively deliver basic goods and services—such as food and medical care—to the population. At least in its early phases, good-governance projects may fall short of requiring full-scale democracy in countries where it does not yet exist; but helping to build sustainable democracies is the ultimate goal of many of these programs.

Transnational networks of nongovernmental organizations provide a growing source of outside influences on the prospects for democracy in nondemocratic or newly democratizing countries. NGOs espousing peace, voting rights, women's rights, press freedom, economic development, environmentalism, anticorruption measures, the elimination of torture, the struggle against racism, and similar causes are organized on a global scale, forming a worldwide civil society. They are using the powers of the Web to publicize information, promote dialogue, and organize international letter-writing campaigns and other projects aimed at pressuring nondemocratic governments to comply with human rights standards. As Sidney Tarrow has observed, since the early 1990s a growing number of transnational activists have emerged who may be labeled "rooted cosmopolitans": they pursue their political causes both in the countries where they are rooted and in the wider world of global political activism. In the process, the number of *transnational social movements* has increased tenfold in the last fifty years, from only about a hundred in the 1950s to more than a thousand today.[15] At the same time, antidemocratic forces are also organized on a global scale, using their own financial resources and websites to influence the course of political development in a host of target countries. Terrorist networks, Islamic extremist movements, international criminal organizations, and similar antagonists of democratic principles compose an international "uncivil society" that has a long reach into states and societies around the world.

A broader question is whether globalization will help or hinder democracy in the developing world. The forces of global economic and technological connectedness have both positive and negative consequences for developing economies, and the coming years should reveal their political effects more clearly.

The evidence is thus *consistent* with the hypothesis. But experience shows that, while external influences may be important, ultimately no foreign government or combination of governments is likely to prove capable of creating or propping up democratic institutions and habits in countries where the domestic conditions for democracy are unfavorable. Ultimately, the sources and nutrients of democracy must be homegrown if democracy is to germinate and blossom to its full potential.

## PATTERNS OF DEMOCRATIZATION

As we pointed out at the start of this chapter, our ten conditions of democracy do not by themselves *cause* a nondemocratic regime to collapse and a democracy to take its place. For such a major transformation to happen, a particular sequence of events must occur. The precise nature and timing of these events will invariably differ from one country to another. No two countries are ever exactly alike, and no two democratization processes are ever exactly alike. Still, there are patterns. So let's look at

**TABLE 9.2**

**European Democracies That Emerged from Monarchies**

| | | |
|---|---|---|
| Belgium | Liechtenstein | Norway |
| Denmark | Luxembourg | Sweden |
| France | Monaco | United Kingdom |
| | Netherlands | |

**TABLE 9.3**

**Contemporary Democracies Derived from British Rule**

| | | |
|---|---|---|
| Antigua and Barbuda | Cyprus (Greek) | New Zealand |
| Australia | Dominica | St. Kitts and Nevis |
| Bahamas | India | St. Lucia |
| Barbados | Ireland | St. Vincent and Grenadines |
| Belize | Jamaica | Tuvalu |
| Botswana | Kiribati | United States |
| Canada | Malta | Vanuatu[a] |
| | Mauritius | |

[a]Governed as a joint British-French condominium.

some general patterns of *how* democratization actually takes place. Keep in mind, though, that even the most widely shared patterns are bound to have exceptions, and every country will have its own idiosyncracies that deviate somewhat from the general mold.

Let's start with some of the oldest democracies in today's world, all of them in Western Europe. These are democracies that have been in existence since at least the end of World War II. Most of these "elderly" democracies are listed in table 9.2. Their common feature is that democracy emerged from some form of monarchy. Each country on the list took its own particular path from monarchy to democracy, and we won't go into these particularities here. (We looked at the Netherlands in chapter 7, and we'll look at the UK and France in Part Two.) It is the commonality of the general pattern that we want to highlight. Another common feature of these democracies is that, in the nineteenth and early twentieth centuries, most of them experienced pressures for democracy from an increasingly assertive middle class (the "bourgeoisie"). These pressures were usually augmented by an industrial working class pushing for inclusion in the political system. The result in most cases was the gradual development of a broad democratic coalition backed by conservative (bourgeois) and social-democratic (working-class) parties.

Another category includes countries that "inherited" democracy from Britain (table 9.3). All these countries were British colonies, possessions, or dependencies at some point in their history. Since achieving their independence from Britain, they have all maintained democratic government in a relatively unbroken pattern down to the present day. (All the countries in table 9.3 had a Freedom House rating of 1 to 2.5 at the end of 2005, qualifying them as "democracies" in this book.) This list includes old democracies like the United States and Canada, along with more recent ones that emerged after World War II. Once again, these countries display plenty of individual idiosyncracies. To state the obvious, democracy in the United States evolved very differently from the paths taken by Canada and New Zealand, not to mention Kiribati and St. Lucia! Nevertheless, the United States is one of "Britain's babies," just like all the other countries on the list. (Israel was a democracy from its inception as a new state in 1948; its territory was formerly part of Palestine under the British mandate.)

Not all of Britain's former charges were equally successful in sustaining democratic institutions. The list of former British colonies that failed to sustain democracy after independence is a long one. Some of them are still not democracies, such as Bangladesh, Egypt, Pakistan, Sudan, and

Zimbabwe. Ghana and South Africa were authoritarian regimes for decades before becoming democracies more recently. Nigeria has been governed mostly by military dictatorships since the mid-1960s. Its elected government under President Obasanjo was a semi-authoritarian regime. Sierra Leone is just coming out of a brutal civil war; it was a semidemocracy in 2005.

Another category consists of countries that developed—or redeveloped—democracy as the result of war and foreign invasion or intervention. Major examples are France, Germany, and Japan, whose stories we tell in Part Two. Italy became a democracy upon its creation as an independent state in 1859. Mussolini's fascist dictatorship put an end to that democratic system in the 1920s, but democracy returned to Italy following the defeat of fascism in World War I. Austria first became a democracy after the defeat of the Austro-Hungarian Empire in World War II. Its current democracy was established in large part as a result of World War II. In the postwar period, several of today's democracies resulted from direct U.S. military intervention against dictators (the Dominican Republic in 1965, Grenada in 1983, and Panama in 1989) or from more indirect forms of U.S. intervention (Nicaragua and El Salvador, which experienced bloody civil wars between left-wing and right-wing political groups in the 1980s).

Now let's focus on countries that have undergone transitions to democracy from either military rule, one-party rule, or rule by a regime centered around a dominant leader (a so-called "strongman") since 1986. Table 9.4 lists the main countries in this category. Most of these countries are still considered *transition countries:* they are still in the process of consolidating democratic institutions and practices. It's possible that democracy may falter in some of them and give way to authoritarianism in some old or new form. Some of the countries on the list were democracies at the end of 2005, some were semi-democracies (with a 2005 Freedom House rating of 3 or 3.5), and some were semi-authoritarian regimes (4–5.5). Many of these countries endured nondemocratic governments of one kind or another for two or more decades before a democratically elected, pro-democracy government took power.

How did democratization come about in this group of countries? At the risk of making a few broad generalizations that gloss over numerous deviations and variations, we can characterize the dominant "ideal type" of democratization pattern in this category as follows:

1. Over time, the authoritarian regime is confronted by opponents who demand a new government based on key elements of democracy. The opposition's main demands tend to be (a) inclusion in political decision making and (b) economic improvements. In some cases a "crisis of inclusion" results from severe discrimination or persecution by the regime against its opponents.
2. The opposition forms organizations (political parties, NGOs); its adherents engage in anti-regime activities (manifestos, demonstrations, political violence, etc.); and international pressures for change mount.
3. The regime tries to co-opt the opposition with minor concessions or rigged elections, or elections to institutions that lack real decision-making authority.
4. Regime leaders realize they can no longer govern or control the situation. In some cases a *catalytic crisis* occurs, involving one or more of the following: the death or retirement of a strong leader; an economic downturn; defeat or stalemate in a war or civil war; mass anti-regime demonstrations or riots; an increase in politically motivated violence; intense international pressure or intervention; the breakup of the regime's ruling coalition (including the defection of military leaders).
5. A "democratic bargain" is struck with the opposition that permits free and fair elections. Elections are held and the opposition wins. The regime either (a) steps aside and allows the opposition to take power, or (b) falsely reports that the opposition has lost, triggering a major crisis that compels the ruling elite to give up power.

*In every country* listed in table 9.4 there was a serious pro-democracy movement or party, demonstrations, unrest, or some combination of these developments. In most countries, democratization got going with the victory of oppositionists at the polls. In several countries a "democratic bargain"

**TABLE 9.4**

**Transition Countries Since 1986 (Former Military, One-Party, and/or One-Leader Regimes)**

| Country | Regime Type | Existence of Pro-Democracy Movement, Party, and/or Demonstrations/Unrest | Did Regime Allow Fair Elections? | Year Opposition Won | Freedom House Rating, 2005[a] |
|---|---|---|---|---|---|
| Benin | One-party | Yes | Yes | 1991 | 2 |
| Cape Verde | One-party | Yes | Yes | 1991 | 1 |
| Chile | Military | Yes | Yes | 1991 | 1 |
| Gambia | Military | Yes | Yes | 2001[b] | 4 |
| Ghana | One-party/leader | Yes | Yes | 2000 | 1.5 |
| Guyana | One-party | Yes | Yes | 1992 | 3 |
| Indonesia | Military/one-leader | Yes | Yes | 1999 | 2.5 |
| Kenya | One-party/leader | Yes | Yes | 2002 | 3 |
| Lebanon | External influence | Yes | Yes | 2005 | 4.5 |
| Liberia | One-leader | Yes | Yes | 2005 | 4 |
| Malawi | One-party/one-leader | Yes | Yes | 1994 | 4 |
| Mali | Military | Yes | Yes | 1992 | 2 |
| Mexico | One-party | Yes | Yes | 2000 | 2 |
| Niger | Military | Yes | Yes | 1993; 1999 | 3 |
| Nigeria | Military | Yes | Yes | 1999 | 4 |
| Paraguay | Military | Yes | Yes | 2003 | 4 |
| Peru | One-leader | Yes | Yes | 2001 | 3 |
| Philippines | Military/one-leader | Yes | Yes | 1986 | 3 |
| Sao Tome and Principe | One-party | Yes | Yes | 1991 | 2 |
| Senegal | One-party | Yes | Yes | 2000 | 2.5 |
| South Africa | One-party | Yes | Yes | 1994 | 1.5 |
| South Korea | Military | Yes | Yes | 1997 | 1.5 |
| Suriname | Military | Yes | Yes | 1991 | 1.5 |
| Taiwan | One-party | Yes | Yes | 1988 | 1 |
| Tanzania | One-party/one-leader | Yes | Yes | 2003 | 3.5 |
| Thailand | Military | Yes | Yes | 1992 | 3 |
| Zambia | One-party | Yes | Yes | 1991 | 4 |

*Note:* "One-party" regimes are run by a single ruling party. "One-leader" regimes are typically headed by an exceptionally well-entrenched individual who exercises personal power over a number of years, at times in conjunction with a ruling party, the military, or both.

[a]From *Freedom in the World 2006* (New York: Freedom House, 2006).

[b]In The Gambia, a military dictatorship transformed itself into a democracy, winning elections in 2001.

was negotiated at a national conference aimed at facilitating fair elections and a transfer of power (Benin, Mali, and Niger are examples). In some of these countries the democratization process proceeded incrementally as the ruling authorities relinquished power gradually, and often grudgingly, over a period of years or even decades (as in Mexico, South Africa, and elsewhere). In some countries there was a protracted civil war that the contending sides were ready to end, at times with international mediation, as in Liberia, Sierra Leone, and (perhaps) Congo.[16] In others there was a catalytic crisis that brought accumulating tensions to a head: fraudulent election results in the Philippines in 1986; a referendum against Chile's strongman, Gen. Augusto Pinochet, in 1988; the decision of Thailand's king to pressure the military to relinquish power in 1992; the death of Nigeria's military ruler, Gen. Sani Abacha, in 1998; an economic crisis and mass demonstrations in Indonesia in 1998; the assassination of former prime minister Rafiq Hariri in Lebanon in 2005; and similarly crucial events elsewhere.

Several military or one-party regimes that lost power to democratization processes *before* 1986 displayed similar patterns. Several of these countries experienced catalytic crises that pushed pent-up opposition to the regime to a tipping point. Greece's military regime collapsed after its attempt to annex Cyprus by force triggered a Turkish invasion of the island in 1974. Political change gathered steam in Portugal in the early 1970s, a few years after the retirement of strongman Antonio Salazar. A highly contentious power struggle between military elements and pro-democracy civilians culminated in the stabilization of democracy in 1982. Democratization got rolling in Spain soon after the death of strongman Francisco Franco in 1975. (Salazar had come to power in 1928 and Franco in 1939.) Argentina's repressive military regime gave up power in 1982 following its defeat in a war with Britain over the Falkland (Malvinas) Islands. Brazil's military unexpectedly lost an election to an opposition candidate in 1985.

Another group of transition countries consists of former communist regimes. Table 9.5 lists countries undergoing transitions to democracy that were once part of the Soviet Union, which ceased to exist at the stroke of midnight on December 31, 1991. Table 9.6 lists former communist countries outside the Soviet Union. Like the countries we've already listed, these former communist states have each taken their own idiosyncratic path to democratization, but some of them also fall into one or more of the patterns we've just observed. We've already referred to the Baltic states in chapter 7, and we'll take a close look at the breakup of the USSR and Russia's troubled democratization process in chapter 20.

After the USSR's collapse, power in Ukraine and Georgia was initially captured by elected governments that proved to be more authoritarian than democratic. A fraudulent parliamentary election result in Georgia in 2003 precipitated mass protests, forcing the country's strongman president, Eduard

TABLE 9.5

**Transition Countries (Former USSR)**

| Country | 2005 Freedom House Rating[a] | Country | 2005 Freedom House Rating |
|---|---|---|---|
| Armenia | 4.5 | Lithuania | 1 |
| Estonia | 1 | Moldova | 3.5 |
| Georgia | 3 | Russia | 5.5 |
| Kyrgyzstan | 4.5 | Ukraine | 2.5 |
| Latvia | 1 | | |

*Note:* The following former Soviet republics are not undertaking serious transitions to democracy: Azerbaijan, Belarus, Kazakhstan, Tajikistan, Turkmenistan, and Uzbekistan.
[a]From *Freedom in the World 2006* (New York: Freedom House, 2006).

TABLE 9.6

**Former Communist Transition Countries (Non-USSR)**

| Country | 2005 Freedom House Rating[a] | Country | 2005 Freedom House Rating |
|---|---|---|---|
| Albania | 3 | Mongolia | 2 |
| Bosnia-Herzegovina | 3.5 | Poland | 1 |
| Bulgaria | 1.5 | Romania | 2 |
| Croatia | 2 | Serbia and Montenegro | 2.5 |
| Czech Republic | 1 | Slovakia | 1 |
| Hungary | 1 | Slovenia | 1 |
| Macedonia | 3 | | |

[a]From *Freedom in the World 2006* (New York: Freedom House, 2006).

Shevardnadze, to resign. A snap presidential election that took place in 2004 was won by Mikhail Saakashvili, leader of the democratic "Rose Revolution." Similar electoral crises ushered in the "Orange Revolution" in Ukraine in 2004 and the "Tulip Revolution" in Kyrgyzstan in 2005.

As communism was falling apart inside the USSR in the late 1980s and early 1990s, powerful forces for change promoted democratization in Central and Eastern Europe. In six states, communist rule effectively collapsed in 1989. In Poland, Czechoslovakia, and East Germany, mass demonstrations forced the ruling elites to permit free elections. Czechoslovakia's nonviolent transition was called the "Velvet Revolution." (In 1993 the country was split into the Czech Republic and Slovakia, the so-called "Velvet Divorce." East Germany merged with democratic West Germany in 1990.) In Hungary, leaders of the ruling communist party announced that there would be free, multiparty elections the following year. A dissident faction inside Romania's ruling elite staged a coup against strongman Nicolae Ceausescu and eventually supported democratization. The Soviet leadership replaced Bulgaria's communist strongman, setting off a democratization process there. In 1990 and 1991, noncommunist parties emerged in these states, the communists transformed themselves into pro-democracy parties, and elections were held that confirmed the transitions of power.

The events in Yugoslavia as its communist system collapsed were described in chapter 5. It is worth reiterating that Bosnia-Herzegovina underwent a painful civil war that required international mediation. And Serbia's postcommunist strongman Slobodan Milosevic was forced to resign after fraudulent election results sparked mass demonstrations against his rule. Meanwhile, Albania's isolated regime under communist strongman Enver Hoxha dissolved in 1990; elections were held in 1992. And in far-off Mongolia, mass protests against the communist regime in 1990 pressured the government to hold free elections.

The countries listed in table 9.6 had all consolidated democracy by 2006.

A comparative examination of transitions to democracy around the world in recent decades reveals still more general patterns. In some cases there was a *pacted transition:* state power was transferred on the basis of a negotiated agreement, or pact, between a weakened nondemocratic government and the leaders of the pro-democracy movement. Another pattern involved a genuine *revolution from below:* a broad-based movement for change shook the foundations of authoritarian rule, confronting the regime with mass protests and, in some instances, violent unrest. Yet another pattern was *democratization from above*. In that pattern, elements of the country's nondemocratic regime became convinced that reforms were necessary, and they either initiated democratization themselves or introduced reforms that ultimately produced democracy (perhaps unintentionally, as in the USSR under Mikhail Gorbachev). Scholars have argued that the way state power is transferred from nondemocratic rulers to pro-democracy leaders has a major impact on the success and quality of the democratization process. But there has been considerable debate about how these patterns work, given the extraordinary diversity of countries that have undergone democratic transitions.[17]

A parsimonious explanation of democratization that seeks to explain a wide range of historical and recent cases has been advanced by Daron Acemoglu and David Robinson. In *Economic Origins of Dictatorship and Democracy*, they argue from a rational-choice perspective that democracy tends to come about when a nondemocratic ruling elite, consisting of a small segment of the population, is faced with a potential revolution and can no longer buy off its opponents with dubious promises of economic rewards. Rather than risk a violent struggle it cannot win, the elite chooses to hold competitive elections. The pro-democracy forces also wish to avoid a costly revolution, and democratization ensues as they are elected to power. Democracy becomes consolidated when the country's elites have no incentive to topple it. The scholars reinforce their argument with evidence of the importance of state institutions, the middle class, civil society, globalization, and other variables that support successful democratization and consolidation processes.[18]

Democracy's extraordinary advances in the past few decades, and the struggles for democracy that are still taking shape, have amounted to a truly global revolutionary process. They have given analysts much to think about and activists much to do. While analysts have turned "transitology" into an academic industry, activists have joined forces around the world to support democratic movements and governments. The two groups can learn from each other, gaining a better appreciation of how democracy comes about and how best to promote it. Government decision-makers concerned with democratization in their home countries and abroad can also benefit from the insights of analysts and the experiences of activists. The ten conditions for democracy presented in this chapter constitute a *framework for comparative analysis* that can be applied to virtually every country in the world. They provide a broad basis for understanding why some countries have succeeded at democracy and others have not.

## KEY TERMS
## (In bold and underlined in the text)

Consolidation
Civil society
Social capital

## NOTES

1. On these points, see Adam Przeworski, *Politics and the Market: Political and Economic Reforms in Eastern Europe and Latin America* (Cambridge: Cambridge University Press, 1991), 26; and Samuel P. Huntington, *The Third Wave: Democratization in the Late Twentieth Century* (Norman: University of Oklahoma Press), 266–67. Huntington suggests that democracy is consolidated when power changes hands in two successive elections. For a critique, see Guillermo O'Donnell, "Illusions about Consolidation," *Journal of Democracy,* 7, no. 2 (January 1996): 34–51.
2. On the importance of elites for democracy, see Juan J. Linz, *The Breakdown of Democratic Regimes: Crisis, Breakdown and Reequilibration* (Baltimore: Johns Hopkins University Press, 1978).
3. Juan J. Linz and Alfred Stepan, *Problems of Democratic Transition and Consolidation: Southern Europe, South America, and Post-Communist Europe* (Baltimore: Johns Hopkins University Press, 1996), 28.
4. See Donald W. Shriver, *An Ethic for Enemies: Forgiveness in Politics* (New York: Oxford University Press, 1995).
5. *Freedom in the World 1998–1999* (New York: Freedom House, 1999), 9.
6. Rustow wrote that national unity "simply means that the vast majority of citizens in a democracy-to-be must have no doubt or mental reservations as to which political community they belong to." It precludes secession or amalgamation with a larger community. See "Transitions to Democracy: Toward a Dynamic Model," *Comparative Politics* 3 (1970): 337–63. Reprinted in Geoffrey Pridham, ed., *Transitions to Democracy: Comparative Perspectives from Southern Europe, Latin America and Eastern Europe* (Aldershot, UK: Dartmouth, 1995), 59–86.
7. Adam Przeworski and Fernando Limongi, "Modernization: Theories and Facts," *World Politics* 49, no. 2 (January 1997): 155–83; Adam Przeworski, Michael E. Alvarez, Jose Antonio Cheibub, and Fernando Limongi, *Democracy and Development: Political Institutions and Well-Being in the World, 1950–1990* (Cambridge: Cambridge University Press, 2000); and Ross E. Burkhart and Michael S. Lewis-Beck, "Comparative Democracy: The Economic Development Thesis," *American Political Science Review* 88, no. 4 (December 1994): 903–10.
8. Barrington Moore, *Social Origins of Dictatorship and Democracy* (Boston: Beacon Press, 1966).
9. Bruce J. Dickson, *Red Capitalists in China: The Party, Private Entrepreneurs, and Prospects for Political Change* (Cambridge: Cambridge University Press, 2003); and Margaret M. Pearson, *China's New Business Elite: The Political Consequences of Economic Reform* (Berkeley: University of California Press, 1997).
10. *Financial Times,* November 7, 1995.
11. Michael Edwards, *Civil Society* (Cambridge, UK: Polity, 2004); Jean L. Cohen and Andrew Arato, *Civil Society and Political Theory* (Cambridge, Mass.: MIT Press, 1994); Chris Hann and Elizabeth Dunn, *Civil Society: Challenging Western Models* (London: Routledge, 1996); John Keane, *Civil Society: Old Images, New Visions*

(Stanford, Calif.: Stanford University Press, 1998); Thomas Janoski, *Citizenship and Civil Society* (Cambridge: Cambridge University Press, 1998); Avishai Margalit, *The Decent Society*, trans. Naomi Goldblum (Cambridge, Mass.: Harvard University Press, 1996); John Ehrenberg, *Civil Society: The Critical History of an Idea* (New York: New York University Press, 1999); and Robert K. Fullinwider, ed., *Civil Society, Democracy, and Civic Renewal* (Lanham, Md.: Rowman & Littlefield, 1999).

**12.** Alexis de Tocqueville, *Democracy in America*, ed. J. P. Mayer, trans. George Lawrence (New York: Harper & Row, 1966), pt. 2, 513–17.

**13.** Robert D. Putnam, *Bowling Alone: The Collapse and Revival of American Community* (New York: Simon & Schuster, 2000); idem, ed., *Democracies in Flux: The Evolution of Social Capital in Contemporary Society* (New York: Oxford University Press, 2002).

**14.** Sarah E. Mendelson and John K. Glenn, *The Power and Limits of NGOs* (New York: Columbia University Press, 2002). Also Nancy Bermeo, *Ordinary People in Extraordinary Times: The Citizenry and the Breakdown of Democracy* (Princeton: Princeton University Press, 2003).

**15.** Sidney Tarrow, *The New Transnational Activism* (New York: Cambridge University Press, 2005), 43–45. See also William E. DeMars, *NGOs and Transnational Networks: Wild Cards in World Politics* (Ann Arbor, Mich.: Pluto, 2005).

**16.** In July 2006, internationally monitored elections took place in the Democratic Republic of Congo, the country formerly known as Zaire, with its capital in Kinshasa. Incumbent president Joseph Kabila was declared the winner, but his chief opponent disputed this result. The elections sought to end a civil war that had raged since 1998, claiming 4 million lives, half of them children. By the end of the year, as fighting continued, it was not clear if democratization would take place. Congo is therefore not included in table 9.4.

**17.** Michael McFaul, "The Fourth Wave of Democracy and Dictatorship: Noncooperative Transitions in the Postcommunist World," *World Politics* 54, no. 2 (January 2002): 212–44. See also Valerie Bunce, "Rethinking Recent Democratization: Lessons from the Postcommunist Experience," *World Politics* 55, no. 2 (January 2003): 167–92, and *Subversive Institutions: The Design and the Destruction of Socialism and the State* (New York: Cambridge University Press, 1999); and Richard D. Anderson, Jr., M. Steven Fish, Stephen E. Hanson, and Philip G. Roeder, *Postcommunism and the Theory of Democracy* (Princeton: Princeton University Press, 2001).

**18.** Daron Acemoglu and James A. Robinson, *Economic Origins of Dictatorship and Democracy* (New York: Cambridge University Press, 2006).

CHAPTER 10

# CONDITIONS FOR DEMOCRACY IN AFGHANISTAN AND IRAQ

The devastating terrorist attacks on the United States that occurred on September 11, 2001, had dramatic consequences for America and the world. Determined to strike back at al Qaeda, the international terrorist network that organized the attacks, President George W. Bush and key administration officials decided that their first priority would have to be the elimination of the terrorists' chief base of operations in Afghanistan, and the death or capture of Osama bin Laden and other al Qaeda leaders. Bin Laden and his chief deputies were living in Afghanistan when they plotted the September 11 attacks and took credit for their execution. Although al Qaeda was a nonstate organization with a global presence, it was symbiotically connected with Afghanistan's Taliban government. The Bush administration's attack on Afghanistan in the final months of 2001 thus targeted both al Qaeda and the Taliban. After the Taliban were swept from power and bin Laden went into hiding, the United States and its chief allies established a new government in that strife-torn country under Hamid Karzai, a widely respected political moderate. In a nationwide vote in 2004, Karzai was formally elected to the presidency. Throughout his time in office, Karzai has shared the Bush administration's overriding long-term goal in Afghanistan: the establishment of a stable, enduring democracy.

Afghanistan was not the only priority in the Bush administration's international response to Islamic terrorism. The next big target was Iraq. Talk of "regime change" aimed at toppling Iraq's dictator, Saddam Hussein, in fact predated the election of President George W. Bush. In 1991 Bush's father directed the CIA to establish conditions for removing Saddam from power. In 1998 Congress passed the Iraq Liberation Act, declaring that U.S. policy should "support efforts to remove the regime headed by Saddam Hussein" and "promote the emergence of a democratic government to replace that regime." This resolution, signed by President Clinton, explicitly stated that Congress was *not* authorizing the use of U.S. military force to unseat Saddam. But three years later, in the wake of September 11, the Bush administration embarked on a course of military action to replace Saddam's regime. The administration's rationale for war centered on three declared aims: to rid Iraq of the large stockpiles of chemical and biological weapons that Saddam was widely believed to possess, along with material that might be used to make nuclear weapons; to extend the war on terrorism to Saddam's regime, which was accused of aiding, training, and harboring terrorists, including al Qaeda operatives; and to build a stable democracy in Iraq. A democratic Iraq, administration officials argued, would serve as a model for other countries in the greater Middle East, providing a viable alternative to both repressive dictatorship and anti-American terrorism. Another, less openly articulated, policy aim was to ensure stable Western access to Iraq's vast oil reserves.

In March 2003, 145,000 American and British troops invaded Iraq and drove Saddam and his ruling elite from power in a mere three weeks. A provisional authority under American leadership soon began working with anti-Saddam Iraqis to build the institutional structures of democracy: elections, a constitution, and an accountable government. But just as quickly, Iraq descended into a nightmare of violence. Remnants of Saddam's regime, foreign al Qaeda agents, career criminals, religious zealots, and various shadowy figures unleashed a deadly barrage of roadside bombs, rocket-propelled grenades, and targeted assassinations that showed no signs of abating by the end of 2006.

Afghanistan and Iraq are very different countries, to be sure; yet they share many similarities. This chapter briefly compares the two states by examining their prospects for democracy. Specifically, it looks at how they measure up against the ten conditions for democracy we presented in chapter 9. After an overview of key historical developments in each country, we will use the ten conditions in *hypothesis-testing exercises* designed to assess the course of democratization thus far, first in Afghanistan and then in Iraq. In each exercise, our *dependent variable* is *democratization*, and the ten conditions are *independent variables* whose presence can be expected to promote democratization, and whose absence can be expected to retard or prevent it.

## AFGHANISTAN

### The Monarchy

Afghanistan's history as a political entity stretches back to Alexander the Great, who conquered it in 329 B.C.E. For long periods up until the eighteenth century, Afghanistan was wholly or partially an appendage of neighboring empires or foreign conquerors. In 1709 a tribal chieftain liberated the area around the town of Kandahar from the Persian Safavid dynasty, giving Afghanistan its own rulers for the first time. In 1747 a king was chosen from one of the two Pashtun clans that were destined to rule the country, with only a nine-month interruption, until 1978. Significantly, Afghanistan managed to avoid conquest and occupation. Despite British and Russian attempts to dominate Central Asia and the passages to India in what was called "the Great Game" of imperial rivalry in this part of the world, Afghanistan escaped colonization in the nineteenth century, safeguarding the sovereignty of its monarchal government over the country's internal affairs. Nevertheless, Britain exercised enormous influence over a succession of Afghan monarchs and essentially controlled Afghanistan's foreign affairs until 1919.

In the first Anglo-Afghan war (1839–1842), the British deposed Afghanistan's king, only to be driven out of the country as the king mounted a successful comeback. The next king sought Russian assistance against Britain, a policy that provoked the British to launch their second war with Afghanistan (1878–80). The British finally managed to depose the recalcitrant king's successor and placed Amir Abdul Rehman on the throne in exchange for his forbearance in allowing Britain to define Afghanistan's boundaries with India and Russia. The "MacMahon line" still divides the region's Pashtun population, with some Pashtuns living in Afghanistan and others in what is now Pakistan. After Amir's heir was assassinated, his grandson Amanullah Khan ascended to the throne in 1919 and immediately declared Afghanistan's complete independence from Britain. The British thereupon initiated the third Anglo-Afghan war, which quickly fizzled with their defeat. A modernizer, Amanullah gave Afghanistan its first constitution, placing the king under the rule of law and establishing the legal equality of all citizens. Amanullah also encouraged Afghan women to study abroad and participate in public life. But his constitutional innovations were never meant to be fully honored, and his social and educational reforms triggered fierce resistance throughout the socially conservative countryside. Unable to suppress the revolt, Amanullah fled abroad in 1929. A general seized power in a coup and ruled as king until his assassination in 1933. The throne then passed to the usurper's nineteen-year-old son, *Muhammad Zahir Shah*.

Zahir Shah sought to modernize Afghanistan's educational system and initiated a political reform program known as "New Democracy." The reforms fell far short of real democracy, however, as the king retained ultimate authority. In the 1950s Zahir's cousin and brother-in-law, Sardar Mohammad Daoud, seized the reins of effective decision-making power, but the king reclaimed them ten years later. Banned from public life, Daoud made another attempt to seize power in 1979. With the aid of Soviet-trained Afghan military officers, Daoud staged a successful coup d'état. Zahir Shah was forced to leave the country, and Daoud abolished the monarchy and proclaimed a republic. From this point on, violence became the principal means of securing power in Afghanistan, and the country slid into a vortex of coups, countercoups, and continuous warfare that lasted more than twenty years.

### The Soviet Invasion

A coup led by a radical faction of Afghanistan's communist party ousted Daoud in 1978. Daoud himself was murdered. The new leaders quickly began fighting among themselves as they plunged the rest of the country into a social revolution based on Soviet-inspired communist principles. One of the coup leaders was assassinated in a plot engineered by his chief co-conspirator, Hafizullah Amin. Amin was determined to orient Afghanistan more closely to the Soviet Union. His government even adopted a new flag modeled on the red flag of Soviet communism. But the regime's attempts to change long-standing social customs provoked strong opposition from Afghanistan's tribal leaders and Islamic clerics. In 1979, with the country careening toward chaos, the Soviet leadership feared that Amin's government was losing control. In December, Soviet troops invaded Afghanistan en masse. KGB agents assassinated Amin and replaced him with Babrak Karmal, who headed a rival communist faction. Soviet military officials indicated that they hoped to restore order very quickly, in a matter of months or possibly even weeks. In the end, Soviet troops stayed more than nine years and eventually suffered bitter defeat.

Although they deployed more than 100,000 troops and controlled the capital city, Kabul, the Soviets were never able to subdue the vast Afghan countryside. Their invasion was countered by determined resistance from several groups known collectively as the *mujahedin*. In addition to taking on tens of thousands of local Afghan fighters, the Soviets also had to contend with warriors who came from other Muslim countries to assist their Afghan brethren in the name of jihad—"holy war." One of these foreign mujahedin was *Osama bin Laden*. The son of one of Saudi Arabia's wealthiest businessmen, bin Laden committed substantial sums of his own money and considerable organizational skills to the mujahedin cause. Compounding the Soviets' problems were the decisions taken by the United States under Presidents Jimmy Carter and Ronald Reagan to provide military and financial assistance to the mujahedin. The United States did not conceal its hope that the Soviet Union, its Cold War archrival, would find itself mired in a long conflict in Afghanistan. Ultimately the United States provided $4 to $5 billion in military equipment and other forms of assistance to the mujahedin. Much of this assistance was channeled through military authorities in Pakistan, and some of it went to bin Laden.

In 1985, Mikhail Gorbachev assumed power in Moscow. An energetic reformer, Gorbachev made an early decision to pull the Soviet military out of the Afghan quagmire. In the following year his government began preparations for withdrawal by replacing Babrak Karmal with another Afghan communist, Mohammad Najibullah. In April 1988 the Soviet Union signed an agreement in Geneva that confirmed its decision to get out of Afghanistan. The first troop withdrawals began the following month, and the last Soviet soldiers departed in February 1989. Their failed war in Afghanistan had cost the Soviets some $45 billion and the lives of more than 16,000 troops. Afghanistan was left in shambles. Close to 1 million Afghans had died in the conflict, out of a total population of 15 to 17 million. Between 2 and 3 million people inside the country were uprooted from their homes, and another 5 million or more had fled Afghanistan as refugees, many of them settling in squalid camps in neighboring Pakistan. In these refugee camps, and in crowded Pakistani border towns like Peshawar and Quetta, the Taliban movement was born.

With Soviet financial support, Najibullah managed to cling to power in Kabul for several more years. But the rest of the country fell apart around him, succumbing to local warlords who were vigorously reasserting themselves. In an effort to prevent Afghanistan's internal disintegration, the United States, the Soviet Union, and the United Nations brokered an agreement on an interim government. But the new government failed to restore central authority during its brief tenure from 1992 to 1996, and Afghanistan descended into civil war. Rival factions divided up the country's territory, and even Kabul became a nightmare of looting and raping as tens of thousands of armed men prowled the streets, spreading anarchy. Having achieved its primary objective of punishing the Soviet Union, the United States now essentially ignored Afghanistan. As the Afghan economy disintegrated, opium and heroin production emerged as sources of income for many Afghans on the brink of ruin. Over the course of the 1990s, Afghanistan would supply more than 90 percent of Europe's heroin.

Into this tumultuous scene stepped the Taliban. The movement emerged in 1994 when a number of devout Afghan Islamists who had become disgusted at the sorry plight of their country gravitated to Mullah Muhammad Omar, a quiet cleric who had been wounded several times in the war against the Soviets. Mullah Omar came from an impoverished Pashtun village near Kandahar, one of the most socially conservative areas in Afghanistan. Women in this part of the country tended to be veiled and confined to the home. Omar himself never completed his formal education, but he had studied theology and ran a religious school. Omar's followers called themselves the Taliban, or "students of Islam."

As his fame spread, Mullah Omar began receiving financial support from Benazir Bhutto's government in Pakistan, which was interested in extending its influence in the region. In 1994, with Pakistani help, the Taliban took control of Kandahar, Afghanistan's second largest city. They gradually subdued other parts of the country, and by November 1996 they were in Kabul. Once installed in power they quickly imposed one of the harshest variants of shariah (Islamic law) ever seen in the Muslim world. Men were forced to grow beards and women were required to wear the burqa, covering their bodies from head to toe. Women were forbidden to attend school or work outside their homes, and many were reduced to begging to support their families. Secular music was outlawed. The Department of the Promotion of Virtue and Prevention of Vice stringently enforced these rules. Violators, including women, were often beaten in the streets. For the worst offenders there were public executions and amputations. Some groups that did not share the Taliban's religious beliefs or ethnic ties were the victims of mass massacres. In a deliberate affront to world opinion, in 2001 the Taliban blew up two large statues of the Buddha that had been carved out of a cliff in the second century. The Taliban also gave virtually free rein to bin Laden, who was one of their major financial supporters. Islamic extremists from all over the world went to Afghanistan for training in terrorism at al Qaeda's camps.

After September 11, 2001, the Bush administration decided that the quickest way to strike at al Qaeda was to completely remove the Taliban from power. As U.S., British, and French aircraft conducted a massive aerial bombardment campaign in the final months of 2001, anti-Taliban forces in Afghanistan, mostly affiliated with the Northern Alliance militias, attacked on the ground. Kabul was taken from the Taliban in November, and Kandahar was taken in December. Although both Osama bin Laden and Mullah Omar escaped capture, the Taliban regime crumbled by the end of 2001. In its place a conference of Afghan leaders meeting in Berlin installed a new interim government headed by Hamid Karzai. Karzai was a cousin of the former king Zahir Shah and a descendant of a Pashtun family that had been politically prominent for centuries. In the 1980s, while living part of the time in Maryland, he helped channel U.S. aid to the mujahedin in their war against the Soviets. A secular Afghan nationalist, President Karzai now faced the daunting task of rebuilding Afghanistan politically, economically, and socially. For his part, eighty-seven-year-old former king Zahir Shah returned to Afghanistan in 2002 after thirty-nine years in exile. He announced that he had no intention of reclaiming the monarchy and that he would support efforts to unite the country.

Against this stormy background, how do our ten conditions for democracy help explain democracy's past failures—and potential success—in Afghanistan?

### Elites Committed to Democracy

As our historical account makes abundantly clear, Afghanistan has never had ruling elites who sincerely advocated democratic principles. Even the parliamentary institutions of Zahir Shah's "New Democracy" in the 1960s lacked the decision-making authority of a truly democratic representative legislature. Moreover, political parties were not allowed, so there were no organized political groups to vie for the people's votes in truly competitive legislative elections. President Karzai and leaders of at least some of the country's main ethnic groups now support democracy in principle. However, tribal leaders and a large number of local officials in Afghanistan's provinces remain determined to uphold traditional laws and customs, in contravention of democratic principles and Afghanistan's new constitutional order. In addition, militia leaders, especially in the north, are more interested in wielding their own local power than in acceding to the authority of the national government. As a result, the central government in Kabul has encountered serious obstacles to its efforts to extend the authority of the Afghan state's new institutions over the entire country.

### State Institutions

Afghanistan has never had a central state strong enough to penetrate the entire country with its laws and policies. The country's governmental system has traditionally consisted of weak central governments coexisting with a multiplicity of local authorities—village chieftains, tribal councils, clan leaders, Islamic clerics, warlords, and the like. The authorities in Kabul tended to play favorites, distributing economic and other benefits to their own preferred ethnic group, clan, region, or party rather than spreading them around fairly among the whole population. Consequently they never enjoyed real legitimacy in the eyes of the entire populace. After the Soviet invasion, the legitimacy of the central state deteriorated even further under a succession of Moscow-imposed rulers and then under the Taliban.

In addition, Afghanistan's past leaders failed to create a professional national army. Efforts to repel British and Soviet invaders tended to involve loosely coordinated operations by local militias or groups like the mujahedin. Thus the Afghan state has lacked the coercive power of an institutionalized military force that is loyal to the central government.

However, Afghanistan has traditionally had an institution that might serve as an incubator of state legitimacy and a possible full-fledged democracy: the *Loya Jirga*. Originally the *jirga* ("circle") was a Pashtun tribal or village council. A more important Grand Council, or Loya Jirga, met in 1747 to choose a new king (shah) for Afghanistan. In subsequent years various Afghan monarchs periodically summoned a Loya Jirga to legitimize their authority or gain advice on important political decisions. In the 1920s the Loya Jirga became institutionalized as the country's highest representative body. In the 1960s Zahir Shah convened a Loya Jirga to debate and amend a new draft constitution for Afghanistan. The resulting constitutional system of "New Democracy" provided for Afghanistan's first bicameral legislature and a new Loya Jirga consisting of appointees representing various groups in Afghan society. But despite the Loya Jirga's importance as a legitimizing device, its democratic authenticity remained limited. Its composition was rarely inclusive: membership was usually overwhelmingly (and often exclusively) male, and confined mostly to Pashtuns, the country's largest ethnic group. Typically the members of the Loya Jirga were handpicked by the monarchal government rather than freely elected. They never had the authority to hold the king accountable or to compel him by majority vote to make specified decisions. Their role was purely advisory, and at times they were cynically manipulated or co-opted by the crown. Daoud and the Soviet-imposed leader Najibullah also convened their own handpicked Loya Jirgas, but their attempts to use the institution to fabricate their legitimacy as rulers ultimately proved futile.

In 2002, President Karzai summoned a new Loya Jirga in an effort to touch base with representatives of Afghan society and acquire an element of legitimacy for his government. Of 1,598 delegates, about a thousand were elected in voting that took place in local districts; the rest were chosen by important groups. After several days of lively debate, Karzai won the approval of 82 percent of the delegates in a secret ballot, formally assuming the presidency of a newly established Transitional Authority. Then in December 2003 a Constitutional Loya Jirga was summoned to consider a draft constitution prepared by the Transitional Authority. After lively debates among 502 delegates and the adoption of a number of amendments, the Loya Jirga approved the amended constitution in January 2004.

The constitution defines Afghanistan as an Islamic republic and Islam as the state religion. Although it guarantees freedom of religion, no laws may be passed contrary to Islamic beliefs. The document also provides legal guarantees of equal rights for men and women, freedom of expression, freedom of assembly, and other basic democratic rights and freedoms on the basis of the rule of law. The constitution establishes a *presidential system* of government (see chapter 8). The president, elected by winning more than 50 percent of the vote in a direct popular election, is simultaneously head of state and head of government, bearing responsibility for the government's policies. There are two vice presidents but no prime minister. Among other duties, the president appoints the government (the cabinet ministers) and supervises its work. The bicameral National Assembly consists of a lower house, the 249-member House of the People, elected directly by the voters; and a less important upper house, the 102-member House of Elders, chosen by provincial and local councils and by the president. The constitution stipulates that at least two women must be elected to the lower house from each province (there would be at least 68 women members in all, or 25 percent of the total membership); half the members of the upper house must also be women. The House of the People has the right to approve the president's nominees for the cabinet.

In October 2004, Afghanistan's first free and inclusive presidential elections took place. Facing sixteen challengers, President Karzai won 55 percent of the vote and survived a post-election investigation of the results. Approximately 75 percent of the country's registered voters turned out to vote. Slightly more than a year later, in September 2005, Afghanistan held its first elections to the House of the People. Using a complicated electoral system called the *single transferable vote*, the election featured 2,800 candidates running under their own names on the ballots rather than under party labels. A checkered array of candidates presented themselves to the electorate, from Karzai allies and other proponents of democracy to provincial warlords, militia fighters, Islamic conservatives, organized crime figures, human rights offenders, and even former communists and Taliban militants. Only about half the country's 12.4 million registered voters took part in the election. Despite a deadly campaign by the Taliban to derail the vote, with some six hundred people killed in the months leading up to election day, and despite incidents of electoral fraud at various polling places, the elections were widely regarded as free and fair. Slightly more than half the delegates elected to the body were Karzai loyalists. Other winners reflected the wide-ranging diversity of the candidates. Women won their allotted sixty-eight seats, but no more. On the same day, Afghans also elected thirty-four provincial councils. And in December 2005 the upper house was selected, with most delegates representing conservative Islamic positions.

Although the democratic election of Afghanistan's main executive and legislative offices has taken place fairly smoothly, the central state institutions are still a long way from asserting full control over the country. To begin with, the national government does not monopolize the means of violence, a fundamentally important requirement of any state that claims legitimacy in the eyes of its population. Provincial militias operate in various parts of Afghanistan, exercising predominant authority in some areas. The Taliban has been mounting a steady comeback in the past several years. Starting with only a few hundred fighters after their overthrow in 2001, by 2006 the Taliban claimed to have twelve thousand armed militants. Although most Taliban activity has occurred in the southern regions around Kandahar, a traditional bastion of Islamic conservatism, the organization has steadily widened its base, claiming responsibility for suicide bombings in Kabul, targeted assassinations of political figures, and other operations. Some two thousand people were killed by the Taliban in 2006. Afghanistan's national army has been too weak to confront these various militias and guerilla groups. It has fallen far short of its goal of 70,000 trained soldiers; desertion rates are high. To maintain a modicum of security, NATO had some 20,000 troops in Afghanistan in 2006, including 1,300 U.S. forces. Under a separate chain of command, the United States had an additional 20,000 troops in place. Raids on Taliban units multiplied in 2006, but the rise of Taliban activity has raised doubts about the adequacy of these troop levels.

The judiciary is another problematic state institution. Afghanistan still lacks an independent judiciary capable of adjudicating the law in accordance with the new constitution. Afghanistan's Supreme Court is dominated by Islamic religious jurists unschooled in civil law. The weakness of government controls in the country's vast provincial hinterlands has placed the administration of the law in the hands of local authorities, many of whom apply customary religious law. Bribery and intimidation of judges are rampant. Despite the constitution's assurance of the equality of men and women, women in much of Afghanistan are still subjected to traditional forms of discrimination and repression, including child marriage, rape, and other forms of violence. In 2005 at least one woman was stoned to death for alleged adultery.

Official corruption has also undermined the effectiveness of the Afghan state. Other abuses of governmental power include arbitrary arrest, torture, extrajudicial killings, the abuse of detainees, and other improper actions on the part of Afghanistan's government, police, military, and intelligence officials.

Afghanistan has registered significant achievements in building the basic constitutional and institutional structures of democracy since 2001. But it has yet to complete its transition to democracy by effectively translating into reality the rights and freedoms that the constitution guarantees on paper.[1]

### National Unity

One of the most serious barriers to democracy in Afghanistan is the country's extraordinary social diversity. Occupying an area slightly smaller than Texas, Afghanistan's population numbered approximately 31 million in 2006. About 90 percent of the inhabitants are distributed among four large ethnic groups, each with its own territorial base. The *Pashtuns* constitute about 42 percent of the total population. They mainly inhabit southern and southeastern Afghanistan, and they share close ethnic ties with Pashtuns living across the border in Pakistan. Most of Afghanistan's monarchs have been Pashtun, as were several communist leaders and most of the Taliban. *Tajiks* comprise about 27 percent of the populace. Most of them live in northeastern Afghanistan next to Tajikistan, which was once a part of the Soviet Union and is now independent. Tajiks figured prominently in the Northern Alliance, the coalition of militias that helped defeat the Taliban in 2001. The *Hazara* constitute about 9 percent of Afghanistan's population. Most of them speak a variant of Persian and are Shiite Muslims, characteristics that give them fairly close ties with neighboring Iran. (About 84 percent of Afghans are Sunni Muslims.) *Uzbeks* make up about 9 percent of the population. Most reside in northern Afghanistan, along the border with Uzbekistan, another former part of the Soviet Union that is now an independent state. Uzbeks also formed part of the Northern Alliance.

About a half dozen other ethnic groups make up the remainder of the population. Most Afghan ethnic groups contain a variety of subgroups. The Pashtuns, for example, include two major confederations of tribes, about 60 tribes, and a large number of clans and other units. A social pecking order distinguishes prominent tribes and clans from less important ones. A person's clan or tribal identity can be more important in Afghan society and political life than the fact that one is simply Pashtun.

Rivalries among the larger ethnic groups have been common throughout much of Afghanistan's history. The Pashtuns' political dominance has often been resented by other groups. Tajiks and Uzbeks who joined the Northern Alliance to combat the Taliban not only were opposed to the Taliban's harsh regime but also were motivated by the fact that the Taliban were mostly Pashtuns. (By no means did all Pashtuns favor the Taliban, however.)

Afghanistan not only has considerable social heterogeneity; it also lacks the unifying gel of a shared national identity. Afghanistan is a land of separate, and often competing, nations; it has not had national unity on the basis of a commonly accepted *Afghan* nationhood. In the past, the diverse communities that composed Afghanistan were able to come together to fight and repel outside invaders. To that extent, there has been a minimal Afghan nationalism. But these groups have not been able—or willing—to forge a sense of internal nationalism based on a strong central state.

The governments that Hamid Karzai has put together since 2002 have been carefully balanced to include cabinet members from Afghanistan's leading ethnic groups. But some local leaders who

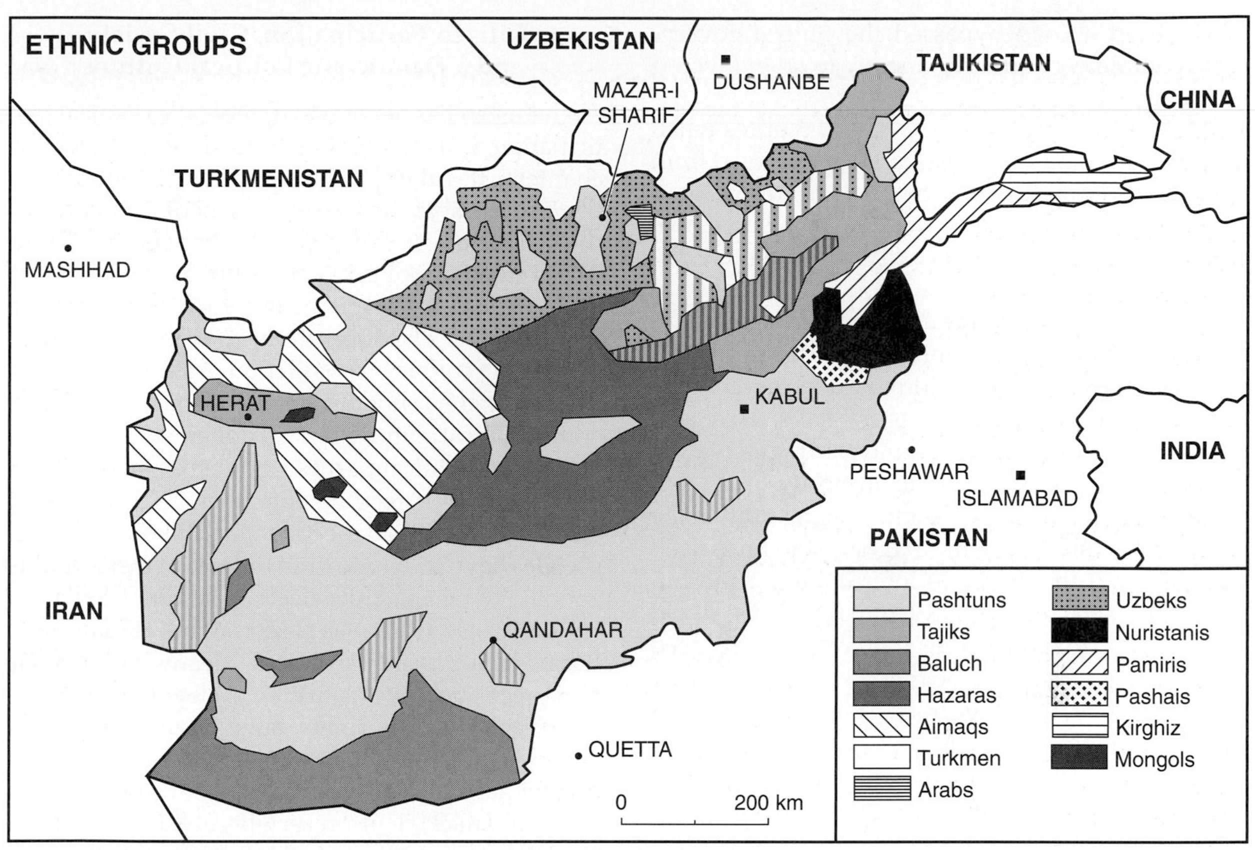


**Geographical Distribution of Ethnic Groups in Afghanistan**
*Source:* Barnett R. Rubin, *The Fragmentation of Afghanistan.* Map by Alain Mango.

represent large ethnic groups like the Uzbeks or smaller groupings like Pashtun tribes have grown restive at the thought of having to acknowledge the primacy of the new central government. Some of these leaders, supported by their own small armies, have asserted their own local authority and openly defied the new government in Kabul.

### National Wealth, Private Enterprise, and a Middle Class

Afghanistan is one of the poorest countries in the world. After more than twenty years of warfare, its economy is shattered. The majority of its people live on the margins of subsistence. Opium and heroin production are still the main sources of income in certain parts of the country. Although the U.S. government has spent hundreds of millions of dollars to discourage poppy growth in Afghanistan, a United Nations study reported in 2006 that opium cultivation had grown 59 percent over the previous year, accounting for more than 50 percent of Afghanistan's national income and 82 percent of the world's poppy cultivation. Afghanistan now supplies about three-quarters of the world's heroin, in spite of tough new anti-drug laws.[2]

Afghanistan never developed an industrial sector of any significance. It has also failed to develop a modern system of private enterprise based on dynamic manufacturing and service sectors. As a consequence, it has failed to develop a large and prosperous middle class. With a weak economic infrastructure, Afghanistan for most of its history has survived on foreign aid. Britain, the Soviet Union, the United States, Pakistan, Saudi Arabia—these and a handful of other foreign governments have taken their turns as Afghanistan's benefactors. Invariably, these external donors tended to play favorites: the British assisted friendly Afghan monarchs; the Soviets aided their communist comrades; Osama bin Laden's terrorist organization provided funds for the Taliban. At times the flow of aid from abroad bypassed the central government completely and went directly to other favored recipients.

Afghanistan's rulers also played favorites when it came time to distribute the aid they received from abroad. As Barnett Rubin has shown, throughout the country's history as a modern state, successive weak central governments actively promoted disunity by distributing these economic benefits to politically favored groups and local strongmen. Instead of integrating the entire population under a state that the citizenry could regard as legitimately their own, Afghanistan's leaders have used economic aid to deepen the country's fragmentation into separate fiefdoms of local authority.[3]

Now that a new government is being built in the wake of the Taliban regime, Afghanistan finds itself once again at the mercy of international contributors of financial aid. A joint United Nations–World Bank study concluded that the country will need $15 billion by the end of the present decade. By 2005 Afghanistan had received $8 billion in international assistance.

Until now, Afghanistan's economically disadvantaged masses have been marginalized from the political decision-making process in Afghanistan, with no real representation in its institutions of government and no effective organization to voice their interests. Unless the poor majority can see some hope of a brighter future, they may ignore democracy or reject it outright.

Women will have to reclaim the gains they registered before the Taliban came to power. (In the 1970s, a majority of Kabul University's students were women. And prior to the Taliban, a substantial proportion of the country's doctors and teachers were women.) The quality of any democracy that may take hold in Afghanistan in the future will be measured to a considerable degree by how much opportunity women will have in its governmental, economic, and social institutions. Despite the new constitution's pledge of gender equality, the gains women have made since the fall of the Taliban have occurred mainly in Kabul. In vast parts of the rest of the country, traditional mores still hold sway, keeping most women confined to their homes and subjected to the application of the harshest interpretations of Islamic law and local customs.[4]

## Citizen Participation, Civil Society, and a Democratic Political Culture

Afghanistan has never had democratic political participation or a civil society of the kind described in chapter 9. Its rulers have never allowed political parties or interest groups to serve as mediators between the central government and the population. To the extent that nonpolitical associations have been permitted to exist, they have not succeeded in creating attitudes of cooperation, tolerance, and trust among the country's population. As a consequence, Afghanistan has not developed the basis of a democratic political culture. Today Afghanistan has a multiplicity of political parties: about sixty parties were registered prior to the September 2005 legislative elections. But President Karzai and like-minded associates have sought to limit the role of these organizations. To that end, the electoral system used in the legislative elections was based on individual candidacies rather than party lists. Meanwhile, Afghan nongovernmental organizations devoted to democracy and human rights have been increasingly active, as have international NGOs. But civil society activists and aid workers have been threatened or attacked in areas where warlords or the Taliban are active; a few have been killed. Trade unions remain weak. The development of a vibrant democratic civil society and a widely shared democratic political culture will probably take decades.

## Education and Freedom of Information

Closely related to the task of building a democratic civil society and political culture is the need for an educational system that inculcates democratic values. Here, too, Afghanistan's record has not been exemplary. Although various enlightened monarchs promoted education, most of it was centered in the capital city of Kabul. The University of Kabul has been Afghanistan's main institution of higher learning, turning out the country's bureaucratic elite and many of its doctors, teachers, and other professionals. But these educational opportunities have benefited only a small minority of the population, mostly in the capital. In the rest of the country, large numbers of people never finished high school or even primary school. Moreover, once the communist-oriented factions took power in the 1970s, the entire education system was turned into a vehicle for ideological indoctrination. The Taliban, for their part, placed their own fundamentalist Islamic stamp on education, and they forbade women to be educated at all or to work outside their homes. Since 2001, academic freedom has prevailed. The constitution guarantees public education to all. It also asserts that the state will devise programs to promote the education of women. Children are now attending school in unprecedented numbers. Nevertheless, the Taliban and other Islamic fundamentalists still seek to prevent girls and young women from attending school; they have shut down schools in some areas for this purpose. Female illiteracy is close to 90 percent. The new constitution also guarantees freedom of the press and other media. Once again, however, signs of progress coexist with practices that diverge from the letter of the law. Hundreds of print publications are now available, and private radio and television stations are on the air. But Islamic fundamentalists and security agents have threatened and used violence against journalists and telejournalists who report unwelcome news or express unpalatable opinions, and this has led some media professionals to censor themselves. As a general rule, there is more freedom and tolerance in Kabul than in the provinces.

### A Favorable International Environment

As it has been for much of its history, Afghanistan is still heavily dependent on external powers. International financial assistance is vital for its economy; the U.S. and NATO troop presence is vital for its internal security. President Karzai and his team have leaned heavily on the United States and its allies, a policy that inevitably arouses the ire of anti-Western political forces. Afghanistan occupies center stage in the global war on terrorism: the inaccessible border region between Afghanistan and Pakistan provides shelter and support for al Qaeda and the Taliban. In 2006, President Karzai and Pakistan's President Musharraf accused each other of not taking sufficient action against terrorists in this border area. At a White House dinner intended to mend fences, the two leaders refused to shake hands. The incident highlighted the pressures that the outside world is placing on the two leaders, as well as the importance the world's democracies attach to the development of stable, effective governments in these countries. As far as Afghanistan is concerned, Barnett Rubin's prophetic warning, articulated several years before the events of September 11, 2001, remains as relevant as ever: "If the international community does not find a way to rebuild Afghanistan, a floodtide of weapons, cash, and contraband will escape that state's porous borders and make the world less secure for all."[5]

In conclusion, Afghanistan has made some observable progress in the quest for democracy, but it is still far from completing its democratization process, and farther still from qualifying as a "consolidated" democracy. Now let us turn to Iraq.

## IRAQ

### British Influence

With roots in ancient Babylon and Mesopotamia, Iraq came under the control of the Ottoman Empire in the sixteenth and seventeenth centuries. When the Ottoman sultan sided with Germany in World War I, British troops fought their way from Basra to Baghdad, evicting the Turks. On the basis of a prior agreement with France to carve up the Middle East, Britain assumed responsibility for most of Iraq in 1920 under a League of Nations "mandate."[6] Initially, Britain planned to enfold Iraq into the British Empire and run it much like India and other colonies. But pressure from President Woodrow Wilson, the liberal Democrat who hoped to "make the world safe for democracy," prompted the British to consider a looser form of domination. Iraqi resentment of any form of British rule was evident immediately, however. "From the beginning," an official British report later concluded, "the idea of a mandate has been abhorrent to nearly all educated elements in the country." Most Shiites followed a decree (*fatwa*) by a Muslim cleric calling for noncooperation with the foreign "crusaders." In 1920, Iraqis unleashed a revolt against the British presence. The country's socially diverse population—Arabs, Kurds, Sunnis, Shiites, urban professionals, and rural tribes—put aside their differences at least temporarily and joined together in what one historian has described as a "national war of independence." Although the British had 133,000 troops in place, it took them six months to subdue the rebellion. More than sixteen hundred British soldiers lost their lives; perhaps ten thousand Iraqis were killed. T. E. Lawrence, the English adventurer better known as "Lawrence of Arabia" for his exploits in support of Arab independence from British imperialism, commented that the "people of England have been led in Mesopotamia into a trap from which it will be hard to escape with dignity and honor. They have been tricked into it by the steady withholding of information." Winston Churchill, Britain's minister of colonial affairs, observed that British authorities had "succeeded in such a short time in alienating the whole country." It was Churchill who presided over the delineation of Iraq's new borders in 1921.[7]

Military casualties and mounting expenses quickly turned British public opinion against the Iraq mandate. By 1922 an overwhelming majority of the members of Parliament opposed keeping troops in Iraq indefinitely. The following year, the British government decided to pull out of Iraq in roughly four years. During that period British authorities essentially abandoned the quest for democracy and created the foundations of an elite-dominated constitutional monarchy under Faisal, the recently deposed king of Syria. Faisal was a Hashemite, the descendant of a family that traced its lineage to the Prophet Muhammad. For centuries the Hashemites had been custodians of the holy sites in Mecca and Medina. Faisal was also a Sunni, and his selection by a foreign power to be the monarch of a country whose majority consisted of Shiites and Kurds was bound to spark frictions. The British knew that Faisal's government did not control the whole country, but they were eager to get out. In 1929 Iraq was admitted to the League of Nations. And in 1932 Iraq formally became an independent state.[8]

Iraq's sovereignty was narrowly circumscribed, however, by agreements that allowed the British government to control the country's foreign policy and to keep a small contingent of troops on Iraqi territory. In addition, the British-controlled Iraq Petroleum Company gained exclusive rights over oil deposits in Iraq's Kurdish region. The British also interfered in Iraq's domestic politics by working through favored clients, mostly Sunni tribesmen and political elites in Baghdad. During the 1930s a succession of military coups and conflicts between Iraq's religious and ethnic communities kept the country in a near-constant state of instability. A large number of Iraqis—perhaps a majority—did not regard the British-imposed Hashemite monarchy as legitimate. Elections to the Iraqi national parliament tended to reinforce the dominance of the country's unrepresentative political elites. Between 1921 and 1936, the same forty Iraqi leaders controlled a succession of twenty-one cabinets. A clique of military officers eventually assumed power, exercising their influence either directly in government or behind the scenes. Meanwhile, the Iraqi military was developing into a source of smoldering anti-British sentiment. Many officers favored greater collaboration among the Arabs of the Middle East against foreign domination, an orientation known as *pan-Arabism*. After World War II broke out, military leaders staged a coup against the monarchy in 1941 and sided with Hitler's Germany and Mussolini's Italy. As Iraqi troops tried to take over a British air force base on Iraqi soil, Prime Minister Churchill's government dispatched troops. British troops once again fought their way from Basra to Baghdad, just as they had in World War I. Lacking support from Iraq's Shiites and Kurds, the largely Sunni military government collapsed and Britain installed a friendlier government for the remainder of the war.

After the war, Britain continued to exert its influence over Iraqi politics. Iraq formally remained a constitutional monarchy, but King Faisal died in 1933 and his son Ghazi, who succeeded him on the throne, died in 1939. Ghazi's heir was only three years old, and during the boy's childhood the monarchy was represented by relatively weak regents. In 1953 the young heir came of age and assumed the monarchy as King Faisal II. Between 1946 and 1958, Iraq was governed primarily by pro-British elites whose support came from Sunni landowners and the Baghdad professional class. Political, economic, and social inequality was rampant. Shiites and Kurds had only minimal representation in the executive and the legislature, even though they constituted the majority of the population. Election laws were frequently rigged to deliver a majority of seats to the ruling elite's supporters. Governments would dissolve parliament or postpone elections at whim, occasionally imposing martial law. Opposition parties were at times permitted, at other times proscribed or disbanded. Though socialist, communist, and pan-Arabist parties attracted some interest, they generally lacked mass support. Demonstrations in favor of workers' rights or other opposition causes were quickly suppressed and rarely had any effect. Land reforms aimed at helping the country's impoverished small farmers were put on hold. The country's most influential politician during these years, Nuri al-Said, at one point sought to create a one-party state modeled on Turkey under Mustafa Kemal Atatürk (see chapter 6). Meanwhile, with Cold War tensions spreading across much of the world, the United States supplanted Britain as the principal Western power in the Middle East. Nuri supported American efforts to keep the Soviet Union from exerting influence in the region. But as these events unfolded, key military officers—mostly Arab Sunnis—became increasingly disgruntled at the pro-British and pro-American policies of civilian Iraqi governments. They also strongly objected to the creation of the state of Israel in 1948. Inspired by pan-Arabist ideology and by the successful military coup in Egypt in 1952, a cabal of officers led by General Abdul Karim Qassem murdered Iraq's king and other members of the royal family, along with Nuri al-Said, in 1958. Power now passed directly to the military.[9]

The 1958 coup was supported by Iraq's Baath (Renaissance) Party, a pan-Arabist movement that had its roots in Syria. Several months later, a twenty-one-year-old Baath recruit named Saddam Hussein committed his first political murder.

### Saddam Hussein

Born in the centuries-old town of Tikrit in 1937, Saddam had a troubled childhood. His father disappeared at about the time of Saddam's birth, and his stepfather enjoyed humiliating and beating him. Saddam was raised by his uncle, a staunch Iraqi nationalist who was imprisoned by the British for supporting the 1941 coup. The author of a book entitled *Three Whom God Should Not Have Created: Persians, Jews, and Flies*, Saddam's uncle had a profound influence on his nephew's political views. Saddam turned to politics after failing the entrance exam for Iraq's leading military academy, joining the Baath Party at the age of twenty. At his uncle's behest, he murdered a political adversary in Tikrit in 1958.

Two years later, Saddam participated in an assassination attempt on General Qassem, whose policies ultimately disappointed his former Baath supporters. The plot failed and Saddam fled the country. In 1963 Qassem was ousted in a coup engineered by the CIA. Soon afterward, Saddam returned to Iraq and gradually gained control over the Baath Party's private militia. During the next several years Saddam emerged as a central figure as the Baath Party seized power and then split into rival factions. Through a succession of coups, assassination plots, and other intrigues, Saddam schemed his way into the highest reaches of power. By 1968 he was the second most powerful man in the country behind his close political ally, President al-Bakr, a relative from Tikrit.

With a firm grip on Iraq's main security apparatus, Saddam solidified his own power base and extended his reign of terror to elements of the Iraqi population. During the 1970s, while maintaining a low profile behind the president, Saddam took charge of key elements of Iraq's economic policies and foreign relations, earning an international reputation as "the strongman of Baghdad." In 1975 he met with France's prime minister, Jacques Chirac, and signed a deal to purchase a French nuclear reactor, promising that it would be used solely for peaceful purposes. In 1981 the Israelis bombed the reactor on suspicions that it was being used to build nuclear weapons.

As Saddam tightened his grip on the levers of political power, he also gained control over economic policy, starting with the crucially important oil sector. In the 1950s, Nuri al-Said's government had cut a deal with the British-owned Iraq Petroleum Company (IPC) to share revenues on a 50-50 basis. The British retained their control of the main oil fields, however. In 1972, Saddam's government nationalized (took over) the IPC in a broadly popular move that reflected widespread Iraqi resentment at foreign domination. Following the war between Egypt and Israel in October 1973 (see chapter 6), Middle Eastern oil-producing countries—including Iraq—took the lead in quadrupling world oil prices. Iraq's annual oil income rose dramatically over the course of the decade, from $1 billion in 1973 to $26 billion by 1980. Saddam spent increasing shares of these revenues on social welfare projects aimed at improving the quality of life for average Iraqis. The construction of hospitals, schools, museums, and other amenities expanded significantly, and small private businesses proliferated as Iraqis had more cash to spend. The middle class grew and prospered, especially in Baghdad; unemployment vanished. The 1970s would be remembered by many Iraqis in years to come as a "golden age"—in economic, if not political, terms.

Nevertheless, Saddam's economic policies always followed distinctly political objectives. Most of Iraq's rising national wealth was lavished disproportionately on Sunni areas; Shiites and Kurds got less than their fair share. And a huge proportion of the country's oil revenues was funneled into Saddam's burgeoning security apparatus. By the end of the 1970s, Saddam had built a police and military security empire comprising an estimated 677,000 members, a total that accounted for 20 percent of Iraq's labor force. The Baath Party grew apace: starting with only 300 adherents in the 1950s, it now had 25,000 members, and 5 million followers. Saddam surrounded himself with a small following of loyalists that included relatives and other associates from Tikrit.

In 1979 Saddam prevailed upon President al-Bakr to resign so that he could assume the presidency. Shortly after his inauguration Saddam convened a meeting of the country's political elite. As cameras recorded the macabre event, more than sixty officials were denounced for conspiracy. When the accused were escorted from the hall to meet their death, the lucky survivors chanted "Long live Saddam!" Within weeks as many as 500 high-ranking Baath Party officials had been executed. Saddam then launched a propaganda campaign exalting himself as the country's supreme ruler. Iraq had become a totalitarian state under a leader whose power knew no bounds. In a particularly gruesome incident, Saddam interrupted a cabinet meeting to shoot one of his ministers. The victim's dismembered body was returned to his wife the next day.

In 1980 Saddam declared war on Iran. He was concerned that the country's new rulers, who were Shiite clerics, were trying to destabilize his government. The conflict dragged on for eight years and consumed an estimated one million lives. Although the United States maintained its formal neutrality in the Iran-Iraq war, it was more concerned with threats from Iran and Syria than it was with Iraq. In 1983 the Reagan administration dispatched its special Middle East envoy, Donald Rumsfeld, to meet with Saddam and reestablish diplomatic relations. The administration was determined to take "necessary and legal" actions to keep Iraq from being defeated. Acting directly or in some cases through other states, the U.S. government saw to it that Saddam's regime was able to obtain anthrax, bacteria, fungus cultures, and other biological weapons, along with equipment capable of producing poison gas. A number of prominent American and European companies were involved in these transactions.[10] On several occasions the Iraqis used gas on Iranian troops. The United States also supplied Saddam with conventional weapons and cluster bombs. After a series of skirmishes in the Persian Gulf, U.S. naval vessels demolished most of Iran's navy, giving Saddam another military boost. And the U.S. supplied Iraq with satellite reconnaissance intelligence about Iranian troop deployments. In return, Saddam allowed the CIA to set up an office in Baghdad.

In the summer of 1988, their populations exhausted, Iran and Iraq made peace. Neither side had gained any territorial advantage.

In addition to fighting the Iranians in the 1980s, Saddam wreaked havoc on Iraqis suspected of disloyalty. The Kurds, who constituted 20 percent of Iraq's population, were a traditional target. Saddam had been fighting Kurdish separatists for years. In February 1988 he launched a ferocious military campaign against the Kurds. Chemical attacks on the village of Halabja in March killed an estimated five thousand men, women, and children. By September some 80 percent of the Kurds' villages were destroyed and perhaps as many as sixty thousand people lay dead. Approximately 350,000 Kurds fled to Iran and Turkey in hopes of escaping the onslaught.

Another victimized group was Iraq's Shiite Muslim community. Shiites were the religious majority in Iraq, composing more than 60 percent of the population. But Saddam and his cohorts were Sunnis. (Iraq's Arab Sunnis constituted little more than 20 percent of the population.) The regime ordered the torture and execution of Shiite clerics and expelled as many as a hundred thousand Shiites from Iraq. During the war, Saddam also ordered the execution of hundreds of Iraqi officers accused of poor performance on the battlefield.

By the end of the war, Iraq's economy was in shambles. The government owed $80 billion to foreign creditors, including neighboring Kuwait and other Arab states. Iraq's "golden age" was over, its middle class destitute. Strapped for cash, Saddam pressured the oil-rich Arab states of the Persian Gulf to boost world oil prices and provide Iraq with cash. When the Gulf states showed reluctance to comply with Saddam's demands, he invaded neighboring Kuwait in July 1990, incorporating it into Iraq. This attack was the opening salvo of the *Persian Gulf War*. The United States, fearful that Saddam would next attack Saudi Arabia and perhaps other states in the region, formed a coalition consisting of more than thirty countries and gained United Nations approval for military action. Starting in January 1991 the United States launched a devastating missile and aerial bombardment of Iraq. In February a massive ground assault by coalition forces evicted the Iraqi occupation force from Kuwait and pushed it back into Iraq. In forty-eight hours of fighting, Saddam's vaunted army suffered 100,000 casualties, his Soviet-built tank armada was largely destroyed, and his crack Republic Guard troops suffered heavy casualties.

Saddam Hussein nevertheless managed to achieve his primary goal: he remained in power. President George H. W. Bush's administration decided not to pursue Iraq's retreating forces back to Baghdad.[11] Saddam's troops were still strong enough at the end of the war to quash a Shiite uprising, killing tens of thousands. The Shiites believed that the United States might help them. But the U.S. government did not want to get involved in the conflict and American troops stood aside, allowing Iraqi forces to attack the rebels. The incident created long-lasting mistrust in the Shia community about American intentions. A mass grave in Al-Hillah, a Shia town, offered grim testimony to Saddam's brutality. In an attempt to deprive Shiite rebels of hiding places, Saddam ordered the draining of the marshes that had been the home of the "Marsh Arabs" in southern Iraq for centuries, destroying in the process an ancient way of life and a historic focal point of Shiism. Saddam next turned on the Kurds, harshly suppressing a new uprising that the Kurds mounted in the aftermath of the Gulf War. Shortly after these events, the United States and Britain established "no-fly zones" over Kurdish and Shiite territory, shooting down Iraqi warplanes that ventured into these areas. The Kurds established their own Kurdistan Regional Government under the Anglo-American umbrella, complete with civil liberties. Their local economy also blossomed, even though Saddam retained control of the region's oil fields.

During the 1990s Saddam survived several assassination attempts and engaged in summary executions of uncounted numbers of people. The Abu Ghraib prison and other gruesome sites became notorious for their torture chambers, where victims were pushed feet-first into wood shredders or suffered other horrible abuses. Human rights groups estimate that perhaps some three hundred thousand Iraqis disappeared in these years.

In 1995 Saddam had himself reelected president in a campaign in which he was the only candidate—scarcely a democratic confirmation of his regime's legitimacy. In the same year his two sons-in-law fled to Jordan and informed Western intelligence officials about Saddam's chemical weapons plants; one of them divulged that Iraq had come close to producing an atomic bomb before the Gulf War broke out. The two fugitives were coaxed by Saddam's regime to return to Iraq, where they were killed on orders from Saddam. Saddam's relatives were not the only ones to flee. During the reign of terror, approximately 20 percent of Iraq's population left the country.

International concern about Saddam's plans for weapons of mass destruction resulted in United Nations Security Council decisions to send inspectors to track down the banned weapons. Saddam's government admitted to possessing 30,000 tons of chemical agents, but in 1998 it terminated its compliance with the UN and the inspection teams were withdrawn. Meanwhile, Saddam spirited away billions of dollars in oil revenues for his private coffers and for the construction of seventy lavish presidential palaces. Most of this money was supposed to provide food and medicine for the population under a United Nations program. Members of Saddam's family, above all his sons Qusay and Uday, shared lavishly in Saddam's regime of personal power and self-enrichment.[12]

After September 11, key members of the Bush administration, including Vice President Richard Cheney, Secretary of Defense Donald Rumsfeld, Deputy Secretary of Defense Paul Wolfowitz, and other officials variously identified as neoconservatives, argued strenuously that the global war on terrorism required "regime change" by force in Iraq. The principal pretext for a military invasion was the assumption that Saddam still possessed chemical and biological weapons and was seeking material for nuclear bombs. After 1998 the Iraqis prevented subsequent UN inspection missions from doing their work. In 2001 the prospect that Saddam might provide some of these deadly substances to terrorists raised apprehensions that future terrorist attacks on U.S. territory, or on other American targets around the world, might prove far more devastating than the 9/11 tragedies.

Under prodding from the Bush administration, the United Nations Security Council on November 8, 2002, passed Resolution 1441, which demanded that Iraq permit weapons inspectors to enter the country within forty-five days. Building on sixteen previous Security Council resolutions requiring Iraq to disarm, Resolution 1441 reiterated the Council's earlier warnings of "serious consequences" if Iraq remained in material breach of its obligations to comply with UN demands. Iraq permitted a UN inspection team under Hans Blix to start its work within a few weeks. In January 2003, Blix reported after more than three hundred inspections that Iraqi authorities had not as yet provided convincing evidence to back up their claims that they had destroyed anthrax, bacteria, and other weaponizable agents whose quantities were known from previous UN inspections conducted in the 1990s. But Blix concluded that the hundred UN inspectors already in place had the ability to conduct daily inspections throughout the country. In subsequent reports he made it known that he wanted the inspections to continue.

The United States lacked reliable intelligence on Iraq's secretive weapons programs.[13] After Blix's report, the Bush administration accused Saddam Hussein of hiding weapons and obstructing the inspections. As the governments of Britain, Spain, Italy, Poland, and a number of other U.S. allies supported President Bush and agreed to send troops to Iraq, the leaders of France, Germany, and Russia opposed armed intervention and sought to block the U.S.-led invasion. Prime Minister Tony Blair, facing mounting anti-war sentiment in Britain, wanted another Security Council resolution explicitly sanctioning war. But President Jacques Chirac announced that France would use its veto in the Security Council to prevent UN approval of military action. Determined to proceed, President Bush declared in an address to the Iraqi people, "The day of your liberation is near." On March 21, 2003, as dawn broke in Iraq, 125,000 U.S. troops and 20,000 British forces launched their assault.

Over the next three weeks the ground campaign, augmented by more than 30,000 bombs dropped from the air, delivered the "shock and awe" that American military commanders had promised. Iraq's 700,000-man army, which included 400,000 Shiite draftees who had little reason to fight for Saddam Hussein, quickly disintegrated. Saddam's elite Republican Guards proved largely ineffective. But American forces encountered unexpectedly fierce resistance from the Saddam Fedayeen, a corps of fanatical defenders of Saddam's regime who were well trained in hit-and-run guerilla operations and adept at blending in with the civilian population. These unconventional tactics turned out to be a portent of the insurrection that would subsequently harass American forces in the years to come.[14] On April 9, American troops swooped into the center of Baghdad and helped friendly Iraqis pull down a large statue of Saddam Hussein. A little more than two weeks later, President Bush stood on the deck of the aircraft carrier *Abraham Lincoln* under a banner proclaiming "Mission Accomplished" and announced that the main combat phase of the war was over. U.S. troops had suffered 138 deaths, the British had lost 33. Tens of thousands of Iraqi soldiers were probably killed, and thousands of Iraqi civilians lost their lives, caught in the bomb blasts that leveled buildings and in the crossfire of ground fighting. An untold number of combatants and civilians were wounded or traumatized.[15]

Despite at least two bomb attacks on buildings where Saddam was reportedly seen, the Iraqi dictator managed to escape. In December he was caught hiding in a hole in the ground and was bound over for trial on charges of mass murder.

No sooner were American troops ensconced in the heart of Baghdad than pandemonium broke loose. Though U.S. forces tightly guarded the oil ministry, looters were left free to plunder other public buildings and private establishments throughout Baghdad. The National Museum of Antiquities was spoliated of thousands of priceless artefacts dating back fifty-five hundred years to Sumerian times. Although ordinary citizens participated in the rampage, venting their pent-up rage at Saddam or taking advantage of the lack of security personnel on the streets, criminal elements may also have been at work. Shortly before the impending U.S. invasion, Saddam had opened his prisons, releasing thousands of criminals and political prisoners.

The Pentagon selected a retired general, Jay Garner, to head the U.S.-led *Coalition Provisional Authority* in post-Saddam Iraq. But when the mayhem that roiled Baghdad showed no signs of abating, and violence began spreading to other cities, the Bush administration replaced Garner with *L. Paul (Jerry) Bremer III*, an energetic former diplomat with experience in counterterrorism. Before he left Washington to take up his new assignment, Bremer was shown a study indicating that the United States would need 500,000 troops to impose order after Saddam's removal from power. In addition to completing the elimination of Saddam's regime by hunting down hundreds of his top henchmen, the troops would be needed for other duties, including policing Baghdad and other population centers; sealing Iraq's borders with Iran, Syria, Jordan, and Saudi Arabia against encroachments from terrorists; and protecting 4,000 miles of pipelines in Iraq. The figure of 500,000 troops was in line with earlier estimates by several U.S. generals in leadership positions. But Secretary of Defense Rumsfeld and like-minded generals believed it was possible to take over Iraq with a far smaller strike force. Moreover, Bush administration planners were convinced that, once Saddam was gone, there would be a quick and orderly transfer of power to an Iraqi government. The president and his team openly repudiated the idea of "nation building" by American peacekeepers; for them, Iraq would not be another Bosnia-Herzegovina (see chapter 6). They had planned before the war to withdraw most U.S. forces within a few months after the end of combat, with the intention of leaving only about 30,000 troops in Iraq by September 2003. They turned down proposals for an international police force and for the emplacement of 5,000 U.S. police personnel. The administration further estimated that, with Iraq's oil exports expected to finance reconstruction, no more than $3 billion in financial assistance to Iraq would be necessary over the course of the next three years.[16]

Bremer arrived in May 2003 as the administration's presidential envoy. He immediately got down to business trying to fashion a viable democratic government that would prove legitimate in the eyes of the Iraqi people. Bremer would have his work cut out for him. He soon realized that the Pentagon's plans to pull troops out of Iraq quickly and ignore the tasks of nation building were a "reckless fantasy."[17] He also agreed that the United States would need about 500,000 troops to impose order on a country whose seething population was heavily armed with guns and explosives. Within months of his arrival, a full-blown insurgency would rear up in the "Sunni triangle," which harbored Saddam loyalists, and in various Shiite areas. The anti-American and anti-British violence would soon be exacerbated by sectarian violence between Sunnis and Shiites. Bremer also found that Iraq would require a financial investment from the United States considerably higher than the $1 billion per year initially earmarked for the next three years. Electrical grids in Baghdad and other parts of the country were in disrepair, resulting in electricity cutoffs that irked Iraqi citizens, especially in the intense summer heat. Water facilities were also damaged, and incessant attacks on oil pipelines by saboteurs limited the amount of oil available for export and the amount of gasoline available to Iraqi drivers. Iraqis recalled that Saddam Hussein had managed to get electricity and other amenities up and running only a few weeks after the Gulf War in 1991, and they wondered why the United States, the most powerful country in the world, could not do the same.

Bremer also quickly learned how difficult it would be to create the foundations of democratic governance in a fragmented society that had never before experienced a democracy worthy of the name. Let's see how our ten conditions for democracy illustrate some of the problems Iraq has encountered.

### Elites Committed to Democracy

After achieving legal independence in 1932, Iraq was governed for the next seventy years by political elites who represented only a small fraction of the population. Opposition leaders were ignored, harassed, imprisoned, exiled, or killed. Saddam

Hussein wiped out or drove into exile an entire generation of potential leaders who advocated any alternative to his murderous rule. One of the most severe problems hampering Iraq's transition to democracy today is the acute shortage of home-grown political leaders dedicated to democratic principles. And Iraq has no charismatic pro-democracy leaders capable of galvanizing a mass following like India's Mohandas Gandhi or South Africa's Nelson Mandela.

Shortly after the Gulf War of 1991, the United States began cultivating a group of political exiles from Saddam's Iraq, along with anti-Saddam militants inside Iraq, in hopes that they might one day form the nucleus of a democratic government after Saddam left the scene. With American support, in 1992 the group formed an umbrella organization known as the *Iraqi National Congress.* From the outset, the U.S. government and Saddam's opponents endeavored to be inclusive of Iraq's main ethnic and religious groups. Sunnis, Shiites, and Kurds were all represented in the National Congress in its first year. Each of these three large social groups was represented by two or more political organizations, however, complicating the task of reaching consensus on goals and strategy. Nevertheless, the Iraqi National Congress right from its foundation dedicated itself to human rights, the rule of law, and a "constitutional, democratic, and pluralistic Iraq."

Personal rivalries, ethnic and religious dissension, and disputes over strategy splintered the organization over the course of the 1990s. The Iraqi National Congress was gradually whittled down to a smaller organization headed by *Ahmad Chalabi* (AHK-mahd CHAAH-lah-bee). Chalabi was a secular Shiite from a wealthy Baghdad family that had left Iraq in 1956 for Britain and then the United States. A math prodigy, he earned degrees from MIT and the University of Chicago. In the 1970s Chalabi established a bank in Jordan, but he was later convicted of violating Jordanian banking laws. With an eye to returning to Iraq some day in a political capacity, Chalabi befriended politicians and Defense Department officials in Washington in the 1990s. Elements of the State Department and CIA were more skeptical of him. It later turned out that Chalabi's contacts in Iraq were a prime source of false information about Saddam's weapons of mass destruction.

In December 2002, as it geared up for the invasion, the Bush administration sponsored a meeting in London of exiles and Iraq-based dissidents to prepare for the imminent collapse of Saddam's government. Several hundred attendees chose a *Leadership Council* consisting of seven key individuals. Chalabi represented his Iraqi National Congress. *Ayad Allawi*, another secular Shiite, headed a group called the Iraqi National Accord. Allawi had once worked in Saddam's regime, but he broke away from the dictator and moved to London, where Saddam's agents nearly succeeded in hacking him to death with an axe. A rival of Chalabi, Allawi worked with the CIA before joining the Leadership Council. Two rival Kurdish leaders—*Massoud Barzani* and *Jalal Talabani*—whose militias had clashed at various times in the 1990s were also on the Leadership Council. Rounding out the seven-member group were an elderly Sunni lawyer representing the small National Democratic Party; a widely respected Shiite dissident of long standing, *Ibrahim al-Jafari*, who headed the Shiite Islamic Dawa Party; and two members of another Shiite Islamic party. The factions represented on the Iraqi Leadership Council—two rival secular Shiite groups, two rival religious Shiite groups, two rival Kurdish groups, and only one Sunni—prefigured the divisions that would plague the U.S.-backed political forces who would seek to create democracy in Iraq.

Moreover, the Leadership Council had no women, Christians, or Turkmen. (Women made up 60 percent of Iraq's population. Christians and Turkomans were small minorities, together accounting for less than 5 percent of the population.) Seeking a larger and more representative group, American and British authorities in July 2003 replaced the Leadership Council with a twenty-five-member *Iraqi Governing Council*, which included the seven members of the Leadership Council along with new participants representing Iraq's diverse society. Bremer worked patiently with Governing Council members during his year in Iraq. All were in principle committed to democracy, but they found it exceedingly difficult to overcome their differences and reach agreement on specific policies. Compromise proved elusive. Decision-making paralysis set in, requiring Bremer to prod the Iraqis into action and broker deals in late-night bargaining sessions. On more than one occasion these agreements would be repudiated by one faction or another a day or two later. Some members expected the United States to confer power instantly on the Governing Council. To this end, Chalabi lobbied influential contacts in the United States on his own behalf. As Bremer remarked, the various Iraqi factions he dealt with viewed the political process as a zero-sum game: one side's gain inevitably meant another side's loss (see chapter 2).

Compounding these problems was the gnawing reality that the members of the Governing Council were largely unknown to many Iraqis who had grown up under Saddam Hussein. Those who had spent long years in exile were held in lower esteem by the population than those who had courageously remained behind in Iraq to endure Saddam's repression. Meanwhile, as time wore on with no improvement in security or basic services, public acceptance of the American authorities—which was fairly high among most Iraqis in the first months after the war—deteriorated rapidly. By 2004, 92 percent of Iraqis viewed the United States and other coalition authorities as "occupiers"; only 2 percent considered them "liberators."[18] As attitudes toward the Americans hardened, public acceptance of the Iraqi leaders who collaborated with them soured as well. The Iraqi Governing Council simply lacked legitimacy in the eyes of a large number of Iraqi citizens. Two of its members were assassinated by insurgents.

Among local elite figures, Grand Ayatollah *Ali Husseini al-Sistani* was perhaps the cleric most widely respected by the country's large Shia majority. The fact that he had remained in Iraq and suffered ill treatment at the hands of Saddam's regime enhanced his reputation. U.S. and British authorities were therefore relieved when Sistani expressed his support for the overthrow of Saddam and urged Shiites to cooperate with the coalition authorities. Sistani believed that the Shiite clergy had committed a historic mistake by withdrawing from Iraqi politics after the 1920 revolt against the British mandate. But he was reluctant to get too close to the Americans or British. He declined to meet personally with Bremer or his successors, preferring to deal with them through intermediaries. Sistani was a "quietist"—a Shiite cleric who believed that religious authorities should not be directly engaged in politics but should instead try to influence the state indirectly, allowing political figures to govern. (For an explanation of Shiite political attitudes, see chapter 13.) Sistani did not want an Iranian-style Islamic Republic for Iraq; he was willing to accept civilian leaders. Sistani's main goals were to make sure that Iraq's Shiites were able to translate their majority status into equivalent political power, and to incorporate elements of Islamic law into the country's legal structure without going to the extremes of an Islamic theocracy. Like other Iraqi leaders, however, Sistani was reluctant to compromise. He would agree to political bargains only to back out of them soon afterward. Several other prominent Shiite ayatollahs shared Sistani's general views.

Not all Shiite clerics went along with Sistani, however. One of the most recalcitrant was *Muqtada al-Sadr*, a Shiite cleric still in his late twenties or early thirties. Despite his youth Sadr commanded respect as the heir of revered Shiite clergymen. In 1980 one of Sadr's cousins, an admired Islamic scholar, was forced to watch Saddam Hussein's torturers rape his sister, then suffered execution as nails were pounded into his forehead. In 1999 Saddam's security agents assassinated Sadr's father, an esteemed ayatollah, shooting him in his car along with Sadr's two brothers. Although these tragedies reinforced Sadr's revulsion toward Saddam's dictatorship, he had no intention of cooperating with American and British authorities. In the summer of 2003 Sadr issued a religious decree (*fatwa*) calling on his followers to wage a jihad (holy war) against the U.S.-led coalition. Drawing on large numbers of impoverished and uneducated youths in the Shiite slums of Baghdad, once known as "Saddam City" but recently renamed "Sadr City," Sadr organized a militia called the Mahdi Army. Over the next several months his armed bands took over mosques and staged demonstrations in several Shiite communities. His actions posed a direct challenge, not only to the coalition authorities, but also to Sistani, whom Sadr viewed as a rival. Sadr's family was Arab; Sistani was of Persian descent. Sadr was implicated in the assassination of another respected Shiite ayatollah. Bremer wanted Sadr arrested and his Mahdi Army disbanded, but the U.S. military, the CIA, and British officials were reluctant to confront him, fearing an uncontrollable backlash. By 2006 Sadr's

Iraqis display ink-stained fingers after voting.

rebellion had grown in strength as Iraq's sectarian violence intensified, with the Mahdi militia sending death squads to attack Sunnis. Thus Iraq's Shiite leadership was by no means united on the desirability of democracy.

Sunnis were especially reluctant to enlist in the cause of democratization. Saddam Hussein had ruled Iraq on the basis of his own handpicked Sunni elite, institutionalized in the Baath Party, the army, and his special security organs. After the Gulf War, Saddam purchased the support of Sunni tribal chiefs in Iraq's rural heartland with handouts and funds for local economic development. Millions of Sunnis and their families owed their livelihood and their privileged status in Iraqi society to Saddam's regime. It therefore came as a shock to many of these people when Bremer, in one of his first major decisions after arriving in Baghdad, ordered the dissolution of the Baath Party and the security organs.

The "de-Baathification" policy was targeted at the party's top leaders, who constituted only 1 percent of its total membership. The policy's aim was to prevent Saddam's most powerful loyalists from returning to positions of authority in the new Iraq. But the Governing Council's initial implementation of the policy went overboard. Tens of thousands of people who had joined the party mainly because it opened career opportunities in the educational system and the civil bureaucracy were barred from future employment for a year or more. Bremer's decision to disband the Iraqi army and other security organs was equally controversial. Bremer was advised by Shiite and Kurdish leaders that their communities would never accept the continuation of the existing Iraqi military and its officer corps. Moreover, the Iraqi army had essentially disbanded itself during the recent three-week war. Bremer and the Governing Council thus decided to create a new Iraqi Army. But hundreds of thousands of Iraqi soldiers, finding themselves destitute, staged demonstrations demanding to be paid. The coalition authorities paid them, but large numbers of displaced Iraqi troops, Republican Guards, and other security personnel joined the nascent resistance movement, taking their weapons with them. Since 2003, the United States has had a difficult time training a new Iraqi Army that is prepared to stand up to the various resistance fighters and sectarian marauders who have turned Baghdad into a killing field, and who have at times taken control of Fallujah, Ramadi, and other cities.

In sum, the effort to build a democratically oriented political elite in post-Saddam Iraq has proved arduous. Although there are respected and capable leaders from Iraq's diverse communities who are committed to a democratic future, they have had a difficult time surmounting their divisions and making compromises. Without a spirit of compromise among a country's political elites, there can be no successful consociational democracy (see chapter 7). And without timely decisions, there can be no effective government. These problems have proved especially debilitating in the quest for new state institutions.

### State Institutions

Since the collapse of Saddam's regime, Iraqis have had the rare opportunity to create a democracy from scratch. It would not be an easy birth. The ethnic and religious divisions represented in the Governing Council resulted in sharp disagreements on fundamental issues. Would Iraq be a unitary state, a federal state, or a loose confederation? Would it be an Islamic or a secular state? From the beginning, Iraq's new government had "stateness" problems concerning the very nature of the state.

A number of Iraqi leaders wanted the United States and its coalition partners to confer power on Iraqis as rapidly as possible, but they differed on how this should be done. After protracted

**Aftermath of Car Bombing in Sadr City District of Baghdad, July 2006**

negotiations, it was finally agreed that the Governing Council would prepare an interim constitution known as the Transitional Administrative Law. This task, marked by considerable wrangling over divisive issues, was completed in March 2004. Working with the Governing Council and UN envoy Lakhdar Brahimi, Ambassador Bremer next orchestrated the selection of an interim Iraqi government under the secular Shiite leader Ayad Allawi. Faced with mounting domestic and international pressure to transfer sovereignty to the Iraqis, the U.S.-led Coalition Provisional Authority formally transferred legal authority to Iraq's interim government on June 1.

The next step big step was the election of a *Transitional National Assembly*, which took place on January 30, 2005. Despite daily attacks by Iraqi insurgents and foreign terrorists led by Abu Musab al-Zarqawi, a Jordanian affiliated with al Qaeda, more than 8.5 million Iraqis courageously trooped to the polls in the country's first post-Saddam elections. After casting their ballots, voters proudly displayed the purple ink on their fingers certifying that they had voted. In the "purple revolution," voters could choose from among 111 parties and multiparty coalitions in filling 275 Assembly seats. The electoral system was a variant of party-list proportional representation, with a hurdle amounting to less than 0.4 percent of the votes cast (see chapter 8). The interim constitution provided that at least 25 percent of the Assembly members had to be women; in the end, women won 32 percent of the seats. The election's biggest winner was a group of Shia parties running jointly as the United Iraqi Alliance. Together these allied parties won 48.2 percent of the vote and 51 percent (140) of the seats. A collection of mostly Kurdish parties, the Kurdistan Alliance, finished second with 25.7 percent of the vote and 27.3 percent (75) of the seats. (The Kurds now constituted about 15 to 20 percent of Iraq's population.) A group of Sunni parties running together as the Iraqi List won a disappointing 13.8 percent of the vote and 14.5 percent (40) of the seats—figures that were out of proportion to the Sunnis' 17 to 20 percent share of the population.

The headline story of the first elections was the low voter turnout in Sunni areas. Whereas 71 percent of Shiite voters and 85 percent of Kurdish voters had cast their ballots, only 6 percent of Sunnis bothered to vote. Many nonvoters heeded the call of influential Sunni leaders to boycott the election. Some were intimidated by warnings of terrorist attacks on voters. Moreover, the nationwide proportional representation system, with Iraq as a whole constituting one large electoral "district," played into the hands of the large Shiite majority. The election results forced Sunnis to confront the reality that, in a democratic Iraq, they would always be in the minority. Following the elections, the Transitional National Assembly elected Kurdish leader Jalal Talabani to Iraq's new presidency, a largely ceremonial position, and the popular Shiite politician Ibrahim al-Jafari to the more important post of prime minister.

The Transitional Assembly's most important duty was to draft Iraq's permanent constitution. Although the deputies agreed that the new Iraq would be a "democratic, federal, representative republic," serious disputes broke out over the role of Islam and the rights of minorities. A number of Shiite delegates wanted the constitution to affirm that Islam was "the" main source of Iraq's laws and that no laws contrary to Islamic law could be passed. But the largely secular Kurdish representatives opposed excessive religious power for the "black turbans" of the Shiite clergy. And women feared that Islamic law would give them fewer rights than they had under Saddam Hussein, subjecting them to discrimination and potentially harsh treatment at the hands of conservative clerics, judges, and husbands. Ultimately, the draft described Islam as "the national religion and a basic foundation for the country's laws" (as opposed to "*the* basic foundation"), and it guaranteed freedom of religion. But it also permitted "experts in Islamic jurisprudence" to become Supreme Court justices, and it allowed individual households to decide whether to use Islamic law in family matters such as divorce, inheritance, and the right of husbands to beat their wives.

Kurds were anxious to retain the wide autonomy they had won in recent years through provisions permitting regional governments. But Sunnis were distraught at their declining power and eager to secure a share of revenues from the oil fields that are located mainly in the Kurdish and Shiite areas. Hence they wished to preserve a centralized state. Sunnis tended to view Iraq as an Arab state with a Kurdish minority, and some of them wanted Arabic to be the country's only official language. Kurds, however, conceived of Iraq as a multinational state with two official languages, Arabic and Kurdish. The final draft reflected the Kurdish position. It even permitted the Kurds to write a constitution of their own that would supersede Iraqi law. Shiites also wanted to enhance their local autonomy.

With U.S. Ambassador Zalmay Khalilzad working behind the scenes to cobble together eleventh-hour compromises, the much-delayed draft constitution included a new clause permitting constitutional amendments to be legislated after the next parliament was elected at the end of 2005. This clause allowed some Sunni leaders to support the draft in hopes of changing it later. Many Sunnis were looking for a way to end their alienation from the emerging political system, which was increasingly dominated by Shiite-Kurdish cooperation. But other Sunnis staunchly opposed the draft, hoping to defeat it in the national referendum to be held on October 15, 2005. By law, if more than two-thirds of the voters in any three of Iraq's eighteen provinces had voted against the constitution, it would have failed. On the day of the referendum, 65.7 percent of Iraqi's registered voters turned out to cast their ballots. Turnout in Sunni areas was much higher than in January. With more than 10 million votes cast, 78.6 percent voted in favor of the constitution and 21.4 percent—mostly Sunnis—voted against it. More than two-thirds voted no in two Sunni-dominant provinces, but not in a third one. The constitution passed.

Iraq's new constitution established a *parliamentary system* of government (see chapter 8). The system rests on a bicameral legislature consisting of the *Council of Representatives* and the *Council of the Union*. The Council of Representatives elects the *president* of the Republic by two-thirds vote. The Council of the Union thus far has minimal powers. The president is the "symbol of the nation's unity" and has largely ceremonial functions, but is authorized to appoint the leader of the majority party in the Council of Representatives to be *prime minister*. If the president's first nominee fails to form a government, the president picks another one. The prime minister has the primary executive responsibility for national policy, serves as commander in chief of the armed forces, and appoints the cabinet, subject to the approval of the Council of Representatives.

With a new constitution in place, Iraqis next went to the polls on December 15, 2005, only two months after the referendum, to vote for their new Council of Representatives. To mollify the Sunnis, the electoral law was changed to permit each province to send a certain number of deputies to the Council, thus assuring Sunni districts of fair representation. Thus Anbar Province, a hotbed of the Sunni insurgency, would send nine deputies to the legislature; Salahuddin Province would elect eight deputies, and so on. (Baghdad would elect fifty-nine deputies.) Within each province, parties and multiparty coalitions were to be elected on the basis of proportional representation. Of the Council's 275 seats, 230 would be elected in this manner. The remaining 45 seats would be distributed to individual candidates who failed to win seats in the provincial elections, a procedure intended to favor small parties. A party had to receive at least forty thousand votes—a threshold less than 1 percent of the votes cast—to win a seat.

In the run-up to the election, the main Shiite and Sunni political forces reorganized their party coalitions. The *United Iraqi Alliance*, the multiparty alliance of Shiite religious parties that had won the most seats in the previous elections, opened its doors to Muqtada al-Sadr's faction, endorsing Sadr's efforts to integrate his militia into Iraq's security forces. This agreement represented a deal between Sadr and *Abdul Aziz Hakim*, the influential

Shiite cleric who headed the multiparty United Iraqi Alliance along with his own group, the Supreme Council for the Islamic Revolution in Iraq (SCIRI). The Hakim and Sadr families had a long history as rivals in the Shiite community, though they were also linked by marriage.[19] The two archrival secular Shiite leaders, Ahmad Chalabi and Ayad Allawi, led separate party coalitions: Chalabi organized a new grouping called the National Congress Coalition, and Allawi led a coalition of secular-oriented Shiites and Sunnis, the *National Iraqi List*. Three Sunni religious groups that had boycotted the January elections formed an electoral alliance called the *Iraqi Accordance Front*. A multiethnic secular group of Sunni parties formed a new coalition called the *Iraqi National Dialogue Front*. The Kurdish secular organizations remained together as the *Kurdistani Gathering*, joined by Christian and Turkmen parties. All told, more than seven thousand candidates were in the running, listed under more than three hundred political groups and nineteen multiparty coalitions and single tickets.

With interest in the election running high despite escalating violence, 12.4 million Iraqis—some 80 percent of registered voters—turned out to vote in the December 2005 elections. Turnout was high in Sunni areas, with many voters having learned a hard lesson from their boycott of the January poll. Once again, the Shiite religious bloc won a solid plurality with 128 seats, only 10 seats short of a voting majority. The Kurdish coalition retained its position as the second largest group in the legislature, winning 53 seats. The Sunnis' Iraqi Accordance Front placed third but won only 16 percent of the seats. Allawi's secular Shiite-Sunni group finished fourth. And the new secular bloc of Sunnis, the Iraqi National Dialogue Front, finished fifth. Chalabi's group did not win any seats. As in January, the three largest party blocs each represented one of the main contending groups in Iraqi society: Shiites, Sunnis, and Kurds. The results of the December 2005 elections are displayed in table 10.1.

As the newly elected Council of Representatives convened in March 2006, the large Shiite religious coalition nominated Ibrahim al-Jafari, the country's prime minister since the January 2005 elections, to remain in his job. But Kurdish and Sunni parties immediately objected, criticizing Jafari as ineffective. Both groups were also intent on limiting the Shiites' growing power. After several weeks of intense pressure, Jafari abandoned his quest for a second term. In his place, the Shiite bloc nominated a little-known member of their own ranks, *Jawad al-Maliki* (jah-WEHD ahl-MAHL-ee-kee). Although he had no previous executive-level experience in the new Iraq, Maliki was quickly confirmed by the parliament as prime minister in April. Born in 1950, Maliki had fled Saddam's Iraq in 1979, spending twenty-three years in exile, primarily in Syria. By agreement among the main parties to end the long political stalemate, the Kurdish leader Jalal Talabani was reelected president of Iraq and a Sunni was selected speaker of the house.

By far the most important factor weighing on Iraq's new state was its inability to secure its monopoly of the means of violence, a fundamental requirement of any state. In 2004 there were 866 terrorist attacks; in 2005 the number rose to 3,500. High-fatality incidents were also on the rise. In September 2005, rumors of a car bomb triggered a stampede of Shiite worshipers, killing nearly a thousand. More than thirteen hundred people died in less than a week in February 2006 in sectarian fighting that followed the bombing of the Shiites' famed Golden Mosque in Samarra. Despite the killing of the terrorist Zarqawi in June 2006, the number of attacks by insurgents and sectarian death squads rose to their highest levels yet in the following summer and fall. Many victims were tortured. Human rights organizations estimated that there was more torture taking place in 2006 than in Saddam Hussein's time. With multiple incidents of

**TABLE 10.1**

**Iraq's Council of Representatives**

(275 Seats; Elected December 15, 2005)

| Party/Multiparty Alliance | % Vote | % Seats | Seats |
|---|---|---|---|
| United Iraqi Alliance | 41.2 | 46.5 | 128 |
| Kurdistani Gathering | 21.7 | 19.3 | 53 |
| Iraqi Accordance Front | 15.1 | 16.0 | 44 |
| National Iraqi List | 8.0 | 9.1 | 25 |
| Iraqi National Dialogue Front | 4.1 | 4.0 | 11 |
| Others[a] | 5.1 | 5.1 | 12 |

[a]Seven parties that received less than 2 percent of the vote each.
*Source:* IFES, www.electionguide.org.

violence occurring on a daily basis, and with sectarian militias proliferating, it was evident that the fledgling Iraqi state could not protect its citizens, a reality that seriously threatened its legitimacy. Iraqis were increasingly turning to their own arms or to tribal justice to exact vengeance on their enemies. The New Iraqi Army was still in training and remained dependent on more than 100,000 American and British forces. The new Iraqi police force was penetrated by militia groups. Iraq's interior minister, a Shiite with responsibility for domestic security, personally incorporated Shiite militias into the police. The police force was also riddled with corruption. And Maliki's government was increasingly dependent on Muqtada al-Sadr, whose political group had twenty to thirty deputies in the legislature and four posts in Maliki's cabinet. Instead of confronting Sadr's Mahdi Army, Maliki in 2006 relied on its support, to the consternation of U.S. and British officials.

At the same time, cases of corruption were multiplying in the civilian government. (See table 4.1 for Iraq's ranking on the Corruption Perceptions Index.) The national judiciary was an emerging bright spot, in part because Saddam had not controlled the judges as mercilessly as he dominated his political and security organs. But Saddam made a mockery of his own trial with disruptive outbursts. Despite the creation of hundreds of local councils, local governments lacked funding and were helpless in the face of terror. These and other discouraging developments made it clear that, in spite of widening elite and public support for the electoral process and parliamentary government, Iraq in 2006 still had a long way to go before it could claim to have functioning democratic state institutions.

### National Unity

As the preceding pages have amply demonstrated, Iraq is a seriously divided country. There are deep splits between its main groups as well as within them. The ethnic split between Arabs and Kurds, with many Kurds longing for complete independence, raises obvious questions about whether there exists an *Iraqi* national identity that bridges over these divisions. Conflicts between religious Sunnis and Shiites show few signs of abating after nearly fourteen hundred years. Sectarian violence is sharpening these differences and breaking up mixed neighborhoods in Baghdad and other places where Sunnis and Shiites once lived together peacefully. There are also divisions within each religious camp. Some Sunni religious authorities want to participate in democratic processes, while others oppose those processes, in some cases supporting the insurgency. On the Shiite side, several contending factions have their own militias and they attack each other. For their part, the Kurds have also been historically divided between rival factions. Christians have long been a persecuted minority in Iraq, and they are divided between Chaldean and Assyrian Christians. Turkmen are another minority. Gypsies have also been subject to persecution. Jews were persecuted and driven out of Iraq both before and after the founding of the state of Israel in 1948, and anti-Israeli sentiment remains high among most Iraqis. There are other small minorities as well. Divisions between religious and secular Iraqis are also very deep. In addition to these ethnic and religious axes of conflict, Iraq's Arabs are further fragmented along tribal lines. There are about 150 tribes in the country, about 30 of which are especially influential. Perhaps as many as half of all Iraqis identify more closely with their tribe than with the national government. Clans and families that are subsumed under these tribes also claim intense loyalties.

In view of these sharp divisions, one has to wonder whether Iraq can endure as a single state. Some people have called for its breakup into separate Kurdish, Sunni, and Shiite entities as the only way out of the spiral of violence.[20] In October 2006 the lower house passed into law a measure that would allow Iraq's provinces to form autonomous regions starting in 2008. Kurdish deputies and most Shiite deputies (including Hakim's powerful SCIRI group) voted for the law, hoping that it will transform Iraq into a loose federation with a highly autonomous Kurdish zone in the north and a Shiite zone in the south, each possessing valuable oil reserves. Sunni legislators bolted from the parliament before the vote was taken, fearing that a federated Iraq with a weak central government will leave the oil-poor Sunni region without adequate access to Iraq's oil revenues. Even Muqtada al-Sadr's Shiite group walked out of the session, voicing objections to the federation plan. Whatever organizational structure Iraqis ultimately adopt, it is evident that the country's internal disunity is obstructing its

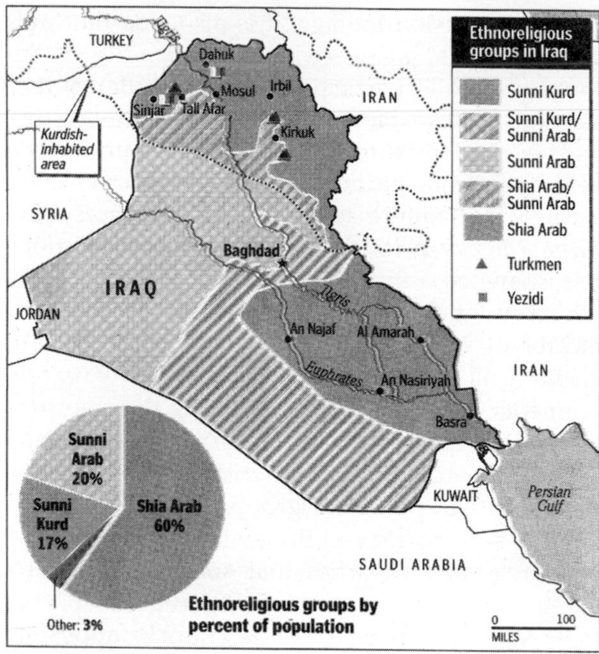


**Iraq's Ethnoreligious Divisions**

path to democracy. Iraq risks the danger of slipping from the tyranny of the Sunni minority over the Shiites and Kurds to the tyranny of the majority over the Sunnis. But one should not discount the possibility that wise leaders and an exhausted population may eventually decide that the give-and-take of democracy is the best alternative to unremitting bloodshed or a new dictatorship.

### National Wealth

Iraq's national wealth is based on "black gold": after Saudi Arabia, it has the world's second largest known oil reserves. It also has large deposits of natural gas. But the Iraq-Iran war of 1980–1988 devastated the economy, forcing the government to borrow nearly $100 billion from abroad. After the Gulf War of 1991, the United Nations imposed economic sanctions on Saddam's regime, further damaging the country's economy. Starting in 1996, the UN's oil-for-food program sought to reduce economic hardships for the Iraqi people, but corruption on the part of the program's managers and Saddam's ruling elite siphoned off oil revenues that were intended to help the population. Meanwhile, world oil prices tumbled. By the time the U.S.-British invasion of Iraq took place in 2003, the economy had been in decline for a number of years. Since the invasion, the turbulence that has rocked the country has further damaged the economy, despite the infusion of tens of billions of dollars in American assistance. Sabotage operations by terrorists have hampered oil production, which is struggling to get above pre-invasion levels. The country's technical infrastructure—including the oil industry, power grids, transport networks, and other vital components—is in severe disrepair. Continuing violence has severely disrupted the economy's recovery. Unemployment is up. Inflation is skyrocketing as goods become scarce and shopping is fraught with danger. Efforts by the United States and other aid donors to rebuild Iraq have made some progress. New schools have been built and the infrastructure is being modernized; the marshes used by the Marsh Arabs have been replenished. But the unstable security situation has slowed these efforts considerably. Iraq's parlous economic predicament can only increase public dissatisfaction with the government's ineffectiveness, inevitably complicating the democratization process.

### Private Enterprise

Saddam Hussein placed considerable responsibility for the economy in the hands of the state and its Baath Party overlords. In the first year after the 2003 invasion, U.S. envoy Bremer issued an order calling for the privatization of most of the Iraqi economy. The all-important oil industry would remain in state hands for the time being, however. Bremer also decreed that foreigners could purchase virtually all of Iraq's assets, a controversial decision that raised fears of a U.S.-led takeover of the country's most productive assets by outsiders. The tumult of the post-Saddam period has significantly slowed down privatization efforts and foreign investment. It is still too early to tell if privatization will promote democracy or transfer control of the economy to foreigners, along with perhaps a handful of wealthy Iraqis, fostering new resentments that may prove harmful to democracy's development.

### The Middle Class

Iraq's rising oil revenues in the 1970s promoted the emergence of a sizable middle class, especially in Baghdad and other urban areas. But the Iran-Iraq war, the Gulf War, the UN sanctions regime, and the corrupt oil-for-food program had a cumulatively devastating impact on Iraq's middle class. As a senior political figure in the Iraqi Governing Council lamented to Jerry Bremer, "It was a tragedy that Saddam destroyed the middle class, the reservoir of moderation." Since 2003, violence and economic hardships have only aggravated conditions for Iraq's shrinking middle class, including business owners, scientists, doctors, lawyers, educators, and civil servants. Most of these people are secular in their political orientation and oppose the rise of religious forces that seek to impose some form of religious authority on the country. Many favor democracy in principle, even though they may have joined the Baath Party in Saddam's era in order to pursue their careers. But in the midst of bombings, kidnappings, and other intolerable realities, Iraqis were leaving their country at the rate of 100,000 a month by 2006. With the exodus of the middle class, a potential bulwark of democracy was disappearing.[21]

### Support of the Disadvantaged for Democracy

The "disadvantaged" in Iraq includes a long list of people who can rightly claim to have suffered discrimination or economic deprivation under Saddam Hussein, and who can make an equally valid claim to a disadvantaged status in the aftermath of Saddam's departure. If we narrow our focus on this group just to those who are economically disadvantaged—the urban and rural poor—it appears evident that support for democracy among them is tenuous at best, and in some quarters nonexistent. Many impoverished and poorly educated people have flocked to the cause of Muqtada al-Sadr and other authority figures who offer handouts from their own coffers and the psychic rewards of combating the American and British occupiers as well as domestic enemies. Some have joined the Baathist insurgents, religious militias, or the roving gangs of career criminals. Without a radical improvement in the economy, it is not likely that the members of Iraq's economic underclass will move toward democracy, unless they are led there by leaders they respect.

### Citizen Participation, Civil Society, and Political Culture

Although the carnage in Iraq's streets can be witnessed every day in front-page photographs and chilling television footage, it is also true that millions of Iraqis, an overwhelming majority of the country's adults, participated in two parliamentary elections and a referendum in 2005, braving the most frightening threats to their safety. Sunnis who held back from participating in the first election learned that failure to vote in a democracy can carry a heavy price. Iraq's post-Saddam elections also spawned a multiplicity of parties, multiparty coalitions, and individual candidates—another indicator of widespread political participation. But virtually all of these parties represent fairly narrow segments of the electorate, reflecting the country's endemic social divisions. Such narrowly representative parties are called *particularistic* parties, because they represent particular groups or interests. Thus far Iraq's democracy-in-the-making has produced few broad-based parties that span the country's ethnic and religious divides. Broad-based parties that seek to maximize their vote count by appealing to a diversity of groups are called *catch-all* parties: they try to catch all the votes they can get. As a general rule, catch-all parties are better for democracy because they tend to bring diverse voters and interests together. Particularistic parties tend to perpetuate conflict. (Particularistic and catch-all parties are discussed further in chapter 11.) Iraq appears to have a long way to go before a major catch-all party attracts widespread popular support.

A growing number of Iraqis are taking part in nongovernmental organizations, interest groups, and other organs of civil society. The U.S.-led Coalition Provisional Authority actively promoted the development of these organizations, and it invited NGOs from the United States and other countries to work in Iraq. Centers for democracy, human rights, and women's rights have sprung up in various parts of the country, along with NGOs like Women for a Free Iraq and the Iraq Foundation for Development and Democracy. Trade unions have also reemerged from under the tight lid of Saddam's repression. Advisors and activists have conducted forums on democracy, attracting thousands of Iraqis avid for information and discussion.[22]

Precisely when these elements of democratic participation will forge a widely shared democratic political culture, based on such indispensable values as tolerance and compromise, remains to be seen. Iraq has never had a democratic political culture.

A succession of leaders have taught the populace to expect little more than deceit, manipulation, prejudice, and brutality from politics. The disturbing realities of aggression and retribution that today coexist in Iraq with elections and parliamentary procedures suggest that the struggle to create a durable democratic culture will be a long one.

### Education and Freedom of Information

In the town of Al-Hillah, a Shiite cleric named Sheik Farqat al-Qizwini hopes to build a new university open to Muslims, Christians, and Jews. The spirit behind this plan reflects the new freedom of thought and expression to be found in Iraq's academic institutions after decades of subservience to Baathist controls. At the same time, there is evidence that political parties in Kurdish and Shiite areas are controlling educational life within their respective regions. Press and broadcast freedom has resulted in more than a hundred print publications and more than a dozen private television stations. Unrestricted Internet usage is on the rise. On the negative side, journalists have been targeted for assassination and threats of violence against media outlets have induced some publications to engage in self-censorship. Academic and press freedoms are vital components of democracy. It appears that in Iraq's conflicted post-Saddam era, there are conflicting signs of unprecedented freedom and ominous opposition to freedom, with correspondingly mixed effects on the future of democracy.

### A Favorable International Environment

Perhaps the most salient factor that distinguishes the attempt to build democracy in Iraq from most other cases of democratization is that democracy came to Iraq from the outside, riding the Humvees of an American and British invasion force. Like Afghanistan, Iraq had virtually no organized political movement dedicated to democracy when the invading forces got there. In the past, the United States had intervened militarily in other countries more than thirty times since the start of World War II, in many cases with the avowed goal of promoting the development of democracy. America's record in these interventions has been decidedly mixed. After World War II, West Germany and Japan developed into stable democracies. But Hitler's Germany and Japan's military-dominated imperial government both surrendered to the United States and its allies; Saddam's government never formally surrendered. Postwar Germany was governed by U.S., British, and French occupation authorities for four years; Japan was under U.S. occupation for seven years. In later decades, U.S. intervention eventually led to democracy in Panama, Guyana, and a few other countries. But there were failures as well, such as South Korea, Vietnam, and Haiti.[23] Political, military, and other conditions in these and other cases varied considerably; none were exactly like Iraq. Whether the United States succeeds in helping the Iraqis become democratized by imposing democracy from abroad remains to be seen. The record, however, suggests that homegrown democracy movements tend to fare better than those implanted from the outside.

Iraq's internal situation is also affected by its location in the vortex of the greater Middle East. Iraq's porous borders have allowed terrorists to infiltrate the country from Syria and Jordan. Iran's Islamic theocracy has meddled in Iraqi politics, providing various forms of assistance to Shiite groups that it favors. The governments of Sunni countries like Saudi Arabia and Egypt are scarcely predisposed to democracy. Opposition to Israel runs high in Iraq, as was evident in Baghdad street demonstrations supporting Hezbollah's attacks on Israel in the summer of 2006. Opposition to Israel generally translates into opposition to the United States. These regional factors tend to counter rather than promote Iraq's democratization efforts.

By the end of 2006, more than 340 American troops had died in Afghanistan and more than 3,000 had fallen in Iraq. The U.S. government had spent upward of $400 billion on these countries. Despite these enormous human and financial costs, both Afghanistan and Iraq still faced stiff challenges to their democratization processes. In 2006 it was still unclear how long American troops would remain in these volatile and unpredictable nations. As the American public and politicians in both parties turned increasingly against an indefinite U.S. military presence in Iraq, a CIA report indicated that the war and occupation there had increased the global terrorist threat. Government sources indicated that

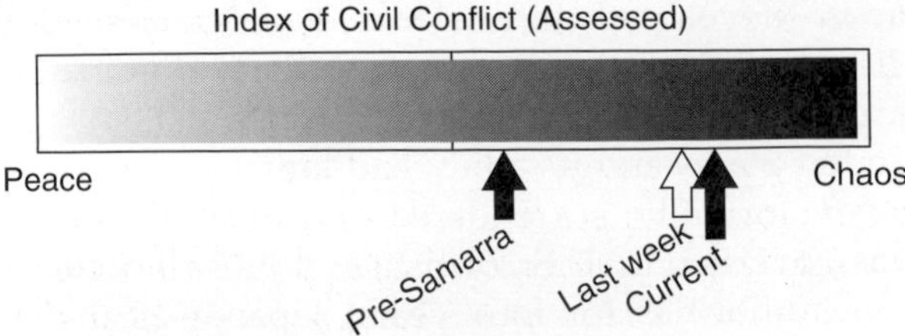


**FIGURE 10.1 U.S. Central Command's Index of Civil Conflict in Iraq**
*Source: New York Times*, November 1, 2006.

the security situation in Iraq would probably worsen in 2007. In October 2006 the U.S. military released a bleak assessment of Iraq's immediate future, illustrated by a barometer showing an accelerating slide toward chaos since the bombing of the Golden Mosque in Samarra in February (see figure 10.1.)[24] Fears that Iraq might share the fate of Lebanon, which endured a sectarian civil war for fifteen years, were in the air. In November, when an Iraqi court sentenced Saddam Hussein to death by hanging for ordering the executions of 148 Shiite men and boys in the town of Dujail in the 1980s, Shiites celebrated the verdict but Sunnis took to the streets to protest it. The execution took place on December 30, 2006.

By September 2006, 71 percent of Iraqis favored the withdrawal of U.S. troops within a year or less, and 79 percent said the Americans were having a negative influence on their country.[25] Civilian casualties were mounting uncontrollably. One study by American and Iraqi epidemiologists estimated that more than 600,000 Iraqis had died in the violence that occurred between the invasion of March 2003 and the fall of 2006.[26]

At this stage, the next developments in the countries examined in this chapter cannot be easily predicted. In the long run, however, this much is certain: the success—or failure—of democracy in Afghanistan and Iraq will ultimately depend on the people of those countries themselves and on those who succeed in leading them.

## NOTES

1. *Freedom in the World 2006* (New York: Freedom House, 2006), 14–22; Human Rights Watch, www.hrw.com; Amnesty International, www.amnesty.org; the International Crisis Group, www.crisisgroup.org; and the U.S. State Department's Bureau of Democracy, Human Rights, and Labor, accessible at www.state.gov.
2. *Washington Post*, September 3 and 19, 2006.
3. Barnett R. Rubin, *The Fragmentation of Afghanistan: State Formation and Collapse in the International System* (New Haven: Yale University Press, 1995). See also idem, *The Search for Peace in Afghanistan: From Buffer State to Failed State* (New Haven: Yale University Press, 1995); and Ralph Magnus and Eden Naby, *Afghanistan: Mullah, Marx, and Mujahid* (Boulder, Colo.: Westview, 2002).
4. Visit HelpAfghanWomen.com and www.rawa.org.
5. Rubin, *Fragmentation of Afghanistan*, 280. See also idem, *Afghanistan's Uncertain Transition from Turmoil to Democracy* (New York: Council on Foreign Relations, 2006).
6. David Fromkin, *A Peace to End All Peace: The Fall of the Ottoman Empire and the Creation of the Modern Middle East* (New York: Avon, 1989).
7. William R. Polk, *Understanding Iraq: The Whole Sweep of Iraqi History, from Genghis Khan's Mongols to the Ottoman Turks to the British Mandate to the American Occupation* (New York: HarperCollins, 2005), 75, 77, 184.
8. Toby Dodge, *Inventing Iraq: The Failure of Nation Building and a History Denied* (New York: Columbia University Press, 2003), 1–41.
9. Charles Tripp, *A History of Iraq*, 2nd ed. (Cambridge: Cambridge University Press, 2002), 30–147. Faisal II's son, Sharif Ali Bin Hussein, survived the attack and was taken to Britain. He returned to Iraq in 2003 and offered assistance to U.S. authorities.
10. For sources, see Polk, *Understanding Iraq*, 132–33, 146.
11. In his memoirs, President George H. W. Bush wrote that he refrained from marching on Baghdad and deposing Saddam in 1991 because the United Nations had not authorized the United States to do so and because he did not want the United States to be "an occupying power in a bitterly hostile land." George Bush and Brent Scowcroft, *A World Transformed* (New York: Knopf, 1988), 489. Defending this decision, Defense Secretary Richard Cheney said in 1991, "Once you get to Baghdad, it's not clear

what you do with it. It's not clear what kind of government you put in place of the one that's currently there now. Is it going to be a Shia regime, a Sunni regime, a Kurdish regime? Or one that tilts toward the Baathists, or one that tilts toward Islamic fundamentalists? How much credibility is that going to have if it's set up by the American military there? How long does the United States military have to stay there to protect the people that sign on for that government, and what happens once we leave?" (Quoted by Richard Reeves, www .uexpress.com/richard reeves/.)

**12.** Con Coughlin, *Saddam: His Rise and Fall* (New York: Harper, 2005) and *Saddam: King of Terror* (New York: HarperCollins, 2002); Efraim Karsh and Inari Rautsi, *Saddam Hussein: A Political Biography* (New York: Free Press, 1991); Samir al-Khalil, *Republic of Fear: The Politics of Modern Iraq* (Berkeley: University of California Press, 1989); and Yitzhak Nakash, *The Shi'is of Iraq* (Princeton: Princeton University Press, 1994).

**13.** A main source of U.S. intelligence turned out to be a fabricator code-named "Curveball." James Risen, *State of War: The Secret History of the CIA and the Bush Administration* (New York: Free Press, 2006), 115–19. Ultimately, no chemical or biological weapons were found in Iraq, nor was there any evidence of radioactive material.

**14.** For an account of the war, see Michael R. Gordon and General Bernard E. Trainor, *Cobra II: The Inside Story of the Invasion and Occupation of Iraq* (New York: Pantheon, 2006), 182–433.

**15.** For an account of the war and its immediate aftermath as experienced by Iraqi citizens, see Anthony Shadid, *Night Draws Near: Iraq's People in the Shadow of America's War* (New York: Henry Holt, 2005).

**16.** On planning for the war and its aftermath, see Thomas E. Ricks, *Fiasco: The American Military Adventure in Iraq* (New York: Penguin, 2006), 3–111. Also Gordon and Trainor, *Cobra II*, 3–163.

**17.** L. Paul Bremer III, *My Year in Iraq: The Struggle to Build a Future of Hope* (New York: Simon and Schuster, 2006), 12.

**18.** Cited in Fouad Ajami, *The Foreigner's Gift: The Americans, the Arabs, and the Iraqis in Iraq* (New York: Free Press, 2006), 26. Another 2004 poll revealed that 80 percent of Iraqis had a negative view of the U.S.-led Provisional Authority (*Washington Post*, May 13, 2004).

**19.** *Washington Post*, April 19, 2006.

**20.** For example, see Peter W. Galbraith, *The End of Iraq: How American Incompetence Created a War Without End* (New York: Simon and Schuster, 2006).

**21.** Adnan Pachachi's remark is in Bremer, *My Year in Iraq*, 379. Also *New York Times*, October 2, 2005, and *Washington Post*, January 23, 2006.

**22.** Larry Diamond, *Squandered Victory: The American Occupation and the Bungled Effort to Bring Democracy to Iraq* (New York: Henry Holt, 2005).

**23.** South Korea, which the United States defended against aggression in 1950–53 at a cost of 37,000 American lives, was ruled by the country's military until the late 1990s. South Vietnam, whose defense resulted in 58,000 American casualties, fell to the communists in 1975. In 1994, after threatening a military invasion, the U.S. government restored Haiti's legitimately elected president to power after he was deposed and exiled in a military coup. But the once-popular president was forced to resign after governing through fraud and intimidation, and his successors have created one of the world's most authoritarian regimes.

**24.** *New York Times*, September 24 and November 1, 2006; Bob Woodward, *State of Denial: Bush at War, Part III* (New York: Simon and Schuster, 2006).

**25.** The poll was conducted by the University of Maryland's Program on International Policy Attitudes for World Public Opinion and released in October 2006. The same poll showed that 92 percent of Iraq's Sunnis and 62 percent of Shiites approved of attacking U.S.-led forces. It also revealed that 95 percent of Shiites and 93 percent of Kurds had a "very unfavorable" view of al Qaeda, while 77 percent of Sunnis had either a "very unfavorable" or "somewhat unfavorable" view of the terrorist network. See www.worldpublicopinion.org/pipa.

**26.** *Washington Post*, October 11, 2006; Eugene Robinson, "Counting the Iraqi Dead," *Washington Post*, October 13, 2006. Other casualty estimates were much lower. See *New York Times*, October 30, 2005.

CHAPTER 11

# PEOPLE AND POLITICS

## Participation in Democracies and Nondemocracies

One of the central premises of democratic theory is that citizens will take full advantage of their opportunities to participate actively in political life. They will make their views known to the governing authorities and hold them fully accountable for their actions. Contrary to these expectations, however, most people who live in democracies choose not to participate very much. One study of political participation in the United States conducted in the 1960s labeled 30 percent of the adult population "apathetics" because they knew virtually nothing about politics. Another 60 percent were labeled "spectators" on the grounds that they paid some attention to politics, though they varied in degree. Many spectators paid only minimal attention to political goings-on. Only about 5 percent to 7 percent could be termed "gladiators" who actively participated in political campaigns in presidential election years; in other years this group of political activists would typically fall to 1 percent to 2 percent of the population. Counting the gladiators and the most politically active spectators, only about 20 percent of the population regularly engaged in discussions about political issues; they were labeled "opinion leaders." These figures have remained substantially the same right up to the present day. In the 1990s, fewer than 10 percent of Americans campaigned for candidates and fewer than 5 percent took part in a political demonstration or protest activity.[1] In other democracies, too, most people do not get actively involved in political life.

Nevertheless, as a general rule a large number of citizens, quite often the majority, will turn out to vote in periodic elections. Voting is the main form of mass participation in virtually all democratic countries. Voter turnout rates differ from country to country, however. As table 11.1 indicates, the United States, on average, ranks next to the bottom of twenty-two major democracies, and at the very bottom in off-year congressional elections.

Why don't people who have the privilege of democratic participation take advantage of it? One explanation was hypothesized by Mancur Olson in his acclaimed book *The Logic of Collective Action.*[2]

## THE LOGIC OF COLLECTIVE ACTION

According to a traditional assumption about democracy, people who are free to engage in open political activity will take advantage of this opportunity by organizing or joining groups that seek to exert pressure on state decision makers in behalf of some common

**TABLE 11.1**

**Electoral Turnout in Selected Democracies**

The figures show average turnout, measured as a percentage of the voting age population, in countries that have had fair elections to the lower house of parliament since at least the 1950s.[a]

| Country | 1950s | 1960s | 1970s | 1980s | 1990s |
|---|---|---|---|---|---|
| Australia | 83 | 84 | 85 | 83 | 82 |
| Austria | 89 | 90 | 88 | 87 | 77 |
| Belgium | 88 | 87 | 88 | 89 | 84 |
| Canada | 70 | 72 | 68 | 67 | 59 |
| Denmark | 78 | 87 | 86 | 85 | 82 |
| Finland | 76 | 85 | 82 | 79 | 69 |
| France | 71 | 67 | 67 | 64 | 61 |
| Germany | 84 | 82 | 86 | 79 | 74 |
| Iceland | 91 | 89 | 89 | 90 | 88 |
| India | 61 | 59 | 61 | 63 | 63 |
| Ireland | 73 | 74 | 82 | 76 | 70 |
| Israel | 79 | 82 | 81 | 81 | 84 |
| Italy | 93 | 94 | 94 | 93 | 90 |
| Japan | 74 | 71 | 72 | 71 | 61 |
| Luxembourg | 62 | 70 | 71 | 63 | 59 |
| Netherlands | 88 | 90 | 85 | 82 | 73 |
| New Zealand | 91 | 84 | 83 | 86 | 79 |
| Norway | 78 | 83 | 80 | 83 | 76 |
| Sweden | 77 | 83 | 87 | 86 | 81 |
| Switzerland | 61 | 53 | 43 | 40 | 37 |
| United Kingdom | 79 | 75 | 74 | 74 | 72 |
| United States | 49 | 56 | 46 | 46 | 43 |
| Presidential years | 57 | 62 | 54 | 52 | 52 |
| Off years | 43 | 48 | 41 | 38 | 37 |

[a]Turnout for *registered* voters tends to be somewhat higher in all countries and significantly higher in the United States (see figure 3.4).
*Source: Voter Turnout for 1945 to 1997: A Global Report on Political Participation* (Stockholm: International Institute for Democracy and Electoral Assistance, 1997), and this organization's website, http://www.idea.int.

group interest or demand. But do they? In *The Logic of Collective Action,* Mancur Olson suggested that people in large groups usually do not behave this way. Rather than join in collective action with like-minded citizens, even people with serious grievances usually do nothing. Personal inaction is often preferred to collective action.

Olson argues that such inaction is a *rational choice* for the individual. Most social scientists define *rationality* as behavior aimed at maximizing (or at least increasing) one's expected gains and minimizing (or reducing) one's expected costs or risks. As applied to the **logic of collective action**, Olson hypothesizes that the average person will reason as follows when making up her or his mind about whether to get involved in some sort of group political activity:

- **The costs and risks of such action may be too high** (one will have to sacrifice time, comfort, or perhaps money, and one may even run the risk of being jailed, beaten, or killed if the activity is illegal).
- If a group has already been formed to militate in behalf of the individual's interests, **one's own contribution may not be all that necessary** anyway ("If 10,000 are demonstrating in the streets or signing petitions, what difference will one more make?").
- If the group fails to change government policy favorably, those engaged in the collective action gain exactly what those who did not engage in it get: nothing. But if the group succeeds, **the nonparticipant shares in the collective gains equally** with the hardy activists who bore the costs and risks of action (lower taxes, extra social security benefits, a more responsive government, and so on).

This logic is particularly applicable in the case of *collective goods:* material or nonmaterial goods that are shared by large segments of the community rather than being divisible among individuals. Social security increases, national security, and an improved environment are examples.

Given these considerations, Olson maintains that most people will opt to be nonparticipating "free riders" who let others do the dirty work of political activity for them. "The paradox," Olson concludes, "is that . . . large groups, at least if they are composed of rational individuals, will *not* act in their group interest." This conclusion is strikingly counterintuitive, since it contradicts the commonsense assumption that rational people will take action in their own self-interest, or in the interest of some group to which they belong, if given the opportunity to do so.

---

Although Olson's rational choice logic explains why many people do not take part in political activity, it does not explain why people *do* participate. In fact, tens of millions of people around the world will at least vote every few years, and millions of others will get more actively involved in politics in one way or another. And though they may constitute a small minority in their own country, significant numbers of ordinary citizens at times feel sufficiently seized by a political issue to get up and demonstrate, sign a petition, or take part in much riskier behavior by challenging the ruling authorities in the streets. Politics is not just a matter of costs and risks; it also offers serious opportunities and benefits.

## FORMS OF PARTICIPATION

Although the *degree* of political participation in democracies can vary considerably, the *forms* of mass participation are generally the same. Typically they include *voting, political parties, interest groups,* and *social movements*. Let's examine these and a few additional modes of popular participation and look at some relevant hypotheses on these topics.

### Voting

The scientific study of elections is called *psephology;* this term comes from the Greek word for "pebble." (In ancient Greek city-states, people voted by depositing colored pebbles into containers.) We are particularly interested in finding *patterns* in electoral behavior. What types of people, for example, vote for the various parties competing for power? One answer to this perennially topical question is that, as a general rule, people tend to vote primarily in accordance with their socioeconomic status: wealthier people tend to vote for the more conservative parties (such as the Republicans in the United States, the Conservative Party in Britain, or the Christian Democrats in Germany), and the less well-to-do tend to vote for left-of-center parties especially concerned with social welfare (such as the Democrats in the United States, the Labour Party in Britain, or the Social Democratic Party of Germany). As with any frequently observed pattern, however, there are bound to be exceptions. In fact, voting patterns in most democracies are affected by a multiplicity of factors. While income levels frequently play a major role in influencing how people vote, so do variables such as party identification, ethnicity, religion, gender, age, and ideology.

There are also numerous factors that affect voter *turnout*. In addition to personal attributes such as one's educational level, interest in the campaign, and sense of political efficacy (Does my vote really matter?), patterns of voter turnout are also affected by such things as voter registration requirements, the tightness of the race, the effectiveness of political parties in getting out the vote, and even the day of the week on which elections are held (Americans vote on Tuesdays, most Europeans vote on Sundays). The generally lower turnouts in the United States compared with other countries listed in table 11.1 are also due in part to the fact that Americans are asked to vote more often, and for more political offices, than their European counterparts are. Elections to the U.S. Congress take place every two years, compared with every four to five years for comparable offices in most other democracies, and in the United States there are more elections for local and regional offices than there are in most other democracies.[3]

**Do Voters Know What They're Doing?** It is a standing premise of democratic theory that voters need to be aware of what they are doing when they vote. Without a minimum level of political knowledge on the part of the electorate, the act of voting may be meaningless and the very notion of popular sovereignty illusory. Democracy thus rests on the assumption that voters are rational. Are they?

According to the standard variant of rational choice theory, individual voters are "rational" to the extent that they

1. know what their own preferences and priorities are (lower taxes, less crime, a cleaner environment, and the like);
2. gather as much information as they can about the various candidates and understand their positions on the issues, and they also understand what the likely consequences will be if this or that candidate gets elected; and
3. vote for those candidates who are most likely to satisfy those priorities once in office.

Some rational choice theorists have maintained that voters are truly rational only when they seek to promote their own material self-interests. This rather narrow definition stresses personal selfishness as an essential ingredient of rationality. Voters with this type of orientation are rational if they vote for candidates who would lower their taxes or increase their social security payments, for example; they are less interested in the general welfare of the community. In a famous study published in 1957, Anthony Downs argued that voters in democracies think and act pretty much like consumers in a market economy: they know what type of product they want, they shop around and gather information about alternative models, they look at how the available products will affect their wallet, and they make a rational selection based on what is best for them. Thus each citizen, Downs hypothesized, "casts his vote for the party he believes will provide him with more benefits than any other." Politicians, for their part, behave like sellers, rationally adjusting their "product lines" (their policies and campaign promises) so as to attract the most "buyers" (voters). Democratically elected governments and opposition parties, Downs wrote, will always act in their own self-interest: they will espouse only those policies that maximize votes, whether or not such policies are good for society in some ideal sense.[4] Do voters really behave this way?

## HYPOTHESIS-TESTING EXERCISE: Are Voters Rational?

### Hypothesis

The hypothesis we are testing is that *voters behave on the basis of strict rationality*, as defined in the preceding paragraphs.

### Variables

The *independent variable* is *strict rationality*. The *dependent variable* is *individual voting behavior*.

### Expectations

If the hypothesis is right, then we would expect voters (a) to know what their own preferences and priorities are, and to emphasize their economic self-interest; (b) to be knowledgeable about the issues and candidates; and (c) to vote for candidates who are the most likely to "deliver" what the voter wants.

### Evidence

A landmark empirical study based on election returns and interviews with voters provided considerable evidence that most Americans were anything but rational in their actual voting activity. *The American Voter*, a comprehensive analysis of elections in the late 1940s and 1950s undertaken by a team of political scientists at the University of Michigan, showed that most Americans did not vote on the issues at all. The single most important variable accounting for how the majority of Americans voted in this period was *party identification*. Those who identified themselves as Democrats tended generally to vote for Democratic Party candidates, and those who identified themselves as Republican tended to vote accordingly. Only about 20 percent of the electorate changed their long-term loyalties from one party to another. This "expressive" explanation of voting behavior stressed the voters' psychological attachments to parties: the choices people made in the voting booth were an expression of their identification with the general long-term orientation of a particular political party (e.g., as "pro-business" or "pro-social welfare"). Voters might also identify with the party's general stance on the issues of the day and with the broad images—positive or negative—they had of the competing candidates. Thus, people did not necessarily vote on the basis of a detailed knowledge of the issues or a strategic comparison of the candidates' positions, as the most stringent rational choice criteria would assume. More recent studies have updated the concept of expressive voting.[5]

Another political scientist suggested that only about 20 percent of the U.S. citizenry are reasonably well informed about political issues, a group known as the *attentive public*. By contrast, the *mass public* has considerably less political knowledge. Additional studies have portrayed most British and French voters in a similar light.[6]

Students of U.S. voting behavior in more recent decades have somewhat altered this unflattering portrait of the average American citizen. While acknowledging that very few voters meet the strict criteria for rationality defined earlier, some scholars argue that high levels of political knowledge and analytical sophistication may not be necessary for voters to make up their minds in a reasonable fashion. Most voters, they contend, have a "gut" understanding of the candidates and issues, derived in part from campaign slogans and other cues they get from politicians and the media. These simple understandings, based on information shortcuts rather than on extensive reading and analysis, are good enough for them to make electoral choices that are logically consistent with their own political preferences, however vaguely they may be articulated. Without being perfectly rational, most voters, according to this view, are not entirely irrational, either. They act in accordance with a kind of *limited rationality* (also called *low-information rationality* or *bounded rationality*).[7]

Some analysts have disputed the notion that Americans and voters in other democracies are as ignorant about politics today as voters may have been thirty or forty years ago. Russell Dalton points out that the time costs of obtaining information about political issues are much lower nowadays than they used to be, thanks in large part to the expansion of television as an easily accessible source of news for most people. In addition, there is now a larger pool of well-educated people who have the political sophistication to process political information intelligently. Many of them no longer need to take their cues from political parties about how to vote: they can make up their own minds. The "cognitive mobilization" of ever increasing segments of the electorate, according to Dalton, thus accounts for the rise in independent voters and for the corresponding decline in party loyalties that has been observed in the United States and Western Europe in recent decades. Other scholars have confirmed the rise of independent-minded "critical citizens" in today's democracies.[8]

Finally, a number of theorists have taken a broader view of rationality than the one suggested by the strict concept stressed in our hypothesis. They maintain that voters can still be considered rational even if their election-day priorities place community goals rather than personal ones at the top of the list. If a voter wants to promote environmental protection or national security, that person may still be considered a rational voter as long as she votes for candidates who openly espouse such goals. Such community-minded individuals would still gain some personal benefit if their general-welfare goals are achieved (such as clean air or a stronger national defense). Even Anthony Downs came around to this broader view of rationality, amending his original position.[9]

### Conclusions

The evidence for the rational-voter hypothesis is *mixed*. Much of it is inconsistent with the strict concept of rationality, which requires a highly knowledgeable, politically sophisticated electorate motivated largely by economic self-interest. But there is ample evidence that is consistent with a *bounded* (or *limited*) rationality that reflects a somewhat less knowledgeable electorate motivated by a variety of interests and preferences.

## Political Parties

Political parties are *organizations that seek to place their designated representatives in governmental positions*. In democracies, parties are the main mechanism for providing voters with a menu of candidates and programs from which to make their electoral choices. Parties in democratic countries permit the periodic *alternation in power* between competing sets of political leaders and policy orientations. As a consequence, parties are indispensable to the functioning of contemporary democracies. But parties can also exist in nondemocratic countries. Hitler's Nazi Party, the Communist Party of the Soviet Union, the Chinese Communist Party, Saddam Hussein's Baath Party, Egypt's National Democratic Party, and a host of others are examples of *ruling parties*. A **ruling party (or power-monopolizing party)** ***typically monopolizes state power and bans (or effectively controls) other parties.*** Two or more competing parties may also exist in semi-authoritarian or authoritarian states, as in contemporary Pakistan and Iran, but the government finds ways to circumscribe their influence. Any understanding of political parties must take account of the variety of roles parties can play under different political conditions and systems. For example:

- *Pro-democracy political parties* accept democratic principles and compete for governmental positions through the electoral process in democracies.
- *Anti-democracy parties* do not accept the rules and principles of democracy. Sometimes anti-democracy parties compete in elections, but their goal is not to promote democracy but to gain power, with the ultimate intention of destroying democracy.
- *Ruling parties* monopolize governmental power in authoritarian regimes; they are also called *power-monopolizing parties.*[10]

One thing that all three party types have in common is that they *seek governmental power.* Whether in the legislature, the executive branch, local government, or some other state institution; whether through democratic electoral procedures or through force and intimidation, parties exist mainly to obtain the power to make authoritative decisions.

**Particularistic and Catch-all Parties** Another distinction that is commonly made when categorizing political parties is that between *particularistic* and *catch-all* parties.

**Particularistic parties** ***are parties that confine their appeal to a particular segment of the population.*** When modern political parties emerged in nineteenth-century Europe and America, they often had a rather narrow appeal. Conservative parties tended to reflect the attitudes of the aristocratic upper classes and the wealthier members of the business class, while working-class parties sought their votes almost exclusively from the laboring masses in urban industrial centers. Agrarian parties promoted the interests of farmers. These parties were defined essentially by their *social class* base. Other particularistic parties had a predominantly religious outlook. These so-called *confessional* parties usually sought the votes of Protestants or Catholics in countries with deep religious divisions. A number of them still exist. Contemporary Europe has quite a few Christian Democratic parties, but their orientation is now defined primarily by socioeconomic appeals and nonreligious political issues rather than by religious considerations. Religion-centered parties are very active in a number of countries, however. Northern Ireland has Catholic and Protestant parties; Hindu and Muslim parties have large followings in India.

Islamic parties exist in a number of countries with large Muslim populations. A few of them have multiple functions in addition to trying to win governmental positions through competitive elections. In Lebanon, Hezbollah (the Party of God) has a political wing that won fourteen legislative seats in the 2005 elections and placed two of its leaders in the government. It also has a well-armed militia that attacked Israel in 2006, precipitating a thirty-three-day war; an international terrorist network that has attacked Jewish organizations around the world; a social welfare system that provides clinics, schools, cash, and other social welfare benefits to Lebanon's large Shia population; and a media operation that propagates its official positions (see chapter 2). Hezbollah receives its weapons and hundreds of millions of dollars a year from the government of Iran. In the Palestinian Authority, Hamas (Zeal) won a majority of seats in the legislature in 2005. It has also engaged in militia and terrorist activity against Israel, and runs a network of social services for Palestinians in the West Bank and Gaza (chapter 6). In Pakistan, an alliance of six Islamic parties won 11 percent of the vote in parliamentary elections held in 2002, becoming the third largest political grouping in the legislature (chapter 5). Campaigning against U.S. intervention in Afghanistan, the alliance won control of the local legislature in Pakistan's Northwest Frontier Province, which borders Afghanistan and provides wide support for al Qaeda. These and other Islamic parties around the world may participate in elections and legislatures, but their support for democratic values and procedures is ambivalent at best. Some of them openly espouse theocratic government based on Islamic law.[11]

Other particularistic parties around the world are organized to promote the interests of national or regional minorities (such as the Scottish National Party in the UK and Kurdish parties in Turkey). Still others focus on a specific issue, such as the environment, women's rights, opposition to the European Union, or the priorities of beer lovers. Ultimately, what matters is whether a particularistic party accepts the rules of democracy—including compromise and cooperation with other parties when necessary to prevent gridlock or the complete breakdown of democracy. The particularistic religious or ethnic parties that are emerging in Iraq and Afghanistan may spell trouble for democracy if they flout these rules.

By contrast, **catch-all parties** ***are parties that seek to widen their base of popular support as much as possible.*** Their primary aim is to win elections and take over the government. Accordingly, they try to catch all the votes they can, drawing them from a diversity of social classes, religions, ethnic groups, and other segments of the population. In the process they usually loosen their commitment to specific groups or principles and adopt more flexible positions capable of broadening their mass appeal. Sometimes catch-all parties are criticized for being so vague about where they stand that the voters can't tell where they stand at all. But it is only by diluting their political consistency and opening their arms to all comers that they can amass the vote tallies they need to outpoll the other parties. Catch-all parties thus tend to be middle-of-the-road, moderate parties. They steer clear of the left and right political extremes, preferring instead to cast a wide net on either side of the political center. Over time, most of the class-based particularistic parties of Western Europe—conservative parties on the right and social-democratic parties on the left—evolved into catch-all parties. Although they may still attract their core voters from a particular tier of the socioeconomic pyramid, most of these parties today appeal to the large middle class and win votes from multiple social sectors, including the rich, the poor, women, and ethnic minorities.

According to one widely held hypothesis, catch-all parties are more supportive of stable democracy than are particularistic parties.[12] Catch-all parties, it is argued, promote moderation and compromise across social classes and other groups in society because they are so inclusive. Particularistic parties stick to their own narrow interests in a conflictual and uncompromising posture. Evidence from democracies in North America and Western Europe provides considerable support for this proposition. Virtually every generalization has its exceptions, however, and so does this one. One of the most viscerally antidemocratic parties in history, the German Nazi party, increasingly became a catch-all party as it fought its way to power through the electoral process in the late 1920s and early 1930s. With stunning rapidity the Nazis increased their share of the national vote from just 2.6 percent in 1928 to more than 37 percent by the summer of 1932, capturing votes from the upper, middle, and working classes, from urban voters and rural voters, from women as well as men, from Protestants and Catholics, and from every age group eligible to vote.[13]

In Western Europe there are *party families* consisting of roughly similar parties that are organized in different countries. Some of them are particularistic parties, like the environment-friendly Green parties that are organized in most countries in the region. Others are more broadly based catch-all parties like the Christian Democrats and their conservative counterparts in various countries, or the Social Democratic parties that exist in virtually all West European countries. The member parties of each family consult with one another and form voting blocs in the European Parliament, the European Union's legislature.

**How Democratic Are Parties?** In 1911 Roberto Michels published a study of Germany's Social Democratic Party, which was perhaps the most outspokenly pro-democracy party in Germany prior to World War I. Michels showed that, despite its democratic ideology, the party conducted its own internal affairs in a distinctly undemocratic fashion, relying on its executive board to make key decisions with scant regard for the opinions of the party's dues-paying members. Michels concluded that, for the sake of decision-making efficiency, all large organizations (including governments) have to be run by a handful of officers, making democracy virtually impossible. He called this tendency the *iron law of oligarchy.*[14]

Political parties in today's democracies display various patterns of internal organization. In the United States, the Democratic and Republican parties are highly decentralized, with separate organizations in each of the fifty states. At the central level, each party has a "national committee," but these executive bodies are primarily concerned with fundraising rather than with formulating party policy on the issues of the day. Neither party has a formal leader who is responsible for articulating the party line on specific issues, and neither one

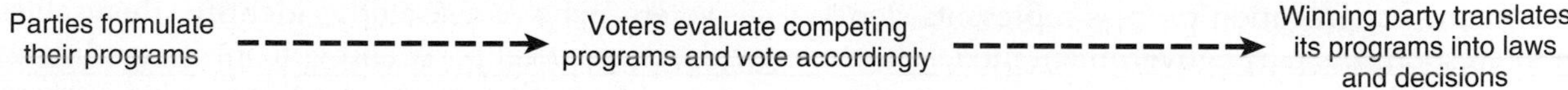


**FIGURE 11.1 Responsible Party Government Model**

is a membership party that invites people to pay dues and take part in party meetings. Individual candidates have the freedom to raise their own campaign funds and stake out their own positions on the issues, and American citizens make their main input in party activities when they vote in primary elections. By contrast, the Labour and Conservative parties in Britain are membership parties. Their dues-paying members are entitled to participate in party meetings and vote for the party's nominees for parliamentary elections. (Like most democracies other than the United States, Britain does not have primary elections to determine party nominees.) In recent years the members of these two large parties have won the right to take part in voting procedures to elect the party chief, who is the party's candidate for prime minister. Both the Labour Party and the Conservatives are more centralized than the Democrats and Republicans in the United States, with a central party headquarters in London that raises and spends most of the money disbursed in political campaigns. Individual candidates for Parliament have less latitude than candidates for Congress to raise their own money or deviate from the official party line on the issues. A number of parties in Europe and elsewhere are similar to the Labour-Conservative model. As we noted in chapter 9, parties that give ordinary citizens meaningful opportunities to participate in party affairs may be considered part of civil society.

But quite a few parties in today's world are nearly as oligarchic as the pre–World War I German Social Democrats described by Michels. Professional political elites and superactivists tend to dominate party politics and policy making in most countries, even in democracies. And it is quite probable that in many—if not most—countries, party professionals and activists tend to be more extreme in their political views than average citizens, a majority of whom tend to be more moderate and less avidly committed to particular positions. Evidence from the United States amply confirms the disjuncture between the extreme views of political activists—whether of the left or the right—and the moderation (or lack of interest) on the part of most Americans.[15]

**Responsible Party Government** For electoral democracy to work effectively, according to some theorists, three essential things must happen. First, the competing parties need to clarify as explicitly as possible what they would do if they are elected to positions of governmental responsibility. Thus each party must formulate a coherent program and spell it out to the voters in advance of election day, specifying where it stands on economic policy, social welfare policy, foreign policy, and so on. Candidates running for office need to reinforce these messages in their campaign appearances. Second, the voters need to compare the competing programs carefully and vote for the candidates most representative of their own views. And third, on taking office the victorious party must translate its campaign programs and promises into governmental action. This three-step model of *responsible party government* is depicted in figure 11.1. But do things really work this way? If fact, several obstacles obstruct the smooth realization of responsible party government.

One problem arises when a political party is internally divided. Such *internal fragmentation* can result from disputes over party policy on domestic issues or foreign affairs; from the multiple class, ethnic, religious, or other constituencies that gravitate to the party; from leadership rivalries; or from other factors. Internal divisions of these kinds often complicate the process of what political scientists call *interest aggregation.*[16]

**Interest aggregation** ***is the process by which political parties gather together (aggregate) the various interests, priorities, and opinions of their leaders and constituents and shape them into common goals and policy proposals.***

The interest aggregation process represents step 1 in the responsible party government model shown in figure 11.1. Some parties perform it more effectively than others. In just about all political parties in today's democracies, however, it is a complicated task that usually involves a considerable amount of negotiation and bargaining among the political elites who guide the party's fortunes. The more complex the process of internal interest aggregation, the more difficult it will be for the party to speak with a clear, unified voice to the voters.

As a consequence, the programs that parties present to the voters may be so vague or internally inconsistent that it's hard to tell exactly what the party will actually do if elected to office. Large catch-all parties are especially prone to these problems. It is quite common in the United States, for example, for candidates nominated for the presidency to casually ignore, or openly repudiate, the "platform" of general principles and specific proposals that is officially adopted at the party's nominating convention.

A second problem is *voter ignorance* and *shifting party alignments*. Step 2 of the responsible party government model assumes that voters have a sufficient comprehension of political affairs to make intelligent decisions in the voting booth. As we've seen, however, voters in most democracies may not be very well informed on the issues. In a recent survey, three out of four Americans could name the Three Stooges, but less than half could identify the three branches of government.[17] (Churchill remarked that "the best argument against democracy is a 5-minute conversation with the average voter.") To complicate matters, in most established democracies political parties are having an increasingly difficult time holding on to a stable core following of voters. *Party loyalty* is in decline in many democracies. In the United States, voter identification with the Democrats and Republicans, so prominent in the 1950s and 1960s, has diminished considerably since then.[18] In Western Europe, party loyalties in the 1960s were very close to what they were in the 1920s. Although they still remain strong in many cases, they have become looser in a number of European countries, and new parties have come into the picture. Party loyalties have also weakened in Japan, India, and other democracies.[19]

Voters who consistently identify themselves with one political party and vote for its candidates from one election to the next are called *partisan voters.* Sometimes certain identifiable groups in society, such as various socioeconomic classes, religious groups, or ethnic groups, have a general tendency to support a favorite party over long periods of time. This phenomenon is called *stable partisan alignment:* the same social groups vote for the same party time after time. But when large numbers of voters disengage their established loyalties to their favorite party and become less partisan and more independent, *partisan dealignment* is said to occur. Partisan dealignment means that once-solid supporters of a particular party no longer vote for that party's candidates automatically. They may vote for certain of its candidates depending on the stance they take on various issues, or they may gravitate to another party, or they may switch back and forth between parties from one election to the next. Voters who move back and forth in this way are called *swing voters.*

Under conditions of partisan dealignment, it becomes more difficult for parties to produce long-term programs that will attract a long-term following. By having to make frequent shifts and revisions in their programs to attract increasingly fickle and unpredictable voters, parties find it harder to represent their constituents' views in a stable fashion and support policy initiatives that may take many years to translate into effective governmental action. In short, party dealignments further complicate the task of establishing responsible party government.

Sometimes the voters may change their habits even more radically. When a large bloc of voters that traditionally votes for one party massively shifts its support to a rival party and sticks with that party over prolonged periods, *party realignment* takes place. In the United States, Southern white Protestant males were once solid Democrats. Since the 1970s, however, they have moved in large numbers to the Republicans. Whereas partisan *dealignment* means simply a *loosening* of traditional party loyalties on the part of *individuals, realignment* means an *enduring shift* from one party to another on the part of large *social groups.* Realignments represent major changes in a society's electoral patterns, in some cases placing new obstacles in the path of responsible party government.

A third set of obstacles is *divided government* or *coalition government*. After the elections take place, it's up to the elected officials to translate their programs and promises into authoritative actions (step 3 of the responsible party government model). This process can be strewn with hazards, however. In some democracies, such as the United States, France, and Russia, the voters may elect a president of one party and a legislative majority of a rival party or parties. As such cases of *divided government* frequently demonstrate, it is usually more difficult to convert the competing proposals of rival parties into government actions than it is to convert the proposals of just one governing party. In democracies that have a parliamentary system of government, as we explained in chapter 8, two or more parties may be forced to form a *coalition government* or a *parliamentary alliance* in order to form a working majority in the legislature. Once again, the more parties that are involved in the decision-making process, the more difficult it is for any individual party to give the voters what it promised.

A fourth obstacle blocking implementation of the responsible party government model is a *lack of party discipline*. Party discipline means that the party's entire legislative delegation votes together unanimously on bills that come up for a vote. Party discipline is traditionally somewhat low in the United States. Members of Congress have usually financed their own election campaigns and are not financially dependent on their party. In addition, the American system of separation of powers gives members of Congress an institutional independence from the presidency. As a result, presidents may not be able to convince legislators in their own party to go along with their policies.

Party discipline is relatively higher in parliamentary democracies like Britain and Germany. Even in these countries, however, the unity of the party's legislative delegation may occasionally break down as individual legislators diverge from their party leadership on roll call votes.

The ideal of responsible party government can be very difficult to achieve in well-established democracies; it can be even more elusive in newly democratizing countries. In countries that are making the transition from authoritarianism to democracy in Eastern Europe, Latin America, East Asia, Africa, and elsewhere, new parties must be formed from the ground up or, in some cases, re-formed on the remains of parties that once existed under earlier democratic regimes. It will most probably take quite a few years before these parties solidify into stable organizations with fairly coherent political orientations, widespread voter recognition, and a core of loyal voters. Some will probably fall by the wayside. If these fledgling democracies are to take root, however, parties will have to play a major role in forging vital links between the population and the state.

**Party Systems** The term **party system** ***refers to the number of parties within a country, their ideological orientations, and various other general patterns.*** We'll consider just two variable features of party systems here: the *number* of parties to be found within a given system, and the ideologically based distinction between *centripetal* and *centrifugal* party systems.[20]

*The Number of Parties* Some democracies are dominated over prolonged periods by one party. These are called *predominant-party systems*. Japan, for example, was governed uninterruptedly by the Liberal Democratic Party (LDP) from 1955 to 1993. Although other parties ran against the LDP in freely contested elections, they were not able to win a parliamentary majority until the LDP suffered severe losses in voter support in the 1990s because of corruption scandals. Mexico was governed by the Institutional Revolutionary Party (PRI) from 1929 until 2000, when Vicente Fox, a challenger from a rival party, won the presidential election. Although several parties had increased their share of the vote from the 1970s onward, the PRI remained Mexico's predominant party until it lost the all-important presidency to Fox.

Very few countries have a predominantly *two-party system*. The United States, of course, is one of them. While third parties have cropped up now and then on the national scene, they have not fared very well in getting their candidates elected to Congress or the presidency. Some people regard Britain as having a two-party system. To be sure, the Conservative and Labour parties have taken turns running the government since World War II without having to take on other parties as coalition partners. But several other parties also exist in the

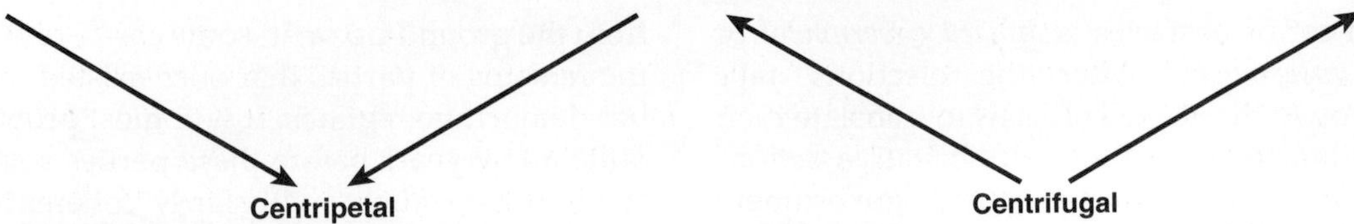


**FIGURE 11.2 Centripetal and Centrifugal Party Systems**

United Kingdom that regularly elect representatives to Parliament, and they occasionally play an important role in shaping the government's policies. Britain might more appropriately be called a *few-party system*. Few-party systems typically have about three to five important parties. Contemporary France, Germany, Japan, and Canada also fall into this category.

Still other countries have real *multiparty systems*. Multiparty systems typically have six or more parties that play a significant political role, electing their candidates to the national legislature, participating in coalition governments or parliamentary alliances, providing critical support in key legislative votes, or obstructing government actions they don't like. The Scandinavian countries, Poland, Israel, and Italy provide examples of multiparty systems.

Some theorists contend that a few-party system is optimal because it gives voters more choice than a two-party system. It also creates more stable party attachments than a multiparty system, which provides too many incentives to desert one party for another. In *Exit, Voice, and Loyalty*, Albert Hirschman argued that voters essentially have two choices when they no longer agree with the policies pursued by their favorite party. Either they can raise their *voice* within the party in an attempt to persuade its leaders to change course, or they can *exit* the party and shift their votes to a rival one. The choice they make will depend largely on their degree of party *loyalty*. Hirschman concludes that the ideal party system will have enough competing parties to give voters acceptable alternatives should they choose to exit, but it will not have so many parties that people will have no incentive to use their voice within their initial party of preference. Hirschman does not specify how many parties would meet these requirements, but he implies that a few-party system with three to five parties would be ideal.[21]

*Centripetal and Centrifugal Party Systems* These terms pertain to the tendencies of party systems to have either predominantly *moderate* or *extremist* parties. ***A* <u>centripetal party system</u> *is one that favors moderate, centrist parties rather than extremist ones.*** The term derives from the Latin for "center seeking." In a centripetal system, the main parties and the majority of the electorate tend toward the center of the political spectrum, making consensus possible. The United States, Britain, and contemporary Germany are a few examples. By contrast, a **<u>centrifugal</u>** *("center fleeing")* **<u>party system</u>** ***is one in which the leading parties and large numbers of voters tend toward the extremes of right or left.*** Germany's Weimar Republic (1919–33) is a prime example of such polarization. During the last few years of its existence, increasing numbers of voters deserted the centrist parties, which favored democracy, and flocked to the German Communist Party on the extreme left and Hitler's Nazi Party on the extreme right. (See figure 11.2.) Students of democratization warn that today's newly democratizing countries face serious gridlock problems if their legislatures are fragmented into a large number of highly polarized parties.[22]

## Interest Groups

**<u>Interest groups</u>** ***are organizations that speak up for the interests and demands of particular groups of people, often with the aim of influencing the state to do something in their behalf.***

Interest groups provide another means of mass participation in democratic political systems. They promote the aims of specific segments of the mass public by exerting pressure on political parties, candidates, and government officials themselves. In the terminology developed by Almond and Powell, ***interest groups perform the function of* <u>interest articulation</u> *when they articulate the interests,***

***demands, and desires of various groups in society.*** Political parties and interest groups are called *intermediate organizations*: they are located in between the population and the state. At least in democracies, one of their aims is to enable citizens to influence state actions.

Not all interest groups are interested exclusively in political activities. In many cases they try to promote their group interests without recourse to government involvement. Trade unions, for example, may work out their problems over pay and working conditions through direct interactions with company executives, employing negotiations, strikes, and other bargaining techniques. In political science we are mainly concerned with the *political* activities of interest groups. When trade unions or business associations ask the state to take their side in a labor dispute or in support of specific governmental economic policies, their actions become decidedly political. In the United States and some other democracies, many interest groups have *lobbies,* which work directly to influence government policy, usually by establishing contacts with government decision makers. In 2005 there were about 11,500 active lobbyists in Washington, D.C.[23]

*Associational interest groups* are organizations that speak up for specific segments of a country's population who share common problems and goals. They are more likely to be found in democracies, which permit freedom of association, than in authoritarian states, which usually do not allow such groups to be established independently of state control. Associational interest groups display considerable variety. Some articulate the *economic* interests of their supporters, such as trade unions and business associations. Others may represent ethnic groups (such as the National Association for the Advancement of Colored People), gender and sexual preference groups (the National Organization for Women; the Gay Alliance), generational groups (the American Association of Retired Persons), religious groups (the Christian Coalition), and specific-issue groups (the National Rifle Association).

*Private institutional groups* are organizations that are organized primarily for some purpose other than political action. Private corporations, such as Exxon or General Motors, and established religious institutions, such as the Roman Catholic Church or the Anglican Church, are examples. Like associational groups, these private groups may also have lobbying offices to represent their interests in contacts with public officials.

No consideration of interest groups can be complete without a reference to groups in society that do *not* clearly articulate their common interests. Even in flourishing democracies, there may be segments of society with identifiable political interests that, for one reason or another, do not succeed in building interest groups or call attention to their grievances through anomic behavior. An example is people who are not covered by any kind of medical insurance in the United States. In 2006, this segment of the population amounted to 46 million people. Their problems were acknowledged by political leaders in both major parties, but they had no formal organization or other mechanism of their own for collectively articulating their concerns. Countries all over the globe have their own examples of unorganized social groups that are not able to articulate their political needs effectively. Day workers, child laborers, abused or oppressed women—these and other politically voiceless people, numbering in the millions, confirm the enormous importance of interest groups precisely because they do not have them.

**Pluralism and Corporatism** Precisely *how* interest groups function can differ markedly from one country to another. There is a basic distinction, for example, between *pluralism* and *corporatism.*

As we noted in chapter 4, pluralism is a concept of democracy that asserts that political power is dispersed among a plurality of groups and interests. It is not monopolized by one particular social group or by a unified power elite. ***Interest-group pluralism*** ***emphasizes***

- ***freedom of association,*** which means that people are free to organize their own interest groups, and
- ***competition for influence,*** which means that interest groups on different sides of an issue freely compete for the attention of legislators and other authoritative decision makers and seek to influence their actions.

This model of interest-group pluralism is best exemplified by the United States. Typically, as Congress considers legislation on a particular issue, interest groups concerned with how the outcome will affect their constituents' bank accounts or quality of life will seek to influence the way individual legislators vote. In the wide-open U.S. system, groups are free to use a variety of persuasive techniques to state their case: television and newspaper advertisements, e-mails and blogs, analytical reports, expert testimony, organized demonstrations, letter-writing campaigns, and so on. Those with direct access to members of Congress (an access purchased, perhaps, with generous contributions to their election campaign war-chests) can buttonhole legislators in face-to-face meetings, at times in the comfortable settings of country clubs, conference resorts, or trendy restaurants. The line between what is legally permitted in these attempts to exercise political clout and what is illegal (or what ought to be illegal) can be a thin one: "influence" is at times barely distinguishable from outright bribery. Instances of corruption, whether blatant or subtle, have not been uncommon.

In some cases the American system of interest-group pluralism can delay legislation for months or even years. It can even prevent Congress from taking any action at all. One illustrative example centers on the Clinton administration's attempt to win congressional approval of a new national health care system in 1993–94. Organizations on either side of the issue besieged senators and representatives, spending tens of millions of dollars to either defeat the Clinton proposal or get it passed. After a year, no congressional majority could be found for the Clinton plan, nor for any alternative. More than 40 million Americans were left uninsured. Despite these and other problems, however, Congress passes thousands of bills every session. In the process, a large number of interest groups have ample opportunity to influence the results. Other democracies have their own variants of interest-group pluralism.

In contrast to the U.S. variant of pluralism, *corporatism* represents a different approach to involving interest groups in the policy process. Defined in very broad terms,

> **corporatism** ***is a system of formal interest-group participation in the state's decision-making processes.***

Different versions of corporatism have existed at different periods of time and in different political systems. Corporatism has been variously conceptualized and embraced by the Roman Catholic Church, fascist dictatorships under Mussolini and Hitler, military dictatorships in Latin America, authoritarian regimes in Portugal and Mexico, and modern democracies like Austria, Germany, and Sweden. These and other proponents of corporatist methods share some ideas in common but diverge, at times considerably, in their application of those ideas.

One of the most widely shared commonalities of corporatist thinking is the notion that *leading representatives of the key groups in society—especially business and labor—should negotiate directly with government officials to work out the country's principal economic and social welfare policies.* We'll confine ourselves in this chapter to sketching out a very generalized model (an *ideal type*) of modern corporatism as it works in several democracies today. Along the way we'll highlight some salient differences between corporatism and U.S.-style pluralism.

Corporatism in contemporary democracies (sometimes called *neo-corporatism*) typically consists of the following institutions and procedures:

1. The main groups in society involved in economic production—notably industry, labor, and agriculture—form large interest groups that represent a large proportion, sometimes the majority, of the people in their respective sector. These large interest groups are called *peak associations.* A peak association for labor will thus represent a high percentage of the country's factory workers. The peak associations tend to be *hierarchically organized;* that is, their national leaders exercise considerable influence over the rank and file at local levels. (In the United States, such peak associations are rare; each industry tends to have its own labor unions that bargain with employers. The AFL-CIO, American labor's large umbrella organization, does not engage in corporatist-style bargaining.)
2. Leaders of the main peak associations, especially those representing the business sector and labor, meet on a regular basis with representatives of the state, who are usually from the executive branch rather than the legislature. The executive branch representatives may include the prime minister, other cabinet ministers, their

PLURALISM

Congress
President
Business firms, groups
Labor unions
Other interest groups
Rank and file

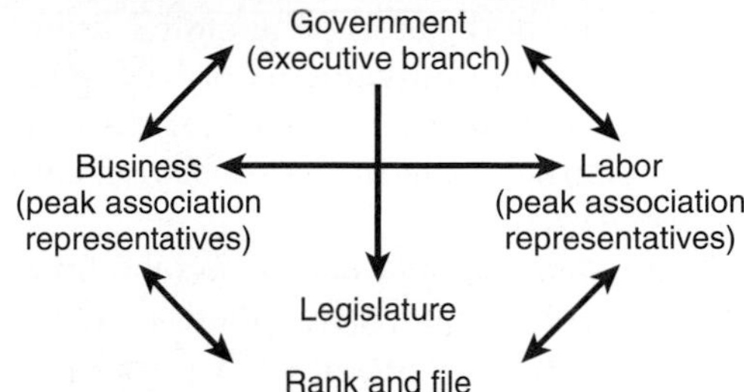


**FIGURE 11.3 Models of U.S.-Style Interest-Group Pluralism and Neo-Corporatism**

deputies, or key bureaucrats in relevant ministries. Under corporatism, the executive branch plays a more important role in dealing with business and labor groups than the legislature does. (In the United States, by contrast Congress tends to play a more active role than the president in dealing with interest groups.)

3. Together these representatives of the main peak associations and the state work out deals on such economic issues as taxes, wages, working conditions, social welfare benefits, and the like. (In the United States, the government usually does not get involved in brokering agreements between unions and employers on wages or working conditions.)
4. Once agreements are worked out, the business and labor negotiators go back to their respective groups and solicit the reactions of their members. If the rank and file does not accept the agreements, they may have to be renegotiated. But the leaders of the peak associations frequently exert pressure on the membership to go along with the deals they have worked out in the tripartite negotiations on the grounds that they are the best possible under present circumstances.
5. If appropriate, the national legislature ratifies the agreed-upon arrangements by passing them into law. In parliamentary systems, the government can usually count on commanding the parliamentary majority to facilitate this procedure. Quite often the parliament's role is limited to voting on a done deal.
6. The peak association leaders then urge their respective members to carry out the agreements. If they fail, the agreements may have to be renegotiated.

Compared with the freewheeling style of American pluralism, neo-corporatism is typically a more orderly and regularized process. Bilateral and tripartite negotiations among business, labor, and government are often an ongoing process. However, corporatism can also be a more closed process than pluralism is. The negotiations tend to take place behind closed doors, centered in the executive branch of government. It is not always as open a process as those fought out in the legislature.[24]

Proponents of corporatist procedures argue that they provide the government with an effective way of keeping the economy running smoothly, based on constant negotiations with business and labor leaders who are armed with broad negotiating powers. (For a description of neo-corporatism in Germany, see chapter 18.) In the United States, however, the government has less direct influence over business or labor. Critics of the American system charge that the U.S. economy is less coordinated and less efficient as a result. Figure 11.3 compares pluralism and neo-corporatism.

## Social Movements

**Social movements** ***consist of segments of the population who engage in significant collective action because they believe that neither the state nor the established political parties or interest groups have adequately addressed their concerns.*** Women, gays, environmentalists, peace advocates, and others have formed social movements in many of the world's democracies, especially since the 1960s and 1970s. Because they view the existing modes of expressing grievances and getting the state's attention as ineffective, social movements often engage in highly contentious forms of political activity: demonstrations, strikes, disruptive behavior, and even revolutionary violence.

What explains why people decide to take time-consuming and potentially risky political action instead of behaving like inactive "free riders"? Students of contentious politics like Sidney Tarrow have argued that, in democracies and nondemocracies alike, social movements tend to form when people who are dissatisfied with the status quo suddenly perceive new opportunities to pressure those in authority. Such opportunities may arise because a potentially more responsive government has come to power, or because economic conditions are conducive to change. People are also prone to act when the costs and constraints of action decline—because the ruling elites are divided or vulnerable, or because their acts of repression are no longer intimidating. And when they are able to make common cause with other aggrieved groups in society, they can build alliances and strong networks of cooperation that permit sustained political activity. National protest movements in eighteenth-century Europe and more recent struggles like the American civil rights movement, labor unrest in Western Europe, the quest for democracy in former communist countries, and peasant protests in contemporary China have many features in common. Social movements are but one facet of the broader phenomenon of *contentious politics*, which has common causal mechanisms and other distinguishing features.[25]

## Patron-Client Relationships

**Patron-client relationships** are another set of ties between political elites and the population. Also known as **clientelism**, this type of relationship ***typically involves a political organization (such as a party) that dispenses benefits or favors to people in exchange for their votes or other forms of support.*** In contrast to mass electoral politics and large-scale interest-group activity, patron-client relationships generally operate on a smaller, more personalized scale. Their origins are rooted in the personal ties that developed in preindustrial societies between local authorities and ordinary villagers or peasants in need of advice, favors, or perhaps a job from authoritative figures. The patrons in these relationships could be the village mayor, a respected landowner, or other local notables who did not necessarily hold official governmental positions. Their clients were those who came forward, hat in hand, with a favor to ask. Patrons who did favors for a large number of clients could accumulate considerable personal power and prestige in the local community.

With the advent of urban industrialism in the nineteenth century and the expansion of electoral democracy that accompanied it in the United States and certain parts of Europe, patron-client relationships moved into the big cities and became politicized. Now it was political figures, particularly those connected with vote-generating urban political machines, who became patrons for all sorts of clients struggling to make a life for themselves in the intimidating maze of mass society: local residents trying to climb out of poverty, recent arrivals from rural hinterlands, immigrants from near and far. With their hands on the apparatus of city, regional, and occasionally national government, politicians and their well-connected associates dispensed jobs, contracts, and other favors to a widening clientele. In exchange for these considerations, the clients provided their patrons with a highly cherished reward: votes. This style of political activity became especially prevalent in the United States and Italy.[26]

Patron-client networks of various types continue to exist today in a number of countries. Quite often it is a powerful political party, one with access to government funds and jobs, that is the principal patron in these relationships. In quite a few cases these relationships are marked by bribery, favoritism, and other forms of corruption. The Congress Party of India, the Institutional Revolutionary Party of Mexico, the Liberal Democratic Party of Japan, and various parties in Greece, Italy, the Philippines, and elsewhere are characterized by "clientelistic" relationships of one sort or another.

## NGOs

As we noted in chapter 1, nongovernmental organizations (NGOs) are *organizations of concerned citizens and experts who seek to inform the public and influence governments, international institutions, private corporations, and other relevant bodies to take action on particular problems.* Most of them are devoted to a specific issue like women's rights, freedom of speech, or peace in the Middle East. NGOs tend to be smaller than interest groups or social movements, but they may act in conjunction with these larger collectivities. Quite often an NGO will consist of a small team of experts who write reports or perhaps consult with decision makers, a core of reliable activists and volunteers, and a larger base of sympathizers connected mainly via the Web. Their funding tends to come from private donors and from governments that support their causes. It is estimated that there are some 2 million NGOs currently active worldwide. Most are based in democracies, but a growing number of them are mushrooming in nondemocratic states, boosted by Internet linkages at home and abroad. By enabling their often far-flung constituents to take part in their activities—through exchanges of information, fundraising drives, and e-mail letter-writing campaigns addressed to governments—NGOs are playing an increasingly important role in expanding political participation on a global scale.[27]

### Mass Participation in Nondemocratic Regimes

Authoritarian regimes usually do not allow much free political participation by the people, if any. Some of them may have the trappings of democracy, such as elections, parties, interest groups, and news media, but the population's ability to use these mechanisms is rarely free; it is typically controlled by the ruling authorities. Mass participation in nondemocratic political systems is usually *coercive participation.* The people, having no parties or interest groups of their own to represent or articulate their desires, are often reduced to an atomized "mass society": an amorphous crowd with no effective organizations to express or aggregate their interests and thus no direct way to influence the actions of the state.[28]

Nevertheless, various authoritarian governments, in the past as well as today, have seen to it that the masses do participate in political activities under the state's direction. Some of these nondemocratic regimes have staged *uncontested elections.* The population may be asked (and in some cases compelled) to approve the existing top leader in an orchestrated "election" or referendum in which the leader is unopposed. Napoleon, Saddam Hussein, and Egypt's Hosni Mubarak are among those who have employed this technique. Alternatively, the people may be asked to vote for handpicked candidates for a national legislature. For each legislative seat there is typically only one candidate, someone chosen by the ruling authorities; the voters have no real choice. In most of these cases, the legislature so elected is of little importance, since the main political decisions are made elsewhere, by the higher-ups in the state's executive machinery. Both the electoral process and the elected organs are purely *symbolic* in nature: the symbols of democracy are present but not the reality. The ruling authorities use these procedures mainly to manipulate and control the public, giving the masses they rule a false sense of participating in the affairs of state. Prior to 1989, the Soviet Union and the former communist states of East Central Europe all had uncontested (or mostly uncontested) elections and powerless legislatures based on this model. Contemporary states using similar procedures include the People's Republic of China and Cuba.

Another form of mass participation utilized in at least some authoritarian states is *mass mobilization.* In addition to being called out to vote in phony elections, the people may also be compelled to take part in mass demonstrations and parades organized by the government, listen to propaganda speeches at their school or place of work, or lend a hand in special barnstorming work projects in the factory, on the farm, or out on construction sites.

It may also happen that authoritarian regimes may enjoy a measure of mass support. Quite a few dictatorships have openly cultivated popular appeal by providing the masses with improvements in their economic welfare, by enhancing their national pride through military conquests or nationalistic propaganda, or by various other means. In some cases these regimes may actually succeed in building a broad base of popularity. Such overtures to the mass population by political elites is known as *populism.* Actually, **populism** has two meanings. When it springs from the people themselves, populism means ***mass anti-elitism.*** It expresses the people's hostility to the overweening power of elites. Sometimes these sentiments can spark significant political activity, like the Populist Party organized in the 1890s by American farmers and workers opposed to the power of big business. When the source of populist ideas is the political elites, populism means ***elite efforts to cultivate the support of the disadvantaged masses.*** Elite-driven populism routinely occurs in democracies as politicians seek to drum up votes among the downtrodden by promising to alleviate their poverty. But it can also occur in authoritarian regimes as dictators try to win mass support, or at least acceptance, by providing the masses with various welfare benefits to alleviate their plight.

In some cases, this strategy of *populist authoritarianism* succeeds in winning broad support for nondemocratic leaders, as long as they manage to improve the lot of the impoverished masses. But the strategy does not always work. Communist leaders in the Soviet Union and in Central and Eastern Europe sought to keep their populations quiet through an unwritten "social compact" stipulating, in effect, that the people would refrain from challenging the regime politically while the regime would provide economic and social amenities in return. Communism failed at least in part because the ruling authorities, saddled with stagnating economies, did not keep their end of the bargain.

If a nondemocratic regime's leaders are truly unpopular and if people categorically reject the political system, they can simply revolt. Anti-regime behavior of this kind takes two basic forms: *dissidence* and *revolution*. Both are risky.

## Dissidence

**Dissidence** ***is antigovernment behavior that falls short of actually toppling the regime.*** It can take many forms, from the distribution of leaflets and other peaceful activities to overt acts of terrorism. While dissidents may nourish the hope that their small sparks of personal opposition will ignite a general conflagration, they are often willing to take extraordinary risks even if they realize that a mass uprising is not an immediate likelihood. Surveillance, incarceration, and torture are often their grim rewards.

Political dissidence is by no means confined to advocates of democracy. Some may wish to replace one form of dictatorship with another. A number of the most prominent political dissidents in recent decades, however, have been outspoken proponents of democratic liberty, courageously taking up the cause of human freedom and dignity against incalculable odds. Mohandas Gandhi, the leader of the movement for India's liberation from Britain, stands out as one of democracy's most inspiring heroes, as detailed in chapter 15. More recent examples include the following figures:

- *Aung San Suu Kyi* (AWN SAN SOO CHEE), winner of the 1991 Nobel Peace Prize for her efforts to bring democracy to Myanmar (Burma), was placed under house arrest by the military regime in 1989. Under intense international pressure the regime formally released her in 1995, but she was arrested again in 2003 and accused of plotting an armed uprising. She was still locked under house arrest in 2006.
- *Shirin Ebadi* (SHEE-REEN eh-baw-DEE), the Nobel Prize–winning human rights lawyer, is president of the Defender of Human Rights Center in Iran, a group declared illegal in 2006.
- *Akbar Ganji*, an Iranian writer, spent six years in prison for "defaming" Iran's theocratic regime. His book *Dungeon of Ghosts* and other writings have exposed the regime's repression and corruption.
- *Chen Guangcheng* (CHUHN GWAHNG-CHUHNG), a blind human rights lawyer in rural China, was sentenced to more than four years in prison in 2006 after organizing a lawsuit

**Aung San Suu Kyi**

**Shirin Ebadi**

to stop the government's population-control policy of forced sterilizations and abortions.

- *Saad Eddin Ibrahim*, an Egyptian scholar and founder of the Arab Organization for Human Rights, was arrested on false charges in 2000 after criticizing Egypt's authoritarian regime; in 2003 he was acquitted and released.
- *Nelson Mandela*, the South African champion of racial equality, was jailed for twenty-seven years before reaching a historic agreement with white leaders that gave nonwhites the vote in 1994.
- *Kim Dae Jung*, a fearless advocate of democracy in South Korea during three decades of authoritarian rule, spent sixteen years in prison, in exile, or under house arrest before being elected president in 1997. He served in that office until 2003.
- *Lech Walesa*, an electrician who led illegal strikes against Poland's communist government in 1980, spearheaded the creation of Solidarity, the communist bloc's only noncommunist trade union. Though Solidarity was temporarily banned and Walesa was arrested, in 1989 they pressured the communist regime to hold elections and subsequently give up power. Walesa served as post-communist Poland's first president from 1990 to 1995.
- *Vaclav Havel*, an acclaimed Czechoslovak playwright, was repeatedly jailed by the communist authorities in the 1970s and 1980s before becoming the first president of postcommunist Czechoslovakia.
- *Wang Dan* was at the top of the Chinese regime's most-wanted list at the age of twenty for his leadership role in the 1989 student demonstrations for democracy in Beijing's Tiananmen Square. Following his arrest he spent four years in prison. Upon his release in 1993 he continued his pro-democracy activities, only to be arrested again. The communist authorities released him to the United States in 1998.
- *Andrei Sakharov*, the father of the Soviet H-bomb, was exiled to the isolated city of Gorky in the 1970s for his pro-democracy views. After being freed by Soviet reformer Mikhail Gorbachev, he was an outspoken champion of democracy during the Soviet Union's final years.

The contributions of these and other courageous dissidents to the cause of human rights and democratic freedom dramatize the importance of leadership in the struggle against oppression. Democratization projects that lack such dynamic and widely recognized leaders tend to have a difficult time energizing mass action in support of change.

### Revolution

**Revolution** ***usually means the overthrow of one system of government and its replacement by a different system.*** Such fundamental changes in a nation's political regime are often accompanied by profound changes in the political attitudes of the masses and elites, a phenomenon often referred to as a *cultural revolution.*

Successful revolutions are rare. The American revolution of the 1770s and 1780s, the French revolution unleashed in 1789, the Russian revolution of 1917, the Chinese revolution that started in 1911 with the collapse of the Manchu dynasty and culminated in the communist takeover of 1949, and the Iranian revolution that toppled the Shah in 1979 are major examples in modern history. More recently, the collapse of communism in the Soviet Union and Central and Eastern Europe and the swing toward democracy in these countries surely qualify as true revolutions. The transformations from authoritarian rule to democracy now taking place in a number of other countries around the world may also be considered revolutionary.

When do revolutions take place? The enormous scholarly literature on revolutions provides several explanations. All of them stress the importance of mass opposition to the existing government and a widespread yearning for something better as a critical element. Though political activists—*revolutionary elites*—invariably lead revolutions, they cannot succeed without establishing some kind of rapport with the masses.[29]

One set of explanations looks at the *psychological sources* of revolutionary violence. The other set concentrates on the *social and political conditions* of revolutionary situations. Any comprehensive understanding of the causes and outcomes of revolutionary tumult requires us to combine both types of analysis.

One psychological approach regards revolutionary activity as a rational choice, arguing that the "logic of collective action," which views most people as politically passive, may not always apply. The people's discontent may be so great that they are willing to shake off their passivity and actively participate in antiregime activity, even if they run the risk of being arrested or shot. Such behavior may be quite rational if there appears to be a "once-in-a-lifetime" chance to get rid of a despised government, the risks are tolerable, and the chances of success look good. Calculations like these may account for the popular uprisings in East-Central Europe that destroyed communism.[30]

Some of the most compelling psychological studies of revolution are rooted in *frustration-aggression theory,* which argues that people turn to violence when they are repeatedly or consistently frustrated in their attempts to achieve their goals. James C. Davies, for example, hypothesized that revolutions are not likely to occur simply because people are poor or oppressed, as common sense might lead us to expect. He made the counterintuitive argument that revolutions are most likely when large numbers of people have experienced recent improvements in their living conditions but are suddenly confronted with a sharp reversal of fortunes as the economy takes a downward turn. In these circumstances, the "rising expectations" that people experienced under favorable economic conditions are rudely frustrated and replaced with fears of reverting back to the deplorable conditions that prevailed before the improvements. The result is a rapid increase in violent behavior, which eventually targets the political regime itself.[31]

One of the most influential students of mass violence and revolutionary psychology is Ted Robert Gurr. His widely read book *Why Men Rebel* centers on *relative deprivation* as the main source of frustration that, at least in some cases, sparks mass violence and can lead to a real revolution. Relative deprivation occurs when people perceive a gap between what they feel rightfully entitled to and what they feel they are actually capable of getting and keeping under existing circumstances. If they are continually frustrated in their efforts to satisfy their basic political, economic, or social goals and if there are no alternative ways of satisfying them, the likelihood rises that they will engage in some form of collective violence against others. Ultimately these frustrations can lead to exceptionally high magnitudes of *political* violence aimed directly at the governing authorities.[32] Other psychological studies have focused on "revolutionary personalities" and individual revolutionaries.[33]

The other category of research on revolutions focuses on the social, economic, and political realities (or "structures") that exist when revolutionary activity explodes. Karl Marx theorized that when a country has achieved an advanced stage of capitalism, society becomes split between a small but wealthy and politically dominant business class (the bourgeoisie) and a large mass of workers and unemployed. Once they fully understand their predicament and achieve "class consciousness," the workers will stage a revolution and wrest control of the economy from the bourgeoisie. Marx's theory of inevitable revolution was not confirmed by subsequent historical events, however.

A more recent "structural" approach explores the causes of the French, Russian, and Chinese revolutions and finds striking political and social similarities among all three cases. At the political level, the prerevolutionary state in France, Russia, and China consisted of a decaying absolutist monarchy that could no longer cope with the pressures posed by stronger foreign rivals. At the socioeconomic level, all three countries experienced violent rebellions by peasants who had become fed up with their inferior economic and social status. Finally, in each of the three cases the revolutionaries mobilized the masses and, upon taking power, set up a powerful centralized state with an intrusive bureaucracy. Authoritarian rule, not democracy, was the immediate result.[34]

Revolutionary activity has by no means subsided in our times. During the 1980s and early

1990s, for example, a fanatical guerilla movement known as the Shining Path conducted a systematic terror campaign in Peru in an effort to take over state power. As many as 25,000 people were killed during the prolonged insurrection. Shining Path attracted most of its adherents from the urban and rural poor during a period of severe hardship for the Peruvian economy. The movement suffered a severe blow in 1992 when its leader was captured and sentenced to prison, but in 2003 it appeared to be making a comeback.[35] Colombia has witnessed a decades-long attempt by revolutionaries to topple its central government. By 1999 the rebels controlled as much as half the country. They started out as Marxists bent on social revolution, but their aims appear to have degenerated into the simple pursuit of power and economic control over the territory they occupy, plus access to the lucrative drug trade. A variety of rebel groups have sought to gain power in Congo, Ivory Coast, Liberia, Sierra Leone, and other African countries, though their ultimate political goals beyond taking power are unclear. For better or worse, history's great revolutions have been guided by major ideologies: nationalism, democracy, communism, fascism, Islamic fundamentalism. Rebels without a cause other than their own lust for power and plunder are scarcely revolutionaries. Most of them are little more than political thugs.

This chapter has examined various forms of political participation. The next one looks at the attitudinal components of political behavior, centering on political culture.

## KEY TERMS
## (In bold and underlined in the text)

Logic of collective action
Ruling party
Particularistic parties
Catch-all parties
Interest aggregation
Party system
Centripetal party system
Centrifugal party system
Interest group
Interest articulation
Interest-group pluralism
Corporatism
Social movement
Patron-client relationships (clientelism)
Populism
Dissidence
Revolution

## NOTES

1. Lester W. Milbraith, *Political Participation* (Chicago: Rand McNally, 1965). See also the second edition, coauthored with M. L. Goel (Chicago: Rand McNally, 1977). Also Sidney Verba and Norman H. Nie, *Participation in American Politics* (New York: Harper & Row, 1972); Michael M. Gant and Norman R. Luttbeg, *American Electoral Behavior: 1952–1988* (Itasca, Ill.: F. E. Peacock, 1991); and Sidney Verba, Kay Lehman Schlozman, and Henry E. Brady, *Voice and Equality: Civic Volunteerism in American Politics* (Cambridge, Mass.: Harvard University Press, 1995).
2. Mancur Olson, *The Logic of Collective Action* (Cambridge, Mass.: Harvard University Press, 1965).
3. One scholar showed that U.S. registration requirements reduced voter turnout by at least 10 percent compared with other democratic countries; see G. Bingham Powell, "American Voter Turnout in Comparative Perspective," *American Political Science Review* 80, no. 1 (March 1986): 17–43. For a discussion of turnout in the United States, see Gant and Luttbeg, *American Electoral Behavior.* For a comparative study, see Sidney Verba, Norman H. Nie, and Jae-on Kim, *Participation and Political Equality: A Seven-Nation Comparison* (London: Cambridge University Press, 1978), 190–91, 234–68. When asked to agree or disagree with the statement "People like me don't have any say about what the government does," 29 percent agreed in 1964, 39 percent in 1980, and 45 percent in 1988; 69 percent disagreed in 1964, 59 percent in 1980, and 54 percent in 1988. The rest did not know or had no opinion. Reported in Gant and Luttbeg, *American Electoral Behavior,* 128. See also Michael Schudson, *The Good Citizen: A History of American Civic Life* (New York: Free Press, 1998); and Kay Lehman Schlozman,

"Citizen Participation in America: What Do We Know? Why Do We Care?" in *Political Science: The State of the Discipline,* ed. Ira Katznelson and Helen V. Miller (New York: W. W. Norton, 2002), 433–61.

4. Anthony Downs, *An Economic Theory of Democracy* (New York: Harper & Row, 1957).
5. Angus Campbell, Philip E. Converse, Warren E. Miller, and Donald E. Stokes, *The American Voter* (Chicago: University of Chicago Press, 1960). The researchers also found that only an extremely small proportion of the electorate (2.5 to 3.5 percent) thought about politics in terms of a coherent ideology, such as "liberal" or "conservative" orientations. Subsequent studies by members of the Michigan group tended to corroborate this depiction of the American voter as essentially uninformed, with little appreciation of the policy implications of the candidates' positions. In a study of the political belief systems of Americans, for example, Philip E. Converse found that they consisted mainly of what he called *nonattitudes*—political opinions that are inconsistent, contradictory, and subject to unpredictable fluctuations over time. Angus Campbell et al., *Elections and the Political Order* (New York: Wiley, 1966); Philip E. Converse, "The Nature of Belief Systems in Mass Public," in *Ideology and Discontent,* ed. David E. Apter (Glencoe, Ill.: Free Press, 1964). For a summary of more-recent treatments of expressive voting, see Randall Calvert, "Identity, Expression, and Rational-Choice Theory," in Katznelson and Miller, *Political Science,* 568–96. See the American National Election Study data at www.umich.edu/~nes/.
6. David Butler and Donald Stokes, *Political Change in Britain,* 2nd ed. (New York: St. Martin's Press, 1974); Philip E. Converse and Georges Dupeux, "Politicization and the Electorate in France and the United States," *Public Opinion Quarterly,* no. 26 (1963): 1–23.
7. See, for example, Samuel L. Popkin, *The Reasoning Voter* (Chicago: University of Chicago Press, 1991).
8. Russell J. Dalton, *Citizen Politics: Public Opinion and Political Parties in Advanced Industrial Democracies,* 3rd ed. (New York: Chatham House, 2002), 19ff, 189–93. See also Russell J. Dalton, Scott Flanagan, and Paul Allen Beck, eds., *Electoral Change in Advanced Industrial Democracies: Realignment or Dealignment?* (Princeton: Princeton University Press, 1984). See also Pippa Norris, ed., *Critical Citizens: Global Support for Democratic Governance* (Oxford: Oxford University Press, 1999); and Pippa Norris, *Democratic Phoenix: Political Activism Worldwide* (New York: Cambridge University Press, 2003).
9. Anthony Downs, "Social Values and Democracy," in *The Economic Approach to Politics: A Critical Assessment of the Theory of Rational Action*, ed. Kristin R. Monroe (New York: HarperCollins, 1991), 143–70. See also Donald P. Green and Ian Shapiro, *Pathologies of Rational Choice Theory* (New Haven: Yale University Press, 1994); and Jeffrey Friedman, ed., *The Rational Choice Controversy* (New Haven: Yale University Press, 1996).
10. For a different categorization, see Kenneth Janda, *Political Parties: A Cross-National Survey* (New York: Free Press, 1980), 5; and his essay "Comparative Political Parties: Research and Theory," in *Political Science: The State of the Discipline II,* ed. Ada W. Finifter (Washington, D.C.: American Political Science Association, 1993), 163–91. A classic is Giovanni Sartori, *Parties and Party Systems: A Framework for Analysis* (Cambridge: Cambridge University Press, 1976). For information on parties around the world, visit www.electionworld.org.
11. On Hezbollah, see Judith P. Harik, *Hezbollah: The Changing Face of Terrorism* (New York: Palgrave Macmillan, 2004); and Ahmad Nizar Hamzeh, *In the Path of Hizbullah* (Syracuse, N.Y.: Syracuse University Press, 2004). On Hamas, see Matthew Levitt, *Hamas: Politics, Charity, and Terrorism in the Service of Jihad* (New Haven: Yale University Press, 2006). On Pakistani parties, see Farooq Tanwir, "Religious Parties and Politics in Pakistan," at www.worldvaluessurvey.org.
12. On catch-all parties, see Otto Kirchheimer, "The Transformation of the West European Party Systems," in *Political Parties and Political Development,* ed. Joseph LaPalombara and Myron Weiner (Princeton: Princeton University Press, 1966), 177–200.

**13.** Thomas Childers, *The Nazi Voter* (Chapel Hill: University of North Carolina Press, 1983); Richard F. Hamilton, *Who Voted for Hitler?* (Princeton: Princeton University Press, 1982).

**14.** Roberto Michels, *Political Parties: A Study of the Oligarchical Tendencies of Modern Democracy*, trans. Eden and Cedar Paul (New York: Free Press, 1962).

**15.** See Morris P. Fiorina, "Parties, Participation, and Representation in America: Old Theories Face New Realities," in Katznelson and Miller, *Political Science*, 510–41.

**16.** Gabriel A. Almond and G. Bingham Powell Jr., *Comparative Politics: A Developmental Approach* (Boston: Little, Brown, 1966) and *Comparative Politics: System, Process, Policy* (Boston: Little, Brown, 1978).

**17.** The poll, conducted by Zogby International, was released in 2006. Consult www.zogby.com.

**18.** Paul Allen Beck, "The Dealignment Era in America," in Dalton, Flanagan, and Beck, *Electoral Change in Advanced Industrial Democracies*, 243. See also Gant and Luttbeg, *American Electoral Behavior*, 63–74.

**19.** Seymour M. Lipset and Stein Rokkan, eds., *Party Systems and Voter Alignments: Cross-National Perspectives* (New York: Free Press, 1967), 50. See also Dalton, *Citizen Politics*, 168–70. On the persistence of party loyalties in Britain, Germany, and the Netherlands, see Bradley M. Richardson, "European Party Loyalties Revisited," *American Political Science Review* 85, no. 3 (September 1991): 751–75.

**20.** For a detailed study, see Giovanni Sartori, *Parties and Party Systems* (Cambridge: Cambridge University Press, 1976).

**21.** Albert O. Hirschman, *Exit, Voice, and Loyalty* (Cambridge, Mass.: Harvard University Press, 1970).

**22.** Stephen Haggard and Robert R. Kaufman, *The Political Economy of Democratic Transitions* (Princeton: Princeton University Press, 1995), 163–74.

**23.** *Washington Post*, January 29, 2006. See also John R. Wright, *Interest Groups and Congress* (Boston: Allyn & Bacon, 1996), 23.

**24.** For introductions to corporatism in theory and practice, see Peter J. Williamson, *Varieties of Corporatism* (Cambridge: Cambridge University Press, 1985) and *Corporatism in Perspective* (London: SAGE, 1989), and Alan Cawson, *Corporatism and Political Theory* (Oxford: Basil Blackwell, 1986). See also Philippe C. Schmitter, "Still the Century of Corporatism?" *Review of Politics* 36 (1974): 85–131; Schmitter and Gerhard Lehmbruch, *Trends Towards Corporatist Intermediation* (Beverly Hills, Calif.: Sage, 1979); Lehmbruch and Schmitter, *Patterns of Corporatist Policy-Making* (Beverly Hills, Calif.: Sage, 1982); Peter J. Katzenstein, *Corporatism and Change: Austria, Switzerland, and the Politics of Industry* (Ithaca, N.Y.: Cornell University Press, 1984).

**25.** Charles Tilly, *Contention and Democracy in Europe, 1650–2000* (New York: Cambridge University Press, 2004); Mario Diani and Doug McAdam, eds., *Social Movements and Networks: Rational Approaches to Collective Action* (Oxford: Oxford University Press, 2003); Jack A. Goldstone, ed., *States, Parties, and Social Movements* (Cambridge: Cambridge University Press, 2003); Doug McAdam, Sidney Tarrow, and Charles Tilly, *Dynamics of Contention* (Cambridge: Cambridge University Press, 2001); Marco G. Giungi, Doug McAdam, and Charles Tilly, eds., *From Contention to Democracy* (Lanham, Md.: Rowman and Littlefield, 1998); and Sidney Tarrow, *Power in Movement: Social Movements and Contentious Politics*, 2nd ed. (Cambridge: Cambridge University Press, 1998).

**26.** Theodore J. Lowi, *At the Pleasure of the Mayor: Patronage and Power in New York City, 1898–1958* (London: Macmillan, 1964); P. A. Allum, *Politics and Society in Post-War Naples* (Cambridge: Cambridge University Press, 1973).

**27.** Sidney Tarrow, *The New Transnational Activism* (New York: Cambridge University Press, 2005); William E. DeMars, *NGOs and Transnational Networks: Wild Cards in World Politics* (Ann Arbor, Mich.: Pluto, 2005).

**28.** A classic work on this subject is William Kornhauser, *The Politics of Mass Society* (Glencoe, Ill.: Free Press, 1959).

**29.** For introductory overviews, see Peter C. Sederberg, *Fires Within: Political Violence and Revolutionary Change* (New York: Harper-Collins, 1994), and A. S. Cohen, *Theories of Revolution: An Introduction* (London: Thomas Nelson, 1975).

**30.** On revolution and collective action, see Michael Taylor, ed., *Rationality and Revolution* (New York: Cambridge University Press, 1988).

**31.** James Chowning Davies, "The J-curve of Rising and Declining Satisfactions as a Cause of Revolution and Rebellion," in *Violence in America,* rev. ed., ed. Hugh Davis Graham and Ted Robert Gurr (Beverly Hills, Calif.: Sage, 1976), 415–36.

**32.** Ted Robert Gurr, *Why Men Rebel* (Princeton: Princeton University Press, 1970). See also Ivo K. Feierabend et al., eds., *Anger, Violence, and Politics* (Englewood Cliffs, N.J.: Prentice Hall, 1972), and Fred R. von der Mehden, *Comparative Political Violence* (Englewood Cliffs, N.J.: Prentice Hall, 1973).

**33.** E. Victor Wolfenstein, *The Revolutionary Personality: Lenin, Trotsky, Gandhi* (Princeton: Princeton University Press, 1971); Bruce Mazlish, *The Revolutionary Ascetic: Evolution of a Political Type* (New York: Basic Books, 1976); Erik H. Erikson, *Gandhi's Truth: On the Origins of Militant Nonviolence* (New York: W. W. Norton, 1969).

**34.** Theda Skocpol, *States and Social Revolutions* (Cambridge: Cambridge University Press, 1979).

**35.** Cynthia L. McClintock, "Why Peasants Rebel: The Case of Peru's Sendero Luminoso," *World Politics* 37, no. 1 (October 1984): 48–84; David Scott Palmer, ed., *Shining Path of Peru* (New York: St. Martin's Press, 1992).

CHAPTER 12

# POLITICAL CULTURE

It is generally recognized that in the United States, certain basic attitudes about political life are widely shared. Americans tend to be rather proud of their political system, for example: they revere their Constitution, prizing it as one of the greatest political documents ever devised. At the same time, their attitudes toward politicians are rather ambivalent. Though Americans generally treat their political leaders with civility, they can be highly critical of politicians and even quite cynical about them.

Americans are also pretty ambivalent about government in general. There is a prevailing aversion to "big government" and excessive governmental intrusion in people's lives. In fact, many Americans do not have a particularly high regard for government. Though only a few Americans are intensely angry about their government, trust in government officials has declined appreciably since the 1960s.[1] Many people regard the government as inefficient and wasteful and hold the private business sector in higher esteem as more effective than politicians or bureaucrats. Most Americans value individual responsibility and personal initiative over excessive reliance on the state. Most favor equality (or equity) of opportunity rather than a state-enforced equality of condition.

In fact, most Americans just don't care about politics all that much. In a mid-1990s survey, only 18 percent of Americans said that politics was very important in their lives, ranking it at the bottom of their priorities after family, friends, religion, work, and leisure.[2] As we noted in the previous chapter, voter turnout in the United States is lower than in most other Western democracies. Still, most Americans perceive themselves as law abiding and have a high respect for law and order. They decisively reject violence as a legitimate form of political action.

Americans value hard work, believing that people are entitled to earn as much money as they can. Private enterprise, while not without problems, is viewed positively by most Americans as basically successful, even though many of them regard large corporations as excessively powerful and impersonal. Socialism is taboo. By and large, Americans tend to be distrustful of excessive power in any form, whether it is the power of government, of large corporations, or of "special interests" representing particular groups in society.

Nevertheless, most Americans believe that it is proper for the government to help take care of people who cannot help themselves. There is a consensus that such large government programs as Social Security, Medicare, and welfare for those unable to work are necessary. Some observers maintain that Americans in recent decades have become so accustomed to expecting various government benefits that an "entitlement" mentality has set in. While they may object to big government in principle, they favor it in practice as long as they can derive some gain from it.

Most Americans favor compromise. They like to get things done, and a refusal to compromise is regarded as a barrier to effective action. Quite a few Americans have become dissatisfied with the two main political parties in recent years because they believe that Democratic and Republican politicians are more interested in opposing each other than in reaching effective agreements that can help the country. This willingness to compromise helps make for moderation in American political life. Most Americans think of themselves as moderates or centrists. Even those who regard themselves as liberals or conservatives tend to shun the more extreme tendencies of these competing orientations. Political radicalism of any kind is generally frowned upon.

Of all the political values Americans hold, freedom usually tops the list. Typically this means freedom from excessive governmental interference, but it is more than that. To most Americans, freedom means that they can come and go as they please and express themselves as they wish, that there are practically no barriers to what they can accomplish, and that the future is full of possibilities. Most Americans are relatively optimistic about the future; there is a continuing belief that all are entitled to fulfill "the American dream": to own one's own house, earn a rising income, and enjoy the pleasures of life, a value extolled in the Declaration of Independence as "the pursuit of happiness." Most Americans are content and optimistic. Surveys conducted in 2005 reported that 58 percent of Americans said they were "very satisfied with their lives" and 65 percent said they expected their lives to improve in the next five years. By contrast, in 2004 only 33 percent of the British, 21 percent of Germans, 18 percent of the French, and 16 percent of Italians were "very satisfied." On average, 44 percent of Western Europeans expected their lives to improve.

Americans are also generally tolerant of the freedoms of fellow Americans, and they have a general commitment to "fair play" and equity. Their tolerance has limits, however. Although there has been substantial progress in the area of racial and ethnic tolerance over the past three decades, racial divisions persist, and many heterosexuals are intolerant of homosexuals. Most Americans favor immigration, boasting that the United States is a "land of immigrants"; but there is unease about the influx of illegal immigrants, who are perceived as enjoying the benefits of American society unfairly.

On the whole, Americans can work together to achieve common goals. A high degree of interpersonal cooperation undergirds American society, giving rise to all sorts of civic, business, cultural, philanthropic, and other associations and volunteer organizations. But many Americans also experience a tension between their desire for freedom and individualism, on the one hand, and close community bonds on the other. Interpersonal trust is declining, especially among younger Americans, as is participation in voluntary associations.

Most Americans are religious. To a greater extent than people in most other economically advanced democracies, they believe in God, attend church regularly, and are profoundly influenced by religious beliefs and moral teachings. (See tables 12.1 and 12.2.)

To be sure, not all Americans subscribe to all these notions. Public opinion survey data, however, show that large numbers of them do, often a majority. In most respects, these surveys have displayed considerable consistency over the last several decades.[3]

## DEFINING POLITICAL CULTURE

The attitudes toward politics that were just described are representative of what political scientists would call the prevailing *political culture* of the United States.

> **Political culture** ***is a pattern of shared values, moral norms, beliefs, expectations, and attitudes that relate to politics and its social context.***

Political culture reflects the ways people think and feel about political life. It consists of clusters of attitudes about authority, government, and society that are accepted by large portions of a country's population, quite often the majority. It includes broadly diffused core *values*, especially those that relate to political ideals and social relations. In some cases, the *ideas of liberal and social democracy—*

**TABLE 12.1**

**Belief in God, 1947–2001**

Percentage of the public who said yes when asked if they believed in God.

| Country | 1947 | 1968 | 1975 | 1981 | 1990 | 1995 | 2001 | Change |
|---|---|---|---|---|---|---|---|---|
| Sweden | 80 | 60 | | 52 | 38 | 48 | 46 | −33.6 |
| Netherlands | 80 | 79 | | 64 | 61 | | 58 | −22.0 |
| Australia | 95 | | 80 | 79 | | 75 | 75 | −19.9 |
| Norway | 84 | 73 | | 68 | 58 | 65 | | −18.9 |
| Denmark | 80 | | | 53 | 59 | | 62 | −17.9 |
| Britain | | 77 | 76 | 73 | 72 | | 61 | −16.5 |
| Greece | | 96 | | | | | 84 | −12.3 |
| West Germany | | 81 | 72 | 68 | 63 | 71 | 69 | −12.0 |
| Belgium | | | 78 | 76 | 65 | | 67 | −11.2 |
| Finland | 83 | 83 | | | 61 | 73 | 72 | −10.8 |
| France | 66 | 73 | 72 | 59 | 57 | | 56 | −10.1 |
| Canada | 95 | | 89 | 91 | 85 | | 88 | −7.2 |
| Switzerland | | 84 | | | 77 | 77 | | −7.2 |
| India | | | 98 | | 93 | 94 | | −4.0 |
| Japan | | | 38 | 39 | 37 | 44 | 35 | −3.0 |
| Austria | | 85 | | | 78 | | 83 | −1.9 |
| United States | 94 | 98 | 94 | 96 | 93 | 94 | 94 | 0.4 |
| Brazil | 96 | | | | 98 | 99 | | 3.0 |

*Source:* Reprinted from Pippa Norris and Ronald Inglehart, *Sacred and Secular: Religion and Politics Worldwide* (Cambridge: Cambridge University Press, 2004), 90.

**TABLE 12.2**

**Must Political Leaders Believe in God?**

Percentage of the public who agree that "Politicians who do not believe in God are unfit for public office."

| | | | | | | | |
|---|---|---|---|---|---|---|---|
| Pakistan | 95 | India | 42 | Lithuania | 20 | *Slovenia* | 11 |
| Indonesia | 89 | *United States* | 39 | *W. Germany* | 18 | *Britain* | 10 |
| Egypt | 88 | Mexico | 39 | *Ireland* | 16 | S. Korea | 10 |
| Morocco | 86 | *Greece* | 37 | Poland | 16 | *France* | 9 |
| Iran | 83 | Argentina | 35 | Bosnia | 16 | *Belgium* | 9 |
| Nigeria | 82 | Chile | 35 | *Italy* | 15 | *Japan* | 8 |
| Jordan | 81 | Ukraine | 34 | *Austria* | 15 | *E. Germany* | 8 |
| S. Africa | 57 | Serbia | 27 | Estonia | 14 | Czech Rep. | 6 |
| Turkey | 57 | Russia | 22 | *Spain* | 12 | *Denmark* | 4 |
| Romania | 52 | Slovakia | 22 | Hungary | 12 | *Sweden* | 4 |
| Venezuela | 52 | *Canada* | 21 | *Finland* | 12 | *Netherlands* | 2 |

*Note:* High-income democracies are in italics.
*Source:* www.worldvaluessurvey.org (2006).

such as individual freedom, equality, tolerance, and social welfare—are the main sources of political values. In other cases *religion* is a source of values. Many political and social values in the United States, such as individual dignity and social equality, have been shaped by the Judeo-Christian heritage. Much like patriotism, religion itself is a *political* value in America, as reflected in the mottos "In God We Trust" and "One nation, under God." Despite the formal separation of church and state, U.S. political leaders routinely invoke the deity in political speeches and call on the citizenry to pray in times of national crisis. Christian denominations like Roman Catholicism, Protestantism, and Eastern Orthodoxy have each made contributions of their own to political and social values in various countries, in some cases by supporting democracy, in others by propping up authoritarian regimes.

Similarly, Confucianism (which is a moral-philosophical tradition that functions like a religion) has exerted a profound influence on prevailing values in countries like China, Taiwan, and Singapore. It is the principal source of what some East Asians extol as "Asian values," which emphasize respect for authority and the individual's responsibilities to the community, while disparaging Western notions of individualism and freedom of expression as dangerous threats to social harmony and political order. Perhaps not surprisingly, apologists of authoritarian regimes in this part of the world have argued that "Asian values" are incompatible with democracy. Islam has had an equally powerful impact on the political culture of numerous countries in the Middle East, Africa, and various parts of Asia, with important political and social implications for the role of women and for the state's responsibility for the enforcement of Islamic law and customs. Hinduism in India and Shinto in Japan have also had profound effects on the ways people view politics in those countries. But religious beliefs and practices are in decline in many countries, reflecting long-term trends toward *secularization*, especially in economically advanced democracies (see table 12.1). We'll discuss some reasons for these trends later in this chapter.

*Nationalism* may also be a source of political values, involving a range of affective attachments to one's country or people that run from quiet patriotism to militant hypernationalism.

Closely related to political and social values are *norms* that define right and wrong in the behavior of public officials, in the substance of government policy, and in the enforcement of legal codes. In some countries, for example, providing gifts to officials in exchange for favors is acceptable, but in others it is condemned as corruption. Public policy relating to abortion and homosexuality largely reflects prevailing (or conflicting) moral tenets within a given country. Some countries, like the United States, have the death penalty; others, like the twenty-seven members of the European Union, have banned it. Governments based on Islamic law—such as the regimes in Iran, Saudi Arabia, Afghanistan under the Taliban, and certain parts of Nigeria—sanction decapitation, stoning, amputation, and flogging as just punishments. Singapore practices caning. And some societies tolerate revenge killings and other customary forms of tribal or village justice.

General *beliefs* about the nature of politics are also components of political culture. People in one culture, for example, may view their political system as essentially transparent and accessible, with state officials sharing information with the public and making decisions in accordance with the public's wishes. The game of politics in this perception is one in which everybody has a chance to win something, and today's losers can be tomorrow's winners. By contrast, people in another political culture may perceive politics in darkly conspiratorial terms as the preserve of distant elites who demand obedience and play favorites. In this view, politics is rigged as a zero-sum game in which the winners take all at the losers' expense. Trust in government is also a critical element of a country's political belief system. Can the people who run the country's political institutions be trusted to be ethical, truthful, and fair, and to act in the best interests of the people rather than in their own self-interest? As we'll see later in this chapter, trust is declining in most of the world's established democracies. Beliefs about politics color the *expectations* people have about how their political system works. In most well-established democracies, people expect elections to take place regularly and they do not expect the military to seize power. In other countries the public's expectations may be quite different. In some political cultures there is a general expectation that political figures and other elites (such as business executives) will abide by the law or suffer serious consequences if they do not. In others, people learn to expect powerful figures to do what they want and get away with it.

Political culture thus involves a combination of things that together shape mass *attitudes* toward politics and the implications of political life. Though some regard political culture as a nebulous concept, because it refers to so many disparate perceptions and feelings, many political scientists believe that it is a real phenomenon of social psychology that can be empirically verified in studies of public opinion.[4]

Most countries have a *dominant political culture*, a collection of attitudes that are broadly shared by the political elites and a large proportion of the population. These dominant or prevailing attitudes frequently cut across social classes, ethnic groups, and other social strata. The attitudes we have just described as elements of the dominant political culture in the United States are broadly representative of "middle America"—the white middle class.[5] To be sure, not everyone in the United States shares all of them. A majority of African Americans have different attitudes than most whites on a host of racial questions, for example. Nevertheless, they share quite a few basic attitudes with whites, including support for the Constitution, individual freedom, private enterprise, equality of opportunity, the importance of education and hard work, and belief in God.

Many, if not most, countries also have one or more *political subcultures*. **A political subculture *is a political culture that deviates from the dominant culture in key respects.*** In the United States, many poor and uneducated people, for example, feel more or less permanently alienated from the American political and economic systems. They may feel a fundamental dissatisfaction with life in general and a sense of being trapped in their circumstances. In some instances these orientations are combined with a hostile attitude toward authority, intolerance of different ethnic groups, and a sense that one has nothing to compromise. In the most extreme cases these attitudes may lead to violations of the law and perhaps a tendency to violence.

### Political Socialization and Psychology

The defining attitudes of a political culture are essentially learned and transmitted in what is called the *political socialization process*. **Political socialization *is the process in which individuals learn about politics and the political culture of their society.*** One's *family* is the *primary agent of socialization. Secondary agents of socialization* include peer groups, schools, churches, places of employment, and other elements of the larger society.

Mass attitudes reflect the attitudes and perceptions of individuals. At the same time, the attitudes of individuals are profoundly influenced by the cultural orientations of the larger society in which they live. Individuals interact with their political cultures in complex ways that are difficult to capture in a single parsimonious theory. While rational choice theorists focus on the incentives and costs that structure individual decisions, some "culturalists" highlight the impact of political culture as an independent variable that shapes behavior.[6] And psychologists have provided insight into cognitive processes that are anything but rational. The perceptions and attitudes of individuals and masses alike can take irrational turns, at times with disturbing political consequences. In *The Authoritarian Personality,* a group of psychologists and political analysts probed the personality factors that inclined certain types of people to be particularly receptive to fascist or racist propaganda. A rigid adherence to conventional values, a low tolerance for ambiguity, a reliance on superstition as opposed to scientific logic, and gullibility as opposed to independent critical judgment emerged as the leading characteristics of the "antidemocratic personality."[7] In another famous study, *The Theory of Cognitive Dissonance,* Leon Festinger reported on experiments showing that many people, when faced with information that contradicts one of their deeply held opinions, preferences, or biases, find ways to ignore or explain away the undesirable messages rather than alter their views in a rational fashion to take account of the facts before their eyes. They also go out of their way to avoid information that they suspect will be "dissonant" with what they are used to believing. Decision makers and the mass public are likewise prone to these misperceptions.[8]

## STUDIES OF POLITICAL CULTURE

The concept of political culture has a venerable tradition. Plato and Aristotle both attached considerable importance to the basic attitudes people have about authority, about how social relationships should be conducted, and about the roles government should play in people's lives. Some of these cultural attitudes, they maintained, favor democracy, while others are incompatible with democratic self-government.

Alexis de Tocqueville placed cultural values and attitudes at the forefront of his famous analysis of democracy in America. In place of our contemporary term *political culture,* he used *mores,* a generic term meaning the broadly shared customs and values of a society. Tocqueville defined mores as "the whole moral and intellectual state of a people," and he was particularly interested in *political* mores, those "habits of the heart" and "mental habits" that helped shape the political behavior of Americans. In his view, American political mores were characterized above all by the love of liberty, an attitude he believed was propagated by both the Protestant and Catholic religions in America, by the educational system, and by the family, with women playing an especially important role. In addition, Tocqueville believed that Americans had a basic good sense about political life that came from generations of experience with social cooperation and local self-government at the village level. He also noted their general "restraint," "moderation," and "self-command."

In fact, Tocqueville regarded these attitudinal factors as even more important in accounting for the success of American democracy than the Constitution and other legal props of the U.S. governmental system. "Laws are always unsteady when unsupported by mores," he wrote. "Mores are the only tough and durable power in a nation." Without the proper attitudes, values, and habits on the part of the population, Tocqueville clearly implied, even the most brilliantly conceived democratic institutions would inevitably rest on shaky foundations. Other students of early American history have also underscored the impact of cultural factors on political developments. Gordon S. Wood, for example, has pointed out that colonial-era concepts of equal dignity were a powerful component of the American Revolution against Britain. "Ordinary Americans came to believe that no one . . . was really better than anyone else," a notion that has made the United States "the most egalitarian nation in the history of the world," despite its history of slavery and great disparities of wealth.[9]

German sociologist Max Weber was also a keen student of political culture. He believed that political and economic institutions could not be understood solely on their own terms. Cultural attitudes deriving from such nonpolitical sources as religion, the family, and rules of logic can also have a profound impact on political and economic reality. In *The Protestant Ethic and the Spirit of Capitalism,* Weber wondered why Protestants tended to dominate the German economy at the turn of the twentieth century, occupying the most important corporate executive positions to a far greater extent than Catholics. His answer was that Protestantism and Catholicism had traditionally taken divergent approaches to religious asceticism (austere living). Whereas Martin Luther had placed a high value on personal engagement in worldly activities and on modestly saving one's wealth, medieval Catholic doctrine preached withdrawal from the worlds of commerce and politics in favor of worshiping God in monasteries. Although these ascetic ideals faded over time, they generated mass attitudes toward economic behavior that endured. In the process, Weber concluded, Protestantism proved more conducive than Catholicism to encouraging entrepreneurial activity and the accumulation of wealth.[10]

A groundbreaking study of political culture was published in 1963 by Gabriel Almond and Sidney Verba. *The Civic Culture* examined political culture in five countries (the United States, Britain, West Germany, Italy, and Mexico). Based on responses to a host of questions about politics, the authors concluded that the populations of each of these countries could be divided into three groups:

1. *Participants,* who generally are knowledgeable about politics and have positive feelings about their governmental system, regarding it as legitimate and worthy of support. They vote regularly and may also get involved in other forms of political activity.
2. *Subjects,* who are less knowledgeable about what is going on in politics. Subjects evince relatively little pride in their political institutions, vote rarely, and have little confidence in their ability to get results out of government, but they are law abiding and can be quite deferential in their attitudes toward governmental authority.
3. *Parochials,* who know practically nothing about politics, especially at the national level. Their world is usually confined to their local community or village. They are basically alienated from their government and apathetic, with very low confidence in their ability to get government officials to help them or to effect political change.

Almond and Verba concluded that all the countries they studied consisted of a mixture of participants, subjects, and parochials. The countries differed, however, with respect to the relative size of the three categories in proportion to the population. At the time the studies were conducted, in the late 1950s, the United States had a high proportion of participants and subjects. Mexico and Italy had high proportions of subjects and parochials, while Britain and Germany fell in between.

Almond and Verba hypothesized that democracy would be most stable in countries possessing what they called a **civic culture**, that is, ***a combination of fairly large numbers of participants and subjects together with a smaller number of parochials.*** In their view, democracy did not require a population consisting entirely of politically active participants. Too many activists, they argued, might destabilize the political system. Democracy would be most stable if, in addition to political activists, the population also included subjects and parochials who did not make too many political demands and who quietly accepted the existing political arrangements. They believed that the United States and Britain most closely approximated this ideal mixture.

Like Tocqueville, Almond and Verba affirmed that a successful democracy requires more than just democratic governmental institutions and laws; it also requires a compatible political culture. "Unless the political culture is able to support a democratic system," they wrote, "the chances for the success of that system are slim." By contrast, the authors hypothesized that authoritarian governments of various kinds (such as communist countries and military dictatorships) would rest on a cultural foundation of subject and parochial attitudes. Politically active participants would be a small minority in such countries, confined mainly to the ruling elite and their most determined opponents. Advocates of the importance of political culture thus contend that authoritarian governments do not rule on the basis of force alone. They stay in power at least in part because large segments of the population share certain attitudes and beliefs supportive of authoritarian rule.

Though some scholars have questioned the assumptions and conclusions of *The Civic Culture,* others have supported their basic contention that attitudes and feelings do play a major role in explaining why some countries have stable democracies and others do not.[11] Let's look at some examples in the following hypothesis-testing exercise.

## HYPOTHESIS-TESTING EXERCISE: Does Political Culture Matter?

### Hypothesis

The hypothesis to be tested asserts that political culture is a factor that affects the existence or success of democracy independently of other factors such as political institutions or economic realities.

### Variables

In this hypothesis, the *dependent variable* is the existence or success of *democracy* and the *independent variable* is *political culture.*

### Expectations

If the hypothesis is correct, then we would expect to find that countries with successful democracies have a political culture characterized by high levels of interpersonal trust and cooperation. Conversely, we would expect that countries in which these and related attitudes are not widely shared by the populace either are not democracies at all or have unstable, ineffective democracies. We would further expect to find that these cultural factors exercise an impact of their own on democracy, independently of such other variables as political institutions or levels of wealth. In testing the hypothesis empirically, we would expect to find evidence of these attitudes in public opinion surveys and various forms of behavior, such as public involvement in voluntary associations.

### Evidence

In several major books and other works devoted to testing this hypothesis, Ronald Inglehart has found considerable evidence that high levels of interpersonal trust and voluntary participation in cooperative associations are strongly correlated with stable democracies. Countries that lack these cultural attributes tend to be less successful at building or maintaining stable democratic institutions. While admitting that the cultural factors associated with democracy are often correlated with high levels of national economic development, Inglehart notes that "wealth alone does not automatically bring democracy." By the same token, he notes that "democracy is not attained simply by making institutional changes or by clever elite-level maneuvering." Rather, cultural factors play a role of their own in affecting democracy's prospects.[12]

In an innovative study, Robert Putnam and his associates examined various explanations of why some regions of Italy have very effective governments while other regions do not. They found that economic

| Submissive | Deferential | Interactive | Alienated | Rebellious |
|---|---|---|---|---|

**FIGURE 12.1 Continuum of Attitudes Toward Authority**

factors were not the principal explanatory variables. The critical difference rested on a key aspect of political culture, namely, the extent to which people trusted one another enough to cooperate in forming associations. Regions with a history of social trust and cooperation were more successful at making democracy work than were those characterized by high levels of suspicion and non-cooperation. The combination of social capital, civil society, and a civic culture forms *civicness*, an essential cultural ingredient of democracy.[13]

Unfortunately, there is little or no public opinion survey data available in most nondemocratic countries. Public attitudes thus cannot be systematically examined in these cases. However, there is ample historical evidence that many authoritarian states have had low levels of participation in private voluntary associations.

**Conclusions**

In a study of some forty-three countries, Inglehart concluded that "political culture does seem to be a central factor in the survival of democracy." There is a general tendency for successful democracies to be undergirded by the cultural attitudes identified in the hypothesis. Putnam and other scholars have also uncovered evidence that political culture can be an important independent variable explaining why democracy works well in some instances but less effectively (or not at all) in others. These findings are largely *consistent* with the hypothesis. But there have been very few works that have tested the hypothesis with the empirical thoroughness of Inglehart and Putnam, and more work needs to be done to see if evidence seriously contradicting their findings can be found.

## Conceptualizing Political Culture

To make the concept of political culture clearer, let's consider some patterns of attitudes and values about political and social life that can exist in different countries. We'll divide these attitudinal patterns into three clusters: (1) *attitudes toward authority;* (2) *attitudes toward society;* and (3) *attitudes toward politics,* especially *the state.* Within each of these clusters, we'll look at specific dichotomies (i.e., paired opposites) that form the outer extremes of possible attitudes people may have. We should recognize, however, that many people, perhaps the majority, do not share these extreme attitudes, but are located at various points in between them. Hence we should conceptualize the various attitudes people have toward a given object (such as the government) in terms of a *continuum,* a line of gradations between one polar extreme and the opposite. Let's clarify these notions with specific examples.

**Attitudes Toward Authority** One possible dichotomy that describes attitudes toward authority is the *submissive-rebellious* dichotomy (figure 12.1). At one extreme, people can be highly submissive toward authority (whether in the family or in the political community). Often this attitude is tinged with fatalism and resignation (e.g., "Nothing can be changed; it is God's will."). At the other extreme are those who reject authority altogether and seek to rebel against it. But there are various stations in between. Without being humbly submissive, people can be *deferential* toward authority, like the "subjects" in Almond and Verba's analysis. These people willingly respect authority but do not seek to deal with it directly. Moving along the continuum, people can be *interactive* with authority: they can share in making the decisions that affect their lives. This interactive attitude is characteristic of what Almond and Verba would call "participants."

Next along the continuum we find *alienated* attitudes toward authority. Alienated people are too discontented to be obligingly submissive or quietly deferential, and they are generally quite cynical about the authority patterns under which they live. But if they do anything at all to express their alienation, the actions they take will usually be sporadic, halfhearted, and ultimately ineffective (such as persistently refusing to vote). At the opposite extreme on this continuum, people with *rebellious* attitudes toward authority are so hostile to the ruling powers that they try to take action against them. In political

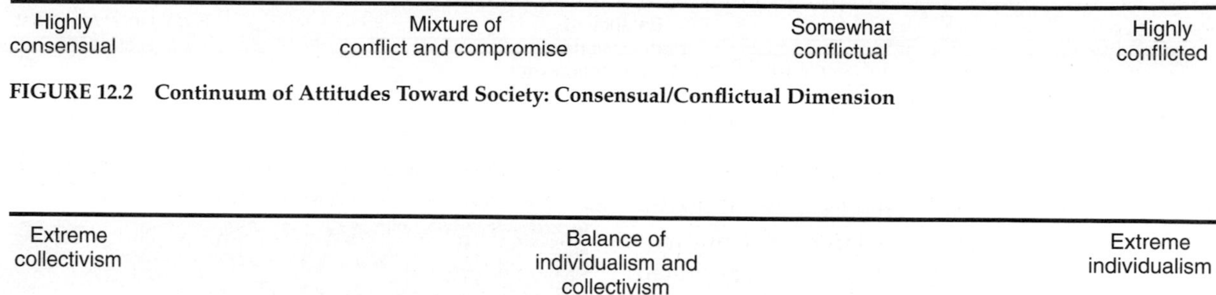


**FIGURE 12.2 Continuum of Attitudes Toward Society: Consensual/Conflictual Dimension**



**FIGURE 12.3 Continuum of Attitudes Toward Society: Collectivist/Individualist Dimension**

life, rebels may undertake such dissident behavior as publicly denouncing the government, or they may actively seek to overthrow it, whether violently or through nonviolent resistance. Highly traditional political cultures, such as Middle Eastern sheikdoms, tend to have a large number of submissive and deferential citizens. Democracies thrive on an interactive citizenry, though some people may feel alienated. Any country with a large number of rebels is probably experiencing violent discontent or civil war.

**Attitudes Toward Society** One continuum of this type is delineated by the *consensual–conflictual* dichotomy (figure 12.2). At one end of the line we find people with highly cooperative attitudes toward other individuals and social groups. They exhibit high levels of tolerance, interpersonal trust, and willingness to compromise. At the other end we find highly conflictual attitudes toward other individuals and social groups, defined by correspondingly low levels of tolerance, interpersonal trust, and propensity to compromise. The continuum shows various gradations in between. Yugoslavia, wracked by ethnic cleansing in the 1990s, and Lebanon, with a plethora of religious groups embroiled in civil strife down to the present day are examples of highly conflictual political cultures. Japan exemplifies a highly consensual one: political decisions typically have to meet with a broad social consensus before they can be finalized. The United States, Canada, the West European democracies, and other successful democratic states generally display a mixture of conflict and compromise, with the conflicts typically dealt with through the democratic process rather than through violence.

Another dichotomy we can expect to find in people's attitudes toward other people is the *collectivist–individualist* dichotomy (figure 12.3). At the far right end, the most extreme individualists have an "everyone-for-himself" mentality. Proponents of *economic individualism* reject government assistance and seek to take care of themselves and their immediate families entirely on their own. If they fail in these efforts, they proudly reject handouts or charity. Such extreme types expect everyone else in society to behave the same way. Proponents of what may be called *expressive individualism* believe that all individuals should have the right to say what they want and live as they please, with scant regard for the larger society. Whether stressing economic or expressive individualism, extreme individualists place the individual at the center of society.

At the left end of this continuum are extreme collectivists who discount individual rights and freedoms in favor of group rights and group activities. Just as extreme individualists may be willing to tolerate a high level of social inequality, at least some extreme collectivists seek to achieve as much egalitarianism as they can in all facets of social life: equality of opportunity, wealth, education, power, and so forth. But collectivism also risks producing the very opposite of political and social equality if authoritarian leaders and parties, acting in the name of the common good, establish a dictatorial regime commandeered by a narrow elite and its privileged supporters. That is what happened in Russia when the Communists took power. In the middle are those

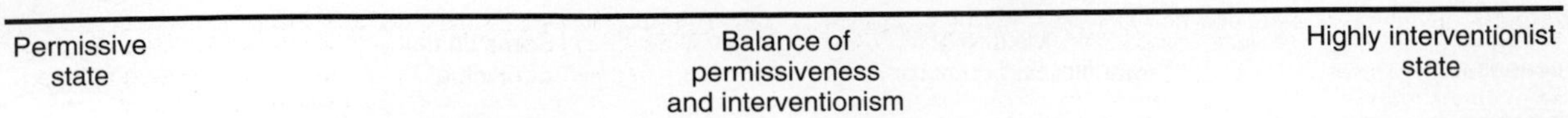

| Permissive state | Balance of permissiveness and interventionism | Highly interventionist state |
|---|---|---|

**FIGURE 12.4 Continuum of Attitudes Toward the State**

who seek a balance between the freedom of the individual and the welfare of the larger community.

Historically, the United States has gravitated somewhat toward the individualist side of this dichotomy, an attitude reflected in the old nostrum, "The government that governs least, governs best." As we pointed out at the start of this chapter, however, most Americans also expect their government to provide various social welfare benefits. This balance of individualist and collectivist values places the United States close to the middle of the continuum, though it still leans toward the pole of individualism. Most European countries are also close to the center, but they gravitate more toward the collectivist side because of public support for their well-funded welfare states. Russia has generally gravitated toward the collectivist side. Hypothetically, individualist cultures are more likely to favor market economies than are collectivist cultures, which would tend to favor strong state intervention in the economy in order to promote social equality.

**TABLE 12.3**

**Attitudes Toward the State in Selected Democracies (1996)**

Percentage who say they "agree" or "strongly agree" that it is the state's responsibility to reduce income disparities between those with high incomes and those with lower incomes.

| | | | |
|---|---|---|---|
| East Germany[a] | 76% | Spain | 60% |
| Russia | 74 | Britain | 54 |
| Israel (Jews) | 70 | West Germany | 49 |
| Israel (Arabs) | 69 | Japan | 48 |
| France | 68 | Canada | 43 |
| Hungary | 66 | Australia | 43 |
| Italy | 65 | United States | 33 |

[a]Consists of the area of the former communist state of East Germany.

*Source:* International Social Survey Program, Role of Government III, 1996. Accessed via the Inter-university Consortium for Political and Social Research: http://www.icpsr.umich.edu.

**Attitudes Toward the State** The main dichotomy in this cluster of attitudes is the *permissive state–interventionist state* dichotomy (figure 12.4). At one end are those who favor a weak government that permits people the widest possible freedom to do what they want. The most extreme permissivists want no governmental interference of any kind in the economy (no taxes!), a minimal government role in maintaining law and order, no national obligation to defend the country; indeed, very few government intrusions of any kind. The most extreme permissivist is basically an anarchist. As one moves along the continuum, one finds increasing levels of support for various governmental tasks, starting with such elemental ones as the maintenance of law and order, regulation of transportation facilities, delivery of the mail, and control over the national defense.

At the other end of the continuum are those who favor maximum governmental intervention in all facets of life, including control over the economy and the regulation of social conflicts. Political elites who favor such an interventionist state may do so, at least in some cases, in order to maximize their own power over the population or over the economy. But ordinary citizens may also prefer an interventionist state, usually because they want the state to protect them against economic fluctuations, ill health, destitution in old age, or other possible hardships, whether natural or human-made. Proponents of the interventionist state may be willing to give up some of their personal freedoms in exchange for the state's assistance. Of course, there are less extreme variants of this protectivist attitude as one moves back toward the center of the continuum.

Various questions have been asked of citizens in different countries to ascertain their attitudes toward the state. The next table and figure show how wide the range of opinion can be among some of the world's economically advanced democracies. Table 12.3 reflects attitudes on the question of whether it should be the state's responsibility to

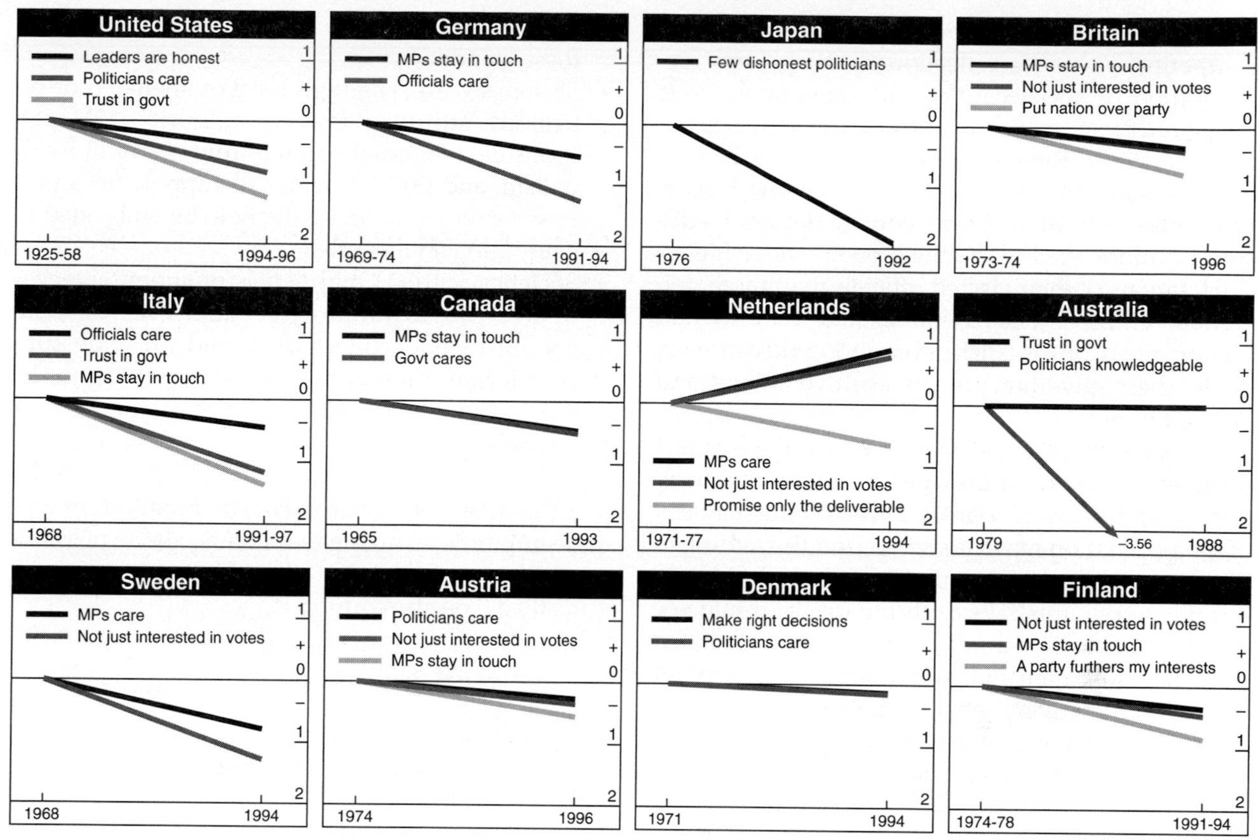


**FIGURE 12.5 Political Confidence, Annual Percent Change**
*Source: The Economist*, July 17, 1999.

reduce income disparities. Figure 12.5 shows a general tendency toward declining trust in a number of established democracies. Surveys conducted in Western Europe in 2004 confirmed these trends. On average, 54 percent of people in the fifteen West European member-states of the European Union tended "not to trust" their national parliaments, 61 percent did not trust their national governments, and 76 percent did not trust their political parties. The British displayed the least amount of trust in their national institutions (only 25 percent trusted the British Parliament and 19 percent trusted the British government). Greeks and Danes had the highest levels of trust in their parliaments (63 percent); citizens of Luxembourg had the highest level of trust in their national government (61 percent).[14]

A recent study of public attitudes in the trilateral world (North America, Western Europe, and Japan) confirmed these trends and proposed some explanations for them. In most of these countries, citizens have perceived an accelerating decline in the capacity of governments to respond to their needs—a phenomenon due, at least in some countries, to globalization. As the intrusion of external economic and political influences from abroad expands, producing unemployment and other unwelcome consequences, domestic governments have less latitude than in the past to act on their own when addressing the population's concerns. Global problems require complicated global efforts, a situation that many people find frustrating. A second cause of declining rates of trust is the growing perception that political leaders have failed in their obligation of fidelity to the public's expectations and interests. Malfeasance in office is one manifestation of this tendency. Another is excessive polarization and unwillingness to compromise on the part of competing parties, a reflection of the general deterioration of social capital and cooperative civic engagement in many of today's democracies. In another study, Russell Dalton found that in economically advanced democracies declining trust is most prevalent among the young, the well educated, and the well-to-do. Such people have higher expectations of their elected officials than more deferential citizens tend to have, and they exhibit higher levels of dissatisfaction and cynicism even when their governments do positive things and avoid failure.[15]

The spectrums of attitudes shown in Figures 12.1 through 12.4 make ample room for political subcultures within a given country. Whereas the majority of the population may cluster around the middle of the spectrum along the authority continuum, favoring interactive relations with the decision makers, some people in the same country may be alienated from the dominant elites or political majority, or may even be actively rebellious. Similarly, whereas a few people may favor "rugged individualism," most segments of society may not. The point is, almost every country will have people whose attitudes can be located at different points along the attitudinal spectrums. At the same time, many countries will show majorities huddled around the midpoint. In short, we should conceive of each country's political culture as consisting of a combination of attitudes on a variety of dimensions. In most cases it would be an oversimplification to suggest that we can locate an entire country at a precise point along any of the continuums we have shown in this chapter.

We can hypothesize that some combinations of attitudes will be more supportive of stable democracy than others are, while alternative combinations can be expected to yield different results. For example, at least hypothetically we can assume that:

- Societies with (1) high levels of interactive attitudes toward authority, (2) a high level of consensual attitudes toward society, (3) intermediate levels of individualism and collectivism, and (4) roughly balanced support for permissiveness and intervention on the part of the state will be more likely to sustain a stable democracy than will societies whose majorities deviate from these standards.
- Societies with (1) a high level of alienated or rebellious attitudes toward authority, (2) high levels of conflictual social attitudes and individualism, and (3) high levels of support for a permissive, weak state are likely to be embroiled in continuing civil conflict.
- Societies with (1) high levels of submissiveness or deference to authority, (2) high levels of social consensus and collectivism, and (3) wide support for an interventionist state are likely to be fairly stable authoritarian states of one kind or another.

Of course, these alternative combinations of attitude mixtures by no means exhaust all the possibilities. We may find some other mixtures as we look directly at specific countries.

## Do Political Cultures Change?

Although most systematic studies of political culture have revealed considerable continuity in the way particular populations think about politics, political culture is rarely static. Attitudinal change is real; all political cultures evolve. In some cases such changes take place slowly, shifting only every two generations or more. But in other cases they occur a bit more rapidly. As noted in chapter 2, members of every generation tend to be influenced by the political events of their youth. When succeeding generations basically adopt the political attitudes of their parents with little or no change, obviously change in political culture will be slight. But when key segments of a particular generation adopt political attitudes at variance with those of the preceding generation, a country's political culture can shift accordingly.

A good example of such generational change occurred in West Germany after World War II. In 1953, some eight years after the defeat of Nazi Germany, only about half the population said that democracy was the best form of government. With the passing of the older generation and the emergence of younger people who grew up after the war, support for democracy rose appreciably. In 1972, 90 percent of West Germans favored democracy.[16] Similar changes are occurring right now in the formerly communist countries of Russia, Poland, the Czech Republic, and others. Attitudes toward authority, society, and the state are in flux, sometimes wildly so. Some people in these countries cling to old habits of mind and behavior and long for a restoration of strong political authority and a state-controlled economy; others (especially younger people) are ready to experiment with democracy and private enterprise.[17]

**Culture Shifts in Modernizing and Postindustrial Societies** Another shift in attitudes has occurred since the 1960s in many Western democracies. As Ronald Inglehart has shown, an increasing percentage of citizens in the United States and Western Europe in the 1960s and 1970s shared what he calls *postmaterialist values.* Instead of being motivated primarily by the need for financial security, as was the case with previous generations, a large number of citizens who came of voting age in these years, particularly those who had a secure economic background and higher education, tended to vote or engage in other forms of political behavior on the basis of broader concerns about the welfare of the community. The goals of urban renovation, environmental protection, and other community-wide considerations increasingly took precedence over personal wealth as a source of political behavior. Subsequent decades showed slight variations in these attitudes in particular countries.[18]

In a subsequent work, Inglehart undertook a sweeping investigation of the hypothesis that "economic, political and cultural change go together in coherent patterns that are changing the world in predictable ways." With an insightful look at the historical record and an analysis of recent survey data from forty-three countries, collected in the World Values Survey, Inglehart found substantial evidence consistent with modernization theory and what he calls "postmodernization."[19]

- *Modernization.* As societies progress from traditional, largely agricultural economies to industrialization, the attitudes and values of the population shift as well. A preoccupation with survival under conditions of acute scarcity gives way to a quest for personal economic advancement. Maximizing one's material security and wealth becomes a top priority.

  As people pursue these economic goals, they seek greater political influence. Whereas premodern societies tend to have authoritarian regimes, the rising prosperity and education levels that accompany industrial modernization promote greater mass political participation. Industrialism and the value changes accompanying it thus promote democracy.
- *Postmodernization.* In the most economically advanced societies of the late twentieth century, industrial economies developed into *postindustrial economies.* The service sector—consisting of government, education, banking and finance, retail stores, and all sorts of consumer services—replaced manufacturing as the main source of economic growth and employment. Personal and national incomes rose appreciably. A well-funded welfare state guaranteed minimal living standards for the less fortunate as well as various other benefits for all (medical insurance, social security pensions, and the like).

  Under these "postmodern" conditions of rising prosperity, the main priorities of a growing portion of the population shift from maximizing material wealth to maximizing nonmaterial forms of personal well-being: a satisfying job, a clean environment, more leisure time, and other postmaterialist values. Politically, these values entail less reliance on the state and declining deference to authority. People want less government intervention in their lives. Voters show greater independence at election time, loosening their traditional ties to the major political parties. Ironically, though their living standards are high, people with postmaterialist values have higher expectations and tend to display fairly high levels of dissatisfaction with their governments.

Gender roles change significantly in postmodern societies. Women are less confined to the home and more inclined to pursue higher education, careers, and political activism. People who embrace postmodern values are also more accepting of gender equality, divorce, homosexuality, abortion, and sexual liberalization than are the members of more traditional countries or less economically advanced segments of society.[20]

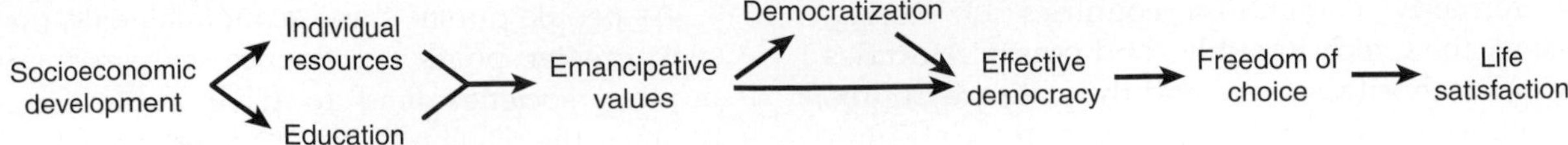


**FIGURE 12.6 The Logic of Human Development Theory**
*Source:* Based on Christian Welzel, Ronald Inglehart, and Hans-Dieter Klingemann, "The Theory of Human Development: A Cross-Cultural Analysis, *European Journal of Political Research* 42 (2003): 341–79.

Attitudes toward religion also change with postmodernism. Pippa Norris and Inglehart have shown that the populations of all economically advanced countries have manifested a general tendency toward secularization over the past fifty years, albeit at varying rates of change (see table 12.1). Belief in God, church attendance, the frequency of prayer, and other indicators of religious commitment have declined steadily in most of these countries as national wealth and educational levels have risen. Differences are also observable between affluent and less affluent citizens inside these countries: on average, the poor are nearly twice as religious as the rich. Even in the United States, an "outlier" country that has consistently remained more religious than most other wealthy democracies, two-thirds of the poor tend to regard religion as "very important" and pray every day, as compared with 47 percent of the highest income group. These and other data suggest that "as lives become more secure and immune to daily risks, the importance of religion gradually fades away." At the same time, however, the number of people around the globe who profess strong religious beliefs has never been higher. A major reason appears to be that countries whose populations have traditional religious attitudes are producing children at significantly higher rates than wealthier countries.[21]

**Human Development Theory** In a pathbreaking study, Inglehart and his collaborators, Christian Welzel and Hans-Dieter Klingemann, go beyond modernization-postmodernization theory and present what they call **human development theory**. Drawing on the work of other scholars, the Freedom House rankings, and the World Values Surveys conducted between 1981 and 2001, the study ***demonstrates causal linkages between economic development, the value of freedom, and democratic institutions.*** The authors begin with the well-established observation that scarce economic resources in poor countries compel people to adopt a cluster of attitudes necessary for survival. These *conformity values* include tight group discipline, distrust and intolerance of others, moral rigidity, and the acceptance of strong hierarchical authority patterns. But as the economy develops and individuals have more resources at their disposal, people become better educated and demand more liberty. Socioeconomic prosperity engenders such *emancipative values* as individual freedom and self-expression, along with greater tolerance for the freedoms and rights of others. As emancipative values spread across the population, popular demands for democracy rise.

When these trends occur in nondemocratic countries, they spark opposition to authoritarian elites and promote democratization. When they occur in countries that already have democratic institutions (including those we label semi-democratic and semi-authoritarian states), people become less willing to put up with limitations on their political influence or with corrupt leaders. In other words, they become less satisfied with the veneer of "formal democracy" and insist on a truly "effective democracy": a democracy that requires the integrity of the elite and ensures the government's accountability to the governed. At the end of this chain of causation (depicted in figure 12.6) come rising levels of *human choice:* people are increasingly free to choose the lives they want to lead. Freedom of choice is a globally shared value. Surveys conducted in 148 countries display a highly significant correlation between the perceptions of how much choice people believe they have, on the one hand, and their overall satisfaction with life, on the other hand.

All of this is good news for democracy advocates. Human development theory tells us that socioeconomic development sets in motion a train of processes that ultimately leads to democracy. But even though the causal connections laid out in the theory are valid across different countries and cultures, they cannot predict exactly when a democratization process, or a move toward "effective democracy," will take place in any specific country. As we saw in chapter 9, transitions to democracy and democratic consolidation depend on a variety of factors, some of which cannot be foreseen in advance. Inglehart and his co-authors acknowledge that their theory is probabilistic in nature: it highlights general tendencies that make democracy *probable* but not inevitable or predictable by a certain point in time. Every country moves along the path to democracy at its own pace, in accordance with its own specific economic, social, and political characteristics. Nevertheless, from human development theory and its supporting evidence come findings of global applicability: Democracy rests on both socioeconomic development *and* the value of freedom. Economic progress *promotes* support for the value of freedom. And as a key attribute of a country's political culture, freedom has a *causative* effect on democratic institutions; it is not simply a product of democratic institutions, as some scholars maintain.[22] Reinforcing these conclusions, Christian Welzel finds that when mass attitudes are shaped by aspirations of liberty, democratization tends to progress. Arguing against democratization theories that downplay mass attitudes, Welzel observes that no other independent variable, including per capita income or social capital, explains democratization processes better than emancipative values and aspirations when they are adopted by large elements of the populace. These findings, Welzel notes, are fully consistent with human development theory.[23]

The division of the world into different countries, regions, and cultures reflects different value orientations. Some countries and regions have societies that tend on average to favor *traditional* values: strong religious beliefs, deference to authority, close family ties, intolerance of diversity, nationalism, and a few others. By contrast, other countries have populations that tend to favor *secular-rational* values, such as weaker ties to religion and family, tolerance, democratic attitudes toward authority, and a cosmopolitan outlook. A second cultural dichotomy centers on the division between societies that emphasize *survival* values, reflecting the constraints of poverty, and those that tend to favor the *self-expressive* values associated with postmodernism. These differences are portrayed in the Inglehart-Welzel Values Map (figure 12.7).

In view of these striking cultural differences, is the world facing a "clash of civilizations"?

**A Clash of Civilizations?** Samuel Huntington has advanced the hypothesis that the main source of conflict in the contemporary world is neither ideological nor economic but cultural in nature, centered in a "clash of civilizations." Defining a civilization as the broadest level of a person's identity, Huntington divides the world into seven (perhaps eight) major civilizations: Sinic, Japanese, Hindu, Islamic, Orthodox, Western, and Latin American. A cohesive African civilization may also be emerging. Each one is rooted in a distinct blend of history and culture. For several of them, religion is the key defining feature. With the disappearance of the ideological rivalries of the Cold War, the principal "fault lines" in world politics are drawn at the borders of these cultural communities. Numerous "fault-line conflicts" between representatives of different civilizations have recently occurred in Bosnia, Sri Lanka, Russia, Kashmir, and other parts of the globe. In addition, the presence of powerful "core states" like China, Japan, India, Russia, and the United States at the head of their respective civilizations makes the prospect of a global civilization war, while "highly unlikely," at least possible, with potentially devastating results. Meanwhile, the West is now at the zenith of its economic and military power, but it is simultaneously entering a period of relative decline, losing ground to Asia in economic terms and to several other civilizations in demographic terms. The Western countries are also meeting stiff resistance from almost all the other civilizations—above all from the "Confucian-Islamic connection"—in their attempts to promote democratization and human rights around the world.

Under these circumstances, Huntington argues, the West must stick to its core democratic values but repudiate the idea that the defining features of Western civilization—Christianity, the rule of law, pluralistic democracy, individualism, and the separation of church and state—are universally applicable. The West's belief in the universality of Western culture, he writes, is false, immoral, and dangerous. Instead of arrogantly foisting these values on the

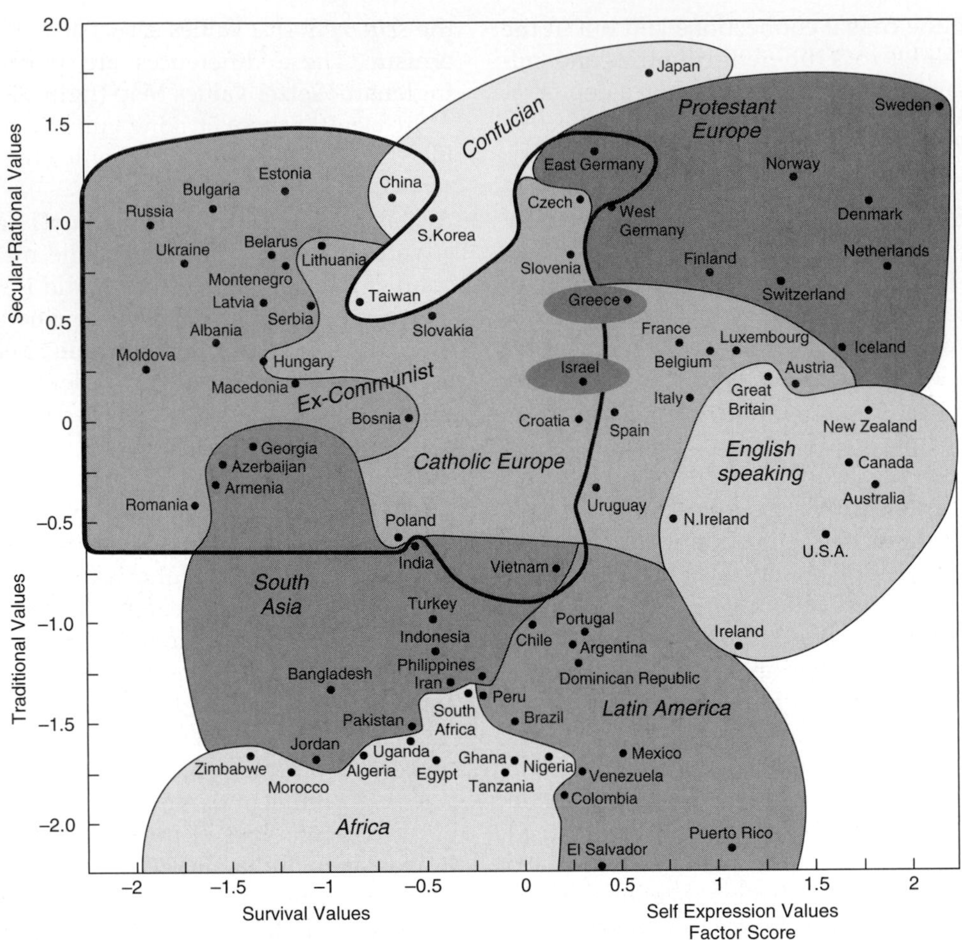


**FIGURE 12.7 The Inglehart-Welzel Values Map**
The numbers represent the scores of countries on the traditional/rational-secular values dimension and the survival/self-expression values dimension.
*Source:* worldvaluessurvey.org.

world, or expecting economic and technological progress to create a single, Western-oriented global culture, Huntington argues, the United States and its European allies should concentrate on solidifying their own unity while encouraging international acceptance of cultural diversity and promoting commonalities among the world's great civilizations. It is "most important to recognize," he concludes, "that Western intervention in the affairs of other civilizations is probably the single most dangerous source of instability and potential global conflict in a multicivilizational world."[24]

Huntington's views have touched off a lively debate. Critics like Norris and Inglehart point out that global opinion surveys conducted up to 2001 revealed markedly little evidence of a clash of *political* values between Western and predominantly Muslim countries. Majorities in both cultures approved of democratic ideals in principle and the way democracy works in practice. The greatest gap between Muslim and Western societies centers on gender equality and sexual liberalization. Even young Muslims retain deeply traditional values on these issues, in contrast to young Westerners. "The central values separating Islam and the West revolve far more centrally around Eros than Demos," the authors conclude. The survey data revealed less support for democratic values and greater support for strong governments in Central and Eastern Europe, the former USSR, Latin America, and East Asia. Thus the survey evidence bearing on Huntington's thesis is mixed.[25]

Another criticism focuses on the fact that states, not civilizations, are the primary elements of organized political activity around the world. Civilizations cannot account very well for the specific forms of government and political life countries have, or for their foreign policy orientations. In fact, every civilization Huntington identifies is characterized by a variety of political regimes, ideologies, parties, and government policies, both domestic and international. For example, Orthodox civilization—Russia, Greece, Romania, and Serbia, among others—has seen kaleidoscopic changes in political regimes just in the past fifty years. Russia, Romania, and Serbia have gone from different forms of communism to different degrees of democracy. Greece has had a military dictatorship as well as democratic governments of both the center-right and the center-left, plus two communist parties. Greece and Romania are in the European Union and NATO; Serbia appears to be heading into those organizations, whereas Russia nurtures its independence. The variety of regime types, domestic political developments, and international orientations in these states is even greater if we go back a hundred years. Much the same can be said for the other civilizations Huntington singles out.

This chapter has shown that political culture has a broad, long-term impact on political life around the world. Chapter 13 examines a more immediate influence on politics and policy: ideology.

## KEY TERMS
## (In bold and underlined in the text)

Political culture
Political subculture
Political socialization
Civic culture
Human development theory

## NOTES

1. In 1964, 22 percent of Americans said they distrusted the federal government. This figure climbed to 62 percent in 1976 and 73 percent in 1980 before dropping to 58 percent in 1988. Cited in Michael M. Gant and Norman R. Luttbeg, *American Electoral Behavior* (Itasca, Ill.: F. E. Peacock, 1991), 144. A poll taken in 1995 revealed that 45 percent of Americans were "satisfied but not enthusiastic" about the way their federal government works, and 41 percent were "dissatisfied but not angry." Only 3 percent were "enthusiastic" and 9 percent were "angry." See the *Washington Post,* May 18, 1995.
2. Russell J. Dalton, *Citizen Politics,* 3rd ed. (New York: Chatham House, 2002), 24.
3. Donald J. Devine, *The Political Culture of the United States* (Boston: Little, Brown, 1972); Herbert McClosky and John Zaller, *The American Ethos: Public Attitudes Toward Capitalism and Democracy* (Cambridge: Cambridge University Press, 1985); Robert N. Bellah et al., *Habits of the Heart: Individualism and Commitment in American Life* (Berkeley: University of California Press, 1985); Gary Wills, *A Necessary Evil: A History of American Distrust of Government* (New York: Simon & Schuster, 1999). For the 2005 Harris survey on U.S. life satisfaction, and the 2004 *Eurobarometer* survey of West Europeans, see www.harrisinteractive.com. See also the attitudinal orientations of various clusters of Americans in the survey conducted by the Kaiser Family Foundation, the *Washington Post,* and Harvard University entitled *Why Don't Americans Trust the Government?* (Menlo Park, Calif.: Henry J. Kaiser Family Fund, 1996). On the intellectual history of contending political cultures in the United States, see Richard J. Ellis, *American Political Cultures* (Oxford: Oxford University Press, 1993).
4. For surveys of concepts of political culture, see Richard W. Wilson, "The Many Voices of Political Culture: Assessing Different Approaches," *World Politics* 52, no. 2 (January 2000): 246–73; and John R. Gibbons, "Contemporary Political Culture: An Introduction," in *Contemporary Political Culture,* ed. J. R. Gibbins (London: Sage, 1989), 1–30.
5. Herbert J. Gans, *Middle American Individualism* (New York: Free Press, 1988).
6. Harry Eckstein, "A Culturalist Theory of Political Change," *American Political Science Review* 82, no. 3 (September 1988): 789–804.

7. T. W. Adorno et al., *The Authoritarian Personality* (New York: Harper, 1950).
8. Leon Festinger, *A Theory of Cognitive Dissonance* (Stanford: Stanford University Press, 1957). See also Robert Jervis, *Perception and Misperception in International Politics* (Princeton: Princeton University Press, 1976); Richard Hofstadter, *The Paranoid Style in American Politics* (New York: Knopf, 1965); and Robert S. Robins and Jerrold M. Post, *Political Paranoia* (New Haven: Yale University Press, 1997). An early classic is Charles Mackay, *Extraordinary Popular Delusions and the Madness of Crowds* (Boston: L. C. Page, 1932).
9. Alexis de Tocqueville, *Democracy in America,* ed. J. P. Mayer, trans. George Lawrence (New York: Harper and Row, 1966), 165, 274, 287–89, 291, 297–301, 309. John Adams remarked that "the source of the revolution" against England was the "systematical dissolution of the true family authority." See Gordon S. Wood, *The Radicalism of the American Revolution* (New York: Knopf, 1991), 145–68, 235–36.
10. Max Weber, *The Protestant Ethic and the Spirit of Capitalism,* trans. Talcott Parsons (London: Routledge, 1992). This work was first published in 1904 and 1905. See also H. H. Gerth and C. Wright Mills, eds., *From Max Weber: Essays in Sociology* (New York: Oxford: 1946).
11. Gabriel Almond and Sidney Verba, *The Civic Culture* (Boston: Little, Brown, 1963). See also Almond and Verba, eds., *The Civic Culture Revisited* (Boston: Little, Brown, 1980), and David Laitin, "The Civic Culture at 30," *American Political Science Review* 89, no. 1 (March 1995): 168–73.
12. Ronald Inglehart, *Culture Shift in Advanced Industrial Society* (Princeton: Princeton University Press, 1990) and *Modernization and Postmodernization* (Princeton: Princeton University Press, 1997). The quotes are on page 215 in the latter work.
13. Robert D. Putnam, *Making Democracy Work: Civic Traditions in Modern Italy* (Princeton: Princeton University Press, 1993). Putnam's findings corroborated the results of an earlier work on Italian political culture by Edward C. Banfield, who found that high levels of distrust among families undermined the effectiveness of local government. See *The Moral Basis of a Backward Society* (New York: Free Press, 1967). See also Christian Welzel, Ronald Inglehart, and Franziska Deutsch, "Social Capital, Voluntary Associations and Collective Action: Which Aspects of Social Capital Have the Greatest 'Civic' Payoff?" *Journal of Civil Society* 1, no. 2 (September 2005): 121–46.
14. *Eurobarometer* 61 (2004), accessible at www.europa.eu.
15. Susan J. Pharr and Robert D. Putnam, eds., *Disaffected Democracies: What's Troubling the Trilateral Countries?* (Princeton: Princeton University Press, 2000). Also Russell J. Dalton, "The Social Transformation of Trust in Government," *International Review of Sociology* 15, no. 1 (March 2005): 133–54.
16. Kendall L. Baker, Russell J. Dalton, and Kai Hildebrandt, *Germany Transformed: Political Culture and the New Politics* (Cambridge, Mass.: Harvard University Press, 1981), 24; David Conradt, "Changing German Political Culture," in Almond and Verba, *The Civic Culture Revisited,* 212–72.
17. The question of cultural change is also addressed in Cynthia McClintock, *Peasant Cooperatives and Political Change in Peru* (Princeton: Princeton University Press, 1991).
18. Ronald Inglehart, *The Silent Revolution: Changing Values and Political Styles Among Western Publics* (Princeton: Princeton University Press, 1977).
19. Inglehart, *Modernization and Postmodernization.* The World Values Survey is a cross-national survey of public values on a host of issues. The first wave surveyed twenty-two countries in 1981–83, the second one covered forty-one countries in 1990–93, the third surveyed forty-three countries in 1995–98, the fourth covered fifty-nine countries in 1999–2001; subsequent surveys have been under way. Consult www.worldvaluessurvey.org and the Inter-university Consortium for Political and Social Research at icpsr.umich.edu.
20. Ronald Inglehart and Pippa Norris, *Rising Tide: Gender Equality and Cultural Change Around the World* (Cambridge: Cambridge University Press, 2003).
21. Pippa Norris and Ronald Inglehart, *Sacred and Secular: Religion and Politics Worldwide* (Cambridge: Cambridge University Press, 2004).

**22.** Christian Welzel, Ronald Inglehart, and Hans-Dieter Klingemann, "The Theory of Human Development: A Cross-Cultural Analyis," *European Journal of Political Research* 42 (2003): 341–79. See also Christian Welzel and Ronald Inglehart, "Liberalism, Postmodernism, and the Growth of Freedom," *International Review of Sociology* 15, no. 1 (March 2006): 81–108; and Ronald Inglehart and Christian Welzel, "Political Culture and Democracy: Analyzing Cross-Level Linkages," *Comparative Politics* (forthcoming), all accessible at www.worldvaluessurvey.org.

**23.** Christian Welzel, "Democratization as an Emancipative Process: The Neglected Role of Mass Motivations," *European Journal of Political Research* 45, no. 6 (October 2006): 871–896. This article, along with Welzel's "A Human Development View on Value Change" and a collection of graphs by Ronald Inglehart, can be accessed at www.worldvaluessurvey.org.

**24.** Samuel P. Huntington, *The Clash of Civilizations and the Remaking of the World Order* (New York: Simon & Schuster, 1996).

**25.** Norris and Inglehart, *Sacred and Secular*. The authors attribute the relatively high degree of religiosity in the United States to fairly high levels of economic insecurity and the growing number of Hispanic Americans. For more critiques of Huntington, see *The Clash of Civilizations? The Debate* (New York: W. W. Norton, 1993).

CHAPTER 13

# IDEOLOGY

In virtually every country in the world, political ideas have played a vital role in shaping the kinds of government that have evolved over time as well as the ways people behave in political life. Because of their presence in such a wide variety of settings, political ideas and the terminology used to express them can be a source of considerable confusion. As we've pointed out before, terms like *liberalism, conservatism,* and *socialism* can have different meanings in different historical or country-specific contexts. One of the purposes of this chapter is to clear up some of this conceptual ambiguity.

To begin with, the term *ideology* itself is used in different ways. In its most informal, everyday usage, ideology frequently means little more than a person's general political orientation. When people say, "Ideologically, I'm a Republican" or "Environmentalism is my ideology," they often mean simply that they identify with the Republican Party or environmental causes in a general way, without necessarily subscribing to a carefully elaborated theory of politics or a particular form of government. But politicians, activists, political scientists, and others who take a more avid interest in politics usually have a more formal understanding of ideology. In its formal definition, **ideology** ***is a coherent set of ideas that typically includes***

1. ***a theory about political relationships and the role of the state***
2. ***a notion of what constitutes political legitimacy and the highest political values***
3. ***an action program indicating the goals, ideals, policies, and tactics to be pursued by the state, political elites, and the masses***

This second definition involves a more systematically thought-out ideological orientation than the first definition does.

Although ideologies are created by sophisticated thinkers and are grasped in their entirety by very few people, they can exert a profound impact on mass political behavior. Political elites are often quite successful at attracting large followings by getting a few key points of their ideologies across to the masses. Most people living in established democracies have not read the works of John Locke or James Madison, but they have learned in the course of their political socialization that democracy entails the right to vote and various other rights and freedoms. Average Muslims are not scholars of the Koran and may have little or no understanding of the complicated doctrinal feuds that have marked their religion's history. Still, they may be swayed by Islamic clerics to adopt any of a variety of political attitudes, ranging from extreme hostility to the non-Islamic world to more tolerant positions.

Throughout history there have been relatively few political orientations sufficiently coherent to be regarded as ideologies. Most flourished in the twentieth century, which is often called "the century of ideologies." In this chapter we'll focus on four of them: *liberalism*, *socialism*, *fascism*, and *Islam*. The sharp differences among these ideological orientations have fueled some of the most bitter conflicts in human history. People have fought and died over ideological beliefs by the tens of millions.

All four ideologies have variants. Sometimes these variations are very similar to one another. Liberals and conservatives in the contemporary United States, for example, are in basic agreement on the Constitution and on the nature of the economy as a mixture of private enterprise and state intervention. But in other cases the diverse tendencies within an ideology can be so disparate as to constitute distinctive ideologies in their own right. At times these internal variants have sparked intense conflict between their adherents, resulting in prolonged debates and in some cases bloody feuds over the ideology's "correct" interpretation. The socialist tradition, for example, produced two fundamentally different strains: Soviet-style communism and Western-oriented social democracy. Islam has produced several competing doctrinal and political orientations.

Any attempt to understand comparative politics in the contemporary world must explore the ideological sources of political life. We must also consider the implications of ideology for the immediate future. Some scholars assert that the intense ideological conflicts of the twentieth century are dying out. Have we reached the "end of ideology"? We'll examine this hypothesis at the end of the chapter.

## LIBERALISM

In today's world, **liberalism** ***essentially means democracy.*** Because this book devotes three full chapters to democracy, we do not need to devote many pages here to a detailed discussion of liberal ideology. It is nevertheless useful at this point to clarify the diverse shadings of meaning that the term *liberalism* has acquired over the course of its historical evolution.

In its oldest and broadest definition, liberalism refers to a system of government that guarantees liberty. This was the original meaning of the term as it emerged in the late seventeenth and early eighteenth centuries in Great Britain and as it developed over the course of the eighteenth, nineteenth, and early twentieth centuries, particularly in Britain, America, and France. In its earliest manifestation, liberalism posed a direct challenge to government by absolute monarchs and aristocracies, expressing the basic idea that the power of the state should be limited and that certain freedoms should be granted to the people by law. From the outset, the essence of liberalism was its opposition to tyrannical state power. It regarded the citizenry, not God, as the source of legitimacy. For its earliest advocates, like Locke, Madison, and Thomas Jefferson, liberalism did not imply mass democracy based on universal suffrage. They espoused a highly elitist concept of liberalism, with the right to vote confined primarily to men of property.

For many early liberals, moreover, the concept of liberalism had both political and economic components. Whereas political liberalism emphasized the concept of government by consent of the governed, economic liberalism stressed the notion that the state should strictly limit its role in the economy, leaving the bulk of the nation's economic activities in the hands of private individuals and companies. Early economic liberalism championed a *free-enterprise* economy. It sought to dismantle the vast edifice of taxes, state monopolies, feudal estates, and other forms of governmental or aristocratic domination of economic life that were common under most monarchal regimes. In their place it favored the free operation of businesses and commercial farming.

As liberal ideas evolved over the course of the nineteenth and twentieth centuries, the notion that a liberal political order requires mass democratic participation gradually asserted itself. Universal adult suffrage finally became a reality during and after World War I as women gained the right to vote in Britain (1918), Germany (1919), and the United States (1920). A host of countries adopted universal voting rights after World War II. As a consequence, liberalism as a political ideology today is synonymous with modern democracy.

The concept of economic liberalism also changed over time, especially during the second half of the twentieth century. Whereas early conceptualizers of economic liberalism advocated only the barest minimum of government involvement in the economy, since World War II most proponents of private enterprise have accepted the view that governments should play a significant role in national economic life. Instead of advocating a completely free-enterprise economic system, they accept a *partially* free-enterprise system. Today's economic liberals acknowledge that governments must collect taxes, regulate banks and stock markets, promote economic growth, and provide various social welfare measures for the population such as education, unemployment insurance, and pensions. Hence we can make a general distinction among economic liberals between *classical liberals,* who favored virtually no governmental intervention in the economy, and *neo-liberals,* who favor a *mixed economy* that combines private enterprise and a large economic role for the state.

### Liberalism and Conservatism in the United States

The interacting concepts of political and economic liberalism resulted in several different strands of liberalism in the contemporary world. In the United States, for example, the term *liberalism* as used in everyday parlance has a narrower, more specific meaning than the generic ones just described.[1] Liberalism in the United States is a variant of the liberal tradition that can be called *social liberalism.* Social liberalism *means active government intervention in the economy and society for the purpose of promoting economic growth, community welfare, and social justice.* With its stress on government activism, this conception of liberalism took shape in Franklin D. Roosevelt's New Deal. Assuming office in 1933 at a time when American political traditions precluded massive governmental interference in the private sector, Roosevelt boldly broke precedent and launched sweeping measures to combat the Great Depression. In the process, proponents of federal government activism in the United States became known as "liberals." They favored a liberal (i.e., permissive) interpretation of the Constitution's injunction to "promote the general welfare."

American social liberals are not socialists, because they do not favor abolishing private enterprise or drastically limiting its scope in favor of a predominantly state-controlled economic system. Historically, American liberals have tended to side with the labor movement in labor-management disputes. They have generally made their home in the Democratic Party.

*Conservatism* in the United States is the heir to the classical liberal tradition of minimal government interference in the economy. During the New Deal decades, many rock-ribbed conservatives viewed Roosevelt's interventions in the economy as heresy. As time went on, and many New Deal programs such as Social Security and the regulation of the private banking system proved their popularity, most conservatives came to accept the notion that the government must play an expanded role in the modern American economy. Contemporary conservatives do not reject government interventionism in principle but tend toward skepticism about its effectiveness in dealing with poverty or ameliorating other social conditions. They usually prefer more limited government activism, less government spending, and greater freedom for the private sector, and they tend to side with the business sector in labor–management relations. In recent decades, modern liberals and conservatives have differed more sharply on such value issues as abortion and school prayer, with "cultural conservatives," often connected with the Christian right, more inclined to take pro-life and pro-prayer positions than liberals are. Conservatives have generally gravitated to the Republican Party.

American conservatives today are divided between those who favor a "realist" conception of foreign policy that would confine the use of military force to protecting vital U.S. national security interests, and *neo-conservatives* who would use force in certain cases to promote "regime change" and democracy—an "idealist" approach previously advocated by Woodrow Wilson and other American liberals.

### Liberalism and Conservatism Around the World

In many countries outside the United States, the term *liberalism* also has two meanings, roughly similar to those employed in the American context.

Throughout much of the world, the first meaning of liberalism is its traditional one: as a generic political orientation, liberalism favors political and economic freedom as opposed to authoritarianism and socialism.

Its second connotation roughly approximates the more specific meaning that the term liberalism has acquired in twentieth-century U.S. politics. Like social liberals in the United States, many politicians and political parties that label themselves "liberal" in Canada, Western Europe, and elsewhere combine staunch support for private enterprise with attitudes favoring a certain amount of state intervention to improve general living conditions. European liberals, for example, constitute a centrist movement positioned in between the more conservative parties on their right and the working-class-oriented social democratic parties on their immediate left.

Conservatism also assumes different meanings in different contexts. In its most literal meaning, conservatism means resistance to any kind of change unless absolutely necessary. In the famous words of Sir Edward Grey, "When it is not necessary to change, it is necessary not to change." If change must come in order to save the country or preserve certain essential values, then it should be gradual rather than abrupt or revolutionary. For Edmund Burke, considered the founding father of British conservative thought, the constitutional order of monarchy, Parliament, and church had proven its legitimacy in Britain over the course of centuries. The accumulated wisdom of tradition, in his view, should not be thrown over in a headlong rush to revolution.[2]

In the United States and other democracies, today's conservatives favor democracy and the market economy. As a general rule, they attach a high priority to promoting private enterprise. European and Japanese conservatives, however, tend to favor a more interventionist state than is typically the case with American conservatives, as we'll see in Part Two.

## SOCIALISM

The origins of twentieth-century socialist movements are to be found in nineteenth-century Europe. Socialism emerged as a reaction to the excesses of the industrial revolution and free enterprise. Over the course of the nineteenth century, the spread of manufacturing in Britain, France, Germany, and other countries rapidly blighted the cities and countryside with grimy factories and squalid slums. For much of the century, governments did virtually nothing to regulate working hours, safety standards, or child labor. Business owners were free to deal with their work force as they wished. Health care and unemployment insurance either did not exist at all or were grossly inadequate. The vast majority of the working class, lacking basic educational opportunities, faced a desperate future with scant hope of improving their lot. Peasants who owned little or no land of their own labored under similarly arduous circumstances for their landlords.

These conditions spawned several variants of socialist ideology. In the first half of the nineteenth century a number of socialist thinkers devised elaborate plans for replacing the free-enterprise system (capitalism) with an entirely different economic system in which the workers, or the people as a whole, would collectively own the factories, farms, mines, and other productive enterprises. Common ownership of the economy (or "communism") would thus replace private ownership. While the schemes proposed by these imaginative thinkers differed in detail, they agreed on one essential point: capitalism was an exploitative and unstable economic system that had to be replaced by a more humane society based on the values of equality and community. These thinkers came to be known as *utopian socialists*, a term that derived from Sir Thomas More's design for an ideal society in his book, *Utopia*, published in 1516. Efforts to establish ideal socialist communities largely failed in Europe, however, and in some cases their adherents journeyed to the United States, creating utopian societies in Texas, Indiana, New Jersey, and other states. Most of these experiments also proved short-lived.[3]

A more enduring approach to socialism was elaborated by *Karl Marx*. Marx was significantly influenced by the utopian socialists, but in the course of his long career as an ideological theorist he developed a far more complicated system of thought that incorporated elements of philosophy, history, economics, sociology, and political theory. Marx turned out to be the principal intellectual source of twentieth-century socialism. But his complex ideas were interpreted in different ways by his contemporaries and subsequent generations.

In its original nineteenth-century conception, therefore, **socialism** was understood as ***a political and economic system in which private enterprise (capitalism) is abolished and replaced by some form of common ownership of factories, farms, and other productive enterprises.***

## Marxism

Summarizing Marx's thought is no easy task. The following brief sections convey some of the essential points of Marxism without underestimating its complexity, ambiguity, and internal inconsistencies.

**History Has Direction** Marx was born in Germany in 1818. After spending a year studying law at Bonn University in 1835–36, he moved to Berlin and became attracted to the ideas of one of the most influential figures in modern philosophy, Georg Wilhelm Friedrich Hegel (1770–1831). Marx was particularly intrigued by Hegel's philosophy of history.

Hegel maintained that human history has an identifiable direction and purpose. He argued that the long-term progression of history moves in accordance with a process he called the *dialectic.* For Hegel, the dialectic meant that history advances through recurring clashes between opposing forces. Conflicting religious beliefs, philosophical ideas, forms of government and society, modes of artistic expression: over thousands of years, these and other elements of the human drama were always and everywhere in contention. The progress of humanity from one historical epoch to the next thus always involved conflict. Hegel termed these ongoing conflicts "contradictions."

Hegel further believed that these contradictions arose because virtually everything creates its own opposite. Just as intense joy produces tears, and masters "create" slaves, every development in humankind's historical evolution—ideas, institutions, technologies, and so on—produces contrary developments. "Contradiction is the root and movement of all life," he wrote. Hegel also believed that humanity would eventually reach a final synthesis, a state of perfection beyond which there would be no more conflicts. He further maintained that this strife-torn but inexorable path of the dialectic toward human perfection was guided to its ultimate destination by God.

Marx was captivated by Hegel's vision of the dialectical process of history. But as an atheist, Marx could not accept Hegel's assumption that God presided over the dialectical process. Hegel was a philosophical *idealist* in the sense that he believed in spiritual, or "ideal," forces like the deity. But Marx was a philosophical *materialist* who rejected spiritual essences. For materialists, human beings and the ideas they create are purely material substances.

**Economics and Class Conflict as the Motor Forces of History** Marx moved to Paris and began his first major treatise on political economy in 1844.[4] In these early manuscripts Marx concluded that *economic* factors constitute the primary material sources of human action. Private property, in particular, stood out as a principal cause of *alienation,* which Marx described as "the self-estrangement of man from himself." He reasoned that as long as there is private ownership of productive enterprises, the workers are engaged in producing objects that do not belong to them. Their employers sell these commodities and pocket the profits, remunerating the workers with wages barely sufficient to keep them alive. The workers are therefore "alienated" from the very products of their labor. The only way out of this inhuman predicament, Marx announced, was communism.

Over the next several years Marx was to refine his central notion that *the principal motive forces in society and politics are economic in nature.* He was joined in this endeavor by *Friedrich Engels* (1820–1895), the son of a wealthy German industrialist, who had become a socialist in his youth. The two became lifelong collaborators: Marx was the creative thinker while Engels contented himself with popularizing his friend's more abstruse ideas. One of their most famous tracts was the *Communist Manifesto,* written in 1847 at the request of a group of German communists and published the following year. In this and subsequent works, Marx developed two critical ideas that defined what dialectical materialism meant in practice.[5]

The first of these ideas was the notion that *economic relations condition everything else that happens in human affairs,* including the type of government a country has as well as its prevailing beliefs and social conventions. For Marx, economics determines, or at least significantly influences, politics. In essence, whoever controls a nation's economy also controls its political system. Thus the state is always manipulated by those who possess economic power.[6]

The second idea that was critical to Marx's concept of dialectical materialism was *class conflict.* Marx maintained that whenever there is private ownership of the "means of production" (factories, the land, technology, and the human labor force), social classes come into being. The relationships between the main social classes under conditions of private property, in Marx's view, are invariably antagonistic. "The history of all hitherto existing society," he wrote in the *Manifesto,* "is the history of class struggles." Thus in the ancient world, the slave-master class and the slave class were locked in hostile confrontation. In nineteenth-century Europe, wherever capitalism was the dominant mode of production, the capitalist class confronted the working class.

When referring to the capitalist class in the industrializing countries, Marx used the term *bourgeoisie.* The term derived from *bourg,* the old German and French word for "town" or "city." (Industrial capitalism in Marx's time was largely an urban phenomenon.) The bourgeoisie consisted of entrepreneurs who owned factories and other productive enterprises, together with other private businesspeople who stood to profit from providing their services in a free-enterprise economy: bankers, lawyers, accountants, and the like. Marx used the term *proletariat* when referring to the industrial working class, which consisted mainly of factory laborers. This term came from the Latin *proletarius,* referring to a member of the non-property-owning lower class of ancient Rome. In Marx's conceptualization, these two classes were destined to clash, much like the "contradictions" in Hegelian philosophy. True to the laws of the dialectic, the bourgeoisie creates the very class that will destroy it. By building factories, the capitalists in effect create the working class. "What the bourgeoisie therefore produces, above all," Marx wrote, "is its own grave-diggers."

As industrial capitalism matures over time, he believed, the "contradictions" inherent in the relationship between bourgeoisie and proletariat inevitably intensify. The rich grow richer while the poor get poorer. The most successful capitalists drive their competitors out of business, a process Marx called *monopolization.* As a consequence, the bourgeoisie shrinks in size, concentrating society's wealth in very few hands. The middle class, consisting of small, independent property owners—shop owners, artisans, small farmers, and the like—are also victimized by the relentless pursuit of capitalist competition. Crushed by aggressive large-scale businesses, the middle class literally disappears, sinking into the working class. As the ranks of the proletariat swell beyond the capitalist system's ability to employ them, the unemployed grow into a vast "reserve army of the proletariat" that Marx called the *lumpenproletariat,* the "proletariat in rags."

Meanwhile, the capitalist elite uses its control over the state to reinforce its subjugation of the proletariat. For Marx, the state is always an instrument of class domination. "Political power," says the *Manifesto,* "is merely the organized power of one class for oppressing another." In capitalist societies, "The executive of the modern state is but a committee for managing the common affairs of the bourgeoisie." In Marx's view, electoral democracy in capitalist societies is a sham that holds out no hope for the working class; it is nothing more than a "bourgeois democracy," thoroughly manipulated by the capitalist class for its own benefit. Legislatures, political parties, politicians—all do the bidding of the captains of industry. Britain, where Marx lived from 1849 until his death in 1883, impressed him as a prime example of such a capitalist-dominated parliamentary system.

Eventually, the proletariat comes to comprise the vast majority of the population wherever advanced capitalism has developed to its full potential. Only about 10 percent of the population ends up owning private businesses. Under these circumstances, the capitalists are outnumbered. Time is then ripe for revolution and socialism.

**The Socialist Revolution** In the *Manifesto,* Marx and Engels declared that the capitalist bourgeoisie is destined to be overthrown in a working-class revolution. Reduced to a small minority of the population, the bourgeois class is incapable of holding back the mounting tide of proletarian resentment. The proletariat, imbued with growing "class consciousness," undertakes "the forcible overthrow of all existing social conditions" in a spontaneous revolutionary outburst. Through the dialectical clash of bourgeoisie and proletariat, humanity is then "lifted up" to the higher historical plane of communism.

Once installed in power, Marx and Engels predicted, the working class dismantles the entire capitalist system. Private ownership of the means of production is forever abolished, the capitalist "expropriators" are expropriated. The workers themselves take possession of factories, farms, and other productive enterprises, reorganizing economic life for the benefit of the people as a whole. With the dissolution of private property and its transformation into "the property of all members of society," all class distinctions then cease to exist. The economic exploitation of one class by another is no longer possible. The proletariat scrupulously refrains from setting itself up as a new dominant class. Communism, in Marx's grand vision, is a truly classless society.

Most important, Marx and Engels affirmed that the abolition of private property is accompanied by the abolition of the "bourgeois" state. Indeed, the seizure of state power will be the first task of the revolutionaries. Having captured the main institutions of government, the proletariat then uses its command of the state to wrest all economic power from the bourgeoisie. In pursuing this task, the workers might have to establish a temporary "dictatorship of the proletariat," but its term would be brief, probably no more than a year.

In fact, once the capitalists have been deprived of their economic power, *government itself ceases to exist as a political institution.* The state, as Engels put it, simply "dies out." While there may still be an "administration" in communist society to take care of basic services, the state is no longer an instrument of class domination. It has no real political power. By abolishing private property, the victorious working class abolishes class conflict; and by abolishing class conflict, which is the driving force of politics, it abolishes politics itself. Under communism, in other words, private property, social classes, conflict, the state, political power, and even politics itself all disappear.

While politics withers away in communist society, economic conditions vastly improve. Marx and Engels prophesied that the great mass of the population would respond to their newfound freedom with a tremendous burst of creativity and productive energy. Although everyone would be expected to work, they would work for society as a whole, not for greedy capitalists. The result would be a superabundance of socially useful goods from which everyone would ultimately benefit. Marx and Engels thus portrayed socialist society (that is, communism) as an idyllic utopia. In Hegelian terms, communism was Marx's vision of the final stage in the long dialectical march of human history. Beyond a few generalities about a classless, stateless society, however, the two founding fathers of modern socialist ideology had very little to say about how communism would actually work. They left no blueprint indicating how the socialist economy would be organized. Nor did they outline a communist "constitution," since there would be no politicized government. They assumed that, without any class conflicts to divide them, the people themselves would find ways to manage their common affairs harmoniously.

**Scientific Socialism** In the *Manifesto,* Marx and Engels proclaimed that the destruction of capitalism and the victory of the proletariat were inevitable. For Marx, the inevitability of socialism was ordained by the immutable laws of History, whose secrets he believed he had discovered. Just as Charles Darwin had discovered the laws of biological evolution, Marx maintained that he had uncovered the laws governing humanity's social evolution. On these grounds Marx always insisted that his theories of dialectical materialism were "scientific." So conceived, History was the source of communism's legitimacy. Accordingly, Marx asserted that the entire course of humankind's historical development, from the most primitive preindustrial societies to the highest stage of communism, was governed by the laws of economic determinism. These laws, moreover, were immutable; no one could change them or get around them.

Both Marx and Engels believed that, as a general rule, industrial capitalism was a necessary precondition to the construction of a successful socialist society over the long term. They did not believe that predominantly agricultural societies were ripe for socialist development, and so they dismissed peasants as incapable of mounting a true socialist revolution. Only the industrial working class had the "class consciousness" necessary to create a stable and enduring socialist society. Consequently they predicted that socialist revolutions would occur only in advanced capitalist countries like Britain, France, and Germany. In their view, nineteenth-century Russia was an unlikely candidate for revolution. Russia's population consisted overwhelmingly of impoverished peasants, not industrial workers, and its capitalist bourgeoisie had not yet formed itself as a dominant class.[7]

These "scientific" predictions would prove wrong. In actual fact, the proletarian revolutions Marx and Engels foresaw as imminent in Britain, France, and Germany in the 1840s never took place in these countries. Communist revolutions did not occur until the twentieth century. Ironically, they triumphed in precisely those countries where industrialism and capitalism were largely undeveloped and where a modern bourgeoisie was weak or absent. Countries like Russia, China, and Cuba were predominantly agricultural societies when the communists came to power. The triumph of what came to be known as *Soviet-style communism* (or *Marxism-Leninism*) in these countries represented only one strand of Marx's legacy, however. In another irony of history, the advanced capitalist societies of Western Europe, which Marx's "laws" regarded as primed for revolution, did not experience socialist revolutions at all. Instead, they developed socialist movements that combined socialist economics with ballot-box democracy, a combination known as *social democracy.*

### Soviet-Style Communism

Communism triumphed in Russia in 1917 under circumstances significantly different from those predicted by Marx and Engels. Russia was still an overwhelmingly agricultural society in 1917. Furthermore, Marx had depicted the revolution as a largely spontaneous upheaval carried out by the masses; he did not portray it as an organized conspiracy led by a handful of revolutionary leaders. But communism came to Russia as a well-orchestrated coup d'état engineered by a highly centralized political party, the Bolsheviks. It was this party, which soon came to be known as the Communist Party, that defined the essence of Soviet-style communism.

The party's principal creator was *Vladimir Ilyich Lenin* (1870–1924). An avid student of Marx's writings from his teenage years, Lenin placed his own stamp on the Marxist tradition by adapting its core ideas to Russia's specific conditions.

Lenin's single most important contribution to Marxist theory, as expostulated in *What Is To Be Done?* (1902), was the notion that the industrial working class in modern Russia and Europe was not capable of launching a spontaneous mass revolution on its own; it had to be led to socialism by a party of professional revolutionaries. Experience had already shown that, instead of risking a potentially disastrous uprising, most workers were content to form trade unions and to seek negotiated compromises with their capitalist employers. But trade unionism, argued Lenin, amounted to acceptance of capitalism; only capitalism's complete destruction could liberate the workers from exploitation. If the workers would not destroy capitalism on their own, a "party of a new type" would have to be formed whose primary task would be to organize and carry out a violent revolution at the first sign of weakness in the capitalist ruling class. This party would be the "vanguard of the proletariat," acting as its "organizational weapon."[8]

For Russia's rulers, that critical moment of weakness occurred amid the turmoil of World War I. With minimal resistance, Lenin's Bolsheviks, organized into a small militia, seized official buildings that had been abandoned by an unpopular government in November 1917. In a brutal civil war that extended into 1921, the Bolsheviks finally vanquished all their opponents. From that point onward, Russia's Communist Party monopolized power in what subsequently became known as the Soviet Union (or USSR, the Union of Soviet Socialist Republics).

The key idea of **Leninism** is ***the primacy of the Communist Party.*** It is the party that leads the revolution; it is the party that governs the country once the revolution has eliminated its foes. Lenin's definition of the "dictatorship of the proletariat"

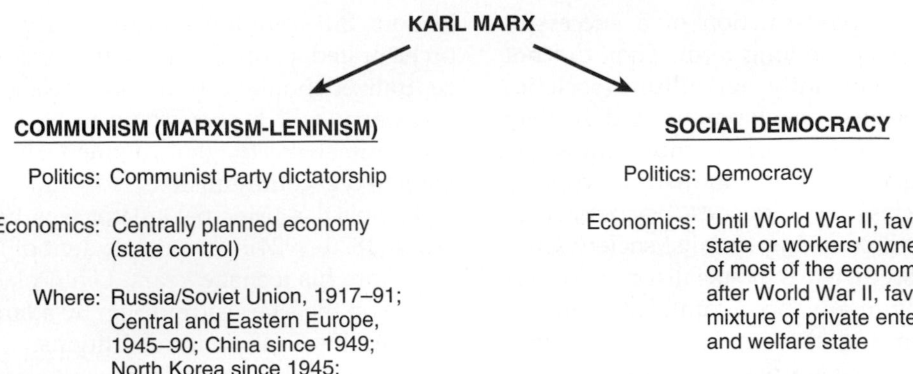


**FIGURE 13.1 Legacies of Marxism**

was distinctly different from Marx's conception of a temporary government in the hands of the masses. "The dictatorship of the proletariat," Lenin affirmed, "is the dictatorship of the party." Far from being a temporary phenomenon, the Communist Party exercised dictatorial rule over the Soviet Union until December 1991, when its power collapsed and the USSR itself disintegrated.

For much of its reign, the party leadership utilized all the coercive mechanisms at its disposal to enforce its will, at times resorting to mass murder. *Joseph Stalin* (1878–1953), who succeeded Lenin following a power struggle within the party hierarchy, brutalized Soviet society by imprisoning millions in concentration camps, killing off the cream of the party elite, and intimidating workers, peasants, intellectuals, and others into submission through the unremitting use of violence. His successors were not as murderous as Stalin on a mass scale, but until the late 1980s they did not shrink from using severe coercive measures to ensure compliance with their dictates.

In another sharp departure from Marx's tenets, Soviet rulers erected a powerful state to undergird their dominance. Instead of dying out, the state swelled into a gargantuan bureaucratic arm of Communist Party rule. The Soviet state was a highly politicized state, moreover; it consisted of party and governmental institutions that joined in propagandizing the population, repressing dissent, and implementing policies over which the people had little or no influence. Its top officials constituted a privileged elite who enjoyed benefits denied to the mass public. This enormous party-state governing apparatus also planned and operated virtually all economic activity in the USSR, presiding over a *centrally planned economy*. (We'll discuss central planning at greater length in chapter 14.)

At no point in its history did the Soviet Union approach the stateless, egalitarian utopia that was Marx's conception of communism. The USSR was called "communist" only because it was governed by the Communist Party. The same can be said for other "communist" countries that came into being after the USSR. These included China, where the Chinese Communist Party took power in 1949 following a long civil war; Poland, Hungary, and other Central and East European states on which the USSR imposed communist party rule after World War II; Cuba, where Fidel Castro's communists won a revolutionary struggle in 1959; and others such as North Korea and Vietnam. All were the heirs, not just of Marx, but also of Lenin. Hence twentieth-century communism, defined in terms of Communist Party dictatorship, was rooted in the ideology of *Marxism-Leninism*. (See figure 13.1.)

### Social Democracy

The second main inheritor of Marx's legacy was **social democracy**, ***which is a combination of economic socialism and political democracy.*** One of the chief incubators of the social democratic tradition was the Social Democratic Party of Germany (known by its German initials as the SPD). Founded in 1875, the SPD's backbone was the

German working class, a disparate mass of mostly blue-collar workers. Deprived of economic and political power by the kaiser's authoritarian regime, Germany's workers looked mostly to the SPD to win them a share of participation in the affairs of government. The ballot box became their main political weapon. Most German workers shunned the path of revolution, sharply contradicting Marx's predictions of an inevitable proletarian uprising.

One SPD leader, *Eduard Bernstein* (1850–1932), drew the implications of this contradiction between Marxist theory and working-class practice with bold clarity. His book *Evolutionary Socialism*, published in 1898, was a point-by-point refutation of key tenets of Marx's thought. For Bernstein, the immediate aim of the socialist movement should not be to mount a violent revolution but to promote democracy. Bernstein defined democracy as "the absence of class government," and he advocated universal suffrage, proportional representation, equal rights for all citizens, and parliamentary control over legislation. He emphatically rejected both the kaiser's militaristic dictatorship and Marx's "dictatorship of the proletariat." And he regarded compromise and moderation as indispensable elements of democratic government. As to socialism, Bernstein conceived of it as a "cooperative society" organized for the benefit of the whole population and guided by the principle of majority rule.

Over the next several decades, the SPD's commitment to political democracy intensified. The party was a mainstay of democratic government during Germany's ill-fated Weimar Republic (1918–33), which died an early death at the hands of Hitler and the Nazis. After World War II a revived SPD became one of the two largest parties in West Germany, a status it still enjoys today in unified Germany. (Former Chancellor Gerhard Schroeder was an SPD leader.) Meanwhile, starting in the 1950s the SPD began retreating from its earlier commitment to economic socialism. It accepted private enterprise and the market as the principal mechanisms of economic production. It has sought to promote the interests of the working class and other constituents by working within the capitalist system through democratic processes.

Other social democratic parties emerged in the industrialized nations of Europe and have undergone a roughly similar historical evolution. They include Britain's Labour Party, France's Socialist Party, and numerous others. Like the SPD, most social democratic parties in today's industrially advanced democracies accept private enterprise and the market economy. Today, social democracy in most democracies is practically indistinguishable from American social liberalism, though many European social democrats favor a larger welfare state than do most U.S. liberals. The United States never developed a successful social democratic party that favored the state's takeover of factories and other productive enterprises.[9]

### Socialism in the Developing World

The varieties of socialism are multiplied when we look at socialist ideas in the developing countries. In Asia, Africa, the Middle East, and Latin America, various forms of socialism have been articulated and adapted over many decades to fit social and economic conditions that are quite different from those that prevailed in nineteenth- or twentieth-century Europe. In most instances, these variants of socialism emerged in countries with little or no industrialization. A proletariat in the European sense has been either very small or nonexistent. Not surprisingly, some of the most creative socialist theorists and political activists in the less economically advanced part of the world did not base their ideas on Marxism but instead on local traditions and circumstances.

One of the most influential Third World socialists was *Julius K. Nyerere* (1922–99), the principal theoretician of what became known as "African socialism." A British-educated Christian from Tanzania, Nyerere rejected Marx's notions of class struggle and devised a Tanzanian variant of socialism rooted in long-standing tribal customs that emphasized the individual's responsibility to the community and the community's responsibility to care for the individual. Out of this tradition he derived the concept of *ujamaa*, or "familyhood." Under Nyerere's leadership as president of Tanzania for more than twenty years, the government abolished private ownership of land and instituted a system of communally owned rural property, touting "self-reliance" as the country's main economic goal.[10] Several African states embarked on roughly similar paths in the 1960s and 1970s. Over time, however, a number of them, including Tanzania, were forced by economic realities to curtail or abandon their lofty goals of agricultural self-sufficiency and full economic equality. Some have reintroduced market economic mechanisms.

Another source of non-Marxist concepts of socialism was the Middle East. Initially, the Muslim Brotherhood, founded in Egypt in the 1920s, had socialist leanings. A coup involving Colonel *Gamal Abdel Nasser* deposed the king of Egypt in 1952 and installed a new regime led mainly by military officers. Nasser elaborated a form of "Arab socialism" that placed heavy emphasis on governmental direction of the economy. These measures were accompanied by efforts to anchor the ideology of Arab socialism in the religious traditions of Islam.[11] Fairly similar concepts of Arab socialism were elaborated in the 1960s in Syria, Iraq, and Libya. As in Nasser's Egypt, they tended to emphasize the state's responsibility for guiding the economy. They also went hand in hand with strong authoritarian governments. The popularity of socialism in the Middle East has waned in recent decades, however, in part because of pressures to open these economies up to market forces and in part because of the collapse of the Soviet Union, which was an occasional ally of several states in the region.

In Latin America, socialist movements have frequently tended to have a Marxist background. Some have been Soviet-oriented Communist Parties, some have espoused violent revolutions of one kind or another (at times with the support of Fidel Castro's communist regime in Cuba), and still others have been social democratic in orientation. One notable example of a radical social democrat was *Salvador Allende*, who was elected president of Chile in 1970. Allende's Socialist Party was committed to democracy but was equally committed to redistributing the nation's wealth from the rich to the poor and to nationalizing large privately owned corporations, including copper mines owned by U.S. companies. Although Allende was not a Soviet-style communist, Chile's Communist Party was part of his governing coalition. Irked by Allende's socialist economic policies and his friendly gestures toward the Soviet Union and Castro's Cuba, the Nixon administration conspired with Allende's domestic opponents to undermine his government. In 1973 a military coup led by Gen. Augusto Pinochet and abetted by the CIA ousted the socialist coalition. Allende was killed in the assault, and democracy itself was extinguished in Chile for the next sixteen years.

Since the collapse of communism in the Soviet Union and East Central Europe, and the failure of socialist economies in the developing world, socialism seems to have receded as a major ideological force around the world. Whether economic and social conditions will lead to its revival some day is an open question.

## FASCISM

Historically, fascism is mainly a European phenomenon that emerged between the two world wars. Its most successful manifestations occurred in Italy, where Benito Mussolini's National Fascist Party held power from 1922 until 1943, and in Germany, where Adolph Hitler and the Nazis ruled between 1933 and 1945. Fascist movements also existed in other European countries during the inter-war period, including France, Hungary, and Romania, but they did not acquire the extraordinary grip on power achieved by their Italian and German counterparts.[12] Fascist-like movements and ideas have also emerged in other parts of the globe in the decades before and after World War II, including the present day. The American Nazi Party, neo-Nazi skinheads in Europe, and white-supremacist Afrikaner groups in South Africa are often singled out as examples of quasi-fascist or neo-fascist organizations in the contemporary era.

In most instances, fascism is a response to a specific combination of problems that face certain societies at a particular juncture in their historical development. Both Italy and Germany had emerged from defeat in World War I feeling humiliated and betrayed, and both had to confront overwhelming economic problems. In both countries, moreover, democracy failed to provide adequate remedies for the nation's misfortunes. Growing numbers of Italians and Germans came to the conclusion that democracy itself was the principal problem. In most instances, neo-fascist movements in today's world also represent extreme responses to social or economic problems for which democratic solutions are either inadequate or completely unacceptable to certain segments of society. Ethnic diversity and long-term unemployment are typical of the problems that spark neo-fascist resentments, particularly among poorly educated white males.

Reduced to its basic elements, **fascism** ***consists of the following four features: hypernationalism, racism, totalitarianism, and mass mobilization through propaganda and coercion.*** To be sure, not all fascist movements have shared all these defining characteristics. The features enumerated here form a composite "ideal type" of fascism extracted mainly from the experiences of inter-war Italy and Germany.

### Hypernationalism

Fascism is rooted in an extreme version of nationalism called *hypernationalism.* Nationalism is the notion that the members of one's nation (or "people") must act together to achieve certain collective goals. In its fascist variant, the nation is exalted as the supreme political value. This conception of nationalism is far more intense than patriotism, which means love of one's country. For many fascists, love of one's own country requires hatred of others, particularly those marked as implacable enemies.

National glory and self-assertion therefore assume the highest priority on the political agenda of most fascist movements. Mussolini was determined to establish an Italian empire through the conquest of Ethiopia in 1936 and other territorial acquisitions during World War II. Hitler sought to subdue all of Europe and the Soviet Union by force of arms, with the express intention of creating a fascist "New Order." Chauvinism is a typical component of the fascist worldview.

Whereas militant nationalism characterizes fascist attitudes toward the outside world, national unity is often the chief priority at home. Both Italy and Germany had achieved statehood only in the second half of the nineteenth century, hundreds of years after Britain and France. Italian and German fascist leaders felt an acute need to solidify bonds of national unity among their people, many of whom still felt more attached to their local region than to the country as a whole. These efforts assumed manic proportions. The fascists sought to forge a common national identity by drumming up hatred of presumed enemies like communists, Jews, and British imperialists. They also demanded unquestioning loyalty to a powerful central state. For Mussolini, Hitler, and other fascists, internal divisiveness breeds external weakness; hence democracy is intolerable precisely because it promotes national discord. Democratic debate and free competition for power inevitably mean that the nation is constantly at war with itself, its domestic fissures deepened by open conflict among social classes, religions, regions, and other segments of the country. Democracy, in this view, is a prescription for national powerlessness, a condition no fascist could possibly accept.

### Racism

At least some fascist and neo-fascist movements have defined the nation primarily in terms of race. Concepts of racial purity and superiority were especially characteristic of German fascism under Hitler. The notion that the Germans were members of a pure-blooded "Aryan race," a completely fabricated idea, was a central tenet of Nazi doctrine. Nazi ideology exalted the Germans as a race of "supermen" and denigrated most other racial categories as "subhumans."

Anti-Semitism assumed ferocious proportions in Nazi doctrine. After World War I, Nazi propagandists used the Jews as scapegoats for Germany's political and economic ills even though Jews comprised less than 1 percent of Germany's population. By the late 1930s the Nazi state had instituted a number of racial laws aimed at publicly humiliating German Jews and depriving them of their means of livelihood. During World War II the determination of Hitler and his principal henchmen to proceed with "the final solution of the Jewish problem" throughout Europe resulted in the Holocaust, the annihilation of some 6 million Jews throughout Europe and the Soviet Union and the infliction of untold suffering on millions of survivors. Anti-Semitism has been a characteristic feature of most other fascist or neo-fascist movements as well, though not all these movements have been as fanatically or blatantly anti-Semitic as the Nazis.[13]

Anti-Semitism is by no means the only form of racism to be found in fascist or quasi-fascist movements. The Nazis denounced just about all racial or ethnic groups not explicitly identified as "Aryan." Depending on local circumstances, racism has also been a defining characteristic of fascist-like movements in other countries as well, spawning hatred and even violence against immigrants and indigenous members of target ethnic groups. Hatred of homosexuals and the physically and mentally handicapped was also part of the Nazi worldview.

### Totalitarianism

Fascist ideology demands a powerful state. The very word "fascism" derives originally from the Latin *fasces,* which in ancient Rome was a staff consisting of a bundle of rods bound together around an axe. The *fasces* would be held aloft on ceremonial occasions as a symbol of national unity and the state's authority.

Once ensconced in office, Mussolini and Hitler established strong totalitarian states. Totalitarianism is an exceptionally intrusive form of authoritarianism in which the state monopolizes control not only over all institutions of government but also over the educational system, the media, science, and the arts, leaving little room for private liberty. Youth groups and even organized religions also come under the watchful eye of the state. Mussolini bluntly asserted that "for the Fascist, all is in the State and nothing human or spiritual exists, much less has value, outside the State. In this sense, Fascism is totalitarian."[14]

The fascists of Italy and Germany also used state mechanisms to secure their control over the economy. Unlike communists and social democrats of that era, who favored abolishing private enterprise, the fascists were willing to permit private firms to do business and make profits. These businesses were subject to all sorts of state regulations, however. To ensure that privately owned companies conducted their operations in accordance with the government's priorities, especially the large industrial concerns, Italian and German authorities created special state institutions, which they called "corporations," in which leading representatives of the business community would meet on a regular basis with state officials to coordinate economic goals and operations. The government established similar corporations to represent the labor force, and all trade unions and other labor organizations were abolished except for those operated by the state or the fascist party. Corporations representing agriculture and other sectors of the economy were similarly organized. This system of *state corporatism* served the central purposes of facilitating the state's supervision of the economy and, not incidentally, of organizing the economy for war.[15]

The fascist concept of totalitarianism, at least in its Italian and German variants, was also characterized by the concept of a *party-state.* The state and the fascist party were fused. The Italian fascists' motto, "Everything inside the state, nothing outside the state, nothing against the state," above all meant that the state and the National Fascist Party were one. Hitler's dictatorial state and the Nazi Party were similarly intertwined, with the Nazis monopolizing all official state institutions.

### Mass Mobilization Through Propaganda and Coercion

Traditional authoritarian regimes, like the old monarchies of Europe, China, and Japan, made little effort to court popularity. The Italian and German fascist parties, by contrast, were authoritarian movements that made decisive efforts to cultivate mass support. Although they rejected democracy as a goal, prior to taking power they took full advantage of electoral democracy to build a wide constituency. Mussolini and Hitler were charismatic orators whose speeches transfixed millions. Their parties proved highly effective at organizing parades, rallies, and other events to galvanize a mass following. The breadth of their appeal, moreover, was multiclass in nature. Though the Italian and German fascist movements started out in the 1920s with a pronounced-working-class orientation, over time they drew support from farmers, the large middle class, and even the wealthiest strata of society. The Nazis, for example, raised their share of the electorate from 3 percent in 1928 to more than 37 percent by the summer of 1932, becoming the largest party in Germany.

In addition to using democratic mechanisms to achieve power, Italian and German fascists freely engaged in coercive techniques in their rush to build and consolidate mass support. The *glorification of violence* against political opponents was another core element of fascist ideology. Mussolini's fascist party explicitly defined itself as a militia. From its earliest years it included "squads" *(fasci)* of black-shirted toughs whose task was to beat up political rivals and fight their way into local city halls, seizing power by force. In October 1922, tens of thousands of armed fascists were massed on the outskirts of Rome, poised for a final assault on the Italian government itself. To avoid a massacre, the king of Italy, acting under his constitutional authority to designate the head of government, named Mussolini as the country's new prime minister. The next day the fascist militia staged a victory parade in the streets of the capital city, an event known as the "march on Rome." The Nazis also employed force in their march to power. Hitler set up a militia in brown shirts, which developed into the notorious Storm Troopers. By 1932, on the eve of the Nazi takeover of power, there were more than four hundred thousand Storm Troopers. In January 1933, German President Hindenburg appointed Hitler the country's new chancellor.

Efforts to mobilize the population, both peaceful and violent, became all the more extensive after the conquest of power. Fascist Italy and Germany were *mass mobilization regimes*, resolved to enlist maximum popular support and stifle all opposition. Both regimes organized continuous propaganda campaigns designed to stir up popularity, appealing not only to national pride but also to the darkest anxieties, prejudices, and yearnings for vengeance on the part of the Italian and German populations. They also engineered massive employment programs and other efforts to improve the economic welfare of large elements of the population. And they did not hesitate to use violence against real or imagined political opponents, with secret police, concentration camps, and torture employed with intimidating effect.

Some scholars contend that fascism was an "epochal" phenomenon unique to inter-war Europe.[16] Nevertheless, it is far too early to consign fascism to the graveyard of history. At least hypothetically, fascist ideas may find a popular resonance wherever other forms of government, including democracy, fail to address the basic needs of the population for economic security, national pride, and social order.[17]

## RELIGION AS POLITICAL IDEOLOGY: ISLAM

At one time or another, all the world's great religions have functioned as political ideologies, articulating explicit political messages and, in some cases, exercising political power. Islam has emerged as the most politically active religious force in the contemporary world. Its centrality in the convulsive politics of the Middle East, in the crucible of international terrorism, and in the global struggle between democracy and authoritarianism raises important questions about some of the most pressing political issues of our time. Specifically, does Islam require theocratic government? Is it particularly prone to violence? And is it compatible with democracy?

### Origins

Although Islam has evolved considerably over the centuries, many of its most widely held beliefs derive from its founder, the Prophet Muhammad. Born sometime around 570 C.E. in Mecca, a religious center in the Arabian peninsula, Muhammad ibn Abdullah was orphaned as a boy and raised by an uncle. Intimations of his spirituality were evident from childhood. Muhammad's marriage to an older widow with a successful business made him a wealthy and respected merchant. In 610 Muhammad informed his intimates that he had received a revelation from God. Three years later he professed his belief in one God (Allah), the same deity worshiped by Jews and Christians. For Muhammad, the adherents of the Jewish and Christian faiths, many of whom resided in Mecca, were "Peoples of the Book" (the Bible). As such they merited special treatment as "protected people," enjoying a higher status than pagan "idolaters." Proclaiming himself a prophet and messenger of God in the grand lineage of Abraham, Moses, David, and Jesus, Muhammad called for the individual's complete surrender to God's will. The word *Islam* is Arabic for surrender; it is etymologically related to *salam,* which means peace. A Muslim is someone who submits fully to God. In his preaching, Muhammad extolled the virtues of moral probity, simplicity, compassion, charity, economic justice for the poor, and peace among all Muslims.

Muhammad's message represented a radical departure from the polytheistic beliefs that were still widely held in the Arabian peninsula. It also threatened the political and economic dominance of local tribal leaders, who sought to kill him. In 622 Muhammad fled from Mecca and emigrated to nearby Yathrib, which became known as Medina.

Muhammad's "migration," known as the *hijrah* (or *Hegira*), formally inaugurated the Islamic era. With about a hundred "companions," Muhammad established the first Muslim community, or *ummah*. A series of battles ensued against the defenders of the old order in Mecca, culminating in the Muslims' victory over the Meccan army in 627. In 630 Muhammad returned to Mecca in triumph and established his political and religious authority there. He acceded to a treaty that brought peace to the war-ravaged peninsula, effectively ending the incessant raids that were a vital source of livelihood for the tribes inhabiting the harsh desert environment. Muhammad's doctrine of Islamic brotherhood prohibited war between Muslims. By the time of his death in 632, Muhammad was the most powerful man in Arabia, simultaneously the leader of a popular new religion and the political head of the Muslim community.

For twenty-one years Muhammad affirmed that he received divine revelations, which he would recite to assembled followers. After his death, his words were gathered from written fragments and oral renditions and compiled in written form as the Koran (or *Quran*—"recitations"). Like holy books in other religions, the Koran was composed from a diversity of sources dating from different times, and its verses are sometimes ambiguous or contradictory, giving rise to different interpretations of their meaning. Another source of Muslim beliefs was the *hadith*, which are anecdotes about Muhammad and his companions. Over time, hundreds of thousands of these orally transmitted stories circulated in the Muslim world; but they lacked an authoritative source to authenticate them, and most were probably fabricated. Islam has no equivalent of the pope, who is the ultimate authority for Roman Catholic doctrine. Hence there is no "official" Islamic doctrine or interpretation of its core beliefs. The interpretation of Islamic religious tenets and Islamic law increasingly fell into the hands of Islamic scholars and legal experts, known collectively as the *ulama*, "the learned men of God." The result has been considerable diversity in the interpretation of Muhammad's legacy and Islamic tradition over the course of the centuries and across the Muslim world. In fact, conflicts within the Muslim community arose shortly after Muhammad's death.

It was not clear who should succeed the Messenger as the next head of the Muslim community, the ummah. A group of Muhammad's companions chose his close friend Abu Bakr as his first "successor" or "representative" (*khalifa*, or caliph). Initially it was agreed that the caliph would be the temporal head of the ummah, but there would be no religious authority. Several Muslims objected to Abu Bakr, however, claiming that Muhammad had personally singled out his cousin and son-in-law Ali as his spiritual and political heir. The schism split the Islamic movement into warring camps. Abu Bakr's faction chose the next two caliphs. When soldiers favorable to Ali assassinated the third caliph, a member of Mecca's prominent Umayyad clan, Ali was elected his successor. His followers were known as "partisans of Ali"—*Shia i-Ali* (Shiites or Shiis). Ali's election was never fully accepted by his opponents, however, and civil war broke out between the two factions. Ali was murdered in 661 and the caliphate reverted to the Umayyads. A second war between Muslims ensued as the Shiites proclaimed Ali's second son Hussain as the next legitimate caliph. Hussain was subsequently killed in a battle in Karbala by rival Muslims in 680. The Shiites were temporarily avenged when the Abbasid faction, advocating succession through Muhammad's bloodline, took over the caliphate in 750 and massacred most of the Umayyad family. The Shiites subsequently fell out with the Abbasids, and the Abbasids then turned on the Shiites, setting the stage for future Shiite revolts.

The internecine conflict over Muhammad's succession persists: there is still no single spiritual or temporal head of Islam. Those who regard Abu Bakr and his immediate successors as the first three legitimate caliphs are mostly **Sunnis**, ***a term meaning Muslims who follow the words and deeds of Muhammad.*** (*Sunna*, meaning custom, refers to the devotional practices and daily habits of the Prophet, which were observed and recorded by his family and friends to serve as instructional models of the exemplary Islamic life.) About 80–90 percent of the world's 1.3 billion Muslims are Sunnis. As we shall see, they are divided into several doctrinal currents. The **Shiites** ***continue to regard only Muhammad's blood descendants as the Prophet's true successors, or imams***. Most of the 170 million Shiites in the contemporary world belong to the

"Twelver" school of Shiism. This school holds that after the death of the Eleventh Imam in 874, the Twelfth Imam was spirited away ("occulted") by God and hidden to spare his life from his Sunni enemies. The mystical doctrine of the "Occultation of the Hidden Imam" asserts that the Twelfth Imam, known as the Mahdi, will one day return to the world to usher in an era of justice. Until then, it is the task of the erudite Shiite clergy to discern his will and lead the faithful on his behalf. Shiites today are heavily concentrated in Iran, where they are 89 percent of the population; in Iraq (60 percent); and in Lebanon (40 to 50 percent).[18]

### Expansion and Decline

Ironically, as these and other feuds unraveled Islam's inner core, the religion itself expanded. Once Muhammad brought peace to the unruly Arabian peninsula, Arab warriors under their new Muslim leadership charged into neighboring areas in search of plunder and territory. By the middle of the seventh century they had conquered Egypt, Palestine, Syria, Cyprus, parts of North Africa, Iran, Afghanistan, and the once formidable Persian empire. In 638 they took Jerusalem, making it Islam's third holiest city after Mecca and Medina. In 711 Muslim invaders entered Spain, parts of which remained under Islamic control until 1492. They advanced as far north as Poitiers, where the French defeated them in 732. By the end of the eighth century the Mediterranean was a Muslim lake. Muslims took over Sicily in the ninth century and held much of it for two hundred years. Baghdad (founded in 762), Cairo, Damascus, Cordoba, and Palermo became flourishing centers of classical scholarship, science, and theology. After suffering major setbacks in the Crusades, which the Catholic Church launched from Europe at the end of the eleventh century in an effort to keep the Holy Land in Christian hands and to control lucrative trade routes, Muslims counterattacked under the Seljuk Turks, retaking Jerusalem in 1187. In the first half of the fourteenth century another Turkish tribe, the Osmanlis, established the first Ottoman government, forming the cornerstone of the most dynamic and expansionist of all Muslim states. After taking Constantinople in 1453 and converting it into their new capital, Istanbul, they extended their sway over most of the Arab world as well as the Balkans and Hungary. In the thirteenth and fourteenth centuries the vast Mongol empire created by Genghis Khan converted to Islam, bringing large tracts of Central Asia into the Muslim world. Shiites established the Fatimid dynasty in Egypt in the tenth century and the Safavid empire in Persia and the Moghul empire in India in the first decades of the sixteenth century. Arab merchants carried Islam across the seas to Africa, Malaysia, and Indonesia.

The Islamic world reached its political apogee in the late seventeenth century. After the Ottoman Turks were defeated in their second attempt to take Vienna in 1683 (the first attempt having failed in 1529), their empire entered into a long process of external retreat and internal decay. Britain and Russia pressed on its flanks, slicing away at the Ottomans' territorial appendages until the end of World War I. Britain's advances into India and Egypt, Russia's expansion into the Caucasus and Central Asia, the French takeover of North Africa, and Europe's colonization of most of black Africa placed large Muslim populations under European or Russian control in the nineteenth century. In 1916, Britain and France agreed to carve up the Middle East, imposing new states on Arab populations in the region. These political defeats were accompanied by a vast cultural divide that widened the gap between Christian Europe and the Islamic world. Although Arab, Turkish, and other Islamic intellects rivaled European scientists until the end of the Middle Ages, Europe in the sixteenth century embarked on a path that led from the Renaissance and the Age of Discoveries to the Scientific Revolution. Because of religious dogmatism and short-sighted political leadership, the Muslim world failed to keep pace with European inventiveness, falling disastrously behind the West in scientific theory, experimentation, and technology—including military technology. (By the late thirteenth century, a "rationalist" school of Islam, stressing human reason and free will, lost out to the "traditionalist" school, which stresses divine revelation and the authority of Islamic law.) In addition, the Enlightenment and the democratic revolutions of the eighteenth and nineteenth centuries in Europe and America had no serious equivalents in the Islamic world. As the West moved in fits and starts toward the rule of law, democratic participation, the separation of church and state, and the emancipation of women, Muslim religious authorities and political elites largely ignored these ideas. The result was a gap not only in the balance of political and military power between Islam and the West, but in political culture as well. In many respects, these cultural gaps endure to the present day. Although modern Islamic states have accepted scientific-technical modernization, many of them have resisted cultural and political Westernization.[19]

## Religion and Politics

Islam was intended to be an all-encompassing way of life. Consequently, Islamic doctrine recognizes no distinction between religion and politics: the ummah is both a religious and a political community in which Islamic law (*shariah*) prevails. Allah, not the people, is the source of legitimacy. Muhammad did not conceive of Islam as a "church" that is organized separately from the state, and he personally disapproved of monarchy, a secular form of government. In its original doctrinal form, Islam thus requires a theocratic government. But with its vast territorial expansion, the Islamic world became fragmented into a variety of states and empires under Muslim rulers who were not religious authorities. The caliphate shifted from one city to another as rivalries intensified and military and political power shifted within the Islamic world. In the process, the caliph's original role as the temporal (political) head of Islam was at times augmented by religious functions, as various caliphs proclaimed their authority as Islam's principal religious leader. Ultimately the caliphate ended up in Istanbul, reflecting the predominance of Ottoman power. In a marked departure from Islamic orthodoxy, the Ottoman Turks established a monarchy under the sultan. Over time the ties between religion and the state grew looser as the Ottoman regime implemented a limited modernization program and the sultans increasingly adopted opulent lifestyles. The leaders of other predominantly Muslim countries took steps of their own to distinguish religion from the state.

Meanwhile, the power of the ulama—the learned Muslim clerics—expanded throughout the Islamic world in matters of religious doctrine and interpretation. Because the Koran did not lay out a body of rules to regulate the daily life of Muslims, it was left to succeeding generations of Islamic thinkers and jurists to formulate and refine Islamic law. And because Islam did not develop an authoritative religious chief (despite the claims of certain caliphs), competing and overlapping schools of religious belief and jurisprudence have proliferated throughout the Muslim world down through the centuries. As a general rule, the Shiite clergy has tended to have a tiered hierarchy, with "grand ayatollahs" outranking ayatollahs, and so on down the ranks. The Sunni clergy is less structured, permitting greater flexibility in religious and political doctrine.

"Traditionalist" Sunni Islam has produced four main schools that are dominant today in different corners of the globe. Most of these Sunni schools have stressed the Prophet's commitment to peace (except for defensive wars) and to coexistence with Christians and Jews; they generally reject terrorism and the killing of women, children, and the elderly for any reason. Traditionalists also view Islamic law as binding on all Muslims, even though the Islamic scholars and jurists who interpret and define the law often disagree with one another. As Reza Aslan has pointed out, "It is practically impossible to reconcile the Traditionalist view of the Shariah with modern conceptions of democracy and human rights." Sunni Islam has also produced a "modernist" (or "reformist") orientation that calls for a separation of religion and the state, with Islamic law separated from the sphere of civil and political life. Some modernists have regarded Muhammad's community in Mecca as an example of such a separation. Modernists have sought to reconcile Islam with Western rationalism and democracy, without necessarily embracing a fully secular state.[20]

In addition to traditionalism and modernism, Sunni Islam has also produced more radical and extreme strains, which are often labeled "fundamentalist" or "Islamist" in the West. Despite some variations, the fundamentalist schools favor a state based on a rigid and puritanical interpretation of Islamic law, including the application of severe restrictions on women and of "eye-for-an-eye" punishments that Muhammad himself did not explicitly condone (such as amputation of a thief's hand). Some fundamentalists favor a theocratic Islamic state; others would permit civil authority, but only if it adheres to a strict code of shariah. Many Sunni fundamentalists also call for the creation of a worldwide Islamic political community. Sunni fundamentalists are deeply opposed to Shiism and most other strains of Islam, regarding their adherents as heretics. Most also oppose the West and Western democratic traditions. Some advocate terrorism.

The most prominent general school of Sunni fundamentalism today is the Salafi school. In Arabic, *salaf* means "the ancient ones" or "the predecessors," a reference to Muhammad's companions. Salafis believe that they are practicing the pure form of Islam developed by the first three generations of Muslims. Salafism has several variants. In Saudi Arabia it is identified with *Wahhabism*, an orientation developed by Muhammad Ibnal-Wahhab (1703–92). Infuriated at the notoriously un-Islamic practices of Ottoman rulers, al-Wahhab called for a return to the religion's roots. In 1744 he formed an alliance with the al-Saud family, a minor desert clan, and together they founded a new state in the Arabian peninsula. Al-Wahhab accepted the temporal authority of the head of the al-Saud family, and the latter agreed to enforce a puritanical interpretation of the Koran and Islamic law. After the collapse of the Ottoman caliphate following World War I, the al-Saud family seized control of Mecca and Medina and publicly executed forty thousand foes. In 1932 the Saudis proclaimed the Kingdom of Saudi Arabia, basing their state on Wahhabist principles. Although the government is controlled by the royal house of al-Saud, the legal system is based on shariah. The Saudi state encourages Islamic religious schools (madrassas) to inculcate Wahhabism's traditional doctrines and values, but the anti-Western messages that are conveyed in many of the madrassas are diametrically opposed to the Saudi government's policy of cooperation with the United States. Fifteen of the nineteen hijackers who participated in the events of September 11, 2001, came from Saudi Arabia, a fact that some observers attribute to the doctrinal influences of Wahhabism.[21]

Another version of Salafist tradition is the Deobandi school, founded in 1867 in the north Indian town of Deoband. Deobandis are active today in Pakistan, where they comprise about 15 percent of the country's Sunni majority, and they formed the backbone of the Taliban movement, another Salafist movement, in Afghanistan. Some of the leaders of Egypt's Muslim Brotherhood have been Salafis. One of them, *Sayyid Qutb* (KUH-tbb), is considered the father of modern Islamic radicalism. Qutb came away from a research trip in the United States in 1948 with an intense hatred of Western political and social freedoms. (He denounced sock hops and jazz as immoral.) The Muslim Brotherhood's current leaders tend to be more moderate in their views. Osama bin Laden and his closest associate, Ayman al-Zawahiri (EYE-mahn al zah-WAH-ree), also subscribe to Salafism, and al Qaeda is a Salafist-inspired movement.

Like Sunni Islam, Shiism also has several different strains. Shiites have advanced three different interpretations of the relationship between religion and politics. Historically, most Shiite clerics have favored a complete withdrawal from politics, preferring instead to concentrate on the purely religious aspects of Islamic law and doctrine. This attitude comes closest to the Western concept of the separation of church and state. A second view permits cooperation between the clergy and the state for the purpose of enforcing Shiite Islamic law through the government of a just ruler. A third approach is even more politically engaged: it actively encourages Shiite clerics to get involved in politics, either by taking over the state themselves and setting up a theocracy, or by openly opposing an unjust, un-Islamic government. Iran's Ayatollah Khomeini was one of the most ardent advocates of this activist stance. Khomeini took the unprecedented step of claiming that he was the infallible representative of the Mahdi (the Hidden Imam) and was therefore entitled to the same power as the Messenger Muhammad in demanding absolute obedience from the people. The question of which of these three Shiite orientations to politics will prevail in the future is of vital importance not only in post-Khomeini Iran but also in post-Saddam Iraq.[22]

Khomeini's Iranian revolution inaugurated a Shiite revival that is still reverberating in the greater Middle East. The rise of Hezbollah in Lebanon and the growth of Shiite militias in Iraq are symptomatic of this great awakening. Both movements are actively promoted by Iran's leaders, who have not concealed their intention of playing an assertive role in the region in opposition to

U.S. interests.[23] During the month-long war between Israel and Hezbollah in the summer of 2006, the leaders of Sunni countries like Egypt, Saudi Arabia, and Jordan initially lined up against Iran, publicly blaming Hezbollah for starting the conflict. But Israel's massive bombing campaign and ground assaults, which killed nearly a thousand Lebanese civilians and drove almost a million from their homes, pushed the Sunni and Shiite leaders together, at least temporarily. Whether this union in opposition to the Israelis would endure was doubtful. The three Sunni states have good ties with the United States, and the fourteen-hundred-year-old doctrinal dispute between the Sunnis and Shiites shows no signs of dissipating.

### Islam and Violence

Violence is no stranger to religion. The history of Christianity, for example, is marked by the Spanish Inquisition, Europe's Wars of Religion, and sectarian violence between Protestants and Catholics in Northern Ireland. In 1095, Pope Urban II preached the First Crusade against Muslims in the Holy Land.[24]

The connection between Islam and political violence has doctrinal roots in the Koran's concept of *jihad.* Muhammad understood jihad (which means "struggle") in several different senses. It can refer to the efforts of individual Muslims or the broader Islamic community to overcome sinful habits ("jihad of the heart") or to speak out against evil and in favor of the good ("jihad of the tongue"). The Prophet also understood jihad in martial terms, as reflected in the so-called "sword verses" and other passages of the Koran that call on Muslims to "kill the idolaters" (pagans) until they embrace the Muslim religion, or to fight the Peoples of the Book until they accept the hegemony of Islam by paying a tax to the Islamic authorities ruling over them. (Muhammad did not require Christians and Jews to be converted to Islam.) These verses espouse "jihad of the sword."[25] But the Koran prohibits the killing of noncombatants. It also prohibits offensive wars ("Do not begin hostilities; God does not like the aggressor.") According to a widely accepted interpretation, it permits only defensive wars undertaken by "the oppressed." Centuries later, Crusaders from Catholic Europe coined the term *holy war* to justify their invasions of the Muslim-controlled Holy Land. It was during this period that Islamic scholars developed a more assertive doctrine of jihad authorizing the House of Islam to take the offensive against non-Muslims (including Christians), who were collectively consigned to the House of War. This "classical" doctrine of jihad was repudiated by subsequent Islamic jurists, but it has been resuscitated more recently by militant fundamentalists like bin Laden, Khomeini, and the leaders of Hezbollah and Hamas. Islamic militants who favor violence against non-Muslims (including the People of the Book) are consequently called *jihadists.*

In 1998 Osama bin Laden and his key associates issued a theological decree *(fatwa)* calling on "every Muslim who believes in God . . . to kill the Americans and plunder their money wherever and whenever they find it" in order to expel U.S. military forces from "the lands of Islam." For most Muslims, bin Laden's appeal represented an extreme concept of jihad that exceeds traditional interpretations of the term. His authority to issue such an order, moreover, has been questioned. Islamic traditions hold that only a qualified Muslim jurist has the authority to issue a fatwa. Whatever its original connotations, jihad is not viewed by most Islamic religious authorities as justifying indiscriminate terrorism against non-Muslims.

A substantial number of the violent conflicts involving Muslim states or terrorists in recent years have occurred for reasons other than the assertion of religious doctrine. Palestinians are struggling against Israel to establish their own sovereign state; most of them do not want an Islamic theocracy. Chechens fighting the Russian government want national independence. Saddam Hussein invaded the Islamic Republic of Iran to capture territory and assert his power in the Persian Gulf region. Bosnian Muslims fought mainly to defend themselves against attacks launched by Bosnian Serbs, the Serbian government, and Croats, while Kosovo's Albanian population fought Slobodan Milosevic's Yugoslav government to regain autonomy rights in Kosovo (or to win Kosovo's independence), not to create an Islamic theocracy. Though the Muslim world today may indeed be heavily engaged in violent conflicts around the globe, few of these conflicts are driven by theological injunctions to engage in all-out holy war against non-Muslims or to create theocratic governments.

In a major study, Robert Pape found that religion is not the root cause of suicide terrorism. After examining 315 suicide attacks occurring around the globe between 1980 and 2003 (prior to the war in Iraq), Pape concluded that nationalism, not religion, was the main explanatory variable driving both the leaders of terrorist movements as well as the individuals who sacrificed themselves in terrorist attacks. Pape argues that the immediate aim of suicide terrorism is "to compel modern democracies to withdraw troops from territories that terrorists consider to be their homeland." The majority of the attacks in this period—76 of the total—were committed by the Tamil Liberation Tigers in Sri Lanka, a Marxist-Leninist group with no religious agenda (see chapter 6). And the immediate aim of Osama bin Laden and the perpetrators of 71 suicide attacks attributed to al Qaeda was to expel American troops from Saudi Arabia and other Muslim states in the Persian Gulf. These U.S. troop deployments, initiated during the Persian Gulf War of 1990–91, were "most likely the pivotal factor leading to September 11," Pape maintains. Similarly, the immediate aim of Hamas-inspired suicide terrorism in these years was to push Israel out of the West Bank and Gaza, and the main aim of Hezbollah's suicide terrorism was to eject Israel from Lebanon. Pape acknowledges that the leaders of al Qaeda, Hamas, and Hezbollah have the broader aim of establishing Islamic states in the Muslim world. But it would be inaccurate, in his view, to ascribe their terror tactics to religion alone. Leaders of terrorist movements play up religious differences with their enemies in order to fan the flames of nationalism among their populations. Moreover, the data show that an "American military presence is a stronger factor than Salafi fundamentalism in predicting who dies for al-Qaeda's cause." The bottom line, Pape concludes, "is that suicide terrorism is mainly a response to foreign occupation."

In light of these findings, Pape recommends that the United States withdraw its troops from the soil of Persian Gulf states—including Iraq—as soon as possible. He urges the U.S. government to return to the policy of "offshore balancing" that it pursued in the 1970s and 1980s, maintaining a strong naval presence in the Gulf in order to protect American access to the region's oil. He also warns that any attempt to impose democracy by force on countries like Iran and Saudi Arabia is likely to trigger more terrorism.[26] Implementing Pape's recommendations, however, may not be enough to stop suicide attacks motivated by demands that go beyond the removal of U.S. troops from Muslim lands (including Afghanistan, not just Persian Gulf countries). Many Islamic terrorists also insist on the liquidation of the state of Israel and the creation of Islamic theocracies throughout the Muslim world, among other things.

### Islam and Democracy

Islamic countries have not readily taken to democracy. The authors of *Freedom in the World* point out that countries with a Muslim majority (or a large Muslim plurality) have generally bucked the historic trend toward political liberalization and democracy that has been evident in much of the non-Islamic world over the past thirty-five years or so. Out of nearly fifty countries around the world with a Muslim majority, two were classified as "free" in 1972. By the end of 2006 there were only three: Indonesia, Mali, and Senegal. Among the Muslim-majority countries of the Middle East and North Africa, not one was "free" in late 2006; six were rated "partly free" and eleven were "not free." In striking contrast, much of the rest of the globe has witnessed more rapid increases in "free" and "partly free" countries since the 1970s.[27]

These realities are partly accounted for by several factors unrelated to Islamic doctrine: the proliferation of military regimes, especially in Africa; the entrenchment of dictators wielding personal power in countries like Iraq (Saddam Hussein), Syria (led by Hafaz al-Assad from 1970 to 2000, and since then by his son Bashar), and Egypt (led by Gamal Abdel Nasser from 1954 to 1970, Anwar Sadat from 1970 to 1981, and Hosni Mubarak since 1981); the persistence of monarchies in places like Saudi Arabia, Jordan, Morocco, and Persian Gulf sheikdoms; and the influence of authoritarian parties like the Baath Party in Iraq. Of forty-seven predominantly or traditionally Muslim countries in 2006, only one—Iran—was an Islamic theocracy.

Nevertheless, Islamic doctrine and traditional practices have fortified resistance to democracy in the Muslim world. Religious intolerance is part of the problem. Most of the world's great religions and religious sects have shown strains of intolerance, directing animosity either at the adherents of other faiths (e.g., Christians vs. Muslims) or at co-religionists (Catholics vs. Protestants, Anglicans vs. Puritans, and so on). Islam is by no means unique in its hostility to other religions or in its internal disputes. However, religious toleration gradually emerged as an important value in the European Enlightenment. Most importantly, religious tolerance was one of the founding principles of American democracy. Many of the immigrants who came to America precisely in order to escape religious persecution at home shared a basic understanding that mutual tolerance and the separation of church and state under a secular government were imperative if they were to avoid a repetition of Europe's bloody religious conflicts. Ultimately, religious tolerance became a cardinal principle of Western democracy.

Although Muhammad did not demand the conversion of Jews and Christians, and he allowed them to live freely in his Muslim community in Medina, he did not regard them as the spiritual or political equals of Muslims. As Islam extended its conquests to areas with substantial Jewish and Christian populations, like Spain and the Ottoman empire, the "Peoples of the Book" were treated harshly by some rulers and favorably by others, but they were always second-class citizens.[28] The treatment of Christians and Jews in Muslim-dominated countries in recent decades has been mixed. In Lebanon, Nigeria, and Sudan there has been considerable sectarian violence between Muslims and Christians, but Jordan and the Palestinian areas have witnessed somewhat greater tolerance of their Christian minorities. Since the intensification of the Arab-Israeli dispute, most Jews have left predominantly Muslim countries like Morocco and Iraq. If democracy is to take hold in the Muslim world, there will have to be genuine tolerance on the basis of political and social *equality* not only for non-Muslims but also for the various currents within the house of Islam.

The treatment of women is another major stumbling block on Islam's road to democracy. Traditional Islamic practice has been more stringent than Muhammad's teachings when it comes to the role of women in social life. After the death of his beloved first wife, Muhammad required only that his subsequent nine wives, but not other women, wear the veil (the *hijab*). And he granted women unprecedented rights of property ownership and inheritance. It was subsequent Muslim caliphs and scholars who adopted demeaning and misogynist attitudes and laws. As a general rule women in traditionally Muslim countries do not enjoy social and political equality with men. In many Islamic societies they are subject to significant restrictions with regard to dress, education, marital rights, property ownership, legal standing, and political activity. As we noted in chapter 2, Steven Fish argues that the status of women in traditionally Muslim countries is *the* single most significant variable associated with authoritarianism in the Muslim world.[29]

Another barrier to democracy in Muslim countries, particularly in those that practice Islamic law, is the legal system. Modern democracies have a civil legal code that is independent of religious authority. Contemporary democracies have also adopted prohibitions against what the Universal Declaration of Human Rights calls cruel, inhuman, degrading punishment. European democracies have abolished the death penalty and the United States has not, but no established democracies permit decapitation, stoning, amputation, or flogging as legitimate punishments for criminal offenses. Such punishments are condoned in Islamic law, and several of them have been routinely carried out in countries practicing shariah—like Iran, Saudi Arabia, and Afghanistan under the Taliban. One notorious case occurred recently in Nigeria. In 2002 Amina Lawall was convicted of adultery by an Islamic court in a Muslim-majority Nigerian state after giving birth to a daughter two years after divorcing her husband. The court sentenced her to death by stoning. The case provoked an international outcry before an Islamic appeals court overturned the single mother's conviction in 2003.

The generalizations we have made in this book about democracy apply to traditionally Muslim countries no less than to non-Muslim countries. Definitionally, democracy must meet at least the minimal criteria that we discussed in chapter 7. Appeals by reformers for "Islamic democracy" and "Islamic pluralism" must consider the full implications of these terms. If a privileged religious group does not accord *everyone*—including the adherents of other religions and women—the same political, legal, and social rights on the basis of inclusion, equality, and nondiscrimination, the political system is not a democracy. If a religious group monopolizes political power and refuses to allow others to vote them out in free and fair elections, and to change the country's laws through fair legislative processes, it's not a democracy. If excessively cruel punishments are imposed for victimless "crimes" or even for real transgressions, it's not a democracy. And if religious laws and practices (other than holidays, perhaps) are imposed on nonadherents against their will, it's not a democracy. Muslims who seek to combine Islam with democracy must confront some difficult questions: Does democracy require a secular state? If it does, then what is "Islamic" about it? And if it does not, then how can an "Islamic" state be reconciled with the democratic principles of equality and inclusion for all?

Ultimately, democracy is most likely to emerge and survive in Muslim countries when a critical mass of elites and elements of the population *want* it and are willing to take risks to get it, whether their purpose is to eliminate tyranny, avert civil war, or share the national wealth more equitably. Any Islamic country will of course have to chart its own path to democracy, based on its history and culture, and creative hybrids of democracy and Islam may very well emerge. Meanwhile, debates about Islamic "exceptionalism," which assumes that Islamic countries cannot build democracies, will likely continue.[30]

Indonesia, the country with the world's largest Muslim population, provides a timely example of the relationship between Islam and democracy.

## ISLAM IN INDONESIA

On a warm Saturday evening in October 2002, bombs went off outside two crowded nightclubs in the popular tourist area of Kuta on the Indonesian island of Bali. More than two hundred people were killed in the blast, including seven Americans and nationals from twenty other countries. The police quickly rounded up the main perpetrators of the attack. All of them were thought to be associated with Jemaah Islamiah (Islamic Community), a secretive terrorist network that seeks to create Islamic states in Southeast Asia. A prime suspect taken into custody was Abu Bakar Bashir, a wispy-bearded Islamic cleric in his mid sixties. Bashir, who ran an Islamic school on the island of Java, had a long history as a Muslim militant. In the 1970s he was jailed for subversion. Subsequently he fled to Malaysia, where he formed contacts with like-minded Islamic radicals, including terrorists subsequently implicated in the Bali bombings. Bashir was suspected of being the spiritual leader of Jemaah Islamiah, an organization allegedly linked to al Qaeda (though there is little hard evidence to prove it). Although Bashir had declared his support for Osama bin Laden and branded the United States and Israel as "terrorists," he denied any connection with al Qaeda and explicitly condemned the Bali nightclub attacks. A court acquitted Bashir of being Jemaah Islamiah's leader. But in a second trial, Bashir was found guilty of complicity in an "evil conspiracy" by giving his approval for the Bali bombings. He received a sentence of thirty months in jail. The others involved in the bomb plot were sentenced to death or life imprisonment.

In August 2003 a suicide bomber set off a car bomb that rocked the Marriott Hotel in Jakarta, killing twelve people (mostly Indonesians). Once again, suspects connected with Jemaah Islamiah were arrested; two of them quickly confessed. In addition, violence between Muslims and Christians has flared up periodically in recent years in several Indonesian provinces. And Jemaah Islamiah is only one of several radical Islamist groups operating in Indonesia. Nevertheless, violence associated with Islamic militants has actually declined substantially since 1999 and 2000, when more than two thousand people were killed in sectarian strife each year. Moreover, there seems to be little support in Indonesia for an Islamic government based on the strict observance of shariah. On the contrary, the country's population and political elites continue to support Indonesia's traditional tolerance of its main religious denominations.

With a population of more than 240 million people, 88 percent of whom are Muslim, Indonesia is the world's largest Muslim country. Since 1999 it has become the world's third largest democracy (after India and the United States). Though problems persist—including endemic corruption and sputtering economic growth—the process of consolidating democracy has made visible strides.

Islam first came to Indonesia from India, brought by traders and itinerant holy men. From the outset, Islamic beliefs and practices in the Indonesian archipelago assumed a hybrid character. Traditional Sunni doctrines from the Arabian peninsula blended with Sufism, a mystical variant of Islam that combines spiritual introspection with poetry and music. As Islam spread across the thousands of islands that make up Indonesia, it fused with preexisting beliefs in each locality, including Hinduism and Buddhism, both imported earlier from India, and traditional animism (paganism). Some of these fusions still exist today.

The Dutch East India Company took over much of Indonesia in the seventeenth century, and when the Dutch government assumed direct control of what it called the Dutch East Indies in 1799, support for Islam hardened into a source of resistance to foreign occupation. Opposition to Dutch rule was particularly fierce in the province of Aceh, located on the northwestern tip of the archipelago. Islam became well entrenched in Aceh, and it remains so to this day.

In 1942 the Japanese invaded the islands and set up an occupation regime, dealing a crippling blow to Dutch colonial rule. The occupation also sparked new life into several indigenous independence movements. After Japan's defeat in 1945, the leader of the Indonesian Nationalist Party, Sukarno, declared Indonesia's independence. (Following Indonesian custom, Sukarno used only one name.) The Dutch tried to reestablish their colonial administration, but the United States objected and threatened to deny the Netherlands the postwar economic assistance it expected to receive under the Marshall Plan. The Dutch pulled out and Indonesia gained its formal independence in 1949. Sukarno soon emerged as the new state's principal leader.

Indonesia's religious diversity, rooted above all in the variety of religious practices of the country's overwhelmingly Muslim population, convinced Sukarno to establish a legal code based on civil law rather than on shariah. Sukarno himself was more interested in consolidating his personal power and in projecting himself as a leader of the world's developing countries than in propagating Islam. As he steered his government away from democracy and created a dictatorship that he called "Guided Democracy," Sukarno formed an alliance with the powerful Indonesian Communist Party. When the Communists attempted to seize power in 1965, the military leadership, backed by anticommunist civilian groups, deposed Sukarno. Approximately half a million Communists and their sympathizers were then killed in a massacre orchestrated by the military hierarchy. Muslims were also intensely opposed to the Communists, and Muslim organizations took an active part in the violent anticommunist backlash.[31]

General Suharto, a top military leader, soon asserted himself as the country's new leader. He was to exercise power for thirty-two years, from 1966 to 1998. Like Sukarno, Suharto was primarily interested in enhancing his own authority. To this end he staged a succession of fraudulent presidential elections, each one carefully rigged to guarantee his victory, and he ruled through an official government party called Gokar. Like many other dictators, Suharto built alliances by providing benefits to favored groups and organizations in return for their political support, or at least their quiescence. Suharto formed alliances with elements of the military as well as with other segments of society, including the country's rising middle class. Thanks to a successful development policy, Indonesia's booming economy started growing at the brisk clip of 7 percent a year, lifting millions of people out of poverty, especially in rural areas. At first, Suharto kept Muslim groups at arm's length. His own religious background was said to be a typically Indonesian melange of Islam and pre-Islamic customs. Members of the military command and the civilian leadership (some of whom were Christian or Hindu) feared that Islamic organizations, with their large mass base, were a potential threat to the regime. But even though Suharto did not initially cultivate Muslim leaders, neither did he move to suppress them. Instead, he co-opted them with minor concessions. In return, most Muslim leaders accepted his regime, however grudgingly.

By the late 1980s, support for Suharto's long dictatorship—his so-called "New Order"—was waning significantly. To shore up his base, Suharto reached out to the Muslim community, actively assisting in the establishment of a new organization for Muslim intellectuals and granting Muslims new concessions. These measures were designed mainly to co-opt Muslim leaders and their mass followings, however, with the aim of keeping the country's large Muslim population under control. A number of prominent conservative Muslims went along with Suharto, and some were rewarded with important posts in the government or the military. But a "modernist" group of Muslim leaders kept their distance from the regime; over time, they increasingly favored a more democratic state based on pluralism, tolerance, and civil society. One of the most independent Muslim leaders was Abdurrahman Wahid, a moderate cleric who became committed to a peaceful transformation of Indonesian politics based on these principles. During the 1990s, Wahid edged closer to an alliance with the anti-Suharto Indonesian Democratic Party, which was led by Megawati Sukarnoputri (MEH-gah-WAH-tee soo-carno-poo-TREE), the daughter of Indonesia's first leader, Sukarno.[32]

As the corruption and nepotism undergirding Suharto's sultanistic regime became increasingly transparent, opposition political parties and NGOs stepped up their demands for greater political liberalization over the course of the 1990s. Suharto moved even closer to Muslim leaders, favoring traditionalist Muslims over more reform-minded modernist Muslims. In the process, he managed to drive a wedge between respected Muslim leaders and their potential allies in the cause of political change. But this strategy came apart in late 1997 and early 1998, when Indonesia's economy was suddenly shaken by the financial shocks emanating from the collapse of Thailand's currency, as described in chapter 1. The economic crisis brought Indonesia's long-simmering political crisis to a dramatic boiling point. The middle class was devastated and turned against the regime. A wave of strikes, student demonstrations, and urban riots destroyed the remaining shreds of Suharto's legitimacy. More importantly, moderate Muslim leaders like Wahid turned away from Suharto, joining forces with oppositionist forces in support of democratization. Suharto resigned in May 1998, handing power over to his vice president.[33]

Legislative elections held in 1999 returned a plurality to a pro-democracy coalition headed led by Megawati Sukarnoputri. The legislature thereupon elected Wahid, her Muslim ally, as president. Megawati, a modern Muslim who did not wear a head scarf or veil, became vice president. Hopes for a stable transition to democracy rose as Megawati and Wahid pledged their support for reform. But rivalries between the two camps frayed their coalition. The ineffective Wahid was impeached in 2001, and Megawati took over the presidency.

In addition to confronting the country's continuing economic slide, Megawati had to deal with one of Indonesia's oldest problems: regional secessionism. On the eastern side of the 3,200-mile-wide archipelago, East Timor had already declared its independence in 1975. The declaration was ignored by President Suharto's government. But after Suharto's ouster, East Timor's largely Roman Catholic population renewed its demands for sovereignty. In a process mediated by the United Nations, East Timor became an independent state in 2002. On the western side of Indonesia, on the island of Sumatra, Aceh province had also been a hotbed of secessionist sentiment for decades. Rebels began fighting for Aceh's independence in 1976. President Megawati responded to the latest armed revolt by declaring martial law and dispatching more troops. As the country's most devoutly Islamic province, Aceh enforces a strict regimen of shariah over its population of more than 4 million Muslims. Couples have been flogged for engaging in "immoral behavior" in public; flogging is also meted out for the consumption of alcohol. Aceh took a devastating hit from the tsunami that jolted the Indian Ocean region in December 2004. Approximately 110,000 Indonesians perished in the tidal wave, mostly in or near Aceh; some 700,000 were left homeless. International relief teams, including military personnel from the United States, were warmly welcomed by rebels from the Free Aceh Movement, who much preferred the foreigners to the dreaded Indonesian army.

In 2004 Indonesia held its first free, direct presidential elections. President Megawati's bid for a strong popular mandate was spoiled when a political outsider of humble origins, Susilo Bambang Yudhoyono (soo-SEE-low BAHM-BAHNG YOO-doe-YO-no), known as SBY for short, forced the president into a second-round runoff. Yudhoyono was the senior minister responsible for security in Megawati's cabinet. Buoyed by widespread antipathy to corruption and unemployment, and aided by an 80 percent voter turnout, SBY handily defeated Megawati in the runoff election. Since assuming office, President Yudhoyono has sought to reach an accommodation with the Aceh rebels and to revive Indonesia's economy. But his small Democrat Party won only 10 percent of the seats in the 550-seat lower house elected in 2004. In search of allies, SBY has found support from two moderate Islam-influenced parties: the Prosperous Justice Party, which won 45 seats, and the Crescent Star Party, with 11 seats. Neither party officially espouses an Islamic state based on shariah. The Prosperous Justice Party increased its share of votes after its leaders moderated the party's religious rhetoric and focused instead on the need to eliminate government corruption, running on the slogan "Clean and Concerned." The party also scored points with voters by providing tsunami relief more rapidly and effectively than the government was able to manage, at least initially.

Despite the Bali bombings of 2002 and subsequent incidents of terrorism, Indonesia today is not on the verge of chaos or civil war. The overwhelming majority of the country's Muslims, including its Muslim leaders and organizations, reject terrorism and support Indonesia's tradition of religious tolerance. Indonesia remains a secular state that officially recognizes five religions: Islam, Hinduism, Buddhism, Catholicism, and Protestantism. Public holidays reflect this diversity. (Other religions and sects experience discrimination, however.) The vote for Islam-inspired parties has in fact declined from 45 percent in the 1950s to 35 percent more recently. Support for radical and terrorist groups is minimal. Moreover, internal disputes are splintering these radical organizations: some of their own adherents object to terrorism. At the same time, support for Islamic beliefs is growing in Indonesia, stimulated by the global rise of Islamic proselytizing and political activism. There is an ongoing debate between traditional and modernist Muslims, in tandem with a debate about how Islam should relate to democracy. Pro-democracy groups like the Liberal Islam Network, which favors the separation of religious and political authority, are playing an active role in these discussions.

The chief conclusion of this section is that Islam has been quite compatible with democracy in Indonesia. Key Muslim leaders actively promoted the democratization process in the 1990s, and most of the country's overwhelmingly Muslim population supported it. They have also supported the democratic process that has developed since then, for all its flaws. Many Muslims regard tolerance, pluralism, and civility as defining features of Indonesia's Islamic tradition, and they want neither an Islamic theocracy nor an all-powerful state. The fate of democracy in Indonesia in all likelihood depends more on how Muslims view the government's efforts to eliminate corruption and improve the economy than on the political status of Islam. And despite occasional deadly attacks by extremists, it appears unlikely that Indonesians will turn in large numbers to the Islamic radicalism of Abu Bakar Bashir, who was released from prison in June 2006.[34]

### Many Islams

A survey of political currents in the Muslim world reveals a wide variety of political orientations and governmental structures.

- *Fundamentalists* (or *Islamists*) advocate the creation of Islamic theocracies, to be governed by clerics in accordance with a strict interpretation of Islamic law. They are vehemently anti-Western. Their ranks include Iran's Ayatollah Khomeini and his like-minded successors, the Taliban, and Osama bin Laden. Some may advocate terrorism.
- *Conservatives* are devout Muslims who favor the implementation of Islamic law, whether in a very austere form or a more moderate version. As a general rule, conservatives tend to be less extreme than fundamentalists in their interpretation of Islam, and they may have a favorable attitude toward the West. Most would oppose terrorism. Some may favor a clerical theocracy (like Iran's former president Khamanei), while others prefer a secular government (like the royal family of Saudi Arabia or Pakistan's former president Zia ul-Haq).
- *Authoritarian secularists* favor a dictatorial state run by secular authorities. As a rule they do not practice shariah. Within these broad parameters there is room for a variety of different religious, governmental, and foreign policy orientations. Some may be devout Muslims; others may only pay lip service to Islamic ideals, manipulating Muslim sentiment to their own ends. Some may be hostile to the West (like Saddam Hussein, Syria's Bashar al-Assad, and Libya's Muammar al-Qaddafi), while others may get along with the West (like Egypt's Hosni Mubarak and Pakistan's Pervez Musharraf). Kemal Atatürk deliberately led Turkey on the path of Westernization. The leaders of the former Central Asian republics of the Soviet Union fall into this category, as do the military or autocratic leaders of various African states and the Mahgreb countries of Algeria, Morocco, and Tunisia.
- *Democratizing secularists* are leaders and political forces in predominantly or traditionally Muslim countries that have embarked on creating or consolidating a secular democracy. Examples can be found in Bangladesh, Indonesia, Mali, Nigeria, Senegal, and Turkey—and perhaps in Bahrain and Qatar, whose monarchs appear to be moving in the direction of constitutional monarchy.

In sum there are "many Islams," with a diversity of political directions. Whether the world's leading Muslim countries can find ways to blend Islam's rich religious and cultural heritage with the requirements of democracy in the years ahead will have a decisive impact on freedom and security throughout the world.[35]

## THE LEFT–RIGHT SPECTRUM

Now that we've surveyed a number of ideologies, we can present a more detailed left–right political spectrum than the one in chapter 2. In view of the complexities of political reality, however, the traditional left–right political spectrum as presented in figure 13.2 should be taken with a grain of salt. Though anarchism is placed on the extreme left,

**FIGURE 13.2 The Left–Right Spectrum**

some extreme right-wing groups in the United States are so antigovernment that they come close to advocating anarchism. Soviet-style communism (as in the former USSR or contemporary China) is placed on the left because of its historical associations with revolutionary socialism. It is virtually indistinguishable from fascism in several key respects, however. Both communist and fascist regimes have been one-party totalitarian regimes with a highly nationalistic foreign policy. Military regimes, for their part, come in left-wing socialist variants (in which the military leaders take up the cause of the working class or the poor) and right-wing variants (in which the military is aligned with a conservative ruling elite). Religiously oriented states, like fundamentalist or traditionalist Islamic states, are placed on the right because of their reactionary tendency to implement religious and political doctrines as they were propounded more than thirteen hundred years ago; but to the extent that they implement social welfare programs for the masses, they resemble the welfarist tendencies of the socialist left. The use of the term *Islamic fascism* to describe Islamic terrorists is inappropriate, however. Although both fascism and Islamic extremism reject democracy and embrace violence, their differences are substantial. Fascism espouses hypernationalism, military conquest, and racism; it scorns religious morality. Islamic fundamentalists want theocratic states. Their nationalism is directed mainly at getting American troops out of the Middle East, not at taking over Western countries. And their animosity toward Jews primarily reflects their opposition to the existence of Israel as a Zionist state in a predominantly Muslim region. It also reflects competing Islamic and Judaic claims of religious superiority. These anti-Jewish attitudes, however vengeful, generally do not stem from anti-Semitic racism. Arabs are themselves Semites.

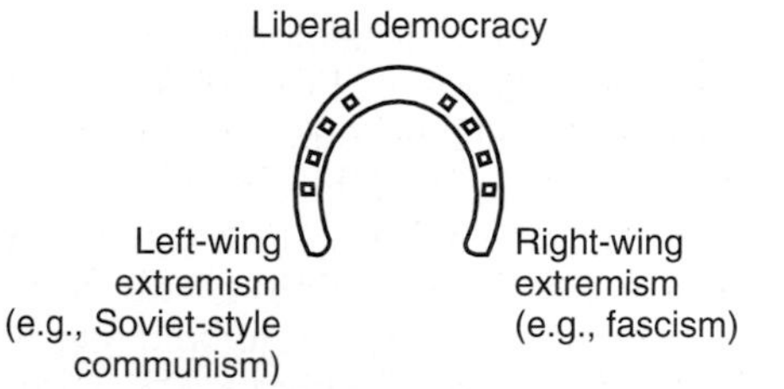


**FIGURE 13.3 A Political Horseshoe**

The similarities that often exist between the extremes of left and right have prompted some observers to suggest that political reality is more accurately represented by a horseshoe (figure 13.3) than by a straight line. The horseshoe depicts the proximity of left and right extremism. Ultimately, both of these graphic representations tend to oversimplify matters. As with virtually every major political phenomenon, ideology must be studied on a comparative basis in order to bring into sharp focus the similarities and differences to be found across place and time.

## HYPOTHESIS-TESTING EXERCISE: The End of Ideology?

A number of scholars have hypothesized that the era of fierce ideological conflict is over. Daniel Bell, for example, argued in the 1960s and 1970s that fundamental changes occurring in the economies of most advanced capitalist countries since World War II were undercutting the basis of the historic ideological clash between capitalism and socialism. Instead of being dominated by industrialism, with its emphasis on manufacturing and manual labor, the post-industrial economies of the United States, Japan, and most West European countries were now driven by the service sector, consisting of financial services (banks, stock markets); consumer services (stores, restaurants, and the like); health and legal services; and so on. Education and technology were becoming the driving forces of economic advancement. As a consequence, Bell argued, the classic confrontation between the capitalist bourgeoisie and the industrial proletariat was essentially dying out. The evidence of recent decades largely confirms Bell's insight.[36]

A more recent "end-of-ideology" hypothesis maintains that the forces of technological advancement and economic globalization since the 1970s have undermined the traditional dichotomy between capitalism and socialism on a global scale. Most of the extraordinary technological innovations of the past several decades, especially in the computer and telecommunications industries, were pioneered by private companies. One of the principal reasons why the Soviet Union collapsed, according to this hypothesis, was that its centrally planned socialist economy proved incapable of keeping up with the accelerated pace of high technology advancement in countries with private enterprise. Meanwhile, the private-enterprise economies long ago ceased being "capitalist" in the sense in which Karl Marx understood the term. The economies of the United States, Japan, and Western Europe today are mixed economies in which the state plays a major role, at times assisting private firms and at times regulating their activities. These countries, moreover, are all welfare states in which the workers have collective bargaining rights and the government provides a host of welfare benefits to the general population. They are also mass democracies.

Our hypothesis asserts that a growing global consensus on the desirability of the democratic mixed-economy model is reducing the scope of ideological conflict both within and between countries around the world.

### Variables

The *dependent variable* is the *end of ideological conflict,* both within countries and among the nations of the world. The *independent variable* is *mixed-economy democracies.*

### Expectations

If the hypothesis is true, we would expect to find a global increase in the number of countries becoming mixed-economy democracies and a decline in competing ideological orientations such as communism, fascism, religious ideologies, and others.

### Evidence

The evidence required to put the hypothesis to a systematic test is vast. The most we can do for now is mention a few facts that touch on the hypothesis and the expectations that flow from it.

The hypothesis finds support in the fact that the centrally planned economies of the former Soviet Union and the communist-ruled states of East Central Europe fell far behind the mixed-economy democracies in developing advanced technologies and maintaining economic growth. As the hypothesis would lead us to expect, Soviet-style communist planning is now being replaced in these countries by private enterprise and other features of the modern mixed economy. Even China, which continues to be governed by a powerful Communist Party, abandoned central planning in the 1980s and now has a considerable amount of private enterprise. A growing number of less developed countries in Asia, Latin America, Africa, as well, have made substantial changes in their economic systems since the 1980s, reducing the degree of state domination of the economy and expanding opportunities for private enterprise. In quite a few cases these economic changes have been accompanied by efforts to establish democracy.[37]

On the other side of the ledger, it is also true that ideological opposition to the prevailing Western model of the mixed-economy democracy continues to exist in various parts of the world. In Russia, for example, the triumph of private enterprise and democracy is still by no means assured. China openly advertises its own model, combining private enterprise with stern authoritarian rule. The desirability of combining private enterprise with some form or another of authoritarian rule has a wide following in other East Asian countries as well. In addition, as we have seen, Muslims around the world have advanced their own ideological alternatives to Western political and economic models. Finally, it cannot be casually assumed that no new ideological orientations will arise in the future. A large proportion of the world's population lives in abject poverty; the blessings of the modern mixed-economy welfare state have eluded them. As Kenneth Jowett has observed, new political ideas and "movements of rage" may yet emerge from these desperate conditions or from other political landscapes where Western ideas are deemed inappropriate or downright unacceptable.[38]

### Conclusions

The sketchy evidence we have just summarized is quite *mixed.* There seems to be a "wave" of democracy and private enterprise billowing around the world, but the long-term success of these efforts is by no means a certainty. Islamic ideology and other orientations still pose a challenge to Western political and economic ideas.

## KEY TERMS
## (In bold and underlined in the text)

Ideology
Liberalism
Socialism
Leninism
Social democracy
Fascism
Sunnis
Shiites

## NOTES

1. See Louis Hartz, *The Liberal Tradition in America* (New York: Harcourt, Brace, & World, 1955).
2. For a biography of Burke, see Conor Cruise O'Brien, *The Great Melody* (Chicago: University of Chicago Press, 1992). See also Burke's critique of the French Revolution, *Reflections on the Revolution in France* (1790).
3. On utopian socialism, see Edmund Wilson, *To the Finland Station* (Garden City, N.Y.: Doubleday, 1940); Robert Heilbroner, *The Worldly Philosophers,* 6th ed. (New York: Simon & Schuster, 1992); and Charles Nordhoff, *The Communistic Societies of the United States* (New York: Hillary House, 1960), first published in 1875.
4. *Economic and Philosophic Manuscripts of 1844,* excerpted in Robert C. Tucker, ed., *The Marx-Engels Reader* (New York: W. W. Norton, 1972), 53–103.
5. *Manifesto of the Communist Party,* in Tucker, *The Marx-Engels Reader,* 331–62.
6. "The mode of production of economic life conditions the social, political and intellectual process in general." From *A Contribution to the Critique of Political Economy,* in Tucker, *The Marx-Engels Reader,* 4. See also Melvin Rader, *Marx's Conception of History* (New York: Oxford University Press, 1979).
7. Engels, "On Social Relations in Russia" (1875), in Tucker, *The Marx-Engels Reader,* 589–99; Marx and Engels, preface to the Russian edition of the *Manifesto* (1882), in Tucker, *The Marx-Engels Reader,* 333–34.
8. V. I. Lenin, *What Is to Be Done?* in *The Lenin Anthology,* ed. Robert C. Tucker (New York: W. W. Norton, 1975), 12–114.
9. Bernstein wrote that the United States "apparently contradicts everything that the socialistic theory has hitherto advanced." In 1906 a prominent German sociologist addressed this curiosity. See Werner Sombart, *Why Is There No Socialism in the United States?* trans. Patricia M. Hocking and C. T. Husbands (White Plains, N.Y.: M. E. Sharpe, 1976). See also Seymour Martin Lipset and Gary Marks, *It Didn't Happen Here: Why Socialism Failed in the United States* (New York: W. W. Norton, 2000). The American Socialist Party fielded presidential candidates between 1900 and 1932 but its candidates never obtained a million votes. For a biography of the party's last major leader, see W. A. Swanberg, *Norman Thomas: The Last Idealist* (New York: Scribner, 1976).
10. Julius K. Nyerere, *Ujamaa—Essays on Socialism* (London: Oxford University Press, 1968).
11. Abdel Moghny Said, *Arab Socialism* (London: Blandford Press, 1972).
12. Stanley G. Payne, *A History of Fascism, 1914–1945* (Madison: University of Wisconsin Press, 1995).
13. Meir Michaelis, *Mussolini and the Jews* (London: Oxford University Press, 1978).
14. Benito Mussolini and Giovanni Gentile, "The Doctrine of Fascism," in *Italian Fascisms from Pareto to Gentile,* ed. Adrian Lyttelton, trans. Douglas Parmee (New York: Harper and Row, 1973), 42. See also Herman Finer, *Mussolini's Italy* (New York: Grosset & Dunlap, 1965), 198, 201. This classic work was first published in 1935.
15. On Mussolini's progression from socialism to fascism, see A. James Gregor, *Young Mussolini and the Intellectual Origins of Fascism* (Berkeley: University of California Press, 1979).
16. Ernst Nolte, *Three Faces of Fascism,* trans. Leila Vennewitz (New York: Mentor, 1969), 282.
17. One leading scholar of fascism, A. James Gregor, has argued that fascist ideas may be

found even in political movements that are not openly identified as fascist, including communist parties in Asia and Latin America and radical groups in the United States. Fascism and twentieth-century communism, he argues, are not mutually exclusive but share certain things, especially nationalism, totalitarianism, and mass mobilization. See *The Fascist Persuasion in Radical Politics* (Princeton: Princeton University Press, 1974).

**18.** For overviews of the history of Islam, see Reza Aslan, *No god but God: The Origins, Evolution, and Future of Islam* (New York: Random House, 2005), and Karen Armstrong, *Islam: A Short History* (New York: Modern Library, 2002).

**19.** Bernard Lewis, *What Went Wrong? Western Impact and Middle Eastern Response* (Oxford: Oxford University Press, 2002).

**20.** Aslan, *No god but God,* 170. See also Mansoor Moadel and Kamran Talatoff, *Modern and Fundamentalist Debates in Islam* (New York: Palgrave, 2002).

**21.** Vincenzo Oliveti, *Terror's Source: The Ideology of Wahhabi-Salafism and Its Consequences* (Birmingham, UK: Amadeus, 2002); Natana J. DeLong-Bas, *Wahhabi Islam: From Revival and Reform to Global Jihad* (Oxford: Oxford University Press, 2004); David Cummins, *The Wahhabi Mission and Saudi Arabia* (London: Tauris, 2006).

**22.** Moojan Momen, *An Introduction to Shi'i Islam: The History and Doctrines of Twelver Shi'ism* (New Haven: Yale University Press, 1985), 191–96. See also Yitzhak Nakash, *The Shi'is of Iraq* (Princeton: Princeton University Press, 1994), and Fouad Ajami, *The Vanished Imam: Musa al Sadr and the Shia of Lebanon* (Ithaca, N.Y.: Cornell University Press, 1986).

**23.** Vali Nasr, *The Shia Revival: How Conflicts Within Islam Will Shape the Future* (New York: W. W. Norton, 2006).

**24.** Jonathan Riley-Smith, ed., *The Oxford History of the Crusades* (Oxford: Oxford University Press, 2002); Karen Armstrong, *Holy War: The Crusades and Their Impact in Today's World,* 2nd ed. (New York: Anchor, 2001).

**25.** Reuven Firestone, *Jihad: The Origins of Holy War in Islam* (New York: Oxford University Press, 1999).

**26.** Robert A. Pape, *Dying to Win: The Strategic Logic of Suicide Terrorism* (New York: Random House, 2005). See also Marc Sageman, *Understanding Terror Networks* (Philadelphia: University of Pennsylvania Press, 2004).

**27.** *Freedom in the World 2003* (New York: Freedom House, 2003), 12. The rankings for 2006 were available at the end of the year at www.freedomhouse.org.

**28.** See, for example, Maria Rosa Menocal, *The Ornament of the World: How Muslims, Jews, and Christians Created a Culture of Tolerance in Medieval Spain* (Boston: Little, Brown, 2002).

**29.** M. Steven Fish, "Islam and Authoritarianism," *World Politics* 55, no. 1 (October 2002): 4–37.

**30.** On democracy and Islam, see Leonard Binder, *Islamic Liberalism* (Chicago: University of Chicago Press, 1988); Charles Kurzman, ed., *Liberal Islam: A Sourcebook* (Oxford: Oxford University Press, 1998); John L. Esposito and John O. Voll, *Islam and Democracy* (New York: Oxford University Press, 1996); Joel Beinin and Joe Stork, eds., *Political Islam* (Berkeley: University of California Press, 1997). See also the articles in the *Journal of Democracy* 13, no. 4 (October 2002): 5–68, and 14, no. 2 (April 2003): 18–49. On "exceptionalism," see *Journal of Democracy* 15, no. 4 (October 2004): 126–46.

**31.** Steven Drakeley, *The History of Indonesia* (Westport, Conn.: Greenwood, 2005); J. D. Legge, *Sukarno: A Political Biography* (New York: Praeger, 1972); Rex Mortimer, *Indonesian Communism under Sukarno: Ideology and Politics, 1959–1965* (Ithaca, N.Y.: Cornell University Press, 1974). The events of 1965 provide the background of the film *The Year of Living Dangerously*, based on the novel by Christopher J. Koch.

**32.** Robert W. Hefner, *Civil Islam: Muslims and Democratization in Indonesia* (Princeton: Princeton University Press, 2000); Donald J. Porter, *Managing Politics and Islam in Indonesia* (London: RoutledgeCurzon, 2002).

**33.** Edward Aspinall, *Opposing Suharto: Compromise, Resistance, and Regime Change in Indonesia* (Stanford: Stanford University Press, 2005); Richard Lloyd Parry, *In the Time of Madness: Indonesia on the Edge of Chaos* (New York: Grove, 2005); Stefan Eklöf, *Indonesian Politics in Crisis:*

*The Long Fall of Suharto 1996–98* (Copenhagen: Nordic Institute of Asian Studies, 1999).

**34.** "Time to Deliver: A Survey of Indonesia," *The Economist*, December 11, 2004. On the tsunami, see *Washington Post*, January 14, 19, 27, and 28 and February 27, 2005. See also Giora Eliraz, *Islam in Indonesia: Modernism, Radicalism, and the Middle East Dimension* (Brighton: Sussex Academic Press, 2004); Bahtiar Effendi, *Islam and the State in Indonesia* (Athens: Ohio University Press, 2003); and the discussion at the conference titled "Islam in Modern Indonesia" organized by the United States–Indonesia Society (February 7, 2002), accessible at www.usindo.org. The website of the Liberal Islam Network is www.islamlib.com.

**35.** Mir Zohair Husain, *Global Islamic Politics* (New York: HarperCollins, 1996). See also Olivier Roy, *Globalized Islam: The Search for a New Ummah* (New York: Columbia University Press, 2004), and Gilles Kepel, *The War for Muslim Minds: Islam and the West*, trans. Pascale Ghazaleh (Cambridge, Mass.: Harvard University Press, 2004).

**36.** Daniel Bell, *The End of Ideology*, rev. ed. (New York: Free Press, 1961), *The Coming of Post-Industrial Society* (New York: Basic Books, 1973 and 1999), and *The Cultural Contradictions of Capitalism* (New York: Basic Books, 1976). See also Chaim I. Waxman, ed., *The End of Ideology Debate* (New York: Simon & Schuster, 1969).

**37.** Daniel Yergin and Joseph Stanislaw, *The Commanding Heights* (New York: Simon & Schuster, 1998).

**38.** Kenneth Jowett, *New World Disorder* (Berkeley: University of California Press, 1992), 275–77.

CHAPTER 14

# POLITICAL ECONOMY

## Laissez-Faire—Central Planning—Mixed Economies—Welfare States

Politics and economics are intimately interrelated. Whether it is a matter of taxes, budget deficits, health care programs, or foreign trade, economic issues are invariably the stuff of intense political controversy and governmental decision making. Especially in today's tightly woven global economy, a sound understanding of economics is more than just useful: it's a survival skill. Consider the following example of how international relationships affect the value of our money.

## A TOURIST'S GUIDE TO INTERNATIONAL ECONOMICS

Most countries have their own currency: the U.S. dollar, the Japanese yen, and the Swiss franc are among the most widely used currencies in the world. Most members of the European Union share a common currency, the euro. Just like stocks and bonds, currencies are bought and sold on world markets by banks and other currency traders. Nearly one trillion dollars' worth of currencies change hands around the globe on a typical business day. And just like stocks and bonds, currencies change their relative value as a result of these global transactions.

A currency's value—its price relative to other currencies—can often be affected by political as well as economic considerations. If currency traders believe that Country X may experience political instability or turmoil such as an unpredictable new government or a civil war, they may sell off their holdings of that country's currency, buying up the currencies of more politically stable countries instead. They may do the same thing if they believe that Country X is about to experience major economic difficulties. When a country's currency is being sold in large quantities in world currency exchanges, its value relative to stronger, more desirable currencies drops, or *depreciates,* significantly.

The result of *currency depreciation* (or *currency devaluation*) can be felt instantly by tourists visiting the country whose currency is declining in value. Suppose you are an American tourist visiting Mexico. When you arrive, the Mexican peso is valued at 3.5 to the dollar. At this rate, you buy 350 pesos for $100. After a few days of dining and shopping, you need more pesos. But in the meantime, Mexico experiences a currency crisis as international traders begin a massive sell-off of pesos. The next time you go to a bank to exchange your dollars, you find to your delight that the peso is now valued at 5 to the dollar. For $100 you can now get 500 pesos in exchange. If the peso continues to slide in value, you may be able to extend your stay or buy more items, since each dollar exchanged buys

**TABLE 14.1**

**Winners and Losers in a Currency Devaluation**

**As the Mexican peso depreciates relative to the U.S. dollar . . .**

| **Winners** | **Losers** |
| --- | --- |
| U.S. purchasers and importers of Mexican goods and services | Mexican purchasers and importers of U.S. goods and services |
| Mexican sellers and exporters to U.S. buyers | U.S. sellers and exporters to Mexican buyers |

more Mexican goods and services than it did upon your arrival. Mexicans involved in the tourist trade eagerly welcome your additional expenditures. Like you, they stand to benefit from the peso's devaluation.

For many Mexicans, however, the peso's depreciation brings unwelcome consequences. Mexicans who buy imported goods from the United States such as computers or autos must now pay out more pesos per dollar's worth of purchase. A $1,000 American-made computer cost 3,500 pesos before the currency crisis; it now costs 5,000 pesos following the Mexican currency's devaluation. At the new rate of exchange, a Mexican consumer or businessperson may decide that it's too expensive to buy the computer at the higher peso price. In that case, the U.S. computer exporter loses a sale. For a U.S.-based company that sells a lot of goods south of the border, the peso's decline can result in a severe loss of customers. The business may be forced to lay off workers or may even go bankrupt.

Imagine the impact of the peso's decline on billions of dollars' worth of economic transactions between the two countries. (In 2006, U.S. exports of goods to Mexico exceeded $134 billion and Mexican exports to the United States exceeded $198 billion.) Large numbers of tourists, consumers, and businesses on both sides of the border are directly affected by the shift: some positively, others negatively. *In virtually every case of currency depreciation, there are winners and losers* (see table 14.1). Those who are economically disadvantaged will exert pressure on the Mexican and U.S. governments to do something about the peso's decline. The economic issue now becomes a political issue: people want governments to take action.

What can governments do in this situation? The most immediate option is for governments to *intervene in world currency markets* by buying pesos. Like stocks, the value of a currency rises the more it is purchased. If the U.S. and Mexican governments spend millions of dollars from their treasuries to buy pesos, the value of the peso will likely rise. It may not go all the way back from 5 to the dollar to 3.5, but at least it will move closer to the latter figure. Most important, the object of the governments' intervention is to stabilize the peso so that it will not fall or rise wildly, but will retain a fairly stable and predictable value against the dollar and other world currencies.

The case just outlined is not fictitious. At the end of 1994, the Mexican peso began falling in value against the U.S. dollar exactly as described. Within a few months the peso plunged from 3.45 to 8 to the dollar. To halt the peso's slide, the Mexican government spent millions of U.S. dollars in its possession (its dollar *reserves*) to buy pesos on world markets. The U.S. government joined with other governments in providing the Mexican government with a $38 billion rescue package to strengthen its economy, in hopes of making the peso more attractive to currency buyers. Though the peso's value rose in response to this assistance, it fell once again in the fall of 1995.

The peso's sudden deterioration had profound political consequences for both Mexico and the United States. In Mexico it triggered a severe economic crisis. The prices of imported goods rose dramatically, hurting businesses and consumers. Prices in 1995 were more than 40 percent higher than the previous year. As many as one million people were thrown out of work in 1995 alone because their employers could no longer afford to pay them. The country's domestic economic growth fell; interest rates skyrocketed to as much as 100 percent. A significant increase in violent crime in Mexico City and other parts of the country was attributed to rising economic frustration. Predictably, Mexicans from all walks of life looked to their government to help them. In the United States, the Clinton administration and the Republican-controlled Congress worked out a response to the Mexican situation because American businesses and consumers have an interest in a stable, fairly valued peso. Approximately seven hundred thousand jobs in the United States depended on trade with Mexico. The United States also had an interest in helping Mexico avoid potentially violent internal unrest as well as a rise in illegal immigrants coming across the U.S. border.

But as the peso fell, Mexico's exports rose more than 30 percent over the next few years. Sales to the United States, which buys 80 percent of the country's export goods, got an additional boost from the North American Free Trade Agreement (NAFTA), which reduces trade barriers between the United States, Mexico, and Canada. The steep rise in Mexico's export industry helped stabilize the economy and boosted growth rates considerably starting in 1996. While wages for industrial workers and other aspects of Mexico's economy deteriorated as a result of the currency evaluation, exports and other sectors improved. Winners as well as losers were still in evidence in Mexico several years after the peso's dramatic fall.

---

Economics is the study of how people and societies choose to allocate the scarce resources at their disposal, such as natural resources, human-made goods, and human services. Accordingly, economists examine such things as the way prices are determined, the impact of taxes, and such other phenomena as production, inflation, unemployment, and the causes of economic growth and decline.

Like political science, economics is a behavioral science: one of its main ambitions is to examine the ways individuals and organizations behave when making economic choices and decisions. And like at least some political scientists, many economists employ *rational choice theory,* the notion that people generally act on the basis of calculated self-interest to increase their anticipated gains and reduce their anticipated costs or risks (see chapter 2). Thus *homo economicus*—economic man—is a rational actor who is able to figure out how to increase his wealth and minimize his losses. Viewed from the larger perspective of an entire society, however, a collection of individual and corporate rational actors may not necessarily produce economic results that maximize everyone's welfare. What is rational for you may be bad for me. If you decide to raise prices for the goods you sell me, you are increasing my costs. Sometimes decisions that are rational for an individual or a particular company may prove harmful for the larger community. If a factory keeps its costs down by refusing to use expensive pollution control devices, the pollutants its chimneys belch into the air not only damage the public's health but raise the community's health care costs in the process. Conversely, it can also happen that economic decisions that are rational for the community as a whole may be deleterious for particular individuals or groups. If the government, for example, decides to trim its budget deficit by raising your taxes, you may not personally appreciate the rationality of its choice.

In short, the economic activities of individuals, private enterprises, and governments very often produce negative consequences for others. Of course, there are times when public and private economic policies benefit just about everyone to a greater or lesser degree. A growing economy can afford better roads, more medical research, cleaner air. These cases are positive-sum games, with many winners. But all too often there are losers as well as winners. This outcome is especially likely when the resources people want—money, land, jobs, and so on—are limited in quantity, an all-too-common occurrence. As a consequence, the allocation of scarce resources in society can sometimes be a zero-sum game. That is, it may be impossible to improve one person's welfare without reducing the welfare of someone else.[1] In other commonly occurring cases, a decision that may improve your welfare in the long run (balanced budgets, for example) may worsen it in the short run (higher taxes).

In these and other social relationships that arise out of economic interactions, conflicts over "who gets what" often result. Whenever conflict occurs over economic issues and the state is expected to deal with them, economics is joined with politics. Every economic system, moreover, is "political" in the sense that it is embedded in laws and procedures that are sanctioned by the state. Whether it is a private-enterprise system, socialism, or some other mode of economic organization, the state invariably makes laws that determine how the economy works in practice. Economics is inseparable from politics.

> **Political economy** ***is the study of how people pursue collective economic goals and deal with conflicts over resources and other economic factors in an authoritative way by means of government.***

In other words, *political economy is about the relationship between the economy and the state and about the various ways people try to use the state to improve their economic welfare.*

Viewed in the most general terms, political economy is interested in two broad sets of questions: (1) *How does economics affect politics?* and (2) *How does politics affect economics?* In question 1, economics is the *independent variable* (the cause or influencing factor) and politics is the *dependent variable* (the effect).

1. *Economics affects politics.* It frequently happens in democracies that many voters, sometimes a majority, "vote their pocketbooks": they vote for candidates who appear most likely to improve their economic well-being. Empirical evidence in the United States shows that, since World War II, incumbent presidents usually win reelection if the economy grows by about 4 percent or more in the four quarters preceding the election.[2] Another example is the tendency for growth in the U.S. economy to stimulate progressive political developments such as the expansion of civil rights, racial tolerance, immigration, and educational opportunities. By contrast, economic downturns have tended to produce cutbacks in social spending and immigration along with outbursts of racism.[3]

In question 2 the variables are reversed: politics is the independent variable and economics is the dependent variable.

2. *Politics affects economics.* In 1996 and 1997, President Bill Clinton signed bills passed by the Republican-dominated majority in Congress designed to balance the annual federal government budget by 2002. This legislation, hammered out in long negotiations that required the Democrats and Republicans to compromise their differences, is credited with promoting one of the longest periods of sustained economic growth and high employment in decades. Other examples of this connection focus on how government institutions like central banks can affect the inflation rate or stock markets, or how the partisan composition of the government can affect the ways the state spends its money and thereby influences the economy. Some comparative studies show, for example, that left-wing governments tend to spend slightly more than right-wing governments.

Because economic transactions and political activity go on all the time, *the relationship between politics and economics is frequently interactive.* That is, economic variables affect political variables, which in turn affect economic variables, which then affect political variables, and so on. A central purpose of political economy is to clarify these interacting relationships.

One of the most important of these relationships is the relationship between *states* and *markets*. Such terms as "markets," "the market economy," and "market forces" refer mainly to the private sector. They apply broadly to the production, buying, and selling of goods and services by private companies and individuals, with prices and salaries determined largely by the forces of supply and demand rather than by government fiat. Political economy examines such questions as, How do government policies affect market forces, and vice versa? Should governments control or regulate the economy, or should markets have fairly free rein? Can there be an acceptable balance between states and markets? The answers to these questions, whether of an empirical or prescriptive nature, will vary from country to country and are often grist for the mill of lively debate within individual countries.[4]

Because political economy encompasses a wide range of specific issues, we'll spread out our conceptual treatment of this topic over two chapters. This chapter looks first at some basic terminology in economics. It then examines three systems of political economy: *laissez-faire capitalism, central planning,* and *mixed economies.* Each one entails a different theory of the relationship between the state and the economy. A prime example of a mixed economy is the modern *welfare state,* which is discussed in the last section of this chapter. The next chapter focuses on countries engaged in early stages of economic development.

## BASIC ECONOMIC CONCEPTS

Grasping the main issues of political economy requires an understanding of a few central concepts in economics. The following definitions are by no means intended as a substitute for a course in economics. Our aim here is simply to provide some rudimentary information about basic economic phenomena and analytical terminology with a view to enhancing your understanding of politics.

The **Gross Domestic Product (GDP)** ***represents the market value of all goods and services produced by a country's economy in a specified period of time.*** It includes the consumption and investment of individuals and private companies as well as government expenditures. It also includes the value of goods and services produced within the country for export abroad, minus the value of imports from abroad. The GDP does not include the income that the country's citizens earn abroad, nor does it take into account the income foreigners earn from investments within the country's borders. Because the GDP excludes the latter two figures, it measures what a country is actually producing *at home.* **Per capita GDP** is the country's GDP divided by its population. Whereas GDP refers to gross production, per capita GDP provides an *average* of the country's domestic product per person. Of course, some individuals and companies produce more than others.

The **Gross National Income (GNI)** equals the total market value of goods and services a country produces at home (the GDP), plus the *net* income received from foreign countries. Net income from foreign countries includes interest payments and dividends paid by other countries, plus the profits earned by the home country's citizens and companies abroad that are sent back (repatriated) to their home country. Similar payments made to other countries are subtracted from these sums. Thus, if the domestic economy of country X generated $10 trillion worth of income at home last year, and residents of X earned $2 trillion abroad and sent it back home, while foreigners earned $1 from their investments in X and repatriated it back to their home countries, then X's GNI last year was $11 trillion. The GNI is essentially the same as the *Gross National Product (GNP),* a term that is now rarely used. **Per capita GNI** is a country's Gross National Income divided by its population. It provides a picture of how much income the country's individuals earn *on average*—but it does not take account of the distribution of national income among the very rich, the very poor, and all those in between.

*Economic growth* refers to *increases in a country's GNI or GDP over a specified period of time.* If a country's national or domestic income falls below the previous period's figure, it experiences negative growth.

**Inflation** means steadily rising prices. The *inflation rate* measures the extent to which the average price for goods in one time period exceeds average prices in some previous period. If the average price for a typical "market basket" of a society's goods and services in 2006 was 10 percent higher than the average price for those same goods in 2005, then the annual inflation rate for 2006 was 10 percent.

Inflation has several different causes. One is an excess in a country's supply of money in circulation. As a result, the money's value declines (or *depreciates*): a single dollar buys less and less. The expression, "Too many dollars chasing too few goods," captures this problem. To remedy it, the government must stop printing more money or significantly reduce the amount it is printing. Governmental decisions affecting the money supply are the main concern of *monetary policy. Monetarism* is an economic theory that emphasizes the links between a country's money supply and such phenomena as inflation and economic growth. One of its most influential exponents was *Milton Friedman* (1912–2006), a Nobel Prize winner.

Prolonged inflation can be ruinous. When the inflation rate tops 10 to 15 percent per year, governments are usually expected to step in and solve the problem. Their efforts are not always successful. Between 1987 and 1991, the annual inflation rate averaged more than 1,000 percent in Argentina and Brazil and more than 2,000 percent in Peru. In 1993 Ukraine had an inflation rate of 8,000 percent. In 1923, Germany's inflation rate topped 1 billion percent! Inflation of this magnitude is called *hyperinflation,* which is usually defined as an inflation rate that exceeds 50 percent per month. Failure to reduce runaway inflation can jeopardize a government's ability to stay in power. Inflation can therefore be just as much a political problem as an economic one.

The *central bank* is the national government's official bank. In the United States it is the Federal Reserve System. In most countries the central bank's main tasks are to determine how much money to print and to provide loans to private (commercial) banks. Central banks may also engage in open market transactions such as buying and selling government bonds. These various actions often have the effect of raising or lowering the nation's inflation rate.

For instance, when private banks borrow cash from the **central bank** for their own lending and investment operations, the central bank charges them interest. If inflation is undesirably high, the central bank may raise the interest rate it charges to commercial banks. The central bank's interest rate is called the *discount rate* or the *bank rate.* Through this action the central bank can indirectly raise commercial interest rates throughout the economy. If the commercial banks must pay higher interest to the central bank, they cover this added expense by charging their own customers higher interest rates for personal or business loans. Higher commercial interest rates discourage prospective borrowers. As interest rates go up, fewer people are willing to take out personal loans for college tuition, auto purchases, home mortgages, or other big expenditures, and fewer businesses are willing to borrow heavily to expand their operations. Less money gets circulated in the economy, the demand for goods declines, and inflation falls. But as a result of this "tight money" policy, business in general may also fall off and unemployment may rise.

Conversely, the economy could be in a recession or a depression. The difference is mainly a matter of degree. A **recession** is a period of low growth, zero growth, or negative growth, resulting in declining business activity, rising unemployment, and perhaps some bankruptcies. A **depression** is much more severe, with prolonged negative growth, massive unemployment, and widespread bankruptcies. In these situations inflation is typically low or nonexistent; prices tend to fall. To stimulate the economy, the central bank may reduce the discount rate or take other action to make money more available to businesses and consumers. If successful, this "easy money" policy revives business activity and reduces unemployment, though prices may rise in the process.

A trade-off exists between inflation and employment: governmental policies aimed at keeping inflation low may at times increase unemployment, while policies aimed at stimulating business and increasing employment opportunities may sometimes increase the inflation rate. The aim of most governments is to sustain both high employment and low inflation simultaneously, but this dual objective is sometimes hard to achieve. Governments therefore frequently have to make difficult policy choices that may adversely affect certain segments of the population for at least the short term, if not longer. Because central banks can have such a powerful influence on the economy, their policies often trigger political conflict.

The question of who controls the central bank is therefore crucial and profoundly political. Some central banks are fairly independent of the executive and legislative branches of government and enjoy ample latitude to make tough decisions that may be good for the economy but unpopular, such as raising interest rates. (The U.S. Federal Reserve bank is an example.) Other central banks are less independent of political decision makers and may have less freedom to make politically unpopular decisions.

A **budget deficit** ***occurs when a government spends more than it takes in.*** When expenditures equal revenues, the government has a *balanced budget.* The U.S. government ran consecutive annual budget deficits from 1969 through 1998. Thanks to a booming economy, the United States finally realized a budget surplus in 1999. But a declining economy and a tax cut sent the deficit soaring above $100 billion in 2002. The costs incurred in bolstering homeland security after September 11, and the money spent on military and reconstruction operations in Afghanistan and Iraq, drove up deficits still higher: the deficit surpassed $426 billion in 2005. Some economists maintain that no government should allow its annual deficit to exceed a certain limit. For advanced economies like the United States and the European Union countries, the recommended limit is usually 3 percent of GDP. In recent years the U.S. figure has been around 3.8 percent of GDP.

The public **national debt** ***is the amount of money the national government owes its creditors at home and abroad.*** When governments do not earn enough revenue from taxes, import duties, or other typical sources, and thereby run up budget deficits, they may have to borrow money from private banks, foreign governments, international lending agencies, or other sources of funds in order to pay their bills. As budget deficits mount from year to year, the amount of money the government must borrow rises accordingly. One way governments borrow money is by issuing bonds (like U.S. savings bonds) or Treasury bills ("T-bills"). The government pledges to reimburse the purchasers of these securities, with interest, after a specified period of time ranging from thirty days to thirty years or more. The accumulated principal and interest owed to the holders of these "debt instruments" are part of the public national debt, along with any other money the government owes to lenders such as the International Monetary Fund or the World Bank.

The U.S. public national debt reached $8.5 trillion in 2006. The U.S. government owes an increasing share of this money to the central banks of foreign governments and to foreign commercial banks. By mid-2006 the U.S. government owed more than $2 trillion to creditors holding government-issued securities like bonds and T-bills. Foreigners held 47 percent of these securities. (In 2000, foreigners held 34 percent of U.S. public debt securities, and in 1995 the figure was 25 percent.) About two-thirds of these foreign holders of U.S. securities were governments. In other words, foreigners—especially foreign governments—have been playing a growing role in financing U.S. government expenditures. Japan currently has the largest amount of U.S. public securities held by one country: in 2006 it held more than $640 billion in U.S. government issues (30 percent of the $2 trillion total). China was next, holding $340 billion in U.S. government securities (about 16 percent of the total). Britain and other EU countries together held the highest share of U.S. public securities.

Is reliance on foreign creditors dangerous? On the positive side, foreign governments, banks, and other investors buy U.S. Treasury securities because they have confidence in the U.S. economy: they can be quite sure that the U.S. government will repay them, with interest, by the promised date. The American economy is so big and its political institutions so stable that there is little likelihood the U.S. government will default on its loans or go bankrupt like individuals or private companies that get over their heads in debt. For the U.S. government, selling bonds and Treasury bills is a quick way to get cash to meet budgetary obligations. For the rest of the world, purchasing U.S. government securities is a safe investment. On the negative side, the U.S. government runs the risk that foreign governments and banks will suddenly stop or reduce their purchases of U.S. securities. Alternatively, they might sell their U.S. holdings in order to buy securities offered by other governments in hopes of reaping a higher return on their investment than the United States might be offering. Such decisions would deprive the U.S. government of vast amounts of money. Japan, China, Italy, and other governments have cut back their purchases of U.S. securities, or sold them, in recent years. In stark contrast to the prodigious U.S. economy, middle-income and poor countries that cannot repay the money they have borrowed abroad may have to be rescued by international agencies like the IMF. In these circumstances they may be compelled to make difficult economic adjustments, such as drastically slashing government spending, as a condition of receiving international assistance.

Another negative consequence of the national debt is that it requires indebted governments to pay interest to their creditors. These interest payments are supposed to be made on time to all creditors, whether domestic or foreign, private or governmental. Paying interest in periodic installments is called *debt servicing.* In 2005 the U.S. government paid out $180 billion in interest, about 7.2 percent of total federal government expenditures for that year. In addition, by borrowing huge amounts of cash from bond purchasers, the government is soaking up money that would otherwise remain in people's hands, to be spent by consumers or invested by businesspeople. Persistent government borrowing, in other words, deprives the national economy of funds that could be more productively utilized, through consumer spending and business investment, to boost economic growth.

Ultimately, there are only two ways to reduce budget deficits and the national debt: slash government spending or raise revenue such as taxes. For especially large debts, both may have to be done simultaneously. Obviously, these choices can be quite painful for large segments of the population.

**Fiscal policy** ***refers to government revenue and expenditure policy.*** The term derives from the old term "the fisc" for the state treasury. Taxation is the most widely used form of raising revenue. One of the most common political controversies surrounding tax questions centers on the fairness of the tax burden. *Progressive income taxes* are generally considered to be fair because they take a rising proportion of income as income rises. The rich must pay at higher rates than lower-income households pay. Critics of this system charge, however, that a "soak the rich" tax policy hinders overall economic growth and employment opportunities because it deprives the most well-endowed consumers and investors in the economy of money they could use to buy goods and services or invest in productive businesses.

*Regressive taxes* take a decreasing percentage of income as income rises. There are several types. Sales taxes, for example, are generally regressive in nature. If everyone in a certain jurisdiction (such as Maryland or France) is subject to the same sales tax rate (say, 10 percent) for certain categories of goods, lower-income people will pay out a higher portion of their income for these taxes than will wealthier people, especially if such necessities as food and clothing are taxed. Low-income people have to spend most of their earnings, whereas the rich can afford to save or invest a portion of their income, and what they do not spend is not subject to sales taxes.

In the United States the federal government has at times imposed national sales taxes on such things as gasoline, alcoholic beverages, and cigarettes. In addition, the fifty states have the right to impose statewide sales taxes. Local communities in the United States, such as cities and counties, also have certain tax powers, as in the case of real estate taxes.

Many countries in Western Europe and elsewhere have a national **value added tax (VAT)** on certain types of goods and services. The VAT is a national sales tax imposed at every point in the production and marketing process of specified goods. Ultimately it is the final consumer who ends up paying the entire tax. By the mid 1990s the average VAT rate was about 20 percent in most countries belonging to the European Union, though the actual rate varied with the item.

Finally, a *flat tax* taxes everyone's income at the same rate (say, 20 percent), regardless of their wealth. In the United States, a national flat tax has been proposed in recent years by both liberal and conservative candidates for president, but never adopted.

The expenditure side of fiscal policy revolves largely around the budget. The process of putting the budget together is typically highly politicized, involving bargaining among multiple actors both inside and outside the state's institutions.

## LAISSEZ-FAIRE CAPITALISM

***The form of political economy with the least amount of governmental interference is known as <u>laissez-faire capitalism</u>.*** *Laissez-faire* (less-ay fair) means "let do" or "leave alone" in French. In effect, the state leaves private individuals alone in their economic activity and lets them do whatever they want. *Capitalism* means private ownership of businesses: in other words, *private enterprise.*

In a completely pure laissez-faire economy, private enterprise is really *free* enterprise: the government plays little or no role in restricting private economic activity. People are free to make as much money as they can by whatever means, subject perhaps to a few laws regulating contracts and penalizing criminal behavior. In such a system there are no taxes to be paid, no health or safety regulations to be concerned about, and no laws requiring employers to pay their employees minimum wages, limit their working hours, or provide them with paid vacations. There are no laws regulating child or female labor. In its most extreme variant, laissez-faire capitalism can be quite beneficial to entrepreneurs, allowing them to concentrate on the rigors of economic competition and the laws of the marketplace. But it can be extremely detrimental to workers and other employees, leaving them unprotected against the demands of their employers. Laissez-faire capitalism prevailed in the United States, Britain, and a few other countries during Karl Marx's lifetime.

Laissez-faire capitalism in its purest form is the most unregulated variant of a market economy. ***A <u>market economy</u> is an economic system in which prices are determined mainly by supply and demand.*** The government, in other words, does not control the price system. The prices of goods and services are established by "what the market will bear": by the independent decisions of sellers and buyers, each seeking to get the most for their money in a market characterized by open competition between businesses. One of the first exponents of this type of economic system was Scottish economist *Adam Smith,* the first major theoretician of laissez-faire capitalism.

### ADAM SMITH (1723–1790)

Smith's groundbreaking work, *An Inquiry into the Nature and Causes of The Wealth of Nations* (or *The Wealth of Nations,* for short), was a passionate plea for the removal of virtually all governmental restrictions on private enterprise.

The idea for which Smith is perhaps most renowned is that the pursuit of every individual's economic self-interest ultimately increases the wealth of society as a whole. Personal gain enhances the common good. Smith believed that individuals are motivated basically by the quest for social status and material wealth in their economic undertakings. Without intentionally striving to do so, however, acquisitive private entrepreneurs end up promoting the general welfare. "It is not from the benevolence of the butcher, the brewer, or the baker that we expect our dinner," he wrote, "but from their regard to their own interest." In a famous image, Smith said that the self-interested economic decisions of individuals would lead to the enlargement of society's welfare as if guided to that end by an "invisible hand." The enterprising individual, he wrote,

> neither intends to promote the public interest, nor knows how much he is promoting it. (He) intends only his own gain; and he is in this, as in many other cases, led by an invisible hand to promote an end which was no part of his intention. . . . By pursuing his interest, he frequently promotes that of the society more effectually than when he really intends to promote it.

Smith therefore recommended that private self-interest be given free rein and that all governmental impediments to "perfect liberty" in economic life be removed.

The freely operating market economy, in Smith's view, would not lead to chaos. On the contrary, it would be a self-sustaining mechanism that would regulate production, prices, wages, and even population through a spontaneous combination of incentives and restraints. While he was too much of a realist to expect an earthly paradise, Smith believed that the market economy, if left unhindered, would function with clockwork regularity to maximize the welfare of all.

At the time Smith was writing, Britain's economy was a complicated mixture of private enterprise and government regulations and monopolies, many of them in place since medieval times. Like other European monarchies of the period, Britain was heavily influenced by the century-old doctrine of mercantilism. *Mercantilism* was the notion that the *state* should expand its direct role in the economy and control foreign trade for the purpose of maximizing national wealth and power. Smith rejected mercantilism. In his view, the government's involvement in the economy had only retarded England's economic growth. Smith denounced royal authorities as "the greatest spendthrifts" in society and praised the hard work and frugality of private individuals for having "maintained the progress of England toward opulence and improvement."

The *Wealth of Nations* still stands as the veritable bible of *classical economic liberalism.* Nevertheless, Smith has often been misinterpreted as a proponent of unrestrained personal greed and a kind of free-market anarchy, devoid of any governmental role at all. In fact Smith strongly maintained that the market economy presupposed a moral order characterized by human benevolence and self-restraint and by a legal system that would effectively punish wrongdoing. In an earlier work, *The Theory of Moral Sentiments* (1759), Smith said that the state must rigidly enforce a strong code of justice. He also stated that the "invisible hand" would eventually produce economic equality. In Smith's view, the main beneficiaries of laissez-faire capitalism ultimately would not be a small entrepreneurial elite but the population as a whole.

Moreover, Smith argued in *The Wealth of Nations* that the state should provide public works that were too unprofitable for private capitalists to undertake (such as roads, bridges, and canals) as well as public education. Smith also expected the state to provide cultural activities to prevent the masses from being spiritually and intellectually "deformed."

Adam Smith was the prophet of modern capitalism.[5] Were his theories valid?

## HYPOTHESIS-TESTING EXERCISE: Was Adam Smith Right?

### Hypothesis and Variables

In Smith's hypothesis that laissez-faire capitalism promotes the wealth of society and economic equality more effectively than state-dominated economies, the *dependent variables* are *national wealth* and *economic equality;* the *independent variables* are *laissez-faire capitalism* and *state-dominated economies.*

### Expectations

Accordingly, we would expect laissez-faire economies to produce higher levels of national wealth and equality than state-centered economies do.

### Evidence

Over the course of the two centuries following Smith's *Wealth of Nations,* capitalism and the market economy became the dominant economic system in much of Western Europe and in the United States. In keeping with Smith's predictions, the wealth of the predominantly capitalist nations expanded significantly. The United States, Britain, France, and other laissez-faire economies generally outperformed economies with higher levels of government intervention. However, Smith's faith in the laissez-faire market system reflected excessive optimism about its ability to provide an equal, or even fair, distribution of goods and services. As the nineteenth century progressed and the industrial revolution advanced in the most dynamic economies, national wealth increased but large segments of the population, in some cases the majority, were mired in poverty. Especially in Europe, which lacked the wide open spaces and other opportunities available to citizens of the United States for upward socioeconomic mobility, the divisions between rich and poor deepened. The ranks of the middle classes increased, but many of these people—shopkeepers, artisans, small farmers, and the like—clung to a precarious existence that alternated between prosperity and bankruptcy.

Smith also failed to foresee with sufficient clarity the extraordinary fluctuations between periods of growth and periods of decline that market economies exhibited. Instead of working with clocklike regularity, free-market capitalism tended to oscillate between spectacular expansions and severe depressions, the latter often triggered by financial panics or stock market crashes. These "boom and bust" tendencies became known as the *business cycle* and soon came to be regarded as a normal fact of economic life. Moreover, Smith's assumption that a widely shared code of ethics, backed by the law, would guarantee that no one would be personally or materially harmed by the free-market economy turned out to be naively idealistic. In fact, the development of capitalism in nineteenth-century Europe was brutal in its impact on the masses, who were left largely unprotected by the state.

In the twentieth century, the Great Depression tolled the death knell of laissez-faire in most countries where it reigned supreme. The result in most economically advanced democracies was the *mixed economy* and the modern *welfare state*. In today's world there are no countries with a purely laissez-faire economy; to varying degrees, governments are involved in all contemporary economic systems.

**Conclusions**

The evidence is therefore quite *mixed.* Although it is largely consistent with Smith's general prediction that laissez-faire economies would generate national wealth more successfully than state-dominated economies, it is quite inconsistent with Smith's assumption that laissez-faire would eliminate poverty and, over time, produce relative equality.

---

Within decades of Smith's dreamy vision of the wealth of nations, a new generation of British economists described the free-market economy in considerably harsher terms. *David Ricardo* (1772–1823) argued that private entrepreneurs had little choice but to squeeze their workers to produce everything they possibly could at the lowest possible wages. In no other way, he maintained, could productive capitalists amass the funds they needed for further investment and business expansion. Ricardo's *iron law of wages* stipulated that the development of the economy, and hence the creation of future employment opportunities, required this pitiless "capital accumulation" process at the expense of the impoverished labor force.[6]

*Thomas Malthus* (1766–1834) maintained that, whereas population grew in a geometric progression (2, 4, 6, 8, . . .), food supplies grew in an arithmetic progression (1, 2, 3, 4, . . .). Consequently, prudence dictated that the masses should not be encouraged by high wages to have lots of children. Excessive overpopulation, according to his calculations, would ultimately outstrip food supplies and provoke mass starvation. It was therefore better to keep working-class wages relatively low. Malthus's calculations turned out to be overly pessimistic, but his dire predictions prompted one observer to label economics "the dismal science."[7]

*Social Darwinism* represented another school of thought that drew stark conclusions from the social divisions created by the progress of capitalist economics. Stimulated by British social thinker *Herbert Spencer* (1820–1903) and American economist *William Graham Sumner* (1840–1910), the social Darwinists argued that, just as animal species had evolved by a process of natural selection, humanity also develops in accordance with the grim law of the "survival of the fittest." (It was Spencer, not Charles Darwin, who coined this term.) Society as a whole would advance only if it encouraged and rewarded individual economic achievement. Spencer firmly opposed all attempts by the state to assist the poor or even educate them. "The whole effort of nature," he wrote, "is to get rid of such [people], to clear the world of them, and make room for better."[8]

Social Darwinist logic made great strides not only among Britain's entrepreneurial elites but in the United States as well. The American economy reflected the principles of laissez-faire capitalism right from its origins. By the late nineteenth century, vast fortunes were accumulated as railroad magnates, steel and oil tycoons, and other infamous "robber barons" plied their trade without the burdens of labor laws or meddlesome governmental regulations. Federal income taxes barely existed until the Sixteenth Amendment to the Constitution was ratified in 1913. Only with Franklin D. Roosevelt's New Deal did laissez-faire economic theory, which had failed to halt the Great Depression, lose its grip on economists and policy makers in the United States. In Europe, meanwhile, the most vocal opponents of laissez-faire economics were socialists who favored abolishing capitalism entirely. In Western Europe, the socialist movement became more moderate over time, as social democratic parties came around to favoring the mixed-economy welfare state. In Russia, however, socialism took on the far more radical form of the centrally planned economy.

## CENTRALLY PLANNED ECONOMIES

The Russian communists seized control of the central government in the autumn of 1917. Over the next several years they consolidated their rule in a bloody civil war against their main opponents. After a brief period in which private enterprise was permitted, the Soviet government under Joseph Stalin began taking charge of the economy in the late 1920s. With rare exceptions (such as tiny family-owned plots of land), all factories, farms, stores, and services came under the all-encompassing control of government agencies. A mammoth planning bureaucracy was erected to organize the production of all manufactured goods. Agriculture was "collectivized" and subjected to bureaucratic supervision. The prices of all products and services were dictated by the planning authorities, whose decrees completely supplanted the market economy's laws of supply and demand. Legally binding plans were issued by the government every year requiring factories and farms to meet official production quotas, usually specified in terms of quantities of goods (pairs of shoes, tons of hay, etc.). A five-year plan set production targets over a longer term.

Beginning with Stalin and continuing under his successors right up to Mikhail Gorbachev in the second half of the 1980s, the Soviet Union had a **centrally planned economy (CPE).** The distinguishing feature of this type of system is ***the fusion of the state and the economy.*** The state and the economy are merged into an integrated whole. In effect, the state "owns" the economy. It is government, not private individuals or companies, that determines what should be produced and in what quantities, how these goods should be distributed, and at what price. Because the state, in effect, commands the entire economic process, the CPE is also called a **command economy.**

In Soviet theory, a fully planned economy was expected to be far more rational in the production and allocation of goods than was a capitalist economy. The market, according to the communists, was chaotic, with countless private individuals and firms making countless decisions in their own personal interest. It wasted resources on unnecessary production and led to inflation, unemployment, inequality, bankruptcies, and depressions. A planned economy, they felt, would avoid these pitfalls. In their view, growth would be higher and faster than under capitalism, and distribution would be fairer.

A planned economy would also facilitate the political elite's control over the population. One of the essential purposes of the state planning system was to stamp out all opportunities for individuals and groups to be independent of Communist Party rule. The extinction of economic freedom was deliberately intended to reinforce the extinction of political freedom.

Industrial production in the Soviet Union grew dramatically in the 1930s under the new planning system, elevating the Soviet Union from a backward agricultural country to an industrial giant in less than a decade. Agricultural production suffered, however, as the collectivization process, in which landholders were forced to hand over their fields, crops, and farm animals to the state, created havoc in the countryside. Additional setbacks occurred during World War II, as the German invasion in 1941 and three years of continuous fighting resulted in the destruction of seventeen hundred Soviet cities and towns and the devastation of the agricultural economy.

The Soviet economy gradually revived after the war, prompting communist officials in the early 1960s to make ambitious claims about overtaking the U.S. economy in the next ten years.[9] Far from accomplishing that grandiose goal, the Soviet economy fell increasingly behind its mixed-economy competitors. Upon assuming the leadership of the Communist Party of the Soviet Union in 1985, Mikhail Gorbachev denounced his predecessors' years in power as an "era of stagnation." Between 1978 and 1985 the Soviet economy had experienced zero growth. As the United States, Japan, and Western Europe charted new directions in high-technology development, the cumbersome Soviet central planning bureaucracy proved no match for the rapid production techniques of private companies competing in global markets. Over the next several years, Gorbachev tried to come up with a new formula for rescuing the central planning system, including the adoption of a modicum of private enterprise, but he never succeeded in devising a more effective economic mechanism. In late 1991, Gorbachev gave up power and the Soviet Union itself ceased to exist. Starting in January 1992, Russia—now an independent country—began moving toward a mixed economy with the introduction of substantial private enterprise and market mechanisms for determining prices. Though the state continues to play a major role in the Russian economy, the centrally planned economy is a thing of the past.

Similar developments have taken place in Central and Eastern Europe since the collapse of communist rule and the installation of democracy. Most of these countries have been quite creative in developing various combinations of public and private economic activity.[10]

For its part, China began dismantling its central planning system long before Russia or

East-Central Europe. The Chinese Communist Party leadership itself inaugurated privatization measures and market reforms starting in the late 1970s. Over the course of the following decade, most of China's industrial enterprises and farms came into private hands. Oddly enough, these massive economic transformations took place in spite of the fact that the communists retained their grip on power, harshly repressing all demands for democracy.

One hypothesis that stands out as particularly relevant in these circumstances states that the process of economic privatization promotes democratization. Our main expectation is that a private enterprise economy creates social groups (such as businesspeople and an upwardly mobile work force) who wish to preserve and expand their freedom in the marketplace by keeping government intervention limited and by making sure that they have a say, through the electoral process and other democratic procedures, in the decisions governments make. Thus if the economic liberalization process succeeds, democracy will succeed in Russia and East-Central Europe, and it may even successfully challenge communist rule in China.

A contrary thesis suggests that the privatization process in formerly communist countries and China ultimately undermines support for democracy. If the economic transformations now under way produce unacceptable levels of inflation, unemployment, inequality, or corruption, large segments of the population and political elites may turn against economic change and, simultaneously, against political change as well. Some may long nostalgically for the "good old days" under central planning when, despite that system's disadvantages, life was more stable and predictable and prices for most basic goods, when available, were cheaper. Driven to despair by economic adversity, many people may demand a strong authoritarian government to impose order on a society they perceive as careening into chaos.

In between these extreme scenarios of triumphant success and catastrophic failure lies a third hypothetical alternative: the dual processes of marketization and democratization may inch along at a rocky pace, with alternating successes and failures, advances and retreats. Though the economic and political transformation processes present great difficulties, the populations and political elites of these countries in this scenario together manage to muddle through, achieving at least some degree of both market economics and democracy.

Whatever happens, it can be confidently anticipated that the development of stable market economic mechanisms and democratic institutions and practices will be a long process, requiring perhaps decades of concerted social and political action. The hypotheses just presented, as well as other ones applicable to these developments, will have to be continually put to the test as time goes on.

## MIXED ECONOMIES

The most widely adopted economic system in the world today is neither laissez-faire capitalism nor full-scale socialism but something in between: the *mixed economy.*

***A mixed economy combines both private enterprise and state involvement in the country's economic affairs.***

There is considerable variety in the forms a mixed economy can take. No single model is faithfully copied by all mixed-economy countries.

For one thing, countries may differ in the relative *degree* of capitalism and state intervention they have. Some grant wider latitude than others to the private sector while holding governmental intervention within bounds (or at least trying to do so). Such factors as the percentage of GDP taken up by central government expenditures and by revenues illustrate the point (see table 14.2).

Mixed economies may also differ in the *forms* of state intervention that they employ. In some cases the government's economic involvement is largely indirect. That is, the state allows private enterprise and market mechanisms to play the main role in the national economy but seeks to influence or adjust private behavior so as to advance certain national economic goals. The central bank, for example, may influence commercial bank interest rates in order to rein in inflation or stimulate growth, or the government may raise or lower taxes in order to advance political or economic goals. In these and other instances of indirect intervention, the state does not directly own enterprises outright but confines its role to influencing or regulating the private sector.

TABLE 14.2

**Central Government Expenditures and Revenues as Percentage of GDP in Selected Economically Advanced Democracies, 2004**

| Country | Central Government Expenditures as % of GDP | Central Government Revenues as % of GDP |
|---|---|---|
| Canada | 18.3 | 19.9 |
| Denmark | 36.5 | 35.2 |
| France | 39.1 | 36.9 |
| Germany | 28.6 | 31.3 |
| Italy | 37.7 | 40.0 |
| Sweden | 38.0 | 37.5 |
| United Kingdom | 36.6 | 39.9 |
| United States | 17.2 | 20.9 |

*Source:* World Bank, *World Development Indicators 2006.*

One of the most widely utilized forms of indirect state intervention in the economy consists of a set of policy mechanisms known collectively as *Keynesianism.* **Keynesianism** ***refers to the state's use of fiscal and monetary measures and public spending to promote growth in an economy dominated by private enterprise.*** Its main architect was perhaps the most influential economist of the twentieth century, *John Maynard Keynes.*

## JOHN MAYNARD KEYNES (1883–1946)

Keynes (canes) was born in Britain the year Karl Marx died. He studied economics at Cambridge University at a time when the teaching of economic theory there had not advanced very far beyond the doctrines of Adam Smith and David Ricardo. The chief stimulus to Keynes's revision of classical economic theory was the Great Depression. The Wall Street stock market crash of October 1929 shattered the foundations of the U.S. economy and exacerbated the problems of other capitalist economies, resulting in bankruptcies, plummeting economic growth, and skyrocketing unemployment around the world. As the years ground on with little improvement, governments as well as the private sector appeared to be at a loss as to how to resolve the crisis. The conventional wisdom of laissez-faire confidently predicted that market forces would generate a recovery in the long run. As Keynes drily observed, however, "In the long run we're all dead."

He argued that the best way to stimulate economic growth during a depression was to increase total spending—that is, *aggregate demand* for goods and services—throughout the economy. As soon as more money was spent for these things, businesspeople would amass enough profits to expand their operations and hire new workers. Unfortunately, Keynes observed, individual consumers do not have much money to spend in a depression. With millions unemployed, much of the population is more likely to be reduced to penury. Starved for customers, businesses stagnate or go bankrupt. Keynes thus reached a startling conclusion: *a free-market economy does not possess the mechanisms needed to recover from a depression on its own.*

If consumers, banks, and businesses do not have sufficient money to spend in the economy so as to spark a recovery, who does? Governments, Keynes replied. By spending additional funds from the national budget, over and above the amounts already being spent, governments can inject spendable money into the economy and thereby "prime the pump" of the private sector. The state can take this action by directly purchasing goods and services from private businesses (such as highway construction equipment or weaponry) or by hiring people for military service or public works projects. By putting cash in the hands of consumers and businesses, Keynes argued, governments would enable individuals to buy more things, thereby increasing the demand for goods, and enable businesses to increase production and hire more employees. Economic recovery would then be under way.

Keynes laid out these ideas in *The General Theory of Employment, Interest, and Money,* published in 1936. By that time, Franklin D. Roosevelt's New Deal had already begun implementing some of them, such as the mass hiring of unemployed workers through the Public Works Administration and the Civilian

Conservation Corps. But in Keynes's opinion, the Roosevelt administration was not spending enough to pump the country out of the depression. Only when the U.S. government engaged in much more massive public spending during World War II did the depression in the United States come to an end.

One problem that disturbed some economists and government officials was that, during the depression, the United States and other governments were already running budget deficits. Keynes's call for even more budgetary expenditures in spite of the deficits was viewed as heresy by classical theorists, who faithfully adhered to the maxim that sound economic policy required balanced budgets. Once again Keynes challenged the accepted wisdom. He asserted that in certain compelling circumstances such as a depression, governments may have to engage in deficit spending in order to improve the overall economy.

> *Deficit spending* is spending by governments even though there is a budgetary deficit that cannot be balanced through ordinary revenue sources (such as taxes). To finance this excess spending, governments must borrow money from individuals or other lenders and pay them interest, thus building up the national debt.

Keynes believed that the money governments spent over budget would eventually come back to the national treasury in the form of enhanced tax revenue, collected from increasingly profitable businesses and a rising number of well-paid employees as the recovery widens and the economy grows.

Though some of his early critics accused Keynes of being a socialist, in fact he always looked upon the private sector as the main source of economic growth and employment. In his view the state's proper role was to stimulate private enterprise, not replace it. He regarded Marxism as "scientifically erroneous."

After World War II, Keynes's principles of government intervention won growing acceptance. By the 1960s the United States, Western Europe, and other countries were routinely using Keynesian mechanisms to "fine-tune" their economies and regulate the business cycle. In more recent decades, however, the economic experiences of many advanced capitalist economies have prompted considerable debate about the pertinence of Keynes's theories. Many contemporary economists argue that national debts have reached such astronomical heights in some countries that additional deficit spending may only hamper future economic growth. A number of economists and public officials also believe that capitalist economies are generally better off with less government intervention rather than more. A number of them cite the warnings of another major theorist, *Friedrich von Hayek* (1899–1992), that excessive government involvement in the economy is "the road to serfdom."[11] Most would agree that we now live in a "post-Keynesian" era in which many of the economic problems we face require solutions different from those Keynes proposed.

Whatever one thinks about Keynes's theories, one thing is certain: the central question today is not *whether* governments should intervene in the economy, but *how much*. By providing a feasible alternative to both laissez-faire capitalism and all-out socialism, Keynes and like-minded economists produced a revolution in economic thinking whose general tenets are widely accepted. Consequently, the so-called *neoliberals* of the contemporary world regard private enterprise and the market as the most effective forms of economic organization, but admit that governments have a major role to play in today's complex economies.[12]

---

In addition to employing indirect forms of economic intervention, governments may engage in more direct forms of activity in mixed economies. In some countries the state may directly own certain enterprises, whether as full owner or as a shareholder in partnership with other investors. These state-owned firms in mixed economies are usually called *public enterprises* or *para-statal enterprises*. Such internationally known firms as Air France and Rolls Royce have been owned by the state, along with giant companies in Italy, Spain, Sweden, Brazil, Mexico, and other countries.

The chief difference between public enterprises and private firms is that the managers and work force of public enterprises are employed directly by the state and the earnings of state-owned companies go into the national treasury. Such enterprises may also receive loans or other forms of financing directly from the state budget. Their proponents regard them as an effective way to combat unemployment and earn revenue for the national treasury so as to help finance general budgetary outlays. Opponents of public enterprises, by contrast, argue that state-owned companies might be less efficient and competitive than private firms. If they do not turn a profit, they may have to be bailed out with state subsidies, thereby draining the national treasury. In some cases, public enterprises may become nests of corruption.

These and other arguments against public enterprises have convinced many of their opponents to push for their privatization. **Privatization** ***means the transfer of state-owned enterprises to private ownership.*** (It is the opposite of **nationalization**, ***which is the transfer of privately owned firms to state ownership.***) The privatization issue has unleashed a storm of political controversy in Britain, France, Russia, Brazil, India, and other countries in recent years.[13]

Another variant of direct state intervention in mixed economies is *bureaucratic coordination* of the economy. In bureaucratically coordinated economies, the state plays a direct and constant role in coordinating the activities of private firms (and, perhaps, the labor market as well) for broad national purposes. There are several different variants of bureaucratic coordination in mixed economies, as the following examples illustrate:

- Contemporary Japan and South Korea have aggressively competitive private firms that cooperate closely with state agencies to promote exports. Such agencies as the Ministry of Finance and the Ministry of Economy, Trade and Industry wield very important bureaucratic power in the Japanese economy, as do their counterparts in South Korea.
- Germany, Austria, and other countries have corporatist systems that involve continuing discussions and coordination among business organizations, labor unions, and government.
- France has a system of "indicative planning" through which the state and private enterprises coordinate general guidelines and expectations of economic development.
- Various African countries have state-managed purchasing boards and other bureaucratic institutions that help coordinate agricultural development or other economic activities.

Today's mixed economies can be measured in a variety of ways. In addition to providing statistics on Gross Domestic Product, Gross National Income, and other widely used measures, economists have also devised methods for calculating the relative *competitiveness* of an economy (that is, its ability to function in the global economy), the degree of freedom that private enterprises have in individual countries, and other yardsticks.[14] In most instances, government policies and political processes play a critical role in affecting the economic bottom lines reflected in these statistics.

Whether guided by indirect or direct methods of state intervention, mixed economies cannot escape politics. This is especially the case nowadays because most countries are *welfare states.* Most welfare states today are mixed economies. While some are authoritarian regimes, the most highly developed ones are in the economically advanced democracies.

## WELFARE STATES

Broadly defined, ***the*** **welfare state** ***is a form of political economy in which the state assumes responsibility for the general welfare of its population,*** especially its most vulnerable elements, through spending on such items as education, housing, health care, pensions, unemployment compensation, food subsidies, family allowances, and other programs.

The term *welfare state* came into vogue in Britain in the 1930s and 1940s. Though it is largely a twentieth-century phenomenon, its roots reach into the previous century. As laissez-faire capitalism advanced and the working-class population expanded, a number of European political theorists and politicians began groping for ways to maintain robust economic growth while at the same time confronting the appalling poverty of the working class and the unemployed.

In Britain the path to the modern welfare state was long and circuitous. One of its early intellectual forebears was the philosopher *Jeremy Bentham* (1748–1832). Bentham is perhaps most famous for his statement that the principal aim of government should be to promote "the greatest happiness of the greatest number." To this end, Bentham maintained that the chief obligation of government was to provide certain services to the population, including basic physical security against crime and foreign enemies, economic subsistence, and the legal protection of property rights, personal reputation, and private contracts. Bentham strongly believed that democracy provided the most effective means for achieving these goals.[15]

Another progenitor of the welfare state was *John Stuart Mill* (1806–73). Mill's essays *On Liberty* (1859) and *Considerations on Representative Government* (1861) established his reputation as a democratic theorist of the first rank. His masterwork, *The Principles of Political Economy,* first appeared in 1848, the same year Marx and Engels published their communist *Manifesto.* Mill's work pointed in a fundamentally different direction from revolutionary socialism, however. Laissez-faire, he wrote, "should be the general practice: every departure from it, unless required by some great good, is a certain evil." He also regarded restrictions on economic competition, as advocated by socialists, as "evil."

But Mill was equally outspoken in his objections to a completely unrestrained free market. He advocated such things as state-funded education, public works, restrictions on child labor, and limited governmental assistance to those unable to work. He also supported the right of workers to organize trade unions and go on strike. To remedy the social inequalities produced by capitalism, Mill favored stiff inheritance taxes aimed at preventing the concentration of wealth in a handful of families. He also favored producers' cooperatives that would compete in the marketplace under the ownership and management of the workers themselves. These ideas flew directly in the face of the British elite's laissez-faire inclinations. Over time, however, Mill's ideas sensitized Britain to the possibility of finding a middle ground between the extremes of unregulated capitalism and revolutionary socialism.[16]

Ironically, it was the highly conservative ruling elite of nineteenth-century Germany that introduced some of Europe's first major social welfare programs. In the 1880s the kaiser's authoritarian government introduced the industrialized world's first government-financed health and accident insurance for workers and its first state-managed pension program. The kaiser and his ministers were no socialists. Their chief incentives for providing social welfare benefits to Germany's working masses were to stave off a potential socialist revolution and to reduce popular support for the Social Democrats.

### The Emergence of the Modern Welfare State: Germany, Sweden, and the United States

In a few countries the twentieth-century welfare state began taking shape in the decades between World War I and World War II. After the kaiser's departure following Germany's defeat in 1918, the German Weimar Republic (1919–33) took the unprecedented step of incorporating generous welfare benefits into the constitution as legally guaranteed social rights. But the entire Weimar system collapsed as the German economy was battered by astronomical inflation in the early 1920s and by a wave of bankruptcies and rising unemployment with the onset of the Great Depression in the early 1930s. Moreover, business, labor, and agricultural leaders were never able to agree on a mutually acceptable balance of economic policies. The failure of the Weimar Republic's political economy provided a perfect opportunity for the Nazi Party under Adolph Hitler to take advantage of widespread frustrations and thereby gain power. While establishing one of the most tyrannical dictatorships ever known, the Nazis also established their own version of the welfare state, one that placed the economy firmly in the hands of a brutal, war-driven elite.

A far more salutary development occurred in Sweden. As the Great Depression took a heavy toll on Sweden's export-oriented economy, leaders of parties and interest groups representing agriculture, labor, and big business made a concerted effort to iron out their conflicts in a grand "historic compromise." In the process, they saved Swedish democracy and established "a model for what all of Europe would do after 1945."[17] Today Sweden and other Scandinavian countries are "cradle-to-grave" social welfare systems, with the state providing a broad spectrum of benefits to workers, farmers, and the sizable middle class.

Across the ocean, Franklin D. Roosevelt's New Deal was forging a new model for the political economy of the United States, one whose basic parameters would also set a pattern for the postwar period. Prior to Roosevelt, the U.S. government had provided only minimal social welfare benefits, mainly to war veterans.[18] The prevailing laissez-faire orthodoxy dictated against governmental interference in the economy and especially against deficit spending. Roosevelt himself initially accepted this view, but later vowed to try anything that might work to bring the U.S. economy out of the depression. Guided by no preconceived blueprint, FDR and his "brain trust" launched a wide assortment of measures aimed at reducing unemployment and reinvigorating the economy. Public works programs, the Tennessee Valley Authority, the Social Security system, and the Wagner Act, which provided legal support for trade unions, were all products of New Deal interventionism. So, too, was the National Recovery Administration (NRA), a corporatist body intended to pull together representatives from business, labor, agriculture, and government in an effort to regulate wages, prices, and production.[19]

Although the NRA was declared unconstitutional by the Supreme Court, and although FDR's critics denounced the New Deal as "creeping socialism," quite a few of Roosevelt's programs remained in place long after the end of his administration. Most important, the New Deal established the legitimacy of significant governmental intervention in the U.S. economy.

## The Postwar Welfare State

The heyday of the welfare state in the economically advanced democracies occurred in the first three decades after World War II. In 1945, Britain's Labour Party won its first majority in the House of Commons. Under Prime Minister Clement Attlee, the Labour government enacted a series of major welfare measures and nationalized several private corporations. (The owners were compensated.) The centerpiece of Labour's legislation was the National Health Service, which guaranteed free medical and dental care to all British citizens while preserving private care for those willing to pay for it. Although the Conservative Party, which had traditionally campaigned against such measures, returned to power in 1951, it did not abolish the National Health Service, which remains a broadly popular institution to this day.

Most other industrially advanced countries also expanded their welfare programs after World War II. In most cases, the social and political underpinnings of the welfare state were the same. From its inception, the democratic welfare state has been based on compromises made by representatives of labor, agriculture, and the business sector as mediated and enforced by a democratically accountable state. The specific agreements reached in Western Europe soon after World War II are sometimes known as the *postwar settlements*.

Particularly rapid expansion of the welfare state took place between 1960 and 1975. This period witnessed fairly continuous economic growth in the advanced democracies. It was during these decades that the economies of the United States, Canada, Japan, and most of Western Europe completed their transformation from industrial economies to *postindustrial economies*, characterized by the fact that more than half the work force was now engaged in the service sector of the economy. As the economically advanced democracies blazed the trails of postindustrialism from the 1960s onward, their governments became increasingly committed to promoting not only education but a host of other programs designed to enhance the welfare of the population and the growth of the economy. Most of these governments utilized Keynesian tax and spending policies designed to keep growth rates climbing while maintaining high levels of employment. As national wealth grew, the amount of money available for social welfare programs rose apace. Government expenditures on an array of social programs in most of these countries rose from 10 to 20 percent of GNP in the 1950s to between one-fourth and one-third of GNP in the mid 1970s.[20] The so-called *Keynesian welfare state* became the dominant mode of political economy throughout the economically advanced world of democratic states.

Not only have government welfare programs assisted the poor and the working class, but they have also benefited the middle class and even the upper class. In various welfare states, people from all income levels have taken full advantage of expanding educational opportunities, health insurance, retirement pensions, and other state-sponsored programs. In countries such as the United States, special tax breaks, such as write-offs for interest paid on home mortgages or other loans, have constituted a form of social welfare benefit for middle- and upper-class property owners.

TABLE 14.3

**Public Social Spending as Percentage of GDP in Selected High-Income Democracies**

| Country | 1980 | 1990 | 1995 | 2003 |
|---|---|---|---|---|
| Belgium | 23.5 | 25.0 | 26.4 | 26.5 |
| Canada | 14.1 | 18.4 | 19.2 | 17.3 |
| Denmark | 25.2 | 25.5 | 28.9 | 27.6 |
| France | 20.8 | 25.3 | 28.3 | 28.7 |
| Germany | 23.0 | 22.5 | 26.6 | 27.6 |
| Italy | 18.0 | 19.9 | 19.8 | 24.2 |
| Japan | 10.3 | 11.2 | 13.9 | 17.7 |
| Netherlands | 24.1 | 24.4 | 22.8 | 20.7 |
| Spain | 15.5 | 20.0 | 21.5 | 20.3 |
| Sweden | 28.6 | 30.5 | 32.5 | 31.3 |
| United Kingdom | 16.6 | 17.2 | 20.4 | 20.1 |
| United States | 13.3 | 13.4 | 15.4 | 16.2 |

"Public social spending" refers to central government expenditures on pensions, health care, unemployment compensation, education, family allowances, income maintenance, and the like.
*Source:* OECD, Social Expenditures Database 2006 (www.oecd.org/els/social/expenditure).

Moreover, both left-wing parties and mainstream conservative parties have tended to agree on the basic principle of the welfare state, though they might disagree on the extent or form of government funding for social welfare measures. Most of these parties in Western Europe, North America, and Japan have recognized that government-funded welfare measures are widely popular and that their electoral fortunes often depend on their ability to provide social benefits to key segments of the population. The main differences among these various political parties and governments have generally been a matter of degree, not principle. The gamut has extended from the extensive welfare systems of Sweden and other Scandinavian countries (commonly known as the *Swedish model*) to the less encompassing, though still significant, welfarism of the United States.[21] (See table 14.3.)

Religion has played a role of its own in shaping various approaches to welfare policy. Kimberly Morgan has shown that from the nineteenth century down to the present day, different patterns of religious attitudes and church–state relations have resulted in different policy choices regarding the role of women in the work force and child-care policies in Europe and the United States.[22]

To be sure, welfare programs cost money. Some populations have been willing to shoulder higher tax burdens than others. Table 14.4 shows the top tax rates in eleven democratic welfare states. Note that the United States is a comparatively low-tax country.

### Farewell to the Welfare State?

Starting in the mid 1970s, doubts about the sustainability of the welfare state began spreading in Western Europe and North America. In October 1973, the world's leading oil exporting countries pushed for the immediate quadrupling of petroleum prices. The sudden price hike dealt a staggering blow to the energy-hungry industrialized democracies, resulting in a relatively new phenomenon dubbed *stagflation,* an unusual combination of economic stagnation and high inflation. (Classical economic theory predicted that, when the economy goes into a recession, prices should fall, not rise.)

Keynesian prescriptions for fine-tuning the national economy, which had registered some visible successes in the previous decade, no longer appeared to work. The budget deficits that many advanced industrial democracies had been running up as government welfare programs proliferated now threatened to get out of hand. Large segments of the population demanded ever-higher government-funded pensions, health benefits, and other forms of assistance to help them keep up with the rising cost of living. But government treasuries were no longer prepared to meet these demands as the decline in economic activity brought in diminishing

**TABLE 14.4**

**Highest Marginal Tax Rates in Selected Democracies, 2004**

| Country | Individual Income: Top Tax Rate (%) | Individual Income: On Income Over ($) | Top Corporate Tax Rate (%) |
|---|---|---|---|
| Belgium | 50 | 30,210 | 33 |
| Denmark | 59 | 51,162 | 30 |
| France | 48 | 60,673 | 33 |
| Ireland | 42 | 35,443 | 13 |
| Italy | 45 | 88,608 | 33 |
| Japan | 37 | 167,395 | 30 |
| Netherlands | 52 | 63,777 | 35 |
| Spain | 29 | 55,962 | 35 |
| Sweden | 25 | 59,756 | 28 |
| United Kingdom | 40 | 51,358 | 30 |
| United States | 35 | 319,100 | 35 |

*Source:* World Bank, *World Development Indicators, 2006.*

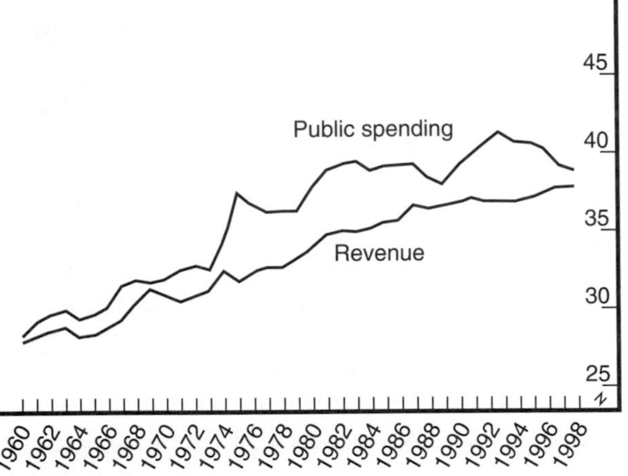


**FIGURE 14.1 Gap Between Public Spending and Public Revenue in Major Industrial Countries* (as Percentage of Gross Domestic Product)**

*Data are from the United States, Japan, the Federal Republic of Germany, France, Britain, Italy, and Canada. (*Source: The Economist,* September 11, 1999.)

tax revenues and necessitated rising amounts of compensation for the growing ranks of the unemployed (see figure 14.1).

Throughout the 1980s and into the 1990s, the idea gained currency in the economically advanced democracies that governments could no longer afford the high deficits and weighty tax burdens typically produced by the modern welfare state. For many people, the welfare state—and government intervention in the economy more generally—seemed to have reached their limits. In the 1980s, conservatives like President Ronald Reagan and British Prime Minister Margaret Thatcher spoke out forcefully in favor of greater reliance on the private sector and less reliance on government. In 1991, the leaders of the twelve West European countries that then constituted the European Community (the forerunner of today's European Union) agreed to restrict their annual budget deficits to no more than 3 percent of GDP as a precondition for adopting the euro. That restriction, along with other criteria, continues to require tough budget control measures on the part of most EU countries.

In spite of belt-tightening policies in a number of countries over the past two decades, the welfare state remains both viable and popular. As table 14.5 shows, government spending on health care accounts for well over half of total health care spending in the wealthiest democracies of North America, Europe, and East Asia (with the exception of South Korea and the United States). And tax revenues still comprise a large share of gross domestic product in most of the welfare states on our list (table 14.2). Indeed, social welfare spending remains broadly popular in most economically advanced democracies, a fact even conservatives acknowledge. (President Reagan *raised* Social Security payments in the 1980s.)[23] At times these welfarist attitudes coexist with support for cutting budget deficits and reducing taxes. Globalization poses additional problems for today's welfare states. While further constricting

TABLE 14.5

**Government Spending on Health Care as Percentage of Total Health Care Spending in Selected High-Income Democracies, 2003**

| Country | Percentage | Country | Percentage |
|---|---|---|---|
| United Kingdom | 85.7 | Italy | 75.1 |
| Sweden | 85.2 | Spain | 71.3 |
| Denmark | 83.0 | Canada | 69.9 |
| Japan | 81.0 | Netherlands | 62.4 |
| Germany | 78.2 | South Korea | 49.4 |
| France | 76.3 | United States | 44.6 |

*Source:* World Bank, *World Development Indicators, 2006.*

TABLE 14.6

**Unemployment in Selected Democratic Welfare States (as % of Labor Force)**

| Country | 1980 | 1985 | 1990 | 1995 | 1999–2001[a] | 2000–2004[a] |
|---|---|---|---|---|---|---|
| Belgium | 9.3 | 10.4 | 6.7 | 9.9 | 7.0 | 7.4 |
| Canada | 7.5 | 10.5 | 8.2 | 9.5 | 6.8 | 7.2 |
| Denmark | — | — | 7.7 | 7.2 | 5.4 | 5.2 |
| France | 5.8 | 10.1 | 9.0 | 11.7 | 10.0 | 9.9 |
| Germany | 2.6 | 7.2 | 4.8 | 8.2 | 8.1 | 9.8 |
| Ireland | — | 16.9 | 13.4 | 12.3 | 4.7 | 4.4 |
| Italy | 5.6 | 8.5 | 9.1 | 11.9 | 10.8 | 8.0 |
| Japan | 2.0 | 2.6 | 2.1 | 3.2 | 4.8 | 4.7 |
| Spain | 10.5 | 21.7 | 16.2 | 22.9 | 14.1 | 11.0 |
| Sweden | 2.0 | 2.9 | 1.7 | 8.8 | 5.1 | 6.5 |
| United Kingdom | 6.2 | 11.5 | 7.1 | 8.7 | 5.3 | 4.6 |
| United States | 7.2 | 7.2 | 5.6 | 5.6 | 4.1 | 5.5 |

[a]Data are for the most recent year available.
*Source: OECD Economic Outlook, June 1999;* World Bank, *World Development Indicators 2003* and *World Development Indicators 2006.*

the resources available to governments for welfare spending, globalization also causes dislocations like unemployment and poverty that raise new demands for government compensation and protection. But as citizens demand more public spending on education, job training, health care, unemployment compensation, pensions, and other items on their social-welfare wish list, the governments they elect will need to figure out how to do more with less.[24] (For unemployment trends, see table 14.6.)

### The Politics of Welfare States

Most democratic welfare states have difficulty coming up with the money needed to meet continuing public demands for welfare services. This has prompted some serious soul-searching about the nature of the state's proper role in economic affairs and, indeed, the very nature of contemporary democracy itself. One disturbing hypothesis suggests that today's mass democracies make such overwhelming demands on their governments for benefits of various kinds that the results can only be uncontrollable budget deficits. These deficits, in turn, stifle economic growth by breeding abnormally high interest rates or inflation, or both. Modern welfarist democracies are therefore by nature self-defeating: they prevent the very increases in national wealth that are needed to meet rising public demands for governmental assistance.

At the same time, the argument continues, democracies place such inordinate pressures on elected officials to "deliver the goods" (better schools, more health care, higher pensions, increased poverty relief, etc.) that politicians cannot get elected unless they make promises that are inevitably unrealistic. Candidates competing in electoral contests seek to outdo one another in making fantastic promises, a process known as *overbidding*. Once elected, political leaders then find that they cannot deliver the goods as promised because of inescapable budgetary constraints or other adverse economic conditions over which they have little or no immediate control, such as sluggish growth rates, or a weak international economy.

Many elected officials find themselves locked into automatic spending commitments for programs already enacted into law. In the United States, the funds available for discretionary spending (that is, money that can be spent at the discretion of the President and Congress) typically amount only to about a third of the federal budget. The remaining two-thirds is already committed to mandatory payments for Social Security, Medicare, and other social welfare measures, plus interest payments on the national debt.

In addition to confronting demands for more benefits, political leaders must frequently confront demands for lower taxes. It is not uncommon that demands for tax relief are raised by the very people who insist on more government assistance for themselves. Mass democracies seem to have no shortage of citizens who feel entitled to various welfare benefits but who are always ready to shift the burden of paying for them to someone else.[25]

As a consequence, democracy once again proves itself to be self-defeating: voters make demands that their government cannot fulfill and for which they are not willing to pay. They take out their frustrations by turning against the incumbent leaders and shifting their support to challengers who make unrealistic promises of their own ("More gain, less pain"). To save themselves, the incumbents may feel compelled to outbid their opponents by providing instant rewards or grandiose pledges to their constituents at election time—tax cuts, higher pensions, and the like—even though the economy can ill afford such favors. Incumbents thus have an interest in promoting a favorable political business cycle, using the powers of their office to tilt economic policy in directions that will enhance their chances for reelection. Irrespective of whether the incumbents are victorious or the vote goes to their opponents, the cycle of broken promises and voter discontent just begins anew.

Elected officials might try to sway voters by tampering with the economy at election time, but some analysts doubt that they have sufficient short-term control over the economy to do so effectively.[26] Nevertheless, there is some evidence that many voters at election time are more likely to be swayed by economic conditions than by other factors impinging on their vote.

There are several variants of these generalizations about the corruptive nature of democratic welfare politics and the "entitlement mentality" accompanying it. One that surfaced in the mid 1970s hypothesized that the increase in mass political participation that had taken place in the United States and various West European countries over the preceding fifteen years (through the enfranchisement of eighteen-year-olds and the increased activism of minority groups), along with the rise in welfare spending that occurred in the same period, had overloaded governments with demands they could not fulfill. The result was a "crisis of governability." Frustrated by the inability of elected leaders and bureaucratic agencies to respond to their demands, growing numbers of citizens in these countries showed signs of having less trust in their governments. Paradoxically, the natural functionings of democracy—mass participation and open interest articulation—were undermining the authority of democratically elected governments in the eyes of the population.[27]

Another set of hypotheses concerning the self-destructive tendencies of modern democratic welfare states was advanced by Mancur Olson. Olson argued in *The Rise and Decline of Nations* (1982) that one of the main variables that accounts for stunted economic growth and the ungovernability of certain democracies is the existence of small special-interest groups that exert a degree of political influence that is disproportionately greater than their share of the population. These groups pressure governments into providing their members with special privileges and benefits at the expense of society as a whole. Ironically, these kinds of pressure groups are more likely to exist in countries that have had a long history of stable democracy, such as Britain and the United States. Successful democracies, in essence, breed the very political forces that undermine an elected government's ability to govern in behalf of all the people. The result, almost inevitably, is the ungovernability of democracies. Democracy, in short, is its own worst enemy.[28]

Other critics of the welfare state point out that it has failed to stamp out poverty, guarantee job security, or eliminate class conflict. Though they vary in degree, virtually all the democratic welfare states of the contemporary world continue to experience hard-core poverty, unemployment, and fairly wide disparities in personal incomes and family wealth. Because today's highly advanced postindustrial economies are particularly dependent on highly educated professionals and a technically skilled work force, income gaps between different socioeconomic classes increasingly reflect gaps in education levels.

Welfare states are also maligned for encouraging excessive dependency on government handouts, a phenomenon that may induce some people to live off welfare payments instead of holding down a steady job. Efforts in the United States, Britain, and other countries in recent years to require impoverished welfare recipients to work in exchange for welfare benefits (or instead of them) reflect the frustration of many taxpayers who believe that income maintenance programs for the able-bodied poor are often abused. "Workfare" programs of this kind are sometimes hampered, however, by a paucity of well-paying jobs for poorly educated or unskilled workers.

Still, many political observers argue that the modern democratic welfare state, for all its faults, is the most stable and humane system of political economy humankind has ever developed. It has combined the freedoms and growth potential of private enterprise with the security of a social safety net that has all but eliminated the terrors of permanent impoverishment and misery. It has provided educational opportunities and community services that were undreamed of only a few generations ago. While admitting that the welfare state's detractors may have some valid points, many of its defenders would say that no superior alternative presently exists or is ever likely to exist. In this view, the democratic welfare state constitutes a model that many countries in the world are striving to emulate, especially former communist countries and others that are now in transition from authoritarianism to democracy.

## KEY TERMS
### (In bold and underlined in the text)

Political economy
Gross Domestic Product (GDP); per capita GDP
Gross National Income (GNI); per capita GNI
Inflation
Central bank
Recession
Depression
Budget deficit
National debt
Fiscal policy
Value added tax (VAT)
Laissez-faire capitalism
Market economy
Centrally planned (command) economy
Mixed economy
Keynesianism
Privatization
Nationalization
Welfare state

## NOTES

1. The term *Pareto optimum* refers to a state of economic equilibrium in which no one's welfare can be improved without reducing someone else's welfare. It was named after the Italian political economist Vilfredo Pareto (1848–1923).
2. Since 1948 the only exceptions to this rule occurred in 1956, when President Eisenhower was reelected despite 1.4 percent growth in the previous twelve months, and 1976, when President Ford was defeated despite 4 percent growth (*Economist*, May 27, 1995, 25–26).
3. Benjamin Friedman, *The Moral Consequences of Economic Growth* (New York: Knopf, 2005).
4. See Herman M. Schwartz, *States Versus Markets* (New York: St. Martin's Press, 1994); and Martin Staniland, *What Is Political Economy?* (New Haven: Yale University Press, 1985). For an overview of recent scholarship on political economy, see James E. Alt, "Comparative Political Economy: Credibility, Accountability, and Institutions," in *Political Science: The State of the Discipline*, ed. Ira Katznelson and Helen V. Miller (New York: W. W. Norton, 2002), 147–71.

5. Adam Smith, *The Wealth of Nations* (Chicago: University of Chicago Press, 1977). For biographic studies, see Jerry Z. Muller, *Adam Smith in His Time and Ours* (Princeton: Princeton University Press, 1993); Ian Simpson Ross, *The Life of Adam Smith* (Oxford: Clarendon Press, 1995); and Athol Fitzgibbons, *Adam Smith's System of Liberty, Wealth, and Virtue* (New York: Oxford University Press, 1995).
6. David Ricardo, *The Principles of Political Economy and Taxation* (New York: E. P. Dutton, 1948). This work was first published in 1817.
7. Thomas Malthus, *An Essay on the Principle of Population* (New York: Oxford University Press, 1994). This work was first published in 1798.
8. Cited in Richard Hofstadter, *Social Darwinism in American Thought*, rev. ed. (New York: George Braziller, 1959), 41, 57.
9. See the *Program of the Communist Party of the Soviet Union*, issued in 1961.
10. David Stark and Laszlo Bruszt, *Postsocialist Pathways* (Cambridge: Cambridge University Press, 1998).
11. Friedrich von Hayek, *The Road to Serfdom* (Chicago: University of Chicago Press, 1956).
12. On Keynes, see Robert Lekachman, *The Age of Keynes* (New York: Random House, 1966); Robert Skidelsky, *John Maynard Keynes: A Biography*, 2 vols. (New York: Viking/Penguin, 1994). For essays on Smith, Malthus, and Keynes, see D. D. Raphael et al., *Three Great Economists* (New York: Oxford University Press, 1997).
13. Daniel Yergin and Joseph Stanislaw, *The Commanding Heights: The Battle Between Government and the Marketplace That Is Remaking the Modern World* (New York: Simon & Schuster, 1998); Harvey Feigenbaum, Jeffrey Henig, and Chris Hamnett, *Shrinking the State: The Political Underpinnings of Privatization* (Cambridge: Cambridge University Press, 1998).
14. See the annual *Global Competitiveness Report*, released by the World Economic Forum, at www.weforum.org, and the *World Competitiveness Yearbook*, prepared annually by the IMD World Competitiveness Center, at www.imd.ch. The Heritage Foundation and the *Wall Street Journal* jointly produce an annual *Index of Economic Freedom*, accessible at www.heritage.org.
15. For a sampling of Bentham's writings, see Bhikhu Pradesh, ed., *Bentham's Political Thought* (London: Croom Helm, 1973).
16. For a comprehensive interpretation, see Alan Ryan, *J. S. Mill* (London: Routledge & Kegan Paul, 1974). For a psychohistory that relates Mill's ideas and personality to his relationships with his father and his wife, see Bruce Mazlish, *James and John Stuart Mill* (New York: Basic Books, 1975).
17. Sheri Berman, *The Social Democratic Movement* (Cambridge, Mass.: Harvard University Press, 1998); Peter Gourevitch, *Politics in Hard Times* (Ithaca, N.Y.: Cornell University Press, 1986), 34.
18. Theda Skocpol, *Protecting Soldiers and Mothers: The Political Origins of Social Policy in the United States* (Cambridge, Mass.: Harvard University Press, 1992).
19. Robert F. Himmelfarb, *Survival of Corporatism in the New Deal Era, 1933–1945* (New York: Garland, 1994).
20. Cited in Christopher Pierson, *Beyond the Welfare State? The New Political Economy of Welfare* (University Park: Pennsylvania State University Press, 1991), 128.
21. For an analysis of different types of democratic welfare regimes, see Gøsta Esping-Andersen, *Three Worlds of Welfare Capitalism* (Princeton: Princeton University Press, 1990).
22. Kimberly J. Morgan, *Working Mothers and the Welfare State: Religion and the Politics of Work-Family Policies in Western Europe and the United States* (Stanford: Stanford University Press, 2006).
23. Pierson, *Beyond the Welfare State?* 168–78. See also Paul Pierson, *Dismantling the Welfare State? Reagan, Thatcher, and the Politics of Retrenchment* (Cambridge: Cambridge University Press, 1994).
24. Christopher Pierson, *Beyond the Welfare State?* 3rd ed. (Cambridge: Polity, 2006); Miguel Glatzer and Dietrich Rueschemeyer, eds., *Globalization and the Future of the Welfare State* (Pittsburgh: Pittsburgh University Press, 2005); B. Vivekanandan and Nimmi Kurian, eds., *Welfare States and the Future* (New York: Palgrave Macmillan, 2005); Gøsta Esping-Andersen et al., *Why We Need a New Welfare State* (New York: Oxford University Press, 2002); Neil Gilbert, *Transformation of the Welfare State: The Silent*

*Surrender of Public Responsibility* (Oxford: Oxford University Press, 2002); and Evelyne Huber and John D. Stephens, *Development and Crisis of the Welfare State: Parties and Policies in Global Markets* (Chicago: Chicago University Press, 2001).

**25.** Shortly after the November 1994 congressional elections in the United States, a survey asked voters to list their chief priorities for the new Congress. The top priority, selected by 62 percent of those surveyed, was protecting Medicare and Social Security. The second most widely named priority, mentioned by 60 percent of the survey respondents, was reducing government spending (*Washington Post*, November 28, 1994).

**26.** James E. Alt and K. Alec Chrystal, *Political Economics* (Berkeley: University of California Press, 1983), 103–25; and Alt, "Comparative Political Economy," 151–52, 163ff.

**27.** Michel Crozier, Samuel P. Huntington, and Joji Watanuki, *The Crisis of Democracy* (New York: New York University Press, 1975).

**28.** *The Rise and Decline of Nations* (New Haven: Yale University Press, 1982).

CHAPTER 15

# THE POLITICS OF DEVELOPMENT

The *developing countries* consist of more than 150 states spread across the globe from Latin America to Africa, from the Middle East to East Asia. Together they are home to 85 percent of the world's population. These countries are also sometimes referred to as the "Third World," a term coined by a French economist in the 1950s. Although it had never been common previously to speak of the "First World" as a euphemism for the economically advanced democracies or to refer to the communist states as the "Second World," it was universally understood that the Third World applied to just about every other country on the planet. Concentrated largely in the southern hemisphere, the Third World is also known collectively as "the South," in contrast to North America, Europe, and Japan, known collectively as "the North." "North–South relations" are relations between the more economically advanced countries and those that are less developed.

Like most blanket terms, such designations as *Third World* or *the South* cover a far greater variety than they imply. In fact, the nations of the developing world exhibit an extraordinary diversity of political systems, social structures, and even levels of economic development. Some are (or have been) democracies. Others are authoritarian regimes of various types, such as traditional monarchies or military dictatorships. Some are fairly homogeneous when it comes to the ethnic composition or religious beliefs of the population; others consist of socially heterogeneous populations. In economic terms, a few developing countries are relatively rich, most are poor, and quite a few are in between.

Most developing states—but not all—have experienced a colonial past (see table 15.1). Few states in these regions managed to escape long-term colonization by the imperialist powers. Even some that avoided colonial rule came under short-term domination by outside powers at one time or another in their history.

Another commonality that most developing states share is their relative economic inferiority to the industrially developed democracies. But here, too, there are exceptions. For example, several Middle Eastern states are rich in oil reserves or other economic assets. In 2006, five of them—Bahrain, Kuwait, Qatar, Saudi Arabia, and the United Arab Emirates—were ranked among the world's high-income countries. An indication of the relative standing of various countries around the world in terms of their overall level of development can be gleaned from table 15.2, which is a partial list of

**TABLE 15.1**

**Colonization Patterns**

| Region or Country | Colonizing Powers | Period of Decolonization |
|---|---|---|
| Latin America | Spain, Portugal | 1810–1820s |
| Caribbean | Britain, France, Denmark, Netherlands, United States | 1950s–1970s |
| Africa | Portugal, Britain, France, Germany Belgium, Italy | 1950s–1960s |
| Middle East; North Africa | Turkey, Britain, France, Spain, Italy | 1920s; 1940s–1950s |
| India; Pakistan | Britain | 1947 |
| Southeast Asia | France, Britain, Netherlands, Japan | 1945–1950s |
| Korea; Taiwan | Japan | 1945 |
| Philippines | United States | 1946 |
| Pacific Islands | United States, France, Japan | 1945–1980s |

**TABLE 15.2**

**Human Development Index, 2003**

Levels of Human Development in Selected Countries Based on Life Expectancy, Literacy Rates, School Enrollments, and Per Capita GDP (Total: 177)

| High | | Medium | | Low | |
|---|---|---|---|---|---|
| **Rank** | **Country** | **Rank** | **Country** | **Rank** | **Country** |
| 1. | Norway (0.963) | 58. | Libya (0.799) | 146. | Madagascar (0.499) |
| 2. | Iceland | 61. | Malaysia | 148. | [a]Cameroon, Lesotho |
| 3. | Australia | 62. | Russia | 151. | Yemen |
| 4. | [a]Canada, Luxembourg, Sweden | 63. | [a]Brazil, Romania | 153. | Haiti |
| | | 73. | Thailand | 154. | Kenya |
| 7. | Switzerland | 75. | [a]Venezuela, Saudi Arabia | 157. | Senegal |
| 8. | Ireland | | | 158. | Nigeria |
| 9. | Belgium | 78. | Ukraine | 159. | Rwanda |
| 10. | United States | 81. | [a]Lebanon, Ecuador, Armenia | 160. | Angola |
| 11. | [a]Japan, Netherlands | | | 163. | Ivory Coast |
| 13. | [a]Finland, Denmark | 84. | Philippines | 164. | Tanzania |
| 15. | United Kingdom | 85. | China | 165. | Malawi |
| 16. | France | 94. | Turkey | 166. | Zambia |
| 17. | Austria | 99. | Iran | 167. | Congo (Dem. Rep.) |
| 18. | Italy | 102. | Palestinian Authority | 169. | Burundi |
| 19. | New Zealand | 110. | Indonesia | 170. | Ethiopia |
| 20. | Germany | 119. | Egypt | 171. | Central African Rep. |
| 23. | Israel | 120. | South Africa | 172. | Guinea-Bissau |
| 28. | South Korea | 127. | India | 173. | Chad |
| 36. | Poland | 135. | Pakistan | 174. | Mali |
| 45. | Croatia | 139. | Bangladesh | 175. | Burkina Faso |
| 52. | Cuba | 141. | Sudan, Congo (Rep.) | 176. | Sierra Leone |
| 53. | Mexico (0.814) | 145. | Zimbabwe (0.505) | 177. | Niger (0.281) |

[a]Tied with same score.

*Source: Human Development Report 2005* (New York: United Nations Development Program, 2005), 219–22. For the calculation of the Human Development Index Value (shown in parentheses), see pp. 340–41. A perfect score equals 1.000.

countries ranked in accordance with the United Nations Development Program's Human Development Index.

## NEWLY INDUSTRIALIZING COUNTRIES

Yet another category of developing countries consists of a small number of relatively successful economies known as the **newly industrializing countries (NICs).** Several of them are in East Asia: South Korea, Taiwan, Singapore, Indonesia, Thailand, and Malaysia. Hong Kong used to be grouped with these East Asian NICs when it was under British authority, but in 1997 it reverted to Communist China. The largest non-Asian countries typically categorized as NICs are Brazil, Mexico, and Argentina. In 2005 these countries had per capita national incomes ranging from $1,280 (Indonesia) to $27,490 (Singapore).

The NICs are characterized above all by the fact that, since the 1950s and 1960s, they have significantly industrialized their economies. They have also expanded the postindustrial service sector, and some have moved into high-technology production. To varying degrees they have been quite successful, but several were severely shaken by the global financial crisis that started in East Asia in 1997 and spread across the globe over the next several years (see chapter 1). The most successful East Asian NICs, once grouped with Japan as the "Asian Tigers" during nearly thirty years of spectacular economic growth, were particularly hard hit by the crisis. Of the Latin American NICs, Brazil's economy was the most severely affected by Asia's financial turmoil.

In addition to sharing certain economic features, all these countries have had problems building stable democracies. We'll examine Mexico and Brazil in chapter 22. The following section looks briefly at the experience of South Korea.

## SOUTH KOREA

With Japan's defeat in 1945, thirty-five years of imperial Japanese rule over Korea came to an end. An agreement between the United States and the Soviet Union to divide the country at the 38° parallel was intended to be temporary, but the division hardened and two Korean states took form. Under Moscow's aegis, North Korea became the People's Republic of Korea, a rigid communist dictatorship led for nearly forty years by Kim Il Sung. Upon Kim's death in 1994, power devolved upon his son, Kim Jong Il, who today presides over a highly repressive, economically moribund state whose leadership appeared determined to build nuclear weapons in 2006. In 1948, South Korea became the *Republic of Korea.*

American hopes for democracy in South Korea were quickly dashed as the first in a series of military leaders imposed dictatorial rule on the fledgling republic. The military's power was immediately reinforced by the *Korean War,* which began with North Korea's unprovoked invasion of South Korea (with Soviet backing) in 1950. A United Nations retaliatory force led by the United States repelled the invasion and restored the status quo ante in 1953. The ensuing military standoff, fortified with huge armies on both sides, tightened the military's grip on South Korea. With the exception of a short-lived elected government in 1960–61, military strongmen governed until the 1990s, at times quite harshly repressing expressions of democratic sentiment. Although 37,000 American troops lost their lives in the Korean conflict, democracy failed in South Korea as the military retained power for most of the next forty years.

The regime's oppressive authoritarianism was accompanied by extraordinary economic dynamism, however. South Korea's military leadership initially attempted to achieve a certain level of economic self-sufficiency, pursuing an "import-substitution" policy aimed at substituting domestically produced goods for costly imports. When this policy failed to generate growth, the government changed course. Starting in the mid 1960s it embarked on a vigorous *export-led growth* strategy. Working closely with the country's leading private companies, organized into some fifty conglomerates known as the *chaebol,* the military leadership and its large civilian bureaucracy catapulted South Korea into the front ranks of the world's export-oriented manufacturing countries by the 1980s. The resulting gains in economic growth were spectacular. In 1950, South Korea's per capita national income was about $100, slightly lower than of India and Ghana; by 1990 it was $3,600. In 2005 South Korea's per capita national income was estimated at $15,830, India's was $720, and Ghana's was $450. South Korea's gross national income of $765 billion was the eleventh highest in the world in 2005.

The South Korean experience strikingly demonstrated that political authoritarianism is not necessarily a barrier to economic growth. Under certain conditions (such as a well-planned export strategy and a robust private sector), an authoritarian regime can successfully promote a vigorous economic development policy.

But such a regime cannot always count on the support of its people, in spite of dramatic improvements in their standard of living. In South Korea, outbursts of democratic fervor periodically challenged the military's hegemony. Prosperity fostered the growth of a middle class that was eager to have a say in political affairs. The state's expansion of educational opportunities produced growing numbers of students and professionals capable of articulating their political demands. In 1980 a student uprising in Kwangju was brutally quashed. The suppression of the labor movement, which enabled private companies to keep their labor costs down, provoked strikes and galvanized support for free labor unions and collective bargaining rights. The rising popularity of Christianity, with Christians eventually constituting 26 percent of the population, expanded the role of churches in the associational life of South Korea's citizenry. In sum, beneath the hard shell of military rule, a vibrant civil society was gathering force. Flagrant corruption in the regime's upper echelons and vocal criticism by democratic governments and human rights organizations around the globe added to the pressures on the military regime to permit fair elections and reinstate democracy.

In 1992, pro-democracy opposition parties won a major victory in parliamentary elections. Later in the same year, democratic reformer Kim Young Sam won the presidency. Pledging to eliminate corruption, widen labor union rights, and reduce the *chaebol*'s excessive influence, the new president took office amid great hopes for a genuine breakthrough to democracy. But South Korea's high-flying economy got caught in the crosswinds of East Asia's financial turmoil; eight large companies collapsed in 1997. To the great disappointment of his followers, Kim Young Sam also failed to make good on his main campaign promises. By the end of his term the country was mired in foreign debts reaching $180 billion, and the government was forced to adopt stringent economic reforms in exchange for a $57 billion rescue loan from the International Monetary Fund.

In these inauspicious circumstances, *Kim Dae-Jung* won the December 1997 presidential election, besting his rivals with 40 percent of the vote. An internationally celebrated human rights activist, Kim had been condemned to death four times by military authorities for his outspoken support for democracy. He also served six years in prison and ten years under house arrest or exile for his political convictions. Although South Korea's economy improved during his administration, President Kim refrained from forcing the *chaebol* to undertake serious reforms. In another disappointment, Kim's bold step of visiting North Korea in hopes of improving economic ties and facilitating family reunions failed to elicit corresponding good will from the North's hardline communist leadership. His government also failed to prevent a wave of layoffs at troubled companies, and by the end of his tenure it was embroiled in corruption scandals. Prohibited by law from running for a second term, Kim stepped down from the presidency in 2003, having failed to accomplish a number of his stated goals. But despite these shortcomings, Kim Dae-jung left office having guided South Korea through a serious economic crisis with its democracy intact. While the country's military ultimately failed to maintain authoritarian rule despite a record of economic success, Kim Dae-jung's administration showed that democracy can survive even in periods of economic duress.

Kim's successor as president of South Korea was *Roh Moo-hyun,* a human rights lawyer who took office in February 2003, having narrowly defeated his nearest rival. President Roh was a left-of-center politician who combined support for the market economy with a popular idealistic message. But his administration got off to a rocky start as several of his aides were accused of corruption. In 2004, the parties opposed to President Roh passed a motion in the national legislature to impeach him for corruption, economic mismanagement, and violations of the election law. Roh resigned the presidency, but a new party formed by his supporters won a slim majority in the next parliamentary elections. The Constitutional Court then overturned the impeachment measure, allowing Roh to return to the presidency. Once again, South Korea's newly reestablished democracy had survived a crucial test with its institutions intact. Signs of economic recovery buttressed support for democracy.

The government's next problem centered on North Korea, which in 2006 exploded an underground nuclear bomb and fired off guided missiles in tests intended to show that it was a nuclear power. But whereas a successful rags-to-riches economic development program had sustained military rule in past decades, a more sophisticated, well-developed economy is sustaining democracy in South Korea now, in spite of rising fears about security.[1] In 2005, South Korea had Freedom House ratings of 1 for political rights and 2 for civil rights.

## UNDERDEVELOPED COUNTRIES

Although the newly industrializing countries are considered developing countries, most countries in the developing world are considerably worse off. Quite a few middle-income countries have major pockets of poverty, especially those in the lower-middle-income range. But the most severely impoverished are the "low-income" countries. In 2005 the World Bank counted fifty-four countries in the low-income group, each with a per capita national income of $875 or less. In 2005 more than a billion people were clinging to the margins of subsistence on less than $1 a day. Another 1.5 billion were trying to survive on incomes between $1 and $2 a day. These 2.5 billion people, making up 40 percent of the world's population, form a global underclass with bleak prospects for climbing out of staggering poverty.

The economic chasm between rich and poor around the world has been widening steadily. The income gap between the richest third of the world's countries, measured in terms of average per capita GNP, grew from about eleven to one in 1970 to just short of twenty to one by 1995. By 2005 the richest 20 percent of the world's population held 75 percent of the world's income; the poorest 20 percent held a mere 1.5 percent of the world's income. The worldwide Gini coefficient, with zero constituting perfect equality and 100 constituting the most extreme inequality, measured 67. (On the Gini coefficient, see chapter 2.) The combined income of the world's 500 wealthiest persons was greater than the combined income of the world's poorest 416 million. But income statistics tell only part of the story. Other current indicators reveal the tragic dimensions of the poorest countries' predicament with even greater harshness:

- More than 10 million children under the age of five die every year—one every three seconds—even though almost all childhood deaths are preventable; 98 percent of these victims are in poor countries.
- Four people die every two minutes from malaria; three of them are children, and most could have been saved with bed nets and timely medication.
- Vaccine-preventable illnesses take the lives of 2 to 3 million children a year.
- More than 850 million people (one-third of whom are preschoolers) suffer from malnutrition, which can have devastating effects on the immune system and brain function.
- More than 38 million people have HIV/AIDS; each year about 3 million die from it and 5 million become infected.
- 500,000 women die every year from pregnancy-related causes, due mostly to inadequate neonatal care.
- More than a billion people lack access to clean water.
- 2.6 million lack access to modern sanitation.
- 115 million lack access to primary school.

Sub-Saharan Africa has been hit especially hard by the grinding effects of poverty and disease. Thirty-three of the region's forty-eight nations are low-income countries. The region accounts for two-thirds of the world's HIV/AIDS cases and 70 percent of the annual fatalities resulting from that affliction. Some 10,000 Africans die *every day* from HIV/AIDS, malaria, or tuberculosis. Life expectancy is diminishing. In the mid 1980s, someone born in sub-Saharan Africa could expect to live 24 fewer years than someone born in a rich country, but the gap was shrinking. By 2005 that figure had grown to 33 years and the gap was widening.[2]

However we choose to draw the dividing lines between middle-income and low-income nations, the fact is undeniable that a large number of developing countries suffer from *underdevelopment*. "Underdeveloped" economies are somewhat different from "undeveloped" economies. Undeveloped economies are ready to grow, like the United States in the mid-nineteenth century.[3] **Underdeveloped economies** ***suffer from chronic, seemingly eternal low growth and mass poverty.***

In an effort to achieve a breakthrough in combating underdevelopment, all 189 members of the United Nations signed the UN Millennium Declaration in 2000, pledging to achieve eight Millennium Development Goals by 2015. These MDGs are listed in table 15.3. Since the adoption of these ambitious goals, there has been some progress in reducing malnutrition and childhood mortality, advancing literacy, and providing greater access to clean water. The number of people living on less than $1 per day fell by about 130 million between

**TABLE 15.3**

**United Nations Millennium Development Goals**

1. **Reducing poverty and hunger.** Halve the number of people living on less than $1 a day, between the baseline year of 1990 and 2015. Halve the proportion of people who suffer from hunger in the same period.
2. **Educating all children.** Ensure that by 2015 children everywhere, boys and girls alike, will be able to complete a full course of primary schooling.
3. **Empowering women.** Eliminate gender disparity in primary and secondary education, preferably in 2005, and at all levels by 2015.
4. **Saving children.** Reduce by two-thirds, between 1990 and 2015, the under-five mortality rate.
5. **Caring for mothers.** Reduce by three-quarters, between 1990 and 2015, the maternal mortality ratio.
6. **Combating disease.** Have halted by 2015 and begun to reverse the spread of HIV/AIDS and the incidence of malaria and other major diseases.
7. **Using resources wisely.** Integrate the principles of sustainable development into country policies and programs, and reverse the loss of environmental resources. Reduce by half the proportion of people without access to safe drinking water. Achieve significant improvement in the lives of at least 100 million slum dwellers by 2020.
8. **Working together.** Develop further an open trading and financial system that is rule-based, predictable, and nondiscriminatory. Address the special needs of the least developed countries and those of landlocked and small island developing states. Deal comprehensively with developing countries' debt problems to make debt sustainable in the long term. Develop decent and productive work for youth. Provide access to affordable essential drugs in developing countries. Make available the benefits of new technologies—especially information and communications technologies.

*Source: World Development Indicators 2006* (Washington, D.C.: World Bank, 2006), 2–19.

the baseline year of 1990 and 2005. But at present rates of progress, projected outcomes will fall short of the Millennium Development Goals in these very same categories. Some countries are moving backward. Eighteen countries had a *lower* Human Development Index value in 2003 than in 1990. At least sixty-five countries, with a combined population of 1.2 billion people, will fail to meet at least one of the Millennium Development Goals until after 2040. Fifty-two countries are retrogressing, or making little progress, in reducing childhood mortality—especially in sub-Saharan Africa, where the Millennium Goals cannot be met at current rates of progress until 2115, one hundred years too late.[4]

Why haven't the chronically underdeveloped countries been able to develop their economies? This pressing question has generated a wide range of answers. The following overview presents a few independent variables that students of economic development have used in their efforts to explain the persistence of underdevelopment in different settings.[5]

## Population

On October 12, 1999, the world greeted the birth of its 6 billionth citizen, according to the calculations of demographers. By the end of 2006, world population surpassed 6.7 billion. Current projections estimate that global population will be about 7.94 billion in 2025 and 9.24 billion in 2050 (see table 15.4). Does "overpopulation" cause poverty? The evidence is rather mixed. On the one hand, *poverty causes overpopulation,* which in turn causes more poverty. People who live in dire conditions must confront the probability that some of their offspring will die as children. To compensate for anticipated

**TABLE 15.4**

**The World's Ten Most Populous Countries**

| Country | 2006 Population (in millions) | Expected Population in 2025 (in millions) |
|---|---|---|
| China | 1,311 | 1,476 |
| India | 1,122 | 1,363 |
| United States | 300 | 349 |
| Indonesia | 225 | 264 |
| Brazil | 187 | 229 |
| Pakistan | 166 | 229 |
| Bangladesh | 147 | 190 |
| Russia | 142 | 130 |
| Nigeria | 135 | 200 |
| Japan | 128 | 121 |

*Source:* Population Reference Bureau, www.prb.org.

childhood mortality, many destitute families tend to have more children than less-deprived families. The population's fertility rate (that is, the average number of children born during an average woman's fertile years) tends to be highest in poor, mainly rural countries—typically above five children. Many poor families overcompensate and have more surviving children than they can afford. (Ironically, areas with high childhood mortality rates tend to have high population growth.) In these circumstances, impoverished parents may not be able to provide all their children with adequate food, health care, or education. Children who grow up in such deprivation tend to remain poor all their lives, producing more poor children in the next generation. The cycle of poverty and overpopulation thus repeats itself.

On the other hand, it cannot be said that the world has "too many" people, or that countries with a high population density are doomed to poverty. There is already enough food in the world to feed *everyone* adequately. The problem is that much of this food rots or goes to waste in wealthy countries; for a variety of reasons, it does not get to the malnourished people of the world in time or in sufficient quantities. Meanwhile, high-density countries like China, South Korea, Singapore, and India have registered extraordinary gains in economic growth. Some of the poorest rural regions of sub-Saharan Africa and Latin America, by contrast, are sparsely populated. (Of course, poverty is also extreme in densely populated urban areas in these two vast continents.) On October 17, 2006, the population of the United States reached 300 million—an increase of 100 million since 1967. Despite its size, the United States has by far the world's largest economy. Nevertheless, even the U.S. economy has attributes of poverty that by some measures are more acute than in poorer countries. The life expectancy of African American children, for example, is lower than that of comparably aged children in China, Sri Lanka, Jamaica, Costa Rica, or the Kerala state of India.[6]

Population can be an explosive political issue. China's communist leadership decreed in 1979 that no couple living in an urban area should be allowed to have more than one child; rural couples may have more than one child only under specific circumstances. Forced sterilization has been imposed on millions of Chinese men, a policy that has raised protests from human rights advocates both inside China and around the world. In parts of countries like China, India, and Pakistan, newborn girls are often killed or sold for adoption as birth control measures.[7] Meanwhile, India's government-sponsored birth control programs, which include sex education and encouragement for voluntary sterilization, are regarded by many observers as inadequate or ineffective. And in countries with large Catholic or Muslim populations, birth control and abortion may be illegal or difficult to obtain.

### Sociocultural Explanations

Some analysts attribute economic underdevelopment to social and institutional structures and to the cultural attitudes and modes of behavior that accompany them. One such school of thought was first conceptualized by Max Weber early in the twentieth century and later adapted by American social scientists in the 1950s and 1960s. It makes a fundamental distinction between *modern* and *traditional* societies.

Modern societies are characterized by a complex social structure consisting of differentiated, specialized professions (doctors, farmers, mechanics, etc.) and organized associations (trade unions and other interest groups), all interacting with one another over a relatively wide geographic area. They also tend to have a network of well-developed governmental institutions, including highly organized bureaucracies and a fairly sophisticated system of laws that regulate political, economic, and social interactions. Modern societies are heavily centered in urban areas and are characterized by fairly high rates of literacy and education.

Traditional societies, by contrast, tend to consist of extended families engaged in primary economic activities, such as subsistence agriculture, within a fairly small area. They display little or no professional differentiation, since one person may perform multiple tasks (farmer, medicine man, priest). There are few, if any, organized associations. They also have much simpler institutional structures. Government, to the extent that it is organized at all, is typically built around elites who wield power arbitrarily, demanding the population's deference while freely engaging in corrupt activities. Most people in traditional societies live in rural areas. Very few are educated or even literate.

Whereas modern societies tend to be secular (even though they may permit religious freedom), rationally organized, and attuned to scientific logic, traditional societies tend to attribute natural phenomena to supernatural forces over which human beings have little control. In modern societies, religion and science coexist. In traditional societies, religious belief or superstition substitutes for scientific rationality. As a consequence, modern societies are able to apply science to the production of sophisticated technology, while traditional societies must make do with fairly primitive technology.

Whereas modern societies are based on impersonal rules that apply to everyone, such as legal codes and the laws of the economic marketplace, social and political relationships in traditional societies are more personalized, with a high value placed on face-to-face relations and personal favoritism. Modern societies are dynamic; change is the norm. Traditional societies are resistant to change: people know their place in the existing social hierarchy and are expected to stay there. Quite often, a sense of resignation precludes even the possibility of change.

Scholars who stress these and related distinctions between modern and traditional societies are often exponents of *modernization theory,* which contends that economic underdevelopment cannot be overcome until the society in question abandons its traditional social and institutional structures, along with their accompanying attitudes and behavioral patterns. Countries as diverse as India, Burma, and various African and Middle Eastern states have been variously viewed as possessing distinct features of traditional society that appear to obstruct their economic development.[8]

The modern-versus-traditional-society dichotomy is not without its critics. Some maintain that the distinction is too sharp, arguing that it is possible for some countries to retain certain elements of their own traditional society while simultaneously adopting specific aspects of modern society. A number of critics accuse Western social scientists of ethnocentric bias because they equate "modern" societies with Western societies. By placing American or West European concepts of modernity on a pedestal as the preferred ideal, they argue, Western advocates of modernization theory implicitly denigrate non-Western approaches to political and economic life and overlook the possibility that individual countries will be able to find their own path to economic growth, independent of their would-be tutors in the West. Another criticism suggests that some less developed countries have already advanced well beyond the simple social and political structures of traditional society but still remain economically undeveloped. Other explanations of economic backwardness are therefore necessary.[9]

## Domestic Economy Explanations

After World War II, most of the nations of Asia and Africa that had been colonized by Britain, France, and other European powers in the eighteenth and nineteenth centuries gained their independence. The process was known as *decolonization.* Flush with their newly won independence, the leaders of many of these decolonized states embraced one form or another of what they generally called socialism. For a number of the freshly independent states, socialism above all meant two things: (1) opposition to Western neo-colonialism, and (2) a powerful role for the state in organizing the national economy.

*Neo-colonialism* and *neo-imperialism* were the terms used by many leaders of the developing world to denounce what they regarded as attempts by Britain, France, the United States, or other Western states to try to dominate their economies and dictate their political orientations even after the formal termination of colonial rule. These anti-Western attitudes often included a rejection of the market-oriented economic approaches of the advanced capitalist states and efforts to forge homegrown models of economic development. Anticolonialism thus implied anticapitalism. In several developing countries, businesses or other property privately owned by Europeans or Americans were expropriated by the state, often without compensation.

In addition to having a distinctly anti-Western bias, socialism in many developing nations meant that the state would play a galvanizing role in guiding the process of national economic development. Throughout the developing world, especially in the decades extending from the 1950s to the 1980s, a considerable number of political leaders and economists subscribed to the view that a state-centered socialist system would promote development far more rapidly and far more equitably than would free-market capitalism. Denouncing capitalism as greedy and exploitative, many of them also placed a sharp emphasis on economic self-reliance and spurned trade relations with the West.

Historically, state-dominated economic systems of one type or another today have been an attractive alternative to Western-style private enterprise for many political leaders and intellectuals throughout the developing world. But the role and effectiveness of the state in economic development has varied considerably. Atul Kohli has identified three ideal types of state organization and activity in the developing world. *Coherent-capitalist states* like South Korea are characterized by a cohesive "rational-legal" central state and a fairly clear distinction between the public (state) sector and private enterprise. Such states tend to be the most successful at promoting economic growth because they are able to organize and carry out coherent government programs aimed at stimulating vigorous private-sector development and promoting foreign trade. At the opposite end of the spectrum are *patrimonial states.* As typified by Nigeria, this pattern features government officials who regard public resources—such as the national treasury and other state assets—as their own personal patrimony, to be plundered for their own benefit or for the benefit of their favored group. Patrimonial states tend to do a poor job of promoting economic development. In between these patterns are *fragmented-multiclass states* like India and Brazil. These states are better organized than patrimonial states, but state authority tends to be highly fragmented because it rests on a very diverse society and its attendant political alliances. States like these find it difficult to pursue a coherent, narrowly focused development strategy because they must meet the demands of multiple social and political groups simultaneously. They are pressured by their supporters to scatter the state's limited resources among conflicting goals, such as promoting industrial growth, subsidizing agriculture, and redistributing wealth to the poor. Though the state has invariably played a major role in the economies of developing countries, Kohli concludes, its effects on economic growth have differed widely around the globe.[10]

Over the course of the 1980s, however, calls for enhancing private enterprise and introducing market mechanisms and more international trade made a strong resurgence. These *neo-liberal* economic policies were favored especially by the Reagan administration in Washington and the Thatcher government in London, as well as by leaders of Washington-based international organizations like the World Bank and the International Monetary Fund. (The governments of the United States, Japan, Germany, Britain, and France dominate World Bank and IMF decision making.) This widening commitment to market economics as a prescription for economic growth in developing countries became known as the *Washington consensus.* It stemmed in part from the failure of a number of heavily state-managed economies to grow. Political elites in a variety of developing countries reached the conclusion that excessive government involvement in the economy had not stimulated growth but retarded it. An effort to privatize at least some government-controlled enterprises followed. Yet another source of the change in attitudes toward capitalism was the undeniable success of the East Asian NICs, at least until the late 1990s. Finally, the collapse of the Soviet Union and its communist empire in Central and Eastern Europe took the wind from the sails of many Third World socialist movements, particularly those that depended on financial or military support from Moscow and its allies.

Although the neo-liberal Washington consensus became the new orthodoxy governing economic policies toward the developing world in the 1980s and 1990s, a number of developing countries have had a difficult time meeting its requirements for *structural adjustment*—the process of trimming budget deficits, removing protectionist trade barriers, eliminating price controls on key consumer goods, privatizing state-owned enterprises, and fulfilling other conditions for receiving IMF financial assistance. Proponents of these measures maintain that they are working, while critics have charged that structural adjustment programs worsen poverty rather than alleviate it. The failure of a number of developing countries to eradicate poverty has led to recent reevaluations of the efficacy of market mechanisms as the predominant engine of growth.

A World Bank report in 2006 noted that Latin America's per capita GDP increased by roughly 1.5 percent a year in the 1990s, but with no significant change in poverty levels. The authors found that poor people cannot actively participate in a market economy because they lack access to credit and insurance. And poor regions cannot attract investment from private companies because they lack basic infrastructure, such as good roads and communications facilities. With the highest income inequality in the world, Latin American countries are also generating social tensions that further reduce incentives for private businesses to invest their money. The result is a vicious circle in which low growth produces more poverty, and more poverty produces low growth.

In addressing these problems, the report broke away from the prevailing Washington consensus by advocating a greater role for national governments in undertaking state-funded poverty-reduction strategies that would supplement (though not replace) private-sector investments. Instead of subsidizing well-to-do people through generous tax breaks and other incentives to invest, the state in these countries should be "an agent that promotes equality of opportunities and practices efficient redistribution [of incomes]," providing money directly to poor regions and families, the authors concluded. Similar sentiments in favor of a larger role for the state in addressing chronic poverty have been expressed by Latin American political leaders representing both the left and the right of the political spectrum. These include recently elected presidents such as Michelle Bachelet of Chile, Felipe Calderón of Mexico, Hugo Chávez of Venezuela, Rafael Correa of Ecuador, Alan García of Peru, Evo Morales of Bolivia, and Daniel Ortega of Nicaragua. It remains to be seen whether these developments signal a trend in the direction of greater complementarity between private and state-directed initiatives to attack global poverty.[11]

In addition to issues relating to how a country organizes its economic institutions, domestic, geographical, and ecological factors invariably play a major role in economic development. Many developing countries have geographical features, climactic conditions, resource scarcities, and other natural conditions that have profound causative effects on their inability to promote economic growth. Sub-Saharan Africa is especially disadvantaged in these respects. Development economist Jeffrey Sachs points out that much of this region lacks navigable rivers, reliable rainfall, and irrigation. Its tropical climate breeds malaria, dengue fever, and other diseases that take a huge toll not only on the population but also on the domestic economy. These and other natural factors, Sachs concludes, are more important than adverse political conditions (such as corruption, civil war, or the lack of democracy), cultural variables (such as "traditional" values), or economic institutions (such as the absence of free markets) in explaining Africa's endemic poverty. Other developing countries are also powerfully affected by the realities of nature.[12]

### International Explanations

As we have repeatedly emphasized, what happens *within* nations is very often affected by what happens *between* nations, and vice versa. Not surprisingly, some explanations as to why certain countries experience significant economic growth while others do not are rooted in the interconnection between internal factors and external ones.

One explanation of this kind is associated with Raul Prebisch, an Argentine economist who served for many years as the head of the United Nations Economic Commission for Latin America. Prebisch and others like him have maintained that one of the chief causes of economic underdevelopment is the prevailing structure of the international economy. Specifically, most Third World countries are at a permanent disadvantage because the *terms of trade* for their imports and exports favor the rich nations of the world. In other words, the products that most poor nations must import (such as oil, technology, autos, and other manufactured goods) cost more than the products they can sell in world markets (which often consist of raw materials or cheap manufactures). The result is lingering economic backwardness. To remedy the situation, Prebisch and like-minded economists in the 1970s called for the negotiation of a New International Economic Order, based on preferential concessions by the advanced states of the North in order to compensate the poorer countries of the South. But this radical reordering of the world trading system has not come about.[13]

Another international explanation for Third World poverty is **dependency theory**. ***This theory asserts that the advanced capitalist countries of the North dominate the world economy and constitute its "core" (or "metropolis").*** The poor countries are relegated to the "periphery" of the world capitalist system. They are treated as mere satellites of the rich industrialized nations and remain economically dependent on them. There are several variants of dependency theory. One variant asserts that capitalists in the core countries sometimes succeed in making alliances with capitalist entrepreneurs and authoritarian political leaders in particular developing countries. The result is a "dual economy" within such countries: a relatively well-to-do capitalist elite with international connections coexists with poverty-stricken masses who are cut off from such privileged contacts.

The dependency hypothesis touched off a lively debate. The neoliberal critique of dependency, for example, affirms that countries that orient their national economy toward active involvement in international trade are more likely to experience growth than countries that cut themselves off from the global economy, whether for ideological reasons (e.g., anticapitalism) or others. As one might expect, neo-liberals point to the Asian NICs as prime examples of export-oriented growth. At the same time, they criticize inward-looking economies based on excessive import substitution or political hostility to trade with the capitalist world as paragons of domestic economic stagnation. One early advocate of dependency theory, Fernando Henrique Cardoso, adopted neo-liberal views in the period leading up to his election as president of Brazil in 1994.[14]

Over the course of the 1990s the neo-liberal approach won acceptance among a growing number of governments in the developing world. By the end of the decade, 110 developing countries were members of the World Trade Organization, compared with only sixty-five members of the WTO's predecessor, the General Agreement on Tariffs and Trade (GATT), in 1987.

Despite undeniable correlations between international trade and economic growth in many countries around the world, wealthy countries continue to prevent developing countries from participating equitably in the world trading system. Most of the gains from trade in the developing world have been reaped by only seven countries. China and other dynamic East Asian states, together with India and Mexico, account for 70 percent of the world's low- and high-technology exports. But the majority of developing countries lack this technological dynamism. Sub-Saharan Africa's exports have been plummeting steadily since the 1960s as a percentage of world trade. The initiation of a new round of international trade negotiations in Doha, Qatar, in 2001 promised major gains for the developing world. But five years later, rich countries continued to impose barriers to the importation of goods from poorer countries; they still subsidized their own farmers at the expense of farmers in the Third World; and they maintained a variety of trade rules detrimental to the less-developed countries. Clearly, the gains from globalization are not being shared by many nations around the world.[15]

Foreign aid is another problematic area. Many developing countries need grants and loans from the wealthier countries to stay afloat. In 1969 a UN commission headed by Lester Pearson, Canada's former prime minister, recommended that North America, Western Europe, and Japan devote 0.7 percent of gross national income in each country to foreign assistance. Most wealthy countries never met that goal. Over the ensuing decades, the United States provided the most foreign aid in money terms, but it ranked among the lowest of the donor countries when its assistance was measured as a percentage of GNI. American aid remained below 0.3 percent of gross income. Much of that aid was military assistance to Israel and Egypt, and a great deal of it came back to the United States because of conditions requiring governments receiving U.S. aid to spend large amounts of it in the United States on equipment and other goods and services needed for development. By 2000 the United States was spending 0.1 percent of its GNI on foreign aid, the lowest percentage among the wealthy countries. With aid allocations falling in other donor countries as well, President George W. Bush joined other world leaders at a conference on development financing in Monterrey, Mexico, in March 2002. The assembled leaders agreed to raise their respective development assistance levels to 0.7 percent of GNI. Over the next two years the U.S. government provided $8 billion in aid (much of it going to Afghanistan and Iraq). Nevertheless, by 2004 its aid assistance had climbed to only 0.16 percent of GNI. Total assistance from the rich countries to the developing world amounted to $78 billion in 2004.[16]

Jeffrey Sachs has done some rough calculations to estimate how much it would cost to lift approximately 1.1 billion people who now live on less than $1 a day to a slightly higher plane of subsistence by 2015. In order for these extremely poor people to meet their most basic needs in terms of nutrition, health care, schooling, and the like, the wealthy countries would have to provide about $80 billion in assistance per year to the developing countries. Half that amount would go to sub-Saharan Africa. The donor countries would also have to provide development agencies like the World Bank with additional funds amounting to $48 to $54 billion each year. Sachs's bottom line thus comes to $135 to $195 billion in assistance per year between 2005 and 2015—amounts that are *less* than the Monterrey target of 0.7 percent of GNI per year from the wealthy countries. Mustering the political will to make these commitments will not be easy, however. In 2005 more than twenty rich countries spent an average of 0.25 percent of their GNI on foreign aid; in the previous year only four countries reached the 0.5 percent figure. Polls show that most Americans believe that foreign aid consumes about 20 percent of the federal budget, when in fact it is considerably less than 1 percent of the budget.[17] In 2005, President Bush asked Congress for $2.5 billion for foreign aid. Congress agreed to $1.5 billion.

Of course, foreign assistance by itself is no panacea for poverty. And development specialists readily admit that some aid is wasted on poorly planned projects, mismanagement, corruption, and other failings that inevitably raise skepticism about the utility of the billions that are spent on foreign assistance. William Easterly, a former World Bank economist, notes that the West has spent more than $2.3 trillion on foreign aid over the last five decades, yet it has failed to provide enough 12¢ medicines and $4 bed nets to prevent malaria, just as it has failed to provide equally simple remedies for other Third World problems.[18] But the need for more foreign aid—along with better oversight—is now accepted by virtually all world leaders.

International debts place additional burdens on developing countries. Over the decades, most of these countries have borrowed heavily from international agencies, foreign governments, and private banks to pay their bills at home and purchase imports. As we noted in chapter 1, by 2002 they had run up total debts amounting to $460 billion. For debtor countries, the interest that comes due on accumulated debts can reach tens or hundreds of millions of dollars annually. Every dollar spent on interest payments represents a dollar that cannot be spent on health care, education, or other basic needs of the population. In recent years a campaign to provide debt relief for poor countries, spearheaded by people like Bono and Pope John Paul II, has resulted in unprecedented agreements by the world's richest countries to cancel at least some of the developing world's debts. Debt relief totaling $35 billion had been provided by 2006.

Poverty in the developing world thus has a number of causative roots in the international economy. But domestic political factors provide additional causes.

### Domestic Political Explanations

Another set of hypotheses accentuates domestic political factors as important independent variables that help explain economic performance. One study, for example, compared the development experiences of more than forty Third World countries between 1950 and 1980. Although the study was conducted by a team of economists, it concluded that political factors such as continuity of leadership and a cohesive sense of nationhood were just as important, and sometimes even more important, than economic factors in accounting for the success or failure of a country's efforts to develop its economy.[19]

More recent studies confirm the importance of governments in fostering—or hampering—economic growth. For example, William Easterly argues that the most crucial factor in determining whether an economy grows rich or stagnates is *incentives*. Individuals, businesses, and others involved in the economic development process will perform at their most productive levels if they can see that their efforts will bear fruit. They need incentives to save, invest, create businesses, and pay taxes. Bad governments stifle these expectations by providing all sorts of disincentives to productive activity. They destroy the value of people's savings by printing excess money and driving up the inflation rate. They destabilize the currency through black-market transactions. They undermine faith in the banking system through lax regulations. They erect barriers to potentially profitable foreign trade by insisting on protectionism. They squander resources by running high budget deficits and foreign debts. And they fail to provide the infrastructure necessary for sustained economic activity, such as roads, telecommunications, irrigation, education, health care, and other basic needs. Worst of all, government corruption casts a pall over the entire development process. When leaders and bureaucrats dispense economic rewards only to a privileged class or ethnic group, or when they steal tax revenues, demand bribes, and misuse foreign aid, potentially productive citizens wallow in poverty. Easterly concludes that bad government is a primary cause of economic stagnation.[20]

Roughly similar conclusions have been reached by studies of the Arab Middle East and North Africa conducted by the United Nations and the World Bank. The studies demonstrate how the region's dictatorships are responsible for persistent economic stagnation. They further indicate that freedom, inclusiveness, accountability, and other aspects of democracy will be essential for future growth.[21]

The need for civil peace is another political requirement for economic growth. Developing countries that are torn apart by civil wars, sporadic ethnic or religious violence, and the breakdown of law and order are typically incapable of maintaining a successful economy.

Acknowledging *good governance* as a factor that can facilitate economic development, the World Bank since the late 1990s has ranked the countries of the world in accordance with six *governance indicators.* These indicators measure the extent of the population's participation in selecting the government, along with freedom of expression, association, and other political freedoms ("voice and accountability"); the degree of political stability and the absence of violence; the effectiveness of the government in providing public services and a timely policy formulation and implementation process; the quality of the state's regulatory policies aimed at promoting private-sector development; the rule of law, including the quality of the police and courts; and control of corruption. Focusing on these criteria of governance has practical policy implications. Researchers estimate that even minor improvements in governance can raise incomes and reduce infant mortality significantly, and can bring about other beneficial effects as well. As a consequence, donor countries are increasingly requiring better governance as a condition of their aid to developing states. Table 15.5 displays the World Bank scores for a number of developing countries in 2005. For the sake of comparison, it also provides the average rankings for the mostly wealthy democracies that belong to the Organization for Economic Cooperation and Development (OECD).[22]

The relationship between economic development and politics is often a complex one, however. As Samuel Huntington pointed out in *Political Order in Changing Societies,* there is always a dynamic interaction between socioeconomic modernization and political development, but the results may vary. As a developing country embarks on the path of modernization and independence, political participation on the part of the masses tends to increase. Literacy, higher education, and urbanization expand, promoting mass political activism. In order to gain popular support, political leaders seek to mobilize the masses, organizing them into supporting various political ideas and programs. At the same time, the state makes a conscious effort to promote the country's economic development. Social change, economic change, and mass political mobilization are the order of the day. These processes typify what Huntington calls *political modernization.*

How the state and other political institutions deal with these changes is problematic. The process of building effective institutions is what Huntington calls *political development.* Successful political development requires the creation of interest groups and political parties that are capable of expressing popular demands and of channeling them into concrete and realistic policy proposals that governments can act upon. It also requires governmental institutions—executives, legislatures, bureaucracies, and so on—that can make decisions efficiently and implement them effectively. Only by being responsive to the newly activated masses can these political associations and institutions hope to gain popular

TABLE 15.5

**Rankings of Selected Countries According to World Bank Governance Indicators, 2005 (Percentile Rank, 1–100)[a]**

| Country | Voice and Accountability | Political Stability/ No Violence | Government Effectiveness | Regulatory Quality | Rule of Law | Control of Corruption |
|---|---|---|---|---|---|---|
| Afghanistan | 11.6 | 2.4 | 9.1 | 5.4 | 1.4 | 2.5 |
| Brazil | 57.0 | 40.6 | 55.0 | 55.0 | 43.0 | 48.3 |
| China | 6.3 | 39.2 | 52.2 | 44.6 | 40.6 | 30.5 |
| Congo (Dem. Rep.) | 7.2 | 1.4 | 1.0 | 4.5 | 1.0 | 3.0 |
| Costa Rica | 76.3 | 70.3 | 64.1 | 68.8 | 65.7 | 66.5 |
| Egypt | 18.4 | 21.2 | 43.1 | 34.7 | 54.6 | 43.3 |
| India | 55.6 | 22.2 | 51.7 | 41.1 | 56.0 | 46.8 |
| Indonesia | 40.6 | 9.0 | 37.3 | 36.6 | 20.3 | 21.2 |
| Mexico | 54.1 | 36.3 | 57.4 | 62.4 | 39.6 | 43.8 |
| Nigeria | 30.0 | 4.7 | 20.1 | 16.3 | 5.8 | 6.4 |
| Pakistan | 12.6 | 5.7 | 34.0 | 27.7 | 24.2 | 15.8 |
| Palestinian Authority | 13.5 | 5.2 | 11.0 | 12.9 | 39.1 | 9.9 |
| South Africa | 70.5 | 41.5 | 75.6 | 67.3 | 57.0 | 69.5 |
| Sudan | 2.9 | 2.8 | 8.1 | 8.4 | 3.4 | 2.0 |
| Turkey | 46.4 | 29.7 | 63.2 | 18.9 | 55.6 | 59.6 |
| Venezuela | 31.9 | 11.8 | 23.0 | 12.4 | 9.2 | 16.7 |
| Zimbabwe | 6.8 | 7.5 | 4.3 | 1.0 | 4.3 | 5.4 |
| OECD[b] | 91.3 | 77.7 | 88.0 | 91.1 | 89.6 | 90.5 |

[a]100 is the best score; the higher the number, the better the performance.
[b]Average scores for 30 OECD countries, including Mexico and Turkey. For a list of members, consult www.oecd.org.
*Source:* info.worldbank.org/governance

legitimacy. If they succeed, the result can be long-term political order and steady economic growth.

But social, economic, and political modernization may explode with such force that it rapidly outpaces the ability of political institutions to keep up with the demands being placed on them. If political development fails to keep pace with modernization, the result can be long-term political authoritarianism and economic decay. "The primary problem in politics," Huntington states, "is the lag in the development of institutions behind social and economic changes." Huntington argues that economic growth does not take place in a political vacuum. It can best flourish in a context of political order and stability, rooted in legitimate political institutions. But one of his implications is that, in modernizing countries, political order may be more difficult to achieve in a democracy than in an authoritarian regime.[23]

Indeed, the question of whether authoritarian states or democracies are more effective at promoting rapid economic growth is still one of the most contentious political issues of modern politics. The authoritarian camp derides democracy as hopelessly inefficient. And the right to vote means nothing, in their view, to populations whose bellies are empty. Democracy's advocates reply that democratic government is more effective than authoritarianism when it comes to generating and sustaining economic growth. Mancur Olson, for example, argued that democracies are more successful than despotic governments at guaranteeing property rights, which are a verifiably important catalyst of economic growth.[24]

Adam Przeworski and his associates provide substantial evidence that, on average, the differences between democracy and dictatorship when it comes to generating economic growth are only marginal. Countries like South Korea under the military or China under the communists have produced phenomenal rates of growth, though other dictatorships have languished. Przeworski and his colleagues conclude that "regimes make no difference for growth"—ultimately, total economic output grows at similar rates in democracies and dictatorships alike.[25] Arguing against these conclusions, other scholars insist that democracy *does* make a difference when it comes to promoting growth; it just takes a longer time for some democracies to produce positive economic results than Przeworski and his colleagues assume.[26]

What about the economy's effects on democracy? Aren't poor countries less likely to create or sustain democracy than rich ones? Chapter 3 provides data relating levels of wealth to varying degrees of democracy and authoritarianism. As the tables in chapter 3 show, the lower we go down the economic pyramid, the less often we encounter democracy. Nevertheless, even countries with very low levels of per capita income—like India—are capable of building and sustaining democracy, as we shall see below.[27]

Amartya Sen underscores the relationship between economic development and democracy with particular forcefulness. In *Development as Freedom,* the Nobel Prize–winning economist redefines the very concept of development in terms of the value of freedom. Instead of focusing exclusively on such economic measures as gross domestic product or per capita income, Sen argues, development should be seen as a process for promoting various kinds of freedom, such as the freedom to live a long and healthy life, the freedom to participate in political and social activities, and the freedom to enjoy educational and cultural opportunities. Sen places human *agency,* centered on the individual as the key "agent" of action and change, at the heart of the development process. Expanding individual freedom is both the principal *means* of promoting development as well as the principal *purpose* of development. The best way to stimulate development, in Sen's view, is to remove the various "unfreedoms" that prevent individuals from realizing their full potential: dictatorship, excessive state controls over the economy, unemployment, inadequate educational facilities, the repression of women, and so on. When people are freed of these constraints, they will expand these and other freedoms all the more. "The people have to be seen as being actively involved in their own destiny," Sen insists. Sen's freedom-based approach to development has directly influenced *human development theory,* as discussed in chapter 12.[28]

Ultimately, there is no single variable that neatly explains underdevelopment, nor is there a single "one size fits all" cure for it. Endemic poverty and economic stagnation have a multiplicity of causes, and their elimination will require concerted efforts on multiple fronts. Political, economic, social, cultural, environmental, medical, and other modes of attack must all be pressed simultaneously. These tasks are both doable and—for the rich countries of the world—affordable. What is needed is a commitment on the part of citizens in both the developing world and the developed countries to support effective actions, and bold decisions by their governments to make them work. In every country, economic development requires political choices.

## INDIA

"At the stroke of midnight, while the world sleeps, India will awake to life and freedom." With those words, Jawaharlal Nehru proclaimed India's independence, which took effect, after centuries of foreign domination, on August 15, 1947.

As independent India's first prime minister, Nehru inherited the world's second most populous nation after China. Nearly 350 million people formed a vast mosaic of religions, languages, classes, and castes, squeezed into an area only about a third the size of the United States. Prior to independence, the country consisted of more than 500 states and subdivisions, most with their own distinct traditions and social patterns. Out of this tangled human web Nehru was determined to shape the structures of an enduring democracy and lay the groundwork for steady economic development.

The challenge was daunting. India's freedom was accompanied by fierce bloodletting between its two largest religious groups, Hindus and Muslims. The confrontation was the result of the breakup of British India into two separate states, India and Pakistan.

After gaining their first foothold in India in 1614, the British gradually extended their domains on the South Asian subcontinent over the course of the seventeenth and eighteenth centuries, ousting Portuguese, French, and Dutch settlers in the process. In 1858, when it officially became a crown colony, British India extended from the borders of Iran and Afghanistan in the north to the southern tip of the subcontinent, opposite the island of Ceylon (now Sri Lanka), another British possession.

Throughout these centuries, the British were at best tolerated but never fully accepted by the population as the legitimate rulers of India. In 1885, a small group of nationalists formed the Indian National Congress, an organization intended to give Indians a greater say in their own affairs and, eventually, freedom. For the next several decades the Congress was largely ineffectual, its membership confined to the country's urbanized, educated elite and its small middle-class following. When **Mohandas Gandhi** became the organization's leader, however, the Congress took on the character of a surging mass movement rooted in India's populous rural villages.

As a young lawyer, Gandhi had worked in South Africa, using Western legal concepts and his own doctrine of *satyagraha* (moral persuasion) in an effort to obtain civil rights and racial justice for the country's Indian minority. After returning to India in 1915, Gandhi began employing the same techniques of persuasion and nonviolent agitation to rouse India's masses against British rule. He organized several demonstrative campaigns of civil disobedience in the 1920s and 1930s, including his famous salt march, a 240-mile trek to the Indian Ocean, where he clutched a handful of salt in defiance of British regulations requiring payment of a salt tax. Gandhi was arrested, and the event became an international sensation. Over the next seventeen years, Gandhi stood out as the charismatic political and spiritual leader of India's impoverished masses and an inspiration throughout the world to oppressed groups seeking to overcome domination through nonviolent means. His followers called him *Mahatma* (Great Soul).

Although a devout Hindu, Gandhi believed strongly in religious tolerance and the national unity of India's diverse peoples. He had no desire to see British India partitioned into separate states after independence. Islamic leaders led by Mohammed Ali Jinnah, however, insisted on the formation of a separate state composed mainly of Muslims. The British authorities agreed. After intensive negotiations it was decided to partition Punjab and Bengal, two northern provinces located 900 miles apart. Each was divided roughly evenly into Muslim and Hindu populations. Portions of these provinces were split off from India to form the new state of Pakistan. A part of Punjab became West Pakistan and a part of Bengal became East Pakistan. The border regions of Kashmir and Jammu were also divided, and the boundary line is still hotly contested. The partition plan resulted in the uprooting of more than ten million people, as Hindus moved to the Indian side of the border and Muslims moved to Pakistan. Periodic outbursts of violence between the two groups in 1947 and 1948 resulted in hundreds of thousands of casualties. Gandhi himself was assassinated by Hindu fanatics infuriated at his efforts to accommodate the Muslims.[29]

Following these unpropitious beginnings, Nehru focused his attention on the political and economic modernization of India. An ardent nationalist and a descendant of the country's select Brahmin caste, Nehru had spent seven years in Britain, where he was educated at Harrow and Cambridge University and admitted to London's prestigious Inns of Court. Although determined to win India's freedom from British rule, he was a great admirer of Western democracy and socialist conceptions of economic justice. He presided over the adoption of India's 1950 constitution, which adopted British-style parliamentary democracy.

Succeeding Gandhi as the leading figure in the Indian National Congress, Nehru helped shape the organization into a political party capable of representing not only India's elites and middle class but also its poor, uneducated masses. Under his guidance, the secular, centrist *Congress Party* quickly dominated India's emerging political system. Aided by a single-member-district/plurality electoral system, the Congress Party in the 1952–67 period managed to convert a popular vote ranging from 45 percent to 48 percent of the ballots into control of about 75 percent of the seats in the House of the People (Lok Sabha), the lower house of the national parliament. (It got roughly similar shares in the 1980s.) In these years the Congress Party evolved into a large grassroots movement as well as the principal party of government at the national level. Its success appeared to be just what Samuel Huntington would have ordered for a country in the throes of modernization: an effective political organization responsive to the newly mobilized masses. Nehru's charismatic leadership and the Congress Party's early dominance helped legitimize India's democratic system among a majority of its citizens. Voter turnout for national elections has averaged about 60 percent of eligible voters since the 1960s.[30]

But neither Nehru nor the party was able to resolve India's two most haunting problems: the immense scope of its economic underdevelopment and the potential explosiveness of its social and regional diversity. Either of these challenges would be enough to keep democracy at bay, or destroy it, in most any other country.

Two years after Nehru's death in 1964, India faced a severe food shortage that compelled the government to appeal to the outside world for immediate assistance. India remained dependent on food imports until 1978. Since then the country has been relatively self-sufficient in food supplies despite a burgeoning population. Nevertheless, poverty has remained ineradicable. The Nehru government's economic strategy of achieving "self-sustained growth" through a combination of private enterprise and government planning yielded some significant gains in national income, but it set India on a course of import substitution and escalating government involvement in the economy that led to waste and inefficiency.[31] For decades, India's industrial growth rates lagged behind those of other developing countries, such as China, South Korea, and Mexico. Early plans to revitalize the agricultural economy were never seriously implemented. India's rural villages, where 85 percent of the population still resides, remain mired in poverty.

Intense social divisions provide a continuing source of political conflict. Socioeconomic divisions are one source of turmoil, but cleavages along religious, ethnolinguistic, and caste lines play an important role of their own.

Today's India is still a predominantly Hindu country: 81 percent of the population adheres to this ancient faith. Muslims comprise about 13 percent of the populace. Even after the partition of British India in 1947–48, some 50 million Muslims remained in India; today they number about 150 million. Approximately 2 percent of Indians are Sikhs, the adherents of a Hindu sect that branched off from traditional Hinduism some five hundred years ago. Christians of various denominations comprise 2.4 percent of the population, and a host of other religions have smaller groups of followers.

Ethnolinguistic distinctions are even more abundant. Though Hindi and English are the main official languages, the constitution recognizes fourteen other official languages. There are twenty-four languages spoken by at least a million people each, and over sixteen hundred dialects. These divisions lead to considerable regional diversity and fragmentation. India's federal structure now consists of twenty-five states and seven union territories, and local distinctions within these subdivisions abound. Separatist movements have flared up in Punjab (with its large Sikh population), Assam and Nagaland in the northeast, in the largely Muslim border areas of Kashmir and Jammu, and elsewhere. Communal violence involving Hindus, Muslims, Sikhs, ethnic and tribal groupings, and ideologically motivated guerilla movements have shaken India's democracy from its foundations down to the present day.[32]

The ties of caste also exert a profoundly divisive effect on Indian society, even though Nehru's government abolished the caste system in legal terms. With deep roots in Hindu cosmology, more than a thousand castes still exist, separated by doctrines and traditions that forbid contact between members of specified castes. A prevailing hierarchy differentiates higher castes from lower ones, with millions relegated to the lowest caste, the untouchables, a group Gandhi sought to dignify by calling them *harijans* (children of God).

Thus far, India's democracy has proved sufficiently resilient to withstand the acute challenges posed by these economic and social realities. The maintenance of democratic procedures and political stability has not been very consistent, however.

In 1966 Nehru's daughter, Indira Gandhi (who was no relation to Mohandas Gandhi), became prime minister. Three years later, deep divisions within the Congress Party over policy issues and personalities split the organization into two parties, one loyal to Mrs. Gandhi and the other opposed to her. Prime Minister Gandhi used her control over political patronage to build a new Congress Party concerned mainly with winning elections rather than serving as the country's prime force for national political integration, as it had in the past.

Meanwhile, long-standing tensions with Pakistan reached a boiling point. In 1971, as 10 million refugees streamed into India in an attempt to flee a civil war, Mrs. Gandhi ordered the Indian army into East Pakistan to put a decisive end to Pakistani control of the area. The Pakistani army quickly surrendered, and with India's blessing, East Pakistan became an independent country, Bangladesh.

On the heels of this triumph, Mrs. Gandhi and her Congress allies won a smashing victory at the polls. In 1975, however, a court invalidated the 1971 elections on the grounds that civil servants had openly aided Mrs. Gandhi's reelection campaign in violation of the constitution. Besieged with demands for her resignation, the prime minister instead declared a state of emergency and suspended normal democratic procedures. She had her chief political opponents arrested and imposed strict censorship on the press. Two years of repressive emergency rule followed. India's fragile democracy appeared finished.

Under intense pressure, Mrs. Gandhi lifted the state of emergency in 1977 and allowed parliamentary elections. Her Congress Party was soundly defeated, garnering only 34 percent of the vote and a mere 28 percent of parliamentary seats. But the new government of M. R. Desai's Janata Dal Party did not last long. With an emotional appeal to India's masses, Mrs. Gandhi led Congress to a decisive comeback. In 1980, her party won two-thirds of the seats in the lower house.

Religious tensions reached new heights in 1984 when Sikh militants demanding greater autonomy for the state of Punjab ensconced themselves in the Golden Temple, a sacred Sikh shrine, and began using it as a base for terrorist operations. Mrs. Gandhi dispatched the Indian army to dislodge the terrorists; more than a thousand Sikhs lost their lives in the raid. The tragedy created an outpouring of resentment among India's 14 million Sikhs. Several months later, Prime Minister Gandhi was assassinated by two Sikh bodyguards. An organized massacre of Sikhs in New Delhi ensued.[33]

The Congress Party then named Indira's son, Rajiv, as prime minister. Rajiv led the party to an impressive electoral victory later in the year. From the outset, however, his government was plagued by mounting sectarian violence in Punjab. Rajiv also failed to heel festering divisions within the Congress Party, which became increasingly factionalized. His efforts to reduce the heavy hand of the government in India's economy also fizzled. By 1985, central government expenditures amounted to more than 35 percent of GNP, up from about 19 percent in 1960. Elections in 1989 swept the Congress Party from power in the aftermath of a kickback scandal, but the next two prime ministers could not establish a stable base of power in the divided parliament. Fresh elections were ordered in 1991, and during a campaign appearance, Rajiv was assassinated by Tamils linked to Sri Lankan guerilla movements. Tamil resentments at the Indian government stemmed from India's unsuccessful military intervention in Sri Lanka several years earlier as well as from ethnic animosities in the southern Indian province of Tamil Nadhu, where the Tamil population was a source of resistence to central government authorities.

The next prime minister, P. V. N. Rao, formed a new Congress-led government following the elections. One of Rao's principal ambitions was to reduce the state's role in the economy by promoting an extensive privatization program. Despite some progress toward this goal, the state's share of the economy remained large. Meanwhile, India's smoldering religious tensions erupted once again as more than 150,000 Hindu fundamentalists demolished a sixteenth-century mosque cherished by Muslims, claiming that it occupied a holy Hindu site. The incident, occurring in the town of Ayodhya, was inspired by the rightist *India People's Party (Bharatiya Janata Party,* or *BJP),* a stridently pro-Hindu organization. Some seventeen hundred people were killed as sporadic confrontations between Hindus and Muslims flared up over the next two weeks. Anti-Muslim violence in Bombay and elsewhere in early 1993 produced an additional thousand casualties. Corruption scandals aggravated Rao's difficulties, along with persistent unemployment and inflation. In the 1996 parliamentary elections the Congress Party suffered a major defeat, with the BJP winning a plurality of seats in the Lok Sabha but not enough to form a government on its own.

The remaining years of the decade witnessed a succession of weak minority governments. In the 1996 elections, Congress's share of seats fell from 47.5 percent to 25.7 percent, rising only to 30.1 percent in the snap elections of 1998. The BJP and its allies raised their share from 21.5 percent in 1991 to 35.4 percent in 1996 and 46.2 percent in 1998. Following the 1998 elections, a BJP-led minority government was formed under Atal Bihari Vajpayee (VAHJ-pay-ee), a moderate in a party noted for its fanatical pro-Hindu attitudes. Vajpayee backed away from the BJP's earlier pledges to build a Hindu temple on the site of the old Ayodhya mosque, but he sought to awaken national pride through a series of nuclear weapons tests several months after taking office. The underground explosions provoked Pakistan into conducting its own nuclear tests and prompted considerable international concern at the prospect of a nuclear confrontation between the two archrivals. Conflicts over Kashmir, most of which is in India, intensified these tensions, and fighting broke out in the summer of 1999 as Pakistani troops invaded the area. Despite India's internal political turmoil, its army evicted the intruders.

In 1999 Vajpayee's multiparty minority government fell apart and lost a vote of confidence. Because no new governing coalition could be stitched together, Indian voters were called to the polls for the third time in as many years. As its new leader the Congress Party chose Sonia Gandhi, Rajiv's widow and an Italian by birth. The choice was roundly criticized by numerous opponents of the Congress Party, and even some Congress members questioned the appropriateness of selecting a non-Indian female as the country's potential next prime minister. "Every drop of my blood says this is my country," Gandhi replied. The elections were spread out over four weeks and provoked sporadic outbursts of violence; more than three hundred people were killed in campaign-related incidents. Only half the eligible electorate voted, an unusually low turnout. When the vote counting was over, Vajpayee and his coalition partners had managed to win a plurality of seats in India's Lok Sabha. But with only a third of the total, they fell far short of a majority. Both the BJP-led coalition and the Congress Party lost seats, while several regional parties, reflecting the enormous importance of local issues in Indian politics, increased their share of votes in parliament. The final result was an even more fractionated lower house than before the elections. Vajpayee, reelected prime minister, formed a government consisting of the BJP and twenty-one smaller parties.

Despite the defection of one of its coalition partners and several defeats in local elections, Vajpayee's BJP managed to hold the government together in the face of explosive Hindu-Muslim violence and another dangerous confrontation with Pakistan. In February 2002, a train carrying Hindu extremists was set ablaze in Godha, in the western Indian state of Gujarat; more than fifty people were killed. The fire, allegedly set by a Muslim mob, incited Hindu attacks on Muslim neighborhoods, businesses, and mosques. About two thousand were killed and a hundred thousand were rendered homeless as local officials and the Gujarat state government, dominated by the BJP, actively cooperated with Hindu extremist groups in organizing the rampage. At the end of the year Gujarat's BJP, campaigning for reelection with a stridently anti-Muslim message, won an overwhelming majority in the state legislature. Tensions with Pakistan escalated in December 2001 when Muslim terrorists fighting for control of the Indian parts of Kashmir, where Muslims are in the majority, staged a raid on India's national parliament. India held Pakistan responsible for failing to rein in terrorist groups based on its territory, and Vajpayee's government placed its troops on high alert. A military standoff between the two nuclear-armed countries lasted for several months before diplomatic intervention and fears of an all-out war calmed the situation.

In anticipation of gaining a third straight electoral victory, Prime Minister Vajpayee called snap elections a few months ahead of schedule in 2004. To his surprise, his BJP party lost more than 40 seats in the House of the People and his allies dropped more than 50. Despite record economic growth of about 8 percent, two-thirds of the voters in India's heavily populated villages were dissatisfied with the government's efforts to improve their conditions. More than two hundred parties fielded candidates, all of them locally oriented parties with the exception of the BJP and the Congress Party. The winner of the three-week electoral contest was Congress, which staged a major comeback under Sonia Gandhi's leadership. Prior to the elections, Congress had joined with several smaller parties in forming the United Progressive Alliance (UPA). The Congress Party won 145 seats outright, and its partners won 75 seats. Vajyapee's BJP won 138 seats, and allied parties won 47. Although the United Progressive Alliance held only about 40 percent of the seats, it was able to form a minority government with the support of India's Communist Party and a collection of smaller parties that agreed to

**TABLE 15.6**

**India's House of the People (Lok Sabha), 2004 (545 seats)**

| Parties | Seats | % of Seats |
|---|---|---|
| United Progressive Alliance | | |
| Congress Party | 145 | 26.6 |
| Other UPA | 75 | 13.7 |
| Left Front (Communist Party and others)[a] | 59 | 10.8 |
| Others[a] | 62 | 11.4 |
| National Democratic Alliance | | |
| BJP | 138 | 25.3 |
| Others | 47 | 8.6 |
| Other parties | 19 | 3.5 |

[a]Declared parliamentary supporters of the UPA government.

vote with the UPA on most bills. These mostly left-leaning parties held 121 seats, more than enough to allow the UPA to govern (see table 15.6).

Shortly after the final vote tallies came in, Sonia Gandhi stunned India by announcing that she would not become prime minister. Cognizant of the opposition within the country, and even within her own party, to having a foreign-born woman lead India, Gandhi stepped aside to allow *Manmohan Singh,* a respected Congress leader, to take the premiership. An economist with degrees from Cambridge and Oxford, Singh had played a critical role in Rao's Congress government in the 1990s, masterminding the government's economic liberalization program. Singh was also India's first Sikh to head the government. Singh put together a coalition government that counted more than twenty parties. Since assuming office in 2004, he has had difficulties building a policy consensus not only within his multiparty cabinet, but also in his dealings with his Communist-led parliamentary partners, who did not always support his policies. But who said governing India is easy?

## HYPOTHESIS-TESTING EXERCISE: India and the Ten Conditions for Democracy

How do India's experiences match up against the ten conditions for democracy we enumerated in chapter 9? In the following hypothesis-testing exercise, we'll test each of these *conditions* as *independent variables* for their impact on *democracy in India,* which is the *dependent variable.* Our expectation is that the presence of these conditions enhances democracy's chances and that their absence reduces them.

### Elites Committed to Democracy

The creators of modern India—Gandhi, Nehru, and their immediate successors—were uniformly committed to democracy, as were most of the elites at the head of the country's major ethnolinguistic and religious groups. Arend Lijphart, who pioneered the concept of *consociational democracy* with respect to countries torn by social strife (see chapter 7), has argued that the consociational model, which stresses the importance of power sharing among the elites representing the main conflicting social groups, explains why democracy survived in India in spite of its teeming social diversity. Lijphart argues that even when India was governed under the Congress Party's large parliamentary majorities, key elements of the consociational model were present at least until the late 1960s.

Subsequently, a breakdown in power-sharing arrangements occurred as Congress lost its grip on the political system and violent political contestation heated up. Even so, Indian elites were careful to retain a sufficient level of power sharing among the country's diverse groups to keep democracy from falling apart entirely. (Indira Gandhi's two-year period of emergency rule in the 1970s was the exception.) In Lijphart's view, these consociational power-sharing efforts best account for the success of Indian democracy.[34] It would appear that consociational power sharing has diminished even further in recent years. Nevertheless, the elites who dominate India's political parties, social groups, and the military do not appear willing to replace it with a non-democratic system. As long as a commitment to this principle endures, democracy itself may endure, strife-torn and turbulent though it may be.

### State Institutions

On the face of it, India appears to be saddled with insurmountable weaknesses in its institutional structures. Fissiparous tendencies rooted in the country's ethnolinguistic and religious heterogeneity are institutionalized in its federal system and exacerbated by separatist movements, creating an enormous "stateness" problem. Dozens of tribal insurgent groups have been fighting incessantly for autonomy or outright independence. Disputes with Pakistan over the Kashmir border complicate matters. Extensive official corruption eats away at public support for state officials and politicians, as do persistent inefficiency and ineffectiveness at all levels of government (see table 4.1). A hundred members of the House of the People were facing criminal charges when elected in 2004. In 2005 the foreign minister resigned after being implicated in the Iraqi "oil-for-food" improprieties (see chapter 1). Political gang warfare wreaks havoc on the electoral process; killings and kidnapings are common in some areas. Police and military personnel routinely abuse their authority, engaging in torture, rape, "disappearances," and murder against insurgents, Muslims, Sikhs, members of the lower castes, women detainees, and other victims. Illegal detentions, the wanton destruction of property, and other abuses have been documented. The judicial arm of the state, while independent, is burdened by a backlog of 30 million cases.

And yet, the central government has thus far managed to hold India's explosive parts together without an all-out civil war or the outright secession of any of its states. Most important, the electoral process retains an enduring legitimacy in the eyes of most Indians. Though turnout is declining at the national level (it fell to 55 percent in 2004), it still exceeds turnout rates in U.S. congressional elections. Political life is lively at the state and local levels; elite and mass support for democracy in principle is widespread. The traditions of parliamentary government adapted from Britain remain intact. And though political contestation is often fierce, no political parties or insurrectionary movements appear poised to impose an authoritarian alternative on the entire country.

## National Unity

Obviously, India is the very opposite of a homogeneous society. In its seven northeast states alone, forty insurgent groups want either autonomy or complete independence. Most are ethnolinguistic or tribal groups. In addition, a relatively small but violent ultra-left communist guerilla movement known as the Naxalites, founded in 1967 in the Naxalbari district, engaged in 1,600 incidents of violence in 2005 alone, displacing tens of thousands of villagers. With about 50,000 cadres spread across a wide "red corridor" in eastern India, the Naxalites seek to mobilize poor peasants, mostly in remote forest areas. Though the movement poses no threat to the central government, its activities have sparked recent countermeasures. Communal violence on the whole was lower in 2005 than in recent years, but tensions persist. Efforts by Singh's government and India's Supreme Court to compel the largely Muslim authorities in Gujarat to prosecute people responsible for the murders and rapes that occurred there in 2002, and to provide restitution to those who were displaced and whose property was destroyed, have met with resistance from Gujarat civil and police officials. Nevertheless, most Indians—including millions of Muslims and the members of India's numerous ethnolinguistic groups—apparently still think of India as a single state, sharing a national identity that bridges the country's myriad divisions. A widely held sense of national unity thus coexists with extraordinary social heterogeneity, religious strife, and separatist tendencies. And most Indians see democracy as the most effective way to keep national unity intact by preventing all-out civil war and permitting the country's various groups to have a say in their own destiny.[35]

## National Wealth

As we observed in chapter 3, India stands out as one of the chief exceptions to the rule correlating national poverty with nondemocratic regimes. With a per capita gross national income (GNI) of a mere $720 in 2005, India is one of the poorest countries in the world by this measure. In 1999–2000, 80 percent of the country's vast population was living on less than $2 a day, and 35 percent were subsisting on less than $1 a day. (By contrast, 47 percent of China's population was living on less than $2 a day, and 17 percent on less than $1 a day.) Women and children are especially harmed by the ravages of poverty. Government programs designed to reduce the causes and effects of chronic underdevelopment have had little impact. At the same time, India's gross national income of $793 billion was the tenth highest in the world in 2005. Its GDP grew at an average rate of 5.8 percent in the 1980s and 5.8 percent from 1991 to 2003, impressive results by any standard. However, Indian officials say that an 8 percent average growth rate is needed in order to provide long-term improvements in living conditions. Thus India's economic status is an ambivalent one: its economy produces considerable aggregate wealth, but not enough to raise the boats of its immense population of more than 1 billion.

India's annual population growth of 1.6 percent is twice that of China's, and India is expected to surpass China in population around 2035. Even if the economy expands by more than 5 percent a year through 2050, per capita GNI will still be very low. Moreover, the economic gains from globalization have been highly concentrated in certain states and urban areas, particularly in the south. Six of India's states, for example, attract almost all its foreign investment.[36] The country's northern states tend to languish in extreme poverty. Efforts to reduce infant and child mortality are losing ground, and India will miss its Millennium Development Goals by 2015. Half of India's children are malnourished; one out of eleven dies before the age of five. Less than half are fully immunized. India's agricultural economy remains a chronic problem: farm output is growing at less than 2 percent a year, and unemployment in the heavily populated rural areas is rising. Prime Minister Singh's government has raised spending on public health, potable water, and rural infrastructure, but the challenges to overcoming decades of underinvestment in these areas are enormous.[37] India's economy thus combines pockets of dynamism with massive poverty. Although poverty of this magnitude would seem to be highly inconsistent with democracy, it has not unleashed a mass outpouring of support for nondemocratic solutions to the country's economic problems.

### Private Enterprise

Efforts to promote private enterprise intensified in the 1990s, especially under Rao's government. Since then, private-sector development has been quite vibrant. A number of government-owned firms have been privatized, and the sums invested in India's stock market nearly tripled in the 1990s. In recent years India has acquired a global reputation as a hub of software production and outsourced services, such as the call-center services increasingly familiar to Americans needing technical support or bank card information. These businesses earned $17 billion in 2004, but that figure represented only 4 percent of India's gross national income. India's much-publicized information technology and business-processing sectors employ only 1.3 million people out of 400 million working Indians. Compared with China, which dominates world manufacturing, India employs only 6.2 million people in its manufacturing sector, fewer than in 1991.[38] At the same time, the state retains a strong economic presence: central government spending actually rose as a percentage of GDP between 1980 (10.8 percent) and 2000 (16.7 percent). Barriers to private-sector development remain, obstructing foreign investment. Nevertheless, neither the persistence of state interventionism nor the uneven growth of private-sector development appears to have affected Indian democracy in any negative way. Proponents of both the state and markets tend to favor democratic methods for obtaining their goals.

### The Middle Class

India's middle class is estimated at 25 percent to 30 percent of the population. In a country with a billion people, that's a sizable segment of society. In conformity with our hypotheses, the Indian middle class has provided a large and consistent bloc of support for democracy. To be sure, many middle-class Indians are gripped by the same ethnolinguistic and religious fervor that characterizes large elements of the rest of the population. On the whole, however, the overwhelming majority of them appear to favor democracy over any authoritarian modes of government, even though they may object to the way democracy works in everyday practice.

### Support of the Disadvantaged for Democracy

If endemic poverty is to constitute a serious threat to democracy, the masses must be mobilized against it as an unacceptable form of government. Thus far, however, no mass political movement has managed to whip up an organized protest of the poor against democracy. On the contrary, political activism is increasingly energized in many of the all-important states in India's federal system.

Although millions of Indian women have made great strides in getting educated and pursuing careers, millions of others are severely disadvantaged, particularly in areas where local authorities turn a blind eye to flagrant abuses. Dowries are outlawed, but thousands of women every year are immolated, beaten, or driven to suicide in dowry disputes. Rapes and other violent offenses are often unreported or ignored by police and judicial officials. Male births inordinately outnumber female births in several states, no doubt because of abortion and infanticide aimed at girls. These practices account for a shortfall of 40 million Indian women. Girls between the ages of one and five are 50 percent more likely to die than boys, and female mortality rates remain higher than those for boys through the age of thirty. Women are often discriminated against in a variety of ways in accordance with Hindu or Muslim traditions. And throughout India, hundreds of millions of women are the victims of the "feminization of poverty," bearing the brunt of subsistence-level living conditions. Gender inequality is thus both a source of flagrant human rights abuses and an obstacle to economic development. To remedy these problems, politically and socially active Indian women have demanded more democracy, not less. Women have entered voting booths and run for office at growing rates, at times pulling even with men. (Women won only 8.3 percent of the seats in the House of the People in 2004, however.) Meanwhile, discrimination against India's 160 million untouchables—now known as *dilats* (the downtrodden)—remains rampant. Child prostitution is also pervasive, and there are reportedly as many as 90 million child laborers toiling in atrocious conditions.[39]

In most cases, however, apathy and resignation, rather than revolutionary unrest, mark the political attitudes of India's destitute masses. In a culture suffused with Hinduism, the eternal mysteries of karma and divine intervention assume a far greater immediacy in the lives of the multitudes than the mundane practicalities of politics. On a less ethereal plane, the simple struggle to survive from one day to the next leaves little time to care about elections and party programs. While support for democracy may not be the consequence, there is little in the way of mass opposition to it, either.

### Citizen Participation, Civil Society, and a Democratic Political Culture

In a country as variegated as India, torn by so many unresolved conflicts, it should not be surprising to find that a thriving civil society shares the social landscape with a notoriously uncivil, violence-prone society. To some extent, the cause of civil society in India has made some noteworthy advances in recent years. There are an estimated one million nongovernmental organizations in India. Women's rights groups are proliferating, and human rights organizations have also become more active. Trade unions are organized and energetic. And civil society has played an especially important role in curbing Hindu-Muslim violence. Ashutosh Varshney has shown that India's periodic outbursts of sectarian violence are largely concentrated in a few cities. Rural India, where two-thirds of the population live, is basically quiet, as are most of India's populous urban areas. Varshney's analysis shows that associational civic groups with mixed Hindu and Muslim memberships—business associations, labor unions, and the like—are often quite effective at halting communal violence in various cities before it gets out of hand. In some cases neighborhood peace committees reinforce these channels of communication. In rural areas, more informal, day-to-day personal contacts across the religious divide are often similarly effective at keeping peace between Hindus and Muslims.[40] India's experiences with civil society are therefore very mixed: some non-state organizations exist mainly to exacerbate social and political conflict, thereby undermining democracy, while others seek to reduce conflict in a democratic spirit.

### Education and Freedom of Information

Here, too, India's record is a tangle of contradictions. The country can boast millions of college graduates and recipients of graduate and professional degrees. Advanced technology and MBA programs are proliferating. The seven Indian Institutes of Technology (IITs) boast of being more selective than MIT or Harvard. Many college grads remain unemployed for years, however. Illiteracy is a mass phenomenon, affecting one-third of males over age fifteen and more than 60 percent of females. By contrast, 87 percent of adult women in China are literate.[41] India's ethnic disputes have found their way into classrooms: in 2002, Vajpayee's government introduced new textbooks reflecting extremist Hindu interpretations of India history. Singh's government has replaced them with texts presenting more balanced interpretations.

India's press freedoms are secure: national and local newspapers and magazines thrive. There is no censorship. Journalists have been physically attacked for their political views, however. The Indian government holds a monopoly on domestic television broadcasting, but foreign-based networks have been allowed to broadcast in recent years. Radio and television stations are mostly in private hands, but All India Radio dominates the airwaves. There are no Internet restrictions.

### A Favorable International Environment

India's external environment is also a source of both negative and positive influences on its democratic order. Its tormented relationship with Pakistan inevitably has an impact on the delicate ties between Hindus and Muslims in India itself. Terrorists bent on Kashmir's separation from India were responsible not only for the December 2001 attack on India's parliament but also for a bombing in Mumbai (Bombay) in 2006 that killed more than 180 people. The Kashmir conflict has cost some 80,000 lives since the early 1990s. Although Prime Minister Singh blamed Pakistan's government for failing to rein in the terrorist groups, he met with Pakistan's President Musharraf in Havana in 2006 to explore ways of dealing with future terrorist activities. India's status as a nuclear power, while a source of pride for most Indians, has prompted warnings by opponents of nuclear saber-rattling that the country should not pursue a potentially dangerous militarism. India is not a signatory of the Nuclear Non-Proliferation Treaty. Nevertheless, the Bush administration agreed to cooperate with India in providing nuclear material for its civilian energy sector. (India is heavily dependent on Iran for energy.) India also has a long-standing border conflict with China, but relations between the two neighboring giants have been improving. India's international environment appears to pose no threat to its democracy.[42]

---

In 2005 India had Freedom House ratings of 2 for political rights and 3 for civil rights. What is most striking about India's democracy is that several of the factors that we tend to think of as potentially crippling for democratic governance—such as ubiquitous poverty, violence-prone social heterogeneity, and a vast cohort of grievously disadvantaged people—have not combined to smother democracy in India once and for all. On the contrary, a commitment to democratic ideals and practices is powerfully present throughout the country. Amartya Sen argues that India's conflicting cultural and intellectual traditions are the very sources of its tolerance for diversity and its widely shared commitment to democracy.[43]

Will India's democracy survive? This question has sparked a decades-long debate between optimists and pessimists. Both must come to grips with the extraordinary complexities of a country that combines high-tech modernity with timeless traditionalism. In the 1960s India developed the capability to produce nuclear weapons. In 1980 it launched the first in a series of space satellites. In 1994 an outbreak of pneumonic plague occurred in the rat-infested city of Surat. Prior to the epidemic, the city government had no program for eliminating the rodents because they are worshiped by Hindus as the companions of Ganesha, an elephant-headed god.[44]

### KEY TERMS AND NAMES
### (In bold and underlined in the text)

Newly industrializing countries (NICs)
Underdeveloped economies
Dependency theory
Mohandas Gandhi

### NOTES

1. On South Korea, see Sung-Joo Han, "South Korea: Politics in Transition," in *Politics in Developing Countries,* ed. Larry Diamond, Juan J. Linz, and Seymour Martin Lipset (Boulder, Colo.: Lynne Rienner, 1990), 313–50; Stephan Haggard, *Pathways from the Periphery* (Ithaca, N.Y.: Cornell University Press, 1990), 51–75, 130–38; Nigel Harris, *The End of the Third World* (London: Penguin, 1986), 31–45; Robert Garran, *Tigers Tamed* (Honolulu: University of Hawaii Press, 1998), 119–36; Dennis L. McNamara, ed., *Corporatism and Korean Capitalism* (London: Routledge, 1999); and *The Kwangju Uprising,* Henry Scott-Stokes and Jai Eui, eds. (Armonk, N.Y.: M. E. Sharpe, 2000). See also Michael E. O'Hanlon and Mike Mochizuki, "Toward a Grand Bargain with North Korea," *Washington Quarterly* 26, no. 4 (Autumn 2003), 7–18.
2. *Human Development Report 2005* (New York: United Nations Development Program, 2005), 1–48, passim.
3. See W. W. Rostow, *The Stages of Economic Growth,* 3rd ed. (Cambridge: Cambridge University Press, 1990).
4. *Human Development Report 2005,* 19–21, 40–45.
5. For an overview, see John Rapley, *Understanding Development: Theory and Practice in the Third World,* 2nd ed. (Boulder, Colo.: Lynne Rienner, 2002).
6. Amartya Sen, "The Economics of Life and Death," *Scientific American,* May 1993, 40–47, and Sen, "Demography and Welfare Economics," *Empirica,* no. 22 (1995), 1–27.
7. *Financial Times,* February 8–9, 2003; *New York Times,* July 20, 2003.
8. Daniel Lerner, *The Passing of Traditional Society* (New York: Free Press, 1958); David E. Apter, *The Politics of Modernization* (Chicago: University of Chicago Press, 1965); Cyril E. Black, ed., *Comparative Modernization: A Reader* (New York: Free Press, 1976).
9. For a critical appraisal, see Irene L. Gendzier, *Managing Political Change: Social Scientists and the Third World* (Boulder, Colo.: Westview, 1985). An early study that recognized a mixture of the traditional and the modern in developing countries is Gabriel A. Almond and James S. Coleman, eds., *The Politics of the Developing Areas* (Princeton: Princeton University Press, 1960).
10. Atul Kohli, *State-directed Development: Political Power and Industrialization in the Global Periphery* (New York: Cambridge University Press, 2004).
11. Guillermo Perry, Omar Arias, Humberto Lopez, William Maloney, and Luis Serven, *Poverty Reduction and Growth: Virtuous and Vicious Circles* (Washington, D.C.: World Bank, 2006). See also Marcela Sanchez, "A New Path on Latin Poverty?" *Washington Post,* February 18, 2006.
12. Jeffrey Sachs, *The End of Poverty. Economic Possibilities for Our Time* (New York: Penguin, 2005), 57–59, 188–209, 311–28.

13. Joseph L. Love, "Raul Prebisch and the Origins of the Doctrine of Unequal Exchange," *Latin American Research Review* 15, no. 3 (1980); Mahbub ul Haq, *The Poverty Curtain: Choices for the Third World* (New York: Columbia University Press, 1976).
14. For examples of dependency theory see Fernando Henrique Cardoso and Enzo Faletto, *Dependency and Development in Latin America*, trans. Marjory Mattingly Urquidi (Berkeley: University of California Press, 1979); André Gunder Frank, *Capitalism and Underdevelopment in Latin America* (London: Penguin, 1970); and Frank, *Critique and Anti-Critique* (New York: Praeger, 1971). On the capitalist world-system, see Immanuel Wallerstein, *The Capitalist World-Economy* (Cambridge: Cambridge University Press, 1979) and *The Politics of the World-Economy* (New York: Cambridge University Press, 1984). For review essays, see James A. Caporoso, "Dependency Theory: Continuities and Discontinuities in Development Studies," *International Organization* 34, no. 4 (autumn 1980): 605–28, and Tony Smith, "Requiem or New Agenda for Third World Studies?" *World Politics* 37, no. 4 (July 1985): 532–61.
15. *Human Development Report 2005,* 113–48.
16. Ibid., 75–85.
17. Sachs, *The End of Poverty,* 290–308.
18. William Easterly, *The White Man's Burden. Why the West's Efforts to Aid the Rest of the World Have Done So Much Ill and So Little Good* (New York: Penguin, 2006). Easterly does not reject foreign aid out of hand, but argues that it can be distributed to needy individuals far more effectively by people who know the local conditions than it can by planners in international agencies.
19. Lloyd G. Reynolds, *Economic Growth in the Third World* (New Haven: Yale University Press, 1985).
20. William Easterly, *The Elusive Quest for Growth: Economists' Adventures and Misadventures in the Tropics* (Cambridge, Mass.: MIT Press, 2002).
21. *The Arab Human Development Report 2004: Towards Freedom in the Arab World* (New York: United Nations Development Program, 2005); and *Better Government for Development in the Middle East and North Africa: Enhancing Inclusiveness and Accountability* (Washington, D.C.: World Bank, 2003).
22. For definitions of the World Bank's six governance indicators and other information, see Daniel Kaufmann, Aart Kraay, and Massimo Mastruzzi, *Governance Matters 2006: Worldwide Governance Indicators,* accessible at www.siteresources.worldbank.org. See also www.worldbank.org/wbi/governance and www.govindicators.org.
23. Samuel P. Huntington, *Political Order in Changing Societies* (New Haven, Conn.: Yale University Press, 1968); Samuel P. Huntington and Joan M. Nelson, *No Easy Choice: Political Participation in Developing Countries* (Cambridge, Mass.: Harvard University Press, 1976).
24. Mancur Olson, "Dictatorship, Democracy, and Development," *American Political Science Review* 87, no. 3 (September 1993): 567–76. Elsewhere, Olson argued that narrowly based political or social groups, like India's caste system, can impede economic development. See *The Rise and Decline of Nations* (New Haven: Yale University Press, 1982). Emphasizing the rule of law, Hernando de Soto contends that the key to capitalism's success in the West and Japan is codified property laws, which many developing countries lack. See *The Mystery of Capital: Why Capitalism Triumphs in the West and Fails Everywhere Else* (New York: Basic Books, 2000).
25. Adam Przeworski, Michael E. Alvarez, Jose Antonio Cheibub, and Fernando Limongi, *Democracy and Development: Political Institutions and Well-Being in the World, 1950–1990* (Cambridge: Cambridge University Press, 2000), 103, 106, 178–79, 212–13.
26. John Gerring, Philip Bond, William T. Brandt, and Carola Moreno, "Democracy and Economic Growth: A Historical Perspective," *World Politics* 57, no. 3 (April 2005), 323–64.
27. Larry Diamond, Juan J. Linz, and Seymour Martin Lipset, eds., *Democracy in Developing Countries* (Boulder, Colo.: Lynne Rienner, 1988), and *Politics in Developing Countries,* 2nd ed. (Boulder, Colo.: Lynne Rienner, 1995). See also Larry Diamond, *Developing Democracy* (Baltimore: Johns Hopkins, 1999), and Stephan Haggard and Robert R. Kaufman, eds., *The Political Economy of Democratic Transitions* (Princeton: Princeton University Press, 1995).

**28.** Amartya Sen, *Development as Freedom* (New York: Random House, 1999).

**29.** On Gandhi and the origins of independent India and Pakistan, see Larry Collins and Dominique Lapierre, *Freedom at Midnight* (New York: Simon & Schuster, 1975). For a biography of Gandhi by a prominent psychologist, see Erik H. Erikson, *Gandhi's Truth* (New York: W. W. Norton, 1969). See also Richard Attenborough's epic film *Gandhi.*

**30.** Myron Weiner, *Party Building in a New Nation: The Indian National Congress* (Chicago: Chicago University Press, 1967); Samuel J. Eldersveld and Bashiruddin Ahmed, *Citizens and Politics: Mass Political Behavior in India* (Chicago: University of Chicago Press, 1978).

**31.** Shashi Tharoor, *Nehru: The Invention of India* (New York: Arcade, 2003).

**32.** Amrita Basu and Atul Kohli, *Community Conflicts and the State in India* (Delhi: Oxford University Press, 1998).

**33.** Katherine Frank, *Indira: The Life of Indira Nehru Gandhi* (London: HarperCollins, 2001).

**34.** Arend Lijphart, "The Puzzle of Indian Democracy; A Consociational Interpretation," *American Political Science Review* 90, no. 2 (June 1996): 258–68.

**35.** On India's diversity, see Robert W. Stern, *Changing India: Bourgeois Revolution on the Subcontinent,* 2nd ed. (Cambridge: Cambridge University Press, 2003). See also Amartya Sen, *Identity and Violence: The Illusion of Destiny* (New York: Norton, 2006).

**36.** "The Tiger in Front: A Survey of India and China," *The Economist,* March 5, 2005. See also "Now for the Hard Part: A Survey of Business in India," *The Economist,* June 3, 2006; and "India's Shining Hopes: A Survey of India," *The Economist,* February 21, 2004.

**37.** *Human Development Report 2005,* 30–31.

**38.** Pankaj Mishra, "The Myth of the New India," *Washington Post,* July 6, 2006.

**39.** *Financial Times,* February 8–9, 2003; *Sun* (Baltimore), September 30, 1999; *Freedom in the World 2006* (New York: Freedom House, 2006), 323–28.

**40.** Ashutosh Varshney, *Ethnic Conflict and Civic Life: Hindus and Muslims in India,* 2nd ed. (New Haven: Yale University Press, 2000).

**41.** On India's educational system, see Thomas Friedman, *The World Is Flat: A Brief History of the Twenty-first Century* (New York: Farrar, Straus and Giroux, 2005), 104–5, 261–62, 465–68.

**42.** Stephen Cohen, *India: Emerging Power* (Washington, D.C.: Brookings Institution, 2001).

**43.** Amartya Sen, *The Argumentative Indian: Writings on Indian History, Culture and Identity* (New York: Farrar, Straus and Giroux, 2005).

**44.** *Washington Post,* September 27, 1994.

PART TWO

# COUNTRIES AND LEADERS

# CHAPTER 16

# THE UNITED KINGDOM OF GREAT BRITAIN AND NORTHERN IRELAND

Population (2005, estimated): 60.1 million
Freedom House Ratings (2005):
Political Rights—1; Civil Liberties—1

Area: 94,251 square miles
(smaller than Oregon)

*Source:* U.S. Central Intelligence Agency.

**Gordon Brown (left) and Tony Blair leave the stage at the end of the Labour Party Autumn Conference on September 28, 2006.**

"I know I look a lot older," Prime Minister **Tony Blair** confessed to several thousand delegates attending the Labour Party's annual conference in 2006. "That's what being leader of the Labour Party does to you. Actually," he continued, "looking round, some of you look a lot older. That's what having me as leader of the Labour Party does to you." For many delegates who joined in the laughter, Blair's jests had the ring of truth. Although Blair had led the party to three successive election victories in 1997, 2001, and 2005—a feat never before accomplished by previous Labour leaders—a large number of party members wanted him to resign as party chief. By resigning as head of the largest party in the House of Commons, Blair would be expected to resign as the United Kingdom's prime minister as well. By tradition in Britain's *parliamentary government,* the official leader of the largest party in the Commons becomes the UK's *head of government*, or *prime minister.* When the party that governs the UK changes its leader, it thereupon selects a new head of government, without necessarily soliciting the voters' approval for the change in immediate new elections.

Pressures on Blair to step down had been mounting since literally the morning after Labour's historic third straight victory in the spring of 2005. Over the course of the following year, the prime minister's public approval ratings sank to 27 percent. Despite enjoying a 66-seat voting majority in the House of Commons, Blair's government suffered some stinging defeats. Its plan to detain suspected terrorists for ninety days was rejected, with forty-nine Labour members voting against it. (Months later the Commons passed a watered-down bill, permitting detentions up to twenty-eight days.) Blair also had to alter his proposal to raise college tuition fees before members of his own party would accept it. Some Labourites disapproved of Blair's plans to invite private companies to play a larger role in health care, transportation, and other areas traditionally regarded by the party as government responsibilities. Financial improprieties and sex scandals forced the resignation of key cabinet ministers, prompting charges of sleaze. In the spring of 2006, disastrous Labour defeats in local elections prompted Blair to reassign several cabinet members, an action characterized by critics as a sign of desperation. And in September, only weeks before Blair joked at the party conference about looking older, eight members of his cabinet dramatically quit their posts in an effort to compel him to set his departure date. The next day, Blair announced that he would resign as party chief—and as prime minister—within a year. "Next year I won't be making this speech," he later told the conference delegates. Blair thus planned to step down in 2007, ten years after assuming office as Britain's first Labour Party prime minister since 1979.

What went wrong? How could Tony Blair lead his party to three overwhelming victories, each resulting in large majorities in the House of Commons, only to be forced from office by members of his own party? One problem that constantly dogged Blair was a matter of leadership style. Many of his critics, both inside and outside the Labour party, accused Blair of being a "control freak": they objected to his practice of tightly keeping the reins of policy making in his own hands, and in those of a few intimate advisors, while shunting to the sidelines other Labour Party personalities and policy organs, including his own cabinet. They also faulted Blair for indulging in too much "spin," accusing him of making bold promises without delivering and of exaggerating his government's achievements.

But by far the most stinging rebuke that many Britons leveled at Blair centered on his support for the invasion of Iraq and on his close ties to President George W. Bush. Opposition to the invasion began spreading even before the fighting began. In February 2003 a million people gathered in London to protest the impending war. On March 18, only a few days before the attack, 139 Labour Party Members of Parliament (MPs) voted against the Blair government's parliamentary resolution calling for the use of "all means necessary," including military force, in Iraq. Forty more Labour members abstained. Fortunately for Blair, the Labour Party had more than 400 representatives. A majority of them voted for the war resolution, enough to pass the measure. Most Conservative Party MPs also supported the nonbinding resolution, which passed by a vote of 412 to 149. The Labour MPs' votes against Blair's resolution constituted the biggest parliamentary revolt by House of Commons members against their own party's government since the nineteenth century. At the same time, a former foreign affairs minister and two junior ministers resigned from Blair's cabinet over the war, and another senior minister resigned soon after the war started. Although more than 70 percent of Britons expressed their approval of the invasion once it got under way and Saddam Hussein's regime was swept from power, support for the venture plummeted rapidly as events in Iraq spun out of control. By summer less than half the British public concurred that the decision to invade was right.

Blair himself was increasingly accused of deception in stating his case for war. Critics charged his government with "sexing up" its assertions that Saddam Hussein's weapons of mass destruction posed a major threat to British security. The prime minister was personally berated in placards denouncing him as "B-liar." Two inquiries cleared the government of outright deception. But the first investigation failed to quell rising public distrust, and the second slighted the government for deliberate ambiguities in its disclosures of intelligence on Saddam's weapons capabilities. The failure to find any weapons of mass destruction in Iraq only intensified suspicions about Blair's truthfulness. By 2004, 39 percent of British respondents in a public opinion poll said that Blair had "exaggerated" the threat posed by Saddam, and 25 percent accused him of knowing all along that Iraq had no weapons of mass destruction and of simply lying about it. As the 2005 election campaign heated up, secret documents were leaked indicating that Blair had not fully shared important information about the Iraq situation with Parliament or the public. Blair himself was subjected to humiliating criticisms in televised meetings with voters during the campaign. And though the 2005 elections returned a large Labour Party majority to the House of Commons, the party dropped 6 percent of the voters it had won in 2001 and lost 47 seats in the Commons to other parties. Doubts about Blair's trustworthiness played a major role in turning many former supporters against the prime minister and his party.

Blair's successor as the Labour Party's new chief—and as the UK's new prime minister—was expected to be **Gordon Brown**. Ever since Blair had formed his first government in 1997, Brown had served as *chancellor of the exchequer,* the stately medieval title of the cabinet minister responsible for the British government's economic policy. Long regarded as the Labour Party's number two behind Blair, and as Blair's main rival for the mantle of party leader ever since the 1990s, Brown had presided over the most successful economy Britain had seen in decades. Thanks to steady growth and low inflation, Britain's GDP surpassed that of France and Germany during the Labour government's first two terms. And Britain's low unemployment rates were the envy of Europe, falling at times to less than half the double-digit figures that persistently troubled France, Germany, and other European economies. Brown garnered much of the credit for keeping the British economy on course for ten years and for changing the long-held public perception that the Labour Party could not manage the economy as well as the Conservatives. But how would Brown perform in the much larger role of prime minister?

For all his detractors' criticisms, Blair would be a hard act to follow. Few could deny his charismatic flair and rhetorical brilliance. Blair was a master of the gladiatorial confrontations with politicians of the main opposition parties, the Conservatives and the Liberal Democrats, that take place in the House of Commons. Blair had played the primary role in leading the Labour Party closer to the center of the

British political spectrum, pulling it away from the state-centered economic doctrines and trade union influences strongly favored by the party's powerful left wing. In shaping what he called the "New Labour Party," Blair set the stage for the landslide electoral victory that restored the Labour Party to power in 1997 after eighteen years of Conservative governments under Margaret Thatcher and John Major. And whatever their failings may have been, Blair's governments could claim real achievements. Not only could they boast of a robust economy; they could also point to measurable improvements in health care, education, and other public services.

Blair also engineered major constitutional changes in the world's oldest continuing democracy. The proper name of what we commonly call "Britain" is the *United Kingdom of Great Britain and Northern Ireland* (or the *UK*). Great Britain consists of England, Scotland, and Wales. Northern Ireland is juridically separate from the sovereign republic of Ireland, which is an independent country. These four regions of the UK all elect representatives to the House of Commons and recognize the monarch as the UK's *head of state.* For much of its history, the United Kingdom has been a *unitary state:* most political decisions have been taken by the central government and Parliament in London, with very little decision-making authority left to regional or local governments. In his first term as prime minister, Tony Blair secured the *devolution* of local decision-making power to newly created legislatures in Scotland and Wales. He also began the process of reviving Northern Ireland's defunct local parliament in the aftermath of the 1998 "Good Friday Accords," which were aimed at ending decades of violent conflict between Protestants and Catholics in that troubled region. In the process, Blair moved the UK closer to the model of a *federal* state (see chapter 8). Another constitutional change was the paring down of inherited memberships in the House of Lords, Britain's unelected upper house of Parliament. And in a country that lacked a written Bill of Rights, Blair's government adopted the European Convention on Human Rights, a comprehensive list of civil rights drawn up by West European governments after World War II, as British law. This measure enabled UK citizens to take their human rights cases directly to British courts instead of having to travel to the European Court of Human Rights in France.

In the wake of the September 11 terrorist attacks in the United States, Blair ultimately got Parliament to tighten legal restrictions on suspected terrorists. Despite charges that his proposals trampled on Britain's traditional civil rights and liberties, Blair regarded them as especially necessary after British-born Islamic terrorists set off bombs in London on July 7, 2005, killing fifty-two people and wounding more than seven hundred. Some of the new rules were applied after a potentially devastating plane hijacking plot was foiled in Britain in the summer of 2006. Blair also moved the UK closer to its partners in the European Union on a number of issues, without surrendering British sovereignty on key foreign policy issues and without giving up the pound in favor of the euro, the common European currency used by twelve other EU member countries. Whether Blair succeeded in recasting the country's traditional stodgy image into "Cool Britannia," as he once proposed, may be debatable. But his governments' successes in shedding Britain's reputation as the economic "sick man of Europe" and as Europe's contentious odd man out—the reputations it bore in the 1970s, 1980s, and 1990s—are beyond dispute. Finally, in spite of all its problems, the Labour Party did win a substantial victory in 2005. Its archrivals, the Conservatives, failed to capitalize on Blair's difficulties.

As these pages went to press, it was far too early to assess Gordon Brown's impact on Britain and its place in the world. This chapter provides an overview of the Britain that Gordon Brown was set to inherit. It begins with a historical survey of British democracy and its political institutions. It then moves on to the main issues, leaders, and institutional arrangements of postwar Britain, demonstrating how quite a few of the problems and attitudes that we find in Britain today have their roots in the political controversies of the past two generations. Along the way, we'll see how the British have dealt with the five main sources of political conflict we identified in chapter 2:

- *Power:* Who has governed Britain? How have contending social groups, parties, and interest groups influenced the state and its policies?
- *Resources:* How has the country's wealth been owned and distributed? What roles have the state and markets played in the British economy?

- *Identity:* How have class, regional, and religious conflicts affected British politics?
- *Ideas:* How did British democracy develop? What does "socialism" mean in Britain?
- *Values:* Should Britain attach a higher priority to individual freedom or to community welfare? How tolerant are the British?

Questions like these cannot be answered without a close look at Britain's past. Let's begin with its long road from monarchy to democracy.

## HISTORICAL BACKGROUND: THE EVOLUTION OF BRITISH DEMOCRACY

In some countries, democracy came about as the result of a fairly sudden turn of events. Examples include the American revolution, the periodic swings between military rule and democracy that have taken place in various Latin American nations, and the outbursts of democracy in Russia and Eastern Europe that accompanied the collapse of communism. By contrast, democracy developed in Britain in a slow, piecemeal fashion that took centuries to unfold. Evolution, not revolution, has characterized the British democratic experience.

Following the collapse of the Roman Empire in the fifth century, England was governed by a succession of monarchs until the middle of the seventeenth century. Though most of them ruled through military force and other forms of coercive power, from the Middle Ages onward there was a growing tendency to justify the crown's legitimacy according to the **divine right of kings**, ***the doctrine asserting that the monarch derived his or her power from God and not from the people.*** The concept of divine right provided the legal basis for **sovereign monarchy**, or **absolutism**, ***which meant that the monarch was the supreme political authority in the land and enjoyed the right to absolute power.*** Rarely, however, did the crown sit easily on the English monarch's head. Challenges to individual claimants to the throne, as well as to royal authority itself, were frequent and sometimes violent. Over the span of centuries, rivalries over the coveted English crown fueled dynastic wars with France and Spain as well as civil wars, palace intrigues, and strategic marriages involving both native and foreign-born noble families.

The first real break with the principle of monarchy occurred in the 1640s. Civil war led to the defeat of the royal army, followed by the trial and decapitation of King Charles I. In 1649, England was declared a republic for the first time in its history. Oliver Cromwell, a commoner rather than a nobleman, ascended to power and ruled as "Lord Protector" under the country's first written constitution. Shortly after Cromwell died, the monarchy was restored in 1660. A monarch has served as Britain's official head of state ever since, though with diminishing effective power.

Other countries have also experienced extended periods of sovereign monarchy. For hundreds of years France, Spain, Germany, Russia, China, and Japan, to mention only a few, were governed by kings, queens, or emperors who asserted their royal preeminence over all other institutions and political forces within their respective realms. In stark contrast to these countries, England began moving as early as the thirteenth century toward a less autocratic form of monarchical power. When viewed in comparative perspective, England's gradual evolution to democracy under the aegis of monarchy stands out as one of very few examples of such a transition. What accounts for it?

As we saw in our discussion of conditions for democracy in chapter 9, the forging of a successful democratic system usually requires a constellation of favorable factors, not just one or two. Britain began developing most of these conditions at exceptionally early stages in its history. They included:

- Parliament, a *state institution* of paramount importance that fostered *elites* opposed to royal absolutism and dedicated to the rule of law
- English nationalism, which took a form that proved especially favorable for the creation of a democratic *political culture*
- *private enterprise,* which promoted *national wealth* and the development of a democratic *middle class*
- political parties that embraced democracy rather than anti-democratic ideologies, bringing *disadvantaged* groups like the working class into the democratic fold; trade unions and other elements of *civil society* also promoted democratic practices
- a system of *education,* centered in universities like Oxford and Cambridge, that fostered freedom of thought, scientific inquiry, and artistic creativity.

Meanwhile, the British have found ways to deal with a number of serious challenges that at various times have threatened to place democracy in jeopardy or severely limited its scope.

- From its very inception the United Kingdom suffered from weak *national unity:* it was formed by force, as England compelled Wales, Scotland, and Ireland to join it in forming a unified state under the English monarchy. In 1922 a self-governing state was created in the south of Ireland, where Catholics had a majority, while six largely Protestant counties remained in the United Kingdom as Northern Ireland. The consequences of the UK's formation are still being addressed through the government's devolution policies.
- Britain's *elites,* though committed to Parliament, took a long time to permit popular sovereignty, granting the vote to the mass citizenry only in the twentieth century.
- Glaring socioeconomic inequalities produced fairly rigid class distinctions that still leave many Britons feeling *disadvantaged* and excluded from the full range of political and social opportunities democracy is expected to provide.
- A frequently tumultuous *international environment* has included more than two centuries of imperialism, two world wars, the Cold War and the complicated post-Cold-War order, with its challenges of globalization and terrorism.

## The Mother of Parliaments

Parliament began in England as an extension of monarchical rule. In 1212 and 1213, King John summoned various clergymen, barons, knights, and other prominent personages "to speak with us concerning the affairs of our realm." The term *parliament* derives from the French *parler,* "to speak." From the outset, however, these elites displayed a marked interest in protecting their own powers and liberties as prelates of the Catholic Church or as leaders of England's counties and villages. In 1215 they prevailed upon King John to sign the **Magna Carta** (the Great Charter), ***a document specifying their rights in such matters as taxation, judicial appointments, and private property.*** The Magna Carta affirmed the *rule of law,* plainly indicating that there were limits to the king's sovereign power and that the monarchy was not above the law. A Parliament summoned in 1265 included representatives of the common elements of society—the equivalent of the middle classes—rather than just the upper ranks of the nobility and church.

These ideas and practices solidified during the fourteenth century as a succession of monarchs called Parliament into session with growing frequency and acknowledged its responsibility in providing advice and passing legislation. In the process the institution became divided into two houses. The "lords spiritual and temporal" consisted of bishops and other members of the cloth, along with earls, dukes, and various members of the country's higher nobility. The "commons" consisted of knights and other elements of the so-called lesser nobility, together with "burgesses," who were prominent citizens from local communities. Typically the crown summoned the **House of Lords** into session by invitation and appointed many of its members to lifetime noble ranks (peerages); eventually, most Lords inherited their seats. The **House of Commons** was usually elected by local property-owning elites in counties and towns. By the late 1370s it was generally accepted that no statutes could be issued without parliamentary consent. The House of Lords was developing into England's highest court, while the Commons acquired the right to approve taxes.

Over the next two centuries Parliament became a permanent fixture of England's governmental system. Even Cromwell relied on parliamentary support, and it was Parliament that restored the monarchy after his death.[1]

Despite its importance, Parliament remained constitutionally subordinate to the crown until the late seventeenth century. England's monarchs insisted that their reliance on parliamentary consent in no way compromised the principle of sovereign monarchy or the doctrine of divine right. They viewed Parliament as an instrument of monarchical rule, not as a democratic substitute for it. Most members of Parliament shared this notion until the dramatic events of 1688–89 brought about a fundamental reordering in the balance of constitutional power in England.

James II, a Catholic, assumed the throne in 1685. England was by now a predominantly Protestant country, however. Its Protestant Reformation had begun in the 1530s when King Henry VIII broke with the Roman Catholic Church and established the Church of England (or Anglican Church), with himself as its head. (To this day the British monarch is still the official head of the Anglican Church, which is the country's *established church.*) James II managed to antagonize virtually all the leading elements of English society through his efforts to restore Catholics to the political prominence they had once enjoyed before the Reformation and through his determination to assert royal powers in the face of widespread opposition to autocratic rule. Acting with extraordinary boldness, the king's opponents invited the Dutch monarch William of Orange to invade England and take power. William was married to James II's daughter Mary, and his own family had distant ties to the English aristocracy. Just as significant, he was a Protestant who proclaimed his willingness to respect the rights of Parliament and the established liberties of English society. Upon William's arrival in England at the end of 1688, King James fled into exile. A special parliamentary assembly thereupon declared that James had abdicated the throne and bestowed the monarchy jointly on King William and Queen Mary. For the first time in English history, Parliament had deposed one king and elected another. A declaration of parliamentary rights issued in early 1689 explicitly forbade the crown from suspending the laws of the land without Parliament's approval.

These events, occurring without bloodshed, are celebrated as England's *Glorious Revolution*. They established a solid precedent for *parliamentary supremacy,* which evolved over the following centuries into the foundation stone of modern British government. <u>**Parliamentary supremacy**</u> ***means that Parliament—not the crown, the courts, or any other institution—is the supreme authority in the British political system.***[2]

Over the course of the eighteenth and nineteenth centuries, Parliament persistently whittled away at the monarch's remaining powers. In the process, Britain's system of government became a *constitutional monarchy*, a system in which the monarch performs the largely symbolic functions of a ceremonial head of state while day-to-day decision making rests firmly in the hands of a prime minister and cabinet, backed by their supporters in Parliament. "The monarch reigns but the government rules" became the standard characterization of this system.

Despite the fact that Parliament and the cabinet today are by far the most important decision-making institutions in the land, the monarch possesses a few traditional political prerogatives that have not been formally abolished. Specifically, the crown retains the legal authority to call parliamentary elections and name the prime minister. Every election to the House of Commons is preceded by an election proclamation by the monarch, and every change of government is accompanied by a "kissing of hands" ceremony in which the queen symbolically designates her prime minister. The fact that the queen now takes these and other actions upon the advice of the leadership of the House of Commons rather than on her own initiative indicates that Parliament has the upper hand in practice. But Parliament has not abrogated these monarchical privileges in legal theory. In the official language of British constitutional law, the basis of Britain's system of government consists of "the queen (or king) in Parliament." In other words, the monarch is *part of* Parliament (but is not a voting member).

Parliament today not only stands politically supreme over a constitutional monarchy; it is also Britain's highest judicial authority. The United Kingdom never developed a Supreme Court like the United States, or a European-style constitutional court that is empowered to declare acts of Parliament unconstitutional. Laws passed by Parliament are thus not subject to judicial review and can be amended or abolished only by Parliament itself.

Meanwhile, the balance of power between Parliament and the *government* (the cabinet plus additional ministers) has undergone its own evolution. By the nineteenth century the Parliament's legislative powers and the cabinet's executive powers had become *fused.* Under the influence of increasingly assertive prime ministers and the rise of political parties, Britain in the nineteenth century possessed an institutional framework in which:

1. the qualified electorate voted for the House of Commons, whereupon
2. the Commons advised the monarch in selecting the prime minister, held the government accountable for its actions, and enacted bills into law.

The Commons also acquired the right to dismiss governments and form new ones, while the prime

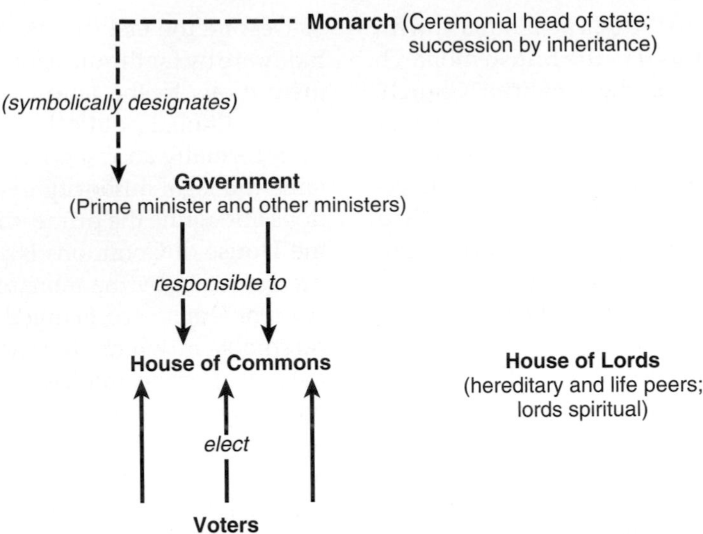


**FIGURE 16.1 Britain's Parliamentary Government**

minister acquired the right to advise the monarch to dissolve the Commons and order new elections. Because Parliament was housed in Westminster Palace, this system of government became known as the *Westminster system.* (See figure 16.1.)[3] Chapter 8 describes this system in general terms. We'll examine how it works in contemporary Britain later in this chapter.

Two additional developments occurring over the nineteenth and twentieth centuries strengthened the democratic aspects of this evolving system: the expansion of the franchise and the ascendancy of the Commons over the House of Lords.

Just as it took centuries for Parliament to become the institutional bedrock of democracy, it also took Britain a long time to confer the right to vote on all its adult citizens. Only in the twentieth century was the franchise extended to virtually all adult males and females.

- Prior to 1832, only males who met stringent property-owning requirements had the right to vote, a group constituting only 5 percent of all adults over the age of twenty-one.
- The Great Reform Act of 1832 extended the franchise to about 7 percent of the adult population, while continuing to limit it to men of property.
- Another voting reform passed in 1867 eased these qualifications somewhat, enabling a segment of Britain's urban working-class males to vote for the first time. Still, only about 16 percent of the total adult population was allowed to vote.
- In 1884 the franchise was widened to include all males over age twenty-one who owned a home, a group comprising about 28 percent of people in that age group.
- Only in 1918, under the impact of the widely shared sacrifices of World War I, were most property qualifications eliminated for males over age twenty-one. At the same time, women obtained the right to vote for the first time, a triumph due in part to the critical role women played in the work force during the Great War. The international environment thus promoted democracy in Britain in the war years. Female suffrage also came about because of decades of militant campaigning for enfranchisement by Britain's "suffragettes." Initially, however, only women over age thirty gained the right to vote; it was not until 1928 that the female voting age was lowered to age twenty-one.
- Though virtually all adults over age twenty-one were now able to vote, graduates of elite universities and various business owners still enjoyed the right to cast *two* votes in parliamentary elections. This plural voting privilege was not abolished until 1948, when the Representation of the People Act formally established the principle

of "one person, one vote" throughout the United Kingdom.
- In 1969 the voting age was lowered to age eighteen, and in 1985 about 4 million British citizens overseas were granted voting rights.

Some individuals, such as the royal family and other titled peers, still have no right to vote.[4]

The gradual extension of the suffrage was accompanied by the increasing authority of Parliament's elected body, the House of Commons, over the House of Lords. Until the early twentieth century the House of Lords retained the right to approve all bills passed by the Commons before they could become law. Because the House of Lords was an unelected body representing the aristocracy and the Anglican Church hierarchy, it constituted the last bastion of nondemocratic rule in a country that was increasingly opening itself up to democratic influences and procedures. In 1911 the Lords lost their veto privilege, retaining little more than the right to delay the enactment of legislation by up to two years. In 1949 their ability to delay legislation was reduced to one year. In 1999, Tony Blair's government effected another major reform of the upper house, to be described later in this chapter.

### Nationalism and Political Culture

A contributing factor in the development of British democracy was the particular brand of nationalism that accompanied Parliament's institutional evolution. As we noted in chapter 6, *nationalism* is a set of political ideas that emphasizes the distinctiveness and unity of one's nation, specifies common interests, and prescribes goals for action, self-government being the most important. In some countries the development of nationalism had pronouncedly anti-democratic accents. Japan, Russia, and Germany stand out as prominent examples. The development of nationhood in these countries, extending from medieval times until well into the twentieth century, was orchestrated largely by aristocratic elites who had no intention of sharing power with elected parliaments. The military establishment, rather than legislative bodies, was their favored institutional partner. In England, by contrast, nationalism from its inception was understood by the country's politically active elites and broad segments of the population in terms that promoted democratic ideals.

Liah Greenfeld points out that England was the first country to develop a modern national consciousness.[5] This national self-conception emerged in the sixteenth century, spurred on by both religious and political developments. One of its chief catalysts was the Protestant Reformation. By 1600, the majority of English people belonged to a church that explicitly defined itself as "Anglican." Protestantism was thus a defining element of the English nation, shaping not just the country's most prominent religious orientation but its basic national identity as well.

Right from its origins, English nationalism was infused with a specific political content. It arose at a time when Parliament was already well established as a vital component of English government, with widespread support among nobles and commoners, Catholics and Protestants. The English concept of national identity included the notion that, at least in principle, the English people were free and equal individuals under the law, with the right to participate in politics and government. The political values of individual freedom, equal dignity, and self-government—values that are at the heart of modern democracy—became defining characteristics of the English nation. Ultimately, what defined the English nation more than anything else was *the way the English governed themselves*. English nationalism, in short, was defined in part by democratic principles.

It therefore gave rise to a political culture that proved highly conducive to the expansion of democracy. As we saw in chapter 13, *political culture* refers to a pattern of shared values, moral norms, beliefs, expectations, and attitudes that relate to politics and its social context. In their classic study of political culture, Gabriel Almond and Sidney Verba described Britain in the 1950s as having a *civic culture:* that is, a cluster of attitudes favoring the rule of law, individual liberty, equal human dignity, and political moderation. They also pointed out that the British tended to be more deferential to established authority than did people in other democracies like the United States. Though these deferential attitudes appear to have declined in more recent decades, the basic contours of Britain's civic culture, including a vibrant civil society, remain largely the same today.[6]

### Private Enterprise and the Middle Class

Another variable that promoted the development of English democracy was the emergence of private agriculture and other business enterprises owned and operated by individuals, families, and corporations independently of the state and its chief partner, the centuries-old aristocracy. These economic processes stimulated the emergence of a property-owning middle class, centrally located in Britain's social pyramid between the wealthy aristocratic elite and the masses of poor peasants and laborers. By acquiring land or businesses of their own, these ambitious entrepreneurs acquired a personal stake in how they were governed. They wanted a say in shaping the laws of the land, especially laws regarding taxes, contracts, and other regulations affecting private property. By electing sympathetic representatives to the House of Commons, they not only advanced their own economic interests; they simultaneously promoted the principle of representative self-government. In their view, the defense of property rights required the assertion of political rights.

An early catalyst to private business activity was the growth of commercial agriculture in the sixteenth and seventeenth centuries. Though the process was frequently violent, its main result was that—unlike Russia, China, and some other countries—Britain entered the late nineteenth century unencumbered by a large, landless peasantry whose discontent might serve as a source of revolutionary ferment. Instead, the country's rich green countryside was cultivated by wealthy estate owners and a rising middle class of commercial farmers. These rural property owners ultimately promoted England's democratization through their support of Parliament and their insistence on voting rights for themselves, along with other legal privileges and freedoms.

The ranks of the propertied middle class swelled with the expansion of private manufacturing and other commercial activities in the sixteenth to eighteenth centuries. By 1800 the English middle class had firmly established itself as the driving force behind a dynamic market economy. As its contributions to the wealth of the country became increasingly indispensable, its influence on Parliament and government decision making grew apace. The social historian Barrington Moore maintained that, without such a capitalist bourgeoisie, there can be no democracy. Countries that failed to develop large-scale private agriculture and industry before the twentieth century—like Japan, Russia, and China—generally failed to develop democracy until much later, if at all.[7]

The expansion of capitalism in Britain was by no means without problems, however. Large numbers of landless peasants, laborers, and others who made up the uneducated mass of British society found it difficult to climb out of the bottom of the social heap in spite of the new opportunities the market economy opened up. Even the middle class led a precarious existence, as the volatile dynamics of the marketplace produced bankruptcies, inflation, and recessions alongside vast personal fortunes and rising national wealth.

These conflicting tendencies intensified in the nineteenth and early twentieth centuries as Britain's industrial revolution, which had taken off in the late 1700s, well ahead of other European countries, flourished and matured. In an economy increasingly functioning according to laissez-faire principles, with minimal government involvement, industrial capitalism generated a huge working class whose fate was determined almost entirely by employers bent on raising profits at all costs. Subsistence-level wages, long working hours, and unsanitary living conditions became the unalterable lot of millions of men, women, and children, with little or no state assistance or protection.[8]

On top of all this, Britain's aristocratic elite, the descendants of blue-blooded families whose lines stretched back centuries, managed to maintain their lofty status at the apex of British society. Though they had ceded place to the business class as the principal creators of England's wealth in the eighteenth and nineteenth centuries, their hereditary titles, accumulated riches, and superior educational attainments at universities like Oxford and Cambridge gave them a social preeminence and political influence that far exceeded their numbers.

The result of these economic and social transformations was a society that by the nineteenth century, if not earlier, was demarcated by increasingly rigid class distinctions. The "class system" became synonymous with social reality throughout Britain (especially in England, where industrialization was the most pronounced). The social class into which one was born largely determined one's life chances, including educational prospects, occupation, and income. Even the middle class became increasingly stratified as industrial capitalism developed in the late nineteenth and early twentieth centuries. Successful owners of large businesses formed an upper middle class whose wealth at times rivaled the inherited millions of the aristocracy, while small businesspeople and white-collar workers occupied lower rungs on the middle-class ladder, at times veering on poverty. Inevitably, such stark class stratification engendered intense conflicts: conflicts over money, jobs, living conditions, and basic fairness. And just as inevitably, these conflicts over "who got what" in British society could not help but become politicized. The privileged upper crust, the plucky middle classes, and the downtrodden workers all looked to the British state for protection and benefits.

In the mid nineteenth century, Karl Marx predicted that any society dominated by the capitalist bourgeoisie was bound to have a government completely in its thrall. Under these conditions, the exploited working masses—the *proletariat*—would eventually take matters into their own hands and stage a revolution, expropriating political as well as economic power from their masters. Their victory would set the stage for socialism, permanently eradicating private enterprise and "bourgeois democracy." In laying out this scenario, Marx had England in mind above all. England was farther advanced along the road of laissez-faire industrial capitalism than any country in the world, with the possible exception of the United States. And yet, contrary to Marx, the proletarian revolution never occurred there, nor did democracy die.

On the contrary, both capitalism and democracy have flourished in the United Kingdom down to the present day. They have continued to survive in spite of persistent social divisions in contemporary British society. What accounts for these results? One of the main reasons why Marx's prognostications did not come true can be found in the ideological development of Britain's leading political parties.

### The Rise of Political Parties

Since the end of World War II, British politics has been dominated by two parties, the Conservative Party and the Labour Party. A third, which now calls itself the Liberal Democrat Party, has played a less important role but still attracts a wide following. With few exceptions, postwar British governments have been *single-party majoritarian* governments, with the Conservatives and Labour alternating in power. There have been no coalition governments since the war. Numerous other parties also exist, but their electoral support is much smaller than that of the three main parties, all of which have roots in the past.

Modern political parties emerged in Britain in the nineteenth century. The two parties that dominated the latter half of the 1900s—the Conservatives and the Liberals—could trace their origins to earlier political orientations rooted in the religious and constitutional disputes of the two previous centuries. The **Conservatives** descended primarily from the **Tories**, a moniker they informally retain today. In the seventeenth and eighteenth centuries the Tories were identified by their devotion to absolutist monarchy, aristocratic rule, the House of Lords, and the established Anglican Church. The Liberals' chief antecedents were the *Whigs*, who tended to favor a more limited monarchy, one whose power would be reined in by the House of Commons acting on the principle of government by consent of the governed. Although the terms *Tory* and *Whig* were originally insults leveled by each side's detractors, in actual practice the two orientations shared certain positions in common.[9] A majority of both groups favored a monarchy of real stature, an authoritative role for Parliament, Protestantism as opposed to Catholicism, and government by propertied elites rather than mass democracy. Both strove to avoid a recurrence of the Civil Wars of the 1640s and recoiled in horror at the French Revolution. These commonalities helped set British politics on a course of moderation, consensus, and compromise that endures to this day.

Party development remained embryonic in the first half of the nineteenth century. The Tories, who began referring to themselves as Conservatives in the 1830s, were divided into competing factions, as were the Whigs. By the end of the century, party ideology and organizational structure began to solidify. The Conservatives under the leadership of Benjamin Disraeli emerged as the chief advocate of the landed aristocracy, while the Liberals under leaders like William Gladstone stepped forward as the main party of the urbanized, business-oriented middle class, championing laissez-faire and free trade. Even these distinctions, however, reflected general tendencies rather than strict demarcations. Most important, both parties accepted the existing constitutional framework of a limited monarchy, cabinet accountability to Parliament, and a restricted franchise confined to property-owning males. At a time when France, Germany, Russia, and Japan experienced authoritarian rule undergirded by the military, Britain's leading parties were wedded to parliamentary government and entertained no thought of military authoritarianism.[10]

At the same time, both Conservatives and Liberals feared the mounting resentments of the working class. Britain's proletariat grew steadily in the nineteenth century. Early government efforts to alleviate their plight did little more than reduce working hours for women and children to about sixty per week. The Poor Law of 1839 actually *decreased* state expenditures for the destitute. None of this legislation addressed the fundamental problem, which was the workers' lack of political power, a weakness that left them completely subservient to their employers. To redress this imbalance, a working-class group known as the Chartists was formed in 1838. Their "Charter" of demands called for universal male suffrage, the secret ballot (as opposed to open elections by show of hands), and salaries for members of Parliament so that politicians other than the superfluously wealthy could afford to hold office. Two petitions to Parliament expressing these wishes were decisively rejected, as neither the Conservatives nor the Liberals in the reign of Queen Victoria were prepared to open the floodgates of democracy to the masses. Both parties were strongly committed to preserving the property rights of land and factory owners. The resulting social conflicts occasionally sparked violence, as strikes, lockouts, and worker demonstrations led to bloody police crackdowns. Most workers, however, hewed the path of peaceful democratic change. Collaboration with sympathetic Liberals like Gladstone yielded a few gains, such as the legalization of trade unions and the right to strike in 1871. But the predominance of business interests in Liberal ranks precluded the critical breakthrough to mass suffrage.

It was therefore incumbent on the workers' movement to establish a party of its own. Accordingly, in 1900 the leaders of several worker-oriented groups held a conference in London and formed the "Labour Representation Committee." After electing twenty-nine candidates to the House of Commons in 1906, this organization renamed itself the **Labour Party**.

From its inception the new party's main source of support came from Britain's trade unions. By 1900 some 1.2 million workers were affiliated with the Trades Union Congress, an umbrella organization formed by unions representing railway workers, factory laborers, miners, and other industrial occupations. Another early source of Labour support consisted of intellectuals, artists, and other middle- and upper-class sympathizers of the labour movement who objected on ethical grounds to laissez-faire capitalism's exploitative tendencies. Such people formed groups like the Fabian Society to give voice to these sentiments.[11]

What is perhaps most significant about the various founding elements of the Labour Party is that their overwhelming majority decisively rejected Marxism, anarchism, and other ideologies calling for violent revolution and the creation of an entirely new social and political order. Most of them believed that working-class demands for political participation and economic justice could be accommodated within the framework of parliamentary democracy and peaceful industrial development under the aegis of the British state. While many of the Labour Party's founders called themselves "socialists," most understood this term to mean a system in which national and local government agencies would play a greater role in the economy for the benefit of the working class, without necessarily eliminating private enterprise altogether. Though many believed that the state should take over the main factories, mines, utilities, and other privately owned industries, very few advocated the wholesale government absorption of all the farms, stores, and other small- and medium-sized businesses that gave millions of British families a personal stake in private property. Only a minority of British socialists favored the gigantic state-run centrally planned economy that the Soviet Union was to set up in the 1930s. Quite a few continued to favor cooperation with the Liberal Party on certain issues, the so-called Lib-Lab orientation.

Just as significant, the early Labourites were true social democrats who believed in ballot-box democracy. They categorically rejected dictatorship. Many of them even professed their loyalty to the monarchy, as long as the crown did not interfere in the workings of Parliament. Far from opposing democracy, the Labour Party and its adherents wanted to extend its blessings to the working masses through universal male and female suffrage. Moreover, a large number of Labour leaders and voters resisted Marxism because its atheistic tenets conflicted with their strong religious convictions.[12] In short, the Labour Party helped enfold Britain's poorest classes into the democratic process. As a result, Britain did not develop a large alienated working class that felt left out of the mainstream of democratic politics. By contrast, France, Germany, and a number of other countries entered the twentieth century with many discontented workers who became radicalized and ultimately supported anti-democratic parties like the communists and fascists.

Another comparison worth noting is that the Labour Party envisioned a much greater economic role for the state than the Democratic Party in the United States tended to favor. Though both parties had deep roots in the labor movement, Labour's call for the nationalization of private companies was not echoed by Franklin Roosevelt's New Deal, which sought instead to revive private economic activity rather than replace it with government ownership. In advocating the takeover of at least some private enterprises by the state, Labour was more socialist than the Democrats ever were.

As the Labour Party gained strength, the Conservatives and Liberals underwent their own evolution in the direction of greater democracy for all. It was a Liberal government under Prime Minister David Lloyd George that conferred voting rights on most males and females in 1918, and it was a Conservative government that expanded female suffrage in 1928. In the 1930s, as the Great Depression wracked the British economy, several Labour leaders joined with Liberals and Conservatives in forming a broad coalition government. Another three-party national unity coalition governed Britain during World War II under Prime Minister Winston Churchill. (Churchill was a Conservative who had once belonged to the Liberal Party.) These crucial developments forged an unshakable consensus among the main parties of the left (Labour), right (Conservatives), and center (Liberals) that the British system of government must consist of ballot-box democracy under a limited monarchy. The three main parties also developed a consensus on Britain's economic system, embracing the general principle that it should be a mixed economy that combines private enterprise with state intervention aimed at stimulating growth and providing for the welfare of the population. Fatefully, this wide consensus on democracy and the mixed economy was precisely what eluded Germany, Italy, Spain, Russia, Japan, and a host of other countries in the first half of the twentieth century, resulting in brutal dictatorships and two world wars. By contrast, Britain emerged from the First and Second World Wars with its democracy strengthened.

## BRITISH POLITICS SINCE WORLD WAR II

Consensus on the fundamental principles of British democracy and political economy has by no means prevented real differences from emerging among the main parties when it comes to the specifics of government policy. Since World War II, Labour and the Conservatives have sparred vigorously over how Britain's mixed-economy welfare state should be managed, while the Liberals underwent profound transformations over this very issue. The question of what role the state should play in the economy has arguably been the single most contentious issue in postwar British politics.

**Labour and the Welfare State, 1945–51** In July 1945, slightly more than two months after Germany's surrender, British voters ousted Churchill's government and swung massively to the Labour Party. With 48 percent of the popular vote and a 146-seat majority in the House of Commons, Labour formed its first majoritarian government under *Clement Attlee* and used its mandate to break new ground in expanding the state's role in the economy. Between

1946 and 1949 the Attlee government nationalized the Bank of England, civil aviation, and the iron and steel industries, along with the country's coal mines, railroads, gas and electricity utilities, and long-distance trucking companies. The owners of these businesses were compensated out of state revenues. In addition, the Labour government established the **National Health Service (NHS)**, ***providing virtually free medical care for the entire population.*** (Private medical care and health insurance remained available for those willing to pay for it.) Other welfare measures included a vastly extended state-funded insurance program to cover unemployment and job-related accidents; maternity allowances; and pensions for widows and retirees, plus direct income assistance for the poorest families. To maintain full employment at a time when Britain's economy was still recovering from the hardships of World War II, the Labour government utilized Keynesian tax-and-spend principles. By 1950 the Labour Party had succeeded beyond all expectations in laying the foundations of Britain's large postwar welfare state, adapting to the realities of British capitalism its long-standing commitment to a social democratic conception of economic democracy.[13]

**Conservative Acceptance of the Welfare State** Despite the unprecedented scope of Labour's nationalizations and welfare measures, Conservative and Liberal politicians generally went along with most of them. Both parties had introduced their own welfare schemes prior to World War II, albeit on a considerably smaller scale.

Accordingly, when the Conservatives were voted back into power in 1951, they did not set out to reverse everything that Attlee's government had accomplished. Though they reprivatized the iron and steel industries and long-distance trucking, they kept the other nationalized companies firmly in state hands. Under prime ministers Winston Churchill (1951–55), Anthony Eden (1955–57), Harold Macmillan (1957–63), and Alec Douglas-Home (1963–64), a succession of Conservative governments significantly expanded spending on the National Health Service, public housing, education, and other welfare services. As one wag put it, "Labour gave us free teeth and the Tories didn't pull 'em out!" To prevent strikes, these Conservative governments acceded to a number of trade union demands for higher wages and other benefits, even though the unions were the principal financial and electoral backers of the Labour Party. And like the previous Labour government, the Conservatives used Keynesian mechanisms such as tax incentives and direct government spending to promote economic growth and reduce unemployment.

While continuing to present themselves as the party most favorable to private business and the middle class, the Conservatives in these years amply demonstrated their adherence to Britain's "postwar settlement," which combined private enterprise with a significant amount of state intervention in the economy. Conservative acceptance of this expansive state role in fact reflected a broad popular consensus in Britain at this time on the need for "collective," that is, state-centered, solutions to national problems as opposed to private initiatives centered in the economic marketplace. The period of British politics extending from 1945 through the 1970s has been aptly described as "the collectivist age," with the value of community welfare predominating over free-market individualism in public and elite opinion to a greater extent than in the United States.[14]

After losing to Labour in the elections of 1964, the Conservatives were voted back into power in 1970. Prime Minister *Edward (Ted) Heath* assumed office with a pledge to preserve the essentials of the welfare state while scaling back some of its more costly programs. He also believed that some of Britain's largest trade unions were abusing their right to strike and should be obligated to keep their agreements with private companies. In 1972, however, unemployment reached one million. At the same time, the coal miners' union declared a nationwide strike for higher wages. Several attempts to reach a settlement fell through, and violence flared up as picketers prevented coal and oil supplies from reaching electric power plants. Strikes by shipbuilders and dockworkers intensified the crisis. Brownouts and heating fuel shortages made for a dark and cold winter. In the face of these challenges, Heath abandoned his previous attempts to confront the unions and instead called on the Trade Unions Congress to join with the government and the main interest group representing the business community, the Confederation of British Industry, in negotiating a series of agreements on pay scales, prices, and production. The unions rebuffed the offer, and Heath called new elections for February 1974 in the midst of a rapidly deteriorating economic situation. "Who governs Britain?"—the unions or the government?—was a central issue of the campaign.

The result was a defeat for the Conservatives but a less than satisfactory victory for the Labour Party. Labour emerged as the largest party in the House of Commons but lacked an overall voting majority. *Harold Wilson* thereupon formed a minority Labour government, but he called new elections in October 1974 that gave his party a slender three-vote majority.

**Labour Divided** Ever since its halcyon days under Attlee's first government, the Labour Party leadership had been split into two increasingly divergent camps. The party's left wing remained faithful to the ideals of economic socialism. Its adherents favored the nationalization of major industries, government spending to ensure full employment, and generous welfare benefits to be paid for by imposing high taxes on private businesses and upper-income individuals. The leftists attached a higher priority to expanding the welfare state than to any other items of the budget, including defense. Their main supporters were Britain's unionized workers. The other Labour group consisted of moderates who shared the left's commitment to the welfare state and trade unionism but warned that government spending needed to be kept within certain limits so as not to generate skyrocketing budget deficits and a mounting national debt. Labour moderates also supported U.S. foreign and defense policies during the Cold War, even though they necessitated significant levels of British military spending.

The first signs of a split between the left and moderate wings of the Labour Party surfaced during Attlee's postwar governments as the costs of Labour's welfare programs soared. Unable to govern, Attlee called snap elections in 1951, which the Conservatives won.

The rift between the Labour left and the moderates intensified over the following years as the Conservatives mounted successive election victories in 1955 and 1959. It was only partially healed when Labour regained power in 1964 under the leadership of Harold Wilson. Wilson, the Oxford-educated son of a factory employee, had been an outspoken representative of the party's left wing in earlier years, but he pursued more moderate policies as prime minister. Wilson held the Labour Party together as it won a new majority in 1966 and seemed poised for yet another victory when he called snap elections in 1970. Unexpectedly, however, the favorable public opinion polls on which Wilson relied turned out to be wrong. To everyone's surprise, the Conservatives came back to power under Ted Heath.[15]

The rise of trade union militancy during Heath's government was cheered by those who believed that Britain's working class was fully justified in demanding a greater share of the nation's wealth. But Labour moderates insisted that the economy could not function unless the unions accepted limits on their wage demands and strike activities. Accordingly, when Wilson reassumed office in 1974 he called for a "social contract" in which the unions would agree to wage restraint in return for government welfare measures. This policy succeeded in calming Britain's troubled industrial relations for the next two years, providing Wilson with a favorable opportunity to announce his retirement.

His successor was *James Callaghan,* a Labour MP since the Attlee years. "Sunny Jim" was quickly forced to shoulder the burdens of the British economy's continuing slide when the pound's depreciating value against other currencies required financial assistance from the International Monetary Fund. The IMF required sharp cuts in welfare expenditures that did not sit well with the Labour left. The pressures on Callaghan intensified during the winter of 1978–79—the "winter of discontent"—as a series of strikes by truck drivers, trash collectors, and other workers inconvenienced the public, prompting widespread fears that the unions were out of control.[16]

Britain's labor unrest was but one symptom of a persistent economic slump that became known as "the English disease." The government's failure to revive the economy and contain trade union militancy led many to conclude that Britain was ungovernable.[17]

As Callaghan wrestled with these troublesome long-term trends, his own troubles were exacerbated by dwindling support in the House of Commons. Defections from Labour ranks and defeats incurred in by-elections (which take place upon the death or retirement of a Commons member) deprived the party of its majority. In order to save his minority government, Callaghan formed a parliamentary alliance with the Liberal Party, which had thirteen seats. The "Lab-Lib" alliance lasted barely a year. In a last-ditch effort to secure a voting majority, Callaghan cut deals with the Scottish Nationalist Party and its Welsh counterpart, which together held fourteen seats. But this new parliamentary alliance was shaken after government-sponsored referendums on devolution in Scotland and Wales failed. With rumors flying that Callaghan's government and its allies no longer commanded a voting majority in the House, the Conservatives supported a no-confidence motion. The tense showdown came late in the evening of March 28, 1979. By the slimmest of margins, 311–310, Callaghan's government was defeated, setting the stage for new elections to the House of Commons only six weeks later.[18]

The result was a convincing victory for the Conservatives, whose combative leader was to serve as Britain's prime minister for the next eleven years: **Margaret Thatcher.**

## PROFILE: Margaret Thatcher

"I am a conviction politician," Margaret Thatcher affirmed as the 1979 election campaign got under way, serving notice that she did not intend to be bound by the prevailing consensus of postwar British politics. One by one, Thatcher repudiated the main tenets of British collectivism.

- Refusing to exalt the state as the mainstay of the British economy, she emphatically favored the private sector as the motor force of job creation. No government, she believed, could overturn the rules of the marketplace.
- She vowed to scale back the soaring costs of welfare by attacking the "culture of dependency." In her view, too many able-bodied citizens preferred government handouts to individual responsibility and hard work.
- Far from favoring the nationalization of private enterprises, Thatcher called for the privatization of nationalized enterprises. She also vowed to promote an "enterprise culture" aimed at encouraging entrepreneurism in a country that, in her view, was permeated with a socialist mentality placing excessive reliance on the state.
- Instead of placating trade unions in an attempt to avoid strikes, Thatcher declared her readiness to confront union leaders whenever their demands were economically unjustifiable or their actions illegal. She also favored greater democracy within trade unions, requiring union leaders to poll their membership before calling strikes. In her view, it was the militancy of a few avowedly Marxist union leaders, not the rank and file, that accounted for Britain's turbulent labor-management relations.
- In a sharp critique of Keynesianism, Thatcher disavowed the principle of boosting government expenditures in an effort to stimulate economic activity. Instead, she embraced *monetarism,* the notion that inflation is fueled by an excess of money placed in circulation by the state's currency authorities. For Thatcher, the battle against inflation took a higher priority over the battle against unemployment, at least in the short run.

These views constituted, in Thatcher's words, a "root-and-branch" reversal of the guiding assumptions of British politics. They also reflected a neoliberal view of economic democracy, one that stressed the liberties of the marketplace and the opportunities of a "people's capitalism" against the Labour Party's more welfarist, egalitarian approach to economic democracy. Thatcher's outspoken decisiveness and buoyant optimism about Britain's possibilities at a

Margaret Thatcher

time of mounting pessimism captured the mood of a growing number of British voters. In May 1979 the Conservatives won a forty-three-seat majority in the House of Commons, and Margaret Thatcher became the first female prime minister in British history.

The daughter of a small-town shopkeeper, Thatcher went to Oxford and quickly got involved in the Conservative Party's student organization. Shortly after graduation in 1947 she decided that she wanted to be a Member of Parliament. After losing her first two electoral contests in 1950 and 1951, she was invited by the Conservative organization of the suburban London constituency of Finchley to compete for the party's nomination in 1959. Although she did not live there, she was eligible to represent Finchley because British law does not require members of Parliament to reside in the district they represent. Thatcher overwhelmingly won the endorsement of the Finchley Conservatives, and in the general elections to the House of Commons held three months later, Thatcher became a Member of Parliament for the first time. In eight subsequent elections she was never defeated.

A tireless worker, Thatcher rose quickly up the ranks of the party leadership. In 1961 she became a parliamentary aide to the minister for pensions and national insurance, in effect becoming a junior minister. In 1970 Prime Minister Ted Heath appointed her to her first cabinet post as education secretary. But she regarded Heath's decision to change his free-market policies in 1972 as a mistake. Vowing never to make such a U-turn, Thatcher declared shortly after taking office, "You turn if you want to; the lady's not for turning." In 1975 Thatcher was elected by Conservative Members of Parliament as their party's new leader. Under her leadership the Conservatives won convincing majorities in the House of Commons in 1979, 1983, and 1987. (Their share of the popular vote, however, remained around 42 percent, as shown in table 16.1 on page 416.) Her overall record was a mixed bag of successes and disappointments.

- *Inflation.* One of Thatcher's biggest successes was her struggle against inflation. In 1980 Britain's inflation rate was 21 percent; by 1982 it was down to 5 percent and in 1986 it fell to 2.5 percent. Her government did not manage to control the money supply as much as it had hoped, however.
- *Growth.* Economic growth rates increased modestly in the 1980s to about 1.9 percent, higher than the previous decade. Business profits and real wages also rose under Thatcher's stewardship, but the gap between rich and poor widened. So, too, did the gap between the prosperous southern parts of Britain and the declining north.[19]
- *Trade unions.* The Thatcher government faced down a yearlong strike in 1984–85 by the National Union of Mineworkers. It also secured legislation holding unions responsible for illegal actions and expanding democratic voting procedures within the unions. By the end of the decade the number of hours lost to strikes had dropped appreciably. A substantial number of British workers supported Thatcher's policies, and the Conservatives won 37 percent of the working-class vote in the 1987 elections.
- *Privatization.* More than twenty-five state-owned companies were sold, in whole or in part, to private bidders. They included British Petroleum, British Airways, British Telecom, and the Jaguar, Rolls Royce, and Rover auto firms. The sales reaped more than £25 billion for the treasury, though critics charged that the sale prices were too low.
- *Unemployment.* The Achilles heel of Thatcher's administration, unemployment soared from 5 percent when she assumed office to more than 10 percent from 1982 to 1987, with more than 3 million people out of work. It began edging downward in 1988, falling to 5.5 percent in 1990.
- *Spending and taxes.* Although one of Thatcher's top priorities was a reduction in government expenditures, state spending *rose* during her tenure in office due to mounting outlays for unemployment compensation, pensions, defense, public safety, and various welfare measures, including the National Health Service. Though the government kept its commitment to lower income tax rates, it raised the value-added national sales tax from 8 percent to 15 percent.
- *Social issues.* Although Thatcher favored abortion rights and the legality of homosexuality, her record on women's issues was mixed. "In politics," she once said, "if you want anything said, ask a man; if you want anything done, ask a woman." Nevertheless, Thatcher did not embrace feminist causes and she filled her cabinets with men. Her campaign to change British political culture by inculcating the values of the "enterprise culture" in place of collectivist values met with only modest success. However, her policy of encouraging low-income families in public housing to buy their homes from the state proved highly popular in the working class.
- *Foreign policy.* Thatcher achieved an international reputation as the "iron lady" for her toughness in foreign policy. In 1982 she sent the British fleet to repel Argentina's invasion of the Falkland (Malvinas) Islands, a small territory off the Argentine coast that had been governed by Britain for nearly 150 years. The successful operation resulted in the collapse of

Argentina's military dictatorship and a Conservative landslide in the snap elections of 1983. A staunch opponent of communism, Thatcher had an especially close partnership with President Ronald Reagan, who shared most of her beliefs, and she played a critical diplomatic role in the West's dealings with the Soviet Union when Mikhail Gorbachev sought to end the Cold War. And her feisty defense of British sovereignty led to frequent conflicts with other members of the European Community. She scoffed at the federalist vision of a supranational "United States of Europe," in which major policy decisions would increasingly be made by politicians and bureaucrats at EC headquarters in Brussels.

Describing herself as "single-minded," Thatcher pursued a take-charge leadership style, firing Conservative cabinet ministers who disagreed with her and mobilizing her loyal grassroots following among party activists in support of her agenda. In 1990, however, the acrimony of opponents within her own party reached the boiling point after her government proposed supplementing the existing real-estate tax system with a head tax on individuals. Dubbed the "poll tax," the plan provoked widespread public disapproval and the vocal hostility of many Conservative politicians. More than 60 percent of the country opposed it, and Thatcher's approval ratings plunged to the lowest levels ever seen for a British prime minister. Taking advantage of her weakness, two Conservative leaders announced they would challenge Thatcher at the annual vote of Conservative members of the Commons to select the party's leader.

Though Thatcher had handily won these elections in past years, usually without opposition, this time she fell short of the minimum votes necessary to win on the first ballot. Convinced that her position was hopeless, she withdrew from the second ballot and announced her resignation as prime minister on November 28. With her support, John Major outpolled her principal rivals and was elected to succeed her as Conservative Party leader. In a subsequent vote in the House of Commons, Major was confirmed as prime minister.

After eleven and one-half years in office, Margaret Thatcher was ousted by her own party's parliamentary delegation. Nevertheless, as the dominant figure in British politics in the 1980s, her successes and failures were bound to leave a lasting imprint on the 1990s and beyond.[20]

**John Major's Governments, 1990–97** Major brought palpable changes in style and policy. A pragmatic consensus-seeker rather than a headstrong ideologue, he consulted representatives of all the diverse currents within his party and included a number of them in his cabinet. One of his first decisions was to abandon the poll tax, a move that won him plaudits among the Conservative Party faithful as well as the general public. He also underscored his government's commitment to improving social services, he dreamed of a "classless society," and he appointed more women to cabinet posts and other high offices than Thatcher ever did.[21]

Though lacking in charisma and saddled with a severe recession, Major led the Conservatives to their fourth straight electoral victory in April 1992. The win was largely unexpected, as the Labour Party under the new leadership of Neil Kinnock was beginning to shed its image as a left-wing movement dominated by militant trade union leaders. The Conservatives lost forty seats, but contrary to the forecasts, they managed to retain a twenty-one-seat majority in the House of Commons.[22] But this majority did not remain solidly behind Major. The newly reelected prime minister soon found himself ensnared in the issue that most sharply divided the Conservative Party: Europe.

Several months after the elections, world currency traders began massively selling British pounds, fearing that they were overvalued in relation to other currencies such as the U.S. dollar and the German Deutschemark. Britain at this time was a member of Europe's Exchange Rate Mechanism (ERM), an agreement among Western Europe's largest economies to keep their currency exchange rates within certain limits, or "bands." As the pound's value deteriorated, Major's government announced its withdrawal from the ERM on a day that became known bitterly as "Black Wednesday." Not only did this decision represent a humiliating admission of the UK's economic weakness, but it also demonstrated that Britain could not necessarily count on Germany or its other European partners to come to its rescue in times of acute economic stress. These implications of the UK's withdrawal from the ERM worried Conservative "Euroskeptics" like Margaret Thatcher, who believed that Britain was already losing its independence by cooperating too closely with its continental European allies. Major spent his next five years in office gamely struggling to maintain party unity in the face of severe internal discord over European issues.[23]

In November 1991, leaders of the twelve countries that composed the European Community at that time held a summit in the Dutch town of Maastricht and agreed to substantially increase their economic and political integration over the decade. Their principal aim was economic and monetary union (EMU), to be anchored in the creation of a single European currency (the euro) and a European central bank to manage it. A treaty to this effect was signed in February 1992. In 1993, with a view to the eventual achievement of these and other cooperative goals, the European Community changed its name to the European Union (EU).

From the outset, Major let his European partners understand that his government was in no position to commit itself to abandoning the pound in favor of an all-European currency. He signed the Maastricht Treaty only after negotiating Britain's right to opt out of the clauses pertaining to European monetary union. He also refused to accept the EU's "Social Chapter," which granted Europe's workers greater rights and welfare benefits than they currently enjoyed in Britain. Major also had doubts about the treaty's sections on establishing a "common foreign and security policy," something he feared would loosen Britain's close political and military ties with the United States. And he vigorously protested the EU's decision to ban the sale of British beef in the other member states following an outbreak of "mad cow" disease, arguing that EU authorities in Brussels were punishing Britain unfairly. Despite these reservations, however, Major himself was nowhere nearly as reluctant to join in the European integration process as the more diehard anti-Europeanists within his own party. He believed that Britain's long-term economic interests required closer trade and financial ties to its EU partners over the coming years, a view strongly endorsed by the pro-European wing of his party.

On a succession of key votes in the Commons on the Maastricht Treaty, as many as twenty-six Conservatives voted against the Major government's bills calling for the treaty's adoption. By 1995 Major was so exasperated at the opposition to his European policies among fellow Conservatives that he resigned as party leader and demanded a vote by the party's House of Commons delegation to reelect or remove him. He won handily, but the internal divisions in his party remained unhealed. Major's woes were exacerbated by a series of scandals. Though the prime minister vowed to go "back to basics" in conducting an efficient and honest government, a dozen cabinet officials were forced to resign for financial misconduct, sexual embarrassments, or other improprieties. Meanwhile, a number of Conservative losses in by-elections, coupled with the defection of several Tories to other parties, reduced the Major government's majority in the Commons to zero by the end of 1996. When the elections of 1997 rolled around, Major and the Conservatives were in no shape to present themselves to the voters as a unified party. Although the economy was perking up, the Conservatives' political luster was tarnished. Just as significant, they now faced a rejuvenated Labour Party headed by its most popular leader in decades: *Tony Blair.*

## PROFILE: Tony Blair

Tony Blair was never a typical Labour Party politician. Unlike such previous party leaders as Harold Wilson, James Callaghan, and Neil Kinnock, Blair stemmed not from the working class but from a relatively well-off middle-class family. His father, a lawyer and university lecturer, was a Conservative Party activist whose moderately Tory views were to exercise a lifelong influence on Tony's political outlook. With the aid of a scholarship, Tony went off to a private boarding school at the age of thirteen and entered Oxford in 1972 to study law. It was only after graduation three years later that he joined the Labour Party.

Born in 1953, Anthony Charles Lynton Blair came of age in the late 1960s and early 1970s, a time of political activism and social rebellion for British youth as it was for the Vietnam War generation of young Americans. A moderately rebellious teenager, Blair became the lead singer of a rock band, Ugly Rumors, while at Oxford. (The name was taken from the back cover of a Grateful Dead album.) But a more serious strain had already taken shape in his personality. When he was ten years old, his father suffered a debilitating stroke, an event that impressed upon young Tony the uncertainties of life. (Blair's mother was to die of cancer only weeks after his graduation from Oxford.) While at the university he deepened his religious faith, entering the Church of England in his second year. Like many students in those years, Blair was also looking for ways to make a positive impact on society, promoting the postmaterialist values of compassion and community welfare in place of self-centered material success. By graduation, Blair combined a moral commitment to social welfare and compassion for the needy with a traditionalist's attachment to God, family, and individual responsibility to the larger community. This combination of "welfarist" and conservative values defined Tony Blair's political viewpoint over the ensuing decades. Blair and political commentators have referred to it as the "third way," a centrist position located in between the socialist orientations of the Labour left and the anti-government inclinations of Margaret Thatcher's market-oriented conservatism.[24]

After leaving Oxford, Blair moved to London and began studying for bar exams in the law offices of a prominent Labour Party activist. There he met Cherie Booth, who had just graduated at the top of her class in law at the London School of Economics. Soon after getting married, they both decided to run for the House of Commons. Tony failed in his first two attempts to secure a nomination in local Labour Party organizations, but in 1982 he was selected as the Labour candidate in a by-election. The constituency was staunchly Conservative, however, and Blair went down to defeat. One year later Blair got another chance to throw his hat in the ring when, after five ballots at the local candidate nomination meeting, he won the endorsement of the Labour Party's organization in Sedgefield. This constituency was located in a former mining area in northeastern England near Durham, where Blair had grown up. It had a long tradition of electing Labour candidates to Parliament. In the 1983 elections Blair won his seat, but the overall results were a disaster for Labour, as Margaret Thatcher led the Conservatives to a decisive victory. Cherie fell victim to the Conservative tide, losing her bid for election to Parliament.

At age thirty, Blair was the youngest Labour member of the newly elected House of Commons. But his youth proved no barrier to rapid advancement. Blair proved more effective than other Labour leaders in convincing the party faithful that fundamental changes had to be made in Labour's ideological orientation if it ever hoped to recapture power. In the process he abandoned his own leftist positions on several issues and accommodated himself—and the party—to selected aspects of Thatcherism.

The 1980s were a decade of disarray within the Labour Party. Following the Conservatives' win in 1979, the leadership passed from the moderate James Callaghan to Michael Foot, who had been a leader of the party's left wing since the 1940s. Under his stewardship the rules for electing the party's leader were substantially changed. In previous years only Labour members of the Commons had the right to choose the head of the party, a practice similar to the Conservatives' procedure. Labour's new rules, adopted in 1981, established an "electoral college" that allotted 40 percent of the vote to trade unions, 30 percent to Labour members of the House of Commons and the European Parliament, and 30 percent to dues-paying party members. This "bloc vote" approach was designed to enhance the influence of Labour's left wing on the party's leadership and policies. Blair opposed this leftward drift, but the left's ascendancy resulted in a 1983 election program that proved disastrous at the polls. The party's share of the vote plunged to 27.6 percent (down from 37 percent in 1979) and Labour lost sixty seats in the House of Commons.

Despite his misgivings, Blair remained in the Labour Party and took an active role in altering its course. He vigorously supported Neil Kinnock, who replaced Foot as party leader after the 1983 elections. Under Kinnock's leadership Labour accepted several of Thatcher's policies, including certain privatization decisions and several of her measures aimed at curbing trade union militancy. Although the proponents of a more moderate Labour Party were now in the ascendancy, their efforts were not enough to overtake the Conservatives. Labour won back some voters in 1987 and 1992 but lost both elections.

After the 1992 defeat, Kinnock stepped down and the party leadership fell on Joseph Smith, another moderate. Smith succeeded in getting the party to change its procedures for electing the party leader. The electoral college established in 1981 was replaced with a new one that gave equal weight to trade unionists, Members of Parliament and the European Parliament, and ordinary party members. The reform eliminated the preferential influence of the unions in Labour's leadership selection process. In the spring of 1994, Smith died suddenly of a heart attack. The party's new election procedures played in Blair's favor and in July 1994 he was formally elected Labour's new leader.

Blair pressed for more reforms. With his prodding a special Labour Party conference in April 1995 voted to reword Clause IV of the party's constitution, which had committed the party to seek "the common ownership of the means of production, distribution, and exchange." This phrase, drafted in 1917, reflected the party's early vision of socialism, with the state taking control of much of the economy. Though this goal was subsequently abandoned in practice, its formal elimination in 1995 was intended by Blair and his followers as another signal to the voters that the Labour Party, now dubbed "New Labour," had decisively broken with its past as a socialist party dominated by trade unions.

Other changes in style and substance followed. In adopting a more accommodating attitude toward business, in affirming the need to keep inflation and taxes low, and in several other areas of domestic and foreign policy, Blair pulled the Labour Party closer to Conservative positions. He deftly balanced these shifts with assurances that a Blair government would be more attentive to community welfare and social fairness than the Conservatives.

With a keen eye to American politics, Blair identified Bill Clinton as a kindred spirit. Clinton's "New Democrat" approach, which stressed education and training for workers as well as tax breaks and other benefits for the middle class, struck a responsive chord in the Blair camp. Like Clinton, Blair knew that union members and non-unionized workers alike had reason to worry about job security at a time of accelerating economic globalization; but he also believed that an open global trading system ultimately creates more jobs and greater national wealth than protectionist trade barriers do. Blair further believed that the interests of all Britons, including workers, would be best served through closer ties to the European Union, a position that encountered some resistance in Labour ranks.

Blair's determination to shift the Labour Party to the center amounted to a major redefinition of the party's ideological self-conception, especially when compared to the 1980s. While many Labourites expressed reservations about Blair's policies, most supported him because he was the most electable leader the party had put forward in years. He did not disappoint. Labour won 43 percent of the vote in 1997 and ended up with a commanding 63.6 percent of the seats in the Commons, one of the most decisive electoral triumphs in British history.[25]

Upon assuming office, Blair attached highest priority to the economy. He selected Gordon Brown, his chief rival within the upper ranks of the Labour Party, as chancellor of the exchequer, giving him full responsibility for the government's economic policies. One of the annual rituals of British politics is the walk the bewigged chancellor takes as he carries his proposed budget, in a red briefcase, to Parliament. The new government quickly announced that it would retain the spending limits of Major's last budget for the next two years. By 2001, the Blair-Brown team had succeeded in bringing Britain's "misery index" (inflation plus unemployment) down to a thirty-year low. While holding income tax rates steady, the government still managed to fund a variety of measures that improved living standards and job opportunities for the poorest 10 percent of the population. More than half the electorate now regarded Labour as the party best suited to run the country's economic affairs, an extraordinary turnabout in the party's image. Another popular policy was Blair's handling of the 1999 Kosovo crisis, with Britain playing a leading role in NATO's diplomatic and military efforts. As polls showed a high likelihood of reelection, Blair called snap elections in 2001, one year ahead of schedule.[26]

**The 2001 Elections** Blair went into the 2001 campaign facing mounting public dissatisfaction. The government's fiscally conservative budgetary policies required a relatively tight lid on spending increases for various social services, including transportation and the highly popular National Health Service, which provides free medical and dental care to all UK residents. (Although private health care and medical insurance are available, about 85 percent of Britons use the NHS.) To keep education expenditures within bounds, Blair had taken the unprecedented step of imposing tuition fees for state-supported colleges, including Oxford and Cambridge Universities. The annual tuition charge of £1,000 (about $1,500) proved highly unpopular. People also objected to new "stealth taxes" on gasoline, cigarettes, liquor, and pensions. In addition, Blair was personally rebuked for being "heavy-handed" in his management of government and party affairs. His attempt to impose his own candidate for mayor of London backfired when Labour voters rebelled and elected Ken Livingstone, a favorite of the party's left wing. Blair was also criticized for trying too hard to "spin" the news and for pandering to public opinion. By election time a majority of voters felt that Blair was more concerned with his personal image than with real issues, and fewer than 40 percent regarded the prime minister and his government as trustworthy.

Fortunately for the Labour Party, the voting public placed even less confidence in the Conservatives. Though Tory leader William Hague castigated Blair for failing to deliver on his promises, he failed to articulate a compelling alternative vision. When all the votes were counted after the polls closed on June 7, Labour had won a smashing second victory, retaining all but six House of Commons seats won

TABLE 16.1

House of Commons Elections, 1945–2005

| | Percentage of Popular Vote | | | | Percentage of Seats | | | |
|---|---|---|---|---|---|---|---|---|
| | Conservatives | Labour | Liberals, Alliance, Lib. Dems | Others | Conservatives | Labour | Liberals, Alliance, Lib. Dems | Others |
| 1945 | 39.7 | 47.7 | 9.0 | 3.6 | 33.3 | 61.4 | 1.9 | 3.4 |
| 1950 | 43.3 | 46.1 | 9.1 | 1.5 | 47.8 | 50.4 | 1.4 | 0.3 |
| 1951 | 48.0 | 48.8 | 2.6 | 0.6 | 51.4 | 47.2 | 1.0 | 0.5 |
| 1955 | 49.6 | 46.4 | 2.7 | 1.3 | 54.6 | 44.0 | 1.0 | 0.3 |
| 1959 | 49.4 | 43.8 | 5.9 | 0.9 | 57.9 | 41.0 | 1.0 | 0.2 |
| 1964 | 43.3 | 44.1 | 11.2 | 1.4 | 48.1 | 50.3 | 1.4 | — |
| 1966 | 41.9 | 47.9 | 8.5 | 1.7 | 40.2 | 57.6 | 1.9 | 0.3 |
| 1970 | 46.4 | 43.0 | 7.5 | 3.1 | 52.4 | 45.6 | 1.0 | 1.0 |
| 1974 (Feb.) | 37.8 | 37.2 | 19.3 | 5.7 | 46.8 | 47.4 | 2.2 | 3.6 |
| 1974 (Oct.) | 35.7 | 39.3 | 18.3 | 6.7 | 43.5 | 50.2 | 2.0 | 4.1 |
| 1979 | 43.9 | 36.9 | 13.8 | 5.4 | 53.4 | 42.2 | 1.7 | 2.5 |
| 1983 | 42.4 | 27.6 | 25.4 | 4.6 | 61.1 | 32.2 | 3.5 | 3.5 |
| 1987 | 42.2 | 30.8 | 22.6 | 4.4 | 57.7 | 35.2 | 3.4 | 3.5 |
| 1992 | 41.9 | 34.4 | 17.8 | 5.9 | 51.6 | 41.6 | 3.1 | 3.7 |
| 1997 | 30.7 | 43.2 | 16.8 | 9.3 | 25.0 | 63.6 | 7.0 | 4.4 |
| 2001 | 31.7 | 40.7 | 18.3 | 9.3 | 25.2 | 62.5 | 7.9 | 4.3 |
| 2005 | 32.3 | 35.2 | 22.1 | 10.4 | 30.7 | 55.1 | 9.6 | 4.8 |

*Source:* John Bartle and Anthony King, eds., *Britain at the Press 2005,* 177, 221.

in 1997. The Conservatives suffered their second historic defeat in a row, gaining only one seat. Charles Kennedy's Liberal Democrats won more than 18 percent of the vote and gained six additional seats. But Britain's plurality electoral system once again relegated the country's third-largest party to an insignificant share of seats in the Commons, a mere 7.9 percent. (For the results, see table 16.1.) Perhaps the most telling figure of the election, however, was the voter turnout rate. Only 59.4 percent of the UK's registered voters went to the polls, the lowest turnout since 1918 and a full 12 percent lower than in the previous election. Blair himself was under no illusions about the voters' discontent. "It has been a remarkable and historic victory for my party," he declared on the morning after the vote, "but I am in no doubt as to what it all means. It is very clearly an instruction to deliver."[27]

**The 2005 Elections** For many British voters as well as for political pundits and the media, the Iraq war and Tony Blair's presumed untrustworthiness were the dominant issues of the 2005 election. As the campaign neared, 63 percent of Britons regarded the government as dishonest. But Blair deflected talk of dishonesty and made no attempt to question his decision to join the United States in the war effort. "If you want me to apologize for the war in Iraq," he told an interviewer, "I'm afraid I cannot say that I'm sorry we removed Saddam Hussein." Defending his war policy, Blair affirmed, "I believe in it." He also insisted that the decision to go to war was vital to British security interests and was not simply a show of support for the traditional Anglo-American "special relationship." "If the Americans were not doing this," he asserted, "I would be pressing them to do so." Blair fiercely resisted the label "America's poodle."

Right from his first months as prime minister, Blair had been alarmed by "scary" intelligence reports indicating that Saddam Hussein was building chemical, biological, and perhaps even nuclear weapons of mass destruction (WMD). Even though British intelligence services concluded by 1998 that Saddam had already destroyed "the vast majority" of his WMD capabilities, there were lingering fears that the Iraqi leader was concealing his existing arsenals and arms production facilities. When President Clinton launched airstrikes on strategic targets in Iraq as Saddam impeded the work of UN inspectors in that same year, Blair ordered British aircraft to take part in the operation. And Britain joined with the United States in enforcing a "no-fly zone" against Iraqi aircraft over Kurdish and Shiite territories in Iraq.

September 11, 2001, was a turning point not only for the United States but for Tony Blair as well. For Blair, "an attack on America was the same as an attack on Britain." Blair also saw Britain, and himself personally, as a bridge between the United States and its increasingly independent European allies. But Blair and the new American president, George W. Bush, came from opposing sides of the left–right spectrum. The prime minister was ideologically and personally much closer to his friend Bill Clinton. And Blair was upset at the new Bush administration's early signs of unilateralism and opposition to European views on the Kyoto Protocol and other issues. Despite these frictions, the prime minister quickly established a close rapport with President Bush, especially after September 11. On September 20, Blair received a standing ovation at a special session of the U.S. Congress after President Bush addressed him with the warm greeting, "Thank you for coming, friend." Both leaders viewed world terrorism as a serious threat to Western security and political values, and both believed that decisive action had to be taken against al Qaeda and their partners in Afghanistan, the Taliban. British forces collaborated with U.S. and French aircraft in ousting the Taliban from power in the final months of 2001. Both Blair and Bush were also alarmed by evidence captured from al Qaeda indicating that the terrorist network was actively seeking to acquire chemical and biological agents as well as radioactive substances for use in making a "dirty bomb." They feared a worse catastrophe than the September 11 tragedy if terrorists were to obtain these materials from Iraq or some other source. Once a new government under Hamid Karzai was put in place in Afghanistan, Blair and Bush turned their attention to the "next phase" in the war on terrorism, centering on Iraq.

Over the course of the following months, the bonds between Blair and Bush drew so close that, according to Secretary of State Colin Powell, they were "essentially inside each other's thinking." Nevertheless, clear differences arose between the British and American approaches to Iraq. For one thing, Bush was heavily influenced by neoconservatives and other influential advisors like Vice President Dick Cheney and Defense Secretary Donald Rumsfeld. These key figures were already inclined *before* September 11 to effect a "regime change" in Iraq. Their preference was to take unilateral military action against Saddam Hussein's regime, without United Nations interference or even cooperation with NATO allies. For Blair and his team, by contrast, the dangers posed by Saddam's weapons of mass destruction were more important than regime change. In a secret document leaked to the British press shortly before the 2005 election, it was revealed that Britain's attorney general, the government's legal advisor, had warned Blair and his cabinet in 2002 that military action against Iraq *for purposes of regime change* would be illegal. (In 2003 the attorney general stated that the invasion could be justified on the grounds that Saddam Hussein had violated several UN Security Council resolutions requiring him to disarm.)

In addition, Blair and his chief lieutenants were insistent that the United Nations needed to be involved in the process of confronting Iraq over its weapons. They further believed that a broad multilateral coalition of states was necessary to build up pressure on Saddam Hussein. Initially they anticipated that President Jacques Chirac of France, Chancellor Gerhard Schroeder of Germany, and President Vladimir Putin of Russia could be persuaded to take part in such a coalition, along with other countries in Europe and the Middle East. Blair further hoped that Saddam could be compelled to reopen Iraq to UN weapons inspectors and cooperate with them unreservedly. Blair believed that if the world could be assured that Saddam possessed no WMD, then war could be avoided. Conversely, if Saddam rejected serious inspections, the justification for war would be unassailable. Finally, Blair wanted to combine pressures on Iraq with new U.S.-backed efforts to get Israel and the Palestinian Authority to reach a settlement of their disputes.

Blair emerged as the only foreign leader who had any real influence on President Bush. It was Blair's arguments that persuaded Bush to tell the United Nations in September 2002 that the United States would work with the Security Council to get the necessary resolutions against Iraq. The result was Resolution 1441, which warned Iraq of "serious consequences" if it refused to comply with UN demands for inspections and the elimination of illegal weapons. But as anti-war sentiment swelled in Britain, especially within the ranks of the Labour Party, Blair convinced President Bush to seek a second Security Council resolution explicitly sanctioning military action. This proposed resolution was withdrawn when President Chirac announced that France would use its veto in the Security Council to block it. Schroeder and Putin also opposed the war. Meanwhile, President Bush responded to Blair's appeals on the Middle East peace process by announcing his support for a Palestinian state. But he disappointed his British ally by rejecting negotiations with Palestinian president Yasser Arafat on the grounds that Arafat supported terrorism.

The British cabinet document leaked during the 2005 election campaign revealed that the Bush administration had made up its mind by the summer of 2002 to proceed with the invasion of Iraq. In early September, Bush told Blair at Camp David that dealing with Saddam's threat would most likely entail war, and that Britain would be expected to provide troops. Blair responded unhesitatingly, "I'm with you." In preparing the British public for military action, Blair's government released two intelligence dossiers intended to substantiate the dangers to British security posed by Saddam's weapons programs. But the first document turned out to contain misleading and insufficiently verified claims about Saddam's military capabilities, and the second was revealed as having been plagiarized from a doctoral dissertation. These and other revelations gave the impression that the government was applying undue pressure on the intelligence community and the attorney general to provide legitimate rationales for war. A defense ministry official was driven to suicide after giving a press interview that resulted in an exaggerated news report about the Blair government's alleged pressures on the intelligence services to overstate their evidence about Saddam's weapons. Meanwhile, neither British nor American intelligence agencies found credible evidence linking Saddam Hussein with the September 11 attacks or indicating that he had provided chemical, biological, or nuclear materials to al Qaeda.

As Blair joined with President Bush in issuing a final ultimatum to Saddam, the Labour Party revolt gathered strength. Robin Cook, Britain's foreign secretary in Blair's first government, resigned from his post as the government's leader in the House of Commons, telling the House that Saddam Hussein "probably has no weapons of mass destruction" capable of being delivered against a strategic urban target. And on March 18, the Blair government's war resolution in the Commons met with unprecedented opposition from Labour Party MPs. Two days later, the invasion of Iraq commenced.[28]

When the mayhem that immediately followed Saddam's ouster deteriorated into an anti-coalition insurgency and sectarian violence, the British public's initial support for the war evaporated. The failure to locate any WMD in Iraq further eroded support for the war. Quite a few Labour Party candidates, each running in single-member districts, lost their seats because of their local constituents' dissatisfaction with Prime Minister Blair. Even so, Labour won a substantial victory. Compared with having 412 members of Parliament and a 167-seat majority over opposing parties in the previous Parliament elected in 2001, the Labour Party ended up with 355 seats and a comfortable 66-seat voting majority in 2005. (The number of seats in the House of Commons was reduced from 659 in 2001 to 646 in 2005.) What explains this historic result?

Two reasons above all account for Labour's success: voter satisfaction with the government's economic policies, and voter dissatisfaction with the Conservative Party as an alternative to another Labour government.

After taking criticism during the 2001 election campaign for failing to "deliver" on public services, Blair and Brown injected new funds into health care, education, and other social programs. The National Health Service saw its budget rise by 7 percent a year starting in 2002. The money spent on new hospitals, clinics, and other facilities succeeded in reducing the number of people on NHS waiting lists for non-life-threatening services, as well as the time spent in these queues. (In 2000, more than a quarter million Britons had to wait more than six months for an operation; by 2005 the list approached zero.) Spending on schools and other social sectors also rose. Despite these expenditures, the British economy retained a low inflation rate (2 percent or less). Interest rates also remained relatively low, stimulating a real estate and consumer spending boom. Unemployment dipped below 5 percent. These successes were instrumental in retaining votes for Labour, even though many citizens continued to complain about the health services and other amenities, and more than 70 percent of Britons claimed that their tax payments were wasted. As the government's economic affairs minister, Gordon Brown reaped much of the credit for these successes. Brown was frequently at Blair's side during campaign appearances. And Blair openly endorsed Brown as his successor, announcing that he would step down as party leader before the next parliamentary elections scheduled for 2010.

The Conservative Party's failure to convince British voters of its viability as an alternative government also played into Labour's hands. Ever since the departure of Margaret Thatcher and John Major from the political scene, the Tories had run into difficulty selecting a leader of stature. Once William Hague resigned as party chief following the 2001 elections, new procedures for choosing his replacement by a ballot of party members resulted in the selection of Iain Duncan Smith, a former career military officer associated with the party's right wing. Duncan Smith failed to present himself as a dynamic leader capable of becoming prime minister, however, and in October 2003 a majority of Conservative MPs voted him out of the leadership. In his place they selected Michael Howard, a former cabinet minister in the Thatcher and Major governments. Though Howard proved an aggressive leader of the "loyal opposition" in his sparring matches with Blair in the House of Commons, he failed to articulate a coherent alternative political vision. As the 2005 campaign approached, nearly 70 percent of British voters said they did not know what the Tories stood for. Anti-EU passions no longer stirred the Conservatives' core voters as they had in the past, nor did Howard's tough stance on immigration win him a large shift in votes. On the all-important issue of Iraq, Howard called Blair a "liar"; but the Tory leader stated explicitly during the campaign that he supported the invasion and Britain's troop presence in Iraq. Polls showed that most voters trusted the Labour Party more than the Conservatives on the economy, health care, and other bread-and-butter social welfare issues. In the end, the Conservatives picked up 32 new seats, winning 198 in all. Despite these gains, it was the party's third worst showing in a century.

The Liberal Democrats won ten new seats in 2005, boosted by their decision under Charles Kennedy's leadership to oppose the invasion of Iraq. These gains fell short of the party's expectations, however. And Britain's single-member-district/plurality voting system, which we'll examine below, once again punished the Liberal Democrats. Despite winning 22 percent of the popular vote nationwide, the party's candidates ended up with only 62 seats in the House of Commons, 9.6 percent of the total number of seats (see table 16.1).

Voter turnout for the 2005 election was 61.5 percent, about 2 points higher than in 2001 but a full 10 points lower than in 1997.[29]

Now that we have surveyed British political developments since World War II, what generalizations can we make about them? One of the oldest hypotheses about voting behavior suggests that people tend to vote in accordance with their class interests. People in the lower levels of the income pyramid can thus be expected to vote for labor- and welfare-oriented parties, while those in the upper echelons vote for conservative parties that pledge to keep taxes low and protect private business freedoms. To what extent does social class explain British voting behavior?

## HYPOTHESIS-TESTING EXERCISE: Social Class in British Politics

### Hypothesis

Social class best explains election outcomes in Britain.

### Variables

The *dependent variable* is *election outcomes.* On what is it dependent? The *independent* (or explanatory) *variable* is *social class.*

### Expectations

If this hypothesis is correct, then we would expect the evidence to show that (1) working-class voters and others at the lower end of the socioeconomic pyramid vote consistently for the Labour Party; (2) upper-income people tend to vote consistently for the Conservatives; and (3) the middle class splits its vote, with the less affluent strata tending toward Labour and the more affluent voting Conservative.

### Evidence

"Class is the basis of British party politics," a political scientist wrote in 1960; "all else is mere embellishment and detail."[30] Indeed, class-based voting patterns were especially evident prior to World War II and up until the 1960s. Between 1945 and 1970, for instance, the Conservatives won a solid 60 percent or more of the votes of nonmanual (white-collar) voters, while Labour won similarly large shares of the manual working-class vote. However, there is also evidence indicating that the impact of social class on voters' preferences is not nearly as one-sided and consistent as our hypothesis would lead us to suspect. For example:

- Even in the 1945–70 period, a substantial number of manual workers (25 percent or more) voted Conservative, the so-called "working-class Tories." Labour won more than a fifth of the white-collar vote in this period.[31]
- In the 1970s there was mounting evidence of party dealignment: a growing number of voters were breaking away from their traditional party loyalties. Labour won a diminishing share of its core working-class following, in part because of disappointment at the Labour government's performance in 1964–70. The Conservatives suffered defections as well, and more voters cast ballots for the Liberals or local parties in Scotland, Wales, and Northern Ireland.
- The heightened ideological confrontations of the Thatcher years sparked more changes. While the Tories held steady at about 42 percent of the nationwide popular vote, they won growing support from manual working-class voters and low-income public housing residents. These votes reflected working-class support for Thatcher's opposition to militant trade union leaders who called strikes without balloting the membership, and for her efforts to help public housing residents purchase homes from the government. In 1983, Labour won only 47 percent of the manual working-class vote; 30 percent went to the Conservatives. The Liberals and their allies, meanwhile, won more middle-class votes from the Conservatives and a growing share of manual workers (22 percent in 1983).
- The 1997 election witnessed a large swing of middle-class voters to Labour and sizable defections from the Conservatives. Tony Blair deliberately pursued a multiclass, "one nation" approach aimed at broadening Labour's middle-class appeal while holding on to its working-class base. This strategy was rooted in the significant changes in Britain's class structure that had occurred over the previous generation. From the 1960s to the 1990s, the number of Britons in middle-class professions rose from about 42 percent of the working-age population to roughly 60 percent, while those engaged in working-class occupations fell from 48 percent to about 41 percent. Voting patterns shifted in accordance with Blair's centrist pitch. In 1992, voters in professional and managerial professions, located in the upper strata of the middle class, cast only 16 percent of their votes for Labour; only 27 percent of average white-collar workers voted for Labour. But in 1997, "New Labour" won 36 percent of the former group and 46 percent of the latter, figures that fell only slightly in 2001 to 30 percent and 38 percent, respectively. Meanwhile, a majority of manual workers continued to vote for the Labour Party in 1997 and 2001, as the class-voting hypothesis would predict.
- In 2005 the Labour Party lost votes in all class categories. The Conservatives and Liberal Democrats each picked up working-class votes at Labour's expense; together their combined share of the skilled workers' vote rose from 44 percent to 52 percent in 2005. But Labour still received about 30 percent of the votes from the professional, managerial, and routine white-collar sectors typically associated with the middle class. All these results run counter to our hypothesis. Nevertheless, Labour in 2005 retained 40 percent of skilled and 48 percent of unskilled manual workers, while the two predominantly middle-class parties together captured more than 60 percent of the professional and white-collar vote—facts that are consistent with the hypothesis.[32]

### Conclusions

The evidence is *mixed.* British elections since 1945 demonstrate that social class indeed accounts for a substantial amount of voting behavior. The Conservatives and Liberal Democrats together have consistently managed to attract well more than half of the middle- and upper-class vote. The Labour Party has always won at least 40 percent of the working-class vote. Nevertheless, British voters in the postwar period have not voted in strict accordance with their social class. The three main political parties, which started out as *particularistic* parties representing specific class interests, developed over the course of the twentieth century into multiclass *catch-all* parties. In conclusion, class does matter in British elections, but class alone does not determine British election outcomes.[33]

## BRITISH DEMOCRACY TODAY: PARTIES, ELECTIONS, AND STATE INSTITUTIONS

It is often said that the UK does not have a written constitution. In fact, the UK does have a constitution, but it is not codified in a single written document like the U.S. Constitution or the constitutions of France, Russia, or numerous other countries. The UK's constitutional laws are instead inscribed in thousands of Acts of Parliament and court rulings that have accumulated over the centuries. And they are reinforced by traditional practices and procedures that also tend to have a long history. As in other democracies, Britain's constitutional arrangements prescribe how the country's governmental institutions are organized and how they should function. They also provide the institutional framework for political competition between parties and other participants in the political process. As we'll see in the pages that follow, the UK's constitutional framework is marked by both enduring tradition and adaptability to changing conditions.

## Parties and Elections

Political parties are vital to the electoral process in all democracies, but especially so in a parliamentary system of government. British parties are more centrally organized than are parties in the United States and play a more direct role in defining policy goals, nominating candidates for office, conducting election campaigns, and coordinating legislative and government activities. The three largest parties—Labour, the Conservatives, and the Liberal Democrats—are particularly well organized. Each has a national headquarters and a bureaucracy, representatives in Parliament (the "parliamentary party"), and local organizations in all House of Commons districts in Great Britain (the "constituency parties"). (Neither Labour nor the Liberal Democrats contest elections in Northern Ireland, while the Conservatives have only a token following there.) Unlike the Democrats and Republicans in the United States these parties also have dues-paying members. Only those members whose dues are paid up are allowed to vote at constituency meetings to nominate candidates for the House of Commons.

**The Party Leader** All the main parties in the United Kingdom have explicit procedures for choosing the party leader, who is the person most likely to become prime minister should the party win a majority of seats in the Commons. By contrast, the two main U.S. parties do not have a formal chief. While a serving president is usually regarded as the leader of his party, he does not carry this title officially. The party that does not occupy the White House may be even less certain as to who its leader is.

Just as important, Britain's parliamentary system requires any prospective prime minister to be a member of Parliament, preferably of the Commons. It is therefore unthinkable that a British politician could become leader of one of the main parties or rise to "the top o' the greasy pole" as head of government without parliamentary experience. Several have also gained executive experience serving in the cabinet prior to assuming party leadership. However, it is quite possible for a political figure in the United States to have no experience whatsoever in national government, in either Congress or the cabinet, and still win election to the highest office of the land. Presidents Carter, Reagan, Clinton, and George W. Bush are recent examples.

British prime ministers are elected by a much smaller group of voters than are U.S. presidents. In Britain, the party leader's name appears on the ballot only in one House of Commons district (constituency). In 1997, 2001, and 2005, Tony Blair was the Labour candidate for Parliament in Sedgefield, and nowhere else. Voters living in other constituencies who favored Blair for prime minister had to vote for the Labour Party candidate running in their own constituency and hope that Labour candidates would win a majority of these single-member constituency contests. By contrast, all American voters have a chance to choose among the competing candidates for president in the general elections.

Every year the Labour Party and the Conservatives hold a conference at which their leaders make major pronouncements and party activists debate policy alternatives. The Liberal Democrats convene twice yearly for these purposes. By contrast, American parties hold national conventions only every four years, mainly to confirm as their nominee for president the candidate who has emerged from the primary elections of the preceding months as the front runner.

**British Parties** The three largest British parties share several features in common, though they differ in details. All three are moderate, mainstream catch-all parties. Labour tends to be a left-of-center party, with its lower-middle-class and working-class base and social-welfare priorities. The Conservatives are right of center, with a large upper-middle-class and upper-class following and strong ties to private enterprise. But these two large parties garner votes from all social classes, especially the large middle class, and their leaders have calculatingly edged closer to the center since the 1990s. The Liberal Democrats position themselves squarely in the center of Britain's political spectrum. All three parties have struggled in recent years to articulate a distinctive message, a task complicated by the fact that they all favor the mixed economy's combination of private enterprise and social welfare, and all favor Britain's alliance with the United States and its membership in the European Union. At the same time, all three parties are internally divided into competing wings and policy tendencies.

The *Conservatives*, who have been formally known as the "Conservative and Unionist Party" ever since the days when they favored the union of Ireland with Great Britain, were Britain's most successful party for much of the twentieth century, producing prime ministers like Winston Churchill, Harold Macmillan, and Margaret Thatcher.[34] Since 1997, however, the Tories have suffered their three worst defeats.

One of their problems is that Tony Blair and the New Labour Party managed to occupy the center ground of British politics by embracing some traditional Conservative goals—such as low inflation, labor union restraint, and business incentives—while pursuing social welfare policies popular among voters in the middle and on the left. Blair stole the Tories' thunder by depriving them of their ability to brand Labour as a high-tax party dominated by trade union militants and pacifists. Another problem has been the Conservatives' failure to find a popular, charismatic leader capable of uniting the party's various wings. After William Hague resigned following the 2001 elections, the Tories instituted new procedures for choosing its leader. In the past, the party chief was selected by the Conservatives' House of Commons delegation (the "parliamentary party"). Under the new rules, Tory MPs would pick two nominees for the leadership post, and then the party's dues-paying members would vote on the final choice by mail-in ballots. When this process was used for the first time in 2001, Iain Duncan Smith won the leadership in a hotly disputed contest. But Duncan Smith proved ineffectual, provoking calls for his resignation. In 2003 the Tories' "1922 Committee," consisting of all the Conservative MPs with the exception of the party leader, removed Duncan Smith and selected Michael Howard as his successor. As the parliamentary party's only nominee, Howard did not require confirmation by the party membership. After Howard resigned in 2005, the Tories chose *David Cameron* as their new leader.

At 39, Cameron had little experience in politics. His background marked him as a traditional blue-blooded Tory. A descendant of King Henry VII, the Tudor aristocracy, and two Conservative MPs, Cameron was sent off to boarding school as a child and rounded out his education at Eton and Oxford. After serving as an aide to Margaret Thatcher and a junior advisor to John Major's chancellor of the exchequer while in his twenties, Cameron gained corporate experience with a large communications firm from 1994 to 2001, when he was elected to Parliament. In 2004 he became the Conservatives' parliamentary spokesperson for education. Cameron was a relative unknown until his three-minute speech at the 2005 party conference won a spirited response from the delegates for its rousing appeal to modernize the party. After being nominated for the leadership by Tory MPs, Cameron won 68 percent of the vote among party members, soundly defeating a more experienced right-winger favored by Thatcher.

Vowing to pursue "compassionate conservatism," Cameron announced plans to steer the Conservative Party closer to the centrist mainstream, much as Tony Blair had led the Labour Party to the center in the 1990s. Cameron also declared that he was "fed up with the Punch and Judy politics of name-calling, backbiting, point-scoring, and finger-pointing" in House of Commons debates. Acknowledging that the Conservatives had "a vast mountain to climb," Cameron hoped to transform a party riven by continuing differences between centrists and right-wingers on taxes, social welfare policy, Europe, and other issues. The Tories also faced declining support among young voters, women, ethnic minorities, college graduates, and even its base of "true blue" supporters from the worlds of business and the professions. And in confronting Tony Blair's presumed successor, Gordon Brown, David Cameron would face a far more experienced opposite number.[35]

As we have seen, the *Labour Party* has undergone profound transformations of its own. Under the informal moniker "New Labour," Tony Blair and his key lieutenants guided the party to unprecedented electoral successes. But the controversies arising from his stewardship as prime minister ultimately compelled Blair to step down as party chief far earlier than he probably would have liked. And the divisions within the Labour Party between Blair-oriented centrists and more left-leaning politicians and voters have by no means disappeared. Opposition to such things as the war in Iraq, college tuition payments, the privatization of traditional social services, and other Blair policies has arisen to a considerable extent from the party's traditional left-of-center base. Although there is little support for a return to trade union militancy or high-tax, high-inflation economic policies, debates about where the party should go under Gordon Brown, a man identified with both the Labour left and New Labour, are likely to intensify in the coming years. Like the Conservatives, the Labour Party must redefine itself in the light of its traditional values and rapidly changing domestic and international environments.

The **Liberal Democrats** are the descendants of the old Liberal Party. The liberals originated as the Whigs and remained the country's second most important party after the Conservatives until shortly after World War I, when they were increasingly eclipsed by the Labour Party. Another antecedent of the Liberal Democrats was the Social Democratic Party (SDP). The SDP got started in 1981 when a number of moderate Labour MPs, distraught at the leftist direction of the Labour leadership, bolted from the party and formed a new one. The Liberals and Social Democrats formed an alliance that won 25 percent of the vote in 1983. Five years later they formally merged as the Liberal Democrats. The party has sought to forge its identity as a centrist alternative to the Conservatives on its right and Labour on its left. After the 1997 elections, the Liberal Democrats sought to make common cause with Blair's New Labour government on issues like electoral and constitutional reform and the euro. But Labour's huge voting majority in the House of Commons enabled Blair to pursue his government's priorities independently of Liberal Democrat support. Nevertheless, the Liberal Democrats continued to support a more proportional electoral system, the replacement of the House of Lords by a democratically elected Senate, and the adoption of the euro. They also held back from supporting Blair's policies on Iraq in 2003.

With only about 70,000 paid members, the Liberal Democrats elect their leader by means of a mail-in ballot of the membership. Paddy Ashdown was elected in 1988 and was followed in 1999 by Charles Kennedy. After leading the "Lib Dems" to small but encouraging gains in the elections of 2001 and 2006, Kennedy was pressured by party leaders into resigning in January 2006 because of a drinking problem. In two rounds of postal-ballot voting, party members elected Sir Menzies "Ming" Campbell, the party's number two, as their new leader.

All three major parties—Labour, the Conservatives, and the Liberal Democrats—have suffered from declines in their membership and core identifiers. The number of dues-paying Conservatives has tumbled from 1.2 million in the halcyon days of Thatcherism in 1982 to about 300,000 by 2005. The Labour Party's membership spiked from 280,000 in 1992 to 405,000 when Tony Blair led the party to a spectacular victory in 1997, but then slid to 215,000 in 2005. And the Liberal Democrats have fallen from 145,000 members during the time of the Liberal-SDP Alliance in 1983 to 73,000 in 2005. The problem is not money: annual dues are at most about £15 (less than $30) in the Labour and Liberal Democrat parties, and typically even less for students and workers. Even well-heeled Conservatives are asked simply to contribute what they can. Though dues-payers have the privilege of participating in the nomination process for House of Commons candidates, as we'll explain below, a diminishing number of British citizens are willing to take part in this process by joining a particular party. In a trend observable in the United States and other long-term democracies, today's voters in Britain are increasingly independent. In 1964, 44 percent of British voters identified themselves as "very strong" adherents of a particular party (typically one of the three main parties), and 40 percent said they were "fairly strong" party identifiers. In 2005, only 8 percent were very strong party identifiers, and 37 percent were fairly strong party adherents; fully 18 percent claimed no party affiliation. In 2005, 8.2 percent of the voters cast their ballots for parties other than the "big three" or for the Scottish or Welsh nationalist parties, the highest percentage of other-party voters since World War II.[36]

Several smaller parties have managed to win seats in the House of Commons fairly consistently. They tend to have weak organizations dominated by a few leaders, with few or no dues-paying members. The more successful of these parties are based outside of England. The *Scottish National Party* (SNP), founded in 1934, advocates independence for Scotland. In 2005 it won 17.7 percent of the Scottish vote and six seats in the House of Commons. Its main competitor is the Labour Party, which won forty-one of Scotland's fifty-nine Commons seats; the Liberal Democrats won six. The *Welsh Nationalist Party,* Plaid Cymru (Plide KUM-ree), founded in 1925, wants more autonomy for Wales (but not outright independence) and greater use of the Welsh language. It polled 12.6 percent of the Welsh vote in 2005 and won only three of the forty seats reserved for Wales in the House of Commons.

Northern Ireland's parties reflect that region's tormented history of sectarian strife between Protestants and Catholics. The Protestants (or "unionists") have an intransigent party, the *Democratic Unionists,* led by the Reverend Ian Paisley; and a moderate party, the *Ulster Unionists,* which has supported the Protestant-Catholic peace process under David Trimble. The Catholics (or "nationalists") are also divided into an intransigent party and a more moderate one. *Sinn Fein* (Shin fane; We Ourselves) is the political wing of the Irish Republican Army (IRA), which has a tradition of terrorism. The *Social Democratic and Labour Party* has been more supportive of the peace process. After sectarian violence erupted once again in Northern Ireland in 1969, the UK government in 1972 suspended the region's local legislature and imposed direct rule from London, policed by British troops. Over the following decades, more than 3,200 people lost their lives in bombings, assassinations, and other acts of violence. With citizens on both sides of the religious divide increasingly eager for peace, Protestant and Catholic negotiators engaged in protracted negotiations mediated by the Clinton administration's envoy, former Senator George J. Mitchell. On Good Friday in 1998, accords were signed aimed at ending the stalemate. After the accords were ratified by 71 percent of Northern Ireland's voters, British rule was supposed to be lifted and the local legislature was supposed to resume its work in the historic building known as Stormont. But these measures were repeatedly rescinded or postponed as the IRA refused to disarm its militants and Protestant hardliners refused to deal with the IRA. Only in 2006, after the IRA certified that it had disarmed, did the Stormont legislature reconvene. Tensions between Protestant and Catholic hardliners remains, however. Northern Ireland is allotted eighteen seats in the UK's House of Commons. In 2001 and again in 2005, the Protestant and Catholic intransigent parties each won seats from the moderate parties. In 2005, Trimble lost his seat to a candidate from Paisley's party.

More than three hundred parties and well over a hundred independent candidates participated in the 2005 elections. Only nine parties and four independents won seats, however. Among the smaller parties, the environmentally oriented *Green Party,* with its support centered mainly in urban constituencies with large student populations, fielded 202 candidates. They averaged 1 percent of the vote but won no seats. The *UK Independence Party,* which favors a referendum on withdrawing from the European Union, ran in 458 constituencies. It won 3.2 percent of the vote but no seats. Several fringe parties on the left (like the British Communist Party) and right (like the anti-immigrant British National Party) also came up short.

One of the four independents who won seats was George Galloway, a former Labour Party MP who was an outspoken critic of the Iraq war. Galloway established a new movement called Respect, but he was the party's only victorious candidate, winning a seat in a London constituency that had the largest proportion of Muslims in Britain. Another was Clare Short, who resigned from Blair's cabinet over Iraq. Other parties that competed unsuccessfully included the Blair Must Go Party, the Legalize Cannabis Alliance, and frivolous entrants like the Monster Raving Loony Party and the Church of the Militant Elvis Party.

**Elections to the House of Commons: The Nomination Process** One of the first things most candidates for elective office must do is obtain the official nomination of a political party. Like most parliamentary democracies, the United Kingdom does not have primary elections. Rather, each party has its own procedures for choosing its nominees to compete in the general elections to the House of

Commons. In the three largest parties it is the party activists and dues-paying party members in each constituency who ultimately select their party's nominee. In the smaller parties that have few, if any, dues-paying members, the nomination process tends to be controlled more tightly by professional party elites.

The Conservatives, the Labour Party, and the Liberal Democrats have roughly similar procedures for selecting their candidates. People who wish to run for Parliament are typically interviewed by a party's selection committee in the constituency they wish to represent. (As noted earlier, MPs do not have to reside in the constituency they represent.) If a constituency is considered fairly safe for one of the parties and the nomination is up for grabs, quite a few apply, sometimes between twenty-five and a hundred. But if an incumbent MP is popular or if a challenging party is not likely to win, there will usually be far fewer applicants for the nomination. The selection committee screens the applicants and draws up a short list, normally consisting of between two and ten applicants. This all-important short-list decision is invariably taken by a very small group of people; constituency selection committees generally consist of only about a dozen local activists in the Conservative Party and around twenty in the Labour Party.

Once prospective nominees have made the short list, they appear before an "adoption meeting" of the local constituency membership. (Conservative Party constituency associations often have a further screening of the short-list candidates, only one or two of whom may be presented to the full constituency membership for final approval.) In the Conservative, Labour, and Liberal Democrat parties, these nomination meetings are rarely attended by more than 200 dues-paying members; in most cases only about 50 to 150 show up to vote.[37] Assuming a generous average turnout of 160 voting members in each constituency, what this means is that slightly more than 100,000 people in each of Britain's two largest parties participate in the nomination process for about 650 House of Commons seats. The Liberal Democrats' nominees are chosen by an even smaller number of members. Far fewer people are eligible to take part in the nomination process in the smaller parties. With about 44 million registered voters in the UK in 1997, it appears that *fewer than 1 percent of British voters participated in the party nomination process* for the House of Commons in that year. The figures for 2001 and 2005 were essentially the same. In the United States, about 30 to 40 percent of eligible voters typically participate in primary elections for the House of Representatives. While many Americans regard these turnouts as lamentably low, they are considerably higher than in Britain and other democracies that do not have primaries.

Meanwhile, the central headquarters of the main parties plays its own role in the selection process. The dossiers of prospective nominees for Parliament are usually scrutinized by the party's central office, and some applicants are personally interviewed. While the national headquarters rarely forces a candidate of its own choosing on a local constituency, all candidates nominated by the constituency parties must be vetted by the party's central organs. As a consequence, candidates for Parliament—as well as serving MPs—tend to be more dependent on their national party leadership than are candidates for Congress in the United States, who compete in primary elections on their own initiative and raise most of their own campaign funding. If a party's national leadership refuses its endorsement of a prospective candidate, that person will not be able to run for Parliament as the party's official nominee. No similar process of interference by the Democratic or Republican national committees exists in the United States, giving candidates and elected members of Congress greater independence from their party leadership than their British counterparts enjoy.

**Campaigns and Campaign Financing** Another salient difference between British and American electoral processes is that the UK does not specify the timing of general elections very far in advance of their occurrence. American law designates the first Tuesday after the first Monday in November every two years for congressional elections and every four years for presidential elections. In Britain the prime minister may ask the queen to call elections to the House of Commons at any time. While British law requires parliamentary elections to take place at least every five years, prime ministers may call anticipated ("snap") elections before the expiration of Parliament's full five-year term. If public opinion polls look favorable for the government, the motivation to call a snap election is especially high. In fact, snap elections are the rule rather than the exception in Britain. Since 1918, John Major's second government (1992–97) has been the only one in peacetime to serve out its full term. Except for the crisis years of 1935–45, all other prime ministers called snap elections.

Once the prime minister gets the queen's symbolic approval and announces the date of the elections, an official campaign period begins that has important legal consequences. In 2005 Blair formally announced on April 5 that the elections would take place in four weeks. Parliament is formally adjourned during this period and ceases to meet; hence no new legislation can be enacted.

Once the campaign is under way, the main parties issue an election "manifesto" that outlines the policies they promise to pursue if elected to form the government. The formulation of these manifestos is taken more seriously by British parties than by the two largest parties in the United States. Presidential candidates in both large U.S. parties are notorious for completely ignoring their party's platform in the ensuing campaign.

Strict spending rules apply during the official campaign period in the UK. It is only during these weeks that parties and candidates may spend money for advertising and related election purposes. Most of the advertisement money is for handouts and billboards, since British law forbids paid political ads on television or radio. The British Broadcasting Corporation (BBC) provides each major party with a limited amount of free air time during the campaign period, while the national treasury picks up the tab for campaign mailings.

One of the most significant differences between British and American elections is that, ever since the passage of the Corrupt and Illegal Practices Act in 1883, British law places limits on how much may be spent in behalf of individual candidates running for the House of Commons. While the precise amount varies from one election to another and depends in part on the number of voters in each constituency, candidates in the 1990s were allowed to spend no more than about £7,500 on average—about $10,000. That amount went up only slightly in 2001 and 2005. Most candidates spent less. In the United States, individual candidates now spend about $1 million in contested primary and general

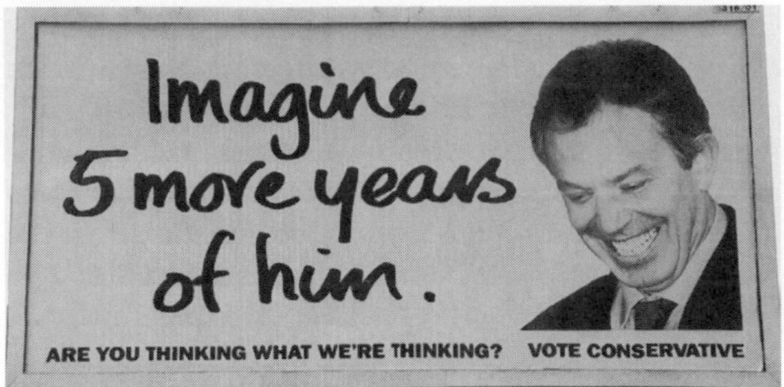


Conservative Billboard in 2005

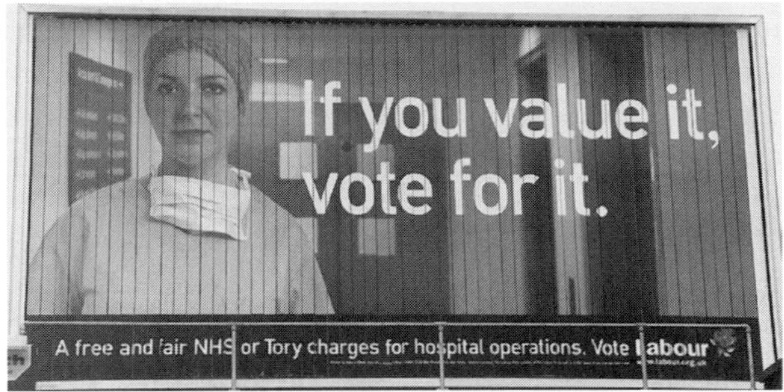


Labour Billboard in 2005

elections to the House of Representatives. The cost of running for the U.S. Senate or the presidency is, of course, vastly higher.

National party organizations, however, may spend large amounts of cash on political campaigns. In recent years these costs have soared, as British parties have adopted American election techniques like hiring ad firms and distributing literature and videos. In 2005 the Conservatives and Labour each spent about £18 million (about $34 million), and the Liberal Democrats spent £4.3 million (about $8 million). The main parties have inevitably found themselves beholden to their chief benefactors, whether they are interest groups or individuals. In British politics as in U.S. politics, money talks. The Conservative and Labour parties have also borrowed heavily to finance their activities, and both parties are mired in debt. In 2000 Parliament passed a law limiting election-year expenditures by a party's organization to £20 million.

All candidates in parliamentary elections are required to put up a deposit of £500. If they fail to garner at least 5 percent of the vote in their constituency, they forfeit the deposit, which reverts to the national treasury.[38]

**Voter Registration and Turnout** Unlike American voters, British citizens are not required to go to a designated location to register to vote. In Britain, voters may register by mail, and election authorities may conduct a door-to-door canvass of some residences before an upcoming election to make sure that all citizens eligible to vote are on the registry. In 2005 it was estimated that about 7 percent of eligible voters in the UK were not registered to vote. This figure was much lower than in the United States, where 30 percent of citizens eligible to vote are not registered.[39]

Voter turnout in Britain has remained consistently higher than in the United States, in spite of the fact that the two countries have similar election procedures for the lower house. Between 1945 and 1997, turnout in fifteen elections to the House of Commons averaged 76.8 percent of registered voters. The 2001 turnout of 59.4 percent was the lowest since World War I. It climbed slightly to 61.2 percent in 2005.

**The Electoral System** The electoral system used to elect the House of Commons is the *single-member-district (SMD)/plurality* method. There is only one round of elections: hence it is a *single-ballot* procedure. The United States employs the same system for elections to the House of Representatives.

The United Kingdom is divided into more than six hundred electoral districts (constituencies). There is no fixed number of constituencies, nor is there a precise limit on the size of their population. A neutral electoral commission fixes the number of constituencies and their boundaries, avoiding the political gerrymandering of districts that occurs in the United States. In 2001 there were 659 constituencies, but the number fell to 646 in 2005 as Scotland lost thirteen seats in the Commons. In recent years the English constituencies have tended to represent about 68,000 voters each, with lower numbers in Scotland, Wales, and Northern Ireland. In the United States, each of the 435 members of the House of Representatives represents, on average, 450,000 eligible voters, but the actual figure varies by state.

*One person is elected to represent each district in a winner-take-all contest.* Because at least three candidates compete in most UK districts, the victor does not have to earn an absolute majority of the votes cast (more than 50 percent) to win; a *plurality* suffices. Each candidate's name is listed on a paper ballot, followed by her or his party affiliation (see figure 16.2). Britain does not use voting machines. In the example in table 16.2, Stephen Hammond was "first past the post" with 41.2 percent of the vote, as described in "The Battle of Wimbledon."

**VOTE FOR ONE CANDIDATE ONLY**

| | | | |
|---|---|---|---|
| 1 | **BARROW**<br>Giles Timothy Barrow<br>Avenue. Morden, Surrey, SM4 4<br>Green Party | Green Party | |
| 2 | **CASALE**<br>Roger Mark Casale<br>Road, Ravnes Park, London, SW20<br>The Labour Party Candidate | Labour | |
| 3 | **COVERDALE**<br>Christopher Joseph Coverdale<br>Woodside, London, SW19<br>Independent | | |
| 4 | **GEE**<br>Stephen Mark Gee<br>Banstead, Surrey, SM7 1<br>Liberal Democrats | LIBERAL DEMOCRATS | |
| 5 | **HAMMOND**<br>Stephen William Hammond<br>Road, Wimbledon, London, SW19<br>The Conservative Party Candidate | CONSERVATIVE | |
| 6 | **MILLS**<br>Andrew Thomas Mills<br>Road, Merton Park, London, SW19<br>UK Independence Party | UKIP | |
| 7 | **WEISS**<br>George Weiss (known as "Rainbow")<br>Street, Hampstead, London, NW:<br>Vote For Yourself Rainbow Dream Ticket | | |
| 8 | **WILSON**<br>Alastair Pitcairn Wilson<br>Close. Tooting, London, SW17<br>Tigers Eye The Party For Kids | | |

**FIGURE 16.2 Sample Ballot**
*Source:* Electoral Services Office, London Borough of Merton.

## THE BATTLE OF WIMBLEDON: Running for the House of Commons in 2005

"And now we have the results for Wimbledon. The candidates will please come forward." It was nearly 2:30 in the morning. The moment of truth after a hard-fought campaign and a long election day was at hand. On the basketball court of a public recreation center,

TABLE 16.2

**Wimbledon Constituency Elections to the House of Commons, 2001 and 2005**

**2001 (Turnout: 64.3%)**

| Candidate | Party | Votes | % of Votes |
|---|---|---|---|
| Casale | Labour | 18,806 | 45.7 |
| Hammond | Conservative | 15,062 | 36.6 |
| Pierce | Liberal Democrat | 5,341 | 13.0 |
| Thacker | Green | 1,007 | 2.5 |
| Glencross | Christian People's Alliance | 479 | 1.2 |
| Bell | UKIP | 414 | 1.0 |

**2005 (Turnout: 68.1%)**

| Candidate | Party | Votes | % of Votes |
|---|---|---|---|
| Casale | Labour | 15,585 | 35.9 |
| Hammond | Conservative | 17,886 | 41.2 |
| Gee | Liberal Democrat | 7,868 | 18.1 |
| Barrow | Green | 1,374 | 3.2 |
| Coverdale | Independent | 211 | 0.5 |
| Mills | UKIP | 408 | 0.9 |
| Wilson | Tiger's Eye | 50 | 0.1 |
| Weiss | Rainbow Dream | 22 | 0.05 |

*Source:* British Election Study, essex.ac.uk/bes

dozens of vote counters seated at long tables had just completed several hours of counting and recounting piles of paper ballots by hand under the watchful eyes of the candidates' representatives. Each ballot was supposed to be marked in pencil by an X next to a single candidate's name, a remarkably low-tech voting procedure that has worked well in Britain for more than a century.

The battle for the Wimbledon seat was a microcosm of the 2005 national elections. Its importance was highlighted by the *New York Times* just a few days before the vote. Roger Casale, the incumbent Labour MP who had won two straight victories, was locked in a tight race with Stephen Hammond, the Conservative who was his main challenger. Casale had defeated Hammond by nearly 4,000 votes in 2001. But the mood in Wimbledon was very different in 2005, as it was in much of the country. Many of the constituency's Labour Party voters were noticeably upset at the war in Iraq and at Tony Blair's apparent disingenuousness. Casale had supported Blair's policies in Parliament, and so he had good reason to anticipate some erosion of his electoral base. Not only did the incumbent worry about Hammond. Casale also feared that disenchanted Labour voters who were not willing to desert him for the Tory Hammond might instead cast their votes for Stephen Gee, the Liberal Democrat. An opponent of the Iraq war and a moderate on social policy, Gee was the wild card in the Wimbledon contest. When the three main contenders joined their five opponents on stage to learn their fate in the early hours of May 6, no one knew who would finish "first past the post" as the Wimbledon race came down to the wire.

Wimbledon is a well-to-do area in southwest London. Its large middle class includes a substantial percentage of small-home owners, while its toniest sections—located around the famous All-England tennis club—are lined with magnificent mansions worth millions. Not surprisingly, it had been a Conservative bastion since 1950. Casale, the grandson of an Italian immigrant and the holder of a master's degree from Johns Hopkins University's international affairs school in Bologna, stood little chance of winning in 1997, but he rode Tony Blair's coattails to victory, pulling off the second widest swing of votes from the Conservatives to Labour in the entire country. "Not even I expected to win," Casale confided.

After Casale pulled off his upset victory, Wimbledon's Tories decided it was time to select a new candidate for the next elections. About 150 people applied for the nomination. Most of them were vetted by the Conservative Party's central office in London for their suitability as potential candidates. Those considered

**Stephen Hammond Campaigning in 2005**

acceptable were put on a list that was then sent to Wimbledon's Conservatives. A series of local Conservative selection committee meetings whittled the list down to about twenty applicants at first, then eight, and finally three. The finalists were subjected to numerous interviews with selection committee members and dues-paying Tory constituents. About two hundred members attended the final selection meeting in the summer of 1999. The person they ultimately chose was Stephen Hammond, a genial 39-year-old investment banker.

Hammond's first order of business was to move to Wimbledon. Unlike Casale, who was a lifelong resident of the area, Hammond did not yet reside there. Hammond spent the next two years making himself known to the community by organizing a variety of citizens' initiatives and going door to door to find out what was on people's minds. Casale, too, understood the importance of close contact with the voters. During his first four years in office, he and his staff had handled twelve hundred constituent cases and answered fifteen thousand letters.

In 2001, the Tories had Casale in their sights. Wimbledon was one of about thirty key seats they hoped to take from New Labour. But in spite of voter grumbling about the Blair government's failure to deliver on its promises of improved social services, Casale and New Labour remained a more acceptable choice than either the Conservative or the Liberal Democrat candidates in the eyes of the highest number of Wimbledon's voters. Winning 45.7 percent of the vote, Casale cruised to a reelection victory (see table 16.2).

Nothing lasts forever in politics, however. Blair's decision to participate in the invasion of Iraq, and Casale's decision to support the prime minister, disturbed quite a few Wimbledon voters. Disaffection with Blair was particularly evident among the district's well-educated, middle-class suburbanites whose postmaterialist values had motivated them to support the Labour Party in previous elections. The Conservatives hoped to profit from Blair's waning popularity, even though the party hierarchy under Michael Howard openly supported the Iraq mission. As Stephen Hammond greeted potential voters in front of Wimbledon's central shopping mall on the weekend before the election, he acknowledged that Howard's support for the war might not help his candidacy. "But subliminally the campaign is about trust," he added, emphasizing that mistrust of Blair was now greater than in 2001, making Casale vulnerable.

Casale encountered some of this anti-Blair sentiment in his "walkabouts" through the constituency. Like his opponents, Casale spent many hours during the four-week campaign knocking on doors and chatting up voters. This personal touch is vital in British constituencies. Unlike American candidates for Congress, who often raise hundreds of thousands of dollars for broadcast advertising and direct mailings, British candidates are subjected to strict limits on the amount of money they can spend on their own campaigns. In Wimbledon that amount in recent years has been about $13,000, but only the Conservative and Labour candidates have come close to raising that much money. Most of it comes from their respective national party headquarters. Individual candidates spread their messages mainly through personal appearances, leaflets, and—increasingly—the Internet; they are not allowed to air television or radio commercials. Moreover, door-to-door campaigning is often the only way of discerning voter sentiment in British electoral districts. Polls taken during UK election campaigns tend to reflect average voter opinion throughout the country, not local opinion at the constituency level. As Casale and his volunteers toured the neighborhoods, friendly welcomes were occasionally offset by complaints about government policies on everything from the war in Iraq and immigration to health care and road paving. Casale himself remarked that many of Wimbledon's citizens were too well off to care about unemployment, welfare subsidies, and other economic concerns of Labour's traditional working-class base.

Stephen Gee, the Liberal Democrat, also sensed that the tide was running against New Labour. With only 150 dues-paying party members in Wimbledon, Gee, the managing partner of a construction company, had been nominated the previous year as the "Lib Dem" candidate at a selection meeting attended by only fifty members. When asked if he expected to defeat his Labour and Conservative rivals, Gee replied that he had at least "an outside chance" of winning. But the Liberal Democrats' opposition to the war gave him a big boost, he averred, adding that his party offered a real alternative to what he called the dishonesty of Blair's government and the racism of the Conservatives' stance on limiting immigration. He therefore expected the Liberal Democrats to win as many as a hundred seats in the new Parliament.

In her stately robe of office, Wimbledon's ceremonial Lord Mayor, who is also the local elections returning officer, approached the microphone, the official tally sheet in her hands. Immediately to her left, the eight candidates stood by nervously. As anticipated, the five candidates with the least likelihood of winning—including representatives of the Green Party and the UK Independence Party, plus three local independents—received only a smattering of votes (see table 16.2). Stephen Gee, the Liberal Democrat, won nearly 8,000 votes, nearly 2,600 more than his party's candidate won in 2001. "Mr. Casale," the mayor then intoned, "15,585"—a drop of more than 3,000 votes since the last elections. And finally, "Mr. Hammond, 17,886." With nearly 3,000 more votes than he had won four years earlier, Stephen Hammond had reclaimed Wimbledon for the Conservatives.

One by one, the candidates came to the microphone and gave a brief speech thanking their supporters and the voters. There was no hoopla or media frenzy. Very few people had been allowed into the hall other than the candidates, their families and aides, the ballot-counters, and a few journalists and other observers. Over the course of the next several hours, scenes similar to the one that had just taken place in the Wimbledon area would play themselves out throughout the United Kingdom, some of them shown live on television. By 3:00 AM, all but a few constituencies had reported.

"We energized our base," the newly elected MP confided, "and we increased our own vote considerably." Meanwhile, the social realities of electoral politics produced a very different result in Mitcham and Morden, the constituency located next door to Wimbledon. With a large population of minorities, immigrants, and working-class voters, Mitcham and Morden handily reelected the Labour Party's Siobhain McDonagh, giving her 56 percent of the vote. It was McDonagh's third consecutive victory in a district whose voters cared less about Iraq and more about the services they received from the Labour government and from their highly responsive member of Parliament. As this election and the battle of Wimbledon demonstrated, voters are savvy and every vote counts. And most Britons would agree that, whether the main issues are national or international, on election day all politics is local.

---

As we saw in chapter 8, one of the chief results of the SMD/plurality system is that it sometimes produces a disparity between a party's percentage of the total vote and its percentage of the seats in the legislature. In Britain these disparities can at times be very wide, generally much wider than in the United States. One of the most glaring examples is the Parliament elected in 1997. With slightly more than 43 percent of the popular vote, the Labour Party won more than 63 percent of the seats—a twenty-point disparity! The results of the 2001 elections were just as striking: Labour won 40.7 percent of the popular vote and 62.5 percent of the seats. In 2005 Labour won 55.1 percent of the seats with just 35.2 percent of the popular vote, the lowest popular percentage ever in the United Kingdom for a single-party majoritarian government. When voter turnout is taken into consideration, Labour won only 21.6 percent of registered voters. The Conservatives' share of seats in the Commons was also higher than their share of the national vote in every election from 1979 to 1992. (See table 16.1.)

While victorious parties have good reason to cheer the results of the British electoral system, less successful parties feel it discriminates against them. The SMD/plurality system punishes small parties. What matters in this system is not the percentage of votes a party gets nationwide, but *how many districts* its candidates win. A small party may have a substantial following spread throughout the country, but its candidates may amass enough votes to win only in a small number of constituencies. The Liberal Democrats and their predecessors, the Alliance and the Liberal Party, provide telling examples, as table 16.1 shows. Not surprisingly, they have called for a new, more proportional system to replace the SMD/plurality system. Tony Blair once promised a referendum on changing Britain's electoral system, but he backed off the idea soon after his party's landslide win in 1997.

*Proportional representation (PR)* means that a political party is entitled to a share of legislative seats that is proportional to its share of the popular vote nationwide. There are several different variants of proportional representation. In a *pure PR system,* such as a *party list* system, a party that gets 30 percent of the vote nationwide would automatically get about 30 percent of the seats. Another variant, which is favored by the Liberal Democrat Party, is the *single transferable vote (STV)* system. This somewhat complicated system rests on multimember election districts and permits voters to rank the candidates in their order of preference. Any of several different formulas may be used to distribute the seats, with the final result being somewhat closer to each party's share of the popular vote than the current plurality system (see table 16.3). If Britain were to adopt some form of PR, it could probably count on a significant reordering of its governing processes. In all likelihood it would be more difficult for one party to win an absolute majority of seats in the House of Commons. Hung

**TABLE 16.3**

**Distribution of Seats under SMD and PR Systems, 1997**

| | Actual Results Under SMD/Plurality | | | Under Pure PR | | Under STV | |
|---|---|---|---|---|---|---|---|
| **Party Seats** | **% of Vote** | **Seats** | **% of Seats** | **Seats** | **% of Seats** | **Seats** | **% of Seats** |
| Labour | 43.3 | 419 | 63.6 | 285 | 43.3 | 342 | 51.9 |
| Conservative | 30.7 | 165 | 25.0 | 202 | 30.7 | 144 | 21.9 |
| Liberal Democrats | 16.8 | 46 | 7.0 | 110 | 16.7 | 131 | 19.9 |
| Others | 9.3 | 29 | 4.4 | 64 | 9.7 | 42 | 6.4 |

*Source:* Bill Coxall and Lynton Robins, *Contemporary British Politics*, 3rd ed. (New York: Palgrave, 2002), 144.

parliaments, in which no party enjoys a majority, would be more common. Single-party majoritarian governments—which have been the norm in Britain since World War II—would accordingly give way to majority coalition governments or minority governments. Although a PR system may provide greater fairness in representing the voters in Parliament, it would also make governments more difficult to form and perhaps more internally divided and unstable as well. A more equitably representative Commons, in short, could increase the chances for governmental gridlock if coalition or parliamentary alliance partners cannot get along. (See chapter 8 for a fuller discussion of PR, coalition governments, and minority governments.)

Britain's single-ballot, single-member-district/plurality electoral system is one of the main reasons why British politics tends to be dominated by the two largest parties. Many observers, in fact, describe Britain as having a two-party system. But other parties are also involved in the political process, indeed considerably more than in the United States. At times these other parties can play a vital decision-making role. As we have seen, Callaghan's government relied on support from the Liberals and non-English nationalist parties. Major required the votes of Northern Irish MPs to get his legislation on the Maastricht Treaty passed and to survive a vote of confidence. Thus it would be inaccurate to describe Britain's party system as similar to the more pronouncedly two-party system that prevails in the United States. Accordingly, we describe the United Kingdom as having a *few-party* system: it has more than two parties, but fewer parties actively involved in the government than one would find in *multiparty* countries like Italy, where four or five parties have routinely joined in governing coalitions or parliamentary alliances. If Britain were to adopt PR, three or more parties would probably play a greater role in government than they do today.

## Parliament

The State Opening of Parliament is one of the most colorful rituals of British political life. Normally it takes place every autumn as Parliament begins a new session, but it also occurs when a new government assumes office soon after parliamentary elections. Garbed in flowing robes and bearing the Imperial State Crown, the Queen strides into the House of Lords, accompanied by peers of the realm in ornate attire. After she ascends her throne, the sergeant-at-arms knocks on the door of the House of Commons with a black rod and formally commands its members to join Her Majesty. With both houses assembled, the monarch then delivers the Queen's Speech, which outlines the legislative priorities her government will pursue in the coming session. While custom prescribes the ceremonial aspects of the occasion, the speech is written entirely by the government. Over the next several days its contents are subjected to a vigorous debate as the two houses get down to business. With the first vote on legislation the government is confirmed in office.

**Commons: The Legislative Process** To become law, a bill usually must be passed by a majority of those present and voting in both the House of Commons and the House of Lords. A bill introduced in one house may not be considered in the other until it is passed; unlike the U.S. Congress, the two British houses do not consider similar legislation simultaneously. Members of both houses have the right to debate bills proposed by the government and, within certain limits, to propose legislation and amendments of their own. The procedures for voting on legislation are also roughly the same in both houses. As the democratically elected house, however, the Commons enjoys important prerogatives not accorded the Lords. These include above all the right to hold the government directly accountable, and to vote it out of office if a majority of the Commons no longer has confidence in the prime minister and cabinet.

The government takes the initiative in drafting most legislation and shepherding it through Parliament. In Britain, as in most other parliamentary democracies, the legislative process rests on the principle of *party discipline.* That is, all the members of a party's parliamentary delegation are expected to vote together unanimously on most pieces of legislation. Should a government's support in the Commons fall below 50 percent on key bills, it could be forced to resign. Consequently, government "whips" stay in close contact with the party's parliamentary membership to ensure a bloc vote, especially on bills the government deems crucial, such as the budget or high-priority manifesto promises.[40]

The concept of party discipline applies no less to opposition parties than it does to the governing party. MPs who vote against their leadership's clearly enunciated position can be penalized, whether by being excluded from party meetings or, in the most extreme cases, by being denied the right to run for reelection as the party's official candidate. Occasionally a party's leaders will relax party discipline and allow their colleagues to vote as they wish on matters of conscience, such as abortion, the death penalty, or gun control. And it sometimes happens that members of Parliament will defy their leadership and vote against its legislation, a reality John Major frequently encountered. Tony Blair also faced a growing number of rebellions by Labour Party MPs in his second term, more than a hundred in 2003 alone. As a general rule, however, British legislators maintain party unanimity about 90 percent of the time, far more often than members of the U.S. Congress.

Once the government has readied a bill, it announces its topic to the Parliament in a first reading. The bill is then debated on the floor of the House in a second reading. Depending on the issue, debates in the House of Commons can be soporifically dull, with few members in attendance, or emotionally charged and bristling with partisan invective. The layout of the Commons lends itself to face-to-face exchanges between the governing party and the parties representing "Her Majesty's loyal opposition." The Speaker of the House presides from a raised chair, facing a center aisle. Since 2000 the Speaker has been Michael Martin, a Labour MP whose position requires general impartiality. (The speaker may vote only to break a tie.) Five rows of green benches rise on either side of the aisle. The benches to the Speaker's right are occupied by the governing party, those to his left by the opposition parties. The seating arrangements are said to date from the sixteenth century, when the Commons met in St. Stephen's chapel, seated in choir stalls located on opposite sides of the altar.

In the front rows of each side sit the parties' top leaders. The government's *front benches* are typically occupied by its ministers, at times led by the prime minister in person. The front benches of "parties opposite" are occupied by their respective leading personalities. Whenever the Conservative or Labour Party is in opposition, its front benches are taken up by ***members of the <u>shadow cabinet</u>, each of whom is assigned a portfolio corresponding to a cabinet post.*** The leader of the chief opposition party is the shadow prime minister, whose main task in Parliament is to challenge the governing prime minister. The shadow defense minister keeps tabs on the government's minister of defense, the shadow foreign secretary "shadows" the cabinet's foreign secretary, and so on. Should fortune bring the opposition party into power, the shadow cabinet will be ready to take office, its members having already immersed themselves in the details of their portfolios while in opposition.

Behind the front benches sit the *backbenchers*, ordinary MPs who have no spot in the government or shadow cabinet. Though they are fully cognizant of their duty to observe party discipline, they tend to be more than simply complacent followers of their party's leadership. Backbenchers have opinions of their own, and they must also consider the interests of the constituencies they represent. Government leaders must therefore conduct frequent consultations with their backbench supporters to make sure that bills under consideration meet with their approval. Opposition leaders must also seek to harmonize their policy positions with their backbenchers' wishes.

After the first debate on a bill, a vote is taken. If a majority supports it, the bill then moves to a committee for detailed scrutiny. British parliamentary committees lack the authority, staff, and financial resources that U.S. congressional committees possess. Until the 1980s the House of Commons had no permanent committees like those in Congress. Instead, it created "standing committees," which are ad hoc bodies formed to consider specific bills, disbanding once their work is done. Since 1980 the Commons has also established more than a dozen "departmental select committees" patterned on the U.S. model, albeit with less intrusive investigatory powers.

It is in the standing committees that most bills are examined and amendments proposed. Government ministers and MPs loyal to the governing party's position generally have the upper hand in these committees. As a result, amendments to government-drafted bills are less frequent than in the U.S. Congress, where legislative proposals—even those with strong presidential endorsement—are often significantly amended before going to the floor for a final vote.

Once the bill comes out of committee in a form the government is willing to accept, it then goes before the whole House for a third reading and the decisive vote. If an initial voice vote is too close to call, a "division" takes place. Members of the house then divide into two lobbies located just outside the chamber. Those voting "aye" scurry into one lobby, those voting "no" into the other. No abstentions are recorded. The Speaker appoints "tellers" to count the votes as each MP files past them. Faithful to tradition, Parliament has resisted the use of electronic voting devices.

Throughout the legislative process, the government's priorities predominate. Well over 90 percent of all government-drafted bills are typically passed into law, often unamended. Even the most controversial measures are often passed quite rapidly. The Attlee government, for example, proposed seventy-five bills in 1945–46. All of them passed in one year, including such sweeping measures as the creation of the National Health Service and the nationalization of several major companies. In 1997, the Blair government's bill to ban all handguns was enacted by the House of Commons shortly after it was introduced. In the United States, by contrast, Congress has never passed universal health insurance legislation, and it took six years to pass the "Brady bill," a handgun regulation measure considerably less comprehensive than Britain's total ban on such weapons. As a general rule, Britain's parliamentary system is more efficient at passing legislation than the U.S. separation-of-powers system. Especially when compared with periods of divided government in the United States, when the president represents one party and the Congressional majority the other, British lawmaking is considerably less susceptible to gridlock.

Individual members of the Commons and Lords have the right to propose their own legislation, called "private members' bills," but only as long as the primary purpose of these bills is not to spend money or raise taxes. The government must approve virtually all spending and taxation legislation. Most private members' bills die, especially if the government is not willing to support them. British MPs thus have considerably less latitude for independent legislative initiative than do members of Congress.

**Parliamentary Questions** One of the most distinctive features of British politics is the practice of allowing members of the Commons to address questions directly to the prime minister and other government ministers. More than 50,000 queries are submitted in writing by MPs in an average year, and most receive a written response. Highly controversial inquiries, however, usually surface in open session during the periods devoted to the ministerial *question time*. By custom, the prime minister and other government ministers must appear before the Commons on a regular basis to answer questions posed by the members. Prime minister's question time now takes place once a week for thirty minutes. (Blair's predecessors took questions in two fifteen-minute sessions weekly.) The highly charged atmosphere surrounding the prime minister's grilling guarantees a packed chamber, with many members obliged to remain standing since the benches cannot accommodate the full House. Since 1989 the proceedings have been aired live on television.[41]

MPs who wish to ask a question must submit a written notice in advance of the session. The submissions are then drawn in lottery fashion to determine the order of questioning. Only about a dozen backbenchers will be able to raise a question in the allotted time, since the leaders of the two main opposition parties are given precedence in confronting the prime minister with several questions, often on different topics. The Speaker recognizes each questioner in turn, struggling to maintain order amidst the bellowing and heckling that typically accompany a sharply worded question. After each question the prime minister rises to a lectern, the "despatch box," and delivers a response. Prime ministers do not know the content of the questions in advance, so their staff prepares them for a variety of likely queries. Still, no amount of preparation can substitute for the cool nerves, quick wit, and debating agility required to answer—or artfully evade—a succession of hostile queries addressed by opposition leaders and backbenchers.

Members of the prime minister's own party also ask questions, usually of a friendly nature designed to elicit a glowing account of the government's achievements. On occasion, however, party disunity shows through when backbenchers raise questions indicating their dissatisfaction with their leader's policies, as occurred when Labour MPs questioned Tony Blair on Iraq.

Margaret Thatcher said that no head of government in the world is as accountable as the British prime minister, largely because of the rigors of question time. No U.S. president has ever had to withstand the grueling ordeal of open questioning in Congress. The U.S. Constitution requires only that the chief executive submit to Congress an annual "state of the union" report. George Washington and the Congress discussed a questioning procedure but it was never instituted.

Other government ministers must also go before the Commons and answer questions, each appearing about once a month. Unlike the prime minister, who is responsible for all the government's policies, the other ministers are questioned primarily on their specific area of responsibility. Even so, the cut and thrust of the process can be unnerving. In 1983 a Conservative undersecretary collapsed while being grilled by Labour MPs and died.

**Votes of Confidence** Perhaps the most compelling indication of the executive's accountability to Parliament resides in the Commons' right to remove the government in a vote of confidence. A confidence motion may be posed either by the opposition (as in 1979) or by the government itself, as in 1994 when Prime Minister Major sought to determine whether his government still enjoyed majority support. The procedure has been used quite sparingly, however. Since 1885 only two British governments have actually been defeated in a confidence vote. Both were Labour minority governments: Ramsay MacDonald's in 1924 and Callaghan's in 1979. This record is remarkable when compared with the more frequent defeats that governments in other democracies have suffered in confidence votes, and it testifies to the enduring stability of British politics.

**Members of the House of Commons** What types of people get elected to the House of Commons? About 40 percent of the MPs elected from each of the three main parties in 2005 came from professional backgrounds, including lawyers (72), civil servants, and academics. Of these, 95 Labour members were college professors or schoolteachers, compared with just 6 Conservatives. Sixty Labour MPs were professional politicians or party workers, and 24 were journalists or publishers; both figures were much higher than the corresponding number of Conservatives from these backgrounds. Some 75 Conservative MPs came from private business, compared with 25 Labour members. Labour's parliamentary delegation also included 35 manual workers, fewer than in past decades but still three times as many as the Conservatives elected. Most Liberal Democrats came from the professions (25) and business (18). One out of four Members of Parliament graduated from Oxford or Cambridge, a substantial number that was nevertheless smaller than in previous decades.[42]

The representation of *women* has undergone slow but observable change over the years. In the seven Parliaments elected between 1964 and 1983, women held as few as nineteen seats and no more than 28 (2.9 percent and 4.3 percent of the total membership, respectively). In 1987 the figure jumped to forty-one members (6.3 percent) and edged a bit higher in

1992. In an effort to increase the number of women in Parliament, Labour in the 1990s adopted a candidate selection procedure aimed at electing women to half the party's seats in the Commons in future elections. In 1997, 121 women were elected (18.5 percent of the total), of whom 101 were in the Labour Party and fourteen in the Conservative Party. In 2001, the number of female MPs fell slightly to 115 (of these, 95 were Labourites). In 2005, 128 women were elected to Parliament (19.8 percent of the total). Ninety-eight were Labour members, 17 were Conservatives, and 10 were Liberal Democrats.

The growing representation of women in Labour's parliamentary ranks coincides with rising numbers of women who voted for Labour candidates in the last two elections. From 1945 until 1979, British women tended to vote for Conservative candidates at higher rates than men—so much so that Labour probably would have formed *every* government in those decades if women had voted the same way as men. Gender differences on election day gradually disappeared in the 1980s as women increasingly abandoned the Tories, apparently out of antipathy to Margaret Thatcher's policies. With Thatcher gone, in 1992 women swung decisively to the Conservatives again, but Labour's efforts to win them back paid off. In 1997, 49 percent of women voted Labour and only 30 percent voted for the Tories. Those figures were exactly the same for male voters. In 2005, 38 percent of women and 34 percent of men voted Labour; 32 percent of women and 34 percent of men voted Conservative.

The House of Commons has not been very representative of the United Kingdom's nonwhite minorities. Britain's history as a colonial power resulted in the creation of the British *Commonwealth of Nations* in 1919. The organization initially sought to regulate relations between the United Kingdom and its colonies, but as Britain relinquished control over most of its dominions it evolved mainly into a forum for promoting economic cooperation. Today the Commonwealth has fifty-three members, most of which are independent states. Until the 1960s, residents of Commonwealth countries had the right to settle in the UK with full citizenship rights. But rising immigration in the 1950s and 1960s, especially from India, Pakistan, Africa, and the Caribbean, sparked resentment among large numbers of white Britons. The Wilson, Heath, and Thatcher governments imposed successive restrictions on immigration. The number of legal and illegal immigrants and asylum seekers wanting to stay in Britain has continued to grow in recent years, prompting the Blair government to work with the European Union to keep the flow within limits.

By 2006 there were some 4.8 million nonwhites living in the UK, about 8 percent of the population. Between 1929 and 1987 there were no nonwhite members of the Commons. Nonwhite representation in the Commons has risen only slightly since 1992. Public opinion polls consistently show that a majority of blacks, Asians, and even whites regard Britain as a "fairly" or "very" racist society. Blair admitted before a hushed Commons in 1999 that "racism still exists in our society" after a report accused the London police and other British institutions of "institutional racism."

**The House of Lords** At the start of 1999 there were 1,294 members of the House of Lords. In accordance with centuries-old custom, the membership has traditionally included various bishops of the Church of England and so-called hereditary peers, who may bequeath their membership to an heir. In early 1999 there were twenty-six "Lords spiritual" and 759 hereditary peers (including sixteen women). Laws were passed in 1876 and 1958 permitting the creation of "life peers," who serve in the House of Lords only for the duration of their lifetime without the right to pass their membership on to their children. Life peers are named by the queen on the advice of the prime minister, usually as a reward for exemplary achievement in political or professional life. In the first months of 1999 there were five hundred life peers (eighty-seven women), including Margaret Thatcher and the composer Andrew Lloyd Webber.

Most members of the nonclerical "Lords temporal" are affiliated with a political party. There were also more than three hundred "cross-benchers" who did not align themselves with any party. Attendance at Lords sessions has often been spotty; traditionally, only a minority of members would show up on an average business day, while a few "backwoodsmen," usually from remote parts of Britain, rarely participated at all.

In 1999, the Blair government prevailed upon the Lords to accept a drastic change: the ranks of hereditary peers were reduced to 92 members. Those permitted to stay on had to be elected by their colleagues in a special vote; the rest were required to relinquish their cherished parliamentary seats, abandoning a patrimony that in some cases stretched back to the fifteenth and sixteenth centuries. In 2006, the House of Lords had 753 members, including 635 Life Peers. A number of additional reforms have been proposed, debated, and voted on in the House of Commons, but none had been adopted by the end of the year. The Conservatives favored replacing the Lords with a new Second Chamber, 80 percent of whose members would be elected. The Liberal Democrats preferred the creation of an entirely elected Senate. The Labour government was considering several options, including an upper house divided in half between elected and appointed members.

Until the next stage of reform takes place, the House of Lords still has the right to vote on legislation passed by the Commons as well as to propose and pass legislation of its own. In the event that the two houses cannot agree on a particular piece of legislation, a compromise is usually worked out. But if no compromise can be reached, the Lords under current procedures may not kill a bill already passed by the Commons. Laws enacted in 1911 and 1949 permit the Lords only to delay the passage of legislation they do not accept, in some cases for no more than one month and in others for up to a year. If the Lords fail to pass the disputed bills within the allotted time, they automatically become law. The House of Commons has invoked this automatic enactment provision only once since 1949.

Although its legislative importance has progressively diminished, the House of Lords continues to have an impact on the legislative process. Between 2004 and 2006, for example, it managed to amend government-sponsored bills passed in the Commons on such controversial issues as anti-terrorism, personal identity cards, acts of racial and religious hatred, and the banning of fox hunting. The Lords also continues to stand at the apex of Britain's legal system. It is the supreme court of appeal for the entire country in civil cases, and for England, Wales, and Northern Ireland (not Scotland) in criminal cases. This juridical function is carried out by a special Appellate Committee, also known as the Law Lords, whose members have had high-level judicial experience. It also includes the Lord Chancellor, who is the Speaker of the House of Lords and the chief of the judiciary. Most of the Appellate Committee's work is carried out by the so-called Lords of Appeal in Ordinary, a group of twelve life peers who have been specifically selected because of their judicial expertise. They are the only salaried members of the House. In stark contrast to the United States, Britain thus has no separation of powers between its legislature and its highest court. However, a government-backed constitutional reform act passed in 2005 created a new *Supreme Court* of the United Kingdom, which will take over the judicial functions of the House of Lords as well as some other judicial responsibilities. The new high court had not as yet begun operating by the end of 2006.

## The Government

In a parliamentary system, the term *government* refers to the chief decision-making body of the executive branch. It is used in the same way people refer to a president's administration in the United States. In Britain the government consists of about a hundred individuals, all of whom must be members of Parliament. Most are members of the House of Commons, but some also come from Lords.

**The Cabinet** The most prestigious twenty or so government ministers constitute the cabinet. Its leader is the prime minister, who also bears the titles of First Lord of the Treasury and Minister for the Civil Service. Most cabinet ministers are formally known as secretaries of state, though a few have more high-sounding titles such the Chancellor of the Exchequer and the Lord Chancellor. Each cabinet member assumes responsibility for a particular functional area, such as foreign affairs, health, or trade and industry, and most preside over a department of civil servants engaged in the bureaucratic tasks of policy planning and implementation within their respective domains. By tradition, two or three cabinet ministers are members of the House of Lords, but the prime minister and all others belong to the Commons.[43] Immediately after winning reelection in 2001, Prime Minister Blair increased the number of women in his cabinet to seven, an all-time high. In 2006 there were eight women in Blair's reshuffled cabinet, including the country's first female foreign secretary, Margaret Beckett.

Although it is customary—and correct—to say that Britain's political system rests on the principle of parliamentary supremacy, in actual practice the government tends to exercise more authoritative power than Parliament enjoys. The government dominates the legislative process, taking the initiative in proposing most bills and invoking party discipline when they come up for a vote. The Parliament may always hold the government accountable for its actions and retains the right to remove it from office in a confidence vote, but on a day-to-day basis it is the government that steers the legislature's activities rather than the other way around.

The prime minister, moreover, steers the government. The head of government possesses an impressive array of powers, all of which derive from customary practice and are not codified in legal statutes. These include the right to appoint and dismiss other cabinet members and top bureaucratic officials, or change their positions, without having to secure Parliament's approval. (The U.S. president may appoint cabinet members and many other officials only with the Senate's approval.) The government has the exclusive right to propose bills affecting revenues (such as taxes) and expenditures. The prime minister may order British military forces into action in wars, peacekeeping missions, and other operations without parliamentary approval. Some observers have suggested that the British prime minister's powers amount to an "elective dictatorship." Though there is more hyperbole than accuracy in this characterization, the fact remains that Britain's prime minister usually has more powers of initiative and greater control over the cabinet and the legislative process than do most heads of government, including the president of the United States.

Leadership styles have varied among Britain's prime ministers. Some have been dynamic leaders determined to seize the policy-making initiative and impose their preferences on their cabinet and party. Others have been more consensus oriented, seeking to balance and coordinate the diverse opinions expressed by other party leaders and the various groups and constituencies connected with their party. Thatcher and Blair are examples of dynamic initiators; Attlee and Major tended to be consensus seekers. Other prime ministers have combined aspects of both leadership styles to varying degrees.

British cabinets tend to meet far more regularly than do cabinets in the United States and to assume a greater collective role in debating and deciding government policy. In Britain the entire cabinet usually meets once a week. While its deliberations are secret, the memoirs of former ministers and occasional leaks to the press reveal that it is a lively institution whose leading members speak up on a range of issues, even those not immediately concerned with their particular functional responsibilities.[44] Budget debates can be especially intense, as the various ministers defend their own department's claims to financial appropriations. The prime minister is not formally bound to follow the cabinet's preferences on any issue, but even a strong-willed leader like Thatcher or Blair cannot stray too far from the cabinet's wishes without risking a potential loss in leadership authority.

Once a decision is made and the prime minister enunciates it, the principle of *collective responsibility* demands that all cabinet minsters fall into line behind the policy in their public statements.

**The Civil Service** Visitors to Parliament and No. 10 Downing Street (the prime minister's residence) soon find themselves on an imposing boulevard called *Whitehall*. Along its wide expanse are some of the most important ministries and agencies of the British government. Just as "No. 10" is synonymous with the prime minister and "Westminster" with Parliament, "Whitehall" connotes the country's bureaucracy, or *civil service*. From the Foreign Office to departments concerned with local government, Britain's civil service is a vital part of the executive branch, playing a critical role in the formulation and execution of the government's policies.

Like many bureaucracies, the civil service is both indispensable and maligned. No cabinet official can do without the expertise of its professional cadres, many of whom have devoted their entire careers to specific policy issues. Quite often an experienced civil servant will know more about a policy matter than the cabinet minister or agency chief who supervises that office. Tensions sometimes arise when the prime minister or cabinet ministers are determined to pursue a policy initiative at variance with the preferences of the senior civil servants who advise them. Although they are expected to be politically neutral, following the government's lead in policy matters and dutifully carrying out its decisions, highly experienced civil servants may on occasion disagree with the government's policy and seek to alter its course, primarily through articulate persuasion rather than bureaucratic sabotage. Both Margaret Thatcher and Tony Blair often relied more heavily on their personal advisors than on civil service experts, especially in controversial policy areas.

The president of the United States has the right to fill some two to three thousand plum positions at the highest levels of the American federal bureaucracy, thus ensuring compliance with presidential policy preferences throughout the executive branch. The prime minister may fill only about a hundred. Career civil servants occupy most of the remaining posts. About seven hundred officials comprise the Higher Civil Service, a prestigious elite heavily populated with "Oxbridge" graduates, mostly males. These highly influential career civil servants owe their positions to professional accomplishment within the bureaucracy, including success in competitive midcareer examinations, rather than to political patronage. From their ranks a smaller group of about sixty to seventy are selected as "permanent secretaries," a uniquely British "elite of the elite" of career bureaucrats who work intimately with government ministers. While it is sometimes criticized as a bastion of elitism with little direct accountability to the population, Britain's civil service also wins wide praise as a model of bureaucratic professionalism and incorruptibility.[45]

### The Monarchy

Although its power has been whittled down to practically nothing and its prerogatives are largely ceremonial, Britain's thousand-year-old monarchy nevertheless fulfills an important function in British politics: it provides a living symbol of the long continuity of the country's history, people, and institutions. In recent years the British royal family has suffered a number of widely publicized indignities and tragedies such as the marital troubles of the queen's sons, Princes Charles and Andrew, and the death of the popular Princess Diana, who was killed in an auto accident in Paris not long after her divorce from Charles. And Queen Elizabeth II has been subjected to criticism for her aloofness from the general public. Nevertheless, both the queen herself and the monarchy as an institution continue to enjoy wide popularity in Britain. Approximately 70 percent of Britons favored retaining the monarchy. However, mounting criticism of the royal family's lavish lifestyle has led to reductions in the amount of public revenue devoted to its upkeep, and in 1992 the queen agreed to pay income taxes.

The distinction between the monarch's *formal legal* powers and her *actual decision-making* powers remains fuzzy in a number of areas. Constitutionally, the monarch is part of Parliament. She retains the formal legal authority to designate the prime minister, dissolve Parliament, and call parliamentary elections. No act of Parliament may take effect as law until the monarch signs a document of Royal Assent. The monarch is the nominal commander-in-chief of the armed forces and the head of the British Commonwealth. In actual practice, however, the monarch is not a *voting member* of Parliament like the members of the Houses of Commons and Lords. Her right to designate the prime minister is limited by the majority party's right to recommend its preferred designee. Her rights to dissolve Parliament and call elections are formalities that are superseded by the prime minister's prerogatives. She cannot refuse her Royal Assent without creating a grave constitutional crisis. (Not since 1707 has a British monarch refused to assent to an act of Parliament.) In actuality it is the government that directs the armed forces in war and peace and sets policy on the Commonwealth.

## GORDON BROWN'S BRITAIN

Born in Scotland in 1951, James Gordon Brown became Britain's longest-serving chancellor of the exchequer since the nineteenth century. A former lecturer at Edinburgh University, his alma mater,

Brown was first elected to Parliament in 1983. He became the Labour Party's shadow chancellor of the exchequer in 1992, just as John Major began his last five years as prime minister.

According to a widely circulated story, Tony Blair agreed before the 1997 elections to give Brown full control of economic policy in a New Labour government if Brown promised not to challenge Blair for the party leadership. Upon becoming chancellor of the exchequer in 1997, Brown initially adopted policies very different from those favored by the more left-leaning Labour governments of previous decades. He gave the Bank of England, the government's central bank, the right to set interest rates independently of political oversight. He also cut personal income tax and corporate tax rates, while retaining for two years the spending limitations he inherited from Major's last government. Brown also postponed Britain's adoption of the euro, a policy approved by the vast majority of British citizens. Brown set five "tests" that needed to be met before Britain would abandon the pound in favor of Europe's currency, subject to voter approval in a referendum. By hewing to conservative monetary and fiscal principles, Brown sought to maintain the positive growth rates Britain had registered since the early 1990s and to remove Labour's stigma as the party of economic instability. After succeeding at these tasks in the Blair government's first term, Brown raised investment in the National Health Service and other public services, raising various taxes in the process.

If, as expected, Brown becomes prime minister in 2007, he will inherit some daunting challenges:

- *Restoring trust* In overcoming the public's distrust of Tony Blair, attitudes shared by many New Labour Party members, Brown would need to establish his own credentials as a trustworthy political leader.
- *Iraq* During the 2005 election campaign, Brown said that he would have made the same decisions Blair had made with regard to Iraq. By late 2006, British forces had suffered more than 120 fatalities in the Iraq conflict. With the vast majority of Britons opposed to the war, Brown would need to make sure that he would not be saddled with the conflict for too long.
- *Terrorism* As the terrorist attacks associated with the Northern Ireland conflict wind down, Islamic terrorism poses new dangers. An al Qaeda plot to set off a bomb in Birmingham was foiled in 2000. In December 2001 a British-born al Qaeda operative, Richard Reid, was subdued on an aircraft headed for Miami while trying to set off explosives hidden in his shoe. On July 7, 2005, four British-born Muslims set off bombs in the London subways and on a bus during the morning rush hour, killing fifty-two. In early 2006 an Islamic cleric based in London was sentenced to seven years in prison for hate crimes and incitement to murder. In the summer, British intelligence agents thwarted a plot by British Muslims to blow up as many as ten airliners. And later in the year, the director general of MI5, Britain's security service, revealed that her agency was tracking some two hundred British terrorist groups involving more than 1,600 known individuals; at least thirty terrorist plots had been discovered. Many of these potential terrorists had ties to al Qaeda in Pakistan. In confronting these threats, Brown's government would need to deal with the feelings on the part of a sizable minority of Britain's 1.6 million Muslims that British policy was directed against Muslims around the world. On these grounds, an estimated 100,000 British citizens regarded the July 2005 bombings as justified. Surveys revealed that 81 percent of Britain's Muslims consider themselves Muslims first and British second; 14 percent voiced "confidence" in Osama bin Laden (though 77 percent expressed concern about Islamic extremism). About a third of the general public in the UK regards immigration from the Middle East and North Africa as a "bad thing."[46]
- *The economy and social welfare* Relying on his long experience in these areas, Brown would be expected to keep the British economy on a steady course of growth (now running at just over 2 percent a year), while holding inflation and unemployment low. At the same time, he would have to find ways to meet the demands of an aging population for improved health care, largely through the tax-funded National Health Service, while recognizing that three out of four Britons are unwilling to pay higher taxes in exchange for better services. He will also have to find ways to fund

Britain's universities in an era of rapidly rising costs for higher education.[47]

- *Constitutional reform* In a country with twelve regions, four of which (Scotland, Wales, Northern Ireland, and London) have elected local governments, Brown may consider the possibility of further devolution in other regions. (In a 2004 referendum, the residents of England's northeast region turned down proposals for a local legislature and executive.) Northern Ireland's contending factions may require continuing attention if the 1998 Good Friday Accords are to work. And reform of the House of Lords will also be on Brown's agenda.
- *Europe* The citizens of the United Kingdom typically have the lowest sense of attachment to the European Union of any EU member state.[48] Most Britons do not want to abandon the pound in favor of the euro, and most probably breathed a sigh of relief when the proposed European Constitution was shelved by French and Dutch voters in 2006, obviating the need for a British referendum. Nevertheless, 85 percent of Britain's commercial laws are now EU laws made in Brussels, and Brown will probably continue the Labour government's cooperation with Britain's EU partners on a host of issues requiring multilateral solutions, such as immigration, counterterrorism, and economic development.

## CONCLUSION

Along with the United States, the United Kingdom is one of the modern world's two oldest continuously functioning democracies. Its success reflects the evolutionary development, over more than three hundred years, of a democratic system modeled on the Temple of Democracy delineated in chapter 7 and promoted by the ten conditions for democracy spelled out in chapter 9. Starting in the Middle Ages, England built the structures of modern democratic government on the foundations of the rule of law and democratic values like freedom from tyranny and the right to private property. Over the centuries these values were supplemented by support for the values of legal equality and equity. The value of political inclusion for Britain's large working class was successfully implemented with the growth of the Labour Party. And racial and religious tolerance also gained support, though these values are always difficult to inculcate universally, as Britain's religious and ethnic conflicts continue to demonstrate today. Nevertheless, during the twentieth century Britain raised and solidified the three functional pillars of democracy—popular sovereignty, based on mass suffrage; civil rights and liberties based on the long traditions of English civil law; and economic well-being, based on private enterprise and a generous welfare state.

Despite its long lineage, British democracy is still evolving. With change on the horizon on a number of important constitutional and social issues, the United Kingdom continues to forge new directions in areas of vital importance to the functioning—and at times the very definition—of democracy.

## KEY TERMS AND NAMES
**(In bold and underlined in the text)**

Tony Blair
Gordon Brown
Divine right of kings
Sovereign monarchy (absolutism)
Magna Carta
House of Lords
House of Commons
Parliamentary supremacy
Conservatives (Tories)
Labour Party
National Health Service (NHS)
Margaret Thatcher
Liberal Democrats
Shadow cabinet

## NOTES

1. R. G. Davies and J. H. Denton, eds., *The English Parliament in the Middle Ages* (Manchester: Manchester University Press, 1981); Conrad Russell, *The Crisis of Parliaments* (London: Oxford University Press, 1971). King Charles I's determination to rule without Parliament in the 1630s provoked intense opposition and helped precipitate the Civil Wars of the 1640s and his own execution in 1649.

2. Stuart E. Prall, *The Bloodless Revolution: England 1688* (Madison: University of Wisconsin Press, 1985).
3. One historian notes that in the years between 1832 and 1867 Britain changed "from a system in which the Crown was the dominant influence in Parliament to a system in which the mass electorate began increasingly to call the tune." See Robert Blake, *Disraeli* (New York: St. Martin's Press, 1967), 259. Though the monarch today still formally names the prime minister, by 1834 the monarch could no longer appoint a head of government unacceptable to the Commons majority. For a classic description of Britain's governmental system in the latter half of the nineteenth century, with comparisons with the United States, see Walter Bagehot, *The English Constitution* (Brighton, UK: Sussex Academic Press, 1997).
4. See Dick Leonard, *Elections in Britain Today: A Guide for Voters and Students*, 3rd ed. (New York: St. Martin's Press, 1996), 12–23. On the suffragettes, see George Klosko and Margaret G. Klosko, *The Struggle for Women's Rights* (Upper Saddle River, N.J.: Prentice Hall, 1999); Barbara Winslow, *Sylvia Pankhurst* (New York: St. Martin's Press, 1996); and Martin Pugh, *The Pankhursts* (London: Penguin, 2002).
5. Liah Greenfeld, *Nationalism: Five Roads to Modernity* (Cambridge, Mass.: Harvard University Press, 1992), chap. 1.
6. Gabriel Almond and Sidney Verba, *The Civic Culture* (Boston: Little, Brown, 1963). On the decline of deferential attitudes in British political culture, see Dennis Kavanaugh, "Political Culture in Great Britain: The Decline of the Civic Culture," in Gabriel A. Almond and Sidney Verba, eds., *The Civic Culture Revisited* (Boston: Little, Brown, 1980), 124–76.
7. Barrington Moore, *Social Origins of Dictatorship and Democracy: Lord and Peasant in the Making of the Modern World* (Boston: Beacon Press, 1966).
8. Eric Hobsbawm, *Industry and Empire* (London: Penguin Books, 1990); E. P. Thompson, *The Making of the English Working Class* (New York: Pantheon, 1964).
9. Originally, a "tory" was an Irish Catholic outlaw. In the seventeenth century the term was abusively applied by opponents of King James II to those who supported his rule and the claims of his Catholic heirs to the throne on the grounds of inherited legitimacy. A "whig" (or "whiggamore") was a Scottish horse thief. It was applied to Scottish Presbyterians and others who wanted Parliament to prevent James from succeeding to the throne, even though he was the legitimate heir. Thus the Tories became identified initially with the traditional principle of royal inheritance and the Whigs with the principle of Parliament's right to alter the succession.
10. For biographies that provide extensive accounts of the times, see Blake, *Disraeli;* Stanley Weintraub, *Disraeli: A Biography* (New York: Truman Talley/Dutton, 1993); Roy Jenkins, *Gladstone: A Biography* (New York: Random House, 1997); and Philip Magnus, *Gladstone* (New York: E. P. Dutton, 1964).
11. See Norman and Jeanne MacKenzie, *The Fabians* (New York: Simon & Schuster, 1977).
12. Henry Pelling and Alastair Reed, *A Short History of the Labour Party,* 11th ed. (New York: St. Martin's Press, 1996); Stanley Pierson, *Marxism and the Origins of British Socialism* (Ithaca, N.Y.: Cornell University Press, 1973).
13. Kenneth O. Morgan, *Labour in Power 1945–1951* (Oxford: Oxford University Press, 1986); Jim Fyrth, ed., *Labour's High Noon: The Government and the Economy 1945–51* (London: Lawrence & Wishart, 1993).
14. Samuel Beer, *British Politics in the Collectivist Age* (New York: Vintage Books, 1969).
15. Harold Wilson, *A Personal Record: The Labour Government 1964–1970* (Boston: Little, Brown, 1971) and *The Governance of Britain* (New York: Harper & Row, 1976); Ben Pimlott, *Harold Wilson* (New York: HarperCollins, 1991).
16. Howard R. Penniman, ed., *Britain at the Polls 1979* (Washington, D.C.: American Enterprise Institute, 1981); Richard Coopey and Nicholas Woodward, eds., *Britain in the 1970s: The Troubled Economy* (London: University College of London, 1996).
17. For a cultural explanation of Britain's economic decline in these years, see Martin J. Wiener, *English Culture and the Decline of the Industrial Spirit, 1850–1980* (Cambridge: Cambridge University Press, 1981).

**18.** Callaghan was deserted by an erstwhile supporter from a Northern Ireland Catholic party and lost the vote of a dying Labour member who was too ill to take part. For his account, see James Callaghan, *Time and Chance* (London: Collins, 1987), 558–63. See also Anthony Seldon and Kevin Hickson, eds., *New Labour, Old Labour: The Wilson and Callaghan Governments, 1974–79* (London: Routledge, 2004).

**19.** In 1979 the bottom tenth of the population shared 4.1 percent of the national income while the top tenth got 20 percent of it. By 1991 the bottom tenth's share was only 2.5 percent while the top tenth's share had grown to 26 percent. Income inequality grew faster in the United Kingdom in the 1980s than in any other economically advanced democracy except New Zealand.

**20.** Margaret Thatcher, *The Path to Power* (New York: HarperCollins, 1995) and *The Downing Street Years* (New York: HarperCollins, 1993); Hugo Young, *The Iron Lady* (New York: Farrar, Straus, & Giroux, 1989); Dennis Kavanaugh, *Thatcherism and British Politics,* 2nd ed. (New York: Oxford University Press, 1990); Christopher Johnson, *The Economy under Mrs. Thatcher, 1979–1990* (London: Penguin, 1991); David Butler, Andrew Adonis, and Tony Travers, *Failure in British Government: The Politics of the Poll Tax* (New York: Oxford University Press, 1994); and Eric Evans, *Thatcher and Thatcherism* (New York: Routledge, 1997).

**21.** Anthony Seldon, *Major: A Political Life* (London: Weidenfeld & Nicolson, 1997).

**22.** Anthony King et al., *Britain at the Polls 1992* (Chatham, N.J.: Chatham House, 1993).

**23.** For Major's own account, see *John Major: The Autobiography* (London: HarperCollins, 1999).

**24.** Tony Blair, *The Third Way* (London: Fabian Society, 1998); Anthony Giddens, *The Third Way: The Renewal of Social Democracy* (Cambridge: Polity Press, 1999).

**25.** On the 1997 elections, see Anthony King, ed., *Britain at the Polls, 1997* (New York: Chatham House, 1998), and David Butler and Dennis Kavanaugh, eds., *The British General Election of 1997* (New York: St. Martin's Press, 1997).

**26.** On Blair, see John Rentoul, *Tony Blair* (London: Little, Brown, 1995) and *Tony Blair: Prime Minister* (London: Little, Brown, 2001); Jon Soepel, *Tony Blair: The Modernizer* (London: Bantam, 1995); and Melanie A. Sully, *The New Politics of Tony Blair* (New York: Columbia University Press, 2000).

**27.** On Blair's government and the 2001 elections, see Anthony King, ed., *Britain at the Polls, 2001* (New York: Chatham House); David Butler and Dennis Kavanaugh, eds., *The British General Election of 2001* (New York: Palgrave, 2002); and Simon Henig and Lewis Baston, *The Political Map of Britain* (London: Politico's, 2002). For additional data, see the 2001 British Election Survey, accessible online at http://www.britishelectionsurvey.com. Another data source is the UK Data Archive, accessible at http://www.data-archive.ac.uk. See also Anthony Seldon, ed., *The Blair Effect* (London: Little, Brown, 2000); Andrew Rawnsley, *Servants of the People: The Inside Story of New Labour* (London: Hamish Hamilton, 2000); Peter Mandelson, *The Blair Revolution Revisited,* (London: Politico's, 2002); and Nicholas Jones, *Sultans of Spin* (London: Gollancz, 1999) and *The Control Freaks: How New Labour Gets Its Own Way* (London: Politico's, 2001).

**28.** Con Coughlin, *American Ally: Tony Blair and the War on Terror* (New York: HarperCollins, 2006); Robin Cook, *The Point of Departure* (New York: Simon and Schuster, 2003); Christopher Meyer, *DC Confidential: The Controversial Memoirs of Britain's Ambassador to the U.S. at the Time of 9/11 and the Iraq War* (London: Weidenfeld and Nicolson, 2005); Philip Stephens, *Tony Blair: The Making of a World Leader* (New York: Viking, 2004); James Naughtie, *Accidental American: Tony Blair and the Presidency* (New York: Public Affairs, 2004); Peter Stothard, *Thirty Days: A Month at the Heart of Blair's War* (London: HarperCollins, 2003); Mark Danner, "The Secret Way to War," *New York Review of Books,* June 9, 2005, 70–74. On Blair's second term, see Anthony Seldon, *Blair* (London: Free Press, 2005), and Anthony Seldon and Dennis Kavanaugh, eds., *The Blair Effect 2001–5* (Cambridge: Cambridge University Press, 2005).

**29.** John Bartle and Anthony King, eds., *Britain at the Polls 2005* (Washington, D.C.: CQ Press, 2006); Dennis Kavanaugh and David Butler,

*The British General Election of 2005* (New York: Palgrave Macmillan, 2005); Pippa Norris and Christopher Wlezien, eds., *Britain Votes 2005* (Oxford: Oxford University Press, 2005); and the British Election Study, www.essex.ac.uk/bes.

**30.** Peter G. J. Pulzer, *Political Representation and Elections in Britain,* 3d ed. (London: Allen & Unwin, 1975), 102.

**31.** Eric A. Nordlinger, *The Working-Class Tories* (Berkeley: University of California Press, 1967).

**32.** Bartle and King, *Britain at the Polls 2005,* 176.

**33.** For a confirmation of this conclusion, see John Bartle, "Left-Right Position Matters, But Does Social Class? Causal Models of the 1992 British General Election," *British Journal of Political Science* 28 (1998): 501–29. See also Andrew Adonis and Stephen Pollard, *A Class Act* (London: Penguin, 1998).

**34.** Anthony Seldon and Stuart Ball, eds., *Conservative Century: The Conservative Party since 1900* (Oxford: Oxford University Press, 1994).

**35.** Chris Philp, ed., *Conservative Revival: Blueprint for a Better Britain* (London: Politico's, 2006).

**36.** Bartle and King, *Britain at the Polls 2005,* 58, 66, 171. The Labour Party's website is www.labour.org.uk; the Conservatives's website is www.conservative-party.org.uk; the Liberal Democrats's website is www.libdems.org.uk.

**37.** Leonard, *Elections in Britain Today,* 97.

**38.** See www.electoralcommission.org.uk.

**39.** U.S. Census Bureau, "Voting and Registration in the Election of November 2000," www.census.gov.

**40.** The term *whip* has two meanings. In addition to referring to the persons charged with keeping a party's legislative delegation in line, a whip also refers to the message sent by the party leadership to its MPs indicating the relative importance it attaches to bills coming up for a vote. Bills of relatively minor importance are underlined once; more significant bills are underlined twice or three times. MPs who vote against a "three-line whip" risk severe disciplinary action by the party leadership.

**41.** A taped broadcast of prime minister's question time is aired weekly in the United States by the C-SPAN network.

**42.** Kavanaugh and Butler, *British General Election of 2005,* 164, 165.

**43.** When Sir Alec Douglas-Home became prime minister in 1963 he was a member of the House of Lords. He thereupon renounced his title and subsequently won a seat in Commons in a by-election.

**44.** For example, David Blunkett, *The Blunkett Tapes: My Life in the Bear Pit* (London: Bloomsbury, 2006).

**45.** David Marsh, David Richards, and Martin J. Smith, *Changing Patterns of Governance in the United Kingdom: Reinventing Whitehall?* (London: Palgrave Macmillan, 2002).

**46.** See the Pew Global Attitudes Surveys released in 2006: "The Great Divide: How Westerners and Muslims View Each Other" (released June 22, 2006), and "Muslims in Europe: Economic Worries Top Concerns About Religious and Cultural Identity," www.pewglobal.org.

**47.** See the annual British Social Attitudes Survey at www.data-archive.ac.uk and www.icpsr.umich.edu.

**48.** In a *Eurobarometer* survey taken in 2004, only 29 percent of British respondents said that EU membership was a "good thing," the lowest among the fifteen West European member states; 37 percent had a "fairly negative" image of the EU, against an EU average of 21 percent. When asked what the EU means to them, the British most frequently mentioned "waste of money," "bureaucracy," and "loss of cultural identity," along with "freedom of movement," reflecting fears that EU enlargement will make it easier for East Europeans to emigrate to Britain. See *Eurobarometer 61* at www.ec.europa.eu.

CHAPTER 17

# FRANCE

Population (2005 est): 60.7 million
Freedom House Ratings (2002): Political Rights—1; Civil Liberties—1

Area: 176,460 square miles
(about two-thirds the size of Texas)

Bretagne = Brittany
Bourgogne = Burgundy
*Source:* U.S. Central Intelligence Agency.

Nicolas Sarkozy

Ségolène Royal

In the fall of 2005, President **Jacques Chirac** solemnly announced that France was experiencing a "deep malaise" and an "identity crisis." Voicing similar sentiments, **Nicolas Sarkozy** (nee-ko-LAH sahr-ko-ZEE), the leader of Chirac's own political party, declared that the country needed "a radical transformation." Repudiating the policies of the very president he had served, Sarkozy called for a complete "rupture" with a political, economic, and social system that, in his view, had produced little more than "stagnation" over the previous thirty years. For her part, **Ségolène Royal** (seh-go-LEHN rwah-YAHL) affirmed on becoming the presidential nominee of France's Socialist Party in 2006 that she embodied "the profound change that people are crying out for."

"Crisis," "rupture," "profound change"—these were the watchwords of French politics as the crucial elections of 2007 approached. When this chapter went to press at the start of the year, the outcomes of the presidential and legislative contests set for the spring were entirely unpredictable. Public opinion reflected a divided and volatile electorate. A tight race was shaping up between the two principal contenders for president: Sarkozy, the leader of the Union for a Popular Movement (UMP), France's main center-right party; and Royal, the candidate of the center-left Socialists. Blogs for and against the various contestants reflected wide interest in the campaign. But no one could be sure until all the votes were counted which of these leading rivals would emerge as France's new president.

French presidential elections typically take place in two rounds. In the first round, virtually any number of candidates may run, subject to certain qualifications. If one of the candidates wins an absolute majority of popular votes (more than 50 percent), that person wins the presidency and there is no need for a second round. But in all the years since this electoral system was first used in France in 1965, no one has ever won a decisive first-round majority. Round two, which takes place two weeks later, is a runoff election between the top two finishers of round one. Although most observers assumed that the 2007 elections would ultimately come down to a second-round face-off between Sarkozy and Royal—"Sarko" versus "Ségo"—the astonishing results of the 2002 presidential elections provided ample warnings that the leaders of France's two largest parties might not both make it into the decisive second round of balloting.

In 2002, most voters and political observers had anticipated a second-round showdown between Chirac, who headed the UMP at the time, and Lionel Jospin, the leader of the Socialist Party. Chirac was winding up his first term as president and was seeking reelection. Jospin was prime minister. Shockingly, Jospin finished third in round one and was eliminated from further contention. In a field of sixteen candidates, Chirac topped the first-round list with a mere 19.9 percent of the vote. Second place went to Jean-Marie Le Pen, the combative seventy-four-year-old organizer of an extreme right-wing party called the National Front. A veteran of previous presidential and legislative elections, Le Pen was renowned for his virulently anti-immigrant opinions. He had once advocated expelling France's immigrants, especially those of non-European descent, and sending them back to their countries of origin. Buoyed by a core of loyal followers and an influx of protest voters registering their dissatisfaction with the mainstream parties, Le Pen finished second with 16.9 percent of the vote. Jospin trailed close behind him at 16.2 percent.

Although Jospin was widely regarded as the standard-bearer of the French left, he was defeated not simply by Chirac and Le Pen but by seven other candidates who represented more extreme leftist tendencies than his own centrist brand of social democracy. Together these seven challengers garnered 26.8 percent of the vote, more than enough to deprive Jospin of second place in round one. Ironically, a significant number of those who had voted for an extreme-left candidate in the first round would have cast their ballots for Jospin had he survived to confront Chirac in the second round. Faced with a choice between President Chirac and the extremist Le Pen, French voters decided overwhelmingly for Chirac in round two. Chirac won 82 percent of the vote, while Le Pen took the remaining 18 percent. As the 2007 elections approached, the French braced themselves for similarly unexpected results.

Round one of the 2007 presidential elections was scheduled for April 22. Round two, if needed, would take place on May 6. About a month later, on June 10, balloting would begin for the lower house of France's parliament, the *National Assembly*. Like the presidency, the 577-seat National Assembly is also elected in two rounds of voting. For these elections, metropolitan (mainland) France and several overseas territories are divided into 577 electoral districts. In accordance with the *single-member-district/plurality* electoral system, one person is elected to represent each district. The American and British variants of this system have a single round of voting on one election day. In the French variant, a candidate for the legislature who wins an absolute majority of votes in round one is declared the winner; no second round is held in such districts. But in districts where no candidate wins an outright majority in the first round, a second round of voting takes place one week later. In these districts, all candidates who won a percentage of the vote equivalent to at least 12.5 percent of the district's registered voters are eligible to compete in the second round. A plurality—the highest number of votes—is sufficient to win in round two.

Inevitably, the National Assembly elections of 2007 would prove just as important as the presidential elections. Not only would the president have to rely on the Assembly to pass bills into law; even more significantly, the French National Assembly has the right to approve the selection of the country's prime minister. Unlike the United States, whose chief executive is the president, and unlike the United Kingdom, whose chief executive is the prime minister, France has *two* executives, not just one. As we pointed out in chapter 8, France has a mixed *presidential-parliamentary system* of government. The chief distinguishing feature of this system is its *dual executive:* France is co-governed by its president, who has real decision-making powers, and by its prime minister, who also has real decision-making powers. The president is formally the country's head of state, while the prime minister is its head of government. To govern effectively, the two executives must try to get along and agree on a common policy agenda. If they do not agree, the result can be *immobilisme,* the French term for gridlock.

If the majority of the deputies elected to the National Assembly (at least 289 out of 577) belong to the same party as the president, the president can safely nominate a like-minded prime minister from his or her own party in the expectation that the party's parliamentary delegation will approve the choice. Thus, if Ségolène Royal is president, and her Socialist Party has won an outright majority in the National Assembly (or if it formed a voting majority with other leftist parties), then President Royal could designate a Socialist prime minister who would win her party's approval in the Assembly. Similarly, if Sarkozy is president, he would need a UMP majority in the Assembly (or a UMP-led majority of center-right parties) in order to win approval of a UMP prime minister. At least in principle, the French political system works at peak efficiency and effectiveness when the president, the prime minister, and the parliamentary majority all belong to the same party. As we'll see, however, even leaders of the same party do not necessarily see eye-to-eye.

But what happens if the French people elect a president of one party and a National Assembly majority of the opposing party and its allies? The majority of the National Assembly is likely to reject a president's nominee for prime minister if they do not like the president's choice. Under these circumstances, the president would be compelled by the logic of French politics to choose a prime minister who represents the opposing parliamentary majority. If Ségolène Royal won the presidency but the UMP and its allies subsequently won control of the National Assembly, President Royal would have been expected to appoint a prime minister from the UMP. Conversely, if Sarkozy won the presidency but the Socialists and their allies took control of the Assembly, Sarkozy would have been expected to appoint a Socialist prime minister. ***When the president is of one party and the prime minister represents an opposing party, the French call this situation*** **cohabitation.** In effect, cohabitation is the French version of *divided government*. In the United States, under a very different political system, divided government occurs when the president belongs to one party and one or both houses of Congress are controlled by the other party. This predicament occurred most recently after the 2006 congressional elections, when the Democrats took over the Senate and the House of Representatives for the final two years of George W. Bush's presidency.[1]

Prior to the 2007 elections, cohabitation occurred three times in France. The first occurrence was in 1986–88, when President François Mitterrand, a Socialist, was forced by a newly elected center-right majority in the National Assembly to select his archrival, Jacques Chirac, as prime minister. The second came in 1993–95, when Mitterrand was again compelled to pick a leader of the rival party, Édouard Balladur, as prime minister. And from 1997 to 2002, President Chirac had to select Socialist leader, Lionel Jospin, as prime minister after the Socialists wrested control of the National Assembly from Chirac's party in the snap elections of 1997. Although these rival leaders avoided political paralysis and even managed to cooperate, none of them regarded cohabitation as a satisfactory method of governing.

The outcome of the legislative elections set for 2007 was hard to predict in advance, though the pendulum of French politics has tended to swing against the incumbent majority in the National Assembly. In five previous legislative elections, starting in 1986, French voters voted out the majority party and its allies and ushered in their opponents. Whatever the results of the 2007 elections, France's new president and prime minister will have to confront an array of problems inherited from President Chirac and his last prime minister, Dominique de Villepin (dough-mih-NEEK duh-veel-PAAN). One set of problems centers on *globalization* and its regional variant, *Europeanization*. France is a rich country, with a gross national income of $2.17 trillion that ranked sixth in the world in 2005. Its per capita GNP of $34,810 ranked fifteenth. Nevertheless, many French people and political leaders are troubled by economic and social pressures emanating from abroad. Economic globalization features unprecedented levels of trade and foreign investment as well as relentless competition between private and state-owned companies in the global marketplace. These market forces are pushing French firms to widen their international activities and reduce operating costs. In the process, French companies are under pressure to merge with foreign-owned firms to form globally competitive corporate giants. In some cases these mergers result in layoffs of workers and staff, boosting unemployment and job insecurity. They can also diminish the executive controls previously exercised by French business owners and managers. As a consequence, antiglobalization sentiments have proliferated on both the left and right sides of the French political spectrum. Prime Minister de Villepin himself stated that globalization "cannot be our destiny." When French survey respondents in their early twenties were asked in 2006, "What does globalization mean to you?" 48 percent replied, "Fear."[2]

Some of these globalization trends are being actively promoted by European Union institutions in

Brussels. In the 1950s, France was a founding member of the European Economic Community, the forerunner of today's European Union. Until the 1990s, France asserted a leading role in the European integration process, acting in close concert with Germany. But the enlargement of the EU to twenty-five states in 2004, plus the addition of two more in 2007, has diminished French influence. Hopes that France might take the lead in fashioning the EU's "common foreign and security policy" foundered when the governments of Britain, Spain, Italy, and several new East European member states backed the U.S. invasion of Iraq in 2003, spurning efforts by France and Germany to block it. The possibility that Turkey may be admitted to the EU in fifteen years or so has raised fears of a further diminution of France's weight. In part for these reasons, a majority of French voters (55 percent), in a referendum held on May 29, 2005, rejected the adoption of the EU's proposed Constitution for Europe. (On the constitution, see chapter 6.) The vote was a stunning blow to the country's mainstream political leaders, most of whom had supported the constitution. Chirac fired his prime minister and replaced him with de Villepin. He also brought Sarkozy, a former cabinet minister, back into his cabinet as interior minister, the position that carries responsibility for maintaining domestic law and order. With the constitution currently on hold, France's new leaders will need to find new ways of dealing with the exigencies of globalization while redefining France's role in a new Europe.[3]

Another set of problems concerns France's ethnic and religious minorities. Out of a total French population of 60 million in 2004, approximately 14 million were born abroad or had at least one parent, grandparent, or great-grandparent who was born abroad. About 5.3 million of these people with foreign roots traced their origins to southern Europe. About 3 million stemmed from one of France's former colonies in North Africa, the so-called "Mahgreb" countries of Algeria, Morocco, and Tunisia. Many others came from sub-Saharan Africa, Vietnam and neighboring parts of southeast Asia, and the Caribbean—areas where France once had additional colonial dependencies. French law prohibits compiling official statistics on religious affiliation, but it is believed that 5 to 6 million Muslims reside in metropolitan France today. Many recently arrived immigrants and their families are crowded into ghetto-like suburbs (*banlieus*) of Paris and other cities. Unemployment rates, especially among youth, run as high as 40 percent of the local working-age population in some of these areas. Crime is a daily occurrence, discrimination and racism are constant realities. In an effort to integrate Muslims more fully into the country's secular education system, the government in 2004 banned the wearing of head scarves and other religious apparel or jewelry in French grade schools and high schools.

One night in October 2005, two Muslim teenagers were electrocuted to death after scaling a wall and falling on cables in an electric power substation located in Clichy-sous-Bois, about an hour's ride from Paris. Witnesses charged that the boys were being chased by police officers. The police denied this account, but accused the boys of trying to dodge a checkpoint where they would have had to show their identity documents. (One of the boys had left his identification papers at home.) Word of the deaths quickly spread around town, sparking anti-police disturbances. Over the course of the next three weeks, full-blown riots jolted more than three hundred towns and suburbs in the Paris region and other areas with concentrations of immigrants. Even central Paris was affected. During this tumultuous period, more than ten thousand vehicles were torched and two hundred public buildings set afire; 4,500 people were taken into custody. Political leaders were taken aback as events spun out of control. President Chirac was silent for ten days before he addressed the public on the mounting turmoil. His comments about France's "malaise" and "identity crisis" came more than a week after that. Prime Minister de Villepin and Interior Minister Sarkozy—rivals for the presidency after Chirac's expected retirement—each promised a crackdown on criminal behavior. De Villepin declared a state of emergency to permit curfews and other preventive measures. Just before the disturbances began, Sarkozy had called for a "war without mercy" against crime in the suburbs. When the riots broke out he initially called the rioters "scum" and "riffraff" who needed to be hosed down, but he subsequently joined with Chirac and Villepin in proposing economic measures to deal with unemployment while deploring the marginalization of France's immigrant population.

Although many of the rioters were already known to French authorities as criminals, their actions reflected widespread anger in immigrant communities. Most of this discontent sprang from the frustrations of everyday life resulting from housing shortages, inadequate medical care, meager job opportunities, police harassment, and the like. Radical Islamic ideology and support for terrorism did not play much of a role in fomenting the riots. Most tellingly, the 2005 turbulence revealed the French political elite's inattentiveness to the grievances of the immigrant community, a problem that will surely be high on the agenda of France's new president and prime minister.

A third set of problems facing France's new leaders are socioeconomic in nature. The country's immigrants are not the only ones facing unemployment: France's overall unemployment rate has hovered around 10 percent since the 1980s. For much of that time, more than 40 percent of the unemployed have been jobless for more than a year—a figure six to nine times higher than in the United States or Canada. In an effort to open up new job opportunities, the government of Socialist Party leader Lionel Jospin reduced average working hours for the vast majority of the country's employees in the private and public sectors to thirty-five hours a week, with pay for forty hours. Supporters of the measure claim that it has created more than three hundred thousand jobs since it took effect in early 2000. Nevertheless, it has not produced a significant long-term reduction in unemployment. Many economists regard the country's highly protective job-security laws as a major impediment to more hiring. French labor laws make it virtually impossible for employers to fire anyone except for gross negligence. Laying off employees to cut labor costs or for incompetence requires costly severance payments. Once hired, most French employees are hired for life. Although this system favorably protects those already employed, it discourages employers from hiring new people. French youth are especially penalized by these labor-market rules. Prime Minister de Villepin stated that the youth unemployment rate in France in 2006 was 23 percent. (Other estimates suggested that the actual rate was closer to 8 percent, only slightly higher than in Britain and Germany.) Quite a few French young people feared that their generation would end up worse off than their patents.[4]

In January 2006, against the advice of most of his cabinet ministers, de Villepin proposed a law establishing a two-year probationary period for newly hired workers under age 26. Employers would have the right to fire these workers during the probationary period under the terms of this "first employment contract." In hopes that the law would stimulate job creation for youth and ultimately lead to permanent employment, de Villepin forced the measure through the National Assembly in just a few weeks. The result was instant turmoil. French trade unions and the country's well-organized unions of college and high-school students quickly denounced the new law, arguing that it would foment more insecurity (*precarité*) and create an easily disposable "Kleenex generation." A series of demonstrations in February and March filled the streets of Paris with hundreds of thousands of protesters. The protest wave billowed across France, spreading to more than a hundred and fifty cities and towns and activating as many as 15 million demonstrators. Most of the country's eighty-four colleges and universities were shut down; the police used tear gas to clear demonstrators from the Sorbonne. Strikes closed businesses and public offices. Ségolène Royal and Socialist Party chief François Hollande strongly denounced the law and called for it to be rescinded. More than 60 percent of the French public opposed it.

Once again, President Chirac tried to stay above the fray, speaking out only a few times. Though he supported de Villepin and his new employment law, Chirac played the traditional role of French presidents by letting his prime minister take the heat for unpopular policies. Even so, Chirac's public approval ratings sank to 20 percent, the lowest of any president in the forty-seven-year history of France's Fifth Republic; only 1 percent said they would vote for him if he ran for reelection. As de Villepin's approval ratings also plunged, dooming his presidential aspirations, Sarkozy held talks with student and trade union leaders and called for the withdrawal of the employment law. He also took Chirac and de Villepin to task by castigating the "opaque decision-making process" that had led to the law's adoption. Finally on April 10, an isolated Prime Minister de Villepin announced he was withdrawing the law, remarking "it was not understood by everyone."

"Rarely has the authority of the state been so undermined," observed a leading French newspaper. Some pessimists went even further, portraying the country as spinning into free fall or drawing ominous parallels with Britain's decline in the 1970s. And some analysts, like Timothy Smith, argued that many of the French use globalization as a convenient excuse for chronic unemployment, income inequality, poverty, and other maladies of the French economy. In fact, Smith contends, these are homegrown problems resulting from policy choices that constrain market forces and reward the rich, the middle class, and comfortably situated pensioners instead of those in need, despite appeals for social "solidarity."[5]

The drama that unfolded over the youth employment law was by no means an unfamiliar story in France. The prime minister's decision to propose a law from on high, without sufficient consultation with those most affected by the legislation; the government's determination to ram its bill through parliament with limited debate; the outpouring of mass opposition to the measure; the public's unwillingness to accept any retreat from the "French model" of government protection for jobs and social-welfare entitlements, despite chronic unemployment, budget deficits, and high taxes; and then the government's humiliating retreat—these and roughly similar events have occurred before in French politics, as we shall see in the pages ahead. They follow long-established French traditions of authoritarian decision making, populist demands for welfare guarantees, and intense contestation that spills out into the streets. They reflect a political culture that mixes support for a strong state with a passion for liberty, elite power with egalitarian ideals. And they stem from a society that includes those who need the state to ensure a basic safety net against poverty and those who want the state to provide the keys to the good life, including tuition-free university education, five-week paid vacations, subsidies for culture and entertainment, and retirement by the age of sixty. Many—perhaps most—French people want a *protected society*, with the state assuming the predominant role in protecting them against the precariousness of the market economy. Many—perhaps most—of the French reject the American and British "liberal" models of political economy, which permit businesses and even the government to fire employees rather easily, and which pad employment rates with low-paying jobs (often without medical insurance, in the United States). In the "Anglo-Saxon" model, people are expected to fend for themselves to a greater extent than in France. In France, the state is expected to take care of people.

Whoever governs France after the 2007 elections will surely have to make some adjustments in adapting the country to the realities of the contemporary world. But France's new leaders will also have to work within the framework of these classic French traditions.

This chapter sets the stage for the government elected in 2007 by analyzing the turbulent history of French democracy, the development of today's Fifth Republic and its institutions, and the principal problems the country's new leadership will face. In the process, we'll examine how France has dealt with the main sources of political conflict that we outlined in chapter 2:

- *Power:* Who has held power over the course of French history? How does the French constitution distribute decision-making powers? How have French leaders used their power?
- *Resources:* What are the respective roles of the state and the private sector in managing the economy? How has France dealt with chronic unemployment and social welfare?
- *Identity:* What does it mean to be French? How have the French dealt with conflicts arising from class, religious, and ethnic diversity?
- *Ideas:* Which are the chief ideological orientations in French politics? What do such terms as *left, right, socialism, communism,* and *conservatism* mean in the French context?
- *Values:* How consensual (or conflictual) is French political culture? How tolerant are the French?

Because so many aspects of French politics today cannot be understood without an appreciation of their historical roots, we'll begin by surveying some key events in the development of French democracy, drawing some instructive comparisons along the way.

## HISTORICAL BACKGROUND: THE EVOLUTION OF FRENCH DEMOCRACY

As we noted in chapter 16, British democracy evolved in a long process that stretched from the origins of Parliament in the 1200s to the full flowering of universal suffrage in the twentieth century.

The French democratic experience was considerably more spasmodic. Instead of a fairly steady evolution, France experienced a convulsive revolution. The French Revolution that began in 1789 was far more radical and violent than Britain's Glorious Revolution a hundred years earlier. Instead of paralleling Britain's gradual expansion of democratic rights in the nineteenth and twentieth centuries, French democracy suffered a succession of failures, giving way to authoritarian regimes of various types. And instead of developing a single concept of democratic governance like Britain's parliamentary system, France tried out several democratic constitutions before settling on its current variant of the presidential-parliamentary model.

In tracing France's tortuous road to stable democracy, we can point to several factors on our list of conditions for democracy that we presented in chapter 9 that distinguish the French political tradition from Britain's. They include the following:

- a long history of nondemocratic *state institutions*, characterized by a strong centralized state and weak parliamentary traditions
- the prolonged influence of authoritarian *elites*
- a prominent role for the state in promoting *national wealth* despite substantial *private enterprise*, especially in nondemocratic regimes
- a concept of French nationalism that, at least until the Revolution, centered on the state and its authority rather than on the people and their liberties, retarding the emergence of a moderate democratic *political culture*
- a *middle class* that did not constitute a steady source of support for democracy but divided its sympathies between democratic and various non-democratic orientations
- prolonged difficulties integrating the working class, the country's main *disadvantaged* class, into democracy, resulting in the political alienation of many workers and the emergence of revolutionary socialist parties
- a turbulent *international environment* that at various times suppressed, destroyed, or threatened to destroy democracy

Though France has traditionally had more *national unity* and ethnic and religious homogeneity than the United Kingdom, and developed an elite system of higher *education* at about the same time as England, these factors alone were not capable of overriding the other factors that made democratic stability much more difficult for the French to achieve than it was for the British. Let's look at these factors in greater detail.

## The French State

*"L'Etat c'est moi"* ("I am the State"). This famous utterance is attributed to King Louis XIV, who reigned from 1651 to 1715. Though perhaps apocryphal, it plainly indicated where power resided in France. A succession of monarchs had ruled the country since the late tenth century, with the Bourbon dynasty establishing itself in 1589. Fancying himself the "sun king," Louis XIV was determined to fortify royal authority through a firm application of the principle of the *divine right of kings:* the notion that God—not the people—was the source of the government's legitimacy. The kingdom he inherited from his father, Louis XIII, was already anchored in centralized state institutions built around the monarch, his ministers, and an expanding cadre of professional bureaucrats. Three successive chief ministers—Cardinals Richelieu and Mazarin, and Jean-Baptiste Colbert—aided the monarchy in fortifying the powers of the French state. Louis XV, grandson of Louis XIV, allegedly expressed his own lack of faith in the ability of the French people to govern themselves by haughtily predicting, *"Après moi, le déluge"* ("After me, the deluge").

In marked contrast to England, the assertion of royal dominance in France was accompanied by the absence of an assertive national parliament. Initially, the French national legislature advanced even more rapidly than England's Parliament in the direction of democratic representation. It originated in 1302, when King Philip IV invited a number of prominent personages to confer with him at a one-day meeting that took place in Notre Dame cathedral in Paris. Those invited included members of what were known in medieval society as "estates." The First Estate consisted of the nobility, the Second Estate consisted of the Roman Catholic clergy, and the Third Estate consisted of the populations of cities, towns, and rural villages. In essence, the Third Estate encompassed the people of France. Their representation in France's nascent national parliament, which became known as the "States General," constituted the first attempts by the

French monarchy to address the population as a whole rather than just the aristocratic and ecclesiastic elites. The next meeting of the States General, held in 1308, included more than five hundred delegates, perhaps as many as half of them coming from the Third Estate.

Over the course of the fourteenth century, meetings of the States General occurred more frequently. In the process, the Third Estate assumed even greater prominence in governmental deliberations than England's equivalent body, the House of Commons. Its representatives tended to come disproportionately from the country's emerging middle class. In 1357 they compelled the king to agree in writing to permit the States General to meet whenever its members wished and to accept its oversight of most of the royal government's activities. This agreement, spelled out in the "Great Ordinance," in principle handed over to the French parliament effective control over the country's governmental affairs. It went much further than the Magna Carta (1215) or the medieval English Parliament did in establishing the bases of a constitutional monarchy, a system in which a national legislature sets limits to the monarch's power. If the Great Ordinance had been followed, France might have achieved in the fourteenth century what Britain did not accomplish until the late seventeenth century.

The French crown was not ready to concede power so rapidly, however. The king quickly disavowed the Great Ordinance, and successive French monarchs called the States General into session with diminishing frequency. After 1439 it did not meet again until 1614. Louis XIV and his immediate successors had no use for it, and the next meeting of the States General was not called until 1789. By that time, popular demands for representation in government had been suppressed for so long that, when at last given a chance for expression, they exploded in a revolutionary frenzy.

**The Revolution** The **French Revolution** was such a shattering series of events that it redefined the significance of almost everything that had come before it in the country's political history. Centuries of royal absolutism, the absence of parliamentary representation, a disaffected nobility with little influence over the monarch and his ministers, financial mismanagement, an unfair tax system, festering urban and rural poverty—these and a variety of additional factors can all be viewed as antecedent causes of the Revolution.

The sorry plight of the government's finances compelled the crown in 1789 to convene the first meeting of the States General in 175 years. Without some form of popular approval, there was little likelihood that King Louis XVI would get the new taxes his lavish administration required. (A major source of the crown's debt was the financial support it had given the American Revolution against England, France's archrival.) From the outset the newly assembled parliament was led by the largely middle-class deputies elected to represent the Third Estate. Shortly after convening, most of the Third Estate's 600-member delegation demanded a constitutional monarchy. The king relented, and the States General quickly reconstituted itself as a unicameral National Assembly. Also known as the Constituent Assembly, the legislature immediately set about the task of drafting France's first written constitution. Its preamble was a "Declaration of the Rights of Man," which enshrined private property along with "resistance to oppression" and citizen participation in the lawmaking process as fundamental civil rights. It formally granted citizenship to all French males over age twenty-five and extended voting rights to those citizens who could meet various property qualifications. Demands for "Liberty! Equality! Fraternity!"—the battle cry of the Revolution—filled the air.

At this juncture in the summer of 1789, France appeared to be moving steadily toward a moderate constitutional monarchy roughly similar to Britain's. But more radical elements, organized mainly in political clubs known as the *Jacobins*, favored abolishing the monarchy altogether and establishing a republic.[6] The Jacobins quickly took political control of the capital city, aided by the poorest classes of Paris, whose smoldering discontent erupted in mass outbursts such as the storming of the Bastille prison on July 14, 1789. (The anniversary is still celebrated as France's national holiday.) Over the next three years, relations between the crown and the Assembly deteriorated. Finally in August 1792, Jacobin elements orchestrated an insurrection in Paris that drove the king from power. A new legislature was elected the following month. Known as the Convention, its members were considerably more radical than the deputies elected to the first National Assembly of 1789 or its successor, elected in 1791. One of the Convention's first acts was to declare France a *Republic* in September 1792.

The Convention's members were divided into extreme radicals, who were seated to the left of the speaker of the house; more conservative elements, seated to the speaker's right; and a majority of delegates in the center whose views were indeterminate or tended to shift. These seating arrangements gave rise to the terms *left*, *right*, and *center* in politics. Though a minority, the left proved highly effective in swaying the Convention's votes. Known as "the Mountain," its delegates persuaded the Convention to put the king on trial. Out of 721 deputies, 394 voted to condemn Louis XVI to death. He died on the guillotine in January 1793.

The king's execution set in motion an orgy of bloodletting known in French history as "the Terror." Over the next year and a half, some twenty thousand "enemies of the people" met their grim fate on the guillotine or in front of execution squads. They included members of the nobility as well as Catholic priests and nuns, victims of the Revolution's anti-clericalism. Outbursts of antirevolutionary activity were ruthlessly suppressed in various parts of France. The Revolution also began consuming revolutionaries. Factional struggles broke out between its most zealous adherents and advocates of a more moderately ordered republic devoted to social peace and respect for property rights. Even heroes of the Revolution died on the scaffold.

As the Terror unfolded, the power of the central government intensified. The radical revolutionaries established a twelve-member Committee of Public Safety that exercised harsh dictatorial rule, sending out "national agents" to impose the central government's will on local governments. The term *Jacobinism* became synonymous with a highly centralized form of government.

The trend toward greater centralization continued even after more moderate factions seized power in July 1794. The next group of revolutionary leaders, solidly middle class and committed to private property rights, abolished the Committee of Public Safety, executed its leaders, and put an end to the Terror. But they also set up a strong executive government of their own, known as the *Directory*. Five Directors were selected by a Council of Five Hundred to govern the country. Voting rights were restricted and parliamentary powers withered.

Though it imposed a measure of tranquillity on an exhausted nation, the Directory could not establish an enduring government. In 1799 it gave way to yet another strong-willed authoritarian regime as General *Napoleon Bonaparte* grabbed power with the support of the French military. Napoleon's coup d'état effectively terminated France's decade of revolution. It had begun with lofty dreams of democracy, defined in the context of eighteenth-century Europe as constituting a limited monarchy, an elected national legislature, limited male suffrage, and private property rights. Within a few years the Revolution had degenerated into dictatorship, fanaticism, and civil strife. The elimination of royal absolutism led not to democracy but to new forms of centralized state power.[7]

**After the Revolution: From Napoleon to the Fifth Republic** Napoleon accentuated these centralizing tendencies. After proclaiming himself "First Consul" of France at the start of his rule, he assumed the crown of Emperor in 1804. A brilliant military commander whose armies brought most of Europe under French domination, Napoleon took an equally domineering approach to domestic affairs. He organized a secret police and pioneered the use of plebiscites to cultivate popular support for his dictatorship. In three such referendums he won the approval of 99 percent of the voters, though the voting procedures were manipulated by the authorities and the official tallies were surely suspect. Another innovation was the creation of a corps of *prefects* charged with ensuring the central government's control over more than eighty administrative departments into which France had been divided during the Revolution. The prefecture system endured with only minor changes until the 1980s, undergirding France's long tradition as a *unitary state*. A unitary state emphasizes the central government's primacy over local governments. (It contrasts with *federalism*, which combines central government authority with significant decision-making powers for local officials.) Even today, despite reforms granting more powers to local governments, France retains the defining features of a unitary state. Prefects still exist, albeit with less power than in the past.

Napoleon's authoritarian rule lasted until his army's defeat in 1814 by an alliance of European powers. Napoleon was sent off into exile, and the victorious allies, whose governments all had monarchs, collaborated with French royalists in restoring the Bourbon monarchy to France. A spirited attempt by Napoleon to reclaim power foundered on the battlefield of Waterloo in 1815, and the *Restoration* of the monarchy was confirmed. The new king, Louis XVIII (a brother of Louis XVI), agreed to a constitution permitting an elected legislature, but his regal powers were substantial. After he died in 1824, his brother Charles X tried even more vigorously to reestablish a sovereign monarchy similar to the *ancien régime* (old regime) that had existed before the Revolution.

But the clock of history could not be turned back to the eighteenth century. Popular agitation resulted in his replacement in July 1830 by a constitutional monarchy under King Louis-Philippe of the house of Orleans. Reigning as the "citizen king," the new monarch was content to leave affairs of state in the hands of middle-class politicians allied with the country's rising business elite. Prime Minister François Guizot explicitly exhorted the country's businessmen, "Gentlemen, get rich!"

In kaleidoscopic fashion, one regime succeeded another. Louis-Philippe's so-called *July Monarchy* lasted only until 1848, when working-class uprisings forced his departure and swept into power a new government devoted to the Revolution's principles of liberty, equality, and fraternity. France's *Second Republic* proved to be as ill-fated as the First Republic of the 1790s. The new leaders proved unable to fulfill their promises to hire the unemployed and improve social welfare. The frustrated working class rose in rebellion once again, and the government resorted to military force to put down the upheaval. With the specter of revolution hanging over the country, the military seized power at the end of 1850 under the leadership of Napoleon's nephew, Louis-Napoleon. A new period of authoritarian rule ensued as the *IInd Empire* reasserted the state's undisputed authority. Like his uncle, Louis-Napoleon (also known as Napoleon III) sought mass approval in manipulated plebiscites but could not survive military defeat. When the French army suffered disaster in the Franco-Prussian War of 1870–71 and Louis-Napoleon was captured, France found itself without a government yet again.

As in 1848, the vacuum was filled in 1870 by devotees of democracy. The *Third Republic* got off to a shaky start, marked by the bloody suppression of a revolutionary uprising in Paris, but it eventually righted itself and promulgated a new constitution in 1875. Its parliamentary system expanded male suffrage, fostered the growth of political parties, and guaranteed civil rights and freedoms, sparking a renaissance in the arts and sciences. But although the Third Republic enjoyed the longest run of any French regime since the Revolution, lasting until 1940, it was no model of governmental stability. Between the 1870s and 1940 it produced no fewer than 108 governments! In the same period Britain had fewer than thirty governments and the United States had seventeen presidents. Vilified by monarchists on the right and revolutionary socialists on the left, at several junctures the Third Republic teetered on collapse.[8]

When Hitler's army invaded France in 1940 and defeated French forces in six weeks, the Third Republic perished and France fell under the grip of Nazi occupation. Initially, the Germans divided the country roughly in half, imposing direct rule in the north and organizing a puppet government under accommodating French officials in the south. The puppet regime, based in *Vichy*, was headed by Marshal Philippe Pétain, a World War I hero who agreed to collaborate with the occupiers in hopes of mitigating the rigors of Nazi rule. The occupation split France into antagonistic camps. *Collaborationists* assisted the Germans; *resistants* took extreme risks in organizing underground opposition to Nazi rule. In 1942 the Germans disbanded the Vichy government and took control of southern France for the remainder of the occupation.

Nazi rule finally ended in 1944 as American and British forces joined with the troops of "Free France" under General *Charles de Gaulle* in driving out the Germans. De Gaulle thereupon installed himself as chief of a provisional government whose principal purpose was to preside over the elaboration of a new constitution. It took two years to accomplish this task, and de Gaulle retreated into retirement once it became clear that his own constitutional design would not win approval. The *Fourth Republic*, formally inaugurated in 1946, was a parliamentary

TABLE 17.1

French Constitutional Regimes

| | | | |
|---|---|---|---|
| Until 1789 | Sovereign monarchies | 1848–1850 | Second Republic |
| 1789–1792 | Constitutional monarchy | 1851–1870 | Second Empire (Napoleon III) |
| 1792–1799 | First Republic | 1870/75–1940 | Third Republic |
| 1793–1794 | Committee of Public Safety | 1940–1944 | German occupation |
| 1794–1799 | Directorate | 1940–1942 | Vichy regime |
| 1799–1804 | Consulate (Napoleon Bonaparte) | 1944–1946 | Provisional governments |
| 1804–1814 | First Empire (Napoleon I) | 1946–1958 | Fourth Republic |
| 1814–1830 | Quasi-sovereign monarchy | 1959 to present | Fifth Republic |
| 1830–1848 | Constitutional monarchy | | |

system with a ceremonial presidency and a bicameral legislature. From the outset it was dogged by governmental instability: a parade of twenty-two coalition governments struggled to exercise power over the next twelve years. Like other unstable French republics before it, the Fourth Republic ultimately fell apart, the victim of its internal conflicts and external disasters.

After failing to reimpose colonial rule on Vietnam and other parts of Indochina after World War II, the Fourth Republic's leaders decided to suppress an independence movement in Algeria that began in 1954. Algeria had come under French control starting in 1830, and its European minority looked to the French government for protection against the Arab–Berber majority. The war ground on inconclusively, splitting French society as devastatingly as the Vietnam War was later to divide Americans. In May 1958 a group of French generals in Algeria, disgruntled at the government's reluctance to prosecute the war more aggressively, staged a mutiny. The Fourth Republic quickly crumbled. A majority of National Assembly delegates voted to confer power on de Gaulle, who came out of retirement with the determination to reorganize the state under a new constitution. The result was the *Fifth Republic,* whose presidential-parliamentary system was approved in a referendum at the end of 1958. With only a few alterations since then, the Vth Republic's constitution remains in force today.

The key points that emerge from the preceding historical account, summarized in table 17.1, are the following:

- France has experienced an extraordinary multiplicity of political regimes over the past 200-plus years. Since the start of the Revolution in 1789 it has had eleven different governmental regimes and fifteen constitutions. This *regime instability* (or *constitutional instability*) contrasts quite starkly with the far less turbulent constitutional development of Britain and the United States.
- French regimes have tended to alternate between more or less democratically organized *republics* and *authoritarian regimes* of one kind or another.
- The first four French republics themselves proved to be highly unstable, exhibiting various forms of *governmental instability.* Here, too, the contrast with Britain and the United States is striking.
- There has been a continuing tradition of *centralized state authority* throughout French history. While the powers of the central government were especially pronounced under authoritarian regimes, even the republics have maintained the institutions of a unitary state and refrained from reconstituting France as a federation.

## French Nationalism

Just as the development of French state institutions diverged sharply from Britain's, French nationalism also displayed palpable differences with British conceptions of national identity. Over the course of the sixteenth and seventeenth centuries, the term *nation* in England became associated with the people rather than the state and with Parliament rather than an all-powerful monarchy. As Liah Greenfeld has shown, French nationalism until shortly before the Revolution revolved overwhelmingly around the state and its crowning authority, the monarchy. Especially during the height of the monarch's absolute power in the seventeenth century, "the nation" referred mainly to the royal government rather than to the people. The people were relegated to the status of servile subjects.[9]

The Revolution made decisive changes in French national consciousness. More than anything else, the Revolution signified the French people's assertion of their right as citizens to constitute the French nation. The word *national*, as used in such terms as *National Assembly* and *national defense*, placed the people of France squarely in the center of the country's political and social life. Popular sovereignty replaced sovereign monarchy. Still, Greenfeld notes that, even during the Revolution, the French conception of popular nationalism continued to differ from Britain's. While the British conceived of their nation as consisting of individuals, the French tended to think of "the people" as a collective entity. This difference mirrored the distinction between John Locke's devotion to individual liberty and Jean-Jacques Rousseau's preference for collective liberty. It was to have long-term implications for political culture. In greater proportions than in Britain or the United States, political elites of both the right and left in France have tended to look to the state more than to private enterprise or society as the chief source of responsibility for the country's economic well-being, a concept known as *étatisme* (statism). Meanwhile, it took centuries to develop a unified French national identity out of the "hexagon" of its diverse regions. As late as the 1860s, local dialects still predominated over French in much of the country.[10]

## Social Class and Democracy

Among the many factors that impeded France's advance toward stable democracy, the political roles played by elites and various social classes stand out as particularly prominent. Once again, a comparison with Britain is instructive.

**The Nobility** In Britain, the nobility contributed to the evolutionary unfolding of democratic institutions and practices: right from the start, it formed a vital component of Parliament. In the twentieth century the House of Lords, the aristocracy's parliamentary preserve, was willing to accept significant limitations on its legislative powers, ceding pride of place to the House of Commons and thus widening popular democracy. Because they were cut in on British democracy, Britain's aristocratic elites supported it. By contrast, the French nobility tended to be cut out of political developments, shunted aside by absolutist monarchs adamantly opposed to sharing power with a national parliament. Feeling neglected and powerless under the monarchy, some nobles joined the Revolution in 1789. (The Marquis de Lafayette, who fought in the American Revolution, was typical.) Even more nobles died on the guillotine, however. From then on, what remained of the French aristocracy was politically marginalized, depriving French democracy of a potential source of elite support.

**The Middle Class** The various strata of the British middle class made indispensable contributions to democracy in England, promoting Parliament along with the Conservative and Liberal parties as the main vehicles for achieving their class interests. The relationship between the middle class and democracy was more complicated in France. By 1789, centuries of exclusion from governmental power had created a split in middle-class ranks between moderates willing to settle for a constitutional monarchy and radicals determined to wipe out the detested monarchy forever. After the Ist Republic was established in 1792, a further split occurred among the largely middle-class Jacobins, as one faction unleashed the Terror and their more temperate rivals replaced them with the Directory. Neither group advanced the cause of stable democracy.

Over the course of the nineteenth century, the French middle class was split between those who favored a republic and more democracy (largely to protect their own property rights) and those who believed that their economic interests were best protected under authoritarian regimes. When democracy finally steadied itself in the Third Republic (1870–1940), it was dominated by middle-class politicians and their followings.

During World War II, the French middle class found itself split once again. While the majority of the population stayed aloof from political action and concentrated on coping with the daily realities of the German occupation, French fascism and the resistance movement each had middle-class support. The two republics that came after World War II have been solidly middle class in orientation.

France's middle class has thus traveled in two political directions: while providing crucial support for democratic institutions at various times, some of its members have also supported non-democratic movements and governments.

**The Working Class** The industrial working class was the main disadvantaged social class in France and Britain in the nineteenth and twentieth centuries. Class conflict between workers and capitalists was sharp in both countries, but Britain managed much earlier than France to contain these conflicts within the structures of parliamentary democracy. Significantly, it was Britain's middle-class parties, the Conservatives and the Liberals, that extended the franchise to working-class voters. But it was the establishment of the Labour Party at the start of the twentieth century that most decisively incorporated Britain's working class into democracy. Britain's Communist Party never gained much support, and the country's trade unions—even those led by radical socialists—have tended to support Labour rather than more extreme parties.

A number of events in French history made for a more radicalized segment of the labor movement than in Britain, with results that are visible to this day. As industrialization intensified in the 1820s and subsequent decades, French manual laborers had to contend with the same wretched conditions as their British counterparts. Especially after the July Monarchy came to power in 1830, the government firmly supported the profit-maximizing ambitions of the capitalist elite. The blatant exploitation of the French working class fueled a rage that boiled over in February 1848. As workers took up arms, King Louis-Philippe fled the country and his regime disintegrated.

The Second Republic was forged in the crucible of this workers' revolution. Its leaders immediately vowed to ameliorate working-class conditions through various welfare measures, including the creation of public sector jobs for the unemployed. The government's promises outran its financial capacities, however. As many as 100,000 workers applied for the jobs, but the state could afford to hire only about 10,000. Short of cash, the Second Republic canceled the employment programs after several months. The workers took to the barricades once again, this time arming themselves against a democratically oriented republic that was ostensibly on their side. Fatefully, it was precisely this republic that crushed the uprising in July 1848, leading many workers to feel betrayed by democracy itself.

An even bloodier sequence of events occurred in 1871, with similar implications for French democracy. As Emperor Napoleon III's government collapsed and France capitulated to Prussia, opponents of the makeshift new regime took control of several parts of Paris and created their own government. Proclaiming themselves the "Commune" of Paris, the insurrectionists included working-class revolutionaries and their supporters who sought to establish a socialist society. But the leaders of the nascent Third Republic, determined to impose their authority on the entire country, dispatched troops to put down the insurrection. As many as fifteen thousand people lost their lives in a bloodbath marked by atrocities on both sides. When the smoke cleared, the Commune was liquidated, but large numbers of working-class citizens and their sympathizers once again felt subjugated by a French government that professed democratic ideals.[11]

In the wake of these events, several socialist parties were formed in France to militate for workers' rights. In 1905 various socialist organizations merged to form a single party that joined the "Socialist International," a group of European socialist parties. The party called itself the "French Section of the Socialist International," known by its French initials as the *SFIO*. Many of its members were social democrats: like Britain's newly established Labour Party, they disavowed revolutionary violence and dictatorship and instead favored improving the lot of workers through ballot-box democracy and trade union activity. In 1920, proponents of a more radical approach to socialism organized the *French Communist Party (PCF)*. Its founders were a disparate group of ideological socialists and pacifists, but the Soviet government in Moscow used its influence to help a pro-Soviet faction take over the party leadership. From the mid 1920s until the late 1980s, PCF leaders generally provided faithful support for Soviet dictates and preferences. The French Communists also dominated a trade union federation, the General Confederation of Labor (CGT), and frequently used it to call strikes and demonstrations against French businesses and governments.

In 1936, as the Great Depression boosted unemployment in France, the SFIO and the PCF won an electoral victory in the lower house of the French parliament that permitted the establishment of a Socialist-dominated government. Known as the *Popular Front*, the Third Republic's first left-wing government produced a spate of laws providing for unemployment compensation, state sector jobs, trade union bargaining rights, paid vacations, and other measures benefiting the country's most disadvantaged groups. France's equivalent of President Franklin D. Roosevelt's New Deal lasted only about a year, however. By 1937, more conservative, pro-business parties used their influence in the legislature's upper chamber to block further reforms. Once again, many French workers had reason to feel let down by French democracy.

This long history of working-class radicalism and disaffection from democratic governments helps explain why France, in contrast to Britain, ended up with a comparatively large Communist Party that was allied with the Soviet Union and militantly hostile to private enterprise. Although PCF leaders increasingly expressed their adherence to democratic principles after World War II, they remained vague about what a "socialist democracy" would look like if they were given the opportunity to establish one in France. During the Fourth Republic, from 1946 to 1958, the French Communist Party was the country's largest political party, routinely capturing about 25 percent of the vote in elections to the national legislature. Some 2 million workers were affiliated with the communist-dominated trade union organization, the CGT.

In 1979 the French Communists could still garner 20 percent of the ballots. The party's vote has dwindled since then, however. In 1997 it got only 3.8 percent of the second-round votes, and in 2002 it won scarcely more than 3 percent. Nevertheless, French Communists continue to play an active role in French politics. In the 1997 parliamentary elections they obtained 6.4 percent of the seats in the National Assembly and three of its leaders were invited by Prime Minister Jospin to participate in his first government. For its part, Britain's Communist Party never got more than 1 percent of the vote after World War II.

**Consequences** The clash between left and right has thus tended to be sharper in France than in Britain, reflecting a somewhat more antagonistic confrontation between the working class and the business community. In the 1970s this situation prompted a French sociologist to describe France as a "stalled society," incapable of resolving its economic disputes because both sides have a fear of face-to-face negotiations. As a consequence, the French government has often had to play a mediating role between business and labor.[12] Inevitably, those in power tend to side with those who elected them, the conservatives supporting business leaders (known collectively as the *patronat*) and the Socialists and their allies supporting labor.

The confrontational nature of labor-management relations in France reflects a more general tendency toward conflict and contention in French history than in British history. Charles Tilly points out in *The Contentious French* that France has experienced a multitude of politically motivated disorders over the past four centuries, largely in reaction to the expansion of the state and the growth of capitalism.[13] (As Charles de Gaulle put it, "How can you govern a nation that has 246 kinds of cheese?") Whereas British political culture has generally emphasized moderation, pragmatic problem solving, and compromise in dealing with its problems, France's more conflictual political culture has placed a greater emphasis on ideological differentiation, demands for radical change, and negotiating intransigence. These attitudinal predispositions have mellowed in recent decades, but a penchant for mass protest remains a vital part of French political culture.

## POLITICS IN THE FIFTH REPUBLIC

After its origins in the Fourth Republic's fatal crisis of 1958, France's Fifth Republic was profoundly influenced by two exceptional political leaders: Charles de Gaulle and François Mitterrand. As the Republic's founder, de Gaulle was the source not only of its constitution but of a political movement—*Gaullism*—that still bears his name. (Contemporary Gaullists like Jacques Chirac are known as *neo-Gaullists* because they have adapted and modernized de Gaulle's seminal ideas.) Mitterrand was the organizer of France's Socialist Party, the party of Ségolène Royal.

## PROFILE: Charles de Gaulle

"All my life," wrote **Charles de Gaulle**, "I have formed a certain idea of France. France cannot be France without grandeur." In a career that stretched from the battlefields of the First World War to the unrest of the 1960s, de Gaulle dedicated his life to rescuing France from international humiliation and fratricidal strife. At times he spoke of embodying in his own person the legitimacy of national political authority. In his own mind, de Gaulle was France.

### From War to War

Born in 1890 into a Catholic family of modest means, de Gaulle decided in boyhood to pursue a military career. In 1910 he entered the French Military Academy at St. Cyr, France's equivalent of West Point. At six feet four inches in height, he struck an imposing figure. Upon graduation he came under the command of Philippe Pétain, a man whose fate was to be linked to de Gaulle's for more than three decades. As World War I broke out in August 1914 and German troops swarmed into Belgium and France, Lieutenant de Gaulle quickly found himself in the thick of the fighting. Wounded in three separate engagements, he was taken prisoner and spent most of the war in German captivity, risking escape five times. Marshal Pétain emerged from the war a national hero, having beaten the Germans in the critical battle of Verdun in 1916.

After the war de Gaulle returned to St. Cyr as a history professor and attended the Ecole de Guerre (War Academy) in Paris, the training ground of the country's military elite. He soon distinguished himself as an original strategic thinker. After World War I, French strategists adopted a defensive doctrine built around the "Maginot line," a heavily fortified barrier designed to block a potential German invasion. De Gaulle criticized this static approach in 1934, arguing for a mobile defensive force more heavily reliant on tanks, planes, and other mechanized weapons. But Pétain and the military hierarchy persuaded the Third Republic's governments to keep the Maginot line intact.

The merits of de Gaulle's advice became painfully evident in the spring of 1940, when Adolph Hitler's armies rapidly devastated French forces. Marshal Pétain assumed control of the government and capitulated. The Germans temporarily allowed Pétain to set up a new French state headquartered in Vichy. Many of Vichy's officials and supporters were openly hostile to democracy and sympathized with fascism. A number of them took part in the roundup of French Jews for deportation to Nazi concentration camps.[14]

**Charles de Gaulle (left) greets Gen. Raoul Salan in Algeria in 1958, shortly before assuming the presidency. Salan was a leader of the military coup that precipitated the collapse of the IVth Republic and was later convicted of plotting to overthrow de Gaulle's Vth Republic.**

De Gaulle repaired to England in hopes of reorganizing French armed resistance to the Germans in conjunction with Winston Churchill's government. In a series of stirring radio broadcasts from London, de Gaulle declared that all Frenchmen still under arms had the "strict duty of refusing to carry out the enemy's conditions." In effect, he dismissed Pétain's government as illegitimate. "At that moment," he later wrote, "it was for me to assume the country's fate, to take France upon myself."

From his London redoubt, de Gaulle created a new French government, known informally as Free France and later as the Provisional Government. Over the next four years he galvanized a Free French army numbering 115,000 troops, based mostly in Britain and in French colonies overseas. A growing anti-German resistance movement in France answered to him as the country's true leader.

Despite these rising manifestations of legitimacy accorded him by French men and women, de Gaulle had a difficult time dealing with his closest allies. Churchill supported Free France, but his failure to inform de Gaulle in advance of certain U.S. and British military operations fueled the General's greatest anxiety, that France would not be treated as an equal by the United States and Britain. President Franklin D. Roosevelt stoked these fears by casually dismissing de Gaulle as an overblown egotist. During the first years of the war the United States maintained diplomatic ties with the Vichy government, much to de Gaulle's consternation.

In laying out his plans for the postwar order, the U.S. president informed de Gaulle that the future would be dominated by the United States, Britain, the Soviet Union, and China; there was no room for France in FDR's grand design. On the eve of the D-Day invasion of Normandy in June 1944, the United States and Britain still withheld formal recognition of de Gaulle's Provisional Government as the legitimate government of France. When de Gaulle complained bitterly to Churchill, the prime minister testily replied, "Every time I have to choose between you and Roosevelt, I shall always choose Roosevelt." The wartime alliance left de Gaulle with a lifelong vision of collusion between the "Anglo-Saxons" (the Americans and the British) to keep France down, a humiliating affront he would never accept.

Despite these conflicts, de Gaulle remained a loyal partner of the anti-Hitler coalition. Several hundred thousand French forces took part in the country's liberation alongside U.S. and British troops in the summer and fall of 1944. In July, following de Gaulle's triumphal visit to the United States, the Roosevelt administration finally accorded his Provisional Government tentative recognition, which it formalized in October.

### The Provisional Government and the Fourth Republic

As soon as French troops entered Paris in August, General de Gaulle assumed the reins of power. From the outset, the new government's main tasks were to reinvigorate France's shattered economy and establish a stable democracy. In addressing the first of these challenges, de Gaulle conferred primary responsibility for stimulating economic activity on the French state. Known as *dirigisme,* this policy stops short of full-scale socialism by allowing ample room for private enterprise. But it encourages state ownership of various enterprises, like railroads and banks, and state coordination of the country's economic activity through planning mechanisms and other forms of intervention in the marketplace.

It was in the political sphere, however, that the Provisional Government concentrated its energies. De Gaulle was firmly committed to democracy, but he did not want France to return to the governmental instability of the Third Republic. He deplored the "regime of the parties" that, in his view, had only heightened France's social and ideological divisions rather than bringing the nation together. He therefore favored a constitution that would counterbalance the powers of the legislature with a strong executive, endowed with real decision-making powers. In de Gaulle's conception, this chief executive would be the "arbiter" and "guide" of French politics, standing above the political parties and social classes as a truly national figure representing the best interests of France as a whole. Needless to say, he conceived of this supreme role for himself.

In effect, de Gaulle was a bridge linking the two warring traditions of French political history: the tradition of authority, order, and stability historically represented by the monarchy, the army, and the Catholic church; and the tradition of "liberty, equality, fraternity" associated with the Revolution and subsequent republican regimes. In the past, France had never succeeded in combining democracy with stability. De Gaulle believed that the only way to achieve a stable democracy was to anchor democratic institutions in a powerful presidency that would guarantee firm and decisive governance. A strong and stable government at home, moreover, was for de Gaulle the precondition of an active foreign policy that would place France in the front rank of the world's most powerful countries.

To his chagrin, the Constituent Assembly elected in October 1945 for the purpose of writing a new constitution did not share his vision, favoring instead a return to parliamentary government without the superexecutive de Gaulle wanted. De Gaulle therefore resigned in January 1946. He was convinced that British-style parliamentary government was ill-suited to France and doomed to certain failure.

Events were to prove him right. The Fourth Republic witnessed a steady succession of revolving-door governments. The lower house of the legislature, elected by proportional representation, was divided among five main parties and several smaller ones. The Communist Party usually had the largest delegation, but most of the other parties refused to deal with it because of its implacable pro-Soviet orientation at a time of mounting Cold War hostilities. (France was a charter member of NATO in 1949, an alliance the Communists vehemently denounced.) De Gaulle and his followers established their own party dedicated to criticizing the Fourth Republic's deficiencies. Governments tended to be shaky coalitions consisting of three or more parties. One government lasted only two days, another merely one. Gridlock reigned.

After World War II, de Gaulle and the Fourth Republic governments that followed him decided to retain control of France's imperial domains. This fateful choice resulted in a protracted struggle in Vietnam, where local communists as well as noncommunists fought to rid their country of French domination. Unable to sustain the fight, France reached a negotiated settlement with the Vietnamese in 1954 that put an end to its political presence in Indochina.

No sooner had the French withdrawn from Vietnam than a new independence movement flared up in Algeria. By virtue of its proximity to France and the presence of more than a million Europeans among its inhabitants, Algeria was France's most prized colonial dominion. The Europeans were outnumbered by twelve million Arabs, however, and in the fall of 1954 an Arab insurgency took arms against French forces. Though a majority of France favored preserving Algeria's colonial status at this time, French military leaders in Algeria believed that the floundering coalition governments in Paris were incapable of providing the support they considered necessary for a decisive military victory. In May 1958 they decided to take matters into their own hands. In a calculated act of insubordination, they engineered the military takeover of France's official government facilities in Algeria. They also proclaimed their own "Committee of Public Safety" to govern the colony. At the heart of the generals' strategy was the hope that their mutiny would precipitate the downfall of the Fourth Republic and motivate their trusted military comrade, General de Gaulle, to come out of retirement and form a "Government of Public Safety" in Paris. Though de Gaulle was informed of the generals' plans, there is no evidence that he participated in the planning of their revolt or approved of its execution. In any event, de Gaulle issued a statement affirming, "I am ready to assume the powers of the Republic."

The Fourth Republic's president, exercising his right to designate the prime minister, thereupon invited de Gaulle to form a new government. De Gaulle agreed, but only on condition that he be granted exceptional powers to govern France by decree for six months, during which his government would have the authority to formulate a new constitution for the voters' consideration. After an intense debate, a large majority of the Fourth Republic's lower house accepted de Gaulle's terms and voted to abolish the Fourth Republic itself. Among those voting against de Gaulle's assumption of power was a future president of the next republic, François Mitterrand.

Though the generals in Algeria assumed that de Gaulle's return signaled a more aggressive approach to crushing the Algerian independence movement, de Gaulle categorically rejected the generals' suggestions that he establish a dictatorship in France. He had no tolerance for a coup d'état and firmly warned the military to obey his orders. In de Gaulle's view, only his firm presence at the helm of the French government could prevent a chaotic civil war and preserve democracy.

### De Gaulle and the Constitution of the Fifth Republic

Meanwhile, de Gaulle got on with the business of framing a new constitution. For this task he assembled a small group of experts led by Michel Debré, a trusted advisor and former member of the French parliament. De Gaulle himself took an active role at every stage in the elaboration of the document. The final draft reflected a combination of a powerful presidency, which was de Gaulle's highest priority, and a prime minister and government who would be answerable to the legislature, as favored by parliamentarians like Debré. Thus the Fifth Republic constitution was a compromise that resulted in two executives, each with significant decision-making authority.

As conceived by its framers, the new constitution's creation of a dual executive was not expected to be troublesome. The president, it was widely assumed, would lay out broad policy guidelines and ensure overall political stability, while the prime minister would take charge of day-to-day governmental activities. But early critics of the proposed constitution, including François Mitterrand, were quick to criticize de Gaulle for seeking excessive decision-making authority. Some warned that the high-powered presidency amounted to an "elected dictatorship," and accused de Gaulle of "Bonapartism"—a reference to Napoleon's military autocracy. But when it was submitted to the people for their judgment in September 1958, de Gaulle's constitution was approved by 79 percent of the voters, a landslide of unprecedented proportions in French democracy. Two months later, de Gaulle's party and its conservative allies outpolled the left-wing parties in elections to the new republic's first National Assembly, ensuring an invincible parliamentary majority in favor of de Gaulle's constitution. And in December, de Gaulle won 78.5 percent of the votes cast in the electoral college established to select the president. In January 1959 he took the oath of office and moved into Elysée Palace, the president's home. He was 68.

From the beginning it was evident that de Gaulle viewed the presidency as the central decision-making office in the Fifth Republic. At times he would announce policy initiatives without even informing his prime minister in advance. "True, there was a government which 'decides the policy of the nation'," de Gaulle later wrote. "But everyone knew that it would proceed from my choice and act only with my blessing." Although the new presidential-parliamentary system was called "semi-presidentialism" by some French political analysts, de Gaulle was anything but a semi-president. On the contrary, he fully intended to be a super-president.

When de Gaulle ordered a referendum in 1962 asking the people to approve the direct popular election of the president, his critics charged that he ignored the constitution's provision requiring him to obtain parliamentary approval before holding a referendum. The legislature thereupon voted to censure Prime Minister Georges Pompidou's government, an act that required the prime minister's resignation. Incensed at the National Assembly's presumptuousness, de Gaulle promptly reappointed Pompidou and dissolved the Assembly, calling new elections. In 1965, when he ran for reelection, de Gaulle barely bothered to campaign. To his surprise he failed to win an absolute majority in the first round. As a result he was forced into a second round with his most serious challenger, François Mitterrand. After campaigning more vigorously, he defeated Mitterrand by 54.6 percent to 45.4 percent.

## Algeria

Only once did de Gaulle resort to invoking the emergency powers outlined in Article 16 of the constitution. Once the Fifth Republic's new institutions were securely in place, de Gaulle announced in September 1959 that he would allow the Algerians to decide for themselves in a referendum how they wished to be governed. The announcement angered French generals opposed to an independent Algeria, prompting them to stage a coup d'état in the colony. De Gaulle went on television in military dress and forcefully declared: "I am the supreme authority. It is I who bear the destiny of the country in my hands. I must, therefore, be obeyed by all French soldiers." De Gaulle's display of command convinced most troops in Algeria to abandon their rebellious commanders. The coup attempt quickly fizzled and some of its leaders were arrested.

But the crisis was not over. Disenchanted French generals and their followers formed an underground conspiracy, the Secret Army Organization (OAS), and in April 1961 they tried once again to seize power in Algeria. At the same time, French police uncovered OAS plans for the military takeover of the French government in Paris. Rumors of a landing by insurgent paratroopers gripped the country. In another riveting television appearance in full military uniform, the president announced that he was invoking Article 16 of the constitution, which permits the president (with parliamentary approval) to call a state of emergency and govern by decree. The insurgency dissolved, and several of its plotters surrendered to French authorities.

As required by the constitution, the parliament continued to meet throughout the duration of the national emergency. Its powers, however, remained in doubt, since Article 16 does not specify exactly what, if anything, the legislature may do during the emergency period. Appeals to President de Gaulle by François Mitterrand and other legislators to clarify the situation were met with majestic silence. The public, meanwhile, solidly backed de Gaulle. Polls showed that 84 percent trusted him to resolve the crisis. Several months after declaring the state of emergency, de Gaulle announced it was over. No French president since him has ever invoked Article 16.

In March 1962, French and Algerian negotiators meeting in Evian agreed on a peace accord providing for a referendum on the colony's status. To legitimize the accord democratically, de Gaulle ordered a separate referendum in France. More than 90 percent of those who went to the polls in France approved the Evian agreements. As the Algerian majority moved toward independence, the OAS intensified its efforts to prevent it. OAS marksmen on at least two occasions came within inches of shooting de Gaulle, at one point shattering his car windows with gunfire.

## De Gaulle's "Policy of Grandeur"

Once the Algerian question was settled, de Gaulle turned to foreign policy matters that, in his eyes, were far more important. "France is not really herself unless in the front rank," he wrote in his memoirs. This meant above all that France must never allow itself to be a mere follower of the "Anglo-Saxons," especially the United States. De Gaulle therefore devised a foreign policy designed to enhance French freedom of maneuver in foreign affairs, while at the same time remaining a member of the NATO political alliance and a dedicated foe of Soviet imperialism. In a series of measures that irked President Lyndon B. Johnson's administration, de Gaulle withdrew French military forces from the unified NATO military command in Europe, which was always headed by an American general, and compelled the United States and NATO to remove their troops and facilities from French soil. While withdrawing from NATO's *military* component, de Gaulle made sure that France remained in most of NATO's *political* decision-making bodies, where it would have a say in the alliance's overall diplomatic and strategic direction. That arrangement was still in effect in 2006.

In 1963 he vetoed Britain's application for membership in the European Community, the forerunner of the European Union, on the grounds that the UK was simply a "Trojan horse" promoting American domination in Europe. In place of a federal Europe, centered in supranational decision-making organs in Brussels, he favored a "Europe of countries," in which the main decisions would always be taken by the organization's member governments. De Gaulle was a proud defender of French national sovereignty and opposed surrendering control over his country's political fate to European technocrats. But even though these and other initiatives antagonized American and British policy makers, de Gaulle remained a reliable ally in times of crisis. De Gaulle fully realized that his policy of promoting French grandeur abroad required political unity and economic strength at home. But precisely these preconditions blew up in his face in 1968.

### 1968

The extraordinary events of 1968 began with a series of small protests by students dissatisfied with conditions in several of the country's large public universities. In March a few dozen students led by Daniel Cohn-Bendit, a charismatic redheaded idealist later dubbed "Danny the Red," took over some lecture halls at the University of Paris campus in the suburb of Nanterre. As the protests continued, students at the Sorbonne in central Paris tore up paving stones and erected barricades. The government ordered the police to clear the area. From this point on, the protests escalated wildly and the brutality of the police inflamed public opinion. As de Gaulle remained stonily silent and his ministers appeared befuddled, some 300,000 students and political opponents of de Gaulle's regime staged a massive demonstration, with many shouting for the president's resignation. De Gaulle responded by casually leaving the next day on a trip to Romania.

On that very day, factory workers at a state-owned factory staged a wildcat strike, setting in motion a nationwide strike movement that soon involved industrial workers and white-collar employees throughout France. Within weeks some 10 million French people were on strike. Factories and offices closed, public services virtually ceased, and the nation's transportation system came to a standstill. Most workers had little in common with the students. Cohn-Bendit and other student leaders spoke of destroying the Fifth Republic and replacing it with a utopian society whose precise contours they admittedly could not define. "Take your dreams for reality!" was one of their slogans. Many drew their inspiration from Mao Zedong, the leader of Communist China. But the striking workers were mainly interested in bread-and-butter issues, not revolution. A slowdown in the French economy over the previous year had reduced their purchasing power and boosted unemployment.

With the entire country sliding toward anarchy, de Gaulle cut his trip short and returned home. "In five days," he thundered at his ministers, "ten years of struggle against rottenness in the State have been lost." But when de Gaulle's televised address failed to quell the turmoil, and when striking workers rejected a negotiated settlement, the president announced that he was dissolving the National Assembly and setting new elections. Shortly after he spoke, a crowd that swelled to more than 500,000 people filled the boulevards of Paris in a massive display of support for de Gaulle. The atmosphere of revolutionary chaos was suddenly broken.

The results of the elections of June 23 and 30 were a triumph for de Gaulle's party and its allies on the right. They won 360 of the National Assembly's 485 seats. Mitterrand's social democratic grouping lost half its seats and so did the Communists. As workers returned to their jobs, the student revolt quietly dissipated in the fine spring weather.[15]

De Gaulle had once more worked his charismatic magic on the people of France, rescuing the country from the brink of disintegration. But at 78, he was not inclined to seek any more titanic challenges. By the following year, with calm restored, there was a growing feeling in the electorate that France no longer needed him. Sensing that the time had come to exit the scene, de Gaulle turned a referendum on reforming the Senate in April 1969 into a referendum on himself. He announced that he would quit if his proposal were defeated. When the results showed 53 percent against his proposed reform, he resigned the presidency the following day. He thereupon withdrew to his Normandy estate to resume the writing of his memoirs and enjoy his retirement with his wife. While at home on November 9, 1970, de Gaulle suffered a ruptured blood vessel and died in less than an hour.

### De Gaulle's Legacy

De Gaulle was a man of many contradictions. Like the Bourbon monarchs, he believed that he personified the French state and that the deluge would surely follow him. And yet he reined in these authoritarian instincts with a principled commitment to popular democracy. Though he occasionally violated the spirit of democracy and even the letter of his own constitution, de Gaulle more than once saved democracy in France from its challengers of both right and left. He detested the routine transactions of everyday parliamentary politics and felt a personal connection with the people of France that went over the heads of ordinary politicians. Though conservative in social matters, in 1944 he gave French women the vote for the first time. His economic policies transcended the traditional categories of left and right, socialist and capitalist. And in an age of impersonal economic forces and mass social movements, he showed how the fortunes of an entire nation can at times rest on the shoulders of a single individual.

Since his death, no one in France has assumed de Gaulle's mantle as one of the world's most extraordinary political leaders. His towering presence continues to hover over French politics. "Gaullism" became a synonym for strong presidential authority at home and foreign policy activism on the world stage. To a considerable extent, most of France today accepts the Gaullist consensus that the Fifth Republic's constitution should remain in force essentially as it is and that France needs to play a role of its own in world affairs, independent of the United States while at the same time allied with it. Although France has changed considerably since Charles de Gaulle's lifetime, its state institutions and prevailing political attitudes remain deeply affected by his powerful imprint.[16]

**De Gaulle's Conservative Successors: Pompidou and Giscard d'Estaing** After de Gaulle's resignation, a special presidential election brought *Georges Pompidou* to the Élysée Palace. (The constitution does not provide for a vice president to fill out the term of a president who vacates the office. New presidential elections must be held within thirty-five days.) Pompidou had been a close associate of de Gaulle's since the liberation of France at the end of World War II. He proved invaluable to de Gaulle as his second prime minister, dutifully deferring to the president in matters of the highest political importance.

When de Gaulle retired, Pompidou won a comfortable victory against a centrist challenger, Alain Poher. Though he was a confirmed Gaullist, Pompidou favored closer cooperation with NATO (though not a complete return to the alliance's integrated command) and withdrew France's veto of Britain's entry into the European Community. With the approval of French voters in a referendum, Britain entered the EC in 1973.

A devastating illness prevented Pompidou from serving out his full seven-year term. Upon his death in 1974, presidential elections were held that signaled major shifts in the French political landscape after sixteen years of Gaullist dominance. No candidate won an absolute majority in the first round. The top two contenders who vied in the runoff election were *Valéry Giscard d'Estaing* (Zhee-scar Deh-STANG) and François Mitterrand. Giscard was a conservative who had served as finance minister under de Gaulle. He had his own small political party that rivaled the Gaullists for the center-right vote. Mitterrand was a veteran of the Fourth Republic and an outspoken foe of de Gaulle's Fifth Republic constitution. His appearance in the 1974 presidential contest appeared more promising than his quixotic 1965 candidacy against de Gaulle because the diverse forces of the French left were now more united than they had been in decades. In 1971 Mitterrand had won the leadership of a new French Socialist Party, and the following year he successfully negotiated a "Common Program" with the French Communist Party for governing France together. The 1974 presidential elections thus presented French voters with a stark choice between opposing left–right visions of how the country should be governed and how its economy should be organized. When all the votes were counted, Giscard d'Estaing narrowly beat Mitterrand, 50.7 percent to 49.3 percent.

Giscard's presidency was largely uneventful, at least when compared to the tumultuous 1950s and 1960s. His government secured the passage of a liberal abortion law, lowered the voting age to eighteen, and promoted women's rights. It also reinstituted the guillotine for capital punishment. Like Pompidou, Giscard mended fences with the United States but refrained from reentering NATO's military command structure. He promoted European unity, forging France's links with West Germany and Britain. Giscard's governing style reflected his emphasis on technocratic competence, especially in monetary and fiscal matters. He jealously guarded the powers of the presidential office and kept the National Assembly in its subordinate position.

Following the Arab-Israeli war in October 1973, the governments of the world's leading oil-producing countries decided to vastly increase the prices they charged foreign oil companies for crude petroleum. Within months, world oil prices were four times higher than before the October Mideast war. The 1973 oil shock was followed by still more oil price hikes over the decade, and the French economy reeled. Economic growth stagnated and inflation soared, an increasingly contagious global phenomenon that economists dubbed *stagflation*. The "thirty glorious years" of steady economic growth that had started after World War II were now over.

Giscard's first prime minister, Jacques Chirac, increased government spending in an effort to stimulate the economy by Keynesian methods. When that approach failed, Giscard replaced Chirac with Raymond Barre, a professor and former trade minister hailed by his admirers as "the best economist in France." Barre reversed the government's course and clamped a tight lid of austerity on the budget, but problems remained. By the time Giscard's term ended in 1981, France was staggering under a 10 percent inflation rate and an unemployment figure of 7.2 percent, the highest in decades. More than 1.5 million people were out of work.[17]

The stage was now set for a reprise of the Giscard-Mitterrand duel for the presidency. This time, however, France's waning economic fortunes played into the hands of the challenger from the left.

**François Mitterrand**

**François Mitterrand** Born in 1916, François Mitterrand was raised in a pious Catholic family of small-business people in provincial France. He joined the army in 1939, and when the Germans stormed into France the following year he was wounded in battle, captured, and shipped off to prisoner of war camps in Germany. He escaped after eighteen months and stealthily made his way home. At a time of limited opportunities, Mitterrand took a position as a minor functionary in the Vichy administration's bureaucracy. But he also sought out the anti-German resistance movement, leading a risky double life.[18] Mitterrand quit his government job in early 1943 and went underground, eventually assuming the leadership of a resistance organization consisting of former French prisoners of war. When he journeyed abroad clandestinely to meet with General de Gaulle in hopes of obtaining assistance for his group, De Gaulle ordered Mitterrand to merge his organization with another one headed by de Gaulle's nephew. Mitterrand initially refused, but on returning to France complied with the General's directives.

In 1946 Mitterrand won election to the newly established Fourth Republic's lower house of parliament. Soon after taking his parliamentary seat, Mitterrand at the age of thirty was invited into the cabinet. Over the ensuing years he served as a minister in eleven of the Republic's twenty-two governments, ultimately rising to such high-level positions as minister of justice and minister of the interior. Despite the Republic's reputation for governmental instability and "immobilism" (gridlock), Mitterrand approved of the constitution and relished the parliamentary game. He also staked out positions that would later prove embarrassing. During the Algerian conflict, for example, he affirmed that "Algeria is France" and voiced support for military action.

It was his stance against de Gaulle in the spring of 1958 that established Mitterrand as an early opponent of the Fifth Republic. As leading officials of the beleaguered Fourth Republic turned to de Gaulle to lead them out of the Algerian impasse, Mitterrand voted against granting him extraordinary powers to write a new constitution, fearing that dictatorship would be the most likely result of de Gaulle's return to power. Over the next several years Mitterrand became France's most outspoken critic of de Gaulle's regime. In 1964 he published a broadside entitled *The Permanent Coup d'Etat*, which systematically attacked de Gaulle's use of personal power as a form of dictatorial rule.

The following year, Mitterrand decided to challenge de Gaulle in the Fifth Republic's first popular election to the presidency. He stitched together a loose coalition of center-left parties and his own political organization, which was more of a club than a party. He also convinced the Communist Party leadership to back him, even though he was a lifelong opponent of communist doctrine and deplored the French Communists' symbiotic connection to the Soviet Union. To everyone's surprise, de Gaulle failed to win an absolute majority in the first round of voting. Mitterrand finished a strong second and won a chance to face de Gaulle in the runoff election. Though he lost to the General, Mitterrand won a major symbolic victory by garnering nearly 45 percent of the vote.

The left's electoral catastrophe of 1968 prompted a reorganization of its party structures. The SFIO renamed itself the Socialist Party in 1969. Mitterrand managed to get himself elected as the party's new chief at a conference of Socialist activists in 1971. While striving to keep the party's conflicting factions together, he moved toward a more pronouncedly anticapitalist position, declaring, "Anyone who does not accept a rupture with the established order and capitalist society cannot be a member of the Socialist Party." Mitterrand's conviction that the left could not take power without the votes of Communist Party supporters reinforced these ideological adjustments. The Socialists and Communists reached agreement on the *Common Program of the Left* only after arduous negotiations, with concessions coming from both sides. The Common Program spelled out a series of measures designed to weaken the hold of private enterprise on the French economy without entirely destroying it. Mitterrand's aims were purely electoral. Shortly after signing on to the Common Program he declared that he hoped to entice three out of five Communist voters to defect to his Socialist Party!

In bolstering his appeal to left-wing voters, Mitterrand exclaimed, "There can be no coexistence between socialism and capitalism." Mitterrand also wanted to reduce the president's term in office to five years, curtail the use of presidential referendums, and eliminate the emergency powers of Article 16, which he called "the dictatorship article." He called for permitting the prime minister to enjoy the full powers granted by the constitution and for strengthening the powers of the National Assembly.

To Mitterrand's chagrin, the left failed to take control of the National Assembly in the elections of 1973 and 1978. Mitterrand suffered another disappointment in 1974, when he lost his presidential bid to Giscard d'Estaing. It was not until 1981 that Mitterrand's time came to take power.[19]

Like the previous presidential elections, the 1981 contest did not produce a victor with an absolute majority in round 1. In the second ballot Mitterrand narrowly defeated Giscard d'Estaing by 51.8 percent to 48.2 percent. Ten days later Mitterrand took office and quickly announced the dissolution of the conservative-dominated National Assembly. Riding a crest of popularity, Mitterrand's Socialist Party defied most predictions and won nearly 55 percent of the seats, giving it full control of the lower house.

Within their first two years in power the Socialists fully nationalized eight major conglomerates, including some of the country's leading firms in telecommunications, electronics, chemicals, steel, and airplane construction, and it nationalized thirty-six banks. The nationalizations cost the state some 39 billion francs (about $8 billion). To improve the lives of French workers, the government raised the minimum wage nine times between 1981 and 1983; added a fifth week of paid vacation; reduced working hours for most categories of workers from forty hours a week to thirty-nine; enhanced trade union bargaining rights; cut the minimum retirement age from sixty-five to sixty; and raised pensions. To finance these and other social programs, the government in 1982 imposed a wealth tax on large fortunes and the following year it raised the average income tax rate from 42 percent to 44 percent. (The average income tax rate in the United States was about 35 percent.)

Mitterand believed that the best way to combat France's rising unemployment was to increase government spending. But this economic strategy turned out to be ill-timed. France was caught in the snares of globalization as the world's fifth largest economy. International economic conditions in the early 1980s were not conducive to the free-spending policies of Mitterrand's new government, which vastly increased budget deficits and the national debt while aggravating France's inflation rate.[20] By 1983 it was also evident that the government's Keynesian spending programs and its nationalization of private corporations were not succeeding in reducing unemployment.

And so the Mitterrand government slammed the brakes on its costly programs and reversed course. It froze wages and prices, cut subsidies to nationalized companies, laid off employees, imposed fees on various social services, and raised taxes. Mitterrand was compelled by events to pursue a conservative austerity policy for most of the next dozen years. He appointed a succession of Socialist prime ministers who shifted the government's policies toward promoting private-sector development. "Profit" and "entrepreneurism" replaced "regulation" and "nationalization" in the Socialist vocabulary.

In 1986, the neo-Gaullist party and its allies won control of the National Assembly, confronting President Mitterrand with the unpalatable necessity of appointing Jacques Chirac—a man he had never met before—as prime minister. In the Fifth Republic's first case of cohabitation, Mitterrand worked out a power-sharing arrangement with Chirac and accepted his plans to privatize more than sixty state-controlled companies. Polls showed that the vast majority of French people wanted the two ideological adversaries to get along and maintain governmental stability. But Chirac had little more success than the Socialists in stimulating the French economy.

Cohabitation came to an end in 1988 after Mitterrand defeated Chirac in the presidential elections and the Socialists led a left-wing comeback in retaking control of the National Assembly. But Mitterrand had to endure another period of cohabitation after the right-wing parties took back the National Assembly in 1993. The Gaullist prime minister, Édouard Balladur, launched a new round of privatizations, dealing another blow to Mitterrand's earlier visions of a socialist economy. Meanwhile, Mitterrand had essentially given up the pursuit of constitutional reform. The man who had been an incessant critic of de Gaulle's presidential authority declared after assuming office in 1981 that he would exercise the "full powers" of the constitution, later asserting that they "suited" him. However, during the two periods of cohabitation, Mitterrand stepped into the background and behaved somewhat like a "semi-president," allowing Prime Ministers Chirac and Balladur to take the lead in formulating national policy. One of Mitterrand's proudest achievements was his party's vote in the National Assembly to abolish the death penalty, a policy he asked Chirac not to overturn.

It appears that Mitterrand's most important legacy was his acceptance on behalf of the French left (or at least a substantial part of the left) of both capitalism and the Fifth Republic's constitution. While the left still favors state intervention to promote the welfare of the bottom sectors of the social pyramid, most of its leaders now also accept the need to promote growth in the private sector. "Socialism" in France—as in most of Europe—has become little more than a euphemism for the modern mixed-economy welfare state, at least in the eyes of all but the extreme left.

In 1996, François Mitterrand died after a long battle with prostate cancer. (It was later revealed by his physician that he had suffered from the disease throughout his presidency.) In the end, his main political contribution to French politics was his willingness to compromise some of the differences between right and left. In the process he established a precedent for the regular alternation of power between center-left and center-right parties, bringing moderation, stability, and "normalcy" to French politics. In a country wracked through much of its history by stormy conflict, this was no mean achievement.[21]

## FRENCH STATE INSTITUTIONS

The *presidential-parliamentary system* of the **Fifth Republic** involves a mixture of presidential authority, a prime minister responsible to the Parliament, and a weak but important legislature. The basic structure of the system is modeled in figure 17.1.

### The Dual Executive

**The President** Initially the Fifth Republic's constitution, formulated under Charles de Gaulle's direction, provided that the *president* would be elected by a special electoral college consisting of some eighty thousand electors. In 1962 the constitution was amended to permit the direct election of the president by the people in a one-round or two-round procedure. Any number of candidates may run in the first round. To be eligible, each prospective candidate must be nominated by at least five hundred elected officials from national or local bodies. In effect, round 1 is a national primary, with all the candidates for president running on the same day. (See table 17.2 for the results of round 1 of the 2002 presidential elections.) If one of the entrants gets more than 50 percent of the first-round

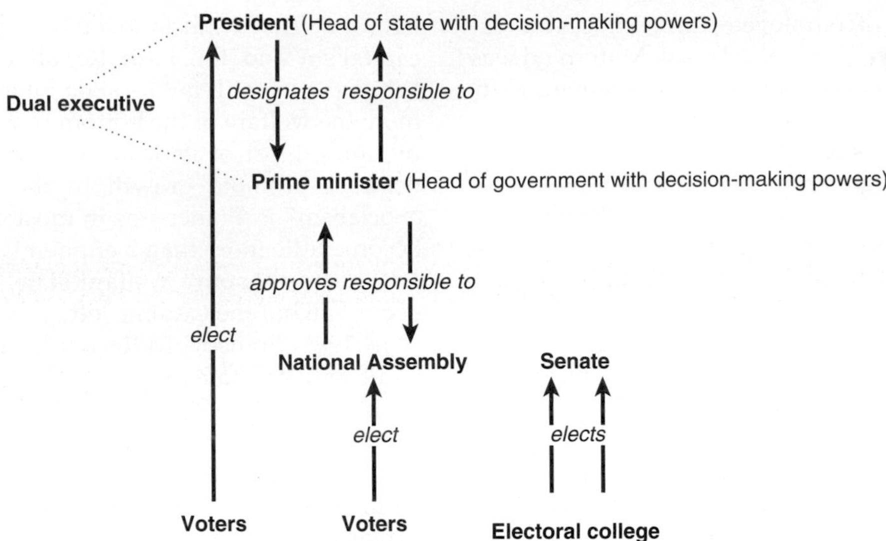


FIGURE 17.1 France's Presidential-Parliamentary System

TABLE 17.2

**First-Round Presidential Elections, 2002**

| Name | Party | % of Vote |
|---|---|---|
| Chirac | Rally for the Republic | 19.9% |
| Le Pen | National Front | 16.9 |
| Jospin | Socialist Party | 16.2 |
| Bayrou | Union for French Democracy | 6.8 |
| Laguiller | Workers Struggle | 5.7 |
| Chevènement | Citizens Movement | 5.3 |
| Mamère | Greens | 5.3 |
| Besancenot | Communist Revolutionary League | 4.3 |
| Saint-Josse | Hunting, Fishing, Nature, Tradition | 4.2 |
| Madelin | Liberal Democracy | 3.9 |
| Hue | French Communist Party | 3.4 |
| Taubira | Walwary (Guyana) | 2.3 |
| Mégret | National Republican Movement | 2.3 |
| Lepage | Convention for a Progressive Alternative | 1.9 |
| Boutin | Forum of Social Republicans | 1.2 |
| Gluckstein | Workers Party | 0.5 |

Valid votes cast: 28,498,471; registered voters: 41,194,689.
*Source: Le Monde,* June 11, 2002.

ballots, he or she is elected president. In the Fifth Republic, no one has ever won the presidency in the first round. Round 2, which takes place two weeks later, is a runoff election between the top two finishers of the first round. Voter turnout tends to be roughly the same in both rounds. French voters whose preferred first-round candidate does not advance into the runoff usually turn out to vote for one of the remaining two candidates. (See table 17.3 for second-round results.)

The president is France's *head of state,* and—thanks to de Gaulle—possesses considerable decision-making powers. These powers are summarized in table 17.4. Unlike the presidents of Germany, Italy, and some other democracies, and like the president of the United States, France's president is far more than just a ceremonial head of state.

The *prime minister* (PM) is *head of government.* The PM is nominated by the president, but must be approved by a voting majority in the National Assembly. As a consequence, the president is well advised to nominate someone who will be acceptable to the parties that control the lower house. As we have seen, when the president's party and its allies dispose of the legislative majority, the president is usually free to pick his or her own personal favorite to

TABLE 17.3

| French Presidential Elections (Second Round Percentages) | | | | | | | | |
|---|---|---|---|---|---|---|---|---|
| 1965 | De Gaulle | 54.5 | 1981 | Mitterrand | 51.8 | 1995 | Chirac | 52.6 |
| | Mitterrand | 45.5 | | Giscard d'Estaing | 48.2 | | Jospin | 47.4 |
| 1969 | Pompidou | 57.6 | 1988 | Mitterrand | 54.0 | 2002 | Chirac | 82.2 |
| | Poher | 42.4 | | Chirac | 45.9 | | Le Pen | 17.8 |
| 1974 | Giscard d'Estaing | 50.8 | | | | | | |
| | Mitterrand | 49.2 | | | | | | |

TABLE 17.4

| France's Dual Executive | |
|---|---|
| **President** | |
| **Election** | Elected by the people. Candidates must be born or naturalized French citizens, at least twenty-three years old, nominated by 500 elected officials (legislators, mayors, etc.). Winning candidate must get absolute majority of voters turning out in first or second round. Until 2002, presidents served a seven-year term, with no limit on the number of terms. In 2000, the presidential term was reduced to five years, starting in 2002. |
| **Powers** | Head of state ("the highest authority of the state"). Likely to be de facto chief decision maker (except in periods of cohabitation).<br>Commander of armed forces. Presides over higher councils and committees of national defense.<br>Names the prime minister. De facto power to force prime minister to resign (except under cohabitation).<br>With prime minister's approval, may appoint and dismiss other cabinet ministers.<br>Chairs cabinet meetings.<br>May veto government ordinances and decrees.<br>May dissolve National Assembly and call new elections, which must take place within twenty to forty days. May not dissolve Assembly again for one year.<br>May *not* veto bills passed by Parliament but may ask the deputies to reconsider legislation.<br>May send messages to Parliament.<br>On the proposal of the government or the two legislative chambers, may submit questions to the voters in referendums on bills dealing with "the organization of the public authorities," European Union agreements, or international treaties requiring ratification.<br>May declare a state of national emergency under circumstances specified in Article 16 and govern by decree.<br>Until 2003, could be impeached (indicted) only for high treason. Under reforms proposed in 2003, can be impeached for "dereliction of his duties manifestly incompatible with the exercise of his mandate," but not for offenses unrelated to presidential functions. Impeachment requires absolute majority of each house of Parliament in an open vote. Upon impeachment, the president must relinquish office in favor of the president of the Senate. The president is tried by a High Court of Justice, composed of various members of the two houses of Parliament. If Parliament votes to remove the president from office, new elections must be held. An ex-president may be tried as a civilian for criminal offenses, but may run for reelection. |
| **Prime Minister** | |
| **Selection Powers** | Designated by the president; approved by majority of the National Assembly.<br>Head of government. PM "shall direct the operation of the government," which in turn "shall determine and direct the policy of the nation." Likely to be chief decision maker in periods of cohabitation, subject to agreements with president.<br>Responsible for national defense. The government "shall have at its disposal . . . the armed forces."<br>Makes appointments to civil and military posts. The government is responsible for the civil service.<br>May replace president as chair of national defense committees and, under exceptional circumstances, may chair cabinet meetings.<br>May seek parliamentary "investiture," that is, vote of approval by National Assembly upon presenting the government and its program.<br>May be dismissed by National Assembly, subject to provisions concerning vote of censure (see later in this chapter). |

serve as prime minister. But when the president's opponents dominate the National Assembly, the president is constrained by political realities to designate a PM from the ranks of the opposition parties. The result is *cohabitation*—the sharing of executive authority between the leader of the right-of-center parties and the leader of the left-of-center parties.

The constitution designates the president "the highest authority of the state" and commander in chief of the armed forces. At the same time, it gives the prime minister and the government the right to "determine and direct the policy of the nation." On paper, the constitution appears to be tantalizingly ambiguous about which of these two officers possesses ultimate decision-making authority. Indeed, the French constitution's text is not a precise guide to determining who calls the shots at the apex of the political system. Executive power in France is often shared on the basis of ad hoc arrangements, especially in periods of cohabitation. All presidents of the Fifth Republic have tended to regard foreign affairs and security policy as their "reserved domain" of responsibility. But all have intruded into domestic matters as well. While they have granted their prime ministers a certain latitude to pursue their own initiatives in economic and social policy, the extent of this ministerial freedom has varied considerably.

President de Gaulle tended to treat his prime ministers as mere executors of his will. President Giscard d'Estaing had a prickly relationship with his first prime minister, Jacques Chirac, and replaced him. President Mitterrand appointed five Socialist prime ministers. In 1984 he replaced Pierre Mauroy, who pursued the socialist economic policies of Mitterrand's first years, with Laurent Fabius, the first in a succession of more conservative prime ministers. (One of them, Édith Cresson, was France's first female head of government.) Acting under the constraints of cohabitation, Mitterrand allowed his neo-Gaullist prime ministers, Chirac and Balladur, wide latitude to conduct their own economic policies, even though those policies dismantled some of the achievements of Mitterrand's early years. (It was Balladur who coined the term *cohabitation.*) President Chirac similarly allowed Prime Minister Jospin a great deal of leeway to elaborate the government's domestic agenda, even though it differed from Chirac's priorities.

**TABLE 17.5**

**Fifth Republic Prime Ministers**

President de Gaulle:
- Michel Debré (1959–62)
- Georges Pompidou (1962–68)
- Maurice Couve de Murville (1968–69)

President Pompidou:
- Jacques Chaban-Delmas (1969–72)
- Pierre Messmer (1972–74)

President Giscard d'Estaing:
- Jacques Chirac (1974–76)
- Raymond Barre (1976–81)

President Mitterrand:
- Pierre Mauroy (1981–84)
- Laurent Fabius (1984–86)
- Jacques Chirac (1986–88)*
- Michel Rocard (1988–91)
- Édith Cresson (1991–92)
- Pierre Bérégovoy (1992–93)
- Édouard Balladur (1993–95)*

President Chirac:
- Alain Juppé (1995–97)
- Lionel Jospin (1997–2002)*
- Jean-Pierre Raffarin (2002–05)
- Dominique de Villepin (2005–07)

*Cohabitation

Ironically, the relationship between president and prime minister has tended to be more enduring under cohabitation than it has been when the two belong to the same party. The president cannot easily dismiss a prime minister of an opposing party, because the National Assembly majority would object. It is much easier for the president to fire a fellow party member or someone from an allied party. The result has been a considerable rotation of premiers (see table 17.5). In a number of cases the president has enjoined the same prime minister to form a new government by reassigning cabinet posts. Between 1981 and 2006, France had twenty-six governments. In that period Germany had nine governments, Spain had eight, and Britain had seven, and the United States had four presidents.

In an effort to prevent cohabitation in the future, the leaders of the two main political parties—Chirac's neo-Gaullists and the Socialists—agreed to amend the constitution in time for the 2002 presidential elections. Until that year, France's president served a seven-year term. In addition, elections to the presidency and the National Assembly (whose members serve a five-year term) took place in different years. As a result, some voters who cast their ballots for a conservative candidate in the presidential elections tended to switch their support to the Socialists in the next National Assembly elections, and vice versa, leaving the presidency in the hands of one party and the National Assembly in the hands of its opponents. Starting in 2002 the president's term of office was reduced to five years. National Assembly elections were due to take place in the same year. It was hoped that, if the National Assembly could serve out its full five-year term without being dissolved for snap elections, presidential elections could henceforth take place in the same year as the National Assembly elections. (Presidential and legislative elections do not take place on the same day, however, but are spaced about a month apart.) The main assumption underlying these reforms was that voters would be more likely to vote for presidential and legislative candidates *of the same party* if the two sets of elections were held close together. If the majority voted for a neo-Gaullist president, they would therefore be likely to elect a neo-Gaullist majority in the Assembly, obviating the need for cohabitation. The Socialists hoped that the same logic would apply to them.

The 2002 elections appeared to verify these assumptions. In May 2002, President Chirac was reelected president. In the following month his neo-Gaullist party, the UMP, won a large majority in the National Assembly. Chirac thereupon nominated Jean-Pierre Raffarin, a UMP political figure, as his new prime minister. After winning quick confirmation in the National Assembly, Raffarin dutifully declared, "I am here to serve the orientations of Jacques Chirac." Following the defeat of the European constitution by French voters in the May 2005 referendum, Chirac replaced Raffarin with de Villepin.

The Fifth Republic's dual executive creates real problems of power sharing. Thus far, French leaders have found ways to deal with these complications without intractable disagreements or prolonged indecision. How France's political system works thus depends as much on the personalities of the leaders as it does on the strictures of the law or the pull of ideology.[22]

**The Government** The American term *cabinet* refers to the various cabinet secretaries who run the main departments of the U.S. government or who enjoy similarly high status. In France the cabinet is called the *government* and its members are known as *ministers*. In the language of the Fifth Republic's constitution, the government is formally called the *Council of Ministers*. Normally the government consists of *full ministers*, who are the most important figures, and *junior ministers* of somewhat lesser rank.

One of the distinctive features of the Fifth Republic is that the government is responsible to two authorities, not just one. It is delicately positioned between the president and the National Assembly and is accountable to both of them. Both the president and the Assembly have explicit or implied rights to choose and dismiss the prime minister and other cabinet ministers. In Britain, by contrast, the government is responsible only to the House of Commons.

The constitution gives the president the authority to name the prime minister. It does not expressly say that the president also has the right to *dismiss* the prime minister, stating only that the head of state "terminates the functions of the prime minister when the latter presents the resignation of the government." Presumably, therefore, the prime minister can always resign but the president has no constitutional authority to compel him or her to do so. Nevertheless, every president of the Fifth Republic has removed prime ministers they no longer wished to see in office. Sometimes a president wants a new PM in order to try out new policies or give the government a fresh look. On occasion a president has sought to deflect public indignation at his own failures by sacking the prime minister as a scapegoat. Whatever the reasons, French presidents at various times have simply told the PM to resign.

As to picking the other cabinet members, the constitution grants the president the right "to appoint and dismiss" them, but only "on the proposal of the prime minister." Here again, actual practice has often diverged from the letter of the law. All five presidents up to 2007 at times took it upon themselves to appoint their own preferred choices to various cabinet positions. As might be expected, the president's ability to impose cabinet choices on the prime minister diminishes considerably under cohabitation. In these awkward circumstances the premier chooses the cabinet, though the president's primacy in foreign and defense policy tends to be respected. During the precedent-setting first cohabitation of 1986–88, President Mitterrand insisted on the right to veto Prime Minister Chirac's choices for foreign minister and defense minister. Chirac complied when Mitterrand rejected his first picks, appointing ministers more acceptable to the president.

**Censure** In addition to being responsible to the president, in practice the government is formally responsible to the National Assembly. Most important, the Assembly has the right to vote the prime minister and government out of office in a vote of "censure," the French equivalent of a vote of no-confidence. The Fifth Republic's provisions for the censure procedure are very exacting. De Gaulle and the constitution's framers were determined to avoid the experience of the Fourth Republic, whose legislature was able to depose a government relatively easily by majority vote, thereby exacerbating the regime's chronic instability. In order to topple a government in the Fifth Republic, the National Assembly must meet the following conditions:

1. A censure motion must be signed by at least 10 percent of the Assembly.
2. The vote may not take place until after a forty-eight-hour "cooling off" period.
3. The motion is adopted only if it is passed by a majority of the full Assembly (289 out of 577). A majority of *those voting* is insufficient; abstentions do not count.

If the censure motion passes, the prime minister must submit his or her resignation to the president, along with that of the rest of the government. Presumably, the president must then select a new PM. In 1962 President de Gaulle flouted this provision when he reappointed Prime Minister Pompidou immediately after the Assembly passed a censure motion against Pompidou's government. To add insult to injury, de Gaulle then sent the Assembly packing and called snap elections. The 1962 incident was the only case of a successful vote of censure against a government in the Fifth Republic, though more than thirty censure motions have been filed. The Socialists filed a censure motion against de Villepin's government after the adoption of his youth employment law in 2006, but lacked the votes to pass it. If a censure motion fails to obtain the necessary majority, its signers may not introduce another one in the same legislative session except under special circumstances.

If the prime minister wishes, she or he may ask the Assembly for a vote of confidence on the government's initial program or on a general declaration of its policies. Although this procedure is not mandated by law, most prime ministers have sought an early vote of support of this kind shortly after assuming office. Known as *investiture,* this practice is followed in a number of parliamentary systems (in effect, the legislature vests power in the government). Alternatively, a government that has already been in power for some time may ask the Assembly to approve its policy orientations. Prime ministers who make such a request typically want to force a divided Assembly to clear the air and decide if the majority backs the government or not. If a government fails to muster a majority in the Assembly on a vote of investiture or a policy declaration, it must resign.

**Question Time** As in Britain, French government ministers—including the prime minister—are required to answer questions posed by members of Parliament. Question periods are held every week in both the National Assembly and the Senate. Most of the questions are in written form, as are most of the ministerial responses. Since 1989 a weekly oral interrogation of a minister or deputy minister has taken place in the Assembly. Thus far, however, the Fifth Republic has not followed the British custom of requiring the prime minister to answer questions spontaneously every week. The president is never required to appear before Parliament.[23]

**Cabinet Membership** The size of the cabinet has varied from as few as twenty-four members to as many as forty-nine. So, too, has its composition. Typically the cabinet includes political leaders from the parties forming the Assembly majority. It may also include other individuals, such as technocrats who have no significant leadership role in a political party but who bring a special expertise to their cabinet portfolio. Some cabinet members, including prime ministers, are graduates of the *grandes écoles,* France's elite graduate schools. These prestigious academies admit only about 4 percent of French university students. Pompidou, Fabius, and Juppé attended the Ecole Normale Superieure, the most prestigious institution for future academics. Giscard and others graduated from the Ecole Polytechnique, founded by Napoleon to train engineers and technicians. Quite a few ministers and deputy ministers, not to mention two presidents, have been products of the *National Academy for Administration (École nationale d'administration,* or *ENA),* an institution established under de Gaulle after World War II to train the country's policy elite. Its graduates are known as *énarques* and include presidents Giscard d'Estaing and Chirac; prime ministers Fabius, Rocard, Balladur, Juppé, and de Villepin; Socialist leaders Ségolène Royal and François Hollande; and a roster of the country's political and business leaders. Various efforts have been undertaken or proposed to broaden the student body's social base beyond the Parisian middle and upper classes.[24]

De Gaulle, Pompidou, and Giscard d'Estaing typically presided over governments consisting of Gaullists and members of Giscard's party. Mitterrand's first prime minister, Pierre Mauroy, had a cabinet comprised mainly of Socialists, but four Communists also held cabinet posts temporarily. Jospin's first coalition government in 1997 consisted of eighteen Socialists, three Communists, and five other leftists. Raffarin's cabinet after the 2002 legislative elections consisted of sixteen ministers (including himself), eleven deputy ministers, and a dozen ministerial officials known as "secretaries of state." Virtually all were drawn from the ranks of Chirac's UMP.

**Incompatibility Clause** Although most cabinet ministers are chosen from the parliamentary ranks of the parties, the Fifth Republic's constitution specifically forbids members of the government from simultaneously serving as elected deputies to either the National Assembly or the Senate. The so-called *incompatibility clause,* which makes cabinet service incompatible with membership in Parliament, was designed to reduce the government's dependence on the legislature and give it greater autonomy than it enjoyed under the Fourth Republic. Members of the French Parliament who are invited to join the cabinet must relinquish their legislative seats. Consequently, candidates for the National Assembly typically run together with a substitute (*suppléant*), whose role is to take over the winning candidate's seat in the legislature if the latter is tapped for a cabinet post. This practice is the exact opposite of the British procedure, which *requires* cabinet members to serve simultaneously as members of Parliament. It is nonetheless permissible, however, for a member of the French government to hold other official positions at the same time. Quite a few government ministers work simultaneously as mayors, members of town councils, regional government officials, and the like. In the past there have been cabinet ministers holding as many as five posts at the same time! In 1987 a new law took effect limiting this "accumulation of positions" (*cumul des mandats*) to no more than two.[25]

### Parliament

The bicameral French Parliament (*Parlement*) consists of the *National Assembly,* its lower house, and the *Senate,* the upper house.

**The National Assembly** The **National Assembly** currently has 577 deputies. As noted at the start of this chapter, each deputy is elected in accordance with a two-round variant of the single member district (SMD) electoral system. An absolute majority is required to win in the first round, a plurality suffices in the second. This system replaced the proportional representation system of the Fourth Republic, which de Gaulle scorned because it resulted in a proliferation of parties in the legislature and in unstable multiparty coalition governments. But the SMD system often leads to disparities between a party's share of the popular vote and its share of legislative seats. In 2002, for example, Chirac's UMP won 47 percent of the popular vote in the second round but captured 64 percent of the seats in the Assembly. Seeking to work the electoral system to their own advantage, President Mitterrand's Socialists introduced proportional representation in 1986, but Chirac's center-right legislative majority changed it back to SMD two years later. (See table 17.6. For an explanation of electoral systems, see chapter 8.)[26]

When electing the National Assembly, registered voters check in with election officials at a polling place in their electoral district (*circonscription*). On a table there are paper ballots, each one bearing the name of a single candidate, along with the name of the candidate's *suppléant,* the person who will take over the Assembly seat if the winner is invited to

TABLE 17.6

National Assembly, 1997 and 2002 (577 seats)

| | 1997 | | | | 2002 | | | |
|---|---|---|---|---|---|---|---|---|
| | % Vote (Round 1) | % Vote (Round 2) | Seats | % Seats | % Vote (1) | % Vote (2) | Seats | % Seats |
| *Left* | | | | | | | | |
| Socialist Party | 23.5 | 38.6 | 246 | 42.6 | 24.1 | 35.3 | 141 | 24.4 |
| Communist Party | 9.9 | 3.7 | 37 | 6.4 | 4.8 | 3.3 | 21 | 3.6 |
| Greens | 6.8 | 1.6 | 8 | 1.3 | 4.5 | 3.2 | 3 | 0.5 |
| Other left | 6.8 | 4.3 | 29 | 5.0 | 5.4 | 3.8 | 13 | 2.3 |
| *Right* | | | | | | | | |
| Neo-Gaullists[a] | 15.7 | 22.7 | 139 | 24.1 | 33.3 | 47.3 | 369 | 64.0 |
| Union for French Democracy | 14.2 | 21.0 | 109 | 18.9 | 4.9 | 3.9 | 22 | 3.8 |
| National Front | 14.9 | 5.7 | 1 | 0.2 | 11.4 | 1.2 | 0 | 0 |
| Other right | 6.7 | 2.4 | 8 | 1.4 | 6.7 | 1.6 | 8 | 1.4 |
| *Others* | 1.4 | — | — | — | 5.2 | — | | 0 |

[a]Rally for the Republic (RPR) in 1997; Union for the Presidential Majority (UMP) in 2002. In 2003, the parties were organized into four parliamentary groups: the UMP group (364 deputies); the Socialist group (149); the UDF group (30); and the group of Communists and Republicans (22). There were 12 belonging to no group.

*Sources:* Inter-Parliamentary Union, *Parliamentary Elections and Developments*, vols. 27 and 31: *Le Monde,* June 12 and June 19, 2002; http://www.francepolitique.free.fr/FAN.htm.

enter the government (see figure 17.2). There is no limit to the number of candidates eligible to run in the first round of balloting. In one district in Paris, for example, there were twenty-seven first-round candidates in 2002, the highest in the country. Twenty-seven stacks of ballots were therefore lined up across the tables. A voter may choose to pick up either the one ballot bearing the name of the candidate she wishes to vote for, or as many other ballots as are available. She then goes into a voting booth, closes the curtain, and inserts a single ballot into an envelope that is provided. (If she puts two or more ballots into the envelope, they are not counted.) Upon exiting the booth, she is rechecked against the voter registry and then deposits her envelope into a ballot box on the table. At this point she may discard any other ballots she may have picked up. When the polls close, the ballots are counted by hand. In 2002, only fifty-eight candidates won their seats by an absolute majority in the first round. The remaining 519 districts required a second round of balloting a week later. In all but ten of these districts there were only two candidates who survived into round two; the other ten districts each had three surviving candidates. Voters in these districts thus had to go to the polls once again (the French vote on Sundays), casting their ballots by the same procedure as in round one.

**FIGURE 17.2 Sample Legislative Ballots, 2002**

**Senate** The **Senate** has 321 members. All are elected to a nine-year term by a special electoral college that represents local governments throughout France. More than a hundred thousand mayors, city council members, and departmental officials constitute the bulk of the electoral body's membership; the 577 members of the National Assembly make up the rest. Historically, the upper house of the French legislature has usually been dominated by local "notables" and rural interests, a phenomenon that has not substantially changed. The Senate has traditionally represented the provincial areas Parisians call *la France profonde*—"deep France."[27] Most senators tend to be conservative and antisocialist in their political leanings.

The Senate normally works with the Assembly in drafting common language for bills their members propose. But if the Senate objects to government-drafted legislation, the government can get around these obstacles by bringing its bills directly before the Assembly for a decisive vote. Thus the French Senate may be able to delay the passage of legislation but not block it completely.

**Parliament's Limitations** The French Parliament's principal distinction is the relatively narrow scope of its importance compared with legislatures in most other democracies. One of de Gaulle's chief purposes in 1958 was to downgrade the Parliament of the Fifth Republic, eliminating the principle of parliamentary supremacy that formed the basis of the Fourth Republic's unstable political system. As a consequence, the Fifth Republic's constitution specifically identifies the policy areas in which Parliament has competence to legislate. All other governmental matters are reserved to the "rule-making" authority of the executive branch, which may issue decrees or ordinances without parliamentary approval. The constitution also spells out additional limits on Parliament's decision-making powers.

Items that fall within Parliament's legislative purview include nationality issues, criminal law, the electoral system, tax rates, and the nationalization of private enterprises. It may also pass civil rights legislation, as the constitution does not contain an enumerated bill of rights.[28] Additionally, Parliament may "determine the fundamental principles" of such things as the organization of the country's national defense, local government, education, property rights, commercial law, and labor law, though the details of these matters may be subject to the government's intervention. Parliament has the exclusive right to declare war and ratify most international treaties.

Aside from possessing these and a few other specified powers, France's Parliament is severely restricted by the overriding authority of the president and the prime minister's government. These restrictions affect both the substance of the law and the procedures used to make it. For example:

- The government, not Parliament, sets the agenda of bills to be considered and their order of priority. It can also limit the time allotted for parliamentary consideration of legislation. (In the United Kingdom, the government and Parliament jointly work out the agenda and calendar, though the government's wishes usually prevail. The U.S. Congress controls its own agenda and calendar.)
- Although members of Parliament have the right to initiate bills, so does the government. Government bills take priority over private members' bills in parliamentary deliberations and have a far greater likelihood of being passed. Typically, fewer than 25 percent of the bills passed during the term of a legislature will have been introduced by legislators independently of the government. (Much the same can be said about Britain. All legislation in the United States is proposed by members of Congress, though some of it may be at the behest of the administration.)
- Members of the French Parliament have no right to introduce legislation or propose amendments to bills that entail an increase or reduction in public expenditures. Only the government may propose spending bills or amendments. (The same is essentially true in the UK, but not the United States.) As a practical matter, the French government can define a wide range of policy issues as spending bills, since virtually every undertaking by the state involves expenses.
- Finance bills, including the annual budget bill, must be passed by the two houses of Parliament within seventy days. Otherwise, they automatically become law by government decree. (Neither Britain nor the United States imposes a time limit on finance bills or provides for their automatic enactment by decree.)

- The government may attach the question of confidence to any bill or part of a bill. In these circumstances, the bill becomes law automatically, *without* a parliamentary vote. The only way Parliament can block such a bill is to pass a censure motion against the government in accordance with the procedures outlined earlier. In effect, the government may adopt a law on its own authority and dare the Assembly to vote it out of office! This "provocation" procedure has been utilized about seventy times by various prime ministers since 1958, always with success. (No similar provision exists in the United States or the United Kingdom.) Prime Minister de Villepin resorted to this rarely used procedure to obtain the adoption of his "first employment contract" law on youth employment in February 2006. As anticipated, the opposition's censure motion against de Villepin's government fell far short of a majority. But the prime minister's decision to have the law adopted as "emergency" legislation in the face of opposition demands for more debate and without a decisive vote in the Assembly only damaged the government's credibility and heightened opposition to the law.
- Under special circumstances, the government may ask Parliament to refrain from passing legislation on matters that are normally reserved to the legislature's lawmaking competence, permitting the government to enact measures in these areas by decree. (Britain has roughly similar "statutory instruments." Though U.S. presidents may issue "executive orders" in certain areas, they cannot ask Congress to give up its legislative prerogatives.)
- The government may limit Parliament's right to propose amendments to bills after they are introduced and may compel Parliament to vote only on amendments proposed by the government. (This so-called "blocked vote" procedure does not exist in Britain or the United States.)
- All legislation goes through parliamentary committees, but they have minimal decision-making powers. Committees may not introduce bills intended to alter the purpose of government bills. By declaring a bill urgent, the government can reduce the time allotted to committee consideration of pending legislation. (Parliamentary committees are also fairly weak in Britain but are more powerful in the United States. In the 1990s French parliamentary committees gained the right to query cabinet ministers about relevant legislation, as in the United States.)

In sum, the French Parliament is much weaker than the legislatures of Britain, the United States, and indeed most other democracies. Its deputies exhibit rather high rates of absenteeism and comparatively low levels of independence from their respective party leaders. Nevertheless, the partisan composition of the Parliament, and particularly of the National Assembly, ultimately determines which parties can form a viable government. In periods of cohabitation, this reality confers on France's legislature a decisive political importance.

## The Constitutional Council

What happens if the executive branch and the legislature cannot agree whether a piece of legislation falls within the lawmaking competence of Parliament or the decree-making privileges of the government? The Fifth Republic constitution provides for a *Constitutional Council* to adjudicate such controversies. At the request of either the government or Parliament, the Council must hand down a definitive ruling within eight days. In addition, the Council has the authority to rule on the constitutionality of so-called "organic laws" that are under consideration in Parliament. Organic laws relate to the operation and legal authority of state institutions. Parliament may not enact any measure in this sensitive area if the Constitutional Council decides it is incompatible with the constitution. In Britain, by contrast, Parliament is supreme: it has the exclusive right to enact bills into law without judicial oversight.

When the Fifth Republic was first established, de Gaulle and his associates wanted the Constitutional Council to act as yet another brake on parliamentary initiative. Rather than applying judicial checks and balances on both the executive and legislative branches as the U.S. Supreme Court does, the Council was conceived by the Republic's framers essentially as a check on the legislature, not on the executive. Three of its nine members are appointed by the president of France, including the head of the Council, who alone is empowered to break tie votes. The other six are appointed by the presiding officers of the National Assembly and the Senate. These nine members serve one nine-year term each, but former French presidents become members of the Council for life. In keeping with the framers' intentions, most Council rulings have in fact supported the government and have run against the preferences of the parliamentary opposition.

Another difference between the Constitutional Council and the U.S. Supreme Court is that the Council has less extensive powers of *judicial review*, which is the authority to invalidate laws as unconstitutional. The U.S. Supreme Court may review laws already in existence, for example, but the Constitutional Council must confine its rulings to draft laws that have not as yet taken effect. Moreover, only the central government or members of Parliament may bring cases before the Council, not local officials or private citizens as in the United States. Nevertheless, since the 1970s the Council has issued a number of decisions widening the civil liberties of the population as against the authority of the state. And in 1974 the constitution was amended to allow sixty National Assembly deputies or sixty Senators the right to bring cases before the Council. Until then, only the president, the prime minister, and the two speakers of Parliament had this privilege. The change has allowed opposition legislators to initiate proceedings, resulting in more cases as well as more rulings that have run against the government's preferences. Both the conservative parties and the Socialists have availed themselves of the extended opportunities to challenge government decisions.

### The Civil Service

Ever since the Middle Ages, the French state has sought to solidify its control over the country through a powerful administrative bureaucracy in Paris. The authority of the civil service not only to implement the law of the land but also to create it through bureaucratic regulations grew stronger in the nineteenth century as Parliament's authority remained comparatively weak. Today the French civil service still wields significant power in virtually every aspect of the country's economic and social life. The scope of its activities extends from economic planning and financial affairs to the worlds of education, scientific research, health care, foreign policy, and a host of other areas. Its personnel, especially some ten thousand functionaries in the highest echelons, enjoy considerable prestige as highly competent policy professionals. Many of them were educated at ENA or other selective graduate schools, and quite a few are socially and politically well connected. Although the state-funded *grandes écoles* are tuition-free, and students may even be paid a stipend, a disproportionate number of those who take the stiff entrance exams tend to come from upper-class and upper-middle-class Parisian families. In every sense of the word, the top layers of the French civil service constitute a true political elite.

One of the distinguishing characteristics of the French civil service is its close interaction with private enterprise. To a far greater extent than in the United States, Britain, or many other democracies, the top managers of state agencies and the directors of major private corporations in France often share similar educational and social backgrounds and switch back and forth from the public sector to the private. This connection between the public and private sectors is reinforced by the large number of *public enterprises* in France—companies that are wholly or partially owned by the French state. A privatization process launched in the 1980s has brought the number of these para-statal enterprises down from 3,500 to about 1,000, but the state bureaucracy remains heavily populated with civil servants engaged in managing their affairs. The French state also cooperates with private firms in a process of *indicative planning*, which aims at forecasting future economic conditions and planning decisions accordingly.

At present, some 5 million people are employed in the public sector throughout France (including teachers and other non-bureaucrats)—one out of every four employed people. Of these, 1 million have been hired since the mid 1980s and about 2.2 million work for the central government. An estimated 57 percent of adults either work in the civil service or are closely related to someone who does—an exceptionally high percentage by European standards. Natural attrition will trim this costly public sector, as about half the civil service is expected to retire by 2013. But though President Chirac confirmed the need to reduce state expenditures, he increased the size of the defense and internal security ministries starting in 2002. And civil service jobs, which are well paid and highly secure, remain popular: three out of four French university students said in 2006 that they would like to work in public administration.[29]

### Local Government and Decentralization

The trends underlying France's long history as a unitary state administered from Paris have not gone uncontested. From its earliest foundations as a national entity, France has always been composed of a diversity of regions, some with their own traditional languages or dialects (such as Brittany, the Basque area, and Alsace). Paris and other large cities experience many of the problems of modern urban centers, while more than twenty thousand small towns still dot the French countryside. Many people living in these areas have sought greater powers for their local governments to manage their own affairs with greater freedom from the central state.

France is divided into twenty-two "regions" (counting Corsica), ninety-six mainland and four overseas "departments," and more than 36,700 "communes" ranging from large cities to rural villages.[30] In 1982 the Socialists enacted a decentralization scheme that increased the powers of various subnational governments without dismantling the predominance of the central state. The reform weakened the traditional powers of France's prefects, who had been since Napoleon's time the central government's agents in the various departments. No longer were they expected to impose the central government's will on the localities; instead, they were to function in a consultative capacity, facilitating communication between the center and the rest of the country. Greater authority was now devolved upon elected councils at the communal, departmental, and regional levels.

These subnational bodies now received the green light to impose various local taxes and assume wider responsibility for local matters in such areas as transportation, the environment, and various economic and welfare functions. Jospin's government permitted wider official usage of local traditional languages, such as Breton in Brittany. Despite these changes, the national government continues to control the bulk of France's tax collections and public spending. It also monopolizes the administration of the entire educational system and plays the predominant role in transportation, the environment, and social welfare. Meanwhile, France does not experience mass separatist tendencies as powerful as those present in Quebec or Scotland, though nationalist movements in Brittany and Corsica that favor greater autonomy or full independence are fairly active.[31]

## POLITICAL PARTIES

Typically, a large number of political parties and groupings put up candidates for office in France, giving voters a wide array of electoral choices. (In 2002 there were more than sixty in the first round of voting in France and its overseas territories.) The two-round SMD electoral system for elections to the National Assembly keeps most of them from winning a greater share of seats than they might otherwise get under proportional representation (PR). Nevertheless, there are more parties represented in the National Assembly today than in the U.S. Congress or the British House of Commons. What explains this efflorescence of parties and independents in an electoral system that tends to punish small parties in the United States and Britain?

Compared to countries like the United States, Britain, and Germany, France still has a substantial number of small parties whose ideas remain tied to the past, reflecting ideological tendencies of the left and right that in most Western democracies either have receded into history or have never attracted a significant following to begin with. Of the sixteen candidates who ran for president in round 1 of the 2002 elections, three were Trotskyites—the intensely anticapitalist heirs of Leon Trotsky, a hero of Russia's communist Revolution of 1917 and an exponent of "permanent revolution" around the world. Together the three ultra-leftists won nearly 3 million votes—10.5 percent of the total. Another candidate represented the Hunting, Fishing, Nature, and Tradition movement, which seeks to preserve the purity of rustic France; he won 1.2 million votes (4.3 percent). To no small extent, the persistence of some of these parties and even smaller splinter groups (especially those on the left) is rooted in continuing debates over "socialism" versus "capitalism"—a discourse that is often conducted in terms reminiscent of the first half of the twentieth century, when the two competing economic systems were regarded as diametrical opposites rather than as adaptable components of the modern mixed economy.

In addition, several small parties are built around a single prominent leader, typically one whose idiosyncratic views do not easily fit into the mainstream parties.

In short, the French party system is dominated by two large mainstream catch-all parties, the center-right neo-Gaullists (currently Chirac's UMP) and the center-left Socialists. But it is also fragmented into a multiplicity of smaller parties and their offshoots. In 2002, candidates from small parties won 64 percent of the first-round vote for president and more than 40 percent of the first-round vote for the National Assembly. New parties are assembled, disbanded, and reconstituted under new names with bewildering frequency. Fourteen parties that fielded candidates in the 1997 elections were not around to compete five years later. By 2002, there were nearly fifty new parties. Most of these mini-parties exist because of attachments—at times quite strong—on the part of millions of French men and women to ideas and attitudes that, in their view, are not supported by the two mainstream parties. As a consequence, neither the two-round direct elections for the presidency, nor the two-round single-member-district/plurality legislative electoral system, has produced an American-style two-party system or a British-style few-party system. Numerous parties continue to exist in France despite the fact that the second round of both the presidential and legislative balloting tends to hurt the small parties and to favor the two largest ones. Analysts have debated whether the political space along the left–right spectrum in France since the late 1980s is characterized by bipartition into fairly stable left–right orientations, or whether the far-right movement headed by Le Pen has resulted in tripartition, with three distinct blocs of parties and voter orientations.[32] Time will tell if a distinct fourth bloc consisting of extreme-left parties and orientations will solidify. In 2002, the newly elected Raffarin government introduced legislation aimed at changing the legislative electoral law so as to prevent three-way "triangular" races in the second round. It remains to be seen in 2007 whether this attempt to mandate two-person runoffs in second-round elections will reduce the presence of small parties.

French parties tend to be categorized as belonging to political "families" of the left and right. The main leftist party (the Socialists) and the main right-wing parties (the neo-Gaullists and the Union for French Democracy) tend to be moderate catch-all parties, avoiding the extremes of all-out socialism or all-out laissez-faire capitalism. They are also dedicated to democratic principles and the institutional framework of the Fifth Republic. These large parties, along with several moderate smaller ones, hug close to the political center, where most of the voters cluster. Hence the Socialists may be considered a center-left party, while the neo-Gaullists and UDF parties are center-right parties. The Communists and a few small leftist parties are situated to the left of the Socialists, while the anti-immigrant National Front is an extreme right-wing party.

**The Right** *The right* in French politics is a term burdened with heavy historical connotations. From the time of the Revolution to World War II, the French right was mainly associated with authoritarianism, imperialism, and in some cases, anti-Semitism. Its principal exponents were monarchists, Bonapartists, the military, the Catholic church hierarchy, the upper classes, and others who never accepted the Revolution. After World War II the right was redefined by de Gaulle and his followers to embrace democracy and the civil liberties promised by the Revolution. Today's center-right parties are "conservative" to the extent that they oppose socialism, embrace private enterprise, and champion French nationalism (though the term *conservative* is not used as widely in France as in the United States or Britain).

But these parties also tend to advocate a strong central state. Deviating from the preferences of American and British conservatives for less government and more private initiative, most politicians of the French center-right openly embrace the principle of government intervention in the economy—through state-owned enterprises, a large civil service, relatively high taxes, and generous welfare spending. They also tend to favor a strong arm for the police and the courts in maintaining law and order. In 2003 President Chirac said, "The state does not have to decide everything," but he also reaffirmed his commitment to the "French model": a combination of private enterprise with a robustly interventionist state sector. Chirac was a very French conservative; he was no Margaret Thatcher.

*The Neo-Gaullists* As the name implies, the neo-Gaullists are the political heirs of Charles de Gaulle. As such, they are devoted above all to the constitutional principles of the Fifth Republic. After de Gaulle's retirement in 1969, their most challenging task was to perpetuate their charismatic leader's legacy by maintaining an effective political organization, a process known to social scientists as the "institutionalization of charisma" (see chapter 5). To that end, over the decades the neo-Gaullists have set up several different parties bearing different names. In 1976, they reconstituted themselves as the *Rally for the Republic* (Rassemblement pour la république, or RPR). As we've seen, during the 2002 elections they formed a broader grouping called the *Union for the Presidential Majority* (Union pour la majorité presidentielle, or UMP). And several months after the elections they converted this enlarged party into the *Union for a Popular Movement* (Union pour un mouvement populaire, again UMP). While the Fifth Republic's institutional framework and a generally center-right political orientation hold them together, the neo-Gaullists display a variety of attitudes on economic policy, social issues, the European Union, and other political controversies, and there are several different currents within their broad-based organization. Since the 1970s, the person who has taken the lead in galvanizing the neo-Gaullist movement, shaping it into viable parties and personifying its various tendencies, has been Jacques Chirac.

**Presidents Bush and Chirac**

## PROFILE: Jacques Chirac

Born in 1932, Chirac experienced World War II as a boy and had vaguely leftist leanings in his teenage years. Craving adventure, he took a job aboard a commercial ship that plied the Mediterranean. In 1953 Chirac spent the summer in the United States, taking courses at the Harvard Business School and working at the local Howard Johnson's. With friends he hitchhiked to California, then made his way to Dallas, New Orleans, the deep South, Washington, and New York. He returned the following year to do research on the port of New Orleans.

Still uncertain about his career, Chirac passed the stiff entrance exams for the National Academy for Administration (ENA) but delayed his matriculation so as to fulfill his military obligation. It was 1956 and the Algerian war was raging. Convinced that Algeria should remain French, Chirac took an immediate liking to military life, volunteering for dangerous operations. After returning to France he completed the rigorous ENA curriculum, finishing sixteenth in his class. In 1959 he returned to Algeria as a junior administrator and over the ensuing year came to accept de Gaulle's position in favor of Algerian independence.

In 1962 a friend managed to get Chirac a position on Prime Minister Pompidou's staff. He quickly established a reputation for competence and high energy, winning Pompidou's praise as "my bulldozer" for his ability to get things done. In 1967 he won election to the National Assembly, but he quickly gave up the seat to take a succession of junior ministerial positions. As the cabinet secretary responsible for the budget, Chirac reported to Finance Minister Giscard d'Estaing and briefed President de Gaulle. After Pompidou became president, he served as minister of agriculture and minister of the interior.

Pompidou's death in 1974 marked a major turning point for Chirac as well as for the Gaullist movement. When Jacques Chaban-Delmas, one of de Gaulle's loyal followers, declared his candidacy for the presidency, Chirac and other Gaullist party figures discreetly supported Giscard d'Estaing, whose bid for the presidency required votes from Gaullist ranks. When Giscard knocked out Chaban in round one and narrowly defeated Mitterrand in round two, he rewarded Chirac by naming him prime minister.

Though Chirac and Giscard were both conservatives, their personalities and political ambitions were bound to clash. Aloof and aristocratic, Giscard subjected his prime minister to petty humiliations. Emotional and populist, Chirac headed the largest party on the right, far larger than Giscard's Republican Party. Without the support of the Gaullists, Giscard would not have been able to govern. The two men also differed on economic policy. In the 1970s Chirac favored a statist economic policy and claimed that the Gaullist party was a party of the "national left." Giscard was by nature uncomfortable with this approach, fearing excessive inflation. Increasing tensions drove the two men apart, and in 1976 Chirac stepped down as prime minister.

Determined to remain a national political figure, Chirac was elected mayor of Paris the following year. More important, he retained his position as chief of the RPR, the neo-Gaullist party. Chirac's next chance to assume national office came in 1986, when the RPR and Giscard's followers won a three-seat majority in the National Assembly. Acknowledging the new right-wing majority, President Mitterrand took the historic step of inviting Chirac to serve as his next prime minister. It was the Fifth Republic's first experience of cohabitation.

The two men scarcely knew each other except as political foes, but Chirac got on better with Mitterrand than he had with Giscard. While Mitterrand insisted on retaining presidential primacy in foreign and defense policy, the prime minister was able to select his own cabinet members. From the outset, Chirac's government reversed some of the Socialists' most important achievements. Whereas the Socialists had nationalized private companies, Chirac and his cabinet set out to privatize some sixty-five state-owned firms. At the same time, Chirac continued to believe that the state needed to retain major responsibilities in guiding the economy.

The presidential election calendar put an end to two years of cohabitation in 1988. Inevitably, Chirac and Mitterrand squared off as the principal leaders of their respective camps. Mitterrand won the final duel in the second round with a convincing 54 percent of the vote. Upon being reelected, Mitterrand dissolved the National Assembly and ordered new elections. When the right-wing parties lost their slender majority, Chirac retreated to his mayor's office. He had to wait another five years before the Gaullists and their allies in the UDF were able to reclaim power at the national level. As unemployment rose and the Socialists became embroiled in a series of financial and campaign funding scandals, the RPR and UDF won an overwhelming victory in the 1993 legislative elections, capturing 84 percent of the seats.

At this point Chirac stepped back and allowed Édouard Balladur, leader of the RPR, to become prime minister as Mitterrand and the right embarked on their second experience of cohabitation. Once again a center-right government set about privatizing state-owned companies, including banks, insurance companies, communications firms, and other valuable economic assets. Still, French business leaders, to a greater extent than their counterparts in the United States or Britain, continued to look to the state for guidance concerning the economy's overall direction.[33] But unemployment maintained its steady rise and Balladur's government, like the Socialists, was tarnished by financial scandals.

The second period of left–right cohabitation came to an end in 1995 with the conclusion of Mitterrand's second term. Jacques Chirac once again found himself poised to stake his claim to the presidency. To his dismay, however, his most pressing challenge came from Édouard Balladur. Although Balladur had been Chirac's chief political counselor, he was convinced that Chirac was not sufficiently popular to win a presidential election. When Balladur announced his intention to run for the presidency, the Gaullist camp became split between his supporters and Chirac's. After a tense first-round campaign, Chirac barely nudged out Balladur, 21 percent to 18 percent. The split allowed Jospin to emerge as the front-runner with only 23 percent of the vote. In the second round of that year's presidential elections, Chirac defeated his Socialist opponent, Lionel Jospin, by 52.6 percent to 47.4 percent. (See table 8.4 for the complete results.)

As president of France, Chirac inherited the massive center-right majority that had been elected to the National Assembly in 1993, with three more years to run before the next regularly scheduled Assembly elections. But after appointing his fellow Gaullist, Alain Juppé, as prime minister, Chirac quickly ran into trouble. The president was compelled to follow the European Union's criteria for creating the euro. Under Mitterrand, France had assumed the obligation of reducing its annual budget deficit to no more than 3 percent of GDP and of cutting its substantial national debt. Chirac, like Mitterrand, was caught in the web of globalization emanating from European economic integration.

To comply with these requirements, Juppé announced new budgetary austerity measures in November 1995. With a view to overhauling the country's state pension system, which was deeply in arrears, he called for raising the eligibility for full pensions from thirty-seven and a half years of employment to forty.

He also raised fees for hospital treatment and other forms of health care and increased health insurance premiums for the unemployed and retirees. In a separate move, the government also announced plans to cut costs in the railway system. These and related measures, which were sprung on the populace with little or no explanation, sparked the most widespread outpouring of mass protest since 1968.

A half million public-sector workers went on strike on the first day, and additional strikes over the following weeks by workers in urban transport, the railways, airports, the postal system, gas and electric utilities, telecommunications, hospitals, and the civil service brought normal life to a halt. Demonstrations in Paris and other cities brought hundreds of thousands into the streets. Juppé's initial reactions to these events were coldly dismissive, reflecting an arrogance many people regarded as typical of the French governing elite. But as economic paralysis loomed, Juppé was forced to enter into negotiations with the trade unions and public-sector employees in an effort to reach a compromise. Some of his austerity plans had to be curtailed or canceled. As Juppé's approval ratings plunged, President Chirac struggled to distance himself from his premier, but his own popularity crumbled as well.

Fearing that the center-right's popularity would sink even lower by 1998, the year of the next regularly scheduled National Assembly elections, Chirac decided in 1997 to call snap elections a year ahead of time. His hope was to retain a large enough majority for the RPR and its allies to pursue their policies of budget cutting and privatization for five more years. His calculations proved wrong, and in June 1997 the left under Jospin's Socialists retook control of the lower house. Now it was Chirac's turn as president to accept the reality of an opposing parliamentary majority. In naming Jospin prime minister, Chirac launched the Fifth Republic's third experience with cohabitation.

The experience was frustrating for the head of state. Just as President Mitterrand had stepped back and allowed Chirac to take the lead in conducting domestic policy as prime minister, President Chirac accorded Jospin a similarly wide latitude. For his part, Jospin pursued a number of policies Chirac supported, including the privatization of a record number of state-owned companies, the reduction of budget deficits and corporation taxes, and cooperation with other NATO countries during the war over Kosovo. But the prime minister also pursued policies that Chirac and his followers strongly opposed. Perhaps the most controversial of these contested initiatives was the decision to reduce the average work week for most employees in France from thirty-nine to thirty-five hours, with employers required to pay their workers for the equivalent of forty hours. The measure, known as the "Aubry law" after its principal advocate, Labor Minister Martine Aubry, was intended to open up jobs for France's large pool of unemployed workers. Despite a booming economy, with annual growth rates between 1998 and 2000 at 3 percent or higher for the first time in decades, France continued to suffer from chronic unemployment. The jobless rate topped 11 percent in the late 1990s, and youth unemployment was roughly double that figure. Jospin also introduced more generous minimum wage laws and other welfare measures aimed at assisting a large—and growing—population of marginalized people living at the fringes of France's fast-growing, high-tech economy. Chirac shared the views of those in the business community who objected to the Aubry law and various other policies emanating from Jospin's government. But despite the vast assortment of presidential powers at his command, he lacked the authority to veto legislation passed by Parliament.

Chirac's frustrations multiplied when judicial magistrates sought to put him on trial to answer allegations that he had misused funds while serving as mayor of Paris. A trial was averted only when a judge ruled that a sitting president could not be tried for offenses unconnected with his presidential duties.

By the time the end of his seven-year term as president rolled around in 2002, Chirac was ready for renewed political combat. His top priority was to put a quick end to cohabitation, a goal that was shared by Jospin and his followers on the left, who were equally dissatisfied with the situation. In order to reduce the likelihood that another left–right split between the president and the National Assembly majority might occur in the future, political figures on both sides agreed to reduce the presidential term of office to five years—the same tenure observed by the National Assembly—so that presidential and National Assembly elections would tend to take place in the same year rather than in staggered fashion.

In preparing for what he thought would be another two-round, head-to-head bout with Lionel Jospin, Chirac encouraged the unification of the center-right into a new political formation. In 2001, leaders of his own party, the Rally for the Republic (RPR), joined with like-minded politicians from the Union for French Democracy and smaller groupings to create a new center-right organization. When Chirac finished first in the initial round of presidential voting in April 2002 (albeit with less than 20 percent of the vote), and Jean-Marie Le Pen stunned the French political universe by outdistancing Jospin for second place, the president and his allies knew that a decisive victory was in the offing. Two days after the first round of balloting, the recently formed umbrella group of center-right politicians constituted itself as a new party, the Union for the Presidential Majority (UMP). With Le Pen discredited in the eyes of the vast majority of French people, and with the leftist voters having no alternative electoral option in the second round, Chirac won a resounding victory on May 5. Fresh on the heels of that triumph, the UMP won more than 60 percent of the seats in the National Assembly in June.

At the age of 70, Chirac the bulldozer had a new lease on political life: at long last he was master of the Fifth Republic's core institutions.[34]

But Chirac's second term was rocked by a succession of failures. His attempts to stop the United States and Britain from invading Iraq in 2003 were ignored by President Bush and Prime Minister Tony Blair and opposed by several old and new EU member states. In 2004 the French electorate, increasingly prone to vote against the party it had just voted into power in the preceding elections, delivered a harsh message to the government in the March regional elections: the UMP lost control of twenty out of twenty-one mainland regions. Three months later, in elections to the European Parliament, UMP candidates won only 16 percent of the vote while the Socialists won 29 percent. Earlier in the year former prime minister Alain Juppé, the man Chirac once called "the best among us," was convicted of misusing public funds when Chirac was mayor of Paris. The next two years were dominated by the events we described at the start of this chapter: the defeat of the government-backed European constitution and the explosion of rage in immigrant communities in 2005, and the withdrawal of the youth employment law in the face of demonstrative public protests in 2006. As Chirac neared the end of his term in 2007, he appeared a forlorn figure, denounced by his opponents on the left and extreme right and repudiated by his own party's chief contender for his mantle as president. In his many years at the pinnacle of power in France, Jacques Chirac learned the hard way how challenging it can be to govern a nation with 246 kinds of cheese.

---

The man who was to take over Chirac's party while rejecting much of Chirac's legacy was *Nicolas Sarkozy.*

## PROFILE: Nicolas Sarkozy

"I want a new relationship between the French people and politics," Nicolas Sarkozy proclaimed, formally declaring his candidacy for the presidency in the 2007 elections. The man who two years earlier had called for a complete "rupture" with the policies of the past now called for a "tranquil rupture." The French people wanted change, he acknowledged; but they also wanted "protection" and a chance to rally together.

Sarkozy's bid for the presidency surprised no one: his political ambition was evident from the earliest stages of his career. Born in 1955, Sarkozy had an immigrant background. His father came to France from Hungary after World War II, and his mother was a descendant of a Sephardic Jewish family that had wandered to Salonika following the expulsion of Jews from southern France in the Middle Ages. After Sarkozy's father abandoned his family, the boy drew close to his maternal grandfather, himself an immigrant who became a confirmed Gaullist and a Jewish convert to Roman Catholicism. (Sarkozy is also Catholic.) Sarkozy later said that his character was shaped by various humiliations he had suffered as a child. His own father, for example, allegedly told him that he would never be French enough to become president when he grew up; France was not the United States. After graduating from law school, Sarkozy attended the *Institut d'etudes politiques* (the Institute for Political Studies) in Paris, a training ground for the country's political elite. But he withdrew prior to graduation, passed the bar exam, and soon embarked on his political career. At the age of twenty-two he was elected to the city council of Neuilly-sur-Seine, the wealthy Paris suburb where he lived. Two years later he was named president of the national RPR youth movement that supported Jacques Chirac's first campaign for the presidency. Chirac lost out in 1981, but Sarkozy's star began rising. Still in his twenties, Sarkozy was elected mayor of his hometown in 1983. In 1988 he was named one of the RPR's national secretaries and won his first election to the National Assembly. During the next several years, with Chirac's backing, Sarkozy climbed steadily up the ranks of the neo-Gaullist party's hierarchy, while his intelligence and dynamism caught the eye of other party leaders. From 1993 to 1995, Sarkozy served as minister for the budget in the "cohabitation" cabinet of the RPR's Édouard Balladur.

When Balladur decided to challenge Chirac in the first round of the 1995 presidential elections, Sarkozy sided with Balladur. Chirac regarded the move as a personal betrayal. After Chirac won the presidency that year, Sarkozy did not serve in any of Chirac's first-term cabinets. Only after Chirac won his second term in 2002 did Sarkozy enter the cabinet as Prime Minister Raffarin's interior minister. That position was tailor-made for Sarkozy, who was now in charge of the politically sensitive issue of law and order at a time of mounting public concern about crime and youth delinquency. Adopting a tough stance, Sarkozy raised the presence of police in high-crime areas and stiffened punishments for offenders. He also strengthened France's anti-terrorism laws, which already accorded French authorities wider investigative and detention powers than their U.S. counterparts possessed. But Sarkozy's interests were not limited to domestic security. In March 2004 he was reassigned to the important post of minister for the economy, finance, and industry. At the same time, Sarkozy was well on his way to realizing his presidential dreams. In November 2004 he was elected by members of the UMP, the center-right umbrella party Chirac had put together in 2002, as its new chief. At Chirac's request, Sarkozy relinquished his cabinet ministry upon assuming leadership of the UMP.

Sarkozy immediately presented himself as the person who would reinvigorate Chirac's party and lead it to victory in 2007. Within a year, the party welcomed nearly 70,000 new members; by 2007 the total membership reached 233,000. To accomplish his goals, however, Sarkozy felt it necessary to distance himself as much as possible from Chirac, whose government was increasingly unpopular. Although he supported the European constitution, Sarkozy broke with Chirac by opposing Turkey's future admission into the European Union—a popular position in France. In June 2005 Chirac restored Sarkozy to his former post as interior minister in the new cabinet headed by Dominique de Villepin. But a month later, as France celebrated Bastille Day, Sarkozy likened Chirac to King Louis XVI on the eve of the French Revolution, accusing the government of "immobilism" and the evasion of reality. In November, with immigrant neighborhoods erupting in flames around the country, Sarkozy issued his call for a rupture with the "debt, unemployment, and stagnation" of the previous thirty years, even though Chirac had been France's president for ten of those years and prime minister for two of them. In the convulsions of the autumn of 2005, and again during the crisis over the government's youth employment law in 2006, Sarkozy sprang into action in search of solutions while his potential presidential rival de Villepin appeared ineffectual and isolated. Sarkozy got the better of de Villepin once again in a subsequent scandal. An intelligence official with ties to the prime minister confessed to giving an investigative judge a list of people accused of channeling illicit money through a financial firm. Sarkozy's name was on the list, but he defended himself against the accusations while de Villepin looked like the villain behind the scenes.

In January 2007 Sarkozy became the UMP's official presidential candidate upon winning 98 percent of nearly 155,000 ballots cast by party members. The outlines of his program were already evident in his previous statements and actions. In addition to his well-known stands on law-and-order issues, Sarkozy favored a U.S.-style quota system in restricting future immigration, with preference given to those with desirable job skills. He also favored efforts to reach out to the country's Muslim community, having previously joined in forming a new organization to represent France's Muslims, the French Council of the Muslim Religion. To this end he favored relaxing French secular traditions by permitting the use of public funds to build mosques. His economic policy was expected to be a pragmatic mixture of new incentives for private enterprise, including tax reductions and adjustments to the thirty-five-hour workweek law, with continued state support for popular social-welfare programs. Sarkozy was wary of being tagged a "liberal," a term that in France implies support for Anglo-Saxon models of market capitalism. It was not likely that he would emerge as France's Margaret Thatcher, exalting private enterprise and bashing welfare-state "socialism." (While expressing admiration for Thatcher, Sarkozy also praised Tony Blair.) Sarkozy's foreign policy would combine cooperation with the European Union with adamant opposition to Turkey's accession to the organization. Sarkozy also favored improved ties with the United States, separating himself from Chirac's neo-Gaullist quest for maximum independence from the U.S. "hyperpower." In a speech in Washington, Sarkozy regretted French "arrogance" over Iraq, alluding to a time when de Villepin was France's foreign minister. President Chirac promptly criticized the remark.

Despite the fact that he represented Jacques Chirac's party, Nicolas Sarkozy was ready to chart his own path in French politics.

---

*The Union for French Democracy* The Union for French Democracy (*Union pour la démocratie française,* or UDF) was founded in 1978 at the instigation of President Giscard d'Estaing. Its initial raison d'être was to support Giscard's presidency. From its inception the UDF has consisted variously of about four or five parties and political clubs.

The UDF's principal problem is that its main constituencies are similar to those courted by the neo-Gaullists. Still, the UDF won a respectable 21 percent of the second-round vote in 1997, electing 109 National Assembly deputies.

But a succession of splits after the 1997 elections seriously reduced the UDF's appeal. The formation of Chirac's UMP in 2002 also cut deeply into its ranks, as a large number of UDF political figures joined the new center-right grouping. UDF leader François Bayroux struggled to maintain the group's independence. But he won only 6.8 percent of the vote in the first round of the 2002 presidential elections, and UDF candidates captured only twenty-one seats in that year's National Assembly elections. Bayroux and his followers are centrists who favor a balance of private enterprise and state-funded welfare, along with a pro-EU orientation. Their chief problem as they headed into the 2007 elections was their inability to distinguish themselves compellingly from like-minded moderates in the UMP and the Socialist Party. By contrast, more than seventy deputies attached to UDF parties were elected under the UMP label.

*The National Front* Perhaps the most controversial party in France is the *National Front* (Front national, or *FN*). The party was established in 1972 under *Jean-Marie Le Pen.* Le Pen had fought as a paratrooper in Indochina. After winning a seat in the Fourth Republic's parliament, he left the legislature to fight in Algeria. When several extreme right-wing factions consisting of Vichyites, anti-Semites, fundamentalist Catholics, die-hard proponents of French imperialism, and theorists of European racial and cultural superiority resolved to form a new party, Le Pen was their man.

In 1987 Le Pen touched off a storm of controversy with his statement that the Nazi gas chambers were just "a point of detail" in World War II, a remark that infuriated France's 600,000 Jews. (After he uttered a similar remark in Germany nine years later, a German court fined him for demeaning the Holocaust.) In 1984 Le Pen won a seat in the European Parliament. In 1988 he shocked the political mainstream again by polling 14.4 percent of the first-round vote for the presidency. In 1995 he increased his presidential support to 15 percent, winning more than 4.5 million votes. And in a succession of elections to the National Assembly, the FN saw its share of the first-round vote rise from 9.7 percent in 1986 to 15.1 percent in 1997. During the 1997 legislative election campaign Le Pen assaulted a female candidate. In 2003 the European Court of Justice stripped him of his seat in the European Parliament for this offense.

In 1998 Le Pen's rivals provoked a split in the National Front. Bruno Mégret, the FN's number two, claimed the party leadership, denouncing Le Pen's reluctance to collaborate with more moderate right-wingers. Ultimately, Mégret split off from the National Front and formed his own party, the *National Republican Movement* (Mouvement national républicain, or MNR).

Le Pen's surprise second-place finish in the first round of presidential balloting in 2002 left the rest of the electorate stunned. Running separately, Mégret won nearly 700,000 votes (2.3 percent of the total). Le Pen's second-round showing of 17.8 percent represented more than 5.5 million votes. But the rapid collapse of the National Front's political fortunes in the National Assembly elections that immediately followed the 2002 presidential contests suggested that Le Pen had a wider appeal than his party, and that his party stood little chance of having a direct effect on legislation. (It won no Assembly seats in 2002.)

The FN's success cannot be explained exclusively by its anti-immigrant positions. The party has also reached out to a wider constituency concerned about taxes, unemployment, crime, AIDS, globalization, and other woes afflicting French society. Its wide electoral base encompasses blue- and white-collar workers, small business owners, affluent voters, and young people. By the late 1990s, 25 to 30 percent of French voters had voted for the FN at least once. In 2002 the party and its standard-bearer made inroads into urban and suburban working-class districts once dominated by the French Communists. But their main electoral support came from France's northeast and northwest corners, where economic decay or pockets of immigrants turned more than 20 percent of the voters to the extreme right. Some 38 percent of the unemployed voted for Le Pen in the 2002 presidential race, and for the first time he scored gains in small communes where immigration was not so noticeable. Many of the National Front's voters may be dyed-in-the-wool bigots. But an indeterminate number of them—perhaps as many as half—are mainly protest voters who are incensed at what they perceive to be the insensitivity of the other parties to their economic distress and social frustrations.

After the 2002 elections Le Pen's daughter Marine sought to "normalize" the FN by making it a potential governing party rather than a relatively isolated extremist organization. But Jean-Marie was by no means ready to step aside. Hoping to play a wild-card role once again, he announced plans to run for the presidency in the 2007 elections, which would take place shortly before his seventy-ninth birthday.[35]

*Other rightist parties* In addition to Bruno Mégret's National Republican Movement, there are several other small right-wing parties and political figures. One of the most notable personalities is *Philippe de Villiers* (duh veel-YAY), a patrician conservative and ENA graduate who served as a junior minister in Jacques Chirac's cabinet in the 1980s. After working within the Union for French Democracy, de Villiers founded a new group, the *Movement for France,* in 1994. Espousing a euroskeptic view of the European Union, he won 4.7 percent of the vote in round one of the 1995 presidential elections. De Villiers did not run for president in 2002, but two years later he and two fellow party members won seats in the European Parliament, where they seek to limit the EU's involvement in the affairs of member states. In 2005 de Villiers was a leader of the campaign to defeat the European Constitution in the French referendum. He raised eyebrows with his claim that EU enlargement was producing an influx of "Polish plumbers" and other cheap laborers from the east who were competing with French jobseekers. Later he published a book warning of the "Islamization of France." De Villiers hoped to win votes from Le Pen and Sarkozy in the 2007 presidential elections.

### The Left

*The Socialists* The main party of the French left today is the *Socialist Party* (Parti socialiste, or PS). Although it is customary to identify socialism with the industrial working class and the underprivileged more generally, the PS has never been a predominantly workers' party or a party of the poor. Ever since its foundation in 1970, it has mainly been a center-left party, attracting those segments of the French middle class who attach a high priority to enhancing social welfare and civil rights for the population as a whole. The party's core voters as well as its dues-paying members and candidates for office include a high proportion of teachers, professors, civil servants, doctors, and other white-collar professionals. Despite the harsh anticapitalist rhetoric of the early Mitterrand years, the PS has also drawn a significant number of votes from private businesspeople and managerial personnel. Less than half its constituency is working class, with most of it consisting of better-paid skilled workers rather than unskilled laborers.

Its main trade union support comes from the two noncommunist federations, the Workers' Force (Force Ouvrière, or FO) and the traditionally Catholic-oriented French Democratic Confederation of Labor (Confédération française démocratique du travail, or CFDT). Neither of these union organizations maintains formal institutional links with the Socialists, however.

Upon becoming prime minister in 1997, Lionel Jospin pursued a middle course that combined private-sector growth with a welfare orientation that was more state-centered than that of his British counterpart, Tony Blair. "My project is not socialist," Jospin declared, while also affirming his "socialist identity" and calling himself a "democratic socialist." Acknowledging the need for more budgetary income, Prime Minister Jospin reaped more revenue by selling off shares of French-owned companies like Air France and France Telecom than all five previous prime ministers put together (including Chirac and Juppé) had managed to do. He kept the state's annual budget deficits within the limits mandated by the European Union, and he explicitly rejected old leftist nostrums about the primacy of the state in the economy. But Jospin also responded to the left wing of his party by supporting a long list of social welfare measures, culminating in the Aubry law that mandated a thirty-five-hour workweek.

Jospin's ouster from the 2002 race after falling third behind Le Pen was a devastating blow. After Jospin's immediate retirement, the party leadership fell to François Hollande, a moderate who had only a few weeks to pick up the pieces before the National

Assembly elections took place. The Socialists were routed, capturing less than a fourth of the Assembly's seats. Several of their star candidates failed to win reelection.

In an effort to reinvigorate the party, Hollande brought a large number of young people, women, and immigrants into the Socialists' executive board, the two-hundred-member National Council. During Chirac's second term he led the Socialists' vigorous opposition to the government's attempts to dilute the thirty-five-hour workweek law and to create a new youth employment law. After shoring up his own leadership position within the Socialist camp, Hollande sought to forge a programmatic consensus in a party divided between its conservative wing, led by former cabinet ministers like Laurent Fabius and Dominique Strauss-Kahn, and its left wing, personified by another cabinet veteran, Martine Aubry. But Fabius broke ranks with other party leaders when he called for the rejection of the European constitution in the 2005 referendum. And none of these leading "elephants" of the party emerged as the Socialists' presidential candidate for 2007. That honor went to Hollande's life partner, *Ségolène Royal.*

## PROFILE: Ségolène Royal

"I am the only one who can win against the right," Ségolène Royal confidently affirmed. She had just won more than 60 percent of the ballots sent in by Socialist Party members in a special poll aimed at picking the party's presidential nominee for 2007. Her rivals, former prime minister Laurent Fabius and former finance minister Dominique Strauss-Kahn, each won about 19 percent. It was a triumphal moment for a relatively new face on the French political scene.

Born in the French colony of Senegal in 1953, the daughter of a colonel, Royal earned the right academic pedigrees for entering the French political elite. She graduated from both the Institut d'études politiques (known informally as the Sciences Po) and the École nationale d'administration. After working as an administrative court judge while in her twenties, Royal held an advisory position on the staff of President François Mitterrand from 1982 to 1988. Her legislative and ministerial career took off quite rapidly after this initial exposure to presidential administration. In 1988 Royal won her first election to the National Assembly, and four years later she was tapped for the post of minister for the environment under one of Mitterrand's prime ministers. Royal held this position for about a year, returning to the government in 1997 as vice-minister of education after the Socialists won control of the National Assembly and Lionel Jospin became prime minister in "cohabitation" with President Chirac. In 2000 she began a two-year stint as vice-minister for family and childhood, a position that was enlarged to include responsibility for the handicapped. In each of these ministerial positions, Royal secured the passage of a number of new laws, including legislation on recycling, school lunch programs, home tutoring, paternity leave, child prostitution and pornography, and the reduction of violence in schools, including measures to combat the bullying of gay students. She also played an instrumental role in legislating the right of gay couples to raise children. (In 2006 she declared her support for legislation to permit gay marriage.) Royal launched campaigns against violence on television and other child and family issues, and she has written several books on these topics.

Royal did not wait very long after the end of Prime Minister Jospin's Socialist government in 2002 before reigniting her political career. In 2004 she ran for the presidency of the region of Poitou-Charantes, a position with responsibility for the local economy and other regional issues. Her decision to run had national implications: the region was the home base of Jean-Pierre Raffarin, President Chirac's prime minister. Unexpectedly, Royal handily defeated her UMP opponent, a Raffarin loyalist.

It was not until the fall of 2005 that Royal publicly expressed her interest in running for the French presidency. After tossing her hat in the ring, "Ségo" became a media sensation. Socialist Party stalwarts like Fabius, Strauss-Kahn, and others whose presidential aspirations were known for years found themselves struggling to catch up with Royal in public opinion polls. None of them could match her star power or the advantage she carried as a lesser-known political figure who did not have a long track record that could be attacked by the press or political opponents. Her appeal attracted some 80,000 new members into the Socialist Party in 2006, swelling party ranks to nearly 220,000. Inevitably, critics began taking swings at her. Some accused her of vagueness in her policy positions, especially with respect to economic policy. Although Royal had joined the rest of the Socialist leadership in condemning de Villepin's youth employment law, she offered few details prior to the 2007 campaign about how she would attack France's persistently high unemployment. Royal's critics were not limited to her opponents in the center-right UMP. Royal raised the hackles of some Socialists when she called for changes in the 35-hour work-week law to permit greater flexibility for workers to spread out their work hours. (The law provided for an annualized average of 35 hours per week. But some workers end up working much longer hours in peak production periods, she noted, while their managers go off on vacation.) Acknowledging public fears of crime and youth delinquency, she called for military-style boot camps specializing in humanitarian activities for disruptive juveniles along with parenting classes for their parents. These proposals provoked charges from the left that she was pandering to law-and-order hardliners on the right. Some women accused her of failing to promote feminist causes vigorously enough. Other detractors accused her of egotism. People on the left wing of her party questioned her admiration for Tony Blair, whom they regarded as too centrist.

At the start of 2006, Royal launched a website called "Wishes for the Future." The site laid out her evolving political program and invited suggestions from the public.[36]

Royal and François Hollande met as students. Though they never married, they have four children and have remained partners under French laws governing civil unions—the same laws that apply to same-sex unions. It is not likely that this arrangement will affect the outcome of the election, given the culture of tolerance that prevails in France. (Sarkozy is divorced, and his second marriage reportedly almost broke up in 2005 amid gossip that prompted him to sue a newspaper.)

After several debates with her chief opponents for the Socialist Party's presidential nomination, Royal in November 2006 won a convincing majority of the nearly 18,000 votes cast by party members. With a razor-thin lead over Sarkozy in public opinion polls taken in 2006, she was poised to become the first woman ever elected president of France. "Now that's a revolution!" she declared.

---

*The Communists* The *French Communist Party* (Parti communiste français, or PCF) has seen its fortunes wane appreciably in recent decades, losing votes to the Socialists and the National Front. In addition, the PCF's trade union partner, the General Confederation of Labor, has experienced a sharp decline in membership and political clout since the 1970s. Finally, the collapse of the Soviet Union in 1991 left the PCF without a clear ideological compass.

Battered by these challenges, the Communists in 1994 picked a new chief, Robert Hue, to replace Georges Marchais, who had dominated the party since 1972. But Hue garnered scarcely more than 3 percent in the 2002 race for the presidency. And in a shocking upset, he lost his National Assembly seat to a Chirac follower who cashed in on the votes of local Le Pen supporters. The Communists came away from the debacle with only twenty-one seats, sixteen fewer than in 1997. The party faces an uphill struggle under its new leader, Marie-George Buffet. Its traditional source of support, the unskilled industrial working class, continues to shrink. Today the PCF's support still remains concentrated in industrial and mining regions, especially the factory areas outside of Paris, which are known as the "Red Belt" because of the party's decades-long control of local governments. But even these areas are increasingly slipping away.

**Other Leftist Parties** As we've noted, there are a number of fairly small leftist groupings, ranging from relatively moderate ones to more extreme groups that purport to favor revolution. Like the larger leftist parties, these mini-groups did not fare well in the 2002 legislative elections, losing sixteen seats. Several ecology-oriented parties and independents are also associated with the left, the largest group being the Greens. The Greens also had a bad year in 2002, losing five of their eight seats. Dominique Voynet, the party's leader and Jospin's environment minister, lost her Assembly seat.

## Women in Politics

Women did not acquire the right to vote in France until 1944, following the country's liberation from German occupation. Even today, women are underrepresented in the French national legislature to a considerably greater extent than in many other democracies (see table 2.4). By the fall of 2003 there were seventy women in the National Assembly (12.2 percent of the total) and thirty-five in the Senate (10.9 percent). In an attempt to raise the number of women taking an active part in politics, a constitutional amendment in 1999 was enacted formalizing "the equal access of men and women to all electoral mandates and elective functions." In the following year, a nearly unanimous National Assembly passed legislation requiring an equal number of male and female candidates for most elections—the first such law in the world. The measure had the approval of both President Chirac and Prime Minister Jospin. (Jospin's Socialists had already adopted a rule in 1996 ensuring that 30 percent of its candidates would be women.)

Although the "parity law" applies to elections to the National Assembly, the leading parties failed to follow its provisions in 2002. Chirac's Union for the Presidential Majority ran women in just 20 percent of the districts where its candidates vied for a National Assembly seat; the Socialists fielded women candidates in only 36 percent of the races it contested. Quite a few of these women candidates were assigned to run in districts where they stood little chance of winning. As a result, the number of women elected in 2002 (71) was only slightly higher than the number elected in 1997 (66), before the parity law was passed. Parties that failed to meet the parity requirement were penalized by having to forego a portion of the state-funded subsidies that supplement private campaign contributions. The parity law does not apply to presidential elections.

Despite these disappointments, the parity law has proved quite successful in boosting the number of women running in municipal elections for city councils. In local elections held in March 2001, nearly twice as many women were elected to municipal councils as were elected before the parity law took effect. About half of the council members in cities with a population of more than 3,500 are now women. The parity law also applies to regional elections, certain Senate elections, and elections to the European Parliament.[37]

## HYPOTHESIS-TESTING EXERCISE: Are France's Institutions Dysfunctional?

### Hypothesis

A mixed presidential-parliamentary system tends to produce the worst possible outcomes: either authoritarianism or gridlock. When the president and the National Assembly majority share the same orientation (whether of the left or right), the president monopolizes power and tends to abuse it. Cohabitation, by contrast, produces gridlock, bringing the lawmaking process to a standstill.

### Variables

The *independent variable* is *the presidential-parliamentary system.* The *dependent variables* are *the concentration and abuse of presidential power* and, alternatively, *gridlock.*

### Expectations

If the hypothesis is correct, then we would expect the evidence to show that (1) whenever French presidents enjoy the support of the majority of the National Assembly, decision making is heavily concentrated in the presidency as opposed to the government and the legislature; (2) presidents then tend to exceed their legal authority, creating the danger of an elective dictatorship; and (3) cohabitation produces an inefficient governmental process bordering on paralysis.

### Evidence

As we've seen, Charles de Gaulle ruled the roost as a super-president, at times even violating the letter of the constitution. Presidents Pompidou and Giscard d'Estaing also governed from the top, concentrating decision making in the presidency. But they were not as imperious as de Gaulle, nor did they overtly exceed or abuse their constitutional authority. President Mitterrand also concentrated decision-making authority in the president's Élysée Palace when the Socialists and their allies enjoyed a parliamentary majority. He used his presidential prerogatives to call snap elections in 1981 and 1988, to rotate prime ministers, and to abruptly change course in economic policy. As a former critic of the Fifth Republic's constitution and of de Gaulle's governing style, however, Mitterrand refrained from abusing his authority. President Chirac used his presidential powers to promote major changes in social and economic policy in 1995 when his party and its allies controlled the legislature, but he and Prime Minister Juppé backed down and withdrew their proposals in the face of massive public opposition. Much the same happened when Chirac and Prime Minister de Villepin introduced the youth employment law in 2006.

The record of three periods of cohabitation demonstrate that the policy-making process is not as inefficient as the hypothesis predicts. President Mitterrand allowed his center-right prime ministers, Chirac and Balladur, ample leeway to pursue their priorities, even when those policies collided with Mitterrand's preferences. President Chirac similarly gave Prime Minister Jospin free rein to enact measures unpalatable to the right (such as the thirty-five-hour law). Despite the frustrations it engenders in the opposing political camps, cohabitation in France has not created paralytic gridlock. Each side has found ways to accommodate the other.

**Conclusions**

Overall, the evidence is *mixed.* When the president's party and its allies control the National Assembly, decision-making power does tend to be concentrated in the president's hands, a finding that is consistent with the hypothesis. Under these conditions, the term "semi-presidentialism" is a misnomer when used as a synonym for the presidential-parliamentary system. (The term was coined by Maurice Duverger, but other French political scientists have rarely used it when characterizing the French system.)[38] When backed by a parliamentary majority, French presidents have asserted their leadership in policy matters, at times treating their prime ministers like scapegoats and replacing them when things go wrong. Still, most French presidents have refrained from the abuse of power. President de Gaulle on occasion may have abused his constitutional authority—though without any taint of personal corruption—but his successors have not stretched the constitution beyond its clear limits. As to cohabitation, the evidence is basically inconsistent with the assumption that it invariably causes gridlock. Much depends on the personal relationship between the president and prime minister. In the three cases of cohabitation that have occurred thus far, Presidents Mitterrand and Chirac moved off to the sidelines and their prime ministers assumed the policy-making initiative. The term semi-presidentialism thus seems appropriate when applied to power-sharing between a president and a prime minister of opposing parties. We'll re-test these hypotheses in chapter 19 to see how they apply to Russia.

## FRANCE AFTER THE 2007 ELECTIONS

However the 2007 presidential and legislative elections may have turned out, France's new leaders will have to deal with a host of accumulating problems. We have already looked at a number of these issues in the preceding pages. Let's wind up this chapter by briefly turning our attention once again to two headline problem areas: the economy and minorities.

**The Economy** As we noted at the start of this chapter, France's per capita GDP ranked fifteenth in the world in 2005. But in 1980 France ranked seventh in that category. Over much of that period, the country's unemployment rates either rose or remained virtually immovable. Annual economic growth has fallen below the OECD average for the past ten years in a row, averaging about 1.6 percent between 2001 and 2005. Average net pay, with inflation taken into account, grew by only 1 percent in the first half of the present decade. French women earned about three-quarters of average male earnings and continued to come against glass ceilings at the upper managerial levels of both the public and private sectors. Tax burdens on individual citizens and on private companies were high by OECD standards, averaging close to 50 percent of national income. France's trade deficit has grown considerably in recent years, along with its public debt and pension deficit. The finance minister stated in 2005 that the country was living beyond its means. Government spending still takes up close to 55 percent of GDP, well above the OECD average of just over 40 percent. Because half the members of the National Assembly are former civil servants, it is unlikely that the French parliament will vote to trim the country's costly bureaucracy. When immigrant communities blew up in 2005, President Chirac sought to douse the flames by creating fifty thousand new civil service jobs for the unemployed.

Most French employees work an annualized average of thirty-five hours a week and benefit from five weeks of paid vacation and an equal amount of sick leave. As a result, they put in fewer work hours than their counterparts in all but two out of twenty-six economically advanced OECD countries. American employees work 27 percent more hours. With an average retirement age of fifty-nine, only one out of six French citizens between the ages of sixty and sixty-four is still employed. In the United States, half the people in that age group are working. Only 53 percent of French people *over fifty* are employed. In 2005 the French labor force was 2.7 times the size of the over-65 population, but by 2025 it will be only half as large, placing even heavier burdens on the pension system. Although tuition is free at France's eighty-four public colleges and universities, and admission is virtually guaranteed except in the highly selective *grandes écoles*, research and development in France has not kept pace with the highest world standards. None of these academic institutions has broken into the world's top forty universities as measured by online faculty publications.

Globalization is transforming French businesses—including state-owned companies—to a greater extent than many people in France would like. When a large Italian energy company tried to take over a privately owned French utility group called Suez in 2006, de Villepin's government arranged Suez's merger with the state-owned energy giant Gaz de France, fending off the takeover bid in the name of "economic patriotism." Even Sarkozy, who favors a more vigorous private sector in France, has applauded the French government's protection of large corporate "national champions" against foreign takeover. These interventionist practices contradict European Union policies favoring cross-border mergers that enhance Europe's competitiveness in the global marketplace. The French government has also resisted enforcing EU rules that require annual budget deficits to be kept at 3 percent of GDP or below. The EU has formally warned France to comply with these strictures or face mandatory fines.

But France also benefits from its participation in the EU. French farmers are especially well compensated out of funds from the EU's Common Agriculture Policy, which subsidizes European agriculture and protects it against competition from the United States and other food-exporting countries. (France has also banned the import of genetically modified food from the United States.) French farm owners and vintners form powerful political lobbies that heavily influence government policies. And French firms are benefiting from globalization, reaping handsome profits from sales and investments abroad while purchasing companies around the world, including American brands. (Trade and investment ties between the United States and France amount to more than $100 billion and employ more than 600,000 people in each country.) The French auto firm Renault, for example, joined forces with Japan's Nissan Motors, and in 2006 the two partners entered into talks on potential cooperation with General Motors. French state-owned companies often fetch hefty prices when the government sells them off or offers partial ownership to outside bidders. To be sure, there are losers as well as winners in these transactions. When the French communications supplier Alcatel purchased the American firm Lucent in 2006, creating a company worth nearly $40 billion, the new management team announced it would reduce its 88,000-strong work force by 10 percent in a cost-cutting measure. For his part, President Chirac displayed his pique at the linguistic implications of globalization. He and two French cabinet ministers walked out of an EU summit in 2006 when the president of France's largest business association, the Enterprise Movement of France (Medef), addressed the meeting in English. English "is the accepted business language of Europe today," the Medef chief said. French citizens are also taking advantages of opportunities in the global economy. Though half the population in 2006 had no faith in the market economy, the number of French men and women who have moved to Britain and other European countries or to the United States in search of better job opportunities has risen more than 40 percent since 1990.

The news is not all grim, by any means. France continues to be a prime choice for overseas investors. With a work force that tends to have a high level of productivity, along with a quality of life that few countries can match, France remains an attractive location for foreign companies and investors. It is also the world's number one tourist destination, drawing upward of 70 million visitors a year, a figure higher than the domestic population. Despite the economy's doldrums, only 6 percent of France's people live below the government's official poverty line, compared with 15 percent in Britain and 18 percent in the United States. Through a variety of insurance programs, the French enjoy universal health care coverage. In the United States, by contrast, 46 million people lacked health insurance in 2006. (Some French physicians have gone on strike in recent years for higher fees, however.) And the French services sector has been booming, accounting for virtually all the new jobs created in recent years. When these and other pluses are added into the mix with the French economy's minuses, it is clear that the country's new leadership will face not only serious challenges but also extraordinary opportunities.[39]

**Minorities** France has more than 4 million foreign-born residents and many more with a parent or grandparent who emigrated from abroad. As we noted earlier, there are between 5 and 6 million Muslims living in France, constituting 8 to 10 percent of the national population. In a country accustomed to defining French identity in ethnic terms, the presence of so many people of foreign origin—especially of non-European origin—creates problems both for *les Français de souche* (people of French stock) and the immigrant community. Young Mahgrebis, who call themselves *beurs* (a play on the French word *Arabes*), have joined with other immigrants in forming groups like "SOS Racisme" that are dedicated to fighting racism. French officials, meanwhile, appear determined to integrate the country's Muslim population into the secular traditions of the French Republic. The separation of church and state was not established in France until 1905, following a long battle between secularists and the proponents of a privileged status for Roman Catholicism. Article 1 of the Fifth Republic's constitution enshrines this principle by describing the republic as *laïque*—"secular." When President Chirac called for a ban on head scarves and other religious attire in French public schools, he pointedly declared, "Secularism is not negotiable." (Ironically, however, French law permits public funding for religious schools, including Muslim schools.)

Fears of terrorism, particularly in the aftermath of September 11, have heightened the urgency of these issues. French police and prosecutors have wider authority to investigate, detain, interrogate, and expel suspected criminals and illegal aliens than their counterparts in the United States possess, and they use it. (France has no habeas corpus law or Miranda rights.) Presumed terrorists are rounded up periodically, and surveillance agents routinely stake out mosques. Allegations of police brutality aimed at immigrants have been publicized by Amnesty International, as has the rise in violence directed against France's Jewish community. The kidnapping, torture, and killing of a young Jewish man in Paris in 2006 by a gang calling itself the "barbarians" raised fears of rising anti-Semitism in the country's Muslim community.[40]

The disturbances in immigrant communities that shook France in 2005 have placed the country on edge, serving notice of an incendiary discontent seething just below the surface of everyday appearances. As we've indicated, members of the French political elite have advocated various measures to address the immigrant minority's sense of alienation from French society. A report commissioned by de Villepin's government provided blatant evidence of discrimination in the hiring practices of French companies. Recommendations to rectify the problem accompanied the report. Conceivably, efforts to improve employment opportunities and living conditions in immigrant communities may evoke a positive response. France's Muslims, who form a large part of the country's minority population, do not seem to be as alienated as their co-religionists in Britain or other European countries. According to surveys conducted by the Pew Research Center, 42 percent of France's Muslims regarded themselves as French citizens first and as Muslims second, while 46 percent saw themselves as Muslims first. But 81 percent of British Muslims considered themselves Muslims first and only 7 percent saw themselves as British citizens first. Muslims in Spain and Germany were also considerably more inclined than French Muslims to see themselves as Muslims first. Some 72 percent of French Muslims (but only 49 percent of British Muslims) saw no conflict between being a devout Muslim and living in a modern society. These attitudes suggest that large numbers of France's Muslims want to be included in French society rather than alienated from it.[41]

Nevertheless, prior to the 2007 elections people of non-European origin were practically absent from the French parliament (except for less than a dozen who represented overseas territories), and they were severely underrepresented in the civil service and corporate management. In 2000, 60 percent of the French said there were too many foreigners in France, and a mere 29 percent said they were "not racist." Despite the joyous celebrations that greeted France's soccer team when it won the World Cup in 1998, the dominance of players of foreign origin like Zinedine Zidane on the championship club had little lasting effect on French racial attitudes. In the following year, 36 percent of French people surveyed believed that there were too many foreign players on the team. And as the French team battled into the World Cup final in 2006, with seventeen minority players out of twenty-three, many French citizens with similar minority backgrounds expressed doubts that the team could bring the country together politically or socially. Integrating France's large minority population into the mainstream of the country's political and economic life will surely be a major test of the country's vaunted traditions of tolerance, inclusion, and equality for many years to come.[42]

## CONCLUSION

As we've seen, France took a long and winding road to stable democracy. The threat of authoritarianism hung over French politics until well into the 1960s. Starting with the Revolution, the French have sought to build a lasting democracy on the values of "liberty, equality, and fraternity." The values of tolerance, nondiscrimination, inclusion, and fairness have been harder to achieve, much as they have been in many other democracies, including the United States and Britain. Despite repeated setbacks, the rule of law has been cemented as a fundamental element of French democracy since World War II. Since then, the French have also largely succeeded in establishing the three functional pillars of the Temple of Democracy that we described in chapter 7: popular sovereignty; guaranteed civil rights and liberties; and economic well-being, centered on a generous welfare state and a vibrant private sector. The wide consensus that now prevails on these basic structural features of democracy has blurred the historic distinctions between right and left in France, despite day-to-day conflict over the details of policy. (By the late 1990s, 86 percent of the French perceived no difference between Socialist and neo-Gaullist governments.)[43] Along the way, the French have also met all ten conditions for democracy that we delineated in chapter 9.

The 2007 elections would give the French people a real opportunity to choose leaders who offer the country new visions and new hopes for change. But it remains to be seen how much latitude a divided and politically assertive public will give their newly chosen leaders as they address the country's problems. Whatever the outcome, this much is sure: in the past fifty years, France has achieved considerable success in overcoming its burdensome legacy of political instability. Though the years ahead may bring renewed friction and vigorous contestation, the French can be confident that they can deal with their conflicts—and enjoy their extraordinary cultural and economic blessings—on the foundations of a solid democracy.[44]

## KEY TERMS AND NAMES
## (In bold and underlined in the text)

Jacques Chirac
Nicolas Sarkozy
Ségolène Royal
Cohabitation
French Revolution
Charles de Gaulle
Fifth Republic
National Assembly
Senate

## NOTES

1. Imagine what might have happened following the 2000 elections if the United States had France's political system. The Democrat Al Gore won 48.38 percent of the popular vote; the Republican George W. Bush won 47.87 percent. Other candidates won the rest. If Gore had defeated Bush in a second round of voting, a Democrat would have occupied the White House. But the Republicans retained control of both houses of Congress in 2000. President Gore then would have been expected to nominate a leading Republican to serve as the government's prime minister. Upon the nominee's approval in the House of Representatives, the Democratic president and the Republican prime minister would then have to govern jointly on the basis of "cohabitation."
2. *Washington Post*, March 25, 2006. On France's "fearful society," see Christophe Lambert, *La société de la peur* (Paris: Plon, 2005).
3. Sophie Meunier, "Globalization and Europeanization: A Challenge to French Politics," *French Politics* 2, no. 2 (August 2004): 125–50; Emiliano Grossman and Sabine Saurugger, "Challenging French Interest Groups: The State, Europe and the International Political System," *French Politics* 2, no. 2 (August 2004): 203–20.

4. *Le Monde,* January 17, 2006; *Financial Times,* March 18–19 and April 11, 2006.
5. Nicolas Baverez, *La France qui tombe* (Paris: Perrin, 2003), *Nouveau monde, vielle France* (Paris: Perrin: 2005), and *Vieux pays, siècle jeune: La France et le monde, 2001–2005* (Paris: Perrin, 2006). For a critical review of "declinist" literature, see Helen Drake, "France in Free Fall? French Perspectives on the Astérix Complex," *French Politics* 2, no. 2 (August 2004): 221–33. Timothy B. Smith, *France in Crisis: Welfare, Inequality and Globalization since 1980* (Cambridge: Cambridge University Press, 2004). See also "The Art of the Impossible: A Survey of France," *The Economist,* October 28, 2006; and *Financial Times,* April 11, 2006.
6. The Jacobins (JACK-o-bins) took their name from an order of friars who were established in the church of St. Jacques (i.e., St. Jacob) in Paris. The Jacobins held meetings in the dining hall of the church convent.
7. The literature on the French Revolution is voluminous. For overviews, see Simon Schama, *Citizens* (New York: Knopf, 1989); William Doyle, *The Oxford History of the French Revolution* (Oxford: Oxford University Press, 1989); and Emmet Kennedy, *A Cultural History of the French Revolution* (New Haven: Yale University Press, 1989).
8. The Third Republic's first president, Marshal Patrice MacMahon, was a monarchist who tried to reestablish authoritarian rule. Electoral victories by pro-Republic forces in 1876 and 1877 prevented him from succeeding and he resigned. In the late 1880s General Georges Boulanger, "the man on horseback," almost took power in a coup. See James Harding, *The Astonishing Adventure of General Boulanger* (New York: Scribner, 1971), and William D. Irvine, *The Boulanger Affair Reconsidered* (New York: Oxford University Press, 1989). Between 1894 and 1906 the Dreyfus Affair, which took its name from a Jewish officer unjustly accused of treason, triggered an intense struggle between the Republic's authoritarian opponents and "Dreyfusards" who supported democracy. Dreyfus served years of hard labor on Devil's Island, a penal colony off the coast of French Guyana, before being exonerated. See Jean-Denis Bredin, *The Affair: The Case of Alfred Dreyfus,* trans. Jeffrey Mehlman (New York: G. Braziller, 1986). Also Sanford Elwitt, *The Making of the Third Republic* (Baton Rouge: Louisiana State University Press, 1975). In 2006 the French government observed the one hundredth anniversary of Dreyfus's pardon. *Le Monde,* July 13, 2006.
9. Liah Greenfeld, *Nationalism: Five Roads to Modernity* (Cambridge, Mass.: Harvard University Press, 1992), 89–188.
10. Pierre Birnbaum, *The Idea of France,* trans. M. B. de Bevoise (New York: Hill and Wang, 2001); Sudhir Hazareesingh, *Political Traditions in Modern France* (Oxford: Oxford University Press, 1994). See also Fernand Braudel, *The Identity of France,* 2 vols., trans. Siän Reynolds (London: Collins, 1988).
11. Edward S. Mason, *The Paris Commune* (New York: Macmillan, 1930). For Karl Marx's views on the Commune, see "The Civil War in France," in *The Marx-Engels Reader,* ed. Robert C. Tucker (New York: W. W. Norton, 1972), 526–76.
12. Michael Crozier, *The Stalled Society* (New York: Viking, 1974).
13. Charles Tilly, *The Contentious French* (Cambridge, Mass.: Belknap, 1986). See also Philip G. Cerny, *Social Movements and Protests in France* (New York: St. Martin's Press, 1982).
14. Robert O. Paxton, *Vichy France* (New York: Knopf, 1972); Michael R. Marrus and Robert O. Paxton, *Vichy France and the Jews* (New York: Basic Books, 1981). See also the film by Marcel Ophuls, *Le chagrin et la pitié (The Sorrow and the Pity).*
15. Alain Touraine, *The May Movement,* trans. Leonard F. X. Mayhew (New York: Random House, 1971); Alain Schnapp and Pierre Vidal-Naquet, *The French Student Uprising, November 1967–June 1968,* trans. Maria Jolas (Boston: Beacon Press, 1971). For a fictionalized account, see the novel by James Jones, *The Merry Month of May* (New York: Delacorte, 1971). See the analysis by Richard Johnson, an American student who witnessed the 1968 events, in *The French Communist Party Versus the Students* (New Haven: Yale University Press, 1972).
16. Charles de Gaulle, *The Complete War Memoirs of Charles de Gaulle,* trans. Jonathan Griffin and

Richard Howard (New York: Simon & Schuster, 1959), and *Memoirs of Hope,* trans. Terence Kilmartin (New York: Simon & Schuster, 1971). See also Jean Lacouture, *De Gaulle: The Rebel 1890–1944,* trans. Patrick O'Brien (New York: W. W. Norton, 1993), and *De Gaulle: The Ruler 1945–1970,* trans. Alan Sheridan (New York: W. W. Norton, 1993); Charles Williams, *The Last Great Frenchman: A Life of General de Gaulle* (New York: Wiley, 1995); Robert O. Paxton and Nicholas Wahl, *De Gaulle and the United States* (Providence, R. I.: Berg, 1994); and Charles Cogan, *Charles de Gaulle: A Brief Biography with Documents* (Boston: Bedford, 1996).

**17.** Valéry Giscard d'Estaing, *French Democracy,* trans. Vincent Cronin (Garden City, N.Y.: Doubleday, 1977); J. R. Frears, *France in the Giscard Presidency* (London: Allen & Unwin, 1981).

**18.** Mitterrand was often accused of covering up his early right-wing views and Pétainist leanings. See, for example, Pierre Péan, *Une Jeunesse française: François Mitterrand 1934–1947* (Paris: Fayard, 1994). See also Catherine Nay, *The Black and the Red: François Mitterrand, the Story of an Ambition,* trans. Alan Sheridan (New York: Harcourt Brace Jovanovich, 1987). For Mitterrand's account of his political development, see *Ma part de verité* (Paris: Fayard, 1969).

**19.** For Mitterrand's thoughts on the 1970s, see *The Wheat and the Chaff,* trans. Richard S. Woodward, Helen R. Lane, and Concilia Hayter (New York: Seaver, 1982). For an account of the "union of the left," see George Ross, *Workers and Communists in France* (Berkeley: University of California Press, 1982).

**20.** For a comparison of Mitterrand's economic policies and Margaret Thatcher's, see Peter Hall, *Governing the Economy: The Politics of State Intervention in Britain and France* (Oxford: Oxford University Press, 1986).

**21.** Julius W. Friend, *The Long Presidency: France in the Mitterrand Years, 1981–1995* (Boulder, Colo.: Westview Press, 1998); Ronald Tiersky, *François Mitterrand: A Very French President* (Lanham, Md.: Rowman & Littlefield, 2003); Mairi Maclean, ed., *The Mitterrand Years* (New York: St. Martin's, Press, 1998); Anthony Daley, ed., *The Mitterrand Era* (New York: New York University Press, 1996); Alistair Cole, *François Mitterrand* (London: Routledge, 1994); Wayne Northcott, *Mitterrand: A Political Biography* (New York: Holmes & Meier, 1992); George Ross et al., eds., *The Mitterrand Experiment* (New York: Oxford University Press, 1987); Jean Lacouture, *Mitterrand: Une histoire de Français,* 2 vols. (Paris: Seuil, 1998).

**22.** A thorough reference work on French institutions is Chagnollaud Quermonne, *La V[e] Republic,* 4 vols., rev. ed. (Paris: Flammarion, 2000).

**23.** Sébastien Lazardeux, "'Une Question Ecrite, Pour Quoi Faire?' The Causes of the Production of Written Questions in the French Assemblée Nationale," *French Politics* 3, no. 3 (December 2005): 258–81.

**24.** ENA graduates only about eighty students a year, École polytechnique about three hundred. By 2002, six out of nine previous prime ministers were ENA graduates, two out of the three most recent presidents, and a large number of cabinet ministers. Two out of three chairmen of the top forty companies listed on the French stock exchange had graduated from either ENA or the École polytechnique. *The Economist,* June 5, 1999; and the *New York Times,* December 18, 2005.

**25.** On the *cumul des mandats,* see the articles in *French Politics* 4, no. 3 (December 2006).

**26.** On France's double-ballot electoral systems, see the articles in *French Politics* 3, no. 2 (August 2005).

**27.** Out of a population of 59 million in 2001, only about 15 million lived in France's ten largest cities (9 million in Paris). There were more than twenty thousand communes having a population of fewer than five hundred people. The number of rural folk fell to 627,000 in 1999, 38 percent less than in 1989 (*Economist,* November 16, 2002). On "deep France," see Richard Bernstein, *Fragile Glory: A Portrait of France and the French* (New York: Plume, 1991).

**28.** The preamble affirms the "attachment" of the French people to the Declaration of the Rights of Man of 1789 and to the rights listed in the preamble to the Fourth Republic's constitution. Article 2 states that the Fifth Republic ensures "the equality of all citizens before the law, without discrimination of origin, race or religion."

**29.** Ezra N. Suleiman, *Elites in French Society* (Princeton: Princeton University Press, 1978); Harvey Feigenbaum, *The Politics of Public Enterprise: Oil and the French State* (Princeton: Princeton University Press, 1985). See also the *Economist,* November 16, 2002 and October 28, 2005.

**30.** France maintains four "overseas departments" (*départements d'outre-mer,* or DOMs): Guadeloupe, Martinique, and Guyana in the Caribbean and the island of Réunion in the Indian Ocean. It also has three "overseas territories" (*territoires d'outre-mer,* or TOMs): French Polynesia, New Caledonia (near Australia), and the Pacific islands of Wallis and Futuna. In addition, it possesses two "territorial collectivities": St. Pierre-et-Miquelon, located next to Canada, and Mayotte, located near Madagascar. These overseas areas, which are not considered part of "metropolitan France," elect twenty-two seats in the French National Assembly. The Mediterranean island of Corsica is part of metropolitan France. It has enjoyed a special autonomous status since 1982 and elects four deputies to the National Assembly.

**31.** Vivien A. Schmidt, *Democratizing France: The Political and Administrative History of Decentralization* (Cambridge: Cambridge University Press, 1990). In 2003, Corsica's voters narrowly rejected the French government's proposal for slightly more local autonomy.

**32.** Gérard Grunberg and Étienne Schweisguth, "French Political Space: Two, Three or Four Blocs?" *French Politics* 1, no. 3 (November 2003): 331–47; Robert Andersen and Jocelyn Evans, "The Stability of the French Political Space, 1988–2002," *French Politics* 3, no. 3 (December 2005): 282–301. See also Andrew Knapp, *Parties and the Party System in France: A Disconnected Democracy?* (New York: Palgrave Macmillan, 2004); and Michael S. Lewis-Beck, ed., *How France Votes* (New York: Chatham House, 2000).

**33.** Vivien A. Schmidt, *From State to Market? The Transformation of French Business and Government* (Cambridge: Cambridge University Press, 1996).

**34.** Philippe Madelin, *Jacques Chirac: Une Biographie* (Paris: Flammarion, 2002); Franz-Olivier Giesbert, *Jacques Chirac* (Paris: Seuil, 1987); John Tuppen, *Chirac's France, 1986–88* (New York: St. Martin's Press, 1991); Jean-Marie Colombani, *Le President de la République* (Paris: Stock, 1998); Raphaëlle Bacqué and Denis Saverot, *Seul Comme Chirac* (Paris: Grasset, 1998); Patrick Jarreau, *Chirac: la Malédiction* (Paris: Stock, 1998). On the UMP's formation, see Florence Haegel, "The Transformation of the French Right: Institutional Imperatives and Organizational Changes," *French Politics* 2, no. 2 (August 2004): 185–202.

**35.** Peter Fysh and Jim Wolfreys, *The Politics of Racism in France* (New York: St. Martin's Press, 1998); Jonathon Marcus, *The National Front in French Politics* (Basingstroke, UK: Macmillan, 1995); Françoise Gaspard, *A Small City in France: A Socialist Mayor Confronts Neofascism* (Cambridge, Mass.: Harvard University Press, 1995).

**36.** Royal's website is www.desirsdavenir.org.

**37.** Karen Bird, "Who Are the Women? Where Are the Women? And What Difference Can They Make? Effects of Gender Parity in French Municipal Elections," *French Politics* 1, no. 1 (March 2003): 5–38; Rainbow Murray, "Why Didn't Parity Work? A Closer Examination of the 2002 Election Results," *French Politics* 2, no. 3 (December 2004): 347–62; Raylene L. Ramsay, *French Women in Politics* (New York: Berghahn, 2003); *Le Monde,* October 25, 2005.

**38.** Gianfranco Pasquino, "Duverger and the Study of Semi-Presidentialism," *French Politics* 3, no. 3 (December 2005): 310–22.

**39.** *The Economist,* November 16, 2002, and October 28, 2006; *Le Monde,* February 25, February 28, and August 12, 2006; *Financial Times,* June 29, 2005, and March 2, March 7, March 27, April 1, April 3, and September 20, 2006; *Washington Post,* December 9, 2005, and February 26 and August 21, 2006. See also the periodic OECD reports on the French economy at www.oecd.org.

**40.** *Washington Post,* February 25, 2006; *New York Times,* March 5 and 26, 2006; *Le Monde,* March 7, 2006. On anti-Semitism in contemporary France, see Michael Wieviorka, ed., *La tentation antisémite: Haines des Juifs dans la France d'aujourd'hui* (Paris: Hachette, 2006).

**41.** See the Pew Global Attitudes Surveys, "The Great Divide: How Westerners and Muslims View Each Other" (released June 22, 2006) and

"Muslims in Europe: Economic Worries Top Concerns About Religious and Cultural Identity" (released July 6, 2006), at www.pewglobal.org.

**42.** *The Economist,* June 5, 1999, and November 16, 2003; *Le Monde,* June 9, 2003; *Financial Times,* November 12, 2005; *New York Times,* August 1, 2003; *Washington Post,* June 11, 2000, November 23, 2001, and January 29 and July 7, 2006. On alienated rappers, see *Washington Post,* November 24, 2005. See also Paul A. Silverstein, *Algeria in France: Transpolitics, Race, and Nation* (Bloomington: Indiana University Press, 2004); and Fadela Amara and Sylvia Zappi, *Breaking the Silence: French Women's Voices from the Ghetto,* trans. Helen Harden Chenut (Berkeley: University of California Press, 2006).

**43.** *The Economist,* July 31, 1999.

**44.** Recent texts include Andrew Knapp and Vincent Wright, *The Government and Politics of France,* 5th ed. (New York: Routledge, 2006); and Anne Sa'adah, *Contemporary France: A Democratic Education* (Lanham, Md.: Rowman & Littlefield, 2003).

CHAPTER 18

# GERMANY

Population (2005 est.): 82.5 million
Freedom House Ratings (2002): Political Rights—1; Civil Liberties—1

Area: 137,826 square miles (about the size of Montana)

The dark line marks the boundary between West Germany and East Germany prior to unification in 1990.

Most people could not believe their ears when they heard the announcement. Unexpectedly, on the evening of November 9, 1989, one of the leaders of East Germany's communist regime mentioned in a televised press conference that East German citizens would henceforth receive immediate and unconditional permission to travel abroad. The statement, delivered almost casually, was a bombshell: it signaled a complete reversal of three decades of stringent communist controls over the travel rights of the East German population. As news of the announcement spread rapidly, crowds gathered on the eastern side of the Berlin wall to see if the official declaration was really true. For several hours they waited while the border crossings remained shut. At last the guards opened the barriers and let them out. A revolution was under way.

Ever since August 1961, when the East German authorities began building the makeshift barriers they subsequently fortified into a massive concrete wall, the two parts of Berlin had been blocked off from each other. The wall ran twenty-seven miles across the center of what used to be the capital of Germany, and it snaked around the perimeter of West Berlin. Armed East German border guards surveyed the barrier from control towers, shooting anyone who tried to escape to the western side. Approximately 160 fatalities attested to their marksmanship. A no-man's-land of mines and barbed wire kept all but the most audacious from getting anywhere near the eastern side of the wall. For years only a small number of East Berliners received permission to visit the western part of the city; these were mostly elderly pensioners or individuals attending a funeral or some special family event. West Berliners were rarely allowed into East Berlin at all until the 1970s.

The division of Germany was one of the most traumatic and dangerous aspects of the Cold War. It resulted from the agreement of the Western allies and the Soviet Union to split Germany into western and eastern Occupation zones following Hitler's defeat, which occurred in May 1945, and to impose a similar east–west division on Berlin. In principle, these divisions were supposed to be temporary; the victorious combatants spoke of eventually reestablishing a single, unified German government. Their failure to agree on the political nature of such a

**Berlin celebrates the opening of the wall in front of the Brandenburg Gate, 1989.**

government, however, produced the divisions that, for the next forty years, appeared to be permanent. The Western allies—the United States, Britain, and France—favored democracy and private enterprise and created a democratic state in their West German Occupation zones. Known as the *Federal Republic of Germany* (the *FRG*), and informally as *West Germany*, it came into existence in 1949 and established its capital in Bonn. The Soviet Union created a dictatorship in its eastern Occupation zone under trusted German communists. The *German Democratic Republic* (the *GDR*, or *East Germany*) was also formally established in 1949.[1] West Germany assumed de facto control over West Berlin and the East German authorities took control over East Berlin.

Over the ensuing decades, divided Germany and divided Berlin gave almost literal meaning to the "iron curtain" that was said to divide the communist part of Europe from the West after World War II. It separated families, partitioned some 80 million Germans into two ideologically antagonistic states, and created a powder keg of confrontation in the heart of Europe that on several occasions threatened to explode into nuclear war. Berlin was especially sensitive. Located deep inside East Germany, 110 miles from the West German border, it was encircled by over 300,000 Soviet troops based in the GDR.

Until the summer of 1961 there were no physical barriers dividing the two parts of the city; hundreds of thousands of Berliners routinely shuttled between West Berlin and East Berlin every day. Between the end of the war and mid 1961, nearly

3 million East Germans who did not wish to live under communism took advantage of this opening to the West, depleting the GDR of one-seventh of its population. To stop this hemorrhage, the East German authorities, with Soviet collusion, began constructing what became the Berlin wall.[2] For the next twenty-eight years, the wall's hulking presence appeared to be an irremovable feature of the German landscape. But all that began to change on the night of November 9, 1989.

For several months the communist party rulers of East Germany had grown increasingly nervous. Their grip on the population, tightened by the most pervasive surveillance network in the communist bloc, was weakening. In 1989 as in 1961, people were leaving East Germany in droves. Ironically, their escape route now was in the east. Thousands of East Germans on vacation in neighboring communist-ruled Hungary took advantage of that country's recently opened border with Austria and simply walked or rode to freedom, their possessions stuffed in a few suitcases. East German vacationers in Czechoslovakia, a more rigidly governed communist state than Hungary, swarmed into the West German embassy in Prague and pressured the West German and Czech authorities to agree to let them leave for West Germany. Between July and October more than 120,000 found a way to get out of East Germany.

Tensions intensified in the fall, as anti-regime demonstrations began taking place in East German cities. Once it became clear that the East German authorities were not prepared to crush the protests with overwhelming force, as they might have done in the past, growing numbers of people were emboldened to take to the streets. In early November more than a million people gathered peacefully in East Berlin in an unprecedented show of opposition to the regime's dictatorial practices.

None of this would have happened without the forbearance of the Soviet Union. Instead of cracking down on these massive displays of anticommunist activity, Moscow had inadvertently precipitated them. After Mikhail Gorbachev assumed the Soviet leadership in 1985, winds of change began blowing from the Kremlin across the entire communist bloc. Gorbachev was a communist reformer. He fully understood that the USSR and the communist states of Central and Eastern Europe were deeply mired in economic and technological inferiority to the West and Japan. He also had no illusions about the fact that the Soviet system of repressive government and state-centered socialism was to blame for the communist world's predicament.

Gorbachev's strategy of reforming the Soviet system was predicated on favorable relations with the United States and its allies. The Cold War, with its exorbitant military expenditures and other costs, had to be ended so that the USSR and its allies could shift their resources to rebuilding their flagging economies. Gorbachev also hoped that friendlier ties with the West and Japan might result in some economic assistance. The use of coercion to suppress demonstrators or stop them from emigrating to the West would inevitably dash these hopes. As a consequence, Gorbachev quietly stood by as more than forty years of Soviet hegemony in Central and Eastern Europe slipped through his fingers over the course of 1989. Communist reformers in Hungary tore down their fortified barrier along the border with Austria, while Poland's communist leaders came to an agreement with the Solidarity trade union leaders on free elections. Those elections virtually removed the Polish communists from power. These developments could not help but have an impact on East German citizens. If the Soviets, Hungarians, and Poles could have change, they felt, why can't we?

It was in the context of these swirling events that the East German leadership, in a desperate attempt to calm the population and restore order, decided to ease the detested travel restrictions. They probably had no idea that, in doing so, they were opening a floodgate. As a state of mass euphoria gripped the country, more than 5 million East Germans crossed the inter-German borders in the first four days after the wall's opening, most of them for the first time in their lives.

The opening of the Berlin wall triggered a chain of events that occurred so rapidly that political leaders could barely keep up with them. While leaders of the two German states cautiously spoke of "stability" and long-term "reform," most East Germans wanted radical change immediately. In March 1990, free elections were held in East Germany for the first time, with dozens of newly formed parties participating. The fledgling party organizations connected with West Germany's three largest parties—the Christian Democrats, the Social Democrats, and the Free Democrats—won more than 75 percent of the East German vote. Their chief goal was the same: the dissolution of East Germany as a separate state and its incorporation into the Federal Republic.

On October 3, 1990—less than one year after the opening of the wall—the two Germanies were unified into an enlarged Federal Republic of Germany. The consequences of this revolutionary development are still affecting Germany today.[3]

One of the East German citizens who walked into West Berlin on that historic night of November 9, 1989, was a thirty-five-year-old scientist named **Angela Merkel** (AHN-gheh-lah MAIR-kl). A research physicist at East Germany's prestigious Academy of Sciences, Merkel was not especially involved in politics. After strolling along a few West Berlin streets separated by the wall from her own East Berlin neighborhood, and after talking with a few strangers who were equally stunned by what was happening, Merkel returned home to get a good night's sleep before rising early for work. For the next several weeks she remained fairly detached from the events erupting around her, unconvinced that everything was about to change forever. Only in the final weeks of the year did she decide to join one of the new political parties that were sprouting up in East Germany. It was a fateful choice. Merkel soon found herself immersed in the transformations driving East Germany's democratization and Germany's unification. To her surprise, politics beckoned as a new career. The East German outsider's rise was extraordinarily rapid. In 2005, Angela Merkel was elected chancellor of the Federal Republic of Germany, becoming the first female head of government in German history.

In many respects the Germany that Chancellor Merkel leads has two political cultures. One is based in the western part of the country, where the habits associated with democracy, private enterprise, and alliances with the United States and Western Europe are deeply ingrained after more than fifty years of experience. The other is in eastern Germany, where people who grew up under communism retain certain values and perceptions deriving from life in an authoritarian socialist state that was officially antagonistic toward the United States and NATO. The "wall in people's minds" still stands. Some eastern Germans (especially older ones) still feel nostalgia for East Germany's simpler lifestyle and cradle-to-grave welfare system—even though the vast majority of them would agree that the economic opportunities and freedoms they have enjoyed since joining the Federal Republic (especially the freedom to travel) have made unification worthwhile. These nostalgic sentiments probably will attenuate over time, but in 2001 fully 75 percent of eastern Germans and 64 percent of western Germans said that the things that separated the two groups still outweighed the things that united them as one people. *Ossies* (Easties) and *Wessies* (Westies) even perceived each other as possessing very distinct character traits. A majority of Ossies saw western Germans as open to the world and adaptable, but also as arrogant, calculating, and greedy. About a third or more of Wessies viewed eastern Germans as "human," but also as inflexible, provincial, dependent—and greedy. And whereas a large majority of western Germans (63 percent) favored the attack on Afghanistan after September 11, 2001, only 42 percent of eastern Germans favored it.[4]

The economic costs of unification have also left their mark. East Germany's economy was in shambles when unification took place in 1990. Its communist-era factories were hopelessly antiquated, its telecommunications system and transportation networks barely serviceable, its housing dilapidated. Between 1990 and 2005 the government of the Federal Republic pumped more than $1.5 trillion into eastern Germany in an effort to modernize its economic infrastructure, reform its educational system, and establish new governmental institutions. A large portion of this money was used to provide jobs or unemployment compensation for people thrown out of work by the liquidation of East Germany's bureaucracy, military, and state-owned enterprises. To pay for these expenditures, average tax rates in the 1990s rose from about 43 percent to 50 percent for people living in western Germany. In addition, private German companies invested their own money—as much as $150 billion in a single year—in the east. The price tag of unification continues to be steep: by 2006 Germany's government was spending close to $100 billion a year in eastern Germany, and it has planned a "solidarity package" amounting to nearly $160 billion for the years 2005–19. Even so, the eastern part of the country is not expected to catch up to western Germany's economy for decades. Unemployment figures in the two parts of Germany testify to their economic differences. The unemployment rate was 19.5 percent in eastern Germany in 2006, double the figure in western Germany. East German workers often work longer hours and earn less money than their counterparts in western Germany.

These problems have exacerbated difficulties in other areas of the economy. Although Germany has the third largest economy in the world after the United States and Japan, and although it overtook the United States in 2003 as the world's largest exporting nation, its economy has been troubled since the 1990s. Unemployment has been persistent. In early 2005 the jobless rate reached 11.6 percent of the labor force. Some 5.2 million Germans were out of work, the highest number since 1932, the year just before Adolph Hitler took power. Germany's economy was also beset with anemic economic growth; high labor costs and high tax rates that discouraged private business investment; soaring payments for health care, pensions, and other social welfare benefits; and mounting budget deficits that have exceeded the European Union's mandatory annual limit (3 percent of GDP) for countries using the euro. Proposals for spending cuts, longer working hours, and other sacrifices regarded by many economists and political leaders as necessary to pull the economy out of its slump have been fiercely resisted by workers, retirees, and other Germans who feared they would lose out, at least in the short term, if such reforms were implemented.

The social and economic transformations that have occurred since Germany's unification have been accompanied by political changes. Like other countries, Germany has had to find its own path to democracy. After World War II, American, British, and French Occupation authorities presided over the establishment of a democratic system in West Germany, a process that proved successful thanks to the support for democracy demonstrated by West Germany's political leaders and a growing segment of its population. That support was reinforced by a commitment to avoid the tragic failure of Germany's first attempt at democracy, the so-called Weimar Republic of 1919–33, and by deep-seated revulsion at the horrors of the Nazi dictatorship under Adolph Hitler (1933–45). The Germans learned from their mistakes.

Today Germany has five main political groupings. Three of them—the center-right *Christian Democrats* (divided into the CDU and the CSU), the center-left *Social Democrats* (SPD), and the middle-of-the-road *Free Democrats* (FDP)—dominated the Federal Republic's political life until 1998, forming stable and effective coalition governments in varying combinations. In 1998, the Social Democrats under the leadership of **Gerhard Schroeder** formed a coalition government with a fourth group, the environmentally oriented *Greens*, who were allied with a former East German democratic movement, *Alliance 90*. Until just after the 2002 elections, the fifth main political grouping was the *Party of Democratic Socialism* (PDS), the pro-democracy descendant of East Germany's former ruling communist party. The PDS subsequently renamed itself the *Left Party*. In 2005 it joined with a splinter group of left-wing dissidents from the Social Democratic Party in forming an electoral alliance.

Like Britain's Labour Party and France's Socialist Party, Germany's Social Democratic Party today is a catch-all party that occupies the political space immediately to the left of the political spectrum's center point. And like their British and French ideological cousins, German Social Democrats today are divided between centrists who favor spending cuts and pro-business policies in order to deal with budget deficits and the pressures of globalization, and more left-leaning political forces who strongly defend the accumulated benefits and protections of the welfare state. *Gerhard Schroeder* was a centrist Social Democrat, cut in roughly the same mold as Tony Blair, Gordon Brown, Lionel Jospin, and Ségolène Royal. During his seven years as chancellor, Schroeder introduced a number of reforms aimed at reducing Germany's unemployment rolls and trimming its budgetary arrears.

The most controversial of these reforms sought to reduce the labor costs incurred by German businesses. As West Germany prospered after World War II, trade unions and business associations reached understandings designed to accommodate the interests of both sides. Employers were interested in preventing strikes and maximizing profits; employees wanted job security, higher wages, and generous benefits. By the 1980s Germany's industrial workers were among the best paid and most well-protected workers in the world. Employers were required to make significant contributions to funds for their employees' health and unemployment insurance, pensions, and other social benefits. Job security was virtually guaranteed by laws that made it prohibitively expensive for employers to fire anyone after the expiration of a six-month probationary period for new workers. Over time, the average workweek fell to less than thirty-eight hours in western Germany. Although these and other arrangements greatly benefited German jobholders, businesses complained they could no longer afford these welfare obligations. By the late 1990s, employers' contributions were running close to 40 percent of the average worker's gross wages, an exceptionally high figure by American, British, and Japanese standards. Such high labor costs, combined with Germany's job-protection laws and limitations on working hours, made it increasingly costly for German businesses to hire new workers. Under pressure from trade unions, labor costs in eastern Germany rose to levels almost as high as those in western Germany. As economic globalization forced German businesses to slash their operating costs in order to compete effectively with American, Asian, and other competitors in the global marketplace, company executives called on the German government to reduce their welfare contribution requirements and allow them greater flexibility to hire and fire workers and adjust their working hours.

Meanwhile, the collapse of communism and the rise of democracy and private enterprise in Poland, Hungary, the Czech Republic, and other states in Germany's eastern backyard after 1990 opened up new opportunities for German businesses to build plants in countries where labor costs were about one-tenth the German average. Shortly after Schroeder became chancellor, a group of Germany's leading corporate executives told him they would move more of their operations outside of Germany if the government did not respond to their pleas for labor-cost reductions and lower corporation taxes.

Germany's labor laws, the forces of economic globalization, and the economic transformations of eastern Germany and East Central Europe thus combined to perpetuate Germany's unemployment problem.

Schroeder responded to these business demands with a number of reforms intended to make it less costly for the private sector to hire new workers. But as in France, many of these cost-cutting measures proved highly unpopular in Germany. They were especially resented in Schroeder's own party, whose commitment to working-class welfare dated back to the nineteenth century. Trade unions, the backbone of the SPD's electoral support, were vocal in opposing the chancellor's reforms. But Schroeder insisted that the reforms, no matter how painful, were vital to reducing unemployment. When he was first elected chancellor in 1998, at a time when more than 4 million Germans were unemployed, Schroeder told voters that he should not be reelected four years later if unemployment had not fallen by then to 3.5 million. Although there were still more than 4 million unemployed in 2002, Schroeder and his coalition partners were reelected anyway. But the next three years proved rough sledding for the chancellor, who took the blame for reforms that seemed only to threaten Germany's social welfare system without reducing joblessness. With his popularity dwindling, Schroeder announced snap elections in 2005, one year ahead of schedule. His main opponent was Angela Merkel, the leader of the Christian Democrats. Merkel promised voters an even stiffer regimen of reforms than the changes Schroeder advocated, vowing to cut unemployment and deficits through more extensive labor-cost reductions and higher sales taxes.

The results of the September 2005 elections to Germany's lower house of parliament, the *Bundestag* (Federal Diet), turned out to be much closer than forecasters had predicted. The two main parties—Schroeder's Social Democrats and Merkel's Christian Democrats—finished neck-and-neck, separated by just 1 percent of the popular vote out of 48 million votes cast. These two rivals lost more than 20 Bundestag seats each compared with their gains in the 2002 elections, a sign of general voter discontent. In the end the Christian Democrats came away with 4 seats more than the Social Democrats (226 to 222). But neither the Christian Democrats nor the Social Democrats emerged as the clear winner. The Christian Democrats won 36.8 percent of the 614 seats in the Bundestag; the Social Democrats won

36.2 percent. Other parties won the remaining seats. The result was a hung parliament, with no single party claiming an absolute majority (at least 308 seats).

Germany has a *parliamentary system* of government patterned on the British system, as described in chapter 8. But Germany's electoral system differs from Britain's. Britain has a single-member-district/plurality system that usually produces a single-party majority in the House of Commons. As a result, Britain has had no coalition governments since 1945. Germany has a hybrid electoral system that combines single-member districts with proportional representation. The final distribution of seats in the Bundestag, however, reflects proportional representation: each represented party gets a share of seats roughly proportional to its share of the national vote. As a consequence, *every government in the Federal Republic of Germany has been a coalition government since 1949*, when the FRG was founded in West Germany. As soon as the results of the September 2005 election were known, jockeying began to form the country's next coalition government.

The political arithmetic of these elections proved more difficult than advanced calculus. None of the traditional coalition partnerships equaled a voting majority in the Bundestag. The Christian Democrats' natural center-right ally, the Free Democrats, won just under 10 percent of the seats—not enough to form a majority with the Christian Democrats (10 + 36.9 = 46.9). The Social Democrats' coalition partners for the previous seven years, the Greens, won 8.3 percent of the seats, not enough to reestablish their "red-green" coalition government (8.3 + 36.2 = 44.5). None of these parties wanted to form a coalition with the only remaining party to win seats in the Bundestag, the Left Party. (The Left Party won 8.8 percent of the seats.) What to do?

A few days after the elections, Chancellor Schroeder and Angela Merkel announced that their parties, although archrivals, would begin talks to form *a Christian Democrat–Social Democrat coalition government*—a so-called **Grand Coalition** of the main center-left and center-right parties. A precedent already existed for this union of opposites: between 1966 and 1969, West Germany was governed by a Grand Coalition of these same parties. It was as though the Democrats and Republicans had agreed to govern the United States jointly, sharing cabinet posts. Neither the Christian Democrats nor the Social Democrats were happy about their predicament. But after nearly two months of intense negotiations they produced a common program for governing Germany, and the Grand Coalition government was formed. The sixteen-member cabinet was shared equally: eight ministries for the Christian Democrats (including Chancellor Merkel) and eight for the Social Democrats. Merkel was sworn in as chancellor on November 22. It was only sixteen years since the night the Berlin wall was opened and she took her first steps into the other—democratic—Germany.

Like any coalition government, the Grand Coalition Merkel heads is built on compromise. Compromise between political parties and their leaders is always difficult; compromise between two rival parties of the left and right is even more difficult. Each side must give up key elements of its policy program. In the process, each side is bound to disappoint some of its own followers. But a public opinion survey conducted right after the election showed that a slim majority of Germans wanted the Grand Coalition to be created. An indeterminate number of voters may have split their two-part vote between the Christian Democrats and Social Democrats with the intention of bringing about a Grand Coalition, hoping that the two parties might work out their differences and agree on the most popular policies. Initially Merkel went out of her way to accommodate the Social Democrats, abandoning some of her chief campaign promises. The Social Democrats also jettisoned some of their main promises in coming to terms with their coalition partners. By early 2006 Merkel had an 83 percent public approval rating, the highest of any German leader in history. Business and consumer confidence rose. The economy perked up in a number of key areas in 2006. Unemployment dipped below 4 million and economic growth exceeded earlier projections. Though Merkel's approval ratings plunged in late 2006 as people demanded faster results, no alternative to the Grand Coalition government appeared possible.

The ability of Germany's largest rival parties to govern the country together may be taken for granted today. But compromise, accommodation, and cooperation were hardly the defining characteristics of German politics before World War II. On the contrary, Germany endured centuries of internal strife and international upheaval—including two world wars—before its contending social groups and political factions were able to sit down together and form effective coalition governments in a stable democracy. In fact, Germany's parties are able to get along today in large part *because* of this shared history of national discord. Germany's unbridgeable domestic disunity delayed the introduction of democracy until after World War I. Internal divisions destroyed that democracy in less than fifteen years and then produced one of the most ruthless and violent dictatorships ever known, the Nazi regime under Adolph Hitler. No reasonable German who is cognizant of the country's past wants to go back to it. Today's Grand Coalition provides vivid testimony of how far the Germans have come in the sixty-plus years since the destruction of the Nazi death machine. The Federal Republic of Germany also stands as a beacon of hope for countries that are currently embroiled in severe internecine conflict, including Iraq, Afghanistan, and Lebanon. No matter how torn apart a country's population may be, a stable democracy based on compromise and tolerance is always a possibility, given the political will to create it. The lessons of German history clearly demonstrate that democracy may be the only way to avoid a repetition of past catastrophes.

This chapter traces Germany's path to its present situation by examining the country's tortuous path to democracy, its division into two states following World War II, and the creation of the "Berlin Republic" after unification in 1990. It also examines the Federal Republic's key government institutions, parties, and political leaders, along with such pertinent issues as the economy, immigration, and foreign policy. Along the way we'll focus on the five sources of political conflict we discussed in chapter 2:

- *Power:* Who has governed Germany? How is power distributed among Germany's political institutions, parties, and social groups today?
- *Resources:* How have economic developments affected the evolution of German politics over the years? What kinds of economic and social welfare reforms are now in view?
- *Identity:* Who is a German? That is, how is Germany dealing with the challenge of building a common identity among east and west Germans, and how is it addressing the issue of citizenship for ethnic minorities? How has Germany defined its role in world affairs?
- *Ideas:* What are some of the legacies of fascism and communism in today's Germany? How stable is German democracy, and who are its main challengers?
- *Values:* How has German political culture changed over time, moving from authoritarian to democratic values and attitudes?

## HISTORICAL BACKGROUND: GERMANY'S DIFFICULT PATH TO DEMOCRACY

Perhaps the most striking feature about German history prior to World War II is that, unlike Britain and France, Germany failed to develop a sustainable democracy. Curiously, democracy failed to develop despite the fact the Germans enjoyed roughly the same level of economic development as the British and French. The Germans' religious and intellectual traditions were just as rich: until Hitler took power, Catholicism, Protestantism, and Judaism co-existed, however precariously, while a constellation of geniuses made brilliant contributions to philosophy, science, literature, music, technology, and other fields of creative endeavor. Germany's first democratic constitution, written in 1919 for the ill-fated Weimar Republic, was perhaps the most progressive constitutional document the world had yet seen. Even so, democracy did not begin to strike lasting roots on German soil until it was implanted by U.S., British, and French Occupation forces in West Germany after 1945.

What accounts for this remarkable failure of democratic ideas and institutions to take hold from within Germany itself? Several factors on our list of conditions for democracy in chapter 9 stand out as especially noteworthy:

- the ambivalence of liberal ideology in eighteenth- and nineteenth-century Germany, which could not overcome *state institutions* characterized by authoritarian governments and a weak parliamentary tradition
- the weakness of support for democracy among German *elites* and the *middle class*
- a preference for a state-dominated economy rather than *private enterprise*

- the antidemocratic and ethnic biases of German nationalism, contributing to a nondemocratic *political culture*
- a *national unity* problem marked by the relative lateness of the creation of a central German state, a process that was finally accomplished by forces opposed to democracy
- difficulties promoting *national wealth* because of the absence of a central German state before 1871, the high costs of World War I, and severe economic problems during the Weimar Republic
- the existence of a large number of *disadvantaged* workers, some of whom gravitated to antidemocratic parties like the Communists and the Nazis
- a violent *international environment* promoted by the hypernationalism of German elites

Although pre-Hitler Germany had a relatively homogeneous population and a superb system of *education* for its elites, these factors alone were not sufficient to build or sustain a democracy. Let's briefly survey these explanatory variables.

### The Weakness of German Liberalism

As we saw in chapter 16, the origins of democracy in Britain stretch all the way back to the emergence of Parliament in the Middle Ages. And as we saw in chapter 17, democracy burst open in France in the Revolution that began in 1789. Similarly, democracy in the United States originated in the democratic institutions and practices of the colonies, with broad support from all social classes.

When these seminal events in the history of democracy took place, Germany had a real "stateness" problem: it did not even exist as a nation-state. Prior to the French Revolution, the German people were divided into more than 1,790 principalities, duchies, city-states, and other governmental entities, each asserting independence from the others. Despite some consolidation, by the early nineteenth century there were still over three hundred German mini-states, most no bigger than towns or rural counties. Virtually all of them were ruled by a prince, a duke, or some other noble lord. Some were predominantly Protestant, others Catholic. The great division of Christendom had in fact started in Germany with Martin Luther and the Protestant Reformation in the sixteenth century, and one of its immediate effects was to reinforce the political division of the German people into a multiplicity of states.

Not until 1848 did German liberalism make its grand entry. In that year the first popular elections ever held among the Germans produced an assembly whose purpose was to discuss political reform and the possible formation of a unified German government. Some eight hundred delegates from thirty-eight sovereign German states met in St. Paul's church in Frankfurt for nearly a year. Their deliberations came to nought. While the more outspoken liberals on the left advocated British-style parliamentary supremacy, conservatives on the right insisted on a supreme monarch. Left-wing liberals called for universal male suffrage, but right wingers preferred a limited suffrage based on property qualifications. Consensus was equally difficult to achieve on religious and economic issues; nor could the delegates agree on the fundamental question of *how* to organize a unified German state under a central government.

In the end, the Frankfurt assembly stitched together a compromise draft constitution calling for the creation of a national German parliament that would share power with a monarch. But its divided members failed to agree on the principle of parliamentary supremacy and could not specify exactly how the new parliament and the king were to share power. When the assembly presented its patchwork document to the king of Prussia in 1849 and invited him to become the first king of a united Germany, he brusquely dismissed the offer. Neither he nor any other reigning German aristocrat wanted anything to do with parliamentarism, however watered down. The Frankfurt assembly thereupon disbanded, never to meet again. The king later ordered his troops to break up the liberal movement in Prussia.

The failure of political liberalism to gain a foothold in eighteenth- and nineteenth-century Germany reflected the narrow social base of its support. In Britain and France the rising middle class, eager to secure its fortunes in private commerce and agriculture, exerted effective pressure for popular sovereignty. But in Germany at that time the commercial middle class was weaker. Of greater significance was the so-called "middle stratum" (*Mittelstand*) of society, whose members consisted mainly of intellectuals and people employed by the state rather than by private enterprise. They included bureaucrats, professors, jurists, and other state employees. Though this class was the principal source of liberal ideas in Germany, many of its members espoused an elitist conception of liberalism that was less concerned with limiting the powers of the state through the rule of law than with placing a strong state in their own hands. They were also less interested in electoral politics and the practical problems of coalition building and governing than in philosophical concepts of reason and intellectual freedom. They also tended to frown on the commercial classes; indeed, German liberals largely rejected Adam Smith's concepts of economic liberty and placed greater faith in a protective state that would dominate the economy. The result was comparatively tepid support for popular sovereignty, representative democracy, limited government, civil rights, or free enterprise.[5]

### German Nationalism

German nationalism took a form that was similarly unsupportive of democratic institutions and liberties. Until the early nineteenth century, as Liah Greenfeld has shown, the notion that the Germans constituted a single, unified nation barely existed.[6] The fragmentation of the German people into numerous political sovereignties promoted narrow local identities and retarded the development of an overarching German national consciousness. People tended to think of themselves as Bavarians, Prussians, Austrians, Saxons, Hanoverians, and the like rather than as "Germans." Germany's Protestant Reformation, moreover, did not have the same liberating effect on elite or mass attitudes as did England's Reformation, at least not in its formative phases. Martin Luther did not conceive of the German people in democratic terms, nor did he promote a common German national identity. Only later did certain strands of German Protestantism promote such democratic values as individualism, equality, and capitalist entrepreneurship.[7]

When nationalist ideas finally took discernible shape in Germany, they arose in the first decade of the nineteenth century as a response to Napoleon's invasion of German territory and his defeat of Prussia, the strongest of the German states, in 1806.

The main advocates of German nationalism tended to be writers and thinkers, professors and journalists: in other words, intellectuals rather than more practically oriented people like political organizers or entrepreneurs. Those Germans who coupled their nationalist appeals with calls for democracy frequently understood "democracy" as necessitating the complete subservience of the individual to the nation as a whole. Such a notion was wholly at variance with the concepts of individual rights and freedoms that are normally considered indispensable values of democracy. By the time German national sentiment gathered sufficient force in the second half of the nineteenth century to bring about a unified German state, the leaders of the unification process were anything but democratic.

### The Creation of the German State

Germany is an example of a "late state": it came together under a single central government much later than Britain, France, or the United States. Late-blooming states tend to share common problems, as the experiences of Germany, Italy, and Japan show. Until the last third of the nineteenth century, all three countries were internally fragmented; the central government was either weak (as in Japan) or nonexistent (as in Germany and Italy). All three countries centralized their governing institutions at approximately the same time, in the 1860s–70s. And all three felt a need to accelerate their economic development as rapidly as possible so as to catch up with the successful great powers. As a consequence, they all relied heavily on the central government to guide the economy, even though private companies were allowed to thrive.

In addition, the governments of these three late states felt compelled to make special efforts to mold a new sense of national identity and loyalty to the central government among their people in place of regional or local identities. People had to be taught to think of themselves as "Germans," "Italians," or "Japanese." The motto *Deutschland ueber alles* called on Germans to put "Germany above everything," especially their local loyalties. Intense nationalism was the result, accompanied by militarism and chauvinistic propaganda. Ultimately these tendencies took the form of imperial aggression abroad and, by the 1920s and 1930s, a fiercely anti-Western fascism. Although Germany, Italy, and Japan were very different in many other respects, dictatorship and hypernationalism triumphed and democracy suffered in all three states.

Indeed, when the Germans dealt with their "stateness" problem by finally coming together as a single nation-state in 1871, it was not democracy that forged their unity but military force. After the liberals' failure to unite the various mini-states under an elected national parliament, the banner of national unity was picked up by the most powerful German state of them all, the kingdom of Prussia. Centered in the plains surrounding Berlin, Prussia under the Hohenzollern dynasty had clawed its way into the ranks of Europe's most important powers over the course of the eighteenth century. By the 1860s it possessed a nascent industrial economy and one of the largest and most disciplined armies on the continent. It also had a dynamic leader, *Otto von Bismarck*, who was determined to create a unified German state under the Prussian monarchy. As chancellor (prime minister) of Prussia, Bismarck—a son of the Prussian nobility—had little use for democracy. On the contrary, he declared his intention to unite the Germans by "blood and iron" rather than by ballots. The creation of a unified German state was a "top-down" affair, orchestrated by authoritarian political elites; the process had virtually no input from the masses down below, thus precluding a democratic approach to nation building. The principal aim of Bismarck and his cohorts was to galvanize Germany into a great power capable of competing with the British and French empires on the world stage.

Bismarck led Prussia into three wars that ultimately resulted in the formation of Germany's first modern state. In 1864 Prussia attacked Denmark and came away with two provinces, Schleswig and Holstein, that remain part of Germany today. In 1866 the Prussians trounced Austria, a rival power that had its own hopes of leading the German people to national unity. And in his boldest stroke, Bismarck led Prussia to victory over France in the Franco-Prussian War of 1870–71. As these wars convincingly demonstrated the effectiveness of Prussian might, Bismarck fanned the passions of German nationalism and won the agreement of more than twenty smaller German states to join together under the Prussian monarchy to form a single Germany. Ironically, the glittering ceremony attending this historic occasion took place not in Berlin but in newly conquered France: in January 1871 the German Empire (or *Reich*) was proclaimed in the palace of Versailles, where King Wilhelm of Prussia was crowned Emperor (*Kaiser*) of Germany.

The new central government that Bismarck now created seemed to have the outward appearances of a democracy. A national legislature, the *Reichstag*, was seated in Berlin; all German males had the right to elect its deputies. In fact, however, the Reichstag's powers were strictly limited and Bismarck's purposes were purely manipulative. One of his principal aims was to keep the liberal movement divided by encouraging the formation of rival parties and factions. Under the constitution, the Reichstag had no right to unseat the government. The chancellor, as head of government, was responsible solely to the kaiser, not to the legislature. (In Britain and France at this time, the reverse was the case: the prime minister and the government were responsible to the legislature, which could vote them out of office.) Whenever the Reichstag showed any signs of opposing his policies, Chancellor Bismarck simply ignored or circumvented its actions. The kaiser's Germany was an authoritarian state, firmly controlled by the Prussian nobility and its main institutional arm, the military.

Not surprisingly, the German state played a prominent role in the economy, even though private enterprise was allowed to flourish. Most industrialists cooperated with state authorities in supplying what the kaiser's regime wanted most: a well-equipped army and navy, an extensive railroad network, and a modern economic infrastructure, all of which were dedicated to enhancing Germany's military prowess and diplomatic influence. Far from favoring mass democracy, the country's leading industrialists joined with the aristocratic owners of Prussia's large rural estates in providing support for the kaiser's dictatorial regime, an alliance known as the "marriage of iron and rye." For their part, a large portion of Germany's owners of small and medium-sized businesses—the backbone of the middle class—in principle favored democratic institutions but were neither able nor willing to organize effective opposition to the prevailing order. Many middle-class Germans, in fact, took pride in the international glory their country had achieved under the kaiser. Finally, many of Germany's most prominent intellectuals and artists looked down on politics as unworthy of their attention and refrained from taking up the cause of democratic values.

The most impassioned proponents of democracy in the kaiser's Germany were the Social Democrats. Founded in 1875, the **Social Democratic Party of Germany** (Sozialdemokratische Partei Deutschlands, or SPD)—the party of Gerhard Schroeder—quickly emerged as the primary advocate for the country's main disadvantaged group, the industrial working class. As German industry expanded, so did the ranks of factory workers, seamstresses, coal miners, and others engaged in the day-to-day rigors of manual labor. Like their counterparts in Britain, France, and other industrializing countries at this time, Germany's workers were relegated to a life of grinding physical toil, squalid living conditions, and the demoralization that comes with prolonged economic exploitation and political powerlessness. When the new German state was founded, no government programs existed to alleviate the plight of the working masses or the unemployed. The Social Democratic Party's mission was to change this situation radically. By 1898 the SPD was the largest party in Germany, winning more than 27 percent of the vote for the Reichstag. In 1912 the party won 34.8 percent.

As the most vociferous exponents of change in Germany, the Social Democrats kept up a constant barrage of criticism of the kaiser's government. In place of authoritarianism they called for parliamentary democracy. In place of profit-driven capitalism they called for a socialist economy based on workers' control of enterprises and state-managed welfare programs. And in place of militarism and global imperialism they espoused pacifism, disarmament, and international cooperation. But despite their sizable support among Germany's voters, their efforts to alter the kaiser's regime failed. Indeed, in a dramatic turnabout, the Social Democratic leadership rallied to the kaiser's side in the feverish first days of World War I. Vowing that they would never "leave the fatherland in the lurch," the party's Reichstag delegates voted for war credits in August 1914. For the SPD, as for most Germans, the spirit of nationalism was overpowering. Democracy in Germany would have to wait until the end of the most brutal conflict the world had yet seen.

### The Weimar Republic

The carnage of World War I lasted four years.[8] With the collapse of the German army imminent, the kaiser abdicated and fled the country. On hearing the news, the leader of the Social Democratic Party proclaimed a Republic from the balcony of the Reichstag. The date was November 9, 1918. Two days later, Germany surrendered. With the sudden disappearance of the entire governmental structure that had ruled the country since its inception in 1871, power in Germany was up for grabs.

As revolutionary communists fought pitched battles with right-wing militias over the following chaotic months, and with both groups fundamentally opposed to democracy, a makeshift German government managed to stage elections to a constitutional assembly in early 1919. The assembly met in Weimar, the hometown of Goethe and the symbolic heart of German culture. After six months of intense deliberation, the assembled delegates adopted a new constitution and thereby created the **Weimar Republic**, so called because of the birthplace of its constitution. Germany was at last a democracy.

The constitution adopted in Weimar in 1919 was in some respects the most democratic in the world at that time. It gave all men and women over age twenty-one the right to vote, securing a victory for women's suffrage that surpassed Britain, the United States, and most other democracies. It also guaranteed certain economic and social rights that were not to be found in the constitutions of other democratic states, including the right to a job or unemployment compensation, decent housing, comprehensive health insurance, allowances for the "protection of motherhood," and a pension. Private property rights were also protected by the constitution, but the state reserved the right to take over privately owned property in the interest of the community (with compensation for the owners). Workers earned a host of new rights, including "equal rights" with their employers in regulating wages and working conditions. In short, the Weimar constitution's framers strove to institute not just popular sovereignty and civil rights (Pillars I and II of democracy), but also a measure of economic democracy (Pillar III).

The structure of the national government was also novel. The constitution created a mixed *presidential-parliamentary* democracy, which today's French and Russian constitutions strikingly resemble. The president of the Republic was directly elected by the people and possessed real decision-making powers. In a risky departure from standard democratic practice, however, the Weimar constitution gave the president extraordinary powers to suspend basic civil rights and liberties during an emergency and to exercise virtually dictatorial authority. As things turned out, the Republic's last president flagrantly abused this authority and used it to rule the country by decree, eventually turning the government over to Hitler and the Nazis. In addition to creating a powerful president, the Weimar constitution's "dual-executive" system also featured a powerful head of government, the *chancellor*, who was nominated by the president and approved by the lower house of parliament.

The Weimar constitution established a bicameral national legislature. The lower house, the Reichstag, functioned much like the British House of Commons, holding the chancellor and the rest of the cabinet accountable. The electoral system used for popular elections to the Reichstag was proportional representation, with no minimum hurdle. This system allowed a multiplicity of small parties, many of them with less than 5 percent of the vote, to win Reichstag seats. A dozen parties or more would typically win Reichstag representation. As a result, it became extremely difficult to form stable governments. No party ever won an absolute majority of seats, making coalition governments inevitable. The inability of the coalition partners to stick together on the basis of compromise proved one of the downfalls of the Weimar system.

The problems that eventually proved fatal for Germany's fledgling democracy began accumulating right from the start. Economic disasters topped the list. The Republic started life under conditions of severe unemployment. Millions of soldiers, beaten and humiliated, straggled home from the front to find the civilian economy in no shape to employ them. As time went on, large numbers of these angry and demoralized troops gravitated to the Nazis' brown-shirted militias, enabling Hitler and his followers to intimidate their opponents in the streets. Many others supported the communists and other extreme left-wing groups militating for a socialist revolution.

Germany's economic woes were aggravated by a steep bill for war reparations imposed by the victorious powers. In 1921, Britain, France, and the United States demanded the payment of $33 billion in gold marks, to be paid out in installments starting immediately. The reparations only aggravated an inflation rate that was already spinning out of control. As the German government printed money around the clock, prices rose more than 300 percent per month. The average inflation rate for 1922–23 was over 1 billion percent! Deft financial maneuvers by the government finally brought the inflationary spiral under control, but millions of Germans in all social classes were financially ruined. The middle class was especially hard hit. Instead of constituting a bastion of support for democracy as in the United States and Britain, large numbers of the middle class in Germany turned away from the Weimar democratic regime and flocked to the Nazis and other antidemocratic groups.

After the Wall Street stock market crash of 1929, the Great Depression spread even more economic misery to Germany. Banks and other businesses plunged into bankruptcy while unemployment skyrocketed, exceeding 30 percent of the work force by 1932. People in virtually every sector of the economy were driven to despair.

These mounting economic and social crises took place in a political environment in which support for democracy remained feeble. The absence of democratic traditions in Germany deprived the Weimar Republic of a solid foundation. Initially, the Republic started out with a broad base of popular support. The three political parties most committed to democracy—the Social Democrats, the Center Party (a largely Catholic-oriented organization), and the middle-class German Democratic Party—together captured more than 75 percent of the vote in 1919. A fourth party, backed by business circles, soon joined their ranks. Leaders of these parties formed a succession of coalition governments, but their common commitment to democracy could not overcome their differences on a host of issues, from economic policy to foreign policy. Conflicts between the representatives of business and labor were particularly intense. To complicate things, all four parties were each *internally* divided on how to deal with the problems besetting the country. Compromise was not a widely shared political value. Other democratic values associated with democracy, such as trustworthiness and tolerance, were also in short supply.

Weimar governments were characterized by instability, inefficiency, and ineffectiveness. Shaky coalition cabinets frequently fell apart and had to be painfully stitched together again, only to succumb to more bickering and breakups. Between 1919 and 1933, Germany had twenty-two governments. Many of them were *minority governments:* that is, they did not have the support of a majority of Reichstag delegates. As a consequence, they could be easily toppled in no-confidence votes posed by their adversaries. The ineffectiveness of these governing coalitions in addressing Germany's problems progressively eroded their electoral base. By 1924 the combined popular vote for the four main pro-democracy parties fell to 48.8 percent, a minority of the electorate. In the fall of 1932, in the last elections held before Hitler came to power, it plummeted to 35 percent.

The electoral fortunes of the antidemocratic parties rose apace. On the left, the German Communist Party increased its electoral support from only 2 percent in 1920 to nearly 17 percent in 1932. During this period its leadership passed into the hands of a pro-Soviet faction, dedicated to abolishing democracy and private enterprise in Germany and establishing a communist dictatorship modeled on the USSR.

On the right, most hardline conservatives who opposed democracy initially cast their support to the Nationalists (formally known as the German National People's Party). This party was essentially a throwback to the kaiser's era. It longed for the restoration of strong authoritarian rule and a powerful military establishment, while harboring bitter resentment of the Western powers for defeating Germany and imposing humiliating surrender terms on the German people. The Nationalists doubled their vote in the first six years of the Republic, peaking at 20.5 percent in late 1924. Their most revered figure, Field Marshal Paul von Hindenburg, was elected president of Germany in 1925 and handily reelected in 1932. At first, Hindenburg endeavored out of patriotic loyalty to keep Germany's new democratic system afloat. In his heart and soul, however, he remained a man of the old regime, a Prussian aristocrat devoted to the army. As the Depression took its devastating toll, Hindenburg used his emergency powers to govern the country by decree, ignoring the Reichstag and relying on a coterie of arch-conservative cronies.

It was **Adolf Hitler** and his *National Socialist German Workers Party*, or **Nazis** for short, who picked up a growing share of the right-wing nationalist vote over time. But the Nazis' support among the German people was by no means confined to old-guard conservatives. Hitler himself was neither a Prussian (he was born in Austria), nor an aristocrat (his background was lower middle class), nor a high-ranking officer (he was a corporal in World War I). But he nourished a fiery German nationalism, fueled by fierce hatred of Britain, France, and the United States and their democratic systems of government. He was also a rabid anti-Semite. Driven by demonic energy and endowed with spellbinding oratorical skills, Hitler built up the Nazi party from obscurity to mass popularity in only a few years. Starting with just 3 percent of the vote in 1924, the Nazis capitalized on the widespread misery generated by the Depression and captured more than 37 percent in the summer of 1932, by far the highest vote ever won by any party in the Weimar Republic.

Electoral support for the Nazis came from virtually every corner of German society. The upper crust, the sizable middle classes, and even a substantial minority of workers (about 25 percent) gave the Nazis their vote. The Nazis won about a third of the urban vote and did even better in rural areas. They were very popular among older voters and had a growing following among Germany's youth. And despite their glorification of violence, they ultimately attracted more female voters than male voters.[9] Hitler's inflammatory oratory combined with the most well-organized election campaign machine in Germany to make the Nazis the most successful catch-all party in the Weimar Republic. (A *catch-all party* is one that seeks to win as many votes as it can rather than concentrating its appeal on a particular segment of the electorate. See chapter 11.) Unlike most catch-all parties, however, the Nazis were not friends of democracy but its vehement opponents. They took skillful advantage of the Weimar Republic's democratic institutions to destroy democracy itself. They also built up their own uniformed militia, numbering 400,000 by 1932, to beat up political rivals and threaten the Republic with a potential coup d'état.

In the summer of 1932, more than half of Germany's voters (51.6 percent) voted for either the Nazis or the Communists, the two most stridently antidemocratic parties in the country. Having few options left, President Hindenburg named Hitler chancellor of Germany in January 1933. The president and his entourage thought they could keep the upstart corporal under control, but Hitler proved more than their match. By the end of the year, democracy was essentially extinguished and Germany was in the grip of a totalitarian fascist dictatorship.[10]

### The Fascist Regime

As we indicated in our discussion of fascist ideology in chapter 13, the Nazi worldview was grounded in *hypernationalism* and *racism*. The German people (*Volk*) were conceived in crackpot anthropological terms as the "Aryan race" and "the master race," while non-Aryans—especially Jews and Slavs—were vilified as "subhumans." (Hitler's alliances with Mussolini's Italy and fascist Japan required the Nazis to mute their anti-Latin and anti-Asiatic bigotry for political reasons.) Shortly after the Nazis took power, German Jews, who represented only 0.9 percent of the population, were accused of ruining the country and subjected to strict limitations on their economic and educational activities. They were also compelled to suffer public harassment and indignities orchestrated by the regime. Gypsies, homosexuals, and the mentally retarded were also targeted for abuse. Once World War II began, these and other groups deemed genetically inferior were packed off to extermination camps and systematically slaughtered.

Nazi rule took the form of a *totalitarian dictatorship*. A single party, the Nazis, monopolized state power; all other parties were outlawed. Hitler exercised supreme personal authority over the party and the state. The Nazi party-state regulated almost every aspect of social life in Germany; its control was virtually total. The educational system, the arts, the media, scientific research, and other aspects of social and intellectual life all came under Nazi supervision.

The state also assumed responsibility for coordinating the economy, though private enterprise was allowed to exist. Nazi governmental authorities set up committees, called "corporations," in which state representatives would meet with leaders of the country's largest businesses as well as with individuals handpicked by the regime to "represent" farmers, workers, and other segments of the economy. This system, known as *state corporatism*, enabled the Nazi party-state to impose its priorities on the country's private entrepreneurs. Hitler and his adjutants were bent on war, so their highest economic priority was to build up a vast military machine, a goal they succeeded in accomplishing in violation of the provisions of the 1919 Versailles Peace Treaty that placed strict limits on Germany's military capacity. State corporatism also enabled the regime to regulate the labor force. All trade unions and other organizations representing workers or farmers were abolished except for those run by the Nazis. Taken together, these characteristics of fascist rule made Nazi totalitarianism considerably more repressive and intrusive than the kaiser's authoritarian regime had been.

Another defining feature of German fascism was *mass mobilization*. Right from their earliest days as a political party in the Weimar Republic, the Nazis under Hitler's firm direction were determined to cultivate broad popularity. They devoted considerable attention to propaganda, using every means at their disposal—marches, rallies, posters, fliers, party newspapers, radio, and film—to drum up mass support. Once they took over the German state, their control over the media and schools permitted them to intensify these propaganda efforts enormously. In addition, the Nazis created a host of organizations—youth organizations, war veterans groups, and the like—to instill their ideas in the population.

Prior to the dark days of World War II, the Nazis enjoyed considerable popular support within Germany. (They were also widely popular in Austria, which Germany annexed in 1938.) The Nazis' well-orchestrated propaganda efforts were not solely responsible for this success. By brazenly flouting the Versailles Treaty, Hitler restored pride to millions of

Germans seething with rancor from their wartime defeat and postwar humiliation. In addition, the Nazi government put a decisive end to the political instability and social chaos of the Weimar Republic. While the Republic's supporters were appalled at the demise of democracy, millions of other Germans were gladly ready to give up their democratic liberties in exchange for political and social tranquillity. Given a choice between freedom and order, millions preferred order. The longing for a strong state and dutiful obedience to official authority were integral elements of German political culture at that time.[11] The Nazis appealed to these attitudes. In elections held in March 1933, shortly after Hitler was named chancellor and under conditions marked by Nazi suppression of opposing parties, the Nazis won 44 percent of the vote: not a majority, but still a substantial figure.

Perhaps most important, the Nazis achieved popularity by arresting Germany's economic slide. With tight control over the state budget, they rapidly addressed the unemployment problem by hiring people for public works projects and for service in the military or in Nazi party organizations. Orders for military matériel and other equipment reinvigorated German industry and kept factories humming, creating jobs for workers and managers. Inflation was brought under control. The Nazis also introduced a series of welfare measures to assist the most vulnerable parts of the population. The Nazi economy represented a kind of militarized Keynesian welfare state: the state stimulated growth and soaked up unemployment by spending large sums of money in the economy (in accordance with Keynes's prescriptions), and much of this money was spent for military purposes (in accordance with Nazi priorities). The years 1936–39 were perhaps the best years the German economy had ever seen up to that point.

Finally, the Nazis gained popularity by engineering a social revolution. Germany's old political elites, heavily populated with aristocrats and the scions of distinguished families, were summarily pushed aside by the Nazis to make way for less pedigreed Germans. The Nazi leaders were overwhelmingly from the middle classes, especially the lower middle class. Once ensconced in power, they opened up positions in the swelling party and state bureaucracies as well as in the army, the educational system, and other institutions to people like themselves.[12]

It was World War II that ultimately destroyed Hitler's "thousand-year Reich," devastating the German economy and inflicting misery on the population. Initiated with Germany's invasion of Poland on September 1, 1939, the war delivered control over virtually all of continental Europe to Hitler and Mussolini before the Nazi military juggernaut was finally vanquished in 1945 by the combined efforts of the United States, the USSR, Britain, and Free France. (As Japan's ally, Germany had declared war on the United States after Pearl Harbor in 1941.) More than 50 million lives were lost in the European theater of the conflict; tens of millions more were uprooted. At the end of the war Germany itself was dismembered: the Soviet Union annexed part of its territory and gave other parts to Poland and Czechoslovakia. The remaining area was then divided among the four victorious allies into Occupation zones, which in 1949 were consolidated into the two separate German states.[13]

As Germans nervously entered the postwar era, uncertain of their political fate, they could look back on the first half of the twentieth century as a succession of catastrophes. Their traumatic experiences could not help but have a powerful impact on their postwar attitudes. Two world wars imprinted an instinctive pacifism on millions of Germans, along with a reluctance on the part of many of them to engage in any display of nationalist sentiment. The tribulations of the Weimar Republic, constituting a paradigm of a failed democracy, left many Germans with a lasting fear of inflation and unemployment, along with an object lesson in what happens when political leaders refuse to compromise their differences. As a consequence, political culture in postwar Germany—particularly in democratic West Germany—was marked by antimilitarism, an embarrassed reticence about patriotism, a strong aversion to economic instability, and a prevailing inclination to political consensus and compromise. Moreover, until the 1960s most Germans wanted little to do with politics; they focused on their jobs and families, leaving political matters in the hands of their new democratic leaders. These attitudes profoundly shaped the development of the Federal Republic.

## DEMOCRACY IN THE FEDERAL REPUBLIC OF GERMANY

### The Formation of Parties

As American, British, and French authorities settled into their respective Occupation zones in 1945, their first task was to lay the foundations for democracy in a country that had just experienced twelve years of Nazi dictatorship. Many Nazi chieftains were put on trial for war crimes in Nuremberg, but thousands of lower-level bureaucrats, jurists, and others involved in the administration of the fascist regime had to be dealt with. Initially the Western occupiers embarked on a program of "de-Nazification," excluding those who had taken part in the Nazi system from the new governmental organs that were being created. This wholesale dismissal of everyone even remotely connected with the fascist government soon proved impracticable, however; there were not enough untainted administrators or judges to fill the positions that needed to be filled in the new administrative system. As a consequence, for several decades the West German bureaucracy and court system included many former Nazi Party members or sympathizers. Fortunately, the vast majority of them adjusted their actions to the new democratic order imposed on them by the victorious Western powers.

Of course, the highest levels of political authority would determine the future of German democracy. It was therefore imperative to set up an effective system of competitive, pro-democracy political parties. With some notable exceptions, Germany's liberals were largely discredited, as their principal leaders had cast their lot with Hitler or antidemocratic nationalists at the end of the Weimar Republic. A new liberal party, the **Free Democratic Party** (Freie demokratische partei, or **FDP**), was formed in 1948 under leaders thoroughly committed to democracy. Though small, this party—also known as the "liberals"—has played a critical role in the Federal Republic down to the present day.

The leadership of the Social Democratic Party of Germany was less corrupted by capitulation to fascism. Several of its most prominent figures spent a large part of the Nazi period in prisons or concentration camps; others had fled the country. At the end of the war, *Kurt Schumacher* emerged from imprisonment and took over the reins of the SPD hierarchy. Schumacher wanted both economic socialism and ballot-box democracy. He believed that a middle path had to be found between American-style capitalism and Soviet-style dictatorship. Though his party later abandoned his socialist economic doctrines, Schumacher helped reestablish the SPD as one of German democracy's staunchest supporters.[14]

During the Weimar Republic, two parties appealing mainly to Catholic voters had provided relatively consistent support for democracy: the Center Party and its Bavarian affiliate, the Bavarian People's Party. After the war, two new parties were established that directed their appeal to West Germany's Catholics and Protestants. The two confessions had roughly equal shares of the population. After experiencing the brutality of fascism and war, many Germans were ready to support parties that subscribed in a general way to such Christian principles as fellowship and reconciliation. One of these new parties, the **Christian Democratic Union** (Christlich-demokratische Union, or **CDU**), set up operations everywhere in West Germany except Bavaria, the largest of West Germany's constituent states. *Konrad Adenauer*, a respected Center Party politician who had served as mayor of Cologne from 1917 until the Nazi takeover in 1933, came out of retirement to head the CDU.

Bavaria, with its state capital in Munich, had a largely Catholic population. It proudly guarded its dialects, its traditional modes of dress, and other distinctly German cultural traditions along with a vibrant sense of independence. (Fittingly, a popular song about Bavaria is sung to the tune of "Deep in the Heart of Texas.") Bavarian politicians wanted to set up their own wing of the newly founded Christian Democratic movement, the **Christian Social Union** (Christlich-soziale Union, or **CSU**). The two parties have generally cooperated as one party and are usually referred to as the "CDU/CSU." The CSU tends to be more conservative than the CDU, however, and rivalries between their leaders occasionally produce frictions. Unless otherwise specified, the label *Christian Democrats* refers to the CDU and CSU together. Together with other like-minded parties in Europe, Germany's CDU and CSU are part of a large "party family" of European Christian Democratic and moderate conservative parties.

Other parties also came to the fore in the first years after Germany's defeat, including a Communist Party, but these three—the Christian Democrats, the Social Democrats, and the Free Democrats—were to dominate politics in the Federal Republic right up to the late 1990s. The Christian Democrats and Social Democrats became *catch-all parties* that reach out to a broad base that includes working-class voters, entrepreneurs, educators, and Germany's large middle class. So wide is their appeal that they are known in Germany as the *people's parties (Volksparteien).* The Free Democrats, the Alliance 90/Greens, and the Left Party tend to have a narrower appeal. The Free Democrats are centrists who position themselves in between the Social Democrats to their immediate left and the Christian Democrats to their immediate left. They mainly attract elements of the business community and the middle class through their neo-liberal economic policies. Though small, with a constituency ranging from 7 to 12 percent of the electorate, the FDP has been a coalition partner of either the Christian Democrats or Social Democrats in almost every government formed at the national level between 1949 and 1998. (The lone exception was the first Grand Coalition government of 1966–69, which we will discuss shortly.) The Alliance 90/Greens grouping tends to focus on environmental issues, and many of their adherents are pacifists who reject the use of force by Germany's military. This party formed a coalition government with the Social Democrats between 1998 and 2005. The Left Party reaches out to working-class voters and those displaced by unemployment and other social problems, particularly those occurring in the former communist East Germany, where the Left Party has its base. Together these five party groupings form what we call a *few-party system.* As indicated in chapter 10, a few-party system has between three and five parties that play a significant role in national politics.

Each of the main party groupings in Germany is identified with a color. The Christian Democrats are black, the Social Democrats and the Left Party are red, the Free Democrats are yellow, and so on. Thus the SPD–Alliance 90/Greens government was called the "red-green coalition."

## The Basic Law and the Federal Republic of Germany's Institutional Framework

As World War II came to a close in 1944 and 1945, the allies in the anti-Hitler coalition had no clear notion of what to do with Germany after the war other than to impose their own control over it. Although the United States, Britain, France, and the Soviet Union eventually agreed on the demarcation of their respective Occupation zones (along with the division of Berlin, a special case), it became increasingly apparent by 1947 that the Soviet Union and the three Western powers were at loggerheads over a wide range of issues in the postwar world.

The ideological clash between Western democracy and market economics, on the one hand, and Moscow's Communist Party dictatorship and centrally planned economy, on the other, was unresolvable. Harsh ideological rhetoric inflamed the atmosphere. The Soviet government's imposition of communist regimes on the countries of Central and Eastern Europe that were under the control of the Soviet army created growing consternation in the West, which had hoped for democracy in Poland, Hungary, Czechoslovakia, and other nations in the region. Kremlin threats against Iran, Turkey, and other countries sparked Western resolve to defend them against a possible Soviet takeover or invasion. As tensions mounted, it became apparent that there could be no agreement on creating a single, unified German government. No formal peace treaty could be signed between the victors of World War II and the vanquished, similar to the Versailles Peace Treaty that had concluded World War I, because there was no agreement on which German government would sign it. Germany was doomed to being divided between the powers that had defeated it.

In 1948 the three Western Occupation governments took a major step toward the creation of a separate West German state by establishing a common currency for all three of their zones. The Soviets retaliated by blockading the land passages between West Germany and West Berlin, provoking the West to respond with the Berlin Airlift. Flying over the blockaded land routes in East Germany, U.S., British, and French planes brought food and other vital provisions to West Berlin until Stalin called off the blockade in 1949. In the midst of the Berlin crisis, the Western powers in July 1948 ordered the German authorities under their control to convene an assembly to write a constitution for a West German government. Most Germans were reluctant to take this step, fearing that a separate constitution for West Germany would dash all hopes of eventually reestablishing a single German state with the borders it had in 1937, before Hitler annexed Austria and parts of Czechoslovakia.

Bowing to Allied pressures, the elected leaders of the various regions into which West Germany was divided at the time selected the members of the constitutional assembly. Thus the body that drafted the Federal Republic's founding document was not elected directly by the people (unlike the assembly that convened in Weimar in 1919). After nine months of deliberation, the assembled delegates produced a document they called a **"Basic Law"** *(Grundgesetz)*. They avoided the term *constitution (Verfassung)* on the grounds that only a reunited Germany could have a permanent constitution. The Basic Law was meant to be temporary, pending reunification. Contrary to the preferences of the Occupation authorities, the Germans did not submit the Basic Law to the West German voters for their approval, again on the grounds that only a reunited German people could vote to legitimize its most important governing instrument. Article 146 stipulated that the Basic Law would expire upon the unification of the Germans and their approval of a "constitution" in a free vote. Rather than submit the Basic Law to only part of the German people in a referendum, its framers secured its ratification by members of the various regional legislatures.

On May 23, 1949, the Basic Law went into effect and the **Federal Republic of Germany** was formally proclaimed in the Western Occupation zones. To this day the Basic Law has never been submitted to the voters for their approval. Consequently, some Germans have called for its replacement by a full-fledged constitution that would gain its legitimacy in a national referendum.

In another sign that the Basic Law was meant to be temporary, its framers established Bonn as the Federal Republic's capital. The choice of this small town instead of a large city like Frankfurt or Munich reflected their hope that Germany's division would not last very long and that, sooner or later, Berlin would once again stand proudly as the capital of a large, united Germany. Even the buildings selected to house important institutions like the parliament and the chancellor's office were modest quarters that could be easily left behind when the time came to move to Berlin. In addition, the Federal Republic proclaimed the Basic Law's validity for *all* Germans, including those in communist East Germany and other parts of former German territory. West Germany's main political parties were all in agreement that the Soviet-imposed communist dictatorship in East Germany was completely illegitimate and that eventual reunification should be a national goal.

## A Federal System

The Basic Law established the Federal Republic as a federal system. *Federalism* is a political system that combines a meaningful central government with a multiplicity of regional or local governments that have specific real powers. (The United States is an example.) After the devastating fascist experience, the Allied Occupation powers and most Germans themselves had no desire to recreate a powerful central government.

The original Basic Law established eleven **Laender** (lender), a term rendered in English as **"states"** (as in "The United States has fifty states."). Three of these states are actually large cities (Berlin, Hamburg, and Bremen). Each *Land* (state) has its own legislature, typically known as the *Landtag* (State Diet), elected every four or five years by the state's voters. The elections are usually staggered; rarely do more than two of them occur on the same day, with some occurring in different years.

All these state legislatures are unicameral. The majority party (or parties) of each newly elected legislature elects a state government, whose chief usually bears the title *minister-president (Ministerpraesident)*. (The three city-states have different titles for their respective legislatures, governments, and heads of government. Berlin's legislature, for example, is called the House of Delegates, its government is the Senate, and its head of government is the governing mayor.) Each state's head of government is roughly analogous to an American governor, though they are elected differently and the extent of their legal powers differs. The position of head of government at the state level is an important one in German politics, at times serving as a stepping-stone to higher office. Just as several U.S. presidents like George W. Bush, Bill Clinton, Ronald Reagan, and Jimmy Carter were previously governors, several German chancellors and candidates for that position once served as minister-presidents of individual German states. Unlike American governors, however, most state leaders in Germany serve simultaneously as members of the German federal legislature, thus participating in national government. Presidents Carter, Reagan, Clinton, and G. W. Bush had never held national office before assuming the presidency.

From the very beginning, the Basic Law conferred extensive powers on each state to regulate education, the administration of justice, the police, and the mass media, including radio and television, within its territory. This decentralization of administrative authority, though effective in providing checks on the power of a potentially intrusive central state, can sometimes prove ineffective when it comes to coordinating governmental activities. Events surrounding the events of September 11, 2001, provide a striking illustration. Three of the four pilots who commandeered the planes hijacked in the United States on that tragic day had previously lived in Hamburg as students and underground al Qaeda operatives. Their activities attracted little notice, in part because Germany's domestic intelligence agency, the Office for the Protection of the Constitution, did not have a central office but was organized on a federal basis, with a local bureau in each of the *Laender*. Many of these individual bureaus were underfunded and lacked expertise in tracking foreign terrorists.[15]

In constitutional law, the legal powers accorded the regional subunits of a federal system are known as "reserved powers," i.e., they are *reserved* to the subunits. In addition to having these considerable reserved powers, the states were given the right to supervise the administration of *federal* laws—laws enacted by the Federal Republic's national legislature and central government—within their respective jurisdictions. Since virtually every law touching on domestic affairs in Germany has an administrative component, the states have their hand in practically every aspect of government administration. Most taxes imposed by the federal government, for instance, are actually collected by the states. Though the fifty states in the United States also have extensive reserved powers, they do not have such sweeping rights to administer federal laws and regulations as their German counterparts do.

The only major policy areas where the states play little or no role concern Germany's international dealings, such as foreign and defense policy. Even in foreign affairs, however, the states are expanding the scope of their authority. In 1992 the Basic Law was amended to give the states a major role in shaping the German government's policies toward the European Union. Fearing that the process of European unification might give EU authorities in Brussels excessive powers to interfere in their internal state affairs (for example, by imposing regulations on their broadcast media), the *Laender* won the right to veto any agreement the German government might conclude with the European Union that intrudes on their local powers.

With the collapse of the communist government of the German Democratic Republic, East Germany was united with the rest of the Federal Republic in 1990 on the basis of a provision in the Basic Law that permitted the incorporation of new states into the FRG. After the 1990 elections in East Germany demonstrated overwhelming popular support for unification, the GDR was reorganized into five states. These five states then entered the Federal Republic in a procedure roughly similar to the way various territories once "joined the union" of the United States of America. Some political forces in both eastern and western Germany objected to this procedure, arguing that Article 146 of the Basic Law mandates a new German constitution and a national referendum on it when unification takes place. Former anticommunist East German dissidents joined with western German Greens and Social Democrats in demanding a new constitution, but their proposals were blocked by their opponents, the Christian Democrats, in the mid 1990s.

*The Federal Republic now consists of sixteen states (Laender).* The former East Germany is often referred to as "the five new states." Local governments in Germany at the county and municipal levels within these states are heavily dependent on money transferred to them from the federal and state budgets.[16]

### The Bundesrat

Perhaps the most striking evidence of the political power of Germany's sixteen states is the special role they play in constituting ***the upper house of the***

***Federal Republic's national parliament.*** This house is known as the ***Federal Council***, or **Bundesrat**.

The Bundesrat directly represents the states. It is chosen *by the state governments*. Unlike the U.S. Senate, its members are *not* directly elected by the people of each state. What this means in practice is that the *majority party (or parties) within each state legislature* selects the state's representatives in the Bundesrat (because it is this legislative majority that forms the state government). Thus, if the Christian Democrats have the majority of seats in the state legislature of Hessen, they will establish Hessen's government and pick its minister-president. That government will in turn send Christian Democrats to represent Hessen in the Bundesrat. In fact, each state's head of government typically serves as a member of its Bundesrat delegation, along with other ministers in the state government. If the Social Democrats and Greens have a combined majority of seats in Hamburg, they will form a coalition government to govern this large city-state, and their government will select people of its own choosing to represent Hamburg in the Bundesrat. The opposition parties in these state legislatures have no role in selecting their state's Bundesrat deputies.

*Each Bundesrat member votes on instructions from his or her state government* and has no personal freedom in deciding how to vote in that chamber. Bundesrat deputies thus have vastly less independence than do U.S. senators, who may vote as they see fit.

Though each state is represented, the Bundesrat's voting procedures are not based on "one state, one vote." Because Germany's sixteen states come in different sizes, the Bundesrat uses a *weighted voting* procedure. The largest states, with a population of more than 7 million each, are each entitled to six votes in the Bundesrat. A state with between 6 and 7 million inhabitants is entitled to five Bundesrat votes; those with between 2 and 6 million people are entitled to four votes; all the rest are entitled to three votes each. Thus the sixteen states that comprise the Bundesrat together dispose of a total of sixty-nine votes, distributed proportionately by size. If the four largest states, with six votes each, choose to vote together, their twenty-four votes are enough to block the passage of any bill requiring a two-thirds majority, such as a proposed constitutional amendment. In these circumstances the four largest states can use their weighted votes to block action favored by the twelve smaller states. Even so, the Bundesrat's malapportionment favors the smaller states, which have more representation per person than the largest states have.

Each state may send as many representatives to the Bundesrat as it has votes; but each state deputation *must vote together as a bloc*. Thus, if Bavaria sends six deputies to the Bundesrat, all six must vote in unison as instructed by the Bavarian state government. These voting members of a state's Bundesrat delegation tend to be ministers in the state's government (cabinet). When Bundesrat sessions mainly involve committee work and no votes are taken, the state governments usually delegate civil servants from the state's bureaucracy to take their place on the committees. Such people tend to be technical experts on policy issues such as budgetary matters, education, the environment, and so on. Sometimes a state's Bundesrat delegation will be instructed not to vote at all. If the state government is a coalition between two parties (say, the Social Democrats and the Christian Democrats) and the partners cannot agree on certain pieces of legislation that come up for a vote in the Bundesrat, they may instruct their delegation in that body to abstain from voting. But abstentions count as nay votes because Bundesrat decisions require a majority of all the votes (at least 35 out of the 69 votes).

Table 18.1 lists Germany's sixteen states, along with their populations and state capitals, the number of votes they are entitled to in the Bundesrat, the year of their most recent election, the parties that governed them in December 2006, and the names of their respective minister-presidents at that time.

What can the Bundesrat do? First of all, the national government must submit its bills to the Bundesrat first and to the Bundestag subsequently. The Basic Law gives the upper house a *veto power* over all bills whose passage into law would require the state governments to implement their provisions. In the formative years of the Federal Republic, it was assumed that very few bills of this type would come up. But nowadays, almost two-thirds of all federal legislation requires the Bundesrat's approval, including tax measures, educational reforms, environmental laws, the regulation of cable television, and the like. If a bill is specifically designated as one that

**TABLE 18.1**

**Germany's Sixteen States**

| State (*Land*) | Population (Millions, 2004) | State Capital | Bundesrat Votes | Last Elections | Government (December 2006) | Head of Government |
|---|---|---|---|---|---|---|
| North Rhine–Westphalia | 18.1 | Duesseldorf | 6 | 2005 | CDU, FDP | Ruettgers (CDU) |
| Bavaria | 12.5 | Munich | 6 | 2003 | CSU | Stoiber (CSU) |
| Baden-Wuerttemberg | 10.7 | Stuttgart | 6 | 2006 | CDU, FDP | Oettinger (CDU) |
| Lower Saxony | 8.1 | Hanover | 6 | 2003 | CDU, FDP | Wulff (CDU) |
| Hessen | 6.1 | Wiesbaden | 5 | 2003 | CDU | Koch (CDU) |
| Saxony[a] | 4.3 | Dresden | 4 | 2004 | CDU, SPD | Milbrandt (CDU) |
| Rhineland-Palatinate | 4.1 | Mainz | 4 | 2006 | SPD | Beck (SPD) |
| Berlin | 3.4 | Berlin | 4 | 2006 | SPD, Left | Wowereit (SPD) |
| Schleswig-Holstein | 2.8 | Kiel | 4 | 2005 | CDU, SPD | Carstensen (CDU) |
| Brandenburg[a] | 2.6 | Potsdam | 4 | 2004 | SPD, CDU | Platzeck (SPD) |
| Saxony-Anhalt[a] | 2.5 | Magdeburg | 4 | 2006 | CDU, SPD | Boehmer (CDU) |
| Thuringia[a] | 2.4 | Erfurt | 4 | 2004 | CDU | Althaus (CDU) |
| Hamburg | 1.7 | Hamburg | 3 | 2004 | CDU | von Beust (CDU) |
| Mecklenburg–West Pomerania[a] | 1.7 | Schwerin | 3 | 2006 | SPD, CDU | Ringstorff (SPD) |
| Saar (or Saarland) | 1.1 | Saarbruecken | 3 | 2004 | CDU | Mueller (CDU) |
| Bremen | 0.7 | Bremen | 3 | 2003 | SPD, CDU | Scherf (SPD) |

[a]Formerly part of communist East Germany.

*requires* Bundesrat approval, the Bundesrat can veto it by majority vote even if the bill has already passed the lower house, the Bundestag.

This legislative power has major political significance, as the government of Chancellor Gerhard Schroeder found out. In state legislative elections held from the time Schroeder came to power in 1998 up to the Bundestag elections of 2005, the Christian Democrats captured or retained a role in thirteen state governments, giving them a majority of votes in the Bundesrat. As a result, Schroeder was forced to shape many of his government's policies with a view to their potential reception in an upper house dominated by his adversaries.

The Bundesrat also gets to vote on some bills that do not directly affect state governments, such as foreign or defense policy. On these issues, a negative Bundesrat vote can be overridden by a vote in the Bundestag. Thus the Bundesrat's approval is not required on all legislation. (In the United States, by contrast, the Senate's approval is required for all legislation.) Still, the Bundesrat can block even these kinds of bills. If the Bundesrat *by a two-thirds majority* rejects a bill that does not require its approval, the Bundestag can pass it only with a two-thirds majority of its own. If it fails to do so, the bill is dead.

The Bundesrat also exercises its influence in committees where draft legislation is often amended before it goes up for a final vote. In addition, Bundesrat members may initiate legislation (always acting on their state government's instructions, to be sure). They even have a right to participate and be heard in plenary sessions of the lower house, the Bundestag, as well as in some Bundestag committees. And each of the states has one representative on the powerful bicameral Mediation Committee, which consists of sixteen Bundesrat and sixteen Bundestag members who may be called upon to amend legislation so that it can pass both houses. In sum, the Bundesrat gives Germany's sixteen state governments a direct role in the national parliament that the fifty state governments in the United States do not possess. It forces the central government in Berlin to pay close attention to the wishes of each state's elected officials, injecting a considerable measure of decentralization into Germany's federal system. So important are the states in Germany's political decision-making process that one student of German affairs has called the Federal Republic's central government a "semi-sovereign state," in large measure because it must constantly share power with the *Laender*.[17]

Sometimes, however, the Bundesrat's ability to kill legislation passed by the lower house of the legislature, the Bundestag, can produce gridlock. When one house is largely controlled by the Social Democrats and the other house is controlled by the Christian Democrats, resulting in a German version of divided government, these rival parties must compromise their differences for legislation to be enacted. At times it can be very difficult—or downright impossible—to find acceptable compromises. With politicians on both sides of the political divide growing increasingly frustrated with this situation, in 2003 a committee consisting of members of both houses of the legislature was formed with the task of recommending changes in Germany's federal structure.

For all its influence, the Bundesrat takes a back seat to the Bundestag when it comes to forming the German government and holding it accountable to the voters' elected representatives. The Bundestag is really the main locus of parliamentary action in the Federal Republic.

### The Bundestag

The ***Bundestag—or Federal Diet—is the lower house of the national legislature.*** In most respects it functions much like Britain's House of Commons or the lower house in other parliamentary systems. Although Germany has a federal structure, its system of national government is a variant of British-style *parliamentary government*. That is, (1) *the people elect the lower house of the legislature,* and (2) *the lower house holds the government accountable* and retains the right to vote the government out of office. (See chapter 8.)

**The Bundestag's Electoral System** Bundestag elections take place at least every four years. Anticipated elections, however, may be called before the expiration of the full four-year term. Members of the Bundestag are elected through a combination of the two main systems for electing a legislature: the single-member-district (SMD) system and proportional representation (PR). *Half the members are elected by SMD, the other half by PR.* Once all the votes are counted, a formula is used to ensure that the final distribution of Bundestag seats approximately resembles proportional representation. This dual system is called a *mixed-member* electoral system, or a *personalized proportional* system. The German variant of this system is a bit complicated, but an understanding of its main features is essential to understanding how political power is acquired in the Federal Republic.

To begin with, a minimum number of Bundestag seats is established prior to the elections. In 1998 that figure was set at 656 seats; in 2002 and 2005 it was reduced to 598.

Half the seats (299 in 2005) are elected by the single-member-district method and are called "direct mandates." For this part of the election, Germany is divided into 299 electoral districts (*Wahlkreisen*), and one person is elected to represent each district in the Bundestag. The remaining half of the Bundestag is elected through a variant of proportional representation. Voters get a paper ballot with two columns (see figure 18.1); each voter gets two votes. The left column lists the *individual candidates* running in the single-member election in the voter's district; they are listed by name and party affiliation. The right column lists the *parties* that are running in the voter's district. Next to each party are the names of some of its most prominent leaders in the voter's home state. In the "first vote," the voter places a mark next to one of the individual candidates in the left column. In the "second vote," the voter marks a party in the right column.

A growing number of German voters nowadays split their vote. In 1998, for example, one-third of the voters who voted for the Greens as a *party* in the second column voted for a Social Democrat *candidate* in the first column. The voters who engaged in this kind of ticket splitting hoped to provide the two parties with enough seats in the Bundestag to form an SPD-Green coalition government. In the same year, 55 percent of those who voted for the Free Democrats in the second column voted for a Christian Democrat in the first column, hoping to elect a Christian Democrat–Free Democrat coalition government. Millions of Germans engaged in such kinds of "strategic voting" in 2002 and 2005 as well.

Each of the sixteen states (*Laender*) is allotted a certain number of delegates it may send to the Bundestag, based on its population. The 299 single-member districts are distributed among the states on a population basis. In 2005, each of these districts averaged out nationally to about 249,000

**Stimmzettel**

für die Wahl zum Deutschen Bundestag im Wahlkreis 81 Berlin - Charlottenburg-Wilmersdorf
am 22. September 2002

**hier 1 Stimme**
für die Wahl
**eines/einer Wahlkreisabgeordneten**

**Erststimme**

| |  |  | |
|---|---|---|---|
| 1 | **Merkel,** Petra-Eveline<br>Kaufm. Angestellte<br>Transvaalstr. 6<br>13351 Berlin | **SPD**<br>Sozialdemokratische Partei Deutschlands | ◯ |
| 2 | **Helias,** Siegfried<br>MdB, Friseurmeister<br>Britzer Damm 77<br>12347 Berlin | **CDU**<br>Christlich Demokratische Union Deutschlands | ◯ |
| 3 | **Rottka,** Natalie<br>Journalistin<br>Krumme Str. 64<br>10627 Berlin | **PDS**<br>Partei des Demokratischen Sozialismus | ◯ |
| 4 | **Eichstädt-Bohlig,** Franziska<br>MdB, Dipl.-Ing., Architektin<br>Droysenstr. 6<br>10629 Berlin | **GRÜNE**<br>BÜNDNIS 90 / DIE GRÜNEN | ◯ |
| 5 | **Dr. Rexrodt,** Günter<br>Dipl.-Kaufmann<br>Chausseestr. 99<br>10115 Berlin | **FDP**<br>Freie Demokratische Partei | ◯ |
| | | | |
| 7 | **Peuker,** Dieter<br>Kaufmann<br>Galvanistr. 14<br>10587 Berlin | **GRAUE**<br>DIE GRAUEN - Graue Panther | ◯ |
| | | | |
| | | | |
| | | | |
| 11 | **Köster,** Heinrich<br>Geschäftsführer<br>Duisburger Str. 19<br>10707 Berlin | **BüSo**<br>Bürgerrechtsbewegung Solidarität | ◯ |

**hier 1 Stimme**
für die Wahl
**einer Landesliste (Partei)**
- maßgebende Stimme für die Verteilung der Sitze insgesamt auf die einzelnen Parteien -

**Zweitstimme**

| |  |  | |
|---|---|---|---|
| ◯ | **SPD** | **Sozialdemokratische Partei Deutschlands**<br>Wolfgang Thierse, Dr. Christine Bergmann, Dr. Ditmar Staffelt, Petra-Eveline Merkel, Andreas Matthae | 1 |
| ◯ | **CDU** | **Christlich Demokratische Union Deutschlands**<br>Günter Nooke, Verena Butalikakis, Roland Gewalt, Peter Rzepka, Siegfried Helias | 2 |
| ◯ | **PDS** | **Partei des Demokratischen Sozialismus**<br>Petra Pau, Dr. Bärbel Grygier, Dr. Gesine Lötzsch, Sandra Brunner, Evrim Baba | 3 |
| ◯ | **GRÜNE** | **BÜNDNIS 90 / DIE GRÜNEN**<br>Renate Künast, Werner Schulz, Franziska Eichstädt-Bohlig, Michael Cramer, Anja Schillhaneck | 4 |
| ◯ | **FDP** | **Freie Demokratische Partei**<br>Dr. Günter Rexrodt, Markus Löning, Hellmut Königshaus, Gabriele Heise, Dr. Hans-Peter Schlaudt | 5 |
| ◯ | **REP** | **DIE REPUBLIKANER**<br>Dr. Konrad Voigt, Wolfgang Seifert, Thomas Weisbrich, Marieluise Jeschke, Reinhard Haese | 6 |
| ◯ | **GRAUE** | **DIE GRAUEN - Graue Panther**<br>Dieter Peuker, Karl-Heinz Augustin, Thorsten Hartje, Helga Nönnig, Armin Behrmann | 7 |
| ◯ | **NPD** | **Nationaldemokratische Partei Deutschlands**<br>Klaus Beier, Albrecht Reither, Andrea Lammok, Horst Sinning, Mike Ducherow | 8 |
| ◯ | **DIE FRAUEN** | **Feministische Partei DIE FRAUEN**<br>Helga Trachsel, Elke Bleich, Ilona Braune, Eva Bornemann | 9 |
| ◯ | **ödp** | **Ökologisch-Demokratische Partei**<br>Kerstin Heinrich, Dr. Eva Börsch-Supan, Dr. Larissa Dloczik, Andreas Schinzel, Heiner Fauteck | 10 |
| ◯ | **BüSo** | **Bürgerrechtsbewegung Solidarität**<br>Helga Zepp-LaRouche, Heiko Ziemann, Monika Hahn, Tombolo Wa Kadima Mukengechay, Ulrike Lillge | 11 |
| ◯ | **HP** | **Humanistische Partei**<br>Michael Steinbach, Johanna Krappmann, Benjamin-Christopher Krüger, Michael Daniel Winkler, Dirk Wanner | 12 |
| ◯ | **KPD** | **KOMMUNISTISCHE PARTEI DEUTSCHLANDS**<br>Werner Schleese, Günther Bandel, Alfred Fritz, Anny Wagner, Alfred Wagner | 13 |
| ◯ | **PBC** | **Partei Bibeltreuer Christen**<br>Klaus Lange, Matthias Gardain, Bernd Matthes, Bettina Lange, Dagmar Briegel | 14 |
| ◯ | **Schill** | **Partei Rechtsstaatlicher Offensive**<br>Prof. Dr. Lothar Staeck, Dr. Christian-Friedrich Eigler, Manfred Ehlert, Claas Weseloh, Valeska Jakubowski | 15 |

**FIGURE 18.1 German Sample Ballot**

*Source:* Statistical Office. "You Have 2 Votes": The left-hand column lists candidates by name for the single-member-district vote. The right-hand column lists parties for the proportional representation vote, along with the names of prominent party leaders.

inhabitants and 170,000 voters. North Rhine–Westphalia, Germany's most populous state, with 18 million inhabitants, sent 130 delegates to the Bundestag in 2005. Of these, 64 were elected directly in single-member districts, and the remaining 66 were elected in accordance with Germany's proportional representation rules. Bremen, a city-state with fewer than a million residents, sent 4 delegates to the Bundestag in 2005—2 elected directly in districts and 2 in the proportional representation vote for parties.

The ballots are counted in each state. Whoever gets the most votes in a single-member district wins that seat in the Bundestag. Angela Merkel, for example, won reelection to her single-member-district seat in Mecklenburg–West Pomerania in 2005. The remaining seats are apportioned *within each state* in accordance with a mathematical formula known as the Hare-Niemeyer system. As a general rule, a party that gets 40 percent of the second-column vote in a state that sends 100 delegates to the Bundestag should in principle get 40 of those delegates. If that party's candidates have won 30 single-member districts within the state in the first-column vote, then it is entitled to ten more Bundestag seats from the state. Who are those ten "second-column" people? They are drawn from each party's "party list" within the state; this list is also known as the party's "state list" (*Landesliste*). Prior to the elections, every party draws up a state list that consist mainly of candidates who are *not* running in the single-member-district contests. Each party rank-orders its candidates on the state list, with its most prominent leaders placed in the top positions. In 2005, Gerhard Schroeder was once again at the top of the SPD's state list in Lower Saxony.

The parties themselves, using their own internal procedures, decide who their candidates in the direct-mandate and party-list votes will be. (Some run on both states.) Unlike the United States, Germany does not have primary elections enabling the voters to choose party candidates prior to general elections. In the main parties, party members have an opportunity to participate in meetings and, in some cases, to vote for the party's candidates and influence party policy on current issues. The main parties also have rules that are intended to increase the number of women elected to the Bundestag. For example, about 40 percent of the Social Democratic candidates and half the Greens are women. Of the 614 Bundestag members elected in 2005, 31.8 percent (195) were women—one of the highest percentages in the world (see table 2.4).

Although the election procedures we have just described may seem complex enough, a couple of additional features of Germany's electoral laws can complicate things even more. As a result, the final election results may not be known until the last votes are counted, making for some white knuckles and queasy stomachs in the wee hours of election night.

One feature is Germany's *5 percent threshold:* a party must get at least 5 percent of the vote *nationwide* in order to get a share of Bundestag seats that is proportional to its share of the popular vote. The Federal Republic introduced the hurdle in the 1950s to prevent a proliferation of small parties in the legislature—a problem that plagued the Weimar Republic. In 2002, the Party of Democratic Socialism (PDS)—the offspring of East Germany's ruling communist party—failed to breach that barrier, winning only 4 percent of the national vote. However, two PDS candidates won direct-mandate victories in Berlin, giving the party two delegates in the Bundestag.[18] In 2005 six parties cleared the 5 percent hurdle, but twenty-four others did not.

One of the most unusual—and politically significant—features of Germany's electoral system is the so-called "overhang mandate" (*Ueberhangmandat*). To refer to the hypothetical example above, if a party wins 40 percent of the second-column popular vote in a state that sends 100 delegates to the Bundestag, then it is entitled in principle to 40 of those delegates (assuming that the party clears the 5 percent hurdle nationwide). But what happens if its candidates win more than 40 seats in that state's single-member-district (first-column) vote? What happens if it wins 45 SMD seats? The answer is that the party may keep those 45 Bundestag seats, and the size of the state's Bundestag delegation is enlarged by five "overhang" seats to 105 deputies. "Overhang mandates" are thus *additional Bundestag seats* that are created when a party wins a percentage of single-member-district seats in a particular state that exceeds its percentage of the popular vote for parties in that state. When this happens, the Bundestag itself is enlarged beyond the limit that was originally fixed before election day.

TABLE 18.2

**Bundestag Elections, September 2002 (Minimum 598 Seats, Increased to 603)**

Turnout: 79.1%

| Parties | Districts Won (1st vote) | % Vote Nationwide (2nd vote) | Final Number of Seats[a] | % of Seats |
|---|---|---|---|---|
| Social Democrats (SPD) | 171 | 38.5 | 251 | 41.6 |
| Christian Democrats (CDU/CSU) | 125 | 38.5 | 248 | 41.1 |
| Alliance 90/Greens | 1 | 8.6 | 55 | 9.1 |
| Free Democrats (FDP) | 0 | 7.4 | 47 | 7.8 |
| Party of Democratic Socialism (PDS) | 2 | 4.0 | 2 | 0.3 |
| Others | 0 | 3.0 | 0 | 0 |

[a]Seats won in first and second votes, plus overhang mandates.
*Source:* Federal Returning Officer, Federal Statistical Office, FRG.

TABLE 18.3

**Bundestag Elections, September 2005 (Minimum 598 Seats, Increased to 614)**

Turnout: 77.7%

| Parties | Districts Won (1st Vote) | % Vote Nationwide (2nd Vote) | Final Number of Seats[a] | % of Seats |
|---|---|---|---|---|
| Christian Democrats (CDU/CSU) | 150 | 35.2 | 226 | 36.8 |
| Social Democrats | 145 | 34.2 | 222 | 36.2 |
| Free Democrats (FDP) | 0 | 9.8 | 61 | 9.9 |
| Left Party | 3 | 8.7 | 54 | 8.8 |
| Alliance 90/Greens | 1 | 8.1 | 51 | 8.3 |
| Others | 0 | 3.8 | 0 | 0 |

[a]Seats won in first and second votes, plus overhang mandates.
*Sources:* www.bundestagsleiter.de; www.bundestag.de.

The precise number of overhang seats—and which parties get them—is practically impossible to predict; the final number cannot be tabulated until just about all the votes are counted. But overhang votes can be critical in determining who wins control of the Bundestag. In 1998, Schroeder's Social Democrats assumed power by winning 13 overhang seats. (The Bundestag was accordingly enlarged from its preelection target of 656 seats to 669. For the 1998 election results, see table 8.4.) On election night 2002, as 45 million ballots were being patiently counted by hand and television prognostications of the outcome fluctuated nervously, it was not until shortly after midnight that Germany knew how the election had turned out. In a cliffhanger, the SPD as a party had won only 6,027 more second-column votes than the Christian Democrats. But the Social Democrats won four overhang seats, enough to remain in power as coalition partners of the Greens. The CSU gained only one overhang seat. The Bundestag was therefore enlarged from 598 to 603 seats, with 302 members constituting the voting majority. With their 306 seats, the Social Democrats and the Greens could put together a slim majority. In 2005 there were 16 overhang votes: 9 went to the SPD, 7 to the CDU.

When all is said and done, Germany's complicated electoral system ultimately produces a distribution of Bundestag seats that amounts to approximate proportional representation for all the parties that surmount the 5 percent hurdle. The percentage of Bundestag seats that these parties obtain tends to be roughly equal to their respective shares of the popular vote nationwide (see tables 8.4, 18.2, and 18.3). By capturing the advantages of candidate recognition that comes with the single-member-district system, together with the fairness in party representation that accompanies proportional representation, Germany has sought to reap the benefits of both systems.

**Forming the Government** Once elections have taken place, the Bundestag's first order of business is to set up a government. The Basic Law authorizes the president of the Federal Republic, the country's ceremonial head of state, to formally propose someone to serve as **chancellor**, or ***head of government***. Like the queen of the United Kingdom, however, the German president has little choice but to designate the person whose party is in the strongest position in the Bundestag to form a government that will be backed by the majority of its members. (We'll have more to say about the presidency in the next section.) If one party holds an absolute majority of the seats, then it will be able to form a majoritarian government with no need to rely on coalition partners. Although majoritarian governments are the norm in Britain, in the Federal Republic there has never been one: every government since 1949 has been a coalition government. But unlike the Weimar Republic, which had a succession of weak *minority* coalition governments, the Federal Republic has enjoyed considerably more stability: all of its coalition governments have started out with the voting support of a majority of Bundestag deputies.

It is up to the parties and their top leaders to work out terms for a governing coalition. Following the 1998 elections, with the SPD holding a large plurality of seats in the new Bundestag (44.5 percent), President Roman Herzog, a Christian Democrat, called on Gerhard Schroeder to form a government. After several weeks of bargaining, the SPD came to terms with the Greens, resulting in Germany's first "red-green" coalition government at the national level. As we've seen, the same two parties reestablished their coalition government after the 2002 Bundestag elections. In 2005 the leaders of the Christian Democrats and the Social Democrats began negotiations on a Grand Coalition within days of the inconclusive Bundestag elections, essentially presenting President Horst Koehler (CDU) with a fait accompli as they reached agreement on a new government under Angela Merkel.

After the coalition partners have agreed to form a government, the Bundestag holds a formal vote for chancellor. Invariably this vote falls along straight party lines, with the coalition partners voting to ensure a majority for the new head of government and the minority parties asserting their opposition. After this *investiture*, the chancellor names the cabinet ministers, usually on the basis of a previous agreement between the coalition parties. The junior partner in most coalition governments is assigned the post of foreign minister, generally considered the second most prestigious position after the chancellor, and several other cabinet ministries as well. In 2005 Franz Muentefering, the SPD leader during the election campaign, took the post of vice chancellor in the Grand Coalition cabinet. Another SPD leader became foreign minister. Once the government is in place, the chancellor presents a formal "government declaration" (*Regierungserklaerung*) to the Bundestag, a policy address indicating the government's main priorities.

The size of the cabinet varies from one government to the next, ranging from as few as sixteen to as many as twenty or more. As noted earlier, the Grand Coalition cabinet created in 2005 had sixteen ministers, eight each for the Christian Democrats and Social Democrats.

One of the chief ways the Bundestag holds the government accountable is by open debate and by enabling its members to pose questions directly to cabinet ministers. Unlike Britain, where the prime minister must face questions in the House of Commons every week, Germany does not require the chancellor to undergo an oral grilling in the Bundestag on a weekly basis. Still, even the chancellor must answer oral questions from time to time.

The most effective form of government accountability to the Bundestag centers in the vote of confidence. As in other parliamentary systems, the Bundestag has the right to vote the government out of office. But in the Federal Republic, the Basic Law imposes strict conditions under which a vote of confidence can be used to unseat the government. In what is called the *constructive vote of confidence*, the opposition not only must form a voting majority against the government: it must also be ready to form a new government under a new chancellor within forty-eight hours of the vote. In view of these obstacles, the confidence procedure has been used only a few times in the entire history of the Federal Republic. On three occasions it has been used by a government that deliberately sought to dissolve itself so as to permit a snap election. The most recent use of this procedure came in 2005, after Gerhard Schroeder decided he wanted to go to the electorate immediately. To terminate his government in accordance with the Basic Law, Schroeder had to engineer his government's defeat in a vote of confidence, instructing the Social Democrats and Greens in the Bundestag to vote against his SPD-Green coalition. After the vote, Schroeder informed Germany's president that he could no longer govern. The president then formally dissolved the Bundestag and set a date for new parliamentary elections.

Government stability in the Federal Republic requires fairly strict *party discipline:* all the members of a party's Bundestag delegation are expected to vote in unison, except on special occasions when the party leadership allows its deputies to vote as they wish. Party discipline is higher in Germany than in the United States. The result is relatively smooth sailing through the Bundestag for bills drafted by the government. Roughly 85 percent of government bills pass the lower house, as opposed to about 40 percent of legislation introduced by individual members. Thanks to party discipline, Chancellor Helmut Kohl was able to maintain his coalition government with a mere ten-vote majority from 1994 to 1998, and the Social Democrats and Greens were also able to govern with a ten-vote majority from 1998 to 2002 and with a four-vote majority from 2002 to 2005.

Another factor that serves to facilitate the legislative process in Germany centers on the unusually close relationships between the cabinet, the Bundestag, and the civil service. To begin with, most cabinet ministers and their deputy ministers are themselves members of the Bundestag; they are therefore well acquainted with the procedures and norms of parliamentary practice. The same has *not* been true of most U.S. cabinet secretaries. Moreover, a sizable number of Bundestag deputies tend to come from the civil service. U.S. law prohibits civil servants from running for office while holding down their bureaucratic positions, but Germany permits it. It even allows civil servants to get promoted within the government bureaucracy while serving in the legislature. Another large group of Bundestag deputies tends to come from trade unions, business associations, and other nongovernmental interest groups involved in the policy-making process. Upward of 70 percent of the Bundestag thus has considerable experience in government or interest groups, giving them professional expertise in their various policy specialties.

## The Presidency

As we've indicated, the federal **president** ***is Germany's head of state.*** The position is largely ceremonial, analogous to that of the British monarch. Germany's president in no way possesses the powers of the president of the United States, France, or Russia. The president's principal duty is to select a party leader to form a government after a Bundestag election, upon the chancellor's resignation, or following the government's defeat in a constructive vote of confidence. This task is usually ritualistic, as the person to be designated as the next chancellor has invariably been predetermined by the alignment of parties in the Bundestag.[19]

The federal president is not elected by the people but by a special Federal Convention (*Bundesversammlung*). This body consists of both the Bundestag and the Bundesrat, plus an equal number of delegates elected by the sixteen state legislatures. The dominant party or governing coalition is usually able to get its candidate elected, but at times the three main party groups—Christian Democrats, Social Democrats, and Free Democrats—reach agreement on an individual they hold in high esteem. Two presidents have come from the ranks of the small Free Democratic Party: Theodor Heuss, the Federal Republic's first president (1949–59), and Walter Scheel, a widely popular FDP leader (1974–79). Both were elected with the backing of one or both of the larger parties. The Federal Republic's other past presidents have included Heinrich Luebke (1959–69), a Christian Democrat; Gustav Heinemann (1969–74), a Social Democrat; and Karl Carstens (1979–84), Richard von Weizsacker (1984–94), and Roman Herzog (1994–98)—all Christian Democrats. In May 1999, the Social Democrats and Greens combined to elect Johannes Rau, a former SPD chancellor candidate against Helmut Kohl. After serving one term, Rau was succeeded in 2004 by *Horst Koehler*, a Christian Democrat.

The president serves a five-year term and may be reelected only once.

## The Federal Judiciary

The Basic Law established an elaborate court system, crowned at the federal level by several superior courts. These include the Federal Supreme Court (*Bundesgerichtshof*), which is Germany's highest court of appeals in ordinary civil and criminal cases, and specialized courts concerned respectively with administrative law, labor law, financial law, and social affairs. By far the most important of these high courts is the **Federal Constitutional Court** (*Bundesverfassungsgericht*). From its inception the Constitutional Court was endowed with the power of *judicial review:* the right to interpret the Basic Law and to strike down as unconstitutional laws passed by the parliament and actions taken by the government. With this considerable discretionary authority, the Federal Constitutional Court has been called the most powerful judicial body in Europe. In some respects its authority surpasses that of the U.S. Supreme Court.[20] (Britain has no comparable supreme court, while France's Constitutional Council has substantially more limited powers.)

Seated in Karlsruhe, the Federal Constitutional Court consists of sixteen justices, most of them former judges or eminent constitutional scholars. Half are appointed by the Bundestag, the other half by the Bundesrat. Each house must confirm a nominee for the Court by two-thirds vote, a supermajority deliberately intended to require the approval of the two largest parties, the Christian Democrats and the Social Democrats. Germany's political leaders have sought to ensure a scrupulous balance on the Court between adherents of the two parties, along with an occasional Free Democratic Party member. Even the main left and right factions *within* the main parties are often represented on the Court. Once seated, however, the justices are expected to be nonpartisan, delivering their rulings on the basis of complete political independence. The Court is divided into two eight-person "senates," each of which is responsible for specific categories of constitutional issues. The president of the Court presides over the first senate, the vice president over the second. All justices serve a maximum twelve-year term.

In assuming ample powers to interpret the Basic Law, the Federal Constitutional Court broke with a long tradition in German legal theory known as "positivism." That doctrine held that the laws were so clearly written and detailed that they did not need much interpretation by the courts. Germany's judges thus had little latitude to define the scope of the law through interpretative rulings, but were expected to rigidly apply the state's official interpretations. As a consequence, many of them blindly followed the antidemocratic legal strictures laid down by the kaiser's imperial government and, later, by Hitler and the Nazis. The founders of the Federal Republic wanted a clean break with the past and endowed the court with broad powers to interpret the Basic Law's provisions on human rights and to protect the country against democracy's adversaries.

For example, the Basic Law begins with the affirmation "The dignity of man shall be inviolable. To respect and protect it shall be the duty of all state authority." The next sentence extols the values of peace and justice in the world. Article 3 mandates equality before the law, including the equality of men and women, and it prohibits prejudice and favoritism on grounds of sex, race, religious and political opinions, and other personal characteristics. The Basic Law further states that all state authority emanates from the people, and it specifies a number of guaranteed rights and liberties. It does not provide a constitutional right to bear arms, however, and Germany's gun control laws are much stricter than American laws. Nevertheless, citizens have the right to "resist any person or persons seeking to abolish the constitutional order," if no alternative to armed resistance exists.

The Basic Law also explicitly bans all political parties whose adherents "seek to abolish or impair the free democratic order" or to endanger the FRG's existence. In the 1950s the Federal Constitutional Court upheld the government's right to ban the German Communist Party and a neo-Nazi party on these grounds. In 2003 the court narrowly rejected the government's attempt to ban another neo-Nazi party after federal and state authorities made legal errors in gathering evidence. But in the same year, the court upheld the government's decision to ban a militant Islamic organization on the grounds that it was engaged in "combative-aggressive" activities against Germany's constitutional foundations. (By early 2003, the German government had banned three Islamic organizations since September 11, 2001, as part of its anti-terrorism campaign.) In upholding these and other constitutional rights and prohibitions, Germany's Constitutional Court has a special responsibility for defending democracy.

Unlike the U.S. Supreme Court, Germany's Constitutional Court does not hear cases. Instead, it is asked to rule on constitutional issues upon the request of the federal government, state governments, or one-third of the members of the Bundestag. Individual citizens may also bring complaints before the Court if they believe their constitutional rights have been violated. The Court itself decides which of these thousands of requests it wishes to adjudicate. Not only does it possess the right to invalidate, approve, or attach conditions to laws already passed; it may also rule on "differences of opinion and doubts" about pending legislation if so requested. Within its vast scope of authority, the Court may rule on jurisdictional disputes between different branches of government and may even rule on sensitive foreign policy matters—areas the U.S. Supreme Court usually avoids on the grounds that they are "political" issues best left to the Congress and the president.

Among the plethora of landmark decisions the Constitutional Court has handed down, one of its most controversial was its invalidation of Germany's 1992 post-unification abortion law, which had departed from the Federal Republic's statute outlawing abortions by adopting East Germany's practice of permitting them. Without banning abortions entirely, the Court called for greater measures to protect the unborn (such as counseling for pregnant women) and abolished funding for abortions through the national health insurance system. In light of this ruling, the legislature passed a new law in 1995 permitting abortions in the first trimester but requiring counseling aimed at the "protection of unborn life." The court practically rewrote Germany's campaign financing statutes in 1992, ruling in favor of more public funding for campaign expenses and imposing tighter limits on tax-exempt donations. In 1990 the court upheld an artist's right to take liberties with the German flag on grounds of freedom of expression. In 1998 it declined to take up the complaint of a citizen who claimed that his rights were being violated by smokers. In 2005 it turned down a challenge to Chancellor Schroeder's efforts to call snap elections. Among its foreign policy rulings, the Court affirmed the government's decisions to deploy military forces in Somalia and Bosnia.

## GOVERNMENTS AND POLITICS IN THE FEDERAL REPUBLIC

### Building a Democratic Political Culture

The Federal Republic started out in an environment marked by considerable skepticism about democracy. In a public opinion survey taken in 1951, West Germans were asked, "When in this century do you think Germany has been best off?" Perhaps unsurprisingly, only 2 percent named the current period. Barely two years after the formation of the Federal Republic, West Germany was still reeling, economically and psychologically, from the war's devastation. But only 7 percent named the Weimar Republic, Germany's previous democracy. No fewer than 45 percent of the respondents identified the kaiser's empire before the start of World War I in 1914 as Germany's best period, while 42 percent said Germans had lived best under Hitler before the start of World War II (1933–39). Another survey taken in 1953 asked whether democracy was the best form of government for Germany; only half the respondents said yes. Another survey conducted in these years revealed that more than a third of West Germans would have supported a bid by a new Nazi party to seize power or would have remained indifferent if it occurred. Another third favored restoring the kaiser's monarchy.

Clearly, democracy had to prove itself to most West Germans. Over the course of the late 1950s and 1960s, however, mass attitudes swung overwhelmingly in democracy's favor. By 1970, 90 percent of West Germans said that democracy was the best form of government for Germany. This shift in the country's political culture was no doubt promoted by the Federal Republic's economic successes. Thanks to Marshall Plan assistance from the United States, effective government actions, and the hard work of millions of Germans, the Federal Republic experienced an economic "miracle" that extended from the second half of the 1950s until well into the next decade. Germans in every social class benefited from the boom, including workers at the lower end of the socioeconomic pyramid as well as the large and growing middle class. The West German government's concept of the **social market economy** ***provided ample room for private enterprise, but it also ensured welfare benefits and social protections*** for workers and others positioned in the less advantaged rungs of society.

By 1959, 42 percent of survey respondents named the contemporary period as the time when Germans lived best, while support for the Nazi era dwindled to 18 percent. Those identifying the Federal Republic as Germany's best period rose even further over the following years, reaching 62 percent in 1963 and 81 percent in 1970. Nostalgia for Hitler or the kaiser waned dramatically; by 1970 these bygone eras were fading fast in historical memory, esteemed by only 5 percent of the population each as the time when Germans lived best. As older Germans passed from the scene, their children and grandchildren acquired a much greater respect for democracy and the prosperity it had brought them in the postwar period. Some twenty-five years after the end of World War II, not only had West Germany undergone a profound transformation of its political and economic systems, it had also witnessed one of the most thoroughgoing transformations in political culture ever documented.[21]

With Germany's dark past providing a lasting shadow over much of its development, the Federal Republic has managed not only to survive but to thrive. As the following brief outline of its political evolution shows, the Federal Republic has been characterized by considerable political stability; a broad consensus on political and economic fundamentals among its main political parties; a record of considerable economic achievement over the long term, despite periodic downswings; and close ties with the United States and the European Union. (For a list of the Federal Republic's governments, see table 18.4.)

**TABLE 18.4**

**Governments of the Federal Republic of Germany**

| Governing Coalition | Chancellor (Party) | Came to Power Following . . . | Opposing Chancellor Candidate (Party) |
|---|---|---|---|
| CDU/CSU, FDP, DP[a] | Adenauer (CDU) | Elections, 1949 | Schumacher (SPD) |
| CDU/CSU, FDP, DP, G[b] | Adenauer | Elections, 1953 | Ollenhauer (SPD) |
| CDU/CSU, FDP, DP/FVP[c] | Adenauer | Elections, 1957 | Ollenhauer |
| CDU/CSU, FDP | Adenauer | Elections, 1961 | Brandt (SPD) |
| CDU/CSU, FDP | Erhard (CDU) | Adenauer retirement, 1963 | |
| CDU/CSU, FDP | Erhard | Elections, 1965 | Brandt |
| CDU/CSU, SPD | Kiesinger (CDU) | Coalition change, 1966 | |
| SPD, FDP | Brandt (SPD) | Elections, 1969 | Kiesinger (CDU) |
| SPD, FDP | Brandt | Elections, 1972 | Barzel (CDU) |
| SPD, FDP | Schmidt (SPD) | Brandt resignation, 1974 | |
| SPD, FDP | Schmidt | Elections, 1976 | Kohl (CDU) |
| SPD, FDP | Schmidt | Elections, 1980 | Strauss (CSU) |
| CDU/CSU, FDP | Kohl (CDU) | Coalition change, no-confidence vote, 1982 | |
| CDU/CSU, FDP | Kohl | Elections, 1983 | Vogel (SPD) |
| CDU/CSU, FDP | Kohl | Elections, 1987 | Rau (SPD) |
| CDU/CSU, FDP | Kohl | Elections, 1990 | Lafontaine (SPD) |
| CDU/CSU, FDP | Kohl | Elections, 1994 | Scharping (SPD) |
| SPD, Alliance 90/Greens | Schroeder (SPD) | Elections, 1998 | Kohl |
| SPD, Alliance 90/Greens | Schroeder | Elections, 2002 | Stoiber (CSU) |
| CDU/CSU, SPD | Merkel (CDU) | Elections, 2005 | Schroeder |

[a]DP = Deutsche Partei (German Party)
[b]G = All-German bloc
[c]FVP = Freie Volkspartei (Free People's Party)

### The Adenauer Era (1949–63)

Few politicians typified the longing for stability most Germans felt after the war more than *Konrad Adenauer*. Born in 1876, Adenauer was in his early seventies when he was encouraged by Western Occupation authorities to assume the leadership of the newly formed Christian Democratic Union. He was one of a small number of conservative politicians untainted by cooperation with the Nazis. As mayor of Cologne from 1917 to Hitler's takeover in 1933, Adenauer had spent the Nazi period in seclusion, tending his rose garden. In his critical role as West Germany's first chancellor, *der Alte* (the old man) exuded a sense of grandfatherly tranquillity, which masked a steely determination to alter the course of Germany's domestic and foreign policies decisively.

Starting in 1949, Adenauer formed a succession of coalition governments with either the Free Democratic Party or smaller, short-lived groupings. Though he favored private enterprise, like many Christian Democrats he also had a strong welfarist orientation, based in Christian doctrine. (Adenauer was Catholic, and the CDU was a confessional—i.e., religiously oriented—party.) Hence he tempered his support for market economics with support for a role for German workers in sharing responsibility with their employers in determining wages, working hours, and other company policies, a concept known as *co-determination (Mitbestimmung)*. Under his leadership a watered-down variant of co-determination was instituted in the coal and steel industries.

Adenauer was particularly interested in foreign policy. Though he joined with most other West German politicians in advocating the country's reunification, his first priority was to integrate the Federal Republic firmly into the West, even if it meant renouncing a potential agreement on reunification with the Soviet Union. He therefore formed a close partnership with France, starting with the European Coal and Steel Community in 1952. West Germany helped form the six-member European Economic Community in 1958 (the forerunner of the European Union), and Adenauer enjoyed a close personal rapport with President Charles de Gaulle. At the same time, Adenauer worked closely with the United States, engineering the creation of a new German army and its integration into NATO in 1955.[22]

It was his success in piloting West Germany's economic revival that won him the most plaudits, however. When he retired from the chancellorship in 1963 at the age of 87, he ceded his place to Ludwig Erhard, the man most responsible for designing the Federal Republic's economic miracle. Starting in the late 1950s and early 1960s, the West German economy took off on a ride of sustained economic growth. In the process, Germany developed what Erhard and the Christian Democrats called a *social market economy:* an economic system that combined a vibrant private sector with welfare benefits for the population. Erhard served three years as chancellor. But, by the mid 1960s the wind was beginning to go out of the economy's sails. As a recession set in, West Germany's workers, heretofore among the most moderate in Europe when it came to wage demands and strike activity, began to grow restive on seeing their gains in living standards slow down. In an unprecedented move, several Christian Democratic leaders proposed sharing power with their archrivals, the Social Democrats, in an effort to head off an economic crisis that might bring unsettling social and political consequences. The result was the first Grand Coalition government.

### The First Grand Coalition (1966–69)

Prior to joining the Grand Coalition cabinet, the Social Democrats went through some major ideological transformations. Under Kurt Schumacher's guidance, the SPD had espoused domestic and foreign policies that clashed diametrically with Adenauer's social market economics and his alliance with the United States. Other voices could be heard within the SPD, however, and after Schumacher died in 1952 they became increasingly influential. Recognizing that the majority of West German citizens did not favor the party's socialist orientations, and fearing that the party was doomed to garnering little more than a third of the vote unless it changed its tune, the Social Democratic leadership held a special conference in the town of Bad Godesberg in 1959 and made some major doctrinal changes. They formally accepted private enterprise and the market as the underlying bases of the Federal Republic's economy. In essence, the Social Democrats now accepted the "social market economy." They also explicitly renounced their previous anti-religious biases and assured Germany's believers that they would be welcome in the Social Democratic Party. (A number of SPD leaders and numerous followers were devout Protestants.) These changes were followed in 1960 by a decision to accept West Germany's rearmament and its membership in NATO. With the completion of these ideological about-faces, the Social Democrats became acceptable partners in the eyes of most Christian Democrats.

Christian Democratic leaders who broached the startling idea of a Grand Coalition reckoned that the SPD might be useful in taming working-class discontent while the economy righted itself. But they hoped that the Christian Democrats would get enough credit for the anticipated recovery that the voters would return them to power in the next elections. As things worked out, it was the Social Democrats who stepped forward as the most dynamic partner in the Grand Coalition. The chancellor, Kurt-Georg Kiesinger, was a Christian Democrat, but the chief credit for the economy's rebound went to the Social Democratic finance minister, Kurt Schiller.

One of the most prominent members of the cabinet was another Social Democrat, Foreign Minister *Willy Brandt.* Brandt had fled Germany during the Hitler years, adopting Norwegian citizenship. Brandt made a rapid rise up the SPD's leadership ranks after the war, serving as mayor of West Berlin in 1961 at the time the wall was built. Like many other Social Democrats, Brandt abhorred the nation's division and longed to see Germany restored to unity in a peaceful, democratic Europe. As foreign minister he undertook some new initiatives to entice the communist countries of East-Central Europe to consider the possibility of peaceful unification, but his forays came to naught. The Soviet Union made it clear that it would not let Poland, Czechoslovakia, or other states under its control take any action on Germany's status independently of Moscow.

In 1969, the Grand Coalition ran its course as the electoral cycle mandated elections to a new Bundestag. Though the tally was close, the SPD managed to form a "small coalition" with the Free Democrats thanks to a tenuous twelve-vote majority over the Christian Democrats. Brandt became chancellor and Walter Scheel, the FDP's reform-minded leader, became foreign minister.

**Willy Brandt kneels at the memorial commemorating the victims of Nazi atrocities in Warsaw's Jewish ghetto, 1970. Brandt was the first West German chancellor to visit Poland after the Nazi Occupation.**

## Brandt in Power (1969–74)

With Brandt's ascendancy, the West German government embarked on its most active pursuit of unification since the founding of the Federal Republic. While keeping the Federal Republic firmly planted in NATO and West European supranational institutions, Brandt devised a new "eastern policy" (*Ostpolitik*) that directly approached the Soviet Union and engaged the East German leadership in face-to-face negotiations, steps regarded as heresy by previous West German governments. In 1970 his government concluded a "renunciation of force" agreement with the Soviets, pledging to resolve all disputes peacefully. Similar treaties followed with communist Poland and Czechoslovakia. All these treaties were consciously aimed at proving West Germany's commitment to reconciliation with the nations Hitler's Germany had brutalized during the war. The SPD-FDP coalition's ulterior motive was to convince the USSR and its allies in the region that they had nothing to fear from a peace-loving, united German state.

Brandt fully assumed that, even with these agreements, Germany's reunification was a long way off, perhaps decades away. In the interval he sought immediate relief for the thousands of German families on either side of the Berlin wall and the inter-German frontier who were forcibly separated by a very real iron curtain. East Germany's hardline communist leadership intensely resisted making major concessions to the West Germans, but under Soviet pressure they relented. In 1972 the two German states agreed to a sweeping set of new regulations that greatly facilitated the ability of West Berliners and other West Germans to visit East Germany. (Alas, East Germans did not win any substantial new rights from their government to visit West Germany.) In yet another set of negotiations, the USSR came to terms with the United States, Britain, and France in formally guaranteeing unhindered passage on the access routes between West Germany proper and West Berlin, thereby removing a source of dangerous frictions.[23]

For these efforts, Brandt won the Nobel Peace Prize in 1971. His place in history was assured the following year when his eastern treaties passed in the Bundestag, narrowly surviving the opposition of the Christian Democrats and a few defectors from the governing coalition parties. (The Federal Constitutional Court affirmed their constitutionality.) Brandt's political luster did not last very long, however. In 1974 it was revealed that an East German spy was working on his staff; the spy's wife was also nabbed for espionage. Though Brandt had been unaware of their true identity, he took responsibility for the mishap and resigned.[24]

### Schmidt's Governments (1974–82)

Brandt's successor was *Helmut Schmidt*, a Social Democrat with a razor-sharp intellect and special expertise in economics and defense policy. Schmidt acquired his fairly conservative version of Social Democratic ideology during the war, through contacts with Labour Party members while he was a prisoner of war in British captivity. He assumed office at a time when his financial skills were critically needed. In 1973, the world's leading oil-producing nations quadrupled the price of oil, triggering a global economic crisis. The United States, Western Europe, and Japan sputtered into recession and suffered an unusual combination of diminishing growth and high inflation, a phenomenon called *stagflation*. As the leader of the SPD's right wing, Schmidt favored relatively austere budget-tightening policies designed to dampen inflation. He also maintained close ties with the leaders of West Germany's trade unions, traditionally the SPD's most reliable supporters, and with leading members of the business community, a connection reinforced by the business-oriented Free Democrats. These consultations paid off, as the unions kept their wage demands within limits and big business strove to maintain production, holding unemployment in check. While inflation rates in other countries spiraled into double digits, the Federal Republic held the line at about 7 percent. It also enjoyed a peaceful labor environment, with few strikes.

Schmidt's attempts to hold the line on government spending did not sit well with the SPD's left wing, which favored higher spending on social welfare. The party's youth organization, the Young Socialists, or Jusos (yuzos), favored even more radical policies aimed at imposing higher taxes on corporations and wealthy individuals and redistributing the nation's wealth to ensure greater socioeconomic equality. Future chancellor Gerhard Schroeder was the head of the Jusos from 1978 to 1980, and certain members of his cabinet were Jusos during these years.

Schmidt's defense policies provoked even greater consternation within the party's left-wing ranks. In the late 1970s the Soviet Union ratcheted up the arms race by installing a new generation of guided missiles, equipped with deadly nuclear warheads, within easy striking distance from West German territory. Schmidt responded by convincing the United States and other NATO partners to develop new counter-missiles of their own in an effort to get the Soviets to reach an agreement that would restore the nuclear balance in Europe at lower levels of missile deployments. In 1979 NATO agreed to start developing its counterweapons, some of which would be based on West Germany's densely populated territory. The NATO decision unleashed one of the most virulent crises of the Cold War. It also touched off a wave of protest within West Germany, as hundreds of thousands of people took to the streets in large demonstrations against the missiles. The effects of the crisis were particularly tumultuous inside the Social Democratic Party, as left-wingers—like Schroeder—and a growing number of moderates joined the opposition to

Schmidt's counter-missile scheme. Schmidt himself became increasingly isolated within his own party.[25]

Conflict with his coalition partners, the Free Democrats, exacerbated Schmidt's difficulties. Although the FDP maintained its governing coalition with the Social Democrats during the 1980 elections, within a year the two parties were squabbling over economic policy. In a reversal of alliances, the FDP in the fall of 1982 announced that it was withdrawing from Schmidt's government and was prepared to form a new governing coalition with the Christian Democrats. The FDP's turnabout in 1982 caused Schmidt's government to lose a constructive vote of confidence in the Bundestag. It was immediately replaced by a new coalition consisting of the Christian Democrats and the Free Democrats, and the chancellorship passed to the leader of the CDU, *Helmut Kohl.*

### Kohl's Governments

Helmut Kohl's historic reputation as "the chancellor of German unity" represented an unexpected personal triumph for a man who lacked Adenauer's stature, Brandt's charisma, or Schmidt's brilliance. Having joined the Christian Democratic Union in 1946 at the age of sixteen, Kohl was elected minister-president of the Rhineland-Palatinate, his home state, in 1969, and four years later he became head of the CDU. In 1976, Kohl failed to unseat the popular Schmidt government in his first bid for the chancellor's office. Then in 1980 he lost a power struggle within the Christian Democratic movement, which chose the head of the Bavarian CSU instead of Kohl to lead the Christian Democratic ticket. The Christian Democrats lost to Schmidt's government once again. But when the Free Democrats pulled out of their coalition with Schmidt's Social Democrats in 1982, Kohl became chancellor at last.

Immediately after assuming power by a vote of the Bundestag, Kohl arranged for snap elections to be held six months later to seek the public's approval. The Christian Democrats and their FDP allies won a solid Bundestag majority, ensuring their government's survival. From 1982 until 1998, Kohl played a critical role in some of the most crucial events of the postwar era. One of his first decisions was to go ahead with the controversial deployment of the new NATO missiles starting in 1983, in spite of substantial public opposition in Germany. The Soviet Union strenuously objected to the deployments, but in 1985 a new leadership team under Mikhail Gorbachev took power in the Kremlin. Kohl and Gorbachev soon struck up a close working relationship that blossomed into a real friendship. In a startling turnabout, Gorbachev and the NATO countries agreed in 1987 to destroy all the intermediate-range missiles they had just installed in the European area over the previous ten years, removing in one bold stroke a major source of East–West frictions. The Kohl-Gorbachev connection also smoothed the way to improvements in Bonn's ties with East Germany's communist regime, which was openly resisting Gorbachev's reform program. Kohl played a leading role in boosting West European integration, putting Germany's weight behind such measures as the Treaty of Maastricht of 1992, which led to the euro and the European Central Bank later in the decade. And Kohl got on well with the three American presidents whose administrations coincided with his years in office. He was in President Ronald Reagan's presence at the Berlin wall in 1987 when Reagan dramatically exclaimed, "Mr. Gorbachev, tear down this wall!" Kohl's ties with President George H. W. Bush assumed a special importance during the complicated negotiations leading to Germany's unification. Kohl also enjoyed his relationship with President Clinton, treating him on one visit to a favorite Rhineland delicacy, stuffed pig gut.

Kohl's center-stage role in Germany's unification process, however, was his greatest triumph. Kohl's bonds with Gorbachev were critical in winning the Soviet leader's acceptance of the liquidation of East Germany's communist state. And Kohl allayed the fears of many Europeans who believed that an enlarged Germany would seek to dominate the region, assuring them that his aim was "a European Germany, not a German Europe."

In December 1990, Kohl led the CDU-FDP coalition to a resounding victory in the first Bundestag elections to be held in unified Germany. But after being reinstated as chancellor, Kohl was forced to admit that reunification would cost much more money than he had led the voters to believe. His campaign promises of "blossoming landscapes" in East Germany proved embarrassingly unrealistic during the arduous post-unification decade. In his next term Kohl sought to build as large a consensus as possible on bearing the costs of modernizing eastern Germany's economy. But rising discontent in both parts of Germany led many political analysts to predict Kohl's defeat in the 1994 elections. Once again, however, Kohl confounded the doomsayers. In 1994 Kohl was elected chancellor for the fifth straight time, though his coalition government had a mere five-vote majority in the Bundestag (338 seats to 333).[26]

Kohl's next four-year term was marked by continuing efforts to build up the eastern German economy while contending with mounting unemployment, exploding social welfare costs, and a troubling loss of Germany's famous economic dynamism. With a mixed record of achievements and difficulties, the embattled Kohl went before the voters once again in 1998, only to lose to a new coalition consisting of the Social Democrats and the Greens. After sixteen years at the helm of the Federal Republic, the chancellor of German unity stepped down.

Kohl found himself at the center of controversy once again as the 1990s came to a close. After investigations revealed that various contributors had provided large sums of cash to the Christian Democrats illegally, Kohl admitted that he had operated a secret party slush fund the entire time he was chancellor and had accepted $1 million in illegal campaign contributions from sources he refused to identify. Ultimately, Kohl was fined $143,000 for what he called a "mistake," but he was not subjected to criminal prosecution. And he maintained his silence about the source of the illegal contributions.[27]

### The SPD-Green Coalition

The formation of the SPD-Green coalition following the September 1998 elections broke new ground in German politics: it marked the ascendancy of Germany's postwar generation to the highest rungs of power. *Gerhard Schroeder,* the new chancellor, was born in 1944. He belonged to a generation that grew up in a democratic country, bearing no guilt for the collapse of democracy in the Weimar period or the crimes of Nazism. (Schroeder never knew his father, who was killed in action during the war; his unmarked grave in Romania was not located until 2001.) *Joschka Fischer,* the Greens' principal leader, was born in 1948. Another pathbreaking aspect of the red-green coalition government was its ideological coloration. After sixteen years of conservative rule under Helmut Kohl, the torch of power had passed to a group of individuals whose past political activism marked them as the most left-leaning leaders the Federal Republic had yet seen. As their policies developed, however, they turned out to be far more moderate than their previous leftist convictions would have foreshadowed. The red-green coalition's decisive shift to the center was carefully guided by its leader, Chancellor Gerhard Schroeder.[28]

Schroeder entered office with a mixture of neo-liberal views favoring private-sector expansion and traditional Social Democratic positions favoring an active role for government in fostering social justice for the less advantaged. The new chancellor was also looking for ways to tame the uncontrolled forces of globalization. His finance minister and political ally, Oskar Lafontaine, the leader of the SPD's left wing, shared most of these views but favored larger infusions of government spending as a means to boosting overall demand and eventually reducing unemployment, a classic Keynesian recipe. When Schroeder opposed this approach under pressure from large German corporations, Lafontaine quit the government and launched a broadside attack on Schroeder's policies.[29]

Schroeder managed to secure his party's approval for several economic reforms that neo-liberal economists considered vital to raising Germany's sluggish economic growth rate (which had been falling to the lowest level in Europe ever since 1994), to reducing unemployment, and to cutting the country's huge national debt. The reforms included major tax cuts for corporations and individuals, efforts to alleviate the country's overburdened pension system, and a short-term employment program aimed at creating a hundred thousand new jobs immediately for young people.

In addition to pursuing a centrist economic course, Schroeder took a firm position in favor of engaging German military forces in world trouble spots. Germany's reluctance to use military force in areas where the country was not overtly threatened rested on a broad national consensus that included all the major parties. After the Dayton Accords brought peace to Bosnia-Herzegovina, Schroeder sent German troops to the region as part of the international peacekeeping contingent. Germany also accepted several hundred thousand refugees from the war-torn area. In 1999, Germany participated in NATO's Kosovo campaign. In the fall of 2001 Schroeder won Bundestag approval to dispatch troops to strife-torn Macedonia as part of a NATO peacekeeping force. And in a move that created heated controversy within his own party and among his coalition partners, the Greens, Schroeder took the bold step of ordering up to 3,900 troops for duty in connection with the U.S.-led war in Afghanistan in the months that followed the events of September 11, 2001, bucking opposition from anti-war Social Democrats and Greens.

The terrorist attacks evoked considerable sympathy for the United States in Germany. Nearly 80 percent of Germans said they were "very shaken" by the attacks. By 2002, Germany had ten thousand military forces deployed abroad—second only to the United States among the NATO allies. After the Taliban's removal, Germany hosted an international conference that led to the establishment of a new Afghan government under Hamid Karzai. And Germany later assumed temporary command of international peacekeeping forces in Afghanistan.

Schroeder's relations with the Bush administration rapidly deteriorated over Iraq, however. As the 2002 elections approached, Schroeder's government lagged ten points behind the Christian Democrats in the polls. Dissatisfaction with the government's economic record was the primary source of voter discontent. Contrary to Schroeder's promise in 1998 to cut unemployment to no more than 3.5 million, 4 million Germans were still out of work. The Christian Democrats were poised to take advantage of the government's plight under their new standard-bearer, *Edmund Stoiber*. Stoiber headed the Christian Social Union (CSU), the Christian Democrats' Bavarian wing. As the chief of Bavaria's government since 1993, he had won acclaim for his state's enviable economic record, especially in high-technology development. It was widely assumed that Stoiber would make a stronger candidate for chancellor than Angela Merkel, the head of the CSU's larger sister party, the Christian Democratic Union (CDU). Merkel reluctantly gave up her bid to lead the Christian Democrats in the 2002 elections.[30]

The Bush administration's resolve to invade Iraq was a major factor in turning Schroeder's reelection campaign around. A majority of Germans opposed the war, in part because of the deep-seated pacifism that still shaped the country's political culture more than fifty years after World War II. Schroeder initially assured President Bush that he would not make an issue of Iraq during the campaign, but he quickly sized up the German public's anti-war mood. Asserting that he would not "click heels" to the United States, the chancellor announced that Germany would provide neither troops nor economic assistance for an invasion of Iraq even if the United Nations Security Council approved military action. When the minister of justice in Schroeder's cabinet likened President Bush to Hitler, Germany's relations with the United States sank to their lowest level in the postwar era. (Schroeder apologized for the minister's "alleged remarks.") For his part, Stoiber declared his opposition to unilateral military action by the United States in Iraq, but added that Germany would have to observe a UN resolution mandating war. (President Jacques Chirac made it clear that France would veto such a resolution in the Security Council, however.) Schroeder's stance against the impending war in Iraq brought a large number of voters back into his camp. Schroeder further capitalized on his rapid response to flood victims in eastern Germany during an exceptionally rainy summer. And his debating skills and charismatic personality enabled him to outshine Stoiber in two televised debates just before the elections.

Election night on September 23, 2002, was a nail-biter: the final outcome was not known until the crucial overhang mandates were calculated. Schroeder's Social Democrats lost 47 seats and edged out the Christian Democrats in the second-column vote count by only 6,027 votes out of nearly 49 million cast. The Christan Democrats won three seats more than they had won in the 1998 Bundestag elections. But the all-important smaller parties determined the ultimate result. The Social Democrats were saved by their coalition partners, the Alliance 90/Greens party, who won 8 new seats, bringing their total to 55 deputies in the Bundestag. With the 251 seats won by the Social Democrats, Schroeder's "red-green" coalition had a total of 306 seats—a slender 4-vote majority. By contrast, the Christian

Democrats' hopes of forming a "black-yellow" coalition government with the Free Democrats (FDP) were dashed when the FDP fell short of its anticipated vote share. The neo-liberal Free Democrats advocated even stronger pro-business reforms than the Christian Democrats wanted.

Immediately after his come-from-behind victory, Schroeder returned to the task of tackling Germany's economic woes. The economy's growth rate in 2002 was a feeble 0.2 percent and the unemployment rate topped 9.6 percent. As noted at the start of this chapter, employers were reluctant to take on new employees for a variety of reasons. Hourly wages in Germany exceeded the EU average. In addition, the costs of the contributions employers had to make to their employees' nonwage benefits package was, according to Schroeder himself, "too high." As in France, German employers could not lay off workers without paying costly severance deals, and they had to keep working hours within agreed-upon limits. German workers tended to get six to eight weeks of paid vacation, plus six weeks of paid sick leave. (On average, Germans worked 25 percent less than Americans.) In March 2003 Schroeder unveiled a package of reforms known as "Agenda 2010." The reforms were based in part on recommendations by a government-sponsored commission headed by Peter Hartz, a Volkswagen executive. Introduced in phases starting in early 2003, the reforms initially sought to improve the state employment agency and create new types of "minijobs" with lower tax and insurance obligations for employers. The final phase, known as Hartz IV, reduced the amount of time unemployed workers could receive full unemployment pay and lowered the monthly stipend for most of those qualified for unemployment compensation.

These and other reforms provoked considerable opposition from the Social Democratic Party's left wing and from trade unions. In mid 2003, Schroeder threatened to resign if SPD deputies blocked passage of his reform program. He also had to work out compromises with the more business-friendly Christian Democrats, who controlled the Bundesrat. Once in effect, these various reform efforts scarcely made a dent in the unemployment rate, and economic growth remained sluggish. The government's budget deficits exceeded 3 percent of GDP, the level mandated for countries using the euro. (Ironically, it was the German government and its powerful central bank, the *Bundesbank*, that had insisted on the 3 percent ceiling when the euro was being created in the 1990s.) With opposition to Schroeder's reforms mounting within his own party and few tangible results to show for them, the chancellor's popularity sank to historic laws. Within less than a year after his reelection, his approval rating was only 20 percent. A succession of SPD defeats in Landtag elections in 2004 and 2005 further weakened Schroeder's stature. In May 2005, when the Social Democrats lost to the Christian Democrats and Free Democrats in North Rhine–Westphalia, Germany's most populous state and an SPD stronghold for thirty-nine years, Schroeder decided it was time to clear the air. In a surprise announcement the very next day, he called for snap Bundestag elections in the fall, one year ahead of schedule. This time his opponent would be *Angela Merkel*.

## PROFILE: Angela Merkel

"I'm an optimist," Angela Merkel declared. "Change doesn't frighten me." That optimism helped Germany's future chancellor meet the challenges of growing up in communist East Germany. Later it led her to embark on a political career that she never could have dreamed possible during the first thirty-five years of her life.

Merkel was born Angela Kasner in 1954 in Hamburg, West Germany. Shortly after her birth, Angela's father, a newly ordained minister in the Evangelical (Lutheran) church—Germany's largest Protestant denomination—was assigned to a small parish in East Germany. The young cleric eagerly took up the task, hoping to minister to Christians in a state whose Marxist-Leninist ideology was avowedly hostile to religion. Although communist authorities staged periodic crackdowns, arresting clergy and closing down churches, Angela's father managed to create a small center for training new ministers in the town of Templin, located fifty miles north of Berlin. His library, complete with Western books despite the regime's stiff censorship system, became a focal point for seminars on theological issues for clergymen throughout East Germany. Kasner was able to pursue his religious activities not only because he understood the boundaries of what was permissible but also because he sought an accommodation with the communist regime. Merkel later observed that her father judged the East German system "somewhat milder and less categorically than I did."

The regime's repressive grip was nevertheless palpable. Angela's mother, an English teacher, was forbidden to teach in the East German school system because her husband was a pastor. On the day the government began building the Berlin wall in 1961, Angela's mother sat in their church and wept. Angela would recall that day as her first memory of a political event. Spies were everywhere. The State Security office, the notorious "Stasi," had the most intrusive network of agents and informers in the communist world. Years later, when Merkel applied for a job, she learned that her Stasi dossier contained details on how often she listened to West German radio and when she received new jeans in the mail from relatives in West Germany—information apparently passed on to the Stasi by her classmates. Like most East Germans, Angela lived a double life, watching West German television stations at home while internalizing the rules of a rigid totalitarian dictatorship when in the presence of teachers or other authority figures.

Life in the German Democratic Republic was not entirely politicized, however. Angela grew up in a supportive, intelligent family and her small town was surrounded by nature. Right from childhood she was a star pupil. Although the East German school system inculcated communist ideology starting in elementary school, it retained the high standards and elitism of Germany's educational traditions. In high school Angela excelled in English, Russian, math, and science, winning prizes in multiple subjects and earning a trip to the Soviet Union to participate in academic "Olympics." After getting her *Abitur* degree upon passing the dreaded comprehensive exams that only a small percentage of German students are qualified to take (whether in East or West Germany), Angela was admitted to the University of Leipzig to study physics. Leipzig was far enough away from Templin to give her the independence she longed for, and the natural sciences were the least politicized field of study in the East German academic system. Even so, Angela joined the communist youth groups required for academic success. Once again Angela excelled, winning praise from renowned professors. Her sharp analytical skills would prove an enormous asset once she got into politics and assumed policy-making responsibilities. Angela graduated from Leipzig in 1978. One year earlier she had married a student, Ulrich Merkel, and following graduation the couple moved to East Berlin. Angela was immediately hired as a researcher at the Central Institute for Physical Chemistry, a branch of the government's Academy of Sciences. She worked there for twelve uneventful years, obtained her doctorate, and filled her nonworking hours with family and friends. Her marriage ended in divorce after four years.

Though she scarcely knew it at the time, the opening of the Berlin wall in November 1989 opened up an extraordinary path to political success for Angela Merkel. Initially, Merkel took no part in the anti-regime demonstrations that fanned across East Germany in the late summer and fall of 1989, nor did she join any of the early protest groups that were emerging from dissident Protestant churches and intellectual circles. "I was really no resistence fighter," she later acknowledged. Several weeks after the wall opened, a colleague took her to a meeting organized by the Social Democrats, but Merkel decided not to join that party. Instead, she joined an East German group called *Demokratischer Aufbruch* (Democratic Awakening), a small gathering of people who were still looking for a coherent orientation and policy program. Like most East Germans in the final weeks of 1989, the group's members assumed that the opening of the wall would of course produce major changes inside East Germany, but they did not expect the rapid liquidation of the German Democratic Republic. Nor did the West German government under Chancellor Helmut Kohl foresee the GDR's imminent collapse or the population's demand for immediate incorporation into the Federal Republic. But when the first competitive, multiparty elections to East Germany's parliament were held in March 1990, parties allied to West Germany's main parties won a decisive majority. All of them favored unification with West Germany at the earliest feasible moment.

After leaving her research institute and placing herself at the disposal of Democratic Awakening, Merkel became the group's unofficial press secretary. As the March 1990 elections approached, the group's leaders decided to form an electoral alliance with the Christian Democrats. After the elections, East Germany's new prime minister was himself a Christian Democrat. On the recommendation of one of Merkel's contacts, the prime minister hired Merkel as the government's deputy press secretary. While learning her new responsibilities literally on the job, Merkel won an instant reputation as one of the best-informed and most approachable figures in the new government. She also accompanied the prime minister at important meetings with foreign leaders to discuss East Germany's fate, putting her English and Russian to good use. Over the next several months, the East German state disintegrated. East Germans stopped using the national currency and instead adopted the more valuable West German marks that were flooding into East Germany thanks to the newly opened borders. When a government can no longer get its citizens to use its own currency, it has clearly lost a large part of its legitimacy. Within a few months it was agreed that East Germany would be dissolved as an independent state and that its territory, divided into five states (*Laender*), would join the Federal Republic of Germany, uniting with the FRG's eleven West German states. The date set for unification was October 3, 1990.

Just two days before that date, Angela Merkel joined the Christian Democratic Union at a special CDU "unification conference" held in Hamburg. While there, she asked one of her colleagues from Democratic Awakening to introduce her to Chancellor Helmut Kohl. The brief chat that took place in the midst of a press reception made a mark on Kohl, who was looking for promising new political figures from East Germany. It did not hurt that Merkel was a woman and relatively young, and that—unlike many other potential leaders from East Germany—she had not compromised herself with the communist regime and its spy network. Kohl invited Merkel to meet with him again in November. Following that meeting, Merkel was given a job in the German government's press and information office. But after only a month in her new position, Merkel decided to run for the Bundestag in Germany's first post-unification elections, held in December 1990. She was nominated by the local CDU to run for a single-member-district "direct mandate" in the eastern German state of Mecklenburg–West Pomerania, an area where she had never before resided. After a brief campaign, Merkel won 48.5 percent of the votes in her district, a plurality that placed her "first past the post" in a field of competing candidates. In four subsequent elections, she consistently won reelection to the same seat.

Only a year had passed since Angela Merkel had left her lab for the political fray, and already she was a member of the German parliament! Her ascent up the political ladder was just as accelerated. Right after the December 1990 Bundestag elections, which returned a new majority for Helmut Kohl's coalition government of Christian Democrats and Free Democrats, the chancellor picked Merkel for his cabinet. She was quickly dubbed "Kohl's girl." Starting in January 1991, Merkel was Germany's minister for women and youth affairs. As in her previous tasks, she proved to be a quick study, mastering the technical details and political subtleties of her position in rapid order. By the end of the year Merkel was elected deputy chairman of the Christian Democratic Union, rising to the leadership ranks of her party. Less than two years later she became the head of the CDU's organization in the state of Mecklenburg–West Pomerania. Following Merkel's reelection to the Bundestag in 1994, Helmut Kohl—newly reelected to his fourth term as chancellor—promoted her to minister for the environment, one of the most politically sensitive posts in the German government. Combining her scientific knowledge with her lifelong love of nature, Merkel tackled her new assignment with her customary verve. She won international respect for her contributions to the UN Climate Conference in Berlin in 1995 and the Kyoto conference on greenhouse emissions in 1997, which resulted in the Kyoto Protocol (see chapter 1).

In 1998 the Kohl government went down to defeat as Gerhard Schroeder led the Social Democrats to victory, forming a coalition government with the Alliance 90/Greens party. As the Christian Democrats took stock of their losses and reorganized themselves, Merkel was elected the CDU's new general secretary, the number two leadership position in the party behind the post of party chairman. Merkel appeared ready to hold this position until the next Bundestag elections, but the investigations into Helmut Kohl's financial improprieties while he was chancellor created an immediate uproar within the Christian Democratic Union. The scandal involved other leading party figures as well, producing a crisis of confidence in the CDU that threatened to hurt the party's chances in upcoming state elections as well as in the next national elections. In December 1999 Merkel published an article in one of Germany's leading newspapers that created a sensation: she openly criticized Kohl, her former mentor, for concealing his illegal activities, and she called on the Christian Democratic party to distance itself from Kohl in the way adolescents leave home and go their own way. When she wrote the article, Merkel knew that the CDU's current chairman, Kohl's close friend Wolfgang Schaeuble (SHOY-bleh), had long been aware of Kohl's malfeasance, a fact Schaeuble had heretofore denied. Merkel's article forced Schaeuble to publicly admit his own role in the scandal. In February 2000, Schaeuble resigned as the CDU's leader. Two months later, the party elected Angela Merkel to succeed him. (The CDU's chairman and other leaders are elected by approximately one thousand delegates who attend the party congresses that take place at least every two years. The party's 600,000 members do not vote directly for their top leaders.)

As the CDU's chairman, Merkel had the inside track to lead the Christian Democrats as their candidate for chancellor in the next Bundestag elections in 2002. But a number of CDU politicians, including popular leaders of CDU-led state governments, were not convinced that Merkel would be the Christian Democrats' most effective candidate. They preferred Edmund Stoiber, the experienced leader of the CSU, the Christian Democrats' Bavarian party. When it became clear to Merkel that key leaders of her own party were prepared to abandon her in favor of Stoiber, Merkel hopped in a plane and went straight to Stoiber's house. She informed the astonished Bavarian party chief that she would gladly support him as the CDU/CSU's candidate for chancellor in the upcoming elections. The surprise visit proved to be a politically astute move on Merkel's part. Stoiber and the Christian Democrats went down to defeat in 2002, losing an early lead in the polls to Schroeder's energetic campaigning. Stoiber went back to Bavaria as its governor. Merkel remained chairman of the Christian Democratic Union, confident that she would be the Christian Democrats' chancellor candidate when the next Bundestag elections rolled around. That opportunity came in 2005. Like everything else in Merkel's extraordinary political life, it came earlier than anticipated.[31]

## The 2005 Elections

**Christian Democrats** Recognizing that unemployment and the financing of social welfare programs were the main issues in voters' minds, the Christian Democrats under Angela Merkel's leadership came forward with a number of specific proposals to address these issues. Several ideas responded directly to the business community's concerns. In an effort to lower the nonwage welfare contributions of German companies, the Christian Democrats took the risk of calling for an increase in the value-added tax (VAT) from its current average of 16 percent to 18 percent. (The VAT is a sales tax; see chapter 14.) Part of the additional revenues that the national treasury would reap from this tax increase would be used to finance some of the welfare benefits of German employees (mainly unemployment insurance), relieving private companies of a portion of these costs. The Christian Democrats also responded to the private sector's calls for more flexible rules making it easier to fire redundant workers and adjust working hours. Many corporate executives also wanted the right to opt out of nationwide collective bargaining agreements between labor unions and business associations that set guidelines for wages and working hours for an entire industry. Such agreements were a central element of postwar Germany's neo-corporatist system of labor-management relations, as we'll see later in this chapter. Merkel favored giving individual companies the right to depart from these industry-wide agreements and negotiate wage and work-time deals with their own employees. The CDU and CSU also went into the election calling for income tax reductions, the closing of tax loopholes, and reforms of health care financing and the pension system.

In foreign policy, the Christian Democrats promised to improve relations with the Federal Republic's long-standing ally, the United States. On a trip to Washington in 2003, Merkel had already sought to distance the Christian Democrats from Chancellor Schroeder's harsh criticism of U.S. policy in Iraq, telling the *Washington Post* that "Schroeder does not speak for all Germans." Merkel accused the chancellor of unnecessarily weakening Western unity in the confrontation with Saddam Hussein, thereby making war more likely. Later Merkel insisted that she did not favor the war itself, and she criticized the Bush administration for excessive optimism in thinking that a military invasion would quickly produce democracy in Iraq. But she stuck to her charge that Schroeder had unnecessarily fractured Germany's ties with its transatlantic partners. With regard to Europe, Merkel and the Christian Democrats favored the proposed constitution for the European Union, voting in favor of its ratification in the Bundestag in the spring of 2005. (Germany did not hold a referendum on the constitution, however.) But Merkel was outspokenly opposed to Turkey's admission to the EU, advocating a "privileged partnership" between Turkey and the European Union instead.

Although Merkel and the Christian Democrats were responsive to the concerns of their traditional supporters in Germany's business sector, and were determined to reduce the government's budget deficits over the coming years, they had little desire to dismantle the German welfare state. Ever since the 1950s, the Christian Democrats favored what they called the "social market economy"—a combination of private enterprise with welfare benefits and protections for the masses of blue-collar and white-collar employees, pensioners, and others who needed assistance in some form or other. In an effort to adapt this German model of political economy to the realities of global market competition and spiraling deficits, Merkel in 2000 had issued her own ideas for a "new social market economy." Not all of her proposals were adopted in the Christian Democrats' 2005 campaign manifesto, but Merkel made it clear during the campaign that she was committed to the social market economy. She argued that there was no radical split between the Anglo-Saxon model that emphasized private enterprise and European models that favored welfare and job protection; the two models, in her view, could be combined. Presenting herself as a pragmatic centrist rather than as an axe-wielding German Margaret Thatcher, Merkel insisted that the reforms she advocated were vital to reducing unemployment at a time when a thousand jobs were disappearing in Germany every day and excessive labor costs were forcing companies to lay off hundreds of thousands of employees. "If I do nothing," she asserted, current trends would lead Germany "into a spiral of decline."

**Social Democrats** In contrast to the Christian Democrats' outreach to the business sector, the Social Democrats' campaign manifesto veered to the left. In view of the internal party feuding and trade union restiveness that had greeted Gerhard Schroeder's reforms, the SPD hoped to reclaim its core constituencies in the working class, the lower middle class, and other groups that relied on state protection of their welfare benefits such as pensioners. Aside from proposals to reduce corporate income taxes, the SPD shied away from pro-business reforms and called instead for preserving labor market regulations pretty much as they were, including limitations on firing workers and adjusting their work hours. The Social Democrats also advocated a new minimum wage law and a mandatory universal health-care system. (Under the existing health-care system, about 90 percent of Germans were enrolled in one of more than two hundred nonprivate health insurance plans, but people in higher-income brackets could opt out of these programs and purchase health insurance privately.) To raise state revenues, they called for a 3 percent income tax surcharge on individuals earning more than 250,000 euros a year (a bit more than $300,000). Like the Christian Democrats, Schroeder and the Social Democrats favored the EU constitution, but they also favored Turkey's eventual admission to EU membership. In addition, they wanted a permanent German seat in the United Nations Security Council, a status that would give Germany veto power in that body. (The Bush administration opposed this idea.)

**The Free Democrats** Under the leadership of Guido Westerwelle, the FDP reaffirmed its traditional links to Germany's private sector and business-oriented middle class. Accordingly, the "liberals" favored changes in Germany's labor laws to give businesses greater flexibility to hire and fire employees and to adjust wages and working hours without much trade union interference. The party also favored corporate and individual tax cuts along with efforts to reduce red tape in the German bureaucracy. The party hoped to win enough Bundestag seats to form a coalition government with the Christian Democrats, and its policy proposals were basically consistent with those of their potential governing partners. But the Free Democrats were somewhat less interested in the "social" aspect of the social market economy than the Christian Democrats were, and they rejected the Merkel-led parties' call for an increase in the value-added tax. In keeping with their traditional commitment to individual civil liberties, they also favored tighter restrictions on the protection of personal information than the CDU and CSU advocated, resisting pressures for more government surveillance in an age of global terrorism. The FDP had about 65,000 members in 2006.

**Alliance 90/The Greens** The Green Party first emerged on the German political scene in the late 1970s. It was an outgrowth of several new social movements that took up the causes of environmentalism, women's rights, antimilitarism, and other issues that in their view were not being properly addressed by the mainstream parties and interest groups. (On new social movements, see chapter 11.) The founders of the Greens were particularly concerned with preserving a green environment and preventing nuclear disasters. They called for the elimination of West Germany's nuclear power plants and the removal of American nuclear weapons from German territory. They were especially active in the peace movement that arose in the late 1970s and early 1980s when NATO moved to install a new generation of nuclear-armed missiles in Germany in response to the Soviet Union's deployment of new missiles aimed at Western Europe. In 1983 the Greens cleared the Bundestag's 5 percent hurdle and sent their first delegates to the German parliament, most of them attired in sandals and jeans. From the outset, however, the Greens were split into two camps. The "fundamentalists" (known as *Fondis*) tended to oppose industrialization itself as environmentally threatening; some of them favored the dismantling of factories and a ban on personal automobiles. The "realists" (*Realos*) wanted stronger environmental protections without destroying the German industrial economy. Germany's unification in 1989–90 caught the Greens by surprise. Their abhorrence of patriotic sentiment as excessively nationalistic clashed with the public mood at the time, and they were voted out of the Bundestag in the elections of December 1990. Following this defeat, the realist wing took control of the party under the leadership of Joschka Fischer.

Alliance 90 at first represented a collection of East German dissidents who were eager for democracy. After the 1990 elections, the group formed an alliance with the Greens, forming a joint party known as *Alliance 90/the Greens*. Under Fischer's leadership, the new party accepted Germany's membership in the NATO alliance and the European Union. When the opportunity presented itself to enter into a national coalition government with the Social Democrats after the 1998 elections, Fischer and other party leaders hammered out a common governing program with Gerhard Schroeder and the SPD leadership. Fischer became foreign minister. In 2000 the partners struck a deal mandating the closure of all of Germany's nuclear power plants by their thirty-second year of operation. (By early 2006, nineteen nuclear plants had been decommissioned, leaving seventeen in operation.) Despite conflict within the Alliance 90/Greens party over German military engagement in Bosnia, Kosovo, Macedonia, and Afghanistan, Fischer managed to rally his party to ensure its participation in the coalition government. The red-green coalition survived its first term intact and won reelection in 2002. Fischer stood out in opinion polls as Germany's most popular politician.[32]

In the 2005 elections, Alliance 90/the Greens campaigned for the implementation of plans to eliminate nuclear power (while Merkel favored a slowdown in this process), along with an emphasis on high-technology investment. The party also proposed some labor-market reforms, but did not go as far as the Christian Democrats or Free Democrats in currying the support of the business community. Although the Alliance 90/Greens party is situated on the left of Germany's political spectrum, it has a largely middle-class following, with a high proportion of educators, civil servants, executives and specialists in technology companies, and social activists who share their agenda. They do not appeal so much to the working class, the unemployed, pensioners, or eastern Germans who are having a difficult time coping with the consequences of unification.

**The Left Party** The **Left Party** is the new name adopted by the Party of Democratic Socialism (PDS) in the summer of 2005. The PDS was hastily formed out of the remnants of the Socialist Unity Party of Germany, the GDR's ruling communist party, as the East German regime was falling apart in 1990. Under the leadership of Gregor Gysi, a dissident East German lawyer who had opposed the communist regime's dictatorial practices, the PDS asserted its acceptance of the rules of democracy. It immediately identified itself as the party that would seek to protect East Germans from unemployment, pension cuts, and other harsh realities of the disappearance of the communist state's welfare system. In 2002 the PDS fell below the 5 percent threshold, but it managed to send two directly elected delegates to the Bundestag thanks to a provision in the electoral law permitting exceptions to the hurdle rule. As in previous elections, the PDS won the overwhelming majority of its votes in the former East Germany. Lothar Bisky, a moderate, succeeded his friend Gysi as party chief.

In 2005 Oskar Lafontaine, the outspoken leader of the Social Democratic Party's left wing, bolted from the SPD in protest of Schroeder's pro-business economic reform policies and formed a new grouping, the Labor and Social Justice Party. As the 2005 snap elections approached, Lafontaine and the Left Party joined forces in an electoral alliance, agreeing not to run candidates against each other. A number of leftist independents also adhered to the new grouping. The electoral partners agreed to decide at a later date whether to merge their groups into a single party. During the campaign the Left Party and its partners adopted a pronouncedly leftist program that called for a minimum wage of $21,000 a year, a 50 percent income tax on all those making more than $75,000 a year, increases in corporate income taxes, and hefty increases in government spending on unemployment, pensions, health care, and other welfare programs.[33] By the end of 2005 the Left Party had about 67,000 members; nearly 90 percent of them resided in the former East Germany.

**Results** At the start of the campaign, Merkel and the Christian Democrats enjoyed a substantial lead in the polls. But Merkel proved to be a maladroit and uninspiring campaigner while Schroeder bounded into the campaign with his customary exuberance. By all accounts Schroeder outshone Merkel in their television debate shortly before the elections. With swing voters now constituting upward of half the German electorate, the outcome of the vote appeared increasingly in doubt as election day neared. The final results confounded the experts' predictions. The two Christian Democratic parties eked out a much narrower victory than anticipated—"knocked down hard," in Merkel's observation. Together they won 35.2 percent of the second-column (party-list) popular vote (a decline of 3.3 percent compared to 2002) and 226 seats in the Bundestag (22 fewer than in 2002). The Social Democrats did slightly better than anticipated, but still fell short of their 2002 results. Their second-vote total of 34.2 percent was 4.3 percent less than they had won in the previous Bundestag elections, and the 222 seats they captured in 2005 represented 29 fewer than in 2002. The total second-column popular vote for the "people's parties"—the Christian Democrats and the Social Democrats—sank to only 53.2 percent of Germany's registered voters, their lowest combined share in the history of the Federal Republic. (In 1972 these parties won 82 percent of the eligible electorate, and in 2002 they won 60 percent.) The Free Democrats picked up 14 seats, not enough to form a coalition government with the Christian Democrats. The Alliance 90/Greens party lost two seats, while the Left Party—bolstered somewhat by Lafontaine's small group—increased its vote totals dramatically. The Left Party more than doubled its share of the party-list vote compared with 2002, and its Bundestag delegation increased from 2 PDS members in 2002 to 54 members in 2005. As in the past, the Left Party won most of its votes in the east. It garnered 25.4 percent of the vote in the former East Germany but only 4.9 percent in western Germany.

Prior to the elections, Christian Democrats and Social Democrats alike brushed aside talk of a possible Grand Coalition government. But the distribution of Bundestag seats provided no other option acceptable to a majority of Germans. A poll of one thousand people taken a few days after the September 18 election revealed that 51 percent would accept a black-red Grand Coalition, but no other color combination of governing coalitions attracted a majority of respondents. Fearing instability, only 17 to 20 percent approved of a minority government under the Social Democrats or Christian Democrats. In the absence of feasible alternatives, leaders of the CDU, the CSU, and the SPD began negotiations on the government none of them really wanted. They completed their work on the Grand Coalition's initial governing program after marathon talks that lasted nearly two months.[34]

### The Second Grand Coalition

The Grand Coalition's program, which ran to 190 pages, reflected major concessions on both sides. Merkel and the Christian Democrats had to retreat from some of their hopes of combating unemployment by reducing labor costs significantly. They also had to give up their plans to grant companies a general right to opt out of industry-wide agreements on wages and working hours. The Social

**Angela Merkel and Gerhard Schroeder after the Formation of the Grand Coalition Government**

Democrats had to give up their proposals to spark economic growth through major increases in government spending. Both sides instead agreed to rein in government spending and raise various taxes so as to bring anticipated budget deficits down to 3 percent of GDP by 2007 and even lower by 2009. This fiscally conservative program included an increase in the value-added tax from 16 percent to 19 percent (1 percent higher than the Christian Democrats had advocated), plus an increase in the top income tax rate for people earning more than $300,000 a year. The two sides also agreed to extend the period of time during which employers may fire new workers from the first six months of employment to the first twenty-four months, but they tightened restrictions on the right of employers to lay off long-term workers. The average retirement age was raised from 65 to 67, but it would not take effect until the age cohort born in 1964 reaches 67 in 2031. (It is expected that by that time there will be only two working-age people per retiree in Germany, less than half the current ratio.) Plans for reforms of the tax code and health insurance were put on hold pending future discussions. A health-insurance reform was worked out toward the end of 2006, reducing employer payroll taxes.

During her first months as chancellor, Merkel reiterated her support for the social market economy and made significant efforts to get along with her Social Democratic partners. Pro-business reformers within the Christian Democratic parties worried that the new chancellor was backing away from her previous commitments to greater flexibility for company executives to deal with their labor issues. But consumer spending and business profits rose, boosting economic growth to a projected 1.8 percent for 2006 (the highest rate since 2000). And the general public reacted positively to Merkel's first six months in office, boosting her approval ratings over 80 percent. In the second half of 2006, however, Merkel's ratings took a nosedive, dropping fifty points. Despite a decline in unemployment rolls, the public was jittery. Optimists hoped that the Social Democrats and Christian Democrats would put aside their differences and reach decisions that effectively addressed the country's problems. But pessimists feared that compromises would be reached only at the lowest common denominator of agreement, resulting in watered-down decisions that increased the population's tax and welfare burdens while having little positive impact. Capturing the public mood, a best-seller bemoaned Germany's fall from superstar status; another book portrayed Germany as an "aimless republic."[35]

For their part, the Social Democrats were also having trouble adjusting to their new situation. Conflicts continued to rage between the party's right wing, which had backed Schroeder's reforms, and its left wing, which favored bolstering welfare-state supports for workers and pensioners. Following the formation of the Grand Coalition government, Gerhard Schroeder resigned from the Bundestag and joined the governing board of a Russian-German consortium established to facilitate the sale of Russian natural gas in Germany. The consortium was dominated by Gazprom, an energy giant partially owned by the Russian government. Franz Muentefering resigned as the SPD's chairman upon entering the Grand Coalition cabinet as deputy chancellor. His immediate successor lasted only a few months before the party settled on Kurt Beck, the head of one of Germany's state governments, as its new chairman. (The SPD chairman is selected by the political professionals and party activists who attend the party congress held at least every two years. In 2006 the SPD had about 560,000 members.)

There was uncertainty, as well, about the future of Germany's well-developed system of neo-corporatism.

## POLITICAL ISSUES IN CONTEMPORARY GERMANY

### Neo-Corporatism and the Economy

As explained in chapter 11, *corporatism* is a form of formal interest-group representation in the state's decision-making process. The form of corporatism that developed in West Germany after World War II was democratic in nature and featured several elements sufficiently distinct from other forms of corporatism that it came to be labeled **neo-corporatism.**

The basic idea is simple: representatives of the main business associations and trade unions—known as "peak associations"—sit down with government officials on a regular basis and map out the country's economic and social welfare policies. The main business associations include the *Federation of German Industry (Bund der Industrie,* or *BDI),* which represents large businesses, plus others that represent smaller businesses and agricultural interests.[36] The main peak association of the labor movement is the *German Confederation of Labor (Deutscher Gewerkschaftsbund,* or *DGB),* an umbrella group consisting of eight major trade unions. Wage parameters, working conditions, paid vacations, welfare benefits, profit margins—these and other labor–management issues have traditionally been largely determined by these tripartite negotiations. The resulting agreements have typically extended nationwide across an entire industry, such as the metal industry or the chemical industry.

After Germany became unified in 1990, some observers predicted that the neo-corporatist system, which worked rather well in West Germany, would fall apart when confronted with the new challenges posed by the integration of East Germany's problem-ridden communist-era economy into an enlarged Germany. As time went on, there were additional predictions that globalization—with its pressures on companies to reduce operating costs and raise efficiency—would damage neo-corporatism even further, perhaps delivering a knockout blow. Have these two hypotheses proven correct?

## HYPOTHESIS-TESTING EXERCISE: Neo-Corporatism in Germany

### Hypotheses

Two hypotheses are being tested. The first is that Germany's unification has caused a decline in neo-corporatist decision-making procedures in Germany. The second is that globalization has caused a similar result.

### Variables

In both hypotheses, the *dependent variable* is *neo-corporatism in Germany*. The first hypothesis posits *unification* as an *independent variable* that is affecting neo-corporatism, causing it to decline. The second hypothesis posits *globalization* as the *independent variable.*

### Expectations

Proponents of the first hypothesis believed that the collapse of East Germany's centrally planned economy and the challenges of transforming it into a social market economy patterned on West Germany would create unemployment in eastern Germany and inequalities between a poorly qualified—and poorly paid—eastern German labor force and a better qualified, better paid western German work force. The resulting labor–management frictions could be expected to spill over into party politics, with pro-business parties like the Christian Democrats and the Free Democrats favoring less reliance on talks with trade unions, and pro-labor parties like the Social Democrats and the Party of Democratic Socialism (the future Left Party) favoring neo-corporatist mechanisms. Following roughly similar arguments, proponents of the second hypothesis expect globalization to increase pressures on businesses to cut labor costs and demand greater flexibility in determining wages, layoffs, work hours, and the like. To this end, individual companies would oppose industry-wide agreements and seek to work out their own arrangements with their employees, thus undermining neo-corporatist deals. Once again, the political parties could be expected to line up for and against these anticipated developments.

### Evidence

With regard to the first hypothesis, labor tensions definitely grew in both eastern and western Germany as unemployment followed in the wake of unification. At least initially, however, the consequences for neo-corporatism were just the opposite of those predicted by exponents of the first hypothesis, as an insightful study has shown.[37] Instead of taking a solidly pro-business stance, the Kohl government actually reinforced corporatist practices. Once eastern German Christian Democrats convinced the chancellor that their party would lose votes if they did not address eastern Germany's discontented population, Kohl moved to achieve a broad consensus on a "solidarity pact" that would siphon large sums of money to the east's troubled economy. Between September 1992 and March 1993, no fewer than forty meetings took place in Kohl's office alone as the government made an energetic effort to find common ground among Germany's main economic interest groups, party leaders, and state governments. Kohl convinced the leaders of several of Germany's leading business associations to provide funds for the eastern German economy and to buy capital equipment from east German factories so as to keep them operating as long as possible. Kohl also negotiated with the heads of important trade unions and won their agreement to moderate the wage demands of workers. In exchange, Kohl promised to keep as many communist-era eastern

German factories in operation as long as possible, rather than putting them out of business all at once and aggravating unemployment. Just as important, Kohl's CDU/CSU-FDP government entered into direct talks with the Social Democratic leadership. The SPD now controlled the Bundesrat, requiring Kohl to come to terms in order to get elements of his solidarity pact passed into law.

After concessions were made by all parties, the government and parliament approved a 7.5 percent "solidarity tax" surcharge on German taxpayers to help pay for the surging costs of propping up eastern Germany's economy. After winning a mere ten-vote majority in the Bundestag in 1994, the CDU/CSU-FDP coalition government was in no position to adopt an all-out confrontationist stance. Cooperation and consultation with the business community, the trade unions, the opposition parties, and the state governments proved vital as painful and politically unpopular decisions had to be made.

As time went on, however, the problems associated with the modernization of eastern Germany's economy multiplied. Unemployment in the former East Germany was twice the rate of western German unemployment, for example. These problems were exacerbated by another source of trouble—economic globalization. As anticipated by the second hypothesis, globalization has placed considerable pressures on Germany's neo-corporatist mechanisms. Chancellor Schroeder dealt with private-sector demands for lower labor costs and greater flexibility in hiring and firing by reaching outside the traditional framework of tripartite business-labor-government negotiations and appointing consultative bodies like the Hartz Commission to propose new solutions. As we have seen, Schroeder ran into difficulties when he tried to get the Bundestag to approve the Hartz proposals. Trade unions and members of his own party considered the proposals too harsh, whereas many business executives considered them inadequate. With unemployment rates unchanged and economic growth stalled, just about everybody regarded the proposals as ineffective.

The solutions to these problems proposed by Angela Merkel and other Christian Democrats would undermine neo-corporatism even further. As noted earlier, today's Christian Democrats favor giving companies greater freedom to opt out of national industry-wide wage agreements worked out through corporatist bargaining procedures, allowing them to cut their own deals with their work force. Merkel also favors reducing the influence of workers' representatives on company boards, striking a blow at the "co-participation" (*Mitbestimmung*) institutions set up in the Adenauer era. Meanwhile, the influence of Germany's labor unions is declining. Strikes by the country's large metalworkers' union, IG Metall, have fizzled in recent years (including a strike after the Grand Coalition came to power). Membership in the German Confederation of Labor has fallen from 12 million in 1990 to 7 million in 2006. Only 20 percent of employees in Germany belong to unions, compared to 29 percent in Britain. This steep drop in membership is due in part to globalization factors. German companies are increasingly outsourcing work to other countries and building plants abroad, including in nearby eastern Europe. In the process, they are laying off workers in Germany. International pressures to cut labor costs are discouraging German businesses from hiring new workers, making it difficult for the trade unions to find new recruits. These trends are driven in large part by the importance of the export sector in Germany's economy. Exports account for 40 percent of Germany's GDP and for 9 million jobs. Virtually all of Germany's small- and medium-size companies are involved in the world economy. The need to maintain the competitiveness of German businesses against foreign companies is thus imperative for the entire German economy. Many German workers are agreeing to wage deals negotiated directly with their employers in exchange for job security, bypassing the unions and their national industry-wide agreements. In the process, businesses are increasingly bypassing the national employers' associations. But a shortfall of skilled workers has induced German companies to import labor from abroad. As many as fifty thousand foreigners come to Germany every year to work in high-technology fields and other areas requiring skills that Germany's shrinking population cannot supply. (India is a prime source of this labor force.) Most of these immigrants are not unionized.[38]

## Conclusions

The evidence for the first hypothesis appears to be *mixed*. Initially, Germany's unification did not put an end to neo-corporatist procedures. Both Helmut Kohl and—for a while, at least—Gerhard Schroeder used traditional tripartite corporatist bargaining procedures. But by the late 1990s, as the problems of the eastern German economy persisted, Schroeder increasingly reached outside these neo-corporatist structures in a quest for new solutions to eastern Germany's plight. The evidence for the second hypothesis seems largely *consistent* with its premise that globalization is undermining German neo-corporatism. Whether neo-corporatist bargaining structures will disappear completely remains to be seen.

### Immigration and Minorities

By 2005 Germany had approximately 6 million foreigners. Together they constituted about 8 percent of the population. About 2 million are descendants of "guest workers" from Turkey who, along with workers from other countries, flocked to West Germany in the 1960s as the Federal Republic's long postwar economic miracle gathered steam. Others are refugees from war-torn Yugoslavia or ethnic Germans who left the Soviet union as it collapsed, uprooting families whose ancestors had emigrated to Russia hundreds of years ago. Still others are asylum seekers from Africa, Asia, and other corners of the globe who seek to escape persecution in their native countries. Nearly 90,000 people a year seek asylum in Germany for these reasons—the highest number seeking entry to any European country. As noted above, tens of thousands of immigrants have come to Germany every year to fill job vacancies. (Germany's fertility rate was 1.4 births per woman in 2004, compared to 1.7 in Britain, 1.9 in France, and 2.0 in the United States.)

Historically, Germans have tended to define their nationality in strictly ethnic terms: to be a German citizen, one had to have German blood. But starting in 2000, a new law took effect that grants German citizenship at birth to children born of non-German parents, as long as one parent has resided in Germany at least eight years. (Every year about a hundred thousand children are born in Germany to non-German citizens.) In addition, the waiting period for acquiring German citizenship through naturalization procedures was reduced from fifteen years to eight.[39]

In 2005 there were more than 3 million Muslims living in Germany, about 3.7 percent of the population. A survey published in 2006 revealed that 66 percent of Germany's Muslims considered themselves "Muslims first" and German citizens second. For their part, 59 percent of Germans regarded immigration from the Middle East and North Africa as a "bad thing"—a much higher figure than in Britain (32 percent) or France (41 percent). And 82 percent of the general public in Germany was concerned about the rise of Islamic extremism in their country (compared with 77 percent in Britain and 76 percent in France). Three out of four Germans believe that Muslims who reside in their country want to be distinct from the rest of society (as opposed to about two-thirds of the British and slightly more than half the French).[40] Germany's Constitutional Court has ruled that German states have the right to enact legislation banning head scarves in public schools.

The rise of international terrorism and the war in Iraq have heightened public concerns. As noted earlier, three of the terrorists involved in the September 11 attacks had previously lived in Germany. According to official estimates, there were approximately 31,000 Islamic extremists living in Germany in 2003. In the summer of 2006, when the World Cup soccer championship was taking place in Germany, police found suitcase bombs in two German trains; the bombs were timed to detonate but failed to go off. Within a few days the authorities arrested two Arab suspects who had been living in Germany before fleeing to Lebanon immediately after setting the bombs. German investigators said that they were having problems keeping up with the many websites used by terrorists. In 2003 a Lebanese-born German citizen named Khaled el-Masri was picked up by U.S. authorities in Macedonia on suspicion of terrorist connections. The American authorities then took him to Afghanistan, where he was held for five months before being released. Masri denied he was a terrorist. The United States informed the German government about the case in 2004, after Masri was released. Germany eventually interceded with the Americans in his behalf, and in 2006, U.S. Secretary of State Condoleezza Rice admitted that a "mistake" had been made in Masri's arrest and detention, offering him an apology and financial compensation.

"Germany is not a classical immigration society," Angela Merkel has reiterated, echoing the words of a report by a government-sponsored commission. During Gerhard Schroeder's years as chancellor, the Christian Democrats used their control of the Bundesrat to impose various restrictions on immigration. Foreigners coming to Germany for work, for example, must have a job already secured before they arrive. On a darker side, violence aimed at foreigners has risen in recent years, perpetrated by a fanatically prejudiced minority. But two ultra-right anti-immigrant parties fell well short of the 5 percent threshold in the Bundestag elections of 2005. In the years ahead, Germany's small but growing ethnic and religious minorities will likely pose challenges not only to the broader population's security but also to its commitment to tolerance and inclusion.

## CONCLUSION

In the decades since World War II, the Federal Republic of Germany has achieved considerable success in adopting the core values of democracy and in solidifying the rule of law, thus creating the foundations of the Temple of Democracy that we described in chapter 7. It has also succeeded in building the three functional pillars of the temple: popular sovereignty (Pillar I), guaranteed rights and liberties (Pillar II), and a high level of economic well-being (Pillar III). Postwar Germany has also fulfilled, in varying degrees, all ten conditions for democracy that we enumerated in chapter 9. One of Germany's biggest problems today centers on the need to forge a broader sense of national unity, one that embraces the "Ossies" of the former East Germany as well as people of non-German origin who wish to be full participants in the country's increasingly heterogeneous society. Another problem is that of ensuring the well-being of the entire populace on the basis of fairness and community welfare while addressing the pressures of globalization and domestic financial challenges. Though they may differ on how these challenges should be addressed, Germany's mainstream political leaders appear to be fully committed to meeting them.

Germany has made extraordinary strides in the postwar era in building and sustaining a viable democratic system. When viewed against the mistakes of the past—especially the failures of the Weimar Republic and the atrocities of Nazism—Germany's success provides important lessons for peoples who seek to replace the terrors of dictatorship with the benefits of stable democracy.

## KEY TERMS AND NAMES
## (In bold and underlined in the text)

Angela Merkel
Gerhard Schroeder
Grand Coalition
Social Democratic Party of Germany (SPD)
Weimar Republic
Adolph Hitler
Nazis
Free Democratic Party (FDP)
Christian Democratic Union (CDU)
Christian Social Union (CSU)
Basic Law
Federal Republic of Germany
States (*Laender*)
Bundesrat
Bundestag
Chancellor
President
Federal Constitutional Court
Social market economy
Helmut Kohl
Alliance 90/The Greens
Left Party
Neo-corporatism

## NOTES

1. John H. Backer, *The Decision to Divide Germany* (Durham, N.C.: Duke University Press, 1978); Norman M. Naimark, *The Russians in Germany* (Cambridge, Mass.: Belknap, 1995); Henry Krisch, *German Politics Under Soviet Occupation* (New York: Columbia University Press, 1972); Ann L. Phillips, *Soviet Policy Toward East Germany Reconsidered* (Westport, Conn.: Greenwood, 1986).
2. Hope M. Harrison, *Driving the Soviets up the Wall: Soviet–East German Relations, 1953–1961* (Princeton: Princeton University Press, 2003).
3. Robert Darnton, *Berlin Journal, 1989–1990* (New York: W. W. Norton, 1991); Charles S. Maier, *Dissolution* (Princeton: Princeton University Press, 1997); Jeffrey Gedmin, *The Hidden Hand* (Washington, D.C.: AEI Press, 1992); Gert-Joachim Glaessner, *The Unification Process in Germany* (New York: St. Martin's Press, 1992); Elizabeth Pond, *Beyond the Wall* (Washington, D.C.: Brookings Institution, 1993); Konrad H. Jarausch, *The Rush to German Unity* (New York: Oxford University Press, 1994); Philip Zelikow and Condoleezza Rice, *Germany Unified and Europe Transformed* (Cambridge, Mass.: Harvard University Press, 1995); Angela E. Stent, *Russia and Germany Reborn* (Princeton: Princeton University Press, 1999).

4. Manfred Guellner, ed., *Was Deutschland bewegt: der forsa-Meinungsreport 2002* (Frankfurt-on-Main: Eichborn, 2002), 36, 205, 212, 213, 218, 221.
5. James J. Sheehan, *German Liberalism in the Nineteenth Century* (Chicago: University of Chicago Press, 1978); Leonard Krieger, *The German Idea of Freedom* (Chicago: University of Chicago Press, 1957).
6. Liah Greenfeld, *Nationalism: Five Roads to Modernity* (Cambridge, Mass.: Harvard University Press, 1992), 369.
7. Joshua Mitchell, "Protestant Thought and Republican Spirit: How Luther Enchanted the World," *American Political Science Review* 86, no. 3 (September 1992): 688–95. On later developments, see Max Weber, *The Protestant Ethic and the Spirit of Capitalism*, trans. Talcott Parsons (London: Routledge, 1992). For a summary of Weber's views, see chapter 13.
8. The Great War took an estimated 10 million lives and left about 30 million wounded. It claimed 10 percent of France's male population and 9 percent of British males under age forty-five. Out of 11 million German troops mobilized, 1.8 million were killed and 4.2 million were wounded. Russia, Austria-Hungary, Italy, and other combatants also took heavy casualties. The United States, whose troops entered the fray in the spring of 1918, suffered 11,500 deaths and 206,000 wounded.
9. Richard F. Hamilton, *Who Voted for Hitler?* (Princeton: Princeton University Press, 1982); Thomas Childers, *The Nazi Voter* (Chapel Hill: University of North Carolina Press, 1983).
10. Sheri Berman, *The Social Democratic Movement* (Cambridge, Mass.: Harvard University Press, 1998); Anton Kaes, Martin Jay, and Edward Dimendberg, eds., *The Weimar Republic Sourcebook* (Berkeley: University of California Press, 1994); David Abraham, *The Collapse of the Weimar Republic*, 2nd ed. (New York: Holmes & Meier, 1986).
11. Erich Fromm, *Escape from Freedom* (New York: Holt, Rinehart, and Winston, 1941); Bertram Schaffner, *Fatherland: A Study of Authoritarianism in the German Family* (New York: Columbia University Press, 1948); T. W. Adorno et al., *The Authoritarian Personality* (New York: Harper, 1950).
12. Kurt Dietrich Bracher, *The German Dictatorship* (New York: Praeger, 1970); David Schoenbaum, *Hitler's Social Revolution* (New York: W. W. Norton, 1980).
13. In addition to being divided into West Germany and East Germany after the war, Germany lost a considerable amount of territory to its eastern neighbors. The Soviet Union, whose armies occupied the region, gave some parts of Germany to Poland, including the cities of Danzig (now Gdansk) and Stettin (Szczecin) and the industrial region of Silesia. The USSR annexed the city of Koenigsberg and its surrounding region, renaming it Kaliningrad. It is still part of Russia. The Soviets also restored the Sudetenland to Czechoslovakia. In 1938 Hitler had annexed this region, with its large German population, winning British and French acceptance of his action at the Munich conference.
14. Lewis Edinger, *Kurt Schumacher* (Stanford, Calif.: Stanford University Press, 1965).
15. Robert Gerald Livingstone, "Germany's Intelligence Failure," *Washington Post*, October 19, 2001.
16. Local government in Germany is based on some 16,000 cities, towns, and villages; all have elected councils and have various responsibilities for schools, fire safety, sanitation, and other activities. All but about 100 of these communities (*Gemeinden*) fall within county (*Kreis*) administrations. Though local and county governments may raise some of their revenue locally, most of it comes in the form of grants from the federal and state governments.
17. Peter Katzenstein, *Policy and Politics in West Germany: The Growth of a Semi-Sovereign State?* (Philadelphia: Temple University Press, 1987). On federalism and other aspects of Germany's institutions, see Oscar W. Gabriel and Everhard Holtmann, eds., *Handbuch politisches System der Bundesrepublik Deutschland*, 2nd ed. (Munich: R. Oldenbourg, 1999).
18. Another provision of the electoral laws is the "three-mandate waiver" rule. If a party fails to clear the 5 percent hurdle *but wins at least three district mandates*, the hurdle clause is waived

and it is entitled to a share of Bundestag seats in proportion to its share of the second vote. If the PDS had won a third district mandate in 2002, it would have been entitled to 4 percent of the seats in the Bundestag, its share of the party-list vote nationwide.

**19.** In the event that the parties cannot agree on a chancellor, the president may have some discretion in picking someone of his or her own choice; even then, however, the Bundestag majority would have to agree. The president co-signs all bills before they become law, but has no veto power; the signature is usually automatic.

**20.** Donald Kommers, *The Federal Constitutional Court* (Washington, D.C.: American Institute for Contemporary German Studies, 1994), and *The Constitutional Jurisprudence of the Federal Republic of Germany* (Durham, N.C.: Duke University Press, 1989).

**21.** David P. Conradt, "Changing German Political Culture," in *The Civic Culture Revisited*, ed. Gabriel A. Almond and Sidney Verba (Boston: Little, Brown, 1980), 212–72; Kendall L. Baker, Russel J. Dalton, and Kai Hildebrandt, *Germany Transformed* (Cambridge, Mass.: Harvard University Press, 1981).

**22.** Konrad Adenauer, *Memoirs*, trans. Beate Ruhm von Oppen (Chicago: H. Regnery, 1966); Charles Williams, *Adenauer: The Father of the New Germany* (New York: Wiley, 2000); Hans-Peter Schwarz, *Konrad Adenauer*, trans. Louise Willmot (Providence, R.I.: Berghahn, 1995).

**23.** On Soviet-German relations from 1963 to unification in 1990, see Michael J. Sodaro, *Moscow, Germany, and the West from Khrushchev to Gorbachev* (Ithaca, N.Y.: Cornell University Press, 1990).

**24.** Willy Brandt, *My Life in Politics* (New York: Viking, 1992), and *People and Politics: The Years 1960–1975*, trans. J. Maxwell Brownjohn (Boston: Little, Brown, 1978); Barbara Marshall, *Willy Brandt: A Political Biography* (New York: St. Martin's Press, 1997).

**25.** Helmut Schmidt, *Men and Powers: A Memoir*, trans. Ruth Hein (New York: Random House, 1989); Jonathan Carr, *Helmut Schmidt: Helmsman of Germany* (London: Weidenfield Nicholson, 1985).

**26.** Karl Hugo Pruys, *Kohl, Genius of the Present*, trans. Kathleen Bunten (Chicago: Edition q, 1996).

**27.** Even though German campaign financing laws provide for substantial public funding for the main parties, a parliamentary investigative committee reported in 2000 that the Christian Democrats had received about $9 million, and the Social Democrats about $500,000, in illegal donations.

**28.** See Volker Herres and Klaus Waller, *Gerhard Schröder: der Weg nach Berlin* (Munich: Econ and List, 1998), and Reinhard Urschel, *Gerhard Schröder: eine Biographie* (Stuttgart: Deutscher Verlags-Anstalt, 2002).

**29.** For Lafontaine's views, see his book, *The Heart Beats on the Left*, trans. Ronald Taylor (Cambridge, UK: Polity, 2000). On the SPD's situation during the Kohl years, see Fritz Scharpf, *Crisis and Choice in European Social Democracy* (Ithaca, N.Y.: Cornell University Press, 1991). See also *The Economist*, February 6, 1999.

**30.** Michael Stiller, *Edmund Stoiber: der Kandidat* (Munich: Econ, 2002).

**31.** Gerd Langgruth, *Angela Merkel* (Munich: Deutscher Taschenbuch Verlag, 2005).

**32.** Joschka Fischer, *Die Rueckkehr der Geschichte* (Cologne: Kiepenheuer & Witsch, 2005); Bernd Ulrich, *Der Unvollendete: Das Leben des Joschka Fischer* (Berlin: Alexander Fest, 2002). Fischer left the Bundestag after the 2005 elections.

**33.** Peter Thompson, *The Crisis of the German Left: The PDS, Stalinism, and the Global Economy* (New York: Berghahn, 2005).

**34.** Eckhard Jesse and Roland Sturm, eds., *Bilanz der Bundestagswahl 2005: Voraussetzungen, Ergebnisse, Folgen* (Wiesbaden: Verlag fuer Sozialwissenschaften, 2006). See also *Der Spiegel*, September 19 and 26, 2005; *Focus*, September 20, 2005.

**35.** Stefan Aust, Claus Richter, and Gabor Steingart, eds., *Der Fall Deutschland: Abstieg eines Superstars* (Munich: Piper, 2005); Franz Walter, *Die ziellose Republik: Gezeitenwechsel in Gesellschaft und Politik* (Cologne: Kiepenheuer & Witsch, 2006).

**36.** The main trade union for service and public sector employees is Verdi, with 2.8 million members. In addition to BDI (Bundesverband der deutschen Industrie), the business community's peak associations include the Federation of German Employer Associations (BDA) and the German Industrial and Trade Conference (DIHT). Germany's 2.5 million farmers are represented mainly by three highly influential associations that together call themselves the "Green Front" (though they are not related to the Green Party). They are the Farmer's League, the Association of Agricultural Chambers, and a cooperative organization, the Raiffeisenverband.

**37.** Razeen Sally and Douglas Webber, "The German Solidarity Pact: A Case Study in the Politics of the Unified Germany," *German Politics* 3, no. 1 (April 1994): 18–46.

**38.** *Financial Times*, January 6, May 19, and August 30, 2006. See also "Waiting for a Wunder: A Survey of Germany," *The Economist*, February 11, 2006.

**39.** William A. Barbieri Jr., *Ethics of Citizenship: Immigration and Group Rights in Germany* (Durham, N.C.: Duke University Press, 1998). Germany's Jewish population, which had numbered 500,000 in 1933, increased from 29,000 in 1999 to more than 100,000 in 2001 (*Washington Post*, September 10 and December 13, 2001; February 20 and May 10, 2003).

**40.** "Muslims in Europe: Economic Worries Top Concerns About Religious and Cultural Identity: 13-Nation Pew Global Attitudes Survey," July 6, 2006, available at www.pewglobal.org.

CHAPTER 19

# JAPAN

DEAN W. COLLINWOOD

Population (2005): 123.2/million
Freedom House Ratings (2002):
Political Rights—1; Civil Liberties—2

Area: 145,882 square miles
(slightly larger than California)

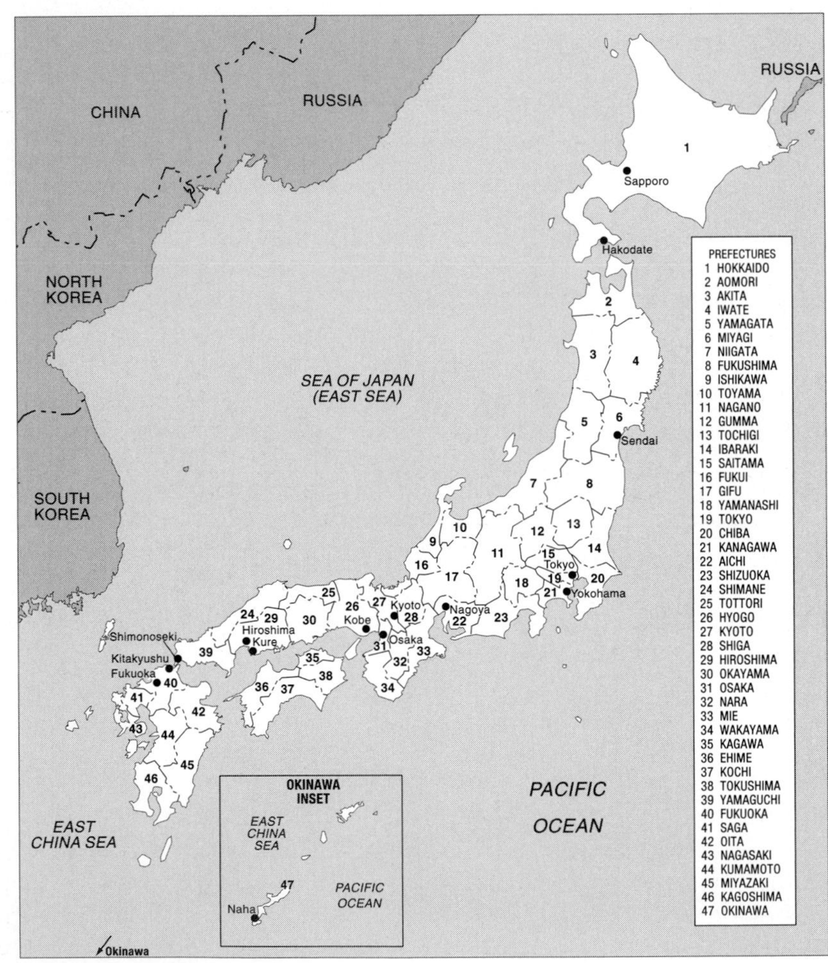


*Source:* U.S. Central Intelligence Agency.

## POLITICAL PARALYSIS IN THE 1990S

When all the votes were finally counted, the result was stunning. In a rare occurrence in Japanese politics, the prime minister and his cabinet had lost a vote of confidence in the House of Representatives, the lower house of Japan's parliament. On June 18, 1993, by a vote of 255 to 220, the House deprived the government of seventy-three-year-old Prime Minister *Kiichi Miyazawa* of its majority, forcing his resignation. Even more shocking, thirty-nine members of Miyazawa's own party, the Liberal Democratic Party (LDP), had joined with the opposition parties in voting against him.

Ever since their party was founded in 1955, the Liberal Democrats had won every national election and formed every government. The opposition parties were so weak that they barely counted. The LDP's dominance of the country's political institutions not only included its sway over the cabinet and the two houses of parliament (known together as the Diet), it also extended over Japan's powerful bureaucracy and most of its local governments. Under the LDP's one-party rule, Japan had risen from wartime defeat and initial postwar poverty to the exalted status of the world's second largest economy after the United States. In 1993 it had a $132 billion global trade surplus, $50 billion of it with the United States. As the economic powerhouse of Asia, Japan fueled the growth of virtually every country in the region. However, after decades of success, Japan's economy had suddenly started to nosedive, placing both the nation and the LDP in unfamiliar trouble. The party's disarray in the Miyazawa no-confidence vote raised the possibility that Japan would soon have a non-LDP government for the first time in thirty-eight years. As Miyazawa, following custom, bowed politely to the House following his defeat and slowly left the chamber, it was evident that change was coming, not just to his own government, but to the prevailing patterns of Japan's political system.

What caused this shred in the fabric of Japanese politics? One factor was the dismal state of the economy. After establishing itself as the world's most active trading nation and catapulting over such strong economies as those of Britain, France, and Germany during the 1960s and 1970s, Japan suffered the sudden collapse of many of its most important financial institutions. Japanese banks had made hundreds of billions of dollars worth of bad loans to corporations and investors with no ability to repay what they had borrowed. The magnitude of these unpaid debts sent shock waves through the economy in Japan and the rest of Asia.[1] But a second factor had an even more devastating effect on the Liberal Democrats' grip on power: corruption.

Only a few months before Miyazawa was forced to endure the fatal vote of no-confidence, the LDP was jolted by the arrest of Shin Kanemaru, one of its most powerful politicians, on charges of tax evasion. Revelations of corruption on the part of LDP leaders were nothing new. Over the previous decades the Japanese had become accustomed to one scandal after another involving bribery, kickbacks, and other forms of corruption on the part of Liberal Democratic Party officials, legislators, cabinet ministers, and even prime ministers. In 1989, for example, two prime ministers in succession were forced to resign, the first for receiving illegal donations from a major Japanese corporation (the Recruit Company), the second for alleged improprieties with a geisha whom he paid to be his mistress. But the arrest of Shin Kanemaru in March 1993 was the straw that broke the camel's back as far as public opinion was concerned.

At age seventy-eight, Kanemaru was the Liberal Democrats' top behind-the-scenes power broker. His influence could make or break LDP politicians as they grappled their way up the ladder of political power. A long list of Liberal Democratic cabinet ministers owed their positions to Kanemaru's nod. His influence remained undiminished despite his 1992 admission that he had received more than $4 million in illegal campaign contributions, a scandal that forced his resignation from the Diet. The following year, the public and many LDP politicians were further disillusioned by the news that investigators had uncovered some $750,000 in gold ingots hidden under the floorboards of Kanemaru's house, plus millions of dollars in cash and bonds stashed away in other places in his homes and offices. Kanemaru died in 1996 before he could be brought to trial, but for a growing number of Japanese, the corruption of the LDP's patriarch typified the party itself and the government it had monopolized for nearly four decades.

Not all Liberal Democrats were corrupt, to be sure. But efforts to reform the party's practices invariably foundered on the staunch opposition of LDP politicians whose careers had profited from illicit behavior. Prime Minister Miyazawa himself, only days before his ouster, was forced to withdraw a reform plan that unleashed a storm of indignation among party officials determined to resist change. But the widespread public hunger for a reordering of the Japanese political system had become irrepressible.

One month after Miyazawa's resignation, new elections were held for the House of Representatives. The weeks preceding the vote witnessed a frenzy of party realignments. Several dozen LDP parliamentarians quit their party to form new ones. Hundreds of thousands of Japanese citizens, normally known for their political quiescence, got involved in clubs and associations organized over the preceding year to promote political change. Many other Japanese citizens, however, were either so confused by the turmoil, or perhaps so fed up with politics, that they stayed away from the polls; only two out of three eligible voters turned out, about 5 percent fewer than in most previous elections.

Nevertheless, when election day came on July 18, the result was a watershed in Japanese politics. For the first time since 1955, the Liberal Democrats lost their lower house majority, winning only 44 percent of the seats. Power passed to a seven-party coalition government headed by *Morihiro Hosokawa,* a fifty-five-year old politician who had once served as a regional governor and who was descended from an old samurai family. He invited no LDP members into his cabinet. Just as astounding, a woman—Takako Doi, a Socialist—was elected speaker of the House, quite a feat in a parliament with 98 percent male membership.

The grandson of a former prime minister, Hosokawa had begun his career in the Liberal Democratic Party but bolted it because of the leadership's resistance to reform. In 1992 he organized the Japan New Party. Dynamic and photogenic (he once played a samurai in a movie), the popular Hosokawa took office amid high hopes for a new beginning in Japanese politics. One of his first acts as prime minister was to issue a formal apology to the world for Japan's "acts of aggression and colonial rule" during World War II, a gesture previous LDP governments had been reluctant to make. His first major piece of legislation was a reform bill that called for the complete overhaul of Japan's lower house electoral system and for significant restrictions on campaign financing. When the bill was rejected by the upper house of the Diet, still dominated by old-guard Liberal Democrats, Hosokawa made compromises to save its essence. The compromises calmed the nerves of politicians accustomed to harmony and consensus in political bargaining—a defining feature of Japanese political culture—and the watered-down reforms cleared both houses in 1994.

But Hosokawa's government did not finish out the year. When Liberal Democrats accused him of improperly using a $970,000 loan for political purposes, and when an investment consultant publicly charged him with lying to the Diet about a large stock purchase, he resigned rather than undergo a politicized public investigation. Hosokawa's successor, another former LDP member, lasted only a few months as his multiparty government squabbled over economic reforms. By the middle of 1994, scarcely a year after the "restructuring" elections, the Japanese government was in a state of paralysis. Its standing in the world, which waited impatiently for a revival of the once mighty Japanese economy, declined. The non-LDP coalition parties proved incapable of governing and broke up. Their failure reopened the door to the Liberal Democrats, who returned limping to power as the coalition partners of none other than the Socialists, their archrivals since the 1950s.

This curious combination of the two parties that were the biggest losers of the 1993 elections did not improve matters. The new prime minister was a genteel seventy-year-old Socialist with no clearly articulated program for governing the country. After six more months of political drift and economic decline, Japan's government changed hands once again in January 1996. This time a Liberal Democrat, *Ryutaro Hashimoto,* took over as prime minister, restoring the highest political office in the land to the party most voters had repudiated less than three years earlier.

"Business as usual" quickly set in. Within a matter of months Hashimoto's government was embroiled in a financial scandal. As his approval ratings plummeted rapidly, the prime minister called snap elections in hopes of cobbling together a workable majority in the House of Representatives. And so in October 1996 Japanese voters went to the polls again, albeit with considerably less enthusiasm than in 1993. Only 59 percent bothered to cast their ballots, a postwar low. The number of people identifying with any of the parties, traditionally more than 80 percent, sank to half the electorate.

The campaign period, which by law may last only twelve days for the lower house and seventeen days for the upper house, had all the elements of a traditional Japanese election process. Typically, candidates in small rural towns and large cities like Tokyo don white gloves to symbolize their devotion to clean government, and they make as many personal appearances as possible. Many of them ride around in vans draped with large-print campaign slogans and equipped with powerful loudspeakers. Parking in front of train stations or busy intersections, they address everyone within earshot. The volume is so loud that no one can escape hearing at least part of their speeches. Every candidate gives such speeches during the campaign. Meanwhile, members of the candidate's *koenkai,* or support group, including relatives and friends, make speeches and telephone calls on behalf of their candidate and glue posters to hundreds of makeshift campaign billboards.

In 1996, for the first time, individual candidates were allowed to run television advertisements. (In previous elections only the national party organizations could do so.) Inevitably, these expenditures drove up the costs of running for office rather than reducing them. In spite of the 1994 reforms that placed limits on the amount of funds individual candidates could raise, the cost of the average campaign rose from $500,000 for a single Diet seat in previous elections to as much as $3 million, exceeding in just two weeks of electioneering what candidates for the U.S. Congress spend in much longer election campaigns.

Many of the 1994 Hosokawa reforms had fallen far short of their original intent. Hopes of promoting a U.S.-style two-party system, with the Liberal Democrats vying against a large opposition party, proved unrealizable. More than a half-dozen parties put up candidates in 1996, and the LDP's most serious rival, the New Frontier Party, was a new upstart party created only two years earlier. The reformers' hopes of encouraging more meaningful debate on the issues during election campaigns also met with disappointment, as most candidates resorted as usual to blaring sound trucks and vague slogans, often laced with vituperative attacks on their opponents. The electioneering became so acrimonious that the largest parties filed suit against each other for violating the new campaign law's prohibition on mudslinging. Furthermore, hopes of bringing new blood into the political elite were only partially fulfilled. While the number of first-time and female candidates rose somewhat, roughly 30 percent of those elected had fathers or grandfathers in previous Japanese parliaments. (For LDP deputies, the figure was 50 percent.)

When the votes were tallied, the LDP ended up with 48 percent of the 500 seats in the House of Representatives. Though short of an absolute majority, the Liberal Democrats took advantage of their opponents' inability to agree on an alternative cabinet and established a minority government under Hashimoto. To pass its bills into law, the new cabinet bargained for the votes of two smaller parties and several independents. For all practical purposes, Japan's political system had reverted back to the one-party dominance of the LDP. And the LDP, for its part, reverted to its old ways of doing business. New scandals came to light, and Hashimoto's efforts to revive the economy had little effect. In 1998, the voters administered another sharp rebuke to the LDP during elections to Japan's upper house, the House of Councillors. Although the prime minister is responsible to the lower house and not to the upper chamber, Hashimoto accepted responsibility for the voters' disaffection and resigned.

In his place as head of government stepped another Liberal Democrat, *Keizo Obuchi.* Obuchi enlarged his government's parliamentary support in the fall of 1999 by inviting two smaller parties, the New Komeito party and the New Conservative party, to form a coalition cabinet with the Liberal Democrats. His efforts to revive the economy were just beginning to bear fruit and his popularity ratings were starting to climb when he suffered a stroke in April 2000. Within days the party bosses who steered the Liberal Democrats' fortunes met behind closed doors and picked a relative unknown, *Yoshiro Mori,* as Japan's new prime minister. Mori's selection represented another throwback to the LDP's traditional practices: Mori was chosen primarily because the leaders of the Liberal Democrats' various factions wanted to reach a quick agreement, not because he stood out as a commanding leader. On the contrary, one of the peculiarities of Japan's postwar political system has been that the LDP's leadership selection process—at least until 2001—has had a pronounced tendency to produce weak leaders. To be chosen head of the party, and thus to become prime minister if the LDP dominated the legislature, a Liberal Democrat had to be acceptable to the party's main factions and willing to accept the policy consensus shared by faction leaders. Assertive politicians with agendas of their own and broad popularity among the voters were anathema to the powerful men who controlled the half dozen or so factions into which the LDP elite was divided. Mori fit the bill nicely: he was a faceless, behind-the-scenes politico with no original policy vision and no popular following. Some degree of public approval was nevertheless useful, and so Mori called parliamentary elections for June 25, 2000—several months ahead of schedule. Though Mori's approval ratings were below 20 percent, LDP leaders were confident that the party itself remained fairly popular, especially in rural areas.

Their calculations proved right, but just barely. The Liberal Democrats lost thirty-eight seats but remained by far the largest party in the House of Representatives. (The full results are shown later in this chapter, in table 19.6.) Soon after the election, the LDP leadership once again agreed on Mori as prime minister and reestablished a coalition government with the New Komeito and New Conservative parties. But Mori remained in office only nine months, resigning in the face of public dismay at some of his political gaffes (such as his statement that Japan was a "divine country with the emperor at its center") and disgust over his scandal-tainted cabinet.

In April 2001, Japan's political establishment was shaken once again when **Junichiro Koizumi** (joo-NEE-chee-ro koh-ee-zoo-me) won a surprise victory as the Liberal Democratic Party's new leader. Although Koizumi possessed the standard pedigree of many LDP politicians—both his father and grandfather had been Diet members—he was regarded as a political maverick with little influence in the upper reaches of the party leadership. Koizumi won because the LDP had recently instituted new voting procedures that allowed ordinary party members to participate for the first time in the selection of their party chief. With wide support in the party's grassroots organizations, along with broad popularity among Japanese voters, Koizumi easily defeated his rival in the balloting, former Prime Minister Hashimoto, who was the favorite of the party's old guard. Koizumi immediately replaced Mori as Japan's prime minister. Koizumi was reelected the LDP's chief in September 2003, and he began his second term as prime minister following snap elections held in November. In late 2005 he was elected again, this time by an overwhelming majority. However, Koizumi, obeying the term limits imposed by his own party's constitution, announced he would step down in 2006. Upon his resignation, he had become the third longest serving prime minister (five and one-half years) since 1945. His successor, **Shinzo Abe** (sheen-zo AH-bay), became the fifty-seventh person to hold the office since constitutional government was established in 1889. At fifty-two, he was also the youngest post–World War II prime minister and the first to have been born after that war. Some observers thought those characteristics would free Abe from the traditional Japanese politician's conservatism, but others countered that Abe would likely be more conservative than his predecessor, in part because of his heritage as the grandson of a war crimes suspect and former right-wing prime minister, Nobusuke Kishi.

## DEMOCRACY AND POLITICAL CONFLICT IN JAPAN

Clearly, the 1990s were a period of real instability in Japanese politics that combined fundamental transformations with the familiar patterns of previous decades. Corruption and waning public trust in government officials were plainly visible. At the same time, profound changes in party structures, the electoral system, and the willingness of voters to become actively involved in promoting reform demonstrated that the pulse of democracy in Japan was beating at an accelerated rate.

It was not always so. For nearly two thousand years Japan's government was, like those of most other Asian countries, anything but an electoral democracy. Though political parties and a legislature appeared in the last decades of the nineteenth century, Japan did not become a democracy until after its defeat in World War II in 1945, when American Occupation authorities essentially imposed a democratic constitution on the country.

Even today, some observers of Japanese politics raise the question of just *how* democratic the country really is. The dominance of a single political party, the Liberal Democratic Party, for more than forty years; the overweening power of the central bureaucracy; the pernicious influence of corruption; and the intra-party faction system that effectively supplants issue-based campaigns have prompted concern that Japan is not very democratic when viewed against the criteria set forth in chapter 7.

In this chapter we shall examine the question of how democratic Japan is today. We will also look at how the Japanese have dealt with the five sources of political conflict we outlined in chapter 2:

- *Power:* Which parties, social groups, and individuals have wielded political power in Japan? Are Japanese political elites today more powerful than in other democracies? Have Japanese leaders abused their power through corrupt practices?
- *Resources:* How did Japan rise from the catastrophe of World War II to become the world's second-largest economy? Why has the economic "bubble" burst in recent years?
- *Identity:* Has Japan's largely homogeneous society been conducive to democracy?
- *Ideas:* What do terms like *conservatism* and *socialism* mean in Japan? To what extent have ideologies influenced the behavior of voters and political parties or movements? Is there a Japanese (or Asian) model of democracy that is different from Western democracy?
- *Values:* What are some of the characteristic features of Japanese political culture? Do the Japanese have essentially the same value structure as other economically developed democracies, or are they significantly different on key questions?

Let's begin with an exploration of Japan's long-delayed acceptance of democracy.

## HISTORICAL BACKGROUND OF JAPANESE POLITICS: WHY NO DEMOCRACY?

In ancient times, the Japanese emperor (*tenno;* literally "heavenly sovereign") was thought to have had the ability and duty to communicate with the gods on behalf of the people.[2] Japanese emperors were believed to rule by divine right, tracing their genealogy back to the Sun Goddess, whose grandson, legend says, descended to earth around 660 BCE to bestow authority on Japan's rulers. Thus, unlike the image of a dictatorial king who ruled the everyday lives of his subjects with an iron fist, the historical picture of the Japanese emperor is that of a very wealthy man concerning himself more with religious and cultural matters than with matters of state. For example, the emperor annually performed rituals to petition the gods for a good rice harvest, and even today the emperor keeps a small rice paddy on the imperial palace grounds in Tokyo where he performs such rituals.

Because the details of running the country, or even making policy, were considered beneath the emperor's dignity, ministers or other representatives appointed by the emperor wielded real political and military power. Regents or emperor substitutes ruled at certain times in Japanese history; in other times, power was in the hands of military generals called *shoguns.* Eventually the ministers, regents, or shoguns developed their own power bases, including their own personal armies, away from the official center of imperial power in the central Japanese city of Kyoto. They became virtual sovereigns in their own geographic domains or fiefs—not unlike lords in feudal England.

Frequent battles erupted between the extended families or clans of rival lords. Each power center attempted to achieve and retain a level of power just below that of the emperor himself (or herself, in ancient times[3]). Thus, in practice, the country's government was usually a military dictatorship superimposed on a thin theocratic base. A pure *theocracy* is government by religious authorities. Although Japan was never a true theocracy, its early history contains evidence of the influence of religion in government and, just as often, of the use of religion by competing warlords to justify or solidify their positions of power.

Occasionally an emperor tried to become a real player in governance or unexpectedly found himself holding more political power than he had anticipated. Between AD 645 and 806, for example, the emperors of Japan directly ruled the country and established a centralized, hierarchical, and heavily bureaucratized system of government. Confucius, a Chinese intellectual and minor political figure who had lived from 551 to 479 BCE, had taught that the anarchy he saw around him in his day could be eliminated by establishing paternalistic kings who would rule over society on the basis of a strict hierarchy. Following this philosophy, a group of Japanese reformers, or "imperial loyalists," began a movement to restore to the emperor the power that had been usurped by ministers and shoguns. (There have been about 125 emperors. The current emperor, *Akihito,* who is Japan's head of state, assumed the office after his father, *Hirohito,* died in 1989.)

Called the **Meiji Restoration** ***of 1868, this reform movement succeeded in ridding Japan of centuries of rule by feudal warlords and began preparing the way for the modern Japanese society we see today.*** The movement was called "Meiji" because that was the reign-name chosen by the emperor of the time, and it was called a "restoration" because the emperor was being restored to his "rightful" position as actual ruler. The Meiji reforms, which began to take shape in the mid 1800s, produced results that probably no one anticipated.[4]

Although the idealists of the Meiji period were preoccupied with the idea of "restoring" the king, more practical minds were primarily interested in bringing an end to 250 years of dominance and strict rule by one of the shogun families, the Tokugawas. Ruling in the name of the emperor since 1600, when they had decisively defeated rivals in a number of major battles, the Tokugawas had come to believe that they could best retain power by closing off Japan from the outside world. By dispersing authority among many clans and lords (the *daimyo*) who were loyal to the Tokugawas, by permitting ***an elite military caste known as*** **samurais** to live off the labor of the peasants, and by almost completely shutting down trade and travel, the Tokugawa system weakened Japan's ability to grow and develop.

Into this closed milieu sailed U.S. naval commander Matthew C. Perry in 1853. His "black ship" was equipped with military gadgets and modern technology, such as a small but fully functional steam engine train, something the Japanese had never seen before. The United States wanted access to Japanese ports to resupply its ships, and it also wanted trade with Japan. Perry therefore demanded that Japan open itself up to foreign vessels. When the Tokugawa government refused, Perry demonstrated America's growing industrial power by firing his weapons into Tokyo Bay; then he invited Japanese leaders onboard to view the amazing gadgets he had brought with him. The Tokugawa government soon realized that it could no longer live in isolation from the rest of the world, and it reluctantly opened Japan to international trade.

Once Japan's technological weakness became apparent to the people a military rebellion against the Tokugawa rulers began. After the government was toppled, the new Meiji Restoration rulers found they still had to suppress resistance from those who had benefited from the *ancien regime:* samurais, farmers, and feudal lords. After prevailing over all these groups in the ensuing five years, the new government officially abolished clan authority in 1871 and eliminated the samurai class, with its numerous privileges, in 1876. Clan fiefdoms were replaced by prefectures under central government control, and a national army was created to replace clan militias. The emperor moved from Kyoto, the spiritual capital, to Tokyo, the political capital (then known as Edo)—the city where the shoguns had ruled for centuries.

Interestingly, it was in approximately these same years that Germans and Italians unified their respective constituent elements—independent principalities, kingdoms, and the like—into national states under central governments. Japan, Germany, and Italy were thus latecomers, compared to Britain and France, when it came to developing a national identity and creating a strong centralized state. Some scholars argue that because such "late states" had to catch up as rapidly as possible to powerful states and empires that were already well established, they were especially prone to the development of strong government authority as a vehicle for economic modernization. In later years, these three late states were also prone to violent aggression against their neighbors.

The Meiji government removed many of the Tokugawa-era controls over the lives of ordinary people. Boundaries between social classes were loosened and restrictions on merchants were removed, allowing for the rise of a solid middle class. The absence of such a middle class during the Tokugawa era was probably one factor that prevented the development of democracy. Of course, building a democracy is not as simple as just having a middle class. For example, once the Meiji leaders took the lid off commercial activity, the merchants began to prosper to such an extent that they wanted nothing—not even democracy itself—to limit their profits. To quicken the pace of modernization, the Meiji government fostered the creation of mammoth business conglomerates. Called *zaibatsu,* these interlocking business behemoths, though private, depended heavily on the government for investment funds and other assistance. They established a close bond between private business and government that remains to this day, thus spawning the modern criticism that Japan is not a country but a company—"Japan, Inc." Modern corporations like Mitsubishi and Mitsui got their start in the Meiji period. Unfortunately, the zaibatsu leaders had little taste for democracy if it interfered with making money, and they began to support an increasingly repressive government. New restrictions on publications and measures designed to prevent workers from organizing collective labor activities were implemented, and the seeds of a new military dictatorship were planted.

## The Rise of Party Politics

When the emperor was restored to power in 1868, he was only fourteen years old and completely unprepared to govern. Therefore, the elites who had masterminded the overthrow of the feudal Tokugawa regime found it easy to constitute themselves as a powerful inner circle around the emperor. In his name they issued declarations on all aspects of political life, shifting more and more power away from the former fiefdoms and toward the central government. For those who had ruled their own local domains for hundreds of years with near sovereignty, these fiats were bitter pills to swallow.

The new government began to tip toward repression in its breakneck push to modernize. In response, urban intellectuals, rural landowners, and former samurai (who were generally quite well educated and later became the backbone of Japan's school system) launched efforts to preserve or salvage their privileges by forming political associations—the precursors of political parties, something never seen in Japan. The rise of these new organizations was extremely significant. For the first time, people of influence were making at least a small effort to ascertain what the population wanted from its government and were attempting to get the government to deliver. The one cause that attracted the most attention was the establishment of democracy.

Some members of the Meiji elite themselves wanted to give democracy a chance. Finding their voices stifled by others in the government, however, they resigned their posts and retaliated by creating political parties. Beginning in 1874, several proto-parties were formed that had as their ultimate goal the establishment of a parliamentary democracy, complete with a constitution (which Japan did not have). Such a thing had probably never occurred to many of those who had helped "restore" the emperor, but it became a persistent demand from a growing segment of the population.

Intellectuals were behind this demand, as were some of the merchants, but many of those pushing for democracy were the former possessors of feudal domains and former samurai who saw a constitution as the only way to prevent the new central government from stripping even more power away from the provinces. The predecessor of today's Liberal Democratic Party was formed in 1874 by, among others, Taisuke Itagaki, who had been a member of the Meiji government but who had resigned in frustration at the antidemocratic politics of his colleagues.

Debate among the educated elite of Meiji society produced varied opinions on the preferred structure of government: some leaders favored a British-style government, others the French model, and still others the Prussian or German model. Many of the Meiji leaders had studied these various forms of government firsthand during official tours of Europe and America in the 1870s and 1880s.[5] One very active participant in these discussions was thirty-two-year-old Hirobumi Ito, the man who would subsequently draft Japan's first constitution and become its first prime minister. After more than fifteen years of studying European and American governmental systems and debating their suitability to Japan, Ito and other democracy advocates drafted a European-style parliamentary constitution. He favored the European models because, among other reasons, most European constitutions allowed for a monarch, whereas the U.S. Constitution did not.

In 1889, twenty-one years after the Meiji rebels overthrew the Tokugawa government, the voices calling for a constitutional government finally prevailed, and Japan's first-ever constitution was promulgated. It took effect upon a declaration by the emperor, not by a vote of the people, for Japan had not yet moved that far along the road toward democratic government. The Meiji Restoration, it must be emphasized, was an *aristocratic* revolution, not a democratic one. It was engineered by upper-class samurai and other authoritarian political elites, not by mass social forces opposed to monarchy and desirous of democracy like those that catalyzed the French Revolution. It would be some thirty years before mass workers' parties such as the Japan Communist Party and the Japan Socialist League would be organized.

In 1889, then, Japan was still far from a democracy. The first election in Japan occurred in 1890, but only half a million people (about 1 percent of the population) voted; suffrage was restricted to males who paid a certain amount of taxes to the government. (Of course, the right to vote was similarly restricted to property-owning males in nineteenth-century Britain, France, and the United States.) Universal male suffrage was not instituted in Japan until 1928, and women did not get the vote until after World War II.

Despite its distance from the ideal democratic model, the first Japanese constitution was extremely significant because, during its formulation, the Japanese had to learn how to organize themselves politically to achieve their goals. Between 1874 and 1890 several political parties or associations were formed: the Public Party of Patriots (later the Liberal Party), the Freedom and People's Rights Movement, the Constitutional Reform Party, and the Constitutional Liberal Party. Most of these parties were created by governmental elites who had become dissatisfied with the excesses of the new Meiji leadership; they were not grassroots mass parties. Those in charge of the Meiji government, in turn, soon realized that they had no alternative but to create parties of their own—"bureaucrats' parties" as they were called—to offset the growing influence of the "popular parties." Unlike in Western democracies, the commoners or ordinary people in Japan were not major players in the years of party formation, although they contributed to pressure for reform by engaging in various forms of civil disobedience. Notwithstanding their origins at the hands of elites, the new parties were a significant step in the direction of mass democracy because parties, by their very nature, reach out for the support of like-minded people.

Japan's new constitution did not specifically mention political parties. Cabinet ministers, including the prime minister, were not selected on the basis of which party had received the largest share of the vote. Indeed, members of the House of Peers (the upper house) were appointed by the emperor entirely from among the imperial family and other nobles, while members of the House of Representatives took office as independents, not as representatives of any political party. Cabinet positions were rotated among members of the four clans that had effected the Meiji imperial restoration, and it was not until 1918 that the first non-pedigreed commoner became prime minister. Nevertheless, party influence steadily increased while clan influence waned. Indeed, the headlong rush by the Meiji government to industrialize Japan and catch up to the West produced so many labor problems that still more political parties were created, including the Social Democratic Party and the Japan Socialist Party, which did, indeed, have roots in the common people.

The Japanese parliament in this period had very little real decision-making authority. Its purpose was mainly consultative, providing the powerful cabinet officials with advice and respectful criticism. It therefore closely resembled the German Reichstag organized in the 1870s under the stern authoritarian rule of the kaiser and his chancellor, Otto von Bismarck. It was considerably less powerful than the British Parliament, which rested on the bedrock principle of parliamentary supremacy, or the U.S. Congress, with its extensive lawmaking powers exercised in conjunction with the president.

## Ideology, Political Culture, and Class Identity in Historical Perspective

With a constitution and the framework of democracy in place, the common people found themselves empowered in a way that they had never before experienced. For the first time, advocates of the democratic values of liberty and equality launched attacks on the guardians of social hierarchy and imperial rule. It was a new era in Japanese political life. That era, called the Taisho Era after the Emperor Taisho, who reigned from 1912 to 1926, covered the years just before World War I until the Great Depression of the 1930s. It was a most unusual time for Japan. Not only did it witness unprecedented ideological conflict; it was also characterized by major changes in the country's mass political culture. The Japanese people had historically thought of themselves as obedient to those above them in the social hierarchy. The impact of Confucianism, imported from China in the fifth century, had created a political culture that stressed respect for authority and deference to the political elites, while Buddhism encouraged a certain detachment from worldly conflict, a passivity that facilitated unfettered leadership by top aristocrats.

But the Taisho Era was remarkably unruly, with various segments of society engaged in passionate debates about equality, democracy, and other core political concepts and values. At times these disagreements turned violent. The conflicts began with a bang in 1913 when a popular protest movement of journalists, opposition parties, and others surrounded the Diet building in Tokyo and demanded the resignation of the prime minister for violating the principles of democratic government. The demonstrators raided pro-government newspaper offices and set fire to police stations. Naming themselves the "Movement to Protect Constitutional Government," the protesters persisted until the prime minister resigned, the first such resignation forced by a popular movement in Japanese history.

With the wartime economy booming, the labor movement began to strengthen. Not only did workers demand a more equitable distribution of company profits, they also wanted recognition as valuable players in society. It was the first time in Japanese history that the masses felt they had a chance to "be somebody." Disgruntled workers organized hundreds of work stoppages, and when the government wanted to raise the price of rice, as many as two million workers and housewives took to the streets in protest. Like workers in other countries at the time, Japanese workers were fighting over core identity issues—in this case, their role in the new social class structure. Shedding their past deference to established authority, many Japanese dared to be openly contentious.

When the economic boom ended after World War I and employers began to lay off workers or reduce their wages, the masses would have none of it. Workers and leftist intellectuals organized the Japan Federation of Labor in 1921, the Japan Communist Party in 1922, and various other leftist groups with names like the Labor-Peasant Party and the Japan Proletarian Party. Many of these associations were short-lived. But it is significant that, for the first time, membership was solicited on the basis of mass interest in political theories or beliefs about the nature of "just" societies, reflecting a growing appreciation of democratic values. Liberal intellectuals argued forcefully to the alarmed elite that the era of privileges and special recognition for the upper classes was over. Realizing that there was no way to contain this clash over values, the ruling elites reluctantly began to make concessions. The government passed a minimum wage law, a tenant-landlord law, and most significant, a universal voting law that gave the vote to all males over age twenty-five.

But just as the political left was making headway, the political right, with far more resources at its command, also began to organize. Its representatives in the Diet rushed through new "antisubversion" laws that gave the police the right to suppress intellectuals and workers. The Japan Communist Party, which favored abolition of the monarchy, was forced underground and severely suppressed in the 1930s.

While workers in the cities were becoming radicalized, rural peasants were organizing themselves into unions to demand rent reductions on farmland. But the farmers' movement showed little strength at the polls, and many farmers' complaints were muted by land reforms initiated in 1939. In the rural areas, the government increased the inculcation of conservative, even militaristic, values in the minds of elementary school children. Respect for imperial institutions and the positive value of social hierarchy were key elements in the students' required moral education. Although the Taisho Era is often referred to as one of popular awakening, in the end the forces of right-wing extremism prevailed, manipulating popular attitudes and setting the stage for the militarization of the government in the 1930s and Japan's wholesale aggression against its neighbors.

During the war years of the 1940s, the military-dominated government virtually abolished all political parties and suppressed, but did not completely extinguish, popular movements that did not support the war effort. When that unhappy era of propaganda and forced obedience to the imperial state ended, the population as a whole seemed less inclined to join any organization that espoused a strong ideological line, whether religious, social, or political. There was a brief flirtation with left-wing parties and radical labor unions during the Allied Occupation (1945 to 1952), but the Japanese people for the most part seemed far more committed to practicality than principle. At war's end, they were physically and emotionally exhausted and disillusioned with government. More than anything else, they wanted stability and normalcy.

### Conflict Between the Military and the Civilian Government

The top Meiji oligarchs, the bureaucracy, and particularly the military had not liked the rise of party politics. Indeed, the beginnings of parliamentary government in Japan in the late 1800s and early 1900s coincided, as it happened, with the rise of Japanese nationalism and military aggression against Japan's neighbors in Asia.[6] If the Japanese had learned one thing from the West, it was that expansionism went hand in hand with being a powerful country. The Japanese understood that countries like England, France, and the Netherlands had tried, whenever possible, to extend their power and national security by subduing weaker nations militarily and politically. Even the United States, which had been founded in opposition to the idea of empire, would take control of Hawaii in 1893, and the Philippines, Puerto Rico, and Guam in 1898. Japan believed that, to avoid a takeover of its territory by Western powers (a process that was occurring in China), it would have to build a strong military that would be capable of both protecting Japan and subduing others.

To prepare for the expansionism that they believed was appropriate for Japan's modern new identity, Japanese leaders began carefully observing the military structures of Western countries. Officers from France were imported to revamp the Japanese army, and British naval officers were brought in to reorganize the navy. Universal military service for Japanese men was inaugurated in 1872. Bolstered by the belief that Japan had now caught up to the West militarily, the Japanese launched an active campaign to acquire an empire. Soldiers took over Okinawa and the Ryukyu Islands in 1879, Taiwan and the Pescadores in 1895, southern Manchuria and Sakhalin Island in 1905, and Korea in 1910. The Japanese handily defeated the armed forces of both China and Russia, thus establishing themselves as a formidable force in Asia.

Initially, not everyone in Japan was pleased with the militarization of the country. By the early 1890s a major battle for resources was under way inside the government. Some Meiji-era party leaders (especially those not connected with the four clans that had launched the 1868 Meiji rebellion) preferred that Japan spend its resources on its social rather than its military infrastructure. Pressure from these leaders produced a national education system in 1871 (using the United States as a model) and a new criminal code (using France as a model). But the military, which had been given enormous power in the new constitution, and was not even required to answer to the Diet, was successful in enlisting support for its motto of "Enrich the Country, Strengthen the Military." Whereas in 1891 and 1892 some of the political parties had successfully forced the resignation of cabinets that had tried to expand the budget for military purposes, by 1894, when Japan was poised to take over Taiwan, most of the opposition to militarization and expansionism had been obliterated in a cloud of nationalistic fervor. The hawks had won the resource allocation debate.

By the 1930s the military had been able to elevate itself to a position of dominance in Japanese governance. Among the reasons for this situation was the universal conscription law of 1872. The former samurai elite who took charge of the military after 1868 took full advantage of conscription to indoctrinate the entire male population with the values of militarism. Military education, including infantry exercises for students from junior high school through university, became mandatory parts of the curriculum. Thus the Japanese people, who had always tolerated a high level of militaristic control of their lives during the era of the shoguns, now found their civilian government reduced to the status of a virtual puppet of the army and navy. Those who resisted the state's militarization often found their lives in danger, as was the case with Prime Minister Tsuyoshi Inukai in 1932. While attempting to keep the army under control and to block its expansionist designs on China, Inukai was assassinated by military officers.

Military control of the country was further strengthened by the February 26 Incident. In 1936, some fourteen hundred soldiers led by junior officers staged a coup d'état in Tokyo. Seizing the center of the city, they killed several top government officials, including the minister of finance, and attempted to kill the prime minister. Their goal was to have the prime minister replaced by a general loyal to their cause. The attempt was eventually suppressed by other units of the military under direct orders of the emperor, but—ironically—the incident actually ended up increasing the military's influence in Tokyo. Under the guise of maintaining public order, the high command persuaded the cabinet to increase the military's budget (and thus its general visibility) and to impose strict censorship on the media. Thus, from the 1930s until the end of World War II in 1945, the Japanese military had de facto control of the government.

In the 1940s several efforts were made to unite all political parties into one large, totalitarian unit called the Imperial Rule Assistance Association (IRAA). Seen by many as the Japanese equivalent of Hitler's Nazi Party, with branches organized all over the country, the military-inspired IRAA was never completely successful in obliterating the influence of civilian political parties. Nonetheless, during the Second World War, political parties were virtually eliminated, and it was the army, navy, and air force that held real power in the country. As for Emperor Hirohito, who reigned from 1926 to 1989, there is evidence that he was considerably more involved in political and military decision-making than he appeared to be at the time.[7]

For many years, the Japanese military machine seemed unstoppable. Troops swarmed over Manchuria in 1931 and much of Southeast Asia in 1941. In 1942, under Prime Minister and General *Hideki Tojo,* Japan launched devastating, simultaneous attacks on the Philippines, Malaya, and Hawaii. By mid 1942, Japan controlled a vast territory from Korea and eastern China in the north, to Indonesia in the south and far out to the islands of the Pacific. This area was what the Japanese leadership called the "Greater East Asian Co-prosperity Sphere," but to the victims of Japanese aggression, the term was just window dressing for nothing less than brutal domination by the "Nazis of Asia."

Japan's luck ran out when the United States and its allies entered the war in 1942. Island by island, country by country, the Japanese were pushed back in bloody battles costing thousands of military and civilian lives. In the Allied attack on Okinawa, for example, 110,000 Japanese soldiers were killed as well as 150,000 Japanese civilians and at least 50,000 Americans. Air raids on the Japanese islands proper ended with the atomic bombing of the cities of Hiroshima and Nagasaki in August 1945, after which the emperor, in a dramatic radio announcement, declared Japan's surrender.

### Japan and the Conditions for Democracy

In sum, Japanese history prior to the end of the Second World War exhibited precious few of the conditions for democracy enumerated in chapter 9. *Political elites* and *state institutions* were thoroughly authoritarian. *National wealth* was low compared to the leading Western countries, while *private enterprise* was dominated by cartels that were highly dependent on the imperial state. The long-suppressed *middle class* remained politically weak. The *disadvantaged* classes of peasants and urban workers occasionally staged protest actions but were not sufficiently organized to effect significant democratic change from below. *Civil society* was undeveloped, with mass-based political parties largely eclipsed by state-oriented bureaucratic parties.

Japan's *political culture* was shaped by Confucian attitudes emphasizing social harmony, consensus, and hierarchy rather than democratic contestation, individual liberty, or constitutional limits to state power. *Education* was an elitist privilege, and the government was able to manipulate the flow of information. Japan's *international environment* was characterized by centuries of isolation followed by decades of aggressive imperialism, both of which reinforced the political influence of the military. Of all the conditions on our list, only Japan's relative level of *national unity* and its ethnic homogeneity might have helped sustain a democracy. But in fact homogeneity probably retarded democracy prior to the end of World War II because the country's political leaders idealized the Japanese people as a superior race descended from the gods, a belief reinforced by the religious doctrines of Shinto. Japan's national identity was thus shaped by the country's ruling elites, not by its people. And its national unity was built around the population's passive acceptance of the elite's myths about the country's divine origins. The prevalence of popular belief in these founding myths was very evident in World War II, as tens of millions of Japanese displayed tenacious loyalty to the emperor and the Japanese state until the very end, enduring extreme hardships that culminated in the atomic bombs that leveled Hiroshima and Nagasaki. It took the complete destruction of Japan's imperial system by U.S. and Allied forces in 1945 to enable the Japanese to refashion their national identity on a democratic basis.

**General Douglas MacArthur and Emperor Hirohito during the U.S. Occupation**

## BUILDING JAPANESE DEMOCRACY

### The Occupation Begins

In August 1945, thousands of tired, hungry, and demoralized Japanese lined the streets of cities throughout Japan to watch their conquerors—the Allied forces—arrive to take over their country. Although most Japanese today agree that losing the war was the best thing that could have happened to Japan, at the time the Occupation was regarded with both fear and a begrudging envy. "What will they do to us?" the people worried, and "What is it that they have or know that gave them the power to defeat our divinely led country?"

The answers to these questions came quickly. Led by U.S. Gen. Douglas MacArthur, some 5,500 Occupation officials, mostly American, began remaking Japan in their own image. They were backed by 150,000 troops. Occupation authorities allowed the emperor to remain in office as Japan's symbolic head of state, but they removed virtually all his political authority. Emperor Hirohito, who had no alternative but to cooperate with the Occupation authorities, issued a statement declaring that he was not personally divine. But in his artfully worded "declaration of humanity," Hirohito did not retract the traditional notion that he and previous emperors were all descended from the Sun Goddess. Meanwhile, Occupation leaders also swept some 200,000 war-era political and military leaders from office and went on to dismantle the military and police apparatus, change the educational and legal systems, introduce sweeping land reforms, weaken the power of the zaibatsu (the business cartels), and encourage the formation of labor unions. Most importantly, they discarded the Meiji constitution of 1889 and replaced it in 1947 with a new constitution modeled heavily, though not exclusively, on the British and U.S. systems of government.[8]

## Japan's Constitution

The new constitution declared that sovereignty resides with the Japanese people and that the emperor, with no powers related to government, derives his position as a symbol of the state "from the will of the people," not from heaven. It established the equality of the sexes in marriage and other matters. It guaranteed various freedoms, such as those of speech, religion, assembly, private property ownership, voting in secret elections, and so on. A significant feature of the new constitution was its declaration that the Japanese people would "forever renounce war," the only such declaration by any country in the world (the famous Article 9).[9] Subsequent legislation gave women the vote for the first time in Japanese history and lowered the voting age to twenty.

The will of the people was to be expressed through a *parliamentary system* of government based on a bicameral legislature, the **Diet**, ***which consists of an elected* House of Representatives *(the lower house) and an elected* House of Councillors *(the upper house).*** The lower house would select a prime minister who, as head of government, would choose the cabinet. The prime minister and a majority of cabinet members would be chosen from elected members of the Diet (who retain their seats while serving in the cabinet) and must be civilians. Terms of members of the House of Representatives were set at four years (unless the House were to be dissolved earlier for some reason) and those of the House of Councillors at six years. The initial electoral regime for the House of Representatives established multimember parliamentary districts, but that system was changed in the 1994 reforms (described later in this chapter). Half the members of the House of Councillors were to be elected every three years by popular vote for a six-year term that is not terminated upon dissolution of the House of Representatives. In the event the House of Representatives is dissolved, a general election must be held within forty days to reconstitute the House. A bill becomes law when it is passed by both houses of the Diet, and it can become law even when the House of Councillors initially rejects it, as long as it is subsequently passed by two-thirds of the members of the House of Representatives.

The power of prefectural and municipal governments was designed to be weaker than those powers are in a federal system, giving the Japanese central government a stronger hand over the forty-seven prefectures and other regional units than, say, the central government has over the states in the United States. An independent judiciary with a Supreme Court and lower courts was also established to adjudicate laws. The Supreme Court, consisting of fourteen judges plus a chief justice, was given the power of judicial review to rule on the constitutionality of laws. The emperor was allowed to appoint the chief justice upon receiving a designation from the cabinet, while the remaining justices were to be appointed by the cabinet and reviewed by voters in a general election. They must retire at age seventy.

The postwar American Occupation lasted seven years, until 1952. At its end, the nation was on the road to economic recovery, sovereignty had been handed over to the Japanese people, and Japan had been reaccepted by the world community as a legitimate nation. The Occupation's reforms had catalyzed the formation of new political parties as well as an explosion of new labor unions (some 5 million workers had joined unions by 1946). Let's review these developments in more detail.

## Political Parties in Postwar Japan

The years immediately following World War II were times of turbulence for Japan's political party system. Aspirants for political office created new parties that echoed what the U.S. government wanted and at the same time reflected the people's desire for change from the militarism of the past. Party names that implied change, such as "progressive" and "liberal," were popular. So were names suggesting an important feature of Japan's political culture, namely the tendency toward communal or group rather than individual action, as reflected in party names like "socialist," "cooperative," and "communist." New parties created by 1952 (many with direct links to prewar parties) are listed in table 19.1.

With many former political leaders purged by the Occupation, the new and reconstituted parties had to draw their leadership from outside the old ruling elites, particularly from the ranks of the

**TABLE 19.1**

**Parties Created During the Postwar Occupation (1945–52)**

Japan Communist Party: established in 1945 with prewar roots
Japan Socialist Party: established in 1945 with prewar roots
Japan Liberal Party: established in 1945 from a faction of an earlier party established in 1900
Japan Progressive Party: established in 1945 from a faction of an earlier party established in 1900
Japan Cooperative Party: established in 1945 with no prewar links
Democratic Party: established in 1947 with roots in Japan Liberal and Democratic Liberal Parties
People's Cooperative Party: established in 1947 with roots in Japan Cooperative Party
Worker-Farmer Party: established in 1948 with roots in Japan Socialist Party
Shakai Kakushinto: established in 1948 with roots in Japan Socialist Party
Democratic Liberal Party: established in 1948 with roots in Japan Liberal Party
Liberal Party: established in 1950 with roots in several other newly formed parties
People's Democratic Party: established in 1950 with roots in several other newly formed parties
Kyodoto: established in 1952 with roots in several other newly formed parties
Japan Reform Party: established in 1952 with roots in People's Democratic Party

business community and the retired bureaucracy. The close relationship that the business community and bureaucracy currently maintain with the Liberal Democratic Party stems, in part, from this Occupation-era necessity (and, in part, from the government-business relationship established during the late 1800s).

After ten years of postwar deal making and power positioning by all parties, a new stability took hold in 1955 that would continue more or less unchanged and unchallenged for nearly forty years. Two parties came to the fore in the Diet: the *Liberal Democratic Party* and the *Japan Socialist Party.*

The **Liberal Democratic Party (LDP),** despite its left-sounding name, ***is a conservative party that has dominated postwar Japanese politics.*** The LDP was formed from two business-oriented conservative parties. It could trace its roots back to the Public Party of Patriots established in 1874 during the early Meiji Restoration. Party leaders used the term "liberal" in its original sense, as supportive of democracy and private enterprise. From its inception the LDP favored business and economic growth over other issues. It was not as concerned with remilitarization and national pride as it was with reigniting the economy and rebuilding the country's industrial infrastructure. To this end, and in keeping with Japanese traditions, the Liberal Democrats placed heavy emphasis on the need for close collaboration between the largest private corporations and the Japanese government. Their support for extensive state involvement in the private sector distinguishes them from conservative parties in the United States and Britain, which have tended to favor less government intervention and more independence for private enterprise.

The LDP also curried the favor of the farm vote by providing subsidies for rice and strenuously resisting the importation of less expensive foreign rice. In foreign policy, LDP leaders favored friendly cooperation with the United States and supported the U.S.-Japan Security Treaty of 1954 that allowed thousands of U.S. troops to be stationed at numerous military bases throughout Japan. Aided by the support of middle-class white-collar "salarymen" as well as the farmers of the countryside, the LDP took control of the government and guided Japan through its stunning economic recovery and rise to world prominence.

The Japan Socialist Party (JSP) assumed the role of chief opposition party. Like the LDP, it too was created in 1955. The JSP traced its roots back to the Socialist Study Society of 1898. It saw itself as the party of ordinary people, a position reflected in the titles of its precursor parties: the Socialist Masses Party, the Japan Proletarian Party, the Labor-Farmer Party, the Japan Commoners' Party, and others with similar left-sounding titles. Despite its "masses" approach, it never garnered enough seats in the House of Representatives to serve as more than an annoyance to the powerful LDP until the late 1980s, as we shall see later in this chapter. In fact, the JSP was never socialist in the sense of favoring less capitalistic approaches to economic life. Many of its supporters were hardly distinguishable in their economic views from those supporting the LDP, except perhaps in their desire to resist joining the establishment.

In the 1950s, many Japanese hoped that the LDP and the JSP would form the backbone of a British-style system that would bring needed stability to Japanese politics. They hoped that these two parties, with their slightly different philosophies of government, would periodically rotate in and out of government like the Conservative and Labour parties in Britain. As it happened, however, the LDP ended up controlling the government for four decades and running the country more or less as a one-party state. The 1960s saw the rise of the *Clean Government Party,* or *Komeito,* a Buddhist religion-based party, but it would not become a major player for nearly three decades. Renamed *New Komeito* in 1999, it became part of an LDP-led coalition government—much to the dismay of the majority of voters, who since the 1930s have been wary of any linkage between government and religion. Extreme right-wing groups wanting the return of Japan's era of military bravado were never able to excite the interest of the war-weary population. Thus the LDP reigned virtually unchallenged.

Some have argued that the LDP's long dominance of Japanese politics and governmental power has diminished democracy because it has narrowed the voters' alternative choices to parties with little chance of winning; thus the LDP has prevented real alternation in power. But others have countered that, despite the absence of a strong opposition in the Diet for several decades, the conservative LDP in fact has represented a variety of viewpoints, since the party itself has been a combination of many interests. This raises the topic of *habatsu,* or intra-party *factions* or cliques.

In a style reminiscent of ancient samurai and the lords they vowed to protect at all costs, the LDP and other parties in Japan are composed of a number of factions, each headed by a powerful, experienced politician. This prominent politician establishes patron-client relationships with younger, less powerful members of the Diet who support him in Diet debates, in voting on bills, in campaigning, and in other ways. In return, he helps find influential positions for his *habatsu* members and helps them get reelected by distributing donated money for use in their campaigns. Younger members find the money to be crucial to their chances of election, because it is with such funds that they pay for the labor and support of their *koenkai,* or support groups.

At any one time, there may be as many as a dozen factions within a single political party. The number of members per faction could be as few as three or four and as many as one hundred or more. Generally, the more members in a faction, the more powerful that faction. The leaders of powerful factions have the best chances of becoming prime minister or heading powerful ministries in the cabinet such as the Ministry of Finance; the Ministry of Economy, Trade, and Industry; or the Foreign Ministry. Generally speaking, decisions about top posts are made with social harmony in mind. That is, cabinet posts are usually distributed in such a way that there is at least one representative from each major faction. When necessary, cabinet members will be replaced for no substantive cause and even after only short tenures in office just to satisfy the power-sharing demands of the *habatsu.*

During the forty years of LDP dominance of the cabinet, when inter-party conflicts were subdued because of the insurmountable power of the LDP, the voting public focused its attention on the factional distribution of power in the LDP government in the same way that voters in other countries were paying attention to the number of seats held by differing parties. From time to time, Liberal Democrats have proposed reforms of the faction system; Prime Minister Koizumi himself spoke out against the system. His efforts had some effect, as the number of unaffiliated LDP Diet members jumped from twenty-five in 2001 to forty-two in 2005 (see table 19.2). But factions in the LDP are not likely to die away completely, because they are a major source of campaign funding. Unfortunately, if the public thought that a fair distribution of cabinet posts by faction was a way to allow varied voices to be heard in the halls of the Diet, they were mistaken. Factions have never been primarily about political ideology, but rather about money and the distribution of power—two of the major sources of conflict in all political systems.

The LDP stabilized Japan for four decades. But it also fostered corruption. In Japan, as in other democracies, the longer a party remains in power,

**TABLE 19.2**

**LDP Factions, 2001 and 2005**

| Faction | Members of Diet 2001[a] | Members of Diet 2005[a] |
|---|---|---|
| Hashimoto | 101 | 77 |
| Mori | 59 | 74 |
| Miyazawa | — | 46 |
| Ibuki | — | 45 |
| Yamasaki | 23 | 29 |
| Tanigaki | — | 16 |
| Komura | — | 14 |
| Kono | 12 | 10 |
| Nikai | — | 6 |
| Eto | 55 | — |
| Horiuchi | 43 | — |
| Kato | 15 | — |
| Komoto | 13 | — |
| Unaffiliated | 25 | 42 |

[a]Both houses, as of November 2001 and September 2005.
*Source:* Various newspapers, 2005, and *The Economist,* April 20, 2002.

the greater the likelihood of unethical practices emerging. By the 1960s, parties looking to clean up government and capture non-LDP centrist voters and brandishing such names as the "Clean Government Party" and the "Democratic Socialist Party" emerged to challenge the dominance of the LDP. The influence of these parties was minimal, however, until the late 1970s and early 1980s, when LDP corruption captured the headlines, and voters started to cast serious glances at the new aspirants for power.

### The Results of One-Party Dominance

The years of one-party LDP rule produced a thick web of behind-the-scenes ***collusion between big business, political parties, and the bureaucracy, sometimes referred to as the "iron triangle."*** So powerful was the influence of the big business elite—known as the *zaikai*—that it could impose its will on the LDP leadership, virtually dictating the selection of prime ministers and other cabinet officials. Buying the votes of politicians became standard practice.[10] Although insiders were aware of the situation, the public got its first extensive exposure to its leaders' dishonesty around the time of the 1976 general election. As is often the case in Japan, the news came from outside the country.

During hearings in the U.S. Senate Committee on Foreign Relations, Lockheed Aircraft Corporation revealed that it had paid millions of dollars in illegal payments to politicians worldwide in return for promises of aircraft purchases by various foreign governments. Prominent among those so paid was Japanese Prime Minister *Kakuei Tanaka.*[11] Tanaka was eventually tried and convicted in Japan, and the corruption scandal mushroomed as reporters found hard evidence of bribery payments from a variety of corporations to many LDP leaders. In addition to the Lockheed Scandal, there was the Recruit Scandal that brought down Prime Minister Takeshita; the Kyowa Scandal; the Sagawa Kyubin Scandal that tarnished LDP strongman Shin Kanemaru, and many others.[12]

## PROFILE: Kakuei Tanaka

On July 7, 1972, fifty-four-year old Kakuei Tanaka walked across the Niju Bridge into the Imperial Palace in Tokyo to receive the emperor's confirmation as the new prime minister of Japan. His elevation to the highest political office in the land was one of the most unusual in Japanese history. Japan is a nation that reveres education, but Tanaka had not even finished high school. Born in 1918 and raised in the hinterlands of Niigata Prefecture by a dissolute father who had gambled away the family income, the new prime minister's image had also been tarnished by his having to manage his first reelection campaign from jail because of his arrest for bribery only a year after his first election to parliament.

Just two years and five months after his assumption of the prime ministership, Tanaka resigned his office amid a swirl of media exposés that alleged bribery involving fantastic sums of money. Tanaka's political career sheds light on the central role of "money politics" and on the place of factions, or *habatsu,* in Japan's political system.[13]

Tanaka started his adult life as a construction worker and contractor. During World War II he made substantial money on projects in Korea and then used those funds after the war to successfully run for national office as a representative from Niigata in 1947. Although positioning himself as a conservative, he favored policies that helped blue-collar workers like himself. In return for their votes, he saw to it that his prefecture's constituents were blessed with new roads, tunnels, and other large construction projects.

**Former Prime Minister Kakuei Tanaka with his daughter Makiko, who would serve as Japan's foreign minister from 2001 to early 2002.**

When Tanaka was arrested for bribery in his first year in office, it was because voters, especially owners of small, blue-collar businesses, gave him their strong support—and apparently illegally gave him their money—because he had decided to vote against the then-Socialist government's attempt to nationalize the coal mines. Eventually his political support group, or *koenkai,* numbered over 95,000 members.

Cleared of the coal mine bribery charge, Tanaka advanced inside the Liberal Democratic Party and was eventually chosen for several cabinet posts. As minister of finance (one of the most powerful posts in Japanese politics), he not only increased his own prefecture's share of government largess (it rose from fifth place to first place out of forty-seven prefectures and similar regional units); he also found ways to line his own pockets. Shadow companies with which he was involved would often buy up land just before it was to be purchased by the government for some public works project. Tanaka had clearly used his political offices to make himself a very rich man. But he had also helped make Japan a very rich country.

As minister of international trade and industry, he started or encouraged such massive projects as the new Tokyo International Airport in Narita, the undersea tunnel linking Hokkaido island with the main island of Honshu, an atomic power plant, a bullet train line to his prefecture, two major highways, and many others. How did he accomplish all this? He used the notorious factional *habatsu* system.

Shortly after Tanaka entered politics, he aligned himself with the Sato faction in the Liberal Democratic Party. Factions or political cliques organized around a senior politician are almost parties within a party, and Eisaku Sato's faction was one of the strongest ever. It supported Sato as prime minister for a tenure of eight years—the longest in Japanese history. With the Sato faction's financial help, Tanaka was elected to the Diet again and again until he eventually became prime minister. Tanaka found ways, apparently often illegal ways, to gather large sums of money that he disbursed to up-and-coming Diet members (and many key bureaucrats) until he had created his own faction of loyal subordinates. Once he became a cabinet member, he made sure that his own faction members received plum cabinet posts. Tanaka was so unabashed about buying support for his projects that he is alleged to have given substantial gifts of money to every member of the Diet in 1974!

Under a cloud of media exposure about his shady financial dealings, Tanaka resigned as prime minister in late 1974. But he remained the strongest LDP faction leader during the 1980s, and his faction remained the largest of all factions. Tanaka himself remained a Diet member even after he gave up his cabinet posts and actively recruited new subordinates, probably in hopes of staging a political comeback. But two events kept him from achieving that goal.

The first was the Lockheed Scandal. As the U.S. Senate investigation revealed, several members of the Japanese government, including Tanaka while serving as prime minister, had received large sums of bribery money from the Lockheed Aircraft Corporation in return for their support for the purchase of Lockheed jet aircraft by Japanese airline companies. More than a dozen people were directly paid off, with Prime Minister Tanaka receiving a $2 million bribe for his support for the deal. The Japanese government eventually indicted sixteen people; all but one were convicted. Tanaka was fined and sentenced to four years in prison, but he appealed his conviction (as did the others) and did not actually serve any time. Moreover, he refused to resign his seat in the Diet. He apparently felt that he had been doing the same thing many other politicians had done and that his approach to governance was, in effect, normal politics in Japan. The opposition, however, demanded a vote on his removal from office. Prime Minister Yasuhiro Nakasone, whose cabinet was peopled by Tanaka faction members, refused to allow the vote, whereupon all the opposition parties boycotted the Diet for over a month, forcing the prime minister to call an election in December 1983.

Although the LDP lost heavily and barely retained a majority in the lower house, Tanaka ran as an independent and was returned to office in 1983—for the fifteenth time—with the highest number of votes he had ever received in his entire political career. Once again, voters in his district, recognizing the pork barrel benefits Tanaka had brought home to them, gave their favorite son their strong support on election day. All the other LDP factions lost heavily. The election had proven once again that Tanaka was the most powerful politician in the country; he was often referred to as the "shadow shogun." With the passage of a little more time, he might have reclaimed the post of prime minister. But two years after his resounding election victory, Kakuei Tanaka, at age sixty-seven, suffered a paralyzing stroke that hospitalized him and ended one of the most extraordinary political careers in Japanese history. He officially retired from politics in 1990.

During the 1970s and 1980s, the combined effects of corruption and inter-factional strife within the LDP produced frequent changes in the office of prime minister (see table 19.3). By the late 1980s, opposition parties felt at last they had a chance to defeat the LDP. Especially hopeful was the Japan Socialist Party led by Takako Doi, the first woman ever to head a major party in Japan. The JSP defeated the LDP in the upper house in the 1989 elections, spurring many disgruntled LDP members to bolt the party and create "study groups" or other precursors of change in the country's party system. New parties sprang up overnight: the Japan New Party, the New Harbinger Party, and the Renewal Party, to name a few. Japanese civil society entered a period of vigorous activity. Suddenly, voters had more than a dozen parties from which to choose candidates. The spate of new choices seemed to overwhelm even the voters' initial interest in Doi's Socialists. For the first time since 1955, the LDP was in trouble.

## JAPAN'S POLITICAL ECONOMY: FROM "JAPAN INC." TO THE "BUBBLE"

Adding to the LDP's problems in the late 1980s and early 1990s was the collapse of the "bubble economy." Beginning in the late 1950s, Japan's economy began a dramatic recovery from the ashes of war. By 1961 annual growth was over 14 percent, more than three times that of most other industrialized economies. With the LDP at the helm, Japan vaulted into second place among the world's economies, overtaking Canada (1960), Britain and France (mid 1960s), West Germany (1968), and the Soviet Union (1991) for that honor. The economy made a dramatic shift from reliance on agriculture to high-quality

**TABLE 19.3**

**Japan's LDP Prime Ministers, 1954–93**

| Prime Minister | Term of Office | Reasons for Rotation out of Office |
|---|---|---|
| Ichiro Hatoyama | 1954–56 | Resigned after concluding treaty with USSR, of which some business leaders disapproved |
| Tanzan Ishibashi | 1956–57 | Illness |
| Nobusuke Kishi | 1957–60 | Resigned after mishandling renewal of controversial U.S.-Japanese security treaty |
| Hayato Ikeda | 1960–64 | Illness |
| Eisaku Sato | 1964–72 | Ousted by Tanaka in intra-party struggle |
| Kakuei Tanaka | 1972–74 | Corruption |
| Takeo Miki | 1974–76 | Resigned |
| Takeo Fukuda | 1976–78 | Defeated in intra-party vote by Masayoshi Ohira |
| Masayoshi Ohira | 1978–80 | Resigned after no-confidence vote against him |
| Zenko Suzuki | 1980–82 | Resigned |
| Yasuhiro Nakasone | 1982–87 | Resigned |
| Noboru Takeshita | 1987–89 | Resigned after recruit bribery scandal |
| Sousuke Uno | 1989 | Resigned after sexual misconduct allegations |
| Toshiki Kaifu | 1989–91 | Resigned after failure to pass reform bills |
| Kiichi Miyazawa | 1991–93 | Resigned upon vote of no-confidence |

industrial production, and by the late 1960s the United States was purchasing about one-third of all of Japan's exports, making Japan America's single most important trading partner.

By the 1980s the economy was so successful that governments the world over were sending experts to Japan to study its industrial management style and other factors they imagined had contributed to the country's phenomenal success.[14] So strong was the economy that Japan's overseas direct investments, plus loans and economic aid, were energizing the entire Asian region. Meanwhile, Japan's economic model of close ties between the state and private corporations was adapted by South Korea, Singapore, Taiwan, and other countries in the region.[15] In 1988, Japan's investments in enterprises in foreign countries (mostly North America) totaled $47 billion. Foreign investment constituted a higher percentage of GNP in Japan than in the much larger United States. In 1993, with an outlay of $11.3 billion, Japan became the world's largest financial aid donor, with 65 percent of its aid going to the Asian region. In the 1990s, Japan was exporting 10 percent of all products exported worldwide (the U.S. share was 13 percent) at a value of $339.5 billion.[16] Unfortunately, Japan was only importing about 6 percent of world imports, creating balance of trade deficits with many countries, especially the United States—a source of great friction. Still, the phenomenal expansion of Japan's export sector was one of the leading catalysts of economic globalization during the 1970s and 1980s.

How much of this meteoric economic growth can actually be credited to the LDP is unclear, for many factors seemed to be at play.[17] For example, Japan's business conglomerates, the zaibatsu, had been broken up by the Occupation authorities after the war. This move allowed new businesses to get started. Moreover, much of Japan's physical infrastructure (roads, factories, railroads, and the like) was destroyed during the Allied bombing. This destruction turned out to be a blessing in disguise, for it permitted Japan to build modern factories equipped with the latest technologies.

Of course, no rebuilding could have been accomplished without massive amounts of capital. In Japan's case, its former enemy became its biggest benefactor. The United States, believing that Japan could serve as a counterweight to China and other emerging communist nations in Asia, provided substantial reconstruction aid. Major Japanese corporations such as Sony got their start with such foreign assistance. It also did not hurt that, at the very moment Japan needed capital, the Korean War erupted next door in 1950. U.S. military funds in the early 1950s helped many Japanese companies get started, including Mazda Motors, which made Jeeps for the Korean War effort.

Of major significance to the country's economic recovery was the Japanese government's lack of expenditures on its own military. Because the post–World War II constitution forbade the Japanese nation from ever again building a war capability, the government was able to redirect funds that "normal" countries usually spend on defense to such areas as education, public works, and support of new industries. Almost everyone, however, agreed that Japan needed some kind of self-defense force, even if it would not have the capability of projecting itself militarily outside of Japan. The problem was how to build such a force without violating Article 9 of the constitution. Eventually, under Prime Minister Miki in 1976, the government established a defense spending limit of 1 percent of GNP. Compared to the United States at the time (6 to 7 percent), Britain (about 5 percent), and France (about 4 percent), that seemed like a small amount. But the size of Japan's economy became so large in the 1980s that the 1 percent figure translated into over $10 billion per year in actual defense dollars, giving Japan one of the largest defense budgets in the industrialized world.[18]

But economic growth, not defense, was the government's emphasis, and soon Japanese industry came to look upon the government as a facilitator rather than a controller of private enterprise. With government support, Japanese industry began an export-oriented growth strategy that privileged gaining market share over realizing immediate profits. The government became an active player in selecting and supporting industries it felt had a good chance of succeeding.

For example, the Ministry of International Trade and Industry (now the Ministry of Economy, Trade, and Industry) regularly targeted particular industries—steel, container ships, automobiles, and so on—for rapid growth through government support. If necessary, it would impose import controls on foreign products in those sectors, thereby protecting Japanese industry from competition. The export strategy of most companies was to obtain growth in market share rather than to pull in immediate profits. Thus, products were priced lower than similar products elsewhere. Japanese investors seemed comfortable waiting for the day when their company's product would dominate the market and then, finally, yield high stock dividends. By contrast, American investors seemed to want immediate profits, and thus the product price had to be high. This situation gave Japanese products the upper hand and caused tremendous consternation in U.S. industry, especially in such sectors as automobiles and steel manufacturing. By 1994, the Japanese were exporting so much more than they were importing that there was a worldwide trade surplus in Japan's favor in excess of $120 billion per year. Moreover, the Japanese people had come to believe that foreign-made products were often inferior to Japanese-made ones and therefore they did not pressure the government to eliminate protectionist measures.

Adding to the strength of Japan's economy was a relatively mild tax burden. Industries targeted for growth were often given tax breaks; even personal income tax was not burdensome. In 1998, Japan's highest marginal individual income tax rate was 50 percent, but it did not take effect until one's income reached more than $230,000, a higher figure than most economically advanced democracies (see table 14.4 for more recent figures). Japan's bottom personal income tax rate has been among the lowest in the industrialized world.

Social factors in which the government had no hand also contributed to the success of the Japanese economy. For instance, workers were used to working six days a week and then saving a large portion of their paychecks. With personal savings rates as high as 25 percent at times, compared to only 3 percent in the United States, banks always had enough funds on hand to make loans for new business start-ups. Workers were also exceptionally loyal to their companies, working overtime without pay and rarely resorting to union activity to resolve disputes. In return for this loyalty, the larger companies promised lifetime employment to their workers and adopted a benevolent, paternalistic stance toward them. It should be noted, however, that smaller companies were never able to promise lifetime employment and that even in larger companies there was always more movement into and out of companies, especially by younger workers, than was commonly thought.

Although there were a number of factors that the government did not control and that contributed to high growth, such as the traditional respect for education and hard work, it cannot be denied that the government worked diligently to promote economic development. Its approach could be described as an imperfect mixture of some of the principles of Adam Smith and John Maynard Keynes. The Japanese leadership believed that private property and capitalism should be the basis of the economy, but they also believed that the state is obligated to guide the development of free enterprises. Consequently, the LDP and the bureaucracy actively worked with the private sector to select industries most likely to achieve dramatic growth. They then provided plenty of capital to those industries and continued to give administrative guidance as necessary. They also quickly erected trade barriers such as import quotas whenever they felt a selected industry was under attack from outside competitors. Thus, despite the reforms initiated by the Allied Occupation in the 1940s, the Japanese government still permitted and encouraged a cartel-like economic structure in certain segments of the economy (today usually referred to as *keiretsu* rather than zaibatsu).

The result of these and other factors (including Japan's reliance on the United States to provide much of its defense) was that Japan's economy grew at an amazing 10 percent a year on average for many years—the fastest growth rate of any country in the world. From small shop owners to corporation presidents, everyone benefited from the economic miracle. So cozy was the government with private enterprise that outsiders began to refer to the whole country as "Japan Inc.," a concept that suggested that Japan's industries and government were one and the same. But this criticism—leveled by foreign companies that were having a hard time breaking into the strong Japanese market—was misplaced, if not downright wrong. Compared to many economies in Europe, for example, the Japanese economy was quite "free." The Japanese had never tried to nationalize major industries as in Britain, France, Germany, and Italy, to name just a few "capitalist" countries. In France, for instance, the government until the 1980s controlled most of the insurance companies, whereas in Japan, insurance companies received strong administrative guidance from the government but were never owned or controlled by it.

Commonly known as **state-guided capitalism**, ***the Japanese economic model*** produced tremendous immediate results, but it also contributed to serious long-term blunders. Determined to keep every state-assisted company afloat no matter what, the government encouraged struggling companies to simply get more loans from private banks and keep going rather than let the free play of the market determine which companies or product lines would survive and which ones would fail. When the banks agreed to make loans to risky companies, they were, of course, putting their own survival at risk. The banks always assumed that, like the companies, they too would get government help if they needed to be bailed out.

By the late 1980s, however, the pile of bad bank loans was too high for even the Japanese government to handle. A decade later, the Ministry of Finance had to admit that Japanese banks were still holding 35 trillion yen (about $300 billion) in bad loans. Inflated real estate prices aggravated the problem, caused in part by land speculation resulting from Prime Minister Tanaka's plan to start major construction projects throughout Japan's previously undeveloped regions. Many Japanese companies had invested heavily in real estate and had used the assumed value of their land holdings to persuade banks to give them loans for industrial expansion, or to support unprofitable but hard-to-sell product lines, or simply to invest in the burgeoning stock market. But property values fell rapidly in a sudden "correction" when the Bank of Japan increased interest rates in 1989. When stock prices plummeted in 1990, wiping out $2.3 trillion in investor money, investors no longer had money to pay back the large loans they had taken out. Dozens of companies went bankrupt and some business leaders committed suicide in disgrace.

### The Japanese Bureaucracy

Japan's economic woes were exacerbated by faulty decisions taken by the government's powerful bureaucracy. Bureaucrats in the Ministry of Finance and the Ministry of International Trade and Industry, for example, did not always do their homework when it came to recommending strategies to the private sector. For instance, one of the reasons that Japan trails the United States and many other countries in the development of computer software and other information industry products is that the bureaucrats strongly advised Japanese industry in the 1970s to give its attention to mainframe supercomputers rather than personal computers, a serious miscalculation. Both the early successes of these ministries and their recent missteps demonstrate the immense impact of "administrative guidance" on the Japanese economy.

Since 1868, a new Japanese prime minister and cabinet has taken office every sixteen months, on average. Many prime ministers have been able to hold on to power for only a few months before the winds of political change have driven them from office. One of the shortest tenures was that of Prime Minister Tsutomu Hata, who took office on April 25, 1994 only to leave just nine weeks later. Factional politics inside the party have often resulted in relatively frequent changes at the top or the reshuffling of cabinet portfolios. Given such a high level of turnover, and considering that many cabinet posts are given to politicians who have no particular knowledge of, or even interest in, the ministry over which they preside, it is not surprising that unelected bureaucrats within the various ministries wield real power. In effect, bureaucrats run the Japanese state. Japan's elected officials—Diet representatives, cabinet members, and even prime ministers—often find that they have very little actual role in the determination of government policy. Until recently, cabinet ministers were generally not even questioned directly in the Diet, but were represented instead by bureaucrats. (The British practice of subjecting the prime minister to questions by members of parliament was not introduced until late 1999.) In Japan, the people's will and that of the nation's elected representatives often take a back seat to the priorities of the bureaucracy.

As in Britain and France, bureaucrats in Japan are often selected from the best universities—in Japan it is predominantly the University of Tokyo—and are required to take rigorous civil service examinations. Passing these exams brings public respect and guaranteed careers in government. Japanese traditions reinforce the prestige of the civil service. Historically, Japanese bureaucrats often came from aristocratic families and worked directly for the emperor. It was often said that, whereas Japanese politicians worked for themselves, the bureaucrats worked for the nation and were therefore above the pettiness of politics.

With the advantage of these historical precedents, today's bureaucrats have built for themselves a mammoth empire that has resisted numerous reform efforts and that seems to push forward consistent policies regardless of which political party is in power. As in France, and unlike in the United States and a handful of other democracies, the bureaucracy is where things happen in Japan. The Japanese bureaucracy is smaller than the bureaucracies to be found in some other industrialized nations, but at 5 million full-time employees, it is a powerful force in Japanese society.

Not counting the thousands of part-time government employees, there are about 120 bureaucrats for every elected official at all levels of government, and about 1,800 bureaucrats per elected official at the national level. In 1999, the Diet passed legislation reducing the number of ministries and agencies from twenty-two to thirteen and set in motion a plan to reduce the number of bureaucrats by 20 percent by the end of 2010. But previous efforts to control, reform, or cut the size of the bureaucracy have usually failed; time will tell if the current effort succeeds.

***One ministry has gained international fame for its role in guiding Japan's economic growth—the Ministry of Economy, Trade, and Industry, or METI.*** (METI was formerly known as the Ministry of International Trade and Industry, or MITI.) METI has been given more responsibility for the growth of small and medium-size businesses. As the prime protector and promoter of Japanese industry since 1949, METI has no exact parallel anywhere in the world. Although it is relatively small, it has tremendous influence through its ability to approve or deny new technological developments, including imports, and to influence the business community through the placement of many of its retired top leaders in the management ranks of Japan's large business conglomerates. Counterpart organizations such as the U.S. Department of Commerce have never had the power or influence of METI, nor would the U.S. business community welcome such a role for it, preferring instead a business style less encumbered (and also less facilitated) by government.

Occupying top honors as ministries go is the *Ministry of Finance,* often considered the most powerful government ministry in the world of economically advanced democracies. Every year the Finance Ministry hires the highest-scoring graduates from Japan's top universities. Sometimes seen as a conservative ministry when compared with the expansionist METI, the Ministry of Finance has actually played a vital role in forecasting potential growth areas for the economy and regulating banking and taxation. Perhaps most important is its role as final decision maker for budget requests from all the other ministries. Other ministries must submit annual budget requests to the finance minister in time for the start of the new fiscal year each April. This gives the Finance Ministry a powerful hand in guiding the economy as it sees fit.

Organizations that cooperate fully with ministry directives, especially private sector companies, may find themselves in the fortunate position of having a ministry official come to work with them after retirement from the ministry. Bureaucrats often retire in their early fifties and seek employment in the private sector, where they can receive more than twice their civil service salary. The company benefits by having on its staff a former ministry official with "insider" influence. This system of retirement to selected private-sector organizations is called *amakudari,* or "descent from heaven," meaning that the official comes from above with his powerful government connections to work in the private sector while at the same time keeping the company in compliance with the bureaucracy's wishes. Similar practices occur in France, another country with an especially influential state bureaucracy and close connections between the state and business.

Japanese civil servants, especially the twenty thousand or so who constitute the core elite, are aware that their education at the best universities in Japan and their power as government officials give them special advantages. They believe that their viewpoint from the pinnacle of power is more objective and fair than that of special interest groups or narrow specialists—and certainly better than that of the elected politicians who are nominally their superiors, but whom they sometimes scorn. Traditionally, many high-level bureaucrats were descended from the Tokugawa-era samurai families. The public image these elites have created with respect to their dedication, hard work, self-sacrifice, and impartiality has remained a fixture of the Japanese bureaucracy ever since. As long as the government has worked well, the public has had little reason to challenge these traditional claims of superiority.

In recent years, however, the bureaucratic veneer has begun to crack.[19] Not only have disgruntled government bureaucrats written scathing exposés about wild parties, lazy workers, and gross inefficiencies, but the general public has become aware that many bureaucrats are simply neither as competent nor as impartial as once thought. Far from making decisions on the basis of the general good, bureaucrats in Japan have been found to be highly susceptible to bribery from the private sector and from regional and municipal officials. Today's newspapers regularly carry stories about *kankan settai,* that is, the practice of local and regional officials spending citizens' taxes on lavish drinking parties and other entertainments, including expensive overseas travel, in order to curry favor with central government officials. Important financial decisions, such as the provision of huge bank loans to certain businesses, have been found to be based on personal friendships (sometimes called "crony capitalism") rather than on creditworthiness, a factor that contributed to the collapse of the bubble economy in 1989 and 1990. Secrecy, rather than transparency, prevails in the bureaucracy's decision-making processes.

Japanese bureaucrats are not known for their attention to the demands of consumer groups or environmental groups, but they seem to respond quickly to big business producer groups such as the Japan Chamber of Commerce and Industry, the Japan Association of Corporate Executives, and the Federation of Economic Organizations *(Keidanren).* With nearly a thousand corporate members and 120 industry-wide associations as Keidanren members, this big business group carries enormous weight inside the government. It has influenced bureaucrats and elected officials to ignore or vote against proposals that would have preserved the environment and protected consumers. In fact, it was at the insistence of the Keidanren in 1955 that the two largest conservative political parties merged to form the Liberal Democratic Party.

Perhaps even worse than unfair influence, graft, and corruption are the growing number of cases in which government officials have shown poor judgment at the expense of the citizens they are supposed to serve. One such case was a potentially disastrous leak at a nuclear power plant in 1997. Rather than inform the public immediately, the bureaucrats decided to keep absolute silence, even though such a decision potentially endangered the lives of many people. A more serious nuclear plant accident occurred in 1999, but this time the government was more forthcoming about the danger to the public. (Nuclear plants generate 35 percent of Japan's electricity.) In another case, HIV-tainted blood was allowed to be sold and used for blood transfusions with the knowledge of bureaucrats from the Ministry of Health. These cases, plus charges of corruption and incompetence against the Ministry of Finance (some of whose officials were arrested in highly publicized police raids) and other ministries, have severely tarnished the image of the central bureaucracy in recent years.

### The Bursting Bubble

The problems that accumulated in Japan's economy in the late 1980s and early 1990s—the collapse of the banking system, the precipitate fall in real estate prices, bureaucratic miscalculations, and related troubles—produced a serious recession from which Japan has not yet recovered. Annual economic growth averaged only 1.4 percent in the 1990s. The high cost of living hit Japanese consumers hard: by the mid 1990s a bag of white rice cost $40 compared to the U.S. price of about $7. And because of Japan's pivotal role in today's globalized economy, its economic crisis inevitably has had a ripple effect on other economies around the world, spawning financial crises in Asia, cutting the profits of companies doing business with the Japanese, and sending stock prices tumbling on Wall Street and other stock exchanges around the world. The high-flying economic system that once appeared unstoppable is now seen as an economic bubble that has burst. Is Japan's economic model a failure?[20]

## HYPOTHESIS-TESTING EXERCISE: The Japanese Economy

### Hypothesis and Variables

According to the tenets of economic liberalism, governments that utilize free-market approaches to economic development will produce more wealth for society than will those that try to dominate the economy through state control or excessive government regulation of the economy.

The *dependent variable* is *wealth,* and the competing *independent variables* are *market capitalism* and *a state-controlled economy.*

### Expectations

We would expect that Japan's economy would have generated more wealth during the period from 1945 to the present, when a form of market capitalism was the rule, than at any period prior to that time, especially the Edo or Tokugawa periods (1600–1868), when the military shoguns attempted to control every aspect of the feudal economy. The style of market capitalism in Japan is a modified version of liberal principles. It combines completely unfettered and unassisted enterprises in large segments of the economy with state-assisted enterprises that receive preferential treatment in financing and in protection from outside competition. None of these state interventions, however, has ever reached the level of state domination of the economy that prevailed in the pre-1868 period or even the level of intervention that a number of West European governments engaged in during the 1960s and 1970s. We would also expect to find lower growth or related problems in areas of the economy where market principles are violated.

### Evidence

By the mid 1960s, the Japanese economy under its combination of market liberalism and state-guided capitalism was able to overtake the economies of several European countries. Today, despite a lengthy economic recession and even some years of negative economic growth, the Japanese economy is still the second largest in the world. During the 1980s and part of the 1990s, Japan generated so much wealth that it was donating more foreign aid to developing countries than was the United States. Japan gave so much aid that a large portion of the gross domestic product of some recipient countries came from Japan.

By contrast, during the Tokugawa era, the Japanese shoguns prohibited all foreign trade except out of one port in Nagasaki, which they controlled themselves. Except for Holland, countries trading with Japan were not allowed even to enter Japan's ports. Furthermore, the shoguns forced their subordinate daimyos, or domain lords, to spend alternating years living in Tokyo, an expensive practice that drained their resources and forced many of them to borrow heavily from rice merchants and samurai. As a result of these controls the economy grew weaker by comparison with its counterparts in Europe and North America. By the mid 1800s, the Japanese realized that their economy and their military were no match for the West, and they had to begin a painful restructuring process.

When weak spots are found in the modern Japanese economy today, it is often at precisely those places where the Japanese have violated market principles in favor of state control. For instance, for many years the government owned and controlled the national railway system. After decades of such control, the system was found to have 277,000 more employees on its payroll than it needed and to have accumulated a public debt in excess of $257 billion. The government eventually resolved the problem by privatizing the system. Likewise, the government has made it a practice for years to provide "administrative guidance" to a variety of industries—that is, to select certain industries for growth and then support them, even at the expense of a truly free market. When lagging sales produced crises in these selected industries, the government encouraged banks to prop up the industries with large loans based on weak collateral. In short, they violated the principle of the free market by supporting companies or products that the consumers did not want. That was one of the causes of the recession of the 1990s and further evidence that the Japanese economy has suffered precisely at those points where the government violated market principles.

### Conclusions

On the whole the evidence is largely *consistent* with our hypothesis. Though postwar Japan has hardly been a laissez-faire economy with no government intervention, its blend of free enterprise, market mechanisms, and state assistance for dynamic private firms has produced far more rapid growth than did the more state-dominated economic strategies that its leaders employed in the past.

TABLE 19.4

**House of Representatives Election Results, 1990 and 1993 (512 seats in 1990; 511 in 1993)**

| | 1990 | | 1993 | |
|---|---|---|---|---|
| **Party** | **Seats** | **% of Vote** | **Seats** | **% of Vote** |
| Liberal Democratic Party | 275 | 46.1 | 223 | 36.6 |
| Social Democratic Party | 136 | 24.4 | 70 | 15.4 |
| Japan Renewal Party | — | — | 55 | 10.1 |
| Komeito | 45 | 8.0 | 51 | 8.1 |
| Japan New Party | — | — | 35 | 8.0 |
| Democratic Socialist Party | 14 | 4.8 | 15 | 3.5 |
| Japan Communist Party | 16 | 8.0 | 15 | 7.7 |
| Other Parties | 5 | 1.0 | 17 | 3.3 |
| Independents | 21 | 4.1 | 30 | 5.9 |

## POLITICAL CHANGE SINCE 1993

### The 1993 Elections

Just as the LDP had been praised for its role in revitalizing the economy, in 1993 it was blamed for its inability to restore it to health. As in other societies, the population rightly perceived that the economy and politics are closely intertwined. In 1993, following the Diet's ouster of Prime Minister Miyazawa, a growing number of former LDP voters decided that it was now time to exit the party rather than raise their voices to try to change it from within. So too did a growing number of LDP politicians, many of whom quit the disgraced party and formed new ones.

In addition to the *Japan New Party,* founded in 1992 by Morihiro Hosakawa, two more parties sprang up just before the elections: the *Japan Renewal Party (Shinseito),* led by former LDP leaders Tsutomu Hata and Ichiro Ozawa, and the *New Harbinger Party* (also translated as the New Pioneer Party), led by another ex-LDP Diet member, Masayoshi Takemura. A number of other parties provided additional choices for the Japanese electorate. On the left were the *Japan Socialist Party* (which wished to be known in English as the *Social Democratic Party*) and the *Japan Communist Party.* In the center were two offshoots of the Socialist Party, namely, the *Democratic Socialist Party* and the *United Social Democratic Party (Shaminren).* Both parties were more moderate than the Socialists, most of whose leaders still rejected the security alliance with the United States. Another centrist group, the *Komeito,* had ties to a Buddhist movement. Several smaller parties and independent candidates complemented the electoral menu.

The results of the 1993 elections (which had the lowest voter turnout in three decades) represented a stinging repudiation of the Liberal Democrats, but no other party emerged as a clear alternative (see table 19.4).

Upon losing control of the lower house, the LDP was forced to turn power over to a broad coalition of old and new opposition parties. In a state of disbelief, the party that had governed Japan without interruption since 1955 now retreated to its new place in the opposition. Although still the largest single party, it had lost control of both houses of the Diet and was no longer able to control its membership.

The hung parliament that followed the 1993 elections ushered in a period of instability and uncertainty that discomfited the Japanese as well as foreign governments. Over the next three years the country had four prime ministers (see table 19.5). Lacking clear direction, the post-1993 coalition governments had little success in tackling the country's mounting economic problems and declining global position. Hosokawa's reformist cabinet, which assumed power immediately after the elections, made good on its promises of electoral reform but dissolved amid hints of scandal. Disagreements over tax policy and other issues plagued the next two coalition cabinets before the Liberal Democrats returned to power in an unlikely partnership with the Socialists in January 1996 under Ryutaro

**TABLE 19.5**

**Japan's Governments, 1993–2006**

| Prime Minister (Party) | Governing Parties | Term of Office |
|---|---|---|
| Morihoro Hosokawa (Japan New Party) | 7-party coalition | July 1993–April 1994 |
| Tsutomu Hata (Japan Renewal Party) | 5-party coalition | April–July 1994 |
| Tomiichi Murayama (Japan Socialist Party) | 3-party coalition | July 1994–January 1996 |
| Ryutaro Hashimoto (LDP) | LDP minority government | January–October 1996 |
| Ryutaro Hashimoto | LDP minority government | October 1996–July 1998 |
| Keizo Obuchi (LDP) | LDP minority government | July 1998–October 1999 |
| Keizo Obuchi | 3-party coalition | October 1999–April 2000 |
| Yoshiro Mori (LDP) | 3-party coalition | April 2000–April 2001 |
| Junichiro Koizumi (LDP) | 3-party coalition | April 2001–November 2003 |
| Junichiro Koizumi | 2-party coalition | November 2003–September 2005 |
| Junichiro Koizumi | 2-party coalition | September 2005–September 2006 |
| Shinzo Abe | 2-party coalition | September 2006–present |

Hashimoto. Corruption and indecisiveness continued to have a wearying effect on domestic public opinion, and there was a widening sense around the world that government in Japan had ground to a halt.

In a desperate attempt to head off mounting criticism and hopeful of establishing a more secure basis for governing without coalition partners, Hashimoto dissolved the House of Representatives and called anticipated elections in the fall of 1996. The House of Representatives is formally dissolved when a dissolution edict from the emperor (actually decided by the cabinet), wrapped in purple paper, is opened and read by the speaker. With the completion of this ceremony, the 1996 race was on.

### The Electoral Reforms Take Effect

The campaign was fought under the new electoral laws enacted in 1994. Under the previous system, Japan's House of Representatives was elected in multimember districts. The country was divided into 129 districts; depending on the district's size, between two and six deputies were elected to represent it in the House. The candidates' names did not appear on the ballot, so voters had to write in their selections. This system required Japanese politicians to do everything they could to enhance their name recognition. Incumbents running for reelection thus had an incentive to deliver highly visible pork-barrel projects to their districts, a practice that at times encouraged corruption in the legislative process. All candidates felt the need to spend lavishly on campaign advertising. (Brazil has a similar system, with roughly similar results.) Ultimately, the pre-1996 electoral system reinforced the Liberal Democrats' lock on power. As the governing party, it had the power to allocate government-funded projects to districts represented by LDP deputies. And as the party with the greatest access to wealthy corporate contributors, the LDP could afford to field several candidates in each district, several of whom might win. By the 1980s it was estimated that running an election campaign for a seat in the Japanese House of Representatives could be five times as costly as running for the U.S. House, with an average reported expenditure of $2.5 million. Prior to 1996, none of this money was allowed to be spent on individual television advertising.[21] Candidates in the larger districts, where five or six Diet representatives were chosen, could win a seat with as little as 20 percent of the vote.

In an attempt to reduce the LDP's advantages and open up the election process to other, less well-funded parties, Prime Minister Hosokawa proposed a sweeping reform of the electoral system as well as stiff limitations on campaign funding. His proposal called for reducing the size of the House from 511 to an even 500 seats and for instituting a two-ballot election process. In the compromise bill that was eventually passed into law, it was agreed that 300 seats would be elected in single-member districts (SMD) on a winner-take-all basis; the remaining 200 would be elected according to proportional representation (PR). For the PR vote, the country was divided into eleven new districts, with parties required to win at least 2 percent of the vote in those districts.

This new system is roughly similar to the "mixed-member" SMD/PR method for electing the lower house of parliament now in use in Germany. It seeks to combine the name recognition factor of single-member districts, where candidates run by name, with the fairness in representation afforded by proportional representation, which allows even small parties to win representation in the lower house. The 2 percent hurdle in each district is aimed at preventing a proliferation of mini-parties. On election day, each voter gets two ballots: one showing the names of individual candidates, the other showing a list of the competing parties. The voter selects one candidate and one party. Voters are therefore free to split their vote, choosing, say, an LDP candidate on the single-member ballot but marking the Japan Socialist Party on the proportional representation list. For years, rural districts have been favored by the multiseat system, but the new SMD/PR system had the potential to alter the balance of power away from the rural areas, giving political advantages to parties whose constituencies are urban workers. This fact was not lost on the LDP, which continues to mull over possible revisions of the 1994 reforms while it increases its activities in urban areas. Even so, the 300 directly elected seats were distributed in such a way as to give rural voters disproportionately greater representation than urban voters. The public, however, wants the LDP to leave things alone for awhile and see how the new system works before attempting any new reforms.

Every Japanese adult age twenty-five or older has the opportunity to run for the House of Representatives. In practice, however, only those who can command large sums of money or who enjoy the advantage of coming from already established political families (sometimes called the "elected nobility") usually succeed at the polls. Hosokawa's original proposals for curtailing campaign funding were fairly stringent. He wanted to ban all donations to individual candidates, requiring donors to make their contributions only to a party's national organization. In negotiations with the Liberal Democrats, Hosokawa retreated from that position and agreed to allow individual candidates to receive up to $4,500 per private sector corporate donor. Obviously, candidates with numerous corporate donors would be able to receive many times that figure, a reality likely to benefit the well-connected Liberal Democrats. (The compromise reform law phased out *all* contributions to individual candidates starting in 1999.) The reform required the disclosure of the source of any donations above $450. (Under the previous system, disclosure was required for donations above $9,000.) It also enabled parties to receive campaign funding from the state. The earlier practice of restricting the official campaign period to twelve days was retained.

## The 1996 Elections

The House of Representatives election of October 20, 1996, took place in a period of flux unprecedented in the lifetime of many Japanese voters. Every week, it seemed, some new political group was freshly born or was joined together from the remains of former parties. And every month it seemed that new alliances were announced, many of which, for ideological reasons, would have been judged unworkable from the start had the electorate taken the time to evaluate them. Voters were bewildered by the sudden array of new parties, most of whose ideological positions were unclear at best. More than a dozen parties, along with a similar number of independent candidates, sought votes in 1996. The resulting confusion may explain the unusually low turnout for the 1996 vote, with only 59.7 percent of the eligible voters going to the polls, the lowest turnout in postwar Japan to date.

The largest new party to take part in the elections was the *New Frontier Party,* an amalgam of nine former parties that was put together in 1994 by two former Liberal Democratic politicians, Ichiro Ozawa and former prime minister Tsutomo Hata. In 1995 Ozawa, an energetic proponent of political and economic reform, bested Hata in an election to choose the party's leader. (In a new twist on party leadership selection procedures, New Frontier allowed all adult citizens to vote for its leader upon payment of a $10 contribution. More than 1.6 million people took part in the vote.) The final results indicated a good showing for New Frontier, which captured 156 seats. But this tally was not enough to

**TABLE 19.6**

**House of Representatives Elections, 1996 (500 seats: 300 chosen by SMD, 200 by PR)**

| Party | Total Seats (%) | SMD Seats | PR Seats |
|---|---|---|---|
| Liberal Democratic Party | 239 (47.8) | 169 | 70 |
| New Frontier Party | 156 (31.2) | 96 | 60 |
| Democratic Party | 52 (10.4) | 17 | 35 |
| Japan Communist Party | 26 (5.2) | 2 | 24 |
| Social Democratic Party | 15 (3.0) | 4 | 11 |
| Sakigake | 2 (0.4) | 2 | 0 |
| Other | 1 (0.2) | 1 | 0 |
| Independents | 9 (1.8) | 9 | 0 |

outdo the Liberal Democrats, who came in first with 239 seats.

Nor was it enough to create a real two-party system, as the authors of the 1994 electoral reforms had wished. Several other parties also won seats in the new legislature, preventing the Liberal Democrats from governing with an absolute majority of seats (see table 19.6). With 47.8 percent of the total seats in the House of Representatives, Prime Minister Hashimoto had to cut deals with smaller parties in order to retain control of the government and pass his bills into law. With the agreement of the Socialists and the small Sakigake Party, along with a few independents, Hashimoto put together a parliamentary alliance that enabled the Liberal Democrats to form a single-party minority government. In full command of the cabinet once again, the LDP was back on top of the Japanese political system.

### Aftermath of the 1996 Elections

Hashimoto's new government found it difficult to take decisive measures to overcome Japan's economic malaise. In 1998, Japanese voters expressed their dismay at the slow pace of change by dealing the Liberal Democrats a rude blow in elections to the Diet's upper house, the House of Councillors.[22] Stung by this shock, Hashimoto decided to resign, even though he was not obligated to do so. His successor was Keizo Obuchi, a member of the same powerful faction as former Prime Minister Tanaka.

An orthodox conservative, Obuchi was one of the least popular contenders for the office of prime minister. By late 1999, Obuchi's approval rating had plunged to just 32 percent. One major complaint against him was his inclusion of the Komeito Party in a three-party coalition government with the LDP and the newly created *New Conservative Party* in October of that year. A political offshoot of a Buddhist denomination known for its strong-arm tactics (the *Sokka Gakkai*), Komeito had been part of the New Frontier Party in the 1996 elections. When New Frontier subsequently broke up, Komeito reconstituted itself as *New Komeito*. But it was still too closely linked to religion to be trusted by the average Japanese voter. Obuchi countered that including New Komeito was politically necessary if the LDP, still weakened in numbers and political clout, was to be able to pass Diet legislation. He put the reform of Japan's fiscal system on hold, postponing tax increases that some critics considered urgent in view of the rising national debt resulting from the government's lavish spending measures. However, signs of the economy's slow recovery were sprouting up when Obuchi suffered a debilitating stroke in April 2000; he died several weeks later.

In his place the kingpins of the Liberal Democratic Party installed Yoshiro Mori, a little-known figure whose principal merit was his acceptability to the party's various factions. (Mori himself belonged to the same faction as Obuchi.) Mori promised to continue Obuchi's economic strategy but he soon found himself the butt of criticism for some embarrassing misstatements.

### The 2000 Elections

With the next elections to the House of Representatives due to be held before the end of 2000, Liberal Democratic Party politicians decided to schedule

TABLE 19.7

**House of Representatives Elections, 2000 (480 seats: 300 chosen by SMD, 180 by PR)**

| Parties | Total Seats (%) | SMD Seats | PR Seats |
|---|---|---|---|
| **Governing coalition parties:** | | | |
| Liberal Democratic Party | 233 (48.5) | 177 | 56 |
| New Komeito Party | 31 (6.5) | 7 | 24 |
| New Conservative Party | 7 (1.5) | 7 | 0 |
| **Opposition parties:** | | | |
| Democratic Party of Japan | 127 (26.5) | 80 | 47 |
| Liberal Party | 22 (4.6) | 4 | 18 |
| Japan Communist Party | 20 (4.2) | 0 | 20 |
| Social Democratic Party | 19 (4.0) | 4 | 15 |
| Small parties and independents | 21 (4.4) | 21 | 0 |

them at the end of June. Their hope was that the LDP's continuing popularity among large segments of the electorate, especially in rural areas where it traditionally ran strong, would be sufficient to overcome Mori's lack of mass appeal. (Mori's popularity ratings hovered between 12 and 19 percent.) They also hoped that the government's massive public works and welfare programs would be gratefully rewarded with votes.

The results of the elections of June 25, 2000, as shown in table 19.7, were no cause for rejoicing for the Liberal Democrats: they lost a considerable number of seats. (Though they had won 239 seats in the previous elections of 1996, their ranks had subsequently swelled to 271 when the New Frontier Party fell apart and a number of its deputies gravitated to the Liberal Democrats.) The public's continuing disaffection was evident in the 60.5 percent turnout, only slightly higher than the record low turnout of 1996. But the final tally was good enough to enable the Liberal Democrats to reconstitute their coalition government with New Komeito and the New Conservative party. With the size of the House reduced from 500 to 480, the Liberal Democrats won 233 seats (48.5 percent of the total). New Komeito won 31 seats (6.5 percent) and the New Conservatives won 7 seats (1.5 percent). ***The largest opposition party,*** the **Democratic Party of Japan (DPJ),** increased its representation from 52 seats in 1996 to 127 seats. The Social Democratic Party (also known as the Japan Socialist Party) improved its showing from 15 seats in 1996 to 19. The Liberal Party, a new party led by Ichiro Ozawa following the breakup of his New Frontier Party, debuted with 22 seats.

Yoshiro Mori emerged from the elections as the renewed choice of the consensus-conscious LDP faction leaders and was duly reinstated as prime minister. He vowed once again to continue the economic policies that he inherited from his predecessor. But a scandal was brewing that threatened to tarnish the Liberal Democrats with fresh charges of corruption. A former LDP construction minister was arrested a few days after the elections and accused of receiving $285,000 in kickbacks, reviving fears that a Liberal Democratic government might once again be immersed in corruption charges.

One of the few signs of change to emerge from the June 2000 elections was a slight increase in the number of women elected to the lower house. Thirty-five women won seats in the House of Representatives, as compared with twenty-three in the previous Diet. In spite of the increase, Japan still had one of the world's lowest percentages of women serving in the lower house of a nationally elected parliament (7.3 percent). Ironically, Japan's reformed electoral system was part of the problem: 300 of the 480 House members are elected in single-member districts. The SMD system places a premium on name recognition, inducing politicians to spend large amounts of money on their campaigns to make themselves known to the public. Few women in Japanese political life possess the organizational and financial backing needed to meet this challenge. Single-member districts also favor incumbents who can remind the electorate of the government benefits they have secured for their constituencies while serving in the legislature. Following Mori's reelection, the LDP selected Chikage Ogi, the leader of the New Conservative Party, as minister of construction. But her cabinet appointment represented a questionable political victory for Japanese women, inasmuch as no male political figures wanted the scandal-tainted post.

As Mori's approval ratings sank to 7 percent by the spring of 2001, it was evident to the LDP hierarchy that a new prime minister was vitally necessary in order to prevent the party from completely losing touch with Japanese voters. Mori agreed to step aside as the party's president and allow other contenders to compete for his position. Following hallowed LDP traditions, the leaders of various factions got together to pick the party's new chief. Their choice fell on Ryutaro Hashimoto, already well known as a former prime minister. Although he had resigned his office in disgrace in 1998, Hashimoto was considered more likely than Mori to succeed as head of government. Hashimoto now controlled the party's largest faction, the one that had been built up by Kakuei Tanaka. He appeared to be headed toward easy confirmation as the LDP's new leader and the country's next head of government.

And then something unexpected happened. In a few frenetic weeks, a veritable revolt welled up from within the LDP's rank and file. A challenger declared his candidacy for the party leadership and threw into doubt the party hierarchy's plans for a smooth transition to Hashimoto. *Junichiro Koizumi,* a veteran Diet member and former health and welfare minister, suddenly presented his party and the country with a real alternative.

Junichiro Koizumi

## PROFILE: Junichiro Koizumi

With his mop of wavy hair, cheerful grin, and boisterous enthusiasm, Junichiro Koizumi bore little resemblance to the typical Liberal Democratic Party elder statesman. At fifty-nine, he still had a youthful bounce, and tastes to match: he was a fan of heavy metal, a popular rock group called Japan X, and Elvis Presley. Unlike most Japanese politicians, he had studied abroad (at the London School of Economics) and he spoke a little English. A glib television personality, Koizumi sent out an e-mail newsletter—under his nickname "Lionheart"—to 2 million subscribers. He was especially popular with women and young voters, and he promised to bring more women and younger people into his cabinet. Breaking with Mori's faction, Koizumi made it known that he opposed the faction system that still kept a tight stranglehold on the LDP, and he declared his readiness to make major changes to break the impasse in economic policy making.

In previous years, Koizumi's bids for the party presidency were written off as futile. But with a view to reconnecting the LDP to Japanese voters, party leaders had instituted new voting procedures to choose the party's president. No longer would a handful of faction chieftains dictate the choice. Under the new rules, local LDP chapters organized in the country's forty-seven prefectures would hold "primary" elections open to party members. After the primaries, LDP legislators would stage their own vote. As the primaries got under way, talk of a "Koizumi revolution" and "Koizumi fever" gripped the country, echoing the excitement of the 1993 Hosokawa campaign. More than 80 percent of the public favored the challenger. With his popularity soaring, Koizumi won 123 of the 141 votes accorded to the local chapters in the primaries. Faced with a clear display of party membership preferences, 175 of the 346 LDP legislators subsequently voted for Koizumi. His combined total was 298 votes, a sum that decisively outdistanced Hashimoto's 155 votes. By opening itself up to greater citizen participation at the grassroots level, the Liberal

Democratic Party was transforming itself from a basically elite-dominated party to one that was beginning to serve, in however limited a fashion, as an arm of civil society. Several days later, the LDP's large parliamentary delegation elected Koizumi prime minister of Japan.

The new head of government instantly fulfilled one of his pledges by appointing to his cabinet five women—a record number—and two men in their forties. (Foreign minister Makiko Tanaka, the daughter of the former prime minister, soon became embroiled in conflicts with ministry officials, and Koizumi dismissed her in early 2002.) Starting out as the most popular prime minister in Japanese history, Koizumi led the LDP to a resounding victory in elections to the upper house, the House of Councillors, in July 2001. After a slow start, he gradually came forward with a spate of economic reform proposals, including plans for deficit reduction, a new tax system, and the privatization of various state-owned companies. Members of the LDP's hierarchy, who controlled the party's huge voting bloc in the Diet, sought to block or water down some of these reforms, and in some cases they succeeded. Faced with the continuing strength of entrenched interests in the LDP, Koizumi held back from attacking the primary source of Japan's economic doldrums: the heavily indebted banks and insolvent private corporations.

By the time Koizumi took office, Japanese banks had outstanding bad loans that were estimated at anywhere from \$280 billion to more than \$600 billion; some estimates topped \$1 trillion. Thirty to fifty large private firms were also over their heads in debts. Some economists urged the government to stop subsidizing still more loans to these institutions, but Koizumi and other LDP leaders were unwilling to permit the high levels of unemployment that would result from widespread bankruptcies. There has been a general consensus in postwar Japan on the need to avoid unemployment. The 2002 unemployment rate, at just over 5 percent, was widely viewed as high enough. Another problem was deflation (falling prices). In the early 2000s, prices were falling at the rate of about 1 percent a year. When combined with the Japanese penchant for saving their money at much higher rates than Americans or Europeans, deflation meant that companies were not earning enough to pay off their debts, expand production, or hire more workers. By 2003 Koizumi had not succeeded in bringing Japan out of its fourth recession in ten years. As we have seen, Japan's economic problems were rooted in the country's *political* system, specifically the "iron triangle" connecting the LDP hierarchy, big business, and the bureaucracy. And Koizumi's "revolution" did not break that combination.[23]

In foreign policy, Koizumi closed ranks with the Bush administration after September 11, 2001. Japan hosted conferences on Afghanistan and made financial contributions to that country's post-Taliban rebuilding effort. As part of its anti-terrorism activity, the Diet in 2001 passed unprecedented legislation permitting Japanese military forces to be sent abroad in peacekeeping missions and other noncombat roles (such as refueling foreign naval vessels.) Although Japan spends a considerable amount of money on its Self-Defense Forces, Article 9 of its constitution, written by Gen. MacArthur, outlaws war and forbids Japanese military deployment outside of Japan. Nevertheless, the United States pressed Japan to engage its forces in global trouble spots in conjunction with U.S. or NATO operations. Koizumi remained attached to the treaties that allow the United States to maintain troops (now numbering about 38,000) in Japan, mostly on Okinawa. Some Japanese politicians have argued that it is time for Japan to abandon its "no war" policy and become a "normal" country with a full offensive military. With mounting American pressure on Japan to shoulder more responsibility for providing security in the Far East, and with the rise of China's military might and North Korea's nuclear ambitions, there was talk of revising Article 9 of Japan's constitution.

LDP lawmakers initiated the slow process of constitutional reform in early 2004. By November 2005, on the occasion of the LDP's fiftieth anniversary, a draft of a new constitution was completed and announced. Of greatest interest were the proposed revisions to Article 9. The proposal left intact the clause declaring that Japan would forever renounce war, but it altered the second clause to permit the Self-Defense Forces (SDF) to obtain clear, legal status under the constitution. Ever since the Self-Defense Forces were created after 1945, pacifists have claimed that the very existence of military forces is a violation of Article 9. The proposed revision would make it clear that the existence of military forces is permitted under the constitution. Other changes would allow the creation of a more muscular Ministry of Defense (instead of a defense agency as at present), allow the SDF to be called an "army," permit the prime minister to be called the commander-in-chief of the military, and allow Japanese troops to be deployed overseas even if there has not been a direct attack on Japan.

Koizumi also sought to maintain good relations with China, a delicate task in view of lingering memories of Japan's harsh treatment of China before and during World War II. Only in 1993 did a Japanese prime minister—Morihiro Hosokawa—first apologize for Japan's aggression against China and other Asian nations. But the Diet did not pass a resolution to this effect for two more years, expressing "remorse" rather than an actual apology. On a visit to China in 2001, Koizumi offered Japan's "heartfelt apology" for its atrocities. The Chinese have also objected to Japanese history textbooks, which gloss over the brutal realities of Japan's wartime behavior. Shortly after taking office, Prime Minister Koizumi provoked criticism in Asia when he visited a shrine honoring Japanese war dead, including some war criminals. But China, with its booming economy, has become one of Japan's main trading partners, and Koizumi was eager to cultivate these ties. He also expressed Japan's opposition to North Korea's attempts to acquire nuclear weapons. While pursuing friendly relations with Russia, Koizumi did not make any progress in convincing the Russian leadership to return four islands—known in Japan as the Northern Territories—that the Soviet Union took from the Japanese in World War II.

Although Koizumi's "revolution" proved modest at best, and his approval ratings fell to about 45 percent, he remained the LDP's most visible politician. For this reason he handily won reelection as the party's president in September 2003. He then led the LDP into parliamentary elections for the House of Representatives in November, facing two serious challenges. The first was the traditional elite within his own party, a group that sought to block his economic reforms. The second was a rejuvenated opposition party—the Democratic Party of Japan—which called for considerably more effective reforms than Koizumi had thus far delivered. For the first time in decades, Japanese voters had the opportunity to choose between two mainstream parties that were equally capable of forming a viable government.

## The 2003 Elections

Koizumi's main rival in the 2003 race was *Naoto Kan,* the leader of the Democratic Party of Japan (DPJ). The DPJ was formed in the late 1990s with the merger of several small parties. With 155 seats, the DPJ was the second-largest party in the House of Representatives in the summer of 2003, but in September its ranks expanded by 22 deputies when it merged with the Liberal Party. As preparations for the impending elections intensified, Kan took the bold step of having his party issue an election manifesto indicating specific actions his government would take if elected. Such detailed campaign manifestos were not common in Japanese politics.

Among other things, the DPJ's program called for "showing the bureaucrats who's boss" by reducing their numbers and by taking public money out of their control by shifting it to local governors. The party's aim was to enact a number of the reforms that Koizumi himself had advocated but had failed to implement because of opposition from the "iron triangle" of special interests that still dominated his own party: the aging representatives of old political families in the LDP, well-entrenched bureaucrats, and the heads of powerful corporations and banks. Kan also hoped to win a large share of Japan's urban vote, echoing the objections of many city dwellers to the expenditure of inordinate amounts of government money in rural areas. Too much of this money was still wasted on needless construction projects whose primary purpose was to court rural support for old-guard Liberal Democrats, another practice Koizumi had failed to stop.

Far-away Iraq was also an issue. Polls showed that more than 70 percent of the Japanese people did not want Japan to send troops to Iraq, something that Koizumi's government and the LDP promised to do in response to requests from the United States. Kan's Democratic Party opposed sending troops to Iraq on the grounds that such action would violate Japan's pacifist constitution. The combination of clearly drawn domestic and foreign policy differences between the two parties made for an exciting race.

As noted earlier, in Japan's two-ballot procedure, Japanese voters choose a political party for the proportional representation vote, and write down the name of a single candidate on the other ballot for the single-member-district vote. The names of the competing candidates are posted in each polling station, and voters carefully copy on their ballot the Japanese characters of their chosen candidate. After all the ballots cast on November 9 were counted by hand, Koizumi's Liberal Democrats came away with 237 seats, ten fewer than in the 2000 elections. Kan's Democratic Party won 177 seats, a gain of 40. But then the horse-trading began. Once the results shown in table 19.8 were in, several candidates who had run as independents

TABLE 19.8

| House of Representatives Elections, 2003 (480 seats: 300 chosen by SMD, 180 by PR) | | | | | |
|---|---|---|---|---|---|
| **Party** | **SMD Seats** | **% SMD Vote** | **PR Seats** | **% PR Vote** | **Total Seats (%)** |
| Liberal Democratic Party | 168 | 43.8 | 69 | 35.0 | 237 (49.4) |
| Democratic Party of Japan | 105 | 36.7 | 72 | 37.4 | 177 (36.9) |
| New Komeito | 9 | 1.5 | 25 | 14.8 | 34 (7.1) |
| Japan Communist Party | 0 | 8.1 | 9 | 7.8 | 9 (1.9) |
| Social Democratic Party | 1 | 2.9 | 5 | 5.1 | 6 (1.2) |
| New Conservative Party | 4 | 1.3 | 0 | (<2.0) | 4 (0.8) |
| Others | 2 | 5.7 | 0 | (<2.0 each) | 2 (0.4) |
| Independents | 11 | — | — | — | 11 (2.3) |

decided to join the LDP. The small New Conservative Party, which had won 4 seats, also decided to join the Liberal Democrats, giving Koizumi's party a post-election total of 245 seats. Meanwhile, other newly elected representatives—including Makiko Tanaka, the outspoken former foreign minister who was elected as an independent—decided to join the Democratic Party. With these new members, Kan's DPJ ended up with 180 seats, making it the first truly strong opposition in years. Finally, the New Komeito party agreed to remain the LDP's partner in a new coalition government. Together the newly enlarged LDP and New Komeito controlled 278 seats out of 480, a comfortable voting majority.

Women registered both gains and losses in the elections. In 2003 there were 149 female candidates for the House. Although that figure was lower than in 1999, a larger percentage won this time, giving women about 7 percent of the seats in the Diet's lower house. A number of women ran as independents, but fifteen were elected as members of the Democratic Party and nine won as Liberal Democrats. Takako Doi, Japan's best-known female politician and a Diet member for thirty-four years, resigned from her post as the leader of Japan's Social Democratic Party following the party's crushing defeat in the November elections. (It fell from 18 seats in 2000 to just 6 seats in 2003.) But when the dust settled and the party's leaders met to choose her successor, they selected Muzuho Fukushima, a 47-year-old lawyer, a member of the House of Councillors for five years—and a woman.

Voter turnout was once again disappointing: 59 percent, one of the lowest rates in Japanese history. The prospect that Japan might finally be heading toward a party system dominated by two mainstream rival parties proved attractive to some voters, particularly those who voted for Kan's Democratic Party of Japan. But disaffection from politics was still widespread. Many voters, it seemed, were concerned about the negative consequences of the economic reforms advocated by both Koizumi and his main rivals in the Democratic Party. They feared that if the government slashed spending for construction projects, social welfare, the bureaucracy, and subsidies for unprofitable private companies, many Japanese might become unemployed or bankrupt, or have a less secure social safety net. Many Japanese admit that such reforms are needed to break the logjam in Japan's economy, but a large number of them are unwilling to take the risks that reform requires. As Prime Minister Koizumi embarked on his second term, he faced an immovable LDP establishment, a vigorous opposition party, and a reluctant public. Clearly he had his work cut out for him.

### The 2005 Elections

It did not help that the 2004 elections for the House of Councillors, Japan's upper house, left Koizumi's party with a smaller majority, while the Democratic Party of Japan gained twelve seats. But the strongest evidence of internal party dissatisfaction with Koizumi's policies came in August 2005 when his proposal to privatize the postal service was defeated in the upper house by rebel LDP members and the increasingly powerful DPJ. The Japanese postal service, in addition to serving as the nation's mail carrier, is Japan's (and perhaps the world's)

**TABLE 19.9**

**House of Representatives Elections, 2005 (480 Seats: 300 chosen by SMD, 180 by PR)**

| Party | SMD Seats | % SMD Vote | PR Seats | % PR Vote | Total Seats (%) |
|---|---|---|---|---|---|
| Liberal Democratic Party | 219 | 73 | 77 | 43 | 296 (62) |
| Democratic Party of Japan | 52 | 17 | 61 | 34 | 113 (24) |
| New Komeito Party | 8 | 2.7 | 23 | 13 | 31 (6.5) |
| Japan Communist Party | 0 | 0 | 9 | 5 | 9 (1.9) |
| Social Democratic Party | 1 | 0.3 | 6 | 3.3 | 7 (1.5) |
| People's New Party | 2 | 0 | 2 | 0.6 | 4 (0.8) |
| New Party Japan | 0 | 0 | 1 | 1.1 | 1 (0.2) |
| Shinto Daichi | 0 | 0 | 1 | 0.6 | 1 (0.2) |
| Others | 18 | 6 | 0 | 0 | 18 (3.8) |

Voter turnout was 68 percent.

largest bank. By 2005 it held about 30 percent of all Japanese personal deposits and a large share of life insurance policies, with assets amounting to 330 trillion yen ($3 trillion). The government subsidized the postal service's interest rates, making them more competitive than the rates offered by private banks and insurers. These subsidies were a drain on the budget. More importantly, a succession of LDP governments had used the postal service's money to finance state-funded construction projects, turning it into a perennial source of favors, kickbacks, and other forms of corruption. Koizumi wanted the postal service privatized so that the trillions of yen deposited there would become part of the free market and handled the same way private banks handle their deposits. His aims were to trim the government's budgetary deficit and—even more boldly—to strike at the very heart of the LDP's well-entrenched corruption system. But some Japanese felt that the privatization plan would endanger the retirement savings they had deposited in the postal service, and they pressured their representatives to oppose it. Old-guard LDP politicians, determined to preserve the traditional practices of Japanese politics, opposed the elimination of such a large source of funding for their pork-barrel spending schemes.

Koizumi defined the vote against the privatization bill as a vote of no confidence in his leadership. Understandably, he was less than happy about the thirty-seven defectors in his own party (including a cabinet minister) who voted against it. Koizumi therefore dissolved the House of Representatives immediately and called snap elections, even though he was not required to call elections for another two years. (The prime minister may call snap elections for the lower house but not for the upper house.) He ordered the LDP politicians who had voted against him on the postal bill to resign from the party, and he dismissed the dissenting cabinet minister from his government. Koizumi also selected high-profile LDP candidates to run against their former party colleagues, increasing the likelihood that the renegades would be defeated. The male candidates chosen for this task were dubbed "assassins"; the women were "madonnas." Like a samurai-era feudal lord, Koizumi made it clear that he would tolerate no disloyalty inside his own party. Some of the rebels ran as independents, while others formed new parties. A total of 989 candidates ran in the 300 single-member districts, and 142 candidates ran in the proportional-representation contest.

It was unusual in Japanese politics for an election campaign to revolve around a single issue; but many people wondered whether that issue was postal privatization, as Koizumi saw it, or Koizumi's leadership itself. Even though Koizumi had antagonized the LDP's old guard by opposing the faction system, and had alarmed others with his proposals to rewrite the Japanese constitution, Koizumi commanded tremendous respect from ordinary voters. In their minds, he was a charismatic figure; unlike his predecessors, he spoke plainly and invested time and energy in reforming the country's political system. When the votes were counted, Koizumi and the LDP had achieved a landslide victory, winning more seats in the lower house than ever before (see table 19.9). The Liberal Democrats now had the two-thirds majority they needed to pass legislation on their own against the objections of the upper house; they would not need the votes of their coalition partner, the New Komeito Party. This result opened up the possibility of calling a constitutional convention to rewrite the constitution, including the famous no-war clause of Article 9.

The LDP's mammoth victory in 2005 produced the return of one-party dominance twelve years after the Liberal Democrats' startling defeat in 1993. Unfortunately for those who wanted a strong two-party system, the LDP's triumph also took seats away from the main opposition party, the Democratic Party of Japan. Naoto Kan, the DPJ's chief, promptly resigned the party leadership after the elections. Even the LDP's coalition partner, New Komeito, lost seats to LDP candidates. The Japan Socialist Party, formerly the LDP's main opponent, and the Japan Communist Party remained more or less where they were, winning a handful of seats.

After the elections Koizumi acted quickly: the Diet passed his postal privatization bill within two months. With this success behind him and with the LDP firmly back in power, Koizumi might have wished he could have stayed in office several more years. But his own party's constitution imposes term limits on how long a person may be party president (and thus prime minister). And so the popular and charismatic Koizumi announced he would resign in September 2006.

Shinzo Abe

### After Koizumi

Koizumi was replaced by the reserved, cautious, and nationalistic *Shinzo Abe.* Abe was first elected to the Diet in 1993. At the time of his selection by the party to the post of party leader, he was serving as chief cabinet secretary. In some respects, Abe's selection represented a new image for a Japanese politician. He was relatively young, he was born after World War II, and he had received part of his education abroad at the University of Southern California. However, Abe's political orientation makes it unlikely that he will be able to mend fences with China and North Korea. He is unapologetic about Japan's role in World War II, he wants to infuse patriotic values into the educational system, and he wishes to pursue his predecessor's plans to rewrite the constitution, including the Article 9 no-war clause. Prior to taking office as prime minister, Abe had been serving as Japan's negotiator with North Korea over the abduction of a number of Japanese nationals. During these talks he showed an uncompromising posture toward the government of Kim Jong-il. North Korea's nuclear bomb test, which took place shortly after Abe assumed power, no doubt strengthened his resolve to maintain a tough stance vis-à-vis the North Korean communist regime.

## CLUES TO ATTITUDES AND BEHAVIOR: IDEOLOGY, POLITICAL CULTURE, AND SOCIAL CLASS

### Does Ideology Matter?

Most Japanese voters do not engage in issue-based political discussion during election campaigns; rather, they evaluate the personality and influence potential of their candidates very carefully. They expect, however unrealistically, to personally meet their favorite for office, and they take that personal relationship very seriously. With personality and personal relationships prevailing in Japanese voters' minds as the key qualifications for office, coherent political ideologies play a less important role as determinants of Japanese voting behavior.

Similarly, ideology is of little significance in explaining the formation of new political parties. Despite the confusion created by the end of absolute LDP dominance, one thing was very clear to Japanese voters as well as to outside observers: profound differences in political philosophy did not seem to constitute the basis for new party formation or party membership. Japan's political parties, heedless of their public image as "conservative," "liberal," "reform," and so on, often "steal" planks from one another's platforms for political expediency.

After the war, a broad consensus developed around the core values of pacifism, democracy, equality of opportunity, private enterprise, and active state intervention in the economy. The Liberal Democratic Party, for all its faults in succumbing to corruption, epitomized these values. With the chief ideological struggles of the past now decisively resolved in favor of democracy, ideology lost its earlier prominence as a source of political conflict. Today only the Japan Communist Party, which won less than 1 percent of the lower house seats in 2005 (and sometimes has no seats in either house of the Diet) seems to be considered enough of an outsider ideologically that the other parties avoid it when seeking coalition partners.

Every country has a collection of individuals or small groups that seem to have perpetual complaints about the government of the day, no matter what it is. Japanese people are used to hearing speakers on the sound trucks of right-wing militarists as they blast each government for its pacifism. And the world watched in amazement as a radical religious group, the Aum Shinrikyo, attempted to kill thousands of passengers in ruthless subway gas attacks in the 1990s. But these groups are small and generally not well organized, and they typically gather only the anger or disgust of mainstream society rather than its support.

In fact, the ideological lines separating Japan's main parties tend to be shadowy. In the postwar years, conservatives have teamed up with Socialists and reform parties have joined ranks with establishment parties in order to form one government after another. Japan's only Socialist premier, Tomiichi Murayama, who governed from 1994 to 1996, did a complete about-face on taking office and repudiated his party's decades-long opposition to the national anthem and to military forces, and he reversed its pacifistic opposition to the security partnership with the United States. The relatively non-ideological atmosphere has not appeared to bother Japanese voters, most of whom seem more interested in a candidate's connections than in his or her convictions. Says one scholar, "nobody in the provinces really cares whether a politician is nominally a socialist or a conservative (or, for that matter, honest): what counts is whether he gets results in pressuring the central government to send some resources to the region."[24] Like the United States and the West European democracies, Japan has experienced the "end of ideology" in the postwar period.

## Political Attitudes and Social Class in Postwar Japan

Even social class differences, which are often the basis for political party membership in many countries and which influenced party formation in the 1920s, have not generally produced sharp ideological conflicts in postwar Japan or coalesced into party structures. As some have suggested, this phenomenon reflects the fact that Japanese society is "vertical": each person, however high or low on the socioeconomic scale, feels obligations to those above or below him or her.

This verticality is particularly evident in the structure of labor unions. Whereas in most countries labor unions constitute a strong symbolic statement of workers' feelings of separateness from the owners and managers of corporations, in Japan they are "company unions." That is, the labor union is an in-house organization with an office inside the company and a budget provided by the company for certain activities and with membership coming only from within the company. Labor leaders feel an obligation to management and vice versa. Organizing an industry-wide strike would be very difficult since union membership does not extend industry-wide.

On the managerial side, managers who can create harmony (*wa*) are considered more praiseworthy leaders than those who are good at winning every contest. In this way, it is believed, the system as a whole can keep happily working for years, and that goal is more important than winning. This very Japanese concept of *wa* is generally shared by most of the population and constitutes a core element of the nation's political culture. It venerates social harmony and consensus as more important values than individualism and self-assertion. That is why, when major political conflict erupts in Japan, it is likely that, behind the scenes, major changes in social relationships are under way, as happened during the Taisho Era.

In addition to the moderating influence of verticality and *wa* in Japanese society, the social class structure today benefits from the Occupation reforms after World War II. Determined to eliminate any source of potential challenge to the rule of law from the military or business conglomerates, the Occupation authorities redistributed large land holdings, broke up many of the business cartels (zaibatsu), and implemented many other social reforms that elevated the status of women and others. As a result of these and subsequent developments, Japanese society today has fewer obvious social class markers than ever before in its history, and the vast majority of citizens consider themselves to be members of the affluent middle class. Japan also experiences less socioeconomic inequality than the United States, Britain, or several other economically advanced democracies. While an income gap assuredly exists between the richest and the poorest, it is narrower than in most other economically advanced democracies. By the mid 1990s a mere 2 percent of Japanese households had incomes below $16,000 per year, and only 2 percent had incomes above $160,000. Everyone else was in the middle, with half of the country's households making an average annual income of between $35,000 and $75,000. Even Japan's top business executives earn considerably less than their American counterparts, a fact the late Sony executive Akio Morita pointed out in criticizing corporate practices in the United States. The top executives at Toyota and Honda earn little more than $300,000 a year, a pittance compared to America's corporate millionaires.

The current Japanese level of social equality is the result not only of modern cultural attitudes created by the Occupation, but also of deliberate efforts by the Japanese government since the end of World War II. Despite their pro-business ethos, the Liberal Democrats established a system designed to reduce inequality by imposing heavy taxes on the wealthiest citizens (who often pay 37 percent of their income in taxes) and on corporations (30 percent), while providing substantial government subsidies to the poor and keeping taxes low for most people. Critics of this policy claim that the country's difficult economic situation will require some changes in these practices, including lower business taxes and fewer subsidies. But fewer subsidies may exacerbate the homelessness problem, which has become increasingly troublesome since the collapse of the economic bubble in the early 1990s. In addition, people are worried about the declining birth rate and the growing senior-citizen population. How can a society with a diminishing birth rate support people who are forced to retire at age fifty-five or sixty and live another thirty years? Japan has the longest life expectancy of any country in the world, and projections show that in 2025, more than 25 percent of the population will be over sixty-five; by 2050, that figure will be 37 percent. In 2005 Japan's population declined for the first time in history, and although births went up slightly in 2006, the average of 1.25 births per woman remains far below the replacement level (2.1 children) necessary to maintain population stability. Since the 1980s Japan has closed four thousand schools because there are not enough children to fill the classrooms. Given this situation, who will support the elderly? Many people worry that Japan's senior citizens will come to constitute a massive but neglected underclass.

Meanwhile, widely shared Japanese social attitudes, stressing strong family ties, respect for authority, and the importance of education, act as cultural brakes on heavy government spending. Some 920 students out of every 1,000 graduate from high school (compared to only 730 out of 1,000 in the United States), and the literacy rate is 99.9 percent.[25] Despite the high price of land and housing, nearly 60 percent of Japanese own their own homes. Only about 1 percent of the population is on welfare, as families often care for their own. Drug addiction is uncommon, resulting in a low crime rate, and murders are several times lower per 100,000 than in the United States (although Japan's murder rate has risen somewhat in the past decade).

Part of the reason for the low murder rate is Japan's strict gun control laws: handguns are illegal, and the use of guns for hunting and sports is strictly regulated. Unwed mothers account for only 1 percent of births (though the abortion rate is traditionally high).

These statistics implicitly explain why the Japanese government does not have to foot a huge bill for crime prevention, the penal system, poverty-stricken children, or literacy programs. The nagging recession of the 1990s eventually produced an unemployment rate of 5 percent—an unusually high rate for Japan, which usually boasts a rate of only about 2 percent. Homeless people have started camping out in train stations, much to the consternation of officials. But these problems are mild in Japan compared to many other societies where the family structure is less supportive. The government continues to provide some of the same benefits found in West European welfare states, such as tuition-free education through college for those able to pass the rigorous entrance exams for the government-funded universities (but not the private universities), as well as universal health insurance in cooperation with industry and private citizens.

## Consensus and Conflict in Contemporary Japan

Despite the powerful webs of consensus that knit Japanese society together, distinct political differences nevertheless exist that occasionally cause problems (though probably less frequently than in other democracies). Sometimes they can lead to violent conflict. Japanese students, for example, have at times staged mass demonstrations in support of such causes as opposition to Japan's security ties to the United States. Rough clashes with the police have ensued, but many of the 1960s demonstrators have now taken their places in the corporate world, and there is little student activism today.

A particularly acute display of public discontent surfaced in the 1970s, when the government announced its intention to build the new Narita international airport in the Chiba area, located one hour east of Tokyo. An idyllic location, with rice paddies and forests surrounding small hamlets, the area was seen by environmentalists and rice farmers as the worst possible place to construct an airport. Demonstrations, riots, and even homemade rocket attacks on airport construction workers revealed deep-seated anger at government policy. Protected by police in head-to-toe battle gear, construction workers were able to complete the massive project, and the government got its way, although not without serious damage to its image.

Such outbursts are rare in Japan. The broad thrust of public opinion gravitates away from extreme ideological positions and inclines toward immediate issues affecting one's livelihood or neighborhood. Interest group articulation tends to be local rather than national, and thus has little ultimate effect on government policy. Consumer movements are particularly short-lived. As one observer has correctly noted, the Japanese are not concerned with "the broad constitutional, environmental or personal liberty issues that tend to interest intellectuals" in other countries.[26] Whether this will always remain so is an open question. Moreover, as Japanese culture as a whole becomes more heavily influenced by the individualistic mindset of the West as opposed to the "good-of-the-whole" philosophy of Confucian-influenced Asian societies, it may be that the Japanese will increasingly find it "natural" to forcefully express their opinions and desires for change.

To be sure, there are several issues that could be cited as sources of disharmony. One is the treatment of minorities. Japan's population is 98.7 percent Japanese. Approximately 3 million Burakumin, whose Japanese ancestors were social outcasts in feudal times, are the targets of unofficial job and housing discrimination, as are members of the indigenous Ainu minority. A more visible problem centers on some 630,000 Koreans, who are subjected to "entrenched societal discrimination," according to a U.S. State Department human rights report.[27] Most of these Koreans were born in Japan, but they are not eligible for automatic Japanese citizenship. Japan's citizenship laws are based on the principle of *jus sanguinis*—the right of blood; automatic citizenship is reserved to those who have at least one parent who is ethnic Japanese. (By contrast, the United States observes the principle of *jus soli*—the right of territory—and confers citizenship on anyone born in its territory.) Moreover, acquiring citizenship through naturalization procedures is considerably more difficult in Japan than in the United States. The Japanese have also been quite reluctant to admit immigrants, even though Japan's birth rate is low and foreign workers may be needed to fill vacant or newly created jobs. Japan grants asylum to only about twenty petitioners a year, far fewer than countries like Germany and Britain accept. Japan's ethnic homogeneity thus appears to be a barrier to expanding the scope of democracy to minorities.[28]

Another potential source of dissatisfaction is the proposed revision of Article 9 of the Japanese constitution, which prohibits war-making capabilities. Former Prime Minister Koizumi's proposal to amend this clause will continue to polarize popular and partisan positions as the country's new prime minister, Shinzo Abe, takes over.

## CONCLUSION

We conclude by returning to the question we raised at the start of this chapter: *how democratic is Japan?* To what extent does Japan conform to the principles shaping the Temple of Democracy, as described in chapter 7?

Since World War II, the Japanese people and their leaders have embraced the core democratic values that underlie democracy. Among the most important of these values, the Japanese score heavily with respect to consensus and compromise. Japanese cultural traditions attach a high value to social harmony, resulting in a relatively high level of civility in the country's political life. The need for consensus can sometimes be self-defeating, however, as when it allows elements of the political elite or Japanese society to block necessary reforms or changes. With respect to the value of tolerance, the Japanese tend to be divided. A large number are tolerant of the small non-Japanese minorities in their midst and are open to sincere cooperation with foreign governments and businesses. But traditional attitudes of intolerance and chauvinism, striking deep chords in the national psyche, are still very much present. Southeast Asians, for example, are not treated with the same civility as Americans or Europeans. While marriages of Japanese with non-Japanese are generally looked down upon, Japanese-Caucasian marriages are more acceptable than, say, Japanese-African marriages.

The Japanese have also accepted the rule of law, transferring political authority from the emperor and his entourage to elected officials who must be held accountable to the law. In the application of this principle, however, Japan has encountered problems.

With respect to popular sovereignty—Pillar I of the Temple of Democracy—it is clear that the Japanese system of government is far from the ideal of "government of the people." More pointedly, it has even strayed from the fundamental principle of government by elites *accountable* to the people. To be sure, since the end of the Occupation, the Japanese people have enjoyed the right to vote for their national and local government officials in free, open, and competitive elections. To that extent, Japan has fulfilled the minimum requirements of an electoral democracy. It was a majority of Japanese voters who repeatedly returned the Liberal Democratic Party to power for nearly four decades, usually passing up the opportunity to elect its opponents. As long as the economy boomed and life was basically good, most Japanese felt they had little reason to vote for change.

But the flagrant violation of the public trust by corrupt LDP officials in the 1990s constituted an indisputable abuse of power, making a mockery of the most elementary principles of popular sovereignty and elite accountability. The corrosive power of money in the electoral and policy-making processes has often abused the general public interest and the will of the citizenry. The extraordinary power of unelected bureaucrats has escaped democratic controls by the people and their elected legislative and governmental representatives. And until the formation of a host of new parties in the 1990s, the main opposition parties were so dogmatic or limited in their appeal that they failed to offer the mass of the population an acceptable alternative to the Liberal Democrats. These and similar realities of Japanese politics have tarnished postwar Japan's struggle to be a full democracy, that is truly representative of its people. In many respects, Japan has had a dysfunctional democracy.[29] To their credit, however, a large number of Japanese political elites and growing numbers of ordinary citizens have taken concerted action in recent years to change the system's most repugnant features. Their efforts, while perhaps only partially successful thus far, provide vivid testimony that the spirit of popular sovereignty and representative democracy is very much alive in a country habituated to one-party rule for most of its postwar history.

As to Pillar II, Japan has done a reasonably good job in maintaining basic political and civil liberties. During the 1950s and 1960s, for example, when students took to the streets in massive demonstrations, some people wondered if the government would take advantage of the unrest to curtail the freedom of assembly rights guaranteed in the 1947 constitution. But the courts upheld the constitutional rights of citizens to assemble. Japan has a vibrant civil society consisting of parties, interest groups, and a variety of NGOs concerned with human rights, the environment, and other issues typical of modern democracies. Though press clubs give some journalists privileged access to policy makers, thereby inhibiting critical reporting, the press has been able to publish articles strongly critical of government leaders or policies, usually without fear of retaliation. The courts have been generally cautious in ruling on cases where basic human rights would be curtailed. Many residents of Japan feel that their level of personal freedom is greater than in other democracies—in part due to gun control and the relatively low violent crime rate and the resulting ability to walk the streets day or night with little concern for personal safety. They believe that "freedom" has gone too far in many countries of the West; they feel that there is sometimes greater freedom within structure, though these attitudes are slowly changing.

Problems remain, however. Although the law guarantees women equality in principle, in fact Japanese women are still subjected to discrimination in a variety of government and private-sector professions. Only one out of seventy high-level Japanese civil servants, and one out of thirty ambassadors, is a woman. Just 10 percent of Japan's corporate managers, and only slightly more than 10 percent of its lawyers, are women. Sexual harassment is common in the workplace. Traditional cultural taboos against shaming one's family or damaging personal reputations discourage many women from reporting cases of abuse. In part for these reasons, Freedom House gave Japan a civil liberties score of 2 in 2005.

Finally, Japan has made enormous strides since the war to achieve a modicum of economic democracy, which is Pillar III of democracy. While the country has by no means achieved real income equality, it has widened equality of opportunity through a superior educational system and professional advancement based on merit, while at the same time producing a level of income differentiation that is less unequal than in many economically advanced democracies. Its principal shortcoming with respect to Pillar III, as noted earlier, is the relative absence of effective democratic checks on the bureaucratic elite's power in the all-important domain of economic decision making.

When we look at Japan in relation to the ten conditions treated in this volume, we again find a mixture of positive and negative elements. Elites, state institutions, and private enterprise all combine support for democratic principles and procedures with such countertendencies as corruption, unaccountability, and other practices that contradict democracy's defining standards. Fortunately, Japan's considerable national wealth and its prosperous middle class have bolstered support for democracy. Its small minority groups, however, continue to be disadvantaged, a result of the large ethnic homogeneity of the population. Political participation has fluctuated, with recent declines in voter turnout counterbalanced by new political activism in civil society. Women are gradually gaining political ground. In addition to their growing prominence in national politics, women hold scores of positions in local and prefectural governments. The educational system is democratic (though textbooks continue to evade the dark chapters of Japan's imperial past), and information flows freely. Internationally, Japan is closely allied with the United States and its democratic partners, and is seeking to overcome the burdens of its past in relations with its Asian neighbors.

Thus we conclude by affirming that, for all its problems, Japan *is* a democracy containing many of the structures and values found in the major industrialized democracies of Europe and North America. It is also obvious that the Japanese people much prefer this system to anything they have experienced in more than two thousand years of history. Not very long ago Japan was so withdrawn from the world that even its own citizens who managed to travel abroad were not allowed to return home for fear they would contaminate the population with unacceptable ideas from overseas. An even shorter historical distance takes us back to a period of military dictatorship at home and ruthless aggression abroad. Today the Japanese can rightfully boast of having democratic institutions that are still just a distant dream in the minds of would-be democrats in many emerging countries of Asia and elsewhere around the world. If such a country can make a dramatic turnabout and establish a democratic system within a relatively few short years, then perhaps those nations that have suffered under internal and external oppression for so long can also make a new start.

## KEY TERMS AND NAMES
## (In bold and underlined in the text)

Junichiro Koizumi
Shinzo Abe
Meiji Restoration
Samurais
Occupation
Diet
House of Representatives
House of Councillors
Liberal Democratic Party (LDP)
Iron triangle
State-guided capitalism
Ministry of Economy, Trade, and Industry (METI)
Democratic Party of Japan (DPJ)

## NOTES

1. For more on the Asian financial crisis of the 1990s, see Dean W. Collinwood, *Japan and the Pacific Rim,* 8th ed. (Guilford, Conn.: Dushkin/ McGraw-Hill, 2006), 10–11.
2. *Nippon Tateyoko [Japan As It Is]* (Tokyo: Gakken, 1997), 171.
3. Women have reigned as empresses ten times in Japanese history. Most reigned between the years AD 500 and 800, although one reigned as recently as the mid 1700s. For more, see *Japan: An Illustrated Encyclopedia* (Tokyo: Kodansha, 1993), 337.
4. W. Scott Morton, *Japan: Its History and Culture,* 3rd ed. (New York: McGraw-Hill, 1994), 149–80.
5. In 1860, the Edo Shogunate organized a tour to the United States for top government leaders. The trip directly exposed government officials to democratic forms of government for the first time in Japanese history, but many of the Edo officials were displaced by the Meiji revolution. Meiji leaders organized another, far more impactful, tour in 1871. Among the results of that tour was the establishment of freedom of religion in Japan and the creation of Japan's first university for women, Tsuda Juku Daigaku, in western Tokyo. See also Dean W. Collinwood, Ryoichi Yamamoto, and Kazue Matsui-Haag, *Samurais in Salt Lake: Diary of the First Diplomatic Japanese Delegation to Visit Utah, 1872* (Salt Lake City: U.S. Japan Center, 1996).
6. Koichi Kishimoto, *Politics in Modern Japan,* 4th ed. (Tokyo: Japan Echo, 1997), 19–24.
7. Herbert P. Bix, *Hirohito and the Making of Modern Japan* (New York: HarperCollins, 2000).
8. John W. Dower, *Embracing Defeat: Japan in the Wake of World War II* (New York: W. W. Norton, 1999).
9. See Kishimoto, *Politics in Modern Japan,* 161–70, for a complete English version of the constitution of 1947.
10. For an analysis of money and politics, see Karel van Wolferen, *The Enigma of Japanese Power* (New York: Random House, 1989).
11. Chalmers Johnson, *Japan: Who Governs? The Rise of the Developmental State* (New York: W. W. Norton, 1995), 184 ff.
12. J. A. A. Stockwin, *Governing Japan,* 3rd ed. (Malden, Mass.: Blackwell, 1999), 57–58.
13. Johnson, *Japan: Who Governs?* 183–211.
14. For more on Japan's phenomenal economic rise, see Ezra F. Vogel, *Japan as No. 1: Lessons for America* (Tokyo: Charles E. Tuttle, 1979).
15. For more on Japan's influence on Asia and the world, see Nishigaki Akira and Shimomura Yasutami, *The Economics of Development Assistance: Japan's ODA in a Symbiotic World* (Tokyo: LTCB International Library Foundation, 1998); Walter Hatch and Kozo Yamamura, *Asia in Japan's Embrace: Building a Regional Production Alliance* (Cambridge: Cambridge University

Press, 1996); and Dennis J. Encarnation, *Rivals Beyond Trade: America Versus Japan in Global Competition* (Ithaca, N.Y.: Cornell University Press, 1992).

**16.** Japan Institute for Social and Economic Affairs, *An International Comparison* (Tokyo: Keizai Koho Center, 1983).

**17.** Collinwood, *Japan and the Pacific Rim,* 24–25.

**18.** Japan Institute for Social and Economic Affairs, *An International Comparison.*

**19.** Taichi Sakaiya, "The Myth of the Competent Bureaucrat," in *Japan Echo,* February 1998, 25–30. For an opposite view, see Peter Drucker, "In Defense of Japanese Bureaucracy," in *Foreign Affairs,* September/October 1998, 68–80.

**20.** For a critical review of Japan's rise to power, see van Wolferen, *The Enigma of Japanese Power.*

**21.** *Washington Post,* October 19, 1996.

**22.** Originally an appointive body, the House of Councillors today is elected by popular vote. Every three years, half of the 252 Councillors are elected to a six-year term. One hundred seats are filled via proportional representation, and 152 seats are filled based on prefectural districts. Japanese citizens age thirty or older may stand for election to the House of Councillors (age twenty-five for the House of Representatives).

**23.** Private savings in Japan averaged 27 percent of GDP between 1995 and 2000, compared with 21 percent in the European Union and 15 percent in the United States. *Financial Times,* May 9, 2001. See also, "What Ails Japan? A Survey of Japan," *The Economist,* April 20, 2002.

**24.** Johnson, *Japan: Who Governs?* 186.

**25.** *Washington Post,* May 4, 1997, and March 16, 1997.

**26.** Stockwin, *Governing Japan,* 111.

**27.** See the U.S. State Department's *Country Reports on Human Rights Practices, 2002,* accessible at http://www.state.gov/g/drl/rls/hrrpt2002/.

**28.** John Lie, *Multiethnic Japan* (Cambridge, Mass.: Harvard University Press, 2001).

**29.** Roger W. Bowen, *Japan's Dysfunctional Democracy: The Liberal Democratic Party and Structural Corruption* (Armonk, N.Y.: M. E. Sharpe, 2003). For more background on the origin and development of Japan's political system, as well as on current political issues, see Gerald L. Curtis, *The Logic of Japanese Politics* (New York: Columbia University Press, 2000); Mayumi Itoh, *The Hatoyama Dynasty: Japanese Political Leadership Through the Generations* (New York: Palgrave MacMillan, 2003); Mike M. Mochizuki, *Strategic Asia 2004–05: Confronting Terrorism in the Pursuit of Power* (Seattle: National Bureau of Asian Research, 2004) (available online at stragegicasia.nbr.org); and Ethan Scheiner, *Democracy Without Competition* (Cambridge: Cambridge University Press, 2006).

CHAPTER 20

# RUSSIA

Population (2005 est.): 143 million
Freedom House Ratings (2002):
Political rights—6; Civil Liberties—5

Area: 6,592,745 square miles
(a little less than 1.8 times
the area of the United States)

The map shows Russia and the other fourteen constituent republics of the former Soviet Union: Estonia, Latvia, Lithuania, Belarus (formerly Belorussia), Ukraine, Moldova (formerly Moldavia), Georgia, Armenia, Azerbaijan, Kazakhstan, Turkmenistan, Uzbekistan, Kyrgyzstan, and Tajikistan. All are now independent states, and all except Estonia, Latvia, and Lithuania belong to the Commonwealth of Independent States.

Six scenes illustrate the dramatic transformations that have swept through Russia since the early 1990s, capping a century of revolutionary change.

In scene 1, **Boris Yeltsin**—the first person ever elected president of Russia by popular vote—stands atop a tank in the heart of Moscow. It is August 19, 1991. On the previous day, a group of senior officials had staged a coup against the government of the Soviet Union and placed its chief, President **Mikhail Gorbachev** (mikh-hah-EEL garh-bah-CHAWF), under house arrest. Under the Soviet constitution, Yeltsin was legally subordinate to Gorbachev. Russia was just one of fifteen "republics" that constituted the **Union of Soviet Socialist Republics** (the **USSR**, or **Soviet Union**). Yeltsin was president only of Russia, while Gorbachev was president of the whole Soviet Union. But Russia, sprawling across eleven time zones and home to half the Soviet population, was the USSR's political heartland. As its popularly chosen president, Yeltsin enjoyed a legitimacy in the eyes of millions of people that Gorbachev, who was never elected by the voters, did not have. As the world watched in amazement, power was literally up for grabs in the USSR, a dictatorship ruled for more than seventy years by the **Communist Party of the Soviet Union (CPSU)**.

The coup leaders included some of the most prominent figures in Gorbachev's regime. Their decision to turn against their supreme leader was motivated by their dismay at the sorry state of the Soviet Union as a result of Gorbachev's policies. In only a few years, Gorbachev's attempts to restructure the Soviet state, revitalize its economy, and reorient its foreign policy had led to the rapid unraveling of Communist Party power at home and Soviet power abroad. Gorbachev had become the head of the Communist Party of the Soviet Union—the most important leadership position in the Soviet Union—in 1985. From his first months at the helm, Gorbachev acknowledged severe problems in the ways the Communists had governed the country for much of the twentieth century. While he did not wish to replace the Soviet system with a full-blown Western democracy, he believed that he could humanize communist rule through the "restructuring" of state institutions. In place of an implacable dictatorship run by a handful of CPSU oligarchs, he called for "democratization" and "openness" in the party's dealings with the population. Without instituting a Western system of competing political parties, he permitted unprecedented elections to legislative and executive bodies. As events were to reveal, the most important of these votes was Yeltsin's election as president of Russia in June 1991, only two months before the coup attempt. Although Gorbachev did not favor a Western-style economic system dominated by private enterprise, he believed he could revive the stagnant Soviet command economy by reorganizing its central-planning mechanisms and introducing elements of a market economy. And although he had no intentions of giving up the Soviet Union's superpower status, Gorbachev decided to end the costly Cold War confrontation with the United States. The consequences of these policies were plain to see: the dissipation of the Communist Party's monopoly of power and the rise of oppositionist voices; economic decline and organizational confusion; and the disintegration of Soviet hegemony in East Germany, Poland, and other countries in Central and Eastern Europe, where communist dictatorships were replaced by Western-oriented democracies. The coup plotters were determined to halt the Soviet system's headlong slide and restore strong authoritarian rule at the top.

**Boris Yeltsin (holding papers) reads a statement denouncing the coup against Soviet President Mikhail Gorbachev, August 1991.**

But Yeltsin unexpectedly took charge of the situation as soon as the coup unfolded. An advocate of even more reform than Gorbachev wanted, Yeltsin was resolved to prevent the conspirators from reestablishing dictatorial rule. Emboldened by Yeltsin's defiance, tens of thousands of Russian citizens staged demonstrations against the coup, and key elements of the military high command refused to support it. Isolated, the plotters capitulated two days later and Gorbachev was released. This event proved to be a watershed in Russian history. It undermined not only Gorbachev's power as president of the Soviet Union but the very existence of the Soviet Union itself.

Scene 2 marks a defining moment in the transfer of real political power from Gorbachev to Yeltsin. At a historic session of the Russian republic's legislature held only days after the coup plot fell apart, Gorbachev was in the process of acknowledging his mistakes when Yeltsin interrupted him to announce that he had just signed a decree suspending all activities of the Soviet Communist Party within Russia. The stunning disclosure effectively ended more than seventy years of the party's monopoly of power in Russia and the rest of the Soviet Union. Gorbachev quietly expressed his disapproval but his words no longer carried weight. Humiliated, Gorbachev resigned as chief of the Communist Party the next day.

Over the next three months the Soviet Union literally fell apart. Shortly after the coup was thwarted, Gorbachev announced that any Soviet republic wishing to declare its independence should be allowed to go free. One by one, the fifteen Soviet republics split off from the USSR and declared their independence. The first to go were the three states on the Baltic Sea that had been forcibly incorporated into the Soviet Union in World War II: Lithuania, Latvia, and Estonia. The Soviet government formally recognized the sovereignty of the Baltic states in September 1990. Ukraine, the second-largest Soviet republic after Russia, also announced plans to secede, followed over the succeeding weeks by all the remaining republics. On December 8, Russian President Yeltsin collaborated with the leaders of Ukraine and Belarus in forming a new grouping, the **Commonwealth of Independent States (CIS).** Two weeks later they were joined by eight more Soviet republics, a development that effectively sealed the fate of the Soviet Union.

Following these events, Gorbachev resigned as president of the Soviet Union on December 25, setting the stage for scene 3: moments later, the Soviet flag was hauled down and the flag of independent Russia was hoisted in its place over the Kremlin, the historic seat of the Russian government. The USSR was passing into history. It officially ceased to exist on December 31, 1991.

As the Kremlin's bells rang in the New Year on January 1, 1992, Russia formally began its new life as an independent state. The ensuing years would bring unprecedented transformations, combining fresh hopes with widespread hardships. The Russian government under President Yeltsin immediately launched economic initiatives designed to transform the still largely state-run economy into a mixed economic system with considerably more private enterprise. Although these measures produced rapid benefits for a few "new Russians" who understood the nature of the changes, most people saw their living standards deteriorate. Prices for a wide range of goods rose astronomically, far outpacing wages. Economic growth remained at a standstill. Hefty loans from the International Monetary Fund and other lenders were needed to keep the economy afloat. Organized crime reared its head as a Russian mafia pursued such illegal activities as gambling and extortion. And a small group of politically well-connected businessmen became instant billionaires, taking over the country's largest banks, newspapers, television stations, and other major assets.

These problems could only sap popular support from Yeltsin's government and undermine the legitimacy of Russia's newborn democracy. But the difficulties of building a solid foundation for democracy in a country where it had never truly existed for very long became all the more evident in 1993, when a confrontation between President Yeltsin and the Russian legislature that had been brewing since the last years of the Soviet era came to a head. As Communist Party legislators opposed to Yeltsin's reform programs dug in their heels and barricaded themselves in the parliament building, Yeltsin called in the army to flush them out. Determined to start anew, Yeltsin scrapped the communist-era constitution and presided over the drafting of a new document that was consciously modeled on France's Fifth Republic. Like Charles de Gaulle's constitution, Yeltsin's constitutional project established a mixed *presidential-parliamentary system,* anchored in a powerful presidency. In December 1993, a majority of Russian voters approved the Yeltsin constitution in a referendum, according it a measure of popular consent.

The promise of a fresh start quickly evaporated. The economy provided the main source of disaffection, as the long-awaited spurt in growth and production consistently failed to materialize. By the end of the decade, nearly 40 percent of the population lived below the official poverty line of $37 a month. Though private businesses increasingly sprouted up and a new middle class was emerging, the penury of the masses glaringly clashed with the accumulating riches of the new capitalist elite. To make matters worse, Russia got caught up in the global financial crisis that originated in Asia in 1997 (see chapter 1). In 1998, as global investors nervously pulled their money out of Russia and other troubled economies, Russia's currency—the ruble—plummeted in value. The economy went into a tailspin, ruining the financial prospects of millions of Russians.

Meanwhile, postcommunist Russia was just as fractionated as the former Soviet Union in its last stages. Its most violent challenge was in Chechnya, a largely Muslim region where a separatist movement launched a guerilla war for independence. Yeltsin sent Russian troops to the breakaway province in December 1994; the bloody confrontation ended with a truce in 1996. The conflict flared up anew in 1999, and troops once again were dispatched to the troubled region.

Yeltsin himself hobbled through the decade in a state of near-permanent illness. A serious heart problem, respiratory illnesses, and other infirmities required him to spend long weeks and months in sanatoria or at home, away from the center of political life in the Kremlin. Although Yeltsin managed to get reelected to a four-year term in 1996, his public approval ratings sank to less than 10 percent. Day-to-day decision making passed from an absentee president to a coterie of shadowy lieutenants, hidden away in the recesses of the Kremlin. Their backroom intrigues and incessant jockeying for power in the president's absence created the impression that a power vacuum existed at the heart of the Russian state.

These problems culminated in scene 4: on December 31, 1999, as the world prepared to greet the new millennium, Boris Yeltsin went on television and stunningly announced his immediate resignation. "Russia must enter the new millennium with new politicians, new faces," he said, asserting that he had already completed his main task, which was to ensure that "Russia will never return to the past."

With Yeltsin's unexpected departure only six months before the completion of his term, the presidency automatically passed to the prime minister, **Vladimir Putin.** A former officer in the KGB—the Soviet Union's notorious spy agency—Putin was practically unknown. President Yeltsin had aroused considerable puzzlement in Russia and around the world in September 1999 with his surprise appointment of forty-six-year-old Putin as Russia's prime minister. Putin's detachment from the secretive Kremlin inner circle, and the calm decisiveness he exuded when announcing his determination to defeat the Chechen rebels for good, won him instant public approval. Yeltsin himself endorsed Putin as his successor. In the fall of 1999, a new political party was organized with the principal aim of providing Putin with greater support in Russia's parliament. Known as Unity, the party scored an unexpected triumph in the December 1999 legislative elections, finishing behind the Russian Communist Party as the second-largest delegation in the State Duma, the legislature's lower house.

Following the terms of the 1993 constitution, new presidential elections had to be held within three months of President Yeltsin's resignation. In March 2000, Putin bested ten rival candidates, winning the presidency with an absolute majority of 52.8 percent in the first round of voting.

Scene 5 dramatizes some of the critical challenges facing Putin's regime. It also illustrates Putin's governing style, providing instructive clues about his conceptions of Russian democracy. On the morning of September 1, 2004, more than thirty armed rebels from Chechnya stormed an elementary school in the nearby Russian town of Beslan. Ceremonies celebrating the first day of the school year had just concluded. More than a thousand children, parents, and teachers were suddenly taken hostage in the school building. Terror gripped all of

Russia as the rebels threatened to kill fifty hostages for every one of their own who might be killed if Russian security forces attacked them. As a tense standoff entered its third day, with Russian troops surrounding the school, bombs went off inside the building and pandemonium broke loose. The rebels began shooting indiscriminately, killing children in the back as they ran, while the soldiers fired away at the rebels. After the guerillas were subdued and the smoke cleared, some 331 people lay dead, half of them children.

The Beslan tragedy had a profound effect on President Putin. "We have to admit that we have failed to recognize the complexity and dangers of the processes going on in our country and the world as a whole," he said, declaring that Russia was embroiled in a "total, cruel, and full-scale war" with terrorism. (Just days before the Beslan incident, two Russian airliners were blown up and a suicide bomber killed ten people at a Moscow subway station.) But Putin was openly criticized for withholding information about the hostage crisis as it was taking place. After it was over, the government admitted it had lied when stating that there were only about three hundred hostages in the school building, and acknowledged that it had refrained from reporting the rebels' demand that Russian forces be pulled out of Chechnya. The government was also initially silent about how many guerillas had attacked the building and how many had been killed. (In 2006 the only terrorist known to have survived the Beslan attack was formally accused in court.) Survivors of the Beslan tragedy faulted Putin for the scale of the carnage that resulted from the all-out gun battle. Some witnesses accused Russian troops of precipitating the catastrophe by shooting first. Putin himself was disappointed in the performance of Russian security officials and called for a "fundamentally new approach" to law enforcement. Responding testily to Western critics who believed the government should have continued negotiations with the hostage-takers, Putin asked, "Why don't you meet Osama bin Laden, invite him to Brussels or the White House?"

The Beslan drama recalled an earlier hostage crisis with remarkably similar features. In October 2002, some fifty Chechen guerillas shot their way into a Moscow theater, taking more than eight hundred people hostage. The rebels demanded an end to the war in Chechnya and large sums of money. As mediation efforts failed and the rebels began shooting hostages, Russian special forces stormed the building, killing more than forty terrorists. But nearly 130 hostages also died from the powerful paralytic gas the Russian troops had pumped into the theater to immobilize the Chechens before the assault. The government also enforced a tight ban on media coverage of the event as it was taking place. When a television station aired live broadcasts of the crisis, the government cut off its transmission. Several months later, it arranged for the dismissal of the station's chief.

The Putin government's attempts to withhold information and muzzle the media in these hostage incidents fit into a larger pattern of measures aimed at limiting freedom of the press. Putin has been considerably less tolerant of public criticism than Yeltsin was. Shortly after Putin assumed office, his administration closed down an independent television network whose principal owner, Boris Berezovsky, was a powerful business tycoon with close ties to Yeltsin. It also wrested control of a separate network from another tycoon, Vladimir Gusinsky. Both Berezovsky and Gusinsky, whose media outlets were vocally critical of Putin, fled Russia after being charged with criminal offenses. The government also arranged the takeover of a number of independent radio stations. Efforts to intimidate journalists or deny them information have proliferated since then.

Scene 6 provides a chilling example of the dangers that journalists face in Putin's Russia. In October 2006 the lifeless body of Anna Politkovskaya, an internationally renowned critic of Putin's government, was found in the elevator of her Moscow apartment building. She had died from a bullet to her head and three to her body. The assailant left the murder weapon at the scene, signifying a contract killing. Politkovskaya was widely known for her reports of abuses by Russian security forces and their allies in what she called the "dirty war" in Chechnya. In 2000 she was arrested, beaten, and forced to undergo a mock execution by military authorities. Russian agents once poisoned her. Her editor revealed that Politkovskaya was about to file a story on the use of torture by pro-Russian Chechens on the very day she was murdered. The next day, police entered her apartment and confiscated her computer files and other material. Politkovskaya's unfinished report was published a few days later.

President Putin made no comment on the case until he assured President Bush in a telephone conversation several days after the murder that the matter would be thoroughly investigated. Subsequently, Putin told reporters during a visit to Germany that the murder "was a dreadful and unforgettable crime which cannot be allowed to go unpunished." But he caustically dismissed Politkovskaya's influence in Russia as "extremely insignificant." Neither Putin nor any other senior government official joined the thousands of mourners who attended a memorial service in Politkovskaya's honor. By the end of 2006, twenty-one journalists had been killed in Russia since Putin was first elected president in 2000. The perpetrators have generally remained at large. Meanwhile, a Russian website posted photos of Russian journalists and human rights activists, describing them as "enemies of the people" and hinting that they could be the next targets of hired hitmen.

Because of these assaults on the press and other limitations on democratic freedoms that we will examine later in this chapter, Russia under Putin has retrogressed in the annual Freedom House evaluations of how governments around the world measure up against criteria for democracy (see chapter 2). In the mid 1990s, Russia under President Yeltsin was doing relatively well, meriting a composite political and civil rights rating of 3.5. That score qualified Russia as a "semi-democracy" in the terms we use in this book. By 2002 Freedom House had dropped Russia to a composite score of 5, and in 2004 and 2005 Russia was ranked at 5.5 (6 for political rights and 5 for civil rights). Accordingly, we now categorize Russia as a *semi-authoritarian* regime.[1]

Unquestionably, the fate of democracy in Russia stands out as one of the most vitally important issues facing today's world. The end of the Cold War, the collapse of the Soviet Union, and the replacement of a Communist Party dictatorship with a regime in transition to democracy have had profoundly positive consequences for Russia's relations with the United States, Western Europe, Japan, and other democracies around the world. These developments have replaced decades of global confrontation and the danger of nuclear war with unprecedented progress in arms control, diplomatic collaboration, and economic cooperation. Any reversion to authoritarian rule in Russia could have a devastating impact on international comity and, conceivably, world peace.

The problems Russia faces in building a real democracy—both immediately and in the coming decades—cannot be grasped without a clear understanding of the country's thousand-year history of authoritarianism. This chapter first surveys Russia's panoramic past under tsars and Communists. It then explores the country's more recent efforts to create a stable democracy. In the process we cover a wide range of issues rooted in the five sources of political conflict we discussed in chapter 2:

- *Power:* How has Russia been governed? How powerful have the ruling authorities been? Have the people ever enjoyed any power? Who has power today?
- *Resources:* How successfully has Russia developed its economy? How have national resources—such as land, oil, money, and other assets—been distributed? How is Russia managing the process of moving from a centrally planned to a market-based economy?
- *Identity:* What have been the roles of class, ethnic identity, and religious identity in Russian politics? How have Russians defined themselves vis-à-vis the outside world?
- *Ideas:* What have such terms as *communism*, *democracy*, and *nationalism* meant in the Russian context?
- *Values:* How have Russians felt about such values as individualism and collectivism, equality and liberty? Do Russians prefer authoritarian governments to democracy?

## RUSSIA'S HISTORICAL TRADITIONS: WHY NO DEMOCRACY?

Throughout its history, Russia was never able to sustain real democratic institutions and practices. Under the tsars (or czars) and their predecessors, Russia deviated substantially from the historical paths to democracy taken by Britain and France. Subsequently, under the Communists, national wealth improved but most of the other conditions for democracy that we discussed in chapter 9 remained far short of fulfillment.[2]

## Tsarism

To begin with, Russia's *state institutions* were entirely or mostly undemocratic from their earliest appearance to the final decade of the twentieth century. Following the invasion of Norman warriors who stormed into continental Europe from Scandinavia in the ninth century, a Norman prince named Rurik established himself in Novgorod ("New Town") around 860, giving rise to a tradition that regards him as the founder of the Russian state. In fact Rurik never presided over a central Russian government worthy of the name. His successors created a more enduring basis of power farther south, in Kiev, the capital of modern Ukraine. The period known as "Kievan Rus" extended from around 882 to sometime in the twelfth century.

A seminal event in Russian history occurred when Grand Prince Vladimir and much of the population were converted to Christianity around 988. Russia embraced the Byzantine variant of Christianity, whose Greek-influenced rituals and doctrines differed from the Western church centered in Rome. In 1054, what became known as the Eastern Orthodox church split off from Roman Catholicism, its adherents refusing to recognize the pope as Christianity's supreme authority. The embrace of Orthodoxy effectively cut Russia off from developments in Western Europe, not only in the religious sphere but in the cultural and political realms as well. An attendant event was the adoption of the Cyrillic as opposed to the Roman alphabet at about the same time. The new alphabet was designed by a monk, St. Cyril, who joined with his brother Methodius in converting the Slavs of Russia and neighboring areas to Christianity.

During the Kievan period a multiplicity of Norman-Slavic princes held sway over the territories that became known as *Rus.* Most of these leaders based their authority on brute force, but Kiev, Novgorod, and other cities established local assemblies, called *veche,* that allowed heads of households to meet on a periodic basis and make effective decisions, a form of direct democracy. These assemblies never governed Russia as a whole, however, and as time went on they fell victim to the superior force of authoritarian rulers.

By the twelfth century, Kiev began to decline as a center of political predominance. The final deathblow came in 1236–37 with the first in a series of invasions by Mongols from Asia. Establishing a regime known as the Golden Horde, the Mongols required the Russian authorities to pay tribute. In 1241 they pillaged Kiev. But they also lent their support to Russian princes willing to acknowledge their preeminence.

Descendants of Rurik gradually consolidated their hold over northern Russia starting around 1300. The ensuing century marked the rise of Moscow as the dominant center of political and military power in the region, a status it solidified following the collapse of Mongol hegemony in the fifteenth century. A burst of territorial expansion accompanied Moscow's ascendancy. By 1600 Russia was as large as the rest of Europe; sixty years later, having absorbed Ukraine, it was the largest country in the world.

Along with relentless aggrandizement came imperial nomenclature. Grand Prince Ivan III (1462–1505) began referring to himself as "tsar," a term derived from Caesar and formerly used by the Byzantine emperors as well as by the leaders of the Golden Horde. His grandson, Ivan IV, formalized the title by proclaiming himself "Tsar of All Russia" in 1547. He later added the title "Lord of All the Orthodox," asserting the tsars' claims to legitimacy on the basis of divine right. Known as *Ivan the Terrible,* Russia's first titled tsar boasted that his powers as "autocrat" of Russia—another of his official titles—far surpassed the authority of European monarchs. Two assemblies that were convened under his rule met briefly and were dissolved. Under no circumstances was Ivan willing to countenance the development of an English-style parliament.

Following a violent period known as "the Time of Troubles" that ensued when Ivan IV's line died out, a special assembly was convened to elect a new tsar. Consisting mainly of Orthodox prelates and nobles, it also included ordinary townsfolk and peasants. In 1613 this assembly elected Michael Romanov, the sixteen-year-old son of the patriarch of the Orthodox church, as the new tsar. The *Romanovs* were destined to rule Russia for more than three hundred years, up to the abdication of Tsar Nicholas II in 1917 only months before the communist revolution. Never again would ordinary Russians be invited to elect their leader until Boris Yeltsin's election in 1991.

The autocratic nature of tsarist power expanded even more pronouncedly under Peter I, better known as *Peter the Great*. Born in 1672, he ascended the throne in 1685. A commanding figure at seven feet tall, Peter compelled even the most distinguished nobles to identify themselves before him as "your majesty's lowliest slave." Russia's commoners (99.7 percent of the population) remained in a state of servitude, completely deprived of rights and subjected to onerous taxes. Compulsory military service and slave labor were integral elements of Petrine Russia.

Having lived in Holland in his youth, Peter clearly recognized Russia's economic inferiority to the West and he was resolved to overcome it. He extended an open hand to scientists and technicians from Germany and other countries and opened a "window on the West" by building the city of St. Petersburg on the Gulf of Finland. Peter's adaptations of Western methods stopped well short of political and social reform, however. Like his predecessors on the Russian throne, Peter had no tolerance of parliamentary bodies or civil liberties. His borrowings were mainly technological in nature, with a pronounced military bent. Peter had every intention of shaping Russia's army and navy into forces to be reckoned with. "We need Europe for a few decades," he said, "and then we must turn our back on it."[3]

Peter's approach created an ambivalence in Russian attitudes toward the West that endured throughout the entire tsarist epoch and that persists to this very day. From Peter's time onward, the defining hallmark of Russian nationalism became its double-edged orientation to Western Europe (and, later, to the United States). On the one hand, Russian leaders and intellectuals have simultaneously recognized and resented their country's economic backwardness vis-à-vis the West. But until quite recently they resisted copying the political freedoms and social structures that underlay Western economic dynamism, preferring instead to pursue their own models (whether tsarist or communist) while asserting their country's spiritual or moral superiority to "decadent" Western norms and practices. The "Slavophile" strain in Russian culture, which crystallized as a body of thought in the nineteenth century, explicitly articulated these notions of spiritual supremacy. As Liah Greenfeld has argued, however, Slavophilism and "Westernism" were simply two sides of the same coin: both were rooted in Russian resentment at the West's achievements and in a gnawing sense of humiliation. Neither concept of nationalism favored the development of democracy.[4]

Several of Peter's successors initiated reforms aimed at loosening up some of the more extreme aspects of the country's political and social rigidity. None, however, permitted real democratization. Empress Catherine II (*Catherine the Great*), who ruled from 1762 to 1796, initiated some administrative reforms, but she opposed sharing power with a parliament modeled on Britain's constitutional monarchy. Like her predecessors, she regarded the vast majority of the populace as mere subjects, unworthy of guaranteed rights.[5]

Her great-grandson Alexander II took the giant step of abolishing serfdom in 1861, freeing tens of millions of peasants from bonded servitude to their landlords. He also allowed the creation of local organs of self-government in villages and cities. Neither of these reforms extended real civil liberties or electoral power to the people, however. Demands for more revolutionary change proliferated, and in 1881 Alexander II was assassinated by a terrorist.

The revolutionary unrest and terrorism that shook Russia in the second half of the nineteenth century only provoked the next tsar, Alexander III, to tighten the regime's grip on power more assertively. Over the course of the 1880s and 1890s, a series of new laws on crimes against the government gave Russia the institutional foundations of a modern police state. With no judicial system to set limits to its practices, the secret police became the principal effective authority in Russia when it came to day-to-day governance. Local government bodies were restricted in their activities, and thousands of people were exiled to Siberia.[6]

In January 1905, military units brutally dispersed a crowd of peaceful petitioners in front of the tsar's palace, an event that set off revolutionary and anarchistic outbursts throughout the country. Faced with the most severe crisis in the history of tsardom, Tsar Nicholas II agreed to the creation of a parliamentary body, the Duma. The first Duma was elected in 1906 under fairly democratic conditions of universal male suffrage. But the tsar issued Fundamental Laws severely circumscribing the Duma's powers and reasserting his own status as "Autocrat of All the Russias." He also instituted a conservative upper chamber of notables to counterbalance the Duma's populist inclinations. The tsar's basic aversion to parliamentarism soon became evident when he dissolved the first Duma in less than three months. The next one did not last much longer. Then in 1907 he unilaterally changed the electoral laws, violating his own constitution. The change resulted in more docile Dumas and no advance toward real democracy. The tsar continued to rely on the old aristocratic elite to govern Russia and opposed a genuine constitutional monarchy.[7] Then in 1917, in the midst of World War I and mounting domestic unrest, Nicholas was forced to abdicate, bringing an end to more than four hundred years of tsarist autocracy.

Reinforcing the tsars' success in maintaining authoritarian state institutions over the centuries was widespread indifference to democracy on the part of Russia's *elites.* Whereas England's parliamentary traditions had originated in the landed nobility, most Russian nobles did not own large estates. Peter the Great kept the nobility subservient, forbidding them to own private property and compelling them to change their residences so as not to develop an attachment to landholdings that might serve as a base of local power, as it had in England. He also compelled them to render lifelong service to the state. When Catherine II allowed the nobility to own land and released them from their service obligations, they gladly accepted these concessions and raised no serious demands for a parliamentary share of power, taking little interest in the consultative assemblies she established.

The first organized challenge to tsarist authority from noble ranks in the nineteenth century was a coup attempt staged in December 1825 by a small group of officers and fellow conspirators who were inspired by the French Revolution to seek a more liberal regime. The "Decembrist" uprising was quickly quashed and its initiators arrested, with scarcely a protest from the noble class.[8] Later, in the 1860s and 1870s, radical university students, largely from noble families, organized a far more serious threat to tsarism. Convinced that Russia's peasant masses needed to be liberated from political and economic oppression, hundreds of young idealists fanned out into the countryside in the summer of 1874 in a concerted effort to stir up revolution. Animated by the slogan "Go to the people," the so-called *populist movement* quickly fizzled, a victim of peasant apathy and the regime's harsh response. Thereafter the populist movement split into two directions: one group embarked on terrorism, the other gravitated to the various socialist movements that proliferated as the century came to a close. Neither of them looked to Western democracy as a source of inspiration, and both groups were relatively small.[9]

Russia's religious elites, consisting of the Orthodox church hierarchy, provided consistent support for tsarism, as did the military elites. Both were props of the tsarist ruling structure and ill-disposed to democracy.

The country's intellectual elites, a group known as the *intelligentsia,* included many people with a passion for improving social conditions. Some were genuinely interested in democracy and formed the basis of the Constitutional Democratic party, which emerged as the largest party in the first two Dumas. Others tended toward the populists or socialists. But a sizable portion of the Russian intelligentsia, perhaps the majority, remained politically inert, exhibiting a greater interest in literature and the arts than in politics.

The absence of *national unity,* reflecting Russia's ethnic, linguistic, and religious *heterogeneity,* also worked against democracy. The state's appetite for territory brought a diversity of non-Russian peoples under tsarist rule—from Poles, Lithuanians, and Finns in the west to Georgians and Armenians in the Caucasus and an array of Turkic groups across Central Asia. These subjugated peoples had as few rights as the Russians themselves and were subjected to military reprisals for acts of insubordination. Any steps in the direction of democracy for these populations could only spell suicide for a polyglot empire. Ethnic Russians also exhibited a noticeable social heterogeneity, rooted mainly in class and status distinctions. Nineteenth- and early-twentieth-century Russian society consisted of the nobility, a midlevel gentry, a large peasantry, a small merchant class, the Orthodox clergy, a small core of professionals, and a growing industrial working class. The tsarist regime played one group against another while striving to keep them all down. Most Russians therefore developed a closer attachment to their own social class than to Russia as a whole, with few espousing a democratic conception of the common good.

A relatively low level of *national wealth* constituted another barrier to democracy in precommunist Russia. Until the communist era, Russia was an agricultural country, with far lower levels of industrialization than in Britain, France, Germany, or the United States. Its agricultural system was grossly inefficient: most landowners were either uninterested in commercial farming or unable to afford it, producing little in the way of a food surplus for sale. Russia was not significantly engaged in international trade, and even its domestic trade was subject to a panoply of government restrictions and disincentives. It was not until the 1860s that a private banking system developed, hundreds of years behind the commercial nations of Europe. Relatively paltry amounts of money circulated among the population, far too little to stimulate economic growth.

A major cause of both the lethargy of Russia's economy and the authoritarianism of its political institutions was the lowly status of *private enterprise.* Until the reign of Catherine the Great in the eighteenth century, the tsars refused to allow the private ownership of land. The tsars themselves literally owned Russia, holding title to all its territory, natural resources, cities, and towns along with virtually all its manufacturing enterprises. In this respect Russia was vastly different from Western Europe, where private property was enshrined in ancient Roman law and respected by monarchs in legal theory and actual practice from the Middle Ages onward. It was largely to defend their property that European (and subsequently American) farmers and businesspeople demanded a say in how they were governed, advancing the cause of representative democracy and political rights through the assertion of their economic rights. In 1785, Catherine II finally permitted members of the nobility to own property. But more than 90 percent of the population, consisting mostly of peasants, did not acquire property rights until the nineteenth century. The tsars who followed her continued to regard the Russian state as their own exclusive preserve—a "patrimonial state."

On the eve of the twentieth century, Russia continued to lag far behind Britain, the United States, France, and Germany in both the level of its industrial development and the scope of its private enterprise. When private industrial capitalism finally emerged in Russia, it did so under the guiding influence of the state. Stimulated by infusions of state investment and direction from above, the economy surged forward at a rate of 8 percent a year in the 1890s.[10] But a depression set in as the twentieth century began, and large segments of Russia's natural wealth and industrial production came under the control of foreign investors. Though Russia had become the fifth-largest industrial economy in the world by World War I, one-third of its industrial investment and half of its bank capital was in foreign hands. The veritable absence of private property in Russia until late in the eighteenth century, and its narrow diffusion and weak development in subsequent phases of tsarist rule, provided slim grounds for the development of a Russian *middle class* that might have militated for democratic reform. As private enterprise expanded at the turn of the twentieth century, Russia's entrepreneurial bourgeoisie remained small by Western standards, and only a portion of its members entered the political lists. With the fortunes of their businesses heavily dependent on state favors, a large number of Russia's businesspeople preferred to lend their support to tsarist authoritarianism rather than threaten it with demands for democracy.

In addition to lacking support from society's elites and middle class, democracy in Russia also failed to capture the allegiance of its *disadvantaged* masses. From the earliest inception of the Russian state to the ultimate demise of tsarism, the vast majority of the country's population consisted of impoverished peasants. Between 1550 and 1650, virtually the entire peasant population became serfs under the dictates of an increasingly centralized Russian autocracy.

Unlike American-style slavery, the landlords did not legally own the serfs, but they controlled them. In actual practice, the serfs were not much better off than slaves. Like slaves, Russian serfs had no rights of any kind. Tsarist law forbade them from moving without permission. Runaways, if apprehended, were to be returned to their landlords. Despite the fact that they were not legally owned by their landlords, they were nevertheless bought and sold as chattel (though Russian landlords tended to refrain from breaking up their families). And yet, in spite of their subjugation, most serfs supported tsarism and displayed little inclination to demand a more democratic regime. Displays of mass rebellion were rare and tended to be spontaneous eruptions directed at the local landlords rather than organized political movements aimed at overthrowing the government. In the 1870s, when the idealistic young populists took to the countryside to spark a revolution, they were shocked to find that the serfs revered their tsar and dismissed talk of an uprising with contempt. The notion that the tsar was a benevolent father, ordained by God to care for his people, was a common assumption in peasant lore.

In February 1861, Tsar Alexander II signed an Emancipation decree abolishing serfdom in Russia. (President Lincoln's Emancipation Proclamation was issued in January 1862.) The decree freed more than 22 million peasants, roughly 38 percent of Russia's population at the time, from their obligation to serve the landlords. (About a hundred thousand Russians were serf-owning nobles.) The newly liberated serfs now became legal persons for the first time, endowed with the right to own property and to vote for newly created local councils. But just as emancipation in the United States abolished servitude in legal terms without providing the former slaves with an accompanying measure of economic self-sufficiency, so the terms of emancipation in Russia imposed new shackles of economic dependency on the former serfs. One-third of the landlords' property was made available to the liberated peasants, but they had to buy it. Unable to meet the demanding schedule of payments to the state and the landlords, many sank hopelessly into debt. Emancipation also failed to provide the full range of civil rights.

Widespread dissatisfaction with these conditions ignited a series of peasant revolts that intensified between 1905 and 1907. Though the government canceled the debts and instituted reforms promoting private land ownership, a smoldering discontent pervaded the Russian countryside. By 1917, self-employed peasants owned two-thirds of the country's farmland, but most were impoverished. Family farms tended to be small and land hunger was rampant, a predicament that induced many peasants to heed the siren call of revolution rather than seek an orderly passage to democracy.

Meanwhile, as Russia's industrial development quickened, a new class of disadvantaged people voiced their indignation. The industrial working class, toiling in the factories that proliferated in the late nineteenth and early twentieth centuries, grew from slightly more than half a million in 1860 to about 3 million by 1914. Although they still constituted only a small portion of the population (estimated at 170 million in 1914), their concentration in and around the country's main urban centers allowed them to join forces. Though trade unions and strikes were not allowed, strikes began taking place in the 1870s and 1880s. In the revolutionary explosion of 1905, workers in St. Petersburg (the capital) and Moscow closed down factories and spontaneously formed workers' councils that were poised to replace government authority until the regime suppressed them. In 1912, 725,000 workers went on strike illegally, followed by more than a million and a quarter in the first half of 1914.

As World War I imposed new hardships on the working population—an increasing number of whom were women—labor agitation intensified. Strikes and mass demonstrations for "bread and peace" convulsed the cities and other areas where workers clustered, such as mines and oil fields.[11] By 1917, Russia's exploited working class was ready for radical solutions. It was the communists who spoke to their grievances more successfully than did the advocates of liberal or social democracy.

Democracy in precommunist Russia was also hampered by the absence of a *civil society* and a *democratic political culture.* One of the defining features of the tsarist era was the gaping chasm that separated the state from society. The heavy hand of tsarist rule remained so oppressive that the people had little latitude to develop viable associations of their own. Virtually all organizations independent of the state—civic associations, trade unions, political parties—were deemed seditious by the ruling authorities. A pervasive sense of resignation and alienation from the government thus settled over the bulk of the population in the nineteenth century. Predictably, the values and behaviors associated with a democratic political culture—participation, cooperation, consensus building, trust, and the like—also failed to blossom in Russia's rocky political soil.

Prior to the nineteenth century, *education* was reserved to the upper nobility and clergy. The expansion of secondary and higher educational opportunities in the second half of the nineteenth century increased the size of the intelligentsia, but the tsarist regime permitted no real outlets for mass participation in the country's political life on the part of its educated strata. The political orientations of high school and university graduates therefore got diverted into a quiescent resignation or a desperate revolutionary radicalism, with only a relative few seeking a moderate democratic constitution. The bulk of the population continued to consist of illiterate peasants, scarcely a promising basis for mass democracy.

The flow of *information* was seriously restricted by the regime. Official activities were tightly guarded state secrets, and the public was fed official versions of the truth as deemed appropriate by the authorities. A censorship system monitored nonofficial publications.

Finally, Russia's *international environment* proved just as obstructive to democracy as its domestic characteristics. Russia was geographically and culturally removed from the crucial developments in European society that promoted the rule of law and the evolution of democratic attitudes and institutions, such as the traditions of Roman jurisprudence, the social obligations of feudalism, the Protestant Reformation, the Enlightenment, and the advancement of bourgeois liberalism. Although the development of democracy proceeded in Britain in spite of the government's aggressive pursuit of imperial expansion and its involvement in the "great game" of power politics in Europe, until World War I Britain did not use conscripted armies. From the time of Peter the Great, however, Russians were impressed against their will into military service to fight for the emperor's personal ambitions rather than for their "country" in any democratic or patriotic sense of the term. When World War I broke out, it only exacerbated the social and political conflicts that had been building up to a revolutionary explosion for decades. Far from promoting democracy, the First World War led Russia to communism.

With respect to all ten conditions for democracy, then, events consistently conspired to inhibit democratic development in Russia over the course of a thousand years. The barriers to democracy would be even more imposing under communist rule.

## Communism

**Marx and the Russian Revolution** If Karl Marx's predictions had been right, Russia would not have experienced a socialist revolution in 1917. As noted in chapter 13, Marx believed that socialism had to be built on the foundations of an industrialized capitalist economy in an advanced state of development. Only a highly industrialized economy could provide a working class large enough to wrest economic and political power from the capitalist bourgeoisie in a spontaneous revolution. But seventy years after Marx and Friedrich Engels authored the communist *Manifesto,* Russia was still a predominantly agricultural nation. Industrial workers and their families barely amounted to 5 percent of the populace in 1917, a far cry from the majority Marx required for a successful proletarian revolution.[12]

Contrary to Marx's expectations, however, a socialist revolution succeeded in Russia. But the Russian Revolution deviated from Marx's predictions in several ways. Instead of being a spontaneous working-class uprising, it was a carefully orchestrated coup d'état, skillfully managed by a revolutionary party that was in turn led by a charismatic personality, **Vladimir Ilich Lenin**. Although it was accompanied by working-class agitation in Russia's largest cities, its timing was due more to the decades-long dissolution of tsarism, the land hunger of the peasantry, and the general turbulence fostered by World War I than to a mass upheaval of the industrial working class. Political power in Russia was seized by a Communist Party elite acting in the name of the workers, not by the workers themselves.

The Russian "dictatorship of the proletariat" was not a temporary affair under the direction of the workers, as Marx had forecast; rather, it turned out to be a *dictatorship of the Communist Party* that endured until the final collapse of party rule in the early 1990s. Rather than withering away, in accordance with Marxist notions, the state in the Soviet Union burgeoned into one of the most oppressive totalitarian regimes ever seen, bolstered by a giant bureaucracy that imposed itself on just about every facet of the country's economic and social life. And instead of becoming a classless society, in conformity with Marx's utopian vision of communism, the USSR developed stark divisions between the mass of society (itself divided into several layers) and a select Communist Party elite (at most 2 percent of the population) who arrogated to themselves a cornucopia of privileges and material goods not available to the wider population.

**Vladimir Ilich Lenin**

**Lenin and Leninism** Lenin, the person most responsible for Russia's deviation from the Marxist paradigm, was not a proletarian but a product of the Russian intelligentsia. His father was a high school principal who was granted noble status at the end of his career. Born in 1870 as V. I. Ulyanov (Lenin was a pseudonym), by eighteen he was a convinced Marxist. Lenin left home in 1895 and moved to St. Petersburg, where he joined a small group of Marxist intellectuals. He was soon arrested by the political police and exiled to Siberia. Following his release in 1900, Lenin fled the country, joining a growing exodus of Russian socialists to Europe, where they formed the nucleus of the newly established Russian Social Democratic Labor Party.

In 1902, Lenin made his first major mark on the socialist movement with the publication of *What Is To Be Done?* The tract boldly staked out several positions that diverged from the tenets of classic Marxism. Whereas Marx regarded the industrial proletariat as the standard-bearers of revolution, Lenin insisted that the workers, if left to themselves, would never mount a revolution; at best they would form trade unions and come to terms with the captains of industry who controlled their lives. And whereas Marx foresaw spontaneous proletarian outbursts, Lenin called for the creation of a "party of a new type": not a mass party concerned with winning votes, like the German Social Democrats or the British Labour Party, but a smaller party consisting of professional revolutionaries who would act as the "vanguard of the proletariat," seizing power whenever the right opportunity presented itself. Armed with its "organizational weapon," such a conspiratorial party might be able to topple the state, along with its economic base, long before capitalism had created a sizable working-class population.

These ideas split the Russian socialists into two groups. ***Lenin's followers called themselves Bolsheviks,*** meaning "the majority." In fact, they constituted a minority of Russian Social Democrats at the start of the century, but the name stuck. Most of the remaining party members, labeled Mensheviks (the minority), regarded Lenin's theses as heresy and remained faithful to Marx's teachings. In their view, Russian revolutionaries were compelled by the laws of history to wait until the advancement of industrial capitalism created an auspicious moment for a spontaneous working-class revolution.

The tumultuous events of 1905 seemed to validate Lenin's propositions. As Russia seethed with revolutionary unrest, Lenin returned home, remaining underground for two years. But the ferment proved premature: the tsarist regime recovered its nerve and crushed the revolutionary outbreaks that flared up spontaneously in Russia's cities and countryside. Lenin returned to Europe, but when he went back to Russia the next time, in April 1917, the situation would be primed for revolution.

As Lenin's train arrived in Russia's capital city, renamed Petrograd during the war, the Bolsheviks could count on no more than 23,000 adherents. Between April and July, their ranks swelled to nearly a quarter million. The war's widespread unpopularity played directly into their hands, sapping the Russian government of what little support it may have possessed. In March, Tsar Nicholas II was persuaded to step down, leaving power in the hands of a Provisional Government consisting of politicians from the conservative right to the moderate left. (Because Russia was still using the Julian calendar, which lagged two weeks behind the more widely used Gregorian calendar, the transfer of power is known in Russian history as the "February Revolution.") Though the new government immediately conferred on Russia's citizens a wide range of democratic rights and freedoms they had never before enjoyed, its decision to prosecute the war hastened its undoing.

One-fourth of Russia's troops deserted the army over the ensuing months. Life on the home front was continuing turmoil: shortages of food and heating fuel intensified public outrage, resulting in strikes, work stoppages, and demonstrations in the cities. Out in the countryside, peasants intensified their demands for more land. In Petrograd and Moscow, workers set up councils to take over the management of their factories and, in a bold challenge to the governing authorities, acted as though they constituted the only legitimate political authority. The Russian word for council is *soviet.* As the crisis deepened, soldiers and peasants formed soviets of their own, electing deputies to join with representatives of the workers' soviets to coordinate their activities.

Bolshevik propaganda deftly exploited these discontents. Lenin and his followers called for an immediate end to the war, land for the peasants, and "all power to the soviets!" By early fall the Provisional Government was virtually powerless. In a methodical coup d'état, Bolshevik militia units moved into the main government buildings in Petrograd, most of which had already been vacated by Russian officialdom. The tsarist regime and the short-lived Provisional Government had each collapsed like a house of cards. The Russian state fell into Bolshevik hands on November 7, 1917. (The date was October 25 on the Julian calendar; hence ***the Bolshevik takeover of power is known as the*** **October Revolution**.)

The Bolsheviks—also known as Communists—promptly pulled Russia out of the Great War, moved the capital to Moscow, and turned their attention to consolidating power at home. Their first moves were calculated to court popularity. During their first months at the helm, the Communists granted independence to nationality groups like the Poles, the Finns, and the Ukrainians, who had been incorporated into the Russian Empire under the tsars. They granted power to the workers' soviets, encouraged peasants to take over land, and allowed previously scheduled elections to a Constitutional Assembly to go forward. The Bolsheviks won nearly 25 percent of the vote in these elections, capturing a majority in Petrograd and Moscow.[13] Then, one by one, the new rulers proceeded to take back most of their concessions: Ukraine was reincorporated into Russia, the soviets came under Communist Party control, farmland and produce were confiscated by the state, and the Constituent Assembly was liquidated the day after its first meeting, consigned to the "dustbin of history."

Private businesses were expropriated by the government in the name of socialism. Nicholas II and his family were executed so as to preclude any return to tsarism. Over the next several years the Bolsheviks (the "reds") fought a bitter civil war against a variety of enemies, known collectively as the "whites." As fighting and famine claimed millions of lives, the Red Army under Bolshevik command finally vanquished its remaining foes in 1921. In 1922 the Union of Soviet Socialist Republics (USSR) was formally proclaimed, uniting under communism the remnants of the Russian empire. The country lay in ruins.

From the outset, Lenin was determined to impose Communist Party authority over all other political and social forces in the country. Driven by a keen sense of power, he believed that the most important question in politics was "Who—whom?" (in Russian, "*Kto—kovo?*"). "Who," in other words, "controls whom?" *The primacy of the Communist Party's power* was the single most characteristic feature of what came to be known as *Leninism.* By Lenin's own candid admission, the dictatorship of the proletariat in Russia effectively meant the dictatorship of the Communist Party.

A second defining aspect of Leninism was what he called *"democratic centralism."* While discussion and debate among party members were supposed to be permitted until a final decision was reached, all were required to follow the policies eventually decided by the top party leaders. In actual practice, internal party democracy quickly dissipated in favor of a top-down structure of command not unlike a military hierarchy.

Violence and a highly centralized state were ruthlessly employed to secure party rule. Accordingly, Lenin set up a powerful secret police—the forerunner of the KGB—and presided over the creation of a large state bureaucracy dominated by Communist Party adherents. Though he recognized that bureaucratic routine threatened to smother revolutionary elan, Lenin was in practice a devotee of strong, centralized state power.

The Soviet system of government that took shape under Lenin's aegis thus revolved around two institutions: the Communist Party of the Soviet Union (CPSU) and the state. The two were so closely intertwined as to be virtually indistinguishable. Both the party and the state had large bureaucracies with overlapping responsibilities for governing the country. And both were topped by small, powerful committees that constituted the leading decision-making bodies in Russia. The highest party committees were the Political Bureau, or *Politburo,* and the *Secretariat.* The highest state committee eventually became known as the *Council of Ministers,* the country's formal executive branch of government. The links connecting the parallel party and state institutions were strengthened by the simultaneous presence of several key individuals in the Politburo, the Secretariat, and the Council of Ministers. In the Soviet system, the Communist Party and the state were fused. Over time, as we shall see, the *party* institutions emerged as more powerful than the state institutions when it came to making the key decisions. Until Mikhail Gorbachev began restructuring this fused party-state institutional system in the late 1980s, its basic structure remained largely intact.

Another feature of Leninism was *tactical flexibility.* After the Civil War, Lenin recognized that the Bolsheviks needed to buy time and rebuild the economy in order to stabilize their authority. In 1921 Lenin initiated a reform known as the *New Economic Policy (NEP),* which reversed the state's efforts to take over the economy, putting socialism on hold. Peasants were allowed to buy and sell land; industrialists and merchants were invited to lease property from the state and run their own businesses, with strong encouragement to turn a profit. The Russian state retained control of what Lenin called "the commanding heights" of the economy: energy and steel production, the communication and transportation systems, and the like. The partial reintroduction of private enterprise was only supposed to be temporary, however. Once economic activity revived, Lenin had every intention of reimposing socialist controls over the economy under the Communist-run central government. But he set no time limit to the New Economic Policy, allowing Russia to have a respite from rigid state controls in hopes of building popularity for the communist regime over time.

The founder of Bolshevism never lived to see the reimposition of socialism in Russia. In 1922 he suffered a debilitating stroke, and in January 1924 he died. He can be rightfully credited with leading the Russian Revolution and creating the bases of Communist Party rule. Although he reinterpreted a number of the central axioms of Marxism to fit Russia's peculiar conditions, Lenin always considered himself a good Marxist. Following his death, Soviet ideology officially became known as **Marxism-Leninism**, ***a concept that combined Marx's revolutionary anticapitalism with Lenin's reliance on the communist party-state.***

One of Lenin's most enduring legacies was to haunt all the Soviet governments that followed him: his failure to establish an orderly procedure for succession to power. Lenin ruled through his charismatic hold over the Communists and unrelenting coercion against his party's opponents. He had no taste for the procedures for transferring power spelled out in written constitutions, especially those in the hated "bourgeois democracies" of the West. Moreover, he designated no successor. As a consequence, a struggle for power within the highest reaches of the Communist Party leadership commenced as soon as Lenin was incapacitated. Through a combination of manipulativeness, guile, and bureaucratic intrigue, the winner of the struggle

**Joseph Stalin**

was **Joseph Stalin**, a man who developed Lenin's legacy of centralization and coercion to unimaginable excesses.

**Stalin** Born in 1879 to an impoverished Georgian family, Stalin studied at a seminary but turned to revolutionary Marxism while still in school. After the Bolshevik seizure of power, Lenin entrusted him with a number of sensitive party and government posts, including that of General Secretary of the Communist Party. Initially, that position was nothing more than a routine bureaucratic office charged with managing the party's records. But Stalin transformed it into a sinecure of personal power, building a loyal following by promoting people to both party and government jobs. Through the calculated use of political patronage, Stalin created a large party bureaucracy, or "apparatus" (*apparat*), dependent on his favors. Toward the end of his life, Lenin criticized Stalin as "too rude" for the post and called for his removal, but the incapacitated Bolshevik was in no physical condition to press his views. Stalin stayed on as General Secretary until he died some thirty years later.

During the 1920s, in the years that followed Lenin's untimely illness and death, Stalin masterfully exploited rivalries and disagreements among the party's top leaders, playing off one faction against another while quietly cultivating his own coterie of loyalists. By the end of the decade he could count on a voting majority in the party Politburo. Utilizing this support, in 1928 and 1929 he engineered the wholesale reversal of the Soviet Union's economic course. The broadly popular New Economic Policy was summarily abandoned, probably much earlier than Lenin would have liked, and the first in a series of five-year plans established the bases of a **centrally planned economy (CPE)** in the Soviet Union. These measures constituted the building blocks of the Soviet model of socialism, which represented another deviation from classical Marxism. Marx, whose descriptions of socialism were inscrutably vague, had left no clear blueprint for building a socialist economy other than to imply that it would *not* be run by a powerful state. The brand of socialism that Stalin and the Communist Party now forced upon the population was a ***command economy controlled by the leadership of an all-intrusive party-state dictatorship.***

Stalin applied his policy with a vengeance. The first Five-Year Plan, introduced in 1928, had set a series of ambitious growth targets to be achieved in various sectors of the economy. In 1929, Stalin suddenly raised these targets astronomically, especially in such critical industrial areas as coal, iron, steel, and electricity production. Although Stalin's plan targets were too unrealistic to be achieved, by the end of the first five-year period the Soviets had nevertheless accomplished one of the most rapid spurts of industrial development in human history. From its inception, however, this forced-pace industrialization policy was guided by a political motivation: to impose stringent controls over the economy for the purpose of retaining the Communist Party's control over Russia's political and social life.

An even more severe policy accompanied the accelerated industrialization drive: the *collectivization* of agriculture. By 1929 there were 25 million private farm households in Russia. In an operation conducted with unparalleled brutality, the Stalinist regime liquidated all privately owned farms and corraled the rural population into newly created *collective farms.* Farm produce was confiscated by government agents, often at gunpoint, for distribution to the cities; animals were also taken from their owners and attached to the collectives. Anyone resisting these measures, or even suspected of potential resistance, might be executed on the spot or rounded up for deportation to the work camps (*gulagi*) that now proliferated in the empty vastness of Russia, forming a great chain that later became known as the "gulag archipelago." Violence in Ukraine was especially widespread. Lacking the means to resist, many peasants killed their horses, cows, and other livestock rather than surrender them. Starvation stalked the countryside as food production plummeted. Stalin's own wife killed herself after speaking out against the horrors gripping the nation. Stalin justified his actions with cynical distortions of Marxist ideology.[14]

By 1934, when the job was done, perhaps as many as 14.5 million Russian peasants had perished in the collectivization campaign, though estimates vary and no precise figure can be authenticated. (Stalin himself told Winston Churchill that collectivization had cost 10 million lives and was more arduous than confronting the German invasion of World War II.) In contrast to the relative success of Stalin's industrialization campaign, however, it took several decades for Soviet agriculture to recover from the catastrophe of the collectivization process.[15]

Having imposed his will on the population and the economy, Stalin next turned his attention to the Communist Party itself. Between 1934 and 1939, he cleansed the party's ranks from top to bottom, dismissing undesirable members and in many cases consigning them to labor camps or firing squads. Known as the *Great Purge,* the process took on the macabre pathology of a witch hunt. An atmosphere of paranoia haunted the party as accusations and denunciations, most of them fabricated, struck terror into the membership from the highest to the lowest echelons. More than 1.6 million members were expelled from the CPSU.

Not even the most powerful Soviet leaders were spared Stalin's wrath. A series of "show trials" subjected dozens of the most senior party officials to public vilification. Many of them had been Lenin's trusted comrades-in-arms during the early days of Bolshevism. Invariably, the show trials ended in a string of death sentences, often carried out immediately. One of Stalin's prime targets was *Leon Trotsky,* the flamboyant revolutionary who was his chief rival. Stalin expelled Trotsky from Russia in 1929 and had him assassinated in Mexico in 1940.[16]

Stalin's terror fanned out from the Communist Party to the general population. According to one estimate, between 1936 and 1938 alone there were 7 million arrests and at least a million executions; in 1939 the camps contained as many as 8 million prisoners. Stalin's deadly reach even extended to the military high command, decimating about a fourth of the officer corps by the eve of World War II. A relentless assault on religion accompanied these brutalities. Clerics were murdered, churches and mosques were destroyed, and atheism was propagated as official communist doctrine. By the end of the 1930s there was little question that Stalin was the unchallenged autocrat of the USSR and that the Soviet system was a paradigm of totalitarianism.[17]

The sufferings of the Soviet masses did not end with the attenuation of the *Great Terror,* however. World War II exacted an even heavier price. Though Stalin managed to delay a German invasion by cutting a deal with Hitler in 1939, the Nazi regime broke the agreement and invaded the USSR with full force in June 1941.[18] By the time the war ended in 1945, more than 22 million Soviet people had died and some 1,700 Soviet cities were destroyed.

Stalin emerged from the war with his powers intact. In fact, the war allowed him to expand his influence beyond Soviet borders. After the USSR's Red Army rolled into Eastern Europe and Germany, Soviet agents and local Communist Party leaders imposed communist dictatorships on East Germany, Poland, Czechoslovakia, Hungary, Romania, and Bulgaria between 1944 and 1948. Later these states were incorporated into a Soviet-led military alliance known as the Warsaw Pact. Yugoslavia and Albania were also taken over by local communists after the war, but they escaped Soviet domination. Victory even brought Stalin a measure of respect and popularity among a portion of the Soviet masses, though the magnitude of this support is hard to estimate. Anyone expecting a postwar diminution of autocratic rule was in for a disappointment, however. The concentration camps remained crowded and the Kremlin voiced suspicions of dark plots. The Cold War added fears of impending nuclear annihilation. Stalin was said by his successors to be planning a new party purge when he died in 1953.

**Khrushchev** Although the Great Purge had expelled or killed nearly 2 million party members, it also opened up new opportunities for eager young recruits as well as for more senior party members who were fortunate enough to survive the onslaught. Most of the men who were to run the Soviet Union from Stalin's death until the mid 1980s rose up the ladder of the party apparatus during the purges and World War II. Stalin's party enticed this generation to its ranks by offering careers, social status, and, for the politically ambitious, the prospect of power.

One of the most ambitious was *Nikita Khrushchev* (khroo-sh-CHOFF). Born to poverty in 1894, Khrushchev joined the party in 1925 as a full-time *apparatchik*—a member of the party apparatus—just as Stalin was gathering effective control over it.

In the early 1930s Khrushchev won swift promotions within the party's Moscow branch and supervised the construction of the city's subway system, a task accomplished by conscripted laborers forced to work in forty-eight-hour shifts. As the Great Purge got under way, Khrushchev wholeheartedly supported Stalin, lauding him as "our leader and teacher" while reviling the show-trial defendants as "fascist dogs" and "degenerates" deserving execution.[19] His loyalty was rewarded with a seat in the powerful CPSU Politburo, where he replaced one of Stalin's purge victims, and an even more spectacular appointment as the party's top leader in Ukraine. In assuming control of the most important Soviet republic after Russia in 1939, Khrushchev stepped into another post freshly vacated by a hapless casualty of the purges. Khrushchev's notoriety among the Soviet people escalated during World War II, when he assumed responsibility for organizing the Ukrainian war effort. One of his sons perished in the battle of Stalingrad.

When Stalin died in 1953 without leaving a designated successor, a struggle for his mantle broke out among his closest associates. Over the next two years, Khrushchev outmaneuvered his chief rivals and emerged as the Soviet Union's top leader by 1955. His behind-the-scenes machinations bore a distinct resemblance to Stalin's rise to power in the 1920s. Moreover, as we've seen, he owed his career to Stalin's blessings. It is thus ironic that Khrushchev's main claim to fame in Russian history derives from his sweeping denunciation of Stalin and his effort to rid the Soviet system of Stalinism's horrors. In a speech delivered in February 1956 at the Twentieth Congress of the Communist Party of the Soviet Union, a gathering of several thousand top party bureaucrats, Khrushchev excoriated Stalin as a madman whose actions had repeatedly brought the Soviet Union to the brink of disaster. Denouncing the "cruel repression" and "mass terror" of the Great Purge as an utterly unjustified breech of legality and berating Stalin for military blunders that had cost hundreds of thousands of lives, Khrushchev denounced the former Soviet dictator's megalomaniacal "cult of personality" and his callous disregard of the people's welfare.

Khrushchev's broadside became known as the *secret speech* because it was delivered behind closed doors. Although it was not published in the Soviet Union until the Gorbachev era, it was read out to CPSU members at local party meetings.[20]

Shortly after Khrushchev's speech, the Soviet Communist Party embarked on a campaign of *de-Stalinization.* Everywhere throughout the USSR, anything bearing Stalin's name was renamed, from streets and schools to the city of Stalingrad (which became Volgagrad). Statues and paintings of Stalin, once ubiquitous, were pulled down. Stalin's body was removed from the Red Square mausoleum it shared with Lenin's and reburied in a nondescript grave beside a Kremlin wall. Khrushchev even allowed writers like Alexander Solzhenitsyn to publish works denouncing Stalin's deeds.[21]

One of Khrushchev's motives in initiating the de-Stalinization program was to buttress his own authority by cultivating support from Communist Party leaders and bureaucrats. In effect, Khrushchev was signaling his assurance that he would never inflict a Stalinist purge on them and that they were safe as long as they supported him in power. But de-Stalinization provoked serious misgivings on the part of a number of high-level Soviet officials. They feared that, by attacking Stalin, Khrushchev had demeaned the party itself in the eyes of the Soviet people and the rest of the world. Several senior party leaders were sufficiently troubled by the anti-Stalin campaign, along with other Khrushchev policies, that they tried to unseat him in 1957. But

Khrushchev rallied his supporters within the party and turned the tables on his opponents, reasserting his grip on power.

Over the next several years, Khrushchev took the initiative in promoting a number of reforms, including adjustments to the central planning system and the shifting of military spending from the army and navy to the newly created missile forces. He proposed changes in the educational system that would have required high school graduates to enter the work force for a couple of years before starting college. Like de-Stalinization, these and other reforms had their critics: admirals and army generals grumbled, and the educational establishment managed to block Khrushchev's work-for-students scheme. Even so, most of Khrushchev's reform proposals were halfhearted at best and did nothing to undermine central planning or diminish the Communist Party's monopoly of power in the Soviet Union. Khrushchev wanted a "thaw" in the system Stalin had created, not its wholesale transformation.

Throughout his life, Khrushchev remained a devout Soviet communist, utterly committed to the authoritarian system he served. He asserted Soviet controls over Central and Eastern Europe and vigorously pursued the Cold War rivalry with the United States. While acknowledging the necessity of avoiding nuclear war, he deployed troops to crush the Hungarian uprising against communism in 1956, approved the Berlin wall in 1961, and put missiles in Cuba in 1962. (On the Cuban missile crisis, see chapter 5.) He was also convinced of the inherent economic superiority of communism over capitalism, vowing that the Soviet Union would overtake the U.S. economy by 1970 and would build the most productive and egalitarian welfare state in the world by 1980.

In the end, however, Khrushchev proved that he was no Stalin. Having antagonized a number of key party officials and bureaucratic agencies with his unsettling reforms, arrogant manner, and occasionally erratic behavior, Khrushchev proved far less adept than his predecessor in maintaining his authority. In October 1964, upon returning to the Kremlin from a trip, he was informed by his Politburo colleagues that he was no longer in power. Chastised by his successors for "hare-brained scheming," Khrushchev became a "nonperson" and was never seen in public again. In 1970, the party newspaper *Pravda* carried a brief notice in its back pages reporting that "pensioner N. S. Khrushchev" had died.[22]

**Leonid Brezhnev**

Many of the events of the next twenty-five years in Soviet politics were reactions to Khrushchev's reformist impulses. His immediate successor, **Leonid Brezhnev,** was opposed to any rash tampering with the basic Stalinist model of firm party rule and central planning. Under his guidance, the Soviet leadership undertook virtually no reforms.

**The Brezhnev Years** Just as Nikita Khrushchev had turned on Stalin, so Leonid Brezhnev turned on the man who had been his chief benefactor during his own climb up the apparatus of the Soviet Communist Party. Thanks to Khrushchev's patronage, Brezhnev had risen from obscurity to the most powerful leadership committees in the USSR. An ethnic Russian, Brezhnev was born in an industrial town in Ukraine in 1906. He joined the party in 1931, at the height of Stalin's industrialization and collectivization campaigns. As the Great Purge combed the ranks of the party, Brezhnev prospered: he won successive promotions during the purge years. During World War II Brezhnev served under Khrushchev as a political officer in Ukraine.

After Stalin's death, Khrushchev entrusted Brezhnev with a succession of important positions. But gratitude is a rare virtue in politics, and its absence was especially conspicuous in the conspiratorial world of the Kremlin. Brezhnev joined the cabal that unseated his benefactor in October 1964. From then until his death in 1982, Brezhnev was the official leader of the Communist Party of the Soviet Union, and thus the single most powerful figure in the USSR.

It was not long before the transfer of power brought noticeable changes in style and substance. Whereas Khrushchev was prone to impromptu declarations and unilateral initiatives, Brezhnev governed as part of a team. Though he shrewdly demoted his principal opponents, he presented himself as the chief spokesman of an oligarchy acting on the basis of consensus. In the policy realm, one of Brezhnev's first departures from his predecessor was his termination of public attacks on Stalin. Brezhnev even allowed positive accounts of Stalin to appear sporadically in the heavily controlled press.

A grim pall of uniformity descended on the country's cultural life. Marxist-Leninist propaganda continued to pervade the entire educational system, with obligatory courses on ideology imposed on Soviet students all the way through graduate school. The official censorship system became even more intrusive than it was under Khrushchev, who had allowed some freedom for anti-Stalinist writers. The Brezhnev regime's censors severely restricted the content of every publication, film, and record made in the USSR or imported from abroad. Political repression as a whole grew even tighter than under Khrushchev. The Brezhnev regime was determined to keep the USSR's small collection of dissidents—mostly writers, artists, and academics—under close surveillance. The dreaded KGB (the Committee on State Security) had carte blanche to investigate, harass, and arrest anyone suspected of engaging in dissident activities, such as writing or disseminating of anticommunist literature. Internationally renowned figures like physicist Andrei Sakharov and writer Alexander Solzhenitsyn were objects of continuing repression. Although the Stalin-era prison camps for the most part had been closed down under Khrushchev, a few still survived under Brezhnev. They were augmented by psychiatric prisons where political dissidents could be subjected to debilitating drug regimens on fabricated diagnoses of mental illness.[23]

The Brezhnevites were also resolved to crack down on any signs of ethnic unrest. Soviet Jews who sought to emigrate to Israel, Europe, or the United States had to contend with endless red tape and prolonged delays, often losing their jobs upon applying for a passport. Many were granted permission to leave only after deals were struck between the Soviet and U.S. governments. One reason for the Kremlin's reluctance to allow Jews to leave was its fear that other ethnic minorities would demand the same privilege. The USSR's population of 260 million at the time consisted of sixteen major nationality groups, each with at least a million people, plus more than eighty smaller nationality groups that together comprised 6 percent of the population. Because the Brezhnev leadership left little doubt that even the slightest signs of ethnic nationalism would be met with swift retribution, there were few outward displays of such dissent. The Russians, who constituted slightly more than half the Soviet population, dominated the country's levers of power.

Lest there be any uncertainty about the government's readiness to use force against challenges to its authority, the Brezhnev regime intervened vigorously on two occasions when communist rule was threatened in its hegemonic preserve of Eastern Europe. In 1968, when a reform movement initiated by the Communist Party of Czechoslovakia unleashed broad popular demands for democracy and closer ties to the West, the Soviets led a massive invasion force to restore hardline communists to power. In 1981, when Poland's Solidarity movement backed the Polish communist regime against the wall, the Soviets stiffened the resolve of Polish authorities to impose martial law and outlaw Solidarity. The Brezhnev government had no intention of losing its controls over Stalin's postwar empire in the region.

This dedication to projecting Soviet power abroad was another defining element of the Brezhnev regime. The Brezhnevites, like their predecessors, were ardent cold warriors. Brezhnev presided over an across-the-board expansion of Soviet military might that boosted spending in all branches of the armed forces. Over the course of the 1970s the USSR outproduced the entire NATO alliance in tanks and various forms of artillery, overtook the United States in the deployment of long-range guided missiles, and installed a new generation of intermediate-range missiles capable of striking Western Europe and Japan within minutes. This unrelenting military buildup occurred in spite of arms control agreements with the United States and talk of "détente," which was supposed to bring about a relaxation in East–West tensions.

Despite the continuing arms race, which required massive expenditures, neither the Soviet Union nor the United States ever achieved a decisive military advantage. Each country possessed thousands of nuclear bombs that they could rain on their adversary by aircraft, land-based intercontinental ballistic missiles, and submarine-based missiles. Each side thus possessed a "second-strike capability"—the USSR or the United States could each absorb a first strike by the other side and still have enough surviving nuclear bombs to obliterate the other side, killing tens of millions of people instantly and rendering the environment uninhabitable for decades through nuclear radiation. Radioactive clouds would then spread a "nuclear winter" over the globe, destroying most of the human race. This "mutual assured destruction" (MAD) kept the peace during the Cold War: whoever attacked first would be committing suicide. Fortunately, the leaders of both the Soviet Union and the United States were sufficiently rational (and nonsuicidal) to understand these realities, and they kept their disagreements from escalating into all-out war.

East–West relations suffered another rude jolt when the Soviet Union invaded Afghanistan in late 1979 to shore up a friendly leadership faction in a country teetering on the brink of civil war. The United States and other NATO countries responded by boycotting the 1980 Olympic Games held in Moscow.

It was the USSR's escalating military expenditures, however, that exacerbated the Brezhnev regime's most pressing problem, the economy. Khrushchev's attempts to tinker with the central planning system were little more than cosmetic in nature; he had no taste for free enterprise. Brezhnev retreated from even these modest changes and shelved plans for future experiments proposed by members of his leadership team. Aside from small private plots that collective farmers were allowed to maintain in order to grow food for their own consumption, the USSR had no private property. Everything from paper clips to space rockets were planned, produced, priced, and distributed by the government under the direction of the State Planning Commission (*Gosplan*). Basic consumer goods and services were heavily subsidized so as to curry favor with the population. Prices for bread, milk, potatoes, and other staples of the Russian diet were kept artificially low; so were prices for beef and pork, which were in shorter supply and quickly sold out. Transportation fares were minimal; rents were cheap; education was free from the lowest to the highest levels. Conversely, many goods were relatively more expensive than in the West. In the 1970s, an ordinary pair of shoes could cost a third of an average monthly wage; new cars were inordinately expensive and potential owners had to wait years before taking delivery.

Although in material terms most Soviet citizens lived better in the Brezhnev years than ever before in Russian history, by the 1970s the economy was stagnating. Between 1978 and 1985, the Soviet Union experienced zero economic growth. Annual increases in military spending took a growing slice out of a diminishing budgetary pie. After Gorbachev came to power and decided to cut military expenses drastically, the Soviets disclosed that their military spending was between one-fourth and one-third of GNP, far higher than the U.S. figure of about 6 percent of GNP.

Meanwhile, the Soviets were falling far behind the West and Japan in high-technology development. The Information Age left the USSR trailing its adversaries by a wide margin, particularly in such sectors as computers, software, and telecommunications. Communication, after all, is not something a dictatorship likes to encourage among its citizens. The Soviet Union's cumbrous planning system moved with bureaucratic lethargy and lacked the financial incentives that lure capitalist entrepreneurs and stimulate innovation. It proved poorly equipped to make the rapid improvements that market-oriented companies must constantly make in order to stay competitive.

Despite these problems, Brezhnev and his colleagues were even less inclined than Khrushchev to change the system they had known all their lives. Triumphalist slogans substituted for realistic self-criticism ("We are steadfastly fulfilling the plans of the 26th Party Congress!"). Rather than institute reforms, they purchased industrial goods from the West, such as pipelines and turbines. Even here, their resistance to capitalism was barely surmountable: Soviet trade with the outside world lagged far behind the averages for most other advanced economies and was conducted mainly with the communist-ruled states of Central and Eastern Europe.

When Brezhnev died in 1982, after nearly eighteen years in office, the ruling elite that clung to power for a few last years was a veritable gerontocracy: most members of the Politburo and other key committees were in their sixties or seventies. Brezhnev's immediate successor as party General Secretary was former KGB chief *Yuri Andropov*, who was sixty-eight when he took over. He was soon overcome by a debilitating illness and died in 1984. The next party chief, *Konstantin Chernenko*, was an old Brezhnev crony who assumed power at eighty-three. He died the following year. An entire generation of Soviet leaders was receding into history, a generation whose political careers and policy outlooks rightfully labeled them as Stalin's successors.[24]

## THE COLLAPSE OF SOVIET COMMUNISM

The accession of *Mikhail Gorbachev* to power brought to the fore not only a new generation but a radically new political orientation as well.

### PROFILE: Mikhail Gorbachev

"We can't go on living like this." Mikhail Gorbachev's words, spoken in March 1985 on the eve of his assumption of power in the Soviet Union, reflected his conviction that the USSR was on the brink of disaster. "By the mid 1980s," he later recalled, "our society resembled a steam boiler." Major changes were absolutely necessary; otherwise, he feared, "an explosion of colossal force would be inevitable."

The inertial forces that had led the USSR to such a catastrophic turning point were plainly visible. Growth rates had fallen by more than half since the early 1970s, leading Gorbachev to characterize the late Brezhnev years as an "era of stagnation." The country's industrial infrastructure, much of it built in the Stalinist epoch, was woefully outdated, and its high-technology lag behind the West and Japan was widening to unbridgeable lengths. Consumer goods were shoddy and scarce, environmental hazards widespread. Public health and even mortality rates were deteriorating. And the population lived in a state of political powerlessness and cultural isolation, demoralized by the regime's routine indifference to its everyday problems. Military expenditures gobbled up nearly 40 percent of the national budget.

The USSR's foreign policy had built a trenchline of confrontation around the world. Soviet troops were still bogged down in Afghanistan more than five years after an invasion that was supposed to have completed its aims within a few months. A major crisis with NATO over guided missiles was in progress: in 1983, several years after the Soviets began installing new missiles on their territory within range of Western Europe and much of Asia, NATO responded by deploying newly designed U.S. missiles in Western Europe, countering Moscow's move. And in Africa and the Middle East, governments and political movements friendly to the USSR received weaponry and other assistance from Moscow, enabling them to pursue their opposition to pro-Western interests and partners. On the whole, world politics was still dominated by Cold War hostilities and by fears that a nuclear holocaust might yet be unleashed by the two superpowers.

#### Youth and Early Career

At fifty-four, Gorbachev was the youngest of the twenty-one men who occupied the highest rungs of power in the Communist Party of the Soviet Union. Born in 1931 to a peasant family in southern Russia, Gorbachev grew up in a poverty-stricken collective farm region. Both of his grandfathers had been arrested on spurious charges during Stalin's terror. Young Mikhail also retained lifelong impressions of World War II. His village was occupied by German troops for several months, and his father fought in a number of major battles before returning home with a leg injury.

In 1950 Gorbachev was admitted to Moscow State University, the most prestigious university in the country. Following graduation in 1955, he returned to his native region of Stavropol, where he became a full-time Communist Party employee. Over the course of the next twenty-three years he remained in Stavropol as a CPSU functionary, rising to the top of the local political heap in 1970 with his appointment as chief of the district's party organization. Khrushchev's secret speech in 1956 was an event of profound importance in Gorbachev's life. In later years Gorbachev stated that he approved of the anti-Stalin campaign as a thoroughly justified attack on the oppressiveness of the Soviet system.

Though Stavropol is located at considerable distance from Moscow, Gorbachev took advantage of its attractiveness as a vacation resort for Soviet leaders to ingratiate himself with leading members of Brezhnev's ruling clique. These ties paid off in 1978, when he was appointed to the party's powerful Secretariat in Moscow and assigned responsibility for overseeing the Soviet agricultural system. His ability to point out shortcomings in the party's agricultural policies without calling the system itself into question won him quick promotions in Brezhnev's oligarchy. Within a year he was appointed a candidate member of the party Politburo, and the following year he became a full (voting) member.

After Brezhnev's death in 1982, his successor Yuri Andropov, who understood the urgent need for economic reorganization, took Gorbachev under his wing and gave every indication that he was grooming the younger man as his eventual replacement. But it was the aged Chernenko who stepped into Andropov's shoes in early 1984. As Chernenko's decrepitude proved an embarrassment to the mighty Soviet Union, Gorbachev increasingly stepped forward as the country's most dynamic spokesman. In 1984 he was chosen to lead a Soviet delegation to Italy and Britain; it was only his second trip outside the Soviet bloc. Prime Minister Margaret Thatcher was instantly impressed with Gorbachev's straightforwardness, assuring the world he was "a man I could do business with."

Gorbachev's crowning moment finally came on March 11, 1985. On the day after Chernenko's death, the party hierarchy elected him General Secretary.

### Starting the Reform Process

Gorbachev ascended the throne of Soviet power with a sure conviction that change was imperative, but with little clear idea of what to do. During his first year in power he adopted the term *restructuring* (*perestroika*) as the masthead of the reform process. But for nearly two years he provided no clear blueprint for a comprehensive economic or political transformation. Right from the start, however, Gorbachev recognized that no perestroika of any kind would be possible without broad public support. Shortly after assuming office he embarked on a series of trips around the country, employing his natural charm and communicative talents in exchanging views with crowds assembled on the streets and in factories. These spontaneous dialogues with the population stood in marked contrast to Gorbachev's distant and incommunicative predecessors and stimulated a groundswell of popular support for the new leader.

Gorbachev knew that any reform process would surely meet with resistance from the party apparatchiks and state bureaucrats who had run the Soviet political and economic system for decades. These officials were collectively known as the *nomenklatura.* Since Stalin's time, the nomenklatura were the occupiers of party and state jobs who were selected from lists of people approved by the Communist Party. This vast group, numbering 18 million by Gorbachev's account, had prospered under Brezhnev, constituting the Soviet Union's power elite. Gorbachev had no illusions about the fact that any serious reorganization of the economy and political institutions would have to upset the nomenklatura's power, privileges, and arrogant disdain for the people's needs and wishes.

Not long after taking office, Gorbachev therefore began combining his call for restructuring with equally persistent appeals for "democratization" and "openness" (*glasnost*). At least during his initial years in power, Gorbachev did not intend democratization to mean the replacement of Communist Party rule by a Western-style electoral democracy with competing political parties. Rather, he meant that the people should be granted greater latitude than in the past to articulate their demands for more effective government and for better treatment at the hands of party and government bureaucrats. Gorbachev's object was to give voice to public discontent as a means of exerting pressure on Soviet officials to support his reform plans. He fully intended to lead and guide the democratization process, channeling public frustration in the directions he desired rather than giving the population complete freedom to replace the communist system.

Gorbachev's concept of openness was similarly limited in its aims. It meant that the party and government elites who controlled the Soviet system should be more forthcoming with information about the true state of the Soviet Union's economic and social problems. Gorbachev wished to share essential information with the public with a view to stimulating open discussion of the country's problems. As with democratization, the aim of glasnost was to exert public pressure for change on the lethargic bureaucratic elite. At least in its initial stages, it was not designed to introduce full-scale freedom of speech of the kind guaranteed by the world's democracies. The explosion of a nuclear reactor in the Ukrainian town of Chernobyl in April 1986 provided Gorbachev with a powerful pretext for promoting his openness campaign. After some hesitation, his government informed the public about the gravity of the situation and opened up the damaged site to foreign technicians. From the outset, Gorbachev's dilemma was how to release the forces of democratization and openness without losing control over them. "What we had in mind," Gorbachev later wrote of his first years in power, "was not a revolution but a specific improvement of the situation."

But improvements were painfully slow in coming. Gorbachev's thoughts on perestroika remained vague, as a book he published on the subject testified.[25] Halfhearted, piecemeal reshufflings of the planning bureaucracy and shifts in its accounting procedures only seemed to generate confusion and opposition among the bureaucrats charged with implementing them, at times provoking outright sabotage. The introduction of market forces, such as privately owned restaurants and other services, remained strictly limited.[26]

As industrial production fell in 1987 and 1988, Boris Yeltsin, Gorbachev's appointee as the Communist Party boss of the city of Moscow, emerged as an outspoken critic of the slow pace of the reform process. But as the radical reformers pressed their attacks on Gorbachev, so did the entrenched party elite and their supporters, now openly in revolt at the changes being forced on them.

### 1989

In an effort to undercut the power of the party apparatchiks and encourage their replacement by reform-minded communists more attuned to his own thinking, Gorbachev called for the creation of a new legislative body, the Congress of People's Deputies, to act as the country's supreme lawmaking organ. Daringly, he insisted that a portion of the new legislature be elected by the people rather than handpicked by the party. Once again, Gorbachev's hope was to energize his reform process through limited democratization without fully relinquishing control over it. Of the 2,250 Congress deputies, 750 were to be elected; the rest (including Gorbachev himself) were to be appointed by the party hierarchy. Candidates for the electoral contests were to be nominated by organizations traditionally dominated by the Communist Party, such as the Communist Youth League and the official trade union organization. Gorbachev thus had good reason to believe that friendly communists would thoroughly dominate the new legislature. To his surprise, the nomination process sparked considerable participation by people eager for far more radical reform than Gorbachev was offering. The country became politically energized as 170 million people were given the right to vote in the first contested elections since 1917. Gorbachev's efforts to effect change from above had awakened long-dormant demands for change from below.

The results of the 1989 elections to the Congress were a shock to the Communist Party elite. Although approved party stalwarts won the majority of contests, dozens of fairly prominent officials were humiliatingly defeated. In a number of races where unpopular officials ran unopposed, the candidates lost when a majority of voters took advantage of their right to vote against them. The winners included reform-minded party candidates as well as academics and others calling for more radical reforms. The most prominent winner of all was Yeltsin, who scored a resounding triumph in Moscow after being demoted by Gorbachev for criticizing the government's feeble reform policies.

From this moment on, Gorbachev increasingly lost control over the reform process. Far more alarmingly, the winds of democratic change swirling in the Soviet Union could not help but have a devastating effect on the communist-run governments of Central and Eastern Europe. Within only a few hectic months, the emergence of democracy in the USSR would sweep away communist rule from the Soviet Union's hard-won postwar empire.

### Gorbachev's Foreign Policy

From its very beginnings, Gorbachev's policy of domestic reform had an important foreign policy component. One of the principal obstacles to economic growth and modernization in the Soviet economy was the stultifying effect of military spending. Gorbachev knew that if the economy was to be rescued, he had to remove the dead weight of the Soviet military-industrial complex on the budgetary process and the powerful political influence of the high command. Changes of this sort inevitably required a radical reorientation in the Kremlin's policies toward the West.

Considering that the Cold War had dominated international politics for forty years, it was extraordinary how rapidly the two contending superpowers resolved so many differences and transformed their relationship from nuclear-armed antagonism to negotiated cooperation and a growing measure of trust.

A quick meeting between Gorbachev and President Ronald Reagan in 1985 broke the ice and established a personal rapport between the two leaders. The first major result of the heady new atmosphere came in December 1987, when the two sides agreed on the elimination of all the intermediate range missiles they had installed in the European theater in recent years (along with Soviet missiles facing Asia). Thus ended one of the most rancorous disputes of the Cold War. For the first time, the superpowers agreed to destroy hundreds of existing missiles, with each side permitting on-site inspection teams from the other side to verify compliance. In 1988, Gorbachev declared his intention of withdrawing all Soviet troops from Afghanistan in the following year (a goal achieved in February 1989) and announced plans to reduce the Soviet military by 500,000 troops within two years.

**Soviet leader Mikhail Gorbachev and U.S. President Ronald Reagan sign the treaty providing for the destruction of Soviet and NATO intermediate range nuclear missiles, 1987.**

But it was in East Central Europe that the Gorbachev phenomenon had its most unexpected consequences. Gorbachev hoped that the ruling communist parties in the area would replace their repressive, Brezhnev-style regimes with more pliable reform-oriented communists like himself. He also gave hints that the USSR would no longer intervene with troops to rescue communist regimes encountering opposition from their populations. He understood that military intervention in Central and Eastern Europe would abruptly snap his cooperative ties with the United States and its allies.

The tumultuous East European revolutions of 1989 began quietly enough. As the year got under way, Hungary's ruling communist party, whose reformist wing was even more radical than Gorbachev's, announced it would hold democratic, multiparty elections the following year. In April, shortly after the first elections to the Congress of People's Deputies in the Soviet Union, the Polish government completed eight weeks of intensive bargaining with representatives of the once-outlawed Solidarity organization. The "round-table agreement" committed the Polish communists to holding elections to a new parliament, with Solidarity permitted to compete for a minority of the lower house seats and all the upper house seats. When the elections were held in June, Solidarity swept into parliament, setting the stage for the complete replacement of communist rule in 1990 with the election of Lech Walesa, Solidarity's leader, as Poland's president.

By far the most dramatic transformation occurred in East Germany, where a hardline communist elite incensed at Gorbachev's reformism clung to power. As thousands of East Germans managed to flee to Western Europe in the summer and spontaneous demonstrations took place in East German cities in the following months, Moscow showed no readiness to support a military crackdown on a society in open revolt against communist power. In November, the East German authorities decided to open the Berlin wall, the fortress-like barrier that had prevented East Germans from traveling freely to West Germany for nearly thirty years. The opening released a surge of pent-up opposition to communism and a desire on the part of most East Germans to be united with West Germany. The communist state, once the most heavily guarded outpost of the Soviet Union's East Central European empire, swiftly disintegrated, permitting the incorporation of eastern Germany into the Federal Republic of Germany in 1990.[27]

The East German example immediately inspired millions of Czechoslovaks to take to the streets of Prague to vent their anger against an equally anti-reformist communist dictatorship. With no signs of imminent assistance from Gorbachev, the Czechoslovak authorities quietly yielded power to democratic forces led by Vaclav Havel, the playwright who epitomized the country's courageous dissident movement. In December, scarcely a month after Czechoslovakia's "velvet revolution," demonstrators in Bucharest shouted down the country's tyrannical dictator, Nicolae Ceausescu, in the middle of a speech. He was immediately arrested by rivals within Romania's communist elite and subsequently executed. Meanwhile, the Soviet Union engineered a behind-the-scenes transfer of power in Bulgaria, replacing an aging communist autocrat with a more flexible party leadership.[28]

To the world's astonishment, the Soviet Union's reformist government had let East Central Europe and the Warsaw Pact military alliance slip through its fingers. In the West, Gorbachev won universal acclaim and was awarded the Nobel Peace Prize. But at home, hardline critics of his reformist policies were mortified. At the same time, proponents of an even more radical reform course set the stage for the USSR's eventual disintegration.

### The USSR Falls Apart

As resistance to Gorbachev stiffened at all levels of the CPSU, Gorbachev sought to shift the locus of decision-making power in the Soviet Union from the party organs, over which he presided as General Secretary, to newly created state institutions like the Congress of People's Deputies. In March 1990 the Congress elected him to a new post as president of the Soviet Union. At no time, however, was Gorbachev ever elected to any of his positions by popular vote. His failure to obtain a mandate from the people was a significant factor in accelerating the collapse of his authority.

Time, however, was running out on Gorbachev's efforts to reform a one-party system that was proving highly resistant to change. The public's patience was also wearing thin as the economy continued to deteriorate. Lacking a clear policy vision, Gorbachev was caught in a tug-of-war between traditionalists who hoped to preserve the central planning system with as few alterations as possible, and an increasingly vocal group of radicals who believed that the system was incapable of being reformed and needed to be replaced by a market economy. Attempts to forge a compromise between a market economy and central planning proved futile. Gorbachev's refusal to permit the privatization of Russia's collective farms was another major disappointment for the market-oriented reformers.[29]

An equally serious problem was the growth of independence movements in key Soviet republics. Gorbachev's democratization policies had mobilized the populations of Lithuania, Latvia, and Estonia to militate for independence, some fifty years after they were annexed by Stalin. Even Communist Party leaders in the Baltic states joined in the liberation movements. After elections held in 1990 brought pro independence forces to power, Lithuania declared its independence and the other two states announced their intention to secede from the Soviet Union in the near future. Separatist movements also sprang up in Georgia, Armenia, and other Soviet republics. Far more ominously for Gorbachev, the Russian Republic, the largest and most populous part of the USSR, was also moving toward greater independence from the central government. In March 1990 Russia elected its own parliament. Two months later, Russian legislators elected Boris Yeltsin as the Russian Republic's top official in spite of Gorbachev's explicit opposition to the move. The Russian legislature then took the bold step of declaring that its laws superseded the laws of the Soviet Union within its territory, a flagrant repudiation of Gorbachev's central Soviet government.

Over the summer months of 1990, Ukraine and several other Soviet republics declared their sovereignty within the USSR. Gorbachev's efforts to halt the Soviet Union's progressive dismemberment proved futile. When Soviet military forces launched attacks in Latvia and Lithuania in early 1991, Gorbachev was roundly criticized in the West and the troops had to be withdrawn. The USSR was crumbling beneath his feet.

In June 1991, the first popular elections ever held for president of Russia gave Boris Yeltsin a strong popular mandate to lead the Russian Republic. It also gave him a popular legitimacy that Gorbachev, who never faced the voters, could not claim. Gorbachev worked assiduously to negotiate an agreement with most of the constituent republics of the USSR to establish a new set of ground rules for the Soviet Union. With the final draft completed, he set off on a fateful vacation in the Crimea in early August.

### The 1991 Coup and Its Aftermath

Gorbachev and his family knew that something was amiss when they were informed that a group of uninvited senior officials had arrived at the Soviet president's vacation retreat. Before receiving the visitors, Gorbachev picked up the phone to call the head of the KGB in Moscow, Vladimir Kryuchkov, only to find the telephone lines cut off. Kryuchkov was in fact the ringleader of a plot to remove Gorbachev from power and reimpose a stern Communist Party dictatorship. The delegation sent to the Crimea by the conspirators instructed Gorbachev to sign a decree declaring a state of emergency throughout the USSR and urged him to resign. According to his own account, Gorbachev refused both ultimata.

From August 18 to 21, the Gorbachevs were prisoners in their official country house: armed guards patrolled the grounds, Soviet warships cruised into the neighboring bay, all communication links were broken. The small band of conspirators included the vice president, prime minister, defense minister, interior minister, the head of Soviet ground forces, the head of the military-industrial complex, Gorbachev's chief of staff, the chief of his personal security detail, and a few others. But right from the outset, the coup attempt went awry.

On hearing the news, Russia's President Yeltsin rushed to the White House, the home of the Russian parliament. Mounting one of the tanks the plotters had ordered into downtown Moscow, Yeltsin denounced the coup as illegal and called on the citizens of Russia to oppose it. Together with a group of Russian officials, he then ensconced himself in the White House while barricades went up outside its doors. At noon he went on radio and appealed to Soviet military forces to refrain from shedding blood. Within a few hours some 25,000 people were forming a protective phalanx outside the parliament. Yeltsin called for a general strike of the whole population.

The coup then unraveled like a bizarre comedy. One of the plotters called a televised press conference only to be bombarded with embarrassing questions. Clearly rattled, his hands shook visibly as his answers were greeted with derision. Another plotter, the prime minister, was drunk. The next day, Yeltsin addressed 100,000 people from the White House balcony, and the crowds surrounding the barricades grew larger. Soviet generals and KGB leaders met to discuss how to disperse the throng, but the high command was divided: a number of commanders and other officers were clearly reluctant to attack the civilians in front of the White House. Later that evening, the plotters made the crucial decision to back away from the use of force. At 3 AM the KGB chief called the White House to inform Yeltsin that the coup was over.

On August 21, a Russian government delegation went to the Crimea to escort Gorbachev and his weary family home. Gorbachev's wife and daughter both suffered nervous disorders as a result of their ordeal. The plotters were arrested, with the exception of two who committed suicide. (All were eventually released without being convicted in court.) On arriving in Moscow, Gorbachev found himself in "a new country": for the first time in their history, Russian citizens had openly defied the coercive power of the state and won a victory for democracy.[30]

For Gorbachev himself, the end of his extraordinary run in office was at hand. Over the next several months, Yeltsin took full advantage of his enormous popularity and orchestrated the final disintegration of the Union of Soviet Socialist Republics. On December 25, Gorbachev resigned the presidency of a country that was about to expire. As the bells tolled midnight on December 31, the USSR formally ceased to exist. Looking back on his experience several years later, Gorbachev wrote, "I never for a moment thought that the transformations I had initiated, no matter how far-reaching, would result in the replacement of the rule of the 'reds' by that of the 'whites'." With the failure of his attempt to reform Soviet communism, the fate of Russia now passed into noncommunist hands for the first time since the October Revolution seventy-four years earlier.[31]

**Gorbachev's Legacy** Unquestionably, Gorbachev left office having granted the Russian people far more freedom than they had ever before enjoyed. Greater freedom of speech and the ability to criticize the ruling authorities without fear of violent retribution; growing freedom of political association and opportunities to vote in competitive elections; freedom of religious worship; freedom to leave the country; freedom to own private property and start a business—these and other liberties that emerged in the course of Gorbachev's tenure, however limited in scope, would have been unimaginable under previous communist leaders. Most of the *political* liberties Gorbachev permitted (as opposed to the economic liberties) were in fact unprecedented in Russian history, if one regards the few brief months of constitutional democracy under the Provisional Government in 1917 as but a momentary aberration.

But no account of Gorbachev's leadership would be accurate without a reminder of the limitations of his initiatives. To the very end of his incumbency, Gorbachev made no serious attempt to subject himself or the nomenklatura to precisely defined laws guaranteeing their public accountability, not even when it was clear that the apparatus was blocking his reforms. He vigorously opposed the establishment of new parties that might challenge the CPSU's monopoly of power. The principle of freedom of speech was never fully codified into law. Gorbachev's economic reforms were just as restricted as his political reforms, carefully calibrated to retain the party's control over the country and, not incidentally, his own primacy within the party.

Unlike Poland and Czechoslovakia, where discredited communist leaders negotiated pacts with their opponents that ultimately led to democracy, there was no "pacted transition" in the Soviet Union. On the contrary, Gorbachev's program of limited reform was imposed on the party and the population from the top down, with no substantive input from the grass roots of Soviet society. Moreover, pro-democracy forces did not enjoy a preponderance of power in Gorbachev's USSR as they did in Poland, Czechoslovakia, Hungary, and East Germany in 1989. As Michael McFaul has pointed out, the relatively even balance of power between moderate reformers, hardline opponents of reform, and advocates of much more radical reform prompted the coup plotters to believe that they could take full control in August 1991—a gross miscalculation. With no compromise possible among these competing groups over such fundamental issues as the nature of the economic system and the relationship between the Soviet Union and its constituent republics, the USSR collapsed in a way that left the prospects for democracy unclear.[32]

In sum, Gorbachev's policies triggered a real revolution in Russian politics, but it was an unintended revolution. It was a revolution pushed forward by the forces of mass expectations for change and elite disarray that he had unleashed but could not rein in. In his heart of hearts, Gorbachev was a *reformer,* not a revolutionary. Perhaps no one better understood the limitations of Gorbachev's approach more deeply than the man who would rise as his most vocal challenger and ultimate successor: *Boris Yeltsin.*

## YELTSIN'S RUSSIA

**Yeltsin's Rise to Power** Like Gorbachev, Boris Yeltsin was born in 1931 into a peasant family. He passed his childhood in grueling poverty, aggravated by the fears that stalked Stalinist Russia. Yeltsin earned a civil engineering degree and subsequently joined the Communist Party in his native region of Sverdlovsk, an industrial city in the Ural Mountains. Party functionaries took a liking to Yeltsin's take-charge instincts, and in 1976 he was appointed chief of Sverdlovsk's Communist Party organization, a position that made him the most powerful political figure in the region. Over the next ten years he quietly built a reputation as one of the Soviet Union's most successful local leaders.

In 1985, Mikhail Gorbachev, newly ensconced as the party's General Secretary, summoned Yeltsin to Moscow and put him in charge of a party Central Committee section that supervised the Soviet construction industry. At the end of the year Yeltsin gained even more prestige when he was named chief of the Communist Party's Moscow city organization. Yeltsin now had the authority to govern the Soviet Union's capital city, the hub of its highly centralized political system. Although Yeltsin's main task was to implement Gorbachev's reform program, it soon became apparent that the two men had radically different concepts of both the scope and the pace of the reform process.

Yeltsin vigorously charged into his assignment, immersing himself in the daily life of the city. Before long he was railing against the privileges of the party elite, who had their pick of special shops, hospitals, cars, and other perquisites of power that the mass of Soviet citizens could only dream about. Convinced that the local party apparatus was riddled with inefficiency and corruption, he fired half its members. In the process, Yeltsin became increasingly critical of Gorbachev himself, viewing him as indecisive and far too reticent to take on the entrenched bureaucrats who were determined to block reform. At a meeting of the Communist Party's powerful Central Committee in 1987, Yeltsin delivered a stinging critique of the party's failure to implement a concrete reform program. He accused Gorbachev of building a "personality cult"—the very same charge that Khrushchev had leveled at Stalin in his famous secret speech of 1956. For his transgressions, Yeltsin was summarily dismissed from his Moscow post and consigned to a demeaning job in the bureaucracy. At this juncture, Yeltsin considered himself a political corpse.

Ironically, Gorbachev's political reforms provided Yeltsin with unexpected openings to revive his political career. In the 1989 elections to Gorbachev's newly created legislature, the Congress of People's Deputies, Yeltsin captured more than 89 percent of the votes in his Moscow legislative district, soundly thrashing his Gorbachev-backed opponent.[33] In the USSR's Russian Republic, Yeltsin made his next, most decisive, moves. In 1990, the various constituent republics of the Soviet Union elected their own legislatures. Yeltsin became a member of Russia's parliament, which soon declared that its laws would henceforward take precedence over Soviet laws throughout the Russian Republic.

Yeltsin then dramatically announced his resignation from the Communist Party. Yeltsin got another boost in June 1991, when he went before the people in the first-ever popular election to Russia's presidency. Deftly playing upon mounting dissatisfaction with Gorbachev's ineffectiveness, he won a convincing 57.3 percent of the vote, besting five rivals.

Scarcely two months after this electoral triumph, the coup aimed at unseating Gorbachev from power suddenly presented Yeltsin with his greatest challenge. Curiously, in a book published before that pivotal event, Yeltsin had asserted that he would support Gorbachev if a coup were ever attempted. "Yes, I shall fight for him," he wrote, "my perpetual opponent, the lover of half-measures and half-steps." Gorbachev was infinitely preferable to the Brezhnevite old guard. Once the coup took place, Yeltsin bravely resisted the plotters in Gorbachev's behalf. In the process, he became the effective leader not only of the coup's opponents but of all those who wanted a clean break with the hard-line communists. After the coup collapsed, Yeltsin pushed Gorbachev to the sidelines. Over the next several months, Yeltsin worked frenetically to dismantle the last vestiges of the Soviet leader's power by dismantling the Soviet Union itself. In December, Russia and eight other Soviet republics formed the Commonwealth of Independent States, a loose organization in which each member state agreed to respect the sovereign independence of all the others. With the Soviet state now a legal fiction, Gorbachev resigned as president of the USSR on December 25, 1991. A few days later, when he returned to his Kremlin office to remove his effects, he found Yeltsin already in his place.[34]

On January 1, 1992, the Russian Federation formally entered the world as an independent country under President Boris Yeltsin.

**Transforming the Economy** Yeltsin and his advisors wasted no time in their attempts to transform Russia's economy from a largely state-run operation to a mixed economy with market mechanisms. To some extent they were guided by prescriptions offered by Western economists, who called for a rapid "shock therapy" approach to restructuring the economy. Advocates of shock therapy—or the "big bang," as some called it—argued that it would be better to change the economic system all at once rather than in a piecemeal process stretched out over a long period of time. But quite a few Russian economists and political leaders feared that an excessively rapid transformation program might trigger social disruptions and political instability. Yeltsin's government therefore began with a partial approach to shock therapy, adopting bits and pieces of the shock therapists' guidelines rather than their entire program. Even so, Yeltsin's initial measures went considerably farther than Gorbachev's, and their effects were shocking enough for many Russians.[35]

On January 2, 1992, the day after Russia formally became an independent state, the government removed government price controls on a host of products and lifted wage controls on various job categories. The new administration also announced substantial cuts in military spending and other items to reduce the budget deficit. Several months later it declared the convertibility of the ruble, permitting it to be exchanged into other denominations in world currency markets. Most important, over the course of its first year in power the new Russian government unveiled an ambitious privatization timetable. Half the state's large and medium-size companies were expected to be privatized by 1995, and all state-owned small industries and consumer services and a considerable portion of the nation's housing were to be in private hands by 1994. A plan to turn Russia's population into shareholders in the newly privatized companies went awry, however. In 1992 the government handed out vouchers to more than 140 million people. The vouchers were investment securities, to be retained or sold like stocks. "We need millions of owners," Yeltsin declared, "rather than a handful of millionaires." But many Russians failed to understand what the vouchers were all about, or they simply did not believe they were worth very much. Some sold them cheaply or gave them away, with shrewd investors and insiders acquiring a disproportionately large share.

From the outset, the Yeltsin government's economic initiatives failed to meet the expectations of the optimists in the president's entourage. Inflation soared 20 to 30 percent per month, finishing out 1992 at 2,500 percent for the year. Though more food and other goods began appearing on store shelves, prices were too high for many Russians, long habituated under the old central planning system to cheap government-subsidized prices for milk, bread, and other staples. Gross domestic product in 1992 was 18.5 percent lower than in the previous year and plummeted another 12 percent in 1993. The Russian government's budget deficits bulged to as much as 20 percent of GDP, a figure more than double the IMF's recommended target. The government lacked the funds to pay millions of people employed in the state sector, while pensions fell far behind the galloping price increases. Unemployment grew to more than 150,000 in 1992, a far cry from the zero unemployment the old communist regime used to boast. By 1994 some 24 million people—more than 16 percent of the population—lived below the government's official poverty line, a subsistence level of $1 to $2 a day. Meanwhile, a small minority of ambitious capitalists, some of them with exceptional political connections or ties to criminal elements, reaped overnight fortunes, resulting in a widening gap between rich and poor. The stresses of economic change and uncertainty had a visible impact on public health.[36]

Not surprisingly, support for market reforms and even for democracy itself began to dissipate during Yeltsin's first years as president of independent Russia. By 1992, only 42 percent of Muscovites identified themselves as part of the "democratic camp," down from 62 percent following the previous year's coup attempt against Gorbachev. Less than two years later, only 25 percent of Russians said they favored market reforms, compared with 40 percent in 1989; a majority described privatization as "legalized theft." Nevertheless, the Yeltsin government persevered in its reform course. By the end of 1994, half the work force was employed by private enterprise, while 70 percent of Russian industry was privatized and over a million small businesses were in operation. It was the *political* aspect of economic reform that was to cause Yeltsin more headaches than the privatization process per se.

**The Politics of Reform** On assuming control of the newly independent Russian state, Yeltsin inherited the legislature that had been elected in the Russian part of the Soviet Union in March 1990, a time when the Communist Party of the Soviet Union still dominated the Soviet political system. Of 1,046 deputies elected to Russia's Congress of People's Deputies that year, only about a hundred were strongly committed to Yeltsin's vision of radical economic transformation, with perhaps another 150 willing to support Yeltsin fairly consistently. Divided into as many as seventeen factions, the Congress included more than 350 hardliners opposed to the wholesale dismantling of the state-controlled economic system. At the end of 1992 the anti-reform majority in the Congress pressured Yeltsin to jettison his young prime minister, Yegor Gaidar.[37]

The clash between President Yeltsin and his anti-reform opponents escalated throughout 1992 and 1993. In April 1993 a referendum gave Yeltsin a boost of popular approval: some 58 percent of those who turned out to vote expressed their confidence in him. Yeltsin dissolved the legislature in September and ordered new parliamentary elections to be held three months later. Yeltsin admitted that his action violated the existing constitution, but he insisted that the April referendum had given him the right to take extraordinary measures to break the country's political gridlock. Incensed at Yeltsin's breach of constitutional authority, hardline politicians declared that Yeltsin was no longer the legitimate president of Russia. They barricaded themselves in the White House, the legislature's home, and named one of their leaders, Vice President Alexander Rutskoi, as Russia's new president.

The crisis threatened to crack the fragile foundations of Russian democracy. After eleven days of confrontation, Rutskoi ordered thousands of anti-Yeltsin demonstrators to storm the state-owned television station, a beacon of pro-Yeltsin propaganda. Fortified with assault weapons and waving Communist Party flags, the crowd next marched on the Moscow mayor's office. Yeltsin responded to this provocation the next day, October 4, by ordering a military attack on the White House. Leading generals decided to support Yeltsin as the only duly elected president of the country. The operation was quick and effective: Rutskoi and others were arrested, and parts of the White House were set ablaze. More than a hundred people were killed in the fracas, with hundreds more wounded.

Yeltsin declared a state of emergency, imposed censorship, and reaffirmed his plan to set new legislative elections for December. The Russian people would also be asked to vote on a new constitution prepared under his direction. In a marked display of anger at Russia's Constitutional Court, which had declared his dissolution of the legislature illegal, Yeltsin pressured the chief justice to resign and summarily fired the court. The manner in which Yeltsin used his manifestly superior power over his opponents in the fall of 1993—imposing a new constitutional order on Russia with practically no public debate—was bound to have long-term effects on the quality of Russia's democracy. It made for a prolonged transition process in which the balance of institutional power would tilt heavily in the direction of a strong presidency, leaving the legislature and the courts in considerably weaker positions.[38]

**The 1993 Elections and Constitutional Referendum** The parliamentary elections and constitutional referendum held on December 12, 1993, returned a mixed result for President Yeltsin. On the positive side, the voters overwhelmingly approved Yeltsin's proposed constitution, with 58.4 percent voting in its favor. The new charter created a dual executive modeled on the French constitution, with a politically active president sharing power with a prime minister. The bicameral legislature, as in France, was kept relatively weak. (We'll discuss the constitution's provisions later in this chapter.) When the new constitution entered into force on January 1, 1994, the so-called Second Russian Republic was born, replacing the First Russian Republic of the previous two years. The vote for the new lower house, the State Duma, was considerably less satisfactory from Yeltsin's point of view. The electoral system involved a combination of proportional representation (with a 5 percent hurdle) and single-member districts: half the Duma's 450 seats were elected under PR and the other half under the SMD/plurality system. (See chapter 8 for a description of these electoral systems.) Thirteen parties fielded candidates, most of them fairly new.

Shockingly, the party to emerge with the largest share of the popular vote was the *Liberal Democratic Party (LDP)*, an arch-nationalist grouping under the leadership of *Vladimir Zhirinovsky*, a flamboyant right-winger with outrageously chauvinistic views. The LDP ended up with sixty-four seats.

Another determined foe of Yeltsin's economic policies was the *Communist Party of the Russian Federation (CPRF;* also known as the *Russian Communist Party,* or *RCP)*. Led by *Gennady Zyuganov*, a party apparatchik since the 1960s, the Communists opposed the rapid economic transformation process but offered no clear alternative program. Professing their acceptance of democracy, they blasted Yeltsin for abusing his authority. Although they had the largest party organization in the country, they captured only forty-one seats, a convincing sign that most Russians wanted nothing more to do with communism. A close ally of the Communists, the *Agrarian Party*, won sixteen Duma seats.

The most outspokenly pro-reform party, *Russia's Choice*, garnered a disappointing sixty-five seats in the Duma.[39] Quite a few voters gravitated instead to moderate parties that were favorable to economic reform in principle but opposed to the accelerated tempo of shock therapy. The most successful was *Yabloko*, a party whose name derived from *Grigory Yavlinsky* and two other co-founders. (*Yabloko* is the Russian word for apple.) Yavlinsky, a Western-oriented economist, advocated a socially harmonious path to reform and opposed Yeltsin's constitution, with its highly centralized presidential power. Yabloko won twenty-seven seats. Two other moderate reform parties together won twenty-six seats.

The divisions in the Duma among these and other contending parties were further complicated by the election of some 136 independent candidates with no party affiliation at all. In the end, about 220 of the Duma's 450 members were opposed to serious economic reform, while even many reformers had reservations about Yeltsin's economic policies and political style. (See table 20.1.) The Duma's checkered political composition was to create insurmountable problems for Yeltsin. The lack of a clear popular mandate for radical reform and the absence of a reliable majority of Duma deputies in Yeltsin's favor resulted in a series of policy flip-flops and political maneuvers that were to plague Yeltsin's presidency until his resignation on New Year's Eve, 1999.

**Chechnya** On December 11, 1994, an invasion force of forty thousand Russian troops stormed into *Chechnya*. The operation sought to put a quick end to a secessionist movement that threatened to

**TABLE 20.1**

**State Duma Elections, 1993 and 1995**

| Party | Seats Won in PR Party List | | Seats Won in Districts | | Total Seats | | % of Seats | |
|---|---|---|---|---|---|---|---|---|
| | 1993 | 1995 | 1993 | 1995 | 1993 | 1995 | 1993 | 1995 |
| Left (socialist) wing | | | | | | | | |
| Communists (CPRF) | 32 | 99 | 9 | 50 | 41 | 149 | 9.1 | 33.1 |
| Agrarian Party | 21 | 0 | 16 | 35 | 37 | 35 | 8.2 | 7.7 |
| People's Power | — | 0 | — | 37 | — | 37 | — | 8.2 |
| Centrists (moderate reformers) | | | | | | | | |
| Yabloko | 20 | 31 | 7 | 15 | 27 | 46 | 6.0 | 10.2 |
| Our Home Is Russia | — | 45 | — | 20 | — | 65 | — | 14.4 |
| Unity and Accord | 18 | — | 3 | — | 21 | — | 4.7 | — |
| Russian Regions | — | 0 | — | 41 | — | 41 | — | 9.1 |
| Women of Russia | 21 | 0 | 2 | 3 | 23 | 3 | 5.1 | 0.7 |
| Others | 14 | — | 16 | — | 29 | — | 6.4 | — |
| Radical Reformers | | | | | | | | |
| Russia's Choice | 40 | — | 25 | — | 65 | — | 14.4 | — |
| Russia's Democratic Choice | — | 0 | — | 9 | — | 9 | — | 2.0 |
| Nationalists | | | | | | | | |
| Liberal Democratic Party | 59 | 50 | 5 | 1 | 64 | 51 | 14.2 | 11.3 |
| Independents and small parties | 0 | 0 | 136 | 14 | 136 | 14 | 30.2 | 3.1 |

*Sources:* Timothy J. Colton and Jerry F. Hough, eds., *Growing Pains: Russian Democracy and the Election of 1993* (Washington, D.C.: Brookings Institution, 1998); and Jerry F. Hough, Evelyn Davidheiser, and Susan Goodrich Lehmann, *The 1996 Russian Presidential Election* (Washington, D.C.: Brookings Institution, 1996). Six seats went unfilled in 1993.

unravel Russia's structure as a federated state. Based largely on the territorial subdivisions of the former USSR, the Russian Federation consisted of eighty-nine administrative units (see figure 20.1). Though most had an ethnic Russian majority, twenty-one of these subdivisions, designated as *republics,* had a non-Russian majority. Most had been incorporated into Russia's expanding empire in the tsarist era. Chechnya was acquired by conquest in 1859. Though the Chechens' origins are obscure, they are a distinct ethnic group practicing Islam. Resistance to tsarist rule earned the Chechens a reputation as the most rebellious people in the empire. The region suffered heavily under Stalin, who deported a half million Chechens and nearby Ingush from their homelands during and after World War II, allegedly because of complicity with the German army.

Right from the first months of Russia's existence as an independent state in 1992, the leadership of the Chechen Republic, an area smaller than Massachusetts nestled in the Caucasus Mountains, began militating for complete independence. Chechnya had a population of about 1.2 million in that year, of whom only about 250,000 were Russians. But any attempt to break out of the freshly established Russian Federation constituted a serious provocation to the central government in Moscow, which had reason to fear that other regions might insist on independence as well if the Chechens succeeded. Moreover, an underground oil pipeline ran through Chechnya, giving it enhanced economic importance.

Yeltsin's administration paid little attention to Chechnya until the summer of 1994, when it sent in troops from the Federal Counterintelligence Service, a successor to the Soviet-era KGB. The Chechens quickly repulsed the small force. On December 2, Soviet planes began bombing Grozny, Chechnya's capital city. With the invasion nine days later, the war was on.

Yeltsin's defense minister assured the civilian leadership that the operation would be "a piece of cake," lasting anywhere from a few hours to a week. It quickly became apparent that the Chechens were dug in for a protracted conflict. Casualties mounted heavily, with estimates running between forty thousand and sixty thousand civilians killed by the

**FIGURE 20.1 Russia's Subdivisions**
*Source:* U.S. Central Intelligence Agency

end of 1995. Several hundred thousand Chechens became refugees; reports of rape and looting by Russian troops were widespread.[40]

Opposition to the war flared up across the political spectrum. Only a few weeks after Russian troops entered Chechnya, public opposition to the war ran as high as 75 percent, while Yeltsin's personal popularity plunged to single digits. Stung by these reactions, Yeltsin moved closer to his more conservative advisors in the intelligence and military wings of his government—centered in his secretive National Security Council—and appeared to turn his back on the reformers.

The mounting strains finally caught up with Yeltsin's health. In the summer of 1995, Yeltsin was hospitalized with cardiac ischemia, a condition brought on by stress and alcohol. In the fall he was hospitalized again for the same problem as the legislative elections of December 1995 approached.

**The Legislative Elections of December 1995** The first Duma was elected to serve only a two-year term. If Yeltsin had hoped to widen his popularity during those two years, he was bound to be disappointed. Between 20 percent and 40 percent of the population lived below the poverty line in 1995. The richest 10 percent earned fourteen times the income of the poorest 10 percent—a gap that had widened appreciably since 1993. Some 40 percent of state employees had not been paid in full or on time. Out on the land, the 1995 grain harvest was the worst in thirty years.

Meanwhile, the privatization process was slowing down. With some of the largest state-owned companies still in government hands, managers, banks, and political insiders worked quietly behind the scenes to acquire large stakes in their privatization. Gazprom, the largest gas company in the world, shifted more than 60 percent of its assets to politically connected insiders, with the state retaining the rest. Hopes for a "people's capitalism" based on widespread stock ownership were giving way to "crony capitalism" and "market Bolshevism." A new breed of powerful tycoons, some with ties to the old Soviet regime and all with carefully cultivated connections with the current political elite, was taking over the "commanding heights" of the Russian economy, including banks, energy firms, mines, television stations, publishing houses, holding companies, and other lucrative assets.[41] In addition, the criminal networks that made up the Russian mafia cast an ominous shadow over the entire economy, extorting protection money from businesspeople, bribing public officials, and extending their criminal operations across Russia and around the world. Crime in general was also on the rise, especially violent crime.[42]

A poll taken in the summer revealed that 78 percent were dissatisfied with their economic status and 62 percent were worse off than in 1990. Although only a third favored the restoration of communist rule (mostly elderly), only 10 percent viewed Yeltsin favorably, while 10 percent said they wanted a tsar and 12 percent favored military rule.[43]

Not surprisingly, the elections held in December 1995 were a sharp rebuke to Yeltsin. The Communists staged a comeback. With slightly more than a third of the Duma, the Communists emerged as Russia's largest party. Opponents of Yeltsin's reform policies held the majority. The radical reformers, now regrouped in the Democratic Choice of Russia party, fared badly, winning only nine seats. The somewhat more moderate reform party, Yabloko, did slightly better with forty-five seats. (See table 20.1.) Perhaps the only positive result from the government's vantage point was that the anti-reform parties had failed to acquire the two-thirds supermajority needed to veto most presidential decrees. Because the constitution conferred considerable decree-making authority and policy initiative on the president, Yeltsin could at least hope to circumvent the legislature in the struggles that loomed inevitably before him. First, however, he would have to win reelection in a troubled electoral environment.

**The 1996 Presidential Election** At sixty-five and in poor health, Yeltsin entered the presidential fray against nine other contenders with surprising vigor. But the first polls showed him trailing his chief rival, Gennady Zyuganov of the Russian Communist Party. Zyuganov appealed to Russian voters nostalgic for "the good old days" of economic stability and international respect in the former USSR.

Recognizing that his chances were slim as long as the bloody Chechen war dragged on, Yeltsin arranged a hasty meeting with a separatist leader and signed a cease-fire, promising Chechnya maximum autonomy within the Russian Federation. Some sixty to eighty thousand people had by now perished in the conflict, most of them civilians. Declaring "the war's over," he went to Chechnya on the eve of the election to demonstrate his political agility and physical stamina. With the state-owned television station at his disposal, Yeltsin dominated the airwaves as the campaign intensified, aided by Western political advertising specialists. He dipped deeply into a lavish war chest of nearly $1 billion in campaign funds, provided largely by a group of tycoons who were determined to stop Zyuganov and the Communists at all costs.

In the first election round held on June 16, 1996, Yeltsin topped the list with 35.3 percent of the vote. Zyuganov finished second, with 32 percent. Mikhail Gorbachev was a forgotten figure, winning only 0.5 percent of the vote (see table 8.7). Because Yeltsin had not won an absolute majority of the votes cast, he was obliged to run head-to-head against Zyuganov in a second round. But several days after his first round triumph, Yeltsin collapsed and dropped out of sight. Panic gripped his entourage as rumors circulated about a heart attack or stroke. He finally reemerged on election day, looking haggard and expressionless as he cast his ballot. But the returns were positive: on July 3, the president edged out Zyuganov by 53.8 percent to 40.3 percent. Nearly 5 percent had voted against both contestants. Yeltsin's margin of victory was surprisingly high in some regions, the result of pressures exerted on local officials to report an exaggerated result in the president's favor.[44]

**Yeltsin's Ills** Yeltsin's 1996 electoral victory marked the high point of his presidency. From then until his resignation at the end of 1999, his declining health required him to spend long periods away from his desk at the Kremlin. Yeltsin's prolonged absences created a void at the highest levels of Russia's political system, stimulating intense rivalries for power among a handful of well-placed intimates in the executive branch—including his daughter. The absence of a legislative majority in the Duma in favor of radical market reforms and amicable relations with the West further constricted Yeltsin's ability to pursue a consistent reform course and a more cooperative pro-Western foreign policy.[45]

The Russian economy veered from one obstacle to the next. Privatization came to a near stop, tax revenues withered, and the budget shrank. Capital flight—the transfer of money to safe havens outside Russia—was estimated at more than $100 billion. Corruption festered, with possibly more than 40 percent of the Russian economy controlled by organized crime. Cronyism remained pervasive, with political and economic power concentrated in the hands of rival "clans."[46] One of the government's few successes was an agreement signed with the Chechens in August 1996 that required Russia to withdraw all its troops while deferring a final agreement on Chechnya's juridical status until 2001.

But Yeltsin's infirmities quickly overshadowed everything. The president was barely able to speak at his inauguration, and several weeks later he announced that he needed heart surgery. The quintuple bypass operation took place in early November and kept Yeltsin away from the Kremlin until late the following month. Within weeks of his return he was hospitalized again for viral pneumonia, followed by other medical problems. In October 1998 Yeltsin formally removed himself from day-to-day responsibilities and entered a sanitarium, returning briefly only to be hospitalized in January 1999 with a bleeding ulcer. His health continued to fluctuate until his retirement at the end of the year.

**Economic Woes** In the power vacuum opened up by Yeltsin's afflictions, ambitious figures jockeyed for influence behind the scenes. About a dozen tycoons had amassed spectacular wealth since the collapse of the USSR by acquiring some of Russia's most lucrative businesses, including television stations,

TABLE 20.2

**Yeltsin's Prime Ministers**

| | |
|---|---|
| Boris Yeltsin | 1991–June 1992 |
| Yegor Gaidar | June 1992–December 1993 |
| Viktor Chernomyrdin | December 1993–March 1998 |
| Sergei Kiriyenko | March 1998–August 1998 |
| Yevgeny Primakov | September 1998–May 1999 |
| Sergei Stepashin | May 1999–September 1999 |
| Vladimir Putin | September 1999–Spring 2000 |

banks, and other holdings. Even the majority of shares in Russia's lucrative energy sector fell into private hands, with the state retaining minority ownership. As the so-called oligarchs grabbed control of the most important branches of Russia's private sector, they also competed with one another for political clout. With Yeltsin almost permanently incapacitated, financial barons like Boris Berezovsky acquired powerful positions at the highest echelons of the Russian government. In effect, the financial oligarchs and a small group of insiders close to Yeltsin were running Russia in secret, with little or no accountability to the legislature or the voters.[47]

Meanwhile, Yeltsin shuffled prime ministers at a dizzying pace (see table 20.2). Several of them got caught in the crosswinds of the global financial crisis buffeting developing economies from Asia to Latin America in 1997 and 1998. After Russia's stock market lost half its value and interest rates jumped to 50 percent, the IMF, the World Bank, and the Japanese government put together a $22.6 billion loan package to prop up the ruble and ward off economic collapse, but it was too late. On August 18, 1998, the government announced a 34 percent devaluation of the ruble and a moratorium on Russia's payments on its international commercial debts. (At the time, Russia's total foreign debt was $200 billion.) The ruble's devaluation spelled economic ruin for millions of Russians as the value of their meager savings collapsed. Many Russians still have not recouped their losses nearly ten years after the 1998 economic catastrophe.

Yeltsin's popularity continued to nosedive. In the spring of 1999 the Communists launched an impeachment process against him for presiding over the Soviet Union's demise and other alleged political offenses. Like French presidents, Yeltsin let his

Vladimir Putin

prime ministers take the blame for the government's problems. He fired one after another before naming a relative unknown, *Vladimir Putin,* to that precarious position in 1999. After Yeltsin announced his resignation on New Year's eve, tearfully acknowledging that "many of the dreams we shared did not come true," he declared his support for Putin in the presidential race set for 2000, a proposal Putin immediately accepted.

**Putin Takes Over** Putin was a graduate of the Leningrad University law school. He had spent his early career from 1975 to 1990 in the KGB, mostly as an agent in communist East Germany. One of his law professors had been Anatoly Sobchak, a liberal reformer who became mayor of Leningrad (later renamed St. Petersburg) and a staunch opponent of the anti-Gorbachev coup in 1991. Sobchak offered his former student a position as the city's unelected deputy mayor, a slot Putin held from 1990 to 1994, the formative years of post-communist Russia. In 1994 the government's privatization chief brought Putin to Moscow, where he initially headed the bureau responsible for Kremlin property and subsequently the office overseeing Russia's eighty-nine regional governors. In the summer of 1998, Yeltsin named him director of the Federal Security Service (FSB), a powerful intelligence agency that succeeded the KGB, and later appointed him to the National Security Council.

Despite the votes of Communists and some radical reformers against him, Putin was confirmed on August 16, only a week after his nomination. He retained his predecessor's cabinet and announced no new policy initiatives, but his government was quickly thrown into a severe crisis. A week earlier, Chechen separatists had invaded the neighboring Russian province of Dagestan and declared their intention of creating an independent state. As soon as Putin took office, he gave the military one week to oust the rebels. Russian forces accomplished their task within the deadline, driving the rebels back into Chechnya. But the skirmishes proved to be the opening salvo in a new round of intense confrontation between the Russian government and the Chechen independence movement. Within weeks a large-scale invasion force was in place, with aerial and artillery bombardments pounding Grozny and rebel strongholds. More than 100,000 civilians streamed out of the battle areas and casualties on both sides mounted rapidly. Putin received strong public endorsement from most Russians for his determination to defeat the rebels, especially after a series of random bombings of apartment buildings and other civilian centers rattled Moscow and other urban areas. The government attributed the attacks to Chechen terrorists. As in the previous round of fighting, hopes for a quick victory proved illusory: Russian troops were still mired in the conflict at the end of 2006.

**December 1999 Legislative Elections** Another immediate challenge confronting the new prime minister was the upcoming parliamentary election set for December. In the months preceding the vote, Russia's fledgling party system underwent a number of changes. Five reform-oriented parties consolidated their forces in a new grouping, the *Union of Rightwing Forces*. Traditionalists led by Moscow mayor Yuri Luzhkov formed a new party, *Fatherland*, dedicated to a "strong state" within the framework of democratic freedoms and a mixed economy. Support for the new party widened when another new grouping, a collection of regional leaders calling themselves the *All Russia Movement,* linked up with Fatherland. Prime Minister Putin's followers took urgent steps to create a new pro-government party called *Unity*. Unity was a curious mix of liberals, Christian democrats, communists, nationalists, and pure opportunists.

TABLE 20.3

**1999 Elections to State Duma**

| Party | % PR Vote | PR Seats | SMD Seats | Total Seats | % Seats |
|---|---|---|---|---|---|
| Communists | 24.3 | 67 | 46 | 113 | 25.1 |
| Unity | 23.3 | 64 | 9 | 73 | 16.2 |
| Fatherland-All Russia | 13.3 | 37 | 31 | 68 | 15.1 |
| Union of Rightwing Forces | 8.5 | 24 | 5 | 29 | 6.4 |
| Yabloko | 5.9 | 16 | 4 | 20 | 4.4 |
| Zhirinovsky bloc | 6.0 | 17 | 0 | 17 | 3.8 |
| Our Home Is Russia | 1.2 | 0 | 7 | 7 | 1.6 |
| Independents | — | — | 114 | 114 | 25.3 |
| Seven small parties | (<2.0 each) | 0 | 9 | 9 | 1.8 |
| Against all candidates | 3.5 | | | | |
| Turnout: 61.7% | | | | | |

*Source:* Richard Rose and Neil Munro, *Elections Without Order: Russia's Challenge to Vladimir Putin* (Cambridge: Cambridge University Press, 2002), 132.

To the surprise of many observers, Unity did quite well, garnering 73 seats. The pro-reform parties all lost seats, with the Union of Rightwing Forces capturing only 29. The Communists won the largest share of popular votes in the party list vote (24 percent) and remained the largest party with 113 seats. The traditionalist Fatherland-All Russia bloc came close to matching Unity's performance (68 seats). Zhirinovsky's party, the Liberal Democrats, was disqualified before the election for failing to meet election law requirements, but Zhirinovsky quickly assembled a new bloc of candidates. His supporters lost seats, falling from 51 in 1995 to 17. The real political coloration of the new Duma ultimately depended on more than 100 deputies elected as independents or as representatives of small parties. (See table 20.3.)

Unexpectedly, a scant two weeks after the Duma elections, President Boris Yeltsin stepped down from the presidency. Once the indispensable hero of Russia's breakthrough to democracy and independence, Yeltsin was a tragic figure as he wiped away tears during his farewell address.[48] By the terms of the constitution, Prime Minister Putin immediately assumed the role of acting president while preparations began for a rescheduled presidential election to be held within three months. In the interval, Putin enlarged his own share of popular support, winning plaudits for his success in providing full financing for Russia's social welfare programs for the first time since independence while simultaneously raising pensions and paying a substantial portion of back wages. His government also achieved a measure of economic stability, aided by a global rise in prices for oil, Russia's most valuable export commodity. Despite more than a thousand Russian army casualties in Chechnya and international criticism for harsh battle tactics, Putin's prosecution of the war against the secessionists remained acceptable to many Russians.

Once his most serious challenger, former Prime Minister Yevgeny Primakov, dropped out of the race, Putin was able to secure a convincing first-round victory, garnering 53.4 percent of the vote. Because of his absolute majority, a second round of voting was not necessary. More than 39.9 million citizens had voted for him. Putin was inaugurated president on May 7.[49] He was reelected on March 14, 2004, winning 71 percent in the first round against five rivals (see table 20.4).

## PUTIN'S RUSSIA

### The Institutional Structure

The constitution approved by Russia's voters in the December 1993 referendum established a mixed *presidential-parliamentary* institutional structure modeled to a considerable extent on the constitution of contemporary France (the Fifth Republic). At the national level it consists of the following:

- a dual executive, with a powerful decision-making *president*, who is head of state, and a

TABLE 20.4

**Presidential Elections, 2000 and 2004**

| 2000 | | 2004 | |
|---|---|---|---|
| **Candidate** | **% of Vote** | **Candidate** | **% of Vote** |
| Putin (Independent) | 53.4 | Putin (Independent) | 71.9 |
| Zyuganov (Communist) | 29.5 | Kharitonov (Communist) | 13.8 |
| Yavlinsky (Yabloko) | 5.9 | Glazyev (Independent) | 4.1 |
| Tuteev (Independent) | 3.0 | Khakamada (Independent) | 3.9 |
| Zhirinovsky (Liberal Democrats) | 2.7 | Malyshkin (Liberal Democrats) | 2.0 |
| Six others | 3.6 | Mironov (Russia's Rebirth-Party of Life) | 0.8 |
| Against all candidates | 1.9 | Against all candidates | 3.5 |

*Source:* Russian Federal Election Commission, www.fci.ru.

responsible *prime minister*, who is head of government

- a bicameral legislature, the *Federal Assembly*, consisting of the *State Duma* (the lower house) and the *Federation Council* (the upper house)
- an independent judiciary, consisting at the national level of the *Constitutional Court*, empowered to rule on the constitutionality of laws and treaties and to settle disputes concerning the competence of state institutions; the *Supreme Court*, the highest court with jurisdiction over civil and criminal law and other cases arising from courts of common pleas; and the *Supreme Arbitration Court*, the highest court authorized to settle economic disputes arising from lower economic arbitration courts. Most of the constitution can be amended only with the approval of two-thirds of the citizenry in a referendum.

**The President** Russia's **president** is elected directly by the people to a four-year term (with a limit of two consecutive terms). A candidate who wins more than half the votes is elected president. If no one wins more than half the votes in the first round, a second round is held between the top two finishers of the first round. ***The president is the country's single most important decision maker.*** In addition to being the "guarantor" of the population's civil rights and freedoms and commander in chief of the armed forces, the president enjoys the right to "determine the guidelines of the domestic and foreign policy of the state," thus possessing considerable authority to initiate and conduct policy. Like France's president, the president of Russia has real political power, in contrast to ceremonial heads of state like the presidents of Germany and Israel. The most important presidential prerogatives in the 1993 constitution include the authority to

- nominate the prime minister for approval by the Duma
- appoint and remove deputy prime ministers and other cabinet ministers upon the prime minister's proposals (and without Duma approval)
- preside over government (cabinet) meetings
- submit bills directly to the Duma
- veto federal laws passed by the Federal Assembly, subject to an overriding vote by two-thirds of the membership of each house
- dissolve the Duma in the event that it rejects three presidential nominations for prime minister or passes a vote of no-confidence in the government
- issue decrees and directives binding throughout the country
- nominate the chairman of Russia's State Bank for approval by the Duma, and nominate the justices of the three high courts for approval by the Federation Council
- place referendums before the voters
- announce a state of emergency in all or part of Russia, informing the Federal Assembly of this decision
- take charge of Russia's foreign and defense policies and sign international treaties

The president may be removed from office only for high treason or some other "grave crime." The procedure requires the Duma to pass formal accusations by two-thirds majority, followed by validation of the charges by the Supreme Court and the Constitutional Court. The Federation Council may then remove the president by two-thirds vote.

In some respects the Russian president's powers are even greater than those of France's president, especially the right to issue decrees and veto bills passed by the legislature. Although the constitution stipulates that presidential decrees may not violate its provisions, it specifies no other limitations to this important prerogative, thus creating a potential for the abuse of power. As we'll see, President Putin has used his presidential powers forcefully, acting at times solely on his own authority to issue decrees and at other times with the support of his sizable majority of supporters in the legislature.

**The Prime Minister and Government** The **prime minister**—more formally, the chairman of the government—also has significant constitutional powers, though they are less sweeping than the president's. Most important, the premier ***is authorized to "determine guidelines" for the government's activities and to "organize its work,"*** a somewhat vaguely worded provision that grants the head of government a certain amount of latitude to initiate and conduct domestic and foreign policy without trespassing on the president's primacy in these domains.

The six prime ministers who served under President Yeltsin had ample latitude to conduct the government's business, but Yeltsin ultimately held them acountable for the country's deteriorating economic situation. President Putin appointed *Mikhail Kasyanov,* a finance expert with close ties to Yeltsin's entourage, to the premiership shortly after the March 2000 presidential elections. Putin's hands-on presidential style kept Kasyanov in a distinctly subordinate position. Just before the 2004 presidential elections, Putin replaced Kasyanov with *Mikhail Fradkov,* 53, a close ally and former trade minister. Putin also reshuffled the cabinet and reduced it from thirty to seventeen portfolios.

The government's most important responsibilities center on the federal budget, which it prepares, submits to the Duma, and subsequently implements. The government is also tasked with ensuring a "uniform state policy" in education, health care, social welfare, the environment, science, and culture. It may also issue "resolutions and directives" within the limits of the law. Other clauses of the constitution more explicitly confine the government's authority to "carrying out" measures concerning defense and foreign policy and the protection of civil liberties, property rights, and public order.

The Russian prime minister and the government are responsible to both the president and the Duma. The president nominates the premier, but the Duma has the right to confirm or reject the nominee by majority vote. If the president's nominee is rejected in three votes, the president must either nominate somebody else or dissolve the Duma and call snap elections. Yeltsin had trouble getting two of his nominees for prime minister confirmed. In the first case he threatened new elections, and the Duma approved his nominee on the third vote; in the second case he backed down and submitted a new nominee more acceptable to the Duma majority. The president has the right to dismiss the prime minister and other cabinet ministers. The Duma has the right to vote the government out of office in a no-confidence vote passed by the majority of its 450 members. If the president opts to reject this vote, the Duma may override his decision by passing another vote of no-confidence within three months. If it succeeds, the president must then either nominate a new prime minister or dissolve the Duma and call snap elections. Snap elections called under these circumstances may not be called again for at least a year.

**The Duma** The **State Duma** ***consists of 450 legislators elected to a four-year term.*** As noted earlier, the 1993 constitution established a hybrid electoral system for the Duma: half of the deputies were elected in single-member districts and the other half were elected by proportional representation on the basis of nationwide party lists. (Germany and Japan have variants of this "mixed-member" system.) This system was used in the Duma elections of 1993, 1995, 1999, and 2003. A 5 percent threshold prevented the proliferation of very small parties in the Duma. But the combination of weak, leader-driven parties, local political loyalties, and other factors resulted in the election of a large number of independent deputies with little or no party affiliation. Just about all of them were elected in the single-member districts. The presence of so many independents confuses voters and can make it difficult to form

TABLE 20.5

**2003 Elections to State Duma**

| Party | % PR Vote | PR Seats | SMD Seats | Total Seats | % Seats |
|---|---|---|---|---|---|
| United Russia | 37.6 | 120 | 102 | 222 | 49.3 |
| Communist Party | 12.6 | 40 | 12 | 52 | 11.6 |
| Liberal Democrats | 11.5 | 36 | 0 | 36 | 8.0 |
| Motherland | 9.0 | 29 | 8 | 37 | 8.2 |
| People's Party | 1.2 | 0 | 17 | 17 | 3.8 |
| Yabloko | 4.3 | 0 | 4 | 4 | 0.9 |
| Union of Rightwing Forces | 4.0 | 0 | 3 | 3 | 0.7 |
| Agrarian Party | 3.7 | 0 | 2 | 2 | 0.4 |
| Other parties[a] | 11.6 | 0 | 6 | 6 | 1.3 |
| Independents | — | — | 68 | 68 | 15.1 |
| Against all candidates | 4.7 | — | — | 3[b] | — |
| Turnout: 55.6% | | | | | |

[a]Smaller parties included Rebirth of Russia (three seats), and one each for New Course–Automobile Russia, Development of Enterprise, and Great Russia–Eurasia Union.
[b]New elections were to be scheduled in three single-member districts where the vote "against all" was higher than the vote for any individual candidate. Results are final as of March 15, 2004.
*Sources:* Central Election Commission, http://gd2003cikrf.ru; "Russia Votes," http://www.russiavotes.org/2003result.htm.

consistent parliamentary majorities without protracted negotiations between the main parties and independents whose votes may be needed to pass legislation.

In his first term, Putin engineered an electoral reform aimed at reducing the number of parties by requiring all parties to have at least ten thousand members, spread out over at least half of Russia's regions. Despite this reform, about seventy independent or small-party candidates were elected in 2003 (see table 20.5). In 2004, shortly after the Beslan terrorist incident, Putin proposed an even more drastic electoral reform. As passed by the Federal Assembly the following year, the new law abolishes the single-member districts and requires the entire Duma to be elected on the basis of party-list proportional representation. The threshold that a party must meet in order to be represented in the chamber was raised from 5 percent to 7 percent. Parties will no longer be allowed to form electoral blocs or alliances in order to surmount the threshold jointly. Other changes to the electoral law include a ban on independent domestic election monitors (with international observers permitted by invitation only); the introduction of electronic voting in some areas; and permission for voters to vote in polling places other than the one in which they are registered without getting the prior approval of their local election officials. These changes were set to take effect in the Duma elections scheduled for 2007. Putin's critics charged that the electoral reforms were deliberately intended to make it more difficult for opposition parties to get elected and easier for Putin and his allies to manipulate the election process and its results. (The pro-democracy Union of Rightwing Forces, for example, is a bloc of small parties that failed to breach the 5 percent hurdle in 2003.) With no viable opposition to the governing party and its allies, there can be no alternation in power between competing parties. Electoral democracy is seriously diminished as a result. Putin's supporters dismissed these criticisms and averred that the pro-Putin United Russia party could lose as many as sixty-five seats under the new voting system in 2007. We'll take a closer look at Russia's party system later in this chapter.

The Duma's chief functions are to hold the government accountable and enact legislation. As noted, it may accept or reject the president's nominee for prime minister, and it may unseat the government in a vote of confidence initiated either by the Duma itself or by the government. It is to the Duma that the president or the government submits bills for adoption into law. In addition, the Duma has the right to lodge accusations against the president for possible impeachment by the Federation Council. (The Duma may not be dissolved once the impeachment process begins, nor may it be dissolved during an emergency period.) And the Duma may approve or reject the president's nominee for State Bank chairman and dismiss the incumbent. In short, the Duma has ample authority to check certain presidential powers and to hold the prime minister and cabinet accountable. Nevertheless, it is a relatively weak body when compared to the U.S. House of Representatives or the British House of Commons.

Among its limitations, the Duma can be dissolved by the president under specified conditions, as we've indicated. Moreover, its members may not propose any financial legislation, such as tax bills or proposals to increase or reduce budgetary spending, without the government's approval. (The lower houses of Britain and France face similar restrictions on finance matters.) The Putin administration has weakened the Duma's influence even further. For example, it terminated the Duma's previous ability to speak directly with government ministries and agencies, a practice that gave the Duma some influence over government activities in the Yeltsin years. Under Putin, the Duma has had to talk with a single representative appointed by the government.

**Federation Council** The **Federation Council** ***consists of two members from each of Russia's eighty-nine republics and regions.*** One is appointed by the local governor, the other by the local legislature. The Council's principal function is to vote on legislation already adopted by the Duma. (Members of the Federation Council who wish to initiate legislative proposals must submit their bills to the Duma.) However, the Council's assent is not always required for a bill to be enacted into law. If the Council rejects a law passed by the Duma and the disagreement cannot be settled by a reconciliation committee of the two houses, the Duma may pass the bill on its own by two-thirds majority. Certain particularly important areas of legislation require the Federation Council's consideration, including the federal budget, tax laws, the ratification of international treaties, and declarations of war. In addition, the upper house has the sole authority to approve or reject presidential decrees declaring a state of emergency or imposing martial law in case of war. The Federation Council also has the exclusive right to remove the president from office once the Duma passes articles of impeachment. Both houses have the right to establish investigative committees.

As part of his attempt to rein in the autonomy of the regions from the central government's authority, President Putin diluted the upper chamber's authority by getting the Duma to pass a law prohibiting the heads of Russia's eighty-nine regional governments from serving in the Federation Council. In their place, regional governments have to appoint less powerful officials to represent them in the Russian parliament. To compensate the regional bosses for their ouster from the upper house of Russia's legislature, Putin created a new body, the *State Council,* which enables these leaders to meet directly with President Putin every three months. The State Council is purely consultative, however, and cannot match the Federation Council's lawmaking authority.

**The Constitutional Court** Of Russia's three highest courts, the Constitutional Court is empowered to interpret the constitution, settle disputes involving the competency of state institutions, and determine whether laws and the activities of state authorities are in compliance with the constitution. The Court's nineteen justices are nominated by Russia's president and confirmed by the Federation Council. Compared with constitutional courts in many other democracies, Russia's Constitutional Court is relatively weak. Its jurisdiction is limited to issues that are brought before it by the president, the government, the legislature, and a few other state institutions. Unlike the U.S. Supreme Court, the Constitutional Court does not hear cases that have been submitted to it by citizens involved in the appellate process. Its powers of judicial review are thus largely dependent on the issues that other state authorities wish to have adjudicated. President Putin's widening authority over the government, the Duma, and the Federation Council gives him wide personal discretion to determine which matters will be submitted to the Constitutional Court for adjudication, and which ones will not. Putin broadened his authority over the Court during his second term when the legislature approved his request for more presidential influence in the selection of the Supreme Qualification Collegium, the body that approves appointments to the Supreme Court and other federal courts. These realities impose serious limitations on the Court's independence from the executive and legislative branches of the Russian government.

Of course, no court system can be effective if state authorities refuse to abide by judicial decisions or if they do not conscientiously enforce court rulings. The laws that governments issue may be authoritative, but the *rule of law* prevails only when state authorities and the citizenry agree to submit themselves to the law. Ten years after Russia's independence in 1992, there were ominous indications that the values and attitudes associated with the rule of law were still lacking. Bribery and other forms of corruption on the part of state officials is rampant. A Russian think tank estimated in 2002 that affluent Russian citizens and businesses spend about $37 billion a year in bribes and kickbacks—mostly to government officials, ranging from traffic cops and bureaucrats to senior administrators. And the sorry state of Russia's finances deprives government agencies of the resources they need to enforce Court rulings effectively. In addition, government prosecutors have undermined the jury system by asserting their right to appeal not-guilty verdicts. Perhaps as many as 50 percent of these verdicts are subsequently overturned. (Double jeopardy is permitted in Russia.) Authorities have used intimidation tactics against defense attorneys who represent clients involved in disputes with the state. There has been a return to the old Soviet practice of incarcerating human rights activists in mental institutions on trumped-up claims of mental illness and forcing them to take debilitating doses of psychiatric drugs. The use of torture and brutality on Chechen rebels and various criminal elements constitute yet another abuse of the state's judicial and penal powers.[50]

**Regional Governments** With the dismemberment of the Soviet Union at the end of 1991, the fifteen "soviet socialist republics" that constituted the Soviet Union all became formally independent. The three Baltic states—Estonia, Latvia, and Lithuania—have made considerable strides toward democracy, entering the European Union and NATO in 2004. The other twelve states—grouped together in the *Commonwealth of Independent States (CIS)*, a loose organization primarily concerned with promoting economic cooperation—have moved much more slowly, or not at all, in democracy's direction. According to the Freedom House composite index for political and civil rights, and the categories we use in this book to characterize countries on the basis of this index, at the end of 2005 there was only one democracy in the CIS: Ukraine moved into the democratic camp with a composite political and civil rights rating of 2.5 as the result of its "Orange Revolution" (see chapter 1). Two CIS countries were semi-democracies: Georgia (3.0) and Moldova (3.5). Georgia raised its score thanks to its "Rose Revolution," which occurred when the Soviet-era leader Eduard Shevardnadze was forced to step down in the wake of mass demonstrations following his transparently fraudulent reelection victory in late 2003. New elections held in 2004 brought a pro-democracy reformer to power. Six CIS states were semi-authoritarian regimes: Armenia, Azerbaijan, Kazakhstan, Kyrgyzstan, Russia, and Tajikistan. In a scenario strikingly similar to what happened in Georgia, Kyrgyzstan rose to a score of 4.5 in 2005 after demonstrations following a fraudulent election forced the ouster of its authoritarian president and the election of an opposition figure. Kyrgyzstan's democratization was dubbed the "Tulip Revolution." And three CIS states had authoritarian regimes (Belarus, Turkmenistan, and Uzbekistan). (On the scoring system, see chapter 2). Several of these countries have fairly large Russian minorities. In all, some 25 million Russians reside in former Soviet republics along Russia's periphery, areas known in Russia as "the near abroad." On numerous occasions the Russian government has asserted its responsibility to speak up for the rights of these external Russian minorities whenever a neighboring government is believed to be discriminating against them.

Russia itself incorporates a diversity of non-Russian peoples who were gathered into the Russian Empire in tsarist times. Approximately 80 percent of the country's population is ethnically Russian. Although most Russians who profess a religion are Orthodox, there are 15 million Muslims (mostly non-Russian) living in scattered parts of the country, roughly 10 percent of Russia's population. Many of the 20 percent of the population who are not Russian are concentrated in administrative subdivisions that might provide a territorial basis for wide autonomy or outright independence. The Russian Federation's structure consists of eighty-nine regional subdivisions, based on the territorial units and nomenclature that prevailed in the Soviet Union. In addition to the cities of Moscow and Leningrad, there are twenty-one republics, forty-nine regions, six territories, ten autonomous areas, and one autonomous region (the Jewish region created in the Stalinist era). Muslims constitute more than one-fourth of the population in eight of these subdivisions, with concentrations of more than 90 percent in places like Chechnya and its neighboring regions of Ingushetia and Dagestan. Russia's Muslim population is growing at a faster rate than its majority Slavic population.[51]

The large numbers of Russians living in neighboring states, together with the non-Russian minorities living in Russia, have saddled the Russian government with what Juan Linz and Alfred Stepan call a "stateness" problem: the problem of defining the country's territorial boundaries and the distribution of decision-making power among its constituent units.[52] Furthermore, Russia's ethnic and religious heterogeneity makes for a fragile sense of national unity. These problems came close to shattering the Russian Federation in its infancy, as regions with a strong sense of their own separate identity began to distance themselves from President Yeltsin's shaky central government. As Chechnya exploded in a violent independence movement, other regions moved more quietly to wrest greater autonomy for themselves while remaining within the Russian Federation. Regions with indigenous sources of wealth and assertive leaders insisted on greater freedom from central authorities to shape their own laws and policies and even to conduct economic relations with foreign countries. Scrambling to hold the federation together, Yeltsin's government negotiated bilateral treaties with a number of these restive regions to clarify their rights and obligations.

In stark contrast to Yeltsin, President Putin moved swiftly to reassert the central government's primacy over the provinces. Within weeks of his election in May 2000, Putin issued a decree reorganizing the country's eighty-nine regions under seven new super-regions known as "federal *okruga* (okrugs)." Putin himself appointed the head of each super-region, with the express purpose of enhancing the central government's controls over regional affairs. There followed other measures aimed at bringing the regions to heel, including the law barring regional chief executives from sitting in the Federation Council (a law that simultaneously stripped them of their parliamentary immunity from prosecution for criminal offenses such as corruption). Another law required the provinces to align their laws with those of the central government and gave the president the authority to replace governors who refused to implement a federal law. Governors who commit crimes can also be replaced by central authorities. Bilateral treaties between the central government and various regions were being phased out in a further effort to subordinate Russia's regional periphery to the Kremlin. And Putin backed his own favorite candidates for election to leadership posts in regional governments. Charges of fraudulent vote counts and other election irregularities have accompanied the victories of some Putin-sponsored candidates.

In his second term Putin launched an even more aggressive assault on regional governors. In September 2004, immediately after the Beslan crisis, he announced a plan to terminate the direct election of Russia's eighty-nine governors by giving himself the presidential authority to select them. (The president's nominee in each region would be subject to confirmation by the regional legislature, but the president may now dissolve that body and call snap elections to it if it rejects his nominee in two successive votes.) The new system significantly strengthens the president's power over Russia's regions, scoring another victory for Putin's policy of recentralizing power in the Kremlin and restricting the centrifugal tendencies of federalism. Prior to this change, some of the regional governors had managed to wield considerable local power, escaping the influence of the large national political parties like Putin's United Russia and suppressing political competition in their respective regions.

Although the reassertion of central authority has been fairly effective in most regions, Chechnya remained troublesome. Major fighting had leveled off by 2003, but 80,000 Russian troops were still stationed in the area. Terrorist raids and suicide bombings by Chechen rebels like the ones described earlier in this chapter have occurred periodically, with deadly results. And as we've already noted, Russian authorities have not hesitated to use torture and other forms of extreme pressure on Chechen captives. In March 2003, the Putin administration held a referendum on a new constitution for Chechnya, promising the region considerable autonomy as a member of the Russian Federation. Russian authorities said the document was approved by 96 percent of the voters, with a turnout of 80 percent, but secessionists boycotted the vote. In October, Akhmad Kadyrov, the pro-Russian head of Chechnya's government, claimed victory in local elections, but the vote took place only after Kadyrov's main rivals were pushed out of the race by his backers in the Kremlin. Rebel leaders dismissed Kadyrov as a puppet imposed on Chechnya by the Putin administration, and they vowed to continue their struggle for independence. Kadyrov was assassinated by Chechen insurgents in May 2004, sparking Russian retaliation. Several high-level rebel leaders were killed by Russian forces in 2005 and 2006. In 2005 the Russian parliament voted to change the name of Chechnya's capital from Grozny to Akhmadkala in honor of Kadyrov, and regional legislative elections were stage-managed to ensure a lopsided plurality for Putin's party. In 2006 former president Kadyrov's son, the head of a pro-Russian militia, became Chechnya's prime minister.[53]

In view of Russia's institutional framework and President Putin's steady accretion of power, can it be said that Russia's presidential-parliamentary system lends itself to the abuse of presidential authority and thereby places democracy itself in jeopardy? Having tried out a similar hypothesis in the case of France in chapter 17, we will now see how it works in Russia.

## HYPOTHESIS-TESTING EXERCISE: Is Russia's Political System Undermining Democracy?

### Hypothesis

A mixed presidential-parliamentary system tends to produce the worst possible outcomes: authoritarianism or gridlock. When the president and the majority in the lower house of parliament share the same political orientation, the president monopolizes power and tends to abuse it. When the president's opponents dominate the legislature, the result is gridlock, and the lawmaking process comes to a standstill. The presidential-parliamentary system is thus especially dangerous for young democracies.

### Variables

The *independent variable* is the *presidential-parliamentary system.* The *dependent variables* are *the concentration and abuse of presidential power* and, alternatively, *gridlock.*

### Expectations

If the hypothesis is correct, then we would expect the evidence to show that (1) when Russia's president enjoys the support of the majority of the National Assembly, decision making is heavily concentrated in the presidency as opposed to the government and the legislature; (2) the president tends to exceed his legal authority of the office, violating democratic principles; and (3) opposition between the president and the legislative majority produces an inefficient governmental process bordering on paralysis.

### Evidence

Not long after his election as Russia's president in 2000, Vladimir Putin put together a fairly stable majority of Duma members who were willing to approve his policies. Starting from his natural base in the Unity party, Putin reached out to the Fatherland–All Russia party (which merged with Unity in the following year), Zhirinovsky's Liberal Democrats, and the Union of Rightwing Forces. He even cut a deal with the Communists, allowing them to take key positions in the Duma in exchange for their votes until he no longer needed them. As Putin's parliamentary support grew, so did his exercise of presidential power. Putin has issued more decrees than Yeltsin did. He moved swiftly against Berezovsky and Gusinsky, whose independent television stations were openly critical of Putin and whose political ambitions directly challenged him. In 2003 Putin's government arrested Mikhail Khodorkovsky, the billionaire chief executive of Russia's largest oil company, along with several of his business allies, charging them with tax evasion and other offenses. Khodorkovsky's political ambitions were viewed as a potential threat to Putin's authority. (His company, YUKOS, was believed to be funding anti-Putin parties, including the Communists.) Khodorkovsky was subsequently convicted of various crimes and sentenced to prison, as we shall see in the next section. Although Putin justified these moves as legitimate attacks on the excessive power of the financial oligarchy, he did not hesitate to curry the support of more favorably inclined oligarchs. And Putin moved vigorously to retain state control over significant sectors of the Russian economy, as we shall see.

Putin also made it clear that he would not tolerate openly critical media. The murder of the crusading journalist Anna Politkovskaya in 2006 was only one among many examples of the downright threatening climate that now surrounds the Russian press, plainly violating the constitution's guarantee of freedom of the mass media. By contrast, President Yeltsin tolerated open criticism of both his policies and himself.

As we have seen, President Putin has also moved boldly to restore the central government's authority over regional governments.

Putin has further reinforced his personal authority by bringing trusted former KGB officials into his administration, along with representatives of the defense establishment and other "power ministries" concerned with national security. These *siloviki* (power people) held nearly 60 percent of the top leadership posts in Putin's administration, a significantly higher percentage than they had under Yeltsin or Gorbachev.[54]

The evidence attesting to Putin's vigorous use of presidential power is fully consistent with our first expectation: it demonstrates an unmistakable concentration of power in the hands of the president. There are also indications that Putin has on occasion exceeded his constitutional authority, in conformity with our second expectation. Nevertheless, public approval for Putin remained consistently high, between 70 and 80 percent. After more than twenty years of turmoil, most Russians appeared to favor political order and a strong state over press freedoms or the formalities of constitutional law. A public opinion poll in early 2000 revealed that three out of four Russians preferred order to democracy, even if it meant infringements of personal freedoms.[55]

President Yeltsin had to contend with a considerably less pliable Duma than his successor has faced. Communists and their allies, archnationalists, regional elites, and other groupings at one time or another opposed at least some of Yeltsin's policy initiatives. As we noted earlier, the Duma challenged two of Yeltsin's nominees for prime minister. Indeed, Yeltsin's prime ministers were never as strong as French prime ministers. In France's Fifth Republic, whose constitution Yeltsin took as his model, prime ministers tend to have the support of a voting majority in the French legislature, whether that majority consists of the president's supporters or the president's opposition (as in times of cohabitation). Yeltsin's prime ministers could never count on the solid support of any party or coalition of parties in the Russian Duma. As a consequence, prolonged wrangling over the budget, economic reform, and other issues sometimes paralyzed the decision-making process. Some bills required so many compromises to get passed into law that they proved ineffective when implemented.

Yeltsin's failing health and long periods of convalescence further complicated the decision-making process. Executive power became lodged in a Kremlin cabal that was accountable neither to the Duma nor to the voters. In the process, conspiratorial figures like Berezovsky and other gray eminences behind the throne amassed enormous fortunes and accrued immense political power with virtually no parliamentary oversight. One political analyst described the Yeltsin regime as an "elective monarchy," even though the "tsar" was unable to wield power for months at a time.[56]

The Yeltsin years were therefore characterized by a weak, fractionated parliament with no stable majority; a succession of weak prime ministers who could not rely on a parliamentary majority; and a president who alternated between decisiveness (when starting the economic reform process, for example) and absenteeism, allowing unelected advisors to wield significant executive power and to engage in massive corruption with virtually no accountability to the legislature or the judiciary. These realities are largely consistent with our third expectation.

## Conclusions

The evidence we have just presented is basically *consistent* with all three expectations emanating from our hypothesis. Under varying conditions, Russia's mixed presidential-parliamentary system has permitted the concentration and even abuse of presidential authority as well as an inefficient, disjointed decision-making process. Far from being a "semi-presidential" system, as it is often called, it can sometimes function as a *superpresidential* system.[57] It therefore seems ill-suited to stabilizing a law-bound democracy in Russia. It certainly has not worked as well in Russia as in France, where democratic traditions are older, parties are stronger, and public opinion is emphatically in favor of democracy. (Even though President de Gaulle occasionally violated the French constitution, he never went as far as Putin in attacking press freedoms.)

Of course, the question must be raised whether Russian democracy would be better off under a U.S.-style presidential system or a British-style parliamentary system. Unless the Russians actually try out these systems, we cannot know for sure how they would work. One recent study showed that the presidential-parliamentary system is not significantly more likely than presidentialism or parliamentarism to be correlated with the breakdown of recently established democracies, though it certainly presents problems.[58] Each of these systems can work differently in different countries; they can even work differently in the same country under different leaders or at different historical junctures. The key point is that, in the end, no system of democracy works properly as long as political elites flout the rule of law, political parties are disconnected from the voters, and mass support for democracy is feeble. On all these counts, Russia still has much to accomplish.

## Socioeconomic Conditions: National Wealth, Private Enterprise, the Middle Class, and the Disadvantaged

Inevitably, economic conditions play a critical role in democracy's success. As we've seen in this chapter, the Russian economy suffered a prolonged depression from the stagnation of the late Brezhnev era to the ruble devaluation of 1998. By the late 1990s, Russia's per capita GDP hovered around $2,700, less than in Thailand, Turkey, or Mexico. President Putin inherited an economy marked by high levels of foreign indebtedness, laggard tax collections, inflation, unemployment, and a host of other problems. But rising prices for oil and natural gas exports fueled significant increases in Russia's gross domestic product. The Russian economy grew by an average of 6.7 percent between 1999 and 2005. Although these growth spurts eased pressures on the domestic economy and led to modest standard-of-living increases for millions of Russians, the country's dependence on natural resources for 80 percent of its exports left it vulnerable to unpredictable price fluctuations for these commodities in world markets. To ensure steady growth in the future, Russia still needed to diversify its economy by promoting the production of manufactured goods; it also needed to attract more foreign investment. Both tasks faced serious political obstacles.

During his first four years in office, President Putin confirmed his commitment to economic reform, including the privatization process, budgetary discipline, the sale of farmland, and related measures. He appointed dedicated reformers to key economic policy posts and sent a welter of reform proposals to the Duma. At the same time, however, Putin failed to keep the pledge he made to Russian voters in the 2000 election campaign that, following his election, "the oligarchs will cease to exist as a class." As we've noted, Putin moved against oligarchs who challenged him politically, but he left other tycoons unmolested as long as they pursued their business activities in conformity with the wider interests of the Russian state. Many of them owned shares in giant corporations that were co-owned by the state, blurring the boundaries between the public and private sectors. Between 2004 and 2007, Putin's government expanded state ownership and direct intervention in the most vital components of the Russian economy, including energy, banking, automobiles, and aviation. In 2006 the national government owned 93 percent of the natural gas industry, 41.3 percent of the electricity industry, and 5.4 percent of the oil industry. Privatization and private-sector development have slowed down.[59] Under Putin's regime, eight giant conglomerates controlled 85 percent of the value of more than sixty large companies. Two oligarchic clans exercised particularly strong political influence in several of Russia's regions, pouring money into regional election campaigns to secure victory for their favored candidates.

This tight concentration of economic and political power, which started under President Yeltsin and intensified under Putin, has emerged as a primary reason for Russia's retreat from democratic consolidation and its descent toward authoritarianism. Steven Fish has argued that the Russian state's continuing—and widening—control over the economy and its overreliance on energy as its main source of wealth are two of the most important independent variables accounting for the retreat from democracy in Putin's Russia. Like Saudi Arabia, Iran, and other oil-rich authoritarian regimes, Russia has some of the key characteristics of a "petrostate." Together with the institutional framework of a superpresidency and a weak national legislature that is incapable of applying checks and balances to executive power, these economic realities are more important than cultural or historical factors in explaining Russia's latest authoritarian tendencies, Fish concludes.[60]

Perhaps the biggest drains on the Russian economy were corruption and extortion. There was widespread bribery of public officials for permits, licenses, and other necessities of doing business, and mafia-like organizations routinely extorted money from private businesses, depriving them of the profits they needed for investments in the future. As a consequence, Russia had one of the worst ratings in Transparency International's 2006 Corruption Perceptions Index (see table 4.1). A World Bank report released in 2002 estimated that 40 to 50 percent of Russia's economy was in the hands of illegal organizations, many of them with close ties to state officials.[61] Inconsistent enforcement of Russia's commercial code created additional barriers to business activity, scaring away foreign investors. Regulations made in Moscow were often ignored in the provinces. Until the rule of business law, including intellectual property rights, is universally observed throughout Russia, the climate for both domestic and foreign investment will remain uninviting. The murder of Andrei Kozlov, the deputy chairman of Russia's state bank, in 2006, provided a grim warning that opponents of corruption faced a dangerous uphill battle. Kozlov was responsible for revoking the licenses of more than forty Russian banks for corrupt practices, and he was widely known for his investigations into money laundering and other illegal banking practices.

The Putin government's arrest and sentencing of Mikhail Khodorkovsky (kho-dor-KOV-skee) sent a chill through the domestic and international business community. While still in his twenties, Khodorkovsky had started out owning a youth cafe in the early days of Gorbachev's economic reforms. That business failed, but the budding entrepreneur quickly learned how to take advantage of loopholes in Russia's emerging commercial laws as he embarked on new ventures. He soon established a large bank and purchased a number of newly privatized factories and plants. Khodorkovsky then parlayed his instant fortune into political influence by joining with other financial moguls in funding President Boris Yeltsin's 1996 reelection campaign. In return, he received majority ownership in an oil company called Yukos, which became Russia's leading oil producer with a market value of $35 billion. Within a few years Khodorkovsky was the richest man in the country; his net worth of $15 billion placed him among the twenty richest people in the world.

After assuming power, President Putin allowed financial oligarchs like Khodorkovsky to keep their fortunes as long as they stayed out of politics. But Khodorkovsky openly criticized Putin at a meeting and gave large sums of money to human rights groups and to anti-Putin political parties like Yabloko. In 2003 he was arrested on charges of fraud, embezzlement, and tax evasion. After a long trial, he and his chief partner were sentenced in 2005 to nine years in prison. (The sentence was reduced to eight years on appeal.) Meanwhile, the government acquired Yukos's prime oil assets and declared the company bankrupt. The Bush administration and European Union countries signaled their alarm at these evident violations of the rule of law, foreign investment in Russia dwindled to new lows, and Putin's chief economic advisor resigned after protesting Khodorkovsky's treatment. Putin tried to calm nervous investors by offering assurances of his commitment to "human rights and freedoms," but his government raised new fears when it ordered several Russian companies to pay massive sums in allegedly unpaid back taxes and extended its Yukos probe to one of the firm's American executives.

As the financial elite tightened its grip on Russia's largest corporations, the development of small and medium-size enterprises continued to lag behind European standards. In Western Europe, such firms employed 50 to 70 percent of adult employees; in Russia, they accounted for only 10 to 16 percent of adult employment.[62] In the 1990s, Russia had less than half the number of small and medium-size firms that were operating in Poland, a much smaller country.

These figures help explain the relatively slow development of Russia's postcommunist middle class. Although the size of the Russian middle class is difficult to specify statistically, a number of investigators have concluded that it constitutes one-fourth to one-third of the population. Professionally, they include such diverse groups as bureaucrats, teachers, scientists, and other state employees; independent professionals such as doctors, lawyers, and accountants; and people owning or working in private companies. Income varies widely among these groups; in effect, there are several layers of middle class, ranging from well-heeled "new Russians" to employees who scrape by from paycheck to paycheck. An indeterminate number of people work in Russia's "second economy"—unlicensed businesses that do not report their income to the tax authorities. A large portion of the emerging middle class was devastated by the 1998 ruble crisis, but they have been slowly regaining their footing. If they find a way to prosper in the coming years, they may grow into a reliable bulwark of democracy; but a great deal depends on how they fare in an unpredictable economic environment.[63]

The disposition of vast numbers of Russians left destitute by the political and economic shocks of the post-Brezhnev decades remains a major question mark. By mid 1999 nearly 38 percent of the population lived below the official poverty line of $37 a month; that figure had fallen to 25 percent in 2002. Maldistribution of wealth has remained a problem, with the bottom 20 percent of the population in 2002 sharing only 6.1 percent of the national income and the richest 20 percent holding almost half of it (see table 2.3). Though the constitution commits the state to a raft of welfare supports, such as free medical care, family allowances, unemployment compensation, disability payments, pensions, and other benefits, the money to finance them has been scarce. The government's wage and pension arrears have been substantial. As economic growth rose with global oil prices between 2000 and 2004, Putin's government made progress in paying state employees, pensioners, and other beneficiaries of government disbursements. But in 2005 the government eliminated a number of benefits for the elderly, such as free transportation and subsidies for housing and prescriptions, replacing them with a meager $7 monthly stipend. These measures provoked protests in various parts of the country, tapping undercurrents of anti-Putin sentiment and influencing the government to modify some of its cost-cutting proposals.

Russia's long economic decline since the late 1970s has taken a heavy toll on the nation's health. A rise in chronic illnesses, HIV and AIDS, alcoholism, suicides, and other life-shortening factors has combined with inadequate health care funding to reduce the life expectancy of Russian males from 70 in 1985 to 59 by 2005. The life expectancy of Russian women has fallen from 74 years in 1985 to 73 years, nine years less than Western European women. Children born in the last five to ten years are measurably smaller than those born two decades ago. As the fertility rate has declined from 2.2 births per woman in 1986–87 to 1.34 in 2005, Russia's population is shrinking by 700,000 per year. The United Nations estimates that, at current rates, Russia's population will drop from 146 million in 2000 to 104 million by 2050. President Putin has called this demographic decline "the most acute problem of contemporary Russia."[64]

### Civil Society and Political Culture

Another important task confronting democratizers in Russia is the development of an active civil society. For a country with virtually no tradition of independent citizen associations, the challenge is to create grassroots organizations from scratch. Political parties can help channel citizens into the political process—but only if they are open to the participation of party members in meaningful ways. Thus far, Russia's main parties have failed to open their policy-making and candidate selection processes to ordinary citizens. Not surprisingly, less than 20 percent of Russians expressed trust in political parties during Putin's first term. Most Russians regarded the parties as nothing more than vehicles designed to serve the personal interests of party leaders. A majority of people surveyed could not clearly distinguish one party from another.

With the exception of the Russian Communist Party, which descended from the Communist Party of the Soviet Union, all parties formed in Russia since its independence in 1992 have been brand new. Just about all these new parties have been built around prominent political personalities rather than around large groups in Russian society, such as social classes or religious denominations. A few parties are committed to human rights and other democratic ideals, while others are more concerned with asserting the power of the Russian state or other aspects of Russian nationalism, but most parties lack distinct ideological convictions. Russia's parties are elite centered and have practically no roots in civil society. The Communist Party claims to have hundreds of thousands of members, but it remains a hierarchy run by its leaders, much as in Soviet times. Until recently, most other parties have been considerably smaller, with only a few hundred, or at most a few thousand, members. Party policy and the selection of candidates for office are largely determined by professional politicians rather than by citizen-activists or membership votes.

The fragmentation of Russia's party system is due in part to the electoral system governing Duma elections and to Russia's structure as a federation of eighty-nine constituent units. In 2001, there were more than two hundred parties. A party (or a bloc of parties that fielded candidates jointly) had to get at least 5 percent of the nationwide vote to elect representatives to the Duma. In four Duma elections starting in 1993, only about a dozen parties or party blocs have cleared that hurdle. The single-member-district vote, however, enabled smaller parties or independent candidates unaffiliated with any party to enter the Duma, sometimes in large numbers. Nearly one-fourth of the Duma members elected in 1999—123 deputies—were independents or the representatives of very small parties. Most of the independent deputies ultimately joined a party, but only after presenting themselves to the voters on election day as independents. Some 23 parties fielded candidates in the December 2003 Duma elections (compared with 26 in 1999 and 43 in 1995); only 4 won seats in the proportional-representation ballot. In the single-member-district contests, there were fifteen candidates per district in 2003 (compared with ten in 1999) and nearly seventy independents were elected.[65]

Russia's federated system exacerbates party fragmentation. More than three out of four deputies elected to serve in the country's eighty-nine regional legislatures do not belong to any of the nationally organized parties. The governors of most regions and other executive-level regional officials are similarly detached from the national parties. Thus the parties represented in Russia's Duma do not speak for the vast majority of political elites in the provinces, another source of the Duma's weakness.

The Duma elections held on December 7, 2003, reinforced these tendencies. The vote resulted in a substantial victory for President Putin's allies, the *United Russia* party. Putin himself—who belonged to no party—had encouraged the formation of the United Russia party, which was formed in 2001 with the merger of the former Unity party with the former Fatherland–All Russia party led by Moscow's powerful mayor, Yuri Luzhkov. Unity and Fatherland–All Russia were "parties of power" par excellence; their merger made United Russia by far the country's largest party of this type. By taking 222 (49.3 percent) of the Duma's 450 seats, United Russia was expected to give President Putin an even greater hold over the Duma than he had previously enjoyed. With Vladimir Zhirinovsky's Liberal Democrats and the *Motherland* party, a nationalist group formed only months before the election, voting together with United Russia and with a number of like-minded deputies, Putin would have the support of two-thirds of the Duma. That figure would give him the supermajority he needs to push through constitutional amendments on such issues as removing the two-term limit on the presidency.

Putin's main opponents—the Communists and the liberal reformers attached to Yabloko and the Union of Rightwing Forces—registered heavy losses in 2003. The Communists fell from 113 seats to 52; the Union of Rightwing Forces declined from 29 seats to 3; and Yabloko went from 20 seats to only 4. The Communists' party-list vote was halved, and the two most pronouncedly democratic parties both slipped under the 5 percent hurdle. (For the results, see table 20.5.)

Henry Hale has described Russia's nascent party system in terms of an electoral marketplace. (For early conceptions of electoral markets, see chapter 11.) In the Russian political market, candidates and voters have been able to make their choices from among a variety of competing parties as well as *party substitutes*. Even though both the Yeltsin and Putin presidential administrations intervened directly in the political market to help the parties they favored and weaken the ones they opposed, dispensing or withholding the favors of political patronage from the central government, local political forces at the regional level have managed to cultivate their own political support outside the framework of the parties. Russia has thus far developed only a "partial party system," Hale observes, because candidates and their constituents have found options other than parties to meet their political needs. Examples of such party substitutes have included local political machines, politically engaged financial-industrial groups, and powerful regional officials who have often formed patron-client relationships with their followers. In many instances these party substitutes have fared better than the parties themselves.[66]

During his second term, President Putin undertook strenuous efforts to revamp the party system. In addition to changing the Duma's electoral system starting in the 2007 elections and curtailing the power of regional governors, Putin actively promoted the development of his United Russia party.

In mid 2006 this "party of power" reported having 1 million members and announced plans to recruit a million more by the 2007 elections. The government also went after parties it opposed. At the end of 2005, the Motherland (*Rodina*) party, the right-wing nationalist group that was becoming Russia's most rapidly growing party under Dmitry Rogozin, was banned from participating in the Moscow city elections after it sponsored an inflammatory advertisement implying that immigrants were "rubbish." In the following year Putin personally arranged Rogozin's replacement by a businessman and orchestrated Motherland's merger with two smaller parties. The leaders duly announced their support for Putin's policies. The government also quashed the National Bolsheviks, a small ultra-right party supported by disruptive skinheads. Meanwhile, the small liberal parties that were unable to surmount the 5 percent hurdle in the 2003 Duma elections managed to capture 11 percent of the vote in the Moscow city elections, boosting their hopes for a comeback at the national level.

Women were significantly underrepresented in the political process. They accounted for only 7.9 percent of the Duma elected in 1999 and 9.8 percent of the one elected in 2003. Women held about 10 percent of the administrative positions in Putin's administration, and in 2006 only one regional governor was a woman—the governor of St. Petersburg, a Putin supporter. It was feared that Putin's electoral law reforms may reduce the number of women elected to the Duma in 2007. Although party-list proportional representation tends to promote the election of women to parliament in Western Europe, Russia's parties have not been inclined to place women at the top of their lists, nor have they established quota systems requiring a certain percentage of their candidates to be women. The new 7 percent threshold and the ban on multiparty electoral blocs are likely to keep small parties concerned with women's issues out of the next Duma in 2007.[67]

Nongovernmental organizations (NGOs)—the main base of civil society—have increased appreciably since Russia's independence. By 2003 there were 300,000 NGOs registered with the authorities, with 2.5 million participants. About one-fourth of these organizations were charitable in nature; others were concerned with the environment, health care, human rights, and other issues. At an extraordinary meeting held in 2001 with five thousand representatives of civic organizations, President Putin asserted that civil society "should evolve independently, feeding on the spirit of freedom." Later he spoke of Russia's need for a "mature civil society" without specifying what he meant. Although Putin cultivated ties with NGOs that served his own political agenda, his administration clamped down heavily on human rights organizations and watchdog groups that were critical of his government. In 2006 Putin got the legislature to pass a new law severely restricting the rights of NGOs funded from abroad. The legislation, clearly aimed at Western human rights organizations that promote democracy, forbids them to engage in "political activity" but does not define that term. Putin himself accused foreign NGOs of funding espionage in Russia. Though business associations have been proliferating, membership in Russia's postcommunist trade union umbrella organization, the Federation of Independent Trade Unions of Russia, is much lower than communist-era levels.

Political attitudes are an important barometer of a country's political culture. Russian attitudes toward politics changed profoundly and rapidly once Gorbachev flung open the windows to greater freedom of expression in the 1980s, but interest in politics quickly subsided during the economic shocks of the early Yeltsin years. Sizable segments of the population clung to nondemocratic attitudes well after independence. In 1991–94, for example, 55 percent said they preferred a leader with an "iron hand," while only 30 percent favored democracy. In 1998, one-third said that they would support a dictator if necessary to restore order, and half said they would not resist a dictatorship to preserve their freedoms. In 1999, approximately half of Russians surveyed said they did not know what democracy is or how it is supposed to work. Only 36 percent believed that elections in Russia were honest.[68]

When asked in 1991 what kind of political system should be relied on to solve Russia's problems, 51 percent favored democracy and 39 percent preferred a "strong leader." When the same question was asked in 2005, only 28 percent favored democracy and 66 percent preferred a strong leader.

The same survey revealed that disillusionment with democracy was especially evident among the "revolutionary generation" that came of age as the Soviet Union collapsed. In 1991, 58 percent of 18- to 34-year-olds preferred democracy to a strong leader. But in 2005 only 29 percent of this same cohort, now aged 32 to 48, favored democracy; 66 percent wanted a strong leader.[69] Xenophobic sentiments are also visible in contemporary Russia: about 60 percent of both younger and older Russians agree with the slogan "Russia for ethnic Russians!" In 2005 approximately 40 percent favored deporting all immigrants and their children.[70] As in previous years, Russians in 2005 overwhelmingly regarded a strong economy as more important than a good democracy. Only 14 percent placed democracy first, whereas 81 percent prioritized economic considerations.[71]

In a 2001 survey, Russians who were indifferent or even hostile to civil liberties outnumbered by more than 2 to 1 those who strongly supported them. Three out of four believed that it is justifiable for the state to violate human rights for the sake of order and public safety—to combat crime, terrorism, or corruption, for example. Surprisingly, Russians aged fifty to fifty-nine were somewhat more supportive of civil rights than were those under thirty.[72]

Surveys conducted in 2002 and 2003 revealed that Russian society was divided into three approximately equal parts: one favoring democracy, another favoring authoritarianism, and the third either completely indifferent or "up for grabs," unable to decide between the two alternatives. Only 31 percent said that "democracy is always preferable"; 35 percent said that "authoritarian government is sometimes preferable." When asked if they would vote for Stalin today if he were running for president, 12 percent said they "definitely" would and 14 percent said they "probably" would vote for him. A minority—41 percent—said they would "definitely" not vote for him, while 19 percent said they would "probably" not vote for him and fully 15 percent were unsure. Young people were only slightly more inclined to reject Stalin than were older Russians, but only a minority of them (48 percent) were definite about it. "Assumptions that a younger generation of democrats will simply replace the older generic communists have little basis in reality," the surveyors concluded.[73]

Political culture can take a long time to change, though cataclysmic events like war or civil turmoil can sometimes hasten its transformation. For now, however, it appears that support for civil rights and democracy is fragile in Russian society.

### Education and Freedom of Information

Russia's new constitution guarantees tuition-free higher education on a competitive basis. Since the fall of communism the country's educational system has freed itself from the shackles of communist ideology and the censorship of politically unacceptable ideas. Russians are now free to pursue artistic creativity and scientific research without government interference. Unfortunately, Russia's economic doldrums have left the educational system seriously underfunded. Moreover, teachers, professors, and researchers—the backbone of the Soviet intelligentsia—were hit very hard by the collapse of the economy in the 1990s. Many of Russia's best-educated people have had a difficult time coping with the country's painful transition to democracy and private enterprise.

As we have seen, freedom of information has been a problematic issue, especially since Vladimir Putin assumed the presidency. In his first state-of-the-nation address in 2000, Putin acknowledged that "without really free mass media, Russian democracy simply will not survive." Print media are more free and abundant than in the days of Soviet censorship. Some six thousand newspapers and four thousand magazines are now available. But the killing of Anna Politkovskaya and twenty other journalists between 2000 and 2006 sends an unmistakable message that the Putin administration, and perhaps others subjected to journalistic investigations, will not tolerate a free press. Most privately owned publications are in the hands of a few tycoons, some with close connections to state authorities. Moreover, the government has taken numerous measures to extinguish the last vestiges of editorial independence. In 2004, for example, it imposed a $10 million legal bill on *Kommersant,* a paper owned by the exiled Boris Berezovsky, after the paper won an antidefamation case against the government. In the same year some six thousand lawsuits were filed by the government against media outlets and journalists accused of libeling state officials. In 2005 the state used its large stake in Gazprom, the energy conglomerate, to acquire the respected newspaper *Izvestiya* from its billionaire owner. This was not the first instance in which Gazprom's media arm was used to bring the print or broadcast media under government control. Later in the year the country's last remaining independent television news anchor was fired. In addition, President Putin aggressively exploited the state's control of broadcast media to boost his candidacy in two presidential elections, denying his opponents equal time. His administration has continuously used the state television networks to manage the news.

Although the constitution guarantees the secrecy of private communications, e-mail transmissions are monitored by the federal intelligence service, a fact that raises concerns among human rights groups and other politically oriented NGOs. Internet usage is still a rarity: only about 4 percent of the Russian population used the Web in 2005, though the numbers are growing by 20 to 40 percent per year.[74]

### The International Environment

From the inception of Russia's postcommunist regime, the international environment has had a mixture of positive and negative consequences for Russian democracy. On the positive side, Russia's democratization—especially in the Yeltsin years—was greeted warmly by the United States, Western Europe, and Japan. These former enemies of the Soviet Union joined with the International Monetary Fund and other international organizations in providing billions of dollars in loans, technical advice, food, and other forms of assistance. The end of the Cold War also brought a major diminution of the nuclear arms race between Russia and the West: both Yeltsin and Putin signed historic arms reduction agreements with the United States that resulted in the destruction of nuclear warheads and guided missiles. In part for these reasons, the power of Russia's military establishment as a bastion of support for dictatorship has diminished appreciably. The United States also financed programs aimed at keeping Russia's nuclear material from being stolen and transferred to other countries seeking to build nuclear weapons. Nevertheless, postcommunist Russia has always had its own national interests, just like any other independent country. Not all of these interests have coincided with those of the West.

Despite generally cordial relations with the United States and its allies during the Yeltsin years, there were frictions over several issues. Yeltsin's government voiced objections to NATO's enlargement, which incorporated into the transatlantic alliance the USSR's former allies in Central and Eastern Europe along with the former Soviet republics of Estonia, Latvia, and Lithuania. The Yeltsin government also had doubts about the NATO bombardment of Serbia, Russia's historic ally, during the war over Kosovo in 1999. (The Russians joined in the NATO-organized postwar peacekeeping mission there, however.)[75] Disputes between Russia and the West have multiplied since Putin became president in 2000. Putin declined to support the U.S.-led invasion of Iraq in 2003, siding openly with France and Germany in opposing the war. The United States has tried to persuade the Putin government to cancel an agreement to sell nuclear reactors to Iran, fearing that the Iranian government will use them to build nuclear weapons instead of limiting their use to electricity generation. The U.S. government has tried to enlist Putin's support at the United Nations for strong sanctions against Iran. Putin made some moves to accommodate U.S. concerns, some of which Russia shares (Russia has no interest in seeing Iran become a nuclear military power); but he did not cancel the reactor deal. The United States and Russia have also engaged in an ongoing rivalry for control over energy resources in the Caspian Sea region.

Putin clashed with the West more directly over Ukraine as the Orange Revolution unfolded. While the United States and the European Union strongly backed the pro-democracy candidate Viktor Yushchenko, Putin's administration supported his opponent, Viktor Yanukovich. The Western allies also objected to the Putin government's use of the "energy weapon" in exerting pressure on the governments of Ukraine and Georgia (see chapter 1). The "color revolutions" that promoted at least a limited amount of democratization in Ukraine, Georgia, and Kyrgyzstan were hailed in the West, but they provoked precisely the opposite reaction in the Kremlin. Putin felt threatened by the wave of democratization on Russia's borders, fearing among other things that they could lead to membership in NATO for Ukraine and Georgia and stimulate pressures for more effective democratization in Russia, thereby undermining his own power. (At the end of 2006, Russia still had troops in Georgia's breakaway regions, despite the Georgian government's demands for their withdrawal.)

In spite of these and other disagreements, Presidents Bush and Putin made special efforts to remain on friendly terms. Bush stated after meeting with Putin in 2001 that he "was able to get a good sense of his soul" and that he regarded Putin as "an honest, straightforward man who loves his country." After September 11, 2001, the two presidents pledged mutual support in the war on terrorism, a commitment that prompted Bush to refrain from condemning Russian tactics in Chechnya and in the hostage incidents that occurred in the Moscow theater in 2002 and Beslan in 2004. After Putin denounced the U.S. decision to invade Iraq, Secretary of State Condoleezza Rice advised Bush to "punish France, ignore Germany, and forgive Russia." Although various Bush administration officials, including Vice President Richard Cheney and Secretary Rice, expressed U.S. concerns about Putin's antidemocratic policies, President Bush himself tended to temper his criticisms of Putin's tightening restrictions on democratic practices.

The leaders of the Western alliance and Russia appear to understand that neither side stands to gain anything from a return to the harsh confrontation of the Cold War. President Putin no doubt wishes to assert Russia's basic interests and independence, but he recognizes that Russia is no longer a military or economic superpower. It is therefore likely that frictions and disputes will continue to mark Russia's relationships with the West, but these discords will be contained within an overall structure of agreement on the need to keep them from getting out of hand. The big question is whether the West can influence the fate of democracy inside Russia. Thus far it appears that President Putin feels a need to assure the West of his commitment to democracy in principle, but he does not seem willing to alter his authoritarian tendencies in practice.

## CONCLUSION

The developments surveyed in this chapter make it clear that, after the Gorbachev era, Russia took a historic leap in the direction of democracy, reversing a thousand years of unyielding suppression of democratic ideals by authoritarian rulers. The adoption of key features of the Temple of Democracy we described in chapter 7—including democratic values like freedom from tyranny, freedom of religion, and a commitment to popular sovereignty—was truly a revolutionary accomplishment. Nevertheless, there have been major shortcomings in Russia's democratic transition. Not all the structural elements of the Temple of Democracy have been constructed successfully, and some of the successes of Yeltsin's first years in power have been dismantled under President Putin. Respect for such values as individual freedom, trust, and compromise is on the wane. The principle of the rule of law has been repeatedly violated by an increasingly heavy-handed national leadership. Popular sovereignty (Pillar I of the temple) has been vitiated by attempts to manipulate the electoral process—first under President Yeltsin and his entourage, and more brazenly by President Putin. Key rights and liberties, especially freedom of the press (Pillar II), have been trampled. For the vast majority of Russians, economic wellbeing (Pillar III) has been absent from the very beginning of postcommunist Russia; the spoils of private enterprise have been snapped up by a handful of politically favored cronies of the country's two presidents. In addition, negative tendencies have marked virtually all ten conditions for democracy presented in this book. As a consequence, Russia's political system slipped in status from a semidemocratic regime to a semi-authoritarian regime in just a little over ten years.

President Putin's rhetoric has matched this retrogression. He has explicitly advocated a "dictatorship of the law," and his advisors have described his government as a "managed democracy."[76] In his second inaugural address following his landslide reelection in 2004, he did not mention the word *democracy* even once. After critics at home and abroad pointed out this omission, Putin referred to democracy repeatedly in a subsequent speech. But he also spoke about the need for a "mature civil society," combining this vague phrase with threats against human rights and pro-democracy organizations. Putin's blatant attempts to intimidate the press, reorganize the electoral process, and harass political opponents have raised troubling questions about what he means by a "mature civil society." In 2005 Putin gave indications that he planned to handpick his successor. Several months after announcing that he would not seek a constitutional amendment permitting him to run for a third term, Putin promoted his chief of staff, *Dmitry Medvedev*, to the post of first deputy prime minister. (Medvedev was simultaneously the chairman of Gazprom.) Defense Minister Sergei Ivanov was promoted to deputy prime minister. Medvedev and Ivanov were immediately touted by political observers as Putin's first and second choices for Russia's next president. Earlier, the government announced that it had launched a criminal investigation into allegations that former prime minister Mikhail Kasyanov had earned illegal profits in a real estate transaction. Kasyanov was already an outspoken critic of Putin's antidemocracy measures and was preparing to run for the presidency in 2008. If convicted, he would not be allowed to run.

For all his faults, Putin is not a Soviet-style dictator or a new tsar. He owes his legitimacy to Russian voters, and in 2006 he enjoyed a sky-high approval rating of 70 percent. His assertion of strong state authority is viewed by millions of Russians as a welcome barrier against a return to the uncertainties and free-fall disorder of the Gorbachev and Yeltsin years. Widespread support for a "strong leader" instead of a more pluralistic democracy props up Putin's brand of *popular authoritarianism*. And though the windows of free expression, electoral honesty, and judicial fairness are closing, Russians today still enjoy more freedoms than they were ever allowed under communism. Among other things, they may still join NGOs and political parties, they may worship freely (though some non-Orthodox faiths are discriminated against), they may travel abroad, they have access to information and culture from around the world, and they are free from the incessant drumbeat of Marxist-Leninist propaganda and the stultifying communist censorship system. In addition, Putin has repeatedly reaffirmed his commitment to private property, a value now regarded by 80 percent of the Russian population as a basic right.

It would be foolhardy to predict what the coming years will bring for Russia. It is far too early to tell whether democracy will flourish or fail, or whether perhaps, in the decades that lie ahead, Russia will oscillate back and forth across the fine line that separates semi-democracies from semi-authoritarian regimes. The unpredictability of Russia's future reminds us of Winston Churchill's famous observation more than half a century ago that Russia is "a riddle wrapped in a mystery inside an enigma."

## KEY TERMS AND NAMES
## (In bold and underlined in the text)

Boris Yeltsin
Mikhail Gorbachev
Union of Soviet Socialist Republics/USSR/Soviet Union
Communist Party of the Soviet Union (CPSU)
Commonwealth of Independent States (CIS)
Vladimir Putin
Vladimir Ilich Lenin
Bolsheviks
October Revolution
Marxism-Leninism
Joseph Stalin
Centrally planned economy (CPE)
Leonid Brezhnev
President
Prime minister
State Duma
Federation Council

## NOTES

1. Freedom House, *Freedom in the World: The Annual Survey of Political Rights and Civil Liberties 1994–1995* (New York: Freedom House, 1995), 477–82; *Freedom in the World 2003* (New York: Freedom House, 2003), 458–65; *Freedom in the World 2005* (New York: Freedom House, 2005), 519–24; and *Freedom in the World 2006* (New York: Freedom House, 2006), 586–92. See also the annual reports on Russia published by

Freedom House in *Freedom of the Press*, www.freedomhouse.org, and by Reporters Without Borders, www.rsf.org. On Politkovskaya, see the *Washington Post*, October 7, 8, 9, 11, and 13, 2006.

2. A classic survey is Nicholas V. Riasanovsky and Mark Steinberg, *A History of Russia*, 7th ed. (New York: Oxford University Press, 2004).
3. Robert K. Massie, *Peter the Great* (New York: Knopf, 1980).
4. Liah Greenfeld, *Nationalism: Five Roads to Modernity* (Cambridge, Mass.: Harvard University Press, 1992), ch. 3 (especially p. 265). She argues that whereas the Slavophiles abandoned the attempt to catch up with the West on the economic and political planes, exalting instead the pristine Russian "soul," the Westernizers favored borrowing technology from the West with the ultimate aim of demonstrating Russia's economic or military capabilities (like Peter the Great) or of eventually overtaking the West (like the communists).
5. Isabel de Madariaga, *Russia in the Age of Catherine the Great* (New Haven: Yale University Press, 1981).
6. Richard Pipes, *Russia Under the Old Regime* (New York: Scribner's, 1974), 281–318.
7. Dominic Lieven, *Russia's Rulers Under the Old Regime* (New Haven: Yale University Press, 1989).
8. Marc Raeff, ed., *The Decembrist Movement* (Englewood Cliffs, N.J.: Prentice Hall, 1966).
9. Franco Venturi, *Roots of Revolution*, trans. M. Haskell (New York: Grosset and Dunlap, 1960).
10. Alexander Gerschenkron, *Economic Backwardness in Historical Perspective* (Cambridge, Mass.: Harvard University Press, 1962).
11. Victoria E. Bonnell, *Roots of Rebellion* (Berkeley: University of California Press, 1983).
12. See, for example, Engels's letter to the Russian revolutionary Peter Tkachov in Robert C. Tucker, ed., *The Marx-Engels Reader* (New York: W. W. Norton, 1972), 589–99.
13. The big winners were the Socialist Revolutionaries, with 40 percent of the vote. The Socialist Revolutionaries were the heirs of the populists and had a large rural following. Though their left wing was quite radical, their large right-wing faction favored Western-style democracy. The Western-oriented liberals, the Constitutional Democrats, won 5 percent.
14. In 1930, Stalin said, "We are for the withering away of the state. But at the same time we stand for the strengthening of the proletarian dictatorship. . . . Is this 'contradictory'? Yes, it is 'contradictory.' But this contradiction is life, and it reflects completely the Marxian dialectic." In justifying the terror, Stalin said that the closer one gets to socialism, the more intense the class struggle becomes. Biographies include Adam B. Ulam, *Stalin* (New York: Viking, 1973); Robert B. Tucker, *Stalin as Revolutionary, 1879–1929* (New York: W. W. Norton, 1973) and *Stalin in Power* (New York: W. W. Norton, 1990); Isaac Deutscher, *Stalin* (New York: Vintage, 1960).
15. Robert Conquest, *The Harvest of Sorrow* (New York: Oxford University Press, 1986).
16. One of the most famous defendants was Nikolai Bukharin. See Stephen F. Cohen, *Bukharin and the Bolshevik Revolution* (New York: Vintage, 1975). His trial formed the basis of the novel by Arthur Koestler titled *Darkness at Noon.*
17. Robert Conquest, *The Great Terror* (Harmondsworth, U.K.: Penguin, 1971); J. Arch Getty, *Origins of the Great Purges* (Cambridge: Cam-bridge University Press, 1985).
18. On August 23, 1939, the Soviet Union and Germany signed an agreement to partition Poland. Several weeks after the German army invaded that country on September 1, 1939, Soviet forces moved into eastern Poland and annexed it. (The annexed territory today is part of Ukraine.) The Germans also handed over Lithuania, Latvia, and Estonia to the USSR.
19. Lazar Pistrak, *The Grand Tactician* (New York: Praeger, 1961).
20. The full text is in *The Anti-Stalin Campaign and International Communism* (New York: Columbia University Press, 1956).
21. Solzhenitsyn's *One Day in the Life of Ivan Denisovich,* published in a Soviet literary journal, was based on his own incarceration in a Stalinist labor camp.
22. Nikita Sergeevich Khrushchev, *Memoirs of Nikita Khrushchev: Commissar (1818–1945)*, trans. George Shriver and Stephen Shenfield (University Park: Pennsylvania State University Press, 2005); N. S. Khrushchev and Sergei Khrushchev, *Memoirs of Nikita Khrushchev: Reformer (1945–1964)*

(University Park: Pennsylvania State University Press, 2006); William Taubman, *Khrushchev: The Man and his Era* (New York: W. W. Norton, 2003); Sergei N. Khrushchev, *Nikita Khrushchev and the Creation of a Superpower,* trans. Shirley Benson (University Park: Pennsylvania State University Press, 2000); and Carl A. Linden, *Khrushchev and the Soviet Leadership, 1957–1964* (Baltimore: Johns Hopkins University Press, 1966).

**23.** Sidney Bloch and Peter Reddaway, *Soviet Psychiatric Abuse* (London: V. Gollancz, 1984).

**24.** Seweryn Bialer, *Stalin's Successors* (Cambridge: Cambridge University Press, 1980).

**25.** Mikhail Gorbachev, *Perestroika* (New York: Harper and Row, 1987 and 1988).

**26.** Anders Åslund, *Gorbachev's Struggle for Economic Reform* (Ithaca, N.Y.: Cornell University Press, 1989); Marshall I. Goldman, *Gorbachev's Challenge* (New York: W. W. Norton, 1987).

**27.** Michael J. Sodaro, *Moscow, Germany, and the West from Khrushchev to Gorbachev* (Ithaca, N.Y.: Cornell University Press, 1990).

**28.** Gale Stokes, *The Walls Came Tumbling Down* (New York: Oxford University Press, 1993); David Pryce-Jones, *The Strange Death of the Soviet Empire* (New York: Henry Holt, 1995).

**29.** Grigory Yavlinsky, Boris Fedorov, Stanislav Shatalin, et al., *500 Days,* trans. David Kushner (New York: St. Martin's Press, 1991). See also Marshall I. Goldman, *What Went Wrong with Perestroika?* (New York: W. W. Norton, 1991).

**30.** On the coup, see Victoria E. Bonnell, Ann Cooper, and Gregory Freidin, eds., *Russia at the Barricades* (Armonk, N.Y.: M. E. Sharpe, 1994).

**31.** Mikhail Gorbachev, *Memoirs,* trans. Wolf Jobst Siedler (New York: Doubleday, 1995). The most substantial monographs are Archie Brown, *The Gorbachev Factor* (Oxford: Oxford University Press, 1996); and Jerry F. Hough, *Democratization and Revolution in the USSR, 1985–1991* (Washington, D.C.: Brookings Institution, 1997). See also Stephen Kotkin, *Armageddon Averted: The Soviet Collapse, 1970–2000* (New York: Oxford University Press, 2003); Mark R. Beissinger, *Nationalist Mobilization and the Collapse of the Soviet State* (New York: Cambridge University Press, 2002); and Steven L. Solnick, *Stealing the State: Control and Collapse in Soviet Institutions* (Cambridge, Mass.: Harvard University Press, 1998). For an insider's account, see Yegor Ligachev, *Inside Gorbachev's Kremlin,* trans. Catherine A. Fitzpatrick, Michele A. Berdy, and Dobrochna Dyrcz-Freedman (New York: Pantheon, 1993). See also Carl Linden, "Gorbachev and the Fall of the Marxian Prince in Europe and Russia," in *Russia and China on the Eve of a New Millennium,* ed. Carl Linden and Jan A. Prybyla (New Brunswick, N.J.: Transaction, 1997), 59–87.

**32.** Michael McFaul, *Russia's Unfinished Revolution: Political Change from Gorbachev to Putin* (Ithaca, N.Y.: Cornell University Press, 2001), 33–117.

**33.** On the formation of opposition movements in this period, see Judith Devlin, *The Rise of the Russian Democrats* (Aldershot, U.K.: Edward Elgar, 1995); Michael Urban, Vyacheslav Igrunov, and Sergei Mitrokhin, *The Rebirth of Politics in Russia* (Cambridge: Cambridge University Press, 1997); and M. Steven Fish, *Democracy from Scratch: Opposition and Regime in the New Russian Revolution* (Princeton: Princeton University Press, 1995).

**34.** Boris Yeltsin, *Against the Grain: An Autobiography,* trans. Michael Glenny (New York: Summit, 1990). See also Andrei S. Grachev, *Final Days,* trans. Margo Milne (Boulder, Colo.: Westview, 1995).

**35.** Martin J. Peck and Thomas J. Richardson, *What Is to Be Done? Proposals for the Soviet Transition to Market* (New Haven: Yale University Press, 1991); Anders Åslund, *How Russia Became a Market Economy* (Washington, D.C.: Brookings Institution, 1995).

**36.** Olga Bridges and Jim Bridges, *Losing Hope: The Environment and Health in Russia* (Aldershot, U.K.: Avebury, 1996).

**37.** Yegor Gaidar, *Days of Defeat and Victory,* trans. Jane Ann Miller (Seattle: University of Washington Press, 1999).

**38.** McFaul, *Russia's Unfinished Revolution,* 121–312.

**39.** See Michael McFaul, "Russia's Choice: The Perils of Revolutionary Democracy," in *Growing Pains: Russian Democracy and the Election of 1993,* ed. Timothy J. Colton and Jerry F. Hough (Washington, D.C.: Brookings Institution, 1998), 115–39. See also Peter Lentini, ed., *Elections and the Political Order in Russia* (Budapest: Central European University Press, 1995).

**40.** Carlotta Gall and Thomas de Waal, *Chechnya* (New York: New York University Press, 1998), and Anatol Lieven, *Chechnya* (New Haven: Yale University Press, 1998).

**41.** Peter Reddaway and Dmitri Glinski, *The Tragedy of Russia's Reforms: Market Bolshevism Against Democracy* (Washington, D.C.: United States Institute of Peace Press, 2001); and David E. Hoffman, *The Oligarchs: Wealth and Power in the New Russia* (New York: Public Affairs, 2002).

**42.** Phil Williams, ed., *Russian Organized Crime: The New Threat?* (London: Frank Cass, 1997); Stephen Handelman, *Comrade Criminal: Russia's New Mafiya* (New Haven: Yale University Press, 1995).

**43.** Jerry F. Hough, Evelyn Davidheiser, and Susan Goodrich Lehmann, *The 1996 Russian Presidential Election* (Washington, D.C.: Brookings Institution, 1996), 40.

**44.** Lilia Shevtsova, *Yeltsin's Russia* (Washington, D.C.: Carnegie Endowment for International Peace, 1999), 180–93. On Zyuganov and his party, see Joan Barth Urban and Valerii D. Solovei, *Russia's Communists at the Crossroads* (Boulder, Colo.: Westview, 1997).

**45.** See George W. Breslauer, *Gorbachev and Yeltsin as Leaders* (Cambridge: Cambridge University Press, 2002).

**46.** According to the Institute of International Finance, a Western organization, Russia by the spring of 1998 had borrowed $99 billion from abroad, but $103 billion had left the country (*Washington Post,* May 30, 1998). Another Western estimate reported $136 billion in capital outflows between 1993 and 1998 (*Financial Times,* August 21/22, 1999). The organized crime figure was estimated by American scholar Louise Shelley, *Financial Times,* March 20, 1997. See also *The Economist,* August 28, 1999, and the views of IMF Managing Director Michel Camdessus is the *Washington Post,* June 17, 1999.

**47.** On the financial oligarchy and Russia's economic development, see Rose Brady, *Kapitalizm* (New Haven: Yale University Press, 1999); Bertram Silverman and Murray Yanowitch, *New Rich, New Poor, New Russia* (Armonk, N.Y.: M. E. Sharpe, 1997); Juliet Johnson, *A Fistful of Rubles: The Rise and Fall of the Russian Banking System* (Ithaca, N.Y.: Cornell University Press, 2000); and Chrystia Freeland, *Sale of the Century: Russia's Wild Ride from Communism to Capitalism* (New York: Crown Business, 2000).

**48.** For his own account of his presidency, see Boris Yeltsin, *Midnight Diaries,* trans. Catherine A. Fitzpatrick (New York: Public Affairs, 2000).

**49.** For Putin's background and ideas upon assuming the presidency, see Vladimir Putin, with Nataliya Gevorkyan, Nataliya Timakova, and Andrei Kolesnikov, *First Person: An Astonishingly Frank Self-Portrait by Russia's President Vladimir Putin,* trans. Catherine A. Fitzpatrick (New York: Public Affairs, 2000).

**50.** Freedom House, *Freedom in the World 2003,* 464; *Freedom in the World 2006*, 591; *Washington Post,* September 30, 2006; and the U.S. State Department's annual reports on human rights practices in Russia, accessible at www.state.gov/g/drl.

**51.** According to a 2002 survey, 58 percent of those polled in Russia identified themselves as Orthodox, 31 percent as atheists, 5 percent as Muslims, and less than 2 percent as adherents of other Christian denominations. It was estimated that there were 600,000 to 1 million Jews in Russia. Freedom House, *Nations in Transit 2003* (New York: Freedom House, 2003), 510. See also the following Policy Memos published by the Program on New Approaches to Russian Security (PONARS): Dmitry Gorenburg, "Russia's Muslims: A Growing Challenge for Moscow"; Judyth Twigg, "Differential Demographics: Russia's Muslim and Slavic Populations"; and Eduard Ponarin, "Russian State Nationalism vs. Local Nationalisms: The Case of Tatarstan," at www.csis.org/ruseura/ponars/pm.

**52.** Juan J. Linz and Alfred Stepan, *Problems of Democratic Transition and Consolidation* (Baltimore: Johns Hopkins University Press, 1996), 28.

**53.** On regionalism, see Mary McAuley, *Russia's Politics of Uncertainty* (Cambridge: Cambridge University Press, 1997); Vladimir Shlapentokh, Roman Levita, and Mikhail Loiberg, *From Submission to Rebellion: The Provinces Versus the Center in Russia* (Boulder, Colo.: Westview, 1997); Kathryn Stoner-Weiss, *Local Heroes: The Political Economy of Russian Regional Governance* (Princeton: Princeton University Press, 1997); and Mikhail Stoliarov, *Federalism and the*

*Dictatorship of Power* (London: Routledge, 2000). On the role of the seven federal okrugs, see Peter Reddaway and Robert W. Orttung, eds., *The Dynamics of Russian Politics: Putin's Reform of Federal-Regional Relations,* vol. 1 (Lanham, Md.: Rowman and Littlefield, 2004). See also Gulnaz Sharafutdinova, "When Do Elites Compete? The Determinants of Political Competition in Russian Regions," *Comparative Politics* 38, no. 3 (April 2006): 273–93; and Grigorii V. Golosov, "What Went Wrong: Regional Electoral Politics and Impediments to State Centralization in Russia, 2003–2004," www.csis.org/ruseura/ponars/pm.

**54.** *Financial Times,* November 1–2, 2003; and Brian D. Taylor, "Power Surge? Russia's Power Ministries from Yeltsin to Putin and Beyond," www.csis.org/ruseura/ponars/pm.

**55.** Peter Baker and Susan B. Glasner, *Kremlin Rising: Vladimir Putin's Russia and the End of Revolution* (New York: Scribner, 2005); Andrew Jack, *Inside Putin's Russia: Can There Be Reform Without Democracy?* (New York: Oxford University Press, 2004); Cameron Ross, ed., *Russian Politics Under Putin* (Manchester, U.K.: Manchester University Press, 2004); Timothy J. Colton and Michael McFaul, "Putin and Democratization," in *Putin's Russia: Past Imperfect, Future Uncertain,* ed. Dale R. Herspring (Lanham, Md.: Rowman and Littlefield, 2003), 13.

**56.** Lilia Shevtsova, *Putin's Russia* (Washington, D.C.: Carnegie Endowment for International Peace, 2003), 59ff.

**57.** McFaul, *Russia's Unfinished Revolution,* 310–12; Shevtsova, *Yeltsin's Russia,* 277ff.

**58.** Sophia Moestrup, *Semi-Presidentialism in Comparative Perspective: Its Effects on Democratic Survival,* Ph.D. dissertation, George Washington University, 2003.

**59.** *Washington Post,* December 14, 2002. See also the 2006 OECD "Economic Survey of the Russian Federation," www.oecd.org.

**60.** M. Steven Fish, *Democracy Derailed in Russia: The Failure of Open Politics* (New York: Cambridge University Press, 2005).

**61.** Freedom House, *Nations in Transit,* 523.

**62.** Center for Citizen Initiatives, http://www.ccisf.org/pep/stabilizes.htm.

**63.** Harley Balzer, "Russia's Middle Classes," *Post-Soviet Affairs* 14, no. 2 (1998): 165–86, and "Routinization of the New Russians?" *Russian Review* 62 (June 2003): 15–36; and Thane Gustafson, *Capitalism, Russian-Style* (Cambridge: Cambridge University Press, 1999), 43–44, 176–79.

**64.** UN population data can be found at http://esa.un.org/unpp. See also *Washington Post*, May 11, 2006.

**65.** Richard Rose and Neil Munro, *Elections Without Order: Russia's Challenge to Vladimir Putin* (Cambridge: Cambridge University Press, 2002); Timothy Colton, *Transitional Citizens: Voters and What Influences Them in the New Russia* (Cambridge, Mass.: Harvard University Press, 2000); and Christopher Marsh, *Russia at the Polls*: *Voters, Elections, and Democratization* (Washington, D.C.: Congressional Quarterly Press, 2002).

**66.** Henry E. Hale, *Why Not Parties in Russia? Democracy, Federalism, and the State* (New York: Cambridge University Press, 2006).

**67.** Freedom House, *Nations in Transit,* 504. See also Valerie Sperling, *Organizing Women in Contemporary Russia: Engendering Transition* (Cambridge: Cambridge University Press, 1999); and "The Fair Sex in an Unfair System: The Gendered Effects of Putin's Political Reforms," www.csis.org/ruseura/ponars/pm.

**68.** Matthew Wyman, *Public Opinion in Postcommunist Russia* (New York: St. Martin's Press, 1997); Vladimir Tismaneanu, ed., *Political Culture and Civil Society in Russia and the New States of Eurasia* (Armonk, N.Y.: M. E. Sharpe, 1995); U.S. Information Agency, *The People Have Spoken: Global Views of Democracy,* vol. 1 (January 1998) and vol. 2 (September 1999).

**69.** "Russia's Weakened Democratic Embrace," Pew Global Attitudes Survey, www.pewglobal.org. For earlier survey data, see McFaul, *Russia's Unfinished Revolution,* 332, 333.

**70.** Mikhail A. Alexeev, "Xenophobia in Russia: Are the Young Driving It?" www.csis.org/ruseura/ponars/pm.

**71.** "Russia's Weakened Democratic Embrace," www.pewglobal.org.

**72.** Theodore P. Gerber and Sarah E. Mendelson, "How Russians Think About Human Rights:

Recent Survey Data," *PONARS Policy Memo* no. 221 (December 2001), http://www.csis. org/ruseura/ponars/policymemos/pm_index.htm.

73. Theodore P. Gerber and Sarah E. Mendelson, "Up for Grabs: Russia's Political Trajectory and Stalin's Legacy," *PONARS Policy Memo* no. 296 (November 2003), http://www.csis.org/ruseura/ponars/policymemos/pm_index.htm.

74. Freedom House, *Freedom in the World 2006*, 590.

75. James M. Goldgeier and Michael McFaul, *Power and Purpose: U.S. Policy Toward Russia After the Cold War* (Washington, D.C.: Brookings Institution, 2003).

76. Timothy J. Colton and Michael McFaul, *Popular Choice and Managed Democracy: The Russian Elections of 1999 and 2000* (Washington, D.C.: Brookings Institution, 2003). See also Herspring, ed., *Putin's Russia: Past Imperfect, Future Uncertain.*

CHAPTER 21

# CHINA

BRUCE J. DICKSON

Population (2005, estimated): 1.3 billion
Freedom House Ratings (2005):
Political Rights—7; Civil Liberties—6

Area: 3.7 million square miles
(between the size of the
United States and Canada)

On the morning of June 5, 1989, a young man blocked a line of tanks moving through downtown Beijing. Holding nothing but a paper shopping bag, he faced off against the first tank in the line. As it tried to maneuver to one side or the other, he would also move to remain in its way. This bizarre little drama lasted for a few minutes until several of the man's friends ran out into the street and removed him from harm's way. The tanks continued on their path.

This vignette—as short as it was, and in the end as fruitless as it was—had a lasting impression on people in China and especially on observers overseas who had been captivated by the pro-democracy movement that gripped China in the spring of 1989. For several weeks, hundreds of Chinese students had staged unprecedented demonstrations in favor of democracy in Beijing's famed Tiananmen Square, issuing a bold challenge to China's communist dictators. Although the pro-democracy movement captured the world's attention and spread to hundreds of other Chinese cities, it was crushed overnight once the government decided to call in troops and tanks to arrest demonstrators and impose martial law. Unlike the Soviet Union and Eastern Europe, where the forces of democratization that were gathering strength at this time would ultimately topple communism, China experienced only a brief outburst of democratic sentiment before the communist authorities forcefully suppressed it. The picture of the man defying the tanks became a symbol of individual bravery in the face of tyranny, of the power of nonviolent protest against the overwhelming power of the state. But it also reminds us of the potential futility of such efforts. Ever since 1989, China's political institutions have remained firmly in the hands of the Communist Party leadership.

**Young man defies tanks as Chinese authorities crack down on the pro-democracy demonstrations in Tiananmen Square, 1989.**

Nevertheless, it cannot be said that China has been standing still since that extraordinary year. There is little dispute that China is a rising power on the world scene. Its diplomatic activities are expanding regionally and globally. Its dramatic economic growth, driven and sustained in large part by foreign investment and trade, has boosted China's impact on the global economy. In 2005 China registered a gross national income of more than $2.26 trillion, vaulting over the United Kingdom as the world's fourth largest economy after the United States, Japan, and Germany. With $1.3 trillion in foreign trade, China was the world's third largest exporting and importing country. Its military is also becoming stronger and more capable of wielding influence beyond its borders. Few people doubt that China is a force to be reckoned with in the world; the only question centers on *how* it will behave as an international actor. Will China be a threat to peace and stability in the Asia-Pacific region, or to American interests in that area or elsewhere in the world? Will it be a threat to the international economy? Or can China's growing power be smoothly incorporated into the international system? The reality of China's ascendancy is self-evident, but the implications of this reality are hotly debated.

In contrast to China's rising international stature, the country's domestic political situation is fraught with tension and turmoil. The **Chinese Communist Party (CCP)**, ***China's ruling party since 1949,*** shows no sign of undertaking fundamental political reforms. Instead, it is determined to remain in power by finding short-term solutions to immediate problems. But the party leadership faces mounting popular protests in the cities as well as in the countryside. Corruption seems to be endemic, and yet the party elite lacks the means or the will to crack down on corrupt officials, despite more than two decades of admitting rhetorically that stopping corruption is a matter of "life or death" for the party. In addition, China is experiencing a surge of popular nationalism: elements of the population are increasingly placing the interests of the Chinese people ahead of the interests of the Communist Party. Criticisms of the communist regime are spreading in cyberspace, as growing numbers of Chinese discuss their country's problems over the Internet. Faced with these challenges, the party has attempted to control the expression of critical views; but success has proven elusive. In contrast to their robust international presence, China's leaders are beset on the domestic scene with a host of problems for which they have no ready answer.

Can these opposing images of international strength and domestic fragility be reconciled? Of course, China is not alone in experiencing a mismatch between its international and domestic levels of political activity. Success in one realm does not readily transfer to the other. Moreover, the standards people use when assessing China's domestic politics vary widely. Many observers both inside and outside China evaluate the political reforms the country's leaders have initiated in recent years primarily in terms of whether they are making China more democratic. But democratization is not the only measure of political development. If we recognize that greater democracy is not the immediate goal of China's leaders, we may conclude that China's domestic environment is not so desperate or fragile after all.

The CCP has been more adaptable and more resilient than it often gets credit for being. It is pursuing a variety of political reforms that are intended to enhance the capacity of the state to govern effectively, if not democratically. It relies on a mix of measures to shore up popular support, resolve local protests, and incorporate those who have benefited from economic reform into the political system. At the same time, it forcefully represses challenges to its monopoly of political power and organization. As a result, public opinion is surprisingly complacent. Although many Chinese are unhappy with their current situation, they remain optimistic about the future. These attitudes are not a recipe for imminent revolution. The ruling elite faces serious problems, but they tend to be chronic rather than dangerously acute. Absent a sudden and unexpected flare-up, they do not pose an imminent threat to the communist regime. Despite the many economic, social, and political changes that are under way in China, the central fact of the Chinese political system remains the same: China is governed by a communist party. Virtually every aspect of Chinese politics—including the policy-making process, relations between state and society, and opportunities for political participation—are derived from that one fact. The top government officials, at the central level and at the local level, are party members. As in the former USSR, the party and the state are *fused* in communist China. Policies are normally debated, decided, and implemented by party members (often in their additional capacity as government officials) with little consultation with nonparty people or organizations. Most large organizations, including universities, factories, and government offices, have party organizations within them to monitor compliance with party policies. The party has a monopoly on political organization and zealously enforces it. Whether organized to represent labor or business, to pursue sports or other hobbies, or to enhance any common interest, every organization must be authorized by the party or else it runs the risk of being disbanded and having its leaders face arrest. The goal of these organizations is not to be independent of the state, which is often the case in a pluralist democracy. Instead, the goal is to be connected to the state, to be "within the system," because everyone knows that to be outside the system means you are powerless.

These realities do not mean that the CCP is monolithic or omnipotent. The history of the CCP's rule in China after coming to power in 1949 and establishing the *People's Republic of China (PRC)* has been marked by occasionally intense conflict over issues of power and policy. Party leaders do not always agree on the proper course of policy or even on the question of who should be in a position of power to make those decisions. The central state often cannot get lower levels of government, from the provincial level to the grass roots, to comply with its current policies. Moreover, the economic and political reforms of the past twenty years have reduced the state's control over the daily lives of most Chinese people, giving them greater independence to switch jobs, change their place of residence, travel, and have access to ideas and sources of information not controlled by the state. These changes have complicated the policy process and relaxed the state's dominance over society, but they have not challenged the CCP's preeminent position in China's political system. In a word, China's party leaders and state officials enjoy a considerable degree of latitude, or *autonomy*, when it comes to making decisions that affect the population, but the population does not have much autonomy from the party and state authorities to act in its own behalf.

The 1989 protests in Tiananmen Square and elsewhere in China demonstrated that there are few legitimate and effective means of political participation for aggrieved individuals and groups in Chinese society. Even though the basic demands of the movement—a crackdown on corruption and inflation, enforcement of the rule of law—were consistent with the government's own policies, the state felt threatened by the spontaneous nature of the movement and the growing popular support it elicited from all walks of life. Moreover, the communist party-state saw the formation of autonomous (but short-lived) student groups and labor unions as a direct challenge to its authority and an unacceptable change in China's political system. Without these types of autonomous groups, there is little accountability for government officials and very limited access to decision-making arenas by people affected by policy decisions. On an everyday basis, *clientelism*—that is, one-to-one relations based on the personal exchange of favors—is very common, and collective action by interest groups and other organizations is extremely rare. (On clientelism, see chapter 11.) Episodes of mass participation tend to be sporadic and unpredictable, prone to rapid escalation and extreme demands that result in a government crackdown rather than a negotiated compromise. The government protects its monopoly on political organization vigorously, without hesitation and without exception. It is motivated by reinforcing sentiments: a deep-rooted cultural fear of instability and the self-interested desire to preserve the Communist Party's power.

These issues reflect the five sources of conflict enumerated in chapter 2, raising a number of related questions about China's past, present, and future:

- *Power:* How is political power organized in China? Who should lead China, and on what basis should they govern? What is the proper relationship between state and society?
- *Resources:* How should China's resources be utilized? Should some regions and individuals be allowed to prosper while others lag behind, or is a more equitable distribution of wealth desirable? What is the proper balance between state regulation and market forces in shaping economic development?
- *Identity:* How many of China's traditions can be carried forward into the modern world? How much can be borrowed from the West without losing a sense of national identity? How is economic development changing the shared identities of regions and professions?
- *Ideas:* How did communism develop in China? Is an authoritarian state necessary to hold the country together during a time of rapid development? Is democracy suitable or viable in China?
- *Values:* Is China's traditional emphasis on the collective needs of the group (family, community, workplace, nation) compatible with individual freedoms? Is rapid economic growth weakening the cultural fabric of Chinese society?

Each of these sources of conflict has generated considerable debate in China, debates that continue to this day. The outcome of these debates will tell us much about where China is heading. To understand the nature of the debates, it is necessary to know where China has been.

## CHINA'S HISTORICAL LEGACIES: WHY NO DEMOCRACY?

A fascination with democracy began in China early in the twentieth century, but the Chinese have never had a democratic government on any meaningful scale for any length of time. Instead, twentieth-century China was governed by a succession of authoritarian governments of the right (mostly nationalists and military leaders) and the left (the communists). These regimes were more concerned with maintaining order and national unity and fostering economic development than with promoting liberty or government accountability.

The first major turning point in the direction of fundamental political change in China came in 1911, when a revolution put an end to the long succession of imperial dynasties that had ruled China almost continually for nearly four thousand years. As one of the world's oldest civilizations, China is believed to have established its first dynasty sometime around 1875 BCE. With the establishment of the Qin (or Ch'in) dynasty in 221 BCE, followed by the Han dynasty (206 BCE to AD 200), the rulers of China embarked on a period of territorial expansion and laid the groundwork for the institutional structures whose basic pattern would endure for much of the ensuing millennia.

Despite long periods of disunity and the breakdown of centralized authority, until the twentieth century China would be governed for most of its history by an imperial bureaucracy emanating from the personal authority of the emperor. The emperor, in turn, typically based his legitimacy on the "mandate of heaven," a Chinese variant of what would later be known in Europe as the divine right of kings. The teachings of **Confucius** (Kung Fu-tzu, approximately 551–479 BCE) provided ethical guidance to imperial rule, emphasizing the hierarchical principles of moral leadership from above and the importance of authority in political and social relationships.

As the centuries unfolded, the most successful dynasties reinforced the system of government they inherited. They appointed scholar-bureaucrats to manage the government's affairs, and they established the central authority of the state over all of China. Nothing in the way of democracy ever emerged from dynastic rule, however: no parliaments or social movements that might pry open the closed world of imperial administration. If we measure imperial China against the ten conditions for democracy specified in chapter 9, it would come up short in virtually every respect.

*State institutions* were authoritarian from the beginning and remained so until the collapse of the dynastic system. The governing *elites* were wholly committed to the imperial system, with its claims to divine legitimation and its Confucian ethos. The nation's *wealth* was based on an agricultural economy, with the imperial tax collection system assuring the state a large share of the national product. Commerce and *private enterprise* were frowned upon until late in the dynastic era, leaving little room for the emergence of a European-style entrepreneurial bourgeoisie or a *middle class*. China's masses, mostly destitute, illiterate peasants, were too dispersed, disorganized, and subjugated by the power of local landlords and ruling authorities to provide a groundswell of support for democracy on the part of the *disadvantaged*.

*Civil society* was dormant, and China's *political culture* was thoroughly imbued with Confucianism's reverence for authority and social harmony. The *educational system* was tightly connected to the state power structure, as the ruling dynasties created a system of rigorous examinations for entry into the prestigious state bureaucracy. Faithful adherence to the Confucian classics, rather than innovation or independence of thought, was the ultimate litmus test for a qualified Chinese official.

The quest for *national unity* also played a major role in strengthening the power of the imperial state. In the seventeenth century, invaders from Manchuria swooped down into China and took over the government, capturing Beijing (Peking) in 1644. China's new rulers, who established the Qing (or Manchu) dynasty, were not ethnic Chinese; they constituted only about 2 percent of the country's population, whose dominant ethnic group was the Han. To impose their authority on a foreign people, they had to fortify the strong arm of the imperial state. The Manchu rulers adopted the system of bureaucratic authoritarianism already in place and ruled through a judicious combination of military power and the cultivation of the leading elements of Chinese society, who in turn obligingly supported imperial rule. The Manchus compelled the Chinese to wear the queue (pigtail) as a sign of submission and never integrated themselves into the population. But they also allowed about a million Han Chinese to earn prestigious degrees and to occupy the vast majority of some forty thousand administrative posts.

The Qing emperors presided over a country with perhaps 300 million inhabitants by 1800, reaching the apogee of their power in the eighteenth century as the arts and invention flourished. The local *international environment* provided another girder of support for the imperial government, as the rulers of China—the "Middle Kingdom"—dominated the East Asian mainland. But a portent of trouble ahead arrived in 1793, when Britain's Lord Macartney called on the imperial court to discuss trade. Shockingly, the visitor refused to kowtow (bow) before the emperor, an affront to the Son of Heaven that signaled far ruder treatment at the hands of foreign intruders in the coming century.

The nineteenth century was a period of catastrophic decline for imperial China. A series of humiliating defeats at the hands of "barbarians" from abroad and organized challenges to imperial rule at home, coupled with the long-term consequences of several centuries of rapid population growth without any increase in the number of officials to govern the now much larger country, resulted in a spiraling process of political disintegration. By the start of the century, Britain was already in command of the tea trade in the southern coastal region of Guangdong (Canton). To finance their purchases, the British imported opium from India and sold it in China for substantial profits, spreading drug addiction among a growing segment of the Chinese population in the process. When the Chinese authorities tried to halt the drug traffic and suspended all trading, the British refused to back down. The "Opium War" began with a naval skirmish in 1839; it ended in 1842 with a British victory as the Chinese government was forced to cede Hong Kong and grant extraterritorial rights to foreigners in China. Another defeat in 1860 compelled the Chinese to open their doors even wider to foreign businesses and diplomatic representatives. These and other "unequal treaties" intensified the government's xenophobia, an attitude shared by many Chinese. Meanwhile, a series of rebellions broke out in China's provinces, further sapping the central government's authority.

In 1894–95, Japan defeated China and took over the Chinese island of Taiwan. A last-ditch effort by China's dowager empress in 1900 to expel the foreigners with the aid of a superstitious peasants' movement known as the Boxers ended in dismal failure as foreign troops fought back, preserving their presence in Beijing.

With China reduced to a shadow of its former glory, a debate broke out over how to rescue the country. Some blamed China itself for its predicament. The more iconoclastic thinkers argued that Confucianism was such an obstacle to China's progress that it had to be entirely abandoned, rooted out of both government and society, and replaced with an alternative system of beliefs. Confucianism valued harmony over competition, stability over change, and deference to authority over individual freedoms. In the eyes of its critics, it was unsuitable to handle the challenges of the modern world, brought on by rapid population growth, urbanization, and the mounting demands from Western powers to open up China to foreign goods, technology, and ideas. They believed there was nothing to be salvaged from China's past; the only way forward was the wholesale replacement of China's tradition with the values and technology imported from the West.

Others did not want to go quite that far and advocated balancing a reliance on Chinese ways as the nation's ethical foundation and Western ways for practical purposes. In the late nineteenth century, conservative writers argued that the solution to China's problems was not the adoption of Western ways, but the exact opposite: they believed that foreign pressures were the cause of China's problems, not their solution, and those pressures needed to be countered with a determined return to orthodox traditions.

Thus began an intense debate in China that has endured to the present: how should China become modern, what parts of its past are compatible with modernity, and what are the reasons for China's current backwardness? Ultimately, the debate concerns what it means to be Chinese at a time when there is little consensus on which elements of the country's traditions should be preserved and which ones should be abandoned.

After nearly a century of humiliation, reformers in the imperial entourage won the upper hand. Their aim was to import Western technological and administrative ideas in an effort to save the monarchy. But their ambitious reform efforts ended when conservative elements in the court, led by the empress dowager (who ruled on behalf of the last emperor of China, then still a young boy), regained control and imprisoned or exiled the erstwhile reformers, returning China to the traditions that were no match for the modern world.

In October 1911, a Chinese army garrison staged a revolt, triggering a stampede of independence movements in China's provinces. The revolutionaries named **Sun Yat-sen**, a reformist intellectual trained in Western schools, as China's president. With their backs to the wall, the imperial officials ruling in the child-emperor's behalf reached an agreement with Sun Yat-sen on the dissolution of the monarchy. In February 1912, the *Republic of China* was established.

Following the collapse of the imperial system, China was governed by a succession of authoritarian governments. The new republican government was weak from the start. It never established its full authority over China's disparate provinces, some of which fell under the sway of local warlords.[1] Rival governments were established in Beijing under the influence of northern warlords, and in Guangzhou under the influence of Sun Yat-sen and his successor, **Chiang Kai-shek.**

Meanwhile, the debate over how far China should go in adapting Western methods gained intensity. The *May 4th Movement* epitomized the critique of Confucianism.[2] It began around 1915, reaching full flower in 1919 after the conclusion of World War I. The hallmark of the May 4th Movement was its critical evaluation of China's condition: too weak to fend off foreign pressures, too restricted by Confucian traditions to adopt more effective policies, and too conservative to consider more innovative ideas in politics, the arts, and basic social values. During the May 4th Movement, Chinese intellectuals advocated the adoption of Western-style liberalism in China. They exalted the superiority of democracy and science over China's Confucian traditions: democracy because it entails a plurality of voices debating the common good rather than the obedience to orthodoxy required by Confucianism; science because it entails empirical investigation of nature and society in the pursuit of truth rather than the sterile application of an outmoded philosophy to rapidly changing times. Their slogan, "Let a hundred flowers bloom, let a hundred schools of thought contend" (a slogan that would be reprised in the 1950s), was itself based on Confucian traditions. China's liberal intellectuals saw the solution to China's problems in the political traditions and systems of government in the West.

That attitude abruptly changed with the end of World War I in 1918. As the allies were deciding what to do with the territories controlled by defeated Germany, China expected that the German concessions in China—territories that had been granted to Germans by a weakened dynastic government—would be returned to Chinese control. Instead, they were given to Japan, a rising Asian power. Chinese who were inspired by the enlightened beliefs that seemed to be the foundation of Western governments were disillusioned by this turn of events. Once it became known that the Beijing government's representatives at the Versailles conference at which these decisions were made had acquiesced in this action, anti-Western protests turned into anti-government protests. This turn of events illustrates another common theme of modern Chinese politics: when Chinese society blames foreign countries for damaging or insulting China, it often also blames its own government for not being strong enough to defend China's interests against foreign threats.

For their part, the leaders of the republican government were in no hurry to embrace Western liberal democracy. Although they abandoned Confucianism, the preference for a single orthodoxy prevailed over the uncertainties inherent in liberalism. Sun Yat-sen, the Republic's leading ideologist, expounded an odd mixture of Western scientific and educational theories, Christianity, Chinese nationalism, and a residual adherence to certain Confucian traditions. His lasting contribution was the establishment of a political party, the **Chinese Nationalist Party**, or **Kuomintang (KMT).** Sun devised the influential "Three Principles of the People" (nationalism, democracy, and social well-being) as the KMT's guiding political doctrine. But despite his concern for the people's welfare, Sun also believed that China was not ready for democracy and advocated a prolonged period of political tutelage to educate and prepare the Chinese people for participation in a future democratic government. Subsequently this notion was used as a rationale to maintain authoritarian controls over the country after the KMT became the ruling party of China in the late 1920s and even after it fled to Taiwan upon its defeat by the CCP in 1949.

This paternalistic belief that the Chinese people are not ready for democracy and unable to govern their own affairs remains influential in China, affecting elites and masses alike. One of the main challenges facing democratic reformers in China today is to convince not only their colleagues in government but also society at large that democracy is valuable and will not generate chaos, a fundamental concern in Chinese political culture.

### The Chinese Communist Party and China's Civil War

After a brief flirtation with liberalism, socialism grew in popularity in China for two reasons. First, it had the ironic appeal of being a Western theory that criticized the West. The writings of Marx and Lenin were used to criticize capitalist and Western imperialist influences in China. Second, the new communist government of the Soviet Union, which took power in 1917, renounced the "unequal treaties" that the previous tsarist government had used, much like the Western countries, to gain trade and other concessions from China in the past. The new Soviet government returned the territories it controlled in China, a gesture that cost very little but that gained the Soviet communist regime tremendous popular appeal within China, especially among urban intellectuals. These events culminated in the formation of the Chinese Communist Party (CCP) in 1921. One of its first adherents was **Mao Zedong** (MAH-OW DZEH-DUH-NG), who would eventually rise to prominence as the party's supreme leader. The son of peasants from Hunan province, Mao developed the unconventional strategy of relying on the potential of the rural peasants, as opposed to urban workers, to lead the revolution in China. His ideas were a leading cause of both the communist victory and enormous political and human tragedies after the CCP became the ruling party in 1949.[3]

Mao Zedong

## PROFILE: Mao Zedong

As chairman of the CCP from the 1930s until his death in 1976, Mao Zedong was the dominant figure in Chinese politics during these years, and unquestionably the leader of the "first generation" of communist leaders. His personality and proclivities shaped the policies of the CCP and—after the communists won the Chinese civil war in 1949—the fate of his nation. No one else enjoyed the charisma and power that let him convert his revolutionary vision into policy, and no one else brought as much tragedy and suffering to his people.

Mao was born in 1893 in Hunan province, the son of successful small farmers. Ironically, his social origins placed him in the landholding class of rural China, the very class he would systematically destroy after the communists came to power. Mao was an avid reader of Chinese history and fiction, and in later years he often drew upon them for military and political strategy. He also was acquainted with the writings of Jean-Jacques Rousseau, Adam Smith, Charles Darwin, and other Western thinkers. After receiving his education at a primary school and a teacher training institute, he followed his favorite teacher to Peking University, where he worked in the library. Although he did not enroll in classes, he attended discussion groups led by Li Dazhao, the director of the library and later one of the founders of the Chinese Communist Party.

After less than a year in the capital, Mao returned to Hunan, where he started a newspaper and organized a student strike against the warlord who had seized control of Hunan. In 1921, he was invited to be one of twelve Chinese to attend the founding of the CCP in Shanghai. (He was not elected to the party's Central Committee or given other leadership posts at that early date, however.) In the 1920s, the CCP was under the influence of the Communist International, an organization controlled by the Soviet leadership under Joseph Stalin. Moscow's rulers counseled the CCP to refrain from revolutionary activities and to cooperate with the Kuomintang in a "united front" until the prospects for a proletarian revolution improved. Mao believed that this strategy was not in keeping with the realities of China's conditions: the industrial work force was still small and the vast majority of the population were engaged in agriculture. But his opposition was generally ignored by other party leaders, who were better educated and more cosmopolitan than the peasant from Hunan.

After returning to Hunan, Mao organized several peasant associations and became inspired by their revolutionary potential. During the coming years, he devised a strategy for a communist revolution that would rely primarily on the peasantry; this approach became known as the "Sinification of Marxism." Although his efforts at leading peasant rebellions in Hunan failed, he never lost faith in his strategy, which seemed heretical to orthodox party leaders.

In 1927, the KMT-CCP united front ended when the KMT led a surprise attack on the CCP and its supporters in Shanghai, killing or arresting and later executing hundreds and perhaps thousands of Communists. Some of the CCP leaders who managed to escape this assault joined Mao and approximately ten thousand supporters at his base camp in the mountains along the Hunan-Jiangxi border, a redoubt that became known as the "Jiangxi soviet." In this remote area they worked on the hit-and-run guerilla tactics that would later become their trademark. But they were not safe for long. In 1934, they were forced to flee the Nationalist (KMT) army, which was steadily encircling them. Thus began the historic *Long March*—a harrowing, circuitous journey of more than six thousand miles across some of China's roughest terrain. When their journey ended more than a year later, only 8,000 of the 100,000 or so people who started the journey still remained. Those who managed to survive, however, enjoyed a bond that would last for decades.[4]

It was only after the Long March started that Mao became the leader of the party. Those who threw their support behind him, such as *Zhou Enlai* (JOE EHN-LIE) and *Deng Xiaoping* (DUH-NG SH-HOW PEENG)*, remained as leaders for years to come, some well into the 1990s. The others, who favored an urban-based revolution and accepted Soviet advice, eventually became marginalized. From the end of the Long March until the victory of the Communists' *People's Liberation Army (PLA)* in 1949, the CCP under Mao's leadership was headquartered in the northwestern town of Yanan, an area so poor that many—including Mao and other party leaders—lived in cave-like homes dug by hand out of the soft soil. Here in Yanan, Mao worked out the military strategy that would bring the communists to victory and, more importantly, the ideology that would consolidate his power over the communist movement.

In the coming years, Mao and the CCP enjoyed growing popularity. Their appeal was based not on their communist ideology but on their ability to take advantage of the nationalism created by the Japanese invasion in the 1930s and by the success of their moderate economic and social policies. Chiang Kai-shek and the Nationalist army refused to fight against Japan, preferring to eliminate the communists before facing the invading armies. The communists instead argued that the KMT-CCP rivalry should be put on hold until Japan was defeated and expelled. Chiang accepted this plan of a second "united front" only after one of his generals kidnapped him and forced him to negotiate with the communists. During this period, the CCP abandoned its revolutionary policies of land reform, which took land away from the gentry and rich peasants and redistributed it to poor farmers. (These policies proved to be unpopular even among the poor, because once the communists left a region, the landlords would forcibly take the land back and punish those who had cooperated with the communists.) To broaden its appeal, the CCP adopted more moderate policies of reducing rents on land and encouraging cooperative efforts to boost production and incomes. Communists also gained support through the disciplined behavior of their troops, who insisted on paying for the food they took and offered to help villagers by repairing the homes they spent the night in. This was in sharp contrast to the behavior of the Nationalists, who were notorious for seizing food and supplies without payment and dragging young men off in chains to become new "recruits" for the army.

It was also in Yanan that the "cult of Mao" began. His writings, speeches, and poetry became the subjects of extensive study and discussion, first among party and military leaders and later throughout society. This veneration of Mao took on near-religious qualities during the Cultural Revolution of the 1960s, when his sayings were collected in the "little red book" that everyone was expected to carry and memorize, when his portrait was hung in all Chinese homes and buildings, and when people performed songs and dances to show their loyalty to Mao. Even today, cars and taxis have pictures of Mao hanging from their rearview mirrors, a rather disconcerting "good luck" charm.

The triumph of the communists led by Mao was based on a combination of policy moderation, nationalistic appeals, and flexible responses to changing conditions. Once in power, however, Mao became less patient in pressing ahead with his ideological goals. He grew suspicious of other leaders who were more

---

*In Pinyin, China's official system of transliteration into the Roman alphabet, *zh* is pronounced "j," *x* is "sh," and *q* is "ch." However, some names (e.g., Sun Yat-sen) are still widely transliterated in the more traditional Wade-Giles system. The pronunciations in parentheses come from the Voice of America's official pronunciation guide (names.voa.gov).

concerned with economic development than with ideological rectitude. One of the mysteries of Mao's rule is why his colleagues, with whom he had worked and lived for decades, were unable or unwilling to organize successfully against him. His charisma was so strong that even those who disagreed with him rarely challenged him directly, nor did they come to the defense of people Mao criticized, even if they shared the same views. In his later years, hobbled by old age, disease, and (according to his physician) years of drug abuse, Mao became increasingly erratic, throwing his support behind one faction of rivals, only to withdraw it soon after. His utterances were nearly indecipherable and open to conflicting interpretations, leading to bitter disputes between individuals and groups who hoped to gain support for their policy prescriptions. All sought Mao's approval in order to legitimize their policies; only in the years after Mao's death was it possible to abandon his goals.

It is often said that without Mao there would be no "New China," and there is some truth to that. The People's Republic might have been established without him—he was not the only communist leader to advocate a rural revolution, nor was he the party's only influential military strategist. But it is impossible to imagine the history of the post-1949 era without him. Despite the fact that his policies brought widespread hardship to his people, Mao Zedong remains a symbol of power and pride for many in contemporary China.

---

The Nationalists' defeat in the Chinese civil war led not only to a change of government in China but also to a fierce debate in the United States over "who lost China?" in the 1950s. Meanwhile, as the Nationalists repaired to Taiwan to relocate their government of the Republic of China, Chiang Kai-shek and his followers hoped one day to retake the mainland. Ever since 1949, Taiwan has been a source of tension in Communist China's foreign policies, especially in its relations with the United States. The United States retained diplomatic relations and a mutual defense treaty with the Republic of China on Taiwan until 1979, when it altered its China policy by recognizing the People's Republic as the sole legitimate government of all China. Although the United States recognizes communist China's claim that there is but one China and that Taiwan is part of it, it continues to sell defensive arms to Taiwan and has an implicit commitment to defend Taiwan against an attack from mainland China.

China's post-1949 split into "two Chinas" (in fact if not in international law) has severely complicated the meaning of Chinese nationalism. What, in fact, is the "Chinese nation"? Nationalism has been an influential force at various times in twentieth-century China, but it has also been a very ambiguous one. There is still little consensus on the values and symbols that define the Chinese nation.

## The Communists Take Over

After the CCP became the ruling party in 1949, it promised a "new democracy" with the active involvement of non-CCP elites and organizations. Two key institutions begun during the civil war years were intended to be the basis of this new democracy. The *mass line* was a process by which concerns and suggestions would come *from the masses* and the policy decisions would be communicated by officials *to the masses*. This cycle of deliberation envisioned a close relationship between the state and society in which society would better understand policy decisions and thereby support them, and the state would better understand the concerns of society and the impact of its policies and thereby devise more effective policies.

The second political institution that was central to China's "new democracy" was the *united front*. The CCP promised to consult and cooperate with non-CCP elites, such as businesspeople, scholars, and even religious leaders, in order to promote China's modernization. The united front promised a policy process that would be consensual rather than conflictual. Today, united front policies are again being publicized to promote cooperation between government and business in China's economic modernization.

Although the mass line and united front policies had some democratic aspirations, in practice they provided at best consultation without accountability. The communist party-state could listen to a variety of viewpoints, but it selected which views would be heard and which would be suppressed. If the state chose to ignore the concerns of society or the suggestions of non-CCP elites, there was little these groups could do to seek redress. If state policies failed, there was no way for the public to replace the policy makers. In fact, the mass line and the united front more often than not have been means of enforcing dictatorship and state domination at the expense of democratic principles and procedures.

Let us now turn to a more detailed discussion of China's political institutions and their performance during the post–1949 communist era.

## CHINA'S POLITICAL INSTITUTIONS

As noted at the beginning of this chapter, the most basic fact of China's political system is that it is ruled by the Communist Party. The party is organized along Leninist lines: like V. I. Lenin's Bolshevik Party, the CCP resembles a military hierarchy, with the chain of command going from the top down. Though lower-level party officials may have a chance to have their views communicated to the party's upper echelons, once a final decision has been taken by the top leaders, all party members are obliged to fall into line behind it. The party elite rules. Virtually every other aspect of China's politics and government, including the policy process and relations between state and society, are derived from that fundamental truth.

### The Chinese Communist Party

At the top of China's political system, and integrated throughout it at all levels, is the Chinese Communist Party. Although it came to power relying on the support of peasants, workers, and soldiers, the CCP today is a broad-based party, drawing its members from all walks of life, including bureaucrats, teachers, and other people in white-collar jobs. It has over 70 million members, a group that is roughly 5 percent of China's population but larger than the population of many countries in the world.

***The most important organization within the CCP is the*** **<u>Politburo</u>.** This body consists of the top two dozen or so leaders in China. Members of the Politburo often hold other important positions in the central government and the military simultaneously. Some local governments, especially Beijing and Shanghai, are also represented on the Politburo. It approves all major policies and personnel changes. Its actual deliberations are clouded in secrecy, but it is believed to make its decisions by consensus rather than majority rule. Within the Politburo there is a subgroup of China's most powerful leaders, known as the *Standing Committee* of the Politburo, which currently has nine members. (See figure 21.1.)

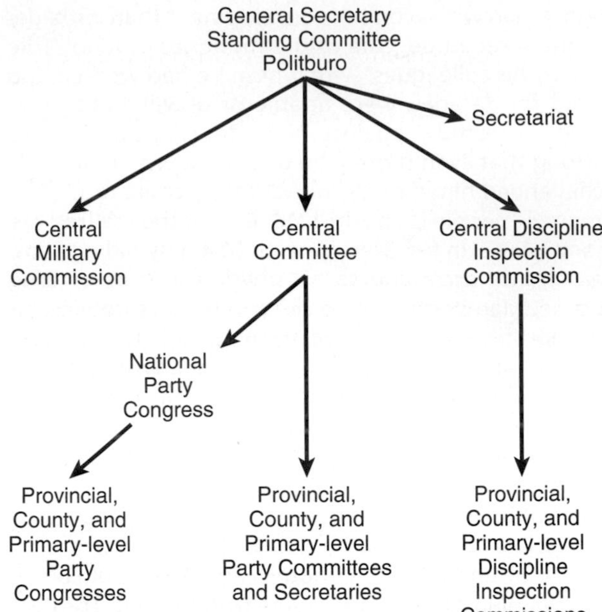


**FIGURE 21.1 Organization of the Chinese Communist Party** The Central Military Commission is the CCP's organization for overseeing the military. The Central Discipline Inspection Commission, and lower-level discipline inspection commissions, are responsible for monitoring the behavior of party members, especially party and government officials. They have the authority to charge and punish those guilty of corruption, malfeasance, and other violations of party policy. Primary-level party bodies are organized at workplaces, schools, neighborhoods, military companies, and small towns.

***The top party official is the*** **<u>General Secretary</u>,** ***currently*** **<u>Hu Jintao</u>** (HOO JIHN-TAOW). Mao Zedong had the title of "Chairman" of the party, but that post was eliminated after his death in 1976 to prevent any leader from accumulating the degree of uncontrolled power that Mao had. The General Secretary is formally in charge of the *Secretariat*, a small organization connected to the Politburo that handles the daily affairs of the party leadership, such as the flow of reports and memos among party leaders and the organization of important meetings.

According to party statutes, the Politburo and Secretariat are supposed to be elected in a sequential process by two larger bodies: the *Central Committee* and the *Party Congress*. The Central Committee is a group of 150 to 200 people that meets once or twice a year to formally endorse important policies and leadership changes that have been approved by the

Politburo beforehand. The members of the Central Committee represent a broader range of the party's top elites, mostly senior party and government officials from around the country. Some discussion takes place, but the Central Committee rarely, if ever, initiates policy or forces the senior leaders to change course. The Central Committee formally elects the Politburo and its Standing Committee, the Secretariat, and the General Secretary. These votes, too, are usually pro forma, as the top leaders invariably decide among themselves how the senior decision-making positions will be distributed.

The Central Committee is formally elected by the national Party Congress, a meeting of more than two thousand party leaders. Although it is supposed to meet every five years, in the past it met on an irregular basis. The Seventh Party Congress met in 1945, and the next ones did not meet until 1956 and 1969. Since then the body has met more regularly: in 1973, 1977, 1982, 1987, 1992, 1997, and most recently, 2002 (the Sixteenth Party Congress). Very little actual debate goes on at these week-long sessions; the Congress typically provides the party leadership with an opportunity to review past achievements and outline the main lines of policy to be pursued in the coming years. Though the Congress takes a formal vote in electing the Central Committee, in fact the Central Committee's membership has already been decided by higher party authorities, leaving the Congress only marginal influence. (For instance, the Sixteenth Party Congress elected 198 Central Committee members from a list of 208 names.)

Party supremacy over the government, the military, and other institutions is achieved through a combination of oversight and personnel appointments. Within all government ministries, factories, schools, and other work units is a party committee that monitors compliance with party directives. The party also nominates or approves all key personnel, from cabinet ministers and department heads to even such relatively low-level positions as heads of university departments and bank officials.

### The State

Structurally, China's government looks very much like a parliamentary system: the governing party appoints ministers and other key government officials, and drafts most legislation. The key difference, of course, is that China's ruling party was not voted into office and does not have to stand for reelection. China's state institutions are highly centralized (see figure 21.2). ***The executive branch is headed by a* <u>prime minister</u> (or <u>premier</u>), *currently* <u>Wen Jiabao</u>** (WUHN JAH-BOW), who appoints officials to head the other ministries and commissions of the government. This group of people comprises the State Council, the equivalent of a cabinet. Almost all top officials in the government are also CCP members, with a few symbolic exceptions to show the party's continued adherence to a "united front" approach to governing. Even nonparty officials, however, are approved and appointed by the CCP. Although the CCP approves the broad principles of policy, the government has the main responsibility for actually implementing policy and monitoring results.

***China's legislative branch is called the* <u>National People's Congress</u>.** It is the weakest of the three main political institutions (the other two being the party and government), although it has been getting more assertive and more influential in recent years. Formerly derided as a rubber-stamp legislature because it unanimously approved all motions proposed by the CCP without dissent or discussion, it now takes an active role in drafting legislation, approving annual budgets, and monitoring the results of reforms. In the past, it met irregularly to ratify party policy; it now has permanent committees with full-time staffs that work year-round. Despite these changes, the National People's Congress is not a democratic or deliberative body. Though its three thousand members are elected by lower-level "People's Congresses," the Communist Party hierarchy carefully supervises their selection. Even those who advocate a more active role for it do not see it as a vehicle for democratization. Instead, they want to make it an institution capable of overseeing the work of the party and government, perhaps delaying or reversing policy decisions made by higher authorities when necessary. They seek to make it a stronger institution, but not necessarily a more liberal or democratic one.[5]

One of the duties of the National People's Congress is to elect the *president* of the People's Republic as China's formal head of state. In March 2003, *Hu Jintao* was elected president, replacing *Jiang Zemin* (jah-ng zuh-MEEN), who had held the post for the previous ten years. The presidency is a

officials had the requisite experience and were therefore relied on, at least in the early 1950s. This practice caused resentment among the CCP's veterans, who felt they had devoted themselves to the revolution and deserved to be given these important positions as a reward. They also resented the party's efforts to recruit better-qualified members and to upgrade the qualifications of existing members. The revolutionaries felt insulted by this emphasis on skills over experience and political reliability.[8]

These conflicts gave rise to one of the most divisive issues in Communist China, the *red versus expert debate*. While we can assume that most, if not all, Chinese leaders shared the same ultimate goals, they disagreed on the proper methods and the pace of change. During the Maoist period (1949–76), many policy debates and power struggles were linked to the issue of whether to emphasize "redness" or expertise. "Reds" were the most ideologically oriented revolutionaries, characterized by their political reliability and ability to mobilize the masses rather than by their technical, administrative, or scientific skills. They believed that economic questions could not be solved until political obstacles (namely anything resembling Western or capitalist values) were eliminated. Consequently, they believed that political factors should determine all policies, whether economic, social, or cultural.

"Experts," by contrast, were more interested in creating a sound, growing economy that would provide the basis for achieving the communists' ultimate goals. They typically had better educational backgrounds than most reds and had not served in the guerilla armies. But the reds questioned the experts' commitment to the CCP and resented their arrogance. Experts in turn resented the intrusion of poorly trained zealots into their complicated work.

The red versus expert debate was closely related to the question of the party's primary goal: whether to promote the country's *economic development* or to be more concerned with *utopianism*.[9] During the Maoist era, China had the political goal of creating a Marxian communist utopia in which there would be no exploitation and in which an abundance of goods and services would be available for distribution to the population on a relatively equitable basis. In the end, the state would wither away, as Marx and Engels had predicted, and its former tasks would be carried out on a voluntary basis by individuals sharing communist values. But China's existing political and economic conditions prevented this utopia from coming about naturally.

Party policy in the Maoist period therefore oscillated between economic development and ideological utopianism. When economic development was the primary goal, party and state policies emphasized production goals and allowed a limited amount of private enterprise and market activity, permitting people to make a little money on the side (thereby creating incentives for more production). They emphasized technical skills in personnel matters and minimized the intrusiveness of political campaigns. In contrast, when utopian goals were paramount, party-state policies prohibited or greatly constrained markets, the "class struggle" against the party's enemies became more coercive and dangerous, and economic growth suffered.

Mao was the champion of both sets of policies, and he often shifted between the two as he felt national conditions mandated. Policy did not change without Mao's consent: his support was necessary for policy decisions, and in fact his change of heart was often sufficient to bring about a change of goals or a change of policies. As a result, during Mao's lifetime China lurched back and forth between these divergent goals of development and utopia. As time went on, Mao seemed to favor utopian goals above all else. Mao wanted to modernize China, but for him, the means were as important as the ends. His supporters often said it was better to be poor and communist than rich and capitalist.

Key episodes in the post–1949 history of China are impossible to understand without appreciating Mao's central role in the political system. In fact, in 1953 the Central Committee passed a resolution that authorized Mao to personally approve all decisions made by the Politburo and Central Committee or else they would be invalid. In 1987 the Central Committee passed a similar secret resolution, this time allowing Deng Xiaoping, Mao's successor as supreme leader, to approve all decisions. Both resolutions violated not only democratic procedures but also the party's traditional norms of consensual decision making. Nevertheless, they reflected the preeminent authority these two men held within China's political system.

During the Maoist period there were three main episodes in which policy shifted from development to utopianism. The first came with the *collectivization* of industry and agriculture in 1955–56. By the mid 1950s, the CCP had consolidated its power, eliminated its rivals, and restored the economy to prewar production levels. It then decided to eliminate all remaining private ownership of land and capital. On the land, some 110 million farm households were converted into about 300,000 communist "cooperatives" under the party's direction. In cities and towns, privately owned factories and other businesses were completely taken over by the communist authorities. Capitalism in China was virtually extinguished by 1956 (although the former owners were often retained as managers). This turning point was of major significance in party policy: the CCP's basis for popular support had been its land reform policies, and now the land that had just recently been given to the poorest peasants was being taken away. However, there was none of the violence that accompanied the land reform of the early 1950s, which in turn was much milder than the Soviet experience under Stalin in the 1920s. The new policies toward industry and agriculture required a greater role for the party. It had to coordinate production and make sure that its policies were followed.

The collectivization of agriculture and industry was followed by the **Hundred Flowers Movement** in 1957.[10] The slogan came from a saying of Confucius, "Let a hundred flowers bloom, let a hundred schools of thought contend." ***It implied that the give and take of ideas was not only healthy but beneficial to the state.*** Mao invited criticisms of the party's performance from experts and intellectuals, confident that his policy successes so far had created considerable enthusiasm and support for the regime. He expected mild criticism of the bureaucratic work style of some party and government officials, in line with his own view that the conservative nature of bureaucracies would inevitably slow progress toward the nation's development. Mao felt that the government was comprised of bureaucrats who, as he put it, behaved like women with bound feet, tottering along taking small steps, afraid to take bold strides.

But when Mao began encouraging people to voice their opinions—an opening seized by intellectuals—what he got instead of mild criticism was a stream of complaints about the fundamental nature of the political system. There were complaints about the absence of democracy, the rule of law, free expression, and free scientific inquiry; complaints about party interference in all walks of life; and above all, complaints about the intrusion of incompetent and illiterate reds in the work of the experts. These were precisely the kinds of criticisms Mao's colleagues feared when they opposed the Hundred Flowers policy.

Mao seems to have been genuinely taken aback by the vehemence of the intellectuals' complaints. Rather than address their concerns, he labeled them "rightists" (akin to being a counterrevolutionary, a very serious crime). He then launched an *Anti-Rightist campaign* to persecute them, replacing many of them with his own political supporters. The sense of betrayal was deep and long-lasting on the part of China's intellectuals. After responding to Mao's personal request to air their views freely, they were ridiculed, persecuted, and in many instances imprisoned. The Anti-Rightist campaign alienated most of China's intellectuals and made them wary of voicing their political views again.[11] Their wariness was not due just to the political culture's emphasis on respecting authority; more important, they had learned from their own experience the high cost of dissent.

Following the Anti-Rightist campaign, the second episode of promoting utopian goals took shape. After disregarding the concerns of China's experts, Mao decided to tap into the latent energy of the masses to create economic growth. The party would encourage people to work harder, not with higher wages, but with propaganda and persuasion. This campaign became known as the **Great Leap Forward** ***(1958–59), the period when the communes were created.***[12] Communes were large-scale economic and administrative units, each combining ten or more villages. Work teams were sent out to mobilize the efforts of peasants and organize their work. Sometimes they would work twenty-four-hour shifts of intensive labor. At first, it seemed that the Great Leap policies were working: most communes reported a bumper harvest, and the counties and provinces began competing with one another to claim the highest production achievements (thus proving that they were the most loyal to Mao). Nightly dinners became banquets at the commune's mess halls as people tried to eat up the excess food, thinking that there was too much to actually harvest and transport to urban areas. But in fact, the harvest was far below the forecast. Much of the grain that would normally have been stored for the winter and for spring planting was eaten in the summer and fall. By 1959, it became clear that the country was in deep trouble. Economic forecasts were drastically cut back. Reports of unrest in the countryside and general unhappiness with the mass mobilization tactics of the Great Leap Forward circulated among the party leadership. The policy excesses of the Great Leap combined with unusually bad weather to create a crisis of huge proportions. During the "three bad years" of 1960–62, close to 30 million people starved to death.

This calamity resulted in a full-scale retreat from the policies of the Great Leap Forward and a period of recovery that lasted for several years.[13] Once again, restoring order and increasing production through proper planning and the use of economic incentives became official policy. Private plots, banned with the creation of the communes, once again were approved. These plots allowed farmers to grow a little extra fruit and vegetables for themselves and to sell some for extra cash. Mao grudgingly tolerated these recovery policies, recognizing that they were necessary to solve the severe crisis facing his country. But he was unwilling to accept them as long-term policies for fear that they would restore capitalism to China and because the reliance on regularized procedures—those favored by experts—minimized the role of his supporters and, not incidentally, his own influence.

By 1965, Mao had several main grievances against his colleagues. For one thing, he felt their policies were leading the country in the wrong direction. The recovery policies sponsored and implemented by such party leaders as Liu Shaoqi and Deng Xiaoping were successful in creating growth and restoring order, but they were leading the country away from the communist utopia Mao envisioned. In 1962, Mao reminded his colleagues, and China more generally, "Never forget class struggle." In other words, the work of economic recovery should not distract people from the true goal of achieving communism.

Another grievance was that Mao was being marginalized. He was no longer consulted in the policy-making process. He complained that Deng had stopped giving him policy briefings and at meetings sat with his bad ear toward Mao. The party chairman referred to himself as a living Buddha: revered but generally ignored.

Indeed, Mao was not happy with his potential successors. With his life running out, Mao wanted to be sure that loyal successors were in place at the top of the party and that a new generation of party members filled with his revolutionary zeal and preference for redness over expertise would be ready to fill posts at all levels of the political system. By the mid 1960s, however, Mao felt betrayed by his heirs apparent, Liu and Deng, and he felt that the next generation of leaders lacked the experience necessary to instill the correct virtues.

These frustrations led him to launch the **Great Proletarian Cultural Revolution**, the third episode of utopianism.[14] Mao became convinced that his own party had lost its revolutionary fervor and had become hostile to himself personally as well as to his policies. Moreover, he felt that the younger generation of China, which had not been tempered in the furnace of the revolution, would benefit from the struggle and the chaos that revolution entails. He therefore encouraged young people, especially students, to form groups of *Red Guards* to attack, verbally and physically, the representatives of the party and state: local leaders, teachers, factory managers, and even high-ranking party leaders and cabinet ministers.

The Red Guards succeeded in attacking people who exercised or symbolized power, along with anyone else suspected of not being loyal to Mao. They fanned throughout China bearing copies of the "little red book" of Mao's choice quotations, haranguing people in lengthy propaganda sessions in factories, on farms, and out in the streets. They broke into party and government offices and released information that supposedly revealed the anti-Maoist activities of the officeholders. They held public "struggle" sessions, in which selected targets were harshly criticized and assaulted. Those being attacked were subjected to beatings, imprisonment, and killings, and some committed suicide. They included many who had fought in the civil war alongside Mao and whose involvement in the CCP went back to the 1930s. Deng Xiaoping, Mao's ultimate successor, was publicly humiliated, removed from his high-ranking party posts, and sent to work as a common laborer for several years. Most schools and government offices closed down, and most regular activities ceased; all but one of China's ambassadors was called home. Economic production ground to a halt.

This convulsive part of the Cultural Revolution came to a close in 1968 after armed clashes between Red Guard groups, each proclaiming to be the most loyal to Mao, broke out all over China. The Red Guards were often given weapons by local troops who supported one side against the other. The result was not so much civil war as complete anarchy: the party and government had collapsed under Red Guard pressure. The Cultural Revolution was not a military coup, but in its aftermath the nation came under effective martial law for several years because the military was the only nationwide organization still intact and able to carry out government responsibilities.

After being nearly destroyed during 1966–69, the party now had to be rebuilt. Although it was weakened by intense factional conflict at all levels, from society's point of view the party was stronger than ever. Virtually every aspect of life had political implications, from opinions about Mao and the party to the clothing one wore, hairstyles, and taste in books and music. Even owning a pet was considered a "bourgeois" affectation. It was a period of political correctness run rampant, with decisions about jobs, housing, access to food, and opportunities to travel or see a play determined by the local party committee.

Just as the Great Leap Forward was an economic disaster, the Cultural Revolution was a political disaster. Many of China's best qualified and most experienced leaders were falsely accused of various crimes, removed from their posts, put in prison, or sent to remote areas of China to perform menial tasks. Eventually many of these people were brought back to their old posts, but they were forced to work alongside the very people who had accused them and caused their suffering.

Each swing toward utopianism enhanced the power of the party and widened the scope of its jurisdiction. By the end of the Cultural Revolution, the CCP had usurped almost all the government's responsibilities and there were no social organizations capable of challenging it. But at the same time, society had grown weary of the incessant political campaigns and frequent policy shifts. People had become disillusioned by a political system that seemed intrusive, arbitrary, inconsistent, and unresponsive to society's desire for higher standards of living. With Mao's death in 1976, an opportunity arose to fundamentally change the style and direction of policy.

## LEGACIES OF THE CULTURAL REVOLUTION

The Cultural Revolution left several different legacies for China's leaders and members of society. The CCP's elites recognized the danger of charismatic authority, as epitomized by Mao, and acknowledged the need for regular institutions to debate and implement policies. Mao had resisted this institutionalization because he felt it would diminish revolutionary zeal, the creative spontaneity of the masses, and his own authority. But most other leaders felt the costs of Mao's preferred methods were too high. China's leaders were also aware of the CCP's failure to improve the lives of most Chinese. Party and government leaders who became victims of the Cultural Revolution and were sent to live and work in the countryside learned firsthand that the political system they had created could be completely arbitrary. They realized it had failed to bring China out of its extreme poverty and that it had thereby lost the legitimacy with which it came to power in 1949.

The Cultural Revolution left lasting marks on Chinese society. People learned that it was acceptable to challenge authority and that it was necessary to think for themselves. Mao's assault on his colleagues and the party as a whole taught Chinese society that it need not, indeed should not, accept the prevailing political orthodoxy as the truth. For the same reason, many people experienced a loss of idealism. They learned too late that the Cultural Revolution was not about revolutionary goals at all, but just a cynical struggle for power among party elites. Contrary to Mao's assumptions, many Chinese came to believe it was not necessary to assume that the leaders always knew what was best or that they had the best interests of society at heart. For a Leninist party, these ideas could only undermine the party's ability to rule. By the time Mao died in September 1976, there was a crisis of confidence, a feeling that the party and the government were no longer legitimate. Even Mao's reputation was tarnished.

With Mao's death, the party was in crisis. Society had grown weary of the continual political witch-hunts and had lost confidence in the party's wisdom. The party itself was divided between the reds, who believed the goals of the Cultural Revolution had to be continued, even intensified, and the experts, who believed the Cultural Revolution had done more harm than good and needed to be abandoned. The economy was shrinking, political instability was rising, and factions within the party prevented any single policy line from being agreed upon and pursued. The end result was a state so weakened by internal divisions that it was unable to adopt and implement a coherent and consistent set of policies, and a society that was unable to influence the policy-making process in any institutionalized way.

This conflict between continuing and ending the Cultural Revolution was resolved a month after Mao's death when the main reds, the so-called Gang of Four (one of whom was Mao's widow) were arrested. After a brief succession struggle, a new consensus emerged: the utopian goals of the Maoist era had to be abandoned for the sake of economic development. This decision was solidified at a historic Central Committee meeting in December 1978. Henceforth, the party would abandon class struggle as its main task (a main rationale for needing a strong party), and the victims of past political campaigns would be rehabilitated. More important, the party would concentrate its energies on the economic modernization of the country and shift its policy choices and selection of personnel with this goal in mind. Throughout the post-Mao period, the party's ability to foster economic growth, rather than its ideology or the charisma of its leader, has been the basis of its legitimacy. While several of the party's leading figures wanted these policy shifts, the man most responsible for initiating them was **Deng Xiaoping**.

## PROFILE: Deng Xiaoping

Just as Chairman Mao was unquestionably the leader of the CCP from the Long March of the 1930s until his death in 1976, Deng Xiaoping was the symbol of the "second generation" of leaders. The numbering of these generations of leaders should not be taken literally. Deng and other leaders of the second generation had careers that extended back into the 1920s and 1930s, but they did not rise to the pinnacle of power until after the deaths of Mao and the other first-generation leaders, such as Zhou Enlai and Liu Shaoqi. Deng was never chairman or General Secretary of the CCP, prime minister, or president, nor did he have indomitable power like Mao's, but he was widely seen as China's paramount leader from 1978 until his death in 1997. His preferences for policies and personnel largely set the tone for the post-Mao era.

Deng was born into a prosperous family in 1904 in Sichuan (Szechuan) province in southwest China. His father was the wealthiest landlord in his area, as well as a political and social leader. He was not a well-educated man, but he emphasized the importance of education to his son, sending him first to Sichuan's largest city, Chongqing, for high school and then to a work-study program in France. In 1920, at the age of sixteen, Deng arrived in Marseilles.

Deng's money soon ran out, and his attention shifted from education to politics. He held a variety of factory jobs in Paris and quickly attached himself to a group of young Chinese workers and students who used their stay in France to debate China's future and form political organizations. One of Deng's first contacts was Zhou Enlai, another worker-student in the program that Deng had initially joined. The two men were destined to remain close allies for decades to come. In 1924, Deng began working for the newspaper of the Communist Youth League of Europe as writer, editor, and typesetter, earning the nickname "Doctor of Duplication." As his activities in communist organizations increasingly came to the attention of French authorities, Deng was subjected to official surveillance. But a police raid on his apartment outside Paris in 1926 was too late: Deng had already left for his next destination, Moscow.

Deng spent eleven months in the Soviet Union, attending special schools the Soviet Communist Party had established for revolutionaries from around the world. At Sun Yat-sen University, the Moscow institute for Asian workers and political organizers, Deng met *Chiang Ching-kuo,* the son of the Nationalist leader Chiang Kai-shek and himself a future president of the

Republic of China on Taiwan. During this period Stalin compelled the Chinese Communists to cooperate with the Nationalists. But by the time Deng returned to China in early 1927, the "united front" was breaking down and the country was already tilting toward civil war. Once Chiang Kai-shek attacked the Communists in Shanghai, killing hundreds, the war began in earnest. Deng himself went to Shanghai that year and spent several years working in the Communist Party's underground operations. In 1929 he moved to southwest China to begin what turned out to be a long career as one of the party's top military leaders.

In 1931 Deng moved to Jiangxi, the base area established by Mao Zedong, and joined him on the Long March, contracting typhoid along the way. He then settled into Shaanxi province, where Mao was trying to impose his will on the party from his base in the caves of Yanan. Promoted to deputy director of the political department of the Communist Party's first army, Deng was now a seasoned political soldier. He was appointed to higher military positions over the next several years as the People's Liberation Army grew to more than 2 million. From 1938 to 1945, Deng led troops in northern China's mountainous regions, launching periodic attacks on KMT and Japanese forces. More importantly, he was Mao's eyes and ears on the front lines, making sure that the political orientation of the military did not stray from the party's (i.e., Mao's) line. In the spring of 1945 he was rewarded for his military and political accomplishments with membership in the party's Central Committee.

When the war against Japan ended and the clash between the communists and Nationalists resumed its earlier intensity, Deng swung into action as one of the party's most successful commanders. After the civil war was over, Deng was given charge of China's vast southwest region, including his native Sichuan and three other provinces containing 150 million people. Then in 1952 he was summoned to Beijing to serve as vice-premier of the Chinese government and in various economic positions under the supervision of his old comrade, Zhou Enlai. In 1954 he won an even more important promotion, gaining the newly created post of secretary general of the Central Committee. Deng was now the chief organizational link between the party leadership in Beijing and its large bureaucracy throughout China. He also entered the party Politburo. Two years later he was a member of the Politburo's Standing Committee, taking his place among the six most powerful people who ruled China.

As Mao plunged China headlong into the whirlwinds of the Hundred Flowers campaign, the Great Leap Forward, and the Cultural Revolution, Deng was unenthusiastic about the radical campaigns but he was called upon to restore the economy afterward. In the early 1960s, he was criticized for using capitalist methods instead of Maoist propaganda to promote economic growth. His response showed his inherent pragmatism: "It does not matter if the cat is black or white; so long as it catches mice, it is a good cat." In other words, whatever made the economy grow was the right policy. Over time, however, Mao began to resent Deng for deviating from his ideological path and for not consulting with him over policy.

During the Cultural Revolution, Deng was castigated as "the number two party leader taking the capitalist road" (number one was President Liu Shaoqi) and removed from all his posts in the party and government. He was placed under house arrest, and then sent to work at a tractor repair plant where he and his wife raised their own food.

When Mao and Zhou Enlai were too ill to handle affairs of state, Mao called Deng back to Beijing in 1973, appointing him vice-premier of the government. Deng took over the daily work of the government, including economic and foreign policy, and with Mao's blessing also took charge of the CCP. By 1975, he had resumed all of the party and government posts he had lost at the beginning of the Cultural Revolution. However, his leftist opponents in the Gang of Four, who included Mao's wife Jiang Qing, remained opposed to Deng and his pragmatic policies. After Zhou died in January 1976, they convinced Mao to once again purge Deng from his posts. Fearing for his life, Deng slipped out of Beijing and went into hiding in south China.

On September 9, 1976, Mao Zedong died; a month later the Gang of Four were arrested. In the summer of 1977, Deng was reinstated to all his former positions in the party and government. In 1981 he became chairman of the party's Central Military Commission. For nearly twenty years thereafter, Deng Xiaoping would be the principal figure in Chinese politics. His policies of "reform and opening up" were responsible for the remarkable economic growth China has enjoyed ever since and for the loosening of political controls over society. This legacy, however, was tarnished by his role in the 1989 popular demonstrations in Tiananmen Square, which Deng condemned as "turmoil" and "planned conspiracy." Because he believed the demonstrations were a threat to economic reform, he supported the decision to impose martial law, which led to the deaths of hundreds and perhaps thousands of peaceful demonstrators and innocent bystanders and damaged both his and China's reputation abroad. To the end of his life, Deng remained firmly committed to the belief that economic modernization required a stable domestic environment and a peaceful international environment, and his policies were designed to ensure both. Twice named *Time* magazine's "Man of the Year," Deng Xiaoping will be remembered for dramatically improving the lives of many in China, but also for disappointing those who believed that political reform should accompany economic reform.

## POLITICS IN THE REFORM ERA

During the 1980s, party leaders identified a series of problems inherited from the Maoist period and attempted reforms to remedy them, but with mixed results.[15]

### Overconcentration of Power

Most Chinese leaders agreed that Mao had wielded too much power. The solution was to create a collective leadership and prevent any one individual from dominating the political system. Although Deng Xiaoping was the paramount leader from 1978 until his death in 1997, he had to work to forge and maintain a consensus behind his policy preferences and was forced to abandon some policies when faced with opposition among his colleagues. He retired from his posts as party vice chairman and vice prime minister in the mid 1980s and from the chairmanship of the CCP's Central Military Commission in 1989. Although he never held the top post in either the party or the government, symbolizing his commitment to collective leadership, he was nevertheless recognized as China's preeminent leader. The title of party chairman was abolished because it was so closely identified with Mao and because there were no suitable checks on the power of the office. Instead, the post of General Secretary was created as the party's top leadership position: the party needed an individual leader, but not one with unchecked authority.

At lower levels, efforts were made to distinguish the party from the government more clearly. The party was to limit itself to making decisions, allowing the government to implement the policies. To this end it was decided to limit the number of concurrent posts held by top party leaders. For instance, during the Maoist period, the top party leader in a province was also its governor, and the top party leader in a city was also its mayor. Beginning in the 1980s, these posts were separated and held by different people.

These efforts had mixed results. For one thing, all key positions were still held by party members (with rare and usually symbolic exceptions), and party committees remained more powerful than their government counterparts. In fact, after the 1989 student demonstrations, the efforts to separate the party and the government were rolled back because party leaders believed the party had become too weak as a consequence.

### Lack of Formal Institutions

Because Mao preferred to rule by virtue of his charismatic authority, formal bodies became virtually meaningless. In the post-Mao period, reforms were implemented that emphasized collective decision making and restored the regular operations of formal bodies. For instance, the Politburo, which had fallen into disuse under Mao, again began to meet regularly, and the National People's Congress, China's nominal legislature, became rejuvenated, passing a variety of laws and overseeing government operations. In addition, the decision-making process has been opened up to a wider variety of people in the post-Mao period. The most important decisions are still made by a handful of people at the top, but now they consult with government officials, experts, local leaders, and others whose opinions are valued or who will be affected by the decision. Instead of decisions being made in secret, regular conferences are now held to share ideas, and drafts of major policies are circulated several times before a final decision is made.[16]

However, Deng and other top leaders continued to intervene in the policy-making process. The personal attributes of individual leaders, their connections with other leaders, and their reputations as revolutionaries were still more important than their formal posts. In fact, during the 1980s and 1990s, a group of "elders" constituted the true center of political power in China even though they had formally retired from their party and government positions. They continued to shape policy and personnel decisions from behind the scenes and through their younger protégés. The clearest example of this was the 1987 decision giving Deng authority over all major decisions. Moreover, there was no legal system to impose limits on the abuse of power by institutions or individuals. It is often said that whereas the United States has the rule *of* law, because even the top leaders are accountable to the legal limits of their power, in China there is only rule *by* law. The party creates laws to help govern the country, but it is above the law. In this type of system, the law is a tool of governance, not a means for protecting the rights and liberties of the citizens.

### Rejuvenation of the Party

At the end of the Maoist era, the party had about 35 million members, up from fewer than 5 million in 1949. From the perspective of Deng and his allies, the composition of the party's membership had several danger signs. Many members were too old. Less than 5 percent of the members were under twenty-five years old, compared to about 25 percent in 1949. The majority were still poorly educated: 45 percent had only a primary education, and 11 percent were illiterate. This educational profile was an improvement over 1949, when 95 percent were illiterate or had only a primary education, but it was hardly exemplary. More important, party members were not educated enough to handle the technical matters required by the new tasks of economic modernization. And most party members had been recruited during periods of utopianism and therefore had dubious political and professional qualifications. In short, by the time Deng Xiaoping took control, party members on the whole were too old, too uneducated, and too radical. This state of affairs led to a change in recruitment policies. The CCP began to target the young and educated, the new elites of the reform era. By 2005, the party had grown to over 70 million members. The proportion of party members with high school or higher levels of education rose from 17.8 percent in 1984 to 56.6 percent in 2004, and 23 percent were under the age of 35. Women constituted approximately 20 percent of CCP members, about the same as in the Maoist years.

These changes led to inevitable conflicts. Veteran cadres resisted the reforms, recognizing that their political skills were being denigrated for the sake of professionalization. There was strong ideological opposition to letting people formerly designated as "rightists" into the party, especially the newly emerging class of private entrepreneurs. In 1989, after the imposition of martial law, the party imposed a ban on the admission of private entrepreneurs into the party and the appointment of entrepreneurs already in the party to official positions. This ban was widely ignored at the local level, however, and after prolonged debate was lifted in 2002. Also after 1989, the party once again began to emphasize political reliability, not simply expertise, as a criterion for recruitment and promotion.

Another challenge to the rejuvenation of the party was that there was less enthusiasm within society to join the party. It was no longer necessary to become a party member to have a successful career. People could now concentrate on acquiring technical skills in school, especially in foreign universities, or open their own business. Party membership was still beneficial, but it was not a prerequisite for prestigious and high-paying jobs. Throughout the reform era, the CCP has continued to lose prestige, and many of its own members do not support it. Society as a whole has lost faith in socialist ideals and no longer responds to ideological appeals. Nevertheless, the party remains an effective distributor of jobs, education, and travel opportunities and provides special access to loans, technology, and markets, along with other valuable goods and services. Party membership is still a valuable asset, even to those who do not believe in communist ideology.

### Weak Bureaucracy

China's officials suffered from the same problems as the party membership as a whole: they were too old, poorly skilled, and more supportive of Maoism than modernization. To address these problems, the party undertook two somewhat contradictory policies: it rehabilitated victims of the Cultural Revolution, and it recruited skilled expertise. The rehabilitation of veteran officials denounced in the Cultural Revolution was designed to build support for reform policies and to push the reds out of their posts. Once the goal of replacing the reds was accomplished, the party introduced a retirement program for veteran officials that would entice them to leave their posts and allow younger and better-educated people to be appointed.[17]

One of the most important transitions has been the recruitment of large numbers of young, highly educated officials to staff the bureaucracy. China is often described as a government of "technocrats," a term referring to bureaucrats with high levels of technical training.[18] This transition was necessary to fulfill the party's main task of the post-Mao era: economic modernization. With the period of class struggle over and the party concentrating on economic modernization, it needed new people with new skills to staff the bureaucracy. The party recruited young, better-educated and better-skilled people to replace the aged veterans, many of whom had first been appointed in the 1950s. It weeded out those who were too old or who lacked the skills necessary to carry out the economic reforms. It established minimum requirements for certain positions, such as a college degree or a specialized degree in engineering or management. In the past, no such requirements existed, and people were appointed not on the basis of their professional merit but on their political virtue. In the post-Mao period, the emphasis has been on upgrading the quality of party and government officials.

### Reconciliation of Party and Society

Party leaders recognized they had lost much of their prestige and public support during the Cultural Revolution by trying to micromanage all aspects of daily life. In the post-Mao period, they have tried to limit the scope of politics. For instance, the party now allows a greater array of plays and music to be performed and literature to be published. Traditional festivals and customs have reappeared, especially in the countryside. New social organizations are allowed to form as long as they are not politically oriented. In recent years, China has witnessed an explosion of chambers of commerce, sports leagues, hobby groups, professional associations for writers, teachers, and businesspeople, and other types of civic and professional groups. It is now possible for citizens to read traditional novels or listen to Western music without accusations of being a counterrevolutionary. The foundations of a civil society are increasingly emerging, albeit under the ever-watchful eye of the communist authorities.[19]

Above all, the party declared that the period of class struggle was over, replaced by a commitment to economic modernization. Those who had been falsely accused and punished during the Maoist period had their records cleared and their derogatory labels *landlord, capitalist, rightist*, and so on removed. Unfortunately, many of the victims of past class struggle campaigns had already died, but even they had their good names restored. In some cases, their families received property or personal belongings back or received a cash settlement.

But not everything has changed. The party still remains the most important institution in the political system. All decisions are made by the party, and there is little opportunity for nonparty people to be involved in the decision-making process. While the party now tolerates a wider assortment of nonpolitical activities, the definition of what is nonpolitical has varied considerably. For instance, religious activities have increased dramatically with official approval, but the state still arrests those religious practitioners whom it sees as stepping over the line between religion and politics. The boundaries are not always clear, but the punishments can be severe for those who cross over. And anything clearly political is strictly prohibited and immediately repressed. Citizens who have tried to create new political parties and autonomous labor unions have been severely punished, losing their jobs and housing, and in some cases, receiving long jail sentences. The CCP, like all Leninist parties, insists on protecting its monopoly on political organization. It does not allow the existence of any organization that it does not approve of or that it perceives as any kind of threat to its power.

## CHINA'S ECONOMIC DEVELOPMENT STRATEGIES

During the more than fifty years of the People's Republic, China's government has pursued three separate strategies of economic development: the Soviet model, self-reliance, and the post-Mao emphasis on markets and "openness."

### The Soviet Model (1953–57)

Following the Communist victory in 1949, China was first concerned with economic reconstruction:

controlling hyperinflation and restoring industrial production to its prewar levels (in 1949, industrial production was only 56 percent of prewar levels). After restoring stability, it adopted the Soviet model of development. The model's main characteristic was a commitment to growth that emphasized heavy industry at the expense of agriculture, light industry, consumer goods, and commerce and trade. In order to achieve this commitment and to promote heavy industry, new central planning institutions were created.

New central ministries were needed to create and implement the plans governing the economy. All key decisions were made at the top in Beijing. Central planning, which did not rely on market mechanisms, required a bureaucracy to run the economy, and the bureaucracy needed experts to do the planning. Production targets were set for each province, which then set targets for lower administrative levels, which then set targets for individual enterprises. Prices were set by the bureaucracy, not by the market forces of supply and demand. Supplies of raw materials, energy, and other inputs to the production process were also determined by planning agencies. Manufactured goods were also distributed according to the plan.

Why did China adopt the Soviet model? The Cold War that began after World War II precluded any other choice. Moreover, the Soviet Union in the 1950s was an example of successful and rapid industrialization. CCP leaders were communist, but they were also nationalistic. They sought rapid development in order to catch up to the West. The Soviet model therefore offered the promise of success plus ideological justification. The Soviet Union was the "elder brother," and China followed its example.

Initially, the Soviet model was largely successful. During the period of the First Five-Year Plan (1953–57), the economy grew by almost 9 percent per year (industrial output grew by 128 percent between 1952 and 1957, agriculture by 25 percent). This success was accomplished not only with the Soviet model, but also with direct Soviet assistance. The Soviet Union sent over ten thousand advisors, blueprints for factories, the machinery and technology for running them, and plans for over 150 major projects in addition to training almost forty thousand Chinese engineers in the Soviet Union. This aid made the Soviet model successful in China.

Not all Chinese leaders were satisfied with the adoption of the Soviet model, especially its emphasis on expertise for planners in the bureaucracy and managers in factories. One reason was practical: the CCP simply did not have enough members with the necessary skills or education.

The second reason some of China's leaders were unhappy with the Soviet model was political: Mao resented the way the Soviet Union treated China as a nation and himself in particular. He and others in China were not satisfied with their reliance on Soviet advice and assistance; they preferred to develop their economy in their own way. Above all, Mao was a revolutionary, and he was not satisfied with planned, incremental progress. He preferred struggle, transformation, turmoil, even violence as a learning experience. He also did not trust intellectuals, who were necessary for the Soviet model to work. The result was a change in economic planning strategy that had major implications for China's development and for its relationship with the Soviet Union.

### Self-Reliance (1957–76)

By the end of the First Five-Year Plan, Mao and other CCP leaders designed a new strategy of "self-reliance," initiated by the policies of the Great Leap Forward and continuing until Mao's death in 1976. Rather than rely on markets or central planning, the Maoist strategy of self-reliance used mass mobilization to tap into China's most abundant resource: its people, not money or machines. The CCP used propaganda and mobilization to create a spirit of team work, emphasizing collective well-being at the expense of personal self-interest. The reward for hard work and successful accomplishments was praise, not money. The careful planning and setting of feasible targets that characterized the Soviet model were replaced with political enthusiasm.

During the Great Leap Forward, local and provincial officials competed with one another in reporting grossly inflated production estimates. The most enduring feature of the Great Leap Forward era was the commune. There were roughly eighty thousand communes altogether, with each commune divided into brigades, and each brigade into teams. (Communes, brigades, and teams corresponded to the traditional townships, villages, and neighborhoods, respectively.) Farming was not done by individuals or families but by teams. Wages were set according to a person's work as well as his or her political attitudes, a very subjective evaluation. There was little financial incentive to work harder, and little available to buy even if money had been plentiful. The self-reliance strategy preserved the low emphasis on consumption that was a key feature of the Soviet model.

Just as China itself was to become self-reliant, each region was supposed to be self-reliant as well. Instead of producing according to its comparative advantage, concentrating on those items in which it excelled, and instead of trading with other areas of the country for other types of food, each area had to provide its own grain, meat, fruit, and vegetables even if the climate was not appropriate. Factories were built throughout the inland areas, often far from transportation lines and sources of energy and other raw materials. This effort was also part of Mao's preference for regional balance and self-reliance, but it led to wasteful duplication and inefficient farming.

Chinese leaders who promoted self-reliance preferred autarky (economic self-sufficiency) in the extreme. They wanted to cut China off from all economic ties to foreign countries, which were suspected of wanting to undermine the integrity of the communist revolution in China. But the war scenario never materialized, and the cost of preparing for it was tremendous.[20]

Self-reliance was an unmitigated disaster. Factories and communes were not required to operate at a profit, and their losses were compensated by the state. As a result, there was no incentive for efficient production. Projects were started in the wrong areas of the country, often without adequate resources, inputs, or skilled labor. These policies cut China off from the outside world, with little trade or other interactions. At a time when other Asian countries were experiencing rapid growth, industrialization, and modernization, China was out of touch with the technological advances of other countries and fell increasingly behind. Self-reliance also had a personal price for most Chinese: wages were frozen after the early 1960s. By 1976, those with fifteen years of experience were earning the same amount as those with much less seniority. However, this egalitarianism did not seem fair to most workers, who resented policies that did not recognize their seniority or personal needs.[21] A greater share of the older workers' wages went to providing housing, food, education, medical care for spouses, children, and elderly parents; many younger workers only had to support themselves, and many lived with their parents if they were not married. For all these reasons, self-reliance led to stagnant growth. The Maoist approach ignored the principles of comparative advantage and material incentives that would have provided more efficient and rapid growth.

### The Reform Era (1978–Present)

By 1978, Deng Xiaoping and his allies were able to consolidate their position and adopt new policies that called an end to the political campaigns and ideologically oriented policies of the past in favor of economic modernization. In the early reform era, this goal was pursued by a variety of experiments, such as promoting private—as opposed to communal—farming, attracting foreign trade and investment through the creation of "Special Economic Zones" along the eastern coast of China, and allowing small-scale enterprises and street vendors to operate. Many of these experiments later became national policy.

Although China's post-Mao leaders agreed that the Maoist policies had to be abandoned, they disagreed about the proper set of policies that should be adopted and the pace at which they should be introduced. Above all, they debated the proper balance between central planning and market mechanisms for regulating the economy. Some saw the early 1950s, when China followed the Soviet model, as a golden era during which the economy achieved high growth rates without having to rely on the market. Others preferred to push ahead to a fully market-oriented economy, believing that a planned economy is too inefficient. Ultimately, this market-oriented group prevailed. Although there has been occasional backtracking from economic reform and international trade since their victory, the reformers have repeatedly regained the initiative and pushed ahead. These policies have transformed China's economy, creating prosperity and a dynamism that were unimaginable in the Maoist era. Although rapid economic growth has created a number of problems, such as regional inequalities, corruption, environmental damage, and occasionally dangerously high inflation rates, support for economic reform remains strong.[22]

The post-Mao economic reforms have had several main goals. First, China's leaders wanted to achieve technological dynamism. They have sought access to Western technology, capital, and management practices essential for modernization.

The reformers also wanted to limit bureaucratic controls. A centrally planned economy needs bureaucratic controls to establish production goals, disseminate materials, monitor results, and redistribute industrial and agricultural goods to consumers and other end users. But these controls also stifle technological dynamism. Markets are needed to enliven the economy via competition and material incentives. Limiting bureaucratic controls requires decentralization: the devolution of decision making to local governments and firms. Deng wanted to make local governments and individual firms responsible for their own profits and losses and reduce subsidies paid by the central government to compensate for their losses. But he also believed that, if they were to be given responsibility, they also had to be given the authority to make decisions they thought best and the right to keep a larger share of the profits. These benefits provided incentives for experimentation and new investments that created the explosive growth seen in China during the past generation.

Another goal of the reforms was to raise living standards. Mao made a virtue out of poverty, but most people want higher living standards and a more comfortable life and are not very enthusiastic about ideological purity. Self-reliance and the resulting poverty and stagnation damaged the prestige of the party and undermined the legitimacy of the government. In the post-Mao period, China's leaders have based their legitimacy on their ability to create economic growth and better living standards rather than on political correctness.

Along with the goals of creating a more vibrant and prosperous economy came a political goal: that of maintaining stability in general and the unquestioned leadership of the CCP in particular. Although most of China's leaders are willing to accept competition within the economy, they do not want a similar logic to seep into the political system. They believe that China must still be ruled by a unified, authoritarian political system in order to provide overall coordination and to keep the country unified. They believe that economic growth cannot be allowed to create political disorder, including demands for democracy. Although some within China (and most foreign analysts) believe that the resulting imbalance between economic openness and political controls cannot be sustained indefinitely, most of China's leaders are worried that introducing more ambitious political reforms would threaten the party's hold on power, creating great uncertainty and potential chaos and undermining the economic gains of the reform era. They view the collapse of the Soviet Union and of communist governments in Central and Eastern Europe as a warning of the dangers of initiating reform before achieving a stable and prosperous economy.

Finally, China's reformers wanted to maintain a peaceful environment in which development could occur. Prior to 1989, when antigovernment demonstrations took place throughout China, Deng and other reformers thought they could enjoy prolonged peace via astute diplomacy, allowing them to divert resources away from military spending toward the civilian economy. Since 1989, military spending has risen sharply, as the party leaders seek to guarantee the support of the military. Moreover, many of China's leaders, especially conservative elites, believe that the power of the United States has risen dramatically since the collapse of the Soviet Union and the end of the Cold War, and they wonder if China should not perhaps give greater priority to security issues, even as it continues its economic modernization. One of the major questions facing the United States and other countries today is whether China still puts a priority on maintaining peace and stability or is preparing to have a more disruptive influence on its neighbors and the international system more generally. The evidence remains ambiguous on this important question, but it has generated an ongoing debate among American policy makers and analysts about the international implications of China's rapid modernization.[23]

If these have been the goals of the economic reforms, what have been the means for achieving them?

TABLE 21.1

China's Economic Growth (Various Years)

| | 1980 | 1985 | 1990 | 1995 | 2000 | 2001 | 2002 | 2003 | 2004 |
|---|---|---|---|---|---|---|---|---|---|
| GDP ($ billions) | 188.2 | 304.9 | 354.6 | 700.3 | 1198.0 | 1325.0 | 1454.0 | 1641.0 | 1932.0 |
| GDP per capita ($) | 192.0 | 290.0 | 312.0 | 581.0 | 949.0 | 1042.0 | 1136.0 | 1274.0 | 1490.0 |
| Exports ($ billions) | 14.3 | 30.5 | 62.2 | 168.0 | 275.7 | 304.7 | 363.5 | 492.2 | 656.8 |
| Imports ($ billions) | 14.8 | 43.0 | 50.8 | 151.8 | 251.7 | 265.0 | 334.4 | 443.1 | 598.8 |
| Foreign direct investment ($ billions) | | 1.0 | 2.7 | 33.8 | 38.4 | 37.4 | 49.3 | 53.5 | 54.9 |

Note: All figures are in current U.S. dollars.
*Source:* World Bank, *World Development Indicators* (successive years), devdata.worldbank.org.

**Increasing Market Forces** China has dismantled the communes, perhaps the most prominent symbol of the Maoist approach to economic development. In their place, new policies have encouraged individual and family farming and allowed farmers to sell their produce on the open market after they sold their quota to the state.[24] China gradually eliminated price controls on most industrial and consumer goods, allowing prices to better reflect supply and demand. State controls over the economy were reduced, including production targets and monopolies on the distribution of supplies and finished goods.[25] In contrast to the Maoist era, economic policies also encouraged consumption instead of enforced savings (although China's savings rate is still much higher than that of most countries) and the production of consumer goods. Finally, comparative advantage was made a priority, allowing regional variation and specialization.

**Increasing Foreign Trade and Investment** China created Special Economic Zones along its coast and "open cities" to encourage greater foreign trade and investment. This approach was part of its comparative advantage strategy: the cities with already developed industrial bases and access to external markets were allowed to exploit their advantages. As a result, coastal areas have developed much more rapidly than inland China, creating much resentment from officials and residents in the disadvantaged areas.[26] Whereas China closed itself off during its self-reliance phase, it now encourages joint ventures and other types of foreign investment. The state no longer has a monopoly on foreign trade: individual enterprises are allowed to make deals on their own.

**Reliance on the Private Sector** China's private sector was virtually eliminated during the 1950s. However, it began to reemerge in the 1980s with the opening of very small scale firms, and it then exploded in the 1990s. In 1990, there were barely ten thousand privately owned firms in China; by 2005, there were 4.4 million. In 1990 the private sector employed only 2.1 percent of industrial staff and workers; by 2005 more than 100 million people were employed in the private sector, comprising 31 percent of the work force. In the most prosperous areas, the private sector is even more dominant. In Zhejiang, a coastal province immediately south of Shanghai, the private sector employs three-quarters of all workers. The private sector produced over half of China's industrial output by 2005, compared to only 9.8 percent in 1990. The state sector, in contrast, has been steadily shrinking, especially since the late 1990s when China's leaders decided to sell off or close many unprofitable and antiquated state-owned enterprises. More and more Chinese are migrating from the countryside in search of jobs in the new private and foreign-invested enterprises. Less than half of the rural population is now engaged in agriculture, and an estimated 100 million workers have joined China's "floating population" of migrant workers.[27]

The results of reform have been both positive and negative (see table 21.1). On the positive side, China has experienced extraordinarily rapid growth. Per capita GDP doubled between 1978 and 1988, and China averaged growth rates of almost 10 percent per year between 1978 and 2005. The fastest growing sectors have been commerce, light industry, and services, the reverse of the Maoist years. There has been tremendous growth in the volume of China's foreign trade and the foreign capital invested in China: the total volume of trade increased from less than $30 billion in 1980 to almost $1.3 trillion in 2004, and the volume of foreign direct investment increased from a negligible amount in the early 1980s to $54.9 billion in 2004 (most of this growth occurred after 1992). As a result of increased trade and foreign investment, technological standards have increased. Factories have been upgraded technologically, allowing them to be more innovative and better able to respond quickly to market demands. For example, China quickly became a major supplier of satellite launches despite several costly accidents. Higher incomes created new markets for a wide variety of consumer goods, better-quality and more fashionable clothing, fresh and processed foods, better entertainment, and tourism within China and abroad. In sum, the living standards for most Chinese are higher now than ever before.

At the same time, a variety of negative consequences also emerged. Most important, the problem of corruption exploded as party and government officials at all levels took advantage of rapid growth, the desire of Chinese and foreign entrepreneurs to develop new projects, and weak laws and regulations to line their own pockets. China now ranks among the most corrupt countries in which to do business, according to surveys of foreign businesspeople (see table 4.1). In 2006, Beijing's vice mayor in charge of building projects for the 2008 Olympics was fired and arrested for alleged corruption. Corruption was the primary cause of the 1989 student demonstrations and it continues to provoke local disturbances. The CCP tends to target cases of corruption that result in large losses of state revenue, such as embezzlement, the use of public funds for private purposes (banquets, homes, cars, etc.), and illegal privatization of state-owned enterprises' assets. In contrast, illegal confiscation of property, excessive collection of taxes and fees, and other abuses of authority by local officials are seen as mere "irregularities" and do not receive the same level of publicity or punishment. Increased enforcement of economic crimes does little to alleviate other forms of corruption that are more obvious to ordinary citizens, and it does not change the public's frustration with widespread corruption.[28]

A related problem arising from rapid economic development has been rising inequality. Although incomes have generally risen, they have not risen equally. There is a growing gap between the city and the countryside and between coastal and inland areas. During the Mao era, China had one of the most equitable distributions of wealth in the world, although most people were equally poor. During the reform era, that picture changed dramatically. In 1980, the beginning of the reform era, China's Gini coefficient was 0.33; in 1995 it had grown to 0.44, and by 2005 the Chinese government estimated it may have increased to 0.47. (On the Gini coefficient, see chapter 2.) In other words, most of the increase in inequality occurred during the early part of the reform era; inequality increased only slightly after 1995. Public awareness of inequality, and the state's complicity in it, has widened over the years, however.

There was a growing perception as well that opportunities to succeed were also unequal. During the 1990s the CCP under Jiang Zemin's leadership pursued an elitist strategy, focusing on private entrepreneurs and coastal areas. During the Jiang era, the number of "red capitalists," private entrepreneurs who belong to the CCP, grew rapidly; by 2005 approximately 35 percent of entrepreneurs were party members.[29] This increasingly close relationship between the party and the private sector has created the widespread perception that the benefits of economic growth are being monopolized by a small segment of the population while the rest are being left behind. Many people now believe that economic success is based on personal connections with party and government officials, not on individual initiative or quality work. As people come to believe that the benefits of the reform policies are unfairly distributed, the legitimacy of the party's policy of letting some get rich first is jeopardized.

Under new leaders Hu Jintao and Wen Jiabao, the CCP has downplayed Jiang's emphasis on the urban elites in favor of the need to promote a more harmonious society. This commitment to China's have-nots has been demonstrated both symbolically and substantively. Premier Wen has frequently visited miners, SARS and AIDS patients, and victims of natural and man-made disasters, even developing a reputation for weeping to show his sympathy. Beyond this, the state has also boosted rural incomes through subsidies, income transfers, and tax relief. One immediate effect has been the return of migrant labor back to the countryside, creating labor shortages in some cities and putting upward pressure on wages and working conditions. It is too early to tell whether these policies are alleviating inequality, but they do reveal the populist orientation of China's current leaders.

Inflation has also been a recurring problem and was another contributor to the 1989 demonstrations. Inflation ate up most of the gains of rapid growth during the 1980s. Since then, inflation has been kept under better control.

The push for rapid growth also created tremendous environmental pollution. China is now the second largest polluter in the world (after the United States), and its emissions grew by 33 percent between 1992 and 2002. Sixteen of the world's twenty most polluted cities are in China, and four of the top ten (including number one) are in Shanxi Province. The World Bank estimates that as many as 300,000 people die every year of respiratory ailments caused by air pollution. Thirty percent of river water is so badly polluted that it is not suitable even for agriculture and industrial use, much less human consumption. China loses more than 10 million hectares of forest land each year, and its deserts are growing by 1,300 square miles each year; 25 percent of China's land is now desert. One study predicted that 30 to 40 million farmers will lose access to adequate land and water in the coming decades and will be forced to migrate. China's pollution problems have become so severe that they have triggered riots in recent years.[30] China's water, air, and land are being damaged by companies that find it cheaper to pollute than to be energy efficient or to dispose of waste properly. A growing number of cars and trucks contribute to this increasingly serious problem. Energy prices are set by the state at below world market levels, giving firms and individuals little incentive to use energy more efficiently.

Rising income levels have also promoted crime. Social ills such as gambling, drug use, pornography, and prostitution have reemerged after being eliminated in the early 1950s. Reports of violent crime, kidnappings, and blackmail have become common. Women in particular have encountered problems during the reform era.[31] They receive lower wages than men for the same work and are often the first to be laid off from state-owned enterprises. They also face physical and sexual harassment in the workplace. Women who migrate to urban areas for factory work are occasionally kidnapped and sold as wives to men in other rural areas.

In addition, another unexpected consequence of economic development has been a spiritual crisis. The emphasis on making money and material interests has taken a toll on Chinese society. Many feel there has been a loss of a commitment to group welfare and collective well-being. China no longer has a shared set of values that binds the country together. First, the communists denigrated the Confucian traditions and promoted the revolutionary virtues associated with Mao; then the post-Mao leaders rejected the values promoted by Mao without offering an alternative ideology or belief system. Deng's emphasis on pragmatism, symbolized by the slogans "seek truth from facts" (as opposed to ideology) and "to get rich is glorious" may have been the basis for policy making, but it did not give people much to believe in.

This nearly exclusive interest in materialism has led to the revival of traditional religious practices and a growing interest in Christianity. Local temples have been rebuilt, usually with public funds, and individual families have rebuilt ancestor shrines. Some Protestant and Catholic churches are officially recognized by the state, but others are "underground churches" that meet in private homes without official approval. Some of these churches are persecuted by local officials, their leaders and parishioners arrested and often mistreated. But in other areas, the churches operate with the tacit approval and even the encouragement of the local leaders. Some churches have rented space from government offices to hold their worship services, while others have borrowed money from the local government to construct their own buildings. Despite foreign criticisms of widespread and systematic persecution of religious practices in China, the number of religious believers has never been higher than it is today. There is no question that religious freedoms still do not enjoy full protection, but at least in some communities the growth in religious faith has come with the knowledge and often the support of local officials. More important, it reflects the search for a meaning to life that goes deeper than just rising living standards.

The most visible manifestation of this longing for a spiritual meaning to life is the rapid rise of *Falun Gong*. This spiritual movement combines meditation and exercises similar to traditional Buddhist and Taoist practices with claims of miraculous healings through the cultivation of a person's inner energy. In addition, it warns of a coming apocalypse and urges its followers to adopt simpler and purer lives in preparation for the end of the world. Falun Gong was banned in 1999 after some ten thousand of its members staged a silent protest, surrounding the party and government leadership compound in Beijing in an effort to seek official recognition. At its peak of popularity, Falun Gong had up to 100 million followers, which would have made it larger than the CCP. Its members included not only retirees and housewives, but also leading party, government, and even military officials. Despite the state's efforts to repress the movement, which included numerous arrests and reports of torture, a determined core of followers continued to engage in public protest, opening banners in public squares and even hacking into satellite and cable television signals to air messages. Public support for the movement waned as its tactics become more extreme. Although there are few signs of continued activity in China, it remains very active abroad. One Falun Gong supporter, posing as a reporter, disrupted an outdoor White House news conference with George Bush and Hu Jintao in 2006. Falun Gong's size and its diverse membership reflect the widespread longing for a deeper spirituality and a return to a society less dominated by corruption and commercialism. The government's repression of Falun Gong, in contrast, reflects its continued insistence on preserving its monopoly on organized power.

**Economic Reform: A Balance Sheet** In the post-Mao era, economic growth has been the primary goal, and equity has been deemphasized. Deng in particular was a fan of rapid growth at any cost. But he was forced to compromise with those who were more concerned about order and stability and believed that the negative consequences of reform required a slower pace of reforms and even a periodic rollback. Even among China's current leaders, many feel that economic equity should not be totally abandoned, because rising resentment against the regions and individuals who are getting rich faster than others may also threaten political stability and ultimately the legitimacy of the CCP. Despite these negative and generally unintended consequences, the benefits of reform—a more dynamic economy, rising standards of living, a flourishing cultural life, greater access to an increasing variety of goods and services, opportunities for entrepreneurship and innovation, improvements in transportation and housing, and so on—have created tremendous popular support for further economic reform. Much of the credit for the reforms' successes goes to **Jiang Zemin**, the man who led the "third generation" of Communist Party leaders who succeeded Deng Xiaoping.

## PROFILE: Jiang Zemin

Jiang Zemin has served as China's president, General Secretary of the CCP, and chairman of the Central Military Commission; thus he was head of state, head of the party, and head of the military. Jiang was promoted to these posts after the 1989 Tiananmen Square demonstrations, and during the 1990s he gradually built his networks of supporters in the central government and military.

Most observers expected Jiang to be a transitional figure. He did not have a strong base of support in the party, and he seemed to lack the personality and vision needed to be a strong leader. In fact, Deng Xiaoping reportedly grew frustrated with Jiang's reluctance to promote economic reform, and he was prepared to replace him in 1992. However, Jiang and his main aide got wind of the plans and quickly restored Deng's confidence in Jiang. They also began maneuvering to replace rivals to Jiang's authority. From 1997 on, there was no other leader prepared to challenge Jiang's position as top leader.

Although Jiang was remarkably successful at accumulating power for himself, he seemed less interested in using that power to promote a policy agenda. Unlike other leaders who had a more consistent and predictable policy perspective, Jiang drifted between the conservative and reformist ends of the policy spectrum. He was intent on being viewed as the equal of Mao and Deng, but he did not have an issue or policy that he consistently championed.

Jiang has been one of China's most colorful leaders. Some have criticized him for being vainglorious, or even eccentric. He can speak several foreign languages and is most fluent in English. He can recite the Gettysburg Address by heart, and halfway through a speech at Harvard University in 1997 he switched from Chinese to English without missing a beat. He has also been known to sing American pop songs, Russian folk songs, and even Italian opera to foreign guests.

Toward the end of his tenure as party general secretary, Jiang promoted a new ideological innovation that was meant to legitimize the CCP's shift from its traditional focus on the working classes to its current pro-business orientation. Known as the *"Three Represents,"* this slogan claimed that the CCP represents (1) "advanced productive forces" (i.e., the urban middle class, entrepreneurs, and high-tech specialists), (2) advanced culture, and (3) the interest of the vast majority of the people. This array of groups and interests was so broad that it could justify just about any set of policies. In particular, it legitimized the recruitment of private entrepreneurs into the party, a practice that had been banned immediately after the 1989 Tiananmen Square demonstrations. Many in China, especially orthodox party members, criticized the slogan—and Jiang—for abandoning the party's traditional base of support among peasants and workers for the sake of the newly emerging economic and technical elites. But Jiang succeeded in getting the slogan added into the Party Constitution at the Sixteenth Party Congress in 2002. He had finally achieved his goal of joining the pantheon alongside Mao and Deng.

Jiang retired as head of the Chinese Communist Party in 2002, as China's president in 2003, and as head of the Central Military Commission in 2004. In 2006 he turned eighty. Although he no longer held any formal positions, he was believed to still wield considerable influence behind the scenes.

## STATE–SOCIETY RELATIONS IN CHINA

### Fundamental Features of State–Society Relations

**One-Party Rule Means No Organized Opposition** The CCP guards its political monopoly quite zealously. One of its primary goals has been to prevent the organization of any group outside its control. To this end the CCP operates a network of party cells throughout the government, the military, and society to monitor compliance with party policies. All labor unions, student organizations, professional associations, and even religious groups must be sanctioned by the government, and their leaders are subject to official approval. Even China's so-called democratic parties have Communist Party cells. Any attempt to form independent organizations is immediately squashed, and their leaders are punished. The party proscribes trade unions, student groups, political parties, and religious organizations like the Roman Catholic Church, which is banned in China because its priests are loyal to the Pope in Rome, not to the leaders in Beijing.

**Communication Between State and Society** China developed the "mass line" concept during the revolutionary period when it was competing with landlords and the Nationalist government for popular support. The ideal of the mass line was that the state would get information from the masses in order to create correct policies and then communicate those policies to the masses. But after 1949, there was no competition for popular support, and the need to solicit public opinion as a guide to policy became less important. The mass line remained, but it became ritualized. Citizens learned the high price of offering contrary opinions and instead learned to recite current slogans.

As in pluralist societies, individuals in China can write letters or visit newspapers or government offices to complain. Most papers have investigative departments to look into reports of official corruption, workplace problems, housing complaints, and so on. So long as people complain only about how they have been adversely affected by the improper implementation of policy, their complaints are likely to be resolved. However, they may not complain about the merits of the policy itself or its general impact.

Moreover, the newspapers and other forms of media are themselves owned by the state, a reality that limits their effectiveness as a form of feedback on the state's performance. Reading the newspaper is a form of political participation in China, as it is in other countries, but after the revolution, reading the paper was frequently a matter of self-preservation. The state often required participation in political study groups after work as a form of thought control. It did not provide objective information but only the party's current propaganda line, thereby imparting important clues about how to think and behave. Even today, Chinese media reports rarely break news of scandal, the abuse of power, poor governmental performance, or other exposés that people living in democracies come to expect of their media.

There is no possibility for organized political action except by officially recognized groups. As part of the economic reform process, the state has created a variety of corporatist-style organizations, especially for businesspeople and enterprise managers, to serve as bridges between state and society. These groups tend to be cooperative with the state and do not seek autonomy or an adversarial role, contrary to the ways we expect such groups to operate in a democracy. However, these groups do seem to communicate the perspective of their members to the state and are no longer confined to simply transmitting the state's position downward to the population, as in the Maoist era. It has been difficult to organize other types of interest groups, such as those concerned with the environment, women's issues, labor, or minority groups. The policy-making process has gradually become more inclusive, allowing a wider range of people and perspectives to be involved, but many voices are still excluded from the process.

**State Autonomy** Because the Chinese party-state allows no organized opposition and imposes limits on the flow of information, it is largely free to decide for itself what policy should be. Decisions are made in secret, and officials are not subject to voter approval; nor are they held accountable to the population through such democratic mechanisms as citizen initiatives, referendums, and the recall of unacceptable officeholders. The results of policy cannot be assessed through citizen feedback because of the lack of information on public opinion and the danger of punishment for excessive criticism of Chinese officialdom. But the state does not always get what it wants: bureaucratic inertia, lower-level resistance, or outright evasion are quite common in China and prevent new policies from being implemented in a timely and proper fashion.[32]

The CCP justifies its autonomy from the population on the ideological grounds that it is a vanguard party with special insights into the laws of history. Therefore, it is uniquely qualified to decide what is best for the nation. Individuals and interest groups are not allowed into the decision-making process—except at the invitation of the party—because they only represent their narrow special interests. Only the CCP, in its own estimation, is concerned with collective well-being and the national interest. On a more basic level, the CCP recognizes that its own rise to power was based on its ability to organize society against the former government, which was unaware of what was going on. The CCP is determined not to be the victim of the same methods that brought it to power. Hence it does not allow alternative voices to be a part of the political process; it has no intention of competing with others for popular support.

**Role of Law** Democracies are based on the rule *of* law: both state and society are bound by the same laws. Many laws are designed to restrict the ability of the state to interfere in the citizens' private lives. The courts (in theory) enforce these laws, preventing the state from infringing on individual rights and civil liberties. These democratic concepts are very foreign in China, whose system is more aptly described as rule *by* law: laws are tools of governance but they do not restrict the scope of the state's actions. A legal code was not adopted until the late 1970s, thirty years after the founding of the People's Republic of China, and many laws and regulations remain secret or are revised at the discretion of China's leaders to meet current needs. Moreover, there is no independent judiciary to mediate public and private disputes; the courts are an arm of the state, not part of a checks and balance system. For major cases, such as for student demonstrators in 1989 or organizers of opposition parties and independent labor unions, verdicts and sentences are determined by the party in advance.

In short, individual citizens have little recourse if they are the target of state actions. And they have often been innocent victims of the state. For instance, during the Great Leap Forward, as many as 30 million people died of starvation as a result of mistaken policies decided without consultation with society, but the recovery policies were similarly undertaken without consultation. There were no demonstrations against the government, no newspapers calling for the resignation of the country's leaders, no calls for nationwide elections. Passive resistance, however, did occur, at times conducted by local officials who did not support the central government's policies or who felt that conditions in their area were so bad that they could not force their people to obey. This was a risky strategy, but local-level resistance was one of the issues that led to the outbreak of the Cultural Revolution in 1966.

## Post-Mao Changes in State–Society Relations

After painting such an ugly picture, we must also recognize how state–society relations improved during the post-Mao period. First, most victims of past political campaigns had their verdicts overturned; they were rehabilitated and assigned new jobs, and the old political labels used to stigmatize them in the past (*rightist*, *capitalist*, *landlord*, and the like) were removed. People were no longer punished for actions that used to be considered political crimes, and they regained their lost reputations and status. The use of mass campaigns as a way of implementing new policies was drastically reduced in number and intensity. Daily life was "depoliticized," and a range of activities that were once prohibited or proscribed were now possible once again. However, the boundary between the permissible and the prohibited was often unclear and subject to change. Finally, there were more opportunities for a lively cultural and social life without political overtones, stimulating an outpouring of new literature, the resurgence of traditional culture, and the importation of Western goods and values (in part as an incentive to make money and to provide a model for China's future). The result was more color and variety, but also fears that China was losing its traditional identity and straying too far from communist ideals.

In addition, Deng Xiaoping's economic reforms undermined the state's control over society. This effect was largely intentional. As noted earlier, Deng Xiaoping and other leaders learned firsthand during the Cultural Revolution about the irrationality and arbitrariness of the political system they helped create. They recognized that the state was too intrusive and only inhibited development rather than fostering it. With more goods and services available on the free market thanks to the reforms, with jobs being created in a small but growing private sector, and with expanding opportunities and even encouragement to make money, citizens became less dependent upon the approval of local officials. During the Maoist period, housing, education, medicine, and welfare were all tied to the workplace; if you were fired, you would no longer have access to any of these things. You would therefore have to cultivate good relations with your superiors, especially the party boss, to make sure you got your share of these scarce goods and services.[33] But the market now gives people more options. The state cannot threaten to withhold things it does not control, and individuals have become less dependent upon the state.

In fact, many local officials are somewhat dependent on local businesspeople. Rewards and promotions are increasingly based on local economic performance, and the fastest growing sectors are not the state-owned enterprises but private firms. Local officials now cooperate with businesspeople to help them succeed—they procure loans, find inputs and markets for goods, give tax breaks, protect local firms from outside competition, and do other similar things to promote economic growth in their communities.

Moreover, the CCP has sponsored the creation of numerous civic and professional associations to both liberalize social life and promote economic development. As the state pulled back from micromanaging society and operating a centrally planned economy, it created new organizations to link the state with key sectors of society. China allowed some organizations even during the Maoist era for officially recognized groups, such as workers, women, and youth, but they were generally seen as "transmission belts" that monitored and enforced state policy toward these groups but had little ability to represent the interests of their nominal members or to influence policy. In the post-Mao era, the state has allowed new organizations to form and has even allowed the older organizations to be more active in representing their members, not simply conveying the official line.[34] China now has a dense variety of associations for businesspeople, for specific professions (e.g., software writers, factory managers, lawyers, etc.), for various religions and traditional practices, and for many others. However, there are still no independent trade unions.

These organizations and the state's relationship with them follow an authoritarian variant of *corporatism* (see chapter 11) as well as the logic of Leninism. Most organizations are created, or at least approved, by the state, and many have government officials as their leaders. For instance, local branches of the Industrial and Commercial Federation, whose members include the largest of China's manufacturing and commercial enterprises, are normally headed by the party official in charge of united front work (which handles relations between the CCP and nonparty individuals and groups), and their offices are often in the government compound. In addition, there is normally only one organization for any given profession or activity. In cases where two groups with similar interests exist in a community, local officials will often force them to merge or will disband one in favor of the other. This practice prevents competition between the associations and limits how many associations are allowed to exist, making it easier for the state to monitor and control them.

Are these new associations like the transmission belts of old, or are they able to truly represent the interests of their own members vis-à-vis the state? The state's strategy in allowing them to exist is to provide an indirect means to maintain its leadership over the economy and society, in contrast to the more direct Maoist approach to state penetration into all aspects of economic and social life. The goal is not to relinquish the state's power but instead to "give up control to gain power."[35] Nevertheless, the associations are not simply loyal agents of the state. Business associations try to balance their mission of representing the state's interests with the desire of their members to have an organized voice to solve business-related problems and even to try to influence the local implementation of policy. The leaders of these associations, even though they are also government officials, often begin to identify with the interests of their members and use the associations as a vehicle to increase their own authority relative to other officials.

In addition, Chinese companies are banding together to form their own associations to lobby the government on technical standards, protection of property rights, and similar common interests.[36] Typically they do not raise broader public policy issues, but their activities may create public space for other groups. For example, homeowners, teachers, retirees, and other groups have their own organizations to promote their collective interests. They are not necessarily politically oriented; but just as all politics is local, local achievements can have broader implications. In particular, these new professional and civic organizations are not based exclusively on where people work or live, or on what community or clan they came from. Because they attract members from diverse backgrounds and experiences, and because individuals can belong to more than one group, they may create the types of social networks that create not only a more orderly society, but also one that seeks more from its government.

This growth of civic and professional organizations in China has created a great deal of excitement among outside observers. Many see these organizations as forming the foundation of a *civil society*, a key component of liberal democratic government.[37] The emergence and spread of such organizations in China may facilitate a transition from authoritarian rule to democracy. But democratization is not the only possible outcome. A key component of civil society is autonomy from the state, and that element is missing in China. In fact, members of these associations do not seek autonomy, because they recognize that, in China's political system, being autonomous means you are powerless and inconsequential. Instead, they want to be embedded in the state in order to increase their influence. The nongovernmental associations serve as links between the state and society: the state is unwilling to allow them autonomy, and the associations do not seek it. China may be undergoing a transition from a corporatism dominated by the state to a more diverse situation that gives greater leeway to the associations and the economic and social interests they represent. Can such a shift in the balance of power between the state and society occur without a more fundamental change in China's political system? That is the question that China's leaders, its citizens, and even foreign observers cannot definitively answer.

After the success of the "Orange Revolution" in Ukraine (see chapter 1) and democratic reforms in other former Soviet states like Georgia and Kyrgyzstan, the Chinese state began to tighten its policy toward a wide array of social organizations, especially those that received international support. The Chinese leadership was worried that an increasingly organized civil society would begin to make political demands. To preempt that potential threat, the government closed down several groups, denied applications to form new ones, and monitored and detained activists. With tens of thousands of NGOs and other social organizations now in China, the state cannot monitor and control all their activities; but it makes examples of some of them to signal the changing boundary between what is permissible and what is not.

But there have been no dramatic *political* changes comparable to the economic and social changes of the post-Mao period. The opportunities for political participation are still limited and the risks remain high. One reason is the legacy of the Cultural Revolution: every episode of mass political participation, whether the goals are greater government responsiveness or more citizen representation, has been categorized by party leaders as similar to the Red Guard activities during the Cultural Revolution and is therefore quickly repressed. This was the case during several episodes we shall consider later in this chapter: the 1978–79 Democracy Wall movement, the student demonstrations in the winter of 1986–87, and the crackdown against the democracy movement of 1989.[38] Unlike South Korea and Taiwan, where demands for political change were gradually accepted and the opportunities for participation within the system gradually enlarged, in China all demands from society have been met with a tightening of party controls and a retreat from political reform. Although there are supporters of political reform within the CCP, they have been on the defensive since 1989. Indeed, there is a fear (among party leaders and society as well) that the post-Mao reforms have created economic and social freedoms that will lead to political instability, and chaos is perhaps the greatest fear in China's traditional political culture.

Consequently, during the 1990s, China's intellectuals became divided into several schools of thought.[39] *Neo-conservatives* advocated a strong state to promote rapid economic growth and maintain political order. Although some in this camp were authoritarians at heart, others were liberals who felt that a period of state leadership was necessary to lay the groundwork for later democratization. *Postmodernists* were critical of the loss of traditional values, the rise of materialism, and the spread of Western influences created by the economic reforms favored by Deng. The *new left* was critical of the transition to a market economy and the inequalities it was creating, but unlike the traditional ideologues in the party it preferred social democratic policies and not the return of central planning and political controls over society. In contrast, the *liberal* viewpoint, which dominated intellectual circles from the May 4$^{th}$ Movement through the 1989 demonstrations, declined in popularity. Its support for modernity and Westernization was rejected by those who argued that the problems facing China were the result, not of an overbearing state, but instead of a state too weak to guide the economy, control local governments, or block foreign influences. The Tiananmen tragedy, the collapse of the Soviet Union, and the increasing influence of international capital in world affairs led many intellectuals to reassess their views toward the state, ironically leading them to dismiss past democratization efforts as hopelessly and dangerously romantic. This dramatic change in thinking gave rise to a popular nationalism that mirrored and in some ways surpassed the nationalistic tone of the official media.[40] A spate of best-selling books decried the evils of Westernization, modernity, and especially the United States. Although the policy of promoting economic growth and privatization remains in place, attention to its often unintended consequences has grown apace.

## POLITICAL PARTICIPATION IN CHINA

In the United States and most democracies, political participation is primarily voluntary and spontaneous. People may join interest groups, donate time or money to a cause they support, sign petitions on various policy issues, write letters to their elected representatives or a newspaper, or take a variety of other actions to make their views known to policy makers and other influential observers. In nondemocratic countries, taking part in these kinds of political participation is often risky or even illegal. Rather than allow spontaneous participation, authoritarian states often mobilize participation to support their policies and strictly limit society's opportunities to influence policy making.

During the Maoist era, most participation was mobilized by the state. China underwent periodic mass political campaigns to both educate society on current policy and promote proper implementation. Often a campaign occurred when policy changed suddenly, as when the Anti-Rightist Movement followed the Hundred Flowers Campaign or when the Cultural Revolution got under way. People were expected to study the new policies and the propaganda that accompanied them, learn the new slogans, internalize the new party line, and change their behavior accordingly. People were not allowed to be passive: it was not enough to be quiet or to avoid politics. The regime engaged in *mass mobilization*, requiring everyone to actively support the new policy in word and deed. However, people were *not* expected to question the new policy or its goals, to compare the results of the new policies with the past, or to criticize their leaders for changing policy. The purpose of the mobilization style of political participation was to have the people publicly affirm their support of the new policy, even if inwardly they did not.

In the post-Mao period, the campaign style of policy implementation has generally been abandoned and the state has tried to be less intrusive in most aspects of social life. There are exceptions, of course: the state resorted to these old tactics after the violent end of the 1989 demonstrations and again beginning in the summer of 1999 against the Falun Gong spiritual movement. The general theme of the reform era has been to have the state pull back from its direct involvement in most areas, including the economy, social life, and even politics. People are no longer required to voice their approval of all policies, to denounce the old policies and the leaders who promoted them, or to refer to the ideology as the measure of correct policies. Instead, they have been encouraged to experiment to find the set of policies best suited to promoting economic development and improved standards of living.

In addition, there are now more opportunities for people to spontaneously participate in political issues. Writing letters to national newspapers to report on local problems, such as corruption or the abuse of authority by local officials, is common. In the post-Mao period the state seems to have taken a greater interest in investigating these allegations than in the past. More recent forms of political participation include lodging complaints, relying on the courts, and voting for local leaders. Chinese citizens are now more able to complain about local conditions to higher levels of government. A village may send a team to the county government to report on excessive taxation or misuse of government funds. What is distinctive about this trend is that the people lodging complaints are becoming better versed in official policy and are using that knowledge to further their cause. For instance, they do not complain that taxes are simply too high: they complain that local officials are demanding taxes higher than what is allowed by the central government. In other words, they do not seek a change in policy, they seek to make local officials actually comply with the existing policies.[41] Once deviations from policies are brought to the attention of higher-level officials, they are very difficult to ignore.

Although the number of complaints and petitions has skyrocketed, the number of successfully resolved cases remains minuscule. The central government has also reportedly ordered local officials to clamp down on local citizens trying to make use of this system, especially those who appeal to provincial and central levels. The growing use of this system, combined with frustrations created when people cannot get the relief they are entitled to, presents a potential challenge to the state. As Samuel Huntington noted, when the level of participation overwhelms the available institutions, instability is likely to rise.[42] If the state cannot reduce the demands that are percolating up, or increase its responsiveness to those demands, the alternative is to have the demands raised outside official channels, as is seen in the growing number of public protests throughout the country.

China is trying to strengthen its legal system, in part to support the push for economic modernization (enforcement of contracts, protection of property including copyrights, etc.) and in part to create more predictability by clearly spelling out which types of conduct are appropriate and which are not. This strengthening of the legal system also gives people the power to defend their interests and protect themselves from capricious actions by their neighbors, other businesses, and even government officials. Private entrepreneurs have turned to the courts to force the government to honor its contracts or to compensate them for confiscating their property. Artists have been known to sue government-owned media for printing libelous accusations against them or for criticizing their works on political grounds. These types of suits are not always successful; China's courts are still not independent of the party–state nor are they neutral interpreters of the law. Almost a hundred thousand lawsuits are brought against local officials each year, but less than 25 percent of them are settled in favor of the plaintiffs. But even this low success rate is enough to encourage more and more to pursue this avenue. As businesspeople, artists, and other groups in society are becoming better educated about the state's own laws and regulations, they are increasingly using them to their advantage.[43]

China's villagers are now able to elect their own leaders. In the past, all local officials were appointed by higher levels of government, which made officials accountable to their superiors but not to the people they actually governed. This system meant, not surprisingly, that many local officials became petty tyrants in local society. Now, villagers can use the opportunity of village elections to replace unpopular or abusive officials.

Village elections have been a controversial experiment, with a range of supporters and opponents. Many of the leaders in Beijing who promoted village elections saw them as a chance to remedy the deteriorating relations between state and society at the local level. Ironically, most of the supporters of village elections belonged to the conservative wing of the CCP and had little interest in promoting democracy. Instead, they sought political stability and saw village elections as a way to address the shortcomings of local leadership.[44] Local officials, particularly in counties and townships with authority over the village leaders, were opposed to implementing elections because they feared that they would not be able to control leaders they did not appoint but who were instead chosen by the people. They worried that it would be even harder to implement unpopular policies, such as tax collection and family planning policies, which limit the number of children per family. (Urban couples are limited to one child. Couples in rural areas may have more than one child under several circumstances: for instance, if the first child is a girl or has severe handicaps, if one of the parents is an orphan or an only child, or if they belong to one of China's minorities.) Much to their surprise, villages that held successful elections where there was real competition between candidates, where the candidates were not simply chosen by higher-level officials, and where voting procedures were fair have done a much better job at policy implementation than elsewhere.[45] Villagers recognize that they cannot change the policies, but they are willing to support their fairer implementation. This development has encouraged other areas also to allow more competitive elections with less intrusion by higher officials. It is still common to hear of incidents in which higher authorities refuse to let a person be a candidate, or throw out the results of elections they do not like, or even refuse to hold elections in the first place. However, national law now requires periodic elections for village chief and village councils, and the Ministry of Civil Affairs is in charge of publicizing and monitoring compliance with the law.

China has been experimenting with local political reforms to make the state more responsive to public opinion, even if it is still not fully accountable. Some local officials now have to receive majority support in a public referendum on their tenure in office in order to be reappointed. China has actively embraced e-government, with many national, provincial, and local government offices having their own websites to disseminate information and receive opinions and complaints. In some public policy areas, China now requires a period of public comment before projects can be approved. Township governments are expected to post annual budget plans, showing both income and expenditures. These types of reforms are still experimental and not fully institutionalized, but they indicate that important political reforms, short of full democratization, may be under way.[46]

These conventional forms of participation are not always effective and are often risky. In a political system with only one political party and limited citizen's rights, the state does not have to be responsive to the wants and needs of society. Most party and government officials are not accountable to the people and are more used to protecting other officials against what are often seen as troublemakers and whistle-blowers. Those making complaints are often subjected to intimidation, arrest, the loss of their job, and occasionally beatings and even death. Nevertheless, some people are willing to appeal to higher and higher levels and even to travel to Beijing, if necessary, in order to seek justice. Politics can be a high-stakes game in China with tremendous costs and benefits for all involved.

Not all types of political participation are so conventional. Mass protests, including strikes, rallies, marches, traffic blocking, and seizure of buildings, increased from fewer than 9,000 in 1993 to more than 87,000 in 2005. Incidents of protest are usually provoked by the government's payments for grain with IOUs instead of cash, by its confiscation of farmland for other uses, by excessive taxation, or by corruption.[47] Even when policies are properly carried out, those unhappy with the consequences have been known to sprinkle broken glass in the officials' rice paddies (which are farmed in bare feet), set fire to the officials' houses, or physically assault them.

Labor unrest is also growing. In addition to strikes, more workers are taking their cases to the courts: lawsuits filed by workers to obtain unpaid wages or contest illegal labor practices multiplied from only 17,000 in 1992 to more than 260,000 in 2004. Local officials respond with a combination of carrots and sticks: they often grant the monetary demands of protesters, paying back wages, medical insurance, and pensions, for example, but they arrest the individuals seen as the leaders of the protest. They also arrest those attempting to form independent labor unions. Still, the number and size of labor protests continues to grow. In 2002, separate protests of over 20,000 workers occurred in two cities in the northeast, China's rustbelt.

Meanwhile, modern technology is providing new opportunities for people to express their views.[48] Internet chat rooms and radio call-in shows in China are full of criticisms of official corruption. Groups such as Falun Gong use the Internet and e-mail to communicate with their followers. The number of Internet users has grown from less than a million in the mid 1990s to 111 million in 2005. China is now second only to the United States in its number of Internet users. The Chinese government has repeatedly issued new regulations aimed at bringing electronic communications by individuals and private companies under tighter control, but the rapid growth and ingenuity of China's Internet users have allowed them to circumvent official firewalls almost as fast as they are put up. The Chinese government not only tries to police the Internet directly, it also enlists others in its efforts. Google willingly censors items on its Chinese search engine, blocking sensitive political issues like the 1989 protests, Falun Gong, and negative articles on Chinese leaders. Microsoft monitors blogs on its servers in China and removes items that may be offensive to the Chinese government. Yahoo has turned over e-mail records that have led to the arrest and imprisonment of several political activists. During the SARS (severe acute respiratory syndrome) crisis of 2003, instant text messaging allowed new, but often incorrect, information to spread rapidly, undermining the state's ability to control the story.

Just as the CCP uses a combination of rewards and punishments to handle protests, it uses a similar strategy to incorporate new economic and social elites into the political system, excluding those with more explicitly political goals. The "Three Represents" slogan, originally coined by Jiang Zemin and enshrined in the party constitution in 2002, provides the justification for admitting "advanced productive forces" (i.e., entrepreneurs, high-tech specialists, professionals, and other new urban elites) into the CCP. The CCP now claims to represent their interests as well as those of peasants, workers, and soldiers, the traditional social base of the party. It also welcomes these new social forces into the party. Entrepreneurs increasingly run in elections for village chiefs and for local people's congresses, and they are frequently appointed to higher-level people's congresses, government posts, and even party committees. Many in the CCP are critical of this trend, fearing that it betrays the party's traditions and undermines its unity. But the inclusion of new urban elites is a result of the CCP's commitment to reform, and the party leadership will undoubtedly reinforce that commitment. It remains to be seen whether the party manages to keep legitimate participation within the existing institutions, or whether the urban elites create pressures for broader democratization that might weaken the CCP's grip on power, thereby putting the CCP's adaptation policies at risk.

At the same time, the CCP still excludes those who pose a direct challenge to the status quo. Attempts to create an opposition party, the China Democracy Party, were blocked and the leaders of the effort sentenced to lengthy jail sentences. Those who seek true autonomy from the state, including labor unions, Christian churches, Falun Gong practitioners, and advocates of free speech and freedom of the press, are normally punished for their efforts. Separatist movements in Tibet and the western province of Xinjiang are harshly suppressed. The state monitors Internet chat rooms, electronic bulletin boards, e-mail, and (according to some) even instant messages to root out subversive content. It routinely limits access to the Internet and the electronic exchange of ideas to stymie dissent. Despite the populist image of party chief Hu Jintao and Prime Minister Wen Jiabao, these leaders reportedly ordered an end to media coverage of "public intellectuals" in order to better control reporting on current affairs.

These trends suggest a change in the CCP's treatment of political activity. Rather than periodic swings between liberalization and retrenchment, the CCP now has a more nuanced strategy of including supportive individuals in the political process but excluding the ideas and individuals it perceives to be threatening. The boundary between threatening and acceptable is not always clear, and those who choose to explore this border often suffer the consequences. Both inclusionary and exclusionary policies are promoted simultaneously, with frequent ebbs and flows in the extent to which each is emphasized.

While noting the changes in political participation that have occurred in the reform era, it is also important to note what has not changed. Although the party is willing to allow experimentation with economic policies, complaints about improper policy implementation, and village elections, it is not willing to allow direct challenges to its authority or demands for changes in the basic political system. During the reform era, three episodes of demands for political reform and even democracy occurred in China, always with the same result: the movements were suppressed, their leaders arrested, and their demands ignored.

### The Democracy Wall Movement (1978–79)

In the immediate aftermath of the Cultural Revolution, a group of intellectuals began putting up posters in an area of downtown Beijing that became known as "**Democracy Wall**."[49] Initially, the protesters were supportive of Deng's efforts to replace the remaining Maoists in the party and government. They wanted to hear official criticism of the Cultural Revolution, of Mao, and of those leaders pledged to remain loyal to his policies. The protesters also called for the rehabilitation of the Cultural Revolution's victims and for political reforms to loosen state controls over society. The movement led to the formation of politically oriented journals and inspired similar developments in other cities. Most of the writers of the posters and the new journals that arose at this time portrayed themselves as loyal citizens who were seeking to reform and improve the political system but not to challenge or replace it. But some advocated positions more radical than even Deng and his allies were willing to permit.

The best-known dissident to emerge in China at the time was *Wei Jingsheng*, who bemoaned the absence of democracy and rule of law in China.[50] He characterized Deng Xiaoping as just another authoritarian ruler who was not chosen by Chinese society and who would not be bound by the public's interest. As the demands of the Democracy Wall protesters moved in this direction, the state initiated a crackdown, arresting leading figures (including Wei) and sentencing some to long prison sentences. It also moved the authorized site of Democracy Wall from a downtown street to a remote park. In 1980, the party removed from the constitution the right to put up wall posters, eliminating one of the few avenues for public criticism of the government. China's leaders were still not willing to be accountable to public opinion.

### Student Demonstrations (1986–87)

During the early 1980s, while dramatic economic reforms were taking place, political reforms were more limited. The political system was not opened to new voices and groups; instead, political reform was primarily administrative and bureaucratic in nature. The number of government ministries, commissions, and offices was reduced (although the number of officials continued to grow), new criteria for appointing and promoting officials were put in place, and mandatory retirement rules were established for officials. Officials debated policy matters more extensively and drew upon feasibility studies and other technical considerations, rather than ideological rhetoric, in making their decisions. These measures had important implications for how well the party and government did their work, but they did not make the state more responsive to popular opinion. The state may have been more efficient, but it was not more democratic.

By the mid 1980s, many in China, especially in academic and intellectual circles, grew frustrated at the slow pace of political change. In December 1986, college students in Shanghai began public demonstrations about poor living conditions on their campuses; these demonstrations soon included calls for more extensive political reform.[51] Reports on these demonstrations spread to other campuses, and other areas of China reported similar outbreaks. Although the official media initially described the demonstrators as patriotic, the leadership soon changed its viewpoint and chose to crack down on the demonstrations without offering political concessions. Moreover, the General Secretary of the CCP, *Hu Yaobang,* was forced to resign his post and to accept responsibility for the outbreak and spread of demonstrations, which other leaders feared might lead to increased instability if not handled forcefully.

### The Tiananmen Crisis (Spring 1989)

Hu Yaobang's death in April 1989 sparked the largest popular demonstrations in post-1949 China. From the point of view of China's leaders, the **Tiananmen Square demonstrations** of 1989—ostensibly about issues such as inflation and corruption—were aimed at overthrowing the government and were seen as a serious threat to their hold on power. The students, workers, professionals, and others who joined in the growing demonstrations in the following weeks were motivated by a variety of concerns. Some were concerned that double-digit inflation was undermining their standard of living, wiping away the gains of a decade of reform. Others were alarmed at the rise of rampant corruption accompanying economic reforms. Both these issues in fact mirrored the government's own position. But others used the opportunity of these demonstrations to demand more fundamental changes in China's political system, calling for labor unions and student organizations free of government and party controls and even for the removal of Deng Xiaoping and Li Peng, the unpopular prime minister who was widely viewed as an opponent of reform. In the end, it was the form of these demands—popular demonstrations without government approval—more than their content that frightened China's leaders and led to the tragic outcome of June 4, when martial law was imposed with deadly force and thousands of people were killed or wounded.[52]

This outcome was not predetermined. It was the result of a long and divisive debate among China's top leaders about how to respond to the demonstrations. In fact, it was the perceived divisions among the elite that fueled the demonstrations, creating expectations that the state might actually give in. The longer the state delayed its response, the more these expectations grew. Some of China's leaders were sympathetic to the demands of the protesters and sought a compromise to bring the demonstrations to a close. Others saw the dramatic surge of protest as a repetition of Red Guard activism, from which they had suffered earlier in their careers, and wanted to nip the movement in the bud. Others were embarrassed by the swelling numbers of protesters and the diversity of people who joined in, including government officials and journalists connected with the official media, people who were responsible for conveying the official line to the public.

The open display of discontent indicated a severe loss of legitimacy for the leadership in Beijing, which appeared incapable of controlling events in Tiananmen Square, the political and symbolic center of China. For more than a month, demonstrators occupied the square and began a hunger strike to dramatize their cause. The willingness of these young idealists to march in defiance of the state's orders, to remain in the square after the declaration of martial law, and to persist in their hunger strike created sympathy and support among other Chinese citizens and foreign audiences, who watched the drama unfold live on their television sets at home. Foreign television crews had arrived in China to cover the visit of Soviet leader Mikhail Gorbachev, but his visit was quickly overshadowed by the growing popular protests. The television crews stayed in China even after Gorbachev departed, providing almost continuous coverage of the protests.

The failure of these demonstrations in Beijing and elsewhere in China to bring about lasting change was due to several factors. First and most important, the party refuses to recognize the legitimacy of any group of which it does not approve and refuses to accept demands for change from outside the limited channels of communications. The political system was created to change society, not to be changed by it, and the party defends its monopoly on political organization quite vigorously. One consequence of this monopoly is that there are no organizations in China with which the state can negotiate a peaceful settlement. There is no equivalent of Poland's Solidarity or the Catholic Church, which in various ways contributed to political change in Central and Eastern Europe, Latin America, and elsewhere. Also, the students, workers, and others who participated in the demonstrations had no durable organization to plan their protests and shape their demands. Organizations formed spontaneously during the demonstrations, but they had little interaction with each other or with the state. The protesters themselves were divided over their agenda: some were seeking the reform of existing policies and institutions, others had more revolutionary ambitions, feeling the system was incapable of reform. Ultimately, it was the CCP's past success in preventing autonomous organizations and its refusal to negotiate even with those making demands that echoed the state's own policies that led to the tragic outcome of the demonstrations.

The Tiananmen legacy was devastating and long-lasting. Hardliners in the party ousted many of the most prominent reformers, including *Zhao Ziyang*, who had been prime minister and later head of the party and who was widely seen as Deng's heir apparent. Diplomatic and foreign economic relations were frozen and are still haunted by the image of tanks and soldiers firing on civilians. For those who participated in the protests, the crackdown led to months and years of anxiety. Some fled the country rather than risk arrest and jail. Some, like student leader *Wang Dan*, were jailed for years. Some had career prospects dimmed because of their involvement. Nearly all were disillusioned by the outcome, convinced more than ever that the party was beyond hope. If it refused to accommodate even the moderate demands of the protesters, it would never sponsor more far-reaching political reforms. Its willingness to use overwhelming force against unarmed demonstrators suggested that it was foolish to try to bring about change through popular appeals. This was a depressing revelation, but one deeply learned. Today, it is difficult to find people willing to talk about the prospects for political reform. To people now focused on business opportunities made possible by the ongoing economic reforms, engaging in idealistic talk about democracy is a waste of time that is better spent on making money. This is, of course, exactly how the CCP wants it. The new social contract in China is built on this trade-off: people who are prospering are unlikely to be rebels.

## CHINA'S LEADERS TODAY

### PROFILE: Hu Jintao

*Hu Jintao* is the leader of the fourth generation of leaders in the PRC. As of 2004, he was concurrently General Secretary of the CCP, president of China, and chairman of the Central Military Commission. On paper, these positions make him the most powerful leader in the country. But in the Chinese political system, political power is derived from informal sources—personal experience, political connections, and family ties—as much as from formal titles. Whether Hu will accumulate the personal authority that should go with his titles will be a test of his leadership in the years to come.

Hu was born into a family of Shanghai merchants in 1943. He graduated from the prestigious Qinghua University with a degree in hydropower engineering in 1964, the year he joined the CCP. During the Cultural Revolution, he volunteered to work in Gansu, one of China's poorest provinces. He remained in Gansu until 1982 in a variety of responsibilities, including party affairs within the department of water resources and electric power, deputy head of the provincial construction commission, and secretary of the provincial branch of the Communist Youth League.

Like many others in the fourth generation, Hu is a technocrat—a bureaucrat with education and work experience in science, engineering, and management. Also, like others in the fourth generation but in contrast to older and younger leaders, Hu has no experience abroad. He did not study or work outside China and apparently he does not know any foreign languages (although he is said to be intensively studying English).

Hu was a beneficiary of Deng Xiaoping's policy of promoting "more revolutionary, younger, better educated, and more professionally competent" officials at the expense of more senior but less skilled leaders. While still in Gansu, he was promoted over the heads of more senior people, and then in 1982 Hu was promoted to the national headquarters of the Communist Youth League in Beijing. He accepted a transfer to Guizhou, China's poorest province, in 1985, and then to Tibet in 1988, serving as party secretary (the top position) in both places. His willingness to accept these hardship posts demonstrated his loyalty to the party, but his record was not distinguished. He seems to have made no notable or long-lasting improvements in these impoverished areas. In fact, for much of his tenure as party secretary of Tibet, he lived in Beijing, reportedly unable to tolerate the high altitude of Lhasa. His most memorable decision in Tibet came just a few months into his tenure there, when he declared martial law to end several months of demonstrations and riots. This decision served as a precedent of sorts for the party leadership's imposition of martial law to end the demonstrations in Tiananmen Square in June 1989.

In 1992, Hu was selected by Deng Xiaoping to represent the fourth generation on the Standing Committee of the Politburo. At the time, Hu was only forty-nine years old. From that time on, he was the heir apparent to Jiang Zemin. In 1997, he was named vice president of China, and the next year he became vice chairman of the Central Military Commission, making him second only to Jiang at the top of the party, the state, and the military. During the next ten years, while waiting for his final promotion to the top of the party, Hu chose to be a loyal supporter of Jiang in order to ensure his continued status as Jiang's designated successor. Unlike Hu Yaobang and Zhao Ziyang, who lost the support of Deng Xiaoping by deviating too far from his charted path, Hu Jintao gave Deng and Jiang Zemin no reason to second-guess his selection as the future leader. He did not build an extensive network of supporters throughout the bureaucracy, nor did he make bold or original policy statements. When he became General Secretary of the CCP in 2002, he did not have an extensive power base, but he did enjoy a favorable reputation for being modest (unlike Jiang), patient (unlike former prime minister *Zhu Rongji,* who was famous for firing local officials on the spot during inspection tours), a good listener,

**Jiang Zemin and Hu Jintao**

and attentive to details. These are all positive assets that may make him a successful leader.

Despite his long experience in leadership posts, including five years as vice president before becoming China's president in 2003, Hu has little experience in foreign affairs. One of the few times he made definitive statements on foreign policy issues came in a televised speech following the accidental bombing of the Chinese embassy in Belgrade by the United States in 1999 during the Kosovo war. Hu deplored the attack, but also called on his Chinese audience to remain calm. Jiang Zemin reportedly chose Hu to deliver this speech because he did not want to be criticized himself for appeasing the United States at a time when nationalist sentiments were rising. On a visit to the U.S. in 2001, Hu's prodigious memory and people skills were on display. Unlike other Chinese leaders, Hu did not rely on written talking points during meetings with American leaders or when fielding questions during public events. But when U.S. officials and reporters compared his comments to the official policy, they found that his comments held close to the party line, even though they had seemed extemporaneous.

The only exception was on the issue of Taiwan, when Hu read from a prepared script, making the point that he was speaking not just for himself but on behalf of the Chinese leadership.

Hu's rise to the top of the Chinese political system highlights some of the regime's key features. Although he has obvious credentials and an impressive résumé, Hu did not distinguish himself as an innovative or successful leader. Instead, the key to his success seems to be the patronage of people in the second and third generations of leaders. Before Hu became General Secretary and president, speculation grew about his potential to sponsor political reforms, but there was almost nothing in his public comments to indicate what his personal beliefs were. He has shown himself to be a loyal subordinate and has avoided making mistakes that might derail his career. As China's top leader, however, he must show that he is capable of charting an independent course. In the months after becoming party leader, Hu made a subtle shift in the "Three Represents" slogan, downplaying the importance of the urban classes (which Jiang championed) and concentrating on the interests of workers and farmers, the party's traditional base of support. When the SARS epidemic broke out, he used the opportunity to fire the minister of health (despite his being Jiang's personal doctor) for covering up the disease. He also ordered a shake-up of top navy officials after a submarine sank, killing all on board. These steps may signal a new and welcome shift toward greater transparency and accountability.

In contrast to Jiang Zemin's elitist approach, Hu Jintao has tried to chart a more populist course. Several motives may underlie his populist orientation. First, Hu spent part of his career in some of China's poorest provinces. He did not make his career in cosmopolitan Shanghai, as did many in Jiang's camp, and he therefore has a better understanding of why some areas continue to lag behind. Second, as part of his effort to consolidate his authority, he needs to distinguish himself from Jiang. In the grand tradition of Chinese politics, Hu has not abandoned the "Three Represents" slogan but has simply redefined it. And third, Hu realizes that Jiang's elitist strategy led to growing inequalities and disenchantment, potentially threatening popular support for the CCP's policy priorities. A slight reorientation of the reform strategy could restore some of the balance lost during the years of rapid growth. These three reasons are quite complementary, and they show why Hu's populist orientation has both political and practical benefits.

But Hu has disappointed those who hoped he would introduce ambitious *political* reform. Instead, he has emphasized enhancing the "governing capacity" of the CCP, requiring an old-fashioned political study campaign for many party and government officials. As we have seen, under Hu's leadership the Chinese state has tightened its control over the media, limited the flow of information and ideas on the Internet, and limited discussion of policy issues by intellectuals. It has also increased its pressure on NGOs, fearful that an emerging civil society may lead to demands for political change. In short, Hu has continued the reform strategy first promoted by Deng Xiaoping: economic liberalization under the political monopoly of the CCP.

This cautious approach to political reform is intended to enhance the survival of both the CCP as China's ruling party and Hu's post as head of the CCP. If he is able to maneuver Jiang's protégés out of their influential posts, and if he does not make major policy mistakes, Hu Jintao is likely to remain China's top leader until 2012, when the fifth generation will take over.

## Other Leaders

Several other leaders of the People's Republic of China today should be singled out for their prominence. *Wen Jiabao*, born in 1943, is China's prime minister (head of government) and a member of the Standing Committee of the Communist Party's Politburo. Like Hu Jintao and others in the fourth generation of leadership, Wen is a technocrat (he was educated as a geologist) who benefited from Deng Xiaoping's policy of promoting young and technically skilled officials. Like party chief Hu Jintao, Wen served in Gansu, one of China's poorest provinces, and he has a deeper appreciation for rural China than do most other leaders.

*Wu Bangguo*, born in 1942, is currently head of the National People's Congress (China's legislature) and also a member of the party's powerful Standing Committee of the Politburo. A graduate of Qinghua University (often referred to as China's MIT), he worked for more than ten years in an electronics tube factory in Shanghai. Because his political career started in that city, he is seen as a member of the "Shanghai gang" associated with former party chief Jiang Zemin. As China's vice premier, Wu has responsibility for the economic and industrial ministries, national defense, state enterprise reform, and other issues. He is a popular leader but is believed to be less enthusiastic about reform than Hu Jintao or Wen Jiabao.

*Zeng Qinghong*, born in 1939, is a member of the Standing Committee of the party's Politburo and a member of the party's Secretariat. He is also China's vice president. Although Zeng has a reputation for political maneuvering, his close ties to former leader Jiang Zemin make him a potential rival to Hu Jintao. If Hu stumbles as party leader, Zeng could step in as his successor.

*Wu Yi*, born in 1938, is the only woman on the Politburo. She also serves as China's vice prime minister. As minister of foreign trade and economic cooperation, Wu was influential in China's negotiations to join the World Trade Organization. Because of her excellent reputation at home and abroad, she was made acting minister of health during the SARS outbreak of 2003, a post she held until 2005. She remains an influential voice on foreign relations and trade issues.

Finally, there is a group of so-called *elders* who have formally retired from their posts but remain influential behind the scenes. Today this group includes people like former party chief Jiang Zemin and former prime ministers Zhu Rongji and Li Peng. Whether they truly retire from politics altogether or try to influence policy through their protégés will partly determine the shape of Chinese politics in the years to come.

## HYPOTHESIS-TESTING EXERCISE: Prospects for China's Democratization

### Hypothesis, Variables, and Expectations

What are the chances that China will undergo democratization in the future? Chapter 9 outlined a series of ten *independent variables* that influence the establishment and survival of democracies and that provide us with a framework for answering this question. *China's democratization,* therefore, is our *dependent variable*. The hypothesized conditions for democracy create a series of *expectations* about their probable effects. As chapter 9 indicates, we can fairly confidently expect most of these variables to promote democracy, while a few others are likely to produce mixed results, depending on local circumstances. Analyzing China's situation against these ten variables provides a useful hypothesis-testing exercise for theories of democratization.[53]

### Evidence

China lacks *elites committed to democracy* in numbers large enough to influence decision making. China certainly does have leaders who favor political reform, even including democratization, but they are wary of being too open in their beliefs for fear of losing their jobs. Ironically, the leaders who were instrumental in promoting village elections were not supporters of democratization: instead, they were concerned with maintaining political order over the restive countryside. Supporters of reform had a potential window of opportunity in 1989, but were outmaneuvered by hardliners.

China has strong *state institutions* that exercise sovereignty over Chinese territories (with the important exception of Taiwan, as noted earlier). But these institutions are, in general, not compatible with democracy. The rule of law, as described earlier, is not protected; the courts and even the constitution are political tools of the state and are strongly influenced by the changing preferences of the leaders rather than by constraints on the state's own actions. The leaders themselves are not accountable to the people, except at the grassroots level. Obviously, the state and those who lead it are the main obstacles to democratization in China.

Insufficient *national unity* is also a problem. Roughly 92 percent of China's population belongs to the Han nationality. However, minority groups, though few in number, occupy strategically important areas of the country. The largest such areas are Tibet, the Buddhist nation that was forcibly annexed in 1949–51; the western province of Xinjiang, which is predominantly Muslim; and inner Mongolia. The periodic activity of independence movements in these areas has provided the Chinese government with a rationale to keep them under control. It denies them autonomy and cracks down on political restiveness, at times quite severely. Thus China's ethnic and religious heterogeneity works against democratization.

Economic reform, however, is bringing about changes that may increase pressures from below for democratic change. For more than two decades, China has experienced rapid growth in its *national wealth*. Its GDP exceeded $2 trillion by 2005, though its per capita income remained low (just over $1,500). This new wealth has been accompanied by other changes that are more intriguing. The growth of *private enterprise* in China has created less state control over the economy and society, and most people are less dependent on the state than at any time since before the communist revolution. The number of private enterprises continues to grow, and most new jobs and economic growth are created by the private sector. However, private entrepreneurs themselves do not seem interested in promoting democracy, at least not now. As in some other authoritarian countries, especially in East Asia, private entrepreneurs in China are partners of the state and benefit from many of its policies. They are indifferent, or even opposed, to calls for political change, a reality strikingly inconsistent with our supposition that private enterprise generally fosters democracy.[54]

But the growth of China's private sector may have indirect effects on potential democratization. It may, for example, give rise to a *middle class* and a *civil society* that will be more supportive of democracy. Here, too, the evidence thus far is limited. China's growing middle class is closely tied to the state and remains generally passive in its political behavior, another reality at variance with our expectations. Its civil society is still undeveloped, largely because the state makes it difficult to organize groups independent of its control. The state has pursued an authoritarian neo-corporatist strategy of setting up business and trade groups to link economic and political elites. Some have hoped that these business associations will develop their own identity and stake out a more independent position and influence policy, but so far their efforts have been focused on narrow business and commercial interests, not on more fundamental political issues. Meanwhile, there are no independent trade unions that might represent the labor force in tripartite neo-corporatist negotiations.

How China's large numbers of economically *disadvantaged* workers and peasants will affect the prospects for democracy is an intriguing question. It seems clear that no mass movement from below is likely to remove the communist authorities at the top. It is nonetheless possible that people favorable to democratic change in the business elite or the middle class may find support from those who have been left out of the private sector's phenomenal growth, or who have been harmed by such things as inflation or the exploitation of low-wage labor.

Attitudinal issues are also important. Many people—including Chinese intellectuals—have argued that Chinese *political culture*, with its emphasis on hierarchy and order and its lack of emphasis on individual rights and interests, is not compatible with democracy. According to this perspective, only after an extensive period of economic growth, rising levels of *education, increased freedom of information*, and greater interaction with the outside world, will China's political culture be suitable for democracy. Literacy levels have been rising, allowing people to absorb more information, and the state is no longer able to control the flow of information as thoroughly as in the past (especially in an age of Internet access and fax machines). Ironically, not only do the new communications technologies allow for more diverse sources of information, but the commercialization of information also allows people to avoid politics more than ever, diverting their attention to other areas of interest.

Not all aspects of this argument stand up to scrutiny, however. The success of village-level elections suggests that people can participate in government even before a democratic culture is created. The gradual democratization of Taiwan—where traditional Chinese values were even more important than on the mainland—shows that democratization creates democratic values.[55] So even though democratic values may be necessary for democracy to survive, they may not be necessary to get the process started.

The *international environment* is an ambiguous factor. Clearly, many countries, including the United States, would like to encourage China's democratization. But this very willingness to promote political change makes the international environment seem threatening to China's leaders. They recognize that foreign governments would prefer that China not remain communist, a direct threat to their hold on power. They see the foreign promotion of "peaceful evolution" toward liberal democracy and a market-based economy as an attempt to undermine their political system.

These attitudes cannot help but create difficult dilemmas for the world's democracies in their policies toward China. Those who wish to promote democracy from outside China have few tools at their disposal. Financial and logistical support for nongovernmental organizations in China often proves counterproductive: it only raises the government's suspicions. Although the United States and other countries often criticize China's human rights record, that issue generally ranks below trade and security in the U.S.–China relationship. (In 2005, U.S. exports to China totaled \$41.8 billion, up from only \$16.3 billion in 2000 and \$11.8 billion in 1995. American imports from China totaled \$243.5 billion in 2005, compared with \$100 billion only five years earlier and \$45.6 billion in 1995.[56]) Moreover, China frequently suspends or cancels dialogues on human rights with the United States and the United Nations when it feels the criticisms are too sharp. Some have hoped that increased foreign trade would help promote political change in China, but American businesses have successfully resisted efforts to attach political conditions to U.S.–China trade. Ironically, international efforts to promote democratization are often criticized by political activists in China. Michael Anti (the pen name of Zhao Jing, a prominent Chinese blogger whose blog was removed from Microsoft's server at the request of the Chinese government) did not welcome congressional hearings on the business practices of Google, Yahoo, Microsoft, and Cisco in China. "I don't feel that the freedom of speech of the Chinese people can be protected by the U.S. Congress," he wrote. Even the best of intentions can backfire.

International support for democratization in China is motivated not only by concerns over the human rights of China's vast population. Many advocates of democratization also believe that a democratic China will be a peaceful China. The communist government's current efforts to strengthen its nuclear arsenal and its occasionally bellicose statements regarding Taiwan provide continuing cause for concern about its military intentions in the Pacific region. In addition, the large imbalance in U.S.-PRC trade in China's favor ($201.7 billion in 2005), and the prospect that China's low-wage economy may attract American firms to relocate there, thus reducing job opportunities in the United States, are concerns that trouble many Americans, regardless of party affiliation.

For their part, the PRC's leaders are suspicious of foreign motives and critical of efforts to meddle in their internal affairs. As we've seen, mistrust of foreigners has deep historical roots in China, and any attempt by outside powers to manipulate the Chinese people or its government invariably strikes a raw nerve, evoking bitter memories of past exploitation. China's pride was fully evident during the celebrations in July 1997 that greeted its assumption of sovereignty over Hong Kong, which reverted to the People's Republic upon the expiration of Britain's ninety-nine-year "lease."[57] Chinese sensitivities were also on view during the Kosovo conflict in 1999 when U.S. warplanes hit the People's Republic's embassy during a bombing run over Belgrade. Washington quickly apologized for the incident, insisting it was an accident. In Beijing, thousands of angry protesters surrounded the U.S. embassy for weeks, chanting anti-NATO slogans; relations between the two governments remained chilly for months afterward. In April 2001, a U.S. EP-3 surveillance plane collided with a Chinese fighter jet off the coast of China, resulting in the death of the Chinese pilot and the detention of the American crew for several days. Popular resentment toward the United States arose again, but did not escalate into the kinds of public demonstrations and attacks on American institutions and symbols (like McDonalds and KFC) that occurred in 1999.

As a general rule, the communist authorities have tried as much as possible to suppress foreign influences. Thus far, efforts to promote democratization from the outside have in fact had the opposite of their intended effect.

### Conclusions

On the whole, some of the conditions for democracy are weak in China, while others are getting stronger. Perhaps the most striking phenomenon is the failure thus far of economic growth and the emergence of a large private sector to stimulate more intense pressures for democratization, a development largely inconsistent with our expectations. Nevertheless, as the spontaneous student demonstrations of 1989's Democracy Spring showed, events can take a sudden turn. Hopes for democracy may still lie just beneath the currently placid surface of Chinese society. The events of 1989 also showed, however, that if democracy is to take hold, it must have the support of key elites, both in the government and in society, who are committed to a democratic transition. So far, China lacks sufficient numbers of those kinds of elites.[58]

## CONCLUSION

As China enters the twenty-first century, many of the most important issues it faced at the beginning of the twentieth century are still unresolved. Is the West the cause of China's problems or part of their solution? Which Chinese traditions and values are appropriate for the modern world? Is democracy suitable to China, given its traditions, distinctive characteristics, and current level of economic and social development? These questions are fundamental ones, and no definitive answer may be possible any time soon. Nor are these questions unique to China: many developing countries face the same dilemmas. Given China's size and potential for future development, however, how China answers these questions is likely to affect not only its future, but the future of its neighbors and perhaps even the international community of nations as a whole. For that reason, China's future is worth watching.

How China develops will also have important implications for the study of comparative politics as well. As the hypothesis-testing exercise on democratization showed, China will be an important test case for many theories in comparative politics. At first glance, China often seems exotic, difficult to understand, an exception to many theories developed on the basis of the experience of Western countries. Indeed, China prefers to portray itself as exceptional and argues that conventional theories cannot capture the country's complexities. But it is only by comparing and contrasting contemporary China with its own past and with other countries that we can gain a clearer understanding of what is truly distinctive and what fits more general patterns of behavior. All countries are unique to some extent, and China no more so than many others. Its ultimate fate will surely tell us a great deal about democracy's potential as a universally applicable system of government and about the capacity of societies to change their political order. For centuries, China has captured the imagination of scholars and policy makers, and it still does today.

## KEY TERMS AND NAMES (In bold and underlined in the text)

Chinese Communist Party (CCP)
Confucius
Sun Yat-sen
Chiang Kai-shek
Chinese Nationalist Party (Kuomintang, KMT)
Mao Zedong
Politburo
General Secretary
Hu Jintao
Prime minister (premier)
Wen Jiabao
National People's Congress
Hundred Flowers Movement
Great Leap Forward
Great Proletarian Cultural Revolution
Deng Xiaoping
Jiang Zemin
Democracy Wall
Tiananmen Square demonstrations

## NOTES

1. Edward A. McCord, *The Power of the Gun: The Emergence of Modern Chinese Warlordism* (Berkeley: University of California Press, 1993).
2. Chow Tse-tsung, *The May 4th Movement* (Cambridge, Mass.: Harvard University Press, 1960).
3. Jonathan Spence, *Mao Zedong* (New York: Viking, 1999); Philip Short, *Mao: A Life* (New York: Holt, 1999); Jung Chang and Jon Halliday, *Mao: The Unknown Story* (New York: Knopf, 2005).
4. Edgar Snow, *Red Star over China* (New York: Grove Press, 1968); Harrison E. Salisbury, *The Long March: The Untold Story* (New York: Harper and Row, 1985).
5. Kevin J. O'Brien, *Reform Without Liberalization: China's National People's Congress and the Politics of Institutional Change* (New York: Cambridge University Press, 1990); Murray Scot Tanner, *The Politics of Lawmaking in Post-Mao China: Institutions, Processes, and Democratic Prospects* (New York: Oxford University Press, 1999); and Randall Peerenboom, *China's Long March Toward Rule of Law* (New York: Cambridge University Press, 2002).
6. *Selected Works of Mao Tse-tung*, vol. 1 (Beijing: Foreign Languages Press, 1965), 28.
7. Frederick C. Teiwes, "Establishment and Consolidation of the New Regime," in *The Politics of China*, 2nd ed., ed. Roderick MacFarquhar (Cambridge: Cambridge University Press, 1997), 5–86.
8. Harry Harding, *Organizing China: The Problem of Bureaucracy, 1949–1976* (Stanford, Calif.: Stanford University Press, 1980).
9. Richard Lowenthal, "Development Versus Utopia in Communist Policy," in *Change in Communist Systems, ed. Chalmers Johnson* (Stanford, Calif.: Stanford University Press, 1970).
10. Roderick MacFarquhar, *Origins of the Cultural Revolution*, vol. 1, *Contradictions Among the People 1956–1957* (New York: Columbia University Press, 1974).
11. Deng Xiaoping was in charge of running the Anti-Rightist campaign. As far back as 1957, Deng was associated with strictly enforcing the limits on free speech and dissent. Despite his emphasis on science and technology in later years and his support for rehabilitating many of the victims of Mao's campaigns (including the Anti-Rightist campaign), he was also opposed to letting the experts turn their expertise into political influence.

12. Roderick MacFarquhar, *Origins of the Cultural Revolution*, vol. 2, *The Great Leap Forward, 1958–62* (New York: Columbia University Press, 1983); David M. Bachman, *Bureaucracy, Economy, and Leadership in China: The Institutional Origins of the Great Leap Forward* (New York: Cambridge University Press, 1991).
13. Kenneth Lieberthal, "The Great Leap Forward and the Split in the Yanan Leadership," in MacFarquhar, *Politics of China*, 87–147.
14. Harry Harding, "The Chinese State in Crisis," in MacFarquhar, *Politics of China*, 148–247.
15. Richard Baum, *Burying Mao: Chinese Politics in the Age of Deng Xiaoping* (Princeton: Princeton University Press, 1994).
16. Kenneth Lieberthal and Michel Oksenberg, *Policy Making in China: Leaders, Structures, and Processes* (Princeton: Princeton University Press, 1988).
17. Melanie Manion, *Retirement of Revolutionaries in China: Public Policies, Social Norms, Private Interests* (Princeton: Princeton University Press, 1993).
18. Hong Yung Lee, *From Revolutionary Cadres to Party Technocrats in Socialist China* (Berkeley: University of California Press, 1991).
19. Timothy Brook and B. Michael Frolic, eds., *Civil Society in China* (Armonk, N.Y.: M. E. Sharpe, 1997).
20. Barry Naughton, "The Third Front: Defence Industrialization in the Chinese Interior," *China Quarterly*, no. 115 (September 1988): 351–86.
21. Martin King Whyte, "State and Society Under Mao," in *Perspectives on Modern China: Four Anniversaries*, ed. Kenneth Lieberthal et al. (Armonk, N.Y.: M. E. Sharpe, 1991), 255–74.
22. Joseph Fewsmith, *Dilemmas of Reform in China* (Armonk, N.Y.: M. E. Sharpe, 1994).
23. A recent example of the "China threat" perspective is Ross Terrill, *The New Chinese Empire: And What It Means for the United States* (New York: Basic Books, 2004); the alternative viewpoint is presented in Andrew J. Nathan and Robert S. Ross, *The Great Wall and the Empty Fortress: China's Search for Security* (New York: W. W. Norton, 1997). A balanced analysis and forecast can be found in David Shambaugh, ed., *Power Shift: China and Asia's New Dynamics* (Berkeley: University of California Press, 2006). An interesting contribution to this debate comes from two collections of essays by young Chinese scholars now teaching in American universities: Yong Deng and Fei-ling Wang, eds., *In the Eyes of the Dragon: China Views the World* (Lanham, MD: Rowman & Littlefield, 1999); and Deng and Wang, eds., *China Rising: Power and Motivation in Chinese Foreign Policy* (Lanham, MD: Rowman & Littlefield, 2004).
24. Jean C. Oi, *Rural China Takes Off: Institutional Foundations of Economic Reform* (Berkeley: University of California Press, 1999).
25. Barry Naughton, *Growing Out of the Plan: Chinese Economic Reform*, 1978–1993 (New York: Cambridge University Press, 1996).
26. Yasheng Huang, *Selling China: Foreign Direct Investment During the Reform Era* (New York: Cambridge University Press, 2005); Thomas G. Moore, *China in the World Market: Chinese Industry and International Sources of Reform in the Post-Mao Era* (New York: Cambridge University Press, 2002).
27. Dorothy J. Solinger, *Contesting Citizenship in Urban China: Peasant Migrants, the State, and the Logic of the Market* (Berkeley: University of California Press, 1999); Rachel Murphy, *How Migrant Labor Is Changing Rural China* (New York: Cambridge University Press, 2002).
28. Yan Sun, *Corruption and Market in Contemporary China* (Ithaca, N.Y.: Cornell University Press, 2004); Melanie Manion, *Corruption by Design: Building Clean Government in Mainland China and Hong Kong* (Cambridge, Mass.: Harvard University Press, 2005).
29. Bruce J. Dickson, *Red Capitalists in China: The Party, Private Entrepreneurs, and the Prospects for Political Change* (New York: Cambridge University Press, 2003).
30. An excellent study of China's environmental problems and fledgling environmental movement is Elizabeth Economy, *The River Runs Black: The Environmental Challenge to China's Future* (Ithaca, N.Y.: Cornell University Press, 2004).
31. Ching Kwan Lee, *Gender and the South China Miracle: Two Worlds of Factory Women* (Berkeley: University of California Press, 1998).
32. Kenneth Lieberthal and David Lampton, eds., *Bureaucracy, Politics, and Decision Making in Post-Mao China* (Berkeley: University of California Press, 1992); Susan Shirk, *The Political*

*Logic of Economic Reform in China* (Berkeley: University of California Press, 1993).

**33.** Andrew Walder, *Communist Neo-Traditionalism: Work and Authority in Chinese Industry* (Berkeley: University of California Press, 1986).

**34.** Gordon White, Jude Howell, and Shang Xiaoyuan, *In Search of Civil Society: Market Reform and Social Change in Contemporary China* (Oxford: Oxford University Press, 1996).

**35.** This is not a new strategy: it was used in the early twentieth century to give chambers of commerce some autonomy but also to have them serve state goals. See David Strand, *Rickshaw Beijing: City People and Politics in the 1920s* (Berkeley: University of California Press, 1989).

**36.** Scott Kennedy, *The Business of Lobbying in China* (Cambridge, Mass.: Harvard University Press, 2005).

**37.** Baogang He, *The Democratic Implications of Civil Society in China* (New York: St. Martin's Press, 1997); Yongnian Zheng, *Will China Become Democratic? Elite, Class, and Regime Transition* (Singapore: Eastern Universities Press, 2004).

**38.** Bruce J. Dickson, *Democratization in China and Taiwan: The Adaptability of Leninist Parties* (London and New York: Oxford University Press, 1997).

**39.** Joseph Fewsmith, *China Since Tiananmen: The Politics of Transition* (New York: Cambridge University Press, 2001).

**40.** Peter Gries, *China's New Nationalism: Pride, Politics, and Diplomacy* (Berkeley: University of California Press, 2004).

**41.** Kevin J. O'Brien and Lianjiang Li, *Rightful Resistance in Rural China* (New York: Cambridge University Press, 2005); Merle Goldman, *From Comrade to Citizen: The Struggle for Political Rights in China* (Cambridge, Mass.: Harvard University Press, 2005).

**42.** Samuel Huntington, *Political Order in Changing Societies* (New Haven: Yale University Press, 1968). For a summary, see chapter 15.

**43.** Neil J. Diamant, Stanley B. Lubman, and Kevin J. O'Brien, eds., *Engaging the Law in China: State, Society, and Possibilities for Justice* (Stanford: Stanford University Press, 2005).

**44.** Daniel Keliher, "The Chinese Debate over Village Self-Government," *China Journal* 37 (January 1997): 63–86; Tianjian Shi, "Village Committee Elections in China: Institutional Tactics for Democracy," *World Politics* 51, no. 3 (April 1999): 385–412; Kevin J. O'Brien and Lianjiang Li, "Accommodating 'Democracy' in a One-Party State: Introducing Village Elections in China," *China Quarterly*, no. 162 (June 2000): 465–89.

**45.** Kevin J. O'Brien, "Implementing Political Reform in China's Villages," *Australian Journal of Chinese Affairs* 32 (July 1994): 33–59.

**46.** This is a hotly debated issue among China specialists. For an optimistic view that China is undertaking important institutional reforms, see Dali L. Yang, *Remaking the Chinese Leviathan: Market Transition and the Politics of Governance in China* (Stanford: Stanford University Press, 2004); for an argument that China's leaders are unwilling to engage in meaningful reform, see Minxin Pei, *China's Trapped Transition: The Limits of Developmental Autocracy* (Cambridge, Mass.: Harvard University Press, 2006).

**47.** Thomas P. Bernstein and Xiaobo Lu, *Taxation Without Representation in Rural China* (New York: Cambridge University Press, 2003); Elizabeth J. Perry and Mark Selden, eds., *Chinese Society: Change, Conflict, and Resistance*, 2nd ed. (London: Routledge, 2003); Peter Hays Gries and Stanley Rosen, eds., *State and Society in 21st Century China: Crisis, Contention, and Legitimation* (London: Routledge/Courzon, 2004).

**48.** Michael S. Chase and James C. Mulvenon, *You've Got Dissent! Chinese Dissident Use of the Internet and Beijing's Counter-Strategies* (Santa Monica, Calif.: RAND, 2002); Yongming Zhou, *Historicizing Online Politics: Telegraphy, the Internet, and Political Participation in China* (Stanford: Stanford University Press, 2005).

**49.** Andrew J. Nathan, *Chinese Democracy* (Berkeley: University of California Press, 1985).

**50.** Wei Jingsheng, *The Courage to Stand Alone: Letters from Prison and Other Writings* (New York: Viking, 1997).

**51.** Orville Schell, *Discos and Democracy: China in the Throes of Reform* (New York: Anchor Books, 1989).

**52.** See Michel Oksenberg, Marc Lambert, and Lawrence Sullivan, eds., *Beijing Spring 1989:*

*Confrontation and Conflict* (Armonk, N.Y.: M. E. Sharpe, 1990); Andrew J. Nathan and Perry Link, *The Tiananmen Papers* (New York: Public Affairs, 2002).

**53.** Martin King Whyte, "Prospects for Democratization in China," *Problems of Communism* 41, no. 3 (May–June 1992): 58–70; Dickson, *Red Capitalists in China.*

**54.** Kellee Tsai, "Capitalists Without a Class: Political Diversity Among Private Entrepreneurs in China," *Comparative Political Studies* 38, no. 9 (November 2005): 1130–58; Dickson, *Red Capitalists in China.*

**55.** Shelley Rigger, *Politics in Taiwan: Voting for Democracy* (London: Routledge, 2002).

**56.** U.S.-China Business Council, at uschina.org.

**57.** Only a portion of Hong Kong's legislature is directly elected, giving Beijing significant influence over its actions. In addition, the chief executive is handpicked by Beijing. This amount of PRC control over Hong Kong affairs has allowed Beijing to block all efforts to promote further democratic reforms.

**58.** A more optimistic assessment can be found in Bruce Gilley, *China's Democratic Future: How It Will Happen and Where It Will Lead* (New York: Columbia University Press, 2004).

CHAPTER 22

# MEXICO AND BRAZIL

JOSEPH L. KLESNER

For nearly three months after the July 2006 presidential elections, thousands of Mexicans repeatedly turned out for raucous public rallies to protest what they saw as widespread electoral fraud perpetrated against their favored candidate, *Andrés Manuel López Obrador* of the *Democratic Revolutionary Party (PRD).* After an intense and oftentimes highly negative campaign, **Felipe Calderón** of the *National Action Party (PAN)* had defeated López Obrador by a margin of only 233,831 votes out of almost 41 million cast—a less than 0.6 percent margin (see table 22.1). López Obrador's legal challenges to the outcome failed when the ruling of Mexico's electoral court produced only very minor changes to the result announced the day after the election. The loser, however, refused to yield, continuing to rally his supporters and proposing to form an alternative government.[1] His intransigence poses enormous challenges to Calderón as he seeks to consolidate the democratic gains of his nation over the past two decades.

Twelve years earlier, in 1994, Ernesto Zedillo, candidate of the *Institutional Revolutionary Party (PRI),* won the Mexican presidential election handily, polling nearly twice as many votes as his closest rival. Zedillo's election was the twelfth in a row won by his party, then the longest-ruling party in the world. Although the PRI had encountered new challenges in the 1980s and early 1990s, no one expected the long-ruling party to yield power anytime soon. However, Zedillo was the last president elected from the PRI. He turned power over to *Vicente Fox* of the PAN when his term ended in 2000. Six years later, the PRI's presidential candidate finished a distant third.

Mexico's transition to a fully democratic regime has come slowly, the result of many efforts by opposition politicians and democracy advocates to pressure the PRI to yield power. It may seem paradoxical that one of the developing world's most economically advanced countries—a country that shares a two-thousand-mile border with the world's oldest democracy—would have embraced democracy so recently. However, formally democratic institutions can sometimes be used to perpetuate undemocratic rule, as you will learn in this chapter. The Peruvian novelist Mario Vargas Llosa, himself a failed presidential candidate in his home country, once called Mexico the world's "most perfect dictatorship." The PRI's adept use and abuse of democratic institutions to prolong its rule forced the opposition to struggle within those democratic arenas—the electoral system, the Congress, and state and local government—to remove the PRI from power. Thus Mexico offers an intriguing example of a country in which *a democratic transition has taken place within the existing constitutional framework.*

In July 2000, Mexicans showed enthusiasm in ousting the long-ruling PRI from the presidency by electing Vicente Fox, but Fox faced major challenges during his six-year administration as he sought to restructure the Mexican political institutions and practices that we will describe in this chapter. His party did not hold a majority of congressional seats, and he found it difficult to convince the other political parties to support his legislative initiatives. The economic downturn experienced by the United States in the aftermath of the September 11, 2001, attacks and the elevated concerns in the U.S. about the security of its borders made Fox's term difficult. His promise to promote rapid economic development foundered because of his nation's economic dependency on its northern neighbor, while his effort to convince the United States to open the border to greater migration of Mexican labor to the States met with hostility from a security-conscious U.S. government.

Meanwhile, half a continent away, Brazilians elected a former metalworker and union organizer as their president in October 2002. In his fourth presidential campaign, **Luiz Inácio "Lula" da Silva** of the *Workers Party (PT)* won an overwhelming victory over the handpicked successor of two-term president *Fernando Henrique Cardoso.* Cardoso, a former socialist and prominent Latin American intellectual, had liberalized Brazil's economy and struggled to streamline the Brazilian political system, but voters suffering the consequences of economic liberalization chose to cast their ballots for Lula, the acknowledged leader of the left, thereby repudiating the Cardoso legacy. However, like Fox, Lula found that his freedom of action was constrained by his country's integration into the world economy. Even as a proponent of the working class he found himself forced to follow fiscally conservative economic policies that he had earlier severely criticized. Nevertheless, Lula remained a popular figure, surviving criticism from the left for his conservative fiscal policies and political scandals within his party to win reelection in 2006.

When Lula and Cardoso were getting their starts in politics in the 1970s as opponents of the existing government, the military was governing Brazil with a firm hand and promoting a model of state-supported capitalism that led to phenomenal economic growth before the oil crises of the 1970s undermined their effort. President João Figueredo, the last military president, turned power over to a civilian in 1985. But democratically elected Brazilian presidents since then have had to contend with widespread poverty, one of the most unequal distributions of income in the world, a tradition of political corruption, rampant crime, and environmental degradation. Like Mexico, Brazil is tied to the world economy and subject to financial instability because of high levels of foreign debt and the fickleness of foreign investors.

**Felipe Calderón**

The challenges confronting Mexico and Brazil are typical of the problems besetting many countries in Latin America. Since becoming independent from Spain or Portugal in the first quarter of

TABLE 22.1

**Mexican Presidential Elections, 2000 and 2006**

| Candidate | Party or Coalition | % of Valid Vote |
|---|---|---|
| | **2000** | |
| Vicente Fox | Alliance for Change[a] | 43.4 |
| Francisco Labastida | Institutional Revolutionary Party (PRI) | 36.9 |
| Cuauhtémoc Cárdenas | Alliance for Mexico[b] | 17.0 |
| Others | | 2.7 |
| | **2006** | |
| Felipe Calderón | National Action Party (PAN) | 36.7 |
| Andrés Manuel López Obrador | Coalition for the Good of All[c] | 36.1 |
| Roberto Madrazo | Alliance for Mexico[d] | 22.7 |
| Others | | 4.5 |

[a]Alliance for Change was composed of the National Action Party (PAN) and the Mexican Green Party (PVEM).
[b]Alliance for Mexico (2000) was composed of the Democratic Revolutionary Party (PRD) and four smaller parties of the left.
[c]Coalition for the Good of All was composed of the PRD and two smaller parties: the Labor Party (PT) and Convergence.
[d]Alliance for Mexico (2006) was composed of the PRI and the PVEM.
*Sources:* Instituto Federal Electoral and Tribunal Electoral del Poder Judicial de la Federación.

the nineteenth century, most countries in Latin America have experienced political instability, often expressed as periodic alternation between democratic structures and authoritarianism, usually in the form of military rule. For example, Brazil had a limited, oligarchical democracy until 1930, when a military coup led to an authoritarian regime that lasted until 1946. From 1946 until 1964, Brazil enjoyed democracy, although the military meddled in politics several times. A military coup ousted Brazil's president in 1964, and the military as an institution ruled until 1985, when democracy returned. Argentina, Peru, and Bolivia have experienced similar cycles of democracy and military rule.

Like Brazil and Mexico, many Latin American nations have joined in the "third wave" of democracy that has swept the world since 1975.[2] However, endemic poverty, corruption, and difficulties in bringing to justice the military officers who committed gross violations of human rights have complicated these democratization processes, along with many other problems. Latin America's new democracies remain in place, but a "third reverse-wave," in which some of them succumb to dictatorship, has become a distinct possibility.

In this chapter we shall undertake a focused comparison of Mexico and Brazil, Latin America's most populous and richest countries. Along the way we'll indicate how they have dealt with the five sources of political conflict outlined in chapter 2:

- *Power:* Which groups have exercised predominant power in these countries? Is power being distributed more broadly among elites and organizations in civil society now that democratization is more widespread than it was twenty to twenty-five years ago?
- *Resources:* How have Mexico and Brazil dealt with the challenges of economic growth, inflation, poverty, and globalization? How wisely have they used their natural resources? How have the fruits of their economic development been distributed to groups in their societies?
- *Identity:* How are problems of ethnic diversity being addressed in Mexico, with its large Indian population, and in Brazil, perhaps the most racially mixed society in the world?
- *Ideas:* How has democracy been conceived in these countries? Is it understood in U.S. or European terms, or is there a specific Latin American model of democracy?
- *Values:* Which values and attitudes have shaped the political cultures of Mexico and Brazil? Are those values compatible with democracy and economic development?

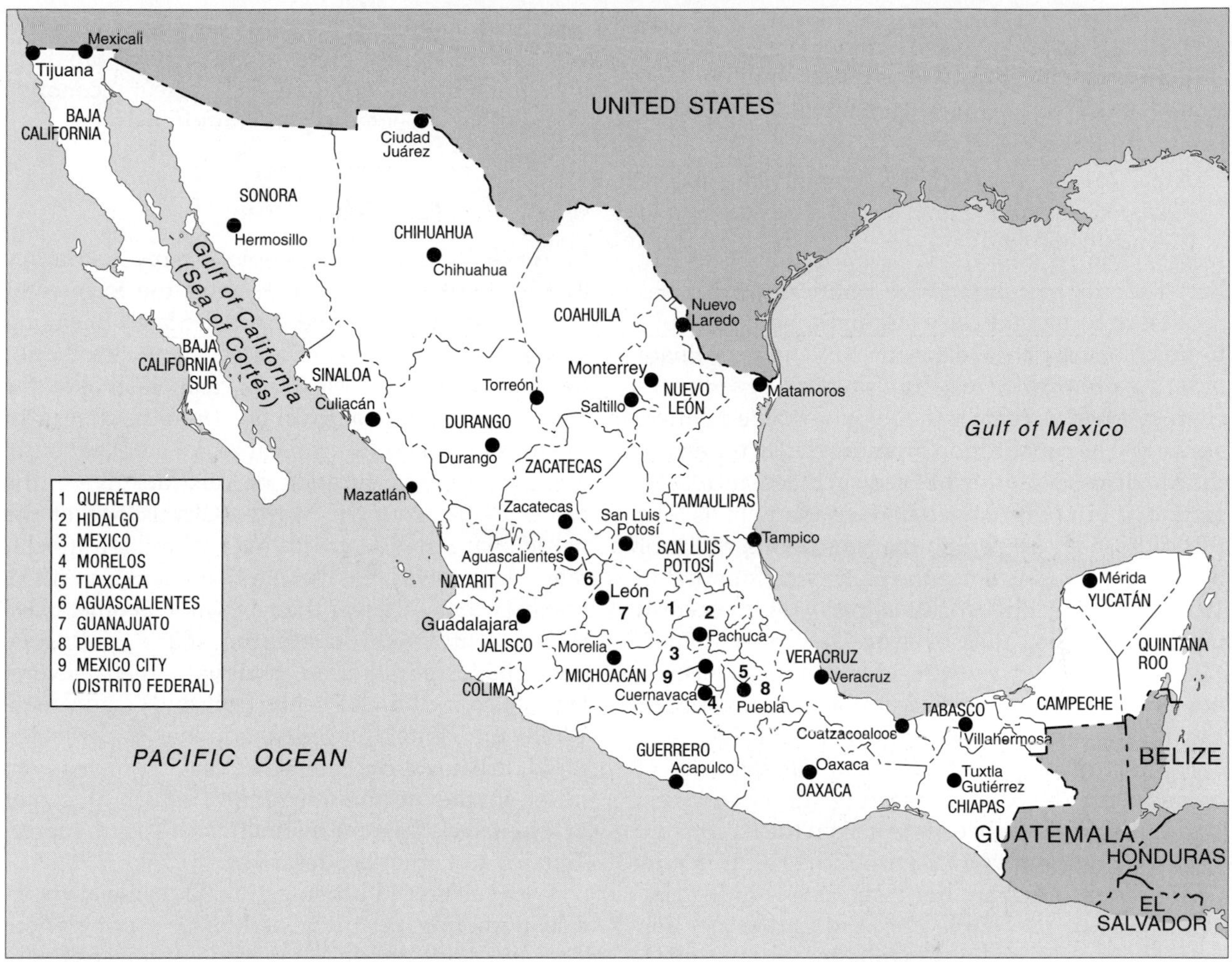


**Mexico**

In addition to looking at these conflicts, we'll assess these two countries' prospects for building and sustaining democracy by relating their experiences to the conditions for democracy and democratization discussed in chapter 9. Central to democracy's viability in Mexico and Brazil are the political institutions that each of these societies has inherited from previous political regimes. Thus we shall pay close attention to the democratic institutions of Mexico and Brazil, institutional forms discussed in chapter 8. Does it matter how the electoral systems of Brazil and Mexico are arranged? What are the power relationships between the Congress and the president in each case? Does federalism function as outlined in the constitutions of Mexico and Brazil?

These and related issues are especially important in Mexico and Brazil. The size and economic potential of these nations are so immense that their fate cannot help but influence future developments throughout Latin America. Brazil and Mexico are the largest Portuguese- and Spanish-speaking countries in the world, respectively. Nearly 188 million people live in Brazil, while the population of Mexico tops 107 million. Together, their 295 million form 50 percent of the population of Latin America and the Caribbean.[3] The actions of the governments of these two nations thus have a direct impact on nearly two-thirds of the population of this hemisphere south of U.S. borders. Further, their economies ranked twelfth (Mexico) and fourteenth (Brazil) in GNI in the world in 2005.[4] To foreign policy makers and to the leaders of banks and other transnational corporations in the United States, what happens in Mexico and Brazil can have major repercussions for U.S. political and economic interests in the hemisphere, as financial crises in Mexico in 1995 and in Brazil in 1998 proved.

## MEXICO

Population (2006, estimated): 107.5 million

Freedom House ratings (2005): Political Rights—2; Civil Liberties—2

Area: 761,602 square miles (roughly the size of Texas, California, New Mexico, Arizona, and Nevada combined)

For students of comparative politics, Mexico has proven to be an endlessly fascinating but difficult-to-describe country. On the one hand, in a continent beset by political crises and upheavals, twentieth-century Mexico demonstrated remarkable political stability. The constitution promulgated at the end of the Mexican revolution has been in place since 1917, amended but not changed in its fundamentals. The PRI, whose leaders sat in the president's chair for over seventy years since the party was founded in 1929, was the longest-ruling party in the world until Vicente Fox took over on December 1, 2000. Mexicans elect a new president every six years; none has refused to hand over power to his successor. Moreover, the PRI oversaw seventy years of economic development—not without setbacks, of course—but the Mexico entering the twenty-first century is profoundly different from the nation that came out of the revolution around 1920. It is now predominantly urban, not rural; it has industrialized; most of its people can read and write; and modern health facilities, sanitation, communications systems, and electricity are available almost everywhere in Mexico today. In many ways, Mexican politics since the revolution can be considered a success story in the turbulent twentieth century.

Yet, for the last three decades of the twentieth century, political observers said that Mexico was in crisis. The end of Mexican stability seemed always just around the corner. The same party ruled for seventy years, making it seem as though no real alternative existed (or was allowed to exist). Formally democratic institutions hid an authoritarian political regime, but only to those who did not look closely. The PRI's challengers only as recently as 2000 defeated the ruling party in the electoral arena; previously, many opponents of the PRI considered guerilla insurrection or other unorthodox challenges to its supremacy. Economic modernization has failed to reach many of Mexico's millions of poor peasants and urban dwellers because of severely inequitable distributions of income and wealth. Apparently often at the edge of breaking into the First World, Mexico's great economic promise has repeatedly gone unfulfilled.

### The Setting

Mexico's 107.5 million people occupy a country that is about a quarter the size of the forty-eight contiguous states of the United States, meaning that the population density is nearly twice that of the United States.[5] Mexico's vastness makes for considerable regional diversity, from the deserts of the north to the semi-tropical regions of the south. The greatest concentration of Mexicans live in the center of the country. Mexico City is one of the world's largest cities, with over 18 million inhabitants. Its growth has been phenomenal: in 1950, Mexico City had fewer than 4 million people.[6] Also in the central region are the states of Puebla, Guanajuato, and Jalisco, and with them several large cities, including Puebla, León and Guadalajara. While the center of the nation has experienced rapid urbanization, the cities have grown even faster in the north, where the industrial center of Monterrey has been joined by Ciudad Juárez, Tijuana, and other border cities.

With such rapid urbanization has come a wholesale uprooting of much of Mexico's population. The cities have grown because many citizens living in the countryside have seen no prospect for employment and prosperity in their families' villages. As they have moved to the cities, neighborhoods have mushroomed in rings around the old central cities, posing enormous challenges to city planners and to those local politicians and administrators charged with providing services and amenities.

At the same time, nearly 25 million Mexicans still live in rural areas, a number larger than the populations of many Latin American countries.[7] Mexico's south has been slower to urbanize than other parts of the country. For all the challenges facing country people moving to large cities like Mexico City, rural conditions are even more rigorous: imagine life without running water, sewage systems or even a septic tank, sometimes even electricity. Millions of Mexicans likewise send their children to rudimentary schools and get along without doctors or emergency room personnel who are on call at all hours.

**Regionalism** Mexico's regions differ in their economic pursuits, too. The northern states, for example, have concentrations of export-oriented industries, such as assembly plants in border cities that have benefited from the North American Free Trade Agreement (NAFTA). Central Mexico, especially the greater Mexico City area, is the site of heavy industry—automobiles and steel, among others—and has not prospered so much from hemispheric economic integration. The south remains more agricultural than the rest of the country and has been especially threatened by the prospect of cheap grain imports from the grain belt of the United States.

One other important regional difference is culture. Like the western states of the United States, Mexico's north has been a frontier region since colonization. Northern Mexicans thus share some characteristics Americans associate with their own west, especially an emphasis on rugged individualism. The much greater influence of the United States on northern Mexico has probably reinforced the individualism of northerners. Northerners have often complained about what they have seen as excessive intervention in their affairs by the Mexican state (located in Mexico City), and they have preferred private enterprise to state ownership of industry. Mexico City residents, in contrast, see themselves as urbane and even cosmopolitan and sometimes view the northerners as too rough around the edges—barbarians of the north. They have been much more inclined to support a large state presence in the economy and in other aspects of social life, perhaps because so many of them work for the state. In many parts of Mexico's south, indigenous peoples remain concentrated in their traditional villages, practicing communal landholding and rejecting private ownership of the land. In states like Oaxaca, Chiapas, and Guerrero, indigenous groups have sought to retain whatever control of their communities' political arrangements they can, arrangements that are sometimes based on longstanding community traditions.

Associated with these different regional economic and political cultures are perceptions of racial differences. Northerners, for example, are more likely to be Caucasians or ***people of mixed European and indigenous heritage*** **(mestizos)**. Southerners are more likely to be of indigenous heritage or mestizos. A latent racism can often be witnessed in statements by northerners of their perceptions of the other regions of the country. For example, some years ago a newly elected governor of the northern state of Aguascalientes couldn't contain himself after his victory, describing the regional differences this way: "The north works, the center thinks, and the south rests."[8]

It is almost impossible to understate the importance of Mexico's proximity to the United States. The countries share a long, often porous border. The bulk of Mexico's trade is with the United States—as much as 80 percent annually. Millions of Mexicans have traveled to the United States to work, visit family members, shop, or just vacation. United States cultural influences have become very powerful in Mexico—many Mexicans look to the United States for their popular culture and for cues about their own futures.

Moreover, the border has served as Mexico's social safety valve: when Mexicans have not been able to find satisfactory employment in their country, they often have gone to the United States, legally or illegally. Many Mexicans come to the United States to work several times in their lives; many others come only once to earn money for an important purchase, like a car or improvements to their home; and still others come to the United States and don't return. Because everyone involved in the U.S.-Mexican relationship knows about this phenomenon, everyone also worries about the consequences of political instability in Mexico, since that would likely increase the flow of Mexicans northward. Mexico's relatively slow economic growth in recent years has meant that more and more Mexicans now move to the United States with the intention of settling there permanently. In his first major policy initiative, President Fox sought to regularize Mexican migration to the United States by asking President Bush to ease immigration restrictions on Mexican laborers who wished to work north of the border. However, the September 11 attacks raised American sensitivities about border security, and Fox's plan has remained on the drawing board, underscoring the asymmetry in relations between the United States and its southern neighbor and the dependency of Mexico on the U.S. economy.

## The Evolution of Mexican Politics

**Prominent Features of Mexican Politics** When students of comparative politics looked at Mexico in the 1970s, they noted that, although Mexicans elected their president, a Congress, state governors, and state assemblies, the political regime had more in common with the military-ruled political systems of South America than it did with the democracies of North America or Europe.[9] As stated in chapter 2, *whereas democracy places the people above the government, authoritarianism (or dictatorship) places the governing authorities above the people.* Mexican authoritarianism had several features. Perhaps the easiest feature to notice was the long rule of the **Institutional Revolutionary Party**, known as the **PRI** (pronounced "pree"). ***The PRI controlled Mexico's presidency and dominated the country's political system as its ruling party from the time it was founded in 1929 until Vicente Fox's victory in 2000.*** Until the 1980s, the PRI did not lose *any* significant elections. Democracy without alternation in power—or the serious prospect of it—could hardly be called true democracy, and no opposition party posed any real challenge to the PRI even as late as the 1970s.

Another feature of Mexican politics that everyone recognized was *presidentialism*. Mexican presidents have been in some ways akin to limited-term dictators. During his six years in office, each PRI president dominated Congress, the judiciary, the military, the states and their governors, the party that elected him, and the media that reported his every move. Observers also agreed that the Mexican political system was highly centralized, despite a constitution that was formally federalist. Mexican *centralism* meant that Mexico City dominated the nation and that the federal government dictated to the states in ways that other federalist societies like the United States or Canada would find unacceptable. Another aspect of the central role of the government in Mexican life was the heavy *state intervention in Mexico's market economy.* The Mexican government held many state-owned enterprises and the economy was highly regulated. Associated with the government's close regulation of the economy was its control of the interest groups spawned by that economy; Mexico was a clear example of *state corporatism.* The labor movement, peasant associations, state employees, small business owners—all were captured in a system of interest representation that channeled their demands through the PRI.

Two other features of Mexican politics also caught the attention of political analysts: *clientelism* and *corruption.* The Mexican political elite was recruited through a system of patron-client relationships "in which the 'patrons'—persons having higher political status—provide benefits such as protection, support in political struggles with rivals and chances for upward political or economic mobility to their 'clients'—persons with a lower political status."[10] *Clientelism* has extended beyond the political class, however, so that many organizations and individuals have found themselves regularly approaching powerful individuals in politics and government agencies to petition for assistance, usually with the expectation that those being helped by powerful patrons will reciprocate by supporting those politicians as they seek to climb the political ladder.[11] It is not surprising that corruption becomes bound up with clientelism, since the favors asked by clients of patrons often involve gaining access to public resources for those clients' private gain. At the same time, the asymmetrical power relationships fostered by clientelism encourage the powerful to demand a great deal of their clients or would-be clients.

How did Mexico come to exhibit these features of political life? As the next sections explain, each feature has some antecedent in Mexican political history.

**Conquest and Colonialism** The makings of the modern Mexican nation came together in the **Spanish Conquest**, ***when Hernán Cortés led his band of 550 Spaniards against the mighty Aztec empire in 1519.***[12] One member of the Spanish band was La Malinche, an indigenous woman who served as translator for Cortés. She also bore him a son, a child who symbolically represents the first Mexican, the first mestizo. Further examples of miscegenation (racial interbreeding) between Europeans and indigenous people, mostly between Spanish men and indigenous women, created a nation whose majority is now mestizo.

During the following three hundred years of colonial rule, Europeans and those of European heritage held complete political control, gaining the fruits of the indigenous people's labors in Mexico's mines and on its landed estates, known as *haciendas.* The idea that Indians were meant to work for white people became firmly embedded in the minds of Mexico's elites. At the same time, indigenous communities were allowed to hold their lands communally and to decide how to farm them through community institutions, an arrangement known as the *ejido.*

**Independence and the Creation of a Mexican Nation** Independence came to Mexico and other Spanish colonies not as a consequence of an uprising of the exploited indigenous peoples and mestizos, but rather because of a conflict between whites born in America and those who came from Spain. However, in the course of Mexico's struggle for independence, the poor and nonwhite became mobilized in a rebellion against the Spanish, a rebellion that began in 1810 but was subsequently put down by troops loyal to the crown.

Political instability characterized the first half-century after Mexico became independent in 1822. Conservatives and Liberals struggled over the definition of the new nation and its political institutions. Conservatives favored a restoration of some form of monarchy, centralized power, and a privileged political position for the Catholic church. Liberals, in contrast, sought a federal republic without an established church, much along the model earlier created in the United States. Battles between Liberals and Conservatives contributed to much political instability, with coups d'état and civil wars leading to very short terms of office for Mexico's presidents. In the thirty-two years from 1823 until 1855, twenty-four men served as president of Mexico, some of them multiple times. General Antonio López de Santa Anna, whom Americans know best as the Mexican commander at the Alamo, was president eleven times.

Meanwhile, Mexico's restive neighbor to the north had proclaimed the doctrine of *manifest destiny,* the notion that the United States should stretch from the Atlantic to the Pacific. Mexico's weakness—a product of its domestic political turbulence—contributed in no small part to the success of the Texas independence movement and to Mexico's defeat in the Mexican-American War, known in Mexico as the War of North American Aggression. In addition, Mexico was invaded by French forces in 1861 while the United States was preoccupied with its own Civil War. After a six-year struggle for independence, liberal forces led by Benito Juárez defeated the French in 1867.

Mexico's unfortunate history of foreign invasion during the nineteenth century played an important role in the formation of Mexican *national identity.* Mexico's colonial heritage had provided little to unite its people: indeed, colonial institutions and practices tended to divide Mexicans into rather rigid social categories based on race. But the struggle against foreign intervention could unite Mexicans of all classes by casting them as victims of foreign aggression. And while Mexico's experiences with the United States reinforced Mexican perceptions of weakness, its successful ouster of the French produced a great national hero—Juárez, who was a Zapotec Indian from Oaxaca—and solidified the conception of Mexico as a republic.

Mexican nationalism became further defined by the nation's experiences in the remainder of the nineteenth and the first decade of the twentieth centuries. General *Porfirio Díaz* led a successful military rebellion against President Sebastian Lerdo under the slogan "Effective Suffrage and No Reelection." After ousting Lerdo, Díaz was duly elected by Mexico's very restricted electorate. He served one term, then stood aside so that one of his political allies could be elected in 1880. But he returned to the presidency in 1884, not to step down until the revolution of 1910. During his long rule, he relied on a small coterie of political followers known as *científicos.*[13] Many of them espoused social Darwinism, the notion that only the fittest would survive in social life (see chapter 14). In the Mexican context, social Darwinists suggested that Europeans or their descendants would be most likely to survive the social struggle, while the indigenous would not. In their view, it would be better for Mexico if the indigenous population remained marginalized.

During Díaz's thirty-five-year rule, Mexico experienced unprecedented economic growth, spurred by major investments in mining and in the railroads. These investments came disproportionately from the United States, and they gave Mexicans of all classes a feeling that they were being cheated out of the fruits of the new economic advances. Americans, in contrast, had been favored in order to attract their investment dollars. In addition, many investors from the United States became large landowners in Mexico and United States banks became major lenders to Mexico's economic elites.[14] In reaction, a strong sense of economic nationalism emerged by the turn of the century.

During Díaz's rule, the poor were further marginalized. In a development parallel to the enclosure movement in England, poor peasants were effectively denied access to their lands. The Liberal Constitution of 1857 had outlawed land ownership by corporate groups. By this provision, the church lost its lands to large landholders, mostly to people associated with the Liberals. But this provision also barred communal property holding in *ejidos,* so individual families in rural villages were given properties previously owned by the entire village. Many such villagers subsequently lost their lands because of economic failures (caused by poor harvests) or were cheated out of them by rich landowners intent on consolidating large estates that increasingly produced commercial crops for the national and international markets. Thus, Mexico's peasantry became more and more proletarianized, forced to become wage laborers on land they formerly owned or to seek employment on the railroads or in the new factories, where wages were low because so many people sought work.

**The Revolution** Mexico's 1910 revolution brought together several different social groups who found themselves dissatisfied by Díaz's regime. The man who initiated the revolution, Francisco Madero, came from a wealthy landowning family in the north. Madero and many like him were angry that Díaz had excluded them from political power and they were frustrated because U.S. investors seemed to get most of the best investment opportunities. Madero remembered Díaz's slogan, "Effective Suffrage and No Reelection," and raised it as his own revolutionary battle cry. Madero's followers were political liberals and economic nationalists, but they were not very interested in serious social reforms.[15]

Other Mexicans sought more revolutionary changes. Among them was *Emiliano Zapata,* a villager from Morelos who led an army of peasants demanding land reform. They wanted to reclaim the land they had lost to investors in sugar plantations and they sought a return of the *ejido,* the system of communal land ownership.

Díaz abdicated the presidency in 1911 and Madero became president later that year. But he was overthrown and assassinated by a counterrevolutionary coup d'état in 1913 that had been orchestrated by the U.S. ambassador, Henry Lane Wilson, who thought Madero was incapable of securing foreign investors' interests. After Madero's assassination, chaos reigned as revolutionaries of all stripes united to defeat the counterrevolutionary leader, General Victoriano Huerta. After ousting Huerta in 1914, however, the revolutionaries fell to fighting among themselves for direction of the new regime.

The revolution became a conflagration: as many as a million Mexicans lost their lives and much property was destroyed. Millions more were mobilized into revolutionary armies that marched or rode (on horses and the railroads) the length and breadth of Mexico, learning thereby what the rest of their country and their countrymen looked like. Although Mexicans were divided during their revolution, a sense of national identity and unity emerged from the struggle, breaking down some of the provincialism that had to that point characterized Mexican society. Those revolutionary soldiers, the majority of them peasants and workers, were now mobilized by their involvement in the revolution and became experienced in using violence against their adversaries. They would not be easily demobilized and excluded from having a political voice after the revolution.

In the end, the revolutionary faction that most closely followed Madero's political philosophy, the Constitutionalists (led by Venustiano Carranza, also a large landowner from the north), emerged as the dominant force. The Constitutionalists defeated the armies of Zapata and Pancho Villa and wrote a new constitution in 1917. Although the Constitutionalists did not favor changes as radical as those proposed by the forces of Zapata and Villa at an earlier convention in 1914, they did include clauses that reserved subsoil rights to the nation, facilitated agrarian reform, permitted labor to organize and to strike, and placed heavy restrictions on the activities of the Catholic church. However, few of these progressive clauses could be implemented immediately because Mexico had to rebuild after the destruction of the revolution and reestablish political stability, a task that took up the entire decade of the 1920s.

## Mexico Under the PRI

In 1928, former president Alvaro Obregón (1920–24) had the 1917 constitution amended so that he could run for another presidential term.[16] Shortly after winning the presidential race, Obregón was assassinated. A political crisis immediately ensued because Mexico has no vice presidency. With Obregón now dead, the most powerful politician in Mexico was the sitting president, Plutarco Elias Calles (1924–28). But Calles could hardly run for reelection, especially given that a reelected president had just been killed. To resolve the crisis and to confront the problem of political instability that plagued Mexico in the 1920s, Calles proposed the creation of a national political party that would unite all "revolutionaries" in one political organization that would resolve the problems of political succession within its own organizational structures. Thus was born the National Revolutionary Party (or PNR), the predecessor to today's PRI. With all revolutionaries united in a single party and agreeing to join forces to support its candidates, a PNR nomination became tantamount to an electoral victory. This scheme proved itself when the PNR candidate, an unknown named Pascual Ortiz Rubio, defeated the well-known philosopher and former secretary of education José Vasconcelos by a margin of 1,948,848 to 110,979 in 1929.[17]

Because Calles stacked the PNR's national executive committee with politicians loyal to him, he was able to continue to control Mexican politics without sitting in the presidential chair, at least until 1935. In 1934, Calles approved the PNR's nomination of General *Lázaro Cárdenas* (LAH-zah-roe KAR-day-nahs) as the party's presidential candidate. Cárdenas embarked on a program of extensive land reforms, finally fulfilling the revolutionary goals of Zapata and other agrarian leaders. When Calles objected to this and other progressive reforms, Cárdenas used his authority as president to exile the former leader. *Presidentialism,* a pattern of executive dominance in the political system that had been firmly established under Díaz and practiced by Obregón and Calles, was thus reestablished in Mexican politics. (For a list of Mexico's presidents, see table 22.2.)

**TABLE 22.2**

**Mexican Postrevolutionary Presidential Administrations**

| President | Years | Vote (%) |
|---|---|---|
| Venustiano Carranza | 1917–20 | 98.1 |
| Alvaro Obregón | 1920–24 | 95.8 |
| Plutarco Elías Calles | 1924–28 | 84.1 |
| Emilio Portes Gil | 1928–29 | appointed |
| Pascual Ortiz Rubio | 1929–32 | 93.6 |
| Abelardo Rodríguez | 1932–34 | appointed |
| Lázaro Cárdenas | 1934–40 | 98.2 |
| Manuel Avila Camacho | 1940–46 | 93.9 |
| Miguel Alemán | 1946–52 | 77.9 |
| Adolfo Ruiz Cortines | 1952–58 | 74.3 |
| Adolfo López Mateos | 1958–64 | 90.4 |
| Gustavo Díaz Ordaz | 1964–70 | 88.6 |
| Luis Echeverría | 1970–76 | 85.5 |
| José López Portillo | 1976–82 | 98.7 |
| Miguel de la Madrid | 1982–88 | 74.3 |
| Carlos Salinas de Gortari | 1988–94 | 50.7 |
| Ernesto Zedillo | 1994–2000 | 50.1 |
| Vicente Fox | 2000–06 | 43.4 |
| Felipe Calderón | 2006–present | 36.7 |

*Source:* Mario Ramírez Rancaño, "Estadísticas electorales: presidenciales," *Revista Mexicana de Sociología* 39, no. 1 (1977): 271–99; Instituto Federal Electoral.

**Cárdenas Fulfills Revolutionary Promises** Cárdenas (1934–40) did more than any other man to build the political regime we have come to describe as uniquely Mexican. In policy terms, Cárdenas engaged in an energetic program of land reform, redistributing more land to Mexican peasants than any other president before or since. He had governed the southern state of Michoacán and understood the desire of indigenous communities to have their land returned to them and to be able to return to a communal ownership of that land. As Cárdenas undertook land reform, he thus preferred to distribute land not to individuals, but to villages set up as *ejidos.* To represent the new beneficiaries of land reform, Cárdenas created the *National Peasant Confederation (CNC),* a peak association of peasant groups.

He also promoted labor organization and militance. During his presidency, the *Mexican Workers' Federation (CTM),* a peak association of labor unions, was formed and won substantial wage increases for industrial workers. In 1938, taking advantage of a labor confrontation between petroleum workers and U.S.- and British-owned oil companies, Cárdenas nationalized the oil industry, thereby creating the giant state-owned enterprise Petroleos Mexicanos (PEMEX). The oil expropriation was the defining moment of Mexican economic nationalism, the ultimate example of Mexico standing up against powerful foreign firms and the countries from which they came, especially the United States. The United States, sensing the coming war in Europe, chose not to get into a confrontation with Mexico about the expropriations. Under Cárdenas, then, the PRI became known as the party that struggled for justice for workers and peasants and that protected the national interest by building state-owned enterprises in crucial economic sectors.

**Political Institutions** In political terms, Cárdenas had a lasting impact. In 1938, the PNR became the Party of the Mexican Revolution (PRM). More important than the name change, however, was an organizational innovation. Cárdenas organized the PRM into four sectors, one for peasants (organized into the CNC), another for the workers (represented by the CTM), a third for state bureaucrats (organized into the *Federation of Unions of Workers in Service to the State,* or *FSTSE*), and a fourth for the military. This organizational structure made the PRM a *corporatist* institution. By incorporating these organizations of peasants, workers, bureaucrats, and the military into the PRM, Cárdenas gave them privileged access to decision makers. At the same time, however, the incorporation of these groups within the party, and especially of their leaders within the PRM hierarchy, made them vulnerable to co-optation and control. In particular, labor and peasant leaders were co-opted (incorporated or taken over) by the PRM's national leadership (and later by the PRI). They were offered personal political opportunities in return for exercising restraint in their demands on behalf of their constituents.

The PRM's corporatist organization also had the advantage of providing the party with an unparalleled capacity to turn out voters on election day. Local representatives of the CNC served as political bosses in their villages, providing the party with new methods for getting rural voters to the polls to vote for the ruling party. Labor union leaders were similarly able to convince their membership to vote for the PRM. With so much of Mexico still rural in the 1930s and 1940s (65 percent of the labor force was involved in agriculture in 1940)[18] and with a considerable number of additional Mexicans incorporated into the official labor movement, the ruling party could easily overcome any challengers. It demonstrated this capacity in the elections of 1940, 1946, and 1952, when mavericks from the ruling party ran for president at the head of hastily arranged parties, but lost by considerable margins.

Under Cárdenas, the powerful position of the presidency within the political regime became cemented too. He built a presidency that could dominate Congress effectively.

The Mexican presidency has held a formidable set of powers, which the Mexican scholar Luis Javier Garrido characterized as *constitutional, metaconstitutional,* and *anticonstitutional.*[19] Garrido argued that the constitutional powers of the presidency were not more extensive than those held by most presidents in other Latin American political systems.[20] However, beyond the constitutionally designated powers, Mexican presidents enjoyed "meta-constitutional powers," a "series of prerogatives [that] corresponds to the 'unwritten norms' of the Mexican system. They allowed the president to centralize his power progressively through a distortion of constitutional mechanisms."[21] Garrido identified ten such metaconstitutional powers, the most important of them being the effective capacity to amend the constitution, the role of "chief legislator," the capacity to designate one's successor to the presidency, and the domination of lower levels of government in the Mexican federal system. The president's anticonstitutional powers, in Garrido's view, were a capacity to violate the legal code and the right to immunity from prosecution.

Such powers set up a characteristic of Mexican politics that scholars have labeled *presidencialismo,* or presidentialism. The president of the United States, of course, has also had great political power, especially since the time of Franklin Delano Roosevelt, and Americans mark political time by presidential administrations in much the same way as Mexicans do. But in the United States, presidents often find themselves unable to be the "chief legislators" because Congress often refuses to pass the bills sent to it by the White House. U.S. congressional committees often write their own legislation without presidential prompting, sometimes openly defying presidential wishes on important policy issues.

The Mexican Congress is charged with the responsibilities of auditing the public accounts of the previous year, approving the budget of the coming fiscal year, and voting on all bills introduced to it by the president or by members of the *Chamber of Deputies* or the *Senate,* the two houses of the bicameral legislature. In the formal rules for making laws established in the Mexican constitution, a bill becomes a law in ways that are similar to the process in the United States. Bills must pass both houses of the Congress; they can be approved or vetoed by the president; and if they are vetoed, the veto can be overridden by a two-thirds vote of both houses. However, until the 1990s, the Mexican Congress had not rejected a presidential bill since the 1930s. U.S. presidents must envy their Mexican colleagues.

How can we explain *presidencialismo,* this seemly unprecedented domination of the legislature and other national institutions by the president? When we take into account the incredible advantages that accrued to the PRI because of its having been the incumbent party between 1929 and 2000 (it could take credit for all the benefits of economic development that came to Mexico in those years) and the mobilizational capacity it enjoyed because of its corporatist organization of peasants, workers, and urban popular groups, we should not be surprised that a PRI nomination was equivalent to an appointment to that "elected" position. This quasi-automatic election ensured by the PRI's endorsement applied not just to presidential candidates but also to candidates for Congress, governor, state assembly, mayor, or membership on municipal councils. If we then remember that postrevolutionary Mexico has forbidden reelection to the many positions just mentioned, it becomes easier for us to understand why the president has been so powerful.[22]

Politicians still cannot develop support bases in constituencies that will return them to office in the way that U.S. politicians can. Each "elected" PRI politician thus had to expect to be looking for a new position, either elected or appointed, within three years (for municipal officers, state assembly members, or federal deputies) or six years (for governors or federal senators). Likewise, because each new president brought a new administration, those appointed to political positions in the bureaucracy knew that they had to plan to be appointed to some new position—probably in another area of the bureaucracy—or nominated for an elected post within six years. Who controlled these appointments and nominations? Ultimately, the president. However, for younger politicians to gain presidential approval, patrons in their *camarrillas,* or political groups, could provide essential support to indicate that an aspiring politician was worthy of appointment to a lesser elected or appointed position. Hence, clientelism became an essential means of ascent in a system in which political recruitment was dominated at the top by the president.

In this situation, the reasons for congressional subordination to the president become clear. Even though the PRI typically had ample majorities in the Congress, which PRI deputy or senator would want to demonstrate opposition to a presidentially initiated bill? What would a vote against a bill proposed by the president accomplish? Since a member of the Congress could not be reelected, why would he care about his constituents' reactions to a bill that might not be favorable to their district? Since his career required getting another position within three or six years, why would he risk antagonizing the president by voting against a presidential initiative?

This logic produced an incredible record of legislative accomplishment for Mexican presidents. As mentioned earlier, between the 1930s and the late 1990s, no presidential bill was turned down by the Mexican Congress. Opposition members of the Congress usually spoke against bills emanating from the presidency, but to little practical effect, especially if the national media paid little attention to their speeches, as was generally true before the 1970s.

Mexico's 1917 constitution also enshrined the concept of the "free municipality": in principle, local governments have had the autonomy to make local laws and policies. But in actual practice, municipalities (equivalent to U.S. counties, the lowest level of government in Mexico) have been subordinate to the federal government in the same way that the Congress has been dominated by the president. This local political subordination to the center developed despite the strong regionalism we described at the outset of this chapter.

Central government domination of the states can be attributed to three factors. First, the federal government raises by far the greatest proportion of tax revenues, which it then "shares" with states and localities. State and local governments thus have had to be careful about their relationship with the federal government, especially with the all-powerful executive, for fear of getting relatively small shares of federal revenues.[23] Second, once the PRI was formed and came to control political recruitment throughout the nation, further political advances for state governors and other aspiring politicians in a state depended on staying in the good political graces of the president. Third, like other elected officials in Mexico, governors cannot be reelected; thus they have been constrained in the degree to which they could build local political machines that would be support bases for resisting central government demands. In effect, because most or all state governors had higher political ambitions in the PRI, the president had the *de facto* power to appoint and remove them. Thus the power of the Mexican presidency extended beyond the federal government to the states and the municipalities.

## HYPOTHESIS-TESTING EXERCISE: Explaining Mexican Authoritarianism

### Hypotheses, Variables, Expectations, and Evidence

Until the 1990s, Mexicans were governed by an authoritarian regime, despite living with a constitution that provided for democratic institutions. Let us briefly review some of the factors discussed in chapter 9 that can best explain Mexican authoritarianism. What follows is a hypothesis-testing exercise in which our *dependent variable* is *authoritarianism in Mexico* (i.e., the absence of democracy) and our *independent variables* are the *ten conditions.* In each case, our expectation is that Mexico's failure to meet each condition enhances the likelihood of authoritarianism. Our evidence is presented in the following sections.

#### *Elites Committed to Democracy*

When Mexico was debating an electoral reform initiative in 1977, the PRI representative to the Federal Electoral Commission said that his party could not support a reform that undermined the two central institutions of postrevolutionary Mexico: the presidency and the "party of the majority," meaning the PRI.[24] This assertion captured the view that the continued rule of their party was more important to the PRI than democracy. The willingness of PRI militants and PRI party leaders to engage in electoral fraud to ensure their party's victories provided further testament to their lack of commitment to democracy.

However, within the PRI political elite there were proponents of democratizing reforms and the rule of law. Many PRI members and leaders wanted to ensure that the party continued to win and thereby to rule Mexico, but they believed it essential that the party win fair and square for its continued rule to be legitimate. The relative moderation of Mexican authoritarianism owed much to this commitment on the part of liberals within the PRI elite.

#### *State Institutions*

Although Mexico's constitution prescribes a set of democratic institutions that would ensure popular sovereignty, the no reelection clause effectively removed the capacity of the electorate to hold elected officials accountable for their actions. Because the PRI so monopolized the electoral process until 2000 and the president so dominated the PRI, Mexico would be better described as having had *presidential sovereignty* instead of popular sovereignty. *Presidencialismo,* which was encouraged by the no reelection principle and by the PRI's control of the electoral process, explains the absence of democracy in Mexico for most of the past century better than any other factor.

#### *National Unity*

Revolutionary nationalism, the ideology prevailing in postrevolutionary Mexico, stressed national unity amidst the nation's diversity. Much earlier than the United States, Mexico adopted a public policy that officially promoted multiculturalism. Far from being homogeneous, Mexico remains a heterogeneous society even five centuries after the Conquest. Indeed, one key element of the official postrevolutionary national identity celebrates the heterogeneity of Mexican society. A trip to the Museum of Anthropology in Mexico City (the largest in the world), where each surviving indigenous group has its own celebratory exhibit, will reinforce the view that Mexico is a multicultural society and that multiculturalism is good for the nation. However, closer analysis reveals a bitter truth: Mexico's indigenous communities have been marginalized by the dominant mestizo culture and exploited both politically and economically. The areas of the country with high densities of people who speak indigenous languages have tended to produce the highest rates of voting for the PRI, at least until recently. Indigenous peoples, who have been poorer and less educated than other Mexicans, have been prime candidates for the kind of coercion that we have just described as being used against illiterates and other less educated people. Although the Mexican state under the PRI voiced a respect for the nation's multicultural heritage, its policies have encouraged the assimilation of Indians into mainstream mestizo culture. Those who have chosen not to be assimilated have been left to the poverty and violence of rural life.

### National Wealth

In Mexico as in other Latin American countries, the growth of national wealth did not bring democracy in the direct way that many political scientists predicted that it would in the 1950s and 1960s. Although Latin America as a region and Mexico as a country have been near the top of rankings of developing countries in terms of income per capita and other measures of wealth since the Second World War, that wealth has been inequitably distributed. Some political scientists have argued that the *maldistribution of income* in Latin America has deterred the spread of democracy because rich elites have too much to lose if the poor use democratic institutions to take power and redistribute that wealth. Many of the richest Mexicans have been PRI supporters over the decades and have encouraged the government to control the political activities of the poor.

### Private Enterprise

As we noted earlier, Mexico was a market economy throughout the twentieth century, but one in which the state has played a large part as "banker and entrepreneur of last resort."[25] In earlier postrevolutionary decades the Mexican state played a crucial role in promoting the development of business by providing subsidized loans, building the infrastructure needed by industry, selling critical manufacturing inputs like energy at subsidized prices, offering government contracts to preferred businesspeople, and protecting the economy from foreign competition. Important segments of Mexican private enterprise became highly dependent for their business success on good relationships with government officials and the continued rule of the PRI. Until the mid 1970s, at least, the business sector did not serve as a counterweight to the authoritarian tendencies of the state. Furthermore, as Mexican development proceeded through the postwar decades, the Mexican state came to directly control larger and larger portions of Mexican enterprise. Many Mexicans owed their very livelihood to the PRI-controlled state, not a situation likely to lead them to support opposition to the PRI.

### A Middle Class

Given the development of the Mexican economy mentioned in the previous section, the middle class hardly has been a homogeneous class. Because Mexico now has 107.5 million people and several large cities, the Mexican middle class has been large enough to have a distinct political impact for many decades. That middle class incorporates people from many different occupations, however: people from the liberal professions (doctors and lawyers), intellectuals, the white-collar salaried employees of large firms and the state, teachers, and small business owners, among others. For some members of the middle class, advancement depended upon the success of the PRI-controlled system, especially those employed by the state. Teachers, for instance, were one of the bulwarks of the PRI's efforts to get out the vote. Others were more critical of the PRI's domination of Mexican politics and criticized the existing political arrangements because of their independence from the state. The middle class has been the support base of the longest-lived of the opposition parties, the National Action Party (PAN), the party of Vicente Fox. On balance, in Mexico the standard hypothesis that the middle class has been in favor of democracy is supported.

### Support of the Disadvantaged for Democracy

Whether the members of the Mexican working class or peasantry have been in favor of democracy or not for most of the postwar years has mattered less than whether they were *able* to support democracy. There exists strong evidence that at times large sectors of the working class sought to break free of the official labor movement. A railroad workers strike in 1958–59 and the growth of an independent union movement in the early 1970s are examples. At other times there were many efforts to create peasant associations independent of the official peasant sector of the PRI. However, the PRI's corporatist organizations for peasants and workers proved very durable. The party was able to co-opt (buy off) the leaders of independent worker and peasant associations, and the government demonstrated a willingness to repress those insurgencies within unions or peasant associations that threatened union leaders who had cozy relationships with the state.

### Citizen Participation, Civil Society, and a Democratic Political Culture

Studies of Mexican political attitudes during the years of the PRI's unquestioned hegemony tended to argue that Mexico had an authoritarian political culture. Early psychoanalytically oriented studies by Mexican intellectuals Samuel Ramos and Octavio Paz (who was later awarded the Nobel Prize for literature) tended to emphasize the *machismo* of Mexican men and to see a collective sense of national inferiority as a national characteristic. These traits, Ramos and Paz argued, promoted political violence and a desire to dominate others, both inhibiting democratic practices.

In the late 1950s, Mexico became a case study in Gabriel Almond and Sidney Verba's famous *Civic Culture* study (see chapter 12). Almond and Verba categorized the respondents to their surveys into "parochials," those who expect nothing from the political system; "subjects," those who look to government for the outputs they can get from it; and "participants," those more inclined to be actively involved on the input side of government.[26] "Participants" would be expected to form the basis of an active civil society and hence to lay the foundations of democracy. However, few participants could be found in Mexico, where about one-quarter of respondents were "parochials" and two-thirds were "subjects." Since few independent organizations could be found in Mexican civil society, one might chalk up that absence to the lack of participant citizens to lead and to join them.

However, the situation may have been more complex than these early studies suggested. So long as people saw the government as a dispenser of individualized benefits via the clientelist networks promoted by the PRI and government agencies, they would not likely organize viable civic organizations or opposition parties to oppose the PRI and the captive organizations it had created (like the official labor and peasant movements). However, perhaps a more fruitful way of explaining Mexicans' "subject" political attitudes is to argue that the structures of government and the official party had been created precisely to encourage individuals to contact elected officials and bureaucratic agencies. The PRI understood that it was cheaper and less politically threatening to provide benefits to individuals (such as the extension of a water line to a petitioner's house or help in obtaining a government job) than to favor large groups of mobilized people who might challenge the PRI's rule. Mexicans who tended to see themselves as "subjects" instead of "participants" were simply reacting rationally to the clientelist institutions that had been created in the 1930s and 1940s. Indeed, other studies conducted in the 1970s concluded that Mexicans held democratic attitudes; if Mexico remained authoritarian, that authoritarianism had to be attributed to factors other than the political culture, such as institutions like the PRI and the presidency.[27]

### *Education and Freedom of Information*

Studies of Mexican voting behavior have consistently reported a close correlation between education levels and voting for the PRI.[28] In parts of the country where illiteracy is high, the PRI has performed much better than in areas populated by more educated people. Why? The simple answer is that less educated people can be persuaded or coerced to vote *against* their interests more easily than is true of more educated people. Perhaps more important, they have been less able to read between the lines for the truth in the esoteric prose that has characterized political reporting in the Mexican press. Thus, they can be strongly urged—or coerced—to vote for PRI candidates by local power holders. Illiterates (who made up 38 percent of the population as late as 1960, and over half the rural population then)[29] have received another voting cue: ballots have included both the name of the candidates' party and the parties' symbols in full color. The PRI's symbol—despite a legal restriction against it—has the same colors as the Mexican flag. So when voting, illiterates have been reminded to do their "patriotic" duty by putting their X over the colors of the flag.

Even the well-educated had to struggle to obtain independent political information and analyses, however, because until the 1970s, the Mexican press censored itself. And until the mid 1990s, television and radio were strongly in the PRI's camp. For years, many articles in newspapers were simply government-written stories placed in the papers in the guise of independent reports. Newspaper reporters often took payoffs from government agencies to place these reports or to write their own favorable articles about those agencies. Newspapers depended on government-placed advertisements to meet their costs and thus they declined to threaten those advertising revenues by writing critically about the government. For many years, newsprint was controlled by a government agency, and thus the government could punish a critical newspaper by delaying its newsprint deliveries or cutting its allocation of newsprint.

Broadcast media were even less critical of the government than the print media were. Like the U.S. government, the Mexican government controls broadcast licenses. This situation alone can explain why Mexican television and radio were very favorable to the PRI in their reporting and unwilling to grant much paid advertising time to the opposition parties. On top of that, Mexican television has been dominated by Televisa, a broadcast conglomerate that accounts for as much as 85 percent of the Mexican viewing audience. Over the years Televisa, in essence, exchanged a strongly pro-PRI, pro-government television news orientation for access to new broadcast licenses in Mexico's growing media market. In short, even in the absence of formal censorship, with a comparatively undereducated population and government-manipulated press and mass media, we should not be surprised that competitive democracy was hindered in its development in Mexico.

### *A Favorable International Environment*

Porfirio Díaz reputedly said of Mexico's international situation, "Poor Mexico! So far from God and so close to the United States!" For much of Mexico's postrevolutionary era the Mexican government has sought to keep the United States at arm's length, but the overpowering influence of the United States has proven impossible to avoid. While the United States government has often made the promotion of democracy a key plank in its foreign policy platforms, that commitment to democracy has often been left aside when other national interests come under consideration. Particularly in view of the already large migration flows back and forth across the two-thousand-mile U.S.-Mexican border, U.S. foreign policy makers have tended to define the chief U.S. national interest in terms of promoting political stability in Mexico rather than democracy, because instability—which could very well result from a democratic revolution—would surely lead to massive refugee flows into the United States. The United States has also benefited from the business opportunities created by a succession of Mexican presidents. In short, official United States foreign policy did not emphasize promoting democracy in Mexico until quite recently.

At the same time, the huge volume of immigration between the two neighbors, most of which is temporary in nature, has meant that millions of Mexicans have been exposed directly to United States culture and the United States political system. Other United States cultural impacts include Hollywood movies, television, and popular music, among other things. Many members of the Mexican political and economic elite have been educated in United States universities. In this interchange, the example of the world's oldest democracy has been conveyed to Mexicans of all social classes. Of course that message has not always been uniformly positive. Many Mexicans who come to the United States as undocumented workers learn about racial discrimination and the circumvention of the law rather than about equality before the law. Yet, on balance, the impact of social interactions between the two nations has promoted democracy in Mexico.

### Conclusions

In the latter decades of the twentieth century there was *mixed* evidence that both supported and undermined the prospects for democracy in Mexico, the country's failure to meet many of the main conditions for democracy is consistent with the notion that, under these circumstances, democracy was not likely to succeed (or come about in the first place), and that some form of authoritarianism was likely to prevail. At the same time, several factors (such as the middle class) held out the possibility that democracy would take hold in the aftermath of Fox's defeat of the PRI. We'll take another look at these ten conditions later in this chapter and see what they tell us about democracy's future in Mexico.

## Economic Development

The political system that Lázaro Cárdenas built survived long after the policy direction he represented no longer held sway. Presidents coming to power after 1940 were much friendlier to business interests than Cárdenas was. After World War II, Mexico began to implement an economic development strategy centered on **import-substituting industrialization (ISI)**, ***which substituted domestically produced goods for foreign imports.*** The country's relatively large and growing population permitted Mexican manufacturers of formerly imported products to have privileged access to a large market of consumers, especially among the middle and working classes of the rapidly growing cities, as long as foreign suppliers were prohibited from selling their goods to Mexico. High tariffs on imported finished goods as well as import licensing and non-tariff barriers to trade effectively promoted Mexico's "infant industries" in the postwar decades, and the economy and industrial employment took off. A class of Mexican industrialists who had close links to the political elite grew out of the ISI policy. To promote industrial development, the state made large investments in infrastructure, especially around Mexico City, where ISI-oriented industries tended to locate. In addition, the official labor movement, which was tightly associated with the PRI, practiced wage restraint. It advocated a philosophy of economic nationalism, promoting the national interest of industrialization in lieu of Marxist-style class conflict.

The result came to be known as the "Mexican miracle." From the mid 1950s until the mid 1970s, Mexico's economy grew at rates of 6 to 7 percent per year, while inflation remained below 5 percent.

Once a largely rural, agricultural nation, Mexico urbanized extremely rapidly in the fifty years between 1940 and 1990. Whereas the country was 22 percent urban in 1940, 72 percent of the population lived in cities by 1990. Government investments modernized the nation's transportation system. Illiteracy, once characteristic of half the population, was nearly eliminated.

Yet the Mexican miracle did not spread its benefits equitably across the population. Because of the emphasis on ISI and the growing urban population, Mexican governments after Cárdenas tended to grant government credit to larger, commercial farmers at the expense of the *ejidatorios* who had been granted land for the community in the agrarian reforms of the 1930s. Continuing poverty among rural villagers coexisted with the income gains of industrialists, the middle classes, and to a lesser extent, organized labor. Meanwhile, new generations of villagers fled their rural poverty, moving to the cities where they lived in the impoverished neighborhoods that mushroomed around Mexico City, Monterrey, Puebla, and other cities.[30] Few of these new urban poor were able to land the jobs protected by the labor movement, so their wages remained low. Many others were unable to land wage-paying jobs at all, becoming itinerant salespeople or domestic workers. Mexico's distribution of income has been among the most inequitable in the world, rivaling that of Brazil, with the richest 20 percent of the population sharing nearly 60 percent of national income, while the poorest half of the society has had to make do with less than 12 percent of the nation's income (see table 2.3). For the poorer half of Mexican society, the years since 1940 have hardly been miraculous.

Another outlet for the rural poor has been emigration to the United States. Emigration has often been called Mexico's "safety valve," a means for venting the pressures associated with a rate of population growth that has outpaced the growth of jobs. Millions of Mexicans have made the trek to the north over the past half century. In the past, most went with the intention of staying only temporarily, just long enough to earn sufficient money to support a growing family, generate the capital to improve the family's housing back home, or invest in a small business or truck or taxi. Many who worked temporarily in agriculture, construction, or manufacturing jobs in the United States would return home. In recent years, however, Mexicans increasingly have come to consider migration as a permanent solution to their lack of economic opportunity at home. Because most Mexicans have family members or friends from their villages or neighborhoods living in the United States, the other side of the border has come to be regarded as less foreign and less forbidding a place to move to. Moreover, they can use those family and neighborhood connections to secure employment, which makes it easier for them to consider bringing their families along. The ratio of young women to young men in the migrant pool has increased in recent years, too.

For Mexico, the earnings of migrants to the United States have served as an important source of foreign exchange. It is not surprising that the Mexican government would therefore prefer to see the border remain relatively open. Yet, as we mentioned above, efforts by President Fox to convince the United States to ease border restrictions on labor migration ran into a wall after the September 11 attacks. Fox is the first Mexican president to have openly admitted that his nation depends heavily on remittances from Mexicans working in the United States, seeking to make a virtue of migrant labor rather than trying to deny the importance of that labor flow.

The Mexican experience with ISI thus brought mixed results, just as it did for most nations that chose to follow an industrialization strategy largely focused on producing manufactured products for the domestic market. The state, as the "rector" of the economy, promoted industrial development that certainly benefited millions of Mexicans, but there were many unexpected consequences of that industrialization. The cities exploded, the rural poor could not be adequately absorbed into the labor force, income remained maldistributed, and eventually, the state developed a large presence in the economy that threatened the private sector.

ISI had its last stand in Mexico in the 1970s. Activist president *Luis Echeverría* (1970–76) sought to reintroduce the populist policies of Cárdenas, including new land reforms, greater government spending on social programs, and more state ownership of industry. He thereby provoked a conflict with the private sector, which ended with massive capital flight and the first devaluation of the peso since the 1950s. His handpicked successor and boyhood friend, *José López Portillo* (1976–82), initially mended relations with the private sector, a move aided by discoveries of large petroleum reserves off Mexico's Gulf coast. However, his government also spent billions of dollars (borrowed from Western banks with future oil revenues as collateral) in order to please nearly all constituencies: businesspeople, the poor, oil and construction workers, and the middle class. When the high oil prices of the late 1970s plummeted in 1981, however, Mexico was faced with a cash flow problem of global proportions. The threat that Mexico would default on its foreign loans in 1982 set off a global debt crisis. Capital flight and another devaluation accompanied the economic calamity, to which López Portillo responded by nationalizing privately owned banks in the last great act of Mexican populism.

Eventually, with the help of the U.S. government, Mexico's foreign debt was restructured. López Portillo's successors, *Miguel de la Madrid* (1982–88) and *Carlos Salinas* (1988–94), finally abandoned the ISI strategy of development, opting instead for incorporation into the rapidly globalizing world economy in an attempt to position Mexico as an exporter of manufactured goods, especially to the United States. Mexico's decisions to join the General Agreement on Tariffs and Trade (GATT) and to become a part of NAFTA cemented the redirection of the nation's economic strategy. (In 1995 the GATT was succeeded by the World Trade Organization.) That new strategy, called **neo-liberalism**, ***has involved the lowering of the nation's barriers to imports, a reduction in state subsidies for staples*** (like cooking oil and tortillas) ***and in expenditures on social welfare, and the privatization of most of the state-owned enterprises accumulated since the 1930s.*** Foreign investment in Mexico, once discouraged by laws that limited foreign ownership of enterprises to 49 percent of a company's stocks, has been welcomed into the country with fewer encumbrances.

Neo-liberalism has led to a dramatic restructuring of Mexican industry. Much new investment has improved the competitiveness of Mexican exporters. Many entrepreneurs have made billions of pesos as new opportunities have come their way, not least by being able to acquire equity stakes (stocks) in newly privatized firms. After nearly a decade of economic depression (and that's not too harsh a label to apply to the 1980s), Mexico's economy began to grow again under Salinas. However, the adjustments associated with the "lost decade" of the 1980s and the economic restructuring of the 1990s have been borne disproportionately by the poor. The end of subsidies for consumer staples hurt the poor much more than it did the middle classes. Bankruptcies by (mostly smaller) firms unable to compete with foreign imports led to layoffs of workers. State employees saw their salary increases lag behind inflation, making their real incomes decline. Overall, real wages may have dropped as much as 41.5 percent between 1983 and 1988.[31] To make up for lost income, families had to send a second or third wage earner out into the work force, or the principal breadwinner had to take on additional income-earning tasks. The size of the "informal sector" of the economy—jobs where income is not reported, such as itinerant sales (street vendors), housekeeping, and repair work—grew in the 1980s. (Of course, the informal economy is, by its nature, nearly impossible to measure.)

The financial crisis at the beginning of *Ernesto Zedillo's* presidency in 1994–95, described in chapter 14, demonstrates that the restructured Mexican economy remained vulnerable to sudden international capital flows associated with the loss of investor confidence, perhaps even more so than in the 1970s and early 1980s. In the year following that downturn, Mexicans suffered yet one more sustained period of unemployment and job changes. The accumulated economic crises of the past quarter century, coming after the apparent successes of the Mexican miracle, have played an enormous role in undermining the legitimacy of the PRI's rule, as we will describe in the next section. For the future, Mexicans certainly will be less confident of the state's ability to guarantee economic progress, a confidence they enjoyed during the heyday of the revolutionary regime's rule.

### Mexico's Protracted Democratization

Although many scholars were impressed with the stability imposed on Mexico by the postrevolutionary PRI elite, the party's monopoly of power has now ended. The Mexico that enters the twenty-first century differs substantially from the Mexico of the third quarter of the twentieth century. A president from a party other than the PRI now sits in the President's chair and no party commands a majority in either house of Congress. As of the beginning of 2006, politicians from the PAN were sitting in the governors' chairs of Aguascalientes, Baja California, Guanajuato, Jalisco, Morelos, Querétaro, San Luis Potosí, and Yucatán. Governors representing the Democratic Revolutionary Party (PRD) ruled in Baja California Sur, Guerrero, Michoacán, and Zacatecas. Almost all of Mexico's largest cities and many of its state capitals, including Mexico City, Guadalajara, Monterrey, and Ciudad Juárez, have been headed by PAN or PRD mayors and city councils. These opposition governments have challenged centralism.[32] Mexicans of all social backgrounds have joined popular organizations and social movements in the past thirty years, attempting to circumvent the clientelist linkages preferred by the PRI and created by organizations associated with it. The top electoral agency in the country, the Federal Electoral Institute (IFE), has gained autonomy from the PRI and the government. Maybe the most spectacular development of all was that a rebellion of indigenous (Indian) people in Chiapas has been able to stand up to the regime for over six years. The *Zapatistas* in Chiapas were not able to get the PRI government to concede to their demands for local autonomy and a new development strategy, but neither was the PRI government willing to destroy them militarily in the way that it would likely have done a generation ago.

What factors account for these changes in the political system? The main sources of change can be summarized in two categories: the *modernization of Mexican society* and major *political failures by the ruling elite* and its party, the PRI.

**Modernization** First, Mexico's economic modernization, a process at work since the 1940s, altered the social structure upon which the PRI's hegemony was based. The Mexico of the 1980s, when political change began to accelerate, had become more urban, more educated, and more influenced by the outside world than had the Mexico of the 1930s when Lázaro Cárdenas built the PRI-dominated regime. Consequently, Mexicans in the 1980s were less subject to the control of the PRI's corporatist organizations, more informed about alternatives to the PRI, and more attracted to the democratic practices observed outside Mexico, especially in the United States. A more complex social structure meant that public policy could not please all Mexicans all the time. As economic development proceeded, support for the opposition grew. In more modern parts of the country, especially in the cities, the opposition performed much better than in the past. However, economic modernization cannot by itself explain the sudden fall in the PRI's electoral fortunes in 1988 and thereafter.

**Policy and Political Failures** Equally important in the erosion of the PRI's dominance was a series of policy and political failures that delegitimated the PRI's rule. The first came in 1968 when a large student movement that began as an objection to government interference in the National Autonomous University (UNAM) developed into a protest against the regime's development strategy. Students and others questioned the government's priorities when it spent millions of dollars hosting the 1968 Summer Olympics in Mexico City while poverty remained widespread throughout the country. A political standoff between students and the government ended tragically when troops fired on a large assembly, killing a still unknown number of protesters. In that event the regime lost the support of the intelligentsia and found its democratic facade torn away.

A second blow to the regime's image came with the debt crisis of the 1980s. The debt crisis revealed that the government had squandered the opportunities presented by the oil boom of the late 1970s. When López Portillo nationalized the banks in order to halt capital flight, he angered much of the private sector and the middle class, leading them into more vigorous electoral activity in support of the PAN. Miguel de la Madrid's administration chose to respond to the debt crisis with an austerity program that became a liberalization project that promoted the business sector. Salinas accelerated the liberalization program. The pain resulting from austerity and liberalization severely afflicted peasants and workers, the very sectors whose support played such a key role in PRI electoral victories. The sudden change in the development strategy also produced severe divisions within the PRI. In

1987, *Cuauhtémoc* (kwah-oo-TAY-mock) *Cárdenas,* the son of the man who had shaped the PRI, defected from the party and declared his candidacy at the head of a union of left-wing parties and groups known as the *National Democratic Front (FDN).* Mexico's "lost decade of the 1980s," during which economic growth stagnated, contributed significantly to the growing dissatisfaction of many sectors of the society with the government.

Moreover, de la Madrid's administration responded poorly to a devastating earthquake that hit Mexico City in 1985, providing too little assistance too late in the view of the millions of capital city residents made homeless by the tremor. Many Mexicans questioned the government's capacity to perform its most important tasks in the aftermath of its tardy response to the earthquake. Those made homeless by the tremor eventually formed their own organizations to help them deal with their predicaments, organizations that pointedly refused to be incorporated into the PRI's organizational structure and that questioned the lack of democratic representation in Mexico City (which was still governed by a presidential appointee).

Cárdenas's presidential candidacy, the first by a PRI maverick since 1952, ruptured the stability of the hegemonic party system. His success at drawing millions to his campaign rallies and then to vote for him indicated significant disaffection from the ruling elite. To defeat Cárdenas, the PRI and the government had to take extraordinary measures, even by their own standards. The electoral authorities' computer allegedly "crashed" on the night of the election, the vote tallies of nearly half of the polling places were never reported, and those ballots were subsequently destroyed. Even then, Carlos Salinas received only half the votes. Consequently, he entered office with the legitimacy of his presidency questioned by substantial portions of the Mexican population, the effective leader of a party whose capacity to carry elections had come under question.

Salinas's presidency became a defining era in Mexico's development. Demonstrating his political acumen, Salinas went right to work to restore the legitimacy he had lost in his contested election. He jailed corrupt union bosses who had unofficially supported Cárdenas's candidacy, including leaders of the powerful petroleum workers union. And he accelerated the privatization of state-owned firms and the reduction of Mexico's high barriers to trade. Quickly Salinas became admired at home and abroad for his forceful leadership.

His two most controversial acts were to create NAFTA and to reform Article 27 of the constitution. We'll discuss NAFTA later in this chapter. The reform of Article 27 essentially put an end to land reform in Mexico. Land reform had been moribund for many years, the spectacular actions of populist president Echeverría notwithstanding. With this reform, Salinas made it possible for the *ejido* land, which was owned in common by local communities, to pass to private investors.

To many, the Salinas presidency had uncomfortable similarities to the reign of Porfirio Diáz. Ignoring the needs of peasants was one of those parallels. Another was a pattern of decisions that seemed to enrich the president's friends. Among those beneficiaries was the Salinas family itself. Raúl Salinas, the president's brother, stashed away tens of millions of dollars in Swiss bank accounts. When these revelations came to light, Salinas quickly became the most reviled of Mexico's ex-presidents. But whether loved or hated, Salinas put an end to ISI and Mexican populism, forcing his country into the new century with a new development model.

## Manifestations of Political Change

Aspects of Mexico's transition to democracy include the rise of two parties (PAN and PRD) that have defeated the former ruling party in important elections, the development of a freer press, and the emergence of many popular organizations and social movements. These forces together have propelled Mexico into a democratic era in which the PRI's string of victories and its control of governments at all levels have come to an end.

**Opposition Parties and Electoral Reform** The first significant electoral reform came in 1977. It relaxed the rules that had previously restricted the registration of opposition parties. It also reserved one quarter of the seats (100 of 400) in the Chamber of Deputies for opposition parties, selected on the basis of proportional representation, and instituted a mixed system for elections to the legislature roughly similar to those used in Germany and

TABLE 22.3

**Recent Elections to the Chamber of Deputies**

| | PAN | | PRI | | PRD | | Others | |
|---|---|---|---|---|---|---|---|---|
| Year | % of Vote | No. of Seats | % of Vote | No. of Seats | % of Vote | No. of Seats | % of Votes | No. of Seats |
| 1991 | 18 | 89 | 61 | 320 | 8 | 41 | 13 | 50 |
| 1994 | 27 | 119 | 50 | 301 | 17 | 70 | 6 | 10 |
| 1997 | 27 | 121 | 39 | 239 | 26 | 125 | 9 | 15 |
| 2000 | 41 | 223 | 39 | 209 | 20 | 68 | 0 | 0 |
| 2003 | 33 | 153 | 37 | 224 | 19 | 95 | 12 | 28 |
| 2006 | 34 | 206 | 29 | 123 | 30 | 158 | 7 | 13 |

The percentages of the vote reported in table 22.3 are the percentages of the total votes received by parties eligible for seats (that is, those receiving more than 2.0 percent of the vote in 1997 and 2000, or 1.5 percent in earlier elections).
In 2000, PAN ran with the Mexican Green Party (PVEM) in the Alliance for Change, with the PAN receiving 208 seats and the PVEM 15. The PRD joined with four smaller parties in the Alliance for Mexico, from which the PRD received 40 seats and the other parties 28. In 2003 the PRI and the PVEM ran in coalition in several states. In 2006 the PRI and PVEM formed the Alliance for Mexico coalition; the PRD, the Labor Party (PT), and the Convergence Party ran in coalition as the Coalition for the Good of All.
*Source:* Instituto Federal Electoral.

Japan. The remaining 300 seats are chosen on the basis of single-member districts. (See chapter 8 for a discussion of these electoral systems.) Opposition parties were stimulated by this reform and by new rules that lowered the requirements for registration as parties. However, since the barriers to entry for new parties were set quite low, the opposition parties of the left remained divided and small. In 1986, the de la Madrid government doubled the number of deputies chosen by proportional representation to 200 (increasing the Chamber of Deputies to 500 seats at the same time). Since then, the PRI and the other parties have negotiated back and forth about how the 200 proportional representation seats should be allotted among the parties. The current formula limits the extent to which a party can be overrepresented in the Chamber of Deputies to 8 percent. In other words, a party must receive at least 42 percent of the national vote in order to obtain an absolute majority of seats in the lower house of Congress.

Other electoral reforms in the 1990s leveled the playing field for the parties, reducing the advantages held by the PRI as an incumbent party. These included making the agency that oversees elections (the IFE) autonomous from the government and reforming campaign financing so that the opposition parties were not at a severe disadvantage compared to the PRI. These reforms were promulgated largely to bolster the legitimacy of the political regime in the aftermath of the crises described earlier. But electoral reform contributed to the effective emergence of challengers to the PRI, especially the Democratic Revolutionary Party (PRD) and the National Action Party (PAN). (See table 22.3.)

*Democratic Revolutionary Party (PRD)* Cuauhtémoc Cárdenas's presidential campaign in 1988 enjoyed the support of a wide range of leftwing parties, some independent and some that had collaborated with the PRI. These parties initially banded together under the umbrella of the National Democratic Front (FDN). When Cárdenas subsequently proposed forming a single, united ***party of the left*** to consolidate and channel the gains of 1988, three collaborationist parties left the FDN. The remaining parties eventually took over the old Mexican Socialist Party and changed its name to the **Democratic Revolutionary Party (PRD).** Although former socialists composed an important contingent of the original PRD at the leadership level, they were gradually overwhelmed by ex-PRI members who defected to the PRD. The PRD has had to deal with a number of internal struggles over ideological and strategic issues as well as personal differences among leaders.

Revolutionary nationalism has motivated most followers of the PRD, but most also recognize that the former policies of economic nationalism and ISI will not lead Mexico to economic prosperity. Although his critics pointed to López Orbrador's populist spending policies when he headed the

Mexico City government and to his criticism of NAFTA to suggest he would represent a return to revolutionary nationalism, his policy proposals stressed fiscal responsibility. PRD militants continue to hold very bad feelings toward the PRI because of the 1988 elections and the repression of many party militants in the years that followed, especially in southern states like Michoacán and Guerrero. The party therefore rejected compromise with the PRI and its governments over election results and legislative proposals for electoral reform.

As a party that came together out of other organizations of the left and from the defection of a substantial portion of the left wing of the PRI, the PRD remains faction-ridden. PRD leaders have had to trade off the need to reward those PRD members who have supported them for many years with the desire to attract new PRD members who come from other organizations—both popular organizations and the PRI itself. Squabbles among leaders have been widely reported in the press, contributing little to the party's public image. These internal weaknesses have made the consolidation of the PRD as the party of the left somewhat disappointing to those who saw a bright opportunity in the 1988 *cardenista* campaign.

In federal elections in both 1991 and 1994, the PRD finished third. It performed much better in the 1997 federal elections and in the first election for the head of government of the Federal District (Mexico City), won by Cárdenas. Compared with the historical performance of the independent left, the PRD's 1994 and 1997 finishes were a significant advance. Fox's performance in the 2000 federal elections dealt a temporary setback to the PRD, which lost more than half of its seats in the Chamber of Deputies (see table 22.3), but in 2003 the PRD made a modest comeback.

The PRD's control of the Mexico City government since 1997 has meant that the party and its popular mayors have been able to reward supporters and lure potential voters with public spending projects. But it remains to be seen whether spending in the capital can effectively convince voters throughout Mexico that the PRD is a credible alternative to either the PAN or the PRI. Like the PAN (see below), the PRD is tending in the direction of a catch-all party that is anchored on the left, but in catching many former PRI activists as well as people from many other progressive currents, it has built into its organization much of the historical fractiousness of the Mexican left.

*The National Action Party (PAN)* In 1985 and 1986, the **National Action Party (PAN)** was subjected to PRI-engineered electoral fraud, prompting its leaders to organize massive demonstrations and hunger strikes in defense of the party's vote. Despite these open displays of discontent, the PAN ***since its founding has been the main party of legal and gradual reform.*** The influx of middle-class and business militants like Fox into the party in the early 1980s (in reaction to López Portillo's nationalization of the banks) may have made the party seem more stridently opposed to state intervention in the economy than ever before, but the PAN has always stood for constraints on state power. Because of its pro-market orientation and its middle-class base, the PAN's opponents often depict the party as being on the right. Although Fox's voting base crossed the whole ideological spectrum, since the 1980s the PAN's following has become concentrated among two: often incompatible segments of Mexican society, social conservatives and supporters of free-market policies.

Salinas's accession to the presidency and the Cárdenas surge presented both the president and the PAN leadership with good reasons to seek accommodation in the 1990s. Salinas needed the PAN to help pass his legislation curtailing state power and initiating economic policy changes that the PAN had favored for decades, while the PAN needed Salinas's acknowledgment of its electoral victories to help meet the growing challenge of Cárdenas and the left. The accommodation between Salinas and the PAN proved highly successful for both sides. When the PAN won the gubernatorial races in Baja California and Chihuahua in 1989 and 1992, respectively, Salinas was able to point to PAN victories as evidence of a political opening to the opposition. The PAN also achieved some electoral reforms, while the PRD was left looking intransigent on this issue.

Overall, as the PAN has advanced electorally, the experience of governing large states and municipalities has produced leaders capable of presenting themselves as realistic presidential candidates in the future, perhaps no one more so than **Vicente Fox**, former governor of Guanajuato and Mexico's president from 2001 to 2006.

## PROFILE: Vicente Fox

Millions of Mexicans hope to remember July 2, 2000, as the day they brought democracy to their country. On that election day, 2.5 million more Mexicans voted for Vicente Fox of the National Action Party (known as the PAN) than voted for Francisco Labastida of the ruling Institutional Revolutionary Party, the PRI. The PRI had controlled the Mexican presidency for seventy-one years, but it was now relinquishing power at last. After the polls closed and the television networks broadcast the results of exit polls that indicated that—unexpectedly—Fox had won, Mexicans streamed into the streets to celebrate what they regarded as a vote for change. They agreed with Fox's campaign slogan: *!Ya!* (Enough Already!).

If one had to choose the profile of the ideal candidate to end the PRI's long lock on the presidency, Vicente Fox would come very close to matching it. Tall, handsome, brash, and successful in business, Fox was a perfect candidate for the first Mexican presidential campaign largely waged by television. While hardly a perfect embodiment of the PAN, a party he had been active in only since 1988, Fox represented perhaps the best of the former businessmen who chose to enter politics in the 1980s to oust what they saw as the increasingly corrupt PRI from office.

Vicente Fox was born in 1942, the grandson of an American immigrant of Irish descent and the son of a Spanish-born mother. His mother's foreign birth disqualified him for the presidency until a constitutional amendment was passed as part of the 1993 electoral reforms to eliminate that obstacle. Fox was educated at Jesuit schools in Mexico and Wisconsin and attended college at Iberoamerican University in Mexico City. He later took an executive education course at Harvard.

Before entering politics, Fox rose through the ranks of Coca-Cola's Mexican and Central American division, eventually becoming its president. However, he declined an offer to take charge of the company's entire Latin American operation, choosing instead to go into a family business in Guanajuato—he and his brother raised vegetables for export and produced shoes. An avid horseman, Fox also owns a ranch.

Manuel Clouthier, the party's rabble-rousing 1988 presidential candidate, drew Fox into the PAN along with many other mostly northern businessmen. These new PAN members shared Clouthier's view that the PAN had to challenge the PRI head on, with no holds barred. For their more audacious approach to opposition politics, these PAN members became known as the barbarians of the north. They were distrusted by PAN leaders in Mexico City who were more comfortable with an elitist approach to opposition politics, seeing their role as a "loyal opposition" more than as true contenders for power.

Vicente Fox hails supporters after winning the presidency.

Fox won a seat in the Chamber of Deputies in 1988. In 1991, he ran for governor of Guanajuato but lost in a highly contested, fraud-ridden election. Eventually, President Salinas had to intervene in post-election conflict, appointing a PAN member (but not Fox) as interim governor. In 1994, Fox ran for governor again and won handily. As governor, he put his efforts into promoting Guanajuato's agricultural and manufacturing industry in international markets, traveling far and wide to open markets and attract investment capital. As governor, Fox was a supporter of NAFTA.

Knowing that the national leadership of his party distrusted him, Fox realized that to win the 2000 PAN presidential nomination he would have to develop popular support early. To help to finance his pre-campaign and to gain new supporters, Fox created an organization called *Amigos de Fox* outside the structure of the PAN. Amigos de Fox represented a major effort to transcend the financial and human limitations of Mexico's opposition parties by building a mass, nonpartisan association dedicated to electing a single politician. Fox sought to court friends among the political elite, too. His campaign team included as advisors several Mexican intellectuals, most notably Jorge Castañeda and Adolfo Aguilar Zinser, leftist political analysts and activists who saw in Fox an opportunity to evict the PRI from the presidency.

Fox led a rollicking campaign, another of his contributions to Mexican politics. He dressed in what we would call Western gear—boots, jeans, an open-collared shirt, a cowboy hat, and a giant "Fox" belt buckle—to emphasize his popular roots and to argue that he had been a working man all his life. Political commentators and his opponents dwelt on what they regarded as the vulgar language Fox used on the stump. Negative campaigning had never been a major element of Mexican electoral politics, but it entered in a massive way in 1999–2000.

Fox was hardly the typical Mexican candidate, and not only because he did not hail from the PRI. A divorced Catholic raising four children—all adopted—when he was campaigning, Fox was romantically linked with his spokeswoman and political advisor, Marta Sahagún. To celebrate his first anniversary in office, Fox married Sahagún, who herself became a prominent contender for the 2006 presidency.

More than anything, Fox's message of change—throwing the rascals out—won him the presidency. Governing Mexico proved more difficult for Fox than campaigning, however. During his term of office, Mexico was saddled with a constitutional structure in which a presidential system coexisted with a congress in which no party held a majority. Fox suffered from comparisons with past Mexican presidents who had enjoyed large majorities in that congress. A pattern of policy making in which PRI presidents dictated to congress had become the norm by which presidential performance was measured. Fox's inability to push through major policy initiatives may have looked like presidential failure when it was little more than a reflection of the existing political constraints. At the same time, President Fox made errors in his handling of both his own party and the PRI. PAN and PRI legislators and their leaders had some incentive to pursue effective public policies because they could then go to the electorate with evidence of their parties' accomplishments in meeting Mexico's urgent challenges. Fox, however, did not effectively court rivals either within his own party or in the former ruling party, with the consequence that major policy and political reform initiatives were left on the drawing board.

In the absence of a majority in the congress, President Fox often chose to play to his strength as a campaigner by going to the people to try to put pressure on the congress to pass his legislative agenda. His presidency was marked by frequent trips outside the capital to trumpet the administration's policy agenda. Like other presidents facing domestic political challenges, Fox tried to focus more attention on his administration's foreign policy initiatives, the most important of which was his effort to gain an agreement on immigration with the United States. Although Fox and George W. Bush got on well—Bush scheduled Fox as the first head of state to visit Washington in September 2001—the aftermath of the attacks of September 11 forced immigration reform off the agenda in the United States until 2006, a major setback for Fox.

Fox's term will not be remembered for policy breakthroughs. Mexicans, however, will remember Fox as the man who ended the PRI's seventy-one-year hold on the presidency.

---

Although primarily a party of the middle class, the PAN could not have won the gubernatorial races it has won without attracting working-class voters. Hence, since 1988 the PAN has converted itself into a catch-all party with a somewhat right-of-center ideology. But this conversion is less the result of changes in ideology than changes in circumstance, principally the rise of the rival PRD.

When he assumed the presidency, Fox appointed many PAN leaders to his cabinet and other key administrative posts. However, because his cabinet selections also included businessmen and leftist intellectuals, Fox's relationship with the party was troubled at times. At the same time, the PAN was regarded as the party in power by most Mexicans; so when they voted in midterm elections in 2003, Mexicans punished the PAN for Fox's inability to achieve the many reforms he had promised when elected three years earlier. The PAN's congressional delegation plunged from 206 members in 2000–2003 to 153 for the 2003–2006 term, but rebounded to 206 for 2006–2009.

*Other Parties* In the past twenty-five years there have been a number of other opposition parties. Some have contested elections either as members of political alliances with one of the major parties or separately. Mexican electoral rules since 1977 have generally favored the development of small parties. A cynical way to look at this phenomenon (but probably the correct way) is to say that the PRI encouraged the fragmentation of the independent parties of opposition by keeping the barriers to creation of new parties low.[33] Those low barriers tended to encourage the fragmentation of the left in the late 1970s and 1980s, until the emergence of the PRD. Only the Mexican Green Party (PVEM), a party whose commitment to the environment is questioned by knowledgeable Mexicans, has proven capable of attracting a significant vote share (over 6 percent in 2003) and acting independently in the Congress.

## The 2006 Elections

The 2006 elections demonstrated that the former opposition parties have now become the main contenders for power in Mexico. The 2006 presidential elections confounded many pundits with their twists and turns, even before the unfolding of the post-election drama described in the introduction to this chapter. A year before the election, Calderón was not expected to be the PAN nominee. However, he took advantage of his status as the consummate PAN insider to win the PAN primary. From well before the beginning of the formal election season in January 2006, López Obrador was viewed as the odds-on favorite. He led in public opinion polls until after the first presidential debate in April 2006. But, overconfident of his lead in the polls, López Obrador chose to skip the first debate, and this cost him his lead. Final pre-election polls yielded results so close as to be within the margin of error. Meanwhile, the PRI candidate, Roberto Madrazo, ran a terrible campaign and finished a distant third.

López Obrador contested the election's outcome from the time the polls closed, calling his supporters into the streets on several occasions to put pressure on the electoral authorities to re-count the votes. He staged an "election by acclamation" in which those present at a rally on Mexico's Independence Day "elected" López Obrador by a show of hands, and he held an "inauguration" ceremony for an alternative government on November 20, the anniversary of the onset of the Mexican Revolution. While López Obrador challenged the preliminary outcome, Calderón waited patiently until the Federal Electoral Tribunal (TRIFE) declared him elected on September 5, two months after the ballots had been cast. Although Calderón eventually prevailed in the legal struggles over the results, he took power while still needing to build a consensus to rule his nation. The PAN failed to take a majority in congress, winning just over 40 percent of the Chamber of Deputy seats. To govern, Calderón will probably have to find a way to cooperate with the PRI, because the former governing party now holds the balance of power in the legislature.

## The Media and Civil Society

**The Media and Politics** The broadcast media's traditional prejudice in favor of the PRI at election time once paralleled its overall uncritical attitude toward the Mexican state and toward close U.S.-Mexican relations. The major private television network, Televisa, which owns major radio stations as well, started out with close ties to former president Miguel Alemán (1946–52). The state owns one of the other major television stations. The uncritical attitude of television news toward the government inhibited public debate about major issues essential to democracy, especially because the majority of Mexicans rely on television and radio for their news. However, campaign finance reforms and new laws mandating that broadcasters provide equal time to all major parties, which took effect before the 1997 midterm elections, weakened some of the excessively pro-government, pro-PRI orientation of the broadcast media. In the 2000 elections the broadcast media finally broke its longstanding practice of favoring the PRI in news coverage. The decision of Televisa and its rival, TV Azteca, to be neutral in their coverage contributed significantly to Fox's successful campaign in 2000.

In contrast to the relatively pro-regime attitudes of broadcasters, the print media have become much more critical of the political system and of specific public policies over the past twenty-five years. Mexico City and the cities of the north have been especially well served by newspapers that have shown a willingness to criticize the government and in which opposition politicians and intellectuals could add their perspectives to the debate about public policy. Newspapers such as *Unomásuno* and *La Jornada* and magazines such as *Proceso* and *Nexos* gave a voice to the left and permitted investigative journalists to publish articles that revealed government corruption and described the way some critical public decisions were made. The Mexico City daily *Reforma,* launched by a media enterprise that published Monterrey's *El Norte,* has set a new standard for investigative reporting in Mexico. Several critical intellectuals have written regular columns for *Reforma, La Jornada,* and *Proceso,* meaning that anti-PRI perspectives got circulated before 2000. However, these newspapers are not the most widely read periodicals in Mexico. Mexico now has a free and critical press, essential to democracy.[34]

**Popular Organizations and Civil Society** Mexico, like several other Latin American countries, has experienced a surge in popular organizations and social movements, especially in the aftermath of the 1968 student movement. These organizations have varied widely in their size, the issues they address, and the extent to which they try to maintain a distance from the government. In the 1980s, popular movements, most of which had sprung up at the grass roots in poor urban neighborhoods as well as among peasant communities, began to make connections among themselves, thus forming networks of similar groups that began sharing ideas and seeking collective responses to the government. Many of those who have studied such social movements argued that they held more promise for a democratization of Mexican life than the political parties and that the flowering of popular organizations witnessed in the past two decades indicates that many Mexicans increasingly wish to create a more participatory society.[35]

Popular organizations typically begin with very local objectives that are closely related to the material needs of their members, such as clean water or other city services, the regularization of land titles, or the government's response to the 1985 Mexican earthquake. Veterans of the 1968 student movement organized many such organizations, but others have sprung up as the result of local leaders' initiatives. Popular movements often have an explicit commitment to internal democracy. Moreover, in both membership and leadership, popular movements tend to redress the gender imbalance otherwise evident in Mexican public life.

In the 1970s and 1980s, popular movements more heavily emphasized socioeconomic issues, and they sought to avoid being captured by the PRI's corporatist structures. Until the 1988 presidential candidacy of Cárdenas, most of these organizations were explicitly abstentionist in electoral politics, seeing electoral politics as an arena of corruption and a distraction from more important local concerns that would never be affected by electoral politics anyway. In 1988, though, after six years of economic austerity under de la Madrid, a time marked by the Mexican government's unusually low responsiveness to the needs of the poor, some popular organizations and their members supported the Cárdenas candidacy, since Cárdenas promised to reject the neo-liberal development model and return Mexico to a concern about social justice.

In addition to the growth of popular movements concerned primarily with the socioeconomic needs of localities, Mexico has witnessed the emergence of movements more focused on human rights and dedicated to fairer elections and a more democratic regime. These organizations have broader membership and a more national scope than the popular movements just described. Middle-class professionals constitute a far larger share of their membership than in urban popular movements.

Human rights associations began to form in the late 1970s and early 1980s and proliferated in number. A relatively freer print media that was willing to report instances of political corruption, police abuse, and political violence; support from international human rights organizations; and a record of assassinations of Mexican journalists all helped to motivate this movement. The Catholic church and church-based groups have also contributed to the development of human rights associations. The Salinas government responded to the growth of attention to human rights by creating a National Human Rights Commission, staffed by highly respected persons committed to human rights who were permitted to investigate reported instances of human rights abuses.

During the 1994 election campaign, civic associations came into prominence because of their role (largely self-appointed) in watching over the electoral process. The best known of these was the *Civic Alliance,* a self-described nonpartisan network of organizations dedicated to protecting the right of Mexicans to have a free and fair electoral process. The development of such associations dedicated to promoting more democratic practices in Mexican politics contributed to a less authoritarian political system. In addition, the open sympathy of many such organizations and human rights groups toward the rebels in Chiapas served to constrain government abuses in putting down that rebellion and has kept the pressure on the government to find a political solution to the armed resistance there.

**Women and Politics** The democratization of Mexican politics has been accompanied by a greater inclusion of women in electoral politics and in the organizations of civil society. When the PRI had a near total monopoly on legislative seats and executive appointments, women's issues received relatively little attention in national politics. The personalism of presidential power in the 1970s and 1980s often meant that the women who managed to be appointed to high office were the family members or mistresses of the president, as under José López Portillo. The opposition's success at gaining congressional seats helped to move onto the national political agenda public policy issues that women's groups valued more highly—such as greater care for victims of sex crimes and more severe penalties for their assailants.

Greater political competition has spurred the parties to present more women candidates for office and to promote more women to important national-level positions. Women rank among the most influential leaders of the PRI and the PRD, and women have served as president or secretary general of those two parties. Among the most powerful leaders of the PRI is Elba Esther Gordillo, head of the teachers union. In addition, Amalia García served as PRD president and Rosario Robles as PRD mayor of Mexico City; both have led important factions of their party. Within the PAN, first lady Marta Sahagún de Fox was often mentioned as a potential presidential candidate.

Having a critical mass of women in the Congress and other positions of power seems essential to raising women's issues onto the national agenda. To that end, Mexico passed an electoral reform in 2002 that required all parties to present women in 30 percent of their congressional candidacies. In the 2003 midterm elections, this resulted in an increase of women elected from 16 percent to 23 percent. Moreover, it appears that the parties, which all complied with the law, did not discriminate against these women candidates by placing them in hard-to-win seats. Thus, women are making progress gaining access to political office.[36]

## NAFTA

On January 1, 1994, the **North American Free Trade Agreement (NAFTA)** came into effect, marking the culmination of President Carlos Salinas's efforts to shift the Mexican economy away from ISI toward a more outward orientation. ***With NAFTA, Mexico is bound by a treaty with the United States and Canada to retain its outward orientation.*** By joining NAFTA, Mexico's political elite made any attempt to reverse the neoliberal economic model much more difficult.

Salinas provided the chief impetus behind NAFTA. When Salinas sought to diversify sources of foreign investment in Mexico during a 1990 trip to Europe, he and his advisors worried that the fall of the Berlin wall would so refocus the attentions of the world's investors that Mexico would be left without the new capital it needed to make its economy competitive in world trade. The United States and Canada had recently signed their own bilateral free trade treaty. At that point, Salinas reluctantly decided that Mexico's economic future lay in the Western Hemisphere. Mexico would commit itself to a future linked to the United States, the overbearing neighbor whose economy had dominated the country for over a century.

Presidential domination of the Congress meant that the Mexican government would quickly approve the concept of a trade agreement, but many sectors of what Mexicans euphemistically call "public opinion"—the views of intellectuals and columnists and the privately stated views of politicians—saw the agreement as including far too many unwise concessions to the United States. On the U.S. side, first George H. W. Bush and then Bill Clinton trumpeted the many new advantages that NAFTA would bring U.S. industry, thereby unintentionally supporting the case of NAFTA's Mexican critics. U.S. critics have been especially concerned about the likelihood that American firms would relocate south of the border, where they believed labor laws and environmental regulations would be much less rigorously enforced. Eventually, to ensure the passage of the 1,100-page NAFTA treaty, the United States and Mexico had to negotiate a set of side agreements that allow for trinational panels of experts to be called to hear complaints about the non-enforcement of any member nation's labor or environmental laws, with the power to issue sanctions against the offending nation.

What does NAFTA mean for the Mexican economy? What does it portend for Mexican politics, especially for the promotion of Mexican democracy? Trade volumes have increased dramatically among the NAFTA countries, more rapidly than their trade with the rest of the world. Direct investment by U.S. firms in Mexico has contributed to trade growth because those firms have located in Mexico specifically to produce goods for export to the United States. However, businesses from Europe and Asia have also sought to get into the Mexican and the NAFTA market by investing there.

Because of the asymmetry in the sizes of the Mexican and the United States economies, we should not be surprised that the impact of NAFTA on Mexico has been considerably greater than on the United States. Some U.S. firms have relocated to Mexico, but they would likely have relocated somewhere else in the world to find lower labor costs, with or without NAFTA. Many Mexicans have suffered job dislocations since NAFTA came into effect; those working in small and medium-size firms have been especially vulnerable to bankruptcies, as have employees of privatized former state-owned firms. Many of these job losses or changes came about in the 1995 economic crisis associated with the peso devaluation of December 1994 (see chapter 14). Those involved in agriculture, especially peasant producers of corn (maize) and beans, have found it difficult to compete against cheap grain imports from the U.S. midwest. Again, to what extent NAFTA has been responsible for causing Mexicans to need to change jobs, as opposed to the overall changes in the economy brought about by Salinas and Zedillo, is not so clear. But some scholars have argued that, during its first ten years, NAFTA failed to create a significant number of jobs in Mexico and had an insignificant effect on job creation in the United States. By contrast, NAFTA's supporters have stressed its achievements.[37]

The renewed ties to Mexico created by NAFTA have engendered a sense of obligation on the part of the United States to promote its neighbor's economic development. A vivid example came during the 1994–95 peso crisis. After 1996, the Mexican economy grew rapidly. Subsequently, the U.S. recession spread to Mexico, making Vicente Fox's first three years as president difficult. The downside of being linked to the North American economy is that an economic downturn in the United States quickly spreads to Mexico. Of course, Mexico is not unique in this regard; globalization has meant that all countries are more affected by world economic trends than they used to be.

Some proponents of NAFTA argued that it would speed Mexico's transition to democracy. Their argument followed the standard account offered by modernization theory: NAFTA would promote a market economy and economic growth in Mexico. As a result, a middle class and economic pluralism would grow there. With a larger middle class and economic pluralism would come more demands for the liberalization of Mexico's political regime. In addition, with the interaction of the cultures in North America, more Mexicans would be exposed to democratic values and adopt them as their own.

Opponents of NAFTA expressed a less sanguine view. They generally argued that the economic dislocations associated with economic integration, especially in the countryside, would lead to political conflicts that the government would choose to repress. Furthermore, they said, the Mexican beneficiaries of economic integration would likely be a small group of very wealthy businesspeople who would become the owners of privatized firms or the Mexican partners of U.S. multinationals. These oligarchs would not want the Mexican masses to have even greater power as the result of democratization.

NAFTA does seem to have put Mexico higher on the agenda of U.S. politicians and political activists. Consequently, Mexican politics have come under greater scrutiny from abroad in the past fifteen years. Changes in communications technologies—satellite television broadcasts and the Internet—have played a significant role in keeping U.S. political figures attentive to Mexico, mostly for the good of democracy. During the course of NAFTA negotiations and the debate about its passage by the U.S. Senate, many linkages were developed between U.S. political activists and Mexican organizations and between U.S. and Mexican business groups. These binational links helped promote the liberalization of the PRI regime.

At the same time, conflict escalated in the Mexican countryside, best illustrated by the rebellion in Chiapas (see the next section) but by no means limited to it. A Mexican student strike in 1999–2000 ended up with a focus on the Mexican development model. In these conflicts, some activists and some representatives of Mexican police forces resorted to violence, and many political observers worried that the government would cover up examples of repression. A balanced assessment, however, ought to note that despite increased political conflict, the federal government generally exercised restraint, although some state and local authorities have been more willing to put down protesters.

## Issues in Mexican Politics

**Rebellion in Chiapas** To respond to their dissatisfaction with political institutions, some Mexicans joined opposition parties that eventually overturned the PRI electorally. Others sought to create new popular organizations that would function democratically and attempt to accomplish some of their objectives at which the national institutions have failed. We see a more extreme reaction with the rebellion in Chiapas.

The Chiapas uprising revealed the cross-cutting pressures on the Mexican elite and its difficult path to democracy. Many of the social reforms of the Mexican revolution had never reached Chiapas, an economically backward state where political violence and *caciquismo*—the rule of local despots (*caciques*)—reached notorious levels. Economic liberalization in the 1980s and 1990s meant that economic elites in Chiapas, such as ranchers and those engaged in lumbering in the rain forest, could benefit greatly by foreign trade. But most Chiapas residents, primarily of Indian heritage, found themselves increasingly marginalized economically, unable to survive on the small plots of land to which they had access and forced to search farther and farther afield for agricultural jobs that paid little. The Mexico City elite was content to allow regional strongmen to govern as they always had, so long as the economic liberalization project was unhindered. Human rights promoters, including Bishop Samuel Ruiz, however, had encouraged the organizing of popular organizations among the long-exploited indigenous communities of Chiapas.

Despite their political oppression, the people of Chiapas had a high capacity to express their democratic orientation and their real economic and political needs. When the Zapatista National Liberation Army (which took its name from Emiliano Zapata) rose up against the government on January 1, 1994, it effectively articulated its differences with the Salinas government and its development project. (It chose the day that NAFTA became effective to indicate its objection to economic liberalization.) The rebels found sympathy for their cause in both Chiapas and around the nation and the world. Indeed, many other popular organizations took up the cause of the Zapatistas in public demonstrations. The national and international press willingly published the communiques of Subcomandante Marcos, the rebels' leader, much to the government's embarrassment.

The Salinas government quickly recognized that in the age of satellite and other international electronic communication, it could not simply crush the Zapatistas militarily. Such a reaction would look too much like the act of a scared authoritarian regime, even though it was by no means clear that anything approaching a majority of Mexicans agreed with the Zapatistas' goals or their methods. Crushing the rebellion would have satisfied the president's neoliberal allies, but it likely would have greatly damaged the regime's reputation on human rights, even more than the rebellion had already done.

In 2000, the PAN's Vicente Fox advocated a negotiated settlement with the rebels as soon as possible. However, although the Congress eventually passed a law to protect the interests of Mexicans of indigenous heritage and permit self-rule for indigenous groups—after significantly watering down Fox's initial bill—the Zapatistas rejected the federal government's overture as a sham. The Zapatistas remain resolutely anticapitalist and antiglobalization. In the new context of democracy, they are much more able to circulate broadly in Mexican society. Marcos, for instance, undertook an alternative "campaign" during the 2006 presidential race, the "Other Campaign," in which he toured the nation broadly articulating the Zapatistas' message, one with which many Mexicans agree.

**Human Rights in Mexico** Vicente Fox's government has made major advances in revealing the extent to which government security forces violated the human rights of Mexican citizens in the past. Fox's administration has published thousands of pages of government documents that describe how the PRI-led governments of the 1960s and 1970s prosecuted a "dirty war" against dissidents and guerillas. Government prosecutors have even sought to indict former president Luis Echeverría on charges related to a massacre of students in 1971 and other charges pertaining to the suppression of the 1968 student movement. Fox also signed a transparency law that makes all government information publicly available. Mexicans can now seek to hold former government officials and members of the military accountable for their violations of human rights.

Despite these gains, however, Mexico continues to have an imperfect human rights record. Most notably, years of political corruption have created an attitude of impunity and disregard of the law by the police and local officials. Drug trafficking only exacerbates a situation in which those who seek to investigate the police, local officials, and the lawbreakers they protect must fear for their lives. More than two hundred Mexican journalists have been murdered in the past fifteen years, and attorneys and human rights activists have also been subject to political intimidation and violence. The inability or unwillingness of local police to solve violent crimes, especially against women, raises issues of fundamental human rights as well. In a notorious example, in Ciudad Juárez, the huge border city across from El Paso, Texas, hundreds of women have been murdered over the past several years without a satisfactory resolution of their cases. Family members and human rights advocates have decried this situation, which puts so many innocent young women's lives at risk. Overcoming this heritage of repression and violence in the many regions of Mexico will remain a top challenge to the incoming Calderón administration.

### Hypotheses on Democratic Consolidation

Does Mexico have a democratic future? With Vicente Fox's election, most Mexicans had good reasons to think that democracy would be their future. Rather than gaze into a crystal ball, let's review our hypotheses on democratization from chapter 9, summarizing as we do the evidence we have just covered.

**Elites** President Zedillo demonstrated a commitment to democracy unparalleled among postrevolutionary presidents. He forced the PRI to accept the opposition victory in the 1997 midterm legislative elections, and he made the party introduce primaries for the selection of gubernatorial candidates, giving away some of the metaconstitutional powers of the presidency. He also recognized Vicente Fox's presidential victory in 2000. Very few high-level members of the PRI would prefer to return to the practices of the 1960s. Since its loss in 2000, the PRI has come to behave much more like an ordinary political party, although the loss of government slush funds has made party financing a significant challenge. Zedillo's disinclination to impose his will on the PRI meant that in many states and localities, his adversaries in the party have engaged in the old-time practices of intimidation and repression.[38] In general, a weaker central government continues to allow regional and local elites to violate the norms of democracy in their quest to expand their power.

**State Institutions** The PRI's loss of the Chamber of Deputies majority in the 1997 elections helped to considerably reduce presidential domination of the Congress. The PRI's loss of the presidency in 2000, along with the failure of Fox's PAN to gain congressional majorities in both 2000 and 2003, means that old-fashioned presidentialism is essentially dead. The parties have attempted to build democratic processes within the Congress, but they will need more time to accomplish that task. So long as reelection is constitutionally proscribed, legislators cannot build legislative careers and serve as powerful committee chairs, who can block presidential initiatives in the way that senators can in the United States. However, Mexican federalism has been bolstered by efforts at administrative decentralization and an increase in the revenue sharing that the federal government grants to the states. Similarly, with parties other than the PRI governing many states and municipalities, a majority of Mexicans can now imagine alternation in power: they can throw the rascals out if they are angry about public services, which they did by electing Fox in July 2000.

**National Unity** If anything, Mexico's indigenous people have become more demanding of their rights. They have found more and more members of the intelligentsia and the political elite willing to espouse their causes too. The Chiapas rebellion has played a critical role in bringing these issues to the attention of the wider world, so that indigenous people have international allies to help support their efforts to gain greater autonomy from the state and the PRI.

**National Wealth** Problems of maldistribution of income continue to cast a shadow over Mexico's path toward democratization. The violent uprisings in Chiapas, Guerrero, and other southern states have their origins in the poverty suffered by millions of Mexicans and in their perception that the neoliberal policies advocated by Salinas, Zedillo, and Fox are intended to make them bear the burden of Mexico's adjustment to globalization, a process they would just as soon not embark upon.

**Private Enterprise** In the past two decades many entrepreneurs have come over to the PAN. The presidential campaign of Vicente Fox, for instance, was funded in part by the organization called Amigos de Fox, in which businesspeople played a key role. These business connections with the PAN should enrich Mexican political pluralism. At the same time, the very wealthy members of the private sector who gained most under Salinas's privatization of the economy have demonstrated little concern for political pluralism; rather, when asked by Salinas to make large contributions to the PRI's campaign war chest for the 1994 race, they willingly offered to ante up the funds.[39]

**The Middle Class** More than any other group, the Mexican middle class has supported political pluralism with its votes. The PAN is a thoroughly middle-class party, and the left-wing PRD draws many of its supporters from the middle class too. To the extent that the middle class continues to grow, democracy in Mexico should benefit.

**Support of the Disadvantaged for Democracy** Although the disadvantaged—the urban poor, the working class, and the peasantry—were controlled by the PRI and its corporatist organizations a generation ago, the socioeconomic changes of the last twenty years have ruptured the PRI's strong control over these social groups. The poor are now able to vote for other parties and to join popular organizations, and they do. But if the clientelism associated with the PRI has declined at the national level, it remains important at the local level and in the relationships that the poor develop with some state agencies. Thus, the disadvantaged might favor democracy overall, but their weakness vis-à-vis the government in their everyday lives may mean that their votes can continue to be bought.

**Citizen Participation, Civil Society, and Political Culture** Mexico now has a much more vibrant civil society, with neighborhood associations, women's groups, and organizations devoted to the promotion of human rights. Mexicans by and large prefer democracy, although there are people who have withdrawn from politics or who have never taken an interest in politics, and these politically alienated Mexicans may support an authoritarian regime as quickly as a democratic polity. Overall, however, in the past three decades the forces for democracy at the grass roots have been bolstered.

**Education and Freedom of Information** Fewer and fewer Mexicans cannot read, so the capacity of democracy's foes to dupe the people is declining from year to year. Information is so much more available and of such high quality today that anyone in Mexico seeking political information would have no difficulty in obtaining it. Of course, Mexicans remain television watchers instead of quality newspaper readers. Even here, however, the last ten years have brought major improvements in the degree of journalistic integrity and the extent to which critical questions are being posed.

**Favorable International Environment** Again, the Chiapas rebellion has brought much world attention to the progress of democracy in Mexico. The globalization of communications now constrains the Mexican government in its actions toward dissident groups. At election time, the world's television cameras were pointed on ballot boxes throughout Mexico, which limited the PRI's ability to undertake electoral shenanigans from 1994 onward. The U.S. government is more involved than ever in providing advice to its Mexican counterpart about how to treat its own citizens. However, many human rights activists have suggested that the U.S. government remains too uncritical of the political elite ruling Mexico.

**Conclusions** Although Mexico faces many significant political and social problems, the past two decades have enabled it to confront them directly. Most important, the forces favoring democracy have grown greatly, having seized on the opportunities granted them by government failures to throw the PRI out of power. In view of the factors we have just reviewed, we can regard Mexico's potential for consolidating a successful democracy as reasonably high. In 2000, Mexico elected a president from a party other than the long-ruling PRI.

Millions of Mexicans themselves took the most important step in consolidating democracy by voting the PRI out of the presidency; they recognized the historic character of their collective act. However, López Obrador's challenge to the 2006 electoral outcome put the integrity of Mexico's electoral institutions into question for a minority of the population. His resort to public protest—direct democracy, in his view, but an attempt to circumvent legitimate democratic institutions, in the perspective of his opponents—has set Mexico back in its quest to consolidate and deepen democracy. Felipe Calderón faces the difficult task of healing the divisions generated by his election while simultaneously addressing the significant policy challenges posed to his nation.

## BRAZIL

Population (2006, estimated): 188 million

Freedom House Ratings (2005): Political Rights—2; Civil Liberties—2

Area: 3.29 million square miles (a little smaller than the United States)

In contrast to the political stability enjoyed until recently by Mexico under the PRI's one-party-dominant rule, Brazil's political history in the twentieth century was marked by political instability. Brazil now is governed under the fifth (or perhaps sixth) distinctly different political regime since the Brazilian imperial monarchy fell in 1889. A nation of great promise, whose leaders have aspired to *grandeza,* or greatness, Brazil enters the twenty-first century having failed to deliver on that promise. A nation vast in population, territory, and resources, it has become in some ways nearly ungovernable. Brazil is by far the most industrialized of the South American countries and has the highest per capita income in the region; but no other major country in the world has an income distribution so unequal, and its politics has been characterized by paradoxes and frustrations.

### The Setting

Brazil occupies more than half the land mass of South America. As the largest Portuguese-speaking country in the world, Brazil has almost 190 million people, making it the world's fifth most populous state. As in Mexico, Brazil's struggle to industrialize led to rapid urbanization in the twentieth century. São Paulo, with almost 18 million inhabitants, rivals Mexico City's size. Its growth has been phenomenal: in 1950, São Paulo did not have as many as 4 million people and was not even Brazil's largest city. (Rio de Janeiro was; its population currently tops 10.5 million.)[40] The Amazon basin, the largest tropical rain forest in the world, remains one of the world's last frontiers. Brazilians and many foreigners have scrambled to exploit its richness—lumber, iron ore, hydroelectric power, and an extraordinary diversity of flora and fauna. In short, Brazil clearly has great potential, and it should be easily understandable that Brazilian leaders would seek to realize that potential by making the country a *grande potência,* a great power.

**Regionalism** Even more than Mexico, Brazil has distinct regions with different political and economic histories. One challenge of any national government is to accommodate these regional differences. Four regions can be identified: the northeast, the southeast, the south, and the Amazon and west. Let's briefly explore their distinct characters.

Sugar production made northeast Brazil the most prosperous region in its eighteenth-century heyday.[41] Sugar production also brought millions of Africans to Brazil in the Atlantic slave trade, creating the multiethnic society Brazil has become. But centuries of sugar cultivation exhausted the soil of the northeast. Combined with cycles of droughts, the decline of the sugar industry has made this region Brazil's poorest one, with per capita incomes at the lowest levels in the country.[42] Yet the northeast remains home to 29 percent of Brazil's population.

In the past two centuries, the southeast has emerged as Brazil's most prosperous region. Brazil's major urban centers, including São Paulo, Rio de Janeiro, and Belo Horizante, are located in the southeast states of São Paulo, Rio de Janeiro, and Minas Gerais,[43] respectively. The foundation for São Paulo's prosperity came from its world renowned coffee industry, which has produced much wealth in the past two centuries. Coffee profits provided the basis for industrial investments in the southeast region, where 44 percent of Brazil's population

**Brazil**

now lives on 11 percent of the nation's territory.[44] Most of Brazil's industry is located in the southeast, including its large automobile industry. The state of São Paulo is home to about half the nation's industries, where per capita income is about twice the national average.

Brazil's southern states border Uruguay and Argentina,[45] and like those Spanish-speaking nations, Brazil's south is largely agrarian. The climate here is temperate, and in the far south, the topography resembles the pampas of the two neighboring countries. The 15 percent of Brazilians who live in the south enjoy a relatively high standard of living.

The part of Brazil that the rest of the world most readily identifies as a distinct region is the Amazon

(Amazonas) and the west.[46] The interest of outsiders has been drawn to the Amazon by concerns about the implications of its development for the world's environment, especially by fears that the greenhouse effect will be exacerbated by excessive clearing of the Amazon rain forest. Many Brazilians have come to share the sense that the Amazon should be saved from the clear-cutting of the forest and from development that would threaten the region's biodiversity and the lives of its indigenous inhabitants. However, in the not-too-distant past the Amazon represented opportunity to Brazilians bent upon economic development and national grandeur. It has been a magnet for northeast peasants and southeast slum dwellers heading for the frontier to break out of their poverty as well as for generals and presidents seeking the resources that could feed Brazil's growing industrial sector with abundant raw materials and cheap sources of energy. This vast region, where only 12 percent of Brazilians live, covers 64 percent of the nation's territory.

A nation of such size and regional variety can be difficult to govern from a central capital, as the experiences of other large nations (Russia, Canada, India, and even the United States) can attest. Yet, without a strong centralized government, such nations tend to fragment when regional political forces strive for autonomy. Brazil's history has reflected the tension between centralism and regional desires to avoid domination by the center. Federalism, or more precisely, the character that federalism will take (the balance between federal power and local prerogatives), thus has been a major theme in Brazilian political development.

**Socioeconomic Development** Brazil, like Mexico, is usually considered a middle-income country. Its economy grew rapidly in the twentieth century, with industry leading the way. Although Brazil retains a substantial agricultural sector—best known for its coffee, but successful in producing other items as well—industrial growth has made Brazil one of the most attractive places for foreign investors to locate. Starting in the 1930s, the Brazilian state followed an *import-substituting industrialization (ISI) strategy* of development. It pursued expansionist fiscal (i.e., tax and spending) policies, protected Brazil's nascent industries against foreign competition (through tariffs and other trade barriers), and made considerable investments in the country's infrastructure (roads, bridges, and the like) and state-owned enterprises. The result was one of the most rapid spurts of economic development in the Third World. In terms of industrial development, Brazil clearly surpasses all its South American neighbors. However, as we shall learn, industrialization may have brought a relatively high per capita income to Brazil, but it has not guaranteed that the proceeds of that development have been fairly distributed.

Associated with rapid industrialization in the twentieth century has been rapid population growth and urbanization. Brazil's population was about 17 million in 1900, but it grew nearly ten times in the twentieth century, now reaching nearly 190 million. As we mentioned, Brazil includes two of the world's largest metropolises, São Paulo and Rio de Janeiro, plus several other cities whose populations exceed one million. At the same time, Brazil retains a large rural society: almost 50 million people live in towns and the countryside. Thus we must recognize that Brazil presents one of the developing world's most complex societies, a society that no political regime can easily govern.

## Brazil's Political Development

**Prominent Features of Brazilian Politics** As in Mexico, we can identify in Brazil a number of distinguishing features of politics that need explaining. In the twentieth century, Brazil was subjected to several instances of *military intervention in politics.* Usually they were of short duration, intended to force the resignation or ouster of an unacceptable president with a view to scheduling new elections. However, the nation was governed for over two decades (1964–85) by the military as an institution, a period that saw the repression of the regime's opponents and an effort to realize Brazil's great power potential.

Brazil, like Mexico, has a history of *state intervention in the economy.* State ownership of industry, state financing of huge infrastructure and development projects, state-subsidized financing of private industry, and state attempts to regulate the market economy characterized the Brazilian political economy

TABLE 22.4

**Brazilian Political Regimes**

| Date | Regime | Regime Type |
|---|---|---|
| 1822–89 | Empire | Constitutional monarchy |
| 1889–1930 | Old Republic | Oligarchical democratic republic |
| 1930–37 | Provisional Government (Vargas) | Dictatorship |
| 1937–45 | Estado Nôvo | Corporatist state |
| 1946–64 | Second Republic | Democratic republic |
| 1964–85 | Military Regime | Military dictatorship |
| 1985–present | New Republic | Democratic republic |

in the last half of the twentieth century. Much of the attention of recent presidents, especially *Fernando Henrique Cardoso,* was given to reducing this large state role. *State corporatism* characterized the government's relationship with economic actors, especially labor and business. Although corporatism is breaking down today—more so for business groups than for labor—past corporatist practices reflected the desire of the Brazilian state to control its economy, especially its labor force.

The centrality of the state in politics is manifested in two other political features that Brazil shares with Mexico: *clientelism* and *corruption.* Brazil's state bureaucracy has been the preserve of clientelism. Political patrons place their clients in positions in the bureaucracy not because of their merits but to reward them for their political loyalty. These patrons also use their connections in the bureaucracy to reward private-sector supporters with state contracts. The many huge construction projects undertaken by the government have provided especially lucrative bonanzas for well-connected "clients" of the political leadership. Clientelism almost naturally leads to corruption scandals when it becomes known how individuals who have benefited from these patron-client relationships have distorted the public interest, using the public purse to finance their private projects. In the most celebrated recent corruption case, President *Fernando Collor de Mello* (1989–92) was impeached in 1992 for the embezzlement of public funds—after running for president on a campaign to clean up corruption.

In contrast to the centralism evident in much of Brazil's political life, there are other forces in the society antithetical to centralism. For our purposes, the two most important are *federalism* and the *fragmentation of the party system.*

Many of Brazil's states have often sought autonomy from a federal government that they worry will govern with the interests of other regions in mind. But central government officials concerned about national security worry that granting too much power to the states may threaten national unity and invite a fragmentation of the federal union. Brazil's more authoritarian regimes have strived to promote unity by establishing central controls over the states. Brazil's more democratic regimes, in contrast, have allowed the states to gather more power to themselves at the expense of the central government.

Related to the dispersion of power associated with federalism is the weakness of the party system, even its fragmentation. Brazilian parties, reflecting the personal aspirations of politicians and regional interests, have proven unusually weak. Politicians have demonstrated little party discipline, displaying instead a marked unwillingness to sacrifice their personal interests for their party's national purposes. Quite a few have proven highly fickle, defecting from the parties that supported them for election and switching to other parties after taking their congressional seats. In this regard, President da Silva's Workers Party has been an exception, demonstrating party unity and discipline.

In this section we'll explore the historical antecedents of these prominent features of Brazilian politics, highlighting how they emerged and how political reformers have sought to address them. (See table 22.4 for a list of Brazil's regimes.)

**Independence and the Empire** In contrast to the wars of independence that rocked Spanish America and contributed to nearly a half century of political instability in Mexico, Central America, and most of

South America in the first half of the nineteenth century, Brazil's independence from Portugal came peacefully and paved the way for a century of political stability and order. Portugal's royal family fled Lisbon before Napoleon's invasion in 1808, moving to Brazil for the duration of the French occupation. When the king, Dom João VI, returned home after Napoleon's defeat, his son, Dom Pedro I, remained in Brazil. In 1822, Dom Pedro I declared Brazil to be an independent empire. He and his son, Dom Pedro II, ruled the *Brazilian Empire* for sixty-seven years (1822–89).[47]

Brazil's imperial constitution of 1824 created the foundations of a centralized state. This constitutional monarchy created executive, legislative, and judicial branches of government. But it also introduced a "moderating power" (*poder moderador*), reserved to the monarchy, which allowed the monarchy to step in and resolve disputes among the branches of government and the political parties. A centralized bureaucracy also emerged during the Empire, but this bureaucracy quickly came to be "colonized" (taken over) by provincial elites seeking to promote their interests. Although the emperor retained exceptional powers, the political system also had some liberal features, including a constitution that was promulgated and carefully observed, regular elections to the legislature, and parties that alternated in power.

The monarchy came to an end in 1889 in a military coup backed by coffee planters from São Paulo. Although several issues precipitated the military's actions, the most significant was a conflict between the government and the planters over the abolition of slavery in 1888. With the end of the Empire, Brazil became a republic with a presidentialist constitution.

**The Old Republic (1889–1930)** The **Old Republic**, as it is now known, was given its birth with the constitution of 1891, when the military chose to limit its role in the political process to that of the "moderating power" formerly held by the emperor. Formally democratic, the constitution became subverted by the oligarchy, the small clique of people who actually wielded real power. Thus the Old Republic can at best be considered a limited democracy. Power was divided between the coffee-rich state of São Paulo and the cattle-raising state of Minas Gerais, hence the pejorative term given to the politics of the Old Republic: *café com leite* (coffee with milk). The dominance of these two states in national politics and their rotation in the office of the presidency was reinforced by another practice called "the politics of the governors."

That procedure allowed the incumbent president to choose his successor and then enforce his decision on the electorate through a vertically downward chain of pressure. The president's choice was imposed on the state governors and *coroneis*, or local political bosses (the Brazilian equivalents of the Mexican *caciques*). The local bosses' task was to turn out the votes on election day, making sure that the president's designated candidate won. *Coronelismo* is a Brazilian variant of clientelism, with local notables (usually landlords) serving as patrons to the less advantaged people in patron-client relationships.[48] Through this process, the southeast region controlled national politics, excluding the south and the northeast from political power. The Old Republic thereby introduced a strong element of federalism into Brazilian politics.

As the success of *coronelismo* implies, the rural underclass could not act independently in politics. Moreover, neither a strong business class nor a large industrial proletariat existed in Brazil at this time. Brazilian politics in the Old Republic was controlled by landowners, the country's economic development driven by the coffee growers' link to the international economy. These rural oligarchs preferred a weak central state. Federalism flourished, with regional governors rather than the central government holding the greater power.

In 1930, the Old Republic faced a crisis in its "coffee with milk" system. Opposition to the hegemony of the São Paulo–Minas Gerais alliance had been mounting in the states of the northeast and south, particularly in Rio Grande do Sul. A group of young army officers also opposed the southeast's hegemony. These two groups were supported by the small but growing urban business class and by the coffee growers, who were hurt by President Washington Luis's policies. When the president violated the established system of rotation in office by choosing someone from his home state as his successor, the main opposition party led a revolt that threatened to overthrow both the president and his designated successor. Alarmed at the increasing polarization of the political elites, the military chose to invoke its "moderating power" and moved in. The officers were convinced that political reforms were necessary, however, and they did not wish to replace a civilian government. Within a few days the junta stepped down in favor of *Getulio Vargas,* the leader of the opposition party, the Liberal Alliance.

**Vargas and the Estado Nôvo (1930–45)** The Liberal Alliance favored an early return to constitutional rule, though segments of the military opposed it on the grounds that elections would only return the old elite to power. In 1934, Vargas approved a new constitution that included elements of both political liberalism and social reformism. But as the global depression jolted Brazil, sending coffee prices tumbling and derailing the first stages of the country's industrialization, the ruling elites had to face a new constellation of opposing forces.[49]

Vargas's Liberal Alliance and the radical junior officers were quickly superseded by two mass-oriented movements, the neo-fascist *integralista* movement and the communist-supported National Liberation Alliance (ANL). Vargas manipulated these two oppositions to make the situation appear to be even more polarized. Since the Brazilian military feared communism every bit as much as it disliked "irresponsible" politicians, the officers invoked their "moderating power" once again, vesting exclusive civilian authority in Vargas. ***Armed with military backing, Vargas established a dictatorship and began constructing his corporatist* Estado Nôvo (New State).**

The period of the *Estado Nôvo* is important for the subsequent development of Brazilian politics because it concentrated power in the central government. In doing so it created three long-lasting effects. First, the corporatist labor legislation of the *Estado Nôvo* gave control of the labor movement to the state, particularly to the minister of labor.[50] This approach provided the government with a means of mobilizing the working class and keeping its demands under control. It deprived Brazilian workers of the right to organize their own unions, and cut off the outlawed communists from their natural working-class base. Second, the state began to take a strong, relatively interventionist role in the direction of the economy and economic development.[51] And third, the New State's centralization of power marked a major political dividing line for many years to come. From here on, Brazilians would be divided between those who favored an interventionist state with a strong executive and those who wished a return to the politics of the Old Republic, with its weaker executive and its diffusion of power to the states and *coroneis.*

Brazil's involvement in the Second World War on the side of the Western Allies undermined any legitimacy that the dictatorial *Estado Nôvo* might have created for itself by stabilizing social conflict. As the military fought alongside the United States and Britain to preserve the world for democracy, the lack of democracy at home became a source of incongruity. Vargas himself recognized the dilemma and therefore planned for the return of democracy by developing a strong following among the corporatized labor movement. Under his leadership, liberal democracy returned to Brazil with the end of the war. But the real key to the return of democracy lay in the perspectives of the military, who held the ultimate source of coercive power.

**The Second Republic (1946–64)** Brazilian populism emerged with the return of democratic rule.[52] In 1951 Vargas was swept back into power by a populist coalition of urban workers in the Brazilian Workers' Party (PTB) and old-time clientelistic politicians in the Social Democratic Party (PSD). His opposition was primarily composed of conservatives who favored laissez-faire policies and a weak central state. Vargas initially steered a delicate path between market-oriented orthodoxy and state-centered economic nationalism, but by 1953 had chosen the latter path, a choice revealed in his support for the creation of the state-owned oil company, Petrobras. Vargas also came to depend more and more on his working-class following. However, when Vargas made *João Goulart* his minister of labor in 1953 to strengthen his support on the left, opposition to his government grew. His chief adversaries were the middle class, which was threatened by inflation, and the thoroughly anti-leftist military, for whom Goulart's pro-worker orientation was an internal security threat.

When the military invoked its moderating power and moved to overthrow Vargas in 1954, he committed suicide. The 1955 elections returned the Workers Party–Social Democratic choice of *Juscelino Kubitschek*, with Goulart as vice president. Kubitschek continued the populist developmental policies of Vargas, perhaps with even more support from national industrialists than Vargas had received. Brazil's economic development proceeded apace, with economic growth rates reaching 8 to 9 percent annually as foreign investment and foreign loans streamed into Brazil. However, this development exacerbated both inflation and trade balance problems, leading the International Monetary Fund (IMF) to propose a stabilization plan in 1958. This stabilization plan threatened Kubitschek's ability to reach his economic development targets and to preserve his reputation and political future. Kubitschek rejected the IMF plan in 1959, to the acclaim of Brazilian nationalists.

The 1961 presidential election was a victory for democratic constitutionalism as the left-wing alliance was defeated by *Jânio Quadros*, the popular governor of São Paulo. Goulart was again elected vice president. However, the apparent gain for democratic legitimacy quickly became a loss when Quadros resigned less than a year after being inaugurated. Goulart was forced to wait fourteen months before taking full presidential power, ruling as a president accountable to parliament.

By the time Goulart assumed the full powers of the presidency, he was faced with a full-blown economic crisis. Inflation was mounting, mobilizing opposition from the working class on the left to the capitalists and upper classes on the right. Balance of payments pressures, reflecting an excess of imports over exports, were inhibiting Brazil's ability to import badly needed industrial goods, thus threatening future economic growth. Furthermore, the working class had gained more autonomy from political control since it was not incorporated into any of the parties.[53] The right favored stabilizing the business climate while the left favored the nationalization of privately owned companies. In this polarized climate, the presence in the presidency of a man who was suspected by the right of leftist sympathies created an unworkable situation. The right would not cooperate with Goulart, so he turned to the left for support.

In fact, Goulart turned so far to the left as to become a serious advocate of land reform. His left turn, however, only confirmed the right's view of him and gave the military a justification to move against him, ostensibly to protect Brazil from communism. In April 1964 the military removed Goulart from power. But rather than arranging new elections as it had when exercising its "moderating power" in the past, the military settled in to rule as an institution.[54]

**Military Rule (1964–85)** The two decades of military rule in Brazil proved less politically disruptive than did other Latin American military dictatorships, especially when compared with the events that followed Argentina's 1976 coup or the 1973 overthrow of Salvador Allende's socialist regime in Chile by a junta led by General Augusto Pinochet. In those nations the military clamped down severely on the left, "disappearing" thousands of progressive activists or suspected activists, effectively banning civilian politics and the public activities of politicians altogether. In contrast, Brazil's military allowed some democratic institutions to survive the fall of Goulart, although the activities of the Congress were greatly restricted and the former political parties were disbanded. Elections continued to be held. It is interesting that the military regime made electoral performance an indicator of its legitimacy. However, the military manipulated the electoral rules so as to ensure a government majority in the Congress, thereby undermining the legislature's legitimacy.

Although government candidates won congressional majorities in 1966 and 1968, high percentages of blank ballots cast doubt on the popularity of the generals in power. After pro-Kubitschek figures won governorships in Minas Gerais and Guanabara in 1966, the military issued Institutional Act No. 2, a government decree that abolished the existing parties. Urban guerilla violence and agitation in the legislature followed the military's failure to carry out a promised liberalization in 1968. These events strengthened the hand of hardliners in the military and helped to touch off the most repressive stage of the regime (1968–74), marked by the issuance of

Institutional Act No. 5, which gave unlimited powers to the president to protect national security.[55] Generally, the military regime strengthened the executive and the central government to the detriment of legislative bodies and the states.

The repression unleashed by Institutional Act No. 5 proved mild by comparison to what the Chilean military did after the 1973 coup and the crimes that the Argentine military perpetrated in its "Dirty War" against "subversion" in the late 1970s. Still, the Brazilian military regime inflicted arbitrary detentions, exile, and torture on its victims. Hundreds disappeared or were killed for their "subversive" politics. It is significant that the Brazilian military entrusted its anticommunist crusade to an intelligence agency, the National Intelligence Service (SNI). However, in the campaign against subversion, the SNI and other intelligence agencies proved too autonomous for the comfort of many military leaders who worried that they could no longer control them.[56]

Throughout the military's rule, factional infighting between hardliners and those military leaders more disposed to an early return to democracy gave the regime's opponents opportunities to push for a liberalization of the political system. By 1974, a major division had appeared between those who wanted to loosen the grips of the state's repression and those who wanted to maintain complete control over society. The more moderate faction prevailed, buoyed in part by fears that the repressive apparatus (the SNI and other internal security agencies) was developing an independence that could eventually allow it to be used against other elements within the military. A "decompression" process began.

One of the military regime's greatest challenges was legitimating its rule. Because it was not born of a true revolution (though the military called its seizure of power in 1964 by that term) and because it was not disposed to the populist, redistributive politics of social welfare for the poor, the Brazilian military could not generate the popular support that Mexico's postrevolutionary rulers enjoyed. In an effort to simulate legitimacy, the military tried to create a two-party electoral competition that would in some ways mirror Mexico's one-party-dominant regime. A pro-regime party was founded called the National Renovating Alliance, or ARENA. A smaller, weaker opposition party, the Brazilian Democratic Movement (MDB), was also encouraged to form. The idea was that, like Mexico's PRI, ARENA would always win. And like the weak opposition parties in Mexico, the MDB would contest elections but lose.

However, when the regime held very strictly controlled elections in 1974 that severely constrained the opposition, the oppositionist Democratic Movement still won. Various efforts to stack the electoral deck in the military's favor after 1974 kept ARENA and its successors in control of Congress, but no one was fooled by the blatant rigging of the contest between regime and opposition. For example, in 1978 the military banned the existing parties (both ARENA and the MDB) in an effort to destroy the MDB before it became too popular. ARENA re-formed as the Democratic Social Party (PDS) while many members of the MDB created the Party of the Brazilian Democratic Movement (PMDB) and returned to their struggle to oust the pro-military party.

In the end, the military's rule created a larger central state presence in Brazilian society, especially in its economy. However, after the spectacular rise in oil prices in the mid 1970s, the pro-growth policies pursued by the military government led it to take on large volumes of foreign debt, which came due in the early 1980s at a time when Brazil could not repay its obligations (just like Mexico). Brazil put off a severe restructuring of its economy for longer than any other major Latin American country, waiting until the mid 1990s, a decade after the military left power, to adopt neoliberal restructuring policies. In the meantime, Brazilian society suffered a decade of hyperinflation.

The military's quest for Brazilian greatness also encouraged it to undertake massive development projects in the Amazon and other parts of Brazil, projects that have proven environmentally disastrous. These projects generally benefited society's "haves" to the detriment of its "have-nots." While the nation's gross domestic product (GDP) grew immensely during the military's two decades (an average of about 7.5 percent annually),[57] the poor gained little. The military saddled its civilian successors with a development model that had exhausted its potential, enormous foreign debts, a bloated central bureaucracy, environmental crises, and the most unequal income distribution of any large country in the world. One had to ask, as civilians returned to power in the mid 1980s without the coercive force of the military behind them, "Would this society be governable?"

### Explaining Brazilian Authoritarianism

Why did democracy fail in Brazil? How could the military manage to rule for two decades? These questions have haunted Brazilians and the social scientists who have studied their society. Let's look at the conditions for democracy laid out in chapter 9 and see if they help us understand Brazil's experience with authoritarianism.

**Elites Committed to Democracy** Various groups with elite status held at best a lukewarm commitment to democracy from the time of the fall of the Old Republic until late into the military regime. Traditional political elites—local elites (the *coroneis*), governors, and political bosses—were willing to work through formally democratic institutions, but they engaged in practices inimical to democracy. Even when operating through political parties and contesting elections, these traditional elites practiced clientelism, regionalism, and personal power.[58] Traditional elites might figure out how to manipulate democratic institutions to promote their interests, but democracy was not their primary goal. In 1964, traditional elites conspired to help bring off the military coup that ousted Goulart.[59]

Military elites have also shown at best conditional support for democracy, at worst outright hostility to it. On the one hand, liberals within the military managed to retain constitutional forms during the military dictatorship, including elections and political parties. (Of course, they permitted only the parties they created rather than the preexisting parties.) These *blandos,* as they were called (the softliners), also pushed to liberalize the regime after 1974. However, the *blandos* were offset by the *duros* (or hardliners), those opposed to democracy. In addition, from the late 1950s onward, the Brazilian military adopted a doctrine of national security and development alleging that threats to the nation's security came from insurgencies and other revolutionary challenges to the state. The military regarded civilian politicians as incapable of confronting these internal security threats.[60] This internal security doctrine, we should note, went beyond the military's earlier notion that it held the "moderating power" in the Brazilian constitutional structure. Although the moderating power might provide a justification for the removal of a chief executive, it did not justify long-term rule by the military as an institution. In either event, however, we can see that military elites could be indifferent to democracy or hostile to it.

One final elite group whose commitment to democracy has been in question were the technocrats who came to staff the large state bureaucracy, especially in those ministries, agencies, and state-owned enterprises charged with promoting national economic development. Many of these technocrats were trained in engineering programs or in neoclassical economics, disciplines that have emphasized the efficacy of rational planning processes. Guillermo O'Donnell has argued that technocrats tended to consider the messy politics of populism, in which politicians like Goulart or Vargas mobilized the urban masses by promising inflationary spending programs (subsidies for staple goods, cheap public transportation, higher minimum wages, and so on), to be threatening to their capacity to plan and administer the economy. Hence, civilian technocrats—many of whose services were indeed retained by the military after they came to power—and military technocrats preferred to see the masses demobilized so that they could more "rationally" operate the economy.[61]

The foregoing suggests that elites in Brazil were historically lukewarm toward democracy, if not hostile to it. Although many found themselves able to prosper under democratic institutions, they were also able to get along well under authoritarianism. Moreover, some elites considered democracy to be inimical to their interests.

**State Institutions** Brazil's two previous democratic regimes came to their ends in 1930 and 1964 as the result of impasses that emerged among the civilian politicians running those regimes. In the

Second Republic, state institutions—the constitutional order—contributed to the political crisis that ended with the military's seizure of power. The Second Republic had a presidential system. Popular candidates could win the presidency even without strong party backing. Unfortunately, Brazil's party system failed to produce reliable majority coalitions for any president. With three major national parties and other regional parties, no single party gained a majority in either house of the bicameral Congress. Federalism encouraged politicians to pay close attention to the needs of local constituencies, often leading them to vote against their national parties on important bills. Without majorities to back their reform measures, presidents were tempted to bypass Congress by issuing decrees or to engage in popular mobilization to gather support. Goulart's use of popular mobilization to push an intransigent Congress into accepting agrarian reform and other populist policies provoked the military to stage its coup in 1964.[62]

**National Unity** Brazil's society is far from ethnically homogeneous. As many as 40 percent of Brazilians can claim some descent from African slaves, and others are descended from native Americans (Indians). On the other hand, in contrast to societies in Eastern Europe and even to some extent the United States, these ethnic or racial differences have had little salience in Brazilian political conflict. Certainly those Brazilians of African heritage are more likely to be among the poor and thus subject to clientelistic control. Myths about "racial democracy" in Brazil have hidden the reality of prejudice, discrimination, and violence against African Brazilians. However, ethnic differences have not been at the heart of political conflict in Brazil and have not therefore promoted dictatorship.

**National Wealth** If the hypothesis that higher levels of national wealth tend to promote democracy were to hold true in its simplest form, we would expect Brazil to be democratic before many of its South American neighbors because its national wealth is the greatest on the continent. However, in addition to a high per capita income, Brazil has a highly unequal distribution of income and wealth, the worst among the world's largest nations. Income inequality is manifested in several ways that have implications for democracy.

In the countryside, where as many as a quarter of Brazilians still live, rural poverty and landlessness permits the local bosses, the *coroneis,* to use their economic power and their connections with the state to dominate the lives of peasants and rural workers. Their domination has kept the rural masses from effectively articulating a preference for democracy, perhaps even from realizing that democracy could be an alternative to authoritarian rule. Nor can the rural poor, often in debt to the *coroneis* and fearful of their willingness to use violence against their opponents, create a real alternative to the control of local government by the political machines of the rural bosses.

The millions of urban poor in the seemingly endless *favelas* (slums) surrounding Brazil's cities serve to remind the rich, who live as well as or better than people do in the world's richest nations, of what could become of their privileged status and their material well-being. Associated with inequality are high levels of crime in Brazil's major cities. Consequently, there has been considerable support from the well-to-do for hardline policies that would clamp down on antisocial behaviors resulting from inequality, even if at the expense of civil liberties.

Even when democratic institutions have been in place, those opposed to redistributive policies have found ways to defeat legislative or presidential efforts to address inequality. In the early 1960s, frustration at the Congress's unwillingness to pass land reform legislation led President Goulart to undertake the populist mobilization of the poor that prompted the military coup. Maldistribution of income often leads to the rise of populist leaders who threaten the middle and upper classes and encourage them to side with military officers against democracy.

**Private Enterprise** Brazil has had a sizable private sector even while the state has owned many large firms in important industries. The private sector worried both about the growth of inflation in the years leading up to 1964 and about the populist mobilization of workers and peasants in which Goulart was engaged at the time of the coup.[63] However, Brazilian entrepreneurs came to join the opponents of the military regime in the 1970s after the economic successes of the early years of the military's rule began to wane. Furthermore, the private sector became frustrated with the growth of the state-owned sector of the economy, as businesspeople thought they were being denied opportunities to make investments in profitable industries because of the state's presence.[64] Thus Brazil's business sector has alternately opposed and supported democracy.

**The Middle Class** Brazil's large middle class consists mainly of the many white-collar employees, self-employed professionals, and small-business owners necessary in an industrial economy. While the middle class might desire the political and personal freedoms associated with democracy, there are other political goals that its members seek as well. Among them are price stability and prosperity. The inflation that came to characterize Brazil in the early 1960s brought the middle class into the coalition supporting the coup. During the later 1960s, especially during the years of the economic miracle (1968–74), support for the military regime by the middle class was high because of the prosperity it enjoyed in those years.[65] However, middle-class support for authoritarianism has been as conditional as its support for democracy. When their interests have been adversely affected by authoritarian rule, as for example when the military's crackdowns on dissidents put their children in prison, members of the middle class have advocated democracy. Brazil's economic difficulties in the later 1970s and 1980s also led the middle class to oppose the continuation of military rule.

**Support of the Disadvantaged for Democracy** The most important point about the support or nonsupport of the disadvantaged for democracy is that, until recently, neither the rural poor nor the urban poor were in a position to act upon a preference for democracy even if they had one. In the later 1950s and early 1960s, the working class had become increasingly politically active under the Workers Party of Brazil (PTB) and President Goulart. But the political mobilization of labor became one of the reasons other groups in society supported the 1964 coup. During much of the military regime, the government sought to use the corporatist labor laws originally written during the *Estado Nôvo* to keep organized labor under control. From 1977 onward, however, a "new unionism" within Brazilian labor played an essential role in opposing the military's continued rule, using strikes to put pressure on the military to leave power.[66] President Lula da Silva was a leader of the new unionism.

Others among Brazil's poor, especially those organized in grassroots social movements, also opposed military rule. Like the unions, however, these grassroots movements were weak or nonexistent in the early years of the military's rule. When in the later 1970s they were able to act, they came to promote democratization of the regime and an expansion of the definition of who ought to be allowed to participate politically. The nonexistence of such organizations in the 1960s, however, made it difficult for the poor to articulate their needs to the state.[67]

**Citizen Participation, Civil Society, and a Democratic Political Culture** As the previous comments should suggest, during the years of the Second Republic, many elements of Brazilian society were what could be described as semi-loyal to the society's democratic institutions.[68] They found themselves willing to desert the nation's democratic institutions when their interests were not served by democracy. Moreover, a major aspect of Brazilian political culture until recently could be labeled *patrimonialism:* the sense that much of society needs political patrons—local bosses, people with connections to state agencies that can provide material resources, even a state that can dole out projects that benefit specific groups or localities. Patrimonialism is necessary, in this view, because people are themselves unable to participate independently in the political system or are unable to accomplish collective projects on their own. Of course, this patrimonial political culture was much cultivated by the *coroneis,* the state governors, and other traditional political elites who came to power with its backing. The military, in contrast, simply sought a nonpoliticized society in which people did not turn to politics to address their needs. They preferred that people focus their attention on the exploits of the Brazilian national soccer team—the world's best in the early 1970s—rather than on national political affairs. Given these attitudes held by elite groups and the pervasiveness of low levels of education among the masses, it should come as no surprise that Brazil had little in the way of an active civil society until well into the 1970s, after the military had been in power for over a decade.

**Education and Freedom of Information** In contrast to the mass media in some of its South American neighbors—for example, Argentina and Chile—but like Mexico, Brazil's mass media have been dominated by television. Television has reached even the many illiterates or semi-literates who populate Brazil's slums, the *favelas.* Brazil's inequalities have historically extended to severe inequalities in education, and the lack of education has led many Brazilians to become trapped in the system of *coronelismo* described earlier in this chapter. Even as late as 1997, 16 percent of Brazilian adults were illiterate and 29 percent of students did not reach the fifth grade. (Mexico had 10 percent illiterate and 14 percent not reaching the fifth grade; Chile had 5 percent illiterate and less than 1 percent failing to reach the fifth grade.)[69] These low levels of educational attainment created a society vulnerable to control by political bosses and easily manipulated by the mass media. Those not subject to the control of political bosses may nevertheless have been constrained in their political choices because the media, especially television, were controlled under military rule and thus disinclined to broadcast the opposition's messages. In short, continuing low levels of education among the poor and the dominance of television among the mass media limited the capacity of Brazilians to formulate and advocate democratic alternatives during the military dictatorship.

**A Favorable International Environment** The United States has had much less influence on South American nations than on Mexico or the small countries of the Caribbean and Central America. However, the United States can influence politics even in more distant nations like Brazil through its diplomacy and its foreign economic assistance programs. During Goulart's presidency, the U.S. embassy conspired with anti-Goulart politicians and provided some intelligence assistance to those conspirators as they aided the military in bringing off its coup. The United States then quickly recognized the new military government. U.S. assistance may not have been critical in bringing authoritarianism to Brazil, but the United States did nothing to stop it.

### Brazilian Economic Development

One of the central tenets of the military's internal security doctrine was the notion that subversion prospered in circumstances in which economic stagnation prevented people from achieving their goals in life. The military thus made the promotion of economic development a high priority in the struggle against communism. Once the military regime had eliminated any evidence of insurrectionary violence in the early 1970s, maintaining healthy economic growth rates became its most important source of legitimacy.

To promote economic development, the Brazilian military embarked on a *state-led growth strategy.* The state took on large roles both in the overall direction of the economy and in investing public money in specific industries. The military's ambitions for Brazilian grandeur led it to lean toward large projects and those that emphasized high technology. As Peter Evans has argued, this approach meant that Brazilian businesspeople often were unable to make the new investments sought by the military government because they lacked sufficient money—the projects were too big for them—or they lacked access to technology. Hence the Brazilian state encouraged foreign investors to enter some of the higher technology industries such as automobiles and petrochemicals. Today several of the world's largest automobile firms have sizable operations in Brazil, including Volkswagen, Ford, and General Motors. At the same time, the state's national development bank channeled investment capital to private firms to encourage them to develop other sectors of the economy. Domestic entrepreneurs came to be involved in important joint ventures with foreign firms so as to facilitate the transfer of technology in pharmaceuticals and computers in the 1970s and 1980s.[70] As Evans argues, in some state agencies, very able administrators learned the skills necessary to encourage development in specific sectors of the economy.[71]

In other areas of the economy, especially where the state considered investment to be of strategic importance, the state itself became the investor, creating state-owned companies (public enterprises) designed to operate under capitalist logic. Though they were owned by the state, they had to observe the market forces of supply and demand in setting prices, and they were expected to earn profits. The state became a large investor in the steel, petroleum, aluminum, mining, and shipbuilding industries, among others. In essence, the Brazilian military propelled the economy further in the direction of import substitution as opposed to free international trade. It sought to produce not only finished light consumer goods in Brazil but also consumer durables (autos, refrigerators, televisions) as well as intermediate goods (steel, petrochemicals) and capital goods (factory equipment). The essence of this strategy was to make Brazil as economically self-sufficient as possible, reducing its dependence on imports to the lowest feasible levels.

However, the large state investments had their costs. The military's economic strategy encouraged the intensive use of energy, especially oil. But Brazil has few deposits of petroleum, making imports mandatory. (Only recently have new discoveries brought Brazil close to energy independence, and in 2005 Bolivia's decision to renationalize its natural gas sector has threatened the access of Petrobras to an important source of energy.) The oil crises of the 1970s, which provided a great opportunity for oil-rich Mexico, threatened to wreck the Brazilian economic miracle. When world oil prices shot up in 1974, so did Brazil's oil bill. Rather than discourage consumption and slow the economy, the generals borrowed from international banks. Large infrastructure projects and borrowing to provide finance capital for the national development bank also contributed to the nation's foreign debt, which reached about $85 billion at the beginning of the 1980s.

Thus the Brazilian miracle emphasized an import substitution model that was capital intensive, technology intensive, and energy intensive. Although this model produced high economic growth rates, the nation's dependence on international sources of capital grew. This pattern of development did not begin to meet Brazilian society's needs in terms of jobs, however, a flaw in the development strategy that had unfortunate consequences for income distribution. While Brazilian incomes may have grown significantly *on average* during the military regime, income distribution became so unequal that Brazil now has one of the worst structures of income distribution in the world (see table 2.3).

In the nearly twenty years since the end of military rule, elected presidents have pledged to liberalize Brazil's economy. Economic liberalization has come slowly to Brazil, however, even while it remains highly dependent on foreign capital for investment and to finance its government debts. Cutting deficit spending has proven very difficult, especially in a democratic regime in which many politicians and interest groups can effectively veto unpopular spending cuts.

### Brazil's New Democracy

In January 1985, Tancredo Neves, a leader of the opposition to the military regime, was elected Brazil's first civilian president in over two decades. His election came as a surprise to the military leadership, which had stacked the electoral college with its own supporters. Neves's vice presidential running mate was *José Sarney,* the leader of the pro-government party, the PDS. On the eve of his inauguration, Neves, a seventy-four-year-old survivor of the Second Republic (1946–64), was hospitalized with an intestinal ailment from which he did not recover. So, on March 15, 1985, José Sarney assumed the presidency. Although Neves and Sarney had been elected indirectly, their successors would be directly elected by the Brazilian people. ***Brazil's new constitution, approved in 1988, inaugurated the* New Republic*, a presidentialist, federal republic.*** (For a list of Brazil's presidents, see table 22.5.)

Although a democratic regime, the New Republic has not spared Brazil from political strife. Sarney and the new Congress were immediately deadlocked over economic stabilization plans during his four-year presidential term. Unable to count on any party to support him in the Congress, Sarney engaged in the widespread use of patronage in exchange for support for his economic policies. But patronage politics ended up undermining the policy coherence of his economic stabilization

**TABLE 22.5**

**Brazilian Presidents Since 1930**

| Name | Term of Office | Mode of Succession |
|---|---|---|
| Getulio Vargas | 1930–45 | Populist dictator |
| Eurico Dutra | 1946–50 | Elected |
| Getulio Vargas | 1951–54 | Elected |
| João Café Filho | 1954–55 | Assumed office as vice president |
| Juscelino Kubitschek | 1956–61 | Elected |
| Jânio Quadros | 1961 | Elected |
| João Goulart | 1961–64 | Assumed office as vice president |
| Humberto Castelo Branco | 1964–67 | Military dictator |
| Artur Costa e Silva | 1967–69 | Military dictator |
| Emilio Garrastazú Médici | 1969–74 | Military dictator |
| Ernesto Geisel | 1974–79 | Military dictator |
| João Figueiredo | 1979–85 | Military dictator |
| José Sarney | 1985–90 | Indirectly elected while vice president |
| Fernando Collor de Mello | 1990–92 | Elected |
| Itamar Franco | 1992–95 | Assumed office as vice president |
| Fernando Henrique Cardoso | 1995–2002 | Elected 1995; re-elected 1998 |
| Luiz Inácio "Lula" da Silva | 2002–present | Elected 2002; re-elected 2006 |

efforts; distributing patronage required federal expenditures at a time when economic stabilization dictated that expenditures be curtailed. Hyperinflation resulted, nearing 2,000 percent before Sarney left office.[72]

When direct presidential elections were held in 1989, *Fernando Collor de Mello,* a former governor of the northeast state of Alagoas with unprecedented skills as a television campaigner, took office on a populist platform of cleaning up corruption in government. Within three years, Collor would be impeached on charges of corruption. A prime example of personalism in politics, Collor had created his own party to campaign for the presidency, but he brought few of his fellow party members into the Congress and commanded very little loyalty there. Amid charges of misappropriating $20 million, he resigned in 1992. His successor was the vice president, *Itamar Franco,* an impulsive politician with little interest in the presidency. Only with the election to the presidency of Fernando Henrique Cardoso in 1994 did Brazil find solid leadership. Lula da Silva entered the presidency with the most unified political party in Brazil behind him and a long track record as an advocate of the interests of Brazil's poor and of democracy. Although Lula da Silva found it difficult to implement his reform agenda because of his commitment to fiscal responsibility and due to opposition in Congress, he remained a popular president and won reelection in October 2006, despite failing to win a majority of votes on the first ballot. Corruption scandals, which forced several members of Lula's cabinet to resign during his first term, dominated the campaign, but Lula's personal connection to the people of Brazil won him nearly 60 percent of the vote on the second ballot.

What were the forces that brought democracy's return to Brazil? Do the institutions put in place in the New Republic promote political stability and a capacity to confront the daunting social and economic problems facing the nation? What are the greatest challenges facing Brazil at the beginning of the twenty-first century?

**Democratization** Democracy came to Brazil only after a long process of political liberalization in which the military regime sought to use democratic institutions to place its allies in positions of power. The opposition fought for democracy on two fronts. The first was the electoral arena, in which an opposition party sought to deny victory to the government's allies. Initially, that party was the Brazilian Democracy Movement (MDB), which later changed its name to the *Party of the Brazilian Democracy Movement (PMDB).* The second front consisted of non-electoral arenas, where grassroots organizations and the organized labor movement fought for the democratization of local government and labor relations. Progress in all arenas came slowly, as the military managed to control the transition to civilian rule and to limit progress in the democratization of society. The government of President *Ernesto Geisel* (1974–79) began a process of "decompression" in 1974. A civilian became president in 1985, but the first direct elections for the presidency did not take place until 1989.

The most severe repression by the military regime coincided with the period known as the *economic miracle* (1968–74). By 1974, after a successful campaign against armed opponents of its rule, the military could not easily claim that repression was necessary to counter subversion, since the subversives had been killed or imprisoned. Moreover, the campaign against urban and rural guerillas had already begun to have an impact on those members of the middle class whose family members were accused of subversion. As mentioned earlier, liberal members of the military also had become worried about the growing autonomy of the state intelligence agency in charge of countering subversion.[73]

Seeking to capitalize on the good feelings associated with the economic miracle and to rein in the hardliners, moderates in the military supported the decompression policy, one element of which involved allowing more open elections for the Congress and governorships in 1974. To the military's chagrin, the opposition Brazilian Democratic Movement defeated the pro-government ARENA. Having opened the electoral process, the moderates in the military could not easily close it down, but they feared losing the Congress to the opposition if ARENA did not have some guarantees that would ensure its victories. Thus began a long series of electoral "reforms" intended to forestall a genuine opposition win. Perhaps the most dramatic of these reforms came in 1979 when the ARENA-dominated Congress voted to dissolve the existing political parties (ARENA included) and to create new rules for party registration designed to fragment the opposition by making the rules for registration easier than they had been in the past. Civilian supporters of the military formed a new party, the PDS, which continued to hold a majority in the Congress, but it became increasingly obvious that it lacked genuine popular support. To retain a government majority in the electoral colleges that chose state governors and the president, the government appointed one member of the senate from each state, so-called "bionic senators."[74]

As economic problems such as the foreign debt crisis and the increasing restiveness of industrial workers mounted in the late 1970s and early 1980s, the government's efforts to stack the deck electorally proved inadequate. The truth was that the military's social support bases had begun to abandon the regime. The military could forestall the advent of a civilian regime, but it could not legitimize its own rule.

Perhaps the most notable allies to abandon the military's coalition in the mid 1970s were businesspeople in Brazil's private sector. Businesspeople had become dissatisfied by the growth of state-owned enterprises during the miracle, an expansion of the public sector that they saw as coming at the expense of investment opportunities that they would be denied. In 1974–76, entrepreneurs led a campaign against the expansion of the state-owned sector. Businesspeople also had become frustrated by what they saw as excessive bureaucratic autonomy under the military; they preferred the more regular access to decision makers promised by democratic institutions.[75] In addition, business leaders found themselves somewhat embarrassed when dealing with business partners or customers in other parts of the world to have to admit that they lived and did business in a military regime. By the late 1970s, business leaders also felt that the military had mismanaged the economy, undermining one of the military's major justifications for being in power.[76]

Other social groups withdrew their support in much the same way that business became disenchanted with the military. Some elements of the middle class such as lawyers and journalists advocated democracy so that their civil liberties would be protected. Given that members of some middle- and upper-class families had been treated as "ordinary" subversives—and thus tortured and held without trial—during the 1968–74 period, the withdrawal of support for the military by many members of the middle class comes as no surprise.[77] The middle class may seek the economic security that dictatorships sometimes provide, but many elements of the middle class value their civil liberties, which dictatorships often trample. Traditional political elites prospered under military rule, but many abandoned the military when it seemed prudent for their political futures.[78]

Meanwhile, the difficulty of producing progressive change through the channels of representation available during the military's rule led many groups among Brazil's poor to create new organizations independent of the political parties or officially sanctioned labor unions. Although grassroots organizations and the "new labor" movement cannot be credited as the only source of democratization in the 1970s and 1980s, they did pose challenges to the military regime. Grassroots organizations ran the gamut of issue areas, from women's organizations to environmental movements to neighborhood associations. Many became active during the military government because no other political organizations—parties or government agencies—gave adequate attention to their members' needs.

Neighborhood associations, for instance, formed to make demands on state and local governments for the extension of public services: utilities, law and order, roads, and schools. These associations perceived that a transition to democracy would be necessary to get the representation that could bring responses to their demands. Popular organizations did not succeed in creating a national movement that shaped the transition process, but they did succeed in raising people's consciousness of the importance of democracy for meeting the needs of ordinary Brazilians.[79] The Catholic church, a progressive force in Brazil, supported grassroots groups and provided a critical voice when few others could be found. Popular movements undoubtedly contributed to the willingness of politicians and representatives of interest groups representing better-off elements of Brazilian society to push for regime liberalization.

The "new union" movement reflected a desire of some segments of the industrial labor force to escape the corporatist organizations of the state-run labor movement. In a wave of strikes begun in 1978–79 by metalworkers led by Lula and eventually extending to many other industries, the new union movement focused attention on the capacity of ordinary people to organize themselves and make demands on the government. The strikes produced only modest gains for workers, and they also demonstrated to the movement's leaders that they needed to create a political organization to focus their efforts at the national level. The *Workers' Party (PT)* was formed after the new law regulating party formation was passed in 1979.[80]

The pressure for democratization increased dramatically in the early 1980s. The most dramatic example of that pressure came in the *Diretas Já* (Direct Elections Now) campaign of 1984. Many opposition politicians, social movements, and labor unions participated in this mass movement, which swept the country. The military resisted the demand for direct elections in 1984, but only after alienating many of its civilian allies, several of whom left the pro-government party to form a party of their own. That new party supported Tancredo Neves, the Brazilian Democracy Movement's candidate in the 1985 indirect elections; together they defeated the military's candidate, thereby ushering out the military regime.

## The New Republic and Its Institutions

Brazil's transition to democracy included the writing of a new constitution, completed in 1988. In many of its fundamental elements, the lengthy new constitution drafted by the Constituent Assembly (245 articles) looks much like the constitution of the Second Republic. The military and President Sarney significantly defeated an effort by reformers to introduce a parliamentary regime in Brazil that would have increased the powers of the legislature by giving it an opportunity to vote no-confidence in the executive (including the cabinet officers in charge of the military branches).[81]

**The Institutional Structure** Roughly patterned on the U.S. Constitution's principle of separation of powers, the New Republic provides for a *president* who is both head of state and head of government (like the U.S. president). The president is now elected directly by the people.

The bicameral *Congress* consists of the *Chamber of Deputies,* the lower house with 513 members drawn from the country's twenty-six states and the Federal District of Brasilia, the national capital; and the *Senate,* the upper house, which has three representatives from each state and the Federal District (eighty-one total). Members of the Chamber of

Deputies serve four-year terms; senators serve eight years. The powers of the two houses are evenly balanced, with both possessing the right to initiate legislation and review the federal budget. Congress may also override presidential vetoes. The *Supreme Court* has the power of judicial review.

Brazil's federal structure gives ample powers to the governors of the twenty-six states and the Federal District. Each state and the Federal District also has a unicameral state legislature. County-level governments called *municipios* are the main institutions of local government.

**The Electoral System and Its Consequences** To most observers, the most notable aspect of relations between the executive and legislative branches is the difficulty that presidents have in putting together majority coalitions for their legislative initiatives. Consequently, Brazilian presidents have found it difficult to accomplish major policy objectives. Weak parties (and the large number of them) play the most important role in producing a governability crisis.

Many of the ills of Brazil's new democracy can be traced to the electoral system put in place with the new constitution. In elections to the Chamber of Deputies, the representatives are chosen in a complex version of the party-list *proportional representation* system. The twenty-six states plus the Federal District serve as the electoral districts. Because the states vary in size, so do state deputations; some have as few as six seats and others as many as seventy. Voters can either vote for a party's label or write in the names of individual candidates, whose names do not appear on the ballot itself. (Japan had a similar system before its 1994 electoral reforms.) The total votes received by the party label or by individuals belonging to a party are then added up. Each party receives a number of seats from that state roughly equivalent to the percentage of the total votes its label and its candidates have garnered. So if the Party of the Brazilian Democracy Movement and its candidates get 35 percent of the vote in São Paulo state, they get roughly 35 percent of that state's total delegation to the Chamber of Deputies.

The actual composition of each party's congressional delegation depends on how many *individual write-in* votes each candidate receives. The candidates with the greatest number of write-in votes are the ones who tend to get elected. To stand a good chance of winning, therefore, candidates must have name recognition; membership in a particular party might help them, but only marginally. Furthermore, in many states there may be several candidates running under a party's name, thus crowding the field.

How does one gain name recognition? A politician seeking office for the first time would benefit from the help of political patrons who might urge their followers to vote for an individual—for example, a governor or senator might tell his followers to vote for a particular deputy candidate. Once a politician has gained a congressional seat, she must figure out how to reward those who have voted for her; she may, for example, direct public spending toward the localities where her votes have been concentrated or intervene to ask for public jobs for constituents. This system strongly encourages pork-barrel politics and clientelism (as in Japan before the reforms). Politicians even attempt to focus the government's spending on those specific localities within their states in which they expect to get the most votes, so they can return from Brasilia (the capital) to those localities and claim credit for the spending. Because pork-barrel politics discourages politicians from developing strong ideological identities and because personal name recognition matters more than a party label does at reelection time, politicians have little incentive to be loyal to their parties and the programs they might put forward. Weak parties result from this electoral system.

**Weak Parties and an Underdeveloped Party System** Given the incentive structure created by the electoral system, we would expect that political parties have a hard time retaining the loyalty of their elected representatives. As table 22.6 shows, at the beginning of the New Republic, Brazilian politicians were notorious for switching parties after they were elected. Politicians jumped from party to party as they bargained for political benefits that they could distribute to their supporters. Parties' fortunes thus rose and fell even between elections, without the voters having rejected a party at the ballot box. If a politician was willing to abandon the party that elected him, would we expect him to vote with the party when crucial issues come before the Congress? Surely not, if it threatened his reelection chances.

TABLE 22.6

**Composition of the Brazilian Chamber of Deputies by Party, 1987–90 Term**

| Party | Feb. 1987 | Sept. 1988 | Jan. 1990 | Oct. 1990 |
|---|---|---|---|---|
| Party of the Brazilian Democracy Movement (PMDB) | 305 | 235 | 200 | 153 |
| Party of the Liberal Front (PFL) | 134 | 125 | 108 | 103 |
| Democratic Socialist Party (PDS) | 37 | 34 | 32 | 35 |
| Brazilian Social Democratic Party (PSDB) | 0 | 48 | 61 | 72 |
| Democratic Labor Party (PDT) | 26 | 28 | 35 | 43 |
| Brazilian Labor Party (PTB) | 19 | 29 | 26 | 32 |
| Workers' Party (PT) | 16 | 16 | 16 | 17 |
| Liberal Party (PL) | 7 | 7 | 19 | 13 |
| Christian Democratic Party (PDC) | 6 | 13 | 17 | 22 |
| Party of National Reconstruction (PRN) | 0 | 0 | 24 | 34 |
| Others | 9 | 24 | 32 | 43 |

*Source:* Adapted from Scott Mainwaring, "Brazil: Weak Parties, Feckless Democracy," in *Building Democratic Institutions: Party Systems in Latin America*, ed. Scott Mainwaring and Timothy R. Scully (Stanford: Stanford University Press, 1995), p. 377.

Weak parties cannot be counted on by party leaders or the president to support major policy initiatives. As a consequence, presidents have had a daunting task before them when they seek to pass legislative bills they consider important: they must constantly cobble together a congressional majority by making deals with groups of legislators or individuals whose votes are essential. Controlling public spending in this context has proven very difficult; legislators expect favors for their votes, usually in the form of budgetary allocations for their home states. That is one reason why inflation plagued Brazil for so long. Significantly, public spending was rarely directed toward major efforts to confront poverty or lessen inequality, for the weakness of the party system ensured that programs threatening the privileges of the better-off segment of Brazilian society simply would not pass the Congress.[82]

Despite incentives against the formation of strong parties, several parties have emerged that have some durability. Fortunately for Brazil, its politicians no longer exhibit the fickleness illustrated in table 22.6, and the party system has become more stable. Not all of Brazil's parties have clear ideologies, but most have something akin to a policy stance on the important issues facing their society. The largest party on the conservative side of the political spectrum is the *Party of the Liberal Front (PFL)*. The PFL can trace its ancestry to the military-backed parties, ARENA and the PDS; it was put together during the 1984–85 transition by PDS members seeking to erase their association with the former military regime. As a party of the right it generally favors reducing the size of the public sector; hence it favors pro-business neoliberal policies. Other parties on the right include the *Brazilian Labor Party (PTB)*, founded by Getulio Vargas's grandniece in the early 1980s, but much more conservative than its namesake during the Second Republic; the *Progressive Party (PPB)*, formed in a merger of the Labor Renewal and Social Labor parties; and several smaller parties. Together these parties of the right or center-right took about 40 percent of the vote in 1998's Chamber of Deputies race, but only about 25 percent in 2002.

On the other end of the political spectrum, the *Workers' Party (PT)* has sought to avoid practicing clientelism as it attempts to represent Brazilian workers and the poor. Its popular leader is now President da Silva. A party that strives to promote internal democracy, the PT has not suffered defections to the same extent as other Brazilian parties. It won nearly 20 percent of the congressional vote in 2002. Unfortunately for the PT's reputation as a party with a different attitude toward corruption and internal democracy, a scandal erupted in 2005 when party leaders were accused of bribing Congress members from other parties to secure their votes on important legislative bills. Top members of the PT's executive committee had to resign. The party's image and that of President Lula were tarnished by the scandal.

TABLE 22.7

**Governors, Senators, and Deputies Elected in 1994, 1998, 2002, and 2006**

| | Governors | | | | Senate | | | | Chamber of Deputies | | | |
|---|---|---|---|---|---|---|---|---|---|---|---|---|
| **Party** | **1994** | **1998** | **2002** | **2006** | **1994** | **1998** | **2002** | **2006** | **1994** | **1998** | **2002** | **2006** |
| Party of the Brazilian Democratic Movement (PMDB) | 9 | 6 | 5 | 7 | 22 | 27 | 19 | 15 | 107 | 82 | 74 | 89 |
| Party of the Liberal Front (PFL) | 2 | 5 | 4 | 1 | 18 | 20 | 19 | 18 | 89 | 106 | 85 | 65 |
| Brazilian Social Democratic Party (PSDB) | 6 | 7 | 7 | 6 | 11 | 16 | 11 | 15 | 62 | 99 | 71 | 65 |
| Brazilian Progressive Party (formerly the PDS) (PPB) | 3 | 2 | — | 1 | 6 | 5 | 1 | 1 | 52 | 60 | 48 | 42 |
| Workers' Party (PT) | 2 | 3 | 3 | 5 | 5 | 7 | 14 | 11 | 49 | 58 | 91 | 83 |
| Democratic Labor Party (PDT) | 2 | 1 | 1 | 2 | 6 | 2 | 5 | 5 | 34 | 25 | 21 | 24 |
| Brazilian Labor Party (PTB) | 1 | — | — | — | 5 | — | 3 | 4 | 31 | 31 | 26 | 22 |
| Liberal Party (PL) | — | — | 1 | — | 1 | — | 3 | 3 | 13 | 12 | 27 | 23 |
| Others | — | 1 | 6 | 5 | 6 | 1 | 6 | 9 | 61 | 21 | 70 | 100 |
| Total | 27 | 27 | 27 | 27 | 81 | 81 | 81 | 81 | 513 | 513 | 513 | 513 |

*Source:* Maria D'Alva G. Kinzo and Simone Rodrigues da Silva, "Politics in Brazil: Cardoso's Government and the 1998 Re-election," *Government and Opposition* 34, no. 2 (spring 1999), p. 259; Tribunal Superior Eleitoral.

Other parties on the left have found breaking into the already crowded party system difficult because of the PT's successes. However, a *Green Party (PV),* a *Brazilian Socialist Party (PSB),* and two communist parties—the *Communist Party of Brazil (PC do B)* and the *Popular Socialist Party (PPS),* formerly the Brazilian Communist Party—contend for votes. The *Democratic Labor Party (PDT),* a populist party led by Goulart's brother-in-law, Leonel Brizola, himself a former governor of Rio de Janeiro before the military regime, gains about 5 percent of the vote.

In the center and center-left of the party system sit the *Party of the Brazilian Democratic Movement (PMDB)* and Cardoso's *Brazilian Social Democratic Party (PSDB).* These parties rival the PFL and the PT in their quest to be the largest party in the nation. Each draws 15 to 20 percent of the vote. While they can be placed in the middle of the ideological spectrum, the PMDB and the PSDB include members on both the right and the left. The PSDB itself was founded by dissidents from the PMDB in 1988 who desired a social democratic alternative in Brazil. However, the PSDB followed centrist policies after Cardoso assumed the presidency in 1994. The PMDB, meanwhile, attracted conservative politicians to its ranks in the 1990s.

Table 22.7 indicates the strength of the most important parties in different electoral settings in the past decade. Note that the largest four parties (PMDB, PFL, PT, and PSDB) do especially well in elections where only one candidate stands, namely, gubernatorial and senatorial races. Other parties that cannot swing a whole state or that can only rarely do so can nevertheless win several federal deputy races. Thereby they gain congressional representation, but with that representation they can make coalition formation all the more difficult in the lower house.

**The Presidency and the Congress** The new constitution gives the president a formidable set of constitutional powers, making the Brazilian presidency on paper among the most powerful in Latin America,[83] with much more sweeping powers than the Mexican presidency. Presidents can veto legislative acts, wholly or partially, and they have exclusive rights to initiate legislation in several important policy areas, including most that deal with public spending. (The Congress can override a presidential veto.) The president can also insist that the Congress take up legislation that he deems urgent within a forty-five-day period. However, to rate the Brazilian presidency's powers on the basis of formal constitutional powers alone would be to ignore other key aspects of presidential power. As we learned by considering the Mexican presidency, if the president has sufficient partisan support in the Congress, he can accomplish feats not envisioned by the constitution. In the Brazilian case, in contrast, insufficient partisan support in the Congress can make it very difficult for the president to accomplish major policy objectives, much as divided government can frustrate U.S. presidents.

To get legislation passed, Brazilian presidents must attempt to hold coalitions together. Since the legislators don't always show party discipline and sometimes even defect from their parties, presidents cannot count on party leaders whipping their members to vote for a presidential initiative. Instead, presidents contribute to the clientelist politics described earlier. They control federal funds and federal jobs, both of which are coveted by members of Congress seeking to satisfy their constituents. Old-fashioned horse trading may be essential to pass laws considered key to a president's agenda. It bears repeating that pork-barrel politics contributes to Brazil's out-of-control federal spending.

Even then, presidents have found it difficult to accomplish major objectives. Scott Mainwaring demonstrated that in nine policy areas critical to economic stabilization and state reform in the 1985 to 1994 period (including the privatization of state monopolies, cutting public sector employment, passing new tax bills, even collecting debts owed to the federal government by private business), Presidents Sarney, Collor, and Franco ran into the opposition of members of Congress who were protecting constituents or supporters and made no progress in those pressing policy areas.[84] Brazil's underdeveloped party system contributes to a legislature more inclined to protect the status quo and vested interests than to promote change or to address major social problems. Presidents are often forced to rule as much as possible by "emergency measures," which allow the president to make laws for thirty days, after which the Congress can either pass or reject the new legislation. Without those measures, presidents would find governing nearly impossible.

## PROFILE: Luiz Inácio "Lula" da Silva

In a society accustomed to selecting the sons of elite families for the presidency, even when they advocate social change, the election of *Luiz Inácio "Lula" da Silva* to Brazil's presidency marks a bold and democratic departure. Born the last of seven children of farmworkers in rural Pernambuco in Brazil's impoverished northeast in 1945, da Silva moved to São Paulo with his mother and siblings when he was seven. There they discovered that his father, who had moved earlier, had a new family. The da Silva children thus began working early to support the now fatherless family, with Lula working as a shoeshine boy before taking on full-time employment at age twelve.

While still in his teens, da Silva became a lathe operator, at times working twelve-hour shifts in São Paulo's metals factories. His first wife died in childbirth due to inadequate medical care. By age 22, Lula's experiences and the encouragement of his older, politically active brother led him to join a union, despite the repressive climate of the military dictatorship.

With his intelligence and boldness, Lula quickly rose to the top of the São Bernardo Metalworkers Union, an important component of what became known as the "new unionism." In 1978–79, mass strikes by metalworkers—led by Lula—put significant pressure on the military to begin its *abertura*, the controlled political liberalization that eventually returned power to civilians in 1985. Lula, however, was jailed for his part in the demonstrations, along with about a thousand other labor activists.

**Luiz Inácio "Lula" da Silva**

**TABLE 22.8**

**Brazilian Presidential Elections, 2002 and 2006**

| 2002 | | | 2006 | | |
|---|---|---|---|---|---|
| **Candidate** | **Party** | **%** | **Candidate** | **Party** | **%** |
| **First Round** | | | **First Round** | | |
| Luiz Inácio "Lula" da Silva | PT | 46.4 | Luiz Inácio "Lula" da Silva | PT | 48.6 |
| José Serra | PSDB | 23.2 | Geraldo Alckmin | PSDB | 41.6 |
| Anthony Garotinho | PSB | 17.9 | Heloísa Helena | PSOL | 6.8 |
| Ciro Gomes | PPS | 12.0 | Cristovam Buarque | PDT | 2.6 |
| Others | | 0.5 | Others | | 0.4 |
| **Second Round** | | | **Second Round** | | |
| Luiz Inácio "Lula" da Silva | PT | 61.3 | Luiz Inácio "Lula" da Silva | PT | 60.8 |
| José Serra | PSDB | 38.7 | Geraldo Alckmin | PSDB | 39.2 |

In 1980, Lula was chosen the first president of the newly formed Workers' Party (PT). The PT's founders conceptualized it as a socialist mass party with democratic operating procedures—a stark contrast to the elite-dominated parties that dot the Brazilian political landscape. Those norms of internal democracy have meant that Lula on two occasions lost when he ran for party president. Yet the PT has been closely identified with Lula, whose charismatic leadership of the metalworkers and then in the movement for democracy won him the following of Brazilian workers, intellectuals, and many others. The PT has successfully incorporated many of Brazil's marginalized groups—homosexuals, blacks, environmentalists, and women, among others.

Lula became a congressional deputy in 1986 and learned the arts of compromise and coalition formation. He became perhaps the best-known politician in Brazil. But in the country's deeply divided society, many people could not conceive of a working-class president. In the 1989, 1994, and 1998 presidential elections, Lula finished second to candidates who clearly represented Brazil's middle and upper classes. His image as a bearded, gruff, T-shirt-wearing exworker may have won him the adulation of workers and the marginalized, but it provoked profound fears in those Brazilians who had much to lose to a candidate who called himself a socialist.

For the 2002 presidential election, Lula chose a different strategy, running from the center and seeking the support of those who had earlier been threatened by him. Lula put on business suits and abandoned his usually combative political rhetoric for a more moderate tone. He reached out to business leaders and the military in an effort to calm the fears of foreign investors and the middle class about what his presidency would mean. And he promised not to overturn the direction of economic policy that Fernando Henrique Cardoso had set—an orthodox development strategy that maintained a floating exchange rate, low inflation, and a budget surplus.

With the fears of the middle class somewhat eased, Lula easily defeated Cardoso's former deputy, José Serra, an economist and a former minister of health credited with devising Brazil's successful efforts to stem the advance of HIV/AIDS, in a runoff election on October 27, 2002 (see table 22.8). Despite worries that a leftist's election would produce an economic meltdown, Brazil fared well in Lula's first months in office—investors did not leave the country, and inflation remained under control.

However, Lula has learned how difficult it can be to govern Brazil. For example, the Landless Workers Movement (MST), once a PT ally, has broken with Lula and organized mass demonstrations because his government has not moved quickly enough to address their demands for land reform. As another example, Lula has followed Cardoso in an effort to reform civil servants' employment contracts and pensions, a huge government expenditure that threatened to produce a ballooning federal deficit. Civil servants who have long been PT supporters strongly resisted any reduction of their privileges. However, Lula was able to pass his reform legislation. He has also run into difficulties keeping his promises to alleviate the extreme poverty that afflicts an estimated 50 million Brazilians, and to implement his "Zero Hunger" program, which seeks to eliminate widespread malnutrition. "If, by the end of my term, all Brazilians are able to eat breakfast, lunch, and dinner," Lula said at his first inauguration, "I will have fulfilled my life's mission." Accomplishing these goals would require, among other things, a commitment to rebuilding Brazil's primary and secondary educational systems. According to the World Bank, two-thirds of the glaring income gap between rich and poor in Brazil is caused by an education gap. Only a third of Brazilian teenagers attend high school, compared to 58 percent in Mexico and 98 percent in South Korea. One of Lula's greatest challenges continues to be to convince members of Congress—and Brazilian taxpayers—to allocate the money needed to address these problems.

Lula's movement to the center reflects the constraints that all societies now face in their political choices. Globalization and dependence on international finance force political leaders to choose their policy prescriptions carefully for fear of producing capital flight and economic crises. Voters are keenly aware of these dynamics, too. Lula's failure in his earlier presidential bids had much to do with the Brazilian voters' unease about selecting a combative leftist to lead their nation. Yet many Brazilians voted for Lula because they sought a change in their nation's direction. Those Brazilians expected Lula to be true to his political party and his working-class origins.

Despite the difficulties in implementing his reform agenda, Lula remained a popular president, even when corruption scandals broke out among his cabinet officers and trusted advisors. Brazil's economy performed well during his first term—productivity and exports rose while inflation remained in the single digits. On top of economic stability, Lula brought modest social reform. A Family Fund program that provides government assistance to nearly a fifth of Brazil's families replaced the failed Zero Hunger plan. Lula also succeeded in raising the minimum wage by 25 percent. Moreover, he has won plaudits for steering a responsible middle course on foreign policy, maintaining strong relationships with both Venezuela's populist president Hugo Chávez and George W. Bush of the United States. He has strengthened Brazil's leadership role in the Mercosur trading bloc in South America. So it is perhaps not surprising that Brazil's voters returned him to office in 2006.

### The 2006 Presidential Elections

Because corruption scandals had tainted Lula's administration in the two years preceding the October 2006 presidential elections, observers noted that Lula's reelection would not be easy, despite his relatively high approval ratings and his broad personal popularity. As the election approached, Brazil's federal structure and multiparty system produced many potential challengers for the sitting president—governors of major states like São Paulo and Minas Gerais and mayors of major cities like Rio de Janeiro and São Paulo. Eventually former president Cardoso's party, the PSDB, put forward São Paulo governor Geraldo Alckmin, with the PFL's senator José Jorge as his vice-presidential running mate. The other noteworthy candidate in the election was Senator Heloísa Helena of the Socialism and Freedom Party (PSOL), a former Lula ally who founded the PSOL and announced her candidacy after the PT expelled her for her vociferous criticism of Lula's turn to economic orthodoxy.

Lula thus faced criticism from Helena on his left and Alckmin on his right. A successful, tax-cutting governor, Alckmin emphasized the corruption scandals that had emerged in the PT and the Lula government as well as what he characterized as Lula's record of slow economic growth. Alckmin's criticism of Lula may have been sufficient to prevent Lula from winning an absolute majority on the first ballot (see table 22.8), but Alckmin failed to win over Brazil's poor majority and the president won easy reelection on the second ballot. Alckmin's vote tally actually declined between October 1 and October 29.

## Issues in Brazilian Politics

**A Robust Federalism**[85] That Brazil's Congress overrepresents small states, most of which are rural states from the northeast and the Amazon, exacerbates a set of structural problems in the Brazilian political system. Those northeastern and Amazonian states depend more on distributions from the federal government than do the southeastern and southern states. Their representatives have parlayed the president's need for their votes in Congress into continuing public spending in their states and localities. Such processes reinforce the sense held by other Brazilians that corruption and backwardness characterize the politics of the north and the northeast.

The 1988 constitution grants significant public funds to state and local governments, but it does not impose greater expectations on those subnational governments for spending on education, health, or infrastructure, the typical responsibilities of subnational authorities. Indeed, about half the nation's tax revenues collected by the federal government is returned to states and municipalities with no mandates about how that money should be spent. Governors and mayors thus have resources they can distribute to help their political clients, including members of the Congress elected from their states. Consequently, governors (who can now be reelected) and mayors can use their influence over members of the Congress to see that their states are favored by federal laws or that their states are recipients of federal spending in infrastructure projects and the like. Development projects in the northeast and infrastructure projects in the Amazon have thus been well supported in the Congress.

The enormous influence of the states was vividly evident in 1998, when the governor of Minas Gerais—Brazil's former president, Itamar Franco—declared a moratorium on his state's $15.3 billion debt to the federal treasury. The unilateral announcement provoked a budgetary crisis that frightened foreign investors and threatened to derail President Cardoso's austerity policies, which were central to retaining the confidence of the IMF. It took all of Cardoso's political skills to resolve the issue.

**Women and Politics** Women's movements emerged with the reduction of political restrictions in the *abertura* in the late 1970s and early 1980s. Women demanded greater political representation and policy initiatives, such as day care and family planning, that would improve their lives. Of course, in many policy areas, such as abortion rights, feminists run up against opposition from the powerful Catholic Church. And we know that the New Republic creates many opportunities for powerful political actors to block policy initiatives.

Overall, Brazil has perhaps the most vibrant feminist movement in Latin America. In addition, during the New Republic the feminist movement has worked with elected officials to pass some of the most advanced measures to promote women's rights.[86] However, women's representation in politics has been marginal in Brazil. Although women have had the vote since 1933, few female candidates have been elected to important positions. For example, in the 1994 Senate race, of the 81 seats open, women won 4 (fourteen women ran for the Senate that year). President Franco had three women in his cabinet, but his successor, Cardoso, appointed only one. Nevertheless, in 1996 Congress introduced a quota of 20 percent for women candidates for municipal office and then extended the system to congressional offices in 1998.[87] As a result, the number of female legislators has grown. Yet nomination does not equate to election, and in 2002 only 6 percent of elected federal deputies, and only 7 percent of senators and governors, were women.[88] Women won 8.6 percent of the Chamber of Deputies in 2006.

**Human Rights in Brazil** Democracy does not guarantee that human rights will be respected. Even though repression of dissidents by the central government went out along with Brazil's military regime, many human rights problems continue in Brazil. A weak central government, the persistence of local political bosses, and highly unequal economic relationships have resulted in forced labor, police brutality, inhumane prison conditions, and extrajudicial killings of activists.

The experience of the Landless Workers Movement (MST) provides a very clear example of human rights abuse in Brazil. The MST is the largest social movement in Latin America; it has struggled for land reform for more than a decade. When its legal efforts to obtain land for the millions of landless rural workers fail, the MST sometimes seizes some of the thousands of acres that large landowners leave fallow. Because of its advocacy of land reform and because it is willing to engage in direct action to address its members' needs, the MST is much reviled by the thousands of large absentee landowners who own so much of Brazil's territory and by their political allies, powerful local *coroneis*.

Despite the size of its membership and the hundreds of lawyers and human rights workers who struggle on the MST's behalf, the MST has been subject to severe repression. More than two hundred activists and peasants associated with the MST have been murdered in the past decade. Rarely are the assassins—often moonlighting policemen—or their employers brought to justice in local courts, and even when they are, local *coroneis* exert such influence over members of juries that convictions are uncommon. Brazilians and international human rights organizations such as Amnesty International and Human Rights Watch continue to pressure for federal legislation that would make it easier to prosecute assassins and other human rights abusers in settings beyond these rigged local courts. In the meantime, though, being an advocate of the poor and the landless can be a very dangerous vocation in Latin America's largest democracy.

## Hypotheses on Democracy and Democratization

Can Brazil's New Republic survive the challenges it faces? Does democracy have a future in South America's giant? Again, let's review our hypotheses on democratization to see if they suggest a bright or a bleak future for Brazil.

**Elites Committed to Democracy** Most important, Brazil's military has apparently withdrawn from politics. If the New Republic has had a notable success, it has been in returning the military to the barracks.[89] Since the transition to democracy, most elite groups seem to support the New Republic, perhaps because the military's rule has been discredited in Brazil as in most of the hemisphere. But the depth of elite commitment to democracy has yet to be tested.

**State Institutions** The institutions of the New Republic provide powerful groups many points of access to defeat measures that threaten their interests. This means that measures designed to reform the economy so as to address the needs of the poor and redistribute income prove nearly impossible to legislate. A legislature composed of weak and undisciplined parties whose members seek all the patronage they can acquire, and a federal system in which states and governors can use their power to defeat measures in the national Congress or resist implementing them at the state and local levels, have made socioeconomic reform difficult to accomplish. A democratic process may be in place in Brazil, but it fails to produce policies that reflect the interests of the majority of society.

Paradoxically, some political scientists argue that the fact that Brazil's political institutions allow conservative groups to veto many reform measures makes those same groups more prone to support democracy. Hence, Brazilian businesses, landowners, and locally powerful figures have become much less inclined to advocate nondemocratic acts, such as military coups or other threats against those in office. So Brazil's democracy may be stable even if the quality of democracy is low.[90]

**National Unity** Brazil's society is not homogeneous, but as we noted earlier, as yet the racial diversity of the nation has not promoted political conflict on racial lines. However, African Brazilians and those of indigenous heritage are increasingly active politically, demanding that their voices be heard too. This new political activism regarding racially or ethnically based issues should be welcomed as one way in which Brazil's new democracy is responding to citizens' concerns.

**National Wealth** Income distribution remains severely unequal in Brazil. However, the opponents of income redistribution seem to have learned how to defeat redistributive measures through the institutions of democracy. For those proponents of redistribution, few alternatives to democracy recommend themselves, however, other than "deepening" democracy, a process not very likely to come to Brazil soon.[91]

**Private Enterprise** The Brazilian state has divested itself of considerable portions of the public sector over the past decade. (The 1999 sale of Telebras, the telecommunications giant, is an example.) In part because of the neoliberal policies followed by the government, business owners do not feel threatened by democratic institutions at this time. Having lived through a military regime that enhanced the public sector of the economy, perhaps at their expense, business has little desire to return to military rule.

**Middle Class** Brazil's middle class seems solidly supportive of democracy.

**Support of the Disadvantaged** Brazil's working class has become the voter base of one of its most important, pro-democratic parties, the Workers Party (PT). The PT has expanded its voter base to others among the urban poor. But poverty is a festering wound in Brazilian cities, where millions live in overcrowded shanty towns. Many of Brazil's poor are prey to criminal gangs, drugs, and flagrant police brutality. (A recent poll indicated that 70 percent of the residents of São Paulo are terrified of the police.) Brazilian court officials estimate that three homeless street children are killed every day in Rio de Janeiro, usually by police acting at the behest of local merchants. A UNICEF report said that more than half of the 17.5 million minors forced to work in Latin America are in Brazil, about a million of them under the age of ten. Childhood prostitution is common.

Rural poverty and political marginalization are also endemic. Land remains heavily overconcentrated in the hands of wealthy farmers; the poorest 30 percent of Brazilians share just 2 percent of the country's arable land, and nearly 5 million people have no land at all. As Latin America's largest social movement, the MST has pushed for land reform and on many occasions has taken matters into its own hands, seizing properties that it regards as underused. These actions have both positive and negative implications for democracy. On the one hand, many applaud the activism of the MST as representing a clear example of the underclass taking political action to rectify perceived injustices. On the other hand, direct action of the type followed by the MST is often illegal, forcing the authorities to respond to such acts by *post facto* land redistribution laws or decrees. In addition, the direct action of the MST threatens landowners, who often respond violently, promoting a breakdown of rule of law. Though the constitution reserves 11 percent of Brazil's land for indigenous Indians, numbering about a quarter million, recent laws have facilitated encroachment on Indian territory for lumbering and mining purposes. Illegal encroachments spark periodic violence with native populations.[92] The rural poor have few allies in Congress, while many remain controlled in clientelist networks run by local political bosses. In spite of these enormous problems, however, a nondemocratic revolutionary movement representing the poor is not in evidence in contemporary Brazil.

**Civil Society and Political Culture** Like Mexicans, many Brazilians remain skeptical about whether democracy can make a difference in their lives. Many doubt that it solves society's problems.[93] However, Brazilian civil society has much more vibrancy than it did a quarter century ago. Many social movements have organized the poor and the middle classes to promote the interests of women, indigenous peoples, and local communities and to save the environment. This more active civil society would not as easily succumb to military rule as Brazil did in 1964.

**Education and Freedom of Information** Although educational levels have improved in the last quarter century, and although there are many more sources of information in today's Brazil, in these dimensions of Brazilian society all is not strongly supportive of democracy. On the one hand, the news media have played an important role in investigating allegations of political corruption, thereby demonstrating a degree of journalistic independence critical for keeping politicians somewhat honest. On the other hand, however, the Brazilian reliance on television for news and the popularity of *telenovelas* (soap operas) among the viewing public does not promise to promote political sophistication in the mass public.

**Favorable International Environment** Since 1964, and especially with the end of the Cold War, the likelihood that the United States and other major powers would support a military coup in Brazil has declined drastically.

## CONCLUSION

In this chapter we have suggested that significant forces are at work in Brazil and Mexico to promote democracy's consolidation. Certainly each nation continues to confront serious social problems and an increasingly challenging international economic environment. However, these societies' relatively recent experiences with less than democratic regimes—a civilian authoritarian regime in Mexico, military rule in Brazil—have led both elites and mass publics to prefer democratic politics. There is wide support for democratic values and the rule of law, the two steps that form the base of the Temple of Democracy sketched out in chapter 7. Mexicans and Brazilians also appear determined to solidify the three pillars that represent democracy's functional components. Popular sovereignty (Pillar I) is evident in the large numbers of people who have voted in elections that, in recent years, have swept popular opposition figures like Vicente Fox and Lula da Silva to the pinnacle of power in their respective countries. It is evident as well in the growth of civil society in both Mexico and Brazil. Legal guarantees of political and civil rights and liberties (Pillar II) are also becoming stronger in the two countries, a far cry from the flagrant abuses of these rights that were defining characteristics of Mexico's former one-party regime and Brazil's military governments. And elected officials in both countries have a keener sense of their obligation to improve the economic well-being of the people they govern (Pillar III) than the authoritarian elites they replaced ever had.

Of course, democracy certainly cannot instantly reverse decades of corruption, injustice, and economic inequality. As noted earlier in this book, democracies are works in progress. The progress Mexicans and Brazilians have made in recent years in surmounting powerful dictatorships and charting paths toward democracy has been truly exemplary, and it may well inspire other countries in Latin America to follow the same course. Democracy does not necessarily solve all problems, as Latin Americans have learned in the past twenty years. The important but yet-to-be-answered question is, do Latin Americans value democracy for its own sake?

## KEY TERMS AND NAMES (In bold and underlined in the text)

### Mexico

Felipe Calderón
Mestizos
Institutional Revolutionary Party (PRI)
Spanish Conquest
Import-substituting industrialization (ISI)
Neo-liberalism
Democratic Revolutionary Party (PRD)
National Action Party (PAN)
Vincente Fox
North American Free Trade Agreement (NAFTA)

### Brazil

Luiz Inácio "Lula" da Silva
Old Republic
New State
New Republic

## NOTES

1. For more details on the 2006 Mexican election, see the symposium of essays "The 2006 Mexican Election and Its Aftermath," *PS: Political Science and Politics* 40, no. 1 (January 2007).
2. Samuel P. Huntington, *The Third Wave: Democratization in the Late Twentieth Century* (Norman: University of Oklahoma Press, 1991).
3. www.esa.un.org/unpp.
4. *World Development Report 2007* (Washington, D.C.: The World Bank, 2006).
5. The U.S. population density was 70.3 persons per square mile in 1990; Mexico's was 124 persons per square mile. See *The World Almanac and Book of Facts 1996* (Mahwah, N.J.: Funk and Wagnalls, 1995).
6. See http://www.worldatlas.com/citypops.htm.
7. United Nations Development Program, Department of Economic and Social Affairs, Population Division, "Urban and Rural Areas 1996," at http://www.undp/popin/wdrends/-20ura/ura.htm.
8. Carlos Antonio Gutiérrez, "Extienden su constancia de mayoria a candidatos ganadores en Aguascalientes," *Excelsior* (Mexico City), August 7, 1998.
9. José Luis Reyna and Richard S. Weinert, eds., *Authoritarianism in Mexico* (Philadelphia: Institute for the Study of Human Issues, 1977).
10. Wayne A. Cornelius, *Mexican Politics in Transition: The Breakdown of a One-Party-Dominant Regime* (La Jolla: Center for U.S.-Mexican Studies, University of California at San Diego, 1996), 39.
11. Jonathan Fox, "The Difficult Transition from Clientelism to Citizenship: Lessons from Mexico," *World Politics* 46, no. 2 (January 1994).
12. For a comprehensive historical overview, see Michael C. Meyer and William L. Sherman, *The Course of Mexican History,* 5th ed. (New York: Oxford University Press, 1995).
13. They were called *cientificos* because they adopted the positivist political philosophies then current in Europe that suggested that pursuing scientific progress would lead to economic and social development, just as it had (according to the positivists) in Europe.
14. John M. Hart, *Revolutionary Mexico: The Coming and Process of the Mexican Revolution* (Berkeley: University of California Press, 1987).
15. Charles C. Cumberland, *Mexican Revolution: Genesis under Madero* (Austin: University of Texas Press, 1952).

16. The 1917 Constitution had forbidden reelection for the presidency and other federal offices. Because "no reelection" had been such an important slogan of Madero, dispensing with the no reelection clause seemed unwise. Thus Obregón, who had held the presidency from 1920 until 1924, had the constitution amended to forbid only "immediate reelection."
17. Meyer and Sherman, *Course of Mexican History,* 591.
18. Pablo González Casanova, *Democracy in Mexico,* trans. Danielle Salti (New York: Oxford University Press, 1970), 226.
19. Luis Javier Garrido, "The Crisis of *Presidencialismo,*" in *Mexico's Alternative Political Futures,* ed. Wayne A. Cornelius, Judith Gentleman, and Peter H. Smith (La Jolla: Center for U.S.-Mexican Studies, University of California at San Diego, 1989), 417–34.
20. Scott Mainwaring and Matthew Soberg Shugart, eds., *Presidentialism and Democracy in Latin America* (New York: Columbia University Press, 1997).
21. Garrido, "The Crisis of *Presidencialismo,*" 422.
22. Daniel Cosío Villegas, *El sistema político mexicano* (Mexico City: Joaquín Mortiz, 1978).
23. Victoria E. Rodríguez, *Decentralization in Mexico: From Reforma Municipal to Solidaridad to Nuevo Federalismo* (Boulder, Colo.: Westview, 1997).
24. Joseph L. Klesner, "Electoral Reform in an Authoritarian Regime: The Case of Mexico," Ph.D. dis., Massachusetts Institute of Technology, 1988, 312–13.
25. Douglas C. Bennett and Kenneth E. Sharpe, "The State as Banker and Entrepreneur: The Last Resort Character of the Mexican State's Economic Interventions," *Comparative Politics* 12, no. 2 (January 1980): 165–89.
26. Gabriel A. Almond and Sidney Verba, *The Civic Culture: Political Attitudes and Democracy in Five Nations* (Princeton: Princeton University Press, 1963), 17–19.
27. John A. Booth and Mitchell A. Seligson, "The Political Culture of Authoritarianism in Mexico: A Reexamination," *Latin American Research Review* 19, no. 1 (1983): 106–24.
28. Joseph L. Klesner, "Modernization, Economic Crisis, and Electoral Alignment in Mexico," *Mexican Studies/Estudios Mexicanos* 9, no. 2 (Summer 1993): 187–224.
29. González Casanova, *Democracy in Mexico,* 217.
30. Howard Handelman, *Mexican Politics: The Dynamics of Change* (New York: St. Martin's Press, 1997), 122.
31. Ibid., 135.
32. Victoria Rodríguez and Peter Ward, eds., *Opposition Government in Mexico* (Albuquerque: University of New Mexico Press, 1995).
33. Klesner, "Electoral Reform in an Authoritarian Regime."
34. Chappell Lawson, *Building the Fourth Estate: Democratization and the Rise of a Free Press in Mexico* (Berkeley: University of California Press, 2002).
35. Joe Foweraker and Ann L. Craig, eds., *Popular Movements and Political Change in Mexico* (Boulder, Colo.: Lynne Rienner, 1990).
36. Linda S. Stevenson, "Gender Politics in the Mexican Democratization Process: Electing Women and Legislating Sex Crimes and Affirmative Action, 1988–97," in *Toward Mexico's Democratization: Parties, Campaigns, Elections, and Public Opinion,* ed. Jorge I. Dominguez and Alejandro Poiré (New York: Routledge, 1999); Lisa Baldez, "Elected Bodies: Gender Quota Laws for Legislative Candidates in Mexico," *Legislative Studies Quarterly* 29, no. 2 (May 2004): 231–58.
37. For assessments, see Robert E. Scott, "The High Price of 'Free' Trade," *Economic Policy Institute Briefing Paper,* November 2003, at www.epinet.org/content.cfm/briefingpapers_bp147; Sidney Weintraub, "Scoring Free Trade: A Critique of the Critics," *Current History* 102, no. 670 (February 2004): 56–60; Jorge G. Castaneda, "NAFTA at 10: A Plus or a Minus?" *Current History* 103, no. 670 (February 2004): 51–55; and Robert A. Pastor, "North America's Second Decade," *Foreign Affairs* 83, 1 (2004): 124–35.
38. Wayne A. Cornelius, Todd A. Eisenstadt, and Jane Hindley, eds., *Subnational Politics and Democratization in Mexico* (La Jolla: University of California at San Diego, Center for U.S.-Mexican Studies, 1999).
39. See the account in Andres Oppenheimer, *Bordering on Chaos: Mexico's Roller-Coaster Journey Toward Prosperity* (Boston: Little, Brown, 1996).
40. See http://www.worldatlas.com/citypops.htm.
41. The northeast is made up of the states of Alagoas, Bahia, Ceará, Maranhão, Paraíba, Pernambuco, Piauí, Rio Grande do Norte, and Sergipe.

42. Rex A. Hudson, ed., *Brazil: A Country Study* (Washington, D.C.: Federal Research Division, Library of Congress, 1997), at http://lcweb2.loc.gov/frd/cs/brtoc.html.
43. Espírito Santo joins São Paulo, Rio de Janeiro, and Minas Gerais as the four southeastern states.
44. Hudson, *Brazil: A Country Study.*
45. The states of Paraná, Rio Grande do Sul, and Santa Catarina form the southern region.
46. The Amazonian states are Rondônia, Acre, Amazonas, Roraima, Pará, Amapá, and Tocantins, while the western states are Goiás, Mato Grosso, and Mato Grosso do Sul.
47. A comprehensive political history of Brazil can be found in Peter Flynn, *Brazil: A Political Analysis* (Boulder, Colo.: Westview, 1978).
48. Eul-Soo Pang, "Coronelismo in Northeast Brazil," in *The Caciques: Oligarchical Politics and the System of Caciquismo in the Luso-Hispanic World,* ed. Robert Kern (Albuquerque: University of New Mexico Press, 1973).
49. Thomas E. Skidmore, *Politics in Brazil, 1930–1964: An Experiment in Democracy* (New York: Oxford University Press, 1967).
50. Kenneth P. Erickson, *The Brazilian Corporative State and Working Class Politics* (Berkeley: University of California Press, 1977).
51. Peter B. Evans, *Dependent Development: The Alliance of Multinational, State, and Local Capital in Brazil* (Princeton: Princeton University Press, 1978).
52. Skidmore, *Politics in Brazil, 1930–1964.*
53. Ruth Berins Collier, "Popular Sector Incorporation and Political Supremacy: Regime Evolution in Brazil and Mexico," in *Brazil and Mexico: Patterns in Late Development,* ed. Sylvia A. Hewlett and Richard S. Weinert (Philadelphia: Institute for the Study of Human Issues, 1982).
54. Alfred C. Stepan, "Political Leadership and Regime Breakdown: Brazil," in *The Breakdown of Democratic Regimes,* ed. Juan J. Linz and Alfred C. Stepan (Baltimore, Md.: Johns Hopkins University Press, 1978); Michael Wallerstein, "The Collapse of Democracy in Brazil: Its Economic Determinants," *Latin American Research Review* 15, no. 3 (1980): 3–40.
55. Maria Helena Moreira Alves, *State and Opposition in Military Brazil* (Austin: University of Texas Press, 1985).
56. Alfred Stepan, *Rethinking Military Politics: Brazil and the Southern Cone* (Princeton: Princeton University Press, 1988).
57. Thomas E. Skidmore and Peter H. Smith, *Modern Latin America,* 3rd ed. (New York: Oxford University Press, 1992), 408.
58. Frances Hagopian describes their rule: "In thousands of municipalities across Brazil, local bosses exploit the economic dependence of their clients on resources they own or control to boost their position and power." See her *Traditional Politics and Regime Change in Brazil* (New York: Cambridge University Press, 1996), 16–17.
59. Ibid., 69.
60. This particular doctrine of national security, taught at the military's Superior War College from the late 1950s onward, justified in their own eyes the military's seizure of power. See Alfred Stepan, *The Military in Politics: Changing Patterns in Brazil* (Princeton: Princeton University Press, 1971); Alves, *State and Opposition in Military Brazil.*
61. Guillermo A. O'Donnell, *Modernization and Bureaucratic-Authoritarianism: Studies in South American Politics* (Berkeley: Institute of International Studies, University of California, 1973).
62. Scott Mainwaring, "Multipartism, Robust Federalism, and Presidentialism in Brazil," in Mainwaring and Shugart, *Presidentialism and Democracy in Latin America;* Stepan, "Political Leadership and Regime Breakdown: Brazil."
63. Skidmore, *Politics in Brazil, 1930–1964.* Brazil.
64. On business and democratization, see Leigh A. Payne, *Brazilian Industrialists and Democratic Change* (Baltimore: Johns Hopkins University Press, 1994).
65. Thomas E. Skidmore, *The Politics of Military Rule in Brazil, 1964–85* (New York: Oxford University Press, 1988), 142–43.
66. Margaret Keck, "The New Unionism in the Brazilian Transition," in *Democratizing Brazil: Problems of Transition and Consolidation,* ed. Alfred Stepan (New York: Oxford University Press, 1989).
67. Scott Mainwaring, "Grassroots Popular Movements and the Struggle for Democracy: Nova Iguaçu," in Stepan, *Democratizing Brazil.*
68. This concept is from Juan Linz, *Crisis, Breakdown, and Reequilibrium,* vol. 1 of *The Breakdown*

of *Democratic Regimes,* ed. Juan J. Linz and Alfred Stepan (Baltimore: Johns Hopkins University Press, 1978).

**69.** United Nations Development Program, *Human Development Report 1999,* 176–77.

**70.** Evans, *Dependent Development.*

**71.** Peter Evans, *Embedded Autonomy: States and Industrial Transformation* (Princeton: Princeton University Press, 1995).

**72.** Mainwaring, "Multipartism, Robust Federalism, and Presidentialism in Brazil."

**73.** Stepan, *Rethinking Military Politics.*

**74.** David V. Fleischer, "Constitutional and Electoral Engineering in Brazil: A Double-Edged Sword, 1964–1982," *Inter-American Economic Affairs* 37, no. 1 (Spring 1984).

**75.** Stepan, *Rethinking Military Politics,* 56.

**76.** Leigh A. Payne, "Brazilian Business and the Democratic Transition: New Attitudes and Influence," in *Business and Democracy in Latin America,* ed. Ernest Bartell and Leigh A. Payne (Pittsburgh: University of Pittsburgh Press, 1995).

**77.** Skidmore, *Politics of Military Rule,* 126–27.

**78.** Hagopian, *Traditional Politics and Regime Change in Brazil.*

**79.** Mainwaring, "Grassroots Popular Movements and the Struggle for Democracy."

**80.** Keck, "The New Unionism in the Brazilian Transition."

**81.** Juan J. Linz and Alfred Stepan, *Problems of Democratic Transition and Consolidation: Southern Europe, South America, and Post-Communist Europe* (Baltimore: Johns Hopkins University Press, 1996), 169.

**82.** Kurt Weyland, *Democracy Without Equity: Failures of Reform in Brazil* (Pittsburgh: University of Pittsburgh Press, 1996).

**83.** Mainwaring, "Multipartism, Robust Federalism, and Presidentialism in Brazil," 65–66.

**84.** Ibid., 99–100. See also Barry Ames, *The Deadlock of Democracy in Brazil: Interests, Identities, and Institutions in Comparative Politics* (Ann Arbor: University of Michigan Press, 2002).

**85.** The term comes from Scott Mainwaring, "Multipartism, Robust Federalism, and Presidentialism in Brazil."

**86.** Mala Htun, "Puzzles of Women's Rights in Brazil," *Social Research* 69, no. 3 (Fall 2002): 373–51.

**87.** *Brazil: A Country Study,* at http://countrystudies.us/brazil/99.htm.

**88.** Ibid., 374.

**89.** Wendy Hunter, *Eroding Military Influence in Brazil: Politicians Against Soldiers* (Chapel Hill: University of North Carolina Press, 1997).

**90.** Kurt Weyland, "Neoliberalism and Democracy in Latin America: A Mixed Record," *Latin American Politics and Society* 46, no. 1 (Winter 2004): 135–47.

**91.** Weyland, *Democracy Without Equity.*

**92.** *Freedom in the World 1998–1999* (New York: Freedom House, 1999), 104–7.

**93.** Linz and Stepan, *Problems of Democratic Transition and Consolidation.*

CHAPTER 23

# NIGERIA AND SOUTH AFRICA

TIMOTHY D. SISK

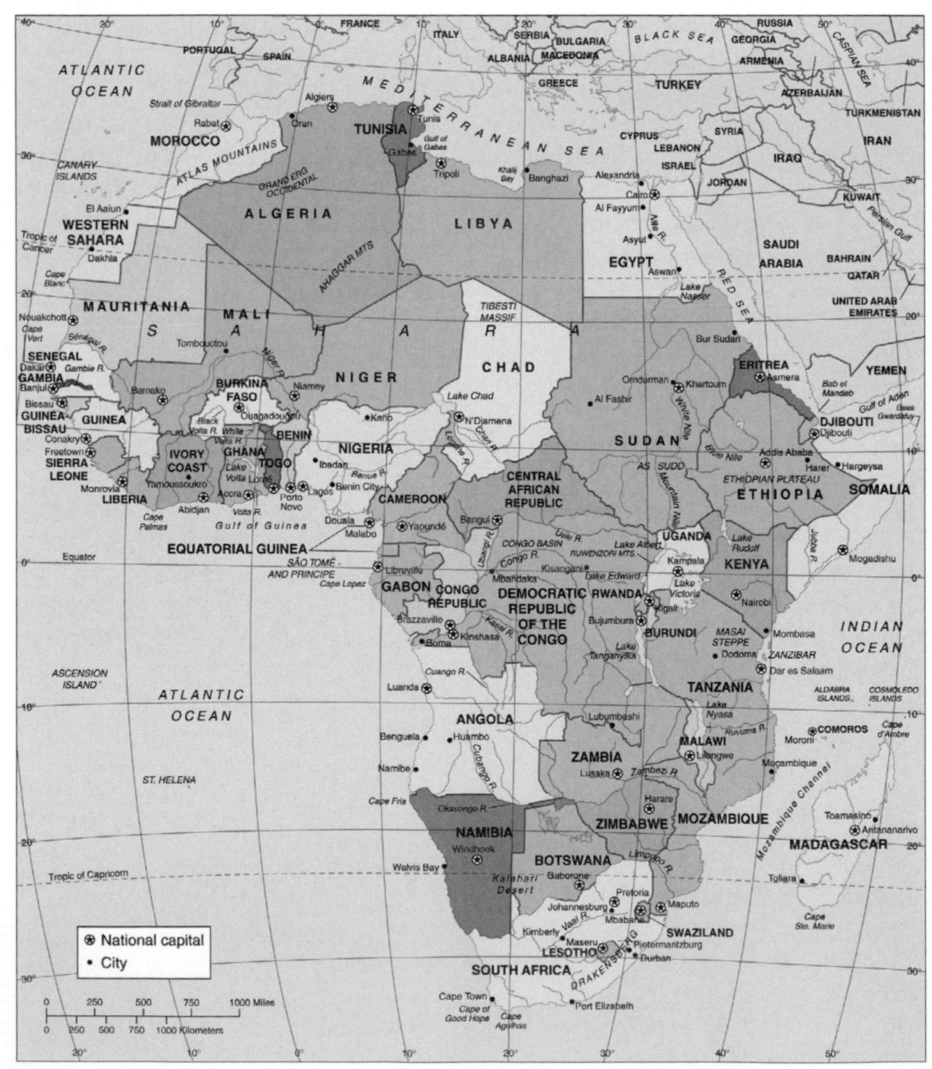

Of the fifty-four countries of sub-Saharan Africa, Nigeria and South Africa—respectively the most populated and the wealthiest of African states—have emerged as pivotal to the continent's future. Nigeria struggles as a democracy, while at the same time also playing a significant political role throughout Africa and globally through its substantial oil exports. South Africa has emerged as an important middle-income country increasingly integrated into the world-economy. It helps stabilize the entire region of southern Africa and is on the verge of substantial economic growth. At the same time, the HIV/AIDS crisis has put a serious strain on its economy and society. Much of the future of Africa depends on the internal politics of these two complicated and vibrant societies.

In both Nigeria and South Africa, democracy continues to be tested. In Nigeria, President *Olusegun Obasanjo* (o-LOO-sheh-goon o-BAH-san-joe) lost a bid in 2006 to seek legislative approval to run for a third term as president in elections scheduled for 2007. Obasanjo's election in 1999 promised to restore democracy to Nigeria after decades of rule by corrupt military leaders. (He was reelected in 2003 with 65 percent of the vote, but the constitution limits the president to two terms in office.) The *New York Times* reported that "Nigeria's experiment in democracy is so frail that many experts believe voters simply must be given reason to believe in it, whatever its flaws."[1] Meanwhile, Nigeria struggles with crime, corruption, ethnic and religious violence, poor human rights abuse records, and spillovers of people and arms from conflicts in its volatile West African neighborhood. In 1990 Nigeria led a West African peacekeeping force in Liberia, which was plunging into civil war. In 2003 Nigerian troops returned to the strife-torn country and helped remove from power Liberia's contentious president, Charles Taylor. These actions paved the way for the election of Ellen Johnson-Sirleaf as Liberia's first woman president in 2005. (Taylor was eventually arrested after fleeing exile in Nigeria.) In May 2006, Nigeria helped broker an agreement intended to bring peace to Darfur in Sudan (see chapter 6). These timely external interventions have not helped Nigeria resolve its internal problems, however. Because of Nigeria's fractious political culture, its strong presidential system, and its dramatic urban and economic stresses, the prognosis for democracy's development in Nigeria remains mixed.

South Africa's democracy has developed more steadily, bolstered by the political culture of bargaining and problem solving that emerged during its celebrated negotiated transition to democracy in 1990–96. The institutional design of South Africa, reflected in the "rainbow nation" constitution of 1996, underscores the country's commitment to tolerance, conciliation, consensus, and basic human rights free of the discrimination that marked the country's apartheid years of strict racial segregation (1948–89). The consolidation of South Africa's multiracial democracy has succeeded in large part because of the political stability the country has achieved under its first two black presidents, *Nelson Mandela* and *Thabo Mbeki* (TAH-bo mmm-BEH-kee). But democracy in South Africa still faces serious challenges. Socioeconomic inequality tops the list: although South Africa has a productive industrialized system, there remains a large underclass of people facing serious physical and health insecurities from the country's low rates of development. Crime, HIV/AIDS, joblessness, illegal immigration, land scarcity, and a youth crisis are among the threats to the consolidation of South Africa's democracy.

Like Nigeria, South Africa has intervened in nearby conflicts to facilitate an end to regional wars. Today, South Africa is dealing with problems stemming from neighboring Zimbabwe, where political tensions and an economic meltdown under Robert Mugabe's dictatorship are creating refugee flows and economic instabilities that are spilling over the border.

This chapter considers the internal politics of these two pivotal African states.

In Nigeria, a country of more than 130 million, military coups have repeatedly ended experiments in democracy, some with popular backing and some with fierce opposition. But in 1999, the military stepped aside and elections in May inaugurated a new period of civilian rule—the Fourth Republic—with Obasanjo emerging as the country's first popularly elected president in fifteen years. Turmoil is spreading in the oil-rich southern part of the country, where rebels are fighting for a greater share of Nigeria's oil revenues and for effective measures to address the environmental and social disruptions that result from local oil exploitation (see chapter 1). There is sporadic violence between Christians and Muslims in a number of Nigeria's federated states, a problem that has plagued Nigeria for decades. Muslim-dominated states reserve the right to apply Islamic law, at times condoning violent penalties for sexual offenses (such as stoning for adultery) that conflict with the civil laws of Nigeria's central government. Political corruption on the part of government officials and politically well-connected private businesses remain a continuing source of the abuse of power. These and other problems haunt Nigeria's troubled process of consolidating democracy.

South Africa, with about 44 million citizens, is a very special case. For centuries a European white minority dominated the African majority, exercising a democracy for themselves while brutally exploiting and oppressing the black majority through the policies of *apartheid* (separateness; pronounced "apart-ide"). Yet voting rights and democracy for all came in April 1994 after negotiations that averted a race war, an achievement seen as a miracle by some and by others as an inevitable consequence of the world's condemnation of racial discrimination. In 2004, South Africa successfully held a third national election, and its democratic system now seems to be durable. The country's democracy will be put to the test in future years, however, as the government struggles to be responsive to the tremendous social and economic challenges it faces.

How will these countries shape themselves, and Africa's future, in the years ahead? By focusing on common challenges to democracy in these countries, we'll gain a glimpse into the possible ways Africa's largest countries will confront challenges to democracy in the twenty-first century. Applying the concepts from chapter 2, we'll look at these dynamics of political conflict:

- *Power:* How did the military usurp power in Nigeria? How did South Africa's white minority, only 17 percent of the population, dominate the nonwhite majority for so many years? How have transitions to democracy affected these power relationships over the years?
- *Resources:* How have chronic poverty and high levels of inequality affected the prospects for democracy in these countries? How is national wealth distributed?
- *Identity:* How have national identities developed in countries with so many disparate social groups? How have ethnic and religious conflicts played out in Nigeria? How has racial diversity affected political life in South Africa?
- *Ideas:* How have countries like Nigeria and South Africa interpreted the concept of democracy? Have other ideologies been developed to justify nondemocratic rule? What ideas will drive the political future of these countries?
- *Values:* To what extent are traditional African values compatible with modern practices of democracy, such as elections? How widespread are such core democratic values as tolerance, compromise, and freedom?

A remarkable finding emerges from our study of Africa's leading states. The idea of democracy, and arguably its practice, is resilient in Africa, even in states that have been torn by political violence. Despite widespread poverty and diversity, democracy has emerged in many African countries, not just Nigeria and South Africa. Increasingly, observers in Africa and abroad argue that *more* democracy—not less—is needed for Africa's states to meet their challenges in the twenty-first century.[2] Today, democracy is viewed as a prerequisite to economic growth and social harmony, the only political system that has a chance of managing Africa's diverse societies.

## AFRICA: FROM CRADLE OF HUMANITY TO CONQUEST AND COLONIALISM

Africa is more than just a continent that is distinguished by its natural boundaries of the Atlantic and Indian oceans and the Mediterranean Sea. It is a large political unit that shares such things as a history of colonial oppression; a new, but still evolving, state system; a subordinate place in the international political economy; and a widespread desire for political and economic change. To understand where Africa's countries are headed today, we must understand their common past.[3]

Current anthropological theories suggest that Africa is the cradle of all humankind. The "African genesis" theory holds that the earliest hominids—the primordial ancestors of the human race—lived in the Great Rift Valley of central Africa and the

Ethiopian highlands. Thus the beginning of African history is the beginning of human history. Africa's history, and its present, are marked by extensive migration, changing structures of authority and governance, evolving boundaries, and changing notions of ethnic and national identity. Great ancient kingdoms developed in Africa, including the Gao in present-day Senegal, the Mali dynasties of the twelfth and thirteenth centuries, and the regal traditions of the Ashanti in present-day Ghana. During these times, Africans interacted with Islamic traders such as the Berbers, and a vibrant system of exchange developed across the sands of the Sahara.

Early in the fifteenth century, Portuguese invaders crossed the straits of Gibraltar and began the European colonization of Africa, a system of domination that lasted until the early 1990s, when independence for Namibia put a final end to *colonialism.* Prior to European rule, traditional authority in the persons of African monarchs and chiefs, rooted in agrarian systems of livelihood, was the dominant mode of governance. These societies led a fairly isolated existence. Colonial rule changed Africa significantly, and its long-term effects down to the present day cannot be overstated.

Over the course of the next several centuries, additional imperial powers invaded Africa. They carved up the continent along artificial and illogical boundaries, manipulated social systems, and created economic legacies that continue to bedevil African countries today. An initial impetus for the colonial exploitation of Africa was the slave trade, in which at least 12 million unfortunate souls were enslaved and sent to the United States alone. Many more never survived the arduous "middle passage" across the seas. Along the coast of Senegal lies Goree Island, once a prison where slaves were auctioned to slave traders in passing ships; today it houses an institute for democracy, development, and human rights.[4] During his visit to Africa in 2003, President Bush singled out modern Senegal as a model of democracy.

With the British decision to abolish slavery in 1833 and with the abolition of slavery in the Americas following the U.S. Civil War, the nature of European subjugation changed. Colonial powers annexed large swaths of Africa in an effort to fuel their industrial revolution with raw materials extracted from the rich natural resources found on the continent. Principally, these resources included cotton, peanuts, cocoa, palm oil, coffee, sisal, and minerals such as copper. Colonization accelerated in the final three decades of the nineteenth century. In 1870 only 10 percent of Africa was colonized; by 1900 only 10 percent was not. At the infamous Berlin Conference of 1884, the major European colonial powers—Britain, France, Belgium, Germany, Italy, Portugal, and Spain—divvied up Africa's territory among themselves. Their basis for determining the boundaries of these colonies was rather arbitrary in terms of existing African social patterns. For the most part, the new entities simply reflected the patterns of military control exercised by the colonial armies of the European imperialist powers: whoever controlled an area took it as a colony. *The borders of most African states today are the legacy of the ill-considered partition of Africa in the mid nineteenth century,* based on the "principle of effective occupation" of territory. These boundaries did not correspond to any geographic, national, or ethnic logic. Ultimately they created many of the problems of ethnic tension that challenge the majority of African countries today.[5]

### Patterns of Colonialism

The discovery of rich diamond and gold deposits in South Africa in the 1860s heightened what became known as the "scramble for Africa." To fully exploit Africa's wealth, colonialism required more effective occupation and social control. Although different in their approaches—the British used "indirect rule" whereas the French, Belgians, and Germans preferred more direct control of territory—the colonial powers engaged in the widespread political manipulation of African societies.

- The *British* relied on agreements with traditional rulers to impose their policies, usually backed up with superior military might. Consequently, we find today that in erstwhile British colonies such as Kenya or Ghana, traditional rulers remain very powerful and territorial control by ethnic groups remains critically important.
- In *French* and *Belgian* colonies, centralized power was more important and it eroded traditional power structures. The French sought to exert

cultural influence through their language policy, and they ruled their colonies as an extension of France itself. Colonial subjects were to become *évolués*, or "people evolving" into Frenchmen. Belgian colonies such as the vast Congo were ruled as the personal property of the eccentric King Leopold II.
- In *Portuguese* colonies, such as Angola, Mozambique, and Cape Verde, assimilation was encouraged and many interracial marriages occurred. As a result, *assimilados* (or mulattos, the products of mixed marriages) became important social groups that blurred the lines between colonial and indigenous rule.[6] Lusophone (Portugese-speaking) countries in Africa today thus have social structures that are remarkably different from those of former British or French colonies, and *assimilados* are still influential leaders in these countries.

Yet another legacy of the colonial period was the stark division of a large part of Africa into Anglophone (English-speaking) and Francophone (French-speaking) colonies. These language differences affect the way today's African countries relate to one another and stymie the development of a common approach to contemporary problems. Former British colonies tend to have special ties with one another, as do former French colonies. For example, former English colonies are active members of the British Commonwealth,[7] while French West African countries have adopted a common currency.

The reliance on African land and labor to grow crops and extract mineral wealth in service to the colonial powers resulted in severe distortions in traditional African societies. The intruders introduced alien concepts and social "fictions" with no indigenous roots in Africa: Christianity, monogamy, formal education, and wage labor, among others. New stratifications based on socioeconomic class came into being, ethnic identities were transformed, and basic economic infrastructures and modes of production were created to serve the single-commodity economies needed by the colonial powers. In southern Africa, European immigrants set up white minority "settler states" that systematically displaced Africans from the land and created a new form of modern feudalism. In many colonies, the imperial powers imposed a "head tax," in which an African peasant had to work for a European plantation owner or an enterprise to pay off debt to the metropolitan state (the colonial power).

After the creation of the Union of South Africa following the British defeat of the Dutch colonists (known as the Boers) in 1902, and after Germany's defeat in World War I, the shape of colonialism in Africa was nearly complete. European plenipotentiaries and bureaucrats ruled the vast continent, and their oppression of the indigenous population was universal. Once Germany lost its colonies after 1918, most decisions affecting the masses of the continent were made in Paris or London, with little regard for their implications for the millions of people whom colonial policy affected.

## Legacies of Colonialism: Explaining Underdevelopment

Colonialism's legacies are thus pervasive throughout Africa some fifty years after the system of domination began to crumble (see table 23.1). These legacies are political, economic, and cultural.[8]

- *Politically*, as noted before, the territorial boundaries of today's countries are the result of the greedy competition among the European powers over arable land, water, blue water harbors, transportation arteries such as rivers, and precious mineral resources.
- *Economically*, the African colonies were reliant on single-commodity, resource-extraction economies. Urbanization was inhibited, subsistence agriculture encouraged, and the development of diversified industrial production was stultified.
- The *cultural* units that had existed prior to colonialism were also affected, and in many regions ethnic and linguistic groups are now divided by artificial lines on a map. As a result, most African countries today are a mosaic of ethnic, linguistic, racial, and religious diversity. One of the consequences is a pattern of distorted social relations. Conflicts in Rwanda, for example, between the minority Tutsi (now 15 percent of the population) and the Hutu (84 percent) were fanned by the Belgian colonists' support for the Tutsi. A Hutu revolt in 1959 ended Tutsi domination. Violence erupted periodically after independence in 1962 as the Tutsi challenged Hutu power. In

**TABLE 23.1**

**The Decolonization of Africa**

| | Independence |
|---|---|
| ***Former French Colonies*** | |
| Algeria | 3 July 1962 |
| Benin | 1 August 1960 |
| Burkina Faso | 5 August 1960 |
| Central African Republic | 13 August 1960 |
| Chad | 11 August 1960 |
| Congo (Republic) | 15 August 1960 |
| Ivory Coast | 7 August 1960 |
| Djibouti | 27 June 1977 |
| Equatorial Guinea | 12 October 1968 |
| Gabon | 17 August 1960 |
| Guinea | 6 March 1957 |
| Madagascar | 26 June 1960 |
| Mali | 22 September 1960 |
| Mauritania | 28 November 1960 |
| Niger | 8 August 1960 |
| Senegal | 20 August 1960 |
| Tunisia | 20 March 1956 |
| ***Former British Colonies*** | |
| Botswana | 30 September 1966 |
| Gambia | 18 February 1965 |
| Ghana | 6 March 1957 |
| Kenya | 12 December 1963 |
| Lesotho | 4 October 1966 |
| Malawi | 6 July 1964 |
| Nigeria | 1 October 1960 |
| Sierra Leone | 27 April 1961 |
| South Africa | 31 May 1961 |
| Sudan | 1 January 1956 |
| Swaziland | 6 September 1968 |
| Uganda | 9 October 1962 |
| Zambia | 24 October 1964 |
| Zimbabwe | 18 April 1980 |
| ***Former Portuguese Colonies*** | |
| Angola | 11 November 1975 |
| Cape Verde | 1 July 1975 |
| Guinea-Bissau | 10 September 1974 |
| Mozambique | 25 June 1975 |
| São Tomé and Príncipe | 12 July 1975 |
| ***Former Belgian Colonies*** | |
| Burundi | 1 July 1962 |
| Congo (Democratic Republic, formerly Zaire) | 30 June 1960 |
| Rwanda | 1 July 1962 |
| ***Former Italian Colonies*** | |
| Eritrea | Seceded from Ethiopia 1991 |
| Libya | 24 December 1951 |
| Somalia | 1 July 1960 |
| Western Sahara | Disputed territory |
| ***Former German Colonies*** | |
| Cameroon | 1 January 1960 |
| Namibia | 21 March 1990 |
| Tanzania | 9 December 1961 |
| Togo | 12 April 1960 |
| ***Not Colonized*** | |
| Liberia, Ethiopia | |

Colonizing countries as of 1914. Modern names used for independent countries.

1994, 800,000 people died in a hundred days in the worst genocide since World War II as Hutus lashed out against the Tutsi.

### African Nationalism: The Pursuit of the Political Kingdom

World War II had significant material and psychological effects on the continent and its people. As a consequence of the war, the colonial powers were weakened and the legitimacy of occupation began to erode; at the same time, the message of the struggle for civil rights in countries such as the United States spread abroad. U.S. presidents such as Eisenhower pressed for decolonization to open Africa's markets to free trade. Encouraged by civil rights activism in the United States, African nationalist movements emerged to resist colonial rule and exploitation. Under the leadership of these movements, demands for independence from the colonial powers grew rapidly in the late 1940s and 1950s. Although there had been prior resistance to colonial rule—notably by the Ashanti Kingdom in the late nineteenth century, the Ndebele-Shona uprisings in current-day Zimbabwe in 1896–97, and the Maji-Maji rebellion in 1905–7—real resistance to

European rule spread with the winds of change that swept rapidly over the continent after World War II. Among the most significant of these new awakenings was the Mau Mau rebellion in Kenya in 1950, in which Kikuyu tribespeople articulated the legitimacy of African aspirations to be free of the colonial yoke.

African nationalism arose from the frustrations of a small but growing *middle class* that deeply resented the fact that the highest positions in commerce, finance, government administration, and even religious organizations were controlled by foreigners, as were the rewards of economic success. African nationalists who emanated from this middle class sought independence from the colonial powers, a goal that would bring them complete control over the state apparatus and territory of their respective countries. Buoyed by the promise of the Charter of the United Nations to promote the "self-determination of peoples," and imbued with the postwar optimism reflected in the 1948 Universal Declaration of Human Rights, African leaders began to agitate for decolonization. Western-educated, skilled professional leaders organized independence movements and petitioned for independence. Tanzania's *Julius Nyerere, Jomo Kenyatta* of Kenya, *Leopold Senghor* of Senegal, *Kwame Nkrumah* of Ghana, and *Kenneth Kaunda* of Zambia, to name a few, articulated philosophies of independence, self-reliance, and economic development for African colonies.

These men were the founding fathers of today's African states, much like Mohandas Gandhi and Jawaharal Nehru, who led India to independence in 1947. Senghor, for example, argued for a rekindling of traditional African values. He coined the term *Négritude* to encompass "the whole complex of civilized values (cultural, economic, social, and political) which characterize the black people." Senghor and other nationalists believed that cultural nationalism could unify countries whose people had little in common other than their suffering to bind them in their postcolonial political units. To achieve this unity, African anticolonial nationalists sought the reins of state power. This drive for power, waged in revolutionary struggles of armed resistance and guerilla warfare in many colonies, was heralded by Nkrumah's dictum, "Seek ye first the political kingdom." At the same time, the United States, in conformity with its own anti-colonial past, pressured the European powers to loosen their control of markets and commerce with Africa.[9]

Independence came rapidly for many countries in the 1960s. Fueled by United Nations General Assembly Resolution 1514 (1960), which called for decolonization and the sanctity of existing borders, the claims of African nationalists could not be denied. By 1957, Ghana's Nkrumah had succeeded in his effort to seize the political kingdom. His Convention People's Party won a pivotal election, assumed power, and forced the British to relinquish control. In 1960 alone, twenty-six African colonies became independent, and by 1969 some forty-two countries had emerged as sovereign states, becoming full-fledged members of the United Nations. In subsequent years, after bitter struggles for independence, Portuguese colonies such as Mozambique and Angola were finally freed in the mid-1970s. The settler societies of southern Africa, such as Rhodesia (now Zimbabwe), Namibia, and South Africa, also came to be ruled by African nationalist movements. Across the continent, in the short historical span of some thirty years, colonial-era flags went down and the flags of newly independent African countries were raised.

As it happened, however, African nationalism in these formative decades of decolonization was not tightly linked to democracy. Unlike leaders in Britain and the United States, where nationalism and democratic tendencies were virtually inseparable from the beginning, most African independence leaders defined their nationalism in pronouncedly anti-Western terms. Upon taking power, most of them quickly abandoned any pretense to Western liberal democratic ideas and practices, establishing authoritarian or semi-authoritarian regimes based on the military or one-party dominance. African democracy was set back for decades as a result.

### From Liberation Struggle to Governance

Initially, the constitutions of the newly liberated states tended to establish the minimal framework of democracy: constitutionalism, the rule of law, and elections. In countries throughout Africa, the anticolonial nationalist movements—such as TANU in Tanzania, KANU in Kenya, and UNIP in Zambia—won elections. With charismatic leaders such as

Nyerere, Kenyatta, and Kaunda, these movements inherited a highly centralized state and highly diverse populations. But contrary to the democratic tenets of political pluralism, which rest on free and open competition among political parties and freedom of expression, some of the most prominent leaders of African independence quickly uprooted the newly sprouting shoots of democracy. Each of them argued that African states needed one-party rule in order to unify their populations and "build nations." Creating new countries required emphasizing common struggles and sufferings; competitive, parliamentary elections, in their view, would tear the nascent nations apart.

The hypothesis that multiparty competition is ill suited to African's multiethnic, impoverished societies because it divides rather than unifies is a common and recurrent theme in Africa's political development.[10] It reverberates throughout the region today. For example, Uganda's President Yoweri Museveni experimented with a system of "no-party" politics, in which candidates for office stand as individuals and are not allowed to assume a party identification. The National Resistance Movement, which he leads, is the guiding force in the country. Although it espouses such democratic notions as market-oriented economics, freedom of expression, and free primary education (a rarity in Africa), it resolutely monopolizes political power. In 2005, voters in Uganda overwhelmingly approved a referendum that endorsed a return to multiparty politics, effectively scrapping the idea of a "no-party" democracy in such a diverse country. At the same time, President Museveni maneuvered a change in the constitution that enabled him to serve a third term, circumventing the provision barring more than two terms in office. In 2006 the government agreed to a deal aimed at ending Uganda's nineteen-year civil war.

While rejecting British-style parliamentarism and other Western models of democracy, most African states in the postcolonial period turned to one form or another of authoritarian or semi-authoritarian rule. In virtually every newly independent African country, the formal institutions of democracy that may have been in place when self-rule began were systematically undermined. Democratic practices and human rights fell prey to political and military elites who sought the reins of office for their own personal power and enrichment. These elites relied on the centralized, bureaucratic structures of the states that they inherited from the colonial powers to become Africa's new dominant class.

### Patterns of Post-Independence Politics

Among the several forms of authoritarianism that emerged in Africa between the early 1960s and the late 1980s, one variant is *semi-authoritarian one-party rule*. Examples include TANU in Tanzania and Guinea's Parti démocratique de Guinée. In these and similar manifestations of this political system, political power is monopolized and guided by famous and generally popular political leaders. The government and party structures operate in parallel, with some similarities to the relationship between party and state in communist Russia and China. These parties have generally voiced socialist rhetoric and have sought to achieve economic development by breaking the bonds of dependency that tied the prosperity of their country to uneven and disadvantageous trade relations with Europe. These parties still exist in most countries. Some of them are still in power despite the introduction of multiparty politics. Elsewhere, as in Zambia, one-party governments were defeated in elections when political liberalization began in the early 1990s.

Zimbabwe experienced a fundamental transformation of its one-party system in 2000 as a relatively new party—the Movement for Democratic Change—won nearly half the parliamentary seats up for election, delivering a stunning blow to the Zimbabwe African National Union (ZANU), the party that had dominated the country for twenty years under President Robert Mugabe. In 2002, Mugabe claimed he had won a hotly contested presidential election against Morgan Tsvangirai, a popular trade union leader and democracy advocate. The election outcome was regarded as fraudulent by Mugabe's opponents, and in 2003 Tsvangirai was put on trial for treason. Mugabe's despotic leadership and the country's rapidly deteriorating economy have prompted some 3 million people to flee the country.

Other countries have had **patrimonial rule**, ***which is rule by a domineering and personalistic elite.***[11] In the Belgian Congo (later known as Zaire and now as the Democratic Republic of Congo), a troubled decolonization process in the 1960s was marked by civil war, UN military intervention, superpower rivalry, and assassinations. Eventually, Mobutu Seso Seko seized power and ruled as a veritable monarch until his despotic regime was toppled by rebels in May 1997. Mobutu's assets at the time of his death were estimated at $8 billion in property and money, while his country had sunk to the bottom of the global list in virtually every conceivable development indicator. A prolonged civil war for control of the country has claimed 3.8 million lives.

In other countries, the military stepped in and took over power. *Military coups* were rampant in Africa from the 1960s through the 1980s: in seventy-four instances between 1952 and 1990, military officers gained power through violence or the threat of it and ruled the country as dictators. In Ethiopia, military officers with pro-Soviet leanings and a Marxist ideology seized power in 1975, replacing the aging emperor, Haile Selassie. Under Mengistu Haile Meriam, the Derg—as the junta was known—unleashed a reign of terror and embroiled the country in devastating civil wars and wars with its neighbors (notably the war with Somalia over the Ogaden desert in 1975). It used its radical Marxist-Leninist ideology to justify dictatorial rule at home and to establish international alliances with the Soviet Union, Cuba, and other communist states. After inflicting untold suffering on the Ethiopian people, Mengistu fled the country in 1991 as rebel forces closed in on the capital, Addis Ababa. Today Ethiopia is edging closer to democracy, though it has suffered from its long war with Eritrea, an independent state that was once a part of Ethiopia.

Some countries, notably Angola and Mozambique, suffered from protracted *civil wars* in which independence movements fought against the Portuguese and among themselves over who would wield power in the independence era. In both instances, the hasty retreat of Portuguese colonizers in 1974–75 left a power vacuum in which the competing local factions vied for dominance. These factions obtained arms and ideological support (and sometimes troops) from their respective benefactors—especially the United States, the Soviets, and the Cubans—who were locked in their global Cold War confrontation. Despite several efforts and peace agreements and UN peacekeeping efforts in the 1990s, Angola's civil war continued for twenty-seven years. Tragically, Angola has the highest proportion of victims of landmines of any country in the world, including some 100,000 amputees. In 1999, an estimated two hundred people died per day in Angola's tragic war. The war finally ended in 2001 when rebel leader Jonas Savimbi was killed on the battlefield. The Ivory Coast, Liberia, and Sierra Leone were also embroiled in civil wars in the 1990s and into the next decade. International peacekeeping missions involving British, French, or (in Liberia's case) American troops were sent to these countries in 2003.

Several countries in Africa—such as Botswana, Mauritius, Gambia, and Senegal—have managed to remain *partial democracies* with constitutional systems, regular elections, and relatively good human rights records.[12] But only in a few instances have elections ever led to the ouster of the ruling party and the assumption of power by an opposition party. For example, in Botswana, Africa's oldest surviving democracy, elections held in 2004 returned to power the only party that has governed the country since independence in 1966. Alternation in power—the periodic transfer of state power from one party to another over a succession of elections—is a key indicator of the vibrancy of democracy as traditionally defined. Unfortunately, it has been largely absent from Africa. The relative success of some of these countries in avoiding the complete collapse of democracy has tended to stem from the responsiveness of the dominant party to ethnic and religious groups. This type of political system has been labeled a **"hegemonic exchange"** ***regime: in exchange for the right to exercise its hegemony over the state and the population, the dominant party provides benefits to the country's main ethnic or religious groups.***[13]

In the 1980s and 1990s, global factors like the collapse of communism in the Soviet Union and Central and Eastern Europe and the new assertiveness of multilateral financial institutions converged with domestic pressures to undermine the alternatives to democracy in Africa. International lending organizations like the World Bank and the International Monetary Fund, along with aid providers like the United States and Western Europe, increasingly insisted on "good governance," private enterprise, and trade liberalization as conditions for future economic assistance. They called on the states of Africa to root out official corruption, reduce state controls over economic activity, and remove tariffs and other barriers to trade with the outside world. They also enjoined them to take more responsibility for their governance, economic development, and human rights records.[14] A worldwide embargo on South Africa in the 1980s placed special external pressures on that country's white minority government to open negotiations with African nationalists with the aim of democratizing the entire country. Under these mounting outside pressures, political practices within individual African countries gave way to new continental and global realities.

In many countries, popular movements arose that demanded space for the development of an autonomous civil society outside the single-party framework. They called for multiparty competitive elections, new constitutional frameworks, an end to corruption, and a more equitable distribution of wealth. In Ghana, Kenya, Malawi, and Zambia, new coalitions of organizations in civil society came together and pressured the incumbent governments to open up the political system to multiparty competition. Africa was clearly caught up in the "third wave" of democratization that spilled across the world in the early 1990s.

Over the course of the decade, nearly all of Africa's fifty-four states underwent dramatic political changes. As we've seen, the pressures for democratization were both external, a condition of further loans and foreign aid, and internal, the result of widespread public disaffection with the status quo.[15] Whether through negotiated agreements ("pacts"), the victory of rebel movements on the battlefield, or the passing of long-time patriarchs, the stereotypical African one-party state became a relic of the past in the early 1990s. Africa has witnessed scores of governments that have come to power seeking to inaugurate a new era. Some have dubbed the period of the 1990s "Africa's second independence."

More than anything, the process of democratization in Africa was characterized by the rush to multiparty elections. Between 1992 and 1994, twenty countries held national-level elections. These elections swept away one-party regimes in the Ivory Coast, Gabon, Mali, and Zambia. In some instances, as in Angola, Eritrea, Ethiopia, Liberia, Namibia, Mozambique, Sierra Leone, South Africa, and Uganda, votes were held to restore and legitimize a new political order after years of civil war and violence. Many Francophone countries held "national conferences" to arrive at new constitutional rules of the game for democratic politics.

The track record of the remarkable attempts at democratization in much of Africa is demonstrably mixed. Some experiments of the 1990s were relatively successful, in that legitimate government was reconstituted and the stage was set for a longer-term evolution to more mature democracy and its consolidation (e.g., frequent or occasional alternation in power by governing coalitions). In Benin, Eritrea, Madagascar, Malawi, Mali, Mozambique, Namibia, South Africa, Uganda, and Zambia, elections have been more or less successful vehicles for ushering in fledgling democracies. But there have been failures, as well. Elections went awry in Angola, Burundi, and Sierra Leone, leading to renewed civil violence, the suspension of human rights, and sharp declines in the standard of living as well as in the prospects for future prosperity. Observers have differed over whether the electoral contests of the 1990s produced greater accommodation among conflicting groups within these countries—especially along ethnic lines—or whether they exacerbated tensions and undermined national cohesiveness.[16]

Among the alternatives to elections as a route to democracy is the promotion of viable *civil societies* in Africa. Some have suggested that popular participation and consensus-building decision-making processes are more suited to Africa's divided societies than are the rough-and-tumble of Western-style competitive elections.[17] John Harbeson suggests that democratization efforts in Africa have relied too much on elections, arguing that "this overemphasis derives from an inaccurate reading of the most widely accepted definition of 'democracy,' upon which much of the contemporary democratic transitions theory appears to rest." He suggests as an alternative that "a broadened conception of democratization will result in a significantly improved understanding of the status and quality of democracy [in Africa] and the prospects for it." African countries should engage in more constitution-making exercises that establish a consensus on the rules of the democratic game before rushing into elections in the absence of that consensus, Harbeson maintains.[18]

**Nigeria**

## The African Renaissance

In recent years, some African leaders have called for a "renaissance." This appeal for a rebirth is a response to disillusioned pessimists who decry the persistence of war, authoritarian rule, and poverty in Africa and the continent's marginalization in the international economy. Led by South Africa's president, *Thabo Mbeki* advocates of a renaissance point to the need for African leaders to take responsibility for the continent's security and economic well-being. As Mbeki put it:

> Renaissance has to be about democracy, peace and stability throughout our continent. It has to be about economic regeneration so that we pull ourselves out of the category "the underdeveloped" permanently. It has to be about vastly improving the quality of life of all our citizens.[19]

There is widespread agreement that, if the hoped-for African renaissance is to occur, the further broadening and deepening of democracy in Africa's fifty-four countries will be necessary. Positive signs include the much-heralded elections in Rwanda in 2003—the first since the 1994 genocide—and the introduction of a new democratically elected government in Kenya. At the same time, the tainted Senate elections held in Zimbabwe in 2005 failed to force Robert Mugabe to step down; instead, Mugabe's forces have perpetrated human rights violations against white former settlers and the government's political opponents in a desperate effort to retain power. Food shortages and starvation have resulted, severely halting progress toward Africa's renaissance.

For Nigeria, and then for South Africa, we will first look at the troubled transitions to democracy that each country has encountered. We'll next look at each country's prospects for consolidating a pluralist political system that protects human rights, manages diversity, and fosters economic development into the twenty-first century.

## NIGERIA

Population (2006, estimated): 132 million
Freedom House Ratings (2006): Political Rights—4; Civil Liberties—4
Area: 356,668 square miles
(more than double the size of California)

Nigeria is an enigmatic case in sub-Saharan Africa. In many ways, this important country of more than 130 million people—20 percent of Africa's population—has long possessed a high potential for developing into a regional and global superpower with national wealth and a strong and vibrant democracy. Nigeria boasts abundant natural resources (especially light sweet crude oil, exports of which account for 30 percent of GDP), a vigorous civil society, highly educated elites, and an enduring commitment to freedom, pluralism, and enterprise among its people. At the same time, the country has been plagued since independence from Britain on October 1, 1960, by poor leadership and a social structure that does not support unity of purpose. Since independence, Nigeria has suffered six successful military coups d'état and many other unsuccessful ones, a brutal civil war, costly military engagements in the region, endemic kleptocracy (rule by theft) and corruption, and deeply ingrained religious and ethnic tensions. That the promise of Nigeria has not been realized remains one of the most important facts of postindependence Africa. The stark reality is that this vast country has been ruled by military leaders longer than by civilian politicians.

### The Mosaic of a Diverse Society

Nigeria is not only Africa's most heavily populated country; it is also one of its most diverse. There are some 250 ethnic groups in Nigeria. The principal division centers on three major ethnic groups that account for some two-thirds of the population: the *Igbo* (or *Ibo*) in the southeast, accounting for about 18 percent of the population; the *Yoruba* in the southwest (21 percent); and the *Hausa-Fulani* group in the northern third of the country (the Hausa comprise about 21 percent of the population, and the Fulani, 11 percent). These divisions reflect linguistic and historical divisions from the precolonial period. Hausa, for example, is a language spoken by several distinct ethnic groups, including the Fulani, the Tiv, the Kanuri, the Nupé, and others. The Igbo, who initially lived in autonomous villages and spoke their own language and dialects, proved especially receptive to Western religious, cultural, and commercial influences. The Yoruba also had their own language.

In addition to having these ethnolinguistic divisions, Nigeria is deeply divided along religious lines. In general, the Igbo are mostly Christian and the Yoruba and Hausa-Fulani mostly Muslim. In all, Muslims comprise about half of Nigeria's population, and Christians about 40 percent. A large number of Igbos are Roman Catholics, but other Christian denominations, such as Baptists and West African Evangelicals, also attract Nigerian adherents. Traditional animism remains widely practiced as well.

While the three largest ethnic groups tend to dominate Nigerian politics, it is important not to overlook Nigeria's numerous smaller minority groups, which often play an important role in regional and national politics.

The current patterns of ethnic awareness had antecedents in the precolonial period, most notably in the Yoruba kingdom, which was an identifiable entity with a shared culture and legal customs for several centuries prior to colonialism. But the effects of colonialism in molding today's social divisions cannot be overlooked. The British, who colonized Nigeria from the mid-eighteenth century to 1960, fostered regional devolution (indirect rule, as described earlier). They promoted the development of regional and ethnic identities in Nigerian political consciousness on the one hand and superimposed a highly centralized administrative system on the other. In many ways, this colonial system set up a tug-of-war among various regional forces in a fight over the central reins of power, creating precedents for postindependence political conflicts.

Like many phenomena in Africa, today's problems have deep roots in colonial misrule. During the British colonial period, the regions of Northern and Southern Nigeria, fused in 1914, were only loosely integrated. Using indirect rule, the British fostered local autonomy in the more Islamic North but offered less autonomy and self-rule to those in the mostly coastal South, where colonial "penetration"—the existence of civil and military administrators—was more extensive than in the hinterlands. But the British also systematically disadvantaged the northern Muslims in terms of education, access to political influence, and economic development, setting up a paradoxical problem that continues to influence Nigerian politics today. Side by side, a relatively politically powerful but economically weak Muslim North competes with a more wealthy but historically less powerful South.

Regionalism fostered by the British has left a poor legacy for nation building in Nigeria. In 1939, the British divided its Nigerian territories into three regions (along with what was then the capital, Lagos, which was administratively separate): the Western (predominantly Yoruba) region, the Eastern (mostly Igbo), and the Northern (generally Hausa-Fulani). After World War II, this regional division evolved into a federal structure. Federalism and related policies in the colonial period set up the basic dynamics that continue to threaten Nigeria's territorial integrity today. It also strongly influenced political organization, such that during the first elections in the early 1950s in the run-up to independence, ethnic parties quickly emerged and gained control of their respective territories.

An important hypothesis worth considering—for then and now—is that ethnically based parties produce such intense competition for power that they consistently undermine opportunities to consolidate democracy. The test for this hypothesis in Nigeria doesn't yield a definitive conclusion. While ethnic politics has plagued every attempt at democratic politics, other factors—namely, corruption stemming from the irresistible temptation to skim national oil export earnings—also account for the recurring breakdown of Nigeria's experiments at civilian rule.

As in much of Africa, rising nationalism in Nigeria in the 1950s forced the British colonizers to expand Nigerian participation in the country's administration, create elected representation, and ultimately move toward independence. The constitution of 1954 reinforced the colonial legacy by formalizing the regions and fostering the hegemony of a dominant ethnic group within each region. If it were simply a matter of constitutional structure, Nigeria might have overcome its ill-considered regional structure that reinforced social tensions. Throughout the years, through legal reforms, the number of states in Nigeria has ballooned—from four in the early 1960s to some thirty-six today—in efforts to change the regional basis of Nigerian politics. Other administrative and technical solutions to resolving ethnic tensions have been tried. Nigeria has witnessed innovative constitutional devices that, on paper at least, try to foster ethnic tolerance and the creation of political alliances across the regional divides. But constitutional "engineering" has not been enough. Nigeria's periods of incipient democracy have been consistently undermined by antidemocratic tendencies and military misrule, much of it driven by avarice and greed.

### The First Republic (1960–66)

Nigeria's first start at democracy after independence led to the creation of two broad political orientations: the Nigerian People's Congress (NPC) and the National Conference of Nigerian Citizens (NCNC). The former had its base in the northern part of the country among the largely Muslim Yoruba and Hausa, while the latter had a more southern base, rooted in the mostly Catholic Igbos. Generally, the NPC was slightly to the right of the center of the political spectrum and the NCNC slightly to the left. A high degree of unity marked the time of independence and the First Republic's initial years. The country's first president was an Igbo (Nnamdi Azikiwe), and its prime minister came from the Hausa-Fulani group (Tafawa Balewa). But corruption and ethnic tensions quickly undermined the civilian regime. In particular, a major dispute over the national census of 1964 (which was to determine the allocation of state spending) heightened antagonisms along ethnic lines. A devastating national strike also undermined the authority and capacity of the government.

Another factor that served to undermine the *First Republic*—and many Nigerian governments since then—is what Richard Joseph terms **prebendalism**, ***or the use of state offices as "prebends" (instruments) for creating wealth and gain for individuals and their ethnic brethren.***[20] This use of the government for wealth-gathering (sometimes known as "rent-seeking") behavior has systematically undermined constitutionalism, which places an emphasis on the statutory functions of an office (that is, its legal competence as set forth in the constitution and other laws). Because prebendalism has become so prevalent, democratic competition in Nigeria, and elections in particular, have been fought with unusual vigor and often violence. Political party organization has often broken down along ethnic lines, threatening to lead the country into disintegration. These problems stalked the First Republic from its inception.

By the time the first independently administered national elections came around in 1964, politics had deteriorated into a sharp struggle along North–South, Muslim–Christian, and conservative–reform lines. The election itself was hotly contested, but eventually the northern-based NPC emerged as the strongest party. Tensions mounted particularly in the Western region, where the Yoruba felt repressed, and these tensions were exacerbated by regional elections. Rising violence further undermined the legitimacy of the country's first experience with democracy. Corruption, too, became endemic, and support for President Azikiwe quickly eroded.

### Military Intervention and Civil War

In an abrupt move, the military intervened in early 1966, murdering the prime minister, the governors of the West and North, and some military officers. Most of the coup-makers were Igbo, including the first head of the military government, Gen. Johnson Aguiyi-Ironsi. His efforts to establish an Igbo-dominated central government and his suppression of the North provoked anti-Igbo reprisals against their ethnic kin in the northern part of the country. In July 1966 Aguiyi-Ironsi was assassinated by rival northern officers, and Lt. Col. *Yakuba Gowon*, a Tiv, emerged as the new military head of state. Fleeing the massacres in the north, more than a million Igbos migrated eastward, and calls for secession—independence—for the East grew substantially.

In July 1967, civil war broke out after a unilateral declaration of independence by the Eastern region's military commander proclaimed the creation of the Republic of Biafra. In the ensuing violence, federal forces battled the mostly Igbo secessionists for three years, but by January 1970 the East had been defeated. At least 600,000 people—perhaps as many as a million—perished in the bitter struggle. Most died of starvation, as government forces cut off Biafra from the outside world. Several countries recognized the breakaway republic, but many others sided with the Nigerian central government. After the Biafran secessionists were defeated, Gowon's policy of forgiveness and national reconciliation managed to keep the country together. He worked hard to foster a new national identity based on ethnic accommodation and tolerance, buttressed by a renewed commitment to federalism and equitable sharing of resources.

Gowon's military rule ushered in a long succession of military governments in Nigeria. Sometimes the military takeover of power has been popular, as civilian administrators squandered their opportunity to govern and lost public support. Often, civilian leaders have brought the country to ruin as a result of factionalism, personal power struggles, corruption, and ethnic favoritism. The military has thus stepped in as the guardian of order, only to rule repressively and in the interests of individual leaders. Almost always, the military in Nigeria has justified its intervention and the suspension of the constitution by promising to lead a transition to restore clean governance and democracy. But more often than not they retracted these pledges and retained their grip on power, burying hopes for democracy under a heap of broken promises.

Gowon headed the Federal Military Government from 1966 to 1975, facing continuing social and economic problems; he was then removed in a bloodless coup and succeeded by Brig. Gen. Murtala Muhammad (1975–76), a Hausa-Fulani from the North. The new military leader purged the government of thousands of corrupt officials. Soon thereafter Lt. Gen. Olusegun Obasanjo, Muhammed's chief of staff, was appointed president by the military leadership after Mohammed was assassinated in a failed coup attempt by disgruntled elements of the military who opposed his corruption-busting campaign. Obasanjo, a Yoruba from the southwest region, was genuinely interested in reestablishing democracy. Governing from early 1976 to the restoration of constitutional government in 1979, he restored order in the military and combated corruption. The Obasanjo-led regime led many Nigerians to believe that the military rulers were truly committed to the restoration of democracy and would respond to popular pressure for it.

Nigeria's fortunes were also buoyed by a rapid expansion of oil production, along with the bounty provided by the escalation in global oil prices during the mid 1970s. Up to 90 percent of Nigeria's foreign exchange earnings were from oil during this highly volatile period. Obasanjo's commitment to the restoration of civilian rule at a time of economic expansion set the stage for a carefully managed, protracted transition to democracy, giving birth to the Second Republic.

### The Second Republic (1979–83)

One of the most important developments in Nigeria's political history was the 1979 constitution, which established several important precedents. One such precedent was the creation of new federal states in an effort to break up the troubled regionalism. Gradually the number of states was increased to twelve, and subsequently to nineteen states. Also important to Nigeria's political evolution was the introduction of the "federal character" clause of the 1979 constitution that required equitable representation among ethnic groups in state institutions (especially the military) and an equitable allocation of Nigeria's oil bounty. This federal character principle retains its importance in today's Fourth Republic.

The constitution featured the creation of a directly elected president with substantial independent powers, a popularly elected National Assembly (lower house), and a Senate with representatives drawn from the states. Many considered the constitution to have been modeled on the U.S. system, although there is no evidence of a direct influence in the constitution-drafting process. The judiciary was fairly independent.

Nigeria's new constitution also featured innovative devices designed to curb the influence of ethnic identity in political organization and leadership. To win the all-important presidential election, a candidate was required to garner an absolute majority of the electorate nationwide and at least 25 percent of the vote in each region of the country. This mechanism provided an incentive for political leaders to eschew narrow appeals to ethnicity and encouraged them to broaden the base of their political organizations to all parts of the country.[21] Political parties were to meet specific and detailed criteria to ensure they did not simply reflect regional or ethnic constituencies. The constitution also provided for compromise on the divisive issue of when Islamic law, the *shariah*, could be used to adjudicate domestic disputes. The careful compromise allowed it to be used in the Muslim northern areas but did not provide for its imposition on non-Muslims elsewhere or in instances where a party to a dispute preferred modern, constitutional legal procedures.

The *Second Republic* was widely seen as a reasonably good start for Nigeria's second attempt at democracy. The election results were disputed; the victor, Alhaji Shehu Shagari, won a nationwide majority, though he may not have garnered sufficient support in all the states. The election commission declared him the winner, however, and this outcome was eventually accepted by most Nigerians. But Shagari was a Hausa-Fulani, a northerner whose assumption of the leadership was resented by those who chafed under the North's domination of the central government. Thus the troubles of the Second Republic began right from its inception.

On the positive side of the ledger, political coalitions crystallized into two blocs, one predominantly right of center, or conservative on domestic social and foreign policy (now organized under the National Party of Nigeria), the other predominantly left-leaning, or more socialist in orientation (the

Unity Party of Nigeria). Yet mounting ethnic violence, especially in Kaduna and Kano states where Muslim-Christian tensions flared, undermined the fragile regime. Once again, impending elections heightened tensions and popular support for democracy quickly waned. Factionalism and political infighting grew rife and increasingly violent.

The prebendal inclinations of politicians were revealed in a number of scandals, often reported by Nigeria's independent press. Ever since the advent of Nigeria's oil wealth in the mid 1970s, for example, control over the central administration had been a point of deep contention and unceasing power struggles. The central government was seen as a funnel through which the nation's oil wealth flowed. Control over the narrow end of the funnel allowed predatory politicians to siphon off the nation's wealth for their own personal enrichment. Corruption, malfeasance, manipulation, neglect and political thuggery undermined the legitimacy of the government and civilian politicians in general. Ultimately it eroded popular support for democracy itself.

When the next presidential elections occurred in mid 1983, they were widely perceived as fraudulent; few believed the Shagari government had been returned to power by the will of the people. Violence ensued among the major political factions, and disillusionment with democracy was pervasive.

### Babangida's Dictatorship

Poor leadership and prebendal politics set the stage for the next military coup. Launched by Maj. Gen. *Muhammad Buhari* in December 1983, it was led by officers who, like some of their predecessors, pledged to restore order, civility, and good governance to Nigeria. They promised a new election to overturn the theft of democracy in the failed elections earlier that year, but it was not to be. Although the military moved quickly to arrest hundreds of corrupt political leaders and made some headway on economic reform, they mishandled the treatment of many individuals in unfair trials, meting out especially harsh punishment to southern politicians. "Ethno-military rule"—the junta was dominated by northerners—also limited the credibility of the government's promises to restore democracy. (Buhari came from the Hausa-Fulani group.) Malfeasance and popular unrest produced a popularly supported usurpation of power by other generals.

This time the coup was led by Maj. Gen. *Ibrahim Babangida,* who would become one of Nigeria's most dictatorial and despised military leaders. Under Babangida, authoritarian repression intensified despite initial expectations that he would lead the country back to democracy.

Indeed, there was a brief period in which the dictator opened up Nigeria's political space, allowing party politics to resume and initiating a halting process of constitution making. From his seizure of power in 1985 to his ultimate political demise in 1993, a process of transition to democracy seemed to be under way. First, Babangida announced a drawn-out transition that was supposed to culminate in a return to democracy in 1990. In 1989 a constitution for the *Third Republic* was drafted that made modest improvements on the 1979 charter. The reforms included clarified the electoral law while retaining the feature requiring the president to draw support from a wide variety of ethnic, regional, and religious groups. The new constitution also expanded the number of states to thirty to further encourage the development of more fluid, multiethnic coalitions. (Babangida himself was a northerner, but he came from a small ethnic group, the Gwari.) Some political prisoners from the Second Republic were released. Yet the dictatorial and kleptocratic nature of the Third Republic could not be denied.

Despite all the trappings of a transition to democracy, at the end of the day the military regime was ruling for its own immediate benefit and wealth. A bloody but failed coup attempt occurred in 1990, which nearly provoked a new civil war. During his rule, Babangida earned a reputation as the most corrupt ruler in Africa, vying for this dubious distinction with the Zairian strongman Mobutu Sese Seko. One of Babangida's most lavish projects was the creation of a new national capital in Abuja, where billions were spent on official buildings, luxury hotels, and hundreds of bridges in a city with no major river. Compared to the former capital of Lagos, Abuja was a gleaming showplace, but its amenities have been enjoyed mainly by visiting foreign dignitaries. The new capital was too expensive for ordinary Nigerians and remains virtually deserted. Under his rule, Nigeria became a pariah state subject to international sanctions. Its external reputation was in shambles, its vast oil wealth was squandered, drug trafficking flourished, and ethnic and religious tensions rose dramatically.

### The 1993 Elections

Babangida's so-called transition to democracy was consistently manipulated and often deferred. Presidential elections were first slated for 1990, but they were shunted aside until June 1993. From the very beginning, the military's pledge to restore democracy lacked credibility. The ruling junta used the protracted and tightly controlled "democratization" process to enhance its power, with a view to remaining the arbiter of national politics even after its military dictatorship came to an end and a democracy governed by civilians took its place.

Among the many ways the military leaders governed Nigeria was their tight control over the registration of political parties. It was the ruling officers who required, through decrees, the creation of two centrist political parties. The military created a left-leaning Social Democratic Party and the more conservative National Republican Convention as a means to control the process of selecting candidates for office as well as the ways the parties would position themselves in the ethnically and regionally divided electorate. These parties were to be loosely based on the party structure of the First Republic, but in reality they were entirely new constructs. In 1992, the government allowed elections to the National Assembly. The voting revealed ethno-regional divisions between the northern groups backing the NRC and the southern and western groups backing the Social Democrats. The Social Democrats won a majority of seats in both the newly reconstituted Senate (earning 55 percent of the seats) and in the lower chamber, the House of Representatives (with 65 percent of the seats). The elections were flawed, however, because of the use of nonsecret voting measures and a very low turnout rate. Subsequent primary elections for presidential candidates were also troubled, with widespread vote buying and rigging. At the end of the troubled process, both presidential candidates turned out to be businessmen with close ties to the Babangida regime, although the SDP candidate, Chief *M. K. O. Abiola*, stood out for his cross-communal profile and broad appeal. The NRC nominated a little-known candidate, Bashir Tofa.

A genuine democratic fervor accompanied the presidential elections when they were finally held in 1993, and Babangida pledged to leave power in August. But the elections of June 12 were fraught with turmoil. At the end of the balloting, ten days after the election, Babangida reneged on his pledge to restore civilian power. He annulled the results of the election when it became apparent that the southern traditional leader, Chief Abiola, had been elected by an estimated 58 percent of the vote. The international community was outraged, Abiola was subject to house arrest, and the country was further driven into isolation and condemnation. Within a few weeks Babangida was forced to leave under pressure, but an "interim" civilian government under Ernest Shonekan fell within months to another military coup, this one led by an especially inept and corrupt military dictator, *Sani Abacha*.

### Abacha's Dictatorship

Abacha, a northerner from the Kanuri group, ruled with an iron fist. Despite modest efforts to recruit credible civilians to his cabinet, he and his subordinates engaged in the systematic theft of the nation's wealth. Like other military leaders before him, he too announced a new draft constitution and pledged to lead the country back to civilian rule. But the military government's deeds spoke louder than its words. Corruption and arbitrary rule reached new depths. Abacha himself is thought to have embezzled billions of dollars from the national treasury, perhaps tens of billions. His cronies also profited handsomely from stolen wealth. A pivotal event in the deepening crisis in Nigeria was the execution on November 10, 1995, of *Ken Saro-Wiwa* and eight other activists who had sought to raise international attention to the plight of an ethnic group in the southeast, the Ogoni, whose area had been desecrated by pollution from the extraction of oil and gas. The executions led to the application of economic and political sanctions against the Abacha regime by the world community and reinforced Nigeria's status as a pariah state. In 1996, the British Commonwealth suspended Nigeria's membership and the United States imposed sanctions on the regime.

Only a bizarre twist of fate allowed Nigeria to find its way out of the abyss. Dramatically, Abacha succumbed to a heart attack on June 8, 1998. Hopes rose that Abiola would now lead a transition to democracy. But exactly one month later, on July 8, Abiola died suddenly in the middle of a meeting with U.S. and Nigerian officials. Abiola's death set off riots by his supporters, many of whom suspected foul play because he was still in detention when he died. (An international investigatory team found no evidence of it.) General Abacha's demise set the stage for a new military government under General Abdulsalami Abubaker, a member of the Hausa-speaking Nupe group. Abubaker realized that the military's ability to retain power was at an end. Popular discontent was at the boiling point. He organized a rapid transition to democracy that featured local elections in December 1998 and presidential elections on February 27, 1999. Abiola's passing set aside the lingering controversy over the aborted elections of 1993. Nigeria now seemed poised for a fresh start.

### From Prisoner to President: Olusegun Obasanjo

With the establishment of an independent election commission and heavy involvement by the international community, the 1999 elections were a major turning point for Nigeria. The presidential vote—widely seen as the most important in the transition—featured Gen. **Olusegun Obasanjo,** the man who had tried to restore democracy in the late 1970s, running for the People's Democratic Party. Until the transition of 1999, Obasanjo was the only Nigerian head of government who had gained power as a military leader (in 1976, when Muhammed was assassinated), only to hand over the reins of government to a civilian leader. Subsequently, in 1995, he was arrested by the military for advocating a return to civilian rule and democracy during the brutal and incompetent rule of Sani Abacha. In a secret trial, Obasanjo was convicted of plotting a coup and remained imprisoned for several years. His main opponent in the February 1999 elections, Olu Falae, was the joint candidate of the Alliance for Democracy and the All People's Party and was alleged to be a favorite candidate of the outgoing military regime.

**President Olusegun Obasanjo**

In a vote deemed somewhat less than free and fair by independent Nigerian and international observers—including Falae, who claimed they were fraudulent—Gen. Obasanjo won a lopsided victory. With the support of a large majority (62.8 percent), mostly in the Southeast and North, Obasanjo enjoyed the backing of some 18.7 million voters from all major ethnic and religious groups. Although Obasanjo is a Yoruba from the Southwest (and a Christian), most Yorubas disliked him because of his past support for the Hausa-led military and his close associations with Hausa leaders during the presidential campaign. The majority of Yorubas voted for Falae, who also comes from their group, and many voiced displeasure with the election results. Nevertheless, Obasanjo's victory represented the first time someone from his region and ethnicity had been elected president with an ethnically mixed base of support. Falae garnered about 11 million votes. Despite the apparent irregularities, the victory of Obasanjo and his party was undeniable. ***On May 29, 1999, the military formally stepped aside and civilian rule at long last returned to Nigeria. The country's* Fourth Republic *was at last a reality.***

Obasanjo was widely believed to be the one leader who could lead Nigeria out of its deep crisis. The country now had the opportunity to restore some legitimacy to its government, to begin developing anew, and to realize its long-lost potential. The obstacles were enormous. Nigeria's tradition of democratic pluralism and constitutionalism had been undermined systematically for years by military officers and inept civilian leaders. Larry Diamond, a renowned scholar of the struggle for

TABLE 23.2

**Rulers of Post-Independence Nigeria**

| Ruler | Dates of Rule | Ethnic Group | How Power Was Attained |
|---|---|---|---|
| ***First Republic, 1963–66*** | | | |
| Nnamdi Azikiwe | 1963–66 | Igbo | Appointed |
| ***Military Rule, 1966–79*** | | | |
| Gen. Johnson Aguiyi-Ironsi | 1966 | Igbo | Military coup |
| Lt. Col. Yakabu Gowon | 1966–75 | Tiv | Military coup |
| Brig. Gen. Murtala Muhammad | 1975–76 | Hausa-Fulani | Military coup |
| Lt. Gen. Olusegun Obasanjo | 1976–79 | Yoruba | Appointed by military |
| ***Second Republic, 1979–83*** | | | |
| Alhaji Shehu Shagari | 1979–83 | Hausa-Fulani | Elected |
| ***Military Rule, 1983–99; Third Republic, 1989–93*** | | | |
| Maj. Gen. Muhammad Buhari | 1983–85 | Hausa-Fulani | Military coup |
| Maj. Gen. Ibrahim Babangida | 1985–93 | Gwari | Appointed by military |
| M. K. O. Abiola | 1993 | Yoruba | Elected; election annulled |
| Chief Ernest Shonekan | 1993 | Yoruba | Appointed by military |
| Gen. Sani Abacha | 1993–98 | Kanuri | Military coup |
| Gen. Abdulsalami Abubaker | 1998–99 | Nupe | Appointed by military |
| ***Fourth Republic (1999–present)*** | | | |
| Olusegun Obasanjo | 1999–2007 | Yoruba | Elected |

democracy in that country, uses the term **praetorianism** to characterize Nigeria's postindependence political system: ***a system in which raw power occupies the pursuits of political leaders and factions, and constitutional rules are manipulated for individual gain.*** Diamond perceptively argues that "the modern state was a resource, devoid of moral content or attachment, to be pursued, occupied, milked—and later plundered—for the individual politician and his support group."[22] Against this inherited weight of the past, the Obasanjo regime had little time to restore the country's vitality. (For a list of Nigeria's leaders, see table 23.2.)

## HYPOTHESIS-TESTING EXERCISE: Democracy in Nigeria

The new civilian rulers of Nigeria's Fourth Republic, which finally got off the ground with the 1999 elections, must deal with a daunting array of challenges. We can usefully assess where Nigeria stands at the start of the new millennium and speculate about its possible future course by measuring it against the ten criteria for democratization discussed in chapter 9.

### Hypotheses and Variables

We hypothesize that democracy's prospects depend to a considerable extent on meeting these criteria. Each *condition* constitutes an *independent variable* that has a presumed impact on whether democracy comes about at all and, if it does, how likely it is to survive the initial democratization process and become consolidated into a stable democracy over the long term. *Democracy, the democratization process*, and *the long-term survival of democracy* are thus the *dependent variables* in our hypotheses; that is, they are *dependent* on the independent variables on our list.

### Expectations

If our hypotheses are correct, we would expect that if a country succeeds in meeting most of the conditions we've set forth, then its prospects for developing a democracy in the first place and sustaining it through the consolidation process rise appreciably. Conversely, failure to meet even a few of these criteria should tend to diminish democracy's chances. How has Nigeria done thus far in fulfilling these conditions, and what are its likely prospects in the future?

### Evidence

#### *Elites Committed to Democracy*

In the past, Nigerian political leaders often substituted military dictatorship for civilian democracy and used state offices to enhance their own personal wealth. The ruling elite under President Obasanjo seemed genuinely committed to democracy, though corruption remained rife in many institutions. In view of the importance of Nigeria's central government in holding the reins of power and national wealth, the commitment of its political elites to democratic rule—above all the military elites—is vital to the survivability of democracy in Nigeria.

### *State Institutions*

State institutions in Nigeria have been well conceived in theory, but in practice have often proved frail and unable to withstand the pressures of ethnic and regional divisions and the temptations presented for officeholders to skim from the national coffers. The strict observance of the rule of law—and the elimination of corruption in particular—will be crucial in the coming years if democracy is to succeed in Nigeria. Similarly, a fair application of federalist principles to the country's diverse regional, ethnic, and religious groupings will also be essential. Institutions alone, however, are not enough to consolidate democracy.

### *National Unity*

As we've abundantly observed, Nigeria's ethnic divisions have been a constant strain on its national unity and attempts at democracy, even though the immediate causes of the downfall of the First and Second Republics were other factors such as corruption and malfeasance. Ominous signs of religious and ethnic strife confronted the new Fourth Republic in its first year. In March 2000 and thereafter, some 800 people were killed in separate clashes between Christians and Muslims as the leaders of Muslim-dominated parts of the North sought to impose Islamic law in their localities and Christians in both the North and South vented their anger. Fortunately Nigeria's political institutions—while not fully consociational as described in chapter 7—have been carefully crafted to help manage ethnic differences. Nigeria's diversity is thus a possible, but not inevitable, barrier to the consolidation of its democracy, depending upon how fairly the central authorities apply the constitution's federalist principles. Multiethnicity in and of itself need not undermine democracy in Nigeria, however.

### *National Wealth*

Nigeria's national wealth is highly dependent on a single commodity, oil. Oil accounts for 95 percent of the government's revenues and the state has reaped hundreds of billions in total revenues since the 1970s. Unfortunately, about $280 billion was squandered by corrupt leaders. By early 2000, buoyant world oil prices helped improve economic performance and increase export earnings. But the volatility of the oil market suggests that Nigeria needs to deal with endemic poverty and structural inequality before its economic bounty can truly contribute to the consolidation of democracy. Nigeria remains one of the poorest countries in the world, with a per capita GNP in 2005 of $560 a year. Oil revenues alone are insufficient to provide a suitable economic base for the consolidation of democracy. The country requires a structural adjustment in the economy, a process that is just as likely to destabilize the democratization process as lead to the consolidation of democracy.

### *Private Enterprise*

The entrepreneurial spirit of many Nigerians is legendary, and the informal economy contributes significantly to the welfare of many citizens. At the same time, rampant corruption limits the ability of private enterprise to grow and prosper. (Nigeria is rated as one of the most corrupt countries on the globe; see table 4.1.) State ownership of the country's oil reserves and nearly all its farmland has facilitated government corruption in the past. Private enterprise contributes to the consolidation of democracy only if the government can effectively root out the deep-seated corruption that limits a flourishing private sector.[23]

### *Middle Class*

The development of a vibrant middle class in Nigeria has been stunted by the poor economic performance engendered by decades of misgovernment by the military. The country's oil wealth, in particular, has not trickled down to support the development of a strong and consolidated middle class. The absence of a secure middle class continues to limit the consolidation of Nigeria's democracy.

### *Support of the Disadvantaged*

Endemic poverty characterizes the lives of most Nigerians today. According to World Bank estimates, nearly 93 percent of the population lived on less than $2 a day in 2003, and 71 percent survived on less than $1 a day. More than a third of children under the age of five were malnourished in the first half of the decade and about 20 percent died before their fifth birthday. Nearly 40 percent of city dwellers lacked access to sanitation. (Nigeria's urban population exploded from 27 percent in 1980 to 41 percent by 1997.)[24] Life expectancy is fifty years. In addition, Nigeria has one of the worst maldistribution of wealth patterns in the world (see table 2.2). AIDS is taking a rising toll—though not as severely as in other parts of Africa. About 5.4 percent of Nigerians were HIV-infected by the end of 1999, with as many as five million AIDS deaths to be expected in the next ten years. AIDS research and medical facilities have received scant funding in Nigeria thus far, however. Agricultural production has fallen far below the country's potential as a producer of cocoa, rubber, cotton, and other valuable commodities, thanks in large measure to inept government policies under the military. The rebellion in Nigeria's southern Delta region, where oil drilling and processing are conducted by foreign-owned companies that have cut deals with the central government, raises the question of whether oil wealth is in fact a curse rather than a blessing for oil-rich countries. The benefits of energy resources do not always reach those most affected by pollution and other negative consequences of oil extraction. Rather than promoting social cohesion in Nigeria, oil wealth inhibits it.

### *Citizen Participation, Civil Society, and a Democratic Political Culture*

Nigeria boasts a vibrant civil society with a plethora of associations and trade unions. The vigor of Nigeria's civil society has been one reason why military regimes have experienced strong pressures for a return to civilian rule. We believe that Nigeria's civil society will contribute to the likelihood that democratic institutions continue to be perceived as the only truly legitimate form of government, bolstering the chances that democracy can be consolidated over time.

### *Education and Freedom of Information*

Illiteracy in Nigeria exceeds 35 percent of the population in some areas. Without a greater emphasis on education and the extension of literacy to a great proportion of the population, Nigeria's chances for long-term consolidation of democracy are slim. Though the country boasts a vigorous free press, the newly elected government will have to take action to lift prior decrees restricting press freedoms and refrain from exercising excessive government controls over the media if democratic liberties are to be fully guaranteed.

### *Favorable International Environment*

Nigeria's external environment has not been especially conducive to supporting democratic institutions; civil wars in Liberia and Sierra Leone, for example, have drawn Nigeria into costly engagements abroad. Yet the broader international community has been very supportive of democracy in Nigeria, and pressure from overseas has been one of the reasons why military regimes have been compelled to return to civilian rule. (President Clinton visited the country in August 2000.) Considerable international assistance—in the form of political party training, election monitoring, and development aid—is critical to the long-term viability of democracy in Nigeria.

## Conclusions

The evidence from Nigeria's checkered experience with democracy since independence, and from its current situation, is quite *mixed*. Positive tendencies coexist with less favorable ones. Political science predictions can by no means plot Nigeria's trajectory with any degree of certainty. Much depends on the ability of the government to manage ethnic tensions, contain political infighting, revive its flagging economy, and especially, root out deep-seated corruption. As a purely speculative prognosis, we can regard Nigeria's chances as doubtful, given the strains to which it will be put.

Nigeria today confronts major social, economic, and political challenges. In the social sphere, tensions are rising from the assertiveness of Muslims who insist on the implementation of Islamic law in their regions, as well as from ongoing sectarian violence between Muslims and Christians. In 2005 and 2006, Muslim sensitivities were aroused all over the world by a Danish newspaper's publication of a political cartoon that caricatured Muhammad; in Nigeria nearly a thousand people died in protest riots. The determination of traditionalists in northern Nigeria's highly conservative Muslim states to implement punishments such as stoning has created frictions with human rights advocates. These and other social conflicts were reflected in the difficult task of conducting a census in 2006, Nigeria's first attempt to count its entire population since achieving independence thirty-five years earlier. Previous attempts were thwarted by the exceptionally sensitive nature of ethnic and religious affiliation in the socially divided country.

In the economic realm, the dramatic rise in crude oil prices in recent years has certainly boosted Nigeria's national wealth. But it has also created sharp resentments in local communities that bear the brunt of environmental degradation but do not get a fair share of the country's oil revenues. Rebels connected with the Movement for the Emancipation of the Niger Delta (MEND) in the Ogoni region are demanding greater central-government accountability. To dramatize their cause, they have kidnapped a number of foreign oil workers.

And in the political arena, Nigeria stands on the brink of crisis. President Obasanjo's failed attempt to win a constitutional amendment that would allow him to run for a third term exposed deep fault lines in Nigeria's political elite. Those cleavages follow historic patterns of religion, region, and ethnic identity. As the 2007 presidential elections approached at the time of this writing, there were serious concerns not only about the prospect of political violence in Nigeria but also about the very survival of the Nigerian federation. The announcements by Muhammad Buhari and Ibrahim Babangida, the former military dictators, that they would run as candidates for the presidency in 2007 could only heighten these concerns.

The consolidation of democracy in Nigeria will no doubt be a lengthy process; there seems to be widespread popular support for the notion of democracy, but not a great deal of satisfaction with the institutions and practices of successive civilian and military governments. It is by no means clear that the rules of the democratic game in this most populous African country are entrenched and that its national unity can be maintained. Clearly the first step in the consolidation process will be to ensure that democratic governance pays direct dividends to a people who have long suffered under corruption, mismanagement, and staggering poverty. Only one thing is for sure: as Nigeria goes, so goes much of West Africa.

## SOUTH AFRICA

Population (2006 estimated): 44.2 million

Freedom House Ratings (2006): Political Rights—1; Civil Liberties—2

Area: 471,444 square miles (about twice the size of Texas)

Democratization in South Africa, Africa's other most important state, has taken a path markedly different from Nigeria's. The dramatic transition from white minority rule and apartheid—the enforced separation of people on the basis of race and ethnicity—to democracy in 1994 reveals a remarkable story of a country that was on the brink of civil war, yet managed to avoid the abyss. In doing so, it embraced a multiracial democracy in which all citizens are entitled to vote and enjoy equal human rights regardless of race or ethnic origin. South Africa's success at

**South Africa**

democratization is a consequence of an unusual confluence of historical events, such as the end of the Cold War, and the equally unique quality of its leadership, particularly Nobel Prize–winning *Nelson Mandela,* the legendary freedom fighter who became the country's first black president.

South Africa's path of transition was the result of extensive negotiation and compromise among its competing political forces.[25] A white minority settler society ruled over the majority black population of South Africa for some 350 years, from the day the first settlers set foot on the Cape Peninsula in 1648. After mounting pressures in the 1980s and 1990s, the ruling regime—led by the **National Party (NP)**, ***which gained power in 1948 and implemented the policies of apartheid***—agreed to a series of extensive negotiations on a new constitution with the leading force in the liberation movement, Mandela's African National Congress. This process was highly turbulent: indeed, some fourteen thousand people died in political violence during this widely heralded "peaceful" transition. But in the end it yielded one of the most progressive democratic constitutions on the globe. Today, South Africa is a highly regarded developing state. Although it faces tremendous challenges in confronting the legacy of apartheid, the country's prospects for the consolidation of democracy are widely considered good. How did a country headed for a brutal war manage to transform itself into a model multiethnic democracy?

## Apartheid, Conflict, and Liberation

**Apartheid** ***means "separateness"*** in Afrikaans, the language of the descendants of Dutch and French settlers of southern Africa known as *Afrikaners*. The policy of apartheid had its antecedents in the domination of the white settlers over the indigenous African peoples that began with the arrival of the first colonists in the late seventeenth century. Yet apartheid was more than just colonial domination; rather, ***it was a systematic division of the country's peoples based on race and ethnic origin.*** The policies of apartheid were intensified by the National Party, led by Afrikaners, after it took power in whites-only elections in 1948; but its roots lay deep in South African history. Indeed, some suggest that the more pernicious effects of apartheid were as much a legacy of British rule in South Africa (extending roughly from 1800 to 1910) as they were the result of the Afrikaners and the National Party. Even so, the post-1948 white-majority regime in South Africa perfected laws of racial domination—especially the exclusion of the country's majority black population from the voting franchise—and it was these measures particularly that led to a black uprising that eventually brought apartheid to an end.

South Africa's historical trajectory is rich and complicated.[26] Originally, the area was a colony of the Dutch East India Company, which needed this southern crossroads of the world as a station for ships rounding the Cape of Good Hope en route to and from the colonies of the West Indies. Shortly after the founding of the Cape Colony in 1648, settlers arrived and the dynamics of a highly diverse society began to emerge. Upon their arrival, the Dutch settlers found indigenous Khoikhoi and San peoples, whom they quickly subjugated using their superior technology, firearms. The settlers imported slaves and indentured labor from Dutch colonies in East Asia and began to implement strict policies of racial segregation. Imperial contests ended Dutch rule by the turn of the nineteenth century, and the British took over the southern African colonies. British suzerainty and policies banning slave ownership led to an uprising by the Dutch-speaking settlers (the Boers), and by 1838 all slaves in the colony had been emancipated. Consequently, the Boers migrated into the vast interior of the subcontinent, in a pioneer march known as the Great Trek. At the same time, however, African tribes such as the Zulu and Xhosa had settled into the east and south, and black-white conflicts and wars erupted on the frontier. In 1838, for example, the well-known battle of Blood River occurred in which Afrikaner commandos (known as Voortrekkers) defeated the army of *King Shaka* of the Zulus.

By the mid nineteenth century, the British controlled the Cape Colony as well as the eastern coastal zone of Natal. The Voortrekkers set up independent republics known as the Transvaal and the Orange Free State. In perhaps the most pivotal historical events in South African history, in 1867 diamonds and later huge gold deposits were discovered in the deep interior of the country; a rush for wealth began. Hundreds of thousands of new European settlers migrated into the Boer republics as tremendous mineral deposits were discovered. Conflict among the whites soon grew over the newfound treasure. The British governor, Sir Cecil Rhodes, sought to undermine the Boer republics and the result was the **Boer War** ***of 1899–1902, in which British control of the entire territory of southern Africa was secured.*** The struggle embittered many Afrikaners: British troops committed untold atrocities, including the incarceration of Boer women and children in concentration camps. Although South Africa became independent in 1910, conflict among the whites and domination over blacks became the hallmarks of South African society.

Steadily throughout the early half of the twentieth century, South Africa's economy boomed from mineral wealth. Meanwhile the Afrikaners, many of whom were farmers or laborers, became increasingly nationalistic. They mobilized against black migrants to the cities who threatened their meager wages and also against English-speaking whites who controlled South Africa's capital, its mines, and the means of industrial production. Blacks were relegated to 13 percent of the land, encompassing the least agriculturally productive parcels. The Afrikaner nationalists, stirring up so-called "poor white" resentments, won progressively larger support among the Afrikaners, who themselves constituted a majority of the whites. They argued for stricter policies of racial segregation and discrimination against the burgeoning black population. They also claimed a Christian basis for their policies, locating its origins in a highly puritan form of Calvinism that they claimed ordained white domination over blacks in South Africa.

### White Domination and Black Protest

By 1948, the Afrikaner-led National Party managed to gain power in an all-white election by employing the political and religious myths that demanded Afrikaner control of southern Africa as a matter of destiny. The policies of apartheid began to be systematically implemented. The entire population was registered by race: African (70 percent in 1960), Colored (mixed ancestry, 10 percent), Indian/Asian (10 percent), and white (20 percent). Mixed marriages and romance across the race bar were forbidden. Racially exclusive areas were demarcated, and blacks were forbidden in cities unless they had a pass that certified their employment. Blacks were assigned separate services such as water fountains, public transportation, and bathrooms, and they were denied education, health services, and other opportunities despite the fact that it was on their backs that a prosperous, modern industrial country was being built.

In the vision of the architect of "grand apartheid," President *Henrik Verwoerd*, South Africa was to be partitioned. The "homelands," or reservations, were created for the ten major black linguistic groups; gradually they became independent black islands in a broader white South African sea. The South African government regarded the homelands as independent states, and their residents were not regarded as South African citizens. Hence they could be classified as migrant workers and were denied unemployment compensation and other benefits. No foreign country ever recognized the homelands' independent status, however. Apartheid was created to systematically exclude the majority black population from citizenship and economic opportunity in its own country.

At the same time that the pernicious policies of apartheid were being implemented, blacks began to develop their own competing national identity, arguing for an end to apartheid policies in their petty form (such as separate amenities) as well as in their more extensive form of "grand apartheid," which set up the system of homelands. On March 21, 1960, in the township of Sharpeville, the first black riots erupted. Blacks burned the passes that they were required to carry; sixty died as the result of police brutality. Today that date is celebrated as Human Rights Day. In a spiral of revolt and repression, black anger grew and the state responded with brutal force. The **African National Congress (ANC)**—*the organizational arm of the anti-apartheid movement*—was banned, along with other black organizations. **Nelson Mandela**, a young ANC activist, was arrested and convicted of treason in the landmark Rivonia trial; he entered prison in 1962. As the protests grew, so did the repression and the whites' commitment to the systematic exclusion of blacks. Although some whites argued for progressive change, most supported the National Party's program of separation and domination. From 1948 to 1984, National Party governments were returned to power with enlarged electoral majorities among whites.

Black protest grew more fervent in the 1970s. By June 1976, widespread riots erupted throughout the sprawling townships that lay astride South Africa's major cities. Beginning in Soweto near Johannesburg, youths set the country aflame, and widespread unrest drew more outside attention to the tragic oppression of the country's majority black population. In 1977 the United Nations imposed an arms embargo on South Africa and the litany of denunciation by the international community against apartheid began. Subsequent sports and cultural boycotts heightened pressure on the white government to reform. Just as the rest of the world was moving away from colonialism, racial segregation, and the denial of human rights in the 1960s and 1970s, South Africa was moving in the opposite direction.

Apartheid could not hold back the economic forces that led desperately poor black laborers to flock to the cities. The country's cities and their environs witnessed a growing influx of blacks—despite brutal government policies of influx control—pushed by the country's tremendous industrial development after World War II and by the diamond and gold wealth extracted from the earth. The government tried various measures to stem the tide of urbanization, such as forced removals and the deeply hated "pass" system, which required blacks to carry cards certifying their employment eligibility. Despite ever-increasing repressive measures, domestic discontent and international condemnation continued to ratchet up the pressure on a recalcitrant and entrenched white minority government.

By the mid 1980s, more comprehensive economic sanctions dried up new foreign investment, technology transfers, and trade opportunities. The once-roaring economy floundered and a recession set in during the early 1980s. About the same time, the first fissures emerged in what had been a brick wall of resistance put up by white South Africans. Under the reformist president P. W. Botha, the South African government began to ease some of the more discriminatory laws of apartheid while reinforcing its commitment to maintaining white dominance in general.

The halfhearted reforms of the 1980s eliminated some of the more overtly discriminatory laws—such as separate public amenities like drinking fountains—but not the foundation of the system, the race-based categories of citizenship. Far from defusing black anger and international disapproval, the reforms led instead to a renewed protest movement and a significant energizing of the international anti-apartheid movement.[27] Widespread protests erupted again in September 1984 in a popular upsurge of demands for democracy, human rights, and full enfranchisement of the black majority. In 1986, the U.S. Congress passed the Comprehensive Anti-Apartheid Act, which included a ban on new investment and promised new sanctions if further reforms weren't enacted. (President Ronald Reagan had opposed the measure on the grounds that it would limit the administration's ability to persuade the white minority government to peacefully cede power.)

Many other countries imposed stiff economic sanctions. With internal and external pressures mounting, the white minority reached a turning point by 1989, the same year that the Berlin wall opened. White leaders could try to defend their indefensible policies of racial domination and face an all-out race war with the majority blacks in their country, or they could seek to reach an accommodation with black leaders such as Mandela before it was too late. Wisely, they chose the latter. Political violence was already high between 1984 and 1989, and without further reforms the black townships would once again explode in protest.

A series of unpredictable events unleashed the process of transition in South Africa. In early 1989, the recalcitrant President Botha suffered a debilitating heart attack. Though he had initiated contacts with Mandela, who was still in jail, Botha was a reluctant reformer who would not take the steps necessary to end the unrest. Later that year, the fall of communism created a situation in which the white minority—which had long claimed that the ANC was controlled by the Soviets in Moscow—could feel comfortable that black rule would not result in the widespread expropriation of property and industry. Botha was succeeded by a man with a reputation as a hardliner, *F. W. de Klerk*, in August 1989.

The stage was now set for a dramatic change of fortune for South Africa. On February 2, 1990, de Klerk shocked white South Africans and the world. He announced the release of Mandela and scores of other political prisoners, lifted the bans on the ANC and other anti-apartheid organizations, invited exiles to return home, and promised to negotiate in good faith the end of apartheid and the dawn of a fully inclusive democracy for all South Africans. Addressing the white minority government's longstanding enemies, de Klerk invited them to "walk through the open door, take your place at the negotiating table together with the government and other leaders who have important power bases inside and outside of parliament. . . . The time for negotiation has arrived." The transition had begun in earnest. Two weeks later Nelson Mandela appeared on the steps of City Hall in Cape Town before a joyous crowd after twenty-seven years in prison.

## PROFILE: Nelson Mandela

Nelson Rolihlahla Mandela is the father of post-apartheid South Africa. He led the independence struggle from his jail cell on Robben Island off Cape Town for nearly three decades, finally emerging from prison to negotiate with the white regime a new constitution that would guarantee voting rights to the majority black population. He served as the country's first president under the new political order from 1994 to 1999. He is extremely popular among all segments of the population—including the white minority—and is hailed as the one individual most responsible for South Africa's dramatic transition to democracy. In 1993, he and F. W. de Klerk were awarded the Nobel Peace Prize for their dedication to a negotiated settlement.

Born July 18, 1918, in a small village in the former Transkei homeland (in today's Eastern Cape province, near Umtata), Mandela was the son of the principal councillor to the Acting Paramount Chief of Thembuland. After his father passed away, he emerged as the Paramount Chief's principal aide, a position that was certain to lead to high office in the traditional tribal hierarchy. At an early age, he dedicated himself to the study of law. To prepare for that path, he was educated in a local mission school. Upon graduation from high school, Mandela entered the University of Fort Hare, where he was for a time suspended for protesting discriminatory racial policies in the country. He eventually migrated to Johannesburg, where he studied law and began his political career by joining the African National Congress in 1942.

In the booming Johannesburg metropolis, Mandela forged ties with other young, intelligent black activists, such as Oliver Tambo and Walter Sisulu, and they banded together to found the ANC Youth League. The League and these fraternal ties became extremely important to South Africa's trajectory; Mandela and his companions espoused an ideology of African nationalism and began to organize and mobilize the ANC to challenge the powerful white minority establishment. The youth organizers eventually were elected to the National Executive Committee of the ANC.

After the end of World War II, when the extreme Afrikaner National Party won elections and began to implement policies of apartheid, Mandela and the ANC became more militant, organizing boycotts, strikes, civil disobedience campaigns, and other acts of noncooperation with the authoritarian regime. Among their demands were full citizenship and direct parliamentary representation for all South Africans regardless of color. In the early 1950s, Mandela helped organize the Defiance Campaign, traveling about the country organizing passive resistance to apartheid. Mandela and the law firm he established with Oliver Tambo were the targets of the government's security forces. In 1952, Mandela created a plan of further nonviolent resistance, particularly against the system of inferior education for blacks (known as Bantu education). In 1955, he was instrumental in the drafting of the Freedom Charter, which committed the ANC to a tolerant, multiracial South Africa with freedom and equality for all. During this time, Mandela was at times banned, arrested, and briefly imprisoned. He was accused of treason in the so-called Treason Trial of 1961, a charge that was eventually dropped.

In the early 1960s, as it became clear that the apartheid government's policies were becoming ever more cruel and discriminatory, Mandela went underground to form the armed wing of the ANC and to launch a struggle for liberation. He later wrote that only the intransigence of the apartheid government—which refused many petitions for reform—led him and his ANC colleagues to turn to violent armed struggle. Mandela became commander-in-chief of Umkhonto we Sizwe, "the spear of the nation." During this time, he constantly evaded the net of the white police who sought to arrest him. Eventually they managed to apprehend him, and he was charged with treason. At the Rivonia trial, as it became known, he conducted his own defense, uttering words that continue to ring in the South African national psyche:

> I have fought against white domination, and I have fought against black domination. I have cherished the ideal of a democratic and free society in which all persons live together in harmony and with equal opportunities. It is an ideal which I hope to live for and to achieve. But if needs be, it is an ideal for which I am prepared to die.

He was convicted, sentenced to life in prison, and spent the next twenty-seven years quietly and clandestinely directing the liberation movement from prison. By the late 1980s, white political leaders were visiting him in prison seeking a negotiated settlement. Finally, in February 1990, he was released. Remarkably, Mandela demonstrated tremendous courage and called for national reconciliation. He embraced white leaders with no sign of bitterness and steadfastly led the ANC through the difficult negotiations that produced a new constitution. With the far-reaching victory of the ANC in the first full-franchise elections in 1994, Mandela was elected president. From 1994 to 1999, he served not only as the country's chief executive, but as its moral force, firmly launching the new republic on a path of tolerance, moderate policies, and national reconciliation. After stepping down at the age of 81 in 1999, he now traveled the world advocating international assistance to help poor children and mediating disputes in other countries. Mandela lives near his birthplace in a quiet rural area, tending his garden and providing moral guidance to his country and the world.

## The Turbulent Transition

The historic events of February 1990 set in motion a transition from apartheid to democracy that was full of hope for a brighter future for all South Africans but that simultaneously unleashed tremendous uncertainty. Initially, the negotiations went well, and an early accord was reached by May of that year that pledged the ANC and the government to a negotiation process that would culminate in the advent of a new, multiracial democracy in which no racial, religious, or ethnic group would dominate another. Individual human rights would prevail over structured domination by a group. All political prisoners would be released, free political activity would be allowed, and negotiations would proceed on convening a constitutional convention to draft a charter that would guide the new democracy into a more peaceful future.

Yet there were significant forces that either were opposed to the end of apartheid altogether or were afraid that the ANC would emerge as a domineering political force despite the promises of toleration and reconciliation contained in the early agreements. In particular, the Zulu-based *Inkatha Freedom Party (IFP)*, led by *Mangosutho Buthelezi*, felt excluded from the negotiations. With the help of clandestine forces in the white-led police and military, IFP cadres instigated violence, especially in the urban areas outside Johannesburg and in the already simmering province of KwaZulu-Natal, which included the traditional Zulu homelands. Although some analysts saw the emerging violence as ethnic—alleging that the ANC was primarily Xhosa—in reality it was a political struggle over power and turf. In the uncertainty of the transition, when apartheid was dead but the new order had not yet been created, when the rules of the political game were in flux, violence among various factions soared. Thousands died in factional fighting and fingers were pointed in all directions.

Political violence soured the initial goodwill that had been generated by Mandela's release. In 1991 and 1992, mass killings, assassinations, clashes among armed militia, and continuing police brutality undermined the incipient talks on democracy. For a while in 1992 it appeared that the talks would fail and a civil war would ensue. Clashes between ANC and IFP supporters left more than two thousand people dead in 1992 alone. Despite a major agreement in December 1991 to curb the violence—the National Peace Accord—the deaths continued to mount and several major incidents scuttled the talks. One particularly traumatic event was the June 1992 Boipatong incident, which left scores of innocent civilians dead after an attack by Zulu migrant laborers on a nearby township. Only after the intervention of the United Nations, which dispatched senior mediator Cyrus Vance, a former U.S. Secretary of State, to investigate the violence, did the country's transition get back on track. As the killing escalated, the realization set in that the country faced a truly stark choice between anarchy and war, on the one hand, and compromise and power sharing on the other.

By late 1992, the violence had shocked the political leaders—especially Mandela and de Klerk—into reaching a series of agreements that formed the essential bargain of the negotiated transition from apartheid to democracy in South Africa. Black South Africans would gain voting rights and other human rights in exchange for assurances to white South Africans that their property rights would be protected. Security force members would receive amnesty for any human rights abuses they may have committed, provided that they supplied all the details on any incidents of abuse. The African National Congress and the National Party would share power after an initial election, and a government of national unity would be installed until a final constitution could be drafted that would guarantee both majority prerogatives and minority rights. South Africa would have a period of democratic power sharing in which decisions were to be taken by consensus among all the major political parties. This pact was sealed in multiparty talks that concluded in June 1993 with an agreement on a new interim constitution and a specific plan for managing the transfer of power at the end of white-minority rule.

The IFP and conservative Afrikaner parties, however, balked at the deal. They demanded greater autonomy for their respective ethnic groups—the Zulus and the Afrikaners—and vowed a campaign of violent resistance unless their demands were met. On the left, opponents of the ANC, organized in the *Pan-Africanist Congress (PAC)*, also objected to the agreement, arguing that it granted too many concessions to the whites. The PAC demanded unfettered majority rule by the blacks. These disaffected parties boycotted the signing of the new interim constitution and pledged to boycott—and possibly disrupt—the momentous elections slated for April 27, 1994, the elections that would end apartheid. Preparations for the culmination of the transition and the hotly contested electoral campaigns generated tremendous tension in late 1993 and early 1994. The far-right whites and the IFP as well as the PAC were poised to spoil the vote.

Mandela's renowned qualities as a conciliator, however, produced a breakthrough in early 1994 that brought the far-right *Afrikaner Volksfront* into the election. Significantly, the Inkatha Freedom Party remained outside the agreement. Preparations for the elections went ahead and a potential showdown loomed. After a bloody confrontation in downtown Johannesburg between the IFP and the African National Congress in which scores died, cooler heads once again prevailed. Deft politicking and international mediation produced a last-minute agreement among Mandela's African National Congress, the National Party government, and the Inkatha Freedom Party, leading to an end to the latter's election boycott.[28] Stickers were placed on the already-printed ballots to include the IFP. South Africa's elections would proceed, and they would be broadly representative of all the country's major political forces.

Remarkably, the elections held on April 26 and 27, 1994, brought South Africa some of the most peaceful days in the troubled country's history. Very little political violence was reported, the vote was relatively free and fair (despite widespread administrative irregularities), and the mood in the country was joyous. The results of the election were as expected: the ANC won a handsome majority of 63 percent of the vote, the NP garnered 20 percent, and the IFP 10.5 percent. All three parties would be in the government of national unity. Nelson Mandela, the great conciliator and guardian of national reconciliation, would be president. De Klerk, along with the number-two leader in the ANC, Thabo Mbeki, would be vice presidents. Buthelezi was offered a cabinet post as home affairs minister, which he readily accepted.

## The New South Africa

The new South Africa was imbued with tremendous hope for reconciliation, economic revival, and newfound legitimacy in the world. Mandela's famous acts of magnanimity toward white South Africans and his Inkatha foes—such as meeting with the widow of the former pro-apartheid president Henrik Verwoerd, donning the cap of the national (and historically all-white) rugby team, appointing Buthelezi acting president while he traveled abroad—did much to consolidate legitimacy for the new government. A new flag and anthem seemed to symbolically unify the nation, and many blacks and whites alike seemed relieved that the tensions generated by the enforcement of apartheid were lifted from the nation's collective shoulders.

**South Africans line up to vote in the country's first multiracial national elections, April 1994.**

The elections of 1994 not only produced a new power-sharing government, they also produced a constitutional assembly that would create a new national charter to permanently guide South Africa's newfound democracy. In a process known for its thoughtful deliberations, its progressive embrace of human rights, and its delicate balance between majority demands and minority fears, the Constitutional Assembly produced a new constitution in 1996. It is in many ways the greatest achievement of the democratization process that today all the major political actors in South Africa see the constitution as a legitimate set of rules for ordering the country's political life.

Yet South Africa faces tremendous economic, social, and political problems. Some are new, but others are a direct consequence of the perverse nature of apartheid. Among the critical challenges the country faces are very high levels of violent crime, economic stagnation, uneven performance in delivering key services (housing, health care, education, water, environmental quality), corruption, tensions over employment and affirmative action, a highly unequal distribution of wealth and income, and a deadly AIDS epidemic. Another significant problem is the lack of a viable opposition. Divisive struggles between labor and industry have also limited the country's "peace dividend," that is, the improvement in economic efficiency resulting from reductions in spending on military and security forces. Power sharing withered away in South Africa in 1996 as opposition parties (except, interestingly, the Inkatha Freedom Party) found their role in government too uncomfortable and chose instead to work from a position of opposition. This situation leaves the ANC in control of the government for the foreseeable future, as the party's electoral majority is secure. Some argue that it may lead to a dominant one-party state. Fortunately, the country enjoys a highly developed civil society that helps mediate social tensions. It includes a well-developed and assertive media, vigorous civic and trade associations, an active multiracial women's advocacy network, and a strong business community.

**Challenges Facing the New South Africa**

- *Reconciling justice and forgiveness for apartheid crimes*. The country created a *Truth and Reconciliation Commission* to review past crimes, hear testimonies, grant pardons for atrocities, and offer recommendations for social healing. Bishop *Desmond Tutu*, the Nobel Peace Prize laureate, chaired the Commission. But few were satisfied with the Commission's final report, issued in early 1999, because it not only condemned the former white minority regime for human rights abuses but also criticized the African National Congress for abuses committed during its liberation war. It also criticized Nelson Mandela's former wife, Winnie Madzhikela Mandela, for her involvement in several killings in Soweto. A lingering question for South Africa is, how can the demands of justice be reconciled with the need for forgiveness?
- *Unemployment and poverty*. South Africa's unemployment level hovers around 30 percent of the working population; half of all black youth are unemployed. About a third of the population lives on less than $2 a day, with about 10 percent subsisting on less than $1 a day. The maldistribution of wealth is one of the worst in the world: in 2000 the wealthiest fifth of the population held 62 percent of the national income, while the bottom 40 percent shared only about 10 percent of the country's income. Some fear that with such widespread poverty, South African society is a cauldron that will eventually boil over.
- *HIV/AIDS and other infectious diseases*. Since 1990, South Africa has witnessed a terrible epidemic of HIV/AIDS. By 2000 it had more HIV-infected people than any other country in the world: approximately 16 percent of its adult population is HIV-positive.[29] In many hospitals, half the emergency room patients test HIV-positive. Government efforts to combat the disease, as well as other threats to public health such as tuberculosis, have been riddled with corruption. Alcoholism is also rampant, posing additional health hazards.
- *Crime*. Johannesburg is the most dangerous city in the world, with a staggering number of murders and other criminal activities. Throughout the country, carjackings, rape, violence against children, robbery, killings of farmers, extortion, and other crimes make South Africa's crime situation one of the worst in the world. In 1998 there were 59 murders per 100,000 people, ten times the U.S. rate. (In 1994 the murder rate was even higher, at 69.5 per 100,000.) More than 6,000 white farmers have been killed since 1994, although it is unclear whether the perpetrators were racially motivated or simply criminals. The police system is crippled with the legacies of apartheid, which have left it wholly illegitimate in many communities. Many South Africans are uncertain if their country can prosper as a democracy with such high crime levels.
- *South Africa's role in Africa and the world*. Now that South Africa is a model of interracial reconciliation and a powerhouse in sub-Saharan Africa, with the largest economy and military force, it is increasingly being called upon to assume a leadership role in world affairs. Already, South African troops have intervened in neighboring states to promote stability, and the country has contributed to regional and international peacemaking and peacekeeping efforts. For example, it has played an important role in efforts to settle the war in the Congo (formerly Zaire), but risks a possible quagmire if its troops are sent there to keep the peace. South Africa has also adopted an open international trade and finance regime, though it remains vulnerable in a

globalized international economy. Foreign investment shot up after the 1994 elections, but investors remain fickle and especially wary of the country's comparatively high labor costs (propelled upward by aggressive trade unions), its crime wave, and creeping corruption.

President Thabo Mbeki

Some expected that the 1999 elections would generate tensions and potentially undermine social consensus in the new South Africa. Fears were raised that if the ANC garnered more than 66 percent of the vote, it could vitiate aspects of the constitution that limited its rule and protected minorities. But the elections revealed that even though the ANC does command a large majority of support in the country—it won handily with just under 66 percent of the popular vote and 266 seats in the 400-member National Assembly—opposition parties are vigorous and the country's system of constitutional checks and balances remains vibrant. The country's judiciary, which has undergone major reforms, has won high praise for integrity, fairness, and a well-earned reputation for safeguarding human rights.

Many analysts around the world were concerned that, without Mandela, South Africa's fledgling democracy would begin to unravel. So far, however, his successor, Thabo Mbeki, a longtime ANC activist who was for many years its representative to the international community, has been able to reassure the outside world and South Africans alike that he can successfully lead the country and carefully balance the need for change with the imperative of stability. Mbeki is a technocratic leader who has taken bold steps to revise the economy and work with business.[30] He has also sought to assuage minority concerns and to carry on Mandela's legacy of balancing social reconciliation with the long-term transformation of South Africa's highly unequal distribution of income. In some ways, Mbeki and South Africa are struggling with the reality that the enormous challenges they now face are similar to those of many other "ordinary" developing countries. These problems are enormous, to be sure, but compared with the difficulties of the past, South Africa is well along the way toward its own renaissance.

In 2004 the ANC won a staggering 69.7 percent of the vote in parliamentary elections, which were widely viewed as free and fair (see table 23.3 on page 792). The party's large delegation in the National Assembly thereupon reelected Mbeki to a second term as president. But all eyes are on the critical elections of 2009, when the transition from Mbeki to his successor will challenge the ANC if opposition parties coalesce against the erstwhile liberation party's dominance. These dynamics will surely put South Africa's fragile democracy to the test. As South Africa prepares for the next big electoral test of its democracy in 2009, when a newly elected parliament will formally elect a successor to President Mbeki, several trends deserve watching. The first centers on the ANC's internal unity and the party's alliance with the trade unions and the South African Communist Party. Left-leaning members of the ANC want to retain these ties, but some believe that the party—which was forged in unity in opposition to apartheid—will face an inevitable split along ideological lines. The second issue to watch is the struggle to succeed Mbeki. In 2005 former deputy president Jacob Zuma was implicated in a corruption scandal and fired by Mbeki, and later that year he was charged with rape of a prominent HIV activist; remarkably, he was acquitted on the rape charge and later his prosecution on corruption charges was also dropped. Zuma has emerged as the champion of young populists who are disaffected over unemployment and grinding poverty, and he has emerged as an important and serious challenger to the more conservative faction of the ANC that is loyal to Mbeki. As long as South Africa

**TABLE 23.3**

**2004 National Assembly Election: Votes and Seats**

| Party | Votes | % | Seats |
|---|---|---|---|
| African National Congress (ANC) | 10,878,251 | 69.68 | 279 |
| Democratic Party/Alliance (DA) | 1,931,201 | 12.37 | 50 |
| Inkatha Freedom Party (IFP) | 1,088,664 | 6.97 | 28 |
| United Democratic Movement (UDM) | 355,717 | 2.28 | 9 |
| Independent Democrats (ID) | 269,765 | 1.73 | 7 |
| New National Party (NNP) | 257,824 | 1.65 | 7 |
| African Christian Democrats (ACDP) | 250,272 | 1.60 | 6 |
| Freedom Front (FF/VF) | 139,465 | 0.89 | 4 |
| United Christian Democrats (UCDP) | 117,792 | 0.75 | 3 |
| Pan-Africanist Congress (PAC) | 113,512 | 0.73 | 3 |

faces its current acute social problems, especially deep inequality, its young democracy will remain vulnerable to populist uprisings.

## HYPOTHESIS-TESTING EXERCISE: Democracy in South Africa

### Hypotheses, Variables, and Expectations

We conclude our analysis of South Africa in the same way we concluded our exploration of Nigeria: with a brief overview of its prospects for democracy in light of the ten conditions for democracy and democratization we developed in chapter 9. Each of these *conditions* constitutes an *independent variable* that, according to our hypotheses, has an impact on the *emergence of democracy and its survival* (*dependent variables*). Our expectation is that the more of these conditions South Africa manages to fulfill successfully, the greater its chances are of sustaining democratic institutions and practices over the long run.

How has South Africa done thus far in fulfilling these conditions, and what are its likely prospects of the future?

### Evidence

#### *Elites Committed to Democracy*

South Africa's governing elite, especially high-level leaders of the ruling ANC, fought for decades against a strong and bitter foe to gain their right to vote and exercise basic human rights. Their commitment to democracy is thus deep and strong. At the same time, civic elites such as white business leaders have dedicated themselves to working with the new black-majority government. Similarly, opposition political party leaders have learned to work very effectively within the new institutions, and they too are committed to democratic processes. It appears that elite attitudes in South Africa are conducive to long-term democratic survival.

#### *State Institutions*

South Africa's new democratic constitution, finalized in 1996, enjoys broad support and is widely respected within the country and abroad. It puts human rights at the forefront of state policy, strikes an admirable balance between majority prerogatives and minority protections, and shows appreciation for the principle of proportionality in representation and in the allocation of state resources. It also recognizes that South Africa must move beyond widespread economic inequality for the long-term survival of democracy. The constitution was broadly debated and is accepted by virtually all segments in South Africa's diverse social mosaic. The government's Commission on Gender Equality enforces the constitution's guarantee of equal rights for women. (About one-third of the National Assembly deputies are female, one of the highest such percentages in the world.) With such a widely accepted and progressive constitution, South Africa's state institutions are aptly designed and should help meet the society's needs for balancing stability and change. (The system of government is described below.)

At the same time, some government bodies—such as some regional governments—suffer from ineptitude and corruption. But on balance, South Africa's institutions contribute to the consolidation of democracy because of broad public support for them and for the principles on which they are based.

### *National Unity*

Ethnic, racial, and religious diversity has been a challenge for South Africa since the very first days of European settlement. Nevertheless, it has emerged from apartheid as one of the most progressive, multicultural countries on the globe, with a widespread commitment to unity in diversity—the "rainbow nation," as some have termed it. Blacks now comprise about 75 percent of the population, whites about 14 percent; about 9 percent are of mixed race and 2 percent are East Indian. Two out of three South Africans are Christian (including 60 percent of blacks), while about 30 percent have traditional animist beliefs. There are also small communities of Muslims (2 percent) and Hindus (1.5 percent). If present trends continue, ethnic and racial diversity will not seriously impede progress toward the consolidation of democracy in South Africa.

### *National Wealth*

South Africa is the strongest regional economy in southern Africa and a significant "newly emerging market" for international investors. Its per capita GNI in 2002 was in the upper-middle-income range at $4,960. Much of the country's current infrastructure and economic development was built on mining as the critical sector—especially gold and diamonds. But mining revenues alone are insufficient to carry today's South Africa into the twenty-first century as a competitive country in the bustling international marketplace. Although natural endowments such as minerals still contribute to economic growth, South Africa will need to develop a more diverse economic base in high-technology industries. At present, its growth rate is only 2 percent to 3 percent per year, not enough to keep up with population pressures that add another 10 percent of job seekers into the employment market virtually every year. National wealth contributes to democracy's success in South Africa, but a prolonged recession could cool public attitudes toward democracy.

### *Private Enterprise*

The private sector remains strong in South Africa, and the ANC's moderate economic policies have begun to woo more international investors. Although domestic and international investors are still nervous about South Africa's long-term economic prospects—especially about the power of the trade unions—the country fosters private industry and, increasingly, a burgeoning tourist economy. South Africa's strong private enterprise sectors contribute to democracy's survival.

### *The Middle Class*

Class distinctions in South Africa are very pronounced, and a solid, multiethnic middle class is just beginning to form. Considerable emphasis has been placed on the development of a black middle class (to include other minority groups disadvantaged by apartheid as well), and signs that such a development is occurring are encouraging. The evidence to date suggests that, over the long term, South Africa will likely develop a fairly broad middle class that will contribute to democracy's survival.

### *Support of the Disadvantaged*

Endemic poverty still grips many South Africans: some 20 percent of the population live below the poverty line. Maldistribution of income makes South Africa one of the most unequal societies in the world (see table 2.3). The country has alarmingly high rates of rural and urban poverty, unemployment, and health issues such as pandemics of AIDS and tuberculosis. The ANC government is committed to building a more viable social safety net even as resource scarcity limits initiatives such as building more houses for people who still live in informal settlements (shantytowns). The likely continued commitment to poverty eradication increases the probability of democratic survival in South Africa.

### *Citizen Participation, Civil Society, and Democratic Political Culture*

One of the consequences of the anti-apartheid struggle has been the strengthening of civic institutions, from neighborhood committees to professional associations, trade unions, women and youth groups, and numerous others. The political culture remains one that emphasizes consensus building and compromise. South Africa's diverse and sophisticated civil society and its newfound tolerant political culture are making major contributions to the survivability of democratic decision making.

### *Education and Freedom of Information*

Transforming the education system in South Africa in recent years has been one of the most difficult challenges for the ANC government. Eighteen percent of the population is illiterate, according to the Development Program.[31] Years of inferior "Bantu education" for blacks, as it was known, have left a system of schools for the majority black population that are riddled with problems. Teachers and resources are extremely scarce and the administrative aspects of education have been dismal. At the same time, the country has a world-class system of higher education and a strong potential for creating new models of community college development. While education policies are improving, the travails of South Africa's education system are a serious impediment to the long-term survivability of democracy. A poor education system limits the opportunities for democratic consolidation in South Africa. Meanwhile, the country also enjoys a vigorous, capable, and independent media sector.

### *International Environment*

South Africa's regional environment remains perilous. Civil wars and instability in neighboring states such as Angola and the Democratic Republic of the Congo seriously threaten regional stability and could draw South Africa into costly military engagements—as combatants or peacekeepers—in the years to come. These wars and regional economic stagnation also limit South Africa's ability to be the economic engine of southern Africa, as it purports to be. At the same time, the broader support among the international community for democracy and development in South Africa remains high. International support for South Africa's nascent democracy will, on balance, bolster the likelihood that it will continue to develop as a democracy.

## Conclusions

South Africa remains a society deeply divided by race, wealth, and ethnicity. Will South Africa's "miracle" transition succumb to the pressures of ethnic and racial extremism, as some competent and highly regarded analysts of politics in deeply divided societies have predicted?[32] Although there are incipient stresses in the newfound social cohesion that was the immediate outcome of the South African transition,[33] the patterns of intergroup bargaining that arose during the 1990–94 transition from apartheid to nonracial democracy are deeply embedded in many sectors of South African society, including its new governmental institutions (see below). Remarkably, this political culture of bargaining, steeped in the necessity of pragmatic moderation that propelled the transition, has been sustained in the post-apartheid era despite the overwhelming electoral predominance of the African National Congress government. Ethnic conflict—which characterizes the vast majority of contemporary civil wars and political violence—still remains a long-term threat to this newborn democracy, if conclusions from the comparative studies of deeply divided societies are any guide.[34] Moreover, there is a growing sense that the multiracial "rainbow-nation" ethos is fading as clouds of ethnic and racial assertiveness appear on the horizon. For example, tensions have flared in the Western Cape province, especially near Cape Town, between blacks and coloreds (those of mixed ancestry). A persistent problem remains that of "white flight," in which skilled whites are emigrating overseas in search of better employment and more security; some estimates are that ten thousand skilled white professionals leave the country every year.

Moreover, South Africa's new constitution, approved in May 1996 (and subsequently amended in response to the Constitutional Court), establishes a system of rules that provide incentives for moderation on divisive ethnic and racial themes. Even though it is essentially a majoritarian constitution, conferring primary governmental responsibility on the majority party or parties, the institutions it has created contain myriad features that may check majority powers and mediate current and potential intergroup conflicts. The judiciary and an independent human rights commission, for example, have helped mediate disputes relating to own-language education and to women's rights, both in the workplace and on reproductive issues. The new political system, over time, will likely encourage the continued integration of South African society, providing institutional remedies and protections to its various minority ethnic and religious groups. For democracy to succeed, a strong civil society and a reinvigorated state (one that has earned legitimacy from its people) will be required, and South Africa appears to be well on the way to securing them.[35]

As long as South Africa's homegrown culture of bargaining, consultation, and intergroup consensus seeking is maintained—however inefficient and laborious such decision making may be—the country's transformation from being the locus of one of the most intractable ethnic conflicts on the globe to one of the world's most promising multiethnic democracies is likely to continue its present, relatively successful, course. This transformation has much to do with the high quality of its leadership, particularly the exceptional efforts of former president Nelson Mandela to keep nation building and reconciliation on the front burner of the country's political life.[36]

In sum, we can conclude that the evidence available thus far is mostly *consistent* with the notion that democracy is gaining a firm foothold in South Africa. These grounds for optimism do not mean that South Africa won't remain deeply divided along ethnic and racial lines. Indeed, as South African political analyst Steven Friedman writes, "The post-1948 legacy of violence and racial polarization seems likely to ensure that a South African democracy will be partial, at least for the next decade. South Africa remains a divided society in which pluralism and compromise presented themselves to political leaders as an unavoidable necessity, not a preferred option."[37] The cleavages of conflict exacerbated by apartheid endure, to be sure. Although the negotiated transition to democracy buried apartheid laws, black-white tensions continue and new, unforeseen social tensions have emerged that deserve careful analysis and preventive, meliorative policies. Racial violence among youth in the mega-cities of Johannesburg and Cape Town have set off alarm bells that the new generation is not fully committed to interracial harmony and ethnic diversity.

*The* critical question for South Africa is whether its political leaders will succumb to the lure of "playing the ethnic card." To what extent, for example, will they try to outbid one another in making extravagant or inflammatory promises to their constituents on sensitive ethnic and racial themes in forthcoming national, local, and provincial electoral contests? And how will the public respond to such overtures?[38]

## SOUTH AFRICA'S GOVERNMENT

South Africa has a *hybrid* democratic political system.

- The *Parliament* is bicameral, consisting of the *National Assembly*, its lower house, and a *National Council of Provinces*, which represents the country's nine provinces as well as local governments. The National Assembly consists of between 350 and 400 deputies, elected to five-year terms on the basis of proportional representation. The National Council has ninety members selected by provincial legislatures and local governments.
- The *President* is the country's head of government and, as a member of the National Assembly, is elected by that body (not by the people). The president presides over the cabinet and appoints the *Deputy President* and other cabinet ministers, and may dismiss them. The National Assembly may remove the president only for malfeasance in office or disability.
- One of the top judicial organs is the *Constitutional Court*, which hears cases on constitutional matters and has powers of judicial review. Its eleven members are appointed by the president upon the advice of the Judicial Service Commission. The *Supreme Court of Appeal* is the highest court in civil and criminal matters.

## CONCLUSION

As we have seen, Nigeria and South Africa both have mixed records when it comes to the ten conditions for democracy discussed in this book. Their records are also mixed when it comes to the structural features of the Temple of Democracy described in chapter 7. Starting with the steps at the temple's base, a majority of the people in both countries seem to have embraced some of the core values of democracy. Above all they value freedom from authoritarian rule—whether in the form of military rule, as in Nigeria, or race-based one-party rule, as in South Africa. Most people in both countries embrace the value of inclusion in the political system on the basis of equality. But Nigeria has had significant difficulties inculcating the values of tolerance and compromise in its diverse, conflict-ridden population. The rule of law may be accepted in principle by majorities in both Nigeria and South Africa, but corruption—especially in Nigeria—undermines this principle in practice. Both countries established electoral democracies in the 1990s, providing an important element of popular sovereignty (Pillar I of the Temple). When it comes to ensuring equal rights and liberties for all (Pillar II), Nigeria is still seriously deficient but South Africa has made somewhat greater strides. South Africa has also outpaced Nigeria in its attempts to improve the population's economic well-being (Pillar III), but both countries are plagued by a grossly uneven distribution of national wealth. According to its 2005 Freedom House rating of 4 for political and civil rights, Nigeria is a semi-authoritarian state. South Africa received a 1 for political rights and a 2 for civil rights, qualifying it as a democracy.

United Nations Secretary General Kofi Annan, who hails from Ghana, has echoed South African President Thabo Mbeki's call for an African renaissance. After witnessing great suffering as a result of the brutal civil war in Sierra Leone, he saw, in the midst of the atrocities of this war, a sense of optimism about Africa emanating from "the resilience and hope that form the reality of Africa today. . . . Never has Africa been more in need of political and financial help," he said. "But never, perhaps, has it been better placed to benefit from it."[39] Africa's fifty-four countries are potentially on the cusp of a new era in which these societies will learn from past mistakes and embrace a course of development and prosperity. Virtually all observers agree that if such a rebirth is to occur, democratic governance will need to be fostered.

Today, Africa's two most important countries—Nigeria, its most populated, and South Africa, its most economically developed—have seen dramatic transitions to democratic rule. The conclusion of this chapter is that consolidating democratic governance in these two countries, which are major players in their regions and throughout the continent, will be a principal prerequisite to realizing the dream of renaissance and renewal for Africa.

## KEY TERMS AND NAMES (In bold and underlined in the text.)

### Africa

Colonialism
Patrimonial rule
Hegemonic exchange

### Nigeria

Prebendalism
Olusegun Obasanjo
Fourth Republic
Praetorianism

### South Africa

National Party (NP)
Apartheid
Boer War
African National Congress (ANC)
Nelson Mandela

## NOTES

1. *New York Times*, April 27, 2003.
2. For the rankings of African states on the United Nations Development Program's Human Development Index (a combination of a number of development indicators), see www.undp.org. For an overview of Africa's contemporary challenges, see Howard W. French, *A Continent for the Taking: The Tragedy and Hope of Africa* (New York: Alfred A. Knopf, 2004).
3. We will concentrate on the states of sub-Saharan Africa in this chapter. Although part of the African land mass and active players in African politics, the Arab states of the Maghreb region—Morocco, Algeria, Tunisia, Libya, and Egypt—are more closely associated with the Mediterranean and Middle East regions.
4. See http://www.refer.sn/sngal_ct/cop/goree/fgoree.htm. For a view of the island during the slave period, visit http://webworld.unesco.org/goree/en/wade.shtml.
5. For an analysis of the project of nation building within the colonial-era borders, see Ricardo René Laremont, ed., *Borders, Nationalism, and the African State* (Boulder, Colo.: Lynne Rienner, 2005).
6. See Gerald Bender, *Angola Under the Portuguese: The Myth and Reality* (Berkeley and Los Angeles: University of California Press, 1978).
7. The Commonwealth consists of former British colonies or dependencies that are now independent countries. Membership is voluntary, and the organization's main function is consultation on such matters as economic cooperation, technical assistance, terrorism, and drug trafficking. At the end of 2006 there were fifty-three member states.
8. See Gus Liebenow, "The Impact of Colonialism," in *African Politics: Crises and Challenges* (Bloomington: Indiana University Press, 1986).
9. See Zaki Laidi, *The Superpowers and Africa: The Constraints of Rivalry, 1960–1990* (Chicago: University of Chicago Press, 1990).
10. This argument was first articulated by Sir Arthur Lewis in his classic book, *Politics in West Africa* (London: Allen and Unwin, 1965).
11. See Robert Jackson and Carl Rosberg, *Personal Rule in Black Africa* (Los Angeles and Berkeley: University of California Press, 1982).
12. See John Wiseman, *Democracy in Black Africa: Survival and Revival* (New York: Paragon House, 1990).
13. See Donald Rothchild and Victor Oloronsula, eds., *State Versus Ethnic Claims: African Policy Dilemmas* (Boulder, Colo.: Westview Press, 1983).
14. See Francis Deng et al., *Sovereignty as Responsibility: Conflict Management in Africa* (Washington, D.C.: Brookings Institution Press, 1996).
15. See Michael Bratton and Nicolas van de Walle, "Popular Protest and Political Reform in Africa," *Comparative Politics* 24 (1992): 419–42.

16. See Harvey Glickman, ed., *Ethnic Conflict and Democratization in Africa* (Atlanta: African Studies Association Press, 1995).
17. See Timothy Sisk and Andrew Reynolds, eds., *Elections and Conflict Management in Africa* (Washington, D.C.: United States Institute of Peace Press, 1998).
18. John W. Harbeson, "Rethinking Democratic Transitions: Lessons from Eastern and Southern Africa," in Richard Joseph, ed., *State, Conflict, and Democracy in Africa* (Boulder, Colo.: Lynne Rienner Press, 1999).
19. Statement at the African Telecom Forum, Johannesberg, May 4, 1990.
20. Richard Joseph, "Autocracy, Violence, and Ethnomilitary Rule in Nigeria," in Joseph, *State, Conflict and Democracy in Africa.*
21. Donald Horowitz, *Ethnic Groups in Conflict* (Berkeley and Los Angeles: University of California Press, 1985).
22. Larry Diamond, "Nigeria: The Uncivil Society and the Descent into Praetorianism," in *Politics in the Developing Countries: Comparing Experiences with Democracy*, ed. Larry Diamond, Juan J. Linz, and Seymour Martin Lipset, 2nd ed. (Boulder, Colo: Lynne Rienner Press, 1995), 419.
23. See the special section on Nigeria in *The Economist*, January 15, 2000.
24. *World Development Report 1998/1999* (New York: Oxford University Press, 1999).
25. See Timothy Sisk, *Democratization in South Africa: The Elusive Social Contract* (Princeton: Princeton University Press, 1995).
26. See Leonard Thompson, *A History of South Africa* (New Haven: Yale University Press, 1990).
27. See Robert Price, *The Apartheid State in Crisis: Political Transformation in South Africa, 1975–1990* (New York: Oxford University Press, 1991).
28. Donald Rothchild notes that international mediation was critical to the success of the South African transition despite the reluctance of the parties to external influence. See his *Managing Ethnic Conflict in Africa* (Washington, D.C.: Brookings Institution Press, 1997), 191–211.
29. See the 2006 *Report on the Global Aids Epidemic* produced by UNAIDS (Joint United Nations Program on HIV/AIDS), at unaids.org.
30. William Mervin Gumede, *Thabo Mbeki and the Battle for the Soul of the ANC* (Cape Town: Zebra, 2005).
31. http://undp.org/hdro.
32. Comparativist scholars such as Arend Lijphart in *Power Sharing in South Africa* (Berkeley: Institute of International Studies, 1985) and Donald Horowitz in *A Democratic South Africa? Constitutional Engineering in a Divided Society* (Berkeley and Los Angeles: University of California Press, 1991) predicted severe ethnic strife if the cluster of political institutions they advocated for South Africa (consociational versus integrative institutions, respectively) were not adopted. Horowitz went so far as to predict "Zulu-Xhosa" polarity as the greatest threat to post-apartheid South Africa. Marina Ottaway in *South Africa: The Struggle for a New Order* (Washington, D.C.: Brookings Institution Press, 1993) referred to the transition from apartheid as a process of conflict generation as much as conflict management and saw ethnic nationalism increasing and threatening any political settlement that might emerge.
33. Sisk, *Democratization in South Africa.*
34. See Donald Horowitz, "Democracy in Divided Societies," *Journal of Democracy* 4, no. 4, (1993): 18–38.
35. See Pierre du Toit, *State Building and Democracy in Southern Africa: Botswana, Zimbabwe, and South Africa* (Washington, D.C.: United States Institute of Peace Press, 1995).
36. See Tom Lodge, *Politics in South Africa: From Mandela to Mbeki* (Oxford: Oxford University Press, 2003).
37. Steven Friedman, "South Africa," in Seymour Martin Lipset, ed., *Encyclopedia of Democracy* (Washington, D.C.: Congressional Quarterly, 1996), 1167.
38. Alvin Rabushka and Kenneth A. Shepsle, *Politics in Plural Societies* (Columbus, Ohio: Charles E. Merrill, 1972).
39. Kofi Annan, "Window of African Promise amid Great Suffering," *International Herald Tribune*, July 31–August 1, 1999.

# CREDITS

## TEXT AND LINE ART

*Page* **24–25** The Universal Declaration of Human Rights reprinted by permission of United Nations, http://www.un.org/Overview/rights.html; **34** From *Freedom in the World 2006* by Adrian Karatnycky. Reprinted by permission of Rowman & Littlefield Publishing Group; **40** From *World Development Indicators 2006,* pp. 76–78. Reprinted by permission of World Bank Publications; **47** From http://www.ipu.org/wmn-e/classif.htm. Reprinted by permission of Inter-Parliamentary Union (IPU); **48** From *Human Development Report 2005* edited by UNDP. Reprinted by permission of Oxford University Press; **109** The results presented in this paper rely on data from the TI Corruption Perceptions Index 2005 provided by Transparency International. Reprinted by permission of Transparency International; **154** From *The Economist*, February 11, 2006, p. 44. Copyright © 2006 The Economist Newspaper Ltd. All rights reserved. Reprinted with permission. Further reproduction prohibited. www.economist.com; **158** From *The New York Times*, February 28, 1988. Copyright © 1988 The New York Times Co. Reprinted by permission; **237** From *Freedom in the World 2006* by Adrian Karatnycky. Reprinted by permission of Rowman & Littlefield Publishing Group; **238 top** From *Freedom in the World 2006* by Adrian Karatnycky. Reprinted by permission of Rowman & Littlefield Publishing Group; **238 bottom** From *Freedom in the World 2006* by Adrian Karatnycky. Reprinted by permission of Rowman & Littlefield Publishing Group; **249** Map by Alain Marigo. Reprinted by permission; **268** From "Military Charts Movement of Conflict in Iraq Toward Chaos" by Michael R. Gordon from *The New York Times*, November 1, 2006; **295** From *Sacred and Secular: Religion and Politics Worldwide* by Pippa Norris and Ronald Inglehart, p. 90. Copyright © 2004. Reprinted by permission of Cambridge University Press; **305** From *The Economist*, July 17, 1999. Copyright © 1999 The Economist Newspaper Ltd. All rights reserved. Reprinted with permission. Further reproduction prohibited. www.economist.com; **306** Christian Welzel, Ronald Inglehart and Hans-Dieter Klingemann, "The Theory of Human Development: A Cross-cultural Analysis" from *European Journal of Political Research,* 2003, p. 341. Reprinted by permission of Blackwell Publishing Ltd.; **354** From *World Development Indicators 2006.* Reprinted by permission of World Bank via Copyright Clearance Center; **359** From OECD, Social Expenditure Data Base 2006. Reprinted by permission of OECD; **360 top** From *World Development Indicators 2006.* Reprinted by permission of World Bank via Copyright Clearance Center; **360 bottom** From *The Economist*, September 11, 1999. Copyright © 1999 The Economist Newspaper Ltd. All rights reserved. Reprinted with permission. Further reproduction prohibited. www.economist.com; **367** From *Human Development Report*, pp. 219–221, 2005 by UNDP. Reprinted by permission of Oxford University Press; **371** From *World Development Indicators 2006*, data taken from pp. 2–19. Reprinted by permission of The World Bank; **379** From info.worldbank.org/governance. Reprinted by permission of The World Bank; **416** From *Britain at the Polls* by John Bartle and Anthony King, pp. 177, 221. Copyright © 2005 CQ Press, a division of Congressional Quarterly Inc.; **427** London Borough of Merton; **629** From *Elections without Order: Russia's Challenge to Vladimir Putin* by Richard Rose and Neil Munro, p. 132. Copyright © 2002. Reprinted by permission of Cambridge University Press.

## PHOTOS

*Page* **4** © Romeo Ranoco/Reuters/Corbis; **7** © Jerome Delay/AP/Wide World Photos; **12** © Efrem Lukatsky/AP/Wide World Photos; **48** © Nic Bothma/epa/Corbis; **112** © Abedin Taherkenareh/epa/Corbis; **135** © Peter Dejong/AP/Wide World Photos; **136** © B.K.Bangash/AP/Wide World Photos; **143** © Corbis; **198** © House of Commons TV/AP/Wide World Photos; **226** © Juda Ngwenya AS/Reuters; **260** © Imad Al-Khozai/Reuters; **261** © Mohammed Hato/AP/Wide World Photos; **286** © Jonathan Karp/Reuters/Corbis; **287** © Vahid Salemi/AP/Wide World Photos; **396** © Scott Barbour/Getty Images; **410** © Bettmann/Corbis; **426 both** Courtesy, Michael Sodaro; **428** Courtesy, Wimbledon Conservatives; **445 left** © Thierry Tronnel/Corbis; **445 right** © Alain Nogues/Corbis; **459** © AP/Wide World Photos; **465** © AP/Wide World Photos; **480** © Brooks Kraft/Corbis; **499** © Reuters NewMedia/Corbis; **530** © Bettmann/Corbis; **541** © Carsten Koall/Getty Images; **562** © Bettmann/Corbis; **567** © Hulton-Deutsch Collection/Corbis; **580** © Bob Strong/Reuters; **585** © Koji Sasahara/AP/Wide World Photos; **594** © AP/Wide World Photos; **605** © Hulton Archive/Getty Images; **608** © Bettmann/Corbis; **611** © Hulton-Deutsch Collection/Corbis; **617** © Miroslav Zajic/Corbis; **628** © Reuters NewMedia Inc./Corbis; **653** © Jeff Widener/AP/Wide World Photos; **659** © AP/Wide World Photos; **693** © Fan Rujun/Xinhau/AP/Wide World Photos; **703** © Omar Torres/AFP/Getty Images; **724** © AP/Wide World Photos; **752** © Reuters/Corbis; **779** © Reuters/Corbis; **789** © AP/Wide World Photos; **791** © AP/Wide World Photos

# INDEX